Norway

Anthony Ham,
Miles Roddis, Kari Lundgren

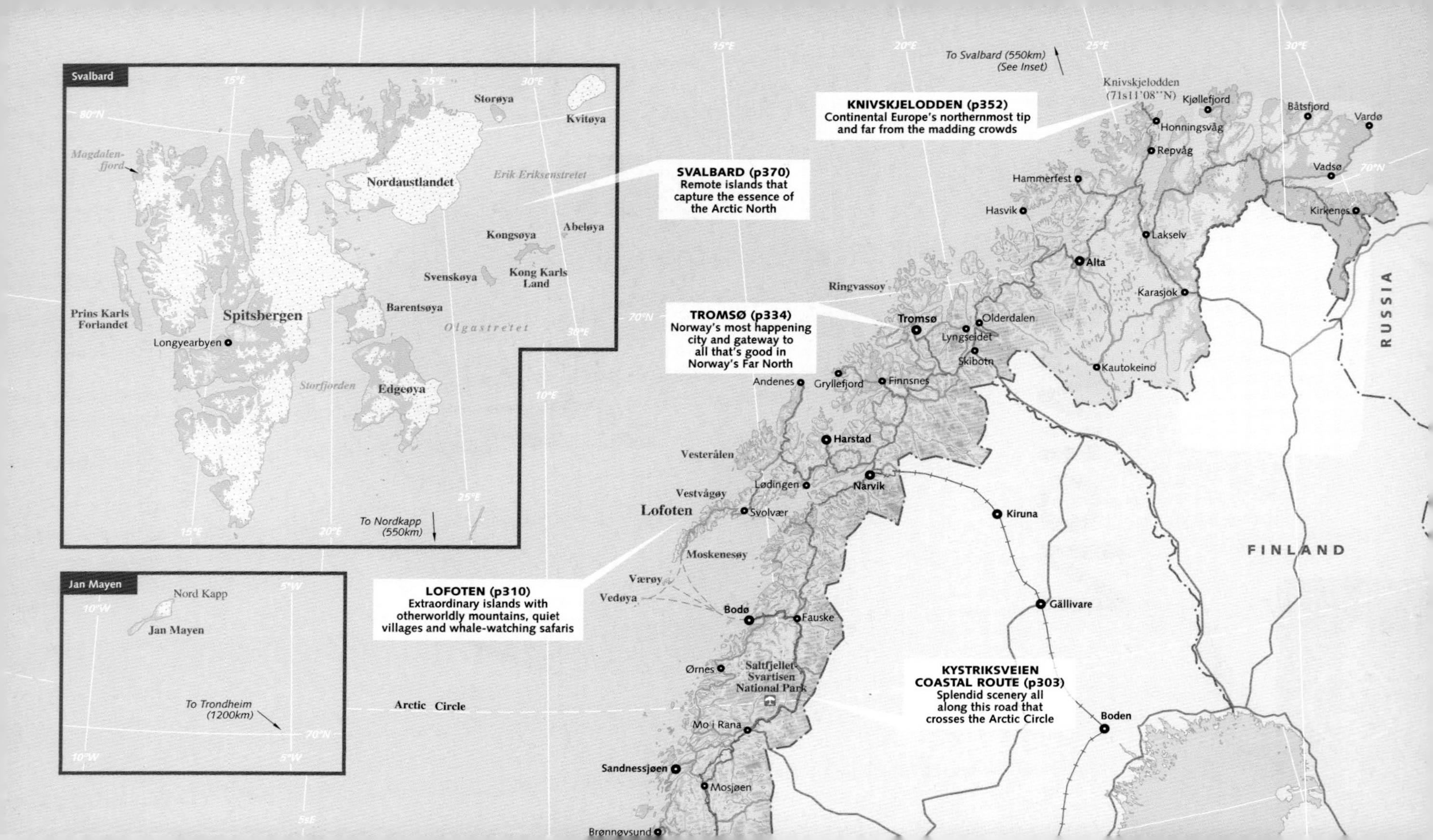

KNIVSKJELODDEN (p352)
Continental Europe's northernmost tip and far from the madding crowds
SVALBARD (p370)
Remote islands that capture the essence of the Arctic North
TROMSØ (p334)
Norway's most happening city and gateway to all that's good in Norway's Far North
LOFOTEN (p310)
Extraordinary islands with otherworldly mountains, quiet villages and whale-watching safaris
KYSTRIKSVEIEN COASTAL ROUTE (p303)
Splendid scenery all along this road that crosses the Arctic Circle
To Svalbard (550km) (See Inset)
Knivskjelodden (71s11'08''N)
Kjøllefjord
Båtsfjord
Vardø
Honningsvåg
Repvåg
Vadsø
Hammerfest
Hasvik
Kirkenes
Lakselv
Alta
Karasjok
Ringvassøy
Tromsø
Olderdalen
Lyngseidet
Skibotn
Kautokeino
Andenes
Gryllefjord
Finnsnes
Harstad
Vesterålen
Narvik
Lødingen
Vestvågøy
Svolvær
Lofoten
Kiruna
Moskenesøy
Værøy
Vedøya
Bodø
Fauske
Gällivare
Ørnes
Saltfjellet-Svartisen National Park
Arctic Circle
Boden
Mo i Rana
Sandnessjøen
Mosjøen
Brønnøysund
RUSSIA
FINLAND
Svalbard
Storøya
Kvitøya
Magdalenfjord
Nordaustlandet
Erik Eriksenstretet
Kongsøya
Abeløya
Svenskøya
Kong Karls Land
Barentsøya
Prins Karls Forlandet
Spitsbergen
Longyearbyen
Olgastretet
Storfjorden
Edgeøya
To Nordkapp (550km)
Jan Mayen
Nord Kapp
Jan Mayen
To Trondheim (1200km)

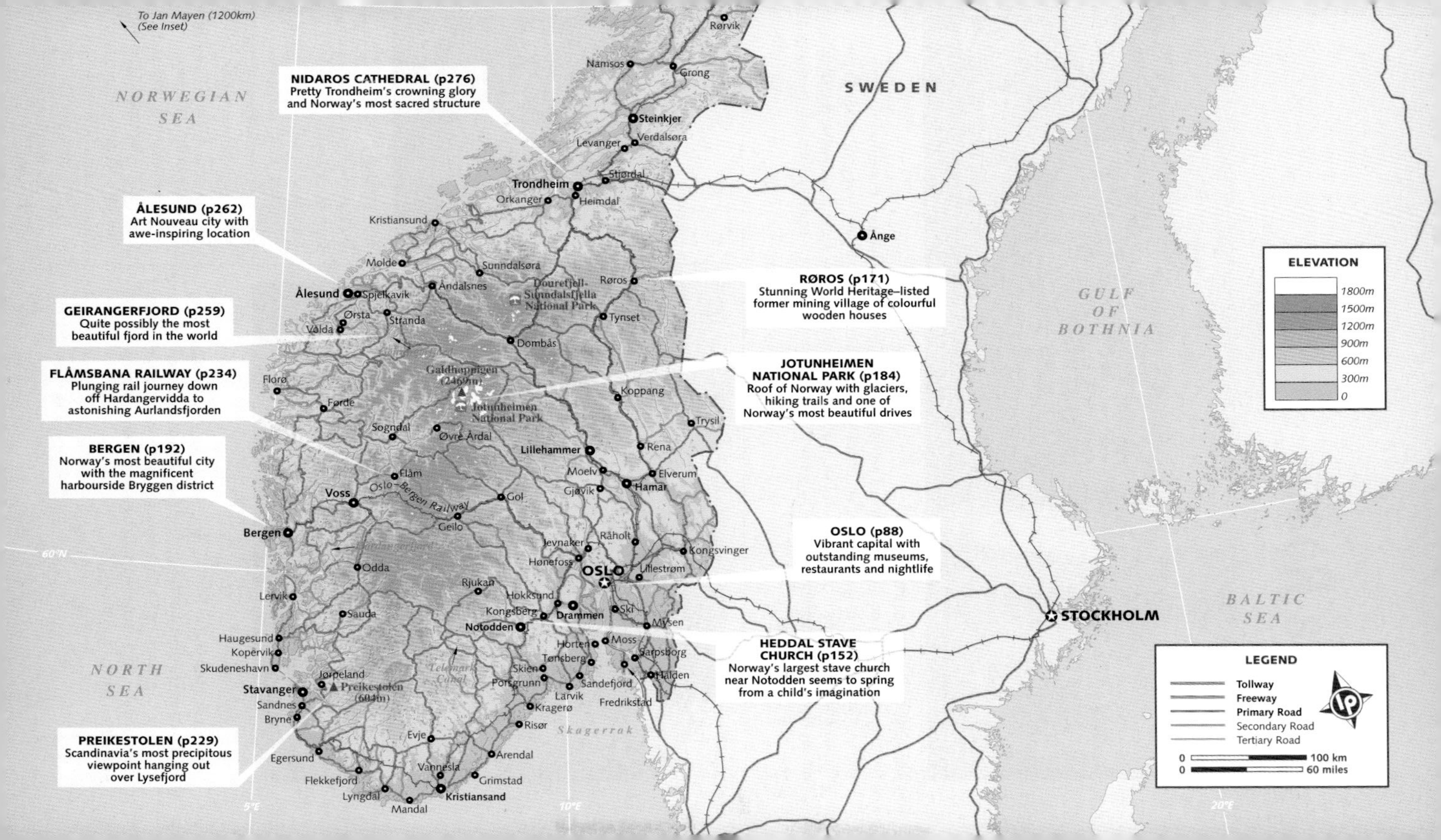

To Jan Mayen (1200km) (See Inset)
NORWEGIAN SEA
NORTH SEA
SWEDEN
GULF OF BOTHNIA
BALTIC SEA
Skagerrak
NIDAROS CATHEDRAL (p276)
Pretty Trondheim's crowning glory and Norway's most sacred structure
ÅLESUND (p262)
Art Nouveau city with awe-inspiring location
GEIRANGERFJORD (p259)
Quite possibly the most beautiful fjord in the world
FLÅMSBANA RAILWAY (p234)
Plunging rail journey down off Hardangervidda to astonishing Aurlandsfjorden
BERGEN (p192)
Norway's most beautiful city with the magnificent harbourside Bryggen district
PREIKESTOLEN (p229)
Scandinavia's most precipitous viewpoint hanging out over Lysefjord
RØROS (p171)
Stunning World Heritage–listed former mining village of colourful wooden houses
JOTUNHEIMEN NATIONAL PARK (p184)
Roof of Norway with glaciers, hiking trails and one of Norway's most beautiful drives
OSLO (p88)
Vibrant capital with outstanding museums, restaurants and nightlife
HEDDAL STAVE CHURCH (p152)
Norway's largest stave church near Notodden seems to spring from a child's imagination
ELEVATION
1800m
1500m
1200m
900m
600m
300m
0
LEGEND
Tollway
Freeway
Primary Road
Secondary Road
Tertiary Road
0 100 km
0 60 miles
Rørvik
Namsos
Grong
Steinkjer
Levanger
Verdalsøra
Stjørdal
Trondheim
Orkanger
Heimdal
Ånge
Kristiansund
Molde
Sunndalsøra
Åndalsnes
Dovrefjell-Sunndalsfjella National Park
Røros
Ålesund
Spjelkavik
Ørsta
Stranda
Volda
Tynset
Dombås
Galdhøpiggen (2469m)
Jotunheimen National Park
Florø
Førde
Koppang
Trysil
Sogndal
Øvre Årdal
Lillehammer
Rena
Flåm
Moelv
Elverum
Gjøvik
Hamar
Voss
Oslo–Bergen Railway
Gol
Geilo
Bergen
Råholt
Jevnaker
Kongsvinger
60°N
Odda
Hønefoss
OSLO
Lillestrøm
Rjukan
Hokksund
Lervik
Kongsberg
Drammen
Ski
Sauda
Mysen
Notodden
Haugesund
Horten
Moss
Kopervik
Tønsberg
Sarpsborg
Skudeneshavn
Skien
Halden
Jørpeland
Telemark Canal
Porsgrunn
Sandefjord
Stavanger
Preikestolen (604m)
Larvik
Sandnes
Fredrikstad
Bryne
Kragerø
Risør
Evje
Arendal
Egersund
Vennesla
Grimstad
Flekkefjord
Lyngdal
Kristiansand
Mandal
5°E
10°E
20°E
STOCKHOLM

On the Road

ANTHONY HAM Coordinating Author

This photo was taken on a cold summer's morning from atop the slag heaps on the outskirts of the former mining village of Røros (p171) in central Norway, which is probably my favourite village in the entire country and which represents all that is good about rural Norway. I love the intimate feel of its timber houses and climbing streets – its sense that the passing years have scarcely changed the essential character of the place.

KARI LUNDGREN

My brother and I visited the Polarship Fram museum (p102) countless times as children, but the thrill of standing at the wheel of a ship once captained by Roald Amundsen and Fridtjof Nansen never seems to fade. And each time I discover something; who knew Amundsen had a Burberry tent?

MILES RODDIS

We'd pitched our tent at a basic, fairly scruffy camp site, not worthy of an appearance in this guide. But gosh, what a view from my shoreside seat of Nordfjord, looking towards Briksdalsbreen (p247)! After barbecuing dinner (fresh fish, of course, recently hauled from the lake), I fired up the laptop and wrote that day's research, inspired by the panorama before me.

See full author bios p435

ACTIVITIES & JOURNEYS

Visiting Norway is inspirational in a way that few destinations in the world can match. The fresh air of the Norwegian wilderness lends itself perfectly to a range of activities-based exploration, while those with less time can see some of the best Norway has to offer on a long summer weekend from Bergen. And then there are the Lofoten Islands, which could just be Norway's most picturesque corner.

Seasonal Activities

During summer there are many opportunities to wed an appreciation of Norway's wild beauty to a sense of adventure. That said, seeing Norway in winter as you ski, or as a team of huskies pulls you cross-country, are experiences you'll never forget. For a rundown of activities, see p388.

❶ Cycle Rallarvegen (Summer)

This exhilarating descent (p189) shadows the famous rail journey from Finse down to the shores of Aurlandsfjorden at Flåm with the advantage that you can stop whenever you want to give yourself (and your brakes) a rest.

❷ Hiking the High Country (Summer)

Summer hiking possibilities are endless, from the stunning but often crowded Jotunheimen National Park (pictured; see the boxed text, p186) to the quieter trails of Rondane National Park (p180), the austere beauty of Hardangervidda (see p188) or the musk-ox–inhabited wild country of the Dovrefjell-Sunndalsfjella National Park (p178).

❸ Glacier Hiking (Summer)

There's something about glaciers that inspires wonder and one of Norway's most memorable summer pastimes is glacier walking. Those that combine accessibility with gravitas include the Hardangerjøkulen glacier on Hardangervidda (p189 and p190), Folgefonn (p219) and Briksdalsbreen (p247).

❹ White-water Rafting (Summer)

The cascading, icy-black waters and white-hot rapids of central Norway are a rafter's paradise during the short season from mid-June to mid-August. Sjoa (see the boxed text, p182) may be a small town but it's famous among rafters the world over.

❺ Parasailing (Summer)

Voss (see the boxed text, p211) and its mountainous, fjord-strewn hinterland is Norway's adventure capital and it's the ideal place to take to the air strapped into a parasail or hurtle towards the earth on a bungee-rope.

❻ Skiing (Year-round)

Cross-country skiing might be Norway's national sport. Trysil (p170) boasts the most extensive trails, while summer skiing is enjoyed at Stryn Ski Centre (p248) and Folgefonn (p219). In winter the downhill slopes of Holmenkollen (p106) and Lillehammer (p168) beckon.

❼ Dog-Sledding (Winter)

Nothing seems quite so appropriate for exploring the frozen wilderness of Norway's north as dog-sledding, an environmentally sound and wonderfully archaic way to get around. Svalbard (p373), Øvre Dividal National Park (p343) and Karasjok (p369) should fit the bill.

Long Summer Weekend

Bergen vies with Stockholm for the title of Scandinavia's most enchanting city. But Bergen also has the rare beauty of the western fjords radiating from its doorstep. With many inbound flights from all across Europe, Bergen makes for a perfect long weekend. If you make it to half of the places covered here, you'll leave spellbound.

1 Bryggen, Bergen

Along with its superb setting, the Unesco World Heritage–listed timber buildings of Bergen's waterfront Bryggen district (p195) are the city's most appealing feature. This living museum is rich in ramshackle charm and the unmistakable echoes of Bergen's golden age. Close by is the Torget Fish Market (p197), with its fresh seafood.

2 Ålesund

With some airlines allowing you to fly into Bergen and out from Ålesund (p262), this engaging city is well worth visiting. Its façades were shaped by the Art Nouveau vision of the early 20th century and its seaside setting is one of Norway's emblematic images.

3 Ulvik

Tucked away in a distant corner of Hardangerfjord, Ulvik (p215) retains a tranquil fjordside air. The views are exceptional and Ulvik's tourist office runs a host of Hardangerfjord tours that help you make the most of your time.

4 Eidfjord

Everything good about Hardangerfjord finds expression in Eidfjord (p216); from Kjeåsen Farm and Viking-era graves to the Hardangervidda Natursenter and Vøringfoss waterfall. The sheer rock-walls and front-row views to this spectacular corner of Norway's fjord network round out a near-perfect picture.

5 Nærøyfjord & Flåmsbana

The 'Norway in a Nutshell' day trip (p201) from Bergen crams more sightseeing into one day than you thought possible. En route, you'll cruise slowly up Nærøyfjord (p237) and take the Flåmsbana railway (p234), one of the world's most breathtaking.

6 Stalheim Hotel

'Norway in a Nutshell' takes you to Stalheim Hotel (p213) for one of the world's most beautiful hotel views, but staying overnight and watching the shadows fill the valley and the sun ignite snowcapped peaks is when you'll really appreciate its charm.

Lofoten Islands

'Fairy-tale landscape' may be a much-overused phrase, but it's the only way to describe the surreal beauty of the Lofoten Islands. The fjords of western Norway are better known, but if we had to choose just one place that will leave you speechless, it would have to be this magical archipelago, which, in summer, is bathed in the crystal-clear light of the north.

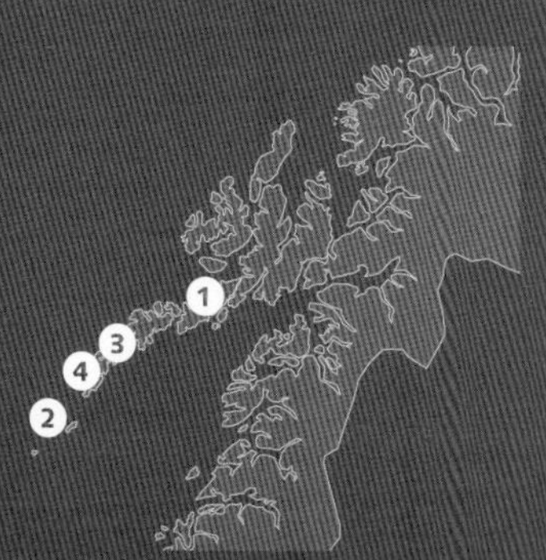

❶ Austvågøy

Most people's entry point into the Lofoten, Austvågøy (p312) is a gentle introduction to the islands' charm. The Raftsund Channel and the dizzyingly narrow Trollfjord provide the backdrop, while the lovely villages of Kabelvåg and Henningsvær offer the perfect bases.

❷ Værøy

Intimate little Værøy (p323), occupying Lofoten's southern reaches, is Moskenesøy's rival for the title of Lofoten's most picturesque island. The combination of vast colonies of sea birds, soaring ridgelines and remote, tiny villages is glorious.

❸ Flakstadøy

Isolated, wind-blown crags along the southern shore are the most eye-catching feature of Flakstadøy (p319), but the old-world beauty of Nusfjord and the utter improbability of surf-worthy waves and white-sand beaches at Ramberg and Flakstad make the island's northern shore breathtaking as well.

❹ Moskenesøy

Tolkien-esque landscapes and glacier-carved land forms lend Moskenesøy (p320) a supernatural beauty that is truly special. The village of Å is the island's soul, while Reinefjord is particularly scenic, as is the country around Vindstad.

A fishing trawler cruises towards the glacier-carved peaks of the Lofoten Islands

Contents

Regional Map Contents

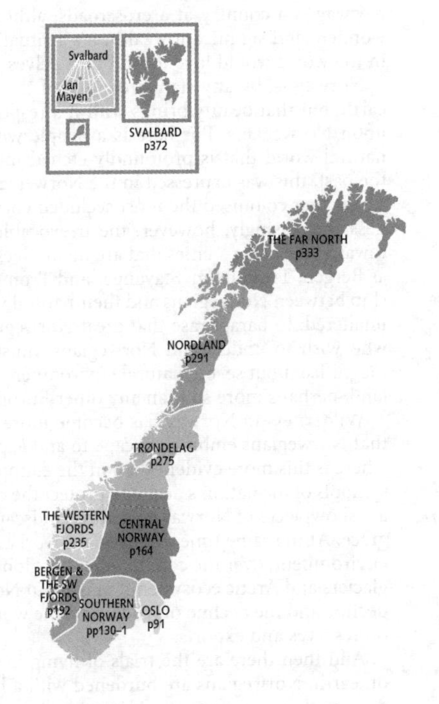

Destination Norway

Norway is a country at a crossroads, although given Norway's natural wonders and significant wealth, it's a situation in which most countries in the world would love to find themselves.

Norway is, by any standards, one of the most beautiful countries on earth, but that beauty brings with it a responsibility that weighs heavily upon Norwegians. For here is a people with an enduring love for the natural world that is profoundly etched into the national character. In the past, this was expressed in the Norwegian tradition of isolated farmsteads that colonised the most secluded corners of the country's wilderness. Increasingly, however, the irrevocable movement of Norwegians towards the cities – cities that are themselves places of great beauty, such as Bergen, Trondheim, Stavanger and Tromsø – has altered the relationship between Norwegians and their natural world. But one thing remains unaltered: to paraphrase that great Norwegian son, Henrik Ibsen, those who wish to understand Norwegians, must first understand Norway's magnificent but severe natural environment, for these are a people of the land, perhaps more so than any other Europeans.

Wilderness in Norway has become more of a leisure pursuit, an idea that Norwegians embrace, escape to and explore with great fervour. Nowhere is this more evident than in the country's national parks – shining symbols of the nation's desire to protect the environment as much as they are showpieces of Norway's peerless landscapes and otherworldly natural grace. At the same time, Norwegians worry about their impact upon the environment, over the consequences of global warming for the country's glaciers and Arctic ecosystems, and about Norway's contributions to this decline and the decline of wilderness the world over due to their massive oil reserves and exports.

And then there are the trials of living in one of the richest countries on earth. Norwegians are burdened with a highly developed social conscience that manifests in far-reaching promises to reduce greenhouse gases, in using its astonishing oil wealth to promote ethical investment abroad and in committing itself to a foreign-aid budget that puts most countries to shame. Where things get complicated is at home, leading to anguished national debates over rising immigration, over the incremental loss of Norway's cultural heritage and over the effects of being cosseted by what is arguably the world's most generous and enlightened welfare system. The country is also divided over whether Norway can continue to go it alone by staying outside the EU, or whether it really should play its part in building a more prosperous and united Europe.

It's not that you'll find many Norwegians complaining about their lot. Nonetheless, you will encounter, again and again, a people wondering about their place in the world.

FAST FACTS

Population: 4.7 million

Raw/real GDP per capita: US$54,465/46,300 (2nd highest in the world)

Inflation: 2.3%

Unemployment rate: 3.5%

Life expectancy: 82.46 years (women) and 77.04 years (men)

Value of Norway's oil-funded Government Pension Fund: US$300 billion

External debt: 0

No of polar bears: around 3000

Maternity/paternity leave on full pay for working parents: 42/five weeks

Ranking on 2006 UNDP Human Development Index: 1

Getting Started

The challenges of Norway's soaring topography and the sheer length of the country – Lindesnes in the south is 2518km from Nordkapp in the far north (leaving aside Svalbard) – mean that preplanning is essential. Norway also doesn't come cheap but careful planning can help ameliorate your expenses. And then there's the simple pleasure of imagining your trip. Bergen and the fjords or the Arctic north? The Lofoten Islands or Jotunheimen? Wonderful, difficult choices all, and ones you really should make before leaving home.

WHEN TO GO

Norway's climate should be your primary consideration. The main tourist season (which coincides with Norwegian and other European school holidays) runs from mid-June to mid-August. During this period, public transport runs frequently, tourist offices and tourist sights are open longer hours and many hotels offer cheaper rates.

That said, Norway is at its best and brightest for much of the period from May to September. Late May is particularly pleasant: flowers are blooming, fruit trees blossoming (especially in Hardangerfjord; p214), daylight hours are growing longer and most hostels, camp sites and tourist sights are open but uncrowded. Be aware, however, that if you've come to Norway to hike (see p391), many routes and huts won't be open until late June or early July. Smaller mountain roads usually don't open until June.

For climate details of major centres across Norway, including climate charts, see p394.

North of the Arctic Circle, the true midnight sun is visible at least one day a year, and at Nordkapp it stays out from 13 May to 29 July. Dates for more places appear on p66.

At any time of the year, be aware that extremes of temperature are always possible; temperatures over 30°C in summer and below -30°C in winter aren't uncommon. Unless you're an avid skier (p393) or hope to glimpse the aurora borealis (see the boxed text, p66), Norway's cold dark winters can be trying for visitors; public transport runs infrequently; most hostels and camp sites are closed; and sights, museums and tourist offices open only limited hours, if at all.

The Norwegian year is also chock-full of outstanding festivals and some of them are well worth planning your trip around. For a list of major festivals, as well as public holidays in Norway, see p22.

DON'T LEAVE HOME WITHOUT...

- sturdy hiking boots – hiking in sandals is a recipe for disaster
- a jacket, jersey (sweater) or anorak (windbreaker) that can readily be carried with you, even in summer.
- a sleeping sheet, a warm, but lightweight sleeping bag and/or your own sheets – most hostels and camping huts charge extra for bed linen
- a rail pass of some description (p406) – why pay full price when you don't have to?
- plenty of patience if you're driving – getting anywhere in a hurry can be a frustrating business (see p415)
- a small pair of binoculars for the views and wildlife-spotting
- mosquito repellent
- airline-style sleeping mask for light-filled Norwegian summer nights

COSTS & MONEY

Norway is expensive. If you stay in camp sites, prepare your own meals and buy discounted transport tickets, you could squeeze by on around Nkr300 per person per day. Staying in hostels that include breakfast (or eating breakfast at a bakery), having lunch at an inexpensive restaurant and picking up supermarket items for dinner, you can possibly manage on Nkr400 per day, but Nkr500 is more realistic.

Staying at hotels that include buffet breakfasts, and eating light lunches and an evening meal at a moderately priced restaurant, you can expect to spend at least Nkr750 per person per day if you're doubling up and Nkr900 if you're travelling alone. Once you factor in transport, sights and alcohol (nightclub cover charges start from Nkr70), you'll struggle to keep below Nkr1000; if you rent a car, Nkr1500 is a more likely minimum. For a run-down on accommodation prices, see p385. See the boxed text, below, for further advice on cost-cutting.

HOW MUCH?

Cup of coffee with pastry Nkr55

Adult entry to museum Nkr40-80

Oslo–Bergen train one-way Nkr298-728

'Norway in a Nutshell' tour from Bergen Nkr820

One-day car rental from Nkr500

TRAVEL LITERATURE

For great predeparture reading or an accompaniment to long, lazy cruises through the fjords, the following books should fit the bill. The Culture chapter also has a detailed run-down of Norwegian literature (p47), music (p49) and films (p55).

The Ice Museum: In Search of the Lost Land of Thule, by Joanna Kavenna, vividly captures our fascination with the Arctic north, with some outstanding sections on Norway.

Norway: The Northern Playground, by Cecil Slingsby, is a classic early-20th-century account of climbing in the Norwegian mountains; it's a gripping account that will appeal equally to nonclimbers.

Fellowship of Ghosts: A Journey Through the Mountains of Norway, by Paul Watkins, is loaded with insight as it tells of the author's solo journeys through Norway's high country on foot.

Isles of the North: A Voyage to the Lands of the Norse, by Ian Mitchell, recounts a boat journey into the Norwegian fjords with musings on Norway's place among modern nations.

Summer Light: A Walk Across Norway, by Andrew Stevenson, is an affectionate and luminous account of a walk from Oslo to Bergen that captures the essence of Norway.

Letters from High Latitudes, by Lord Dufferin, evokes a mid-19th-century sailing trip around the Arctic, including Jan Mayen Island,

NORWAY ON THE CHEAP

Norwegian prices are high by anyone's standards, but here are a few tricks for saving your kroner.

- Plan your eating strategy well (see p56)
- Camp (p386) – camp sites are economical and open-air camping is also possible
- Carry a student or senior citizens' card (p397) to get discounts on entry fees
- Plan ahead and buy *minipris* tickets (p419) or train pass (p406) for train and some bus journeys
- If renting a car (p414), do so across the border in Sweden
- Join Hostelling International (HI; p387), Den Norske Turistforening (DNT; p386) or hotel pass networks (p388) for accommodation discounts

Svalbard and mainland Norway, with references to the more romantic aspects of Norwegian history.

Arctic Dreams, by Barry Lopez, is a classic, haunting treatment of Arctic regions, with many references to Sami culture.

Rowing to Latitude: Journeys Along the Arctic's Edge, by Jill Fredston, documents the harsh richness of Norway's arctic coasts by an author who rowed her way almost along its length.

INTERNET RESOURCES

Norway has colonised the internet and listed here are a few of our favourite websites; there are hundreds more listed throughout the book. Look especially for tourist-office websites that tend to be excellent.

Bergen Tourist Office (www.visitbergen.com) An example of what to expect from tourist-office websites across the country.

Fjord Norway (www.fjordnorway.com) Everything you need to know about Norway's star attraction.

Lonely Planet (www.lonelyplanet.com) Latest travel news, succinct summaries on Norway, postcards from other travellers and the Thorn Tree bulletin board.

Norway.Com (www.norway.com) Comprehensive tourist-oriented site with a practical focus.

Norway Guide (www.norwayguide.no) An excellent site that gives a detailed rundown on Norway's top sights.

Norwegian Tourist Board (www.visitnorway.com) Comprehensive site ranging from the practical to the inspirational.

'Norway's environment remains one of its main drawcards'

TRAVELLING RESPONSIBLY

A single trip might not seem particularly environmentally significant, but Norway's environment remains one of its main drawcards and one that millions of travellers who visit Norway every year have a responsibility to protect.

So what can you do to limit your environmental footprint? For a start, take advantage of Norway's excellent public transport system. Trains cover southern and central Norway, particularly between major centres, while buses make up the shortfall in most places where the trains don't reach. For general information on train and bus travel see the Transport chapter (p413). The Hurtigruten Coastal Ferry (p412) is another form of transport that may equate to less emissions than if the potential travellers chose to travel the equivalent distance by car.

One of the more exciting programmes in recent years is the *National Geographic*–inspired Geotourism charter; for more information, see the boxed text, p85.

Ecofriendly Travel Choices

Look out for ecofriendly places to stay and eat (see p21). Norway also has a wealth of environmentally sound activities (see p388), among them hiking, white-water rafting, skiing, cycling and dog-sledding, many of which cater for those with a commitment to minimal impact or 'slow' travel. For ways to further minimise your impact upon the environment when hiking, see the boxed text, p390. Most tourist offices also rent out bicycles for a reasonable fee.

Carbon Offset Schemes

Aviation is the fastest growing contributor to climate change, although mile for mile, the amount of carbon dioxide emitted for one person driving a car is about as much as that for one per passenger on a plane. However, the problem with flying is not only the carbon emitted (and

TOP 10 NORWAY

SCENIC JOURNEYS

In Norway, getting somewhere can be half the fun and few countries can boast such a fine array of scenic journeys. Some have been designated as National Tourist Routes (see the boxed text, p414).

- Oslo–Bergen railway (p209)
- Norway in a Nutshell (p201)
- Hurtigruten coastal ferry (p412)
- Romsdalen by rail (p178)
- Peer Gynt Vegen (see the boxed text, p168)
- Sognefjellet Road (p184)
- Arctic Highway (p291)
- Kystriksveien Coastal Route (p303)
- E10 across Lofoten (p310)
- Senja (p342)

WILDERNESS AREAS

Travellers who value pristine wilderness will love exploring the following stirring landscapes:

- Svalbard (p370) As deep as you're likely to get in the Arctic north
- Møysalen National Park (p331) Pristine alpine coastal scenery.
- Hardangervidda (p188) Wild high plateau of severe beauty
- Rondane National Park (p180) Cathedral-like mountains with otherworldly forms
- Dovrefjell-Sunndalsfjella National Park (p178) Home of the musk ox, diverse birdlife and wonderful scenery
- Femundsmarka National Park (p175) Forests and lakes with a taste of Sweden
- Jostedalsbreen (p244) Mainland Europe's largest icecap, a glorious world of glaciers
- Jotunheimen National Park (p184) Roof of Norway with trails winding among glaciers and snow-capped peaks
- Saltfjellet-Svartisen National Park (p296) Icefields, rugged peaks and rolling moor country
- Øvre Dividal National Park (p343) Roadless frontier country awash with lakes, forests and views

SIGHTS FOR CHILDREN

Many of Norway's sights (and its trolls!) seem to spring from a child's imagination and will appeal to kids as much as adults. But for some, kids take centre stage.

- Kristiansand Dyrepark (p142)
- Hunderfossen Familiepark (p168), near Lillehammer
- Atlantic Ocean Park (p263), Ålesund
- Musk-ox and elk safaris (p179)
- White-water rafting, Sjoa (see the boxed text, p182)
- The myths of Seljord (see the boxed text, p158)
- Dog-sledding (p389) and visiting a Sami camp (p173), Røros
- Children's Art Museum (p107), Oslo
- Children's Museum (p225), Stavanger
- Midnight Sun (p66)

other greenhouse gases, such as water vapour), but at high altitude these have a greater effect on climate change.

Most forms of transport emit carbon dioxide to some degree so the idea of offsetting schemes is to enable you to calculate your emissions so that you can invest in renewable energy schemes and reforestation projects that will reduce the emission by an equivalent amount of carbon dioxide. Some schemes focus just on emissions caused by flights, while others also help you work out emissions from specific train, car and ferry journeys. One place to try is **Climate Care** (in the UK ☎ 01865-207000; www.climatecare.org). For more information on climate change and travel, see the boxed text, p404.

Remember, however, that paying to offset your emissions is nowhere as effective as choosing to travel in a way that minimises your emissions in the first place.

Responsible Travel Schemes

Arctic Menu (www.arktiskmeny.no) A commitment among around 40, often family-run restaurants to using local, natural ingredients; see p293.
Den Norske Turistforening (DNT; www.turistforeningen.no) The Norwegian Mountain Touring Club encourages ecofriendly exploration of Norwegian wilderness areas.
Miljøfyrtårn (www.eco-lighthouse.com) Environmental certification for small- and medium-sized companies, although you'll need to contact them to find out which businesses qualify.
Miljømerking (www.ecolabel.no) An accreditation system for environmentally sound practices set up by the Nordic Council of Ministers; the Norway page has 23 (mostly top-end) hotels that meet the strict standards. Look for the Swan label at participating hotels and businesses.
National Geographic Centre for Sustainable Destinations (www.nationalgeographic.com/travel/sustainable/index.html) Follow the links to 'Programs for Places' where there are details on Norway's participation in the Geotourism programme.
Save Our Snow (www.saveoursnow.com) Use the searchable directory to find out what, if anything, ski resorts are doing to green up their act.
Vossafjell (www.vossafjell.com) Geotourism-based activities and presentations in western Norway.
World-Wide Opportunities on Organic Farms (www.wwoof.it) Learn about biodynamic and organic living in return for a few hours' work.

Events Calendar

The Norwegian year overflows with festivals. We've listed the major ones that draw international or Norway-wide audiences, but dozens of local festivals are covered in the regional chapters.

JANUARY–FEBRUARY

RØROSMARTNAN 2nd-last week of Feb

Norway's largest winter festival dates to 1644 and runs Tuesday to Saturday; it continues today in Røros (p173) with cultural programmes, street markets and live entertainment.

MARCH–APRIL

SAMI EASTER FESTIVAL

Easter among the indigenous Sami people in Kautokeino (p367) sees celebrations to mark the end of the polar night with reindeer racing, the Sami Grand Prix and other traditional events.

VINTERFESTUKA Mar

All through its long winter, Narvik (p300) looks forward to this week-long festival of cultural events with music, local food and people scanning the horizon for the sun.

HOLMENKOLLEN SKI FESTIVAL mid-Mar

Draws Nordic skiers and ski jumpers from around the world with skiing events and cultural programmes just outside Oslo (p108).

MAY

CONSTITUTION DAY 17 May

Celebrated with special fervour in Oslo (p108) where locals descend on the Royal Palace dressed in the finery of their native districts.

NIGHT JAZZ FESTIVAL (NATTJAZZ) late May

This fine Bergen (p202) festival is one of the happiest as the city's large student population gets into the swing.

BERGEN INTERNATIONAL FESTIVAL late-May–Jun

One of the biggest events on Norway's cultural calendar, this two-week Bergen (p202) festival showcases dance, music and folklore presentations.

JUNE–JULY

VIKING FESTIVAL early Jun

Karmøy Island (p221) returns to Norway's historical roots with Viking feasts, processions and saga evenings.

MIDDLE AGES FESTIVAL Jun

Locals in period costume and Gregorian chants in the glass cathedral of Hamar (p169) are the highlights of this popular local festival.

MIDNIGHT SUN MARATHON Jun

A midnight marathon could only happen in Norway and Tromsø (p337) is the place to try the world's northernmost 42km road race. In January the city also runs the Polar Night Half Marathon.

MOLDE JAZZ mid-Jun

With 100,000 spectators, world-class performers and a reputation for consistently high-quality music, this jazz festival in Molde (p268) is one of Norway's most popular.

EXTREME SPORT WEEK late Jun

Adventure junkies from across the world converge on Voss (p212) for a week of skydiving, paragliding, parasailing and base jumping; local and international music acts keeping the energy flowing.

KONGSBERG JAZZ FESTIVAL late Jun–early Jul

Kongsberg's (p151) jazz festival, which is Norway's second-largest, lasts four days and pulls in some of the biggest international names. As it follows the Molde Jazz festival, this is a great season for jazz lovers.

FJELLFESTIVALEN early Jul

Åndalsnes (p257) hosts what could be northern Europe's largest gathering of mountaineers and rock-climbers, swapping stories and inching their way up the sheer cliffs.

ST OLAV FESTIVAL late Jul

This nationwide commemoration of Norway's favourite saint is celebrated with special gusto in Trondheim (p282) with processions, medieval markets, Viking dress-ups, concerts and, in Stiklestad (p287), a prestigious four-day pageant.

HOLIDAYS

- New Year's Day (Nyttårsdag) 1 January
- Maundy Thursday (Skjærtorsdag) March/April
- Good Friday (Langfredag) March/April
- Easter Monday (Annen Påskedag) March/April
- Labour Day (Første Mai, Arbeidetsdag) 1 May
- Constitution Day (Nasjonaldag) 17 May
- Ascension Day (Kristi Himmelfartsdag) May/June, 40th day after Easter
- Whit Monday (Annen Pinsedag) May/June, 8th Monday after Easter
- Christmas Day (Første Juledag) 25 December
- Boxing Day (Annen Juledag) 26 December

AUGUST

RAUMA ROCK early Aug

Central Norway's largest pop gathering is held in Åndalsnes (p257) over two days, with everything from indie to hard rock.

NOTODDEN BLUES FESTIVAL early Aug

Nondescript Notodden (p152) comes alive with an outstanding blues festival.

INTERNATIONAL CHAMBER MUSIC FESTIVAL early Aug

Stavanger (p225) is the venue for this stately festival; some concerts take place in Stavanger Cathedral.

NORDLANDS MUSIC FESTIVAL early–mid-Aug

Bodø (p308) celebrates 10 days of music from symphony orchestras to jazz trios, folk groups and rock bands.

OSLO INTERNATIONAL JAZZ Aug

A worthy member of Norway's coterie of terrific jazz festivals, this one takes over Oslo (p108) for six days of live music.

VOSS BLUES & ROOTS FESTIVAL late Aug

If you're around the western fjords in August, head for Voss (p212) and one of Norway's better music festivals.

SEPTEMBER

DYRSKU'N FESTIVAL 2nd weekend Sep

Seljord's (p158) premier annual festival centres on Norway's largest traditional market and cattle show; it attracts 60,000 visitors annually.

LILLEHAMMER JAZZ FESTIVAL mid-Sep

This former Olympic city farewells the summer with the last major jazz festival of the Norwegian year; like any ski town, Lillehammer (p163) rocks (so to speak) during festival time.

OCTOBER–DECEMBER

BERGEN INTERNATIONAL FILM FESTIVAL mid–late Oct

Arguably Norway's most important film festival, Bergen (p202) becomes a film-lover's paradise with subtitled movies in cinemas across the city.

UKA Oct-Nov

Norway's largest cultural festival means three weeks of concerts, plays and general celebration led by Trondheim's (p282) 25,000-strong student population.

Itineraries

CLASSIC ROUTES

NORWAY IN MICROCOSM

Two Weeks

After a couple of days exploring the many galleries and museums of **Oslo** (p93), take the scenic Oslo-Bergen railway, billed as one of the most spectacular rail journeys on earth. From Oslo, the line climbs gently through forests, plateaus and ski centres to the beautifully desolate and vast **Hardangervidda Plateau** (p188). At Myrdal, take the Flåmsbana railway down to **Flåm** (p234), from where fjord cruises head up the incomparable **Nærøyfjord** (p237), which can also serve as a gateway to the larger fjord network of **Sognefjord** (p234). Travel via Gudvangen to nearby **Voss** (p209), where thrill seekers love the easily accessible activities on offer.

Voss serves as a gateway to the splendid scenery of **Hardangerfjord** (p214), where **Ulvik** (p215) and **Eidfjord** (p216) stand out among Norway's most worthwhile fjord-side towns. Away to the south, **Stavanger** (p222) is one of Norway's most appealing cities and a base for trips to **Lysefjord** (p229), including the walk up to the dramatic Preikestolen (Pulpit Rock). Swinging back to the north, perhaps detouring via **Rosendal** (p220) and charming little **Utne** (p219), takes you to beautiful **Bergen** (p192) with its stunning timbered houses and cosmopolitan air.

Oslo to Bergen can be done in two days as part of the 'Norway in a Nutshell' tour. But a week is advisable as you travel through fabulous countryside by train, ferry and bus. Stavanger, Lysefjord and Hardangerfjord add another week to the journey before returning to Oslo, a trip that covers around 1700km.

THE HEART OF NORWAY

10 Days to Two Weeks

The dramatic high country of Central Norway is quite simply spectacular and, provided you're willing to rent a car for part of the time, it offers some unparalleled opportunities to explore the region's quiet back roads; serious cyclists could also follow many of the same routes for a slower, but spectacular, journey. A short train or bus ride from **Oslo** (p88), **Lillehammer** (p163) hosted the 1994 Winter Olympics and it remains one of central Norway's most pleasing spots with a wealth of Olympic sites. Continuing north, **Ringebu** (p182) has one of Norway's prettiest stave churches, but having a car enables you to take the quiet Rv27, which draws near to the precipitous massifs of the **Rondane National Park** (p180), before continuing northwest to Unesco World Heritage–listed **Røros** (p171), one of Norway's most enchanting villages with painted timber houses and old-world charm. From Røros, it's an easy detour north to **Trondheim** (p275), a delightful coastal capital.

Turning to the south, head past **Oppdal** (p175) and **Dombås** (p177), both gateways to the **Dovrefjell-Sunndalsfjella National Park** (p178), which is a base for musk-ox safaris in summer. From Dombås, consider a side-trip by train or down the E136, which leads through the heart of **Romsdalen** (p178) with its sheer rock walls. Returning to the main road south, head to **Otta** (p179), where the E15 branches west to **Lom** (p182), the starting point for the **Sognefjellet Road** (p184), which leads through the extraordinarily beautiful **Jotunheimen National Park** (p184). From Turtagrø, head up a scenic road to **Øvre Ardal** (p186), then twist your way across to **Jotunheimvegen** (p186) and then the wonderfully quiet **Peer Gynt Vegen** (see the boxed text, p168) and then back down to Lillehammer.

You could accomplish this 1600km journey in 10 days, but two weeks would enable you to linger a little longer. This would be especially worthwhile in Røros and Trondheim. Although buses and trains run along the main north–south routes, you'll need a car to explore the quiet back roads.

TAILORED TRIPS

UNESCO WORLD HERITAGE–LISTED NORWAY

The drafters of Unesco's World Heritage list must have been tempted simply to list the whole country! As it is, they have chosen six sites that, if you visit them all, will see you travelling through large swathes of northern and western Norway.

Norway's first listing happened back in 1979, when Bryggen, comprised of 58 of the wonderful old trading warehouses beside the harbour of **Bergen** (p195), was added to the list. Difficult as it is to believe now, Unesco's recognition of Bryggen's priceless cultural and architectural heritage came when it was by no means certain that it would be saved from demolition – see the boxed text, p198.

While Bryggen is the most accessible, and hence most popular, of Norway's Unesco-listed sights, it is followed closely by the western fjords of **Geirangerfjord** (p259) and **Nærøyfjord** (p237). These two fjords always rank highly on many travellers' list of favourite fjords (including ours) and chances are that you've seen photos of these exceptional fjords long before you arrive as they're among Norway's most archetypal images.

The same can be said for the **Urnes Stave Church** (p243), set deep in the heart of the western fjords. Dating from the 12th century, this is one of the oldest stave churches in Norway, not to mention one of the most beautiful, with its setting alongside Lusterfjord and the flourishes and flights of architectural fancy for which stave churches are renowned.

Norwegian villages don't come much more picturesque than the former mining settlement of **Røros** (p171), west across the towering peaks of the Norwegian interior from the fjords. Colourfully painted timber-clad houses climb up the Røros hillside like an evocation of all that is quaint about rural Norwegian architecture. Unlike so many other Norwegian villages, Røros retains its 15th-century ambience, albeit with an artsy vibe and a gritty charm bequeathed by centuries of mining operations, the remnants of which remain as some of the most intriguing attractions.

The north's contribution to the Unesco list begins at **Vesterålen** (p324), otherwise known as the Vega Archipelago. This rarely visited cluster of islands just below the Arctic Circle made the list primarily for the cultural heritage of its fishing communities. Here you'll find the all-too-rare sense (for Norway) of a place time forgot and yet to be discovered by mass tourism, which carries significant appeal.

Far, far away to the north, it's a long, but astonishingly beautiful haul up to **Alta** (p344), home to an astonishing collection of thousands of rock paintings and carvings. The fusion of artistic sophistication and a childlike vision of the world adds up to a fascinating history lesson on the lives of the ancients. With the oldest paintings dating back to 4200 BC, the open-air gallery takes in every aspect of late Stone Age life, from hunting scenes and fertility symbols to reindeer and crowded boats.

THE ARCTIC NORTH

The mystique of the extreme north has drawn explorers for centuries. Here is a horizonless world seemingly without end – a frozen wilderness that inspires the awe reserved for the great empty places of our earth. Welcome to Norway's Arctic north, as much a territory of the mind and a land of the spirit as a place of rare and stark physical beauty.

There are many routes from the south into this wonderful land, from the seagoing **Hurtigruten coastal ferry** (p412) to the beautiful routes of the inland **Arctic Highway** (p291) or the coastal **Kystriksveien** (p303). Whichever route you take, a detour to the **Lofoten Islands** (p310) offers a taste of the splendour of what awaits you north of the Arctic Circle.

Less trodden by tourists are the trails that lead to the **Vesterålen** (p324) archipelago, home to landscapes even more untamed than those of Lofoten, while the artists' colony at Nyksund and the whale-watching opportunities off Stø provide some focus for your exploration.

If the solitude of island life has you craving company, **Tromsø** (p334) is the perfect antidote. Arguably Norway's liveliest large town, Tromsø is a university town *par excellence* and its Polar Museum captures the spirit of Arctic exploration while the surrounding peaks host a wealth of summer and winter activities. Tromsø is also an ideal base for excursions offshore to pretty **Karlsøy** (p341) or inland to the **Lyngen Alps** (p341), which are rugged and supremely beautiful with many glaciers and craggy summits. You could visit **Senja** (p342) for a day, but it's far better to stay overnight to truly embrace the quiet of northern Norwegian nights.

The Arctic sense of a world without limit is easy to understand in the forests and lakes of **Øvre Dividal National Park** (p343), while the rock carvings of **Alta** (p344) should also not be missed.

As far north as you can go in Norway without setting out to sea, **Nordkapp** (p350) is high on novelty value, if somewhat overwhelmed by visitors, while further west the **Nordkyn Peninsula** (p355) has much to explore and nearby **Tana Bru** (p356) is one of the best places in the world to go salmon fishing.

But Arctic Norway is so much more than landscapes and activities and to understand why, head to Inner Finnmark, the heartland of the Sami people. **Kautokeino** (p365) is a long-standing centre of Sami culture, and its cultural centre and museum are ideal places to provide cultural context to your visit. Hiking in the **Reisa National Park** (p367) is a possibility, but only for the seriously fit, while **Karasjok** (p367) is the undisputed capital of Sami Norway, filled with fascinating sites of Sami patrimony.

Finally, it may be a challenge and expensive to visit, but there's nowhere in Norway quite like **Svalbard** (p370) for its end-of-the-earth feel. This old whaling centre supports a rich array of Arctic wildlife, including reindeer, polar bears and a few brave whales, not to mention epic glaciers, icebergs and icefields, but perhaps its greatest reward for those who get here is Magdalenefjord, where turquoise seas meet the polar north.

History

Norway may have become the epitome of a modern, peaceful country, but its history is soaked in blood. How one led to the other is one of world history's great epics. It is a story peopled with picaresque characters and always revolving around recurring grand themes – a battle against the hostile elements, the advanced and adventurous spirit of the Vikings, the undercurrent of Christianity and the perennial struggle to be taken seriously as a sovereign, independent country.

DARKNESS & ICE

Some of the most lasting impressions travellers carry with them after visiting Norway – a land of snow and ice, a bountiful coast, extreme climatic conditions and a thinly populated land – have been present here since the dawn of Scandinavian civilisation. Indeed, the human presence in Norway was for thousands of years overshadowed by Norway's geography and climate, which have strong claims to being the most enduring personalities of Norwegian history.

During the last ice age, Norway was barely inhabitable. If Norway was less than hospitable, it was a paradise compared to northern Russia at the time and, as the ice began to melt, it was from the east that the first major, lasting migration to Norway took place when, around 11,000 years ago, the Komsa, who would later become the Sami (p42), arrived in Norway's Arctic north.

As the climate warmed and Norway became increasingly habitable, migrations of the Nøstvet-Økser people of central Europe began arriving along the southern Norwegian coast, drawn by relatively plentiful fishing, sealing and hunting. Wild reindeer also followed the retreating ice, moving north into the still-ice-bound interior, and the hunters that followed them were the first humans to traverse the Norwegian high country. Their presence was, however, restricted to itinerant, seasonal camps and there remained few human footholds in an otherwise empty land dominated by glaciers and frozen wastes.

Little is known about the nomadic, hunter-gatherer Nøstvet-Økser people who were most likely tall, blonde-haired, blue-eyed and spoke a Germanic language, the predecessor of modern Scandinavian languages.

Over the millennia that followed, settled cultures began to take root, to the extent that during the later years of the Roman Empire, Rome provided Norway with fabric, iron implements and pottery. The iron tools allowed farmland to be cleared of trees, larger boats were built with the aid of iron axes and a cooling climate saw the establishment of more permanent structures built from stone and turf. By the 5th century Norwegians had learned how to smelt their own iron from ore found in the southern Norwegian bogs. Norway's endless struggle to tame its wild landscape had begun.

TIMELINE

12,000 BC

The last ice age thaws and Norway takes on its present physical form with a new body of water separating the country from the rest of northern Europe.

9000 BC

The hunting culture of the Komsa, the forerunner of the Sami, arrives in northern Scandinavia and establishes the first permanent settlements in Norway's Arctic north, where they remain to this day.

2500 BC

The wonderfully named Battle-Axe, Boat-Axe and Funnel-Beaker people, named after the stone tools they used, enter southern Norway from Sweden. They traded amber for metals, particularly bronze, from mainland Europe.

HERE COME THE VIKINGS

Few historical people have captured the imagination quite like the Vikings. Immortalised in modern cartoons (*Asterix* and *Hägar the Horrible* to name just a few) and considered the most feared predators of ancient Europe, the Vikings may have disappeared from history, but as a seafaring nation with its face turned towards distant lands, they remain very much the forerunners of modern Norway. But who were these ancient warriors who took to their longboats and dominated Europe for five centuries?

The word 'Viking' derives from *vik*, an Old Norse word that referred to a bay or cove, a reference to Vikings' anchorages during and after raids.

Conquest & Expansion

Under pressure from shrinking agricultural land caused by a growing population, settlers from Norway began arriving along the coast of the British Isles in the 780s. When the boats returned home to Norway with enticing trade goods and tales of poorly defended coastlines, the Vikings began laying plans to conquer the world. The first Viking raid took place on St Cuthbert's monastery on the island of Lindisfarne in 793. Soon the Vikings were spreading across Britain, Ireland and the rest of Europe with war on their minds and returning home with slaves *(thrall)* in their formidable, low Norse longboats.

Explore North (www.explorenorth.com/vikings.html) is the ultimate site for wannabe Vikings, with extensive links to Viking history and sagas, Norse gods, Norse mythology and a delicious smattering of conspiracy theories.

The Vikings attacked in great fleets, terrorising, murdering, enslaving, assimilating or displacing local populations. Coastal regions of Britain, Ireland, France (Normandy was named for these 'Northmen'), Russia (as far east as the river Volga), Moorish Spain (Seville was raided in 844), and the Middle East (they even reached Baghdad) all came under the Viking sway. Well-defended Constantinople (Istanbul) proved a bridge too far – the Vikings attacked six times but never took the city. Such rare setbacks notwithstanding, the Viking raids transformed Scandinavia from an obscure backwater on Europe's northern fringe to an all-powerful empire.

For all of their destruction elsewhere, Vikings belonged very much to the shores from which they set out or sheltered on their raids. Viking raids increased standards of living at home. Emigration freed up farmland and fostered the emergence of a new merchant class, while captured slaves provided farm labour. Norwegian farmers also crossed the Atlantic to settle the Faroes, Iceland and Greenland during the 9th and 10th centuries. The world, it seemed, belonged to the Vikings.

THE VIKING FOOTPRINT

Traces of the Viking presence in Norway can still be seen at Tønsberg (p129), Kaupang (Larvik; p132), Spangereid (see the boxed text, p146), Eidfjord (p216), Kinsarvik (p218), Haugesund (p220), Karmøy Island (p221), Balestrand (p240), Giske (p266) and Leka (p289). And two of the best Viking museums are the Viking Ship Museum (p102) in Oslo and the Lofotr Viking Museum (p318).

AD 787

The earliest account of Norse seafaring appears in the *Anglo Saxon Chronicle* for 787, describing how three ships came to Britain, piloted by sailors who were described as Northmen.

793

The dawn of the Viking age comes when Vikings plunder St Cuthbert's monastery on the island of Lindisfarne, off the coast of Northumberland in Britain.

872

Harald Hårfagre (Harald Fair-Hair) fights his fellow Viking chieftains in the Battle of Hafrsfjord and unites Norway for the first time. Some 20,000 people flee to Iceland.

Harald Fair-Hair

Harald Hårfagre (Harald Fair-Hair), son of Svarta-Hvaldan (Halvdan the Black), was more than the latest in a long line of great Viking names. While most Viking chieftains made their name in foreign conquest, Harald Fair-Hair was doing something that no other leader had managed before – he united the disparate warring tribes of the Viking nation.

Harald's greatest moment came in 872 at Hafrsfjord near Haugesund when he emerged victorious from one of world history's few civil wars to be decided at sea. When the dust settled, Norway had become a single country.

A History of the Vikings, by Gwyn Jones, has been critically acclaimed for its comprehensive details of the Viking era, with vivid accounts of Viking exploits.

The reign of Harald Hårfagre was such an odd and entertaining time that it was recorded for posterity in the *Heimskringla*, the Norwegian kings' saga, by Icelander Snorre Sturluson. According to Snorre, Harald's unification of Norway was inspired by a woman who taunted the king by refusing to have relations with a man whose kingdom wasn't even as large as tiny Denmark. Through a series of confederations and trade agreements, he extended his rule as far north as what is now Trøndelag. His foreign policies were equally canny, and he even sent one of his sons, Håkon, to be reared in the court of King Athelstan of England. There is no record of whether the woman in question was sufficiently impressed. Harald died of plague at Avaldsnes on Karmøy Island (p221) around 930.

According to some linguists, Viking gods gave their names to the days of the week in English – Tuesday (Tyr's Day), Wednesday (Odin's Day), Thursday (Thor's Day) and Friday (Freyr's Day).

The king who unified the country could do little about his own family, however. He married 10 wives and fathered a surfeit of heirs, thereby creating serious squabbles over succession. The one who rose above them all was Erik, his last child and only son with Ragnhild the Mighty, daughter of the Danish King Erik of Jutland. The ruthless Erik eliminated all of his legitimate brothers except Håkon (who was safe in England). Erik, whose reign was characterised by considerable ineptitude, then proceeded to squander his father's hard-won Norwegian confederation. When Håkon returned from England to sort out the mess as King Håkon den Gode (Håkon the Good), Erik was forced to flee to Britain where he took over the throne of York as King Erik Blood-Axe.

The Prose Edda: Nose Mythology, by Snorre Sturluson, is the ultimate source of Norse mythology through the sagas first penned in the 10th century.

Christianity & the Viking Decline

The Vikings gave Norwegians their love of the sea and it was during the late Viking period that they bequeathed to them another of their most enduring national traits – strong roots in Christianity – although this overturning of the Viking pantheon of gods did not come without a struggle.

King Håkon the Good, who had been baptised a Christian during his English upbringing, brought the new faith (as well as missionaries and a bishop) with him upon his return to Norway. Despite some early success, most Vikings remained loyal to Thor, Odin and Freyr. Although the missionaries were eventually able to replace the names of the gods with those of Catholic saints, the pagan practice of blood sacrifice continued una-

995

Olav II builds Norway's first Christian church at Mosterhamn on the island of Bømlo, in the Hardanger region, marking the spread of Christianity throughout western Norway.

997

Trondheim is founded at the mouth of the Nid River and, as the first major settlement in the country; it becomes the first capital of the fledgling kingdom.

c 1000

Almost five centuries before Columbus, Leifur Eiríksson, son of Eiríkur Rauðe (Eric the Red), explores the North American coast, which he names Vinland, meaning the 'land of wine'.

bated. When Håkon the Good was defeated and killed in 960, Norwegian Christianity all but disappeared.

Christianity in Norway was revived during the reign of King Olav Tryggvason (Olav I). Like any good Viking, Olav decided that only force would work to convert his countrymen to the 'truth'. Unfortunately for the king, his intended wife, Queen Sigrid of Sweden, refused to convert. Olav cancelled the marriage contract and Sigrid married the pagan king, Svein Forkbeard of Denmark. Together they orchestrated Olav's death in a great Baltic sea-battle, then took Norway as their own.

So ferocious were the Vikings that the word berserk comes from 'bare sark', which means 'bare shirt' and refers to the way that ancient, bare-chested Norsemen used to fight.

THE KEYS TO WORLD DOMINATION

Like so many successful empires that would follow them onto the world stage, the Vikings' success was built upon the twin pillars of tradition and innovation. For the Vikings this was manifested in a fanatical belief that the gods were on their side, and on a mastery of the seas that relied on technology centuries ahead of its time.

The main god that provided strength to the Viking cause was Odin (Oðinn), the 'All-Father' who was married to Frigg. Together they gave birth to a son, Thor (Þór), the God of Thunder. Why did this matter? Put simply, Vikings believed that if they died on the battlefield, the all-powerful Odin would take them to a paradise by the name of Valhalla where Viking men could fight all day and then be served by beautiful women.

Not surprisingly, it was considered far better for a Viking to die on the battlefield than in bed of old age and Vikings brought a reckless abandon to their battles that was extremely difficult for enemies to overcome – to die or to come away with loot, the Vikings seemed to say, was more or less the same. Equally unsurprising was the fact that the essential Viking values that emerged from their unique world-view embodied a disregard for death, strength, skill in weapons, heroic courage and personal sacrifice.

But the Vikings were as much the sophisticates of the ancient world as they were its fearless warriors. Viking ships were revolutionary, fast, manoeuvrable vessels capable of withstanding torrid and often long ocean journeys. Longboats were over 30m long, had a solid keel, flexible hull, large, square sails and could travel at up to 12 knots (24km/h); they enabled the Vikings to launch and maintain a conquest that would go largely unchallenged for 200 years.

Perhaps the most curious aspect of Viking voyages, however, was the navigational tool they employed to travel through uncharted territory. Norse sagas mention a mysterious device known as a *solarsteinn*, (sunstone), which allowed navigation even when the sky was overcast or the sun was below the horizon and celestial navigation was impossible.

It is now generally agreed that the *solarsteinn* was a crystal of cordierite, which is found around Scandinavia and has natural polarising qualities. When observed from below and rotated, light passing through the crystal is polarised blue when the long axis is pointed toward the source of the sunlight. Even today, jet planes flying over polar regions, where magnetic compasses are unsuitable, use a sky compass that determines the position of the sun by filtering sunlight through an artificial polarising lens.

1024

Olav II founds the Church of Norway and establishes it as Norway's state religion throughout his realm, a situation that continues right to this day.

1030

After being sent into exile by King Canute (Knut) of Denmark in 1028, King Olav II returns, only to be killed during a popular farmers' uprising in Trøndelag at the Battle of Stiklestad.

1049

Harald III (Harald Hardråda, or Harald 'Hard-Ruler'), half-brother of St Olav, founds Oslo (Christiania) and uses it as a base to launch far-ranging raids across the Mediterranean.

Heroes of The North: Stories From Norwegian Chronicle, by F Scarlett Potter, reads like a who's who of the ancient Norwegian world, with names such as Harald Fair-Hair and St Olav peppering the text.

Christianity was finally cemented in Norway by King Olav Haraldsson, Olav II, who was also converted in England. Olav II and his Viking hordes allied themselves with King Ethelred and managed to save London from a Danish attack under King Svein Forkbeard by destroying London Bridge (from whence we derive the song '*London Bridge is Falling Down*'). Succeeding where his namesake had failed, Olav II spread Christianity with considerable success. In 1023 Olav built a stone cross in Voss (p210), where it still stands, and in 1024 he founded the Church of Norway. After an invasion by King Canute (Knut) of Denmark in 1028, Olav II died during the Battle of Stiklestad in 1030. For Christians, this amounted to martyrdom and the king was canonised as a saint; the great Nidaros Cathedral (p276) in Trondheim stands as a memorial to St Olav and, until the Protestant Reformation, the cathedral served as a destination for pilgrims from all over Europe (see the boxed text, p280). His most lasting legacy, however, was having forged a lasting identity for Norway as an independent kingdom.

Of the kings who followed, none distinguished themselves quite as infamously as Harald III (Harald Hardråda, or Harald 'Hard-Ruler'), half-brother of St Olav. Harald III raided throughout the Mediterranean, but it was a last hurrah for the Vikings. When he was killed during an ill-conceived raid in England in 1066, the Viking air of invincibility was broken. Snorre Sturluson's *King Harald's Saga* loosely follows the events of Harald's life.

Den Kongelige Norske Sankt Olavs Orden (www.saintolav.com) has everything you ever wanted to know (and many things you didn't) about St Olav; the 'History of Norway' section is good for understanding the history of the Norwegian monarchy.

NO LONGER INDEPENDENT

The Vikings may have been fast disappearing into history, but Viking expansionism, along with the coming of Christianity, planted the seeds – of success, of decline – for what was to come. As Norway's sphere of international influence shrank, Norway's neighbours began to close in, leaving this one-time world power having to fight for its independence.

Trouble Abroad, Trouble at Home

In 1107 Sigurd I led an expedition of 60 ships to the Holy Land. Three years later, he captured Sidon, in modern-day Lebanon. But by this stage foreign conquest had become a smokescreen for serious internal problems. Sigurd died in 1130 and the rest of the century was fraught with brutal civil wars over succession to the throne. The victorious King Sverre, a churchman-turned-warrior, paved the way for Norway's so-called 'Golden Age', which saw Bergen claim the title of national capital, driven by Norway's perennial ties to foreign lands and, in particular, trade between coastal towns and the German-based Hanseatic League (see p192). Perhaps drawn by Norway's economic boom, Greenland and Iceland voluntarily joined the Kingdom of Norway in 1261 and 1262, respectively.

But Norway's role as a world power was on the wane and Norway was turning inward. Håkon V built brick and stone forts, one at Vardø to

1066

The Viking age draws to a close after Harald III dies at the hands of King Harold of England at the Battle of Stamford Bridge during an unsuccessful incursion into England in 1066.

1261

Greenland joins the Kingdom of Norway, followed a year later by Iceland, reflecting Norway's growing influence over the affairs of Europe's far north.

1319

Magnus, the successor to Norway's Håkon V, becomes King of Sweden and unites Sweden and Norway. This ends Norwegian independence and the royal line of Harald Fair-Hair and begins two centuries of decline.

protect the north from the Russians, and another at Akershus, in 1308, to defend Oslo harbour. The transfer of the national capital from Bergen to Christiania (to become Oslo) soon followed. When Håkon V's grandson Magnus united Norway with Sweden in 1319, Norway began a decline that would last for 200 years. Once-great Norway had become just another province of its neighbours.

In August 1349 the Black Death arrived in Norway on board an English ship via Bergen. The bubonic plague would eventually kill one-third of Europe's population. In Norway, land fell out of cultivation, towns were ruined, trading activities faltered and the national coffers decreased by 65%. In Norway, as much as 80% of the nobility perished. Because their peasant workforce had also been decimated, the survivors were forced to return to the land, forever changing the Norwegian power-base and planting the seeds for an egalitarianism that continues to define Norway to this day.

By 1387 Norway had lost control of Iceland and 10 years later, Queen Margaret of Denmark formed the Kalmar Union of Sweden, Denmark and Norway, with Eric of Pomerania as king. Margaret's neglect of Norway continued into the 15th century, when trade links with Iceland were broken and the Greenland colonies mysteriously disappeared without trace.

In 1469 Orkney and Shetland were pawned – supposedly a temporary measure – to the Scottish Crown by the Danish-Norwegian King Christian I, who had to raise money for his daughter's dowry. Just three years later the Scots annexed both island groups.

Buffeted by these winds of change Norway had become a shadow of its former self. The only apparent constant was the country's staunch Christian faith. But even in the country's faith there were fundamental changes afoot. In 1537, the Reformation replaced the incumbent Catholic faith with Lutheran Protestantism and the transformation of the Norway of the Vikings was all but complete.

The History of Norway – From the Ice Age to Today, by Øvind Stenersen and Ivar Libæk, provides more than enough historical detail for most travellers and is available at larger bookshops in Norway.

The mystery behind the disappearance of the Greenland colonies is examined in Jared Diamond's *Collapse*.

Sweden and Visions of Norway: Politics and Culture 1814–1905, by H Arnold Barton, offers a detailed analysis of the enmity and uneasy neighbourliness between Norway and Sweden in the pivotal 19th century.

Denmark & Sweden – The Enemy

Talk to many Norwegians and you're likely to find that there's no love lost between them and their neighbours, Denmark and Sweden. Here's why.

A series of disputes between the Danish Union and the Swedish crown were played out on Norwegian soil. First came the Seven Years War (1563–70), followed by the Kalmar War (1611–14). Trondheim, for example, was repeatedly captured and recaptured by both sides and during the Kalmar War an invasion of Norway was mounted from Scotland (see the boxed text, p180).

In two further wars during the mid-17th century Norway lost a good portion of its territory to Sweden. The Great Nordic War with the expanding Swedish Empire was fought in the early 18th century and in 1716 the Swedes occupied Christiania (Oslo). The Swedes were finally defeated in 1720, ending over 150 years of warfare.

1369

Bubonic plague (the Black Death) arrives in Bergen and quickly spreads throughout the country, forever altering Norway's social fabric.

1469

The Orkney and Shetland islands, along with the Isle of Man, are sold to the Scots, bringing to an end centuries of Norwegian expansion.

1537

The Reformation that sweeps across Europe and causes the separation between the Catholic and Protestant churches reaches Norway, whereafter the incumbent Catholic faith is replaced with Lutheran Protestantism.

Despite attempts to re-establish trade with Greenland through the formation of Norwegian trading companies in Bergen in 1720, Danish trade restrictions scuppered the nascent economic independence. As a consequence, Norway was ill-equipped to weather the so-called 'Little Ice Age', from 1738 to 1742. The failure of crops ensured a period of famine and the death of one-third of Norwegian cattle, not to mention thousands of people.

During the Napoleonic Wars, Britain blockaded Norway, causing the Danes to surrender on 14 January 1814. The subsequent Treaty of Kiel presented Norway to Sweden in a 'Union of the Crowns'. Tired of having their territory divided up by foreign kings, a contingent of farmers, businesspeople and politicians gathered at Eidsvoll Verk in April 1814 to draft a new constitution and elect a new Norwegian king. Sweden forced the new king, Christian Frederik, to yield and accept the Swedish choice of monarch, Karl Johan. War was averted by a compromise that provided for devolved Swedish power. Norway's constitution hadn't lasted long, but it did suggest that Norwegians had had enough.

INDEPENDENT NORWAY

Norway may have spent much of the previous centuries as a subservient vassal to foreign occupiers and its days as a world power had long ago ended, but not all was doom and gloom. It took almost a century after their first constitution, not to mention nine centuries after Harald Fair-Hair first unified the country, but Norwegians were determined to once and for all become masters of their own destiny.

Henrik Ibsen and the Birth of Modernism: Art, Theater, Philosophy, by Toril Moi, is ideal for those looking for the Norwegian context of Norway's favourite playwright and the times in which he lived.

A Confident Start

During the 19th century, perhaps buoyed by the spirit of the 1814 constitution, Norwegians began to rediscover a sense of their own, independent cultural identity. This nascent cultural revival was most evident in a flowering of musical and artistic expression led by poet and playwright Henrik Ibsen (p50), composer Edvard Grieg (p50) and artist Edvard Munch (p51). Language also began to play its part with the development of a unique Norwegian dialect known as *landsmål* (or *Nynorsk*). Norway's first railway, from Oslo to Eidsvoll, was completed in 1854 and Norway began looking at increased international trade, particularly tied to its burgeoning fishing and whaling industries in the Arctic north.

Norway was still extremely poor – between 1825 and 1925, over 750,000 Norwegians re-settled in the USA and Canada – but the wave of national identity would not be stopped.

In 1905 a constitutional referendum was held. As expected, virtually no-one in Norway favoured continued union with Sweden. The Swedish king, Oskar II, was forced to recognise Norwegian sovereignty, abdicate and re-instate a Norwegian constitutional monarchy, with Haakon VII on the

1720

After almost 150 years of conflict on Norwegian soil (the Seven Years' War, the Kalmar War and the Great Nordic War) Sweden is finally defeated, although Danish and Swedish influence over Norway's affairs remains strong.

1814

After Denmark's defeat in the Napoleonic Wars, Norway is presented to Sweden in the so-called 'Union of the Crowns'. Disgruntled Norwegians draft their first constitution, an event still celebrated as Norway's first act of independence.

1905

Norwegians voted overwhelmingly for independence and against union with Sweden. Norway becomes independent with its own constitutional monarchy presided over by King Haakon VII. This royal line continues to occupy the Norwegian throne.

throne. His descendants rule Norway to this day with decisions on succession remaining under the authority of the *storting* (parliament). Oslo was declared the national capital of the Kingdom of Norway.

Newly independent Norway quickly set about showing the world that it was a worthy international citizen. In 1911 the Norwegian explorer Roald Amundsen reached the South Pole. Two years later Norwegian women became among the first in Europe to be given the vote. Hydroelectric projects sprang up all around the country and prosperous new industries emerged to drive the increasingly healthy export economy.

Having emerged from WWI largely unscathed – Norway was neutral, although some Norwegian merchant vessels were sunk by the Germans – Norway grew in confidence. In 1920 the *storting* voted to join the newly formed League of Nations, a move that was opposed only by the Communist-inspired Labour Party, an increasingly militant and revolutionary party that dominated the *storting* by 1927. The 1920s also brought new innovations, including the development of factory ships, which allowed processing of whales at sea and caused an increase in whaling activities, especially around Svalbard and in the Antarctic; for more information on whaling, see p76.

Trouble, however, lay just around the corner. The Great Depression of the late 1920s and beyond almost brought Norway to its knees. By December 1932 there was 42% unemployment and farmers were hit especially hard by the economic downturn.

The first Allied victory of WWII occurred in late May 1940 in Norway, when a British naval force re-took Narvik and won control over this strategic iron ore port. It fell again to the Germans on 9 June.

Norway at War

Norway had chosen a bad time to begin asserting its independence. The clouds of war were gathering in Europe and although Norway had been spared the ravages of WWI, it could not escape for long.

By the early 1930s Fascism had begun to spread throughout Europe. Unlike during WWI, Norway found itself swept up in the violent convulsions sweeping Europe. In 1933 the former Norwegian defence minister Vidkun Quisling formed a Norwegian fascist party, the *Nasjonal Samling.* The Germans invaded Norway on 9 April 1940, prompting King Håkon and the royal family to flee into exile (see the boxed text, p170), while British, French, Polish and Norwegian forces fought a desperate rearguard action. For further insights into the Norwegian resistance to the Nazi occupation, see the boxed text, p100.

Six southern towns were burnt out and despite some Allied gains the British, who were out on a limb, abandoned Arctic Norway to its fate. In Oslo, the Germans established a puppet government under Vidkun Quisling, whose name thereafter entered the lexicon as a byword for those collaborators who betray their country.

Having spent centuries fighting for a country to call their own, the Norwegians didn't take lightly to German occupation. In particular, the Norwegian resistance network distinguished itself in sabotaging German

War and Innocence: A Young Girl's Life in Occupied Norway, by Hanna Aasvik Helmersen, is an open-eyed account of Norway during WWII as seen through the eyes of an eight-year-old girl.

1911

Norwegian explorer Roald Amundsen becomes the first person to reach the South Pole, highlighting a period of famous Norwegian explorers going to the ends of the earth.

1920

Norwegian territory is extended for the first time in centuries with the signing of the Svalbard Treaty. In the same year Norway's *storting* (parliament) votes to join the newly formed League of Nations.

1940

On 9 April Nazi Germany invades Norway, greeted by the fascist Defence Minister Vidkun Quisling. King Håkon and the royal family flee into exile, first to the UK and then Washington, DC, where they remained throughout the war.

designs, often through the assistance of daring Shetland fishermen who smuggled arms across the sea to western Norway. Among the most memorable acts of defiance was the famous commando assault of February 1943 on the heavy water plant at Vemork, which was involved in the German development of an atomic bomb (see the boxed text, p153).

For its size, Norway plays a disproportionately important role in international conflict resolution (pushing UN treaties to ban land mines, for example) and it has become an effective mediator in the Middle East and Sri Lanka.

The Germans exacted bitter revenge on the local populace and among the civilian casualties were 630 Norwegian Jews who were sent to central European concentration camps. Serbian and Russian prisoners of war were coerced into slave labour on construction projects in Norway, and many perished from the cold and an inadequate diet. The high number of worker fatalities during the construction of the Arctic Highway through the Saltfjellet inspired its nickname, the *blodveien* (blood road).

Finnmark suffered particularly heavy destruction and casualties during the war. In Altafjorden and elsewhere, the Germans constructed submarine bases, which were used to attack convoys headed for Murmansk and Arkhangelsk in Russia, so as to disrupt the supply of armaments to the Russians.

In early 1945, with the Germans facing an escalating two-front war and seeking to delay the Russian advance into Finnmark, the German forces adopted a scorched-earth policy and devastated northern Norway, burning fields, forests, towns and villages. Shortly after the German surrender of Norway, Quisling was executed by firing squad and other collaborators were sent off to prison.

The Oil Years

Although there were initial fears in the post-war years that Norway would join the Eastern Bloc of Communist countries under the Soviet orbit – the Communist party made strong gains in post-war elections and even took part in coalition governments – the Iron Curtain remained firmly in place at the Russian border. More than that, Norway made a clear statement of intent in 1946 when it became a founding member of the UN. Ever conscious of its proximity to Russia, the country also abandoned its neutrality by joining NATO in 1949. Letting bygones be bygones, Norway joined with other Scandinavian countries to form the Nordic Council in 1952.

Norway: Elites on Trial, by Knut Heidar, may be a bit dry and academic but it remains one of the finest and most detailed descriptions of modern Norway, with an emphasis on its evolving relationship with the EU.

There was just one problem: Norway was broke and in desperate need of money for reconstruction, particularly in the Arctic north. At first, it appeared that the increasingly prosperous merchant navy and whaling fleet would provide a partial solution. Norway struggled through (post-war rationing continued until 1952) as best it could.

That would soon change in the most dramatic way possible. Oil was discovered in the North Sea in the late 1960s and the economy boomed, transforming Norway from one of Europe's poorest countries to one of its richest; for more information on Norway's oil bounty, see the boxed text, p41.

Since oil transformed the Norwegian economy, successive socialist governments (and short-lived conservative ones) have used the windfalls (alongside

1945

On 7 May the last foreign troops on Norwegian soil, the Russians, withdraw from Arctic Norway, leaving Norwegians to pick up the pieces after the devastation wrought across the country by the retreating German army.

1946

Norway becomes a founding member of the UN. This membership would later provide a platform for Norwegian foreign policy with Norway an important mediator in numerous international conflicts, including the Middle East and Sri Lanka.

1949

Norway joins NATO and aligns itself with the USA despite fears in the West that left-leaning Norway would turn towards the Soviet Union.

WHERE IS NORWAY NOW?

Stable, comfortably wealthy and a respected international citizen, Norway nonetheless stands at an important crossroads in its history. For one thing, Norway continues to agonise over whether it should join the European Union (EU) and, casting an eye over Norwegian history, it's not difficult to understand why Norwegians remain wary of forming unions of any kind with other countries. Having narrowly voted against membership in 1972 and again in 1994 despite Norwegian governments pressing for a 'yes' vote, Norway remains on the outside looking in. As a result, Norwegians neither receive the benefits of membership (government estimates suggest that Norway loses US$180 million a year by not joining), nor are they fulfilling their responsibilities. You'll meet Norwegians who bristle with indignation at the mere thought that directives on daily life should be made from Brussels (or anywhere else for that matter), even as many – particularly urban-dwellers and southerners – recognise that Norway cannot remain forever isolated. Recent polls suggest that a slim majority of Norwegians supports joining.

Immigration (see p45) is another issue that dominates Norwegian political debates. Norway has been transformed from a nation of emigrants to one where 8.9% of Norway's people were born overseas. The uneasiness that this demographic transformation has brought threatens to revolutionise Norway's political landscape. Although the Labour Party remains in power as it has for much of Norway's independent history, albeit in a red-green alliance with the Socialist Left and Centre Party since 2005, there are signs that the political baseline is shifting right. In the 2005 elections, the (Progress Party) Fremskrittspartiet won 22% of the vote after advocating a crackdown on immigration and opposing EU membership. As a result, many Norwegians worry that other elements of Norway's famed tolerance and egalitarianism may be under threat. There are also fears that if Norway is to remain competitive in the international economy, the famously relaxed lifestyle of Norwegians may need to change; one recent study showed that Norwegians on average work less than 160 days per year.

And then there's oil, the black gold that made modern Norway possible. With a rapidly rising oil fund for future generations soaring beyond US$300 billion (see the boxed text, p41), and with abundant reserves of natural gas, Norway has fewer reasons than most oil producers to worry about the days when the oil runs out. Even so, Norwegians, as they will freely tell you, feel decidedly guilty about their wealth and worry that their laudable attempts to be model environmental citizens will be forever undermined by exporting so much oil. Some of that guilt is assuaged by the fact that Norway is also one of the largest per capita donors of foreign aid, but all the uncertainty over Norway's place in the world is frequently enough to cast a shadow over the normally sunny dispositions of Norwegians. Perhaps the concerns stem from the fact that for the first time since Viking days, Norway is confronting such issues from a position of considerable strength and independence.

high income taxes and service fees) to foster one of the most extensive social welfare systems in history, with free medical care and higher education, as well as generous pension and unemployment benefits. It adds up to what the government claims is the 'most egalitarian social democracy in Western Europe'.

Late 1960s

Oil is discovered, transforming Norway from the poor man of northern Europe into one of the richest countries in the world. Oil revenues have provided the basis for an all-encompassing system of social welfare and generous foreign aid.

1994

Norwegians vote against joining the European Union (EU). The 'no' vote (52%) draws on the concerns of traditional family farms, fishing interests and the perceived loss of national sovereignty that membership would supposedly bring.

2005

A 'red-green' coalition wins parliamentary elections, overturning a conservative-led coalition government that had won power in 2001.

The Culture

THE NATIONAL PSYCHE

Norwegians are at once fiercely independent and keen to engage with the world and this can lead to contradictions. For example, you may come across staunch environmentalists who take pride in their government's controversial stance on commercial whaling, seeing threats not to the animals but to a traditional Norwegian industry and Norwegian freedom of action. You'll find even more who agonise over whether Norway should join the EU, fearful of the sovereignty they will lose, yet aware that they have a responsibility to engage with their neighbours to the south and east. But above all else you'll find Norwegians who speak numerous languages, have travelled widely and who love nothing more than to welcome visitors to their country.

Norwegians love the great outdoors and they take very seriously the ancient law of *allemansretten* (literally 'every man's right'), whereby public access to wild areas is guaranteed, even in long, dark winters when they take to the wilderness on cross-country skis. That's not to say they don't welcome summer – they do, they almost worship it, aware that it may only last for two months. Norwegians are generally good-natured, but in summer they positively glow with infectious good humour.

A strong egalitarian streak runs through Norwegian society as does an awareness of the country's history. Ostentatious displays of wealth are frowned upon, partly because many older Norwegians remember a time when life was a struggle and the country was poor. Although some complain that the old ways of community and solidarity are disappearing, most Norwegians agree with international assessments that Norway is easily the world's most livable country.

LIFESTYLE

Norway consistently comes first on the UN Human Development Index, which ranks countries according to a range of quality-of-life indicators.

Work & Family Life

If government support for the family is your yardstick, Norway may be the best country in the world in which to have a family. In the early 1970s the foundation of Norway's family welfare system was to provide 'a mother's wage', protecting a woman's right to remain at home without relying on her husband's income. Such measures remain in place, but the focus has broadened and now includes everything from paid leave (Norwegians are entitled to five weeks a year) to heavily subsidised childcare.

THE ECONOMICS OF CHILDBIRTH IN NORWAY

Paid maternity leave A compulsory six-week minimum, with full-pay provisions extending to 42 weeks (t longest in Europe) or 12 months on 80% pay.

Paid paternity leave A four-week minimum (soon to be increased to five weeks); if the weeks aren't taker weeks are lost to both parents.

Further leave entitlements Each parent is entitled to an additional one-year's unpaid, job-protected lea (civil servants get three) or to work part-time on full pay for up to two years.

Government grants for children Government grants of over Nkr33,000 upon the birth of a child and fa allowance income-support during the child's life.

LUXURY PROBLEMS

Scarcity has a long history in Norway: it drove the Vikings to pillage, immigrants to set sail for America and left Munch in such an existential funk that he painted *The Scream*. But with the discovery of oil in 1969 Norwegians went from penny-poor to flush overnight, quite the predicament for a country of committed egalitarians.

So how has this newfound wealth affected the country? Here two members of the older generation remark on the changes they've noticed in the past 50 years. Kate Waagaard, born in 1935, comes from Nes i Ådal, in the Valdres district north of Oslo; and Finn Skoien, born in 1936, is from Hønefoss, also in Valdres.

Are things better? Well, more money is certainly being spent. The quality of life has improved and there are higher living standards and low unemployment. And Norwegians use a lot more money than we used to – building more cabins, going on vacations, eat out more – but prices are going up too. (Finn)

People are more open with their money and have a lot more to show. When I first went to England after the war, I went to pick berries for the summer. That was a big trip for me, but today people take exotic trips to places like the Maldives. (Kate)

What are a few everyday changes you've noticed? Cars. A four-wheel drive was a rarity. Not anymore. Rowboats have been replaced by Riva speedboats (US$500,000 and up). (Finn)

A *hytte* (a cabin or hut) is now a large, multibathroom cabin, complete with all amenities. Telephone service has improved! It used to take years to get a phone installed. (Kate)

As told to Kari Lundgren

Perhaps because of these unparalleled levels of support, Norway has one of the highest fertility rates in the Western world (1.81 children per family). Another side effect is that the Norwegian workplace is extremely child-friendly. As one Norwegian mother told the BBC in 2006, 'There's just a completely different level of acceptance among employers here. It's not uncommon to put a telephone conference on hold, because you can hear a baby crying in the background.'

There have nonetheless been changes in family demographics in recent years, with the average age (28.6) of first-time mothers increasing, a decline in marriage rates (5.5 per 1000 people), a rise in de facto relationships (almost 50% of children are born outside wedlock), and an increase in the numbers of single mothers (around one-quarter of children grow up in single-parent households).

These new realities, most of which are protected under the welfare system, have begun a perceptible shift away from the traditional nuclear family, which has always provided the bedrock of Norwegian society. Partly this change is because of the greater choice that rising Norwegian incomes (US$54,465 per capita in 2006, the second-highest in the world) have enabled, and partly because of a decline in churchgoing among the young. Perhaps the most noticeable impact has been not upon immediate family units – which have diversified rather than been replaced, and the double-income-two-kids model remains the norm – but on traditional, extended families whereby the requirement to care for elderly relatives seems to have transferred from family members to the state.

Norway has an ageing population, an official retirement age of 67, pensions guaranteed for the remainder of a person's life and an average life expectancy nudging close to 80 years. It does, however, have an advantage over other countries wondering how they'll meet their pension obligations as the pool of taxpayers shrinks: the Government Pension Fund (see the boxed text, p41).

Education

Education is compulsory (and has been since 1889!), with the public system heavily funded and private schools actively discouraged. Students at secondary level can choose between traditional academic programmes and vocational training. Many also choose to study in cities other than their home town, contributing to a situation wherein children leave home and become relatively independent much earlier than in most southern European countries. Education, including university studies, is free.

Although the marginal income tax rate is 28%, in practical terms this becomes around 36% for middle-income earners and 49.3% for high-income earners

Conscious efforts have been undertaken to preserve Sami traditional culture (p42) – Sami students take cultural studies and can do some coursework in the Sami language. Non-Norwegian speakers also have access to subsidised special education programmes.

There are six main universities, in Oslo (the oldest), Bergen, Trondheim, Tromsø, Ås and Stavanger. There are also around 40 regional and specialist colleges.

Traditional Culture

Apart from vestiges in remote rural areas, Norway's cultural traditions are visible only in the country's excellent folk museums (see the boxed text, p42) or during folk performances (such as in Bergen; see p207).

One of the most enduring elements is the *bunad*, the elaborate regional folk costumes. Each district has developed its own unique designs, which exhibit varying degrees of colour and originality. Although they remained in everyday use until after WWII in traditional regions such as Setesdalen and parts of Telemark, they're now something of a novelty and are dusted off mainly for weddings and other celebrations.

The intricate embroidery work on these lovely creations was traditionally performed by shepherdesses and milkmaids while tending their livestock. Nowadays, these elaborate costumes are produced only by a few serious seamstresses and embroiderers, and the purchase of a *bunad* represents a major financial commitment. The Norwegian Folk Museum in Oslo features displays of these memorable costumes, but the best place to observe them is in Oslo during the 17 May National Day celebrations, when men and women from all over the country turn up in the traditional dress of their regions.

ECONOMY

Norway's economy is one of Europe's star performers. Annual growth rarely drops much below 3%, while high world oil prices, massive trade and budget surpluses, a negligible unemployment rate and the absence of external debt suggest that the economic good times are here to stay.

It wasn't always thus. Norway at the end of the 19th century was one of Europe's poorest countries and grim economic conditions led to the unprecedented wave of emigration from Norway to the USA (see p46). The situation gradually improved, although in 1950 Norwegian income levels (now second only to Luxembourg) were half those of the USA and ranked below Argentina and Venezuela. It was not until the late 1960s, when oil was discovered, that Norway's economy began to experience stellar growth. For an insight into how that change has been experienced by ordinary Norwegians, see the boxed text, p39.

Norway is the world's third-largest oil exporter and oil accounts for 36% of Norwegian government revenues; agriculture, fisheries, hydroelectric power and tourism are other important industries. What that means for a government ruling over Norway's almost five million Norwegians is an unprecedented ability to look after its citizens with massive spending on

SAVING FOR A RAINY DAY

Most countries with significant oil reserves look with concern towards the day when the oil runs out. Not so Norway.

Suddenly flush with oil money in the 1970s, Norway's government began by developing the country's infrastructure, after which the profits were used to pay off the country's debt, an aim achieved in 1995. Thus it was that in 1996, the government established the Norwegian Petroleum Fund. The aim? To safeguard the wellbeing of future generations of Norwegians, more specifically by putting aside enough money to pay for the health and pension costs of Norway's ageing population. The reserve fund, whose name was changed in 2006 to the Government Pension Fund, is now the largest public fund in Europe with a value of over US$300 billion. Some estimates suggest that the fund will swell to US$900 billion (US$180,000 for every Norwegian) within a decade.

But this is not just any investment fund. For a start, the fund's managers may only invest outside Norway, a measure designed to avoid overheating the local economy. As such Norway has become one of the largest investors in the world. 'We basically own a slice of the world,' was how Henrik Syse, head of the fund's corporate governance department at Norwegian central bank, described it to the *International Herald Tribune* (IHT) in 2007.

The fund's managers are also bound by a strict ethical code when choosing where to invest. Companies (such as Wal-Mart) and countries (eg Myanmar) accused of human rights violations have been excluded from the fund as have mining and other companies accused of severe environmental damage. Discussing the policy of socially responsible investing, Gro Nystuen, a human rights lawyer who oversees the ethics council that vets the investments, told the IHT that 'Norwegians feel bad about having all this money. Our job is to make the Norwegian people feel less guilty.'

However, for all the government's efforts to ensure that Norway's oil wealth secures the country's future, an increasing number of Norwegians has begun to question whether some of the money should be used *now* to improve Norway's often ageing infrastructure, especially roads and an overburdened health system. According to Bernt Aardal, research director at the Institute for Social Research in Oslo, the growing concern stems from 'the dissatisfaction of increasing expectations. There are always unsolved problems in a society. And as the money pile grows, the tolerance for living with these problems gets smaller.'

Further, the success of the Fremskrittspartiet has given many food for thought. As the only party to criticise the handling of the oil fund, the Fremskrittspartiet (which is also known for its anti-immigration stance) won almost a quarter of the vote and became the second-largest party in parliament after the 2005 elections.

health, education and public welfare, not to mention an abundance of jobs in a perpetually booming economy.

POPULATION

Norway has one of the lowest population densities in Europe (around 12 people per square kilometre, compared to 246 in the UK). Although still true to its roots as a rural society of remote and rural farmsteads, there's an irreversible trend of urbanisation underway and 47.3% of the population now live in urban areas (compared with 23.4% in 1975); this figure is expected to rise to 55.9% by 2015.

Nordic

Most of Norway's population is considered to be of Nordic stock; these people are thought to have descended from central and northern European tribes who migrated northward about 8000 years ago (see p28). The Nordic physical stereotype – a tall sturdy frame, light hair and blue eyes – does have some basis in fact with nearly 70% of Norwegians having blue eyes, a greater number than anywhere else in the world outside Scandinavia.

NORWAY'S TOP FOLK MUSEUMS

Maihaugen (p165), Lillehammer
Norwegian Folk Museum (p102), Oslo
Setesdalmuseet (p160), Setesdalen
Hardanger Folk Museum (p219), Utne
Romsdalen Museum (p267), Molde
Sverresborg Trøndelag Folk Museum (p277), Trondheim

A 2007 study found that Norway has more per-capita millionaires – 55,000 or one in every 85 Norwegians – than any other country in the world.

Sami

Norway's 40,000 indigenous Sami people (formerly known as Lapps) are the country's largest ethnic minority and can reasonably claim to be Norway's longest-standing residents. Now primarily inhabiting the far northern region of Finnmark (scattered groups live in Nordland, Trøndelag and other regions of central Norway), this hardy, formerly nomadic people has for centuries occupied northern Scandinavia and northwestern Russia. The total population of around 60,000 Sami forms an ethnic minority in four countries – Norway, Sweden, Finland and Russia (see the map, above). The Sami refer to their traditional lands as Sápmi or Samiland.

Reindeer herding, once the mainstay of the Sami economy, was successfully modernised in the 1980s and 1990s and is now a major capital earner. In addition to reindeer herding, modern Sami engage in fishing, agriculture, trade, small industry and the production of handicrafts. For more information on Sami culture, see the boxed text, p357, and consider visiting the Sami museums of Vájjat Sámi Musea and Ceavccageadge (p356), between Tana Bru and Vadsø, as well as the Sápmi Park and Sami National Museum (p368) in Karasjok. To find out more about modern Sami music see p52.

POLITICAL ORGANISATIONS

The first session of the Norwegian Sami Parliament (see the boxed text, p44 and p368) was held in 1989. The primary task of the parliament, which convenes in Karasjok and whose 43 representatives are elected from Sami communities all over Norway every four years, is to protect Sami language and culture.

The Norwegian Sami also belong to the **Saami Council** (www.saamicouncil.net), which was founded in 1956 to foster cooperation between political organisations in Norway, Sweden, Finland and Russia. In Tromsø in 1980, the Saami Council's political programme adopted the following principles:

> We, the Sami, are one people, whose fellowship must not be divided by national boundaries. We have our own history, tradition, culture and language. We have inherited from our forebears a right to territories, water and our own economic activities. We have an inalienable right to preserve and develop our own economic activities and our communities, in accordance with our own circumstances and we will together safeguard our territories, natural resources and national heritage for future generations.

The Norwegian Sami also participate in the **Arctic Council** (www.arctic-council.org/saami.html) and the World Council of Indigenous Peoples (WCIP), which encourages solidarity and promotes information exchange between indigenous peoples in the various member countries. The **Nordic Sami Institute** (☎ 78 48 80 00; www.nsi.no) at Kautokeino was established in 1974 and seeks to

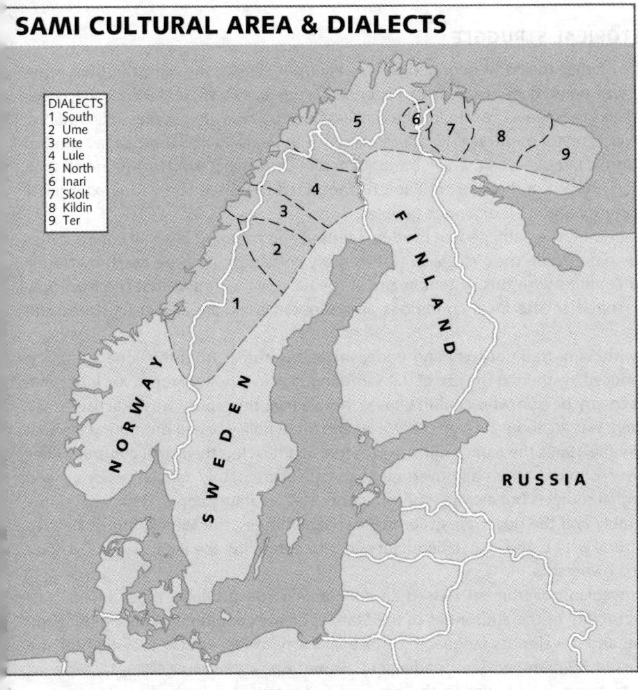

To be officially considered Sami, a person must speak Sami as their first language, consider themselves a member of the Sami community and live in accordance with that society, or have a parent who satisfies either condition.

promote Sami language, culture and education, as well as promote research, economic activities and environmental protection. It's funded by the Nordic Council of Ministers.

SAMI RELIGION

Historically, Sami religious traditions were characterised mainly by a relationship to nature and its inherent god-like archetypes. In sites of special power, particularly prominent rock formations, people made offerings to their gods and ancestors to ensure success in hunting or other endeavours. Intervention and healing were affected by shamanic specialists, who used drums and small figures to launch themselves onto out-of-body journeys to the ends of the Earth in search of answers. As with nearly all indigenous peoples in the northern hemisphere, the bear, as the most powerful creature in nature, was considered a sacred animal.

Historically, another crucial element in the religious tradition was the singing of the *joik* (also spelt *yoik*; literally 'song of the plains'). So powerful and significant was this personal mantra that the early Christian missionaries considered it a threat to their efforts and banned it as sinful. Although most modern Sami profess Christianity, elements of the old religion are making a comeback.

SPORT

Skiing is etched deep in the Norwegian soul, not least because for thousands of years skis were the only practical means of winter transport in much of Norway. Not surprisingly, Norway is a leading winter-sports country. At the 1998 Winter Olympics, Norway finished second on the medal table,

THE SAMI'S HISTORICAL STRUGGLE

Although it's believed that the Sami migrated to Norway from Siberia, the oldest written reference to the Sami was penned by the Roman historian Tacitus in AD 98. In AD 555 the Greek Procopius referred to Scandinavia as Thule (the 'furthest north'), and its peoples as *skridfinns*, who hunted, herded reindeer and travelled about on skis. The medieval Icelandic sagas confirm trading between Nordic peoples and the Sami; and the trader Ottar, who 'lived further north than any other Norseman', served in the court of English king Alfred the Great and wrote extensively about his native country and its indigenous peoples.

During medieval times, the Sami people lived by hunting and trapping in small communities or bands known as *siida*. While the 17th- and 18th-century colonisation of the north by Nordic farmers presented conflicts with this system, many of the newcomers found that the Sami way of life was better suited to the local conditions and adopted their dress, diet, customs and traditions.

Around 1850, with Sami traditions coming under increasing threat from missionary activity, reforms were introduced, restricting the use of the Sami language in schools. From 1902 it became illegal to sell land to any person who couldn't speak Norwegian; this policy was practised zealously. However, there was an about-turn after WWII when official policy began promoting internal multiculturalism. By the 1960s the Sami's right to preserve and develop their own cultural values and language were enshrined across all government spectra. Increasingly, official policy viewed the Sami as Norwegian subjects but also an ethnic minority and separate people. Their legal status improved considerably and the government formed two committees: the Samekulturutvalget to deal with Sami cultural issues; and the Samerettsutvalget to determine the legal aspects of Sami status and resource ownership.

In 1988 the Norwegian government passed an enlightened constitutional amendment stating: 'It is the responsibility of the authorities of the State to create conditions enabling the Sami people to preserve and develop its language, culture and way of life.' It also provided for the creation of an elected 39-member Sami parliament, **Sameting** (www.samediggi.no), to serve as an advisory body to bring Sami issues to the national parliament (similar bodies also exist in Finland and Sweden).

In early 1990 the government passed the Sami Language Act, which gave the Sami language and Norwegian equal status. Later the same year, Norway ratified the International Labour Organisation proposition No 169, which guaranteed the rights of indigenous and tribal peoples.

Although Sami rights are supported by most parties across the political spectrum, the Sami's struggle continues. The right-wing Fremskrittspartiet, which won 22.1% of the vote in 2005, has called for the Sami parliament to be abolished.

matching its 1994 medal tally when it was the host nation. The success turned to domination in 2002 when Norway topped the medal table, but no-one quite knows what happened in Torino in 2006, when Norway trailed in 13th with just two gold medals. As you can imagine, the sudden decline was reported as close to a national tragedy. Among Norway's enduring Olympic legends are: Sonja Henie, the Olympic figure skating gold medallist who won gold in 1928, 1932 and 1936; speed-skater Johann Koss who won three gold medals at the Viking Ship Arena in Hamar in 1994; and cross-country skier Bjoern Daehli who, at the 1998 Olympics, won his seventh gold medal, making him the most successful athlete in Winter Olympics history.

In winter, big ski-jumping events normally take place at Holmenkollen (p106) near Oslo, and other winter events occur at the Olympic venues in Hamar (p169) and Lillehammer (p163).

Football is another hugely popular winter sport. After briefly climbing to 2nd in FIFA ranking in 1993, the Norwegian men's football (soccer) team had, by July 2007, fallen to 35th. The failure to qualify for the 2002 and 2006

World Cups has cast a pall of gloom over the sport in Norway. Ole Gunnar Solskjær, Tore Andre Flo and John Carew are among Norway's most famous football exports, while Trondheim's Rosenberg won the domestic league 13 consecutive years from 1992 until 2004, and again in 2006.

The Norwegian women's national team has strutted the world stage with much greater success, clinching the Women's World Cup in 1995 and the gold medal at the Sydney Olympics in 2000; it now ranks fourth in the world rankings. Their best-known players were Heidi Stoere, who played 151 times for Norway between 1980 and 1997; and Bente Nordby, the goalkeeper who saved US superstar Mia Hamm's penalty en route to a famous tournament victory.

The word 'slalom' derives from the Norwegian words *sla låm*, or 'slope track', which originally referred to a Nordic ski competition that wove over hill and dale, dodging thickets!

MULTICULTURALISM

Norway has become an increasingly multicultural society in recent years, even as Norway's complicated approach to immigration sends out numerous conflicting messages (see p37). Immigration is strictly controlled and only bona fide refugees (ie those who have been granted refugee status with the UN elsewhere), not asylum seekers, are admitted. While there's an argument to be made that the policy is, especially given Norway's wealth, mean-spirited and geared towards maintaining social homogeneity, it's also true that few nations contribute as much money to foreign aid and refugee programmes as does Norway.

Such strategies notwithstanding, Norway was at last count home to 415,000 immigrants, or 8.9% of the population (compared to 1.4% in 1950). More than half of Norway's immigrants come from non-Western countries, especially Pakistan, Somalia, Bosnia, Kosovo, Vietnam, Sri Lanka and Turkey. In 2006 alone a record 45,800 immigrants arrived in Norway, a 30% increase from 2005. One-quarter of all immigrants have settled in Oslo, which is easily Norway's most multicultural city with 20% of its population born outside Norway; nowhere is this more evident than in Oslo's Grønland district, behind the Oslo S train station.

Although many non-Western immigrants came to Norway as refugees, a subtle shift has occurred from refugee-driven immigration to more family-reunion and labour immigrants (especially from Poland); this phenomenon has partly been driven by the often-acute labour shortages caused by Norway's almost nonexistent unemployment.

As in many European countries, Norway is involved in an often anguished debate over the country's cultural mix, with most Norwegians torn between traditional notions of fairness and the perception of a rapidly changing society. Norway's first racially motivated murder occurred in 2001 when a mixed-race youth was stabbed to death outside his Oslo home; 40,000 Norwegians took to the Oslo streets to protest. There was more hand-wringing in 2004 when the Norwegian prime minister Kjell Magne Bondevik rejected a plan to turn empty, disused churches into mosques, claiming that it was not 'the most natural' solution. In 2005 the Fremskrittspartiet, which advocates far stricter limits on immigration, became the second-largest party in the Norwegian parliament; its characterisation of immigrants as responsible for increasing crime rates was denounced as xenophobic by all other political parties.

Other survey results are less clear, with a recent poll showing that 41% of Norwegians agreed with the statement that 'most immigrants abuse the system of social benefits', even as 63% thought that 'most immigrants enrich the cultural life in Norway' and 86% said that 'all immigrants in Norway should have the same opportunities to have a job as Norwegians'.

A PRAIRIE HOME COMPANION

The unofficial voice of Norwegian American culture is the radio show *A Prairie Home Companion (PHC)*. First broadcast in 1974 in the heavily ethnic-Norwegian state of Minnesota, it's now one of the most popular shows on the US National Public Radio network and a two-hour Saturday evening ritual for some three million listeners in Norway, equal to two-thirds of the population of Norway!

Comedic sound effects and interludes of old-time and folk music frame skits with characters such as Guy Noir Private Eye and the cultured cowboys Dusty and Lefty; faux advertisements pitch Bertha's Kitty Boutique (for persons who care about cats) and the Ketchup Advisory Board. The annual joke show teems with titters about Norwegians and *PHC* is not above occasional excretory humour.

The show's Norwegian heart is the weekly news from Lake Wobegon (also a classic book by the same name), a tiny, fictional town in Minnesota's wind- and snow-swept north, where 'all the women are strong, all the men are good looking, and all the children are above average'. Taciturn Norwegian bachelor farmers observe the world from the Chatterbox Café, and locals ice-fish, eat *lutefisk* (dried cod) and fill the Church of Our Lady of Perpetual Responsibility. The town's best-known landmark is the Tomb of the Unknown Norwegian, and its leading civic organisation is the Sons of Knute. *PHC*'s Norwegian-ness is all the more remarkable given that its host, originator and chief writer, Garrison Keillor, is of Scottish descent.

For the latest news from Lake Wobegon, check out http://prairiehome.publicradio.org/.

Emigration from Norway

No discussion of multiculturalism would be complete without mentioning Norwegian emigration (800,000 to the USA and Canada alone in the 19th and early 20th centuries). Across the world you'll find people with Norwegian ancestry, with particularly high concentrations in Minnesota and surrounding US states. If your story is a part of Norway's history, check out **Cyndi's List** (www.cyndislist.com/norway.htm), a website loaded with links for tracing your Norwegian heritage.

Norway has one of the highest percentages of well-educated immigrants in the world: 40% have received higher education, with little difference between Western and non-Western immigrants.

Other sources of help include the **Norwegian Emigrant Museum** (p169; Norsk Utvandrermuseum; ☎ 62 57 48 50; www.museumsnett.no/emigrantmuseum) in Hamar and the **Norwegian Emigration Centre** (p223; ☎ 51 53 88 60; www.emigrationcenter.com) in Stavanger; the latter has a full list of links on its 'Contacts' page.

RELIGION

Around 83% of the Norwegian population nominally belongs to the Church of Norway, with the remainder (mostly in Oslo) comprising other Christian denominations, including around 40,000 Catholics, as well as 75,000 Muslims (85% of whom live in Oslo) and 1500 Jews.

For information on the Sami religion, see p43 and for a discussion of the growing numbers of Muslims in Norway, see p45.

Christianity

Christianity in Norway dates back thousands of years and one of the country's earliest kings, Olav II was canonised by the Catholic Church. However, modern Norwegian Christianity has been most influenced by German reformer Martin Luther, whose doctrines were adopted in Norway in 1537.

Today the Church of Norway is the national denomination of Protestant Evangelical Lutheranism and the Norwegian constitution states: 'All inhabitants of the Realm shall have the right to free exercise of their religion. The Evangelical-Lutheran religion shall remain the official religion of the State. The inhabitants professing it are bound to bring up their children in the same.' So much for complete freedom of religion!

Similiar to the UK, the King of Norway is also the official head of the Church. This power was dramatically exercised in 1961, when King Olav V appointed the country's first woman priest and again in 1993, when King Harald V sanctioned the first female bishop. In the 1970s a bishop and quite a few priests quit after the *storting* (parliament), with royal sanction, passed a liberal abortion law.

While the average Norwegian attends church about twice a year and the organisation funds missions around the world, as many as 5000 Norwegians leave the official church annually, most of them advocating a separation of church and state.

WOMEN IN NORWAY

According to the UN's Gender-Related Development Index, Norway is the best place in the world to be a woman. In addition to a raft of beneficial social welfare provisions (see p38), Norway has a female labour force participation rate of nearly 80%, well above the EU and Organisation for Economic Cooperation and Development (OECD) average (60%); some 79% of married women with children under the age of six work in paid employment, although more than half of these work part-time. In the 1993 election all three party leaders were women, and, after the 2005 elections 37.9% of national MPs were women, the fifth-highest in the world after Rwanda (48.8%), Sweden (47.3%), Costa Rica (38.6%) and Finland (38%). Norwegian women have an average life expectancy of 82.46 years, one of the highest in the world.

Despite such positive statistics, there remain areas where Norwegian women are far from equal with their male counterparts. Women's real annual incomes (US$33,034) still lag behind those of men (US$43,950) even though equal pay is mandated by law under gender equality legislation.

In March 2002 the government announced that 40% of board members of companies would have to be women, although the law has yet to have much impact with women still constituting just 9% of board members in public stock companies; less than 25% of senior leadership positions in universities are held by women and just 23% of executive managers in Norway are female. Domestic violence also remains a serious problem; in 2004 a study suggested that one in six adult Norwegian women had suffered some form of domestic violence.

Accessible yet serious-minded, Gender .no (www.gender .no) is easily the best resource on issues of gender equality in Norway.

When it comes to immigrant women in Norway, the government has been faced with a new set of controversies, especially relating to female circumcision. In 2007 Norway announced that it would stop families from travelling abroad if officials believe that the purpose of the trip is to circumcise a female family member. The move received considerable support in Norway after it was revealed that at least 185 girls from Norway had been circumcised in a Somali village.

ARTS

For detailed coverage of Norwegian architecture, see p78.

Literature

MEDIEVAL NORSE LITERATURE

Norwegian literature dates over a thousand years to the sagas of the Vikings. The two mainstays of the genre are skaldic poetry (*skalds* – the metaphoric and alliterative works of Norwegian court poets in the 9th and 10th centuries) and *eddic* poetry (named after the *Edda,* the most important collection of medieval Icelandic literature). The latter, which combines Christian with pre-Christian elements, is the most extensive source of information on Norse mythology, but it wasn't written down until Snorre Sturluson recorded it in the 13th century, long after the Christianisation of both Norway and Iceland. Its subject matter includes the story of the origin, history and end of the world, instructions on writing poetry, and a series of disconnected aphorisms attributed to the god Oðinn. Apart from the *Edda* itself, there are three forms of eddic poetry: legendary sagas, heroes' sagas and didactic poetry.

THE GOLDEN AGE

The late 19th and early 20th centuries were the golden age of Norwegian literature. Although most of the attention centres on Henrik Ibsen (1828–1906; see the boxed text, p50), it was Bjørnstjerne Bjørnson (1832–1910) who in 1903 became the first Norwegian writer to win the Nobel Prize for Literature. Best known for his story *Trust and Trial* (1857), Bjørnson's work documented vignettes of rural life (for which he was accused of romanticising the lot of rural Norwegians). His former home at Aulestad (p168) is open for visitors.

The hugely controversial Knut Hamsun (1859–1952) won the Nobel Prize in 1920. His greatest novels include *Hunger* (1890), *Mysteries* (1892) and *The Growth of the Soil* (1917). However, Hamsun's elitism, his appreciation of Germanic values and his idealisation of rural life led him to side with the Nazis in WWII, forever darkening his reputation with Norwegians. Only now is he being recognised as belonging to the tradition of Dostoevsky and Joyce.

Sigrid Undset (1882–1949) received the Nobel Prize in 1928 and is the most significant female writer in Norwegian literature. Undset began by writing about the plight of poor and middle-class women; between 1920 and 1922 she published the *Kristin Lavransdottir* trilogy, which was set in 14th-century Scandinavia and was later turned into a film (see p54). Her former home in Lillehammer (p165) is open to the public.

Twentieth-Century Norwegian Writers, by Tanya Thresher (ed), is ideal for those wanting to learn more about Norway's recent literary history and looking for little-known English-language titles.

CONTEMPORARY LITERATURE

One of the best-known modern Norwegian writers is Jan Kjærstad (b 1953), whose *The Seducer* (2003) combines the necessary recipes for a best-seller – a thriller with a love affair and a whiff of celebrity – with seriously good writing. It won the 1999 Nordic Prize for Literature among other international prizes.

Another increasingly world-renowned author is Jostein Gaarder (b 1952) whose first bestselling novel, *Sophie's World* (1991), sold over 15 million copies worldwide. Other Gaarder works include *The Solitaire Mystery* and *The Christmas Mystery*, which are similarly written in the voice of a child protagonist.

Other popular and well-known novelists include Erik Fosnes Hansen (b 1965), Lars Saabye Christensen (b 1953) and Dag Solstad (b 1941), who is the only Norwegian author to win the Norwegian Literary Critics' Award three times. Herbjørg Wassmo (b 1942) has also won numerous international prizes and her 1989 *Dina's Book*, set in 1840s Norway, was turned into a film *I am Dina* (2002), starring Gerard Depardieu; her acclaimed *The House with the Blind Glass Windows* is set in and after WWII. In the crime fiction genre, Gunnar Staalesen and Karin Fossum have devoted international followings.

Another name to catch international headlines is journalist Asne Seierstad, whose *The Bookseller of Kabul* was a runaway international success. Her more recent *A Hundred and One Days* is a first-hand account of the fall of Saddam Hussein.

FOLK TALES & LEGENDS

Nowhere else in Europe does a tradition of folk tales and legends survive to quite the extent it does in Norway.

Mythical Creatures

The most Norwegian of Norway's supernatural beings is the troll, which emerged in Norway at the close of the last ice age. Trolls inhabit gloomy forests, moonlit lakes, deep fjords, snowy peaks and roaring waterfalls. They're creatures of shadow and darkness; any troll who is exposed to direct sunlight turns to stone.

Trolls, who can live for hundreds of years, come in all shapes and sizes, but nearly all have four fingers and toes on each hand and foot, as well as long, crooked noses and bushy tails. Some have multiple heads, with up to three eyes per head. They also have a strange predilection for harassing billy goats and a violent aversion to church bells. Despite having a short fuse and getting decidedly cranky, they're generally kind to humans.

A larger version of the troll was the **giant**, and according to legend, the world was created from the body of the giant Ymir of Jotunheimen (home of the giants), after his death at the hand of the Norse god Oðinn.

Elves, which normally live stream-side in the deepest forests, also come in both good and bad varieties. They only emerge at night, and it's said that the sites of their nocturnal festivities and dances are marked by luxuriant rings of grass.

Other elusive creatures include **hulder**, which steal milk from summer pastures; the frightening **draugen**, a headless fisherman who foretells drownings with a haunting wail; and the **vetter** (wights), who serve as the guardian spirits of the wildest coastlines. Serpents also existed in Viking mythology, but at least one is still with us today – the mysterious Selma the Serpent (see p158). For more information on Norway's fairy-tale characters, see the boxed text (p107).

Folk Tales

The valleys in western and northern Norway are rich sources of folk tales, sagas and myths, many of them explaining curious geographic features.

In one story, a lonely island-dwelling giantess shouted across the water to a giant named Blåmann (Blue Man) on the mainland, asking him to marry her. He agreed, provided she brought the island along with her. Sadly, by the time she'd packed, the sun rose and she turned to stone, as did Blåmann, who'd stayed out too long waiting for her. The island became known as Gygrøy (Giantess Island), but local fisherfolk renamed it Landegode (Good Land), lest the giantess take offence. Landegode's distinctive profile is a familiar landmark on the ferry between Bodø and Kjerringøy, while poor old Blåmann is now an ice-cap.

Another legend involves Hestmannen (the Horseman), who attempted to shoot the princess Lekamøya with an arrow when she wouldn't marry him. Her father, the king of Sømna, threw down his hat as a distraction, and the result was Torghatten, a hat-shaped peak that looks as if it's been pierced through, on Torget island south of Brønnøysund. Hestmannen himself is a knobbed peak on the island of Hestmanna, located further north near Mo i Rana.

Music

CLASSICAL MUSIC

The 19th century was an extraordinarily rich time for Norwegian music, for it was then that Edvard Grieg (see the boxed text, p50), who is regarded as one of history's greatest composers, emerged. Of arguably equal importance, however, was the virtuoso violinist Ole Bull, known throughout Europe as the 'Nordic Paganini'. Bull is credited with critically encouraging the careers of Edvard Grieg and Henrik Ibsen, bringing the Hardanger folk fiddlers to Bergen concert halls and reviving Europe-wide interest in Norwegian folk music.

CULTURAL ICONS

Norway's cultural life in the 20th century may have been dominated by its enviable list of literature Nobel Laureates (p48) and outstanding sportsmen and sportswomen (p43), but three figures from the 19th century – playwright Henrik Ibsen, composer Edvard Grieg and painter Edvard Munch – tower over Norway's cultural life like no others. Their emergence came at a time when Norway was forging its path to independence and pushing the creative limits of a newly confident national identity. More than just artists, Ibsen, Grieg and Munch are an expression of the Norwegian soul.

Henrik Ibsen

Born in Skien, Henrik Johan Ibsen (1828–1906) became known as 'the father of modern drama', but to Norwegians he was the conscience of a nation. Norwegians are extremely proud of Ibsen, but from 1864 until 1891 he lived in disenchanted exile, decrying the small-mindedness of the Norwegian society of the day. Although in 1863 he wrote *The Pretenders*, which takes place in 13th-century Norway with King Håkon Håkonsson expressing anachronistic dreams of national unity, the enormously popular *Peer Gynt* (1867) was Ibsen's international breakthrough. In this enduring epic, an ageing hero returns to his Norwegian roots after wandering the world and is forced to face his own soul.

His other best-known plays include *The Doll's House* (1879), the highly provocative *Ghosts* (1881), *An Enemy of the People* (1882), *Hedda Gabler* (1890) and, his last drama, the semi-autobiographical *When We Dead Awaken*.

Throughout his life, Ibsen was always more than a chronicler of Norwegian society and saw himself as the very reflection of 19th-century Norwegians: 'He who wishes to understand me must know Norway. The magnificent but severe natural environment surrounding people up there in the north forces them to keep to their own. That is why they become introspective and serious, they brood and doubt – and they often lose faith. There, the long, dark winters come with their thick fogs enveloping the houses – oh, how they long for the sun!'

Top places to catch up with Ibsen's work are:

- Ibsen Museum (p94), Oslo
- Ibsenhuset Museum (p138), Grimstad
- Henrik Ibsenmuseet (p153), Skien

Edvard Grieg

Norway's renowned composer, Edvard Grieg (1843–1907) was so disappointed with his first symphony that he scrawled across the score that it must never be performed! Thankfully, his wishes were ignored. Grieg was greatly influenced by Norway's folk music and melodies and his first great, signature work, *Piano Concerto in A minor*, has come to represent Norway as no other work before or since.

There are fine philharmonic orchestras in Oslo, Bergen (dating from 1765), Trondheim and Stavanger; and the Norwegian Opera Company (established in 1958) is based in Oslo. In addition to Grieg, watch out for works by his contemporaries Halfdan Kierulf and Johan Svendsen, or more recent composers such as David Monrad Johansen, Geirr Tveitt, Fartein Valen, Pauline Hall and **Ketil Bjørnstad** (www.ketilbjornstad.com). Modern Norwegian compositions often bear unmistakable traces of folk music roots, including works by Hanson, Kvandal and Søderlind.

CONTEMPORARY JAZZ & FOLK MUSIC

If the country's jazz festivals (see p22) are any indication, Norway has a thriving jazz scene, with world-class annual events in Molde, Kongsberg, Oslo, Bergen, Lillehammer and Arendal among others. Jazz saxophonist Jan Garbarek is one of the most enduring Norwegian jazz personalities. Other

Two years after the concerto Grieg, encouraged by luminaries such as Franz Liszt, collaborated with Bjørnstjerne Bjørnson, setting the latter's poetry and writing to music. The results – *Before a Southern Convent, Bergliot* and *Sigurd Jorsalfar* – established Grieg as the musical voice of Norway. This was followed by a project with Henrik Ibsen, setting to music Ibsen's wonderful novel *Peer Gynt*. The score found international acclaim and became his – and Norway's – best-remembered classical work.

By 1885 he had developed a formidable repertoire (including *Ballad in G minor, The Mountain Thrall, Norwegian Dances for Piano* and the *Holberg Suite*), and he and his wife Nina moved into the coastal home at Troldhaugen, close to Bergen, from which he set off on numerous concert tours of Europe. According to his biographer, Aimer Grøvald, it was impossible to listen to Grieg without sensing a light, fresh breeze from the blue waters, a glimpse of grand glaciers and a recollection of the mountains of Western Norway's fjords.

Places to check out:

- Troldhaugen (p199), Bergen
- Open-air concerts (p207), Bergen
- Grieghallen (p207), Bergen

Edvard Munch

Edvard Munch (1863–1944), Norway's most renowned painter, was a tortured soul: his mother and elder sister died of tuberculosis and his younger sister suffered from mental illness from an early age. Munch's first great work, *The Sick Child*, was a portrait of his sister Sophie shortly before her death. In 1890 he produced the haunting *Night*, depicting a lonely figure in a dark window. The following year he finished *Melancholy* and began sketches of what would become his best known work, *The Scream*, which graphically represents Munch's own inner torment.

In 1892 Munch buried himself in a cycle of angst-ridden, atmospheric themes collectively entitled *Frieze of Life – A Poem about Life, Love and Death*. Beyond the canvas, his obsession with darkness and doom cast a long shadow over his life. Alcoholism, chronic emotional instability and a tragic love affair culminated in the 1907 work, *Death of Marat*, and, a year later, he checked into a Copenhagen mental health clinic for eight months.

After leaving the clinic, Munch settled on the coast at Kragerø. It became clear that Munch's post-clinic work was to be altogether different, dominated by a sunnier, more hopeful disposition dedicated to humans in harmony with their landscape.

Best places to see Munch's work (just don't take them with you, eh?).

- National Gallery, Oslo (p93)
- Munch Museum, Oslo (p103)
- Bergen Art Museum (p198)

well-known names include Karin Krog, Bugge Wesseltoft, Nils Petter Molvær, Silje Nergaard, Solveig Slettahjell, Espen Larsen and Sidsel Endresen.

Folk music is another central pillar of Norwegian music, and the Hardanger fiddle – which derives its distinctive sound from four or five sympathetic strings stretched out beneath the usual four strings – is one of Europe's best-loved folk instruments. Some of the hottest folk acts include: Tore Bruvoll and Jon Anders Halvorsen's traditional Telemark songs *(Nattsang)*; the live Norwegian performances of Bukkene Bruse (heavy on the Hardanger fiddle; *Spel*); Rusk's impressively wide repertoire of music from southeastern Norway *(Rusk)*; Sigrid Moldestad and Liv Merete Kroken, who bring classical training to bear on the traditional fiddle *(Spindel)*; while Sinikka Langeland's *Runoja* draws on ancient runic music. For a wonderful overview of traditional Norwegian folk music, the 2007 CD *Norway: Traditional Music* excavates long-lost music from the vaults of Norwegian Public Radio.

Music from Norway (www.musicfromnorway.com/default.aspx) is a thorough overview of Norwegian music with biographies and informative summaries of the most popular musical forms.

The haunting music of the Sami people of northern Norway is also enjoying a revival. Recent Sami artists such as Aulu Gaup, Mari Boine Persen and Nils Aslak Valkeapääs have performed, recorded and popularised traditional and modern versions of the traditional *joik* (personal songs); Boine in particular has enjoyed international airtime. For further information on the role of music in Sami culture, see p43.

Jazz Basen (www.jazzbasen.no/index_eng.html), the internet's true home of Norwegian jazz, covers festivals and an extensive list of jazz artists to watch out for.

Fiddling for Norway: Revival and Identity, by Chris Goertzen, looks at the revival of folk-fiddling in Norway, the history of Norwegian folk music and its influence on the world folk music scene.

POPULAR MUSIC, ELECTRONICA & HEAVY METAL

One Norwegian fan of A-ha told us that the group is the Norwegian equivalent of Abba from Sweden or U2 from Ireland. While that may be stretching things a little (especially the comparison to U2), no-one can deny the band's enduring success. After making it big in the 1980s, they remain in fine voice and released their eighth studio album, *Analogue*, in 2006. Band member Magne Furuholmen is more than just a musician; see the boxed text, p54.

Electronica is another Norwegian speciality. Although much of the energy surrounding Norwegian electronica has shifted to Oslo in recent years, the so-called 'Bergen Wave' was largely responsible for putting Norway on the world electronica circuit in the first years of the 21st century. **Röyksopp** (www.royksopp.com) in particular took the international electronica scene by storm with their debut album *Melody A.M.* in 2001 and they've never really left the dance-floor charts since. The Bergen Wave was not just about electronica and also produced internationally acclaimed bands **Kings of Convenience** (www.kingsofconvenience.com) and **Ephemera** (www.ephemera.no).

In recent years Oslo has taken up the mantle with *Sunkissed*, produced by Oslo label **Small Town Super Sound** (www.smalltownsupersound.com) and spun by G-Ha and Olanskii – it's quite simply the hottest thing to hit Norwegian dance music since Röyksopp. Other electronica acts causing a stir include Kim Hiortøy, Magnet (aka Even Johansen; www.homeofmagnet.com) and Bjorn Torske.

One popular young singer who's starting to make waves internationally is Maria Mena, whose 2004 album *White Turns Blue* (released as *Mellow* in Norway) marked her out as a name to watch.

Norwegian metal is another genre that Norway has taken to heart and, again, Bergen tends to be the home city for much of the action. There you'll find Hulen (p208), an almost mythical venue among European heavy

INTERVIEW WITH ESPEN LARSEN, JAZZ MUSICIAN

Espen Larsen's CDs include *Alone Together, Jazzsnadder* and *Hope.*

Which city is Norway's jazz capital? I have to say Oslo because they have many different scenes. Cosmopolite is a great scene, but hr.Nilsen.Oslo [a live-music venue] also has its own jazz festival.

Who are the best-known Norwegian jazz musicians? The best known jazz musician outside Norway is I guess, the saxophonist Jan Garbarek. Close behind him you have Bugge Wesseltoft, the pianist, keyboardist and owner of the Jazzland label (under Universal music). For the younger audiences I guess Jaga Jazzist is well known.

Who are the most exciting young jazz musicians in Norway? There are too many to mention, but I would like Solveig Sletthhjell & Slow Motion Orchestra to get more attention outside Norway. Also Come Shine is a great example of a great band with a great singer in front.

Which are your favourite music festivals in Norway? Kongsberg Jazz Festival, Canal Street Jazz & Blues Festival (Arendal), May Jazz Festival (Stavanger), Vossajazz (Voss), Night Jazz Festival (Bergen) and Molde International Jazz Festival.

As told to Anthony Ham

INTERVIEW WITH BERNT ERIK PEDERSEN, MUSIC EDITOR, *DAGSAVISEN*

Which city is Norway's musical capital? There isn't really any competition: no other Norwegian city can match Oslo for the amount and diversity of bands, venues, clubs, hangouts, record labels, shops, media, ie the things that makes a music city great. For gigs Oslo can match most major European cities, with top international acts almost every night. For innovation I'd rate Tromsø as Norway's most influential music city. The house/techno/electronica-revolution came to Tromsø first, and Tromsø's influence on the current Norwegian music scene is huge, although most of the major players have now moved from Tromsø.

Which are your favourite music festivals in Norway? Oslo's Øya-festival (http://oyafestivalen.com) is not to be missed, with a good mix of mainstream and underground sounds, Norwegian and international. The new Hove festival in Arendal looks good for indie rock. And NuMusic in Stavanger is an excellent, innovative festival for electronica, hip-hop, noise etc. For travellers outside the summer season there is always good fun to be had at the Oslo World Music Festival, early November.

If you had to choose your five favourite Norwegian musical acts across any genre, from any era, who would they be? Röyksopp, Radka Toneff, Geir Jenssen aka Biosphere, deLillos, Lasse Marhaug.

Who are the Norwegian heirs to Röyksopp when it comes to electronica? I've recently come to the conclusion that Hans-Petter Lindstrøm is a genius. His productions are crisp, clean and wonderfully starry-eyed. 'I Feel Space', indeed! A lot of current dance music producers are influenced by the post-disco sound of the early '80s, few others make this stuff sound as fresh and contemporary as Lindstrøm. Watch him go!

Who are Norway's most exciting jazz prospects? Piano/keyboard etc-player Morten Qvenild has that magic touch where everything he is involved in just seems to sound better than everything else. There is a particularly dramatic, melancholy feel to his playing: In The Country, Susanna & The Magical Orchestra and Solveig Slettahjells Slow Motion Quintet are his main projects. There are a lot of extremely interesting bands and artists working within the increasingly blurred boundaries between jazz, improv, noise, electronica, avant-rock and contemporary music – ie Arve Henriksen, Lasse Marhaug, Puma, Paal Nissen-Love, and most artists associated with the Rune Grammofon label.

Who will be, in your opinion, the next A-ha or Kings of Convenience when it comes to international success? Soul-influenced rock singer/songwriter Thomas Dybdahl, maybe. But he doesn't really 'do' hits.

Has Norway's landscape played an important role in determining the direction of Norwegian music? If so, how? Norwegian nature has definitely shaped the Norwegian mentality, and subsequently Norwegian music. It is a cold, sparsely populated country, on the outskirts of Europe, where nature can be almost hostile. This has a tendency to turn people, perhaps particularly musicians and artists, into melancholic, outsider individualists. Internationally acclaimed Norwegian artists as diverse as A-ha, Röyksopp, Jan Garbarek, Geir Jenssen, Mari Boine all share a certain windswept melancholy.

As told to Anthony Ham

rock fans. While you're in the area, head for Garage (p207) another rock-heavy venue where former rocker and current caretaker 'Denis' will fill you in on everything you needed to know (and many things you didn't) about Norwegian rock.

Norwegian Black Metal (www.norsksvartmetall.com) has everything you ever wanted to know about Norway's own genre of metal.

Painting & Sculpture

Nineteenth-century Norway gave birth to two extraordinary talents: painter Edvard Munch (see the boxed text, p51) and sculptor Gustav Vigeland (see p99).

During the early 20th century, the impressionist Henri Matisse inspired several ardently decorative Norwegian artists such as Axel Revold, Per Krohg,

NOT JUST A SINGER

Magne Furuholmen may be known better as the guitarist and keyboard player in the group, A-ha, but there's a more serious side to this talented artist. Furuholmen held his first solo exhibition in London in 2007, with 40 monoprints that experiment with what the exhibition's catalogue notes described as, 'a constant game with the structures of language'. He has also exhibited around Europe and in Oslo's Henie-Onstad Art Centre, showcasing his skills with woodcuts, sculpture and other visual arts. Furuholmen's most prominent piece of art is the sculpture of blue vases, in the open square immediately northeast of the tourist office in Bergen.

Alf Rolfsen and Henrik Sørensen, known collectively as the 'fresco brothers'. During the postwar years, the brooding forests of Jakob Weidemann, the constructivist paintings of Gunnar S Gundersen, and the literal (nonfigurative) sculptures of Arnold Haukeland and Åse Texmon Rygh dominated the visual arts scene.

Of the crop of contemporary Norwegian artists, Olav Jensen, Anne Dolven, Ørnulf Opdahl, Bjørn Tufta, Håvard Vikhagen, Odd Nerdrum and Andres Kjær have all created a minor stir with their return to abstract and expressionist forms, with harsh depictions of the Norwegian landscape the norm. Norwegian sculptors who've distinguished themselves include Bård Breivik, Per Inge Bjørlo and Per Barclay.

For the best overview of Norwegian art, visit the National Gallery (p93) in Oslo, the Rogaland Art Museum (p225) or the Bergen Art Museum (p198). The best collections of contemporary Norwegian art are on display at National Museum of Contemporary Art (p93), the Astrup Fearnley Museum (p93) and the Henie-Onstad Art Centre (p104), all of which are in Oslo.

Theatre & Dance

Traditional folk dancing and singing is enjoying something of a resurgence and numerous festivals feature roundels, *pols*, *reinlenders*, polkas and mazurkas. Today, troupes of *leikarringer* (folk dancers) practise all over the country and compete in *kappleiker* (dance competitions), which attract large

TOP NORWEGIAN FILMS

- Kristin Lavransdatter (1995; director Liv Ullmann) Based on the novel by Sigrid Undset and set in 14th-century Norway.
- The Bothersome Man (2006; director Jens Lien) An absurdist fable set in a loveless and claustrophobic IKEA-world.
- Blue Angel (1994; director Marius Holst) A 1995 Berlin Festival winner for its depiction of childhood conflicts in Oslo.
- Frida (1991; director Berit Nesheim) A searing portrayal of adolescence.
- Håkon Håkonsson/Shipwrecked (1990; director Nils Gaup) Disney-funded tale of a 19th-century Norwegian Robinson Crusoe who set off for the South Seas.
- The Pathfinder (1987; director Nils Gaup) Based on a medieval legend and presented in the Sami language.
- The Witch Hunt (1981; director Anja Breien) Won awards at the 1982 Venice Film Festival.
- Nine Lives (1957; director Arne Skouen) Oscar-nominated tale of a soldier on the stormy northern coast of Norway during the German occupation.

audiences. The best place to catch performances of live folklore in summer is Bergen (p207).

Oslo, Bergen and other larger towns have theatre, opera and ballet companies. Classical performances take place in summer in Bergen, including a number of evocative outdoor settings, but elsewhere most are in winter, when outdoor activities are limited, and sadly, few visitors are around to enjoy them.

For information on Henrik Ibsen, Norway's finest playwright, see the boxed text, p50.

Cinema

Norway has a small but internationally acclaimed film industry. Pioneering the industry's claims to international recognition were the Oscar-nominated Nils Gaup and Arne Skouen. Other, more recent directors to catch the eye include Marius Holst, Berit Nesheim, Anja Breien and Jens Lien.

Of the movies filmed in Norway, *Black Eyes,* by Russian director Nikita Michalkhov, was set in the spectacular landscapes around Kjerringøy in Nordland, while Caspar Wrede's *One Day in the Life of Ivan Denisovich* was filmed in Røros.

Food & Drink

Norwegian food *can* be excellent. Abundant seafood and local specialities such as reindeer are undoubtedly the highlights, and most medium-sized towns have fine restaurants in which to eat. The only problem (and it's a significant one) is that prices are prohibitive, meaning that a full meal in a restaurant may become something of a luxury item for all but those on expense accounts. What this does is push many visitors into eating fast-food meals in order to save money, at least at lunchtime, with pizzas, hot dogs and hamburgers a recurring theme. As a result, you may end up leaving Norway pretty uninspired by its food. It's not only foreign visitors who feel the pinch – it's often claimed, backed by authoritative research surveys, that Pizza Grandiosa, a brand of frozen pizza, is in fact Norway's national dish.

Striking a balance between eating well and staying solvent requires a clever strategy. For a start, most Norwegian hotels and some hostels offer generous buffet breakfasts ensuring that you'll rarely start the day on an empty stomach; if you take full advantage, you'll need only a light meal for lunch. Some hotels also lay on lavish dinner buffets in the evening – they're generally expensive, but excellent if it's your main meal of the day. Another key is to think in krone and avoid converting the Norwegian price into your home currency, otherwise you really might wind up emaciated.

STAPLES & SPECIALITIES

Meat

Norwegians love their meat and some of the most memorable meals for carnivores will involve Norway's signature species. Roast reindeer *(reinsdyrstek)* is something every nonvegetarian visitor to Norway should try at least once; despite its cost (starting from around Nkr275), you'll likely order it again as it's one of the tastier red meats. If you're fortunate enough to be invited to a Sami wedding, you might also come across a traditional reindeer stew *(bidos)*. Another popular local meat is elk *(elg)*, which comes in a variety of forms, including as a steak or burger.

Other meat-based dishes that Norwegian chefs excel at preparing include *bankebiff* (slices/chunks of beef simmered in gravy), *dyrestek* (roast venison) and *lammebog* (shoulder of lamb). Not surprisingly given the Norwegian climate, meats are often cured, one variety of which is *spekemat* (cured lamb, beef, pork or reindeer, often served with scrambled eggs). Further

TRAVEL YOUR TASTEBUDS

Norway has its share of strong-tasting culinary oddities that the brave among you may wish to try:

- whale steak *(hvalbiff)* – a reasonably common sight on restaurant menus and in harbourside markets (eg in Bergen); eating it is an act of defiance to your environmental credentials.
- brown cheese – *Gudbrandsdalsost* is made from the whey of goat's and/or cow's milk and has a slightly sweet flavour despite its off-putting caramel-coloured appearance.
- reconstituted cod, mackerel or saithe balls – more common in homes than restaurants and something of a staple for older folk.
- cod tongues – enormously popular in Lofoten and, strangely enough, nowhere else.
- fermented trout – some Norwegians swear by it, but some Lonely Planet authors are happy to leave them to it.

FOOD IN A TUBE

A Parisian orders a *café au lait*, a Londoner kippers. In New York it might be a bagel, in Tokyo rice. Comfort food or culture shock, they're all breakfast, and for Norwegians it comes in a tube.

The question mark at hotel breakfast buffets, and nothing to do with dental hygiene, cream cheese and *kaviar* (sugar-cured and smoked cod roe cream) packaged in a tube have been Norwegian favourites for decades. There are two especially popular Norwegian brands: the Trondheim-based Mills, best known for its *kaviar*, and the older Kavli in Bergen. A dairy established in 1893, Kavli began exporting cheese to the US in the early 1920s and launched its first tube of Primula cream cheese in 1924 – quite the ground-breaking event in the cheese-processing world. It now produces bacon, ham, salami, shrimp, tomato, mexicana and jalapeño flavoured cheeses, all packaged in the familiar tube.

Though both spreads are good alone and part of a well-rounded-Norwegian *frokost* (breakfast), *kaviar* is especially popular coupled with Norvegia cheese or a few slices of boiled egg.

dishes include *kjøttpålegg* (cold meat cuts), *fårikål* (lamb in cabbage stew), *syltelabb* (boiled, salt-cured pig's trotter), *lapskaus* (thick stew of diced meat, potatoes, onions and other vegetables) and *pytt i panne* (eggs with diced potato and meat).

Seafood

One Norwegian contribution to international cuisine that you shouldn't miss is salmon. Where other Norwegian foods will quickly empty your wallet without adequate compensations for taste, salmon (*laks*; grilled or smoked, in which case it's called *røykelaks*) remains blissfully cheap, although this applies only to farmed salmon; wild salmon is considerably more expensive. The quality is consistently top-notch. An excellent salmon dish, *gravat laks* is made by marinating salmon in sugar, salt, brandy and dill and serving it in a creamy sauce.

In 2000 Norwegian chefs came third in an international cooking competition known unofficially as the 'culinary Olympics'. Taking four gold medals, Norway was beaten only by Sweden and Singapore.

Other Norwegian freshwater seafood specialities that are recommended include brown trout (only in the south), perch, Arctic char, Arctic grayling, bream, tench and eel.

The most common ocean fish and seafood that you're likely to eat are cod (*torsk* or *bacalao*; often dried), boiled or fresh shrimps, sprat, haddock, mackerel, capelin, sand eel, ling, ocean perch and coalfish. The ugly but inexplicably lovable catfish is, sadly, rather delicious, as is the blenny. Herring (once the fish of the poor masses and now served pickled in onions, mustard or tomato sauce) is still served in some places, but it's becoming rarer while wild stocks recover. Norwegians are huge fans of *fiskesuppe*, a thin, creamy, fish-flavoured soup.

Other dishes to watch out for include: *fiskebolle* (fish balls), *fiskegrateng* (fish casserole), *gaffelbitar* (salt- and sugar-cured sprat/herring fillets), *klippfisk* (salted and dried cod), *sildesalat* (salad with slices of herring, cucumber, onions etc) and *spekeslid* (salted herring, often served with pickled beetroot, potatoes and cabbage).

Roots web (www.rootsweb.com/~wgnorway/recipe.html) has easy-to-follow recipes of traditional Norwegian foods passed down through generations of people of Norwegian descent.

Other Specialities

Potatoes feature prominently in nearly every Norwegian meal and most restaurants serve boiled, roasted or fried potatoes with just about every dish. Other vegetables that turn up with sometimes monotonous regularity are cabbage (often stewed), turnip, carrot, swede (rutabaga), cauliflower and broccoli.

The country's main fruit-growing region is around Hardangerfjord, where strawberries, plums, cherries, apples and other orchard fruits proliferate.

The most popular edible wild berries include strawberries, blackcurrants, red currants and raspberries; blueberries (huckleberries), which grow on open uplands; blue, swamp-loving bilberries; red high-bush and low-bush cranberries; and muskeg crowberries. But the lovely amber-coloured cloudberries *(moltebær)* are highly prized and considered a delicacy. They grow one per stalk on open swampy ground and in Norway some cloudberry patches are zealously guarded. Warm cloudberry jam with ice cream is simply fantastic!

Authentic Norwegian Cooking by Astrid Karlsen Scott has an emphasis on the practical and has been endorsed by none other than Ingrid Espelid, the Betty Crocker or Delia Smith of Norway.

Norwegian cheeses have come to international attention as a result of the mild but tasty Jarlsberg, a white cheese first produced in 1860 on the Jarlsberg estate in Tønsberg. And for the sweet tooths among you, widely available rich, cream-filled cakes will animate your tastebuds time and again.

DRINKS

If Norway has a national drink, it's coffee. In fact, it's almost universally drunk in such staggering quantities that one can only wonder how people can remain so calm under the influence of so much caffeine. Most Norwegians drink it black and strong, but foreigners requiring milk and/or sugar are normally indulged.

Teas and infusions are also available all over the country, as are the usual range of fizzy drinks and mineral water; they're much cheaper in supermarkets.

Alcoholic Drinks

Beer is not far behind coffee in the popularity stakes. It's available in bulk at eminently reasonable prices from the beer outlets of the state monopoly shops known as Vinmonopolet (fondly known as just 'pole'), the only place where wine and spirits may be purchased.

Beer is commonly sold in bars in 400mL (from Nkr55) or 500mL (from Nkr65) glasses (about 30% and 15% less than a British pint, respectively). The standard Norwegian beer is pils lager, with an alcohol content of around 4%, and it's still brewed in accordance with the 16th-century German purity law. The most popular brands are the lagers Ringsnes in the south and Mack in the north. Munkholm is a fairly pleasant alcohol-free beer. Note that when friends go out drinking, people generally buy their own drinks rather than rounds, which is scarcely surprising given the prices.

Norway has no wine-growing tradition of its own, but Norwegians increasingly drink wine with meals. According to one study, wine makes up one-third of Norway's alcohol intake, compared to just 12% in 1974. Quality restaurants increasingly offer extensive wine lists with wines from across Europe (especially Spain, France, Germany and Italy) and further afield (Australia, Chile, South Africa and California). In some cities (especially Bergen and Oslo), wine bars are all the rage.

NORWAY'S BEST COFFEE

Norwegians drink more coffee per person than anyone else in the world. Here are the places where you'll understand why:

Stockfleths (p111), Oslo
Åpent Bakerei (p111), Oslo
Det Lille Kaffe Kompaniet (p207), Bergen
Dromedar Kaffebar (p207), Bergen
Café Det Lindvedske Hus (p137), Arendal
Bacalao (p314), Svolvær

AQUAVIT

Only the Norwegians would make an alcoholic drink from potatoes. The national spirit, aquavit (or *akevitt*) is a potent dose of Norwegian culture made from the potato and caraway liquor. The name is derived from the Latin *aqua vitae*, the 'living waters'. Although caraway is an essential ingredient, various modern distilleries augment the spicy flavour with any combination of orange, coriander (cilantro), anise, fennel, sugar and salt! The confection is aged for three to five years in 500L oak barrels that have previously been used to age sherry.

Perhaps the most esteemed version of this libation is *Linje Aquavit*, or 'line aquavit', which first referred to stores that had crossed the equator. In the early days, ships carried oak barrels of aquavit abroad to trade, but the unsold barrels were returned to Norway and offered for sale. When it was discovered that the product had improved with age and travel, these leftovers became highly prized commodities. Today, bottles of *Linje Aquavit* bear the name of the ship involved, its route and the amount of time the barrels have aged at sea.

CELEBRATIONS

Food is central to Norwegian celebrations and this is particularly true at Christmas when special dishes include: *rømmegrøt* (a delicious sour-cream variant upon porridge); *rupa* (ptarmigan or grouse); *lutefisk* (a glutinous dish of dried cod or stockfish treated in lye solution that's definitely an acquired taste and extremely popular among Norwegians living overseas); *pinneribbe* (mutton ribs steamed over birch or juniper branches); and pork roast, which stems from the Viking tradition of sacrificing a pig at yuletide. Raisin buns and a variety of sweet biscuits, including *strull*, *krumkake* and *goro*, are what children get excited about. The almost-universal Christmas drink is *gløgg*, which roughly translates as 'grog', but is far more exciting in reality with its blend of cinnamon, raisins, almonds, ginger, cloves, cardamom and other spices with juice, which may or may not be fermented. Many people also imbibe *juløl*, or 'holiday beer', which dates from the Viking days, when it was associated with pagan sacrifices; as with the *lutefisk*, not all foreigners fully appreciate it. Die-hard alcohol fans celebrate the season with generous quantities of Norway's own potato power brew, aquavit (see the boxed text, above).

WHERE TO EAT & DRINK

Hotel breakfasts in Norway often consist of a gargantuan buffet that includes English, American, Continental and Scandinavian options all on one groaning table. If you're staying somewhere where breakfast is not included, your best bet is a bakery where bread, pastries, sandwiches and bagels are well-priced.

If you love fresh fish, any of Norway's fish markets are fabulous places to eat; buy what you want as a takeaway and find a quiet vantage point alongside the water. Among the best are in Bergen, Trondheim and Kristiansand.

Norwegians love to eat out and just about every town in Norway has at least one sit-down restaurant. Although it's more usual to eat a light lunch and save the main meal for dinner, many Norwegian restaurants, especially in larger towns, serve cheaper lunch specials (often around Nkr70). These are often filling and well-sized for those wanting more than a sandwich. Sometimes these are signed as a *dagens rett* (daily special).

Meals at moderately priced restaurants are typically Nkr80 up to Nkr150. More upmarket restaurants tend to have high standards, with prices for main dishes rarely below Nkr180 and often considerably higher. If money is no object, some such places offer three- to five-course meals (from Nkr250 up to Nkr695), which are usually of the highest quality.

NORWAY'S TOP RESTAURANTS

- Bagatelle (p111; Oslo) – Norway's only restaurant with two Michelin stars; for an interview with chef Eyvind Hellstrøm, see the boxed text, p111.
- Fossheim Turisthotell (p184; Lom) – Founded by renowned chef Arne Brimi; his legacy of wild trout, reindeer, elk and ptarmigan lives on.
- Enhjørningen (p205; Bergen) – The freshest seafood in Bergen's charming Bryggen district.
- Finnegaards Stuene (p205; Bergen) – A new addition to Norway's culinary scene with old-style quality and traditional dishes.

Cheap Eats

If you're trying to save a bit of money, shop in supermarkets, Norway's last bastion of reasonable prices; for nationwide opening hours, see inside the front cover of this book. Aside from the usual packaged foods, some supermarkets have reasonably priced delicatessens where you can pick up salads or grilled chickens. These delicatessens also sell smoked or cured meats that make an excellent filling for a sandwich or roll. If you buy your bread from a bakery and the rest of the items from a supermarket, you'll end up saving bucket loads of krone over the course of your trip. Major supermarket chains that you'll find across the country include Rimi, Spar, Co-op and Rema 1000.

Every Thursday from September to May, many Bergen restaurants serve *raspeballer*, a powerful traditional meal with salted meat, potatoes and mashed turnip – an acquired taste perhaps, but hearty winter food.

Salads and other snacks are also available from convenience stores and petrol stations. Your standard snack for a quick lunch is usually a hot dog *(pølse)*, of which you'll find various varieties; garnish and sauce cost no extra and if you buy a drink with it you'll often pay just Nkr35 to Nkr45. Petrol stations also often have a small choice of paninis and rolls that are similarly priced and far more healthy. *Gatekjøkken* (food wagons or kiosks) also serve hot dogs, burgers, chips, pizza slices and the like, and the better ones will also offer fish and chips and a range of sandwiches.

If you're by the coast, fish markets (p59) are often well-priced and that receive large numbers of tourists usually have a range of ready-to-go snacks, such as fish balls or takeaway platters of salmon and other fishy wonders.

Pizzas feature prominently in the local diet. Peppe's Pizza is Norway's standout pizza chain with creative pizzas (from Nkr159) that are a cut above the rest and servings large enough for two; its lunchtime buffets are even better value. Another similar chain is Dolly Dimple's.

VEGETARIANS & VEGANS

Norwegians are not the most vegetarian of people. That said, most restaurants offer some vegetarian options. Sometimes this may just be a cheese-and-onion omelette or a pasta with cream sauce, but increasingly you'll find creative salads (although vegans won't appreciate the widespread use of cheese) and a range of crepes or pancakes to add some variety to your diet. The predominance of potatoes on most Norwegian restaurant menus almost always provides a fall-back option. In general, the rule is that the larger the town, the wider your choices of vegetarian fare. In Oslo, Bergen, Stavanger and Trondheim, you'll find plenty of European-style cafés with a range of vegetarian choices and even vegetarian restaurants. Tapas restaurants are a recurring theme in larger towns and most have vegetable-only options. Pizza restaurants also always have at least one vegetarian dish.

Nordic Plate (www.nordicplate.net) is an initiative by Scandinavian governments to provide a comprehensive site on Norwegian food with recipes and resources for teachers.

EATING WITH KIDS

Norwegians pride themselves on policies and attitudes that are child- and family-inclusive (see p38), and this extends to eating out. Even in many

THE TROUBLE WITH ALCOHOL

Norway must be one of the few countries in the world where the population actually voted *for* prohibition (in a 1919 referendum)! The ban on alcohol remained in force until 1927, by which time half the Norwegian population was involved either in smuggling or illegally distilling home brew, including no doubt many who had voted in favour of the ban. The state monopoly system (state alcohol outlets are called Vinmonopolet) emerged as an alternative method of restricting alcohol, but even today it seems to have had little effect on the amount of illegal distilling that continues. If you're offered any homemade swill, remember that the effects can be diabolical!

Alcohol sales are strictly controlled and a few towns have even implemented virtual prohibition. In some places, including parts of Telemark, drinking beer in public incurs a Nkr2000 fine and/or prison time!, although we're yet to hear of any tourist doing time for enjoying a quiet pint.

As such, Norway's official attitude toward alcohol borders on paranoia, especially as alcohol consumption by Norwegians is among the lowest in Europe, although whether this is because of the strict laws or in spite of them it's difficult to tell. Yes, Norwegian alcohol consumption has increased from 3.4L per person per week in 1960 to 6.2L in recent years, but these figures are still barely more than half the consumption levels in Germany or the UK. That said, there is a disturbing recent phenomenon whereby average alcohol consumption among Norwegian 15- to 20-year-olds doubled from 1995 to 2001. Apart from the figures themselves, what has parents and the government worried is the increasing tendency toward binge drinking. As one young bartender explained to us, prohibitive bar prices for drinks has forced many young Norwegians to buy alcohol in bulk from Vinmonopolet outlets, drink at home ('foreplay' according to the local vernacular) until midnight when they go out to drink in bars. The legal drinking age is 18 years for beer and wine and 20 for spirits.

of the most upmarket restaurants, children will be made to feel welcome and, as a result, Norwegians are often seen eating out as a family group. Many restaurants offer children's menus with smaller portions and prices to match. And most of those that don't are willing to serve a smaller portion if you ask.

In practical terms, high chairs are generally available as a matter of course and most places are happy to improvise with baby-changing areas if they don't have dedicated facilities in the toilets (which some do).

For more information on travelling with children in Norway, see p394.

HABITS & CUSTOMS

The Norwegian day starts with coffee (always!), a boiled egg and some sort of bread or dry crispbread (normally Ryvita) topped with cheese, cucumber, tomato and a type of pickled herring.

For lunch, most people opt for a sandwich or a slice of bread topped with sardines, shrimp, ham, olives, cucumber or egg. In the mid-afternoon Norwegians often break for coffee and one of the highlights of the day, waffles with cream and jam. Unlike the firm Belgian waffles, which are better known abroad, Norwegian waffles are flower-shaped, soft and normally strongly flavoured with cardamom.

The main meal is eaten between 4pm and 6pm. Usually the only hot meal of the day, it normally includes a meat, seafood or pasta dish, with boiled potatoes, a scoop of vegetables and perhaps even a small salad or green garnish. Note that Norwegians often take full advantage of long summer days and eat out considerably later.

Norwegian National Recipes: An Inspiring Journey in the Culinary History of Norway by Arne Brimi can be hard to track down, but there's no finer study of Norwegian food covering all regions and it's written by one of Norway's premier chefs.

EAT YOUR WORDS

If menus in Norway make you break out in a cold sweat, turn to p425 to start learning some elementary Norwegian.

The Norwegian Kitchen by K Innli (ed) brings together over 350 favourite recipes of members of the Association of Norwegian Chefs.

Useful Phrases

Table for..., please.
Et bord til..., takk. — et boo-rr til... tuhk

Can I see the menu, please?
Kan jeg få menyen, takk. — kuhn yay for me-nü-yön tuhk

I'd like today's special, please.
Jeg vil gjerne ha dagens rett, takk. — yay vil ya-rrnö hah dah-göns rret takk

What does it include?
Hva inkluderer det? — vah in-kloo-de-rre rde?

Is service included in the bill?
Er bevertninga iberegnet? — arr bö-vart-ning-uh ee-bö-rray-nöt?

Not too spicy, please.
Ikke for sterkt krydra, takk. — ik-kö fo shtarrkt krrüd-drruh tuhk

I don't eat meat.
Jeg spiser ikke kjøtt. — yay spi-sörr ik-kö cher-t

I don't eat chicken or fish or ham.
Jeg spiser verken kylling eller fisk eller skinke. — yay spee-sörr varr-kön chül-ling el-lörr fisk el-lö shing-kö

Food Glossary

MEAT & POULTRY

kjøtt — meat
kylling — chicken
oksekjøtt — beef
pølse — sausage
sauekjøtt — lamb/mutton
skinke — ham
svinekjøtt — pork

VEGETABLES

grøn(n)saker — vegetables
løk — onion
potet — potato
sopp — mushroom
tomat — tomato

SEAFOOD

brisling — sprat/sardine
fisk — fish
hellefisk — halibut
lysing — hake
makrell — mackerel
reker — shrimp
sild — herring
torsk — cod
tunfisk — tuna

FRUIT

ananas — pineapple
appelsin — orange
banan — banana
druer — grapes
eple — apple
frukt — fruit
jordbær — strawberries

DAIRY PRODUCTS

fløte — cream
ost — cheese
smør — butter

DESSERTS, CAKES & COOKIES

goro — variety of biscuit
is — ice cream
kake — cake
krumkake — variety of biscuit
pannekake — pancake
shillingsboller — pastry bun
sjokolade — chocolate
strull — variety of biscuit
syltetøy — jam

DRINKS

hvitvin — white wine
jus — fruit juice
kaffe — coffee
melk — milk
øl — beer
rødvin — red wine
te — tea
vann — water

Environment

Norway and the environment are like everyone's model couple – from the outside, they seem like a perfect match even if you suspect that they conceal the occasional dark secret. Indeed, the story of how Norway has been acclaimed for promoting environmental sustainability while being one of the world's largest producers of fossil fuels (oil is the elephant in the room) is a fascinating tale. Add to the mix some of Europe's most dramatic landscapes and most stirring geographical forms and it quickly becomes clear that Norway is one of the most important places to watch in these days of creeping environmental uncertainty.

THE LAND

The Norwegian mainland stretches 2518km from Lindesnes in the south to Nordkapp in the Arctic north with a narrowest point of 6.3km wide. Norway has the highest mountains in northern Europe and a land mass of 385,155 sq km. But these facts only hint at the country's spectacular natural history. The secret lies in the sheer diversity of Norwegian landforms, from glacier-strewn high country and plunging fjords to the tundralike plains of the far north.

State of the Environment Norway (www.environment.no) is a comprehensive site covering everything from biodiversity and international agreements to statistics and Svalbard.

The Coast

Seeming to wrap itself around Scandinavia like a protective shield from the freezing Arctic, Norway's coastline appears to have shattered under the strain, riven as it is with islands and fjords (long, narrow inlets of the sea bordered by high, steep cliffs) cutting deep fissures inland. Geologists believe that the islands along Norway's far northern coast were once attached to the North American crustal plate – such is their resemblance to the landforms of eastern Greenland.

Some of the islands along the far northern coast – notably Lofoten and Vesterålen – are largely comprised of granite and gneiss. Further north, Svalbard is geologically independent from the rest of Europe and sits on the Barents continental plate deep in the polar region. While the remainder of Norway's icefields struggle to survive, Svalbard still experiences dramatic glaciation. Sedimentary rock layers in Svalbard include fossils and coal.

Regardless of how Norway's geology evolved, the process has certainly proved profitable. In the North Sea lie two rift valleys that contain upper Jurassic shale bearing the rich deposits of oil and gas that are now being exploited, making Norway one of the world's largest exporters of petroleum products.

BIGGEST & HIGHEST

- Jostedalsbreen (p244) is continental Europe's largest icecap
- Sognefjorden (p234), Norway's longest fjord at 203km (second only to Greenland's Scoresby Sund), is 1308m deep, making it the world's second-deepest fjord (after Skelton Inlet in Antarctica). Hardangerfjord (p214) is 800m deep and is, at 179km, the second-longest fjord network in Norway and the third-longest in the world.
- Galdhøpiggen (p184; 2469m) is the highest mountain in northern Europe
- Hardangervidda (p188), at 900m above sea level, is Europe's largest and highest plateau

Inland

Norway's interior is dominated by fjords, plateaus, the high country of mountain massifs and the Arctic landscapes of the north. For detailed coverage of these signature landforms, see p82.

Rockfalls are a rare, if ever-present threat in Norway's fjord country. In 1934, a rockfall triggered a 62m-high tsunami in Tafjord, causing devastation to fjord-side communities.

WATERFALLS

Norway contains some of the highest waterfalls and glacial streams in the world, hardly surprising given its combination of mountains and wet climate. Some authorities place the glacial stream Utigårdsfossen, which flows into Nesdalen and Lovatnet from Jostedalsbreen (not readily accessible to tourists), as the third-highest waterfall in the world at 800m, including a single vertical drop of 600m. Other Norwegian waterfalls among the 10 highest in the world are: Mongefossen in Romsdal (774m; now dry due to hydroelectric developments); Espelandsfossen (703m; Hardangerfjord); Mardalsfossen (655m; Eikesdal); and Tyssestrengene (647m in multiple cascades; p219), near Odda. Vøringsfossen (p217) is one of Norway's most-visited natural landmarks.

GLACIERS

Perhaps it's their sheer scale or the sense they leave us of a world in motion. Or maybe it's because glaciers have become a barometer for the health of the environment. Whatever the reason, few natural landforms inspire quite the same awe as glaciers and they are undoubtedly among the stand-out natural highlights of Norway, covering as they do some 2600 sq km (1% of Norwegian territory). But this is a far cry from the last Ice Age when Norway was one great icefield. The bulk of the ice melted about 8800 years ago, leaving behind the fjords (see p82) while only a few remnant icecaps and valley glaciers remain in Norway, although Svalbard is an obvious exception.

A stunning 99.3% of Norway's electricity comes from hydro power sources, with zero from nuclear power and just 0.4% coming from fossil fuels.

Not only are glaciers a stunning tourist attraction, but they also serve an important purpose in Norway's economy: 15% of Norway's electricity derives from river basins below glaciers.

Concerns about shrinking glaciers and icesheets in the Arctic have taken on added urgency in recent years as the impact of global warming takes hold. Some of Norway's glaciers retreated by up to 2.5km in the 20th century. The glacier of Austre Brøggerbreen in Svalbard ranks high among the world's glaciers in terms of thinning ice, having lost 15.3m since 1977, while Midre Lovenbreen (Svalbard; 12.3m) and Hellstugubreen (central Norway; 11.7m) aren't far behind. In 2006 Norway experienced its fourth-hottest summer on record, following on from above-average temperatures in 2002 and 2003, thereby accelerating the melting of Norway's glaciers. Inland glaciers are considered to be at far greater risk than Norway's coastal glaciers. A few Norwegian glaciers have grown in recent decades – the thickness of the ice on the Nigardsbreen glacier grew by 13.8m from 1977 to 2007 – although such stories are the exception and do little to diminish the otherwise gloomy outlook.

Glaciers & Climate Change by J Oerlemans can be a tad heavy-going, but it does tell you everything you need to know about why glaciers have become a cause célèbre for environmentalists across the world.

Jostedalsbreen (p244) is mainland Europe's largest icecap and it feeds some of Norway's largest glaciers, among them Nigardsbreen (p246), Briksdalsbreen (p247) and Bødalsbreen (p248). Another spectacular example is Folgefonn (p219). If you're keen to hike atop a glacier, or if you want to learn more about glaciers at one of Norway's glacier museums, turn to p391 for details.

WILDLIFE

Despite sparse wildlife populations compared with neighbouring Sweden and Finland – Norway's unique settlement pattern, which spreads the human population thinly, limits wildlife habitat and restricts numbers – there's still plenty to see, including reindeer, elk, lemming and musk oxen.

Animals

LAND MAMMALS

If you plan carefully, there are plenty of opportunities to see Norway's larger land mammals.

From the forests of the far south to southern Finnmark, *elg* (elk; moose in the USA) are fairly common, although given the Norwegian fondness for elk meat, they wisely tend to stay clear of people and roads. Places that offer elk safaris include Oppdal (see p176), Dombås (p177), Evje (see the boxed text, p159) and Hovden (p161).

After being hunted to the brink of extinction, the downright prehistoric *moskus-okse* (musk oxen) were re-introduced into Dovrefjell-Sunndalsfjella National Park from Greenland in the 1940s and have since extended their range to the Femundsmarka National Park near Røros. For more information on the species, and the best places to join a musk-ox safari in summer, see p179.

Wild *reinsdyr* (reindeer) exist in large herds across central Norway, usually above the tree line and sometimes as high up as 2000m. The prime viewing areas are on the Hardangervidda Plateau, where you'll find Europe's largest herd (around 7000), but sightings are also possible in Jotunheimen, Dovrefjell and the inland areas of Trøndelag. The reindeer of Finnmark are domestic and owned by the Sami, who drive them to the coast at the start of summer, then back to the interior in winter. The smaller *svalbardrein* (Svalbard caribou) is native only to Svalbard.

The smaller mammal species that are more difficult to see include: *hare* (Arctic hares); *pinnsvin* (hedgehogs; mainly in southern Trøndelag); *bever* (beavers; southern Norway); *grevling* (badgers); *oter* (otters); *jerv* (wolverines); *skogmår* (pine martens); *vesel* (weasels); and *røyskatt* (stoats).

Lemen (lemmings) occupy mountain areas through 30% of the country and stay mainly around 800m altitude in the south and lower in the north. They measure up to 10cm and have soft orange-brown and black fur, beady eyes, a short tail and prominent upper incisors. If you encounter a lemming in the mountains, it may become enraged, hiss, squeak and attempt to attack!

Northern Lights: The Science, Myth, and Wonder of Aurora Borealis by Calvin Hall et al combines hard science with historical legend to help unlock one of Norway's great mysteries.

MARINE MAMMALS

The seas around Norway are rich fishing grounds, due to the ideal summer conditions for the growth of plankton. This wealth of nutrients also attracts fish and baleen whales, which feed on the plankton, as well as other marine creatures that feed on the fish.

Minkehval (minke whales), one of the few whale species that is not endangered, measure around 7m to 10m long and weigh between five and 10 tonnes. They're baleen whales, which means that they have plates of whalebone baleen rather than teeth, and migrate between the Azores area and Svalbard.

Between Ålesund and Varangerhalvøya, it's possible to see *knolhval* (humpback whales), toothed whales that measure up to 15m and weigh up to 30 tonnes. These are among the most acrobatic and most vocal of whales, producing deep songs that can be heard and recorded hundreds of kilometres away.

Spekkhogger (killer whales), or orcas, are the top sea predators and measure up to 7m and weigh an astonishing five tonnes. There are around 1500 off the coast of Norway, swimming in pods of two or three. They eat fish, seals, dolphins, porpoises and other whales (such as minke), which may be larger than themselves.

ARCTIC PHENOMENA

The Aurora Borealis

There are few sights as mesmerising as an undulating aurora. Although these appear in many forms – pillars, streaks, wisps and haloes of vibrating light – they're most memorable when taking the form of pale curtains wafting on a gentle breeze. Most often, the Arctic aurora appears as a faint green or light rose but, in periods of extreme activity, can change to yellow or crimson.

The visible aurora borealis, or northern lights, are caused by streams of charged particles from the sun, called the solar wind, which are directed by the Earth's magnetic field towards the polar regions. Because the field curves downward in a halo surrounding the magnetic poles, the charged particles are drawn earthward. Their interaction with electrons in nitrogen and oxygen atoms in the upper atmosphere releases the energy creating the visible aurora. During periods of high activity, a single auroral storm can produce a trillion watts of electricity with a current of one million amps.

The Inuit (Eskimos) call the lights *arsarnerit* ('to play with a ball'), as they were thought to be ancestors playing ball with a walrus skull. The Inuit also attach spiritual significance to the lights, and some believe that they represent the capering of unborn children; some consider them gifts from the dead to light the long polar nights and others see them as a storehouse of events, past and future. Norwegian folklore attributes the lights to old maids or dead maidens dancing and weaving. The lights were seen as a bad omen and a sign that God was angry, and people who mocked the superstition risked incurring the ire of God.

The best time of year to catch the northern lights in Norway is from October to March, although you may also see them as early as August. Oddly enough, Svalbard is actually too far north to catch the greatest activity.

Midnight Sun & Polar Night

Because the Earth is tilted on its axis, polar regions are constantly facing the sun at their respective summer solstices and are tilted away from it in the winter. The Arctic and Antarctic circles, at 66° 33' north and south latitude respectively, are the southern and northern limits of constant daylight on their longest day of the year.

The northern half of mainland Norway, as well as Svalbard and Jan Mayen island, lie north of the Arctic Circle but, even in southern Norway, the summer sun is never far below the horizon. Between late May and mid-August, nowhere in the country experiences true darkness and in Trondheim, for example, the first stars aren't visible until mid-August.

Conversely, winters here are dark, dreary and long, with only a few hours of twilight to break the long polar nights. In Svalbard, not even a twilight glow can be seen for over a month. During

The long-finned *grindhval* (pilot whales), about 6m long, may swim in pods of up to several hundred and range as far north as Nordkapp. *Hvithval* (belugas), which are up to 4m long, are found mainly in the Arctic Ocean.

The grey and white *narhval* (narwhal), which grow up to 3.5m long, are best recognised by the peculiar 2.7m spiral ivory tusk that projects from the upper lip of the males. This tusk is in fact one of the whale's two teeth and was prized in medieval times. Narwhal live mainly in the Arctic Ocean and occasionally head upstream into freshwater.

For more whale species see p69. For the best places for whale spotting, see p393.

Norway also has bottlenose, white-beaked, Atlantic white-sided and common dolphins, while seals are commonly seen near the seashore throughout Norway and some inland fjords. The main species include *steinkobbe* (harbour seals), *havert* (grey seals), *ringsel* (ringed seals), *grønlandssel* (harp seals), *klappmyss* (hooded seals) and *blåsel* (bearded seals). The much larger *hvalross* (walruses), which in Norway lives only in Svalbard, measures up to nearly this period of darkness, many people suffer from SAD syndrome, or 'seasonal affective disorder'. Its effects may be minimised by using special solar spectrum light bulbs for up to 45 minutes after waking up. Not surprisingly, most northern communities make a ritual of welcoming the sun the first time it peeks above the southern horizon.

Town/Area	Latitude	Midnight Sun	Polar Night
Bodø	67° 18′	4 Jun to 8 Jul	15 Dec to 28 Dec
Svolvær	68° 15′	28 May to 14 Jul	5 Dec to 7 Jan
Narvik	68° 26′	27 May to 15 Jul	4 Dec to 8 Jan
Tromsø	69° 42′	20 May to 22 Jul	25 Nov to 17 Jan
Alta	70° 00′	16 May to 26 Jul	24 Nov to 18 Jan
Hammerfest	70° 40′	16 May to 27 Jul	21 Nov to 21 Jan
Nordkapp	71° 11′	13 May to 29 Jul	18 Nov to 24 Jan
Longyearbyen	78° 12′	20 Apr to 21 Aug	26 Oct to 16 Feb

Fata Morgana

If the aurora inspires wonder, the Fata Morgana may prompt a visit to a psychiatrist. The clear and pure Arctic air ensures that distant features do not appear out of focus. As a result, depth perception becomes impossible and the world takes on a strangely two-dimensional aspect where distances are indeterminable. Early explorers meticulously laid down on maps and charts islands, headlands and mountain ranges that were never seen again. An amusing example of distance distortion, described in the enigmatic book *Arctic Dreams* by Barry Lopez, involves a Swedish explorer who was completing a description in his notebook of a craggy headland with two unusual symmetrical valley glaciers, when he discovered that he was actually looking at a walrus.

Fata Morganas are apparently caused by reflections off water, ice and snow, and when combined with temperature inversions, create the illusion of solid, well-defined features where there are none. On clear days off the outermost coasts of Lofoten, Vesterålen, northern Finnmark and Svalbard, you may well observe inverted mountains or nonexistent archipelagos of craggy islands resting on the horizon. It's difficult indeed to convince yourself, even with an accurate map, that they're not really there!

Also unsettling are the sightings of ships, large cities and forests where there could clearly be none. Normal visibility at sea is less than 18km, but in the Arctic, sightings of islands and features hundreds of kilometres distant are frequently reported.

4m and weighs up to 1450kg; their elongated canine teeth can measure up to 1m long in the males. Although once heavily hunted for their ivory and blubber, their Svalbard population has increased to around 1000 since they became a protected species in 1952.

Polar Bears International (www.polarbearsinternational.org) is dedicated to the *isbjørn* (polar bear), with educational information, details on threats and campaigns to save it, and great photos.

FISH

Centuries of fishing have severely depleted fish stocks among species that were once the mainstays of the Norwegian economy. *Sild* (herring), *hellefisk* (halibut) and *lysing* (hake) have all been over-fished and are no longer abundant, though the situation has improved in recent years. Among freshwater fish, *laks* (salmon) are the most widespread and a large sport-angling community ensures that the stocks are kept as widespread as possible. However, diseases have, on occasion, spread from farmed fish to the wild stocks, creating major problems in some areas. See the boxed text, p389, for information on how to protect salmon, while a more extensive rundown on the impact of Norway's fishing industries on the environment can be found on p73. To learn more about salmon, visit the Wild Salmon Centre (p238) in Lærdalsøyri.

BEST BIRD-WATCHING SITES

Femundsmarka National Park (p175) Falcons.
Fokstumyra Marshes (p178) Over 100 species of bird nest here.
Gjesvær (p353) Offshore colonies of puffins, skuas, razorbills, kittiwakes, gannets and white-tailed eagles.
Øvre Pasvik National Park (p363) Siberian jays, pine grosbeaks, redpolls, smews and ospreys.
Runde (p261) Near Ålesund, with over 350,000 nesting pairs of sea birds.
Stabbursnes (p354) Wetland birds including some exotic species and ospreys.
Svalbard (p377) Puffins, little auks, purple sandpipers, Brünnich's guillemots.

BIRDS

Norway is an excellent destination for ornithologists. The greatest bird populations are found along the coastline, where millions of sea birds nest in cliff faces and feed on fish and other sea life. The most prolific species include terns, *havsule* (gannets), *alke* (razorbills), *lundefugl* (puffins), *lomvi* and *teist* (guillemots), *havhest* (fulmars), *krykkje* (kittiwakes), *tjuvjo* and *fjelljo* (skuas) and *alkekonge* (little auks). The standout species among Norway's host of wading and water birds include the *storlom* (black-throated wading birds), *smålom* (red-throated divers; called 'loons' in North America), *horndykker* (horned grebes), *åkerrikse* (corncrakes) and Norway's national bird, the *fossekall* (dippers), which make their living by diving into mountain streams.

Norway is also home to at least four species of owls: *jordugle* (short-eared owls); *spurveugle* (pygmy owls); *snøugle* (snowy owls); and *hubro* (eagle owls).

Marine Mammals of the North Atlantic by Carl Christian Kinze is an excellent field guide to Norway's 51 marine mammals.

The most dramatic of Norway's raptors is the lovely *havørn* (white-tailed eagle), the largest northern European raptor, with a wingspan of up to 2.5m; there are now at least 500 nesting pairs along the Nordland coast, Troms and Finnmark. The same number of *kongeørn* (golden eagles) inhabit higher mountain areas. The rare *fiskeørn* (ospreys) have a maximum population of 30 pairs and are seen only in heavily forested areas around Stabbursdalen (p355) and Øvre Pasvik National Parks (p363).

ENDANGERED SPECIES

Centuries of hunting and accelerating human encroachment have pushed numerous animal species to the brink of extinction, although some have begun to make a recovery thanks to bans on hunting.

Bjørn (brown bears) have been persecuted for centuries, and Norway's only permanent population is in Øvre Pasvik National Park (p363) in eastern Finnmark.

US government scientists estimate that two-thirds of the world's polar bears (now 22,000) will disappear by 2050 due to diminishing summer sea ice.

Isbjørn (polar bears), the world's largest land carnivore, are found in Norway only in Svalbard, spending much of their time on pack or drift ice. Since the ban on hunting came into force in 1973, their numbers have increased to around 3000, although they remain extremely difficult to see unless you're on a cruise around Svalbard. Despite weighing up to 720kg and measuring up to 2.5m long, polar bears are swift and manoeuvrable, thanks to the hair on the soles of their feet, which facilitates movement over ice and snow and provides additional insulation. A polar bear's diet consists mostly of seals, beached whales, fish and birds, and only rarely do they eat reindeer or other land mammals (including humans). Polar-bear milk contains 30% fat (the richest of any carnivorous land mammal), which allows newborn cubs to grow quickly and survive extremely cold temperatures. For more information on polar bears, see the boxed text, p374.

As in most places, *ulv* (wolves) aren't popular with farmers or reindeer herders and hunters, and only a few still exist in the country (around Hamar and in Finnmark). A rare forest-dweller is the solitary lynx, northern Europe's only large cat.

Sadly, many years of whaling in the North Atlantic and Arctic Oceans have reduced several whale species to perilously small populations. Apart from the minke whale, there's no sign that the numbers will ever recover in this area.

The endangered *seihval* (sei whales), a baleen whale, swim off the coast of Finnmark and are named because their arrival corresponds with that of the *sei* (pollacks), which come to feast on the seasonal plankton. They can measure 18m and weigh up to 30 tonnes (calves measure 5m at birth). The annual migration takes the *sei* from the seas off northwest Africa and Portugal (winter), up to the Norwegian Sea and southern Barents Sea in summer.

Finhval (fin whales) measure 24m and can weigh 80 tonnes. These whales were a prime target after the Norwegian Svend Føyn developed the exploding harpoon in 1864 and unregulated whalers left only a few thousand in the North Atlantic. Fin whales are also migratory, wintering between Spain and southern Norway and spending summer in northern Norway.

Spermsetthval (sperm whales), which can measure 19m and weigh up to 50 tonnes, are characterised by their odd squarish profile. They subsist mainly on fish and squid and usually live in pods of 15 to 20. Their numbers were depleted by whalers seeking whale oil and the valuable spermaceti wax from their heads. The fish-rich shoals off Vesterålen attract quite a few sperm whales and they're often observed on boat tours.

Possibly the largest animal to ever inhabit the earth, the longest blue whale ever caught measured 33.58m; 50 people could fit on its tongue alone.

The largest animal on earth, *blåhval* (blue whales), measure around 28m and weigh in at a staggering 110 tonnes. Although they can live to 80 years of age, 50 is more common. Heavily hunted for its oil, the species finally received protection, far too late, from the International Whaling Commission in 1967. Prior to 1864, there were between 6000 and 9000, but only a few hundred

THE TRUTH ABOUT LEMMINGS

Few creatures have been so unjustly maligned as the humble lemming. We've all heard tales of countless lemmings diving off cliffs to their deaths in a ritual of mass suicide. Some people also maintain that their bite is fatal and that they spread disease.

All you need to know about lemmings? Actually, no. Firstly, although lemmings can behave aggressively and ferociously (sometimes even when neither threatened nor cornered), there's no evidence that their bite is any more dangerous than that of other rodents.

As for their self-destructive behaviour, lemmings are known for their periodic mass movements every five to 20 years, when a particularly prolific breeding season results in overpopulation. Thanks to the increased numbers, the vegetation is decimated and food sources grow scarce, forcing swarms of lemmings (the last plague was in 2001) to descend from the high country in search of other, less crowded high ground. Most meet an undistinguished fate, squashed on roads or eaten by predators and domestic animals. Indeed, for a couple of years following a lemming population surge, there will also be an increase in the population of such predators as foxes, buzzards and owls.

Quite often, however, the swarms head for the sea, and often do face high cliffs. When the press of their numbers builds up near the back of the ranks, the leaders may be forced over the edge. Also, inclement weather when crossing fjords or lakes can result in mass drownings. As unpleasant as the phenomenon may be, particularly for the lemmings, there's no evidence to suggest that lemmings are prone to suicide.

Not all lemmings join the rush to near-certain death. The clever, more aggressive individuals who remain in the hills to guard their territories grow fat and happy, living through the winter under the snow and breeding the following year. Females as young as 15 days can become pregnant and most individuals give birth to at least two litters of five each year, thereby ensuring the survival of the species.

remain in the world's oceans (although some Norwegian estimates put the number at around 11,000). Recent evidence suggests that a few hardy blue whales are making a comeback in the northeast Atlantic.

Grønlandshval (bowhead whales), or Greenland right whales, were virtually annihilated by the end of the 19th century for their baleen, which was used in corsets, fans and whips, and because they are slow swimmers and float when dead. In 1679 Svalbard had around 25,000 bowheads, but only a handful remains and worldwide numbers are critically low.

Thanks to the polar bear's rich diet, its liver contains enough vitamin D to kill a human who might be stupid enough to eat it.

To read about Norway's controversial stance on commercial whaling, see p76.

NATIONAL PARKS & RESERVES

At last count, Norway had 37 national parks (including seven in Svalbard) and around 15% of the country lies within protected areas; eight national parks have been added since 2003 alone. In some cases, they don't protect any specific features, but rather attempt to prevent development of remaining wild areas. As a result, park boundaries don't necessarily coincide with the incidence of spectacular natural landscapes or ecosystem boundaries, but simply follow contour lines around uninhabited areas. The focus is very much on preservation, rather than on the managed interaction between humans and their environment, although a few interpretation centres do exist. For a list of the major Norwegian national parks, see p72, while all national parks are marked on the map, above.

Compared to their counterparts in the USA, Britain and elsewhere, Norwegian national parks are low profile and pleasantly lack the traffic and overdeveloped tourist facilities that have turned parks in many countries into little more than transplanted (or seasonal) urban areas. Some parks, particularly Jotunheimen, are increasingly suffering from overuse but, in most parks, erosion, pollution and distress to wildlife are kept to a minimum.

Regulations governing national parks, nature reserves and other protected areas are quite strict. In general, there are no restrictions on entry to the parks, nor are there any fees, but drivers must nearly always pay a toll to use access roads. Dumping rubbish, removing plant, mineral or fossil specimens, hunting or disturbing wildlife, and using motorised off-road vehicles are all prohibited. For advice on responsible hiking, see the boxed text, p390.

Further national park information is available at local tourist offices and from the **Directorate for Nature Management** (☎ 73 58 05 00; www.dirnat.no) in Trondheim.

ENVIRONMENTAL ISSUES

Norway is often held up as a stellar example of a responsible environmental citizen. Most of such praise is deserved, even as Norway's record in confronting the most important environmental issues is, like most countries, riven with contradictions. On the one hand, the Norwegian government has made an unprecedented commitment to cut its greenhouse gas emissions and the fjords were voted first for environmental sustainability out of 115 major tourist destinations by *National Geographic Traveler* magazine in 2004. At the same time, Norway is one of the world's largest oil exporters and a major player in the fishing industry.

When it comes to Norway's micromanagement of the environment, there is much to be praised. Industrial waste is highly regulated, recycling is almost universal, there's little rubbish along the roadsides and general tidiness takes a high priority in both urban and rural environments.

And yet, loss of habitat has placed around 1000 species of plants and animals on the endangered or threatened species lists (see p68). Although

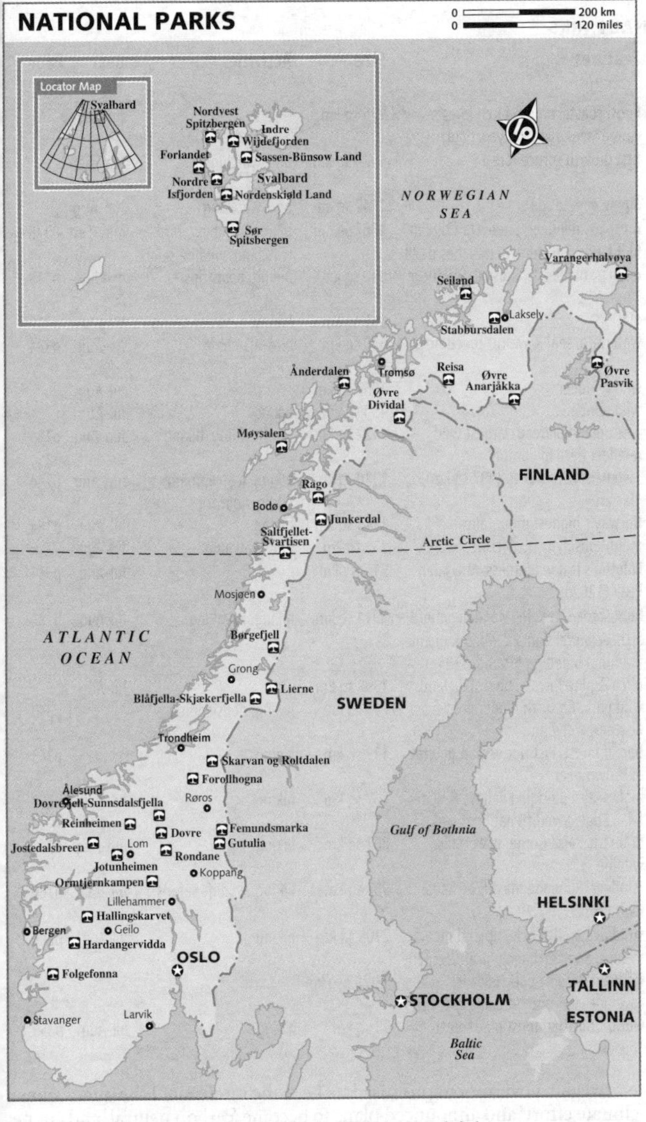

many animals are now protected, sport-hunting and fishing are more popular here than in most other European countries. Norway's unpopular stance on whaling and sealing has raised international ire and resulted in boycotts on Norwegian products.

'Norway's unpopular stance on whaling and sealing has raised international ire'

Climate Change

Global warming is by no means a solely Norwegian problem, but few countries have committed to doing as much about it as Norway. In 2007 the

MAJOR NATIONAL PARKS

National Park	Features	Size	Activities	Best Time	Page No
Ånderdalen	bogs, coastal pine & birch forests (some trees over 500 years old)	125 sq km	-	Jul-Aug	
Blåfjella-Skjækerfjella	first growth spruce forest	1924 sq km	bird-watching	May-Sep	
Børgefjell	alpine vegetation	1447 sq km	bird-watching	Jun-Aug	
Dovrefjell-Sunndalsfjella	musk ox, reindeer, Snøhetta (2286m) highlands, Fokstumyra marshes p178	4367 sq km	hiking, climbing, bird-watching, wildlife safaris	May-Sep	p178
Femundsmarka	glaciers, highlands, musk ox, reindeer	390 sq km	hiking, boat trips	mid-Jun–Aug	p175
Folgefonna	glaciers	545 sq km	hiking, summer skiing	May-Sep	p219
Forlandet	waterbird, seal & walrus breeding grounds	640 sq km	bird-watching	Jul-Aug	p384
Forollhogna	wild reindeer	1062 sq km	-	Jul-Aug	
Hallingskarvet	wild reindeer	450 sq km	hiking	Jul-Aug	
Hardangervidda	vast upland plateau, largest wild reindeer herd in Europe	3422 sq km	Nordic skiing, hiking	Jun-Aug	p188
Jostedalsbreen	Jostedalsbreen icecap (487 sq km), glaciers	1310 sq km	hiking, ice-climbing, kiting, boat trips	Jun-Aug	p244
Jotunheimen	Norway's highest mountains	1145 sq km	hiking	Jul-Aug	p184
Lierne	mountains, lynx, wolverine, bears	333 sq km	bird-watching	Jul-Aug	
Møysalen	Lofoton's last wilderness, Møysalen Peak (1262m)	51.2 sq km	-	Jul-Aug	p331
Nordvest Spitzbergen	Kongsbreen icefield, Magdalenefjord, archaeological sights, caribou & marine mammal breeding groundsp384	9914 sq km	hiking, kayaking	Jul-Aug	p384
Øvre Anarjåkka	birch & pine forests, bogs, lakelands	1399 sq km	-	Jul-Aug	
Øvre Dividal	wild park, Arctic rhododendron & heather, wolverine	743 sq km	hiking, dogsledding		p343
Øvre Pasvik	boreal forest, last Norwegian habitat of brown bear	119 sq km	hiking		p363
Rago	high peaks, plunging valleys & waterfalls, abuts Swedish national parks	167 sq km	hiking	Jul-Aug	p298
Reisa	dramatic Reisa Gorge, waterfalls, wildlife	803 sq km	hiking	Jun-Aug	p367
Rondane	reindeer, Rondane massif, archaeological sites	963 sq km	hiking, wildlife safaris	Jun-Aug	p180
Saltfjellet-Svartisen	straddles Arctic Circle, upland moors, icecaps, Sami archaeological sitesp296	2105 sq km	hiking	Jul-Aug	p296
Sør Spitsbergen	Norway's largest park, 65% ice coverage, sea-bird breeding grounds	13,282 sq km	-		
Stabbursdalen	world's northernmost pine forest	98 sq km	hiking	Jul-Aug	p355

Norwegian government promised to 'be at the forefront of the international climate effort' and announced plans to become 'carbon neutral' and cut net greenhouse gas emissions to zero by 2050. This will mostly involve offsetting its annual 54 million tonnes of emissions by purchasing carbon credits on international markets. The government also agreed to cut actual emissions by 30% by 2030. For all such good news, it is worth remembering that the average Norwegian emits 11 tonnes of greenhouse gases, three or four times the world average although in line with most other developed countries. Environmental groups have also criticised the moves as hypocritical, with

Greenpeace arguing that 'Norway should take responsibility for the 500 million tonnes of emissions caused by its exports of oil and gas'.

Climate change in Norway is most evident in the worrying signs that its glaciers may be under threat; see p64. Other touchstones of environmental health are more encouraging, with a detailed 2007 study of Arctic plant life on Svalbard by the University of Oslo (published in the prestigious journal *Science*) suggesting that the plants have proved more resilient than first thought, adapting and largely weathering the big climate swings of the past 20,000 years.

Fishing & Marine Resources

Norway's most controversial environmental issues involve marine mammal hunting, fishing rights and declining fish stocks.

'Climate change in Norway is most evident in the worrying signs that its glaciers may be under threat'

COMMERCIAL FISHING

In a draft report by the World Wildlife Fund (WWF) in 1998, it was found that Norwegians place three or four times as much pressure on the environment as the average global citizen and were 'the most environmentally destructive people on earth', thanks largely to their consumption of marine fish; the national catch amounts to 250kg of fish per Norwegian per year, over 10 times the world average. For the Norwegian government's response, see p74.

It's fair to say that Norwegians usually view the critical depletion of fish stocks in Norwegian waters as much through the prism of economic self-interest as they see it as a strictly environmental concern. Throughout recorded history, the seas off the Norwegian coast have provided bountiful fishing opportunities and thereby providing a critical backbone to the Norwegian economy. Still Norway's second-largest export earner, it was one of the country's few commercial resources in the days before oil – an essential context to understanding many of Norway's environmental policies as they relate to marine life.

Fishing and aquaculture (fish farming) remain the foundation of Norway's coastal economy, provides work for almost 22,000 people in the fishing fleet, and a host of secondary industries such as shipbuilding, fish feed, processing, packaging, fishing gear and the transportation of fish products. With an annual catch of around 2.5 to three million tonnes, Norway is the 10th-largest fishing nation in the world and it is the world's largest exporter of seafood.

A major factor in the success of Norwegian offshore fisheries has been the warm Gulf Stream waters entering the northern seas, although this varies from year to year. The larger the volume of warm water, the greater the growth of plankton in the far north and the greater the amounts of food available to fish and marine mammals.

Until about 25 years ago, deep-sea fishing in the area was pretty much a free-for-all. Ideal ocean conditions, wedded to the development of sonar, which located schools of herring and other commercially valuable fish, ensured that during the 1960s the Norwegian fishing community enjoyed particularly high catches. Such a bounty, however, was unsustainable, and by the late 1970s, herring stocks were nearly wiped out. In addition, overfishing depleted stocks of cod all across the North Atlantic.

Stung into action by the threat to tens of thousands of livelihoods, on 1 January 1977 Norway established a 200 nautical mile offshore economic zone, which was extended to Svalbard later that year and to Jan Mayen in 1980. The country now has agreements with the EU, Russia, the Faroe Islands, Iceland, Greenland and Poland to set quotas.

Almost three decades of conservation measures later, including strict quotas, the herring fishery industry is again thriving. Cod fishing regulations are now in place, although it will be many years before the numbers return.

INTERVIEW WITH HENRIETTE WESTHRINS, CURRENT STATE SECRETARY, MINISTRY OF ENVIRONMENT

Norway has been praised for its environmental protection. Is such praise justified? Yes and no: Norway has lots of nature and few inhabitants, so Norwegians can take better care of the country than many others. Each Norwegian individually, however, has about the same impact as people in other European countries. Facts about every aspect of the Norwegian environment are on our website (www.regjeringen.no). Take a look at our environmental status reports and our indicators of sustainable development on our website. You may also wish to consult NGOs such as www.wwf.no. I think you will find that we are doing a lot, but we also need to do much more.

Which areas of environmental policy does the Norwegian government need to improve? I want to reduce our own emissions and make Norway climate neutral, stop the loss of biological diversity, and eliminate emissions of persistent toxics. I want a better urban environment: less pollution, less noise, protect the green spaces and have more bike routes.

Which areas of environmental policy does the Norwegian government deserve praise for? Our new management plan for the northern ocean, the Barents Sea, with ecosystem-based management of biodiversity, strict emission controls and monitoring as well as areas out of bounds for oil exploration until more knowledge has been gained. The right of everyone in Norway to walk freely in nature, regardless of who owns the land, and that, with some exceptions, motorised vehicles are not allowed off the roads. More ambitious climate aims than the Kyoto treaty prescribes and a major effort to capture and store CO_2.

How does Norway resolve the contradiction between being one of the world's largest oil producers and its claims to be a good environmental citizen? Oil and gas extraction accounts for about one-fifth of our CO_2 emissions and just above one-fifth of our current GDP. Yes, that puts our CO_2 emissions per person up above the EU average. But our policies eliminate any national feast of exorbitant consumption. The oil era will be over relatively quickly, so the income is placed in a fund for the future and only 4% of the income is used over the annual state budget. The wealth that comes from our indirect export of CO_2 emissions gives us a global duty to take on ambitious climate aims.

Norway aims to become 'carbon neutral' and cut its net greenhouse gas emissions to zero by 2050. What types of things is the Norwegian government doing to reach this goal? We have both national and international emission reduction aims. Our road map sets out what can be done in the next few years in industry, transport, buildings and all other sectors of Norwegian society. If we can also progress by footing the bill for reducing emissions in other countries we will do so.

Audited greenhouse credits are not an escape hatch; it is an effective way of transferring technology to poor countries while reducing global emissions. The government appointed a commission to assess how our emissions could be drastically reduced. It concluded that the necessary changes are not even very costly. Look at its 2006 review of 'Natural resources and the environment' (www.ssb.no/english/subjects/01/sa_nrm).

The aquaculture industry, which has thrived for at least two decades and was born out of the depletion of wild fish stocks, concentrates mainly on Atlantic salmon and trout, but there have also been experiments with Arctic char, halibut, catfish and scallops. Currently, fish farming amounts to around 500,000 tonnes of fish per annum, but the export of pen-raised salmon and trout constitutes 55% of the value of Norway's fish exports.

This ready-made alternative to ocean fishing does carry attendant and potentially serious consequences. The main drawback is that diseases in captive stock have spread to wild populations whenever fish escape from the pens, thereby threatening wild populations. Tightened government regulations have reduced escapes in recent years, but it remains an issue of major concern.

Do current tourist numbers pose a threat to the sustainability of the fjords? Our coastline is 2650km long. If we include fjords, bays and islands we have 83,300km of seafront, so there is plenty of space and a large number of fjords. In a few fjords there are at times queues of cruise ships and cars, which does cause raised levels of local air pollution, but not at a level that can cause long-term damage. Still, we have already introduced some restrictions. We do not have massive concrete hotels strung along each beach. We are also strengthening the rules prohibiting building closer than 100m from the shoreline so as to protect people's access to the sea.

In 1998 a World Wildlife Fund (WWF) report claimed that Norwegians were the most environmentally destructive people on earth, primarily for their consumption of marine fish. Have things improved? As far as I know, that report was revised and in the end Norway got better grades. Some of the data for the comparisons – on fish, climate and water – was wrong, some was misinterpreted. Yes, we use lots of water, but unlike many other countries, we use only a tiny part of the annual rainfall. We use lots of electricity, but 99.9% is renewable energy.

We harvest about 2.5 million tonnes of marine life out of a world catch in the mid-80 millions. Yes, it is more than our share of the global population. This is, of course, because we have a very, very long coastline. Fish cross borders, so we have to cooperate with our neighbours in setting quotas. In particular cod, herring and mackerel have been overfished in the past, so sustainable quotas for all species are high on our list of priorities.

WWF did not just look at what each country does inside its borders, it examined the global footprint. Norway, like all other rich countries, has large imports and uses lots of resources abroad. If producing countries do not have strong policies, their environmental damage will be added to our account. Norway can consume with less impact and we can campaign for stronger environmental rules. The government tries both. We have consistently called for stronger international conventions.

What is the biggest environmental challenge facing Norway? Climate change is a serious global threat and a threat to Norway. With large territories in the Arctic we are particularly concerned. As an oil-producing country, Norway has a greater responsibility than many others.

What advice would you give to travellers to Norway who want to ensure that their impact upon the environment is minimal? You might take a ferry or the train to get here. Most tourists already travel by efficient public transport, but if you are fit and ready for a challenge, hike in the hills and mountains, rent a bike or a kayak and explore Norway by muscle power. You can enjoy the great outdoors without paying anyone. Get a set of maps. Or become a member of the **DNT** (www.turistforeningen.no) and follow its red painted 'T' signs from hut to hut across the mountains.

Norway has some more targeted tax regimes than others. Can you explain this further? Norway has introduced taxes on CO_2 emissions, pesticides and waste and we have mandatory deposit-return systems for bottles, cans, cars and electrical goods. I believe that this culture of sharing burdens to achieve national aims is one of our strongest assets.

As told to Anthony Ham

SEALING

Seal hunting, perhaps because of its shocking visual images, has been a lightning rod for condemnation by animal lovers and environmentalists around the world. In Norway seal hunting is restricted to two species, the harp seal and hooded seal, and the purpose is ostensibly to cull a growing population. This is mainly driven by the needs of the fishing community; it wishes to restrict the competition between fishing boats and marine mammals that depend on fish and eat up to 2.5kg per day. Sealing also provides a livelihood for people in Norway and several other North Atlantic countries.

Sealing occurs on a small scale, mainly for fur and meat, but it is argued that it's a cruel business. To mitigate protests, regulations limit seal hunters to

A DANGEROUS ENVIRONMENTAL HAZARD – MOOSE FARTS

Global warming. Fossil fuels. Moose farts... Although it doesn't quite roll off the tongue as a serious threat to the environment, a moose with gas can actually be more dangerous to the environment than your average family car.

According to a report in London's *Times* newspaper in August 2007, by doing nothing more than farting and belching every year a single adult moose releases the methane equivalent of 2100kg of CO_2 emissions, equal to about 13,000km of travel in a car. Or, to put it another way according to Reidar Andersen, the scientist at the Technical University in Trondheim who came up with this startling fact, 'shoot a moose and you have saved the equivalent of 36 flights between Oslo and Trondheim'. With an estimated 120,000 wild moose roaming the Norwegian wilds – the Norwegian authorities authorised a nationwide hunting quota of 35,000 in 2007 – that adds up to a disturbingly high output of methane, not to mention a heightened state of nervousness among otherwise innocent moose.

The Whaling Season - An Inside Account of the Struggle to Stop Commercial Whaling by Kieran Mulvaney is a passionate account of whaling by an experienced Greenpeace activist.

only two tools: a rifle and a *hakapik*, or gaff; the former is for adult seals and the latter for pups (which may not be hunted while suckling). Hunters are also required to take courses and shooting tests before each sealing season.

WHALING

No Norwegian environmental issue inspires more international fervour and emotion than that of renewed whaling in the North Atlantic.

In 1986, as a result of worldwide campaigns expressing critical concern over the state of world whale populations, the International Whaling Commission (IWC) imposed a moratorium on whale hunting. Although it has largely held, two key elements in recent years have placed the moratorium under considerable threat.

The first has been the decision by the three major whaling nations – Norway, Japan and Iceland – to either resume commercial whaling or, in the case of Japan and Iceland, to threaten to withdraw from the IWC and engage in a full-scale resumption of commercial whaling unless the moratorium is replaced by a management plan that allows some whaling.

Follow the whaling debate at Greenpeace UK (www.greenpeace.org.uk), the Whale and Dolphin Conservation Society (www.wdcs.org), the High North Alliance (www.highnorth.no), Norwegian Ministry of Fisheries (www.regjeringen.no/en/dep/fkd.html?id=257) and the International Whaling Commission (www.iwcoffice.org).

Norway resumed commercial whaling of minke whales in 1993 in defiance of an international whaling ban. While Norway supports the protection of threatened species, the government contends that minke whales, with a northeast Atlantic population of an allegedly estimated 100,000, can sustain a limited harvest. The Norwegian government, after an unanimous vote, issued a quota of 1052 in 2006, a 30% increase on the previous year's quota and more than half the number of minke whales Norway hunted every year before the moratorium was imposed. Greenpeace, which has for decades been at the forefront of anti-whaling campaigns, described the increased quota as a 'meaningless provocation of the international community'.

The second development threatening world whale stocks is a concerted campaign that has seen nations with no history of whaling – including Mauritania, Ivory Coast, Grenada, Tuvalu and even landlocked Mongolia and Mali – joining the commission. The result has seen a change from nine pro-whaling votes out of 55 in 2000 to an almost-50% split among its 73 members currently (a 75% majority is required to change IWC policy). Allegations that prowhaling votes have been rewarded with development aid have not been denied by the Japanese.

Norway, for its part, sees the moratorium as unnecessary and outdated. It counters historical evidence indicating that whalers in this region hunted

(Continued on page 85)

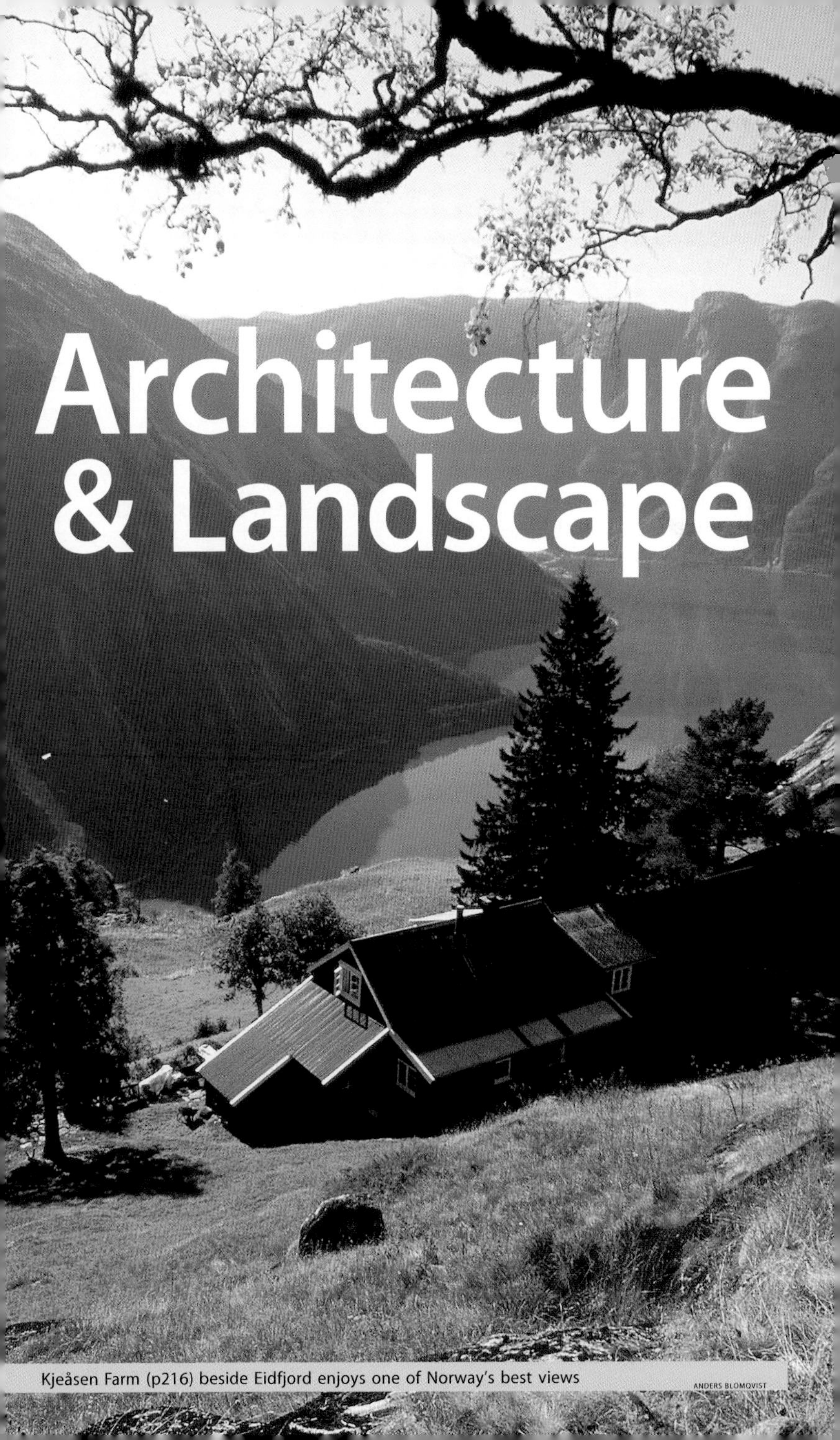

Architecture & Landscape

Kjeåsen Farm (p216) beside Eidfjord enjoys one of Norway's best views

ANDERS BLOMQVIST

Traditional Architecture

A number of Norway's architects have clearly been inspired by the country's dramatic landscapes, while recognising the need to build structures capable of withstanding the harsh dictates of Norway's climate. The results are often stunning: from rustic turf-roofed houses, whose design dates back almost two millennia, to Norway's signature stave churches, soaring religious architecture and creative adaptations of Sami symbols and some Arctic landforms.

Timber and stone are the mainstays of traditional Norwegian architecture; nowhere is this more evident than in the delightful former mining village of Røros (p171), where many of the colourful timber houses date back to the 17th and 18th centuries. In the far north, where both wood and stone were in short supply, the early nomadic Sami ingeniously built their homes of turf, which provided excellent insulation against the cold. While the rural sense of style revels in its rustic charm, Norway's urban architecture strives for a more modern aesthetic, with clean lines and minimalism all the rage.

For an overview of Norwegian architectural styles, it is well worth visiting Maihaugen (p165) in Lillehammer, or any of the excellent folk museums dotted around the country.

top 10 ARCHITECTURE

- **Arctic Cathedral (p335), Tromsø**
- **Art Nouveau Ålesund (p262)**
- **Bryggen (p195), Bergen**
- **Heddal Stave Church (p152)**
- **Miners' Cottages (p171), Røros**
- **Nidaros Cathedral (p276), Trondheim**
- **Sami Parliament (p368), Karasjok**
- **Stavanger Cathedral (p223)**
- **Urnes Stave Church (p243)**
- **Viking Ship Sports Arena (p169), Hamar**

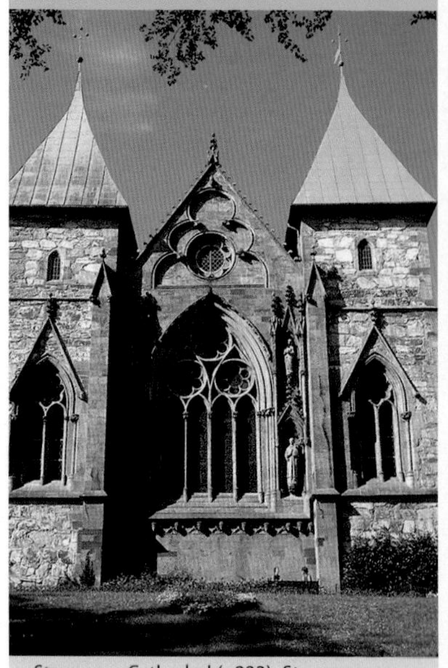

Stavanger Cathedral (p223), Stavanger
ANDERS BLOMQVIST

STAVE CHURCHES

If Norway can be said to have made one stand-out contribution to world architecture, it is undoubtedly the stave church. Seemingly conceived by a whimsical child-

An old turf-roofed farmhouse at Sunnmøre Museum (p263), Ålesund

like imagination, the stave church is an ingenious adaptation to Norway's unique local conditions. Originally dating from the late Viking Age, these ornately worked houses of worship are among the oldest surviving wooden buildings on earth, albeit heavily restored. Named for their vertical supporting posts, these churches are also distinguished by detailed carved designs, dragon-headed gables resembling the prows of classic Viking ships and by their undeniably beautiful, almost Asian, forms. Of the 500 to 600 that were originally built, only about 20 of the 28 that remain retain many of their original components. The most exquisite stave churches include those found at Heddal (p152), Ringebu (p182), the Fantoft Stave Church (p200) near Bergen and, the oldest of them all, the Unesco World Heritage–listed Urnes Stave Church (p243). More are listed in the index of this book. For more information about the construction of stave churches, see the boxed text, p240.

Ringebu's 13th-century stave church (p182)

Contemporary Architecture

Due to the need to rebuild quickly after WWII, Norway's architecture was primarily governed by functionalist necessity (the style is often called *funkis* in the local vernacular) rather than any coherent sense of style. Nowhere is this exemplified more than in the 1950, red-brick Oslo Rådhus (p95). As the style evolved, functionality was wedded to other concerns, such as recognising the importance of aesthetics in urban renewal (for example in Oslo's Grünerløkka district), and ensured that architecture once again sat in harmony with the country's environment and history.

It is with the latter concept that Norway's architects have excelled, especially in the Arctic north. Tromsø's Arctic Cathedral (p335), designed by Jan Inge Hovig in 1964, mimics Norway's glacial crevasses and auroral curtains. Another beautiful example is the Sami Parliament (p368) in Karasjok, where Arctic building materials (birch, pine and oak) lend the place a sturdy authenticity, while the use of lights to replicate the Arctic night sky and the structure's resemblance to a Sami *gamma* (tent) are extraordinary. The creative interpretation of historical Norwegian shapes also finds expression at the Viking Ship Sports Arena (p169) in Hamar.

Tromsø's Arctic Cathedral (Ishavaskaredralen; p335) featuring an auroral-curtain structure

CHRISTIAN ASLUND

The Nidaros Cathedral (p276) of Trondheim was built over the grave of St Olav

WAYNE WALTON

INTERNATIONAL INFLUENCES

Fused with the distinctive styles of Norway's own architectural flourishes are influences borrowed from elsewhere. The most uniform example of this is the Art Nouveau (Jugendstil) style that so distinguishes the harbourside districts of Ålesund (p262). Dating from the early 20th century, these buildings take on additional local charm with the clearly discernible use of symbols from traditional Norwegian mythology such as turrets, spirits and gargoyles. Other international architectural trends are evident in most larger religious buildings, which exhibit strong Anglo-Saxon influences, while the Gothic-style Nidaros Cathedral (p276) in Trondheim and the Romanesque Stavanger Cathedral (p223) bear strong traces of European architectural trends that prevailed at the time of their construction.

A harbourfront warehouse, Ålesund (p262)

JON ARNOLD IMAGES LTD / ALAMY

Signature Landscapes

FJORDS

Norway's signature landscape, the fjord, ranks among the most astonishing natural landforms anywhere in the world. The Norwegian coast is riven with these inlets distinguished by plunging cliffs, isolated farms high on forested ledges and an abundance of ice-blue water. Norway's network of fjords is so vast – and each fjord so rich in its own character – that you could spend months exploring the fjords and never grow tired of the sheer wonder and beauty of it all.

top 10 FJORDS

Eidfjord (p216)
The most spectacular branch of Hardangerfjord

Geirangerfjord (p259)
Precipitous, popular and one of Norway's signature images

Hardangerfjord (p214)
Rolling hills and lovely villages climbing up from the bank

Jøssingfjord (p147)
Surprisingly vertiginous, if less spectacular, fjord in the flatlands of the south

Lysefjord (p229)
Plunging cliffs, cruises and death-defying lookout points

Magdalenefjord (p384)
Remote Svalbard fjord that you'll probably have all to yourself

Nærøyfjord (p237)
One of Norway's narrowest and prettiest fjords

Sognefjorden (p234)
Norway's longest (and one of the most beautiful) fjord network

Trollfjord (p313)
Breathtakingly steep fjord on Lofoten

Vestfjord (p311)
Sheltered bays and pretty villages separating Lofoten from the mainland

A waterfall tumbles into Trollfjord (p313), Lofoten

WAYNE WALTON

The ice-strewn waters and glaciers of Magdalenefjord (p384), Svalbard

GRAEME CORNWALLIS

So inseparable is the idea of Norway from its fjords that it can be easy to forget that the fjords are a relatively recent phenomenon in geological terms. Although Norwegian geological history stretches back 1.8 billion years, the fjords were not carved out until much later. During the glacial periods over this time, the elevated highland plateaus that ranged across central Norway subsided at least 700m due to an ice sheet up to 2000m thick. The movement of this ice, driven by gravity down former river courses, gouged out the fjords and valleys and created the surrounding mountains by sharpening peaks and exposing high cliffs of bare rock. The fjords took on their present form when sea levels rose as the climate warmed following the last Ice Age (which ended around 10,000 years ago), flooding into the new valleys left behind by melting and retreating glaciers. Sea levels are thought to have risen by as much as 100m, creating fjords whose waters can seem impossibly deep.

Not surprisingly Norway's fjords have many admirers. In 1870 representatives from the gentlemen's clubs of London travelled to the fjords to search for the region's famous blue ice so as to provide cachet as well as coolness in the clubs' drinks. Somewhat more recently, in 2004, *National Geographic Traveler* magazine voted Norway's fjords the world's most sustainable major tourist destination. A year later, Unesco inscribed Geirangerfjord and Nærøyfjord on their World Heritage List because they 'are classic, superbly developed fjords', which are 'among the most scenically outstanding fjord areas on the planet'. And then there are travellers who are drawn again and again to the water's edge or along a narrow trail hundreds of metres above the shoreline, to marvel at the silent, pristine drama of these remarkable cathedrals of ice and rock.

ARCTIC NORTH

If the fjords have drama, Norway's Arctic north has an irrevocable sense of mystery. From Svalbard (p370), equidistant from the North Pole and Norway's Nordkapp in the north of the mainland, to the expansively beautiful Arctic Highway (p291) that carries you from the south into Arctic Norway, Norway's far north is rich in phenomena that seem to spring from a

A polar bear *(isbjørn)* rests on an ice floe, Svalbard (p370)

JONATHAN

child's imagination. The first thing you'll most likely notice is the endless horizon that never quite seems to frame a landscape of austere, cinematic beauty. In its most extreme form, this disorienting sense of a world without limit is known as *Fata Morgana* (see the boxed text, p67) whereby all sense of distance and perspective is lost. Or perhaps what you will remember most is the astonishing night sky in winter when the weird and wonderful aurora borealis (see the boxed text, p66), also called the northern lights, can seem like an evocation of a colourful ghost story writ large. The midnight sun and seemingly endless polar night (see the boxed text, p66) can be similarly disorienting, adding a strange magic to your Norwegian sojourn. Another integral element in Arctic Norway's appeal is the soulful presence of the indigenous Sami people (p42), they of the reindeer herds and proud cultural traditions – for what could be more mysterious than a people who choose to live in such an inhospitable environment. Also part of Norway's Arctic mix is Europe's only population of polar bears on Svalbard, a lichen-strewn tundra landscape, as well as its perfect architectural adaptations to the local environment (p80). For the best of Norway's Arctic highlights, see p27.

HIGH COUNTRY

If you think Norway is spectacular now, imagine what it was like 450 million years ago when the Caledonian Mountain Range, which ran along the length of Norway, was as high as the present-day Himalayas. With time, ice and water eroded them down to their current form (some capped with Europe's largest glaciers and ice fields) that covers more than half the Norwegian land mass – great news for tourists and adventure-seekers, less so for farmers with less than 3% of Norwegian soil suitable for agriculture. Norway's highest mountains are in the Jotunheimen National Park (p184) where Galdhøpiggen soars to 2469m. Nearby Glittertind (2465m and shrinking) was for a long time the king of the Norwegian mountains, but its melting glacier sees its summit retreat a little further every year. For an itinerary that takes you through some of the best of this high country, turn to p25.

(Continued from page 76)

their prey to the verge of extinction, by claiming that modern whalers have a better and more informed perspective, that they adhere to a sensible quota system and now adopt more humane methods of killing. The Norwegians claim that they support only traditional, family-owned operations and have no intention to return to industrial whaling. Many Norwegians also feel that conservationists are mainly city folk who have a sentimental relationship with animals, which is based on an unrealistic projection of human ideas and emotions onto wild sea creatures. Japan and Norway resumed trading in whale meat in 2004 and it tends to be the export market that drives the industry rather than domestic consumption, although whale meat is openly sold in fish markets (especially Bergen) – a good moment to decide where you stand on the issue.

In addition to hunting, a major threat to Norwegian whales comes from chemical pollution, particularly the polychlorinated (PCBs), which are suspected of damaging cetacean reproductive and immune systems, a phenomenon which has already led to numerous deaths from viral infections.

GEOTOURISM

One of the more exciting ecofriendly tourism ideas in recent years, Geotourism is an initiative of **National Geographic's Center for Sustainable Destinations** (NGCSD; www.nationalgeographic.com/travel/sustainable/index.html). The programme's centrepiece is the Geotourism Charter (click on 'Programs for Places' in the website and then in the Norway section); Norway is one of only three countries to have thus far signed the charter.

The Geotourism Charter's Global Statement of Principles is built around 13 commitments, all of which focus on preserving not only the environment, but also on a country's diversity of cultural, historic and scenic assets, as well as stressing community involvement. In Norway, the scheme is administered by the state-owned **Innovation Norway** (www.innovasjonnorge.no/Om-oss/Innovation-Norway/ or www.innovasjonnorge.no/reiseliv) and we spoke to Bjørn Krag Ingul, the senior advisor to its geotourism programme.

What are the first projects to begin under the Geotourism Charter? We have developed a guide on what geotourism is and how to implement it in local communities and are working on a major educational program for the travel industry in Norway, to increase the level of competence within the trade. In autumn 2007 we launched a national competition in product development, where geotourism principles are one of the main criteria for getting money, as well as financing courses for about 600 cooks on how to make local food based on local ingredients. We are also funding two pilots – one in Geiranger and Nærøyfjord and one with the Historical Hotels and the Good Life company. Both pilots aim to implement the geotourism principles in the region and within the businesses. But geotourism is still fairly new in Norway so it will take some time to implement it.

Will there be any way for visitors to participate in the projects? They can participate in the activities happening at the destinations of course and some companies also provide guidelines where the tourist must follow strict environmental rules when they visit.

Is tourism at its current levels good for the fjords or does it pose a threat? I think the fjords can handle even more visitors. The threat is if it grows out of hand, especially the cruise traffic ,which can be a problem in the future if it isn't handled right.

If you could give one piece of advice to visitors about how they should respect the local environment when visiting Norway, what would it be? My advice would be to learn about the region you are going to visit before you go, learn about the culture and history, and learn what activities you can join. You should also of course be careful not to spill garbage or pollute nature unnecessarily.

As told to Anthony Ham

For a Norwegian perspective on whaling, stop by the Whaling Museum (p131) in Sandefjord along Norway's southern coast.

Forestry

Although no forestry operation can be entirely environmentally sound, currently Norway has one of the world's most sustainable forestry industries and much of the visible damage to the forests is due to agricultural clearing and timber over-exploitation between the 17th and 20th centuries. Government-protected wilderness areas account for less than 1% of Norway's forests, well below the international standard of 5%. More than 1000 forest-dwelling species are considered to be endangered and areas of old-growth forest are extremely rare.

One remaining stand of old-growth Norwegian forest that has caught the attention of environmentalists is Trillemarka-Rollagsfjell, about 100km west of Oslo and covering 205 sq km. Environmentalists have called on the Norwegian government to set aside the area as a protected reserve to shelter the endangered species that reside in the forest; among these species are the lesser spotted woodpecker, tree-toed woodpecker, Siberian jay and golden eagle, as well as threatened plant life.

'Norwegians strongly support sorting of household waste for collection and recycling'

Today, Norway's forests set aside for cultivation cover around 25% of the country. Currently, numerous small forestry operations, mostly in eastern Norway, cut about 8.5 million cu metre annually. Clear-felling is practised in some areas but it's reasonably rare. In general, operations employ selective cutting to prevent soil erosion and unsightly landscape degradation. In addition, companies immediately re-seed the cuts, planting a total of around 50 million seedlings annually.

Wilderness Areas

Norway may have one of the lowest population densities in Europe, but due to its settlement pattern, which is unique in Europe, and favoured scattered farms over villages, even the most remote areas are inhabited and a large proportion of the population is rural-based. This factor, combined with a national appreciation – in summer, some would say that this appreciation is elevated to the level of obsession – of fresh air and outdoor recreation, has ensured that most Norwegians have kept some contact with nature.

It also means that, despite appearances, areas of true wilderness are rare. The natural world has been greatly altered by human activities in Norway and the landscape is crisscrossed by roads that connect remote homes, farmsteads and logging areas to more populated areas. All but a couple of the country's major rivers have been dammed for hydroelectric power, many Norwegian families own holiday homes beside lakes, around ski slopes or in areas of natural beauty, and even the wild-looking expanses of Finnmarksvidda and the huge peninsulas that jut into the Arctic Ocean serve as vast reindeer pastures. As a result, apart from the upland icefields and the national parks, real wilderness is limited to a few forested mountain areas along the Swedish border, scattered parts of Hardangervidda and most of Svalbard.

Recycling

Norwegians strongly support sorting of household waste for collection and recycling, and travellers are encouraged to do likewise. A deposit scheme for glass bottles has been a success and about 96% of beer and soft-drink bottles are now returned. Supermarkets give money back for returned aluminium cans and plastic bottles (usually Nkr1 to Nkr1.50). There is also a prepaid recycling charge on automobiles sold in Norway, which ensures that they're turned into scrap metal rather than roadside eyesores when their life is over.

Since the early 1970s, however, the average level of household waste generated per person has nearly doubled to around 375kg, a rise that coincides with the golden years of Norway's oil-fuelled prosperity boom. Despite Norway's generally impressive environmental record, the reaction to this increase from governments and ordinary Norwegians was slow – by 1992, just 9% of household waste was recycled – although the figures have since become a source of national pride: around 50% of household waste, and two-thirds of industrial waste is now recycled, while Norway is a world-leader when it comes to recycling electrical and electronics products. Methane from waste nonetheless still accounts for 7% of Norway's greenhouse gas emissions and Norwegians consume more than 130,000 tonnes of plastic packaging every year.

Oslo

Hemmed by a 'fjord' and kilometres of woodland, Norway's capital is an easy-going city with an eclectic architectural mix of old, new and just plain 1960s that is hard not to like. The perfect size for exploring on foot, the city boasts world-class museums, a lively nightlife and plenty of outdoor activities for the energetic.

Most visitors will find themselves struggling to choose between Oslo's numerous museums, which offer something for almost every taste: a face-to-face with the haunting image of Edvard Munch's *The Scream* at the National Gallery, a chance to stand in the shoes of an Olympic ski-jumper at the Holmenkollen Ski Museum, or a window into history and culture at the unforgettable Viking Ship, Polarship Fram or Folk Museums on Bygdøy. And Oslo is certainly the cosmopolitan heart of Norway, with a rapidly growing café and bar culture, top-notch restaurants, and nightlife options ranging from world-class opera and jazz to indie rock.

But many Oslo residents, being avid hikers, skiers and sailors, will fondly tell you that what they love most about their city is how easy it is to leave the city life behind. Located at the head of the Oslofjord (which actually isn't a fjord, but is pretty anyway), Oslo is one of Europe's largest capitals in terms of area (450 sq km) but smallest population-wise. As a result, it is the only European capital that boasts cycling, hiking, ice-skating, kayaking, sailing and skiing, all within its city limits and a short train ride away.

HIGHLIGHTS

- Walk in the footsteps of Henrik Ibsen down Karl Johans gate for coffee at the **Grand Café** (p110)
- Eat ice cream as you stroll with the locals in the **city centre** (p93) and wave a Norwegian flag on 17 May, Norway's **national day** (p108)
- Pick summer blueberries and go winter skiing in Oslo's **Nordmarka** (p105)
- Come up with ways to cheat security at the **Munch Museum** (p103) then start the afternoon in one of **Grünerløkka's cafés or bars** (p112) and find yourself still there early the next morning
- Reconsider parenthood while looking at the works of Gustav Vigeland at **Vigeland Park** (p99)
- Examine the ships and charts of the Viking Ship, Kon-Tiki and Polership Fram Museums on **Bygdøy** (p101)
- Enjoy an impromptu dinner of shrimp on the docks at **Aker Brygge** (p112)

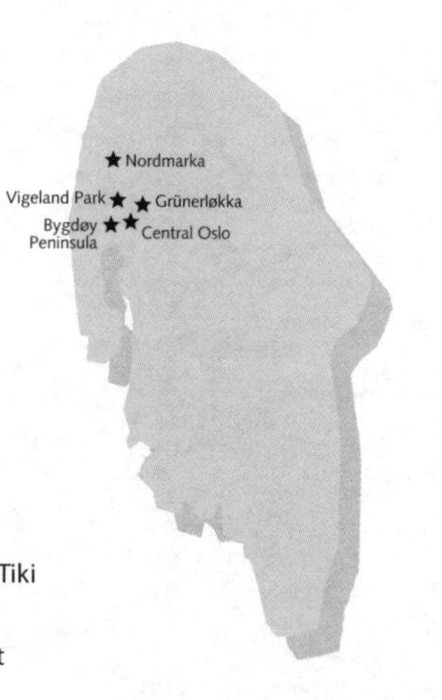

POPULATION: 548,000	HIGHEST ELEVATION: FJELLSJØKAMPEN 812M

HISTORY

The name Oslo is derived from the words *Ás*, the Old Norse name for the Norse Godhead, and *lo*, meaning 'pasture', yielding roughly 'the fields of the gods'.

The city was originally founded in 1049 by King Harald Hardråda (Harald Hard-Ruler; see p32), whose son Olav Kyrre (Olav the Peaceful) set up a cathedral and a corresponding bishopric here. In the late 13th century, King Håkon V created a military presence by building the Akershus Festning (Akershus Fortress; see p98) in the hope of deterring the Swedish threat from the east. After the mid-14th-century bubonic plague wiped out half of the country's population, Norway united with Denmark and, from 1397 to 1624, Norwegian politics and defence were handled from Copenhagen. Oslo slipped into obscurity and, in 1624, it burned to the ground. It was resurrected by King Christian IV, who rebuilt it on a more easily defended site and renamed it Christiania, after his humble self.

For three centuries, the city held on as a seat of defence. In 1814 the framers of Norway's first constitution designated it the official capital of the new realm, but their efforts were effectively nullified by Sweden, which had other ideas about Norway's future and unified the two countries under Swedish rule. In 1905, when that union was dissolved and Norway became a separate kingdom, the stage was set for Christiania to flourish as the capital of modern Norway. It reverted to its original name, Oslo, in 1925 and the city has never looked back.

ORIENTATION

Oslo's central train station (Oslo Sentralstasjon or Oslo S) sits at the eastern end of the city centre, with the Galleri Oslo Bus Terminal not far away to the northeast. From Oslo S the main street, Karl Johans gate, forms a ceremonial axis westward through the heart of the city to the Royal Palace. Most sights, including the harbour front and Akershus Festning, are within a 15-minute walk of Karl Johans gate, as are the majority of hotels and pensions. Many of the sights outside the centre, including Vigeland Park and the Munch Museum, are just a short bus or tram ride away. The Bygdøy Peninsula is a mere 10-minute ferry ride across the harbour.

Maps

The tourist offices distribute a detailed and free city plan. Unless you're heading out to the suburbs, it should be sufficient. On the reverse side is a map of the T-bane (metro) system and an inset covering Holmenkollen.

INFORMATION

Bookshops

Ark Bokhandel (Map pp96-7; ☎ 22 47 32 00; www.ark.no; Øvre Slottsgate 23-25; closed Sun) Good English-language and stationery section; branches around town.

Nomaden (Map pp96-7; ☎ 23 13 14 15; www.nomaden.no; Uranienborgveien 4; closed Sun) Travel books, maps and gear.

Norli (Map pp96-7; ☎ 22 00 43 00; www.norli.no; Universitetsgata 20-24; closed Sun) Largest bookshop in Norway.

Ringstrøms Bookshop (Map pp96-7; ☎ 22 20 00 13; www.ringstrom-antikvariat.no; Ullevålsveien 1; closed Sun) Secondhand and antiquarian books and CDs.

Tronsmo (Map pp96-7; ☎ 22 99 03 99; www.tronsmo.no; Kristian Augusts gate 19; closed Sun) Alternative bookshop with feminist, gay, lesbian and political works.

Emergency

Ambulance (☎ 113)

Fire (☎ 110)

Police (Map pp96-7; ☎ 112; Hammersborggata 10)

Internet Access

Arctic Internet Café (Map pp96-7; ☎ 22 17 19 40; Oslo S; per 30/60min Nkr35/60; 8am-midnight)

Deichmanske Bibliotek (Municipal Library; Map pp96-7; ☎ 22 43 29 00; Arne Garborgs plass; free access limited to an hr, unlimited wi-fi; 10am-6pm Mon-Fri, 9am-2pm Sat Jun-Aug; 10am-7pm Mon-Fri, 10am-4pm Sat Sep-May)

IT-Palasset (Map p93; ☎ 22 46 21 12; www.it-palasset.no; Majorstua T-bane, Sørkedalsveien 1; per hr Nkr60; 10am-midnight Mon-Fri, 11am-midnight Sat & Sun)

Use-It (Map pp96-7; ☎ 22 41 51 32; Møllergata 3; free access; 9am-6pm Mon-Fri, 11am-5pm Sat Jun-Aug; shorter hrs rest-of-year)

WI-FI ACCESS

Free wi-fi is popular in many of Oslo's cafés; the tourist office keeps a list of options. Most ask that you buy something before logging on.

Kaffe & Krem (Map pp96-7; ☎ 22 83 25 10; Haakon VII gate)

Nobel Peace Center (Map pp96-7; 48 30 10 00; Aker Brygge) At an important sight.

QBA (Map p93; ☎ 22 35 24 60; Olaf Ryesplass 4; Grünerløkka)

Tea Lounge (Map p93; Thorvold Meyersgate 33; Grünerløkka) A bar we recommend.

OSLO IN....

Two Days

Start your day with a quick stroll through the centre of town, passing by the elegant **Stortinget** (Parliament building; p95), the **National Theatre** (p115) and **Oslo Cathedral** (p94), all along the busy pedestrian thoroughfare of Karl Johans gate. Stop for a coffee at the **Grand Café** (p110), Henrik Ibsen's favourite haunt, before ducking into the nearby **National Gallery** (p93) on Universitetsgata for a representative dose of artwork by Edvard Munch or, for the bookish, wander up Henrik Ibsensgate to the **Ibsen Museum** (p94).

Try an al fresco, pier-side lunch of peal-and-eat shrimp on **Aker Brygge** (p112) from one of the local fishing boats. For dessert combine a pastry stop at **Pascal** (p112) with a visit to the adjacent **Nobel Peace Center** (p94). From Aker Brygge, take a ferry to **Bygdøy** (p101) and spend your afternoon learning about the exploits of Norway's greatest explorers at the **Polership Fram** or **Viking Ship Museums** (p102). Or head to the open-air **Folk Museum** (p102) to see buildings and exhibits from across Norway.

By night, head to the bars, cafés and restaurants of Oslo's Greenwich Village, **Grünerløkka** (p112), and/or treat yourself to a great view and opulent service at the **Holmenkollen Park Hotel** (p110).

Four Days

Follow the two-day itinerary, but with the extra time you can linger in the medieval **Akershus Castle** (p98) and visit the **Norwegian Resistance Museum** (p99). You will have time to wander among the bold, earthy statues of Emil Vigeland at **Vigeland Park** (p99) and stop in at the **Vigeland Museum** (p100).

The energetic might try spending an afternoon walking, skiing or biking in the **Nordmarka** (p105), or simply take the T-bane up to **Frognerseteren** (p113) for a good view and some apple cake. The **Holmenkollen ski-jump** and adjacent **Ski Museum** (p104) are worth a stop on the way back down.

Make space in your schedule for an evening at one of the harbour-side restaurants on **Aker Brygge** (p112) or for the truly gourmand try Oslo's two-Michelin star **Bagatelle** (p111).

One Week

With a week in Oslo, you'll have a chance to take in some of the city's more specialised (or simply bizarre) museums, wander well beyond the well-beaten track of Karl Johans gate or take a day trip.

The **Historical Museum** (p94) and **Munch Museum** (p103) in particular are worth a stop and the **Astrup Fearnly Museum** (p93) proves that Norwegians are not as conformist as they may seem. On a sunny day, families might enjoy a ferry ride and picnic among the 12th-century ruins on **Hovedøya** (p106). The quirky 18th-century homes of the **Damstredet District** (p99), the bazaars in **Grønland** (p112) and the up-and-coming **Gamlebyen** (p99), are all distinctive neighbourhoods within 10 minutes of the city centre.

Both the **Oscarsborg Fortress** (p118) at Drøbak and the cobbled streets of Gamlebyen, the old quarter of **Fredrikstad** (p120), are well worth a day trip.

Laundry

A Snarvask (Map p93; ☎ 22 37 57 70, 41 42 92 53; Thorvald Meyersgate 18; wash/dry Nkr35/30; 🕑 10am-7pm Mon-Fri, 10am-3pm Sat)

Selva Laundry (Map pp96-7; ☎ 41 64 08 33; Ullevålsveien 15; wash Nkr40-90, dry Nkr30; 🕑 8am-9pm)

Left Luggage

Oslo S has various sizes of lockers priced from Nkr20 to Nkr30 per 24 hours.

Libraries

Deichmanske Bibliotek (Map pp96-7; ☎ 22 43 29 00; 4 Arne Garborgs plass; 🕑 10am-6pm Mon-Fri, 9am-2pm Sat Jun-Aug; 10am-7pm Mon-Fri, 10am-4pm Sat Sep-May) The largest public library in Norway, it has a reading room with foreign newspapers and magazines.

National Library (Nasjonalbiblioteket; Map pp96-7; ☎ 81 00 13 00; www.nb.no; Drammensveien 42; 🕑 8.30am-3pm Mon-Fri May-Sep, 8.30am-3.45pm

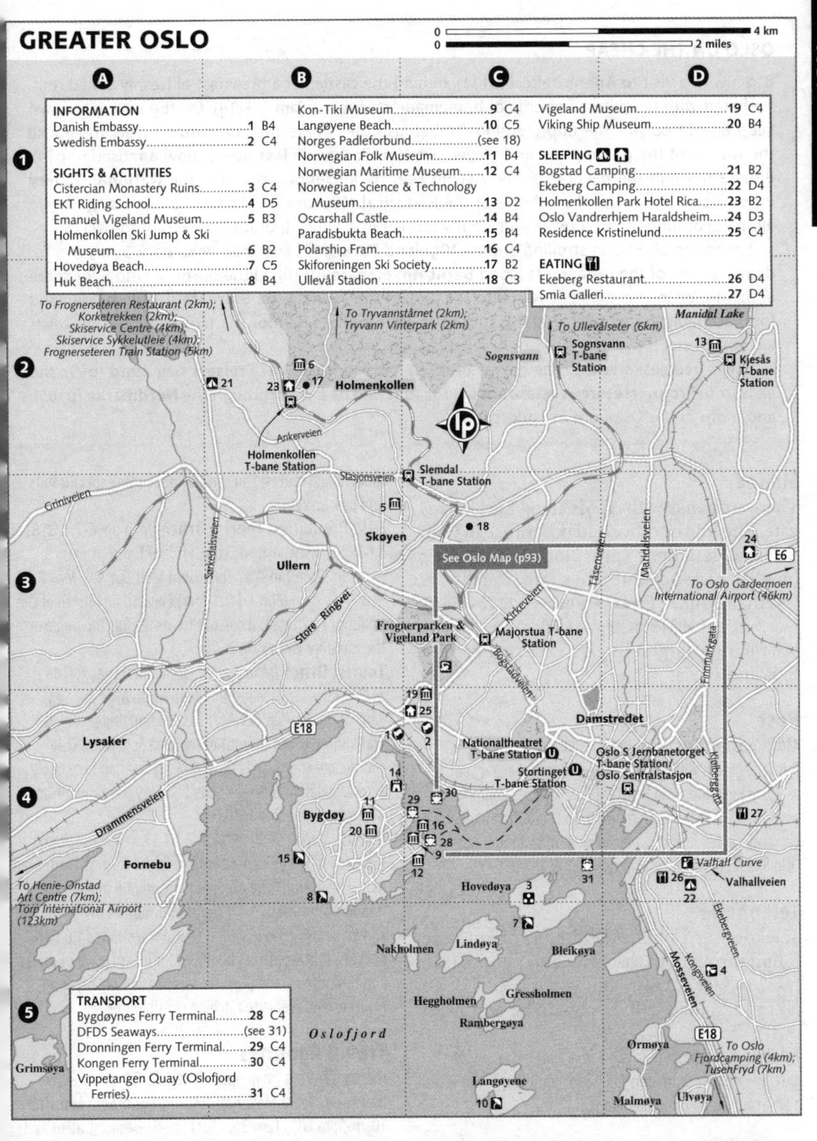

Mon-Fri Sep-May) Contains the world's largest collection of material about and by Henrik Ibsen.

Medical Services

If you're pressed for time (and not worried about the expense) the Oslo Kommunale Legevaketen clinic has a list of private doctors they recommend.

Jernbanetorget Apotek (Map pp96-7; ☎ 22 41 24 82; Fred Olsens gate) A 24-hour pharmacy opposite Oslo S.

Oslo Kommunale Legevakten (Oslo Emergency Clinic; Map pp96-7; ☎ 22 93 22 93; Storgata 40; 24hr) Casualty and emergency medical clinic.

Tøyen Tannlegevakten (Map p93; ☎ 22 19 18 00; Kjølberggata 29; 7-10pm Mon-Fri, 11am-2pm & 7am-11pm Sat & Sun) Recomammended dental practice.

OSLO ON THE CHEAP

Begin with a visit to **Åpent Bakeri** (p111), behind the castle, for a breakfast of freshly baked rolls, slathered with unlimited amounts of homemade strawberry jam (Nkr14). On the walk into town keep an eye out for the unpretentious Nobel Institute, where the committee meets to choose the winner of the peace prize, and playwright **Henrik Ibsen's last home**, now a museum (p94). Browse through the galleries at the **Astrup Fearnly Museum** (opposite), the **National Gallery** (opposite) or check out the exhibits at the **Historical Museum** (p94) near the university; they're all free. For lunch snag a *polse* (hot dog) wrapped in a *lumpe* (potato flour wrap) for Nkr15.

Spend the afternoon strolling around **Vigeland Park** (p99) and then head back into town for dinner at one of the restaurants along **Bernt Ankersgate** (p110) a little north of Oslo S for some authentic Vietnamese (mains Nkr60 to Nkr105). In the evening, try **Stargate** (p114) in Grønland for reasonably priced beer (Nkr35). Tuck in at **MS Innvik** (p109) for the night and let the waves lull you to sleep.

Other freebies: a visit to the graves of Ibsen and Munch at **Vår Frelsers Gravlund** (p99); the view from **Frognerseteren restaurant** (p113), followed by a walk through the **Nordmarka** (p105); and a dip in the Oslofjord at **Huk** (p106).

Money

There are banks with ATMs along Karl Johans gate. The tourist office and post office in Oslo S exchange money (into Norwegian kroner only) at a less advantageous rate (usually 3% less than banks). **Forex** (Map pp96-7; ☎ 22 41 30 60; www.forex.no; Fridtjof Nansens plass 6 & Oslo S; 🕑 9am-6pm Mon-Fri) is the largest foreign exchange service in Scandinavia.

Post

Main post office (Map pp96-7; ☎ 23 14 90 00; cnr Prinsens gate & Kirkegata) To receive mail, have it sent to Poste Restante, Oslo Sentrum Postkontor, Dronningens gate 15, 0101 Oslo, though pick it up using the Kirkegata entrance. You'll find convenient post office branches at Oslo S, Solli plass and on Grensen (all Map pp96–7).

Telephone

Telekort card phones and coin phones are found throughout the city. Coin phones take Nkr1 to Nkr20 coins, but you'll need at least Nkr5 for a local call. Faxes can be sent from post offices.

Telehuset (Map pp96-7; ☎ 81 54 44 00; Haakon VII gate 1; 🕑 7am-9pm Mon-Fri, 10am-6pm Sat) If you want a SIM-card for your mobile phone.

Tourist Information

Den Norske Turistforening (DNT; Norwegian Mountain Touring Club; Map pp96-7; ☎ 22 82 28 22; www.turist foreningen.no; Storget 3; 🕑 10am-5pm Mon-Wed & Fri, 10am-6pm Thu, 10am-2pm Sat, open 1hr earlier in summer) Provides information, maps and brochures on hiking in Norway and sells memberships, which include discounted rates on the use of mountain huts along the main hiking routes. You can also book some specific huts and pick up keys.

Oslo Promotion Tourist Office (Map pp96-7; ☎ 81 53 05 55; www.visitoslo.com; Fridtjof Nansens plass 5; 🕑 9am-7pm Jun-Aug, 9am-5pm Mon-Sat Apr, May & Sep, 9am-4pm Mon-Fri Oct-Mar) Located just north of the Rådhus (Town Hall). Look out for its useful *Oslo Guide* or the monthly *What's On in Oslo*.

Tourist Office (Map pp96-7; Jernbanetorget 1, Oslo S; 🕑 8am-11pm May-Aug, 8am-11pm Mon-Sat Sep, 8am-5pm Mon-Sat Oct-Apr) Easy to find under the glass Trafikanten tower in front of the Oslo S; handles Oslo-specific questions, sells the Oslo Pass and can help book accommodation. Also sells city bike day pass and 24-hour Audio Tor i-pod tour (p107).

Use-It (Map pp96-7; ☎ 22 41 51 32; www.use-it.no; Møllergata 3; 🕑 9am-6pm Mon-Fri Jul & Aug, 11am-5pm Mon-Fri Sep-Jun) The exceptionally helpful and savvy Ungdomsinformasjonen (Youth Information Office, better known as Use-It) is aimed at (but not restricted to) backpackers. It makes (free) bookings for inexpensive or private accommodation and provides information on anything from current events to hitching possibilities.

Travel Agencies

Kilroy Travels (Map pp96-7; ☎ 02633; www.kilroy travels.no; Nedre Slottsgate 23; 🕑 10am-6pm Mon-Thu, 10am-5pm Fri, 11am-3pm Sat) Specialises in student and youth travel and discounted stand-by tickets.

SIGHTS

Whether you're artistic or literary, a peacenik or a history enthusiast, an explorer or an athlete, chances are there is a museum in Oslo tailor-made for you. Most are clustered around the city centre, on Bygdøy or near Vigeland Park.

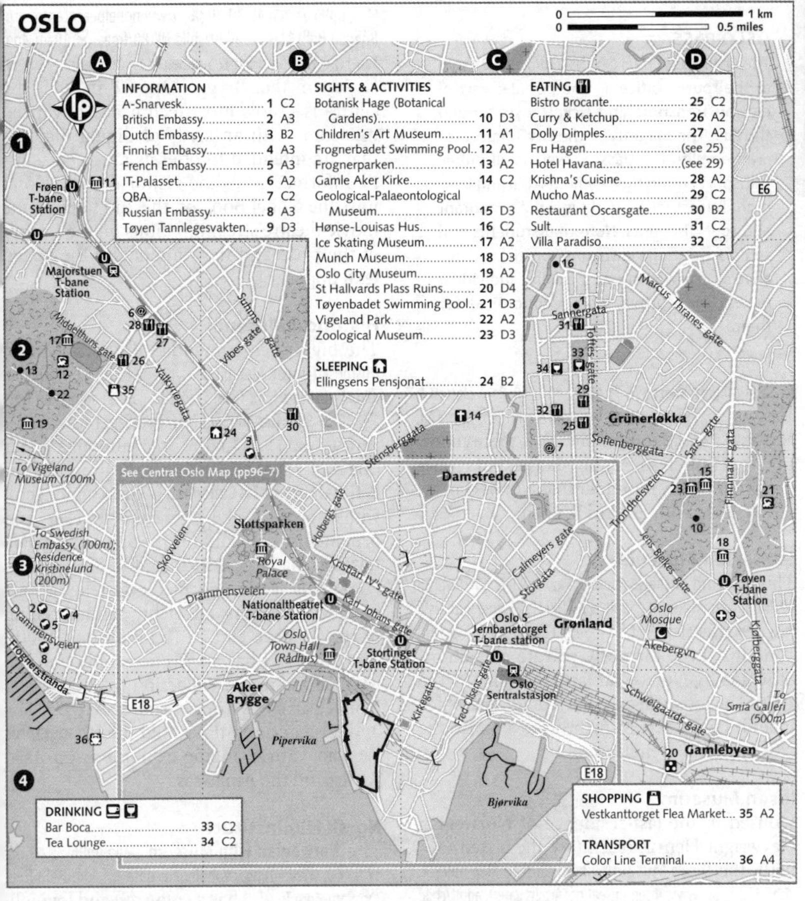

Central Oslo

ART GALLERIES & MUSEUMS

National Gallery

One of Oslo's major highlights is the **National Gallery** (Nasjonalgalleriet; Map pp96-7; ☎ 21 98 20 00; www.nasjonalmuseet.no; Universitetsgata 13; admission free; 🕐 10am-6pm Tue, Wed & Fri, 10am-7pm Thu, noon-5pm Sat & Sun). It houses the nation's largest collection of Norwegian art, including works from the Romantic era and more-modern works from 1800 to WWII. Some of Edvard Munch's best-known creations are on display, including his most renowned work, *The Scream*; see the boxed text, p103. There's also an impressive collection of European art with works by Gauguin, Picasso, El Greco and many of the impressionists: Manet, Degas, Renoir, Matisse, Cézanne and Monet.

For more on Edvard Munch, see p51.

Astrup Fearnley Museum

With its often steamy content, this **museum** (Astrup Fearnley Museet; Map pp96-7; ☎ 22 93 60 60; www.afmuseet.no; Dronningens gate 4; admission free; 🕐 11am-5pm Tue, Wed & Fri, 11am-7pm Thu, noon-5pm Sat & Sun) certainly begs the question, 'what is art?' Don't miss the gilded ceramic sculpture *Michael Jackson and Bubbles*, by Jeff Koons.

National Museum of Contemporary Art

Featuring the National Gallery's collections of post-WWII Scandinavian and international art is the **National Museum of Contemporary Art** (Museet

OSLO PASS

The **Oslo Pass** (1/2/3 days Nkr210/300/390), sold at the tourist office, is one popular way of cutting transport and ticket costs around the city. The majority of the city's museums are free with the pass, as well as all public transport within the city limits (barring late-night buses). Other perks include restaurant and tour discounts. Note that students and seniors get large discounts on ticket fares anyway, so walking and buying individual tickets may prove more economical for them.

for Samtidskunst; Map pp96-7; ☎ 22 86 22 10; Bank plassen 4; admission free; ⏰ 11am-5pm Tue, Wed & Fri, 11am-8pm Thu, noon-5pm Sat & Sun). Some of the 3000-piece collection is definitely an acquired taste, but it does provide a timely reminder that Norwegian art didn't cease with Edvard Munch.

Stenersen Museum

This **museum** (Stenersenmuseet; Map pp96-7; ☎ 23 49 36 00; Munkedamsveien 15; adult/child Nkr45/25, free with Oslo Pass; ⏰ 11am-5pm Wed & Fri-Sun, 11am-7pm Tue & Thu) contains three formerly private collections of works by Norwegian artists from 1850 to 1970. The museum and much of the art, which includes works by Munch, were a gift to the city by Rolf E Stenersen.

Ibsen Museum

Housed in the last residence of Norwegian playwright Henrik Ibsen (see the boxed text, p50), the **Ibsen Museum** (Ibsen-Museet; Map pp96-7; ☎ 22 12 35 50; www.ibsenmuseet.no; Arbins gate 1; adult/child Nkr25/70, free with Oslo Pass; ⏰ guided tours 11am-6pm & hourly, 11am-5pm Tue-Sun May-Sep, 11am-4pm Tue-Sun Sep-May) is a must-see for Ibsen fans along with his birthplace of Skien (p153) and Grimstad (p138), where the eminent playwright spent his formative years. The study remains exactly as he left it and other rooms have been restored in the style and colours popular in Ibsen's day. Visitors can even glance into the bedroom where he uttered his famously enigmatic last words *'Tvert imot!'* ('To the contrary!'), before dying on 23 May 1906.

Nobel Peace Center

Norwegians take pride in their role as international peacemakers, which explains the central location of the new **Nobel Peace Center** (Fredssetner; Map pp96-7; ☎ 48 30 10 00; www.nobelpeacecentre.org; Brynjulf Bulls plass 2; adult/child Nkr80/free; ⏰ 10am-4pm Tue-Fri, 11am-5pm Sat & Sun Sep-May; 10am-6pm Mon-Fri Jun-Aug) in Aker Brygge. Opened in 2005, the centre is Oslo's most technically advanced museum, with an array of digital displays that are intended to offer as much or as little information as the visitor desires. Don't miss the Nobel Book on the 2nd floor or the movie theatre streaming films on the history of the prize and its winners (see the boxed text, opposite).

Historical Museum

The highly recommended **Historical Museum** (Historisk Museet; Map pp96-7; ☎ 22 85 99 12; www.khm.uio.no; University of Oslo, Frederiks gate 2; admission free; ⏰ 10am-5pm Tue-Sun mid-May–mid-Sep, 11am-4pm Tue-Sun rest-of-year) is actually three museums under one roof. Most interesting is the ground floor **National Antiquities Collection** (Oldsaksamlingen), with displays of Viking-era coins, jewellery and ornaments. Look out for the 9th-century **Hon treasure**, the largest such find in Scandinavia (2.5kg). A section on medieval religious art includes the doors and richly painted ceiling of the Ål stave church (built around 1300). The 2nd level has an Arctic exhibit and the Myntkabinettet, a collection of the earliest Norwegian coins from as early as AD 995. The 2nd level and top floor hold the **Ethnographic Museum**, with changing exhibitions on Asia, Africa and the Americas.

Norsk Filminstitutt

The **Norwegian Film Museum** (Map pp96-7; ☎ 22 47 45 00; www.nfi.no; Dronningens gate 16; admission free; ⏰ 9am-4pm Tue-Fri) has a colourful and lovingly presented selection of displays on the history of filmmaking, clips of old films (from silent, black-and-white shorts, to WWII documentaries) and pictures of Norwegian stars. Classic movies are screened regularly in the theatre on the 2nd floor.

HISTORIC SIGHTS

Oslo Cathedral

Dating from 1697, the **Oslo Cathedral** (Domkirke; Map pp96-7; ☎ 22 31 46 00; Stortorget 1; admission free; ⏰ closed for renovations till 2009) is worth seeing for its elaborate stained glass by Emanuel Vigeland (brother of Gustav) and painted ceiling (completed between 1936 and 1950). The exceptional altarpiece, a 1748 model of the Last Supper and the Crucifixion by Michael Rasch, was an

THE WORLD'S MOST PRESTIGIOUS PRIZE

Most Nobel prizes – physics, chemistry, medicine, literature and economics – are awarded every October in Stockholm, but the most prestigious prize of all, the peace prize, is reserved for Oslo. In his will in 1895, Alfred Nobel, the Swedish founder of the prize and inventor of dynamite, instructed that the interest on his vast fortune be awarded each year 'to those who, during the preceding year, shall have conferred the greatest benefit on mankind.'

It is unclear why Nobel chose Norway to administer the peace prize, but whatever the reason, it is a committee of five Norwegians, appointed for six-year terms by the Norwegian Storting (parliament), that chooses the winner each year. Their meetings, held in a room of the Nobel Institute that is decorated with the pictures of winners past, from Mother Teresa (1979) to Mikhail Gorbachev (1990) and Al Gore (2007), are closed-door affairs presided over by the chairman of the Norwegian Nobel Committee, professor Ole Mjøs. Meetings are also attended by the institute's director, Geir Lundestad. Appointed director in 1990, Lundestad filled us in on some prize history and discussed his pet project the new **Nobel Peace Center** (Map pp96-7; www.nobelpeacecenter.org); see opposite for details of the centre.

What's the difference between being nominated and short-listed for the peace prize? Anyone can be nominated, from President George Bush to Madonna, and this often causes a huge outcry, but there is a big difference from being nominated to being selected as the winner! We start from almost 200 candidates in February. The list is cut down to 30, then five and the rest of the time is spent focusing on the qualifications of the candidates on the shortlist.

Is the committee ever criticised for being too secretive? The committee is transparent, but it is true that the list of nominees is closed for 50 years and no minutes are kept, though some of the members keep notes, which they have made public.

How has the nature of the prize changed while you've been director? The definition of peace has slowly broadened to include elements that reflect the changing world. Human rights, for example, was initially a very controversial interpretation when it [the prize] was given in 1960 to South African activist Albert Lutuli. The environment was added as a road to peace in 2004 and there is always pressure to widen the definition further.

Describe the ideal candidate? Many see the prize as a declaration of sainthood, but winners are often just more or less ordinary people that have tried to do something useful for peace. Their efforts have been heroic, but they are all very different. At the same time, they share a vision and they have the courage to carry it out.

What is special about the new Fredssetner? The new peace centre is where we tell the story of all the laureates. It is the most electronically advanced museum in Oslo and the idea is that people can choose to learn as much or as little as they want to find out. It is up to you.

As told to Kari Lundgren

original feature of the church (from 1700), but it was moved all over the country before being returned from Prestnes church in Majorstue in 1950. The organ front and pulpit were both part of the original construction. Occasional concerts are held in the church (Nkr100).

The bazaar halls (Basarhallene; Map pp96–7), around the back of the church, date from 1858 and are currently used by summer handicraft sales outlets.

Stortinget

Built in 1866, Norway's yellow-brick **parliament building** (Map pp96-7; ☎ 23 31 35 96; www.stortinget.no; Karl Johans gate 22; admission free; guided tours in Norwegian & English 10am & 1pm, in German 11.30am Jul & Aug, Sat only rest-of-year), right in the city centre and staring up the hill towards the royal palace, is one of Europe's more charming parliaments.

Oslo Rådhus

This twin-towered **town hall** (Rådhus; Map pp96-7; ☎ 02 180; Fridtjof Nansens plass; adult/child Nkr40/free, free Sep-May or with Oslo Pass; 8.30am-5pm May-Aug, 9am-4pm rest-of-year), completed in 1950 to commemorate the city's 900th anniversary, houses the city's political administration. Something of an Oslo landmark, its red brick functionalist exterior is unusual, if not particularly imaginative. The entrance is lined with wooden reliefs from Norse mythology and the interior halls and chambers are decorated with splashy

CENTRAL OSLO

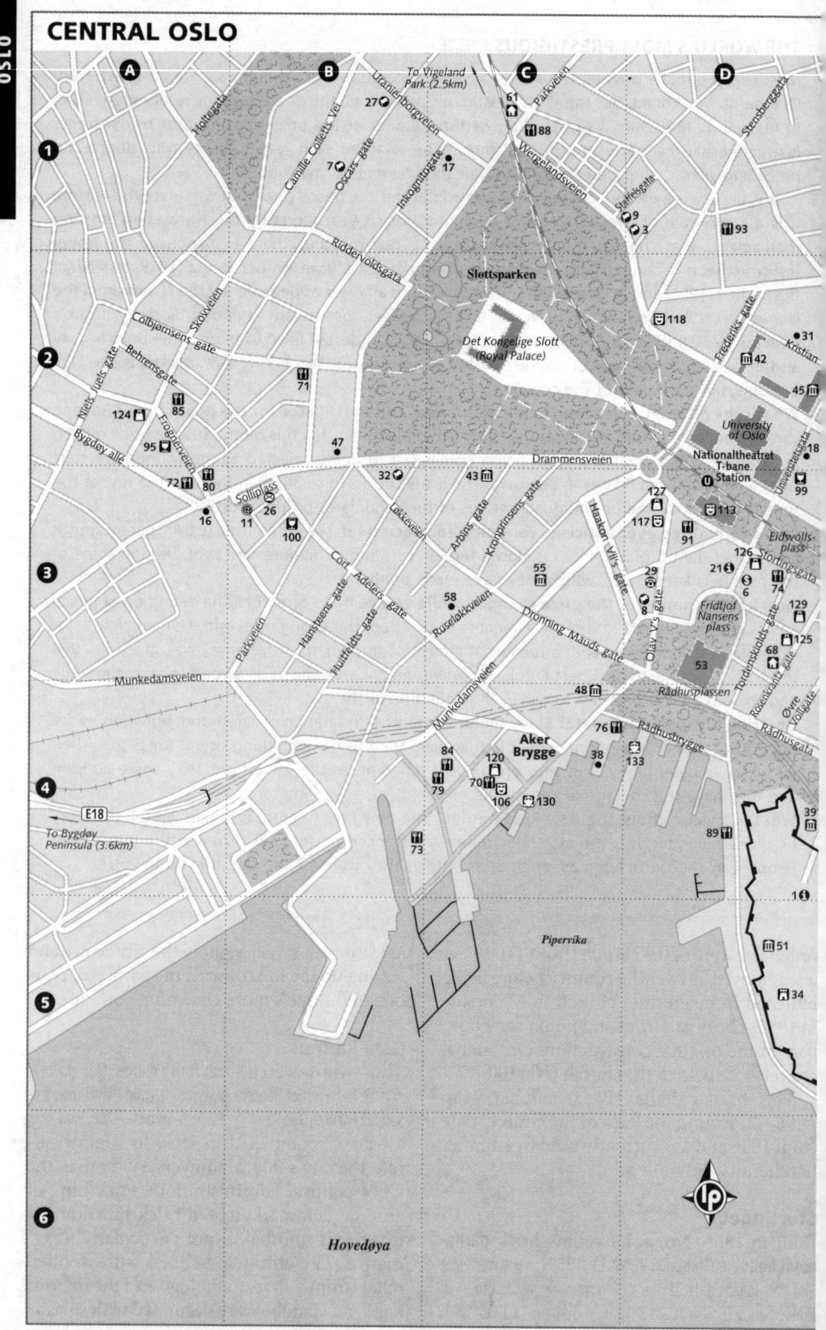

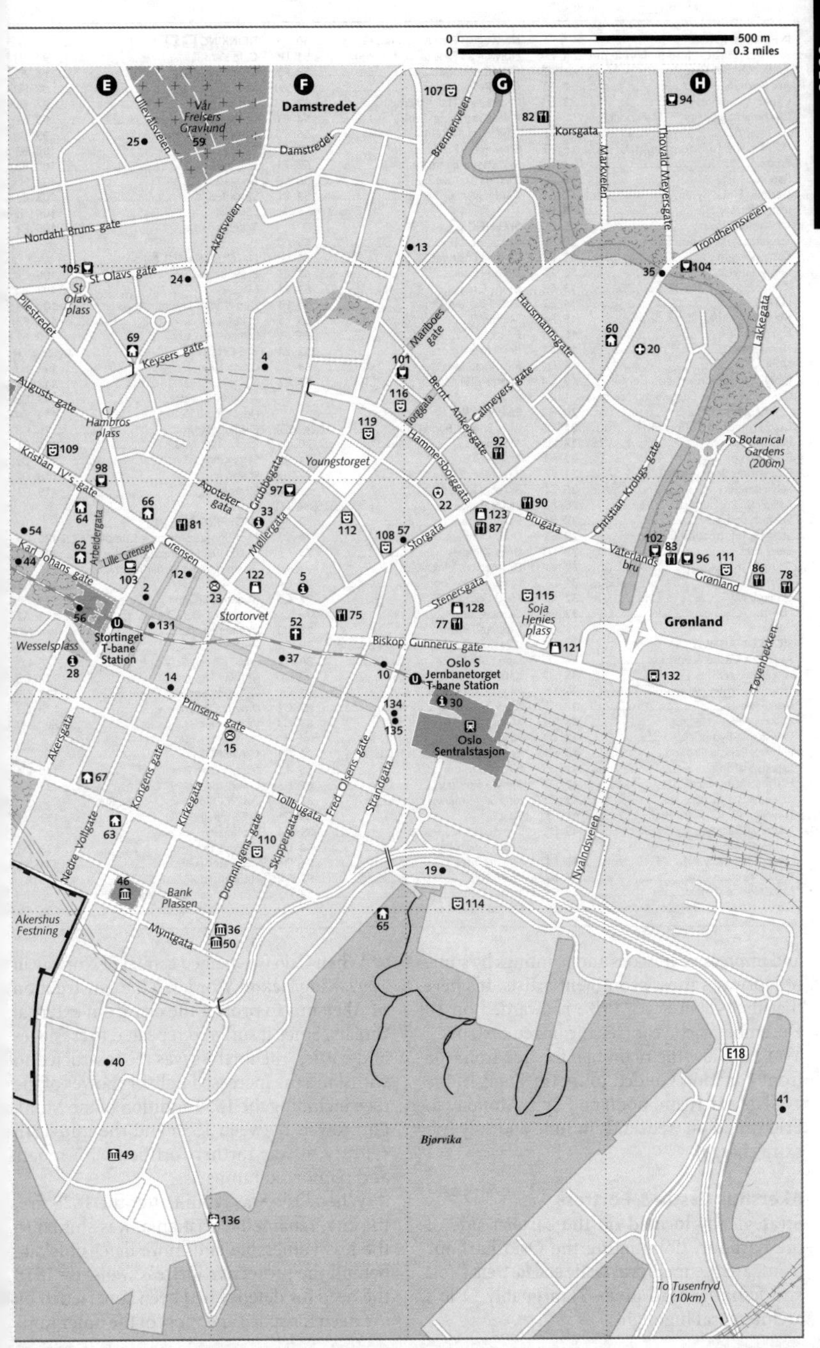
0 500 m
0 0.3 miles
Vår Frelsers Gravlund
Damstredet
Ullevålsveien
Nordahl Bruns gate
Akersveien
St Olavs gate
St Olavs plass
Pilestredet
Keysers gate
Augusts gate
CJ Hambros plass
Kristian IV's gate
Arbeidergata
Lille Grensen
Karl Johans gate
Grensen
Apotekergata
Grubbegata
Møllergata
Youngstorget
Torggata
Hammersborggata
Mariboes gate
Brenneriveien
Korsgata
Markveien
Thorvald Meyersgate
Trondheimsveien
Hausmannsgate
Calmeyers gate
Bernt Ankersgate
Storgata
Brugata
Christian Krohgs gate
Vaterlands bru
Grønland
Lakkegata
To Botanical Gardens (200m)
Stortorvet
Stortinget T-bane Station
Wesselsplass
Biskop Gunnerus gate
Stenersgata
Soja Henies plass
Oslo S Jernbanetorget T-bane Station
Oslo Sentralstasjon
Tøyenbekken
Prinsens gate
Akersgata
Kongens gate
Kirkegata
Tollbugata
Fred Olsens gate
Strandgata
Dronningens gate
Skippergata
Nedre Vollgate
Bank Plassen
Myntgata
Akershus Festning
Nyalndsveien
E18
Bjørvika
To Tusenfryd (10km)

INFORMATION
Akershus Fortress Information Centre 1 D4
Arctic Internet Café (see 30)
Ark Bokhandel 2 E3
Canadian Embassy 3 D1
Deichmanske Bibliotek (Municipal Library) 4 F2
Den Norske Turistforening (DNT) 5 F3
Forex (see 30)
Forex 6 D3
German Embassy 7 B1
Irish Embassy 8 D3
Japanese Embassy 9 D1
Jernbanetorget Apotek 10 F3
Kaffe & Krem 11 B3
Kilroy Travels 12 E3
Kvinnefronten 13 G1
LLH 14 E3
Main Post Office 15 F4
National Library 16 A3
Nomaden 17 C1
Norli 18 D2
Opera House Information Centre 19 G4
Oslo Kommunale Legevakten (Oslo Emergency Clinic) 20 H2
Oslo Promotion Tourist Office 21 D3
Police 22 G3
Post Office 23 F3
Ringstrøms Bookshop 24 E2
Selva Laundry 25 E1
Solli Plass Post Office 26 B3
Spanish Embassy 27 B1
Storting Information Centre 28 E3
Telehuset 29 D3
Tourist Office 30 G4
Tronsmo 31 D2
US Embassy 32 B3
Use-It 33 F3

SIGHTS & ACTIVITIES
Akershus Castle & Fortress 34 D5
Anker Bridge 35 H2
Astrup Fearnley Museum 36 F5
Bazaar Halls 37 F3
Båtservice Sightseeing 38 C4
Christiania Bymodell 39 D4
Fortress Parade Ground 40 E5
Gekko Klatring 41 H5
Historical Museum 42 D2
Ibsen Museum 43 C3
Narvisen Outdoor Ice Rink 44 E3
National Gallery 45 D2
National Museum of Contemporary Art 46 E4
Nobel Institute 47 B2
Nobel Peace Center 48 C4
Norwegian Armed Forces Museum 49 E6
Norwegian Film Museum 50 F5
Norwegian Resistance Museum 51 D5
Oslo Cathedral 52 F3
Oslo Promenade (see 53)
Oslo Town Hall (Rådhus) 53 D3
Paléet Shopping Centre 54 E3
Stenersen Museum 55 C3
Stortinget (Parliament) 56 E3
Syklistenes Landsforening 57 F3
Victoria Terrace 58 C3
Vår Frelsers Gravlund 59 E1

SLEEPING
Anker Hostel 60 H2
Cochs Pensjonat 61 C1
Grand Hotel 62 E3
Grims Grenka 63 E4
Hotell Bondeheimen 64 E3
MS Innvik 65 F5
P-Hotel 66 E3
Perminalen Hotel 67 E4
Rica Victoria Hotel 68 D3
Thon Hotel Munch 69 E2

EATING
Aker Brygge Food Court (see 120)
Albertine 70 C4
ApÅpent Bakeri 71 B2
Bagatelle 72 A3
Bagel & Juice (see 103)
Baltazar (see 37)
Beach Club 73 B4
Dolly Dimples 74 D3
Dolly Dimples 75 F3
Dr Kneipp's Vinbar (see 82)
Fisherman's Coop 76 C4
Food Court 77 G3
Grand Café (see 62)
Grønland Bazar 78 H3
ICA Gourmet Supermarket & Café 79 C4
Japo Sushi 80 A3
Kaffistova (see 64)
Life 81 E3
Markveien Mat & Vinhus 82 G1
Mithas The Sweethouse 83 H3
Pascal (see 48)
Peppes Pizza 84 C4
Pizza da Mimmo 85 A2
Punjab Tandoori 86 H3
Rimi Supermarket 87 G3
Rust 88 C1
Solsiden 89 D4
Teddy's Soft Bar 90 G3
Theatrecafeen 91 D3
Thien Nga 92 G2
Tullins Café 93 D1
United Bakeries (see 81)

DRINKING
Café Kaos 94 H1
Champagneria 95 A2
Dattera Til Hagen 96 H3
Justisen 97 F3
London Pub 98 E2
Onkel Donald Kafé-Bar 99 D3
Palace Grill 100 B3
Robinet 101 F2
Stargate 102 H3
Stockfleth's 103 E3
Süd Øst 104 H2
Tekehtopa 105 E2

ENTERTAINMENT
Black Box 106 C4
Blå 107 G1
Den Norske Opera 108 F3
Elsker 109 E2
Filmens Hus 110 F4
Fire Oslo (see 119)
Gloria Flames 111 H3
Mono 112 F3
National Theatre 113 D3
New Opera House 114 G4
Oslo Spektrum 115 G3
Rockefeller Music Hall 116 F2
Saga Kino 117 D3
Spasibar 118 D2
Stratos 119 F2

SHOPPING
Aker Brygge Shopping Complex 120 C4
Galleri Oslo Shopping Centre 121 G3
Glasmagasinet Department Store 122 F3
Gunerius Shopping Centre 123 G3
Hassan og Den Dama 124 A2
Heimen Husflid (see 64)
Husfliden 125 D3
Juhls' Silvergallery Oslo 126 D3
Norway Designs 127 D3
Oslo City Shopping Centre 128 G3
Unique Design 129 D3
Vinmonopolet (see 128)

TRANSPORT
Aker Brygge Pier 130 C4
Color Line Ferries 131 E3
Galleri Oslo Long-Distance Bus Terminal 132 H3
Rådhusbrygge Quay (Boat Terminal) 133 D4
Stena Lineas 134 F4
Trafikanten 135 F4
Vippetangen Quay No 2 (Stena Line & DFDS Ferries) 136 F6

and impressive frescoes and paintings by some of Norway's most prominent artists. It's here that the Nobel Peace Prize is awarded on 10 December each year (see the boxed text, p95). You can view the main hall for free from the front corridor. Guided tours (in English) are available at 10am, noon and 2pm Monday to Friday and on weekends in June and July (no extra charge).

Akershus Castle & Fortress

Strategically located on the eastern side of the harbour, dominating the Oslo harbour front, are the medieval **castle and fortress** (*slott* and *festning*; Map pp96–7), arguably Oslo's architectural highlight.

When Oslo was named capital of Norway in 1299, King Håkon V ordered the construction of Akershus to protect the city from external threats. Since it suffered repeated fires, sieges and battles, the fortress was reconstructed to withstand the increased fighting power of the day, including the 1559 addition of the Munk gun tower. Between 1580 and the mid-18th century, it was further fortified with moats and reinforced ramparts.

When Oslo was rebuilt after the 1624 fire, the city, renamed Christiania, was shifted to the less vulnerable and more defensible site behind the protective fortress walls. By 1818 the need for defence had been superseded by the need for space and most of the outer rampart was destroyed to accommodate population growth. From 1899 to 1963 it underwent major renovations and, nowadays, the park-like grounds serve as a venue for concerts, dances and theatrical productions – a far cry from its warlike origins and a welcome departure from its grim history. Note, however, that this complex remains a military installation and may be closed to the public whenever there's a state function.

In the 17th century, Christian IV renovated **Akershus Castle** (Akershus Slott; ☎ 23 09 35 53; adult/child Nkr50/10; 🕑 10am-4pm Mon-Sat, 12.30-4pm Sun May–mid-Sep; guided tours 11am, 1pm & 3pm Mon-Sat, 1pm & 3pm Sun) into a Renaissance palace, although the front remains decidedly medieval. In its dungeons you'll find dark cubbyholes where outcast nobles were kept under lock and key (one dungeon still holds a rather miserable-looking model wrapped in sackcloth), while the upper floors contained sharply contrasting lavish banquet halls and staterooms.

The castle chapel is still used for army events, and the crypts of King Håkon VII and Olav V lie beneath it. The guided tours are led by university students in period dress and, while not compulsory, they do offer an entertaining anecdotal history of the place that you won't get by wandering around on your own.

Entry to the expansive **fortress** (admission free; 🕑 6am-9pm) is through a gate at the end of Akersgata or over a drawbridge spanning Kongens gate at the southern end of Kirkegata. After 6pm in winter, use the Kirkegata entrance.

The **Akershus Fortress Information Centre** (Map pp96-7; ☎ 23 09 39 17; 🕑 9am-5pm Mon-Fri, 11am-5pm Sat & Sun mid-May–mid-Aug; closes 1hr earlier rest-of-year), inside the main gate, has an exhibit entitled *New Barricades*, which recounts the history of the Akershus complex. Staff also offer guided tours of the **castle grounds** (🕑 10am, noon, 2pm & 4pm Mon-Fri, noon, 2pm & 4pm Sat & Sun Jun-Aug). At 1.30pm you can watch the changing of the guard at the fortress.

Also within the fortress complex, adjacent to a memorial for resistance fighters executed on the spot during WWII, is the **Norwegian Resistance Museum** (Norges Hjemmefront Museet; Map pp96-7; ☎ 23 09 31 38; www.nhm.mil.no; adult/child Nkr30/15; 🕑 10am-5pm Mon-Sat Jun-Aug, 10am-4pm Mon-Fri, 11am-4pm Sat & Sun Sep-May). The small, but worthwhile museum covers the dark years of German occupation, as well as the jubilant day of 9 May 1945 when peace was declared. Artefacts include a set of dentures that belonged to a Norwegian Prisoner of War in Poland, and were wired to receive radio broadcasts, underground newspapers, numerous maps and photographs. The museum is a must see for WWII history enthusiasts (see boxed text, p100).

DAMSTREDET

The quirky 18th-century wooden homes of the **Damstredet district** and the nearby **Telthusbakken** (Map pp96-7) are a nice change of pace from the modern architecture of the city centre. Once an impoverished shantytown, Damstredet has become a popular residential neighbourhood for artists. To get there, walk north on Akersgata and turn right on Damstredet gate. Telthusbakken is a little further up Akersgata, also on the right. On the way, you'll pass **Vår Frelsers Gravlund**, the graveyard where Ibsen, Munch and Bjørnstjerne Bjørnson are buried.

GAMLEBYEN

The ruins at Sørenga and St Hallvards plass in Gamlebyen east of central Oslo date back to the 12th and 13th century and the city centre might still be here today had the 17th century King Kristian IV not decided to move to Akershus Festning after a devastating fire. Long one of Oslo's poorest neighbourhoods, Gamlebyen remains a bit rough around the edges, but is changing rapidly, a trend that is likely to continue given its proximity to the **New Opera House** (Map pp96-7) on Bjørvika.

Frognerparken & Vigeland Park

Frognerparken, which has as its centrepiece **Vigeland Park** (Map pp96-7; 🕑 year-round), is an extraordinary open-air showcase of work by Norway's best-loved sculptor, Gustav Vigeland (see the boxed text, p101). Vigeland Park is brimming with 212 granite and bronze Vigeland works. His highly charged work ranges from entwined lovers and tranquil elderly couples to contempt-ridden beggars. His most renowned work, *Sinataggen* (the 'Little Hot-Head'), portrays a London child in a mood of particular ill humour.

It's a great place to visit in the evening after other sights have closed.

Near the southern entrance to the park lies **Oslo City Museum** (Oslo Bymuseum; Map p93; ☎ 23 28 41 70; www.oslobymuseum.no; Frognerveien 67; adult/child

THE NORWEGIAN RESISTANCE: 'NEVER AGAIN!'

The day the German army marched into Oslo – April 9, 1940 – Gunnar Sønsteby watched them parade down Karl Johans gate, mounted his bicycle and disappeared into the woods to join the resistance.

At the time, there wasn't really anything to join. After 125 years of peace, Norwegians watched bewildered as their country was occupied in less than 60 days and their king and cabinet were forced into exile. But by the end of the war, there were 40,000 homespun resistance soldiers, 60 underground newspapers and the Norwegian *hjemmefront* (resistance) could take credit for some of the war's most successful acts of sabotage.

These actions came at a cost. Over 50,000 Norwegians were arrested for political reasons during WWII, not a small number for a country of only three million, and 9000 were sent abroad. Of these, 1400 Norwegians, half of them Jewish, would never return.

With that in mind, we posed a few questions about the resistance to Ivar Kraglund, director at **Oslo's Resistance Museum** (see p99).

If resistance fighters had to escape, where did most of them go? Almost 50,000 people escaped to Sweden, some on their own and others with guides. Once there, many received military training. By the end of the war, there were 13,000 Norwegians that had been trained in Sweden and who were carrying Swedish weapons.

Did any famous acts of sabotage take place? The most important attack was on the heavy water plant at Vemork in 1943 (see p153). It is probably one of the most famous sabotage attacks of WWII and the museum has the only remaining water cell from the factory that I know of.

And what happened to Gunnar Sønsteby? He became the leader of the 'Oslo gang' and one of Norway's most famous resistance fighters. He's probably best known for his attack on the registration offices in 1944, which made it impossible for the Germans to send Norwegian recruits to the front.

What other reminders of the resistance are there in Oslo? In addition to the Resistance Museum keep an eye out for the haunting, grey Victoria Terrasse near Oslo centre, which was commandeered by the Gestapo. At the time, it was known as the *skrekken hus* (house of fear). And a little further on, at Solli plass (Map pp96–7), there's a bronze statue of Sønsteby and his bicycle.

As told to Kari Lundgren

Nkr40/20, free with Oslo Pass; ⌚ noon-4pm Wed-Sun, noon-7pm Tue) housed in the 18th-century Frogner Manor (built on the site of a Viking-era manor); it contains exhibits of minor interest on the city's history.

Frognerparken itself attracts Oslo locals with its broad lawns, ponds, stream and rows of shade trees. On a sunny afternoon it's ideal for picnics, strolling or lounging on the grass.

To get there, take tram No 12 or 15, marked Frogner, from the city centre.

VIGELAND MUSEUM

For an in-depth look at Gustav Vigeland's work, visit the **Vigeland Museum** (Map p91; ☎ 23 49 37 00; www.vigeland.museum.no; Nobels gate 32; adult/child Nkr45/25, free with Oslo Pass; ⌚ 11am-5pm Tue-Sun Jun-Aug, noon-4pm Tue-Sun Sep-May), opposite the southern entrance to Frognerparken. It was built by the city in the 1920s as a home and workshop for the sculptor, in exchange for the donation of a significant proportion of his life's work, and it contains his early collection of statuary and monuments to public figures, as well as plaster moulds, woodblock prints and sketches. When he died in 1943, his ashes were deposited in the tower and the museum was opened to the public four years later. Visiting the artist's private apartments on the 3rd floor is possible, but must be arranged in advance (tours per group cost Nkr700 on top of the cost of admission).

EMANUEL VIGELAND MUSEUM

Part gallery, part mausoleum, this spooky **museum** (Map p91; ☎ 22 14 57 88; www.emanuelvigeland.museum.no; Grimelundsveien 8; adult/child Nkr30/15, free with Oslo Pass; ⌚ noon-4pm Sun, noon-5pm during summer) is dedicated to the life work of Gustav Vigeland's brother Emanuel (1875–1948). A pioneer in fresco painting, Emanuel is considered by many to have been the superior artist of the two brothers. The showpiece of the museum is the 800-sq-metre fresco *Vita* depicting human life from conception to death. To get there, take the T-bane (line 1) to Slemdal. For a taste of the artist's work nearer the city centre, check out the stained glass in the Oslo Cathedral.

ICE-SKATING MUSEUM

This **museum** (Skøytemuseet; Map p93; ☎ 22 43 49 20; Middelthuns gate 26; adult/child Nkr20/10, free with Oslo Pass; ⏲ 10am-2.30pm Tue & Thu, 11am-2pm Sun) is dedicated to speed and figure skating in Norway. Featured are historical skating apparatus and information on such Norwegian champions as speed skater Johann Olav Koss – 'Koss the Boss' – and figure skater Sonja Henie. It makes a nice complement to the Olympic sites in Lillehammer (p163) and Hamar (p169).

Bygdøy Peninsula

The Bygdøy Peninsula (Map p91) holds some of Oslo's top attractions. You can rush around all the sights in half a day, but allotting a few extra hours will be more rewarding.

Although only minutes from central Oslo, Bygdøy maintains its rural character. The royal family has a summer home here, as do many of Oslo's well-to-do residents.

Ferry No 91 (☎ 23 35 68 90) operates from early April to early October, making the 15-minute run to Bygdøy (adult/child Nkr20/10, free with the Oslo Pass) every 30 to 40 minutes from 8.45am, with the last crossing returning from Bygdøy at around 6.30pm in April and September, 9.15pm in summer; earlier final departures the rest of the year. Keep an eye out for the king's ship KS *Norge* on the ride over, as well as the King and Queen's royal yacht clubs (*Kongen* and *Dronningen*), which face one another on either side of the Frognerkilen. The ferries leave from Rådhusbrygge 3 (opposite the Rådhus) and stop first at Dronningen ferry terminal, from where it's a 10-minute walk to the Norwegian Folk Museum (p102) and a 15-minute walk to the Viking Ship Museum (see p102). Beyond the ships it's a further 20 minutes' walk to Bygdøynes where the Kon-Tiki, Polarship Fram and Norwegian Maritime Museums (see p102) are clustered; the route is signposted and makes a pleasant walk. Alternatively, the ferry continues to Bygdøynes. You can also take bus 30 to

GUSTAV VIGELAND

The Norwegian sculptor Gustav Vigeland (1869–1943) was born to a farming family near Mandal in the far south of the country. As a child and teenager he became deeply interested in Protestantism, spirituality, woodcarving and drawing – a unique combination that would dominate his life's work. In 1888 Vigeland secured an apprenticeship to sculptor Brynjulf Bergslien. The following year he exhibited his first work at the State Exhibition of Art. It was the break he needed, bringing his talents to national and international attention.

In 1891 he travelled to Copenhagen and then to Paris and Italy, where he worked with various masters; he was especially inspired by the work of French sculptor Auguste Rodin. When his public grants ran out he returned to Norway to make a living working on the restoration of the Nidaros Cathedral in Trondheim and producing commissioned portraits of prominent Norwegians.

In 1921 the City of Oslo recognised his talents and built him a spacious studio in which to work (see opposite;, it's now a museum.

The highlight of Vigeland Park is the 14m-high granite *Monolith*, which crowns the park's highest hill. This incredible production required three stone carvers working daily from 1929 to 1943 and was carved from a single stone pillar quarried from Iddefjorden in southeastern Norway. It depicts a writhing mass of 121 detailed human figures, both entwined with and undermining each other in their individual struggle to reach the top. The circle of steps around it supports rows of stone figures. The figures, together with the pillar, have been interpreted in many ways: as a phallic representation, the struggle for existence, yearnings for the spiritual spheres and transcendence of cyclic repetition.

Leading down from the plinth bearing this column is a series of steps supporting sculptures depicting people experiencing the full range of human emotions and activities. The numerous sculptures dominating the surrounding park carry the artist's themes from the realist to the ludicrous. The result is truly one of Norway's artistic highlights and, best of all, there are no signs admonishing you to keep your distance.

the Folk Museum from Jernbanetorget, next to Oslo S.

MUSEUMS

Norwegian Folk Museum

Norway's largest open-air museum and one of Oslo's premier attractions is this folk **museum** (Norsk Folkemuseum; Map p91; ☎ 22 12 37 00; www.norskfolke.museum.no; Museumsveien 10; adult/child Nkr79/25 mid-May–mid-Sep, Nkr70/25 rest-of-year, free with Oslo Pass; 🕑 10am-6pm mid-May–mid-Sep; 11am-3pm Mon-Fri, 11am-4pm Sat & Sun rest-of-year). The museum includes more than 140 buildings, mostly from the 17th and 18th centuries, gathered from around the country, rebuilt and organised according to region of origin. Paths wind past old barns, elevated *stabbur* (raised storehouses) and rough-timbered farmhouses with sod roofs sprouting wildflowers. The Gamlebyen (Old Town) section is a reproduction of an early-20th-century Norwegian town and includes a village shop and old petrol station; in summer (daily except Saturday) you can see weaving and pottery-making demonstrations. Another highlight is the restored stave church, built around 1200 in Gol and shifted to Bygdøy in 1885.

The exhibition hall near the main entrance includes exhaustive displays on Norwegian folk art, historic toys, national costumes (including traditional clothing used for weddings, christenings and burials), the Sami culture of Finnmark, domestic and farming tools and appliances, as well as visiting exhibits. Sunday is a good day to visit, as folk music and dancing is staged at 2pm (in summer). Other daily summer highlights include carriage rides (noon to 4pm) and children won't want to miss a chance to feed the farm animals at 1pm.

It's the definitive guide to traditional Norwegian culture – don't miss it.

Viking Ship Museum

Even in repose, there is something intimidating about the sleek, dark hulls of the Viking ships *Oseberg* and *Gokstad,* which is why visitors to this unforgettable **Vikingskipshuset** (Map p91; ☎ 22 13 52 80; Huk Aveny 35; adult/child Nkr40/20, free with Oslo Pass; 🕑 9am-6pm May-Sep, 11am-4pm Oct-Apr) often find themselves whispering. Only a few boards and fragments remain of a third ship, the *Tune,* built around the same time as the *Gokstad* and excavated in 1867 from the Oslofjord region. All were built of oak in the 9th century; the ships were pulled ashore and used as tombs for nobility, who were buried with all they expected to need in the hereafter: jewels, furniture, food, servants, intricately carved carriages and sleighs, tapestries and fierce-looking figures.

The impressive *Oseberg,* buried in 834, is festooned on prow and stern with elaborate dragon and serpent carvings. It measures 22m and required 30 oarsmen. The burial chamber beneath it held the largest collection of Viking Age artefacts ever uncovered in Scandinavia, but had been looted of all jewellery. The sturdier 24m-long *Gokstad,* built around 890, is the finest remaining example of a Viking longship, but when it was unearthed its corresponding burial chamber had also been looted and few artefacts were uncovered. In addition to the three ships, the museum contains a good general exhibit on Vikings.

Polarship Fram Museum

Nature is often the best architect. Which is why, when the well-known shipbuilder Colin Archer was asked to design a ship whose hull could withstand the crush of the polar ice, he looked no further than an egg for inspiration. Launched in 1982, the **Polarship Fram** (Map p91; ☎ 23 28 29 50; www.fram.museum.no; adult/child Nkr50/20, free with Oslo Pass; 🕑 9am-6pm mid-Jun–Aug, shorter hrs rest-of-year), captained by both Fridtjof Nansen and Roald Amundsen, spent much of its life trapped in the polar ice. From 1893 to 1896 Nansen's North Pole expedition took the 39m schooner to Russia's New Siberian Islands, passing within a few degrees of the North Pole on their return trip to Norway.

In 1910 Amundsen (see the boxed text, p383) set sail in the *Fram* (meaning 'forward'), intending to be the first explorer to reach the North Pole, only to discover en route that Robert Peary had beaten him to it. Not to be outdone, Amundsen turned the *Fram* around and became the first man to reach the South Pole. Otto Sverdrup also sailed the schooner around southern Greenland to Canada's Ellesmere Island between 1898 and 1902, travelling over 18,000km.

You're allowed to thoroughly explore the ship, peek inside the cramped bunkrooms and imagine life at sea. In addition, there are detailed exhibits complete with maps, pictures and artefacts that bring the various expeditions to life, from Nansen's attempt to ski across the North Pole to Amundsen's discovery of the Northwest Passage and the fateful rescue attempted that ended in his disappearance.

Kon-Tiki Museum

A favourite among children, this worthwhile **museum** (Map p91; ☎ 23 08 67 67; www.kon-tiki.no; Bygdøynes; adult/child Nkr50/25, free with Oslo Pass; 9.30am-5.30pm Jun-Aug, shorter hrs rest-of-year) is dedicated to the balsa raft *Kon-Tiki*, which Norwegian explorer Thor Heyerdahl sailed from Peru to Polynesia in 1947. The museum also displays the totora reed boat *Ra II*, built by Aymara people on the Bolivian island of Suriqui in Lake Titicaca. Heyerdahl used it to cross the Atlantic in 1970. For a full rundown on the life of this extraordinary explorer who achieved a lot in his lifetime, see the boxed text, p132.

Norwegian Maritime Museum

The author Roald Dahl once said that in Norway, everyone seems to have a boat, and there is no better place to explore that theory than at the **Norske Sjøfartsmuseum** (Map p91; ☎ 24 11 41 50; www.norsk-sjofartsmuseum.no; Bygdøynesveien 37; adult/child Nkr40/free; 10am-6pm mid-May–Aug; 10.30am-4pm Fri-Wed, 10am-6pm Thu Sep–mid-May). The museum depicts Norway's relationship with the sea, including the fishing and whaling industry, the seismic fleet (which searches for oil and gas), shipbuilding and wreck salvaging. Outside the museum there's a seamen's memorial commemorating the 4700 Norwegian sailors killed in WWII, and alongside is Roald Amundsen's ship *Gjøa*, the first ship to completely transit the Northwest Passage (from 1903 to 1906). Other features of the museum include Norway's largest collection of maritime art, a dried cod display and a film with scenic footage of the Norwegian coastline.

OSCARSHALL CASTLE

This **castle** (Oscarshall Slott; Map p91; ☎ 22 56 15 39; Oscarshallsveien), designed by Johan Henrik Nebelong to reflect a blend of Romantic and English neo-Gothic styles, was constructed as a residence for King Oscar I from 1847 to 1852. It's probably the least interesting of Bygdøy's attractions, but is worth a brief detour to view from the outside if you're passing by.

Grünerlokka Area

MUNCH MUSEUM

Edvard Munch (1863–1944) fans won't want to miss the **Munch Museum** (Munch-museet; Map

PLEASE DON'T STEAL THE ARTWORK...

On 12 February 1994, the day of the opening ceremony of the Winter Olympics in Lillehammer, Norwegians woke to the news that arguably the nation's most prized cultural possession, *The Scream*, by Edvard Munch, had been stolen from the National Gallery in Oslo. There was nothing hi-tech about this deeply embarrassing incident – a patrolling police officer discovered the theft (carried out by breaking a window and using wire cutters) when he found a ladder propped up against the gallery wall. In place of the painting was a note: 'Thanks for the poor security.'

The nation was appalled, even more so when the authorities received a ransom demand of US$1 million from people with ties to the anti-abortion movement. A Lutheran minister who had helped plan anti-abortion protests during the Olympics claimed that the painting would be returned if Norwegian national TV broadcasted a graphic film showing a foetus being aborted.

Finally, after almost three months, the Norwegian police discovered four fragments of the painting's frame in the northern Oslo suburb of Nittedal. Within days, Edvard Munch's masterwork, which was painted on fragile paper, was found undamaged in a hotel in Asgardstrand, about 60km south of Oslo. Three Norwegians were arrested and the country breathed a huge collective sigh of relief.

Fastforward 10 years. On 22 August 2004, two masked, armed men walked into the Munch Museum, threatened a guard, detached another version of *The Scream* (Edvard Munch painted four versions) as well as another Munch masterpiece, *The Madonna*, and made off in a getaway car, all within five minutes and in front of startled gallery visitors. No alarms went off, the police took 15 minutes to arrive and, astonishingly, the paintings were uninsured (gallery officials claimed that the paintings were simply priceless).

Two years and nine days later, the police recovered both paintings, though restoration work has delayed their return to the gallery. Most Norwegians and museum staff seem keen to put the embarrassing episode behind them. Nonetheless, the bristling security provides a somewhat ironic, after-the-fact reminder to keep your hands to yourself.

p93; ☎ 23 94 35 00; www.munch.museum.no; Tøyengata 53; adult/child Nkr65/35, free with Oslo Pass; ⌚ 10am-6pm Jun–mid-Sep; 10am-4pm Tue-Fri, 11am-5pm Sat & Sun mid-Sep–May), which is dedicated to his life's work and has most of the pieces not contained in the National Gallery. Security is high in the museum since the 2004 theft of *The Scream* and *The Madonna*, though both paintings were recovered in 2006 (see boxed text, p103). The museum provides a comprehensive look at the artist's work, from dark *(The Sick Child)* to light *(Spring Ploughing)*. With over 11,000 paintings, 4500 watercolours and 18,000 prints and sketching books bequeathed to the city by Munch himself, this is a landmark collection. To get there, take the T-bane to Tøyen, followed by a five-minute signposted walk.

ZOOLOGICAL MUSEUM & GEOLOGICAL-PALAEONTOLOGICAL MUSEUM

By Oslo's botanical gardens, the university's **Zoological Museum** (Zoologisk Museum; Map p93; ☎ 22 85 17 00; Sars gate 1; adult/child Nkr40/free; ⌚ 11am-4pm Tue-Sun) has well-presented displays of stuffed wildlife from Norway and elsewhere, including a special exhibit on Arctic wildlife. The adjacent **Geological-Palaeontological Museum** (Geologisk Museum; Map p93; ☎ 22 85 17 00; Sars gate 1; adult/child Nkr40/free; ⌚ 11am-4pm Tue-Sun) contains displays on the history of the solar system and Norwegian geology, as well as examples of myriad minerals, meteorites and moon rocks. The palaeontologic section includes a 10m-long iguanodon skeleton and a nest of dinosaur eggs.

BOTANICAL GARDEN

Oslo's 15-acre **Botanical Garden** (Botanisk Hage; Map p93; ☎ 22 85 17 00; Sars gate 1; admission free; ⌚ 7am-8pm Mon-Fri, 10am-8pm Sat & Sun Apr-Sep; 7am-5pm Mon-Fri, 10am-5pm Sat & Sun Oct-Mar) features over 7500 plants from around the world. There are also plants from the Oslo fjords, including four that are almost extinct in nature. Specimens in the aromatic garden are accompanied by text in both print and braille.

GAMLE AKER KIRKE

This medieval stone **church** (Map p93; ☎ 22 69 35 82; Akersbakken 26; admission free; ⌚ noon-2pm Mon-Sat), located north of the centre on Akersbakken, dates from 1080 and is Oslo's oldest building. Lutheran services are held at 9am and 11am on Sunday. Take bus 37 from Jernbanetorget to Akersbakken then walk up past the churchyard.

Outer Oslo

HENIE-ONSTAD ART CENTRE

In Høvikodden, west of the centre, lies one of Norway's best private art collections, the **Henie-Onstad Art Centre** (Henie-Onstad Kunstsenter; Map p119; ☎ 67 80 48 80; www.hok.no; Høvikodden; admission free; ⌚ 11am-7pm Tue-Thu, 11am-5pm Fri-Sun), founded in the 1960s by Norwegian figure skater Sonja Henie and her husband Niels Onstad. The couple actively sought out collectible works of Joan Miró and Pablo Picasso, as well as assorted impressionist, abstract, expressionist and modern Norwegian works. When you've seen enough art you can head downstairs for a look at Sonja's various skating medals and trophies. From Jernbanetorget, take any bus heading towards Sandvika and get off at Høvikodden.

HOLMENKOLLEN SKI JUMP & MUSEUM

The **Holmenkollen Ski Jump**, perched on a hilltop overlooking Oslo, offers a panoramic view of the city and doubles as a concert venue. During Oslo's annual ski festival, held in March, it draws the world's best ski jumpers.

At the Holmenkollen ski jump, the **Ski Museum** (Map p91; ☎ 22 92 32 00; www.skiforeningen.no; Kongeveien 5; adult/child Nkr70/35; ⌚ 9am-8pm Jun-Aug, 10am-2pm Oct-Apr, 10am-5pm May & Sep) leads you through the 4000-year history of Nordic and downhill skiing in Norway. There are exhibits featuring the Antarctic expeditions of Amundsen and Scott, as well as Fridtjof Nansen's slog across the Greenland icecap (you'll see the boat he constructed from his sled and canvas tent to row the final 100km to Nuuk). Recently redone exhibits on the 2nd floor cover the more modern aspects of skiing and include a glimpse of the royal family on skis.

Admission to the Ski Museum includes a visit to the **ski-jump tower**. Part of the route to the top of the tower is served by a lift, but you're on your own for the final 114 steep steps. Outside, the **ski-jump simulator** (adult/child Nkr50/35) is good for a laugh, but don't try it if you have a weak stomach. To get to the museum, take T-bane line 1 to Holmenkollen and follow the signs uphill.

NORDMARKA

The woodland north of the Holmenkollen ski jump, known as Nordmarka (see p119), is a prime destination for hiking, mountain biking, sledding and skiing and is also the geographical centre of the city. For skiers, there is **Tryvan Vinterpark**, Oslo's largest skiing area with 14 slopes and six lifts. In the summer, the **Tryvannstårnet observation tower** is a good place to start a hike or a bike trip. The 118m-tall tower is no longer open for visitors, but the view from its base is still fantastic. Make sure to take a container for picking blueberries in summer. From the Holmenkollen T-bane station, take the scenic ride to the end of the line at Frognerseteren and look for the signposted walking route.

ACTIVITIES

Avid skiers, hikers and sailors, Oslo residents will do just about anything to get outside. That's not too hard given that there are over 240 sq km of woodland, 40 islands and 343 lakes within the city limits.

Climbing

The best local climbing is on the pre-bolted faces of Kolsåstoppen, which is accessible on T-bane line 3 to Kolsås. Otherwise, there is a good indoor climbing wall at **Gekko Klatring Oslo** (Map pp96-7; ☎ 99 28 21 21; www.gekkoklatring.no; Bispegate 16; before/after 3pm Nkr50/85; 🕑 10am-10pm Mon & Thu, noon-10pm Tue & Wed, 10am-10pm Fri, 10am-6pm Sat, noon-8pm Sun).

Cycling

Renting a bicycle in Oslo (see p117) is harder than it should be, but once you have one, the city is easy to get around. The tourist office has free cycling maps, with *Sykkelkart Oslo* tracing the bicycle lanes and paths throughout the city, and *Idrett og friluftsliv i Oslo* covers the Oslo hinterland. It also has a pamphlet *Opplevelsesturer i Marka,* which contains six possible cycling and/or hiking itineraries within reach of Oslo.

Two especially nice rides within the city (suitable to do on an Oslo city bike) are along the Akerselva up to Lake Maridal (Map p91; 11km) and in the woods around Bygdøy (Map p91). The trip to Maridal will pass several waterfalls, a number of converted factories at the edge of Grünerløkka and cross several of Oslo's more unique bridges, including the Anker or *eventyr* (fairy-tale) bridge (see the boxed text, p107). Cyclists should be sure to stop for coffee and a waffle at **Hønse-Louisas Hus** (Map p93; Sandakerveien 2; 🕑 11am-6pm). This can also be done on foot by taking the T-bane to Kjesås and following the path back into the city. Cycling, or walking, around Bygdøy is far more pastoral and provides ample opportunity for swimming breaks. There is a bike rack in front of the Folk Museum. For more serious cycling take T-bane line 1 to Frognerseteren and head into the Nordmarka.

For Norway-wide cycling information and for more detailed maps for the Buskerud region (the area surrounding Oslo), contact **Syklistenes Landsforening** (Map p91; ☎ 22 47 30 30; post@slf.no; Storgata 23C; 🕑 10am-5pm Mon-Fri). It is a local club and not really set up for tourists, but members are happy to help if they can. Ring the bell 10m to the right of the door if it looks closed.

Hiking

A network of 1200km of trails leads into Nordmarka from Frognerseteren (at the end of T-bane line 1), including a good trail down to Sognsvann lake, 6km northwest of the centre at the end of T-bane line 5 (Map p91). If you're walking in August, be sure to take a container for blueberries and a swimsuit to cool off in the lake (bathing is allowed in all the woodland lakes around Oslo except Maridalsvannet and Skjersjøen lakes, which are drinking reservoirs). The pleasant walk around Sognsvann itself takes around an hour, or for a more extended trip, try hiking to the cabin at **Ullevålseter** (☎ 22 14 35 58; www.ullevalseter.no), a pleasant old farmhouse that serves waffles and coffee. The round trip (about 11km) takes around three hours.

The Ekeberg woods to the southeast of the city centre (take bus 34 or 46 from Jernbanetorget to **Ekeberg Camping** (Map p91) or tramline 18 or 19 towards Ljabru to Sjømannskolen) are other nice places for a stroll. During the summer weekends, it's a popular spot for riding competitions and, more recently, cricket matches. There is an Iron Age heritage path through the woods, and for a piece of architectural history don't miss the **Ekeberg Restaurant** (Map p91), one of the earliest examples of functionalism. On the way down, stop at the **Valhall Curve** (Map p91) to see the view that inspired Edward Munch to paint *The Scream*.

Avid hikers may want to stop by the **DNT office** (Map pp96-7; ☎ 22 82 28 22; www.turistforeningen.no; Youngstorget 1; ⏰ 10am-4pm Mon-Wed & Fri, 10am-6pm Thu, 10am-2pm Sat, open 1hr earlier May-Sep), which maintains several mountain huts in the Nordmarka region and can provide information and maps covering longer-distance hiking routes throughout Norway.

Ice-Skating

At the **Narvisen outdoor ice rink** (Map pp96-7; ☎ 22 30 30 33; Karl Johans gate), you can skate for free whenever it's cold enough to freeze over (around November to March). Skates can be hired from the ice rink for around Nkr40.

Skiing

Oslo's ski season is roughly from December to March. There are over 2400km of prepared Nordic tracks (1000km in Nordmarka alone), many of them floodlit, as well as a ski resort within the city limits. Easy-access tracks begin right at the end of T-bane lines 1 and 5. The **Skiservice Centre** (☎ 22 13 95 04; www.skiservice.no; Tryvannsveien 2), at Voksenkollen station, one T-bane stop before Frognerseteren, hires out snowboards and Nordic skis. The downhill slopes at **Tryvann Vinterpark** (☎ 40 46 27 00) are open in the ski season. **Skiforeningen** (Ski Society; Map p91; ☎ 22 92 32 00; www.skiforeningen.no; Kongeveien 5) can provide further information on skiing options, or check out www.holmenkollen.com.

Swimming

ISLANDS & BEACHES

If the weather hots up, there are a few reasonable beaches within striking distance of central Oslo. Ferries to half a dozen islands in the Oslofjord region leave from Vippetangen Quay, southeast of Akershus Fortress. Boats to Hovedøya and Langøyene are relatively frequent in summer (running at least hourly), while other islands are served less often. The last ferry leaves Vippetangen at 6.45pm in winter and 9.05pm in summer.

The southwestern shore of otherwise rocky Hovedøya (Map p91), the nearest island to the mainland, is popular with sunbathers. The island is ringed with walking paths to old cannon emplacements and the 12th-century **Cistercian monastery ruins**. Take boat 92 or 93.

South of Hovedøya lies the undeveloped island of Langøyene (Map p91), with superb swimming from rocky or sandy beaches (one on the southeastern shore is designated for nude bathing). Boat 94 will get you there.

The Bygdøy Peninsula has two popular beaches, **Huk** (Map p91) and **Paradisbukta** (Map p91), which can be reached on bus 30 from Jernbanetorget to its last stop. While there are some sandy patches, most of Huk comprises grassy lawns and large smooth rocks ideal for sunbathing. Separated into two beaches by a small cove, the beach on the northwestern side is open to nude bathing. If Huk seems too crowded, a 10-minute walk through the woods north of the bus stop leads to the more secluded Paradisbukta.

SWIMMING POOLS

Oslo has two outdoor municipal swimming pools: **Frognerbadet Swimming Pool** (Map p93; ☎ 23 27 54 50; Middelthus gate 28; adult/child Nkr69/33, free with Oslo Pass; ⏰ mid-May–mid-Aug) in Frognerparken (entry via Middelthus gate) and **Tøyenbadet Swimming Pool** (Map p93; ☎ 23 30 44 70; Helgesens gata 90), which is near the Munch Museum.

OSLO FOR CHILDREN

A springtime afternoon spent counting baby carriages in Oslo highlights just how child- and parent-friendly the city is (or at least gives a sense of how long the winters are).

Most Oslo parents will tell you that the best activities are often the simplest and free. There are no rules against climbing the statues at Frognerparken, for example, or chasing your little sister around the garden's 3000m mosaic labyrinth. The park also has one of the city's best playgrounds. Nearer the centre, the cannons and fortifications at Akershus Fortress are great for sparking the imagination. And it would be a pity to leave Norway without picking up a copy of Norwegian folktales (see boxed text, opposite).

More organised summer activities include taking a **Thomas Train City Tour** (☎ 91 62 53 03; www.thomas-toget.no; ⏰ 11am-5pm Mon-Sat mid-Jun–Aug) or the **Oslo Toget** (☎ 67 97 20 60; www.oslotoget.no), which both do a half-hour loop around the city centre in cheerfully painted open-air trains. Tours begin every half-hour in front of the Paléet shopping centre (Map p93) and Aker Brygge shopping complex (Map pp96–7). There is a Christmas train in December.

For a more rural experience, try the **EKT Riding School and Husdyrpark** (EKT Rideskole and Husdyrpark; Map p91; ☎ 22 19 97 86; www.rideskole.no;

SNIPP, SNAPP, SNUTE

Norwegian trolls come in all shapes and sizes. There is the Nokken, a slimy creature who lives in mountain ponds, and the Huldra, a stunning temptress who seduces young men before dragging them into the woods (unless they can first drag her to a church). There are even lucky trolls who grant wishes to fishermen who treat them nicely.

The antics of these fantasy characters, as well as the princesses and farms boys that managed to outwit them, are as essentially Norwegian as the fjords and Vikings. But it is only due to the work of two Buskerud locals – Peter Asbjörnsen and Jörgen Moe – in the early 1800s that they were ever written down at all. Inspired by the popular work of the Grimm brothers, the two men began with what they knew best: the folktales told in the woods and valleys surrounding Oslo. Comic, cruel, moralistic, ribald and popular from the moment they were published, these stories set the tone for some of Norway's greatest authors including Henrik Ibsen and Bjørnstjerne Bjørnson.

The tales, most often illustrated with the distinct sketches of Erik Werenskiold and ending with the words *'Snipp. Snapp. Snute. Så er eventyret ute'* (Norwegian for 'The End'), remain popular and easy to find. In Oslo keep an eye out for the bronzes that decorate the Anker (or *eventyr*; meaning 'fairy-tale') Bridge (Map pp96–7) on Storgata. No trolls, but you will see four other famous characters from Asbjörnson and Moe's stories: Peer Gynt, the Polar Bear King, Kari Woodencloak and Little Freddy and his Fiddle.

For more on Norwegian folklore, see p49.

Bekkelagshøgda 12; pony rides Nkr30; 11am-6pm daily May-Sep, shorter hrs rest-of-year) in the Ekeberg forest southeast of the city centre. There are sheep, goats, pigs and rabbits, as well as Norwegian fjord ponies. Take tram 19 toward Ljabru to Sportsplassen and walk 15 minutes uphill until you reach the farm. The **Folk Museum** (p102) also has regular events that are geared towards children.

In the winter, try sledding down the 'legendary' **Korketrekkeren** (cork screw) toboggan run. The 2000m long track drops 255m and began its life as a bobsledding run for the 1952 Olympics. Sleds can be rented at the **Akerforeningen** (☎ 22 49 01 21; www.akeforeningen.no; adult/child Nkr80/50; 9am-9pm Mon-Sat, 10am-6pm Sun during winter) next to the Frognerseteren restaurant. To get there take the T-bane to Frognerseteren and follow the signs downhill.

A popular rainy day distraction is the **Norwegian Science & Technology Museum** (Norsk Teknisk Museum & Telemuseum; Map p91; ☎ 22 79 60 00; www.tekniskmuseum.no; Kjelsåsveien 143; adult/child Nkr80/40, free with Oslo Pass; 10am-6pm Mon-Fri, 11am-6pm Sat & Sun mid-Jun–mid-Aug; shorter hrs rest-of-year) near Lake Maridal, which has Norway's first car and tram, water wheels, clocks and enough gadgetry to keep the whole family busy for a few hours at least. Or if you have a particular affinity for your friends' refrigerator art displays, visit the **Children's Art Museum** (Barnekunstmuseet; Map p93; ☎ 22 46 85 73; www.barnekunst.no; Lille Frøens vei 4; adult/child Nkr50/30; 11am-4pm Tue-Thu & Sun late Jun-early Aug, shorter hrs rest of-year, closed early Aug–mid-Sep) near the Frøen T-bane station.

Finally, **TusenFryd** (Map p119; ☎ 64 97 64 97; www.tusenfryd.no; Vinterbro; height over/under 120cm Nkr240/290; 10.30am-7pm mid-Jun–Sep, shorter hrs rest-of-year), an amusement park 10km south of the city, is enormously popular with kids from the whole Buskerud region. The park offers carousels, a fantasy farm and an excellent wooden rollercoaster, which creates zero gravity 12 times each circuit. You'll find it just off the E6. The TusenFryd bus departs from the Galleri Oslo bus terminal nine times from 10am to 4pm daily (adult/child Nkr30/15).

TOURS

The best Oslo tours offer juicy cultural and historical morsels (or a boat trip), while also giving the visitor the flexibility to explore at their leisure.

our pick **AudioTor** (☎ 98 82 93 23; www.audiotor.no) rents out iPods with information on various sites around Oslo so you can tour the city at your own pace. The iPods, available from the tourist office (one-/two-day rental Nkr149/249), have a selection of itineraries covering major attractions such as Vigeland Park and Holmenkollen. They offer all the basic history, practical details, a pronunciation guide, as well as a variety of interesting information most Oslo dwellers don't even know.

City Sightseeing (☎ 22 78 94 00; www.citysightseeing.net; ⏰ mid-May–mid-Sep) is Oslo's version of the hop-on hop-off phenomenon. Tickets cost Nkr165/85 per adult/child, are valid for 48 hours, and cover the overwhelming proportion of city sights, which you can explore at your own pace. The tourist office has a list of stops that this tour company goes to. Another option is to go on a 1½-hour evening city walk starting from in front of the Rådhus (Town Hall) with **Oslo Promenade** (adult/child Nkr80/free; ⏰ 5.30pm Mon, Wed & Fri Jun-Aug). The guides are knowledgeable and entertaining, making this a good option for getting an insider's view of Oslo.

For a more comprehensive package, or if you want to get out on the water, try **Båtservice Sightseeing** (Map pp96-7; ☎ 23 35 68 90; www.boatsightseeing.com; Pier 3, Rådhusbrygge), which does a tidy 7½-hour city tour to the Bygdøy museums, Vigeland Park and the Holmenkollen ski jump, plus a cruise of the Oslofjord for a reasonable Nkr515 (late May to early September only). Shorter tours are available.

If the weather is clear, there are few more dramatic ways of seeing the city than by seaplane. **Fonnafly** (☎ 67 10 50 50; www.fonnaflyoslo.no; Nkr790) does a 20-minute Oslo on Top tour (minimum three people) that flies over the Holmenkollen ski jump and the city centre.

FESTIVALS & EVENTS

Oslo's most festive annual event is surely the 17 May **National Constitution Day** celebration, when Oslo residents, whose roots spring from all over Norway, descend on the Royal Palace dressed in the finery of their native districts. Other festivals of note include the **Holmenkollen Ski Festival** (www.holmekolen.com; ⏰ mid-March) featuring Nordic skiers and ski jumpers from around the world and skiing events and cultural programmes, **Summer Parade** (last weekend in July), the six-day **Oslo International Jazz Festival** (www.oslojazz.no; ⏰ Aug) and the **Øya Festival** (www.oyafestivalen.com; ⏰ Aug).

For details on these and other festivals, visit www.visitoslo.com.

SLEEPING

Oslo has a good range of accommodation, including a growing number of small bed and breakfasts, which offer more character than the chain hotels.

Budget

CAMPING

Oslo Fjordcamping (Map p119; ☎ 22 75 20 55; mail@oslocamping.no; Ljansbrukveien 1; tent with/without car Nkr130/150) Oslo Fjordcamping enjoys a peaceful location 6km southeast of the city centre but the facilities have seen better days. To get there take bus 83 from Oslo S.

Bogstad Camping (Map p91; ☎ 22 51 08 00; www.bogstadcamping.no; Ankerveien 117; 4-person tent with/without car Nkr245/170, 4-person cabins from Nkr440; ⏰ year-round; 🅿) Located at the edge of the Nordmarka, Bogstad Camping is ideal for enjoying the Oslo outdoors. However, as one of northern Europe's largest camp sites, it can get very busy. The facilities include showers, communal kitchen and there is a nearby kiosk and restaurant. It's 9km north of the city centre. To get there take bus 32 from Oslo S (30 minutes approx).

Ekeberg Camping (Map p91; ☎ 22 19 85 68; www.ekebergcamping.no; Ekebergveien 65; 4-person tent with/without car Nkr245/170; ⏰ 1 Jun-1 Sep; 🅿) Nestled on a scenic knoll southeast of the city, Ekeberg Camping promises one of the best views over Oslo. It can get seriously crowded and facilities (kitchen, laundry, convenience store and showers) aren't as well maintained as they could be. Take bus 34 or 46 from Jernbanetorget to Ekeberg Camping (10 minutes). Prices rise by 10% in peak periods.

Those who prefer wild camping can take T-bane line 1 to Frognerseteren at the edge of Nordmarka or line 5 to Sognsvann. You can't camp at Sognsvann itself, but walk a kilometre or two into the woods and you'll find plenty of natural camp sites where you can pitch a tent for free.

HOSTELS

Anker Hostel (Map pp96-7; ☎ 22 99 72 10; www.ankerhostel.no; Storgata 55; 4-/6-bed dm with bathroom Nkr215/195, s/d from Nkr510; 💻) This traveller-savvy hostel boasts an international atmosphere, spick-and-span rooms, a laundry, luggage room, kitchen and small bar. Breakfast costs an extra Nkr75 and linen costs Nkr50. The location is not scenic but it is convenient, with Grünerløkka and the city centre only a five-minute walk away.

Oslo Vandrerhjem Haraldsheim (Map p91; ☎ 22 22 29 65; oslo.haraldsheim.hostel@vandrerhjem.no; Haraldsheim-

IN SEARCH OF THE CHEAPEST BED

Cheap beds in Oslo come at a premium, but there are four good services to help you track one down:

- **Use-It** (Map pp96-7; ☎ 22 41 51 32; www.use-it.no; Møllergata 3), the Oslo Youth Information Service will help with bookings at hostels and private homes (dorms from Nkr120); there's no minimum stay and bookings are free.
- **Oslo tourist offices** (Oslo S & Fridtjof Nansens plass 5; see p92) also book rooms in private homes (two nights minimum stay; booking fee Nkr50) for prices a little cheaper than the hostels, as well as hotel rooms at discounted rates.
- **Den Norske Turistforening** (Map pp96-7; DNT; Norwegian Mountain Touring Club; ☎ 22 82 28 22; www.dntoslo.no; Storgata 3) has lists of around 40 locally owned huts in Nordmarka. Among them are better-known staffed huts where beds must be booked in advance and DNT members/nonmembers can expect to pay Nkr185/240; most of these huts are at least 10km from the centre.
- **Bed & Breakfast Norway** (☎ 22 67 30 80; www.bbnorway.com) is the best source for finding a room in one of the capital's B&Bs.

veien 4; dm from Nkr220, s/d with shared bathroom Nkr355/495, all incl breakfast; 💻) A pleasant, if hard to find, hostel 4km from the city centre. It has 24-hour reception and 270 beds, mostly in clean four-bed dorms. There are kitchen and laundry facilities. Linen costs Nkr50. Take tram 12, 15 or 17, or bus 31 or 32 to Sinsenkrysset, then walk five minutes uphill.

Perminalen Hotel (Map pp96-7; ☎ 23 09 30 81; www.perminalen.no; Øvre Slottsgate 2; 4-/6-bed dm with bathroom Nkr335, s/d Nkr360/499; 💻) Perminalen has a barracks feel, but tidy rooms and a central location make up for the pension's sterile, dormitory atmosphere. Prices include linen and a simple breakfast, which you can eat outside in the summer.

Ellingsens Pensjonat (Map p93; ☎ 22 60 03 59; www.ellingsenspensjonat.no; Holtegata 25; s/d with shared bathroom Nkr330/540, s/d with bathroom Nkr460/650) Located in a quiet, pleasant neighbourhood, this homey pension offers one of the best deals in the capital. The building dates from 1890 and many of the original features (high ceilings, rose designs) remain. Rooms are bright and airy, with refrigerators and kettles. It's a popular place so reservations are a must in the summer.

Midrange

Cochs Pensjonat (Map pp96-7; ☎ 23 33 24 00; www.cochspensjonat.no; Parkveien 25; s/d with shared bathroom Nkr420/580, with bathroom from Nkr520/680) Opened as a guesthouse for bachelors in the 1920s, Cochs has sparsely furnished, clean rooms at an ideal location behind the Royal Palace. The rooms at the back overlooking the Slottsparken are especially spacious. There is a luggage room and it offers a discounted breakfast buffet at a coffee shop around the corner for Nkr59.

P-Hotel (Map pp96-7; ☎ 80 04 68 35; www.p-hotels.com; Grensen 19; s/d Nkr645/745; 💻) P-hotel offers some of the best prices in central Oslo, which does something to make up for the hotel's otherwise sterile character. A breakfast in a bag, delivered to your door is included and there is free wi-fi access.

MS Innvik (Map pp96-7; ☎ 22 41 95 00; www.msinnvik.no; Langkaia; s/d Nkr425/750) A car ferry turned theatre/B&B, MS Innvik offers a memorable, if slightly cramped, sleeping experience. On a sunny day, breakfast can be enjoyed on deck with a clear view over the fjord and across to Oslo's new opera house at Bjørvika. To get there take the footbridge over the E18 south of the central station.

our pick **Residence Kristinelund** (Map p91; ☎ 40 00 24 11; www.kristinelund.no; Kristinelundveien 2; s/d with shared bathroom Nkr590/790, with bathroom Nkr690/970; 💻) In a pretty 19th-century building, on one of Oslo's more exclusive streets, the Kristinelund provides some respite from the bustle of the city centre. Breakfast is served in a sunny room facing the garden, rooms are well kept and the staff is both helpful and friendly. The location is especially nice if you plan to spend several days in Oslo, as Bygdøy, Vigeland Park and the city centre are all within a short walk or bus ride. To get there take bus 20, 30, 31 or 32 (towards Bygdøy) from Jernbanetorget and get off at Olav Kyrres plass. Kristinelund is the white house on the corner.

Thon Hotel Munch (Map pp96-7; ☎ 23 36 27 00; www.thonhotels.no; Brugata 7; s/d mid-Jun–mid-Aug, also Sat & Sun Nkr595/795, breakfast buffet Nkr50; 💻) One of 13 Thon hotels scattered around Oslo, the Munch has the amenities of a good budget hotel-chain and an all-out breakfast buffet.

Hotell Bondeheimen (Map pp96-7; ☎ 23 21 41 00; www.bondeheimen.com; Rosenkrantz gate 8; s/d weekdays mid-Jun–mid-Aug from Nkr750/830, Sat & Sun Nkr750/990, rest-of-year Nkr1095/1295; 💻) This central hotel has attractive rooms and helpful staff. The older rooms (with 1980s Scandinavian pine-wood furniture) are slowly being renovated and all are highly recommended.

Rica Victoria Hotel (Map pp96-7; ☎ 24 14 70 00; www.rica-hotels.com; Rosenkrantz gate 13; s/d mid-Jun–mid-Aug & Sat & Sun Nkr695/945, rest-of-year Nkr950/1290; 💻) This straightforward business hotel, located between Aker Brygge and Karl Johans gate, is also a winner.

Top End

Holmenkollen Park Hotel Rica (Map p91; ☎ 22 92 20 00; www.holmenkollenparkhotel.no; Kongeveien 26; s/d mid-Aug–mid-Sep Nkr1160-1410; s/d rest-of-year Nkr1680/1930; P 💻 🏊) Founded in 1891 as a sanatorium by Dr Ingebrigt Christian Lund, this hotel offers luxury, great views and some history. Not to mention a vast breakfast buffet, complete with organic produce.

Grand Hotel (Map pp96-7; ☎ 23 21 20 00; www.grand.no; Karl Johans gate 31; s/d summer Nkr1245/1495, rest-of-year Nrk1710/1960; P 💻 🏊) Brimming with period character, the regal Grand Hotel has long been considered the benchmark of true elegance in Oslo. The rooms are beautifully appointed and classy without being overdone. It's also highly recommended.

Grims Grenka (Map pp96-7; ☎ 23 10 72 00; www.grimsgrenka.no; Kongens gate 5; s/d from Nkr2150; 💻) It's Oslo's answer to the exclusive, cosmopolitan experience offered by boutique hotels in London and New York. Grims Grenka, opening in 2008, will have minimalist, modern-designed rooms, a hipster rooftop bar, an Asian-fusion restaurant and a great location.

EATING

In the past, eating out in Oslo was an expensive luxury that residents reserved for special occasions. Luckily, this began to change in the late '90s (see boxed text, opposite) and today there are good restaurants, cafés and supermarkets all over the city.

While there are some excellent restaurants on Akers Brygge and along Karl Johan, a five-minute walk towards Majorstua T-bane station or Grünerløkka offers more variety and better prices.

For the ultimate snack try a *polse* (hot dog) in a *lumpe* (potatoe cake) for Nkr15 or a waffle with sour cream and strawberry jam.

Central Oslo

RESTAURANTS

Rust (Map pp96-7; ☎ 23 20 22 10; Hegehaugsveien 22; snacks & light meals Nkr36-59, mains Nkr119-129) On a cobblestone side street, Rust has plenty of outdoor seating and loads of blankets for when it gets cold. Good for a quiet cocktail, burgers (Nkr129), hearty salads (Nrk119) or tapas late into the night.

Thien Nga (Map pp96-7; ☎ 22 20 44 41; Bernt Ankersgate 6b; starters Nkr40-50, mains Nkr60-105) Thien Nga is one of several good Asian-food choices on this street. Ignore the Greek ambience; the food is authentically Vietnamese.

Krishna's Cuisine (Map p93; ☎ 22 60 62 50; Kirkeveien 59b; lunch Nkr65, dinner Nkr70-90) Upstairs across from the Majorstua T-bane station, Krishna's is one of Oslo's best vegetarian options, serving up enormous platefuls of vegetarian curries for both lunch and dinner.

Tullins Café (Map pp96-7; ☎ 22 20 46 16; Tullins gate 2; snacks & light meals Nkr69-108) This dimly lit café offers a little bit of everything, from salads and burgers to pasta and stir-fry dishes. It's a favourite among students.

Curry & Ketchup (Map p93; ☎ 22 69 05 22; Kirkeveien 51; curries Nkr74-110) With decorations reminiscent of a Tiki bar or garage sale, Curry & Ketchup dishes out piping hot naan (Nkr23) and fragrant portions of Indian classics such as chicken tikka masala and palak paneer (Nkr74), not to mention good mango lassis for Nkr35. The service is notoriously bad, but the good atmosphere makes up for it.

Grand Café (Map pp96-7; ☎ 23 24 20 18; Karl Johans gate 31; lunch Nkr92-215) At 11am sharp, Henrik Ibsen would leave his apartment on Drammensveien (now Henrik Ibsens gate) and walk to the Grand Café for a lunch of herring, beer and one shot of aquavit (alcoholic drink made from potatoes and carroway liquor). His table is still there and you don't have to eat herring if you go, though it is on the menu (Nkr88).

BAGATELLE

Eyvind Hellstrøm still remembers the thrill of the day he first hosted the discerning taste buds of the Michelin inspectors at **Bagatelle** (Map pp96-7; ☎ 22 12 14 40; www.bagatelle.no; Bygdøy allé 3) in 1984. Two stars later, Hellstrøm continues to apply lessons learned in the exacting kitchens of Paris and Lyon, to glam up old favourites and create something entirely his own. His restaurant represents the pinnacle of fine dining in Norway, serving modern European cooking with an emphasis on local and, when possible, organic ingredients. He filled us in on his restaurant and the city's blossoming dining scene.

'The Oslo dining scene has completely changed. I remember when I came back from France there were few fresh markets. They just didn't exist. Getting the products to make great cooking was so difficult. Now, the customers are more open to gastronome. Even members of the old class are changing their habits, going to restaurants and trying new cooking.

'If there is a trend, it is towards Asian restaurants and towards sushi bars. Young people like these casual places and I think that's good. It's easy, informal and it gets people used to eating out. It's an introduction for young people to go to more elaborate places like Bagatelle and discover new styles of cooking.'

And what Norwegian dish simply cannot be missed? Fresh cod and I even like *lutefisk* [a glutinous dried cod dish], which is my Norwegian speciality. We had the great pleasure of introducing *lutefisk* at the Ritz in Paris and the French people appreciated it because the texture is very different. It's best with a light red wine, but start with beer and aquavit in the traditional way.

Which are the up-and-coming stars of the Oslo dining scene? Try **Restaurant Oscarsgate** (Map pp96-7; ☎ 22 46 59 06; www.restaurantoscarsgate.no; Oscarsgate 2) for a good mix of know how and craziness.

As told to Kari Lundgren

Theatercafeen (Map pp96-7; ☎ 22 82 40 50; Stortingsgaten 24/26; small dishes Nkr98-154, mains Nkr190-318) A favourite with Norwegian families during Christmas and on17 May, the Theatercafeen, directly across from the National Theatre, presents Norwegian classics in posh Viennese surroundings. Favourites include the reindeer steak with mushrooms and whortleberries (Nkr305).

Pizza da Mimmo (Map pp96-7; ☎ 22 44 40 20; Behrensgate 2; pizza Nkr105-135) The best pizza in Oslo is served in this family-run basement restaurant; book ahead on weekends.

Baltazar (Map pp96-7; ☎ 23 35 70 60; Dronningens gate 27; starters Nkr110-130, mains Nkr150-280) Located in the bazaar halls of the cathedral, Baltazar serves up Italian classics, homemade pasta and good wine. During the summer (when the owners are in Lucca, Italy), the main restaurant is closed and lunch is served at Trattoria Cappuccino in the leafy courtyard behind the cathedral.

CAFÉS

Fact: unaided by Starbucks, Norwegians drink more coffee per capita than any other nationality. And while most coffee drinking happens at home, preferably alongside waffles, in Oslo, there is a good selection of coffee bars. Most cafés offer toothsome open-faced sandwiches to snack on, topped with *gulost* (yellow cheese) or mayonnaise and shrimps. *Boller* (raisin rolls) and *skolebrød* (pastry with vanilla cream filling) are also popular.

Stockfleths (Map pp96-7; Lille Grensen) Founded in 1895, the award-winning Stockfleths is one of Oslo's oldest coffee shops. It also serves thick slices of wholegrain bread with brown cheese, a favourite Norwegian snack.

our pick Åpent Bakerei (Map pp96-7; ☎ 22 04 96 67; Inkognito terasse 1) A neighbourhood café that serves coffee in deep, cream-coloured bowls and has unbeatable breads and pastries. A freshly baked roll (Nkr14) topped with homemade *røre syltetøy* (stirred jam) and enjoyed on the bakery's patio, makes for one of Oslo's best and least expensive breakfasts.

QUICK EATS

Bagel & Juice (Map pp96-7; ☎ 22 42 38 70; Lille Grensen; bagels Nkr31-58; breakfast & lunch) Terrific bagels and a huge range of fresh juices.

Japo Sushi (Map pp96-7; ☎ 22 55 55 11; Frognerveien 1; bento boxes Nkr79-155) Given that Norwegians cheerfully down pickled herring for breakfast, it shouldn't be too surprising that Oslo has some good sushi. Japo is one fast option of many.

United Bakeries (Map pp96-7; ☎ 22 41 27 53; 1st fl, Paléet shopping centre; 8am-8pm Mon-Fri, 8am-7pm Sat, 10am-5pm Sun) Offers quiche, salads and gourmet sandwiches (Nkr89).

Other recommendations:

Dolly Dimples (Map pp96-7; ☎ 04 440; Stortingsgata 12; pizzas from Nkr124) Reliable Norwegian pizza chain, with a number of locations around the city, including Kirkeveien 64 and Storgata 2.

Kaffistova (Map pp96-7; ☎ 23 31 80 00; Grensen 19; snacks Nkr68-120, mains Nkr80-160) A centrally located Norwegian-inspired cafeteria.

Life (Map pp96-7; ☎ 22 42 96 00; Akersgata 32; 9am-6pm Mon-Fri, 10am-4pm Sat) Sells organic produce and wholesome snacks.

Aker Brygge

Aker Brygge, the old shipyard turned trendy shopping complex west of the main harbour, has a **food court** (11am-10pm) with various eateries and a variety of waterside restaurants.

If the weather is nice, the local meal of choice is peel-and-eat shrimp, eaten dockside with a fresh baguette, mayonnaise and just a touch of lemon. In the summer, you can buy shrimp from the **Fisherman's Coop** (Map pp96-7; ☎ 22 42 02 75; Rådhusbrygge 3/4; 7am-5pm Tue-Sat; shrimp per kg Nkr120) or, on Thursdays, keep an eye out for one of Norway's richest men, Kjell Inge Røkkes, who can be found selling shrimp from his boat *Trygg*.

Albertine (Map pp96-7; ☎ 22 83 00 60; Stranden 3; snacks Nkr34-95, light meals Nkr78-170, mains Nkr189-225) One of the oldest waterfront eateries, Albertine offers bistro-style food and a front-row seat to watch the world go by.

Pascal (Map pp96-7; ☎ 22 55 00 20; Brynjulf Bulls plass 2; starters Nkr90-140, mains Nkr180-215) Next door to the Nobel Peace Center, Pascal is best known for its French pastries. Former US president Bill Clinton came here for coffee. It also offers a savoury Francophone lunch and dinner menu.

our pick **Solsiden** (Map pp96-7; ☎ 22 33 36 30; Søndre Akershus Kai 34; starters Nkt125-155, mains Nkr185-295; May-Sep) Solsiden means 'sunny side' in Norwegian, which explains why this place is so popular among sun-craving Oslo-dwellers. Located on the opposite side of Pipervika from Aker Brygge, Solsiden serves up some of the city's best seafood and has an ideal view over the fjord.

Other recommendations:

Beach Club (Map pp96-7; ☎ 22 83 83 82; Bryggetorget 14; burgers Nkr85-135; breakfast, lunch & dinner) Great for a sunny afternoon, it serves a full American breakfast (Nkr105).

ICA Gourmet Supermarket & Café (Map pp96-7; Holmens gate 7; 9am-10pm Mon-Fri, 9am-8pm Sat) Well-stocked supermarket.

Peppe's Pizza (Map pp96-7; ☎ 23 31 12 80; pizzas from Nkr134)

Around Oslo S & Grønland

Teddy's Soft Bar (Map pp96-7; ☎ 22 17 36 00; Brugata 3A; light meals around Nkr75; lunch & dinner Mon-Sat) Teddy's Soft Bar is a local institution and has scarcely changed since it opened in the 1950s. On offer are light, typically Norwegian meals – try the *pytt i panne* (Nkr88), which is essentially eggs with diced potato and meat.

Mithas The Sweethouse (Map pp96-7; ☎ 22 17 03 03; Grønland 2A) Sells delectable Iranian sweets.

Punjab Tandoori (Map pp96-7; ☎ 22 17 20 86; Grønlandsleiret 24; lunch specials Nkr75, mains around Nkr60) Good-value Indian and Pakistani food is easy to find anywhere around the Grønland T-bane station. This place has simply presented Indian fare – curry, dahl, samosas and tasty curries.

Anyone aged over 18 can buy beer at Oslo supermarkets until 8pm from Monday to Friday and 6pm on Saturday. For wine or spirits, you'll have to be at least 20 years old and visit the **Vinmonopolet** (Map pp96-7; Oslo City Shopping Centre; 10am-5pm Mon-Wed, 10am-6pm Thu, 9am-6pm Fri, 10am-2pm Sat). There are others at Kirkeveien 64, Møllergata 10 and Elisenbergveien 37.

The Grønland district and the back streets east of Storgata are brimming with inexpensive ethnic supermarkets where you'll find otherwise unavailable items such as fresh herbs and African, Asian and Middle Eastern ingredients.

Regular supermarkets also abound around Oslo. Only the small ones classed as kiosks can open on Sundays. Some of the more central choices include the following:

Grønland Bazaar (Map pp96-7; ☎ 22 17 05 71; Tøyengata 2) Middle Eastern–themed shopping centre.

Rimi Supermarket (Map pp96-7; Storgata 32; 8am-10pm Mon-Sat) All-purpose grocery chain; other branches can be found at Oslo S and Gunerius Shopping Centre.

Grünerløkka

Oslo's Greenwich Village, while always lively and frequented by a well-dressed, youthful crowd, is especially pleasant in the summer when life spills out onto the sidewalks from the numerous cafés, bars and restaurants around Olaf Ryes plass.

Mucho Mas (Map p93; ☎ 22 37 16 09; Thorvald Meyers gate 36; chips & salsa Nkr62, burrito Nkr143) What it lacks in authenticity, Mucho Mas more than makes up for in cheese and portion size. The full Mexican repertoire is on offer, including tacos, nachos and burritos (which are enormous); all dishes are offered in meat or vegetarian versions. Well-priced beer helps put out the fire.

Sult (Map p93; ☎ 22 87 04 67; Thorvald Meyers gate 26; starters Nkr59-69, mains Nkr179-215) The polished green-and-black colour scheme of Sult perfectly captures the Grünerløkka vibe with an imaginative menu replete with superb fish and pasta dishes often using local and organic ingredients. It's always packed so get there early and wait for a table in the attached bar appropriately called Tørst (meaning 'thirsty'). There are free tapas on Fridays.

Fru Hagen (Map p93; ☎ 22 38 24 26; Thorvald Meyers gate 40; mains Nkr118-137) The low-key and always full Fru Hagen, 'Mrs. Garden', serves sandwiches and burgers, all with a healthy side portion of vegetables. Its location facing Olaf Ryes plass also makes it good for people-watching.

Bistro Brocante (Map p93; ☎ 22 35 68 71; Thorvald Meyers gate 40; lunch specials Nkr59-129, starters Nkr96-102, mains Nkr192-199) Next door to Fru Hagen, this informal French-inspired café serves fantastic salads (Nkr98 to Nkr115), quiche (Nkr93) and even *coq a vin* (Nkr192). The outdoor tables are at a premium in summer.

Markveien Mat & Vinhus and Dr Kneipp's Vinbar (Map pp96-7; ☎ 22 37 22 97; starters 135-155, mains Nkr240-290, 3 courses Nkr495) With a hint of truffle oil or a dash of dill, the cooks at Markveien make Norwegian cooking unforgettable. The restaurant focuses on using local seafood and meat, as well as organic produce, to create their delectable dishes. If you're not in the mood for the formal dining room, slide into one of the dark wooden booths at Dr Kneipp's next door for finger food or a sumptuous dessert, not to mention an amazing wine list.

Other recommendations:

Hotel Havana (Map p93; Thorvald Meyers gate 38; 🕑 10am-6pm, Mon-Fri) International deli with everything from French cheese to Belgian chocolates. The chorizo and manchego sandwiches (Nkr55) are an especially good bet.

Villa Paradiso (Map p93; Olaf Ryes plass 8; ☎ 22 35 40 60; pizzas from Nkr99) No-frills Italian food (mostly pizzas), pleasant service and family friendly.

Vålerenga & Ekeberg

Smia Galleri (Map p91; ☎ 22 19 59 20; Opplandsgata 19; starters Nkr85-95, mains Nkr185-215) Smia Galleri is one of those places Oslo residents are so fond of they almost hate to share it. The leafy patio is perfect on summer afternoons and there's jazz on Thursday evenings. If they have it, try the rhubarb crumble with wild strawberry sorbet. It takes about 15 minutes to get there: from Oslo S, take bus 37 towards Helsfyr T-bane station and get off at Vålerenga.

Ekeberg Restaurant (Map p91; ☎ 23 24 23 00; Kongsveien 15; starters Nkr95-138, mains Nkr145-275) An early example of functionalist architecture, the 1929 Ekeberg Restaurant once attracted long lines of spectators eager to be seen enjoying a beer outside this angular, painfully white nonconformist building. After falling into disrepair in the 1980s, the restaurant was renovated and reopened with a classy menu and slick bar. If nothing else, go for the view.

Holmenkollen Area

Frognerseteren restaurant (Map p91; ☎ 22 92 40 40; www.frognerseteren.no; 🕑 11am-10pm Mon-Sat, 11am-9pm Sun) There are three good reasons to visit Frognerseteren: the apple cake (Nkr50), the view and the building. The apple cake is billed as the best in Oslo and the view, from over 400m above sea level, is as good as it gets. As for the building, with dragon heads and enough wood trim to rival the most ornate Swiss chalet, it is the epitome of the Viking revival–style popular in the 1860s.

DRINKING & ENTERTAINMENT

The tourist office's free monthly brochure *What's On in Oslo* lists current concerts, theatre and special events, but the best publication for night owls is the free *Streetwise*, published annually in English by Use-It (p92).

Bars & Clubs

Going out in the world's most expensive city requires a bit of skill, but high prices certainly don't keep the locals at home. Quite the opposite: Oslo is more vibrant, busy and nonchalantly proud of its up-and-coming status than ever. And the manageable size of the city makes it easy to figure out where to be on any given night.

OSLO

GAY & LESBIAN OSLO

Oslo is a liberal, gay-friendly city in an already liberal country, which makes for a relaxed gay/lesbian scene. Favourite watering holes include: the mixed scene at **Elsker** (Map pp96-7; Kristian IV gate 9), which has, according to local Øyvind Gjengaar, a 'kind of Eurovision schläger-musical profile'; and the dark basement at **London Pub** (Map pp96-7; ☎ 90 83 98 58; www.londonpub.no; CJ Hambros plass 5; cover charge Nkr50), Oslo's oldest gay bar. The parties at **Fire Oslo** (Map pp96-7; www.fireoslo.com; at Stratos, Youngstorget 2; cover Nkr100 or Nkr150) are also popular.

At the end of June, don't miss **Skeive Dager** (☎ 22 41 11 33; www.skeivedager.no), Oslo's Gay Pride week complete with a parade, art exhibits, concerts and other events. And the first Sunday of every month is Gay Sunday at the **Norske Filminstitutte** (Map pp96-7; ☎ 22 47 45 00; www.cinemateket.no).

For more information, the *Streetwise* guide published by Use-It (p92) has a 'Gay Guide' covering cafés, pubs, clubs, bookstores and other activities. Or for a truly insider scoop, ask someone to translate the weekly guide from *Blikk* (www.blikk.no), Oslo's gay/lesbian magazine.

Note that many Oslo night spots have an unwritten dress code that expects patrons to be relatively well turned out – at the very least, don't show up in grubby gear and hiking boots. For most bars and clubs that serve beer and wine, you must be over 18 years of age, but many places, especially those that serve spirits, impose a higher age limit. On weekends, most Oslo night spots remain open until at least 3am.

Beer prices for half-litres typically range from Nkr50 to Nkr65, but some places (usually grim and inhabited by wary elbow-on-the-bar locals) charge as little as Nkr30 for those travellers watching their kroner. **Stargate** (Map pp96-7; Grønland 2; half-litre Nkr36) is a decent and central dive.

Some of the most popular places close to the city centre can be found around the Youngstorget, also the political hub of Oslo. **Justisen** (Map pp96-7; ☎ 22 42 24 72; Møllergata 15), frequented by lawyers and politicians, is good for a peaceful beer in classic surroundings and has outdoor tables. **Robinet** (Map pp96-7; ☎ 22 20 01 50; Mariboes gate 7), to the north of the square, is a tiny, retro bar packed with musicians and media types.

Grab a stool at the well-polished wooden bar at the ex-pharmacy **Tekehtopa** (Map pp96-7; ☎ 22 20 33 23; St Olavs plass) – that's pharmacy spelled backwards in Norwegian – for decent beer or a bite to eat. Another popular central location is the long-standing **Onkel Donald Kafé-Bar** (Map pp96-7; ☎ 23 35 63 10; Universitetsgata 26).

The well-heeled crowd of Oslo west can be found sipping Cava in **Champagneria** (Map pp96-7; ☎ 21 94 88 02; Frognerveien 2; ⏲ 11am-1am Mon-Sat, noon-1am Sun) or cocktails at the New Orleans–style courtyard bar at **Palace Grill** (Map pp96-7; ☎ 23 13 11 40; Solli gate 2), also an excellent restaurant, both near Solli plass.

The city's best neighbourhood bar scene is along Thorvald Meyers gate and the surrounding streets in Grünerløkka. Try working your way through the cocktail list at the hip **Café Kaos** (Map pp96-7; ☎ 22 04 69 90; Thorvald Meyers gate 56) or minimalist **Tea Lounge** (Map p93; ☎ 22 37 07 05; Thorvald Meyers gate 33b). **Bar Boca** (Map p93 ☎ 22 04 10 80; Thorvald Meyers gate 30) is famous for its bloody marys, among other things.

In Grønland, the back garden at **Dattera Til Hagen** (Map pp96-7; ☎ 22 17 18 61; Grønland 10) is especially busy in the summer, as is the swanky riverside patio of **Süd Øst** (Map pp96-7; ☎ 23 35 30 70 Trondheimsveien 5; ⏲ 11am-midnight Mon & Tue, 11am-1am Wed & Thu, 11am-2am Fri & Sat).

Live Music

An upbeat place is the rock club **Mono** (Map pp96-7; ☎ 22 41 41 66; www.cafemono.no; Pløensgate 4), which is known for being ahead of the curve on booking good indie bands. In Grønland, **Gloria Flames** (Map pp96-7; ☎ 22 17 16 00; www.gloriaflames.no; Grønland 18) is a popular rock bar.

West of the centre, the Russian, cowboy-themed and just plain bizarre **Spasibar** (Map pp96-7 ☎ 22 11 51 90; www.spasibar.com; St Olavs gate 22) has live music, food, beer, art and a garden overlooking the Slottsparken. To get there go through the Kunstacademe on Wergelandsveien and go towards the back of the yellow building.

Finally, it would be a pity to leave Oslo without checking out **Blå** (Map pp96-7; ☎ 40 00 42 77; www.blaaoslo.no; Brenneriveien 9c), which features on a global list of 100 great jazz clubs compiled by the savvy editors at the US jazz magazine *Down Beat*. As one editor put it, 'to get in this list means that it's quite the club'.

Concerts

Keep your ear to the ground in summer to hear about outdoor concerts at Vigeland Park – a weird-and-wonderful venue.

The city's largest concert halls, **Oslo Spektrum** (Map pp96-7; ☎ 22 05 29 00; www.oslospektrum.no; Sonja Henies plass 2) and **Rockefeller Music Hall** (Map pp96-7; ☎ 22 20 32 32; www.rockefeller.no; Torggata 16), once a bathhouse, host a wide range of artists and events.

Den Norske Opera (Map pp96-7; ☎ 81 54 44 88; www.operaen.no; Storgata 23; tickets from Nkr300) is Oslo's opera company and stages opera, ballet and classical concerts every month, except for July. As of 2008 it will be performing in the city's new Opera House at Bjørvika, complete with humidified air for resonance and screens with subtitles in eight different languages on the back of each seat. More casual concerts in the public roof garden are also planned.

You may also want to check out the alternative dance and theatre scene at the café-style **Black Box** (Map pp96-7; ☎ 22 10 40 20; www.blackbox.no; Stranden 3), in the Aker Brygge complex.

The **National Theatre** (Nationaltheatret; Map pp96-7; ☎ 22 00 14 00; www.nationaltheatret.no; Stortingsgata 15) is Norway's showcase theatre venue and has a lavish rococo hall. It was constructed specifically as a venue for the works of Norwegian playwright Henrik Ibsen, whose works are still performed here.

Cinema

Saga Kino (Map pp96-7; ☎ 82 03 00 00; Stortingsgata 28) The six-screen Saga Kino cinema shows first-run movies, including Hollywood fare, in their original language; the entrance is on Olav V's gate.

Filmens Hus (Map pp96-7; ☎ 22 47 45 00; Dronningens gate 16) Filmens Hus screens old classics and international festival winners most days.

SHOPPING

Oslo excels in upmarket shopping and there are many fine shops on Grensen and Karl Johans gate. For art, try the galleries on Frognerveien, exclusive boutiques head to Hegdehaugsveien or Skovveien and for funky shoes or T-shirts go no further than Grünerløkka. **Oslo City Shopping Centre** (Map pp96-7; Stenersgata) and the more glamorous **Glasmagasinet Department Store** (Map pp96-7; Gensen) are good for mainstream shopping.

Husfliden (Map pp96-7; ☎ 24 14 12 80; Rosenkrantz gate 19-21) Husfliden is a larger shop selling quality Norwegian clothing and crafts, as well as a popular place to buy a *bunad* (national costume).

Vestkanttorget flea market (Map p93; Amaldus Nilsens plass; 🕑 10am-4pm Sat) If you're happy with pot luck and sifting through heaps of junk, take a chance here. It's at the plaza that intersects Professor Dahls gate, a block east of Vigeland Park and it's a more than pleasant way to pass a Saturday morning.

Hassan og Den Dama (Map pp96-7; www.hassanogdendama.no; Skoveien 4) One of many boutiques on Skoveien, this shop has clothing, shoes and jewellery produced by Scandinavian and international designers.

Norway Designs (Map pp96-7; ☎ 23 11 45 10; www.norwaydesigns.no; Stortingsgata 28) Features beautifully designed glassware, stationery, clothing and watches within a stone's throw of the National Theatre.

Other recommendations:

Heimen Husflid (Map pp96-7; ☎ 23 21 42 00; www.heimen.net; Rosenkrantz gate 8) Clothing and crafts.

Unique Design (Map pp96-7; ☎ 22 42 97 60; Rosenkrantz gate 13) Good for sweaters.

Juhls' Silvergallery Oslo (Map pp96-7; ☎ 22 42 77 99; Roald Amundsens gate 6) Fine silver and crafts.

GETTING THERE & AWAY

Air

Oslo's Gardermoen International Airport (Map p119; ☎ 91 50 64 00; www.osl.no) opened in October 1998 and has a motorway and high-speed rail link to the city centre (see p116). For details of international services, see p403.

Domestic flights also depart from here and include services (with sample one-way fares) to Ålesund (Nkr459), Bergen (Nkr374), Røros (from Nkr498, daily except Saturday), Stavanger (Nkr374), Tromsø (Nkr708) and Trondheim (Nkr374).

KLM, Widerøe, SAS Braathens and Ryanair also operate 'Oslo' services to/from Torp Airport (Map p119), some 123km southwest of Oslo. See p116 for details on how to get there.

Boat

For details of international ferry services, see p408.

Ferries operated by **DFDS Seaways** (Map p91; ☎ 21 62 10 00; Vippetangen 2) connect Oslo with Denmark from the Vippetangen Quay off Skippergata. Bus 60 stops within a couple of minutes walk of the terminal.

Color Line Ferries (Map p93; ☎ 81 00 08 11; www.colorline.no; Color Line Terminalen, Hjortnes) runs to/from Hirtshals (Denmark) and Kiel (Germany); boats dock at Hjortneskaia, west of the central harbour. Take tram 10 or 13 from Oslo S, or the Color Line bus, which leaves Oslo S one hour before boat departures.

Bus

Long-distance buses arrive and depart from the **Galleri Oslo Bus Terminal** (Map pp96-7; Schweigaards gate 8, Galleri Oslo); the train and bus stations are linked via a convenient overhead walkway for easy connections.

Nor-Way Bussekspress (☎ 82 02 13 00 or 81 54 44 44; www.nor-way.no) has the biggest range of services. International services also depart from the bus terminal.

Car & Motorcycle

The main highways into the city are the E6 from the north and south, and the E18 from the southeast and west. Each time you enter Oslo, you must pass through (at least) one of 19 toll stations and pay Nkr15 to Nkr25.

Hitching

When leaving Oslo it's generally best to take a bus or train to the outskirts of the city and start hitching from there.

To hitch to Bergen, take bus 161 to its final stop and wait beside the E16 towards Hønefoss. For Trondheim, take T-Bane line 5 (direction: Vestli) to Grorud and wait beside Rv4, which connects to the E6. For the south coast and Stavanger, take bus 31 or 32 to the Maritim petrol station. For general information see p418).

Train

All trains arrive and depart from Oslo S in the city centre. It has **reservation desks** (Map pp96-7; 6am-11pm, international 6.30am-11pm) and an **information desk** (☎ 81 50 08 88), which provides details on routes and timetables throughout the country.

There are frequent train services around Oslofjord (eg Drammen, Skien, Moss, Fredrikstad and Halden). Other major destinations include Stavanger via Kristiansand, Bergen via Voss, Røros via Hamar, and Tronheim via Hamar and Lillehammer.

For details of international schedules and prices, see p406.

GETTING AROUND

Oslo has an efficient public transport system with an extensive network of buses, trams, underground trains (T-bane) and ferries. In addition to single-trip tickets, day and transferable eight-trip tickets are also available. Children aged four to 16 and seniors over 67 years of age pay half price on all fares.

The Oslo Pass (see the boxed text, p94) includes access to all public transport options within the city, with the exception of late-night buses and trams. Bicycles can be carried on trams and trains for an additional Nkr11. The automatic fine for travelling without a ticket is a rather punitive Nkr750.

Trafikanten (Map pp96-7; ☎ 177; www.trafikanten.no; Jernbanetorget; 7am-8pm Mon-Fri, 8am-6pm Sat & Sun) is located below Oslo S tower and provides free schedules and a public transport map, *Sporveiskart Oslo*.

To/From the Airport

Flybussen (☎ 177; www.flybussen.com) is the airport shuttle to Gardermoen International Airport 50km north of Oslo. It departs from the bus terminal at Galleri Oslo three or four times hourly from 4.05am to 9.50pm. The trip costs Nkr120/220 one-way/return (valid one month) and takes 40 minutes. **Flybussekspressen** (☎ 177) connects Gardermoen with Majorstua T-bane station (Nkr160), Bekkestua (Nkr180), Ski Skole (Nkr185) and other places, one to four times hourly.

FlyToget (☎ 81 50 07 77; www.flytoget.no) rail services leave Asker station in the far southwest of the city for Gardermoen (Nkr190, 49 minutes) every 20 minutes between 4.18am and midnight, with departures also from the National Theatre and Oslo S. In addition, most northbound **NSB** (☎ 81 50 08 88) intercity and local trains stop at Gardermoen (Nkr75, from 26 minutes, hourly but fewer on Saturday).

To get to/from Torp Airport in Sandefjord, 123km southwest of Oslo and serviced by Ryanair among others, take the **Torp-Expressen** (☎ 48 30 10 00177, 81 50 01 76; www.torpekspressen.no; adult/child Nkr150/80) bus between Galleri Oslo bus terminal and the airport (1½ hours). Departures from Oslo leave three hours before scheduled Ryanair departures, and leave from Torp after Ryanair flights arrive. Although the service operates primarily for Ryanair passengers (the bus will wait if the flight is delayed), passengers on other airlines may also use it. At other times, you'll need to take the hourly Telemarksekspressen bus (or a taxi; from Nkr150, 10 minutes) between the airport and Sandefjord train station from where there are connections to Oslo.

Bicycle

The best place to rent bicycles is the **Skiservice Sykkelutleie** (☎ 22 13 95 04; www.skiservice.no; Tryvannsveien 2; per day around Nkr295) in the Nordmarka. To get there by public transport take T-bane 1 towards Frognerseteren and get off the Voksenkollen station (the 2nd-last stop).

One alternative if you don't plan on going too far is **Oslo Citybike** (☎ 22 02 34 88), a network of bikes that cyclists can borrow for up to three hours at a time from bicycle stands around the city. Access cards (Nkr70) can be purchased from the tourist office and last for 24 hours, but bikes must be exchanged or returned to a rack within three hours or you will loose your deposit (Nkr500). They're convenient and well maintained; just don't forget to get a map of the bike stand locations around the city, as the rack you were planning to use may be full.

For ideas on where to cycle, see p105.

Boat

Ferries to the Oslofjord islands sail from Vippetangen Quay (Map p91), see p106. For details of ferries to Bygdøy, see p101.

The express boat **Princessin** (☎ 22 87 64 20; www.nbds.no) connects Oslo with Drøbak (Nkr72, 1½ hours, three weekly) and other Oslofjord stops en route: Ildjernet, Langåra and Håøya (which is a holiday spot offering fine swimming and camping). It departs from Aker Brygge pier.

Bus & Tram

Bus and tram lines lace the city and extend into the suburbs. There's no central local bus station, but most converge at Jernbanetorget in front of Oslo S. Most westbound buses, including those to Bygdøy and Vigeland Park, also stop immediately south of the National Theatre.

The frequency of service drops dramatically at night, but on weekends, night buses N12, N14 and N18 follow the tram routes until 4am or later; there are also weekend night buses (201 to 218). These services are called Nattlinjer and cost Nkr45 per ride (no passes are valid).

Tickets for most trips cost Nkr20 if you buy them in advance (at 7-Eleven, Narvesen, Trafikanten) or Nkr30 if you buy them from the driver. A day pass costs Nkr60.

Car & Motorcycle

Oslo has its share of one-way streets, which can complicate city driving a bit, but the streets are rarely as congested as in most European cities.

Metered street parking, identified by a solid blue sign with a white 'P', can be found throughout the city. Payment (up to Nkr44 per hour) is usually required from 8am to 5pm Monday to Friday, and until 3pm Saturday. At other times, parking is free unless otherwise posted. The city centre also has 16 multistorey car parks, including those at Oslo City and Aker Brygge shopping centres; fees range from Nkr70 to Nkr200 per 24-hour period.

Note that the Oslo Pass includes parking at all municipal car parks; instructions for display come with the pass.

Taxi

Flagfall starts from Nkr39 plus Nkr12 to Nkr18 per kilometre. There are taxi stands at Oslo S, shopping centres and city squares, but any taxi with a lit sign is available for hire. Otherwise, phone **Norgestaxi** (☎ 08000) or **Oslo Taxi** (☎ 02323), but note that the meter starts running at the point of dispatch! Oslo taxis accept major credit cards.

T-Bane

The five-line Tunnelbanen underground system, better known as the T-bane, is faster and extends further from the city centre than most city bus lines. All lines pass through the Nationaltheatret, Stortinget and Jernbanetorget (for Oslo S) stations.

AROUND OSLO

DRØBAK

pop 11,500

Once Oslo's winter harbour, Drøbak is a cosy little village by the water's edge, home to enough clapboard timber buildings to warrant a day trip from the capital.

The helpful **tourist office** (☎ 64 93 50 87; Hanegata 4; 🕑 8.30am-6pm Mon-Fri, 10am-4pm Sat & Sun mid-Jun–mid-Aug) by the harbour has a wealth of information on Drøbak, including *Walks*

Around Drøbak (free) to assist your rambling through the village.

In town, there are several small eateries around the pretty Torget Sq and along nearby Storgata.

Sights

Drøbak is known as Oslo's 'Christmas town' and is renowned for its public decorations. There's also a Christmas shop, **Tregaardens Julehus** (☎ 64 93 41 78; www.julehus.no; Torget 4; 🕑 10am-5pm Mon-Fri, 10am-3pm Sat Mar-Oct; 10am-7pm Mon-Fri, 10am-3pm Sat Nov; 10am-8pm Mon-Fri & 10am-4pm Sat Dec-Feb), which has a Father Christmas post box for kids.

Saltvannsakvarium (☎ 64 93 09 74; www.akvarium.net; Havnegata 4; adult/child Nkr30/10; 🕑 10am-7pm May-Aug, 10am-4pm Sep-Apr) lays claim to the title of the world's only *lutefisk* museum. Not far away, the small **Drøbak Båtforenings Maritime Samlinger** (☎ 64 93 09 74; Kroketønna 4; adult/child Nkr10/free; 🕑 11am-7pm May-Aug) is a museum of maritime paraphernalia.

Not to be missed is the imposing **Oscarsborg fortress**, which lies on an offshore island and dates back to the 1600s. It was the Oscarsborg batteries that sank the German warship *Blücher* on 9 April 1940, an act that saved the King and the Norwegian government from being captured. The fort museum was renovated in 2005 and open-air concerts and complete operas are held here throughout the summer. There is even a hotel, spa and restaurant on the island if you want to extend your stay. **Ferries** (www.oscarsborgfestning.no) to the island (adult/child Nkr70/40; 45 minutes) depart 14 times daily from the harbour from mid-June to mid-August.

Getting There & Away

The hourly bus 541 travels between Oslo and Drøbak (Nkr62, one hour). Alternatively in July, the express boat **Princessin** (☎ 22 87 64 20; www.nbds.no) does one trip (Nkr72) from Oslo's Aker Brygge pier daily Wednesday to Sunday (three times weekly in August), allowing 1½ hours in Drøbak before returning to Oslo.

The new tunnel under Oslofjord, between Drøbak and Drammen, charges Nkr55 each way for a car (motorcycles free).

DRAMMEN

pop 58,700

Drammen is an industrial centre of more interest to businesspeople than tourists. With heavy port machinery and factories, it hardly jumps out at you as being worth a stop. It does, however, have a couple of quirky elements – Drammen was the start of the Royal Road to Bergen and it was the original home of the potato alcohol aquavit – which may warrant a detour. The **Drammen Kommune Offices** (☎ 03008; www.drammen.kommune.no; Engene 1; 🕑 9am-5pm Mon-Fri) can provide further information.

Sights & Activities

Drammen has several buildings of note all of which are clustered close together in the old centre around the main thoroughfare Bragernes Torg: the historic **Stock Exchange** (Bragernes Torg), which now houses a McDonald's; the restored **Rådhus** (Engenes 1), the city hall, a former courthouse and jail; the **fire station** (Bragernes Torg), now a bank; the lovely **Drammen Theatre** (☎ 32 21 31 00; Gamle Kirkeplass; 🕑 events only), built in 1870, burned down in 1993 and reopened in 1996; and the Gothic-style **Bragernes church** (Bragernes Torg) built in 1871.

You can also see the house (from the outside only) where aquavit was first produced in 1804, on Sommerfrydveien by merchant Johan Godtfried Schwencke in response to a royal decree that corn not be used to produce spirits. In late autumn, Drammen holds a national aquavit competition in which celebrities judge which is the best brand.

To get beyond the industry, take a trip up the 1650m-long **Spiralen tunnel** (Map p119) to the 200m-high Bragernes for a lovely view, as well as good waffles (Nkr35) at the Spiralentop Café. And if you still can't quite face the drive back down the six-spiral tunnel – reminiscent of a never-ending indoor parking lot – go for a walk in the Drammensmarka. Bus 41 does the trip three times daily from Bragernes Torg (Nkr20, 15 minutes) on weekends during the summer.

Getting There & Away

Trains run to Oslo every 30 minutes (Nkr83 35 minutes) and buses depart once or twice every hour (Nkr75, 35 minutes).

AROUND DRAMMEN

Another interesting excursion will take you to Åmot, where the **Royal Blåfarveværk** (☎ 32 78 67 00; www.blaa.no; hourly tours Nkr35; 🕑 11am-6pm mid-June–mid-Aug, 11am-5pm Tue-Sat, 11am-6pm Sun rest of-year) was established by King Christian VII in 1773 to extract cobalt for the production

AROUND OSLO

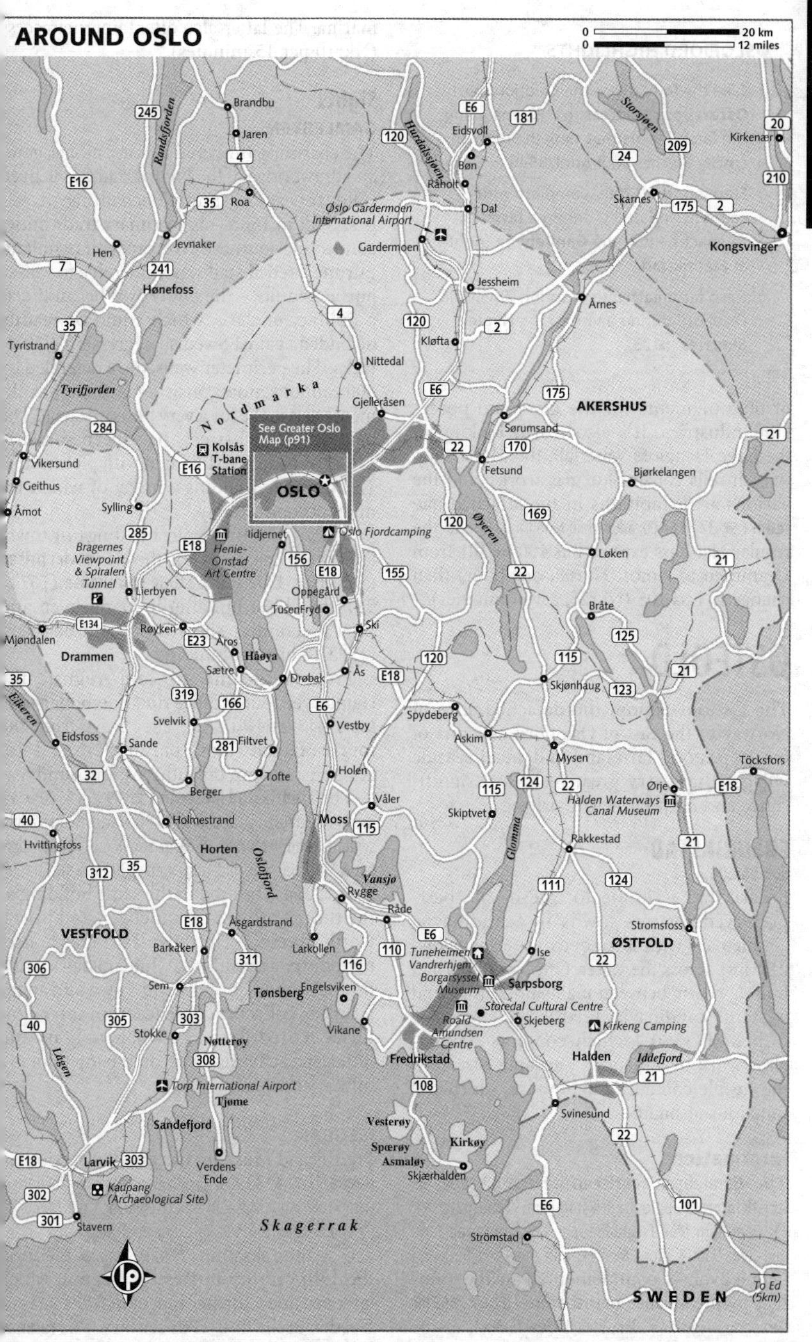
0 20 km
0 12 miles
See Greater Oslo Map (p91)
OSLO
Nordmarka
AKERSHUS
VESTFOLD
ØSTFOLD
SWEDEN
Skagerrak
Oslofjord
Tyrifjorden
Randsfjorden
Hurdalssjøen
Storsjøen
Øyeren
Glomma
Vansjø
Iddefjord
Eikeren
Lågen
Brandbu
Jaren
Roa
Jevnaker
Hen
Hønefoss
Tyristrand
Vikersund
Geithus
Åmot
Sylling
Kolsås T-bane Station
Henie-Onstad Art Centre
Bragernes Viewpoint & Spiralen Tunnel
Lierbyen
Mjøndalen
Drammen
Røyken
Åros
Håøya
Sætre
Drøbak
Svelvik
Sande
Eidsfoss
Filtvet
Tofte
Berger
Holmestrand
Hvittingfoss
Horten
Åsgardstrand
Barkåker
Sem
Stokke
Nøtterøy
Tønsberg
Torp International Airport
Tjøme
Sandefjord
Larvik
Verdens Ende
Kaupang (Archaeological Site)
Stavern
Eidsvoll
Bøn
Råholt
Dal
Oslo Gardermoen International Airport
Gardermoen
Jessheim
Kløfta
Nittedal
Gjelleråsen
Iidjernet
Oslo Fjordcamping
Oppegård
TusenFryd
Ski
Ås
Vestby
Holen
Våler
Moss
Rygge
Råde
Larkollen
Engelsviken
Vikane
Fredrikstad
Vesterøy
Spærøy
Asmaløy
Kirkøy
Skjærhalden
Tuneheimen Vandrerhjem
Borgarsyssel Museum
Roald Amundsen Centre
Storedal Cultural Centre
Sarpsborg
Skjeberg
Ise
Kirkeng Camping
Halden
Svinesund
Strömstad
Spydeberg
Askim
Skiptvet
Mysen
Rakkestad
Halden Waterways Canal Museum
Ørje
Töcksfors
Stromsfoss
Skjønhaug
Fetsund
Sørumsand
Løken
Bråte
Bjørkelangen
Årnes
Skarnes
Kirkenær
Kongsvinger
To Ed (5km)
245
4
E16
35
7
241
284
E16
285
E18
E134
E23
319
166
281
32
40
312
35
E18
311
306
305
303
308
40
E18
303
302
301
E6
181
120
24
209
20
210
175
2
4
120
2
E6
175
22
170
21
169
120
156
E18
155
22
21
125
120
115
E18
21
E6
123
115
124
22
E18
115
21
111
124
E6
110
116
22
108
21
22
E6
101

OSLOFJORD HIGHLIGHTS

- Take the ferry down the Oslofjord past **Oscarsborg Fortress** (p118), imagining the fateful shots that sank the German cruiser *Blücher* on 9 April, 1940
- Step into the 1700s, complete with cannons and duels, during a historical re-enactment in the **Gamlebyen** (right) at Fredrikstad
- Gasp for breath after a spring dip in the Oslofjord during a visit to the **Hvaler Skerries** (p123)

of blue pigments for the glass and porcelain industries. It's also worth looking at the large Haugfoss waterfall, the Mølla shop (which sells cobalt-blue glasswork), and the various art exhibitions in the attached **museum** (☎ 32 78 67 00; adult/child Nkr60/free). Take the regular Nettbuss express bus 100 or 101 from Drammen to Åmot (Nkr68, one hour) then change to bus 105 (Nkr26, seven minutes).

ØSTFOLD

The Østfold region, the detached slice of Norway to the east of Oslofjord, is a mix of forest, pastoral farmland and small seaside villages that carry great historical significance and are well worth visiting.

FREDRIKSTAD

pop 96,600

Fredrikstad is home to one of the best-preserved fortress towns in Scandinavia, Gamlebyen with a modern waterfront district just across the water. Once an important trading centre between mainland Europe and western Scandinavia, Fredrikstad also has a cathedral (1880), which contains stained-glass work by Emanuel Vigeland; bizarrely, the steeple contains a lighthouse, which still functions at night.

Information

The **Gamlebyen tourist office** (☎ 69 30 46 00; turistkontoret@opplevfredrikstad.com; Tøhusgata 41; 9am-5pm Mon-Fri, noon-5pm Sat & Sun mid-Jun–mid-Aug; 9am-4.30pm Mon-Fri mid-Aug–mid-Jun), in Gamlebyen is complemented in the summer by the smaller **tourist office** (☎ 69 39 65 00; Dampskipsbrygga; 8am-9pm 15 Jun-15 Aug), at the marina. The latter also offers internet access (Nkr10 per 15 minutes).

Sights

GAMLEBYEN

The charming timbered houses, moats, gates and drawbridge of the Fredrikstad Gamlebyen (Old Town) are simply enchanting. It was first built in 1663 – as a primary trade outlet connecting southern Norway with mainland Europe, Fredrikstad was vulnerable to waterborne assaults – the Old Town began life as a military enclave, which could be readily defended against Swedish aggression and attacks. The perimeter walls, once defended by 200 cannons, now consist of grassy embankments that make for a very pleasant stroll. The narrow cobbled streets have been similarly preserved and are still lined with picturesque 17th-century buildings, many of which remain occupied today.

Among the finest old buildings in town look out particularly for the **old convict prison** (Salveriet; 1731); the **stone storehouse** (1674-91), the oldest building in Gamlebyen and now a ceramics showroom; and **Balaklava** (1783), a historic building.

From mid-June to mid-August, the Gamlebyen tourist office runs one-hour **guided tours** (adult/child Nkr75/35). They leave from the tourist office at 11am, 1pm and 3pm, and also at noon and 4pm on Saturday and Sunday.

The **Fredrikstad Museum** (☎ 69 95 48 500; www.fredrikstad.museum.no; combined ticket with Isegran adult, senior or child Nkr40/20; 9am-5pm Mon-Fri, noon-5pm Sat & Sun mid-Jun–mid-Aug; 9am-4.30pm Mon-Fri mid-Aug–mid-Jun) is housed in the same building as the tourist office in Gamlebyen and is well worth a browse. The downstairs area houses temporary exhibitions, while upstairs you'll find scale models of the Old Town and an interesting collection of relics from three centuries of Fredrikstad's civilian, military and industrial activities. Also on the top floor is a military museum.

ISEGRAN

Fredrikstad Museum has another section on **Isegran** (☎ 69 33 20 03; www.isegrn.no; combined ticket with Fredrikstad Museum adult/senior or child Nkr40/20; noon-5pm Tue-Sun mid-Jun–mid-Aug), an isle across the Glomma. Norse sagas mention the 13th-century fortress of Isegran, which later became a further line of defence against Sweden in the mid-17th century. The **ruins** of

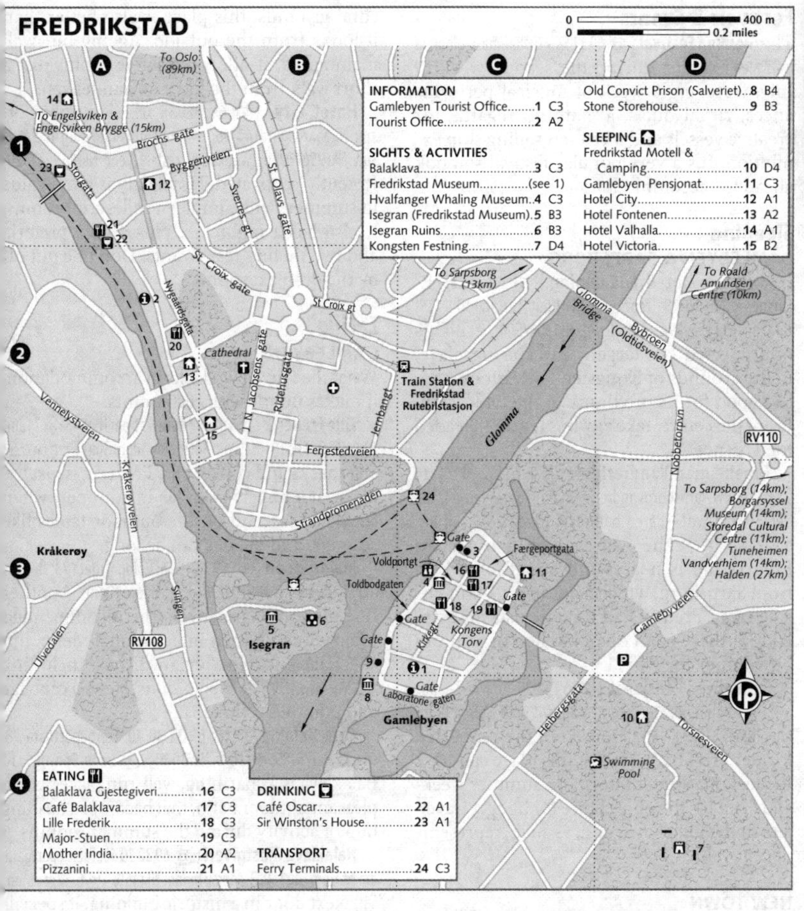

a stone (originally wood) tower remain visible at the eastern end of the island. It's also the site of a small museum on local boatbuilding (from the time when boats were lovingly handcrafted from wood). Boats run between Isegran and Gamlebyen or the modern centre (Nkr6). By road or on foot, access is from Rv108, about 600m south of Fredrikstad city centre.

HVALFANGER (WHALING) MUSEUM

This small whaling **museum** (☎ 69 32 44 21; Tolbodgaten; admission Nkr10; ⏲ noon-4pm Wed-Sun Jun, Sat & Sun Aug-Sep) is run by proud old men only too keen to show you around the old photos, the formidable whaling guns once used in the Antarctic, and the even more formidable penis of a blue whale. No English is spoken and all labels are in Norwegian.

KONGSTEN FESTNING

On what was once called 'Gallows Hill' stands the flower-festooned **Kongsten Festning** (Kongsten Fort). Dating from 1685, it once served as a lookout and warning post for the troops at nearby Gamlebyen. Although it can get overrun on summer weekends, this otherwise lonely and appealingly unkempt spot is a fun place to scramble around the turrets, embankments, walls and stockade, or just sit in the sun and soak up the silence. It's a 10-minute walk southeast of the Gamlebyen drawbridge (turn off Torsnesvien at Fredrikstad Motell & Camping).

Festivals & Events

The **Glomma Festival** (☎ 69 31 54 77; glommas@glommafestivalen.no) runs during the second week in July, featuring a week of musical performances, ritual duels, a 'bathtub regatta' for creative vessels and a veteran sailing ship exhibition. It's a very popular festival so book ahead for accommodation.

Sleeping

GAMLEBYEN & SARPSBORG

Fredrikstad Motell & Camping (☎ 69 32 03 15; Torsnesveien 16-18; tent with/without car Nkr100/155, caravan Nkr155-190, motel s/d Nkr400/500; P) This multifaceted but largely uninspiring place, in the grounds of Kongsten Fort, is nonetheless good for its proximity to the Old Town. From the centre, take any bus (eg 362) headed for Torsnes.

Tuneheimen Vandrerhjem (Map p119; ☎ 69 14 50 01; www.sarpsborgvandrerhjem.no; Tuneveien 44; dm Nkr250, s/d with shared bathroom Nkr425/630, all incl breakfast; P) The nearest youth hostel to Fredrikstad is near Tunevannet lake, 1km from Sarpsborg, which is in turn a 14km bus ride from Fredrikstad. Linen costs an extra Nkr55; there is an open kitchen or you can buy dinner for Nkr115.

Gamlebyen Pensjonat (☎ 69 32 20 20; www.gamlebyen-pensjonat.no; Smedjegaten 88; s/d with shared bathroom Nkr378/5094; P) Housed in the renovated former artillery barracks, this place can have the feel of a student dorm on summer weekends, but it's the only choice for budget travellers in the Old Town and, as such, represents decent value.

NEW TOWN

Hotel Fontenen (☎ 69 30 05 00; www.hotelfontenen.no; Nygaardsgata 9-11; s/d Nkr795/995) One of the best-value midrange places in town, this place has pleasant rooms, good breakfasts and a family feel. The polished floorboards and views of the cathedral (ask for a room at the front) are among the highlights.

Hotel Valhalla (☎ 69 36 89 50; www.hotelvalhalla.no; Valhallsgate 3; s/d Nkr695/995 mid-Jun–mid-Aug & Sat & Sun; Nkr750/1090 weekdays rest-of-the-year) High on a hill overlooking the town, but within easy walking distance of the centre, the lovely old wooden house has comfortable, tidy rooms and good views.

Hotel Victoria (☎ 69 38 58 00; www.hotelvictoria.no; Turngaten 3; s/d mid-Jun–mid-Aug & Sat & Sun Nkr895/1020, weekdays rest-of-year Nkr1240/1365) Opposite the cathedral grounds, this place is also better than it looks from the outside. Ageing but well maintained, it offers attractive rooms just a short walk from the ferry to Gamlebyen.

Hotel City (☎ 69 38 56 00; www.ricahotelcity.no; Nygaardsgata 44-46; s/d mid-Jun–mid-Aug & Sat & Sun Nkr956/1056, weekdays rest-of-year Nkr1195/1320) Recently renovated, Hotel City is good value in summer, with simple, nondescript rooms. It also has a nightclub, plus a pub, pizzeria and two quality restaurants. Don't be put off by the drab exterior.

Eating

GAMLEBYEN

What the Old Town lacks in accommodation it makes up for with restaurants.

Lille Frederik (Torvgaten; burgers from Nkr54; 🕒 11am-10pm Mon-Fri, 10am-10pm Sat, noon-10pm Sun) For burgers, snacks and coffee, Lille Frederik is just the place. It's hugely popular in summer, when snackers descend on the outdoor tables like seagulls, and queues can be long.

Major-Stuen (☎ 69 32 15 55; Voldportgata 73; starters Nkr75-95, mains Nkr205-285; 🕒 noon-10pm) Another fine place in Gamlebyen, the recommended Major-Stuen has an international menu, but specialises in Norwegian dishes, including whale meat with fried onions, stewed cabbage and potatoes (Nkr225).

Café Balaklava (☎ 69 32 30 40; Færgeportgata 78; snacks Nkr79-89, desserts Nkr30-45; 🕒 noon-9pm) Café Balaklava is a charming, well-run place, with a pleasant outdoor patio, that becomes a bustling hub of activity during the summer months.

Balaklava Gjestgiveri (☎ 69 32 30 40; Faergeportgata; mains from Nkr150, 3-course dinner Nkr450; 🕒 6-11pm Mon-Sat) Next door in a historic building, it specialises in excellent, more upmarket, Norwegian beef and fish dishes.

NEW TOWN

The Fredrikstad waterfront between Storgata and the water is lined with all manner of restaurants and bars, most with pleasant outdoor terraces ideal for a summer's afternoon or evening.

Pizzanini (☎ 69 30 03 00; Storgata 5; pizzas Nkr99-275, pasta Nkr129-149; 🕒 noon-1am Sun-Thu, noon-2am Fri & Sat summer, 3pm-midnight winter) When other restaurants stand empty, this place always buzzes due in part to its young vibe and extensive well-priced menu.

Mother India (☎ 69 31 22 00; Nygaardsgata 17; mains Nkr140-195; 🕒 4-11pm Mon-Sat, 2-10pm Sun) This atmospheric Indian restaurant gets the thumbs up from locals and travellers alike for its attractive décor and good food.

Engelsviken Brygge (☎ 69 35 18 40, Engelsvikveien 5, Engelsviken; 3-course dinner around Nkr350) Excellent quayside seafood restaurant, 15km northwest of Fredrikstad. The high-quality food includes crab, mussels, catfish and halibut.

Drinking

The following have breezy outdoor tables in summer.

Café Oscar (☎ 69 36 99 20; Storgata 5; noon-1.30am Sun-Thu, noon-2.30am Fri & Sat) With a buzzy vibe, Café Oscar offers cover bands from 10.30pm Wednesday (free) and from 11.30pm Friday and Saturday (cover charge Nkr60). Beer costs Nkr59.

Sir Winston's House (☎ 69 36 99 10; Storgata 17; 3pm-3am Wed-Fri, noon-3am Sat, 2pm-2am Sun) Beside the river, this English-style pub serves fish and chips for Nkr95, and you can choose between 10 draught beers. On weekends it also offers DJ music (mostly 1960s, but some contemporary) and dancing.

Getting There & Away

Intercity buses arrive and depart from the **Fredrikstad Rutebilstasjon** (☎ 177, 69 35 72 00) at the train station. Bus 200 and 360 run to/from Sarpsborg (Nkr30, 25 minutes, twice hourly). Nor-Way's Oslofjordekpress has one to seven daily services between Oslo and Fredrikstad (Nkr155, 1¼ hours), with most buses continuing to Hvaler; there are also regular **Flybussekspressen** (☎ 177, 82 02 13 00; www.flybussekspressen.no) services from Fredrikstad to Oslo Gardermoen International Airport (Nkr240, 2¼ hours, every hour or two).

Fredrikstad lies on the **NSB** (☎ 81 50 08 88; www.nsb.no) rail line between Oslo and Göteborg. Trains to/from Oslo (Nkr166, one hour) run about 10 times daily, and also go to Sarpsborg and Halden but note that southbound international trains require a mandatory seat reservation.

Getting Around

To cross the Glomma to Gamlebyen, you can either trek over the high and hulking Glomma bridge or take the *Go'vakker Randi* ferry (Nkr6) from Strandpromenaden. It operates from 5.30am to 11pm on weekdays (to 1am on Friday); from 7am to 1am on Saturday and from 9.30am to 11pm on Sunday.

The ferry (adult/child Nkr10/5, two minutes) shuttles across the river Glomma to the main gate of Gamlebyen regularly between 5.30am and 11pm.

For a taxi, phone ☎ 69 36 26 10. Bicycle hire is available from the two tourist offices.

AROUND FREDRIKSTAD

Hvaler Skerries

Norwegian holidaymakers and artists love the Hvaler Skerries, an offshore archipelago of 833 forested islands and islets guarding the southern entrance to Oslofjord. The main islands of **Vesterøy**, **Spjærøy**, **Asmaløy** and **Kirkøy** are connected to the mainland by a toll road (Nkr55) and tunnel. Bus No 365 (Nkr58) runs all the way from Fredrikstad to Skjærhalden, at the far end of Kirkøy.

Hvaler **tourist office** (☎ 69 37 50 00; Skjærhalden; 10am-8pm mid-Jun–mid-Aug) can point you in the direction of the numerous sights dotted around the islands.

Above the coastline of Akerøy island, accessible only by ferry (taxi boat) from Skjærhalden, clings a well-preserved 17th-century coastal **fortress**, renovated in the 1960s. Admission is free and it's always open.

The mid-11th-century **stone church** (Skjærhalden; noon-4pm Jul, noon-4pm Sat 2nd half of Jun & 1st half of Aug) on the island of Kirkøy is one of the oldest in Norway. The church hosts a week-long music and arts festival in July.

The tourist office has a list of fully equipped private houses and chalets in Hvaler available for between Nkr400 and Nkr700 per day or Nkr2700 and Nkr4500 per week. **Hvaler Kurs & Konferansesenter** (☎ 69 37 91 28; Skjærhalden; apt from Nkr500) offers excellent apartments for rent.

All year, the M/S *Hollungen* and M/S *Hvalerfergen II* sails roughly every hour from Skjærhalden and through the Hvaler Skerries (Nkr45, one hour). Alternatively, you can sail with the scheduled tour ferry M/S *Vesleø II* between Skjærhalden, Koster (Sweden) and Strömstad (Sweden) from mid-June to mid-August for Nkr135/95 per adult/child return.

Roald Amundsen Centre

The renowned and noted polar explorer Roald Amundsen, who in 1911 was the first man to reach the South Pole, was born in 1872 at Hvidsten, midway between Fredrikstad and Sarpsborg. Although the family moved to Oslo when Roald was still a small child, the family home in Hvidsten, which was the base for a small shipbuilding and shipping business, is now the **Roald Amundsen Centre** (Map p119; ☎ 69 34 83 26; museum & guided tour adult/child Nkr30/10; ⌚ 5-7pm Wed, noon-2pm Sun mid-Jun–mid-Aug), which is dedicated to the man's life and expeditions. Standing surrounded by these quiet fields of southern Norway, it seems perhaps not so surprising that Amundsen set off to seek adventure so far from home. The centre is signposted about 11km east of Fredrikstad, along the Rv111 towards Sarpsborg.

Storedal Cultural Centre

This **cultural centre** (Map p119; ☎ 69 16 92 67; www.storedal.no; Storedal; adult/child Nkr35/free; ⌚ 9.30am-5pm Mon-Fri May, 9.30am-5pm Tue-Fri, noon-6pm Sun Jun-Aug) is 11km northeast of Fredrikstad. King Magnus the Blind was born here in 1117; he took the throne at 13 years of age and earned his nickname at 18 when he was blinded by an enemy in Bergen. A later owner of the farm, Erling Stordahl, who was also blind, developed a monument to King Magnus, as well as a centre dedicated to blind and other disabled people. The most intriguing feature is the *Ode til Lyset* (Ode to the Light), a 'sound sculpture' by Arnold Haukeland and Arne Nordheim which, using photo cells and a computer in the farmhouse, transmutes the slightest fluctuations in natural light into haunting, ever-changing music. To get there, follow Rv110 east for about 9km from Fredrikstad; the centre is 2.1km north of the main road.

Borgarsyssel Museum

This excellent Østfold county **museum** (Map p119; ☎ 69 11 56 50; www.ostfoldmuseet.no; Gamlebygaten 8, Sarpsborg; adult/child Nkr40/free; ⌚ 10am-5pm Tue-Fri, noon-6pm Sat & Sun mid-May–Aug) lies in the town of Sarpsborg (14km northeast of Fredrikstad). The open-air display contains 30 period buildings from various parts of the country and includes a vast collection of cultural art and artefacts. There's also a **herb garden**, a **petting zoo** and the **ruins** of King Øystein's St Nikolas church, constructed in 1115 and destroyed by the Swedes in 1567. From Fredrikstad, trains and buses run frequently to Sarpsborg.

Oldtidsveien

People have lived and worked in the Østfold region for thousands of years, and numerous examples of ancient stone works and rock paintings lie along the Oldtidsveien (Old Times Way), the old sunken road between Fredrikstad and Sarpsborg. At Solberg, there are three panels with around a hundred figures dating back 3000 years. At Gunnarstorp are several 30m-wide **Bronze Age burial mounds** and several **Iron Age standing stones**. The site at Begby includes well-preserved renditions of ships, men and animals, while Hunn has several **stone circles** and a series of **burial mounds** dating from 500 BC to AD 800. The **rock paintings** at Hornes clearly depict 21 ships complete with oarsmen. The sites are signposted off the E6, just south of Sarpsborg, but they may also be visited on a long day walk or bike ride from Fredrikstad.

HALDEN

pop 28,000

The soporific border town of Halden, at the end of Iddefjord between steep rocky headlands, possesses a hugely significant history as a cornerstone of Norwegian defence through centuries of Swedish aggression. With a pretty little harbour filled with yachts, a looming fortress rising up behind the town and a sprinkling of decent restaurants, this place makes a worthwhile detour.

The Halden **tourist office** (☎ 69 19 09 80; www.visithalden.com; Torget 2; ⌚ 9am-4.30pm Mon-Fri mid-Jun–mid-Aug, 9am-3.30pm Mon-Fri rest-of-year), just off Torget, has some useful information. In summer, there is a second office at the fortress, **Infosenter** (⌚ 10am-5pm May-Aug).

History

Halden served as a garrison during the Hannibal Wars from 1643 to 1645. From 1644 it was fortified with a wooden stockade. In the 1658 Roskilde Treaty between Sweden and Denmark, Norway lost its Bohuslän province (and Bohus fortress), and Halden was left exposed as a border outpost requiring heavy defences. When attacks by Swedish forces in 1658, 1659 and 1660 were scarcely repelled, the need for a better fortification became apparent, resulting in the fortress, which was begun in 1661.

In the midst of it all, in 1659 and 1716, the Halden resistance resorted to fire to drive out the enemy, a sacrifice honoured with a mention in the Norwegian national anthem, which includes the lines: '...we chose to burn our nation, lest we let it fall'. The fires also serve as a centrepiece for a museum on the town's history in the fortress.

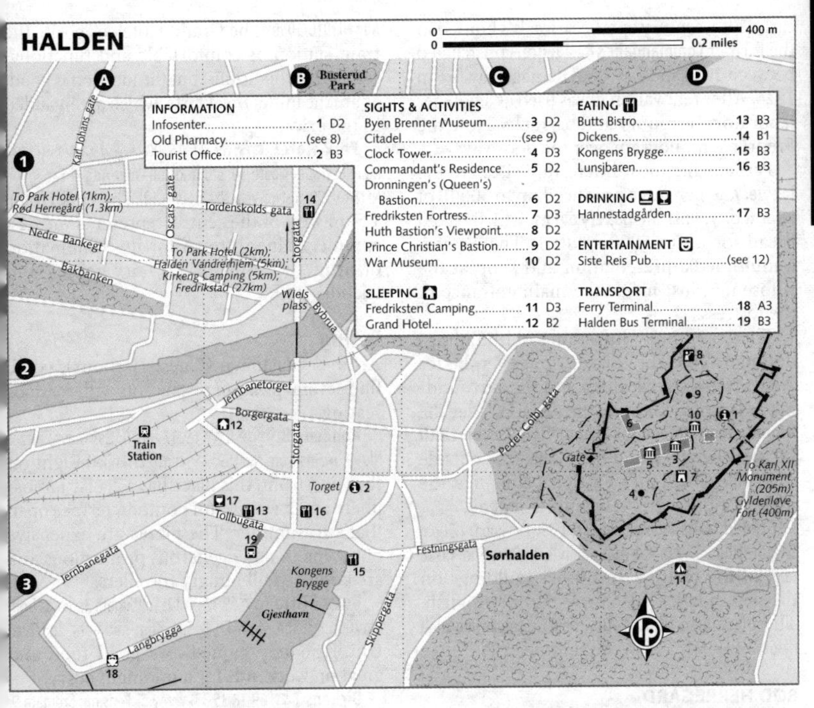

Further attacks from the Swedes continued into the 19th century. In the first few years of the 20th century, Fredriksten Fortress was armed with increasingly powerful modern cannons, turret guns and howitzers. However, this firepower was removed during the 1906 negotiations for the dissolution of the Swedish–Norwegian union and the town nestled into life as a quiet seaside village.

Sights

FREDRIKSTEN FORTRESS & MUSEUMS

Crowning the hilltop behind Halden is the 1661 **Fredriksten Fortress** (Fredriksten Festning; ☎ 69 18 54 11; www.halden.museum.no; adult/child Nkr50/10, incl all museums; 🕙 10am-5pm daily 18 May-Aug & Sun in Sep), which has resisted six Swedish sieges and never been captured.

To reach the fortress from the town, a half-overgrown cobbled footpath climbs from the top of Festningsgata in Sørhalden (a neighbourhood of 19th-century sea captains' cottages), up the unkempt lilac-covered slopes. The road for cars leads up from the same street.

On 28 July 1660 King Fredrik III of Denmark issued a declaration ordering a more sturdy fortification above Halden. The pentagonal citadel, as well as the adjoining Gyldenløve Fort to the east, Stortårnet and Overberget, was constructed across two parallel hills from 1661 to 1671, and augmented between 1682 and 1701. Its crowning event came on 11 December 1718, when the warmongering Swede King Karl XII was shot dead on the site (a monument now marks the spot).

The museums in the castle grounds cover various facets of the fortress' history. Downhill from the main entrance, the **War Museum** contains military artefacts and a variety of information on Halden's experiences of war from 1660 onwards, including details on the Norwegian independence movement in 1905. A tunnel leads up into **Prince Christian's Bastion** – the main vantage point for the fortress defenders. A broader sweep of Halden's history is outlined in the **Byen Brenner Museum** ('City in Flames' Museum) exhibition about halfway down the main thoroughfare. Displays in the **old pharmacy** describe the history of pharmacology from early Norwegian folk remedies to early-20th-century apothecaries. It's housed in the former **Commandant's Residence**, constructed between 1754 and 1758 and damaged by fire in 1826. After renovation it was used as a powder laboratory, armoury and barracks. Note the Fredrik V monogram over the doorway.

Perhaps the most interesting sites are the **brewery**, which once produced up to 3000L of beer a day, and the **bakery ovens**, which baked bread for up to 5000 soldiers. There's also a multimedia presentation and shop at the Infosenter, just inside the main entrance of the fortress.

There are many intriguing old buildings dotted around the fortress, but even better are the **views** over Halden and the surrounding hills from alongside the cannons near the **Dronningen's (Queen's) Bastion**, **Clock Tower**, **Huth Bastion's Viewpoint** and the **citadel** (the outside of Prince Christian's Bastion). Note that the high bastions are barely fenced, if at all.

Guided tours (adult/child Nkr50/25; noon, 1.30pm & 3pm daily mid-Jun–11 Aug, noon & 1.30pm Sun 12-26 Aug) of the fortress and other buildings on the grounds are in Norwegian or English. There are also **ghost tours** (child/accompanying adult Nkr50/25; May-Aug) in the summer.

RØD HERREGÅRD

Rød Herregård **manor** (69 18 54 11; Herregårdsveien; tours adult/child Nkr50/10; tours noon, 1pm & 2pm Tue-Sat mid-Jun–mid-Aug, noon, 1pm & 2pm Sun May–mid-Jun, noon, 1pm & 2pm Sun mid-Aug–Sep), dating from 1733, has fine interiors, notable collections of both weapons and art, and one of the best gardens in Norway. It's 1.5km northwest of the town centre and is well signposted.

Sleeping

Fredriksten Camping (69 18 40 32; Fredriksten Festning; tent with car Nkr150, 4-/5-bed cabins Nkr400/800; P) A great location amid the trees and adjacent to the fortress makes this well-run place a winner. It also offers minigolf and, after the fortress closes and the crowds disappear, a quiet green spot to pitch a tent.

Halden Vandrerhjem (69 21 69 68; www.vandrerhjem.no; Brødløs; dm/s/d/tr Nkr150/250/395/450; mid-Jun–mid-Aug) The family-run hostel, at the suburban Tosterød school, offers standard rooms in pleasant surroundings on the edge of Halden. Take bus 102 to 104 from Busterud Park (marked Gimle).

Grand Hotel (69 18 72 00; www.grandhotell.net; Jernbanetorget 1; s/d Fri & Sat 755/910, Sun-Thu mid-Jun–mid-Aug Nkr910/1050) The Grand Hotel, opposite the train station, is comfortable and functional rather than luxurious, but the location is good, as are the buffet breakfasts, which are included in the price.

Park Hotel (69 21 15 00; www.park-hotel.no; Marcus Thranes gate 30; s/d mid-Jun–mid-Aug & Sat & Sun Nkr840/990, rest-of-year Nkr1160/1410) The Park Hotel, 1.5km west of the centre, represents the best summer value in town for its combination of attractively furnished, airy rooms and friendly staff.

Eating

Around Gjesthavn (Guest Harbour), you'll find several pleasant restaurants with outdoor seating.

Kongens Brygge (69 17 80 60; Gjesthavn; pizzas Nkr99, mains from Nkr169; lunch & dinner) Right on the waterfront, this place has a cruisy atmosphere and a wonderful pontoon terrace open that's in summer. The pizzas are expensive but come in quite generous proportions and are bound to fill hungry travellers.

Butts Bistro (69 17 20 12; Tollbugata 3; mains from Nkr100; 3pm-4am Fri & Sat, 3pm-midnight Sun-Thu) Unfortunately named, but good food and great on weekends for a midnight curry.

Dickens (69 18 35 33; www.dickens.no; Storgata 9; mains from Nkr110; lunch & dinner) The very popular Dickens offers a choice between outdoor seating (summer only) or the dining room in a 17th-century cellar.

Drinking & Entertainment

Hannestadgården (69 19 77 81; Tollbugata 5; nightclub cover Nkr50; beer garden 3pm-3am Mon-Fri & 1pm-3am Sat, nightclub 10pm-3am Fri & Sat) This multipurpose nightspot has an atmospheric beer garden, a piano bar, boisterous nightclub and regular concerts throughout summer.

Dickens (69 18 35 33; Storgata 9; www.dickens.no) If you prefer laid-back music on a lazy summer's afternoon, head to Dickens where there's (free) jazz in the courtyard from 1.30pm to 3.30pm on Saturday during July and August.

Getting There & Away

Trains between Oslo and Halden (Nkr211, 1¾ hours) via Fredrikstad run hourly from Monday to Friday and every second hour on weekends. An average of four trains daily continue on to Göteborg and Malmö in Sweden. The long-distance bus terminal sits right at the harbour, with regular services (less on weekends) to Oslo and Fredrikstad.

AROUND HALDEN

Halden Canal (Haldenkanalen)

East and north of Halden, a canal system connects the town with Göteborg, Sweden, for all but one short dry section (1.8km). The highlight is the Brekke Locks, a system of four locks between Femsjøen and Aspern (on the Halden–Strømsfoss run), which raise and lower the boats a total of 26.6m.

Canoe hire is available from **Kirkeng Camping** (Map p119; ☎ 69 19 92 98), 5km northeast of town in Aremark, if you prefer to explore under your own steam. You can pick up a boating and recreation map from the tourist office in Halden.

Otherwise, you can take a ride on the tourist cruise boat **M/S Turisten** (☎ 93 06 64 44; www.turisten.no), which follows the Haldenkanalen between Tistedal (just east of Halden) and Strømsfoss (adult/senior/child return Nkr250/200/150, 3½ hours). The boat leaves Strømsfoss at 11am and begins its leisurely return from Tistedal at 3pm on Wednesday and Friday to Sunday from mid-June to mid-August. To reach the town of Tistedal, take bus 103 or 106 (Nkr32, 18 minutes, twice hourly except late Saturday afternoon and Sunday). You'll need to drive to Strømsfoss to do the return trip.

Southern Norway

Norway's southern coastline has always drawn Norwegian tourists in summer droves. It's not difficult to see why, with coastal villages all dressed in white looking out across an island-studded sea.

Many of the villages are quite beautiful, especially Grimstad, Risør, Kragerø and Flekkefjord, and can make for picturesque stepping stones en route from Oslo to Stavanger. The region also offers a chance to see a different kind of Norway from fjords and high plateaus – not to mention the fact that you're more likely to meet Norwegians on holiday than just about anywhere else in the country. Kristiansand, Larvik and especially Arendal are also agreeable larger towns. Apart from everything else, the kids will never forgive you if you don't take them to Kristiansand Dyrepark, one of Norway's best children's theme parks. However, unless you're planning to be in the country for a long visit, think carefully about whether this is really the Norway you came to see, especially given the price hikes that most towns along the coast insist on in summer.

Venture inland and you'll begin to experience increasingly dramatic landscapes but without the masses of tourists that gravitate towards the west and north in summer. The quiet valley of Setesdalen is rich in forested hillsides, traditional culture and high-energy thrills such as white-water rafting. Kongsberg promises a journey deep into the earth at its legendary silver mines, while nearby Notodden has Norway's largest stave church. Telemark, especially at Dalen and troll-haunted Seljord, is also beautiful. But the place we love above all others in the region's interior is Rjukan, in part for its epic historical stories, but more as the gateway to some of Norway's most scenic high country – the Hardangervidda National Park and the spectacularly formed mountain of Gausta.

HIGHLIGHTS

- Stroll through the narrow streets of the 'white town' of **Grimstad** (p138)
- Take the quiet but beautiful **coastal road** (p147) between Flekkefjord and Egersund
- Climb to the summit of **Gausta** (see the boxed text, p157), Norway's most beautiful mountain
- Admire the exquisite roof lines and paintings in the stave church at **Heddal** (p152)
- Scour the surface of **Seljordvatn** (p158) in search of Selma the Serpent

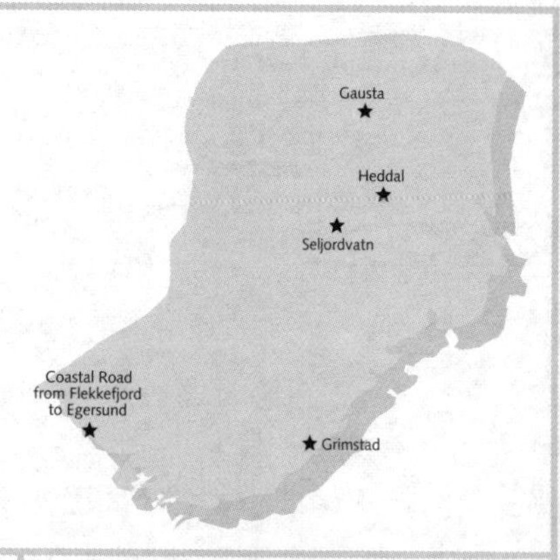

- POPULATION: 652,000
- HIGHEST ELEVATION: GAUSTA 1881M

THE COAST

You probably didn't come to Norway for the beaches, but if you did, expect to be accompanied by masses of local tourists drawn by reasonable beaches and picturesque islands. The towns along the coast are pretty, if way overpriced in summer.

TØNSBERG

pop 37,493

Tønsberg is the oldest town in Norway, although so distant are its origins that few interesting remnants remain in what is now a largely modern town. There are nonetheless a few Viking-era ruins and a decrepit castle that together make Tønsberg worth a brief detour as you head along the coast.

The **tourist office** (☎ 33 35 45 20; www.visittonsberg.com; Nedre Langatte 36; ⏰ 9am-7pm Mon-Sat, 9am-3pm Sun mid-Jun–early Aug, 9.30am-3.30pm rest-of-year), at Tønsberg Brygge waterfront, produces the excellent *Tønsberg Guide*.

History

In the *Saga of Harald Hårfagre* (p30), Snorre Sturluson mentions that Tønsberg existed prior to the Battle of Hafrsfjord, which took place in 872. Tønsberg celebrated its 1100-year anniversary in 1971. When King Harald Hårfagre divided the kingdom in the 9th century, he appointed his son, Bjørn Farmann, to rule over Vestfold and the court at Tønsberg became the seat of royal power. In the late medieval period it served as one of three Hanseatic trading posts in Norway, with ties to northern Germany. The town was destroyed by fire in 1535, after which it fell into decline. By the 17th century the town had recovered and by 1850 Tønsberg had the largest merchant fleet in Norway.

Sights

TØNSBERG CASTLE

The remains of **Tønsberg Castle** (Castrum Tunsbergis; ☎ 33 31 18 72; admission free, tower adult/child Nkr20/10; ⏰ tower noon-5pm late Jun–mid-Aug, shorter hrs rest-of-year), spread across the 63m-high hill behind the town, was the largest fortress in Norway in the 13th century. In 1503, the Swedes destroyed the fortress and little remains of the castle itself. Nonetheless, the modern (1888), 17m-high **Slottsfjellstårnet tower** provides a good viewpoint over the ruins. In front of the tower there's a bronze model of how the castle looked in 1500. Parts of the 600m-long outer wall remain intact, while the extant medieval stone foundations include **King Magnus Lagabøte's Keep**, the 1191 **Church of St Michael**, the **hall of King Håkon Håkonsson** and various **guard towers**. The park is always open.

RUINS

Atop the hill in the Haugar district are the **Viking-era grave mounds** of kings Olav and Sigrød. In the park off Kongsgaten lie the ruins of **Kongsgården**, the old royal court of King Håkon Håkonsson where the kings of Vestfold were elected; while at Storgaten 17 are the ruins of the medieval **Church of St Olav**, which dates from 1207, as well as St Olav's monastery and several Viking-age graves. You'll need a lot of imagination to make sense of it all.

VESTFOLD COUNTY MUSEUM

At the foot of Slottsfjellet (Castle Rock) at the northern end of town is **Vestfold County Museum** (Vestfold Fylkesmuseum; ☎ 33 31 29 19; www.vfm.no; Farmannsveien 30; adult/child Nkr50/10; ⏰ 10am-5pm Mon-Sat, noon-5pm Sun mid-May–mid-Sep), a five-minute walk northwest of the train station. Highlights include displays on the excavation of the impressive *Oseberg* Viking ship (now shown in Oslo's Viking Ship Museum, p102), a collection of historic period-furnished farm buildings, and a section on Tønsberg's whaling history, including skeletons of both a sperm whale and a blue whale. The latter, measuring 23m long, is the largest whale skeleton on display in the world.

Sleeping

Furustrand Camping (☎ 33 32 44 03; fax 33 32 74 03; Tareveien 11, Tolvsrød; tent sites Nkr110 plus per car/person Nkr40/30, cabins from Nkr500) Campers should head 5.5km east of the centre; take bus 111 or 116 to Tolvsrød (Nkr20). It has a beachfront location and reasonable facilities.

Tønsberg Vandrerhjem (☎ 33 31 21 75; tonsberg.hostel@vandrerhjem.no; Dronning Blancasgata 22; dm Nkr195-220, s/d with shared bathroom Nkr375/525, s/d with bathroom Nkr475/625; P 💻) This exceptionally well-run and friendly hostel is well equipped, clean and tidy and just a five-minute walk from the train station. Prices include a good breakfast.

Thon Hotel Brygga (☎ 33 34 49 00; www.thonhotels.no; Nedre Langgate 40; s/d from Nkr770/970; 💻) This modern waterfront hotel has pleasant (if

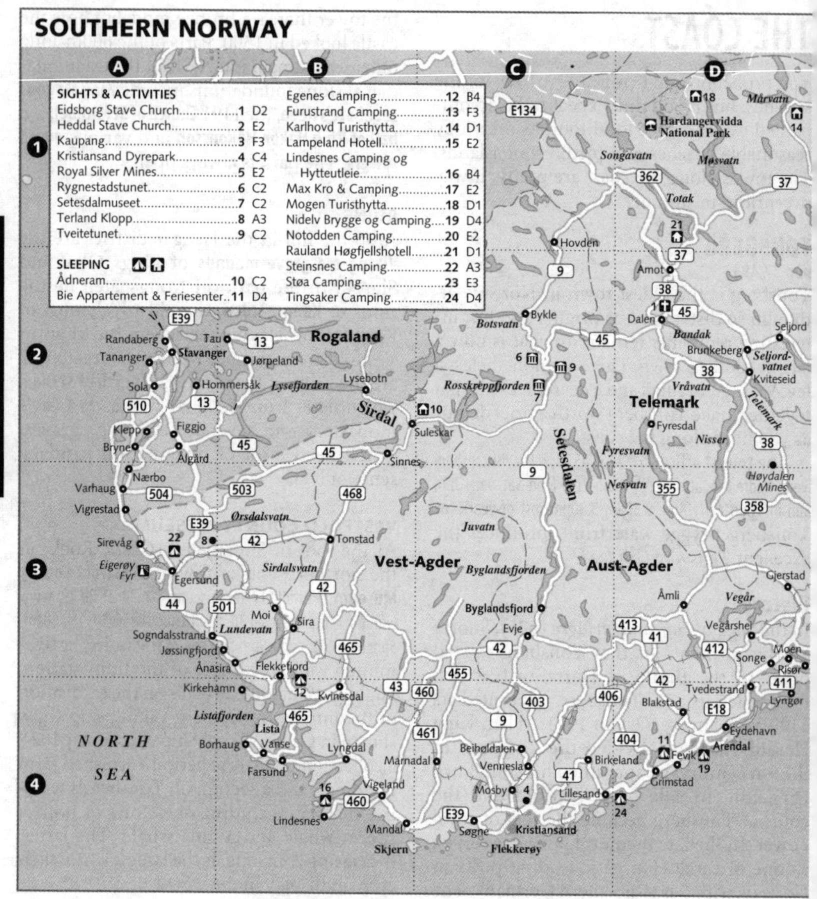

smallish) rooms and great breakfasts, and is popular with families.

Quality Hotel Tønsberg (☎ 33 00 41 00; www.choice.no; s/d from Nkr750/950; 💻 🅿) Another excellent option, this branch of the Quality Hotel chain has stylish (in a Nordic minimalist kind of way) rooms by the waterfront.

Eating

Tønsberg has dozens of decent restaurants, with the best atmosphere along the water.

Himmel & Hav (☎ 33 00 49 80; Nedre Langgate 32; tapas buffet Nkr215, mains Nkr135-264; 🕐 11am-3am) This place is recommended for its excellent fish and seafood dishes. Great live music can also be heard at night on summer weekends.

Brygga (☎ 33 31 12 70; Nedre Langgate 35; mains Nkr179-245; 🕐 11am-3am) A step upmarket from the neighbouring Himmel & Hav, this is Norwegian and international cuisine at its most pleasant, particularly on the outdoor terrace.

Esmeralda (☎ 33 31 91 91; Nedre Langgate 26C; salads Nkr75-100, mains Nkr175-229; 🕐 10.30am-3am) This long-standing local favourite is brisk, bright and breezy with economical light meals on the terrace.

Getting There & Away

The **Tønsberg Rutebilstasjon** (☎ 33 30 01 00; Jernbanegaten) is a block south of the train station. Nor-Way Bussekspress buses run to/from Kristiansand (Nkr330, 4½ hours, one

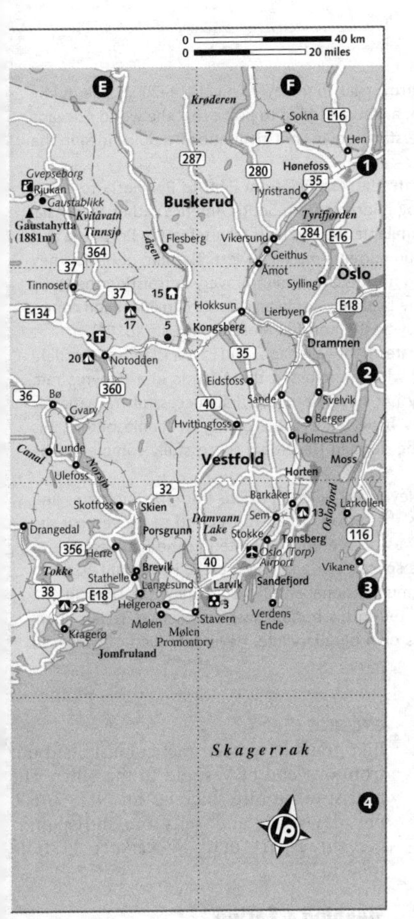

to two daily) via most coastal towns en route, including Larvik (Nkr81, one hour, two daily), and also run to Oslo (Nkr149, 1¾ hours).

Intercity trains run hourly between Tønsberg and Oslo (Nkr184, 1½ hours) or south to Larvik (Nkr84, 34 minutes).

SANDEFJORD

pop 41,897

This former whaling capital is worth a detour to one of only a couple of museums dedicated to whaling in the world.

The Sandefjord **tourist office** (☎ 33 46 05 90; www.visitsandefjord.com; Thor Dahls gate 1; 9am-6pm Mon-Fri, 10am-4.30pm Sat, 12.30-4.30pm Sun mid-Jun–early Aug, 9am-4pm Mon-Fri rest-of-year) is just back from the waterfront.

The impressive **Whaling Museum** (Hvalfangstmuseet; ☎ 33 48 46 50; www.hvalfangstmuseet.no; Museumsgaten 39; adult/child Nkr50/25; 10am-5pm mid-Jun–mid-Aug, shorter hrs rest-of-year) charts the history of Norwegian whaling, with photos, equipment and information on marine life. The museum's exhibits are complemented by the 1950s whaleboat **Southern Actor** (9.30am-5pm late Jun–mid-Aug), which is moored at the harbour; entry is by the same ticket. There's also the striking sculpture **monument to whalers** by the water.

Most buses running between Oslo and Kristiansand stop in Sandefjord.

LARVIK

pop 41,364

Larvik is one of the largest towns along Norway's south coast. Although it has some good museums, its main attractions are Norway's most accessible excavations from the Viking era. The town's main historical claim to fame is as the home town of Thor Heyerdahl (see the boxed text, p132), one of Norway's premier explorers.

The helpful **tourist office** (☎ 33 13 91 11; www.visitlarvik.no; Storgata 48; 8.30am-6pm Mon-Sat, 1-4pm Sun mid-Jun–early Aug, 8.30am-4pm Mon-Fri rest-of-year) is opposite the ferry dock and also offers internet access (Nkr20 per 10 minutes)

Bibliotek (☎ 33 17 10 50; 10am-7pm Mon, 10am-4pm Tue-Fri, 10am-2pm Sat) offers free, time-limited internet access.

Sights & Activities

LARVIK MUSEUM

This four-part **museum** (☎ 33 17 12 90; adult/child combined ticket Nkr40/10) is spread across the town.

The classic baroque timber **Herregården manor house** (Herregårdsletta 6; noon-4pm Wed, Sat & Sun, guided tours 12.30pm, 1.30pm & 2.30pm mid-Jun–mid-Aug, Sun only Jun–mid-Sep) was constructed in 1677 as the home of the Norwegian Governor General, Ulrik Frederik Gyldenløve, the Duke of Larvik; as the illegitimate son of King Fredrik IV of Denmark, Gyldenløve was given a dukedom and packed off to Norwegian obscurity. It's furnished in 17th- and 18th-century style.

Larvik Maritime Museum (Kirkestredet 5; noon-4pm Tue-Sat mid-Jun–mid-Aug & Sun Jun–mid-Sep), in a 1730 brick structure immediately east of the harbour, is home to maritime art and a number of impressive model ships. There's

THOR HEYERDAHL

Larvik's favourite son was the intrepid and controversial Thor Heyerdahl (1914–2002), the quirky scientist, anthropologist and explorer who spent a lifetime trying to prove that the world's oceans were vast highways that were essential to understanding ancient civilisations, a novel idea in the hallowed halls of scientific research.

In 1947 he sailed 6000km in a balsawood raft, the *Kon-Tiki*, from Peru to Polynesia to prove that the South Pacific may have been settled by migrants from South America rather than Asia. His theories were supported by discoveries of similar fauna and cultural artefacts in Polynesia and South America and by the fact that Pacific Ocean currents run east–west. The film of his journey won an Oscar in 1951 for best documentary and his medal-winning bravery in resisting the Nazis only added to his legend. His book describing the expedition sold an astonishing 60 million copies worldwide. The actual *Kon-Tiki* ship is on display at the Kon-Tiki Museum in Oslo (p103).

After being one of the first Europeans to excavate on the Galapagos and Easter Islands, Heyerdahl again grabbed international attention in 1970 when he crossed the Atlantic in a papyrus raft. His purpose was to prove that Columbus may not have been the first successful transatlantic navigator and that the ancient Egyptians may have made the crossing millennia before. His first raft, *Ra*, sank soon after setting out, but the dogged Heyerdahl successfully completed the crossing in *Ra II*.

In 1978, at the age of 64, the indefatigable Heyerdahl sailed the *Tigris* from the Euphrates and Tigris Rivers, down the Persian Gulf and across the Indian Ocean to Djibouti to prove how the ancient Sumerians travelled widely. When he was prevented from entering the Red Sea due to local conflicts, Heyerdahl set fire to his ship in a spectacular anti-war protest. Heyerdahl was also a fervent internationalist; his crew was always multinational and his boats flew the UN flag.

On Heyerdahl's 75th birthday in 1989, a statue in his honour was unveiled at Tollerodden, east of Larvik's harbour. It's sculpted in Larvik's own blue larvikite. Heyerdahl died of cancer in northern Italy on 18 April 2002.

also a small exhibition on the nearby Viking town of Kaupang (see below).

Verkensgarorden (Nedre Fritzøegate 2; noon-4pm Tue-Sun mid-Jun–mid-Aug, noon-4pm Sun rest-of-year) has tools and implements from a local 17th-century sawmill and ironworks. There's also a permanent geological exhibition documenting the evolution of blue larvikite, a beautiful, locally quarried 500-million-year-old type of granite.

Kaupang (admission free; noon-5pm Tue-Sun mid-Jun–mid-Aug), 5km east of Larvik, was a former Viking town built around AD 800 and occupied until 960. It is believed that up to 1000 people lived here in its heyday. For us, this is the most interesting of Larvik's sights. Although most of the original artefacts are now in Oslo, the custodians of the site make the most of what they have with a small exhibition, four Viking tents and knowledgeable guides in Viking dress on hand to show you to nearby Viking graves and to explain Kaupang's past. On Wednesday (family day) and weekends, they cook Viking soup and bread. The guides can also tell you where to find other Viking cemeteries in the Larvik area.

CYCLING

Bike trails have been meticulously laid out from one end of Vestfold to the other. The tourist office hires bicycles for Nkr150/600 per day/week and sells the indispensable three-part map *Sykkelkart Vestfold* for Nkr100.

Sleeping & Eating

our pick **Lysko Gjestegaard** (33 18 77 79; www.lysko-it.no; Kirkestredet 10; s/d from Nkr550/750; P) This quiet guesthouse occupies possibly Larvik's most charming location, with a lovely old timbered house opposite the Maritime Museum at the eastern end of the harbour. Prices don't include breakfast.

Greven Hotell (33 18 25 26; www.hotel-greven.no; Storgata 26; s/d from Nkr640/810) With considerable charm, this renovated 1903 hotel represents a good choice right on the waterfront.

Quality Hotel Grand Farris (33 18 78 00; www.choice.no; Storgata 38; s/d from Nkr750/1040; P) Also overlooking the water, this is Larvik's finest; its supremely comfortable rooms may help you forgive the fact that it's an architectural eyesore.

Both the Greven Hotell and Quality Hotel have good restaurants; the former mainly does Italian dishes. Otherwise, try **Ferdinands Lillekjøkken** (☎ 33 13 05 44; Storgata 32; mains from Nkr139; ⏰ dinner) for steak and seafood, or **Bøkekroa Restaurant** (☎ 33 18 10 53; Bøkeskogen; ⏰ lunch & dinner May-Aug) which has live jazz on Friday nights.

Getting There & Away

Nor-Way Bussekspressen buses pass through Larvik en route between Seljord (Nkr199, 2¼ hours, up to three times daily) and Tønsberg (Nkr81, one hour). For other destinations along the coast, you may need to change at Tønsberg or Arendal. Local trains run hourly between Oslo S (Central Station) and Larvik (Nkr253, two hours). The train and bus stations are side by side on Storgata.

Color Line operates ferries to Fredrikshavn in Denmark (see p408).

AROUND LARVIK

The low-lying Brunlanes Peninsula southwest of Larvik has a few moderately interesting towns, though they are packed in summer with Norwegian holiday-makers, who flood the coastal camp sites.

Stavern

pop 5643

The pleasant little town of Stavern, just south of Larvik, has pedestrian streets lined with cafés and small private galleries, making for a pleasant stroll. Highlights include the mid-18th-century fort, **Fredriksvern Verft**, surrounded by block houses that once formed part of the fortress defences. Also worth visiting is the colourful 1756 **church** (☎ 33 19 99 75; Kommandør Herbsgata 1; admission free; ⏰ 11am-1pm Tue-Fri), Norway's first naval house of worship.

Stavern is the start of the popular and attractive 33km-long Kyststien **coastal walk** to Ødegården on the western coast of Brunlanes. The Stavern **tourist office** (☎ 33 19 73 00; Havnegata 3; ⏰ 10am-4pm Wed-Sat, 1-4pm Sun mid-Jun–early Aug) provides the route map *Kyststien i Larvik* for Nkr85.

For accommodation, try the very pleasant **Hotel Wassilioff** (☎ 33 11 36 00; www.wassilioff.no; Havnegata 1; s Nkr900-1150, d Nkr1100-1300), which offers considerable comfort just across the park from the water; at the latter, you pay an additional (and extremely steep) Nkr200 for sea views.

To get to and from Larvik (Nkr26, 15 minutes, hourly), use bus 1.

Mølen

The Mølen Promontory is something of a geological oddity. It forms the end of the ice age **Ra moraine** (rock and silt pushed ahead of the glacier and deposited as a new landform) which extends from the lake Farrisvatn (which the moraine dammed) to the southwestern end of Brunlanes. The 230 stone cairns and heaps of boulders, which are laid out in parallel rows, are Iron Age burial mounds.

DAMVANN

Some 20km north of Larvik is the beautiful, haunting lake of Damvann surrounded by forests. Popular legend claims it to be the home a witch called Huldra, a woman of such exquisite beauty that it is said that any man who looked upon her was doomed. On Sunday in July, a modern-day version of **Huldra** (Ellen Dalen; ☎ 33 11 25 17) serves meals here from noon to 4pm. Access is difficult without a car; the nearest bus stop is at Kvelde (6km from the lake) on Numendalslågen Rd.

KRAGERØ

pop 10,481

One of the favourite summer retreats for Norwegians, Kragerø has narrow streets and whitewashed houses climbing up from the water's edge. Kragerø has also long served as a retreat for Norwegian artists, and Edvard Munch (see the boxed text, p51) spent a few restorative fishing holidays here and called Kragerø 'the pearl of the coastal towns'. A statue of Munch stands on the spot where he painted a winter sun over the sea.

Information

The modest **tourist office** (☎ 35 98 23 88; www.visitkragero.no; Tovgaten 1; ⏰ 9am-7pm Mon-Fri, 9am-6pm Sat, 10am-5pm Sun mid-Jun–mid-Aug, shorter hrs rest-of-year) is at the bus station. The **public library** (Bibliotek; off Tovgaten; ☎ 10am-6pm Mon & Thu, 10am-2pm Tue, Wed & Fri mid-Jun–mid-Aug, longer hrs rest-of-year) offers free, time-limited internet access; it's between the tourist office and the pretty main square.

Sights & Activities

There's not much to see here; the offshore island of Jomfruland (p134) is Kragerø's most popular attraction. For a great view

SOUTHERN NORWAY

over the town and its skerries, climb from Kragerø Stadium to the lookout point on **Steinmann Hill**.

The **Berg-Kragerø Museum** (☎ 35 98 14 53; Lovisenbergveien 45; adult/child Nkr50/free; noon-6pm Jun–mid-Aug) on the shore of Hellefjord, 3km from the centre, is a 120-hectare estate with a country residence dating from 1803. There are gardens, walking tracks and a gallery for visiting art and history exhibits.

You can also take a **rail-bicycle ride** along the 13km railway between Sannidal and Merkebekk. Rail-bikes (*dressin*, or bicycles on bogies) cost Nkr75/225 per hour/day. Book through Støa Camping (below) or ask at the tourist office.

Sleeping & Eating

Kragerø Vandrerhjem (☎ 35 98 57 00; kragero.hostel@vandrerhjem.no; Lovisenbergveien 20; dm/s/d Nkr325/550/650; mid-Jun–mid-Aug) Prices at this fine HI hostel, about 2km north of town, include breakfast, and it serves dinner for Nkr100.

Støa Camping (☎ 35 99 02 61; spar.kivle@ngbutikk.net; Sannidal; tent sites from Nkr130, cabins from Nkr275) Støa Camping is uninspiring but more than adequate, and conveniently connected to the town by bus 607 (Nkr26, 12 minutes).

Victoria Hotel (☎ 35 98 75 25; victoria@aco.no; PA Heuchtsgata 31; s/d mid-Jun–mid-Aug Nkr1165/1365, rest-of-year Nkr965/1165; P) An example of the overpriced summer hotels along the southern coast, the Victoria nonetheless has the best rooms in town. Some rooms have balconies overlooking the wharf and the whole place was tastefully renovated in 2007. But unless you're earning a Norwegian salary, you may feel a little bit cheated for what you're paying.

El Paso Western Saloon (☎ 35 98 15 32; PA Heuchtsgata 31; pizzas from Nkr189, mains Nkr129-239) An incongruous fusion of the Norwegian seaside with the badlands of west Texas, this place serves steaks, burgers, pizzas and OK Mexican fare.

Getting There & Away

Trains from Oslo or Kristiansand stop at Neslandsvatn, where most are met by a bus to Kragerø. Buses run up to five times daily to Oslo (Nkr250, 3½ hours) and Kristiansand (Nkr200, 2½ hours), although you may have to change in Tangen on the E18.

AROUND KRAGERØ

Jomfruland

Norwegian tourists love the island of Jomfruland, just off the coast from Kragerø. Measuring around 10km long and up to 600m wide, the island is covered by forest and encircled by mostly sandy beaches. The landmark old (1869) and new (1937) **lighthouses** (☎ 35 99 11 79; adult/child Nkr20/10; noon-4pm Mon-Sat, noon-6pm Sun mid-Jun–mid-Aug) can be visited.

The appealing **Jomfruland Camping** (☎ 35 99 12 75; www.jomfrulandcamping.no in Norwegian; Åsvik brygge; tent sites from Nkr120, caravan sites with electricity Nkr190, 4-bed cabins from Nkr450) is near the Åsvik brygge ferry terminal.

Kragerø Fjordbåtselskap (☎ 35 98 58 58) ferries between Kragerø and Jomfruland (Nkr54, 50 minutes) run up to four times daily in summer.

RISØR

pop 6873

Risør, the 'White Town on the Skagerrak', is one of southern Norway's prettiest. Centred on a U-shaped harbour with colourful fishing boats and private yachts, and surrounded by historic white houses (dating from 1650 to 1890), this is a great place to wander and soak up the rustic charm for a few days. If you get bored by long, lazy days by the water, you probably shouldn't be here.

The town **library** (Kragsgate 48A; 11am-3pm Mon-Fri, 11am-2pm Sat mid-Jun–mid-Aug; longer hrs rest-of-year) offers free internet access. The **tourist office** (☎ 37 15 22 70; www.risor.no; Kragsgata 3; 10am-6pm Mon-Fri, 10am-4pm Sat, noon-6pm Sun mid-Jun–mid-Aug) is 50m west of the harbour.

Sights & Activities

RISØR SALTWATER AQUARIUM

The interesting **Risør Saltwater Aquarium** (Saltvannsakvariet; ☎ 37 15 32 82; Dampskipsbrygga, adult/child Nkr50/30 mid-Jun–mid-Aug, Nkr30/20 rest-of-year, 11am-6pm mid-Jun–mid-Aug, shorter hrs rest-of-year), on the quay in front of the Risør Hotel, is a small showcase of saltwater fish, crustaceans and shellfish common to Norway's south coast. Highlights include baby lobsters and the colourful cuckoo wrasse.

RISØR MUSEUM & RISØR KUNSTPARK GALLERY

For the lowdown on local geology, fishing and the 275-year history of Risør, check out the **Risør Museum** (☎ 37 15 30 85; Prestegata 9; adult/family

Nkr30/50; ⌚ 9am-4pm Mon-Fri, 9am-2pm Sat mid-Jun–mid-Aug). Ask for a loan of the explanatory booklet in English. Adjacent to the museum is the **Risør Kunstpark Gallery** (⌚ 9am-4pm Mon-Fri, 9am-2pm Sat mid-Jun–mid-Aug), which displays works by artists inspired by Risør's charm.

RISØR ART CENTRE

This innovative **art centre** (Risør Kunstforum; ☎ 37 15 63 83; www.kunstforum.no in Norwegian; Tjenngata 76; ⌚ mid-Jun–mid-Aug) runs a range of courses ranging from making handmade paper to watercolour painting. Courses start from Nkr1500 for three days, up to Nkr3500 for seven days; accommodation/course packages are also available.

BOAT HIRE

To explore the offshore islands under your own steam (or horsepower), **Risør Båtformidling** (☎ 37 15 25 50) rents out small motorboats, while **Sørlandet Feriesenter** (☎ 37 15 40 80) also rents larger motorboats and canoes.

Festivals

To get summer rolling, the town hosts the **Risør Chamber Music Festival** in the last week of June, with a growing cast of local and international performers in attendance. On the first weekend in August Risør hosts the **Risør Wooden Boat Festival** (Trebåtfestival), which encompasses boat races, concerts and kids' activities; getting accommodation at this time can be difficult.

Sleeping

Moen Camping (☎ 37 15 50 91; fax 37 15 17 63; Moen; tent sites Nkr100, cabins Nkr300-550) This well-run and well-equipped place is Risør's closest camp site, 11km west of town off the E18. Regular buses (Risør to/from Arendal, Kristiansand and Oslo) run past the entrance.

Risør Kunstforum (☎ 37 15 63 83; www.kunstforum.no in Norwegian; Tjenngata 76; s/d/tr Nkr450/600/700) This appealing place, 1km west of the harbour, offers simple but adequate rooms with do-it-yourself breakfast, but the real attractions include art and sculpture classes (above).

Risør Hotel (☎ 37 14 80 00; www.risorhotel.no; Tangengata 16; s/d from Nkr895/1195 mid-Jun–mid-Aug, Nkr600/900 rest-of-year) Although probably the pick of a very limited choice, the Risør Hotel lacks the attention to detail you'd expect for this price. The waterfront location is, however, a winner.

Det Lille Hotell (☎ 37 15 14 95; www.detlillehotel.no; s/d per night from Nkr1240/1565, per week from Nkr8840/9800) This interesting choice offers self-catering suites and apartments dotted around town. Most are in delightfully restored homes with period furnishings and ideal if you plan to spend a week here; daily rates are cheaper outside the peak summer season and always cost less the longer you stay. Highly recommended for a splurge.

Eating

Around, or just back from the harbour, you'll find several moderately priced cafés and restaurants.

Brasserie Krag (☎ 37 15 04 50; Kragsgata 12; mains Nkr79-215; ⌚ lunch & dinner) This recommended restaurant has a fairly diverse selection on the menu and a laid-back ambience.

Brygge Pizza (☎ 37 15 00 99; Strandgata 2; pizzas from Nkr129; ⌚ lunch & dinner) One of the few places with tables out on the water and reasonable prices makes this a good option for those counting their kroner.

Risør Hotel (☎ 37 14 80 00; Tangengata 16; mains Nkr75-189; ⌚ lunch & dinner) This restaurant has a lovely elevated terrace overlooking the water and good snacks and meals, as well as a more expensive à la carte menu.

Getting There & Away

Local buses link Risør with the rail line at Gjerstad (Nkr60, 45 minutes) several times daily. Nor-Way Bussekspress buses between Kristiansand (Nkr150, three hours) and Oslo (Nkr315, 3¾ hours) connect at Vinterkjær with local buses to/from Risør (Nkr29, 20 minutes).

AROUND RISØR

The Skerries just offshore are a popular excursion from Risør. The southernmost island of **Stangholmen**, with a pretty lighthouse dating from 1855, is the most popular; this may be due in part to the fact that it's the only one of the islands with a restaurant, **Stangholmen Fyr Restaurant & Bar** (☎ 37 15 24 50; mains from Nkr215), which is in the lighthouse.

Any of the islands can be reached by ferries and water taxis. In summer, **ferries** (☎ 37 15 24 50) leave Tollbubrygga for Stangholmen (Nkr40 return, twice hourly) from 10am to at least midnight.

LYNGØR

pop 120

Tiny Lyngør, consisting of several offshore islets near the village of Gjeving, isn't shy about the fact that it won the 1991 European competition for the tidiest town on the continent. Even if it weren't for that distinction, this picturesque little settlement would be worth a visit. Part of its charm lies in the fact that visitors can't bring their vehicles across on the ferry.

If you want to enjoy Lyngør after the day-trippers have returned to the mainland, **Knatten Pensjonat** (☎ 37 16 10 19; Odden; s/d from Nkr575/775) is a simple *pension*. It's a touch overpriced, but you're not exactly spoiled for choice. It's 300m from Holmen Quay.

Seilmakerfruens Kro (☎ 37 16 60 00; Ytre Lyngør; pizzas around Nkr150; lunch & dinner) offers the most reasonably priced eating choice on the island, with decent pizzas and a few à la carte specialties.

The **Lyngør Båtselskap ferry** (☎ 41 45 41 45; adult/child Nkr28/17) between Gjeving, Holmen and Lyngør leaves up to seven times daily on weekdays, four times on Saturday and at least once on Sunday. For further information on ferries to Arendal, see opposite.

ARENDAL

pop 40,057

Arendal's main appeal lies in its undeniable buzz throughout summer around the harbour (known as Pollen), with outdoor restaurants and bars next to the water and a fairly full calendar of festivals. Large enough to have an array of amenities but not too big to overwhelm, it's a nice place to spend a few days. The old district of Tyholmen, which features many timbered houses, adds considerable charm, while those seeking greater communion with the sea than a harbour-side café can offer will find the offshore islands of Merdø, Tromøy and Hisøy to be worthwhile excursions.

Information

Library (☎ 37 01 39 13; Torvet 6; 10am-6pm Mon-Sat) Free, time-limited internet access.

Planet X-Pec (Ostregata 9; internet per hr Nkr35; noon-2am Mon-Thu, noon-midnight Fri-Sun) Internet access opposite the Ting Hai Hotel.

Tourist office (☎ 37 00 55 44; www.arendal.com; Sam Eydes plass; 9am-7pm Mon-Fri & 11am-2pm Sat Aug-Jun, 9am-7pm Mon-Fri & 11am-6pm Sat & Sun Jul)

Sights

TYHOLMEN

Rising up behind the Guest Harbour (Gjestehavn) is the old harbour-side Tyholmen district, home to beautiful 17th- to 19th-century timber buildings featuring neoclassical, rococo and baroque influences. In 1992 it was deservedly awarded the prestigious Europa Nostra prize for its expert restoration. Tyholmen was once separated from the mainland by a canal, which was filled in after the great sailing era.

One Tyholmen highlight, by the water's edge, is the striking **town hall** (Rådhus; ☎ 37 00 55 44; Rådhusgata 10; by appointment), Norway's tallest wooden building. Originally a shipowner's home dating from 1815, it became the town hall in 1844. The interior is accessible for groups, but the façade is elegant for those who can't get inside.

MUSEUMS

The **Aust-Agder Museum** (☎ 37 07 35 00; www.aaks.no in Norwegian; Parkveien 16; adult/child Nkr30/15; 9am-5pm Mon-Fri, noon-5pm Sat mid-Jun–mid-Aug, shorter hrs rest-of-year) was first conceived in 1832, when the town authorities asked their globetrotting sailors to be on the lookout for items that may be of interest back home. The results are housed in the county museum, along with relics of Arendal's shipbuilding, timber and import-export trades. The most interesting exhibits are those covering the ill-fated final journey of the slave ship *Fredensborg*, which went down off Tromøy in 1768; sadly those African slaves who survived were rewarded by being sold in the Caribbean.

Also well worth a visit is **Arendal Town Museum** (☎ 37 02 59 25; Nedre Tyholmsvei 14; adult/child Nkr30/10; 10am-3pm Tue-Fri, 10am-2pm Sat Aug-May), largely because it is a rare opportunity to see inside one of Arendal's charming old burghers' houses (Klöckers Hus).

Festivals & Events

There's always something going on in Arendal, with open-air concerts by the water quite common on weekends. Other summer highlights include:

Sørlandet Boat Show (www.baatmesse.com in Norwegian; late May)

Hove Festival (www.hovefestivalen.no; late Jun) Rock festival drawing international acts to the island of Tromø.

Summer Market (www.arendal-sentrum.no, in Norwegian; mid-Jul)

Canal Street Jazz & Blues Festival (www.canalstreet.no; late Jul) World-class jazz.

Sleeping

Arendal has a good sprinkling of midrange hotels, but those on a tight budget will need to head out of town.

Nidelv Brygge og Camping (☎ 37 01 14 25; home.no.net/svs012 in Norwegian; Vesterveien 251, Hisøy; tent sites Nkr110 plus per adult/child Nkr20/10, caravan sites Nkr120, cabins Nkr300-750) On the Nidelv River at Hisøy, 6km west of Arendal, this reasonable camp site can be reached on any bus (Nkr28, every half-hour) bound for Kristiansand or Grimstad. If you're driving, take the Rv420. Some cabins have river views and there's a restaurant and grocery store on site.

Ting Hai Hotel (☎ 37 02 22 01; ting@online.no; Østregate 5; s/d Nkr695/995) Simple, spacious and reasonably priced rooms with little character are what you'll find at this place a few blocks up from the harbour. The corner rooms are the best. There's a Chinese restaurant downstairs and you get the impression that's its primary focus.

Thon Hotel Arendal (☎ 37 05 21 50; www.thonhotels.no; Friergangen 1; s Nkr775-1375, d Nkr995-1575; 💻) It might not have the waterfront views, but this outpost of Thon Hotels is just 50m from the water's edge. Typical of the Thon chain, the rooms are modern, large and comfortable.

Clarion Tyholmen Hotel (☎ 37 07 68 00; www.choice.no; Teaterplassen 2; s/d from Nkr990/1190) Undoubtedly Arendal's best hotel, the Clarion combines a prime waterfront position with attractive, semiluxurious rooms in a restored old building that seeks to emulate Tyholmen's old-world ambience.

Eating & Drinking

There's no need to stray too far from the harbour and indeed you may find yourself spending much of your day and evening by the water.

our pick Café Det Lindvedske Hus (☎ 37 02 18 38; Nedre Tyholmsvei 7b; snacks & light meals Nkr40-105; 🕓 11am-11pm Mon-Thu, 11am-1am Fri & Sat, noon-11pm Sun) With its mellow atmosphere and 200-year-old décor, this lovely place does light meals (grilled sandwiches and pasta), great coffee and has the ambience of a sophisticated but casual art café. The kitchen closes at 9pm, whereafter music of the Stan Getz kind takes over. A terrific place.

Café Victor (☎ 37 02 18 38; Nedre Tyholmsvei 7b; light meals Nkr49-99; 🕓 10am-midnight Jun-Aug, 10am-5pm Mon-Sat Sep-May) In a prime waterfront position, Café Victor is another cool choice. Apart from the antique ceiling, the décor is sleek and modern, the service friendly and the food (sandwiches and pasta) and coffee excellent.

Castelle Bar & Restaurant (☎ 37 00 14 14; Langbrygge 5; mains Nkr89-129; 🕓 noon-11pm Sun-Thu, noon-3.30am Fri & Sat) Perhaps the classiest bar/restaurant by the Pollen harbour, Castelle is a chic place and a cut above the beer-and-yobbo culture that sometimes afflicts other waterside bars in Arendal. Meals are light (sandwiches, good burgers and pasta) and most drinks are possible, from 0.5L beer (Nkr64) to cocktails (Nkr99).

Madam Reiersen (☎ 37 02 19 00; Nedre Tyholmsvei 3; starters Nkr79-125, lunch mains Nkr115-125, dinner mains Nkr219-235) One of the better restaurants ringing the Pollen harbour, Madam Reiersen is good value for lunch, especially its seafood platter (Nkr145). Then again, we did enjoy the crisp-fried Norwegian Arctic char (Nkr225) for dinner.

No.9 Kaffe & Platebar (☎ 37 02 77 92; Langbrygge 9; coffee Nkr19-34; 🕓 10am-5pm Mon-Sat, noon-5pm Sun, until 7pm Jul) Another classy little café, No.9 is the work of Espen Larsen, a local jazz musician who sells a range of (mostly jazz) CDs and plays them while you sip your coffee or snack on a pastry – the perfect accompaniment to a lazy Arendal afternoon.

For an outdoor drink in summer, **Fiskebrygge** (☎ 37 02 31 13; Nedre Tyholmsvei 1; 🕓 9am-2am Wed-Sun Apr-Sep) has a fine location on the waterfront and serves a range of beer (from Nkr50) and cocktails (from Nkr89).

Getting There & Away

M/S Merdø (☎ 90 97 43 61; www.skilsoferga.no, in Norwegian) sails from Arendal (Pollen) to Lyngør (Nkr250 return) and Hisøy (Nkr120 return) regularly in July, with fewer departures for the rest of summer. It also sails to Merdø (adult/child Nkr25/15) several times daily in July.

Nor-Way Bussekspress buses between Kristiansand (Nkr115, 1½ hours, up to nine daily) and Oslo (from Nkr225, four hours) call in at the Arendal Rutebilstasjon, a block west of Pollen harbour. Local Timekspressen buses connect Arendal with Grimstad (Nkr42, 30 minutes, hourly) and Risør (Nkr83, 1¼ hours).

Getting Around

Sykkelsport (☎ 37 02 39 60; cnr Nygaten & Vestre gates) rents bicycles for Nkr100 to Nkr150 per day – a great way to explore the islands and reach the bathing beaches on Hisøy and Tromøy.

AROUND ARENDAL

The 260-hectare island of **Merdø**, just off Arendal, has been inhabited since the 16th century. One peculiarity is that the island bears the remnants of vegetable species introduced in the ballast of early sailing vessels. The **Merdøgård Museum** (☎ 37 07 35 00; adult/child Nkr25/10; noon-4.30pm mid-Jun–mid-Aug), housed in a historic 1736 sea captain's residence, is decked out in period furnishings.

The favoured bathing sites are on Tromøy, Spornes, Hisøy and Hove. The nearest access to Spornes is on the bus marked 'Tromøy Vest/Øst', but you'll still have a 15-minute walk. Alternatively, take a bike on the **M/S Skilsøy ferry** (☎ 37 00 55 44), which sails frequently between Arendal and the western end of Tromøy (Nkr17, 10 minutes).

On the islets of **Store** and **Lille Torungene** rise two grand lighthouses that have guided ships into Arendal since 1844. They're visible from the coasts of both Hisøy and Tromøy.

GRIMSTAD

pop 19,536

Unusually for a town along the coast, Grimstad is at its most beautiful in the pedestrianised streets that lie inland from the waterfront; these streets are some of the loveliest on the Skagerrak coast. Grimstad has a number of interesting calling cards: it was the home of playwright Henrik Ibsen and has a good museum; it is the sunniest spot in Norway, with an average of 266 hours of sunshine per month in June and July; and Grimstad also has an unmistakably young vibe, thanks to its large student population.

History

Grimstad's low-key atmosphere, peacefulness and charm belie its past importance: between 1865 and 1885 it was one of the greatest shipbuilding centres in the world. The oak forests that grew on the surrounding hillsides were chopped down and sawn into timbers to supply the booming industry; at one point the town had 40 shipyards and 90 ships were under construction simultaneously.

During the same period, a land shortage caused local farmers to turn to fishing and many an inland farm homestead doubled as a shipbuilding workshop. By 1875 Grimstad had a home fleet of 193 boats.

Information

Guest harbour (Gjestehavn; ☎ 37 04 05 93; www.grimstadgjestehavn.no) Public toilets, showers and a laundry (all open to land-lubbers).

Library (☎ 37 29 67 90; Storgata 44; 10am-5pm Mon-Fri, 11am-2pm Sat) Free, time-limited internet.

Tourist office (☎ 37 25 01 68; www.grimstad.net; Sorenskrivergården, Storgata 1A; 9am-5pm Mon-Fri, 10am-4pm Sat Jun & Aug, 9am-5pm Mon-Fri, 10am-4pm Sat & Sun Jul, 8.30am-4pm Mon-Fri Sep-May)

Sights

IBSENHUSET MUSEUM

Norway's favourite playwright, Henrik Ibsen (see p50), arrived here in January 1844. The house where he worked as a pharmacist's apprentice, and where he lived and first cultivated his interest in writing, has been converted into the **Ibsenhuset Museum** (Grimstad By Museum; ☎ 37 04 04 90; www.gbm.no in Norwegian; Henrik Ibsens gate 14; combined ticket with Grimstad Maritime Museum adult/child/student/senior Nkr50/20/35/35; 11am-5pm mid-May–Aug). It contains a re-created pharmacy and many of the writer's belongings and is one of southern Norway's more interesting museums, with everything you needed to know from Ibsen's life and work. There's also a library with the writer's complete works. His 1861 poem *Terje Vigen* and his 1877 drama *Pillars of Society* take place in the Skerries offshore from Grimstad.

The eager young custodians of the museum, who can be found in the museum shop and ticket office across the street, can arrange **tours** (☎ 37 04 04 90; without/with museum entry Nkr50/75) of the town's other Ibsen landmarks, as well as sights associated with well-known Norwegian author Knut Hamsun (p48), who lived at nearby Norholm from 1918 to 1952.

GRIMSTAD MARITIME MUSEUM

This important **museum** (Sjøfartsmuseet; ☎ 37 04 04 90; Hasseldalen; adult/child/student/senior combined ticket with Ibsenhuset Museum, Nkr50/20/35/35; 11am-5pm Mon-Sat, 1-5pm Sun May–mid-Sep), in the office of the 1842 Hasseldalen shipyard, provides a glimpse into Grimstad's history during 'the days of the white sails'. While you're there it's worth climbing the short track from the end of Batteriveien up the Binabben hill for a view over Grimstad. Make sure you visit the Ibsenhuset Museum first or the combined ticket won't work.

QUARRY THEATRE

One of the more unusual cultural experiences in Grimstad is run by Kristiansand-based **Agder Theater** (☎ 38 07 70 50; www.agderteater.no in Norwegian; tickets Nkr300), which performs in an old quarry up to six days a week in summer. After a hiatus in 2007 the troupe was due to return to performing in 2008; the tourist office has a programme of upcoming performances. The quarry, 4km north of town, became infamous during WWII when red granite blocks for Hitler's 'Victory Monument' were taken from here; the monument was, of course, never built.

Sleeping

For camping, there are at least six nearby camp sites that are listed on the tourist office's **website** (www.grimstad.net), while **Grimstad Hytteutleie** (☎ 37 25 10 65; www.grimstad-hytteutleie.no; Grooseveien 103) can book holiday cabins in the area for one night (from Nkr375) or for longer stays.

Bie Appartement & Feriesenter (☎ 37 04 03 96; www.bieapart.no; off Arendalsveien; tent sites Nkr200, cabins Nkr500-1200;) The nearest camping option is friendly, well equipped and 800m northeast of the centre along Arendalsveien.

Grimstad Vertshus & Kro (☎ 37 04 25 00; www.grimstad-vertshus.no in Norwegian; Grimstadtunet; s/d from Nkr595/750) This friendly, cosy place is a fair hike into town. Given the shortage of other midrange places nearby, it's reasonable value although the rooms are quite simple.

Norlandia Sørlandet Hotel (☎ 37 09 05 00; www.norlandia.no/sorlandet; Televeien 21; s/d from Nkr790/990;) This modern hotel, around 3km west of the harbour, has fine rooms in a quiet woodland setting. Some of the upper rooms have views of the ocean.

our pick **Grimstad Hotell** (☎ 37 25 25 25; www.grimstadhotell.no; Kirkegata 3; s/d mid-Jun–mid-Aug Nkr775/1250, rest-of-year Mon-Thu Nkr1295/1545, Fri-Sun Nkr850/1100;) The stylish and very comfortable Grimstad Hotell is the only in-town hotel and comes with loads of charm that spans a number of converted and conjoined timber houses. It's the sort of quiet place where you wonder if anyone else is staying here, only to discover there's no table free at breakfast.

Eating & Drinking

our pick **Apotekergården** (☎ 37 04 50 25; Skolegata 3; mains from Nkr215; noon-midnight) The highly recommended Apotekergården is an excellent gourmet restaurant with a breezy outdoor terrace and a cast of regulars who wouldn't eat anywhere else. It can be difficult to get a table here in summer.

Haven Brasserie (☎ 37 04 90 22; Storgata 4; pastas, pizzas & starters Nkr82-198, meat & fish mains Nkr168-295; noon-midnight Mon-Sat, 1pm-midnight Sun) One of the few restaurants in town that allows you to sit at a table by the water, this appealing place serves Italian-inspired dishes as well as seafood like tiger prawns, monkfish and grilled salmon.

Platebaren (☎ 37 04 21 88; Storgata 15; baguettes Nkr27-35, salads Nkr49; 9am-5pm Mon-Fri, 9am-4pm Sat Jun-Aug; shorter hrs rest-of-year) This highly recommended coffee bar spills out into the street in summer and is a terrific place to tuck into decent-sized snacks (baguettes, bacon and eggs etc). Even better are the milk shakes (Nkr30), while coffee lovers swear by the iced coffee with ice cream (Nkr35).

Bryggerhuset (☎ 37 09 18 60; Storgata 32; lunch specials Nkr60; 10am-5pm Jun-Aug; shorter hrs rest-of-year) This engaging little café-cum-crafts shop serves terrific coffee, bakes its own bread and offers home-made food like crepes and waffles.

Viet Thai (☎ 37 04 15 80; Storgata 36; starters from Nkr35, mains Nkr75-120; 11am-11pm) If you're craving something a little more international, Viet Thai is cheap, extremely popular and servings are large. It also does cheaper lunch specials.

Café Ibsen (Henrik Ibsens gate 12; 10am-4pm Mon-Sat) Come here for delicious pastries. It's opposite the Ibsenhuset Museum.

Café Galleri (☎ 37 32 06 30; Storgata 28; 5pm-3am Sun-Thu, 3pm-3am Fri & Sat) The centre of Grimstad's nightlife has DJs, jam sessions and a crowd that seems to spring from Grimstad's woodwork on the most unlikely of nights.

Getting There & Around

The Grimstad **Rutebilstasjon** (☎ 37 04 05 18) is on Storgata at the harbour. Nor-Way Bussekspress buses between Oslo (Nkr300, five hours) and Kristiansand (Nkr85, one hour) call at Grimstad three to five times daily. Nettbuss buses to/from Arendal run once or twice hourly (Nkr45, 30 minutes).

You can hire bicycles from the tourist office for Nkr30/100 per hour/day; the daily rate drops to Nkr80 for more than one day. Child seats cost Nkr20 and those with boats moored in Gjestehavn pay just Nkr25 a day.

LILLESAND

pop 9109

Lillesand, between Kristiansand and Arendal, has a whitewashed village centre of old houses, and although nothing much happens here, that can be charming in itself. There's a **tourist office** (☎ 37 40 19 10; Rådhuset; ⌚ 9am-6pm Mon-Fri, 10am-4pm Sat, noon-4pm Sun mid-Jun–mid-Aug) in the town hall in summer. For summer boat tours through the offshore islands, contact **Brekkesto** (☎ 37 27 14 33; www.brekkesto.com).

Sleeping & Eating

Tingsaker Camping (☎ 37 27 04 21, fax 37 27 01 47; tent & caravan sites with car Nkr150, cabins Nkr750-950) This crowded camp site, on the shore 1km east of the centre, is a typical seaside holiday resort with camping, caravans and a range of overpriced cabins. It's nothing special but it's the cheapest place in town.

Lillesand Hotel Norge (☎ 37 27 01 44; www.hotelnorge.no; Strandgata 3; s Nkr990-1090, d Nkr1390-1590, starters Nkr95-115, mains Nkr165-255; 💻) This boutique hotel has been thoughtfully renovated to reflect the original 1837 splendour and overflows with period touches, particularly in the public areas. There are rooms dedicated to King Alfonso XIII of Spain and author Knut Hamsun, both of whom stayed here, and there's an antiquarian library and good restaurant.

Getting There & Away

The most pleasant way to reach Lillesand in summer is by boat from Kristiansand (see p145). There's also an hourly Nettbuss to Kristiansand (Nkr55), Grimstad (Nkr45) and Arendal (Nkr70).

KRISTIANSAND

pop 77,840

Kristiansand, Norway's fifth-largest city, calls itself 'Norway's No.1 Holiday Resort'. That can be a bit misleading: sun-starved Norwegians do flock here in the summer, but for everyone else it serves more as a gateway to the charming seaside villages of Norway's southern coast and the inland region of Setesdalen (p159). The claim also reflects a newfound confidence that has seen the city clean up its environmental act (it was until a decade ago infamous for its pollution). Kristiansand does have an interesting small harbour, an attractive old town, some good museums and an outstanding children's park.

Orientation

Central Kristiansand's *kvadraturen*, the square grid pattern measuring six long blocks by nine shorter blocks, was conceived by King Christian IV who founded the city in 1641. As a result of this planning, this is one of the easiest Norwegian cities to find your way around. The rail, bus and ferry terminals form a cluster west of the city centre. Pedestrianised Markens gate serves as a focus for the central shopping and restaurant district, while the fish market is at the southern tip of the town centre.

Information

You can change money at the **post office** (cnr Rådhus & Markens gates) or at all the major banks (there are several on Markens gate), one of which is **Nordea** (Markens gate 16).

Gjestehavn (Guest Harbour; ☎ 38 02 07 15; per wash/dry Nkr40/40) Has laundry facilities.

International Internet Café (cnr Gyldenløves gate & Vestre Strandgate; per hr Nkr30; ⌚ noon-10pm Mon-Sat, 2-10pm Sun) Skype-enabled internet access.

Kristiansand Library (☎ 38 12 49 10; Rådhus gate 11; ⌚ 10am-7pm Mon-Thu, 10am-5pm Fri, shorter hrs mid-Jun–Aug) Free, time-limited internet access.

Kristiansand og Oppland Turistforening (☎ 38 02 52 63; www.kot.no in Norwegian; Kirkegata 15; ⌚ 9am-3.30pm Mon-Wed & Fri, 9am-5pm Thu) Maps and information on hiking, huts and organised mountain tours in southern Norway.

Tourist office (☎ 38 12 13 14; www.sorlandet.com; Vestre Strandgate 32; ⌚ 8.30am-6pm Mon-Fri, 10am-6pm Sat, noon-6pm Sun mid-Jun–mid-Aug; 8.30am-3.30pm Mon-Fri rest-of-year)

Sights

CHRISTIANSHOLM FORTRESS

The most prominent feature that sits along the Strandepromenaden is the distinctive **Christiansholm Fortress** (Kristiansand Festning; ☎ 38 07 51 50; admission free; ⌚ grounds 9am-9pm mid-May–mid-Sep). Built by royal decree between 1662 and 1672 to keep watch over the strategic Skagerrak Straits and protect the city from

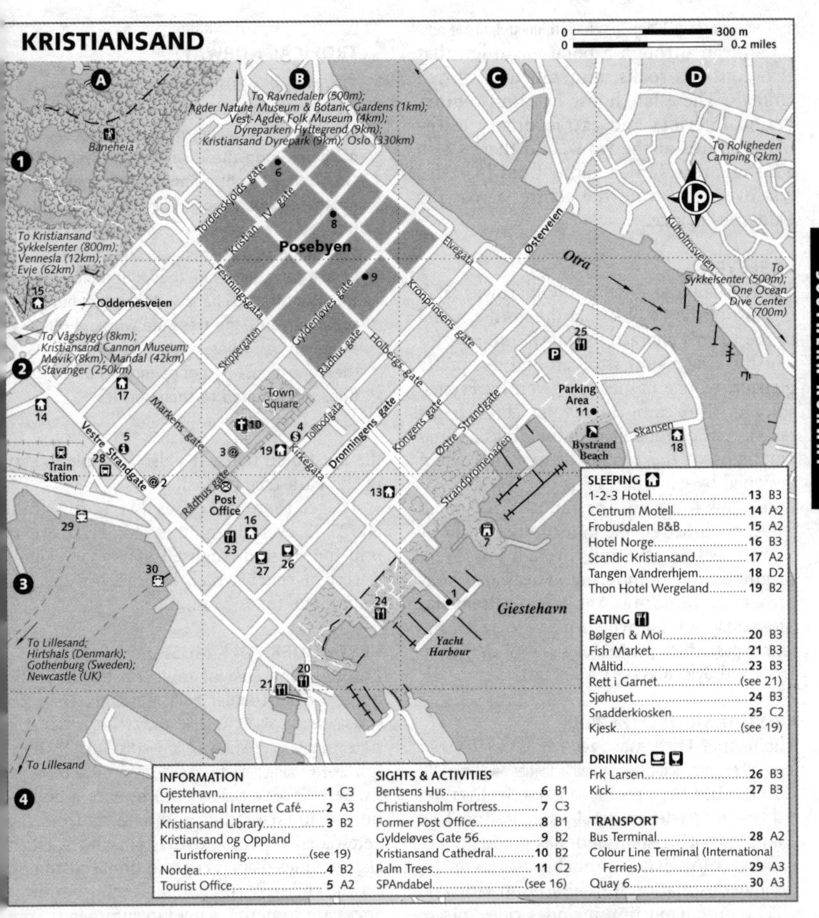

pirates and rambunctious Swedes, the construction featured walls up to 5m thick and an armoury buried within a concentric inner wall, all of which came at a price: 1550 local citizens were taxed to fund the project and coerced into labour. It was connected to the mainland by a bridge over a moat (filled in during the 19th century) deep enough to accommodate tall ships. The fortress served its purpose – it was never taken by enemy forces. The original roof was destroyed by fire in 1872 and a new roof with glass clerestory windows was built. A ring of eight bronze cannons, cast between 1666 and 1788, still menaces the offshore skerries. Free guided tours run on Sundays from mid-June to mid-August.

KRISTIANSAND CATHEDRAL

Built in 1884 in late gothic style, the **Kristiansand Cathedral** (Domkirke; ☎ 38 10 77 50; Kirkegata; admission free, tower Nkr20; ⌚ 10am-4pm Mon-Fri, 10am-2pm Sat mid-Jun–mid-Aug), with seating for 1800 people, is Norway's third-largest church. Guided tours (adult/child Nkr20/10) of the cathedral, including the tower, run at 11am and 2pm Monday to Saturday in summer, and there are organ recitals at 1pm Tuesday to Saturday during the same period.

AGDER NATURE MUSEUM & BOTANIC GARDEN

The winding paths through the established 50-hectare park at **Gimle Estate** (☎ 38 09 23 88; Gimleveien 23; adult/child Nkr50/15; ⌚ 11am-5pm mid-Jun–mid-Aug; 10am-3pm Tue-Fri, noon-4pm Sat rest-of-year) lead through a botanic garden that also contains rocks, minerals and stuffed animals. The estate house has 19th-century period interiors and extraordinary teeth-like columns at the front, and there's also a historic rose garden dating from 1850. It's just over 1km from the centre, across the Oddernes bridge.

POSEBYEN

The Kristiansand Posebyen (Old Town) takes in most of the 14 blocks at the northern end of the town's characteristic *kvadraturen*. It's worth taking a slow stroll around this pretty quarter, whose name was given by French soldiers who came to *reposer* (French for relax). A scale model (with buildings around 1m high) of the city as it appeared when designed by Christian IV is on view at Vest-Agder Folk Museum. The annual *Kristiansand* guide, published by the tourist office, includes a good section 'A Stroll through Posebyen' to guide your wandering. The most well-preserved buildings include **Bentsens Hus** (Kronprinsengs gate 59), which dates to 1855, the **former post office** (Kronprinsengs gate 45) dating to 1695 and **Gyldenløves gate 56** (1802).

KRISTIANSAND DYREPARK

The former **Kristiansand zoo** (☎ 38 04 97 00; www.dyreparken.com; admission incl all activities adult Nkr110-290, child Nkr90-230, depending on season; ⏰ 10am-7pm mid-Jun–Aug; shorter hrs rest-of-year), off the E18 10km east of Kristiansand, has gradually expanded into what is probably *the* favourite holiday destination for children in Norway.

The funfair portion includes rides, pirate ship cruises, Captain Sabretooth's Treasure Trove and enchanted houses, while the zoo portion offers a surprising variety of specimens, including the near-extinct golden lion tamarin and a new African lion enclosure. If you want to enjoy the water park, be sure to bring a swimming costume.

The real highlights, however, are the **Northern Wilderness** (Nordisk Vilmark), where visitors are transported over the habitat of moose, wolves, lynx and wolverines on elevated boardwalks; and **Cardamom Town** (Kardamomme By), named for a key ingredient in Scandinavian waffles, a fantasy village based on the popular children's stories of Thorbjørn Egner. The town has been carefully laid out exactly as it appeared in the illustrated book. It's also possible to stay in the park (see opposite).

To get there, take bus M1 (adult/child Nkr25/13, every 15 minutes Monday to Friday mid-June to mid-August, less often weekends & rest-of-year), which leaves from the bus station and takes 25 minutes.

TROPICAL NORWAY?

Kristiansand's claims to be a beach resort are aided by the fact that it has what locals claim to be Norway's only palm trees, five of them along the town beach (Bystrand). OK, so they're potted and rather small and, no, there's not a coconut anywhere in sight. But they are palm trees nonetheless and that alone makes them special in Norway. In fact, so valuable are they that the city authorities take no chances. At the first hint of summer's end, the trees are whisked off to the town hall where a glass house protects these most cosseted of palm trees in conditions more suited to their species.

VEST-AGDER FOLK MUSEUM

Located 4km east of town on the E18, the open-air **Vest-Agder Folk Museum** (Vest-Agder Fylkesmuseum; ☎ 38 10 26 80; www.vestagdermuseet.no in Norwegian; Vigeveien 22B; adult/child Nkr40/15; ⏰ 10am-6pm Tue-Fri, noon-6pm Sat-Mon mid-Jun–mid-Aug, noon-5pm Sun May–mid-Jun & mid-Aug–Oct) houses a collection of 40 farmsteads and hamlets from the Setesdalen region and Kristiansand itself. It also includes displays of traditional costumes, art and children's toys. Folk dancing performances are sometimes held in summer at 5pm on Wednesdays. There's also a scale model of Kristiansand Old Town.

SETESDALSBANEN

The 78km-long narrow-gauge railway between Kristiansand and Byglandsfjord was opened in 1896 to link Setesdalen with the coast. It was used to transport nickel from the Evje mines, and local timber and barrel staves that were used in the salting and export of herring. Although competition from the normal-gauge state railway forced its closure in 1962, the **Setesdalsbanen Railway** (☎ 38 15 64 82; www.setesdalsbanen.no; adult/child return Nkr100/50; ⏰ departures 11.30am, 1.15pm & 3.10pm Sun mid-Jun–August, 6.05pm Thu & Fri Jul) still runs steam- or diesel-powered locomotives along the last 6km between Grovane (2km north of Vennesla) and Beihøldalen; the journey takes 25 minutes one way. NSB trains run up to four times daily from Kristiansand to Vennesla (Nkr31, 12 minutes), while bus 30 does the same trip (Nkr35).

KRISTIANSAND KANONMUSEUM

The **Kristiansand Cannon Museum** (☎ 38 08 50 90; www.kanonmuseet.no; Møvik; adult/child Nkr60/30; 🕑 11am-6pm mid-Jun–mid-Aug, shorter hrs rest-of-year), 8km south of town, preserves the Germans' heavy Vara Battery, which, along with an emplacement at Hanstholm in Denmark, ensured German control of the strategic Skagerrak Straits during WWII. At each end, four 337-tonne, 38cm cannons, reportedly the second-heaviest guns in the world and with a range of 55km controlled traffic along either end of the strait, while the unprotected middle zone was heavily mined. In the autumn of 1941, over 1400 workers and 600 soldiers occupied this site. Visitors to the museum can see the big guns as well as bunkers, barracks and munitions storage (including some daunting 800kg shells).

BANEHEIA & RAVNEDALEN PARKS

Baneheia and Ravnedalen, both north of the city centre, offer greenery and a network of lakeside **hiking** and **skiing tracks** for those keen to escape the city for a while. Both parks were created between 1870 and 1880 by Kristiansand's city chairman, General Oscar Wergeland. Over a 30-year period, he oversaw the planting of 150,000 coniferous trees and transformed the area into a recreational green belt.

Activities

One Ocean Dive Center (☎ 91 62 85 25; www.oneocean.no; Strandåsen 22; one/two dives Nkr500/850, equipment rental per day Nkr500-750) is a professional centre that runs dives to wrecks, which include a downed plane and even a minesweeper. It's to be found just across the water east of the town centre.

Opened in 2007, **SPAndabel** (☎ 38 17 41 74; www.spandabel.no in Norwegian; Tollbodgata 6; 🕑 10am-6pm Mon, Tue & Sat, 10am-8pm Wed-Fri) in the Hotel Norge (see following) is a luxurious spa centre that offers a range of pampering from Nkr495 up to Nkr1250.

Sleeping

Kristiansand can be expensive for what you get, which may be nothing unless you book early for summer, especially during the July school-holiday period when prices soar. One unwelcome Kristiansand quirk is the 10am check-out time in some places.

Roligheden Camping (☎ 38 09 67 22; www.roligheden.no in Norwegian; Framnesveien; tent sites Nkr130 plus per person Nkr30, 4-person cabins from Nkr750; 🕑 Jun-Aug) Tent campers are in luck at this well-run camp site at a popular beach site 3km east of the centre. Take bus 15 from the centre.

Tangen Vandrerhjem (☎ 38 02 83 10; www.kristiansand-vandrerhjem.no; Skansen 8; dm incl breakfast Nkr230, s Nkr350-495, d Nkr450-550; 🕑 Jan-Nov; P 💻) The huge Kristiansand HI hostel lives in a rather bland warehouse (10-minutes' walk northeast of the fortress) and is home to simple, tidy rooms and friendly staff.

Centrum Motell (☎ 38 70 15 65; www.motell.no; Vestre Strandgate 49; s Nkr420-520, d Nkr520-695; 💻) We wouldn't normally recommend a place nestled in a car park between an overpass and the train station, but Kristiansand's pricey accommodation scene makes this good budget value, especially if you throw in free wireless access. Rooms are simple with bunk beds.

Frobusdalen B&B (☎ 91 12 99 06; www.gjestehus.no; Frobusdalen 2; s/d Nkr500/700) Probably the most personal place to stay in Kristiansand, this small B&B in an old timber home a 10-minute walk northwest of the centre is rustic, cosy and friendly.

1-2-3 Hotel (☎ 38 70 15 66; www.123-hotel.no; Østre Strandgate 25; s/d mid-Jun–mid-Aug Nkr695/895, rest-of-year Nkr530/695; 💻) It's hard to know what to make of this place, which styles itself as a self-service hotel. With its electronic check-in (there's no reception except to pay), meagre breakfast and 10am check-out, we wonder if this hotel exists more for the convenience of its owners than guests. Then again, the price is good for Kristiansand and the rooms are light, airy and comfortable.

Thon Hotel Wergeland (☎ 38 17 20 40; www.thonhotels.no; Kirkegata 15; s Nkr1095-1295, d Nkr1295-1495; P 💻) It doesn't get any more central than this attractive, modern hotel right next to the cathedral. The high-standard rooms with hardwood floors have a touch more charm than some others in the Thon Hotels chain.

Hotel Norge (☎ 38 17 40 00; www.hotel-norge.no; Dronningens gate 5; s/d Nkr1295/1495 mid-Jun–mid-Aug, Nkr725/925 Fri-Sun, Nkr1375/1575 Mon-Thu rest-of-year; P 💻) It can sometimes be difficult to distinguish many of Norway's chain hotels so we welcome the effort taken here. The all-important mattresses are extremely comfortable, and there's a rooftop sun lounge, private bakery and a spa centre (p143).

Scandic Kristiansand (☎ 21 61 42 00; www.scandic-hotels.com; Markens gate 39; s Nkr880-1485, d Nkr1080-1685; P) If you value style as well as substance, the Scandic Kristiansand has both. The rooms and public areas are stylish, rooms have all the requisite bells and whistles, and the hotel adheres to the strictest environmental standards. A good package.

Dyreparken Hyttegrend (☎ 38 04 98 00; booking@dyreparken.no; fantasy house Nkr630-2500) One of Norway's more unusual sleeping options are the self-catering fantasy houses, that sleep up to five, in the Dyrepark (see p142). These charming products of a child-like imagination are fantastic for kids, but very often booked out in summer. Prices include admission to the park.

Eating

Snadderkiosken (☎ 38 02 90 29; Østre Strandgate 78a; dishes Nkr18-88; 8.30am-11.30pm Mon-Fri, 11.30am-11.30pm Sat & Sun) We don't normally direct you to the fast-food kiosks that are everywhere in Norway, but Snadderkiosken is one of the best of its kind in Norway. Near the town beach, it has an extensive and great-value menu, with things such as hearty meatballs and mashed potatoes or grilled chicken with rice and salad.

In summer the most atmospheric places to eat are in the small, remodelled harbour around the **fish market** (☎ 38 12 24 50; 7am-4pm Mon-Fri, 7am-2.30pm Sat) where you'll find the freshest and best-value seafood. Two restaurants in particular stand out.

our pick **Bølgen & Moi** (☎ 38 17 83 00; Sjølystveien 1A; light meals Nkr55-169, restaurant starters Nkr75-145, mains Nkr220-279; 3pm-midnight Mon-Sat) The best restaurant around the fish market harbour, the supercool Bølgen & Moi does a sublime fish and shellfish soup (Nkr145) and a tasty range of fish and seafood dishes as well as set menus (from Nkr385). In summer the outdoor tables are packed and it's a good place for a drink after the kitchen closes.

Rett i Garnet (☎ 38 12 24 03; Fiskebrygga; lunch mains & snacks Nkr59-139, mains Nkr129-239; 11am-late Mon-Sat, noon-late Sun) Not quite as classy as Bølgen & Moi but with good food, this place next to the fish market entrance is also all about seafood, serving trout, mackerel, salmon and monkfish. It also does a terrific seafood platter (minimum two persons) for Nkr265 per person.

Sjøhuset (☎ 38 02 62 60; Markens gate; light meals & snacks Nkr75-169, starters Nkr85-115, mains Nkr179-269; 11am-11pm) Along the waterfront next to the yacht harbour, this long-standing restaurant of quality is another fine choice for lovers of the fruits of the sea.

Måltid (☎ 47 83 30 00; Tollbodgata 2B; lunch dishes Nkr69, tapas Nkr30; 11am-6pm Mon-Thu, 11am-11pm Fri & Sat) Part delicatessen, part restaurant and part wine bar, this outpost of casual sophistication is terrific. The tapas idea may come from Spain, but the food is Norwegian with so many tempting plates on offer and the waiters more than happy to help choose your tapas platter. For a light lunch the pasta salad or sandwiches are good options.

Kjesk (☎ 38 10 86 10; Kirkegata 15; light meals Nkr45-145; lunch & dinner Mon-Sat) Also recommended, Kjesk is a very cool coffee bar with great food.

Drinking & Entertainment

Apart from the places around the fish market where the outdoor tables are difficult to snaffle on a summer's evening, there are a couple of decent places for a drink.

our pick **Frk Larsen** (Markens gate 5; 11am-midnight Mon-Wed, 11am-3am Thu-Sat, noon-midnight Sun) Our favourite drinking hole in Kristiansand, this trendy place has retro-chic fusion décor, a mellow ambience by day and late-night music for an 'in' crowd on weekend nights. The cocktail bar opens at 8pm.

Kick (☎ 38 02 62 44; Dronningens gate 8; 3pm-late) This outdoor café morphs into a disco with a DJ as the night wears on. It's one of the most popular hang-outs for young people and there's occasional live music on weekends.

Getting There & Away

BOAT

For information on ferries to Denmark, Sweden and the UK, see p408.

BUS

Departures from Kristiansand are shown in the table below.

Destination	Departures	Cost	Duration
Arendal	up to 9 daily	Nkr115	1½hr
Bergen (via Haukeligrend)	one daily	Nkr450	12hr
Evje	7-8 daily	Nkr100	1hr
Flekkefjord	2-4 daily	Nkr220	2hr
Oslo	up to 9 daily	Nkr199-300	5½hr
Stavanger	2-4 daily	Nkr355	4½hr

CAR & MOTORCYCLE

With a vehicle, access to the E18, north of the centre, is via Vestre Strandgate; when arriving you'll most likely find yourself along Festningsgata. For parking in the city centre, the open-air **parking area** (cnr Østre Strandgate & Elvegata; per 24 hr Nkr50), east of the centre, is easily the cheapest.

TRAIN

There are up to four trains daily to Oslo (Nkr580, 4½ hours) and up to five to Stavanger (Nkr390, 3¼ hours).

Getting Around

Unlike many Norwegian towns, Kristiansand is mercifully flat and the downtown area is easily negotiable on foot. Alternatively, for bicycle rental, **Sykkelsenter** (☎ 38 02 68 35; Grim Torv 3; per day/week Nkr150/500) has a range of bikes on offer.

AROUND KRISTIANSAND

The Skerries

In summer, Kristiansand's archipelago of offshore skerries turns into one of the country's greatest sun-and-sea destinations for Norwegian holiday-makers. The most popular island, **Bragdøy**, lies close to the mainland and boasts a preservation workshop for wooden ships, nice walks and several bathing sites. In the distance, you'll see the classic lighthouse **Grønningen Fyr**.

Ferries (Nkr17) to the island run from Vågsbygd, around 8km south of central Kristiansand, three times daily Monday to Friday, with an additional sailing on Saturday, and three on Sunday.

M/S Øya (☎ 95 93 58 55; www.lillesand.net) sails from/to Lillesand (Nkr215/110 per adult/child one way, Nkr360/180 return, three hours) once daily except Sunday from late June to early August. The departure point was uncertain at the time of research (either south of the fish market or from Quay 6) – check at the tourist office.

MANDAL

pop 14,200

Norway's southernmost town, Mandal is famous for its 800m-long beach, Sjøsanden. About 1km from the centre and backed by forests, the Copacabana it ain't, but it is Norway's finest stretch of sand, just crying out for a sunny Mediterranean climate.

The **tourist office** (☎ 38 27 83 00; www.regionmandal.com; Bryggegaten 10; ⏰ 9am-7pm Mon-Fri, 10am-4pm Sat & Sun Jun-Aug, 9am-4pm Mon-Fri Sep-May) is along the waterfront.

Sights

The moderately interesting town **Bymuseum** (☎ 38 27 30 00; Store Elvegata 5/6; adult/child Nkr20/free; ⏰ 11am-5pm Mon-Fri, 11am-2pm Sat, noon-4pm Sun late Jun–mid-Aug), which displays a host of historical maritime and fishing artefacts and works by local artists, is elevated above the mundane by impressive exhibits of works by Mandal's favourite son, Gustav Vigeland (see the boxed text, p101).

The family home of Norway's finest sculptor has been converted into a small museum and exhibition space, **Vigeland Hus** (☎ 38 27 83 00; adult/child Nkr30/free; ⏰ noon-4pm Tue-Sun mid-Jun–mid-Aug). The house has been decorated in a style approximating that of the sculptor's early days and his workshop has been transformed into a gallery.

Festivals

The second week in August, when Mandal hosts the **Shellfish Festival** (www.skalldyrfestivalen.no), is a great time to be in town: there's fresh seafood everywhere and a range of musical performances.

Sleeping & Eating

Accommodation in Mandal tends to be rather expensive.

Sjøsanden Feriesenter (☎ 38 26 14 19; www.sjosanden-feriesenter.no; Sjøsandveien 1; tent sites without/with car Nkr130/150, d Nkr350-650, 2-6-person self-catering apt Nkr500-800) Being just a few metres away from the beach, Sjøsanden distinguishes this well-run place from the other camp sites in the vicinity. It even has its own water slide.

First Hotel Solborg (☎ 38 27 21 00; www.firsthotels.no/solborg; Neseveien 1; s/d from Nkr795/975, main courses Nkr165-279; 💻 🏊) This flash hotel, only a 10-minute walk west of the beach, boasts an indoor pool, the best restaurant in town and a bar and Saturday disco called Soldekket. Oh yes, and the rooms at this place aren't at all bad either.

Dr Nielsen's (☎ 38 26 61 00; Store Elvegate 47a; mains from Nkr79) Any cravings for Greek salads and grilled meats will be satisfied at this place, which also does pasta, chicken and some fish dishes. Every other restaurant in Mandal does seafood and not much else.

Getting There & Away

The Mandal Rutebilstasjon lies north of the river, just a short walk from the historic district. The Nor-Way Bussekspress coastal route between Stavanger (Nkr335, 3½ hours) and Kristiansand (Nkr88, 45 minutes) passes through Mandal two to four times daily.

LINDESNES

As the southernmost point in Norway (latitude 57° 58' 95" N), Lindesnes (literally 'arching land peninsula') provides an occasional glimpse of the power nature can unleash between the Skagerrak and the North Sea. Even better, as the brochures point out, 'the camera angles are better than at Nordkapp' (2518km away).

Rising above the cape is the evocative **Lindesnes Fyr** (☎ 38 25 77 35; www.lindesnesfyr.no; adult/child Nkr50/free; 🕑 11am-5pm May–mid-Oct, shorter hrs rest-of-year), a classic lighthouse. In two of the buildings you'll pass as you climb to the cape there are exhibitions on the history of the lighthouse, while the visitors centre next to the gate has more plus an informative video about the site. The first lighthouse on the site (and the first in Norway) was fired up in 1655 using coal and tallow candles to warn ships off the rocks. The current electrical version, built in 1915, is visible up to 19½ nautical miles out to sea. Be wary of strong winds: one Lonely Planet author lost his sunglasses in a sudden gust.

Sleeping

Lindesnes Camping og Hytteutleie (☎ 38 25 88 74; www.lindesnescamping.no; Lillehavn; tent sites Nkr135, cabins Nkr210-790) You'll find excellent modern facilities at this place, on the shore 3.5km northeast of Lindesnes Fyr. There's a small kiosk and kitchen facilities and it also organises boat hire.

Lindesnes Gjestehus (☎ 38 25 97 00; liveueland@hotmail.com; Spangereid; B&B per person from Nkr350) About 11km north of the cape lies this simple but cosy guesthouse.

Getting There & Away

Buses from Mandal (Nkr58, one hour) travel to the lighthouse via Spangereid on Monday, Wednesday and Friday.

FLEKKEFJORD

pop 8860

Flekkefjord is a quiet place with a pretty old town (the town's history dates back to 1660 when it competed for power with Kristiansand). It's also famous for having virtually no tidal variation (typically less than 10cm between high and low tides). Along with Egersund (p148), it's one of the more enjoyable towns to base yourself on this stretch of coast.

The small **tourist office** (☎ 38 32 69 95; flekkefjord@regionlister.com; Elvegata 9; 🕑 9am-5pm Mon-Fri, 10am-3pm Sat mid-jun–mid-Aug, 9am-4pm Mon-Fri rest-of-year) should be your first port of call.

Sights

Before setting out to explore the town, collect the pamphlet *A Tour of Flekkefjord* from the tourist office. The richest source of old architecture is the **Hollenderbyen** (Dutch Town)

HERE WERE VIKINGS

From the 8th to the 11th centuries, Norway's coastline was the domain of Vikings, but the cape at Lindesnes, where the waters of the Skagerrak and the North Sea collided, proved a challenge even to these formidable seamen. Their solution? In a spirit of creative engineering that Norway's road builders would later emulate when faced with daunting geographic forms, the Vikings carved a **canal** (www.spangereidkanalen.no, in Norwegian) across the Lindesnes Peninsula at Spangareid (once a home port of Viking chieftains) to avoid the dangerous seas of the cape. In summer 2007, a replica canal was opened to recreate the Viking detour. Close to the site, the excellent historical centre **Vikingland** (☎ 38 25 76 61; www.spangereidvikingland.no; Spangareid; adult/child Nkr70/40; 🕑 11am-5pm mid-Jun–mid-Aug) offers Viking exhibitions, a Viking cruise and tranquil Viking sports such as axe-throwing.

If the Vikings have caught your attention, there's another site nearby that you'll want to seek out. At Penne, west of Farsund and close to Borhaug, are some remarkable **rock paintings** dating from the Viking era, including representations, at once child-like and sophisticated, of Viking ships. For more information, contact the **Farsund tourist office** (☎ 38 39 08 39; farsundtourist@eunet.no, ahga@farsund.kommune.no (outside summer); 🕑 Jun-Aug).

istrict, with its narrow streets and old timer buildings. **Flekkefjord Museum** (☎ 38 32 81 40; www.flekkefjordmuseum.no in Norwegian; Dr Kraftsgata 15; dult/child Nkr20/free; 🕑 noon-5pm Mon-Fri, noon-3pm Sat Sun Jun-Aug) is housed in a home from 1724, ut with 19th-century interiors.

One feature that stands out is the unuual octagonal log-built **Flekkefjord church** (☎ 38 32 43 00; Kirkegaten; admission free; 🕑 11am-1pm Mon-Sat Jul), which was consecrated in 1833. Designed by architect H Linstow (he of the Royal Palace in Oslo), the octagonal theme continues throughout, with the columns, steeple and baptismal font all conforming to the eight-sided form.

In 2007 Flekkefjord trialled a system of small-town ambassadors, a loose collection of around a dozen locals who offer information and even a look inside their Flekkefjord homes. It's a novel idea that we hope catches on. Contact the tourist office if you want to find them.

Sleeping & Eating

Egenes Camping (☎ 38 32 01 48; www.egenes.no; tent sites without/with car Nkr90/110 plus per person Nkr20, caravan sites Nkr120, cabins Nkr400-900) This spectacularly located camp site is beside Lake Seluravatnet, 1km off the E39 and 5km east of Flekkefjord. There's boat and canoe hire and a good-value café (mains around Nkr75). Buses running from Flekkefjord (Nkr25, 10 minutes) towards Kristiansand pass within 1km of the site. Water-sports equipment is also available.

Maritim Fjordhotell (☎ 38 32 58 00; www.fjordhotellene.no; Sundegaten 9; s Nkr775-1095, d Nkr995-1350) Flekkefjord's largest hotel has a great waterfront position, stylish rooms and a decent restaurant (mains from Nkr125), although the architecture is a real eyesore.

Grand Hotell (☎ 38 32 53 01; www.grand-hotell.no in Norwegian; Anders Beersgt 9; s/d Nkr845/1045) For the most character and personality that you'll find in Flekkefjord, the Grand Hotell perfectly suits this old town. Housed in a delightful white timber-clad building, the hotel's rooms have a certain old-world charm.

Pizza Inn (☎ 38 32 22 22; Elvegata 22; snacks Nkr65-115, pizza/pasta from Nkr169/125, mains Nkr129-179; 🕑 daily) This pleasant harbour-side restaurant has breezy outdoor tables to pass a summer's afternoon or cosy booths for a winter's evening. The service is good, as is the food. The entrecôte with salad (Nkr129) is a good deal.

Fiskebrygga (☎ 38 32 04 90; Elvegata 9; 🕑 10am-4pm Mon, Tue & Sat, 10am-6pm Wed & Fri, 10am-7pm Thu) Possibly the nicest place in Flekkefjord for a light meal, this café-style restaurant next to the tourist office does fish and chips (Nkr99), marinated spare ribs (Nkr129), delicious cakes (Nkr39) and ice cream. It has a certain urban sense of style, which is lovely in quiet little Flekkefjord.

Getting There & Away

The Nor-Way Bussekspress bus between Kristiansand (normal/express Nkr175/220, two hours) and Stavanger (Nkr220, two hours) passes through Flekkefjord. Buses run to Jøssingfjord three times daily except Sunday (Nkr61, 40 minutes).

FLEKKEFJORD TO EGERSUND

If you have your own vehicle, forsake the E39 and take the coastal Rv44 to Egersund – one of southern Norway's most beautiful drives. You'll pass through barren, bouldered hills with a few forested sections and lakes, before descending to **Jøssingfjord**, around 32km west of Flekkefjord; it's the site for breathtaking, perpendicular rock scenery, including a fine waterfall. Two 17th-century houses, known as **Helleren**, have nestled under an overhanging cliff since the 18th century and were definitely not for the claustrophobic. Despite the danger of falling rocks, the overhang did provide protection from the harsh Norwegian climate. The houses are open year-round.

Some 30km southeast of Egersund and 2.5km south of Hauge i Dalane, **Sogndalsstrand** should not be missed for its picturesque timber homes and warehouses that jut out over the river. The houses feature on the covers of tourist brochures across the region and they're well worth seeking out as it's a quiet, beautiful place. The homes date from the 17th and 18th centuries. If this small village has won your heart, consider staying at the **Sogndalsstrand Kultur Hotell** (☎ 51 47 72 55; www.sogndalstrand-kulturhotell.no; s/d Nkr820/1190, a lovely place with cosy rooms and an excellent little restaurant (meals with wine are priced from Nkr315).

For more information on scenic lighthouses and other attractions along this route and the entire coastal road from Kristiansand to Haugesund, visit the excellent www.nordsjovegen.no.

EGERSUND

pop 13,594

One of the prettiest towns along this stretch of coastline, Egersund is a serene place strewn with old timber houses that tell the story of its long history; intriguing rune stones found in nearby Møgedal are among the oldest written forms found in southern Norway. It's a quiet place to wander and to soak up the small-town ambience of the southern Norwegian coast.

The **tourist office** (☎ 51 46 80 00; www.eigersund.kommune.no; Jernbaneveien 2; ⏰ 10am-6pm Mon-Fri, 10am-4pm Sat & Sun Jun-Aug) is fine for local information, but it's only open in summer.

Sights

From mid-June to mid-August, **guided walking tours** (per person Nkr20; ⏰ 1pm Sat) of Egersund leave from the tourist office.

DALANE FOLK MUSEUM

The **Dalane Folkmuseum** (☎ 51 46 14 10; www.museumsnett.no/dalmus; Slettebø; adult/child Nkr20/10; ⏰ 11am-5pm Mon-Sat, 1-5pm Sun mid-Jun–mid-Aug, 11am-5pm Sun only rest-of-year) is divided into two parts. The more interesting main section features eight historic timber homes at Slettebø, 3.5km north of town just off the Rv42. The other section is the **Egersund Fayance Museum** (⏰ same hrs), a walkable 1.5km northeast of town. It displays the history and wares of Egersund Fayance, the ceramic and porcelain firm that sustained the entire district from 1847 to 1979.

HISTORIC BUILDINGS

Some 92 homes, nearly two-thirds of the original town, were gutted by fire in 1843, after which Egersund was reconstructed with wide streets to thwart the spread of future fires. Most buildings in the old town date from this period. **Strandgaten**, a street of timber houses constructed after 1843, is well worth a stroll. **Skrivergården** (Strandgaten 58) was built in 1846 as the home of the local magistrate Christian Feyer. The small town park opposite served as his private garden – half his luck. **Strandgaten 43** is arguably more beautiful and has what's known as a 'gossip mirror', which allowed the inhabitants to keep an eye on the street. The **Bilstadhuset** (Nygaten 14) still has its original timberwork and includes a sailmaker's loft upstairs. None of the houses are open to the public, but the tourist office hands out a leaflet, *Strolling in Egersund*, which has a map and informative commentary.

EGERSUND KIRKE

There has been a church in Egersund since at least 1292. The cute, current manifestation **Egersund Kirke** (Torget; admission free; ⏰ 11am-4pm Mon-Sat, 10am-3pm Sat, 12.30-3pm Sun mid-Jun–mid-Aug) dates back to the 1620s; the carved altarpiece, a depiction of the baptism and crucifixion of Christ by Stavanger carpenter Thomas Christophersen and painted by artist Peter Reimers, dates back to 1607 and the baptismal font is from 1583. The cross-shaped design, intimate balconies and wonderfully decorated pew doors are all worth lingering over. An English-language sheet handed out at the door details the church's history.

VARBERG

Fine **views** over the town centre are to be had for those who climb to the summit of Varberg, the hill with the prominent TV mast. The path to the top takes about 20 minutes from the centre of town.

Sleeping & Eating

Steinsnes Camping (☎ 51 49 41 36; fax 51 49 40 73; Tengs; tent sites Nkr120 plus per person Nkr30, cabins Nkr250-500) Egersund's most convenient camp site is 3km north of town alongside a rushing stream; buses heading for Hellvik will get you there. In a very Norwegian touch, it sells salmon-fishing permits.

Hauen Camping (☎ 51 49 23 79; www.hauencamping.no; tent sites Nkr120 plus per person Nkr30, cabins Nkr450-550) Spotless pine-clad huts here have a wilderness feel to them and the communal facilities are well-kept. It's along the coast road, 7km west of Egersund.

Anne's B&B (☎ 51 49 37 45; www.annes-bb.no; Sjukehusveien 45; d Nkr500-600; ⏰ Apr-Oct; 🏊) This family-run B&B 2km northeast of the town centre offers the most personal stay in town, with simple but traditionally styled rooms and the added bonus of a swimming pool. It's just off the Rv44 on the road into town and close to the Dalen Folkmuseum.

Grand Hotell (☎ 51 49 18 11; www.grand-egersund.no; Johan Feyersgate 3; s Nkr605-1190, d Nkr805-1150; 💻) The Grand Hotell is a lovely old 19th-century building with stylish, renovated rooms, although you pay more for those in the picturesque old but refurbished wing. The corner rooms (eg 307 in the old wing and 224 in the newer section) are the best on offer. It also has a good restaurant, with lunch specials priced at Nkr59 to Nkr135 and a dinner buffet for Nkr195).

Shopping

Egersund Terracotta og Keramikk (☎ 51 49 15 96; Strandgaten 44; 9am-4.30pm Mon-Wed & Fri, 9am-6pm Thu, 9am-2pm Sat) Three generations of potters have been moulding and selling ceramics here since 1946. What's on offer is authentic local ceramics, not tourist kitsch.

Getting There & Away

Trains to/from Kristiansand (Nkr274, two hours) run three times daily, with eight daily services to/from Stavanger (Nkr133, one hour). **Fjord Line** (☎ 55 54 87 00; www.fjordline.no) runs international ferries between Bergen and Hanstholm in Denmark via Egersund, but it's not available for transport between Bergen and Egersund. For details on international ferries, see p408.

AROUND EGERSUND

For details of the picturesque route between Egersund and Flekkefjord, see p147.

If you're driving along the Rv42 west of Egersund, **Terland Klopp**, 15km northeast of town, is a lovely 60m-long bridge from 1888. Constructed in 21 stone arches, it has been proposed for inclusion on Unesco's list of historical monuments.

Eigerøy Fyr (Midbrødøy; adult/child Nkr20/10; 11am-4pm Sun mid-Jun–mid-Aug), the majestic 1855 lighthouse on Midbrødøy, is near the southwestern tip of Eigerøy island. Still one of the most powerful lighthouses in Europe, it has great views at any time, but especially on stormy days. Take the Nord Eigerøy bus from the Rutebilstasjon and get off at the sign 'Eigerøy Fyr' on the Rv502 (Nkr27, 15 minutes). From there, it's a 30-minute walk down the Fyrvegen road to the lighthouse.

THE INTERIOR

Inland from Norway's southern coast, quiet mountain valleys like Setesdalen and the magnificent peak of Gausta, close to Rjukan, are wonderful places. Another highlight is the lake-studded Telemark region, connected by a canal with pretty Seljord – home to the Nessie-esque Selma the Serpent.

KONGSBERG

pop 23,644

At first glance, you might not be tempted to give Kongsberg a second look as you rush on to towns of greater renown. But Kongsberg has plenty of reasons to stop, among them the interesting Kongsgruvene (Royal Silver Mine) and one of Norway's best jazz festivals in June or July. With cascading rapids running through the heart of town, it's also one of the more agreeable towns in this part of Norway.

History

The history of Kongsberg begins and ends with silver, which was discovered by two children with an ox in 1623 in the nearby Numedal Valley. Their father attempted to sell the windfall, but the king's soldiers got wind of it and the family was arrested and forced to disclose the site of their discovery. Kongsberg was founded a year later and in the resulting silver rush it briefly became the second-largest town in Norway, with 8000 inhabitants including 4000 miners. Between 1623 and 1957, 1.35 million kilograms of pure thread-like 'wire' silver (one of the world's purest forms of silver) was produced for the royal coffers. Kongsberg is still home to the national mint, but the last mine closed in 1957.

Orientation & Information

Kongsberg is neatly split into old and new sections by the falls of the river Numedalslågen. The new eastern section takes in the tourist office, transport terminals, hotels and some restaurants. In the older section west of the river lie the museum, church and HI hostel.

The **tourist office** (☎ 32 29 90 50; www.visitkongsberg.no; Schwabesgt 2; 9am-7pm Mon-Fri, 10am-2pm Sat & Sun late-Jun–mid-Aug, shorter hrs rest-of-year) is excellent.

Sights & Activities

KONGSBERG KIRKE

Norway's largest baroque **church** (☎ 32 73 19 02; Kirketorget; adult/student/pensioner/child Nkr30/20/20/20; 10am-4pm Mon-Fri, 10am-1pm Sat, 2-4pm Sun mid-May–mid-Aug, shorter hrs rest-of-year), in the old town west of the river, officially opened in 1761. The rococo-style interior features ornate chandeliers and an unusual altar that combines the altarpiece, high pulpit and organ pipes on a single wall. From June to August there are organ recitals held here at 8pm every Wednesday.

SOUTHERN NORWAY

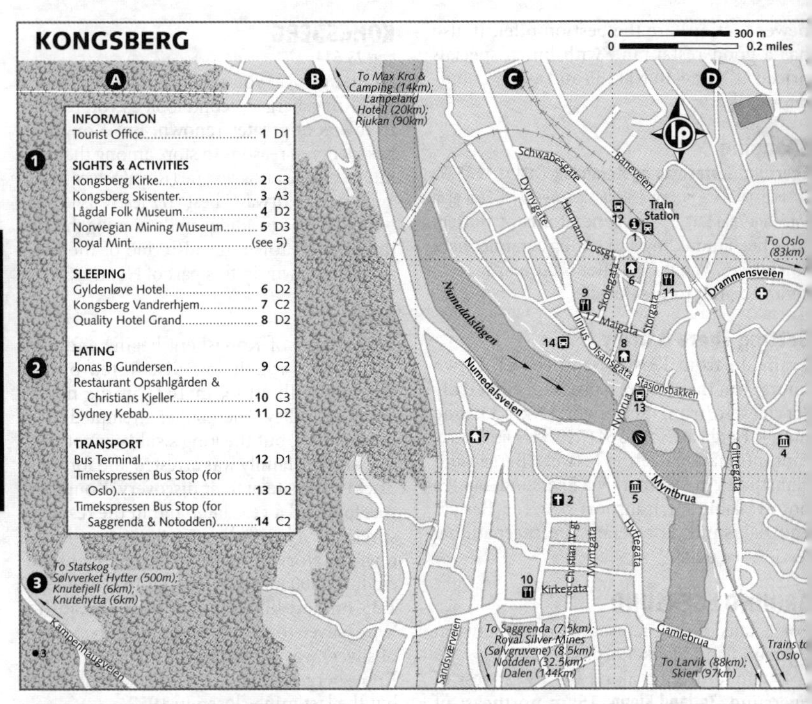

NORWEGIAN MINING MUSEUM

This worthwhile **mining museum** (Norsk Bergverksmuseum; ☎ 32 72 32 00; www.bvm.museum.no; Hyttegata 3; adult/child Nkr50/10; 10am-5pm mid-May–Aug, noon-4pm Sep–mid-May), in an 1844 smelter, tells the story of mining in Kongsberg with relics, models and mineral displays; the old smelting furnaces still survive in the basement. In the same building, other sections include the **Royal Mint**, which was moved from Akershus Fortress in Oslo to the source of the silver in 1686, as well as a skiing museum and other local exhibitions.

LÅGDAL FOLK MUSEUM

This **folk museum** (Lågdalsmuseet; ☎ 32 73 34 68; www.laagdalsmuseet.no in Norwegian; Tillischbakken 8-10; adult/child Nkr40/10 mid-Jun–mid-Aug, admission free rest-of-year; 11am-5pm mid-Jun–mid-Aug, shorter hrs rest-of-year), a 10-minute walk southeast of the train station, houses a collection of 32 period farmhouses and miners' cottages, an indoor sampling of re-created 19th-century workshops and a local WWII resistance museum. In summer there are guided tours at 11am, 1.30pm and 3.30pm.

ROYAL SILVER MINES

The profusion of silver mines in Kongsberg's hinterland is known collectively as Sølvgruvene. The main shaft of the largest mine plunges all of 1070m into the mountain to a depth of 550m below sea level. The easiest way to visit the mine is the **mine tour** (adult/child Nkr130/60; hourly 11am-4pm Jul–mid-Aug, shorter hrs mid-May–Jun, Sep & Oct) that leaves from the signposted Kongsgruvene, 700m from Saggrenda (8km south of Kongsberg along the road to Notodden). It begins with a 2.3km **rail ride** along the *stoll,* a tunnel that was painstakingly chipped through the mountain in order to drain water from the mines. Constructed without machinery or dynamite – the rock was removed by heating it with fire, then throwing water on the rock to crack it – the tunnel moved forward at 7cm per day and took 73 years (1782 to 1855) to complete. Inside, visitors are guided around equipment used in the extraction of silver, including an ingenious creaking and grinding lift and work area on 65 wet and slippery ladders.

Bring warm clothing as the underground temperatures can be a chilly 6°C. The admis sion price includes a bus ride from outside Kongsberg's tourist office.

Other possibilities that require advance bookings and at least 10-15 people include **two-hour guided walks** (per person Nkr250) through the 5km-long Underberg mine and the **rope-and-torch tour** (☎ 32 72 32 00; cb@bvm.museum.no; Nkr800), which begins with a 1km walk through Crown Prince Fredrik's tunnel. You must then abseil by torchlight down 112m into the mine (after a 'crash' course in abseiling).

HIKING & SKIING

Kongsberg's best hiking and cross-country skiing is found in the green, forested Knutefjell, immediately west of the town. The Kongsberg tourist office sells the map *Kultur-og Turkart Knutefjell* (Nkr80), which details the hiking and skiing tracks.

Festivals

Kongsberg's four-day **Kongsberg Jazz Festival** (☎ 32 73 31 66; www.kongsberg-jazzfestival.no in Norwegian) is Norway's second largest (after Molde; see p268) in late June or early July. It has a reputation for avant-garde performers and in 2007 drew big international names like the Joshua Redman Trio, Dee Dee Bridgewater and Wilco. In the lead up to the festival, there's a small **festival shop** (Nymoens torg 2-4; variable hrs) in the town centre.

Sleeping

Max Kro & Camping (☎ 32 76 44 05; fax 32 76 44 72; Jondalen; tent/caravan sites Nkr130/150, 4-/6-bed cabins Nkr400/600) The nearest camp site to town is 14km northwest of town along the Rv37. To get there use the twice-daily Kongsberg–Rjukan bus (Nkr26, 15 minutes).

Kongsberg Vandrerhjem (☎ 32 73 20 24; www.kongsberg-vandrerhjem.no; Vinjesgata 1; dm/s/d incl breakfast from Nkr260/570/710; P) Kongsberg's youth hostel bridges the gap between budget and midrange with comfortable rooms in a quiet but accessible part of town.

Gyldenløve Hotel (☎ 32 86 58 00; www.gyldenlove.no; Hermann Fossgata 1; s/d mid-Jun–mid-Aug & Fri-Sun year-round Nkr825/975, Mon-Thu rest-of-year Nkr1275/1550;) One of Kongsberg's best hotels, the Gyldenløve has spacious rooms with some pleasing stylistic flourishes and polished floorboards.

Quality Hotel Grand (☎ 32 77 28 00; www.choice.no; Christian Augustsgata 2; s/d from Nkr920/1060;) Although a touch more expensive than the Gyldenløve Hotel, the Quality Hotel Grand, near the river, is a comfortable establishment.

Lampeland Hotell (☎ 32 76 20 46; www.lampeland.no in Norwegian; Rv40; s Nkr890-1020, d Nkr995-1130, with Fjord Pass Nkr585/740, internet per hr/12hrs Nkr30/120) This lovely hotel, 20km north of Kongsberg on the Geilo road, has plenty of charm (apart from its roadside locale) and is super value if you book through Fjord Pass. It's also one of the more environmentally friendly hotels in the area.

Eating

Sydney Kebab (☎ 32 76 88 58; Storgata 1; kebabs Nkr49-89, falafel Nkr49; until 4am Sat & Sun) If you're saving money on food, you can still eat a hearty meal at this pleasant little kebab shop.

Jonas B Gundersen (☎ 32 72 88 00; Nymoens torg 10; pasta Nkr69-159, pizza from Nkr169) At this good restaurant the menus look like vinyl records, there's an unmistakable New Orleans jazz feel and the food includes imaginative salads and mostly Italian dishes.

Restaurant Opsahlgården & Christians Kjeller (☎ 32 76 45 00; Kirkegata 10; starters Nkr79-115, mains Nkr179-229; restaurant 3-10pm Mon-Fri, café 3-10pm Mon-Fri & 2-10pm Sat) A few doors down from Kongsberg Kirke, this fine dining restaurant is complemented by a pleasant café where lighter meals are available at the outdoor tables in summer.

Getting There & Around

Hourly trains connect Kongsberg with Oslo (Nkr153, 1½ hours). **Nettbuss Telemark Timekspressen** (☎ 177) buses connect Kongsberg with Oslo (Nkr160, 1½ hours), Saggrenda (Nkr48, 10 minutes) and Notodden (Nkr82, 35 minutes) at least hourly throughout the day.

The tourist office hires out bicycles for a cost of Nkr250 for the first day, then Nkr150 per day.

THE TELEMARK CANAL

The 105km-long Telemark Canal system, a series of lakes and canals that connect Skien and Dalen (with a branch from Lunde to Notodden), lifts and lowers boats a total of 72m in 18 locks. The canal was built for the timber trade from 1887 to 1892 by up to 400 workers. For some useful tourist information, check out the website www.visittelemark.com.

A SLOW BOAT THROUGH TELEMARK

Every day from June to mid-August, the ferry M/S *Telemarken* travels along the canals of Telemark between Akkerhaugen, 24km south of Notodden, and Lunde (adult/child Nkr250/125, 3¾ hours). It leaves Akkerhaugen/Lunde around 10am/1.45pm. If you only want to sail one way from Lunde to Akkerhaugen, buses leave from Notodden for Lunde (Nkr103, one hour) late morning and from Akkerhaugen to Notodden at around 5pm (6pm on weekends).

Every day between late June and mid-August, the sightseeing boats M/S *Victoria* (built in 1882) and M/S *Henrik Ibsen* (built in 1907) make the leisurely 11-hour journey between Skien and Dalen (adult/child Nkr420/210). Round trips, including one way by boat and return by bus (three hours), cost a total of Nkr680/340. Return tickets for all boats are 50% cheaper. For most of June, there are four weekly departures while trips run weekly from mid- to late May and from mid-August to early September. Dogs receive a 50% discount.

For further information, contact **Telemarkreiser** (☎ 35 90 00 30; www.visittelemark.com).

A great way to see the canal is by canoe, kayak or bicycle, and the ferries will transport your own boat/bicycle for Nkr100/50 between Skien and Dalen.

Notodden

pop 12,221

Unless you're here for the hugely popular **Blues Festival** (☎ 35 02 76 50; www.bluesfest.no) in early August, drive straight past industrial Notodden and keep going until you reach the marvellous imposing Heddal Stave Church, about 5km west of town on the E134. Otherwise, the only reason to pause in town is the Notodden **tourist office** (☎ 35 01 50 00; www.notodden.kommune.no; Teatergate 3; 🕒 8am-3pm Mon-Fri).

SIGHTS

The fairytale **Heddal Stave Church** (☎ 35 02 00 93; www.heddal-stavkirke.no; Heddal; adult/child Nkr40/free, entry to grounds free; 🕒 9am-7pm mid-Jun–mid-Aug, shorter hrs rest-of-year) is the largest and one of the most beautiful of Norway's 28 remaining stave churches.

The church possibly dates from 1242, but parts of the chancel date from as early as 1147. It was heavily restored in the 1950s. As with all stave churches, it's constructed around Norwegian pine support pillars – in this case, 12 large ones and six smaller ones, all topped by fearsome visages – and has four carved entrance portals. Of special interest are the lovely 1668 'rose' paintings on the walls, a runic inscription in the outer passageway and the 'Bishop's chair', which was made of an old pillar in the 17th century. Its ornate carvings relate the pagan tale of the Viking Sigurd the Dragon-slayer, which has been reworked into a Christian parable involving Jesus Christ and the devil. The altarpiece originally dates from 1667 but was restored in 1908, and the exterior bell tower was added in 1850.

The displays downstairs in the adjacent building (where tickets are sold) describe the history of the church. For more information on stave church architecture, see the boxed text, p240.

From Notodden, bus 301 goes right by; otherwise take any bus heading for Seljord or Bondal.

The **Heddal Rural Museum** (Bygdetun; ☎ 35 02 08 40; www.museumaust.no; Heddal; adult/child Nkr20/free 🕒 11am-5pm mid-Jun–mid-Aug), 300m from the stave church, includes a collection of houses from rural Telemark.

SLEEPING

Notodden Camping (☎ 35 01 33 10; www.notodden camping.no; Reshjemveien; tent sites without/with car Nkr110/130, caravan sites Nkr150 plus per person Nkr50, cabins Nkr380-490) Notodden Camping is an acceptable site 3km west along the E134, then 200m south on Reshjemveien. You'll be lucky to find a square inch of space at festival time. Take a bus from the centre in the direction of Seljord.

Nordlandia Telemark Hotel (☎ 35 01 20 88; www.norlandia.no/telemark; Torvet 8; s Nkr735-1115, d Nkr1115-1270) If you must stay in Notodden, here you'll find a modern hotel room and a reasonable breakfast in a bland building in the town centre.

GETTING THERE & AWAY

Between the towns of Kongsberg and Notodden, Timekspressen buses run once or twice an hour (Nkr82, 35 minutes).

Skien

pop 50,696

Industrial Skien has little to detain you, unless you're setting off along the Telemark Canal (see the boxed text, opposite) or you're a fan of the great Norwegian playwright Henrik Ibsen.

The **tourist office** (☎ 35 90 55 20; www.grenland.no; Nedre Hjellegate 18; 8.30am-7pm Mon-Fri, 10am-4pm Sat, 11am-4pm Sun mid-Jun–mid-Aug, 8.30am-4pm Mon-Fri rest-of-year) is moderately useful, although it doesn't have much to work with here.

SIGHTS

Author, playwright and so-called 'Father of Modern Drama', Henrik Ibsen (see p50) was born in Skien on 20 March 1828. In 1835 the family fell on hard times and moved out to the farm Venstøp, 5km north of Skien, where they stayed for seven years. The 1815 farmhouse has now been converted into the excellent **Henrik Ibsenmuseet** (☎ 35 52 57 49; Venstøphøgda; adult/student/senior/child Nkr50/20/20/20; 10am-6pm mid-May–Aug). There are some terrific audio-visual displays in the former barn, while guides (some of whom are Ibsen actors) show you around the family home. Ask also about Ibsen theatre performances here or at the tourist office, or check out the programme at the **Theater Ibsen** (☎ 35 90 50 50; www.teateribsen.no; Hesselbergsgt 2), which is in the town centre, a block back from the harbour.

SLEEPING & EATING

Skien Vandrerhjem (☎ 35 50 48 70; skien.hostel@vandrerhjem.no; Moflatveien 65; dm/s/d Nkr175/425/600) This well-equipped hostel is open year-round and has tidy rooms. Breakfast costs Nkr50 extra.

Thon Hotel Høyers (☎ 35 90 58 00; www.thonhotels.no; Kongensgate 6; s/d from Nkr890/1090) Right next to the harbour, this family-run place is an excellent choice with spacious, light and airy rooms.

Clarion Hotel Bryggeparken (☎ 35 91 21 00; bryggeparken@comfort.choicehotels.no; Langbryggene 7; s/d

THE HEROES OF TELEMARK

In 1933 in the USA it was discovered that 0.02% of all water molecules are 'heavy', meaning that the hydrogen atoms are actually deuterium, an isotope that contains an extra neutron. Heavy water weighs 10% more than normal water, boils at 1.4°C higher and freezes at 4°C higher than ordinary water. Why does that matter? Because such properties are sufficient to stabilise nuclear fission reactions, making heavy water invaluable in the production of an atom bomb.

During WWII in Norway the occupying Germans began building a heavy-water production plant at Vemork, near Rjukan. In response, Allied insurgents mounted Operation Grouse in October 1942 when four Norwegians parachuted into Sognadal, west of Rjukan. They were to be joined a month later by 34 specially trained British saboteurs who would arrive in two gliders at Skoland near Lake Møsvatnet, but one tow plane and its glider crashed into a mountain, and the other glider crashed on landing. All the British survivors were shot by the Germans.

Undeterred, the Norwegian group changed its mission name to Swallow and retreated to Hardangervidda, where they subsisted through the worst of the winter. On 16 February 1943 a new British-trained group called Gunnerside landed on Hardangervidda. Unfortunately a blizzard was raging and they wound up a long 30km march from their intended drop site. By the evening of 27 February the saboteurs were holed up at Fjøsbudalen, north of Vemork, waiting to strike. After descending the steep mountainside along the now-famous Sabotørruta (Saboteurs' Route), they crossed the gorge to the heavy-water plant, wire-clipped the perimeter fence and planted the explosives, which largely destroyed the facility. Some of the saboteurs retreated on skis to Hardangervidda then fled into neutral Sweden, while the rest remained on the plateau, successfully avoiding capture.

The plant was rebuilt by the Germans, but on 16 November 1943, 140 US planes bombed Vemork, killing 20 Norwegians in the process. The Germans abandoned any hopes of producing heavy water in Norway and decided to shift their remaining stocks to Germany. On 19 February 1944, the night before the ferry carrying the supplies was due to sail ferry across the lake Tinnsjø, the saboteurs placed a timed charge on the boat. The following night, the entire project was literally blown out of the water.

In 1965 this intriguing story was made into the dramatic (albeit historically inaccurate) film *The Heroes of Telemark,* starring Kirk Douglas.

Nkr1445/1645) Also right on the water, this modern place may lack the personal touch, but the rooms are modern and very comfortable, if ridiculously overpriced. It also has a decent restaurant and waterfront café.

GETTING THERE & AWAY

Nor-Way Bussekspress buses run to Notodden (Nkr137, 1¾ hours) and Rjukan (Nkr245, 3¼ hours) once or twice daily. NSB trains run every hour or two to Larvik and Oslo (Nkr275, 1¾ hours).

Dalen

pop 828

Settled by a lake and surrounded by steep forested hills, pretty little Dalen is a jumping-off point for ferries along the Øst Telemark Canal system. The **tourist office** (☎ 35 07 70 65; www.visitdalen.com; 9am-7pm Mon-Fri & 10am-5pm Sat & Sun mid-Jun–Aug, 9am-3.30pm Mon-Fri rest-of-year) is in the village centre.

High above town on the Rv45 to Høydalsmo is the quaint, 14th-century **Eidsborg Stave Church** (guided tours Nkr40) dedicated to St Nicolas and with a single nave. The grounds are open year-round.

SLEEPING & EATING

Buøy Camping (☎ 35 07 75 87; www.dalencamping.com; tent sites Nkr125-205, campervan Nkr145-215, 4-bed cabin from Nkr465) This is a reasonable camp site with cabins.

Dalen Hotel (☎ 35 07 90 00; www.dalenhotel.no; s/d late May-early Oct Nkr1095/1750, rest-of-year Nkr895/1500, mains Nkr85-235) The ornate Dalen Hotel, with its faint resonance of a stave church, first opened in 1894 and lies 1km from Dalen Brygge. Although looted by the Nazis in WWII, it remains a comfortable place to soak up an old-world atmosphere, although more so in the public areas than the rooms. Room 17 is said to be haunted.

RJUKAN

pop 6120

Strung out for 6km along the valley floor of the steep-sided Vestfjorddalen and in the shadow of what is arguably Norway's most beautiful peak, Gausta (1881m), Rjukan is a picturesque introduction to the Norwegian high country if you're coming up from the south. Apart from the scenery, Rjukan is also an activities centre with winter skiing, summer hiking and bungee jumping all possible.

History

This hydroelectric company town was founded in 1907 and, then years later, the industry supported 10,000 residents. In the early days, the administrators' homes occupied the highest slopes, where the sun shone the longest; below them were the homes of office workers and in the valley's dark depths dwelt the labourers. The builders of the Måna Kraftverk hydroelectric plant on the eastern limits of town clearly had an eye for records: its daunting wooden stairway consists of 3975 steps (it's the world's longest and is open to very fit visitors).

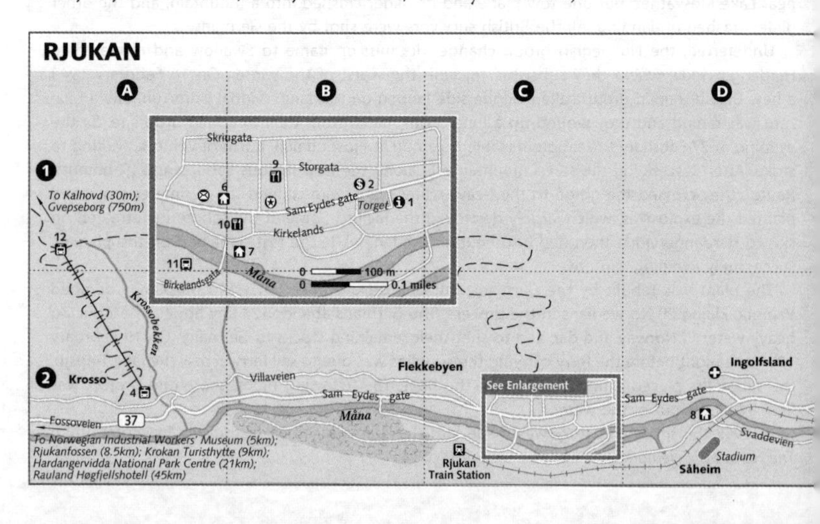

Information

The **tourist office** (☎ 35 08 05 50; www.visitrjukan.com; Torget 2; 9am-7pm Mon-Fri, 10am-6pm Sat & Sun late Jun-late Aug, 9am-3.30pm Mon-Fri rest-of-year) is the best of its kind in Telemark with loads of information and knowledgeable staff. Ask if the Hardangervidda National Park Centre, 21km west of Rjukan, has reopened as it was due to in 2008.

Sights

NORWEGIAN INDUSTRIAL WORKERS' MUSEUM

This **museum** (Norsk Industriarbeidermuseet; ☎ 35 09 90 00; www.visitvemork.com in Norwegian; adult/child Nkr65/35; 10am-6pm mid-Jun–mid-Aug, shorter hrs rest-of-year), 7km west of Rjukan, is in the Vemork power station, which was the world's largest when completed in 1911. These days it honours the Socialist Workers' Party, which reached its height of Norwegian activities in the 1950s. You won't want to miss the 30-minute film *If Hitler Had the Bomb,* describing the epic events of war-time Telemark (see the boxed text, p153), nor the miniature power station in the main hall. There's also an interesting exhibition about the worldwide race in the 1930s and '40s to make an atom bomb. It consists of short films, touch screen exhibits, photos and dioramas.

Disabled travellers and seniors over 65 are permitted to drive up to the entrance; everyone else must park at the swinging bridge. In summer, a **bus** (adult/child Nkr20/10; 10am to 4pm mid-June to mid-August) runs up from the car park to the entrance. Otherwise, it's a 15-minute, 700m climb on foot.

KROSSOBANEN

The **Krossobanen Cable Car** (☎ 35 09 00 27; adult one way/return Nkr40/80, child Nkr15/30, bike Nkr30/60; 10am-8pm mid-Jun–Aug, 10am-6pm Sat Sep, 10am-4pm Oct–mid-Jun) was constructed in 1928 by Norsk Hydro to provide its employees with access to the sun. Long since renovated, it whisks tourists up to Gvepseborg (886m) for a view over the deep, dark recesses. The best panoramas are from the viewing platform atop the cable-car station. It also operates as the trailhead for a host of hiking and cycling trails; see the boxed text (p157) or ask at the tourist office for details.

GAUSTABANEN

One of Norway's most extraordinary cable railways, **Gaustabanen** (☎ 35 08 05 50 or 90 08 82 49; adult one way/return Nkr200/350, child Nkr100/150; 10am-4pm late Jun–mid-Aug, 10am-4pm Sat or Sun mid-Aug–late Oct) runs 860m deep into the core of Gausta before a different train climbs an incredible 1040m, alongside 3500 steps at a 40-degree angle, to 1800m, just below the Gaustahytte, not far from the summit. Built by NATO in 1958 at a cost of US$1 million to ensure it could access its radio tower in any weather, it was recently opened to tourists. Taking the railway is an incredible experience, although not for the claustrophobic. The railway's base station is 10km southeast of Rjukan.

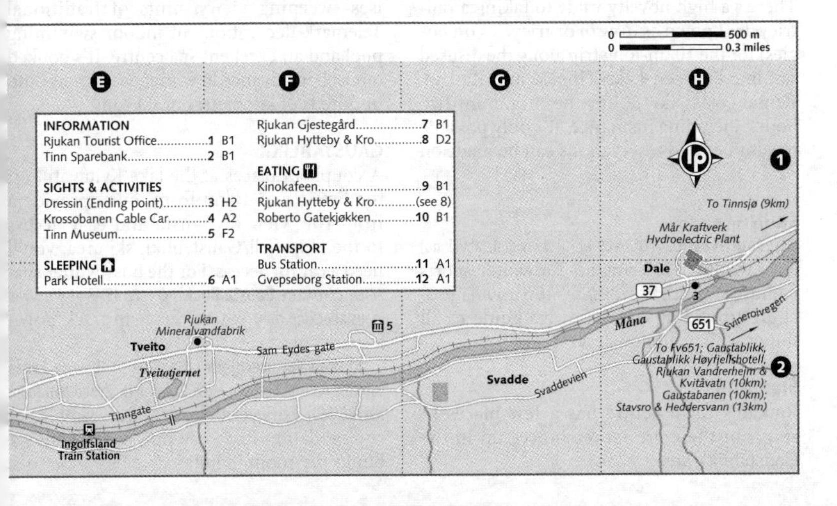

TINN MUSEUM

This quiet little **folk museum** (☎ 35 09 22 33; Sam Eydesgt 299; adult/child Nkr40/20, combined ticket with Norwegian Industrial Workers Museum Nkr85/40; ⏲ noon-6pm mid-Jun–mid-Aug, noon-3pm Mon-Fri May–mid-Jun & mid–end-Aug), at the eastern end of town, traces rural Norwegian architecture from the 11th century to the early 1900s. Highlights include doorways of stave churches and old textiles.

RJUKANFOSSEN

Believed to be the highest **waterfall** in the world in the 18th century (Angel Falls in Venezuala now has that claim), the 104m-high Rjukanfossen is still a spectacular sight, even if most of the water has been diverted to drive the Vemork power station. To get the best view, take the Rv37 heading west and park just before the tunnel 9.5km west of town; a 200m walk leads to a fine viewpoint.

Activities

For more on hiking and cycling, see p157.

BUNGEE JUMPING

Described as Norway's highest land-based **bungee jump** (Nkr490; ⏲ 11am-1pm Sat & Sun, 5-6pm Tue & Thu Jul-Sep, 11am-1pm Sat mid-May–Jun), this 84m leap into the canyon from the bridge leading to the Norwegian Industrial Workers' Museum is Rjukan's highest adrenaline rush. Book through the tourist office.

RAIL-BIKING

There's a high novelty value to taking a rail-tricycle (known as *dressin* or tricycles on bogies) for the 10km-long trip along the disused rail line between Lake Tinnsjø and Rjukan. Rental costs Nkr130 for the minimum two hours, including insurance. It's only possible in summer and reservations can be made on ☎ 45 48 38 99.

SKIING

The **tourist office** (☎ 35 09 14 22; www.gaustablikk.no) has a wealth of information for winter-sports enthusiasts, with its *Gaustablikk Skisenter* brochure providing the definitive guide to all things white and powdery.

Sleeping

Rjukan's town centre has a few places to stay, but there are more choices up in the Gaustablikk area.

RJUKAN & WEST

Rjukan Gjestegård (☎ 35 08 06 50; www.rgg.no in Norwegian; Birkelandsgata 2; dm Nkr195, s/d with shared bathroom Nkr305/485) This central guesthouse occupies the buildings of the old youth hostel. The rooms here are simple but fine enough, there's a guest kitchen and the location is good if you want to be in town. Breakfast costs Nkr60.

Rjukan Hytteby & Kro (☎ 35 09 01 22; www.rjukan-hytteby.no; Brogata 9; 2-/4-/6-bed cabins Nkr690/890/990, motel s/d Nkr690/790) Probably the best choice in town, Rjukan Hytteby & Kro sits in a pretty spot on the river bank and has simple, tidy huts that seek to emulate the early-20th-century hydroelectric workers' cabins. The motel rooms have less character but are fine.

Park Hotell (☎ 35 08 21 88; www.parkhotell-rjukan.no in Norwegian; Sam Eydes gate 67; s Nkr645-790, d Nkr845-940, junior ste Nkr995-1095) Obviously once a moderately grand old hotel, the Park Hotell desperately needs an overhaul. The tired rooms are a tad musty. On the plus side, you are in the town centre.

Krokan Turisthytte (☎ 35 09 51 31; fax 35 09 01 90; near Rv37; 4-bed cabins Nkr400-600) Around 10km west of Rjukan, this historic place was built in 1869 as DNT's first hut. You're housed in museum-like 16th-century log cabins and it serves traditional meals. Ring ahead as there's not always someone here.

Rauland Høgfjellshotell (☎ 35 06 31 00; www.rauland.no in Norwegian; Rv37; s Nkr750-1140, d Nkr1380-1780; ⏲ Jun-Apr;) Around 45km west of Rjukan, this excellent mountain hotel promises sweeping views, hints of traditional Telemark decoration, an indoor swimming pool and an excellent spa centre. It's booked out well in advance in winter as it opens onto hundreds of kilometres of ski runs.

GAUSTABLIKK

A couple of places at the lake Kvitåvatn, off the Fv651 and 10km from town, provide a front-row view of Gausta and easy access to the Skipsfjell/Gaustablikk ski area; you'll need a car for access. For the busy winter season, contact **Gausta Booking** (☎ 45 48 51 51; www.gaustabooking.com) which can help track down a spare hut.

Rjukan Vandrerhjem (☎ 35 09 20 40; www.kvitaavatn.dk; Gaustablikk; dm Nkr260, s/d with shared bathroom Nkr380/560) This youth hostel offers simple accommodation in a cosy pine lodge with six bunks per room in huts.

HIKING & CYCLING FROM RJUKAN

To get an idea of what's possible, visit the tourist office to pick up the free *Rjukan – Cycling & Hiking Guide,* which has 23 route suggestions.

Gausta

From the summit of beautiful Gausta (1881m) you can see a remarkable one-sixth of Norway on a clear day. The popular two- to three-hour, 4km hiking track leads from the trailhead of Stavsro (15km southeast of Rjukan) up to DNT's **Gaustahytta** (1830m), next to the rather ugly NATO radio tower. The summit is reached by walking along the rocky ridge for a further half-hour. A 13km road link, but unfortunately no public transport, runs from the far eastern end of Rjukan to Stavsro (altitude 1173m) at lake Heddersvann. **Taxis** (☎ 35 09 14 00) charge around Nkr300 one-way. Allow all day for the hike, which leaves plenty of time for exploring the summit. The tourist office distributes a map of the Fv651, but the *Turkart Gausta Området* is a better option and is available for Nkr50.

More difficult, three- to four-hour routes to the summit also run from Rjukan itself and from the Norwegian Industrial Workers' Museum (p155).

If you can't make the hike, the summer Gaustabanen service (p155) takes you almost to Gaustahytta.

Hardangervidda

From Gvepseborg, the summit of the Krossobanen cable car, good walking or cycling tracks strike out onto the Hardangervidda plateau (p188), home to Europe's largest herd of wild reindeer. The main, eight-hour route, which can also be used by cyclists, leads north nine hours to **Kalhovd Turisthytte** (☎ 35 09 05 10), where you can either catch a bus or hike nine hours down to **Mogen Turisthytte** (☎ 35 07 41 15), where you can catch the Møsvatn ferry (Nkr190) back to Skinnarbu, west of Rjukan on Rv37; ferry timetables are available from the Rjukan tourist office. For those seeking greater guidance, the tourist office organises guided expeditions for hikers and cyclists (adults Nkr700 to Nkr1300, children Nkr400 to Nkr700). Serious hikers can also strike out north from Kalhovd, deep into the high Hardangervidda.

Alternatively you can follow the marked route which begins above Rjukan Fjellstue, around 10km west of Rjukan and just north of the Rv37. This historic track follows the Sabotørruta (Saboteurs' Route), the path taken by the members of the Norwegian Resistance during WWII (see the boxed text, p153). From late June until mid-August, the tourist office can also arrange guided hikes along this route.

The best map to use for any of these hikes is Statens Kartverk's *Hardangervidda Øst,* at a scale of 1:100,000 and available from the tourist office (Nkr125).

our pick Gaustablikk Høyfjellshotell (☎ 35 09 14 22; www.gaustablikk.no; s/d from Nkr840/950, half-board from Nkr940/1480) With a prime location overlooking the lake and mountain, this expansive mountain lodge is one of Norway's better mountain hotels. The rooms are quite modern and many have lovely views of Gausta, while the evening buffet dinner is a lavish affair. Geared towards a winter skiing crowd (prices rise considerably in winter when advance reservations are necessary), it's also a great place in summer. Half-board rates (highly recommended) are only available for stays of two nights or more; otherwise book through Fjord Pass for a cheaper one-night rate.

Eating

Kinokafeen (☎ 40 85 60 48; Storstulgate 1; lunch specials Nkr89-120, dinner mains Nkr159-279; lunch & dinner) Kinokafeen, at the cinema, has a pleasant ambience. The lunch dishes (pasta and steaks) are the best value.

Roberto Gatekjokken (off Sam Eydes; snacks from Nkr35; lunch & dinner) A cut above most Norwegian roadside kiosks, this well-run little place offers fish and chips (Nkr45), hamburgers (Nkr41 to Nkr116), steak sandwiches (Nkr47) and taco wraps (Nkr35). Eat at the shady adjacent tables.

Rjukan Hytteby & Kro (☎ 35 09 01 22; Brogata 9; pizzas from Nkr130, mains Nkr59-159) Offering simple but hearty cafeteria-style food, this place along the river does everything from pizzas to baked potatoes.

Gaustablikk Høyfjellshotell (☎ 35 09 14 22; lunch specials from Nkr69, dinner buffet Nkr335; lunch & dinner) Even if you're not staying here, this mountain hotel's enormous buffet is worth the trip up the mountain.

Getting There & Around

A daily express bus connects Rjukan to Oslo (Nkr280, three hours) via Kongsberg (Nkr177, two hours). More regular buses head to Notodden from where there are better connections.

Rjukan's linear distances will seem intimidating, but the local Bybuss runs from Vemork to the eastern end of the valley. Bike hire at the tourist office costs Nkr50/200 per hour/day.

SELJORD

pop 2933

Lakeside Seljord is known mainly as the home of Selma the Serpent, the Nessie-type monster that inhabits the depths of the lake Seljordvatn (see the boxed text, below). Other creatures of legend call the nearby hills home and hikers can also seek out the feuding troll women, Ljose-Signe, Glima and Tårån; personally we haven't seen them but locals assured us that they're there. Seljord was also the inspiration for some of Norway's best-known folk legends, including Asbjørnsen and Moe's *The Three Billy Goats Gruff*, known the world over.

The **tourist office** (☎ 35 06 59 88; www.seljordportalen.no; 8am-6pm Mon-Fri, 9am-3pm Sat mid-Jun–mid-Aug, 8am-8.30pm Mon-Fri rest-of-year) has lots of local information and revels in good troll stories.

Sights

The charming Romanesque stone **church** (admission free; 11am-5pm mid-Jun–mid-Aug) was built in the 12th century in honour of St Olav; it's at the northern end of town. In the grounds, between the church and the churchyard wall, are two impressions reputedly made by two mountain trolls who were so upset by the encroachment of Christianity that they pummelled the site with boulders.

Festivals & Events

On the second weekend of September, Seljord holds the **Dyrsku'n Festival**, which started in 1866 and is now Norway's largest traditional market and cattle show, attracting 60,000 visitors.

Sleeping & Eating

Seljord Camping og Badeplass (☎ 35 05 04 71; www.seljordcamping.no; tent sites Nkr150, cabins Nkr400-1200) This pleasant camp site beside the lake is the

SELMA THE SERPENT

The first evidence of Selma the Serpent's existence dates back to 1750, when Gunleik Andersson-Verpe of nearby Bø was 'attacked by a sea horse' while rowing across the lake. Nearly every summer since (Selma, like Norwegians, comes out of her shell in summer), witnesses have sighted the fins and humps of this fast-moving lake creature, which reportedly measures the size of a large log, or slightly bigger. Some have described it as eel-like, while others have likened it to a snail, a lizard or a crocodile and have reported lengths of 25m, 30m and even 50m. Amateur videos filmed in 1988 and 1993 reveal a series of humps in the water, but their grainy nature renders the evidence deliciously inconclusive. Researchers have suggested that the lake is too small to support creatures more than about 7m long.

As with Scotland's famous Nessie, Selma has fuelled local folklore and drawn tourists to search the surface of the deep, pine-rimmed lake Seljordvatn (14km long, 2km wide and 157m deep) for evidence. In 1977 and again in 1988, Swedish freelance journalist Jan-Ove Sundberg scanned the lake with sonar equipment, underwater cameras and even a mini-submarine and detected several large objects moving in unison, then separating in several directions. According to Sundberg, 'The serpent does not fit any species known to humanity. It has several qualities not seen before, such as travelling on the surface at high speed and moving vertically up and down. It shows a back or a head or a neck or all three for long periods above the surface and travels very fast, maybe up to 25 knots.'

When we asked one local whether he believed in Selma's existence, he replied, 'I have never seen her, but I believe she exists and my children won't swim in the lake.' We didn't see her either, but...

dock for monster boats on Seljordvatn (fares vary with the number of passengers) and it has a telescope to help you spot Selma.

Seljord Hotel (☎ 35 06 40 00; www.seljordhotel.no in Norwegian; s/d Nkr900/1100, starters Nkr90-105, mains Nkr225-275) This lovely old wooden hotel dates back to 1858 and is one of the nicest hotels in this part of Norway. Rooms have period touches and are individually named, each with its own story. It gets points also for having the same rates all year, which is very unusual in Norway. The restaurant is Seljord's best, with gourmet local cuisines – there are five meat or fish mains to choose from and each is a work of art. It also does cheaper lunch dishes.

Sjøormkroa (☎ 35 05 05 02; mains Nkr89-149) You'll get a standard cafeteria meals (hamburgers, Wiener schnitzels and the like) in this odd serpent-shaped building, on the E134 next to the lake.

Getting There & Away

Nor-Way Bussekspress (Haukeliekspressen) buses connect Seljord with Notodden (Nkr132, 1¼ hours) and Oslo (Nkr296, 3¼ hours) up to four times daily.

SETESDALEN

The forested hillsides and lake-filled mountain valleys of Setesdalen, one of Norway's most traditional and conservative regions, remain little frequented by travellers, although they are becoming increasingly popular with outdoor enthusiasts.

Evje

pop 3315

The riverside town of Evje, surrounded by forests and rolling hills, serves as the southern gateway to Setesdalen. It's famous among geologists for the variety of rocks found here – a mineral park, nickel mine and the chance to prospect for your own rocks are among Evje's primary attractions. Quiet little Evje is also a first-class base for white-water rafting and other outdoor activities.

The **information centre** (☎ 37 93 14 00; www.setesdal.com; 10am-6pm Mon-Fri, 10am-3pm Sat & Sun mid-Jun–mid-Aug, 10am-noon Mon-Fri rest-of-year) occupies the same old log building as the bus terminal. Ask also about permits for mineral prospecting.

SIGHTS

Budding geologists will find plenty to get excited about in Evje. First stop should be the small **Evje Og Hornnes Museum** (☎ 37 93 07 94; adult/child/student/family Nkr20/free/15/40; 11am-4pm mid-Jun–late Aug), 2km west of town and across the river in Fennefoss. Displays include more than a hundred different types of mineral found in the nearby hills, as well as exhibits on local nickel mining and rural life in Setesdalen.

For displays of local and worldwide minerals, the well-run **Setesdal Mineral Park** (☎ 37 93 13 10; www.mineralparken.no; Hornnes; adult/child Nkr85/50; 10am-4pm mid-May–Oct) is every rock collector's dream come true, with a wonderful world of colour and quartz, with many items for sale. It's about 10km south of Evje.

A summer visit to **Flåt Nikkelgruve** (Flåt Nickel Mine; ☎ 37 93 03 71; www.flaatgruve.com; adult/child/family Nkr80/50/210; guided tours 1pm Jul-early Aug), once Europe's largest nickel mine with a shaft 440m deep, takes you deep into the earth on a fascinating underground tour that's not for the claustrophobic. Temperatures down there drop to 5°C so wear warm clothes. It's 3.3km off the Rv9; the turn-off is around 2km north of Evje.

SOUTHERN NORWAY

ENERGETIC IN EVJE

TrollActiv (☎ 37 93 11 77; www.troll-mountain.no; 9am-8pm Apr-Oct), around 6km north of Evje, is the centre of most of Evje's high-energy thrills. White-water rafting (per person Nkr400) is its forte, but it also organises riverboarding (Nkr400), rock-climbing courses (Nkr750), river kayaking (Nkr750), paintball (Nkr550), waterskiing (Nkr350) and more sedate pastimes that include fishing safaris (Nkr250) and nightly beaver and elk safaris (adult/child/family Nkr260/210/820). There's also a climbing wall (per hour Nkr200), family rafting trips (per person Nkr350) and kids' activities packages that include climbing, archery and canoeing (Nkr250). As if that weren't enough, it also rents out canoes (Nkr300), inline skates (Nkr150) and mountain bikes (Nkr300).

Viking Adventures Norway (☎ 37 71 00 95; www.raftingsenter.no), in town, offers most of the same activities for similar prices.

Reached via the same road as the nickel mine, **Evje Mineralsti** covers five small mines for those who aren't satisfied by rocks found by other people. Digging for your own requires a **permit** (adult/child/family Nkr40/70/140), which is available at the site or, sometimes, from the information centre in town.

SLEEPING & EATING

Odden Camping (☎ 37 93 06 03; www.oddencamping.setesdal.com; tent sites without/with car Nkr70/110 plus per adult/child Nkr10/5, caravan sites Nkr120, 2-8-bed huts Nkr300-1000) This large, recommended camp site is extremely well run and can be found in a postcard setting by the water just 200m south of town. It can get crowded in summer.

Neset Camping (☎ 37 93 42 55; www.neset.no in Norwegian; tent sites from Nkr150 plus per person Nkr10, 4-8 bed cabins Nkr400-800) Also in a picturesque lakeside spot, Neset Camping is 13km north of Evje.

TrollActiv (Evje Vandrerhjem; ☎ 37 93 11 77; www.troll-mountain.no; tent sites/tepees per person Nkr60/90, caravan sites Nkr120, dm/d Nkr150/410; 💻) This energetic activities centre (p159) doubles as Evje's youth hostel, 6km north of town. It's modern and well run and the place to be if you're planning any one of the many activities on offer.

Hotel Dölen (☎ 37 93 02 00; www.hoteldolen.no; Evje; s/d from Nkr695/995, mains Nkr129-235; 💻) Last time we were here, we just couldn't bring ourselves to include this place, Setesdalen's oldest hotel, because the rooms were so run-down. Thankfully, Monika and the wonderfully named Roar took over and are slowly overhauling the hotel. The newly renovated rooms have an old-world charm, while those yet to be renovated are all about tired 1970s décor; there's free wireless throughout. The restaurant is possibly Evje's best, with dishes such as Arctic trout (Nkr147), reindeer heart (Nkr85) and 'reindeer à la Rudolph' (Nkr155); it also has a popular Sunday buffet (Nkr175) in summer. The lakeside terrace is lovely, while Roar, a former country musician, sings in the bar on some weekend nights.

Revsnes Hotell (☎ 37 93 46 50; www.revsneshotell.no; Byglandsfjord; s/d from Nkr795/995, 3-course dinner Nkr225; 💻) Still Evje's best hotel, the Revsnes is 12km north of town by the lovely lake Byglandsfjorden. The rooms are large and modern, and most have wonderful big windows overlooking the water. It's also a family-run place and you'll be made to feel welcome.

Pernille Cafeteria (☎ 37 93 00 69; mains Nkr99-139; 🕒 8am-6pm Mon-Fri, 8am-4.30pm Sat, 10am-7pm Sun) Right in the heart of Evje, this upstairs place is popular with locals although the menu is not Norway's most inspirational. Expect burgers and Bolognese alongside a few Norwegian dishes.

Dragon Inn (☎ 37 93 09 19; starters from Nkr45, mains Nkr105-159; 🕒 3-9pm Tue-Thu, 3-10pm Fri & Sat, 1-9pm Sun) Just south of the centre, the Dragon Inn serves reasonable Chinese specialities.

GETTING THERE & AWAY

Nor-Way Bussekspress buses that travel between Kristiansand (Nkr110, one hour) and Haukeligrend (Nkr263, three hours) run via Evje at least once daily. If you're continuing on to Bergen, change at Haukeligrend. Heading north from Evje, car drivers will be stung with a Nkr30 toll that pisses us off every time we pass.

Setesdalsmuseet

This fine collection of folk **museums** (☎ 37 93 63 03; adult/child/family Nkr30/free/60; 🕒 11am-5pm mid-end Jun & Aug, 10am-6pm Jul) along Rv9 is a good way to break up your journey through Setesdalen.

Coming from the south, Rysstad's main **Setesdalsmuseet** is a fine, refurbished exhibition space displaying period interiors and cultural artefacts. Around 10km further north is **Tveitetunet** (Valle), a log farm with a storehouse dating from 1645. Best of all is **Rygnestadtunet**, 9km north of Valle, where the farm has a unique three-storey storehouse (from 1590) and an extraordinary collection of 15th-century painted textiles. Local legend has its owner as Evil Åsmund, who served as a mercenary around Europe and brought back looted weapons and artwork from his travels. Staff may be dressed in traditional costume.

Bykle

pop 902

The distinctive log-built **Bykle Kirkje** (☎ 37 93 81 01; admission Nkr20; 🕒 11am-5pm mid-Jun–mid-Aug) is one of the smallest churches in Norway and all the more delightful because of it, with painted stalls, altar and organ. The building and altar date from 1619; roses on the front of the galleries and traditional rose paintings on the wall were added in the 1820s, although some of the paintings date back to the 15th century.

There's also a lovely signpost-guided **walk** above the Otra River, 5km south of town. The route, which takes about 30 minutes, dates from at least 1770 and was once the main route through Setesdalen.

Hovden

pop 450

Watching over the northern end of Setesdalen, Hovden is a winter ski resort, although there are some activities during summer. The **Hovdenferie** (☎ 37 93 93 70; www.hovden.com; ⌚ 9am-5pm Mon-Fri, 10am-2pm Sat, noon-4pm Sun) provides a full run-down on what's possible, including **rafting** (from Nkr375), **canyon walks** (Nkr450), **elk safaris** (adult/child Nkr300/200) and **helicopter rides** (from Nkr450).

In summer, for fine views you can reach the summit of **Mt Nos** (1176m) by taking the **chairlift** (adult/child Nkr80/60; ⌚ 10.30am-2pm Jul, 10.30am-2pm Wed & Sat Aug, 10.30am-2pm Sat Sep).

Hovdenferie's **Sentralbooking** (☎ 37 93 93 75; post@hovden.com) service can connect you with the dozens of nearby ski huts, flats, chalets and hotels that offer good-value deals. **Hovden Fjellstoge & Vandrerhjem** (☎ 37 93 95 43; www.hovdenfjellstoge.no in Norwegian; dm/s/d incl breakfast Nkr250/450/590, meals around Nkr100) is housed in a traditional-style wooden building with a grass roof, while **Quality Hovden Høyfjellshotell** (☎ 37 93 88 00; www.hovdenhotell.no, in Norwegian; s/d from Nkr850/1050), at the top end of the town, is Hovden's finest.

In addition to the hotels, you'll find a range of meal options at the **Furumo Kafé** (☎ 37 93 97 72).

The daily Nor-Way Bussekspress bus between Kristiansand (Nkr332, 3¾ hours) and Haukeligrend passes through Hovden; from the latter there are connections to Bergen.

SIRDAL

Sirdal is the access route to the scenic descent through 27 hairpin bends to Lysebotn (p231). From the well-appointed DNT hut at **Ådneram**, at the top of Sirdal, hikers can reach Lysebotn in nine hours (follow the road for the last 4km). The road is open only from mid-June to mid-September.

For tourist information and details of wilderness tours, horse riding and dog-sledging, contact **Sirdalsferie** (☎ 38 37 78 00; www.sirdalsferie.com; Tjørhom).

Sinnes Fjellstue (☎ 38 37 11 21; www.sinnes-fjellstue.no in Norwegian; Sinnes; s/d from Nkr575/775) is a tidy mountain lodge offering accommodation in summer time.

The Nor-Way Bussekspress Suleskarekspressen connects Stavanger (Nkr187, two hours) and Oslo (Nkr539, 7½ hours) via Fidjeland, 7km south of Ådneram, daily from June to September.

Central Norway

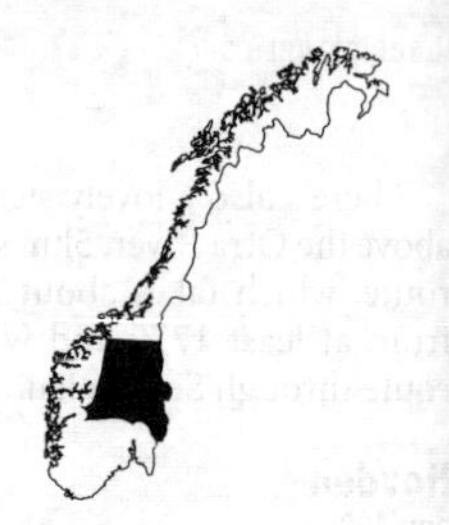

Most people come to Norway for the fjords, and go you should, but the high country of central Norway is an equally extraordinary place. It's home to what is easily the finest mountain scenery in northern Europe, unrivalled hiking, high-thrills white-water rafting and two of Norway's most appealing towns.

Røros could just be Norway's most charming village, a fact acknowledged by Unesco, which inscribed this centuries-old mining town of timber houses and turf-roofed cottages on its World Heritage list. Further south, Lillehammer may belong to a more modern era but after hosting the 1994 Winter Olympics it has drawn a steady stream of visitors hoping for some Olympic magic of their own in the Olympic museum, ski jump and the Olympic bobsled run; its pretty lakeside setting and Maihaugen, Norway's best folk museum, also have strong appeal.

If stave churches capture the fairy-tale magic of Norway for you, there are two fine examples at tranquil Ringebu and Lom; the latter is also a crossroads town for some of Norway's most scenic drives and rides, including the breathtaking Sognefjellet Road, which runs over the mountains and deep down into fjord country.

Connecting these sites are quiet back roads and challenging hiking trails that lead through some of Norway's most rewarding national parks – Rondane, Dovrefjell-Sunndalsfjella, Jotunheimen and the desolately beautiful Hardangervidda, which drops suddenly within sight of the fjords. Within the parks' boundaries you may find wild reindeer, musk ox and elk. Oppdal and, particularly, Sjoa are two important centres for white-water rafting.

HIGHLIGHTS

- Return to the past in the charming Unesco World Heritage–listed **Røros** (p171)
- Trek along the highest trails in Norway in the endlessly beautiful **Jotunheimen National Park** (p184) or drive or maybe cycle over **Sognefjellet Road** (p184)
- Wet your pants while white-water rafting in **Sjoa** (see the boxed text, p182)
- Climb the Olympic ski jump at **Lillehammer** (opposite)
- Search for the prehistoric musk ox in **Dovrefjell-Sunndalsfjella National Park** (see the boxed text, p176)
- Spot your first reindeer on **Hardangervidda** (p188)

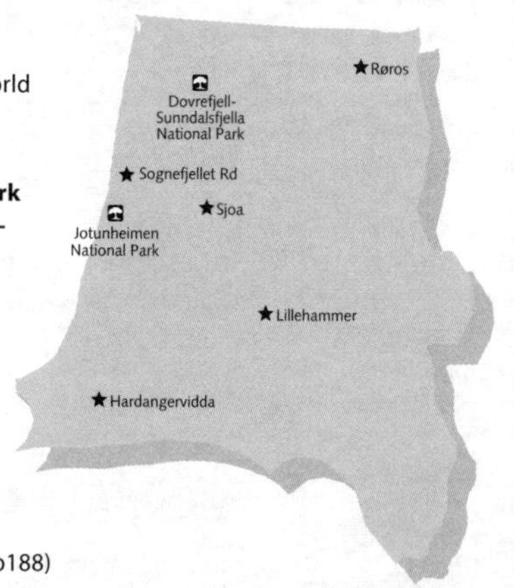

- POPULATION: 620,000
- HIGHEST ELEVATION: GALDHØPIGGEN 2469M

CENTRAL NORWAY

EASTERN CENTRAL NORWAY

LILLEHAMMER

pop 25,537

Long a popular Norwegian ski resort, Lillehammer became known to the world after hosting the 1994 Winter Olympics. These Olympics, overwhelmingly considered a great success, still provide the town with some of its most interesting sights. Lying at the northern end of the lake Mjøsa and surrounded by farms, forests and small settlements, it's a laid-back place with year-round attractions, although in winter it becomes a ski town *par excellence.*

The four-day **Lillehammer Jazz Festival** (☎ 81 53 31 33; www.dolajazz.no in Norwegian) is held in mid-September; tickets go on sale from 1 July each year. In March there's a popular women-only ski race; contact the tourist office for details of these and other events.

Orientation & Information

Central Lillehammer is small and easily negotiated. Most of the Olympic sites and the folk museum Maihaugen are a 30-minute walk uphill from the centre. The main (pedestrianised) street is Storgata, two blocks east of the Skysstasjon (the bus and train stations).

Bibliothek (Library; ☎ 61 24 71 40; Wiesegate 2; 11am-6pm Mon-Thu, 11am-3pm Fri & Sat) Free, but time-limited internet access.

Lillehammer og Omland DNT (☎ 61 25 13 06; www.turistforeningen.no/lillehammer; Storgata 34; 10am-3.30pm Tue-Thu) Hiking and skiing maps, mountain hut information and mountain hiking trips.

Lillehammer tourist office (☎ 61 28 98 00; www.lillehammerturist.com; Lillehammer Skysstasjon; 9am-8pm Mon-Sat, 11am-6pm Sun Jun-early Aug, shorter hrs rest-of-year) Offers 15-minutes of free internet.

Sights & Activities

OLYMPIC SITES

After Lillehammer won its bid for the 1994 Winter Olympics, the Norwegian government ploughed over two billion kroner into the town's infrastructure. Most amenities remain in use and visitors can tour the main Olympic sites over a large area called the **Olympiaparken** (☎ 61 25 11 40; www.olympiaparken.no; 9am-8pm Jun-Sep, shorter hrs Oct-May).

For the Olympic Bobsled Run, see p168, while the Olympic ski slopes are covered on p168.

Lygårdsbakkene Ski Jump

The main **ski jump** (K120) drops 136m with a landing-slope angle of 37.5°. The speed at takeoff is a brisk 91km/h with a record leap of 136.5m. During the Olympics, the site was surrounded by seating for 50,000 spectators and it was here that the opening ceremony was held; the tower for the **Olympic flame** stands near the foot of the jump. There's also a smaller jump (K90) alongside where you'll often see athletes honing their preparations.

The **ski jump chairlift** (adult/child return Nkr40/35; 9am-8pm 9 Jun-19 Aug, 9am-5pm 26 May-8 Jun & 20 Aug-9 Sep, 11am-4pm Sat & Sun 15-30 Sep) ascends to a stunning panoramic view over the town. Alternatively you can walk for free as long as the 952 steps don't prove too daunting. The chairlift price includes entry to the **Lysgårdsbakkene ski jump tower** (9am-8pm 9 Jun-19 Aug, 11am-4pm 11-25 May & 10-30 Sep, 9am-5pm 16 May-8 Jun & 20 Aug-9 Sep), which costs Nkr15/12 on its own for an adult/child. Here you can stand atop the ramp and imagine the experience with all the pre-jump nerves.

To experience the men's downhill race (and the Olympic bobsledding course) without putting your life at risk, try the nerve-jangling **simulator** (adult/child per 5 min Nkr45/35; same hrs as chairlift) at the bottom of the jump.

A combined ticket (adult/child Nkr65/50) is also available for the chairlift, tower and simulator.

To reach the summit by car, take the road that leads past the Olympic Museum north out of town. The turn-off (signed as 'Lysgårdsbakkene') comes after 2.8km.

LILLEHAMMER'S COMBINED TICKETS

If you plan to visit a number of sites while in Lillehammer, consider the **combined ticket** (adult/child/student & pensioner Nkr260/130/210), which includes entry to the Maihaugen Folk Museum, the Norwegian Olympic Museum, Bjerkebæk and Aulestad (p168). A ticket covering Maihaugen and Bjerkebæk costs Nkr150/75/120, while a combination of any other two generally costs Nkr130/55/105, slightly less from September to May.

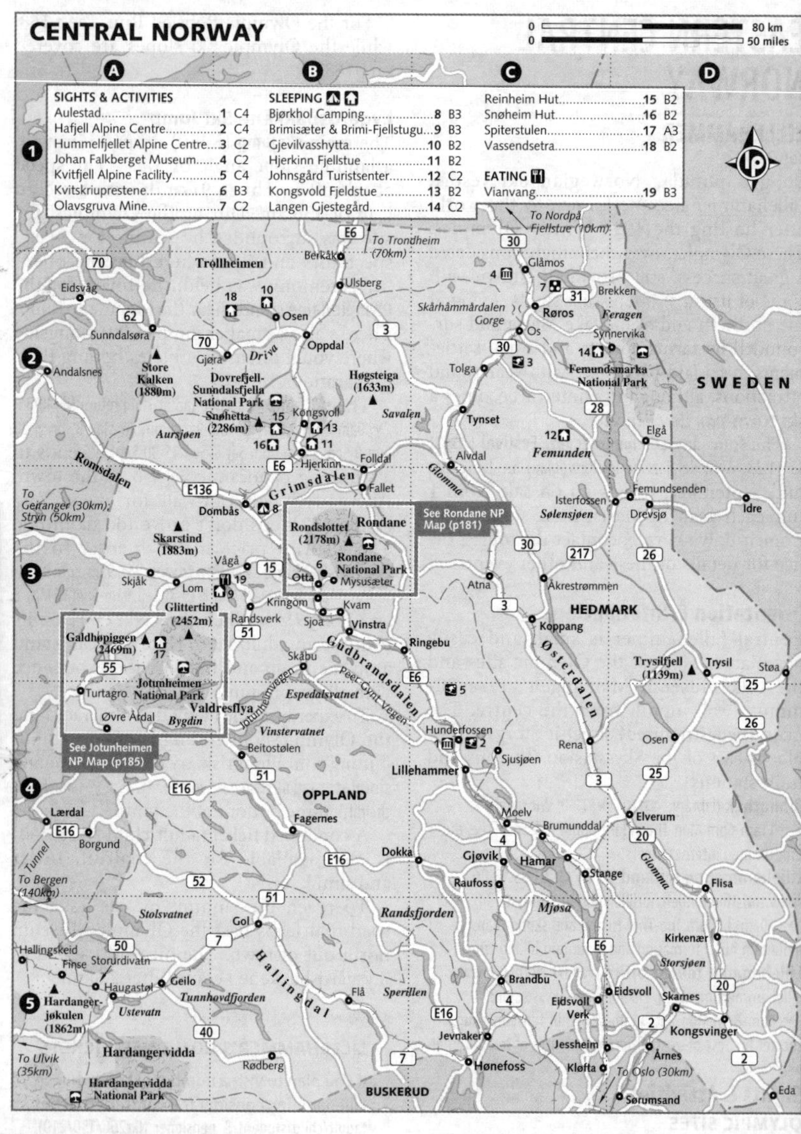

Norwegian Olympic Museum

The excellent **Olympic museum** (☎ 61 25 21 00; www.ol.museum.no; Olympiaparken; adult/child/student/senior Nkr75/35/60/60; ⏰ 10am-5pm Jun-Aug, 11am-4pm Tue-Sun Sep-May) is at the Håkons Hall ice-hockey venue. On the ground floor there is a well-presented display covering the ancient Olympic Games as well as all of the Olympic Games of the modern era, with a focus on the exploits of Norwegian athletes as well as the Lillehamer games. The exhibition is updated every two years.

Upstairs, you can look down upon the ice-hockey arena, which is circled by corridors with displays and video presentations from the Lillehammer games.

MAIHAUGEN FOLK MUSEUM

Norway's finest folk museum is the expansive, open-air **Maihaugen Folk Museum** (☎ 61 28 89 00; www.maihaugen.no; Maihaugveien 1; adult/child/student/senior/family Nkr80/40/70/70/200; 10am-5pm Jun-Aug, 10am-4pm Sep & mid-end May, 11am-4pm Tue-Sat, 11am-6pm Sun Oct–mid-May). Rebuilt like a small village, the collection of around 180 buildings includes the transplanted Garmo stave church, traditional Gudbrandsdalen homes and shops, and 27 buildings from the farm Bjørnstad. The three main sections encompass rural and town architecture, with a further section on 20th-century architecture. The life's work of local dentist Anders Sandvig, it also houses temporary exhibitions in the modern exhibition hall and a permanent exhibition 'We made the road', a fascinating journey through Norwegian history.

BJERKEBÆK

Bjerkebæk (☎ 61 28 89 00; www.maihaugen.no/bjerkebek; Sigrid Undsetsveg 1; adult/child/student/pensioner Nkr100/50/80/80; 10am-5pm Jun-Aug, 11am-4pm May & Sep) celebrates the life of Sigrid Undset, one of Norway's most celebrated authors; she won the Nobel Prize for Literature in 1928. Her home has been restored with memorabilia from her life.

LILLEHAMMER ART MUSEUM

This **art museum** (Lillehammer Kunstmuseum; ☎ 61 05 44 60; www.lillehammerartmuseum.com; Stortorget; 2; adult/student/pensioner/child Nkr60/50/50/free; 11am-5pm daily mid-Jun–mid-Aug, 11am-4pm Tue-Sun rest-of-year) is not only architecturally striking, it also covers Norwegian visual arts from the early 19th century to the present. Highlights of the permanent collection include some of Norway's finest artists (including Edvard Munch) and some local painters.

NORWEGIAN VEHICLE MUSEUM

Tucked away behind the stream in central Lillehammer, the **Norwegian Vehicle Museum** (Norsk Kjøretøyhistorisk Museum; ☎ 61 25 61 65; Lilletorget 1; adult/child Nkr40/20; 10am-6pm daily mid-Jun–mid-Aug, 11am-3pm Mon-Fri, 11am-4pm Sat & Sun rest-of-year) is for car buffs, featuring everything from sleighs to vintage cars and motorcycles.

Sleeping

Thanks to the Olympics, Lillehammer has a more varied range of accommodation than most other Norwegian towns.

BUDGET

Lillehammer Camping (☎ 61 25 33 33; www.lillehammer-camping.no; Dampsagveien 47; tent/caravan sites from Nkr125/220, 2-bed cabin from Nkr550; year-round) Camping is available here on the lakeshore, a typical urban site with cooking and laundry facilities, water-sports equipment, children's play areas, a Viking camp and cable TV.

Lysegaard (☎ 61 26 26 63; lysgaard@c2i.net; Lysegaard; s/d Nkr200/400; Jun–mid-Aug) A converted farmhouse up the hill, this place also represents great value, although for most of the year it serves as a base for budding Olympic skiers.

Gjeste Bu (☎ /fax 61 25 43 21; gjestebu@lillehammer.online.no; Gamleveien 110; s/d from Nkr275/450) This friendly guesthouse has a range of accommodation, shared kitchen facilities and apartments that are ideal if you'll be in town a while. Breakfast costs extra as does bed linen (Nkr50). If you understand its pricing system, let us know.

our pick **Lillehammer Vandrerhjem** (☎ 61 26 00 24; www.stasjonen.no; Jernbanegata 2; dm/s/d/tr Nkr315/590/790/900, 5-7-bed apt Nkr1500, all incl breakfast;) If you've never stayed in a youth hostel, this one above the train station is the place to break the habits of a lifetime. The rooms are simple but come with a bathroom, bed linen, and free wireless internet and free internet access. The service is arguably Lillehammer's friendliest and there's a spick-and-span communal kitchen.

MIDRANGE & TOP END

Birkebeineren (☎ 61 26 47 00; www.birkebeineren.no; Birkebeinervegen 24; s/d Nkr690/980, 2-/4-bed apt Nkr1080/1515; P) This very good place, on the road up to the bottom of the ski jump, offers a range of accommodation to suit different budgets; prices fall the longer you stay.

Gjestehuset Ersgaard (☎ 61 25 06 84; www.ersgaard.no; Nordseterveien 201; s/d with shared bathroom Nkr420/590, s with bathroom Nkr590, d with bathroom & view of farm/lake Nkr720/850; P) High on the hill overlooking Lillehammer, this fine old place has a rural patrician air and pretty rooms in refurbished farm buildings. It's quiet, loaded with character and the views are superb.

Clarion Collection Hotel Hammer (☎ 61 26 73 73; cc.hammer@choice.no; Storgata 108; s/d with half board from Nkr950/1050;) This upmarket hotel has extremely comfortable rooms right in the heart of town. There's free wireless connection and the light evening buffet is another selling point.

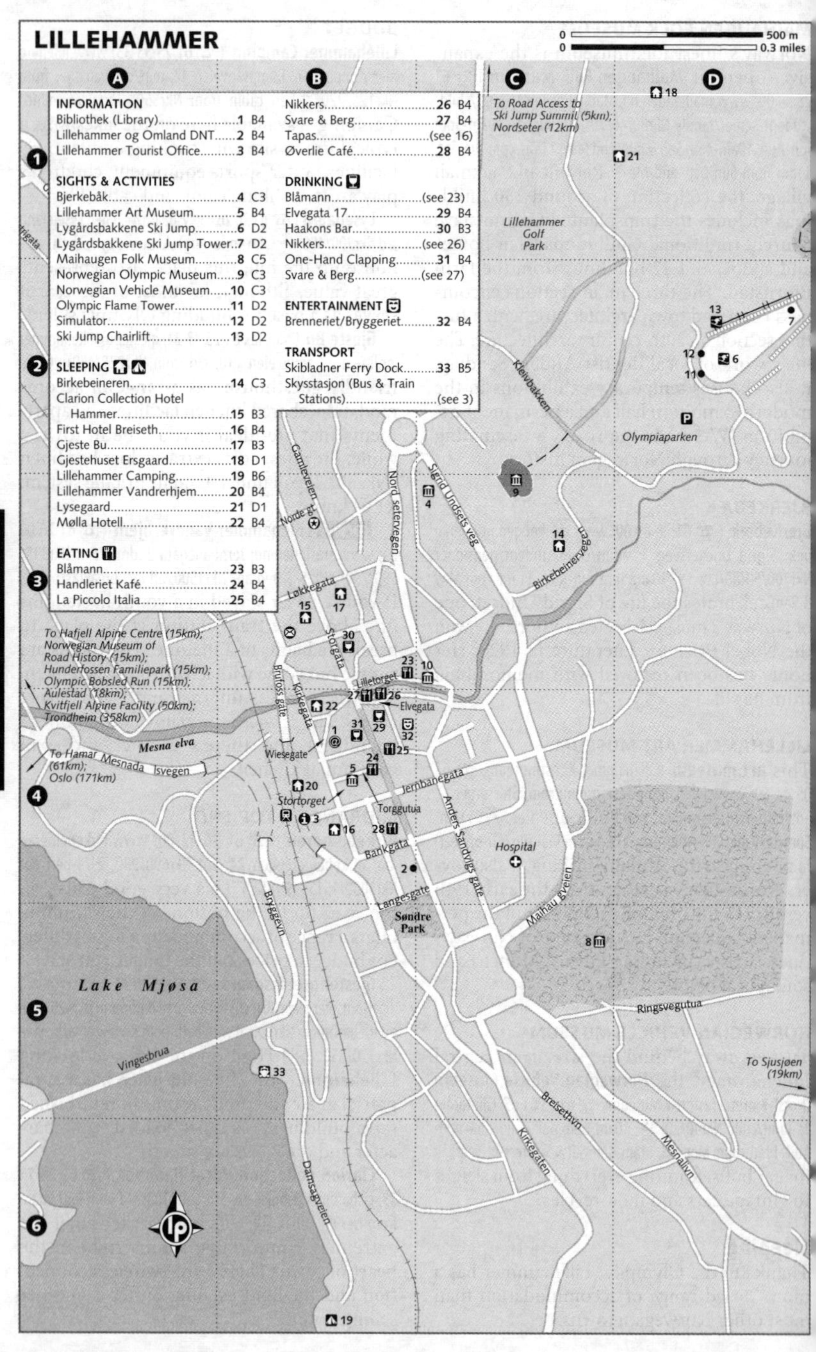
LILLEHAMMER
0 500 m
0 0.3 miles
A B C D
1 2 3 4 5 6
INFORMATION
Bibliothek (Library)....1 B4
Lillehammer og Omland DNT....2 B4
Lillehammer Tourist Office....3 B4
SIGHTS & ACTIVITIES
Bjerkebåk....4 C3
Lillehammer Art Museum....5 B4
Lygårdsbakkene Ski Jump....6 D2
Lygårdsbakkene Ski Jump Tower..7 D2
Maihaugen Folk Museum....8 C5
Norwegian Olympic Museum....9 C3
Norwegian Vehicle Museum....10 C3
Olympic Flame Tower....11 D2
Simulator....12 D2
Ski Jump Chairlift....13 D2
SLEEPING
Birkebeineren....14 C3
Clarion Collection Hotel Hammer....15 B3
First Hotel Breiseth....16 B4
Gjeste Bu....17 B3
Gjestehuset Ersgaard....18 D1
Lillehammer Camping....19 B6
Lillehammer Vandrerhjem....20 B4
Lysegaard....21 D1
Mølla Hotell....22 B4
EATING
Blåmann....23 B3
Handleriet Kafé....24 B4
La Piccolo Italia....25 B4
Nikkers....26 B4
Svare & Berg....27 B4
Tapas....(see 16)
Øverlie Café....28 B4
DRINKING
Blåmann....(see 23)
Elvegata 17....29 B4
Haakons Bar....30 B3
Nikkers....(see 26)
One-Hand Clapping....31 B4
Svare & Berg....(see 27)
ENTERTAINMENT
Brenneriet/Bryggeriet....32 B4
TRANSPORT
Skibladner Ferry Dock....33 B5
Skysstasjon (Bus & Train Stations)....(see 3)
To Road Access to Ski Jump Summit (5km); Nordseter (12km)
Lillehammer Golf Park
Olympiaparken
Kleivbakken
Sigrid Undsets veg
Nord setervegen
Gamlevegen
Birkebeinervegen
Løkkegata
Storgata
Lilletorget
Elvegata
Brufoss gate
Kirkegata
Wiesegate
Stortorget
Torggutua
Jernbanegata
Bankgata
Anders Sandvigs gate
Hospital
Langesgate
Søndre Park
Maihaugveien
Bryggevn
Ringsvegutua
To Hafjell Alpine Centre (15km); Norwegian Museum of Road History (15km); Hunderfossen Familiepark (15km); Olympic Bobsled Run (15km); Aulestad (18km); Kvitfjell Alpine Facility (50km); Trondheim (358km)
To Hamar (61km); Oslo (171km)
Mesna elva
Mesnada
Isvegen
Lake Mjøsa
Vingesbrua
Damsagveien
Breisethvn
Kirkegaten
Mesnalivn
To Sjusjøen (19km)

CENTRAL NORWAY

First Hotel Breiseth (☎ 61 24 77 77; www.breiseth.com; Jernbanegata 1-5; s Nkr798-1190, d Nkr998-1398; P) This upmarket hotel opposite the train station has a range of attractive rooms, some of which reflect the hotel's august 110-year history while others are modern. Our only complaint? If the youth hostel can afford free wireless connection, we resent having to pay for it here.

Mølla Hotell (☎ 61 05 70 80; www.mollahotell.no; Elvegata 12; s/d Nkr895/1095; P) Built from the shell of an old mill, this fully refurbished hotel is one of Lillehammer's more original hotels, with mill machinery existing alongside flat-screen TVs. The rooftop bar has fine views and the architecture is distinguished.

Eating

Handleriet Kafé (☎ 61 25 63 40; Torggutua; menu Nkr115; 10.30am-6pm Mon-Fri, 10.30am-4pm Sat) With the air of an English tea room, a wide-ranging menu of light meals and pastries and a pleasant outdoor terrace, this lovely old café just down the hill from Storgata is terrific.

Øverlie Café (☎ 61 25 03 61; Storgata 50; meals from Nkr50; 11am-11pm) Filling, inexpensive meals (eg meatballs and mashed potatoes) are the order of the day at this unpretentious pavement-side café.

La Piccolo Italia (☎ 61 05 45 10; Storgata 73; pasta from Nkr75, pizzas from Nkr75) This good Italian place spills over onto the pavement when the weather's warm. The food is authentically Italian and prices are reasonable.

our pick **Svare & Berg** (☎ 61 24 74 30; Elvegata; baguettes & sandwiches Nkr64-129, salads Nkr89-139, soups Nkr84-119; 11am-11pm Mon-Wed, 11am-midnight Thu, 11am-2am Fri & Sat) Right by Lillehammer's bubbling brook, this very cool café-bar-restaurant serves tasty light meals and great coffee. It's a popular spot for locals.

Blåmann (☎ 61 26 22 03; Lilletorget 1; snacks from Nkr75, lunch soup/full buffet Nkr65/135, mains Nkr195-330, children's meals Nkr35; 11am-11pm) This recommended spot has a clean-lined interior and a trendy menu that encompasses Mexican dishes, crocodile in Sichuan sauce, kangaroo and reindeer!

Nikkers (☎ 61 27 05 56; Elvegata 18; lunch Nkr75-125, baguettes from Nkr65, mains from Nkr139) Known as the place where a moose has apparently walked through the wall (look outside for the full effect), it serves international cuisine and has a pleasant outdoor terrace. The ambience is somewhere between English pub and Oslo café.

Tapas (☎ 61 24 77 88; Jernbanegata 1-5; tapas Nkr45-75; 6-11pm Mon-Thu, 6pm-midnight Fri & Sat) For a change of scene, try this Spanish-flavoured bar, which plays Latin music, does good tapas and has a pleasant, buzzy ambience when it's full.

Drinking & Entertainment

Bars are an integral part of the Lillehammer experience, especially during the ski season.

One-Hand Clapping (☎ 61 25 12 22; Storgata 80; 9.10am-5pm Mon-Wed, 9.10am-6pm Thu & Fri, 9.10am-3pm Sat) This very cool little coffee shop does superb coffee (from Nkr25), as well as croissants and chocolate cake (Nkr20) to die for. The two easy chairs on the pavement are prime people-viewing spots if you're fortunate enough to snaffle one.

Elvegata 17 (Elvegata 17; 2-11pm Mon-Thu, 2pm-2am Fri & Sat, 8pm-2am Sun) Lillehammer's trendiest little bar, Elvegata 17 draws a 20-something crowd. Mellow by day, it gets livelier as the night wears on.

Blåmann (☎ 61 26 22 03; Lilletorget 1) The downstairs Lille Blå of this stylish restaurant is informal, supercool and a great place to spend a summer's afternoon writing postcards. There's great coffee and drinks and it stays open until 2am on weekends.

Other restaurants which double as attractive bars include Nikkers, Svare & Berg and Tapas.

Haakons Bar (Storgata 93; 11am-3am) During the day Haakon's Bar is the preserve of elbow-on-the-bar locals and very slow. After the sun sets, it kicks into action, becoming a crowded and agreeable place to drink. It can get a little raucous during the ski season.

Brenneriet/Bryggeriet (Elvegata 19; 6pm-3am) This pub, nightclub and disco appeals to a varied clientele from the just-legal to time-worn veterans. It's not the classiest place in Norway, but it can be fun if your musical tastes aren't too discerning.

Getting There & Away

Lillehammer Skysstasjon (☎ 177) is the main transport terminal for buses, trains and taxis. There are Nor-Way Bussekspress services to/from Oslo (Nkr290, three hours, three to four daily) via Oslo's Gardermoen Airport (Nkr245, 2¼ hours). To/from the western fjords, buses pass through Lillehammer several times daily. There's also one daily run to/from Bergen (Nkr515, 9¼ hours).

PEER GYNT VEGEN

Of all the beautiful mountain roads of Central Norway, one stands out for its combination of scenery and storytelling: **Peer Gynt Vegen** (www.peergyntvegen.no; toll Nkr60; ⌚ Jun-Sep). Running for 60km from Skei to Espedalen, it takes you along the trail followed by that ill-fated, fictional character created by Henrik Ibsen and offers unrivalled views of the Jotunheimen and Rondane massifs en route. Climbing up to 1053m above sea level, it passes the Solbrå Seter farm where Gudbrandsdal cheese was first made in 1863 and an early August concert of Edvard Grieg's Peer Gynt finds its spiritual home at Gålåvatn lake. To reach Skei, head north of Lillehammer along the E6 and at Tretten take the turn-off for the Rv254. At Svingvoll, Peer Gynt Vegen branches off to the northwest.

Lavprisekspressen buses run less often but are cheaper (from Nkr149), and include Oslo, Trondheim and many towns in between.

Rail services run between Oslo (Nkr310, 2¼ hours, 11 to 17 daily) and Trondheim (from Nkr299, 4¼ to seven hours, four to six daily).

For details of the *Skibladner* paddle steamer, see the boxed text, opposite.

AROUND LILLEHAMMER

Hunderfossen

Some 15km north of Lillehammer, just off the E6, is Hunderfossen, home to the **Norwegian Museum of Road History** (Norsk Vegmuseum; ☎ 61 28 52 50; www.vegmuseum.no in Norwegian; Hunderfossen; admission free; ⌚ 10am-6pm mid-May–Aug, 10am-3pm Sep–mid-May), which tells the story of Norway's battle to forge roads through its challenging geography. Up the hill and part of the same complex, the **Fjellsprengnings-museet** (Rock-blasting Museum) is a 240m-long tunnel that gives you a real insight into the difficulties of building a tunnel through the Norwegian mountains. The walk, guided with lighting, models and video commentary, takes around 30 minutes.

Nearby is the **Hunderfossen Familiepark** (☎ 61 27 55 60; www.hunderfossen.no; Hunderfossen; adult/child Nkr280/235; ⌚ 10am-8pm 23 Jun-5 Aug, closed 3 Sep-25 May, shorter hrs rest-of-year), one of Norway's best parks for children with water rides, 3-D presentations, fairy-tale palaces and wandering trolls.

Also in Hunderfossen, you can career down the **Olympic Bobsled Run** (☎ 61 27 75 50; Hunderfossen; admission to grounds Nkr15; ⌚ 11am-6pm daily 30 Jun-19 Aug, 11am-6pm Sat 28 April-26 Jun & 25 Aug-16 Sep, 11am-6pm Sat & Sun 2-24 Jun, shorter hrs rest-of-year) aboard a **wheelbob** (adult/10-11-year-old-child Nkr190/95) under the guidance of a professional bobsled pilot. Wheel bobs take five passengers and hit a top speed of 100km/h. The real thing, **taxibobs** (adult around Nkr950; ⌚ Nov-Easter), take four passengers, reach an exhilarating 130km/h and you won't have much time to get nervous – you're down the mountain in 70 seconds. Bookings are advisable during winter.

In summer there are up to five buses a day from the Lillehammer Skysstasjon (adult/child Nkr35/20, 30 minutes) to Hunderfossen, with less frequent departures the rest of the year. A considerable uphill walk is involved to reach the bobsled run.

Olympic Ski Slopes

Lillehammer has two Olympic ski slopes. **Hafjell Alpine Centre** (☎ 61 27 47 00; www.hafjell.no), 15km north of town, hosted the downhill events, while the **Kvitfjell Alpine Facility** (☎ 61 28 36 30; www.kvitfjell.no), 50km north of town, was dedicated to cross-country. Both offer public skiing between late November and late April and are connected by bus from the Lillehammer Skysstasjon.

Aulestad

Bjørnstjerne Bjørnson won the Nobel Prize for Literature in 1903 and lived on a farm at **Aulestad** (☎ 61 22 41 10; www.maihaugen.no/aulestad; Follebu; adult/child/student/pensioner Nkr 35/75/60/60; ⌚ 10am-5pm Jun-Aug, 11am-4pm mid-end May & Sep), 18km northwest of Lillehammer. It has been lovingly restored, although you'll need your own vehicle to get here. For details on an entry ticket combined with sights in Lillehammer, see the boxed text, p163.

HAMAR

pop 27,909

For a town that would never win a beauty contest, Hamar has a surprising number of attractions. Most date from the 1994 Winter Olympics in Lillehammer when Hamar hosted a number of events, but there are also some good museums.

The **Hamar Regional Tourist Office** (☎ 62 51 75 03; www.hamarregionen.no in Norwegian; 8am-6pm Mon-Fri, 10am-6pm Sat & Sun mid-Jun–mid-Aug, 8am-4pm Mon-Fri rest-of-year) is at the Viking Ship Sports Arena.

Sights

VIKING SHIP SPORTS ARENA

Hamar's stand-out landmark is this **sports arena** (Vikingskipet; ☎ 62 51 75 00; www.hoa.no in Norwegian; Åkersvikaveien 1; entry Nkr30; 8am-6pm Mon-Fri, 10am-4pm Sat & Sun late Jun–mid-Aug, shorter hrs rest-of-year), a graceful structure with the lines of an upturned Viking ship. The building, which hosted the speed skating during the Winter Olympics, holds 20,000 spectators, encompasses 9600 sq metres of ice and is 94.6m long. Both in scale and aesthetics, it's an impressive place. From late July to mid-August, the ice is open to the public for ice-skating (Nkr80).

NORWEGIAN RAILWAY MUSEUM

Established in 1896 to honour Norway's railway history, this open-air **railway museum** (Norsk Jernbanemuseum; ☎ 62 51 31 60; www.norsk-jernbanemuseum.no in Norwegian; Strandveien 163; adult/child Nkr70/40; 10.30am-5pm daily Jul-19 Aug; 11am-3pm Tue-Sat, 11am-4pm Sun 20 Aug-Jun), lies on the Mjøsa shore. In addition to lovely historic stations, engine sheds, rail coaches and steam locomotives, you'll learn about the extraordinary engineering feats required to carve the railways through Norway's rugged terrain.

HEDMARK MUSEUM & GLASS CATHEDRAL

West of town (1.5km), the extensive open-air county **museum** (Hedmarkmuseet; ☎ 62 54 27 00; www.domkirkeodden.no; Strandveien 100; adult/child/pensioner Nkr70/30/55; 10am-5pm daily mid-Jun–mid-Aug, 10am-4pm Tue-Sun mid-May–mid-Jun & mid-Aug–mid-Sep) includes 18th- and 19th-century buildings, a local folk-history exhibit featuring the creepy Devil's Finger, the ruins of the castle, and the extraordinary showcase 'glass cathedral' (Domkirkeodden). The cathedral, whose ruins stand poignantly beneath the glass-and-steel roof, and castle dominated Hamar until 1567, when they were sacked by the Swedes. Take bus 6 from the town library (Nkr32, hourly).

NORWEGIAN EMIGRANT MUSEUM

Around 10km east of town, the fine open-air **Norwegian Emigrant Museum** (Norsk Utvandrermuseum; ☎ 62 57 48 50; www.museumsnett.no/emigrantmuseum; Åkershagan; admission free; 9am-3.30pm Tue-Fri, 10am-4pm Sat, noon-4pm Sun Jun-Aug, 9am-3.30pm Tue-Fri Sep-May) focuses on exhibits and archives from Norwegian emigrants to America from the 1880s. There's also a research library open to members (Nkr150).

Festivals & Events

On the second weekend in June, Hamar hosts the **Middle Ages Festival** (www.middelalderfestival.no) with locals in period costume and Gregorian chants in the glass cathedral. In the first week of September, the **Hamar Music Festival** (www.musicfest.no in Norwegian) attracts a growing band of international acts.

Sleeping & Eating

Vikingskipet Motell og Vandrerhjem (☎ 62 52 60 60; www.vikingskipet-motell.no; Åkersvikavegen 24; s/d Nkr690/790, 2-bed apt Nkr1190) Opposite the Viking Ship Sports Arena, this is an excellent choice with simple but very well-kept rooms and terrific self-contained apartments.

Seiersted Pensjonat (☎ 62 52 12 44; www.seiersted.no; Holsetgata 64; s/d Nkr450/695;) Central Seiersted Pensjonat offers a family atmosphere, nicely decorated rooms and wireless access. Dinner is available from Nkr75.

Scandic Hamar (☎ 21 61 40 00; www.scandic-hotels.com/hamar; Vangsveien 121; s/d from Nkr720/920;) With sleek-lined Scandinavian design, a gymnasium and convenient location, Scandic Hamar could just be Hamar's best address.

WORLD'S OLDEST PADDLE STEAMER

Skibladner (☎ 61 14 40 80; www.skibladner.no), the world's oldest paddle steamer, is a wonderfully relaxing way to explore lake Mjøsa. First built in Sweden in 1856, the boat was refitted and lengthened to 165ft (50m) in 1888. From late June until mid-August, the *Skibladner* plies the lake between Hamar, Gjøvik and Lillehammer. Most travellers opt for the route between Hamar and Lillehammer (one way/return Nkr220/320, 3½ hours) on Tuesday, Thursday and Saturday, which can be done as a return day trip (from Hamar only, Nkr320). Jazz evenings aboard the steamer cost Nkr450, including food (but not drinks).

Rack rates are expensive but there are always good deals happening on its website.

Stallgården (☎ 62 54 31 00; cnr Bekkegata & Torggata; lunch Nkr75-89, snacks & light meals Nkr70-160, mains Nkr179-260; 11am-11pm Mon-Sat) The downstairs café here is particularly popular for its outdoor tables in summer, while the upstairs restaurant is more formal.

Getting There & Away

Frequent trains run between Oslo (Nkr205, 1¼ hours, once or twice hourly) and Trondheim (Nkr585, five hours, four or five daily) via Lillehammer. Trains also head to Røros (Nkr425, 3¼ hours, one to three daily). Lavprisekspressen buses go to Oslo (from Nkr149) and Trondheim (from Nkr199) one or two times a day.

ELVERUM

pop 19,620

With a name like Elverum, you might expect a whiff of magic, but in reality this is a pretty nondescript town set amid the vast and lush green timberlands of southern Hedmark county. Its excellent forestry museum is the main reason to stop here en route elsewhere.

Elverum's **tourist office** (☎ 62 41 31 16; www.elverum-turistinfo.com; Storgata 24; 9am-6pm mid-Jun–mid-Aug, shorter hrs rest-of-year) is centrally located and brimful of information.

Sights

The expansive **Norwegian Forestry Museum** (Norsk Skogmuseum; ☎ 62 40 90 00; www.skogmus.no in Norwegian; Rv20; adult/child/student & senior incl Glomdal Museum Nkr80/40/60; 10am-6pm mid-Jun–mid-Aug, 10am-4pm rest-of-year), 1km south of central Elverum, covers the multifarious uses and enjoyments of Norwegian forests. It includes a nature information centre, children's workshop, geological and meteorological exhibits, wood carvings, an aquarium, nature dioramas with all manner of stuffed native wildlife (including a mammoth) and a 20,000-volume reference library.

The open-air **Glomdal Museum** (☎ 62 41 91 00; adult/child/student & senior incl Forestry Museum Nkr80/40/60; 10am-4pm mid-Jun–mid-Aug), across the bridge from the Forestry Museum, is a collection of 90 historic buildings from the Glomma valley.

Sleeping & Eating

Elverum Camping (☎ 62 41 67 16; www.elverumcamping.no; Halvdans Gransvei 6; tent sites Nkr150, 2-bed cabin with/without bathroom Nkr900/450) This decent place is in a green setting south of the Norwegian Forestry Museum.

Glommen Pensjonat (☎ 62 41 12 67; Vestheimsgata 2; s/d from Nkr400/450) A simple but friendly guesthouse, Glommen Pensjonat lies 500m west of the town centre. It's a good choice for a more personal touch than most hotels.

Elgstua (☎ 62 41 01 22; Trondheimsveien 9; s/d from Nkr700/950) Although a little overpriced for its simple rooms, Elgstua is a traditional place that gets good reports from travellers.

Forstmann (☎ 62 41 69 10; mains from Nkr125; lunch & dinner mid-Jun–mid-Aug) The fish-and-game restaurant at the Forestry Museum serves good traditional Norwegian cooking.

Getting There & Away

The Nor-Way Bussekspress 'Trysil Ekspressen' runs between Oslo (Nkr205, 2½ hours) and Trysil (Nkr107, 1¼ hours) via Elverum seven times daily.

TRYSIL

pop 6782

Surrounded by forested hillsides close to the Swedish border, and overlooked by Norway's

THE DARK DAYS OF WWII

Elverum played a proud but tragic role in the Norwegian resistance to the Nazis. When German forces invaded Norway in April 1940, King Håkon and the Norwegian government fled northwards from Oslo. They halted in Elverum and on 9 April the parliament met at the folk high school and issued the Elverum Mandate, giving the exiled government the authority to protect Norway's interests until the parliament could reconvene. When a German messenger arrived to impose the Nazis' version of 'protection' in the form of a new puppet government in Oslo, the king rejected the 'offer' before heading into exile. Two days later, Elverum became the first Norwegian town to suffer massive bombing by the Nazis and most of the town's old wooden buildings were levelled. By then the king had fled to Nybergsund (close to Trysil), which was also bombed, but he escaped into exile.

largest collection of ski slopes, little Trysil is well worth a detour with year-round activities taking you off into the wilderness.

Although Trysil lives and breathes winter **skiing**, for the rest of the year you can do just about anything to keep active, from canoeing to canyoning or the more sedate pastime of fishing. Perhaps the most rewarding activity in summer is **cycling** with at least six cycle routes from 6km to 38km; route maps are available from the tourist office, while bike hire is available from **Trysil Hyttegrend** (see below; 1-/3-/6-days Nkr200/375/575). For horse-riding, contact **Trysil-stallen** (☎ 62 45 10 55; www.trysil-stallen.no; half-/full-day Nkr450/700).

Trysil Tourist Office (☎ 62 45 10 00; www.trysil.com; Storvegen 3; 9am-6pm Mon-Fri, 10am-2pm Sat & Sun 25 Jun-12 Aug, shorter hrs rest-of-year), just off the northern end of the main street, has loads of useful information.

Sleeping & Eating

Trysil Hyttegrend (☎ 90 13 27 61; www.trysilhytte.com; Øränset; 4-bed huts per day/week from Nkr450/1500; P) By the water's edge 2.5km south of town, this excellent site has many drawcards, with wireless internet, a wood-fired sauna and plenty of activities on offer.

Trysil Hotell (☎ 62 45 08 33; www.norlandia.no/trysil; Storvegen; d from Nkr830; P) One of the few Trysil hotels to open year-round, this good hotel is right in the centre of town. It also has a good restaurant.

Getting There & Away

The Nor-Way Bussekspress 'Trysil Ekspressen' connects Trysil with Oslo (Nkr225, four hours) via Elverum (Nkr107, 1¼ hours) seven times daily.

NORTHERN CENTRAL NORWAY

RØROS

pop 5671

Norway's outstanding folk museums that recreate the past are no substitute for Røros, a charming Unesco World Heritage–listed village set in a small hollow of stunted forests and bleak fells. This historic copper-mining town (once called Bergstad, or mountain city) is home to colourful wooden houses that climb the hillside and a strong community spirit. The Norwegian writer Johann Falkberget described Røros as 'a place of whispering history'. It makes for a good tourist brochure cliché, although in this case it happens to be true as Røros remains one of the most enchanting places in Norway.

History

In 1644 a local, Olsen Åsen, shot a reindeer at Storvola (Storwartz). The enraged creature pawed at the ground, revealing a glint of copper ore. In the same year Røros Kobberverk was established, followed two years later by a royal charter that granted it exclusive rights to all minerals, forest products and waterways within 40km of the original discovery.

The mining company located its headquarters at Røros due to the abundant wood (fuel) and the rapids along the river Hyttelva, which provided hydroelectric power. The use of fire in breaking up the rock in the mines was a perilous business and cost Røros dearly. Røros first burnt to the ground during the Gyldenløve conflict with the Swedes between 1678 and 1679, and the smelter was damaged by fire again in 1953. In 1977, after 333 years of operation, the company went bankrupt.

Information

Biblioteket (☎ 72 41 94 24; Fargarveien 4; 2-7pm Mon, Wed & Fri, 11am-4pm Tue & Thu, 11am-2pm Sat) Free, but time-limited internet access.

Tourist office (☎ 72 41 11 65; www.rorosinfo.com; Peder Hiortsgata 2; 9am-6pm Mon-Sat, 10am-4pm Sun mid-Jun–mid-Aug, 9am-3pm Mon-Fri, 10.30am-12.30pm Sat rest-of-year)

Sights

For details of the Olavsgruva Mine and Johan Falkberget Museum, see p175.

HISTORIC DISTRICT

Røros' historic district, characterised by the striking log architecture of its 80 protected buildings, takes in the entire central area. The two main streets, **Bergmannsgata** (it tapers from southwest to northeast to create an optical illusion and make the town appear larger than it is!) and **Kjerkgata**, are lined with historical homes and buildings, all under preservation orders. If you follow the river Hyttelva upstream, you'll reach the historic smelting district and its tiny turf-roofed **miners' cottages**.

CENTRAL NORWAY

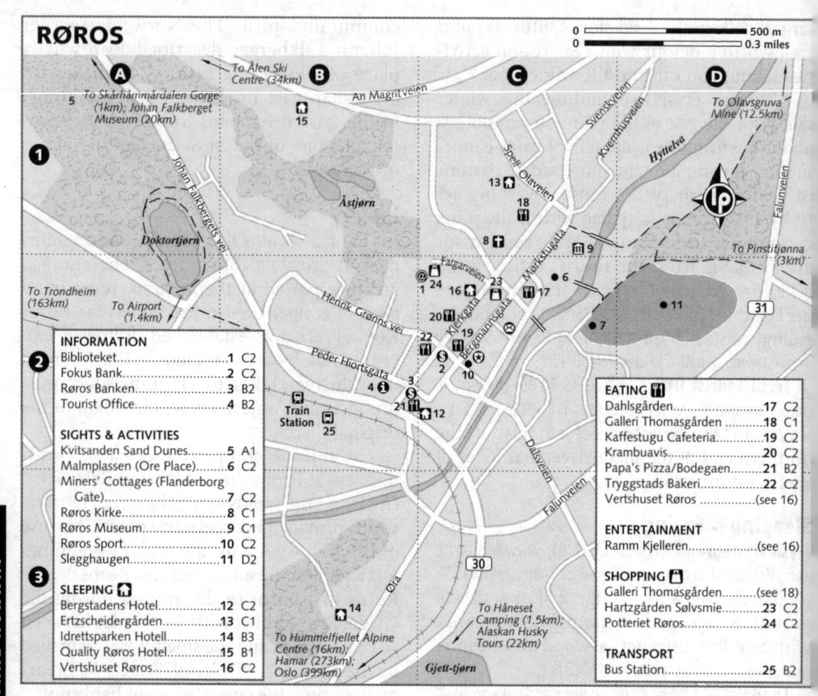

If Røros looks familiar, that's because several films have been made here, including Røros author Johan Falkberget's classic *An-Magrit*, starring Jane Fonda. Flanderborg gate starred in some of Astrid Lindgren's *Pippi Longstocking* classics and Røros even stood in for Siberia in *A Day in the Life of Ivan Denisovich*.

RØROS KIRKE

Røros' Lutheran **church** (Kjerkgata; adult/child Nkr25/free; 10am-5pm Mon-Sat, 1-3pm Sun mid-Jun–mid-Aug, shorter hrs rest-of-year) is one of Norway's largest with a seating capacity of 1640. Constructed in 1650, it had fallen into disrepair by the mid-18th century and from 1780 a new baroque-style church was built just behind the original at a cost of 23,000 *riksdaler* (one *riksdaler* is the equivalent of Nkr4, and at the time miners earned about 50 *riksdaler* per year).

The posh King's Gallery at the back, identified by both royal and mining company logos, has never hosted a king; visiting royals have always opted to sit among the people. Unusually, the pulpit sits over the altarpiece, while the organ (1742) is the oldest Norwegian-built organ still functioning.

Until 1865 the building was owned by the mining company and this is reflected in the church art. By the altar you'll see the grizzled Hans Olsen Åsen, credited with the discovery of Røros copper, among other company dignitaries. There are also paintings of the author Johan Falkberget and the original 1650 church.

For five weeks from early July to early August, the church hosts **organ recitals** (adult/child Nkr50/free; 6pm Mon-Sat), sometimes accompanied by orchestral musicians from across Europe.

RØROS MUSEUM

Housed in old smelting works, which were central to Røros' *raison d'être* from 1646 until 1953, this **museum** (72 40 61 70; Malmplassen; adult/child/senior/student/family Nkr60/30/50/50/140; 10am-7pm mid-Jun–mid-Aug, shorter hrs rest-of-year) is a town highlight. The building was reconstructed in 1988 according to the original 17th-century plan. Upstairs you'll find geological and conservation displays, while downstairs are a large balance used for weighing ore, some well-illustrated early mining statistics, and brilliant working models of the mines and the water- and horse-powered smelting processes. Displays of copper smelting are held at 3pm from Tuesday to Friday from early July to early August.

Outside the museum entrance spreads the large open area known as the **Malmplassen** (Ore Place), where loads of ore were dumped and weighed on the large wooden scale. Just across the stream from the museum are the protected **Slegghaugan** (slag heaps) from where there are lovely views over town.

In summer your entry ticket entitles you to a free guided tour at 11am, 12.30pm, 2pm or 3.30pm; the last is in English.

Activities

Hiking (and, in winter, **nordic skiing**) possibilities abound across the semiforested Røros plateau; ask the tourist office for advice. Note, however, that many areas remain covered in snow well into the summer. **Hummelfjellet Alpine Centre** (☎ 62 49 71 00; www.hummelfjell.no in Norwegian), 16km south of Røros, has two lifts and six slopes, while **Ålen Ski Centre** (☎ 72 41 55 55), 34km northwest of town, boasts two lifts and four slopes.

A 1km walk northwest from central Røros will take you to the sand dunes of **Kvitsanden**, the largest in Scandinavia. Scoured, transported and deposited there by water flowing under an ancient glacier, they're more novel than beautiful.

Another kilometre to the west is **Skårhåmmårdalen**, a gorge with sand-lined pools, which offers **swimming** on hot days and appears as if it might harbour trolls.

The tourist office has details of **cycling**, **canoeing**, **horse riding** and **ice -fishing** for trout. For summer cycling, you can rent a mountain bike from **Røros Sport** (☎ 72 41 12 18; Bergmannsgata 13).

Tours

In winter, **Alaskan Husky Tours** (☎ 62 49 87 66; www.huskytour.no in Norwegian; Os) organises two-hour excursions by dog-sled (adult/child/12-18-year-old Nkr590/190/290) or horse-drawn sleigh (Nkr600 per hour for four people); in summer dog-cart trips offer an all-you'll-get-at-this-time-of-year substitute. Its office is in Os, 22km southwest of Røros, but reservations can be made at the tourist office in Røros. You can also join a winter day trip to the Southern Sami tent camp at Pinstitjønna, 3km from Røros, where you'll dine on reindeer and learn such unique skills as ice-fishing and axe-throwing. The three-hour tour costs around Nkr500 per person (minimum 10 people).

The tourist office runs excellent **guided walking tours** (adult/child Nkr60/free; 🕒 tours 11am Mon-Sat May–mid-Jun & mid-Aug–mid-Sep, 10am, 11.30am, 1pm, 2.30pm Mon-Sat, noon & 2pm Sun mid-Jun–mid-Aug, 11am Mon-Sat 1-19 Jun & 16 Aug-10 Sep, 11am Sat rest-of-year) of the historic town centre; the summer tours at 1pm Monday to Saturday and 2pm Sunday are in English or German.

Festivals & Events

The biggest winter event is **Rørosmartnan** (Røros Market), which began in 1644 as a rendezvous for hunters who ventured into town to sell their products to miners and buy supplies. Thanks to a royal decree issued in 1853 stipulating that a grand market be held annually from the penultimate Tuesday of February to the following Saturday, it continues today. Nowadays it's celebrated with cultural programmes, street markets and live entertainment.

In August every second year (2009, 2011 etc), Røros stages a nightly three-hour **rock opera** in Swedish entitled *Det Brinner en Eld*, or 'Fiery Call for Peace'. It recounts the invasion of Trøndelag by Sweden in 1718, covering the occupation of Røros and the subsequent death of thousands of soldiers on their frozen trek homewards to Sweden. It's enacted on the slag heaps in the upper part of town.

Other annual events:

Femund Race (www.femundlopet.no/eng/) One of Europe's longest dog-sled races starts and ends in Røros in the first week of February.

Winter Chamber Music Festival (www.vinterfestspill.no) Concerts held in Røros Kirke in the first week of March.

Sleeping

The tourist office keeps a list of summer cabins and guesthouses, some within walking distance of town, from around Nkr2500 to Nkr4000 per week in the high season.

Håneset Camping (☎ 72 41 06 00; fax 72 41 06 01; Osloveien; tent or caravan sites Nkr130 plus per person Nkr25, 2-/4-bed cabins Nkr320/420) Simple but well-kept cabins are available at this excellent site, with cooking and laundry facilities, a common room and TV; it's about 2km south of town.

Idrettsparken Hotell (☎ 72 41 10 89; www.idrettsparken.no in Norwegian; Øra 25; tent/caravan sites from

Nkr100/155, cabins from Nkr420, hotel s/d from Nkr665/990, dogs Nkr100; P) The family-run Idrettsparken Hotell, 500m south of the train station, has a range of options for most budgets.

Erzscheidergården (☎ 72 41 11 94; www.erzscheidergaarden.no; Spell Olaveien 6; s/d from Nkr790/990; P 💻) This appealing 16-room guesthouse is up the hill from the centre and behind the church. The wood-panelled rooms are loaded with personality, the atmosphere is Norwegian-family-warmth and the breakfasts were described by one reader as 'the best homemade breakfast buffet in Norway'. We're inclined to agree.

our pick **Vertshuset Røros** (☎ 72 41 93 50; www.vertshusetroros.no; Kjerkgata 34; s/d from Nkr760/990, 2-/3-/4-bed apt Nkr1060/1305/1640; P 💻) Located in a historic building on the main pedestrian thoroughfare, the Vertshuset Røros is another wonderful choice. The all-wood rooms are generously sized, have numerous period touches such as wooden beds with columns and arguably the most comfortable beds in town. If only all hotels in Norway had this much charm.

Bergstadens Hotel (☎ 72 40 60 80; www.bergstaden.no in Norwegian; Osloveien 2; s Nkr850-1395, d Nkr990-1495) This long-standing Røros hotel has pleasant, mostly modern rooms that won't win too many originality awards. Service can be a little impersonal.

Quality Røros Hotel (☎ 72 40 80 00; www.choice.no; An Magrit veien 10; s/d from Nkr845/1090) The Quality Røros is at the top end of town and has well-appointed rooms with a touch more character than most chains but far less than the smaller Røros hotels.

Eating

Røros has some good restaurants, and most places have good-value lunchtime buffets or specials on offer.

our pick **Vertshuset Røros** (☎ 72 41 24 11; Kjerkgata 34; snacks Nkr71-119, starters Nkr81-145, mains Nkr195-270) Our favourite restaurant in town, Vertshuset Røros is both classy and casual with a small but select menu. For dinner, we couldn't bring ourselves to order the 'heart of reindeer', but the fillet of the same beast was sublime. Fresh mountain trout is another highlight. It's pricey, but easily worth it at least once.

Papa's Pizza/Bodegaen (☎ 72 40 60 20; Bergmannsgata 1; child's/small/large pizza Nkr49/90/170, pasta from Nkr129) Papa's, at the bottom end of Bermannsgata, serves decent pizza, fish and meat dishes. Its outdoor tables have views up this historic street.

Krambuavis (☎ 72 41 05 67; Kjerkgata 28; starters Nkr69-122, mains Nkr134-215) This is an excellent choice with large servings, friendly waiters and good food, which ranges from Mexican to spare ribs and fish dishes.

Kaffestugu Cafeteria (☎ 72 41 10 33; Bergmannsgata 18; lunch specials Nkr82-135, mains Nkr75-165; ⏰ 10am-5pm Mon-Fri, 9am-5pm Sat. 11am-5pm Sun) This informal cafeteria in a historic central building offers a good range of coffee, pastries, snacks and light meals. Its lunchtime specials are a little heavy on the potatoes, but the elk burger is good.

There are also many small coffee shops (some of which are attached to crafts and souvenir shops):

Dahlsgården (☎ 72 41 19 89; Mørkstugata 5; ⏰ 10am-5pm Mon-Fri, 10am-4pm Sat, noon-4pm Sun summer, shorter hrs rest-of-year)

Galleri Thomasgården (☎ 72 41 24 70; Kjerkgata 48; ⏰ 10am-5pm Mon-Fri, 10am-4pm Sat, noon-4pm Sun summer, shorter hrs rest-of-year)

Tryggstads Bakeri (☎ 72 41 10 29; Kjerkgata 12; ⏰ 8.30am-7pm Mon-Fri, 9am-4pm Sat, noon-5pm Sun) Great coffee and baked goodies.

Entertainment

Ramm Kjelleren (☎ 72 41 24 11; Kjerkgata 34; ⏰ 7pm-1am Wed, Fri & Sat) This wonderfully atmospheric place occupies the bank vaults of a building dating from the mid-1700s. Cool bar staff, great decoration and a buzzy ambience when full make for a great evening out. It offers (free) live music on Friday night at around 9pm.

Shopping

Given its unaffected ambience, it isn't surprising that Røros has attracted dozens of artists and artisans.

Galleri Thomasgården (☎ 72 41 24 70; Kjerkgata 48; ⏰ 10am-5pm Mon-Fri, 10am-4pm Sat, noon-4pm Sun summer, shorter hrs rest-of-year) At the worthwhile Galleri Thomasgården, potter Torgeir Henriksen creates rustic stoneware and porcelain. You'll also find the wonderful nature-inspired wood carvings of Henry Solli. The player piano is one of only two in Norway and dates back to 1929.

Potteriet Røros (☎ 72 41 17 10; www.potteriet-roros.no in Norwegian; Fargarveien 4; ⏰ 10am-4pm Mon-Fri, 11am-5pm Sat) Here you'll find pottery based on traditional designs from all over Trøndelag, although there are also some creative mod ern interpretations. The pottery workshop next door is open to the public and staff are always happy to explain the history behind each design.

Hartzgården Sølvsmie (☎ 72 41 05 50; Kjerkgata; 🕑 10am-6pm Mon-Fri, 10am-4pm Sat, noon-5pm Sun summer, shorter hrs rest-of-year) Of special interest is this silversmith's shop, where you'll find locally handcrafted silver jewellery with an emphasis on Viking themes, as well as a small historical jewellery exhibit.

Getting There & Away

Røros has one **Coast Air** (www.coastair.no) flight to/from Oslo (from Nkr471) daily except Saturday. For tickets and information, contact **Røros Flyservice** (☎ 72 41 39 00; www.roros-flyservice.no).

Røros lies on the eastern railway line between Oslo (Nkr199, five hours, six daily) and Trondheim (Nkr159, 2½ hours); for Oslo, you may need to change in Hamar. The daily bus to Oslo (Nkr395, six hours) leaves at 12.40am.

AROUND RØROS

Olavsgruva Mine

The **Olavsgruva mine** (☎ 72 41 11 65; Kojedalen; adult/child/senior/student/family Nkr60/30/50/50/140; 🕑 guided tours 11am, 12.30pm 2pm, 3.30pm & 5pm mid-Jun–mid-Aug, shorter hrs rest-of-year) is 13km north of Røros. The moderately interesting exhibition is made worthwhile by **mine tours,** which pass through the historic Nyberget mine, dating from the 1650s. The modern Olavsgruva mine beyond it was begun in 1936. The ground can get muddy and the temperature in the mine is 5°C; bring a jacket and good footwear. To get to the mine, use your own wheels or take a taxi (Nkr450 return).

Johan Falkberget Museum

Røros' favourite son, author Johan Falkberget (1879–1967), grew up at Trondalen farm in the Rugel valley. His works (translated into 19 languages) cover 300 years of the region's mining history. His most famous work, *An-Magrit,* tells the story of a peasant girl who transported copper ore in the Røros mining district. The **museum** (☎ 72 41 46 31; Ratvolden; adult/child Nkr60/30; 🕑 11.30am-3pm Tue-Sun Jul-early Aug, 11.30am-1.30pm Tue-Sun early Aug–mid-Sep) is beside the lake Rugelsjø, 20km north of Røros. Guided tours run at noon Tuesday to Sunday, with an extra one at 1.30pm in July. To get there, take a local train to Rugeldalen station, where a small walking track leads to the museum.

FEMUNDSMARKA NATIONAL PARK

The national park that surrounds Femunden, Norway's second-largest lake, was formed in 1971 to protect the lake and the forests stretching eastwards to Sweden. Indeed, the landscapes here are more Swedish in appearance than recognisably Norwegian. The park has long been a source of falcons for use in the European and Asian sport of falconry and several places in the park are known as Falkfangerhøgda, or 'falcon hunters' height'. If you're very lucky, you may also see wild reindeer grazing in the heights and, in summer, a herd of around 30 musk oxen roams the area along the Røa and Mugga Rivers (in winter they migrate to the Funäsdalen area). It's thought that this group split off from an older herd in the Dovrefjell area and wandered all the way here (see the boxed text, p179).

Sleeping

The two main sleeping options are **Johnsgård Turistsenter** (☎ 62 45 99 25; www.johnsgard.no; Sømådalen; tent sites Nkr130, 4-bed cabin from Nkr170), 9km west of Buvika; and **Langen Gjestegård** (☎ 72 41 37 18; fax 72 41 37 11; Synnervika; s/d from Nkr250/450), a cosy turf-roofed farmhouse near the lake.

Getting There & Away

The historic ferry M/S *Fæmund II* is more than a century old and sails daily between mid-June and late August from Synnervika (also spelt Søndervika), on the northern shore of lake Femunden, to Elgå (six hours return). At the height of summer, the boat sometimes continues on to Buvika and even Femundsenden, at the lake's southern tip. A timetable is available from Røros tourist office (p171).

From mid-June to late August, buses leave Røros train station for Synnervika 45 minutes before the boat's departure. Buses for Røros later meet the boat at Synnervika. You can reach the southern end of Femunden on the Trysil Ekspressen buses (change in Trysil for Engerdal/Drevsjø).

OPPDAL

pop 6531

Oppdal isn't the most architecturally distinguished town in central Norway, but the beauty of its surrounds more than compensates. Oppdal is also an activity centre

OPPDAL ACTIVITIES

White-water Rafting

The nearby, wild and white Driva promises excellent rafting runs from May to October. The outdoor adventure company **Opplev Oppdal** (☎ 72 40 41 80; www.opplev-oppdal.no in Norwegian; Olav Skasliens vei 12) organises trips, from the relatively tame Class I-II family trips to full-day Class III-IV trips that provide substantial thrills. Prices range from Nkr590 to Nkr830 per person per day.

The same company also offers canoe rental (from Nkr320 per day), river surfing (Nkr830) and rock climbing (Nkr830).

Musk Ox & Elk Safaris

To see the decidedly prehistoric musk ox (see the boxed text, p179), take one of the five- to six-hour **safaris** (adult/child Nkr285/175; 9am mid-Jun–mid-Aug) organised by Oppdal Booking (see below).

The humble elk can also be tracked down by taking an elk safari, which leaves on Wednesday evenings (Nkr250, two to three hours) in summer and can be booked through the tourist office.

Hang-gliding

To get an aerial view of scenic Central Norway, a tandem hang-glide could be just what you need. To find out more, contact **Walter Brandsegg** (☎ 72 42 21 30; walter@brandsegg.no); costs start from around Nkr550 per person.

Skiing & Snowboarding

The three-part Oppdal Skisenter climbs the slopes from Hovden, Stølen and Vangslia, all within easy reach of town. The smaller Ådalen ski area nearby has two lifts. Vangslia is generally the easiest, with a couple of beginners' runs, while Stølen offers intermediate skiing and Hovden has three challenging advanced runs. Lift passes for one/two/three days cost Nkr295/540/760. The season runs from late November to late April.

par excellence and that's why most people come here.

The **tourist office** (☎ 72 40 04 70; www.oppdal.com; 9am-6pm Mon-Fri, 10am-4pm Sat & Sun mid-Jun–mid-Aug, shorter hrs rest-of-year) has information on local activities and the wider attractions of central Norway.

Oppdal Booking (☎ 72 40 08 00; www.oppdal-booking.no; 8am-4pm Mon-Fri mid-Jun–mid-Aug, 8am-6pm daily mid-Jan-Easter, shorter hrs rest-of-year) is a central reservations service for accommodation and activities including trips to see musk ox; booking fees apply.

Sleeping & Eating

If you're unable to find a bed, contact Oppdal Booking or the tourist office for assistance.

Oppdalstunet Vandrerhjem (☎ 72 42 23 11; oppdal.hostel@vandrerhjem.no; Gamle Kongsvei; dm/s/d Nkr150/370/450; May-Nov) This place, 1.5km northeast of central Oppdal, offers good hostel accommodation on a gentle rise overlooking the valley.

Quality Oppdal Hotel (☎ 72 40 07 00; www.choice.no; Olav Skasliens vei 8; s/d Nkr1250/1450) Part of the Choice Hotels network, this comfortable hotel offers pleasant rooms that are overpriced, but easily the best in central Oppdal; prices sometimes drop in summer.

Sletvold Apartment Hotel (☎ 72 40 40 90; booking@sletvold-stolen.no; Gamle Kongsvei; s/d from Nkr805/1015) If you don't mind being on the town's northern fringe, this fine place (part of the Norlandia hotel network) represents excellent value with tidy, appealing rooms, some of which have views down the valley.

Møllen Restaurant & Pizzeria (☎ 72 42 18 00; Dovreveien 2; pasta & kebabs Nkr79-139, small/large pizza from Nkr85/159, mains Nkr135-215) In the town centre alongside the E6, this is a good choice if you feel like a sit-down meal that's a cut above hamburgers, but with a reasonable price tag.

Café Ludvik (☎ 72 42 01 40; Inge Krokanns vei 21; mains Nkr69-159) The popular Café Ludvik is also good, though with a touch less class. It serves a range of inexpensive light meals, including beef dishes, omelettes and pasta. It's 300m south of the centre.

Perrongen Steak House (☎ 72 40 07 00; starters Nkr89-115, mains Nkr115-245) This place, in the Quality Oppdal Hotel, has the best food and he most sophistication of any place in town. Reindeer steak goes for Nkr255.

Getting There & Away

The best access to Oppdal is via the four or five daily train services between Oslo (Nkr199 to Nkr674, five hours) and Trondheim (Nkr199 to Nkr213, 1½ hours). Oppdal lies on the twice-daily Nor-Way Bussekspress route between Bergen (Nkr686, 12½ hours) and Trondheim (Nkr210, two hours). Cheaper Lavprisekspressen buses (from Nkr149) also pass through once or twice daily en route between Oslo and Trondheim.

TROLLHEIMEN

The small Trollheimen range, with a variety of trails through gentle mountains and lake-studded upland regions, is most readily accessed from Oppdal. You can either hitch or hike the 15km from Oppdal up the toll road (Nkr30) to **Osen**, which is the main entrance to the wilderness region. The best map to use is Statens Kartverk's *Turkart Trollheimen* (1:75,000), which costs Nkr120 at the tourist office in Oppdal.

A straightforward hiking destination in Trollheimen is the hut and historic farm at **Vassendsetra**. From Osen (the outlet of the river Gjevilvatnet), 3km north of the main road to Sunndalsøra, you can take the boat *Trollheimen II* all the way to Vassendsetra (Nkr150 return). From July to mid-August it leaves from Osen daily at noon and from Vassendsetra at 3.30pm. Alternatively, it is possible to drive or hike 6km along the road from Osen to the DNT hut, **Gjevilvasshytta**, and follow the lakeshore trail for another 12km until you come to **Vassendsetra** (☎ 72 42 32 20; fax 72 42 34 30; dm for DNT members/nonmembers Nkr150/230, breakfast Nkr75/125, dinner Nkr160/200; ⌚ Jul & Aug). About midway you'll pass several outstanding sandy beaches, with excellent summer swimming.

The popular three-day 'Trekanten' hut tour follows the impressive Gjevilvasshytta–Trollheimshytta–Jøldalshytta–Gjevilvasshytta route; contact Oppdal Booking (opposite) for details.

DOMBÅS

pop 2812

Dombås, a popular adventure and winter-sports centre, makes a convenient break for travellers between the highland national parks and the western fjords. That said, there's more choice of activities to the north in Oppdal (p175), while for rafting you should head to Sjoa (p182).

Dovrefjell National Park Centre (Dovrefjell Nasjonalparksenter; ☎ 61 24 14 44; dombaas@nasjonalparker.org; Sentralplassen; admission free; ⌚ 9am-8pm mid-Jun–mid-Aug, shorter hrs rest-of-year) is an adjunct to the **tourist office** (☎ 61 24 14 44; www.dovrenett.no; ⌚ 9am-8pm mid-Jun–mid-Aug, 9am-4pm Mon-Fri rest-of-year).

Sights

The **Dovregubbens Rike Trollpark** (☎ 61 24 12 90; www.trollpark.com; Sentralplassen; adult/child Nkr40/20; ⌚ 10am-7.45pm Mon-Fri, 10am-6.45pm Sat, 11am-6.45pm Sun mid-Jun–mid-Aug, 10am-4pm Mon-Fri, 10am-2pm Sat rest-of-year) brings to life the legendary Norwegian trolls and the 'Realm of the Mountain King' (the Dovre massif), inhabited by the friendliest and most powerful troll. There's also a film explaining local natural history and various displays, from stuffed animals and prehistoric hunting techniques to the creation of national parks in the region.

Tours

Moskus-Safari Dovrefjell (☎ 99 70 37 66; www.moskus-safari.no) offers a range of well-run, guided tours including:

Elk Safari This tour (Nkr250) departs from the tourist office from mid-June to mid-August Tuesday to Thursday; advance booking required.

Hiking to Snøhetta This five- to seven-hour (Nkr450) guided hike to the summit of Snøhetta (2286m) runs on Saturday from mid-June to mid-August, requires a minimum of five people and reservations are essential.

Musk Ox Safari This five-hour tour (Nkr300) departs at 9am from the tourist office from 10 June to at least the end of August and weekends in September. No advance booking is necessary.

Sleeping & Eating

Bjørkhol Camping (☎ 61 24 13 31; www.bjorkhol.no; Bjørkhol; tent/caravan sites Nkr90/110, 2-/4-bed cabin with shared bathroom from Nkr240/350, 2-bed cabins with bathroom from Nkr550) One of Norway's best-value and probably friendliest camp sites is 7km east of Dombås. The facilities are in excellent nick and a bus runs several times daily from Dombås.

Trolltun Gjestegård & Dombås Vandrerhjem (☎ 61 24 09 60; www.trolltun.no; hostel dm/d/f Nkr200/550/600, hotel s/d Nkr670/960) This excellent place is 1.5km northeast of town, up the hill from the E6. The setting's lovely, the rooms tidy and the meals reasonably priced. A good choice.

Norlandia Dovrefjell Hotell (☎ 61 24 10 05; www.norlandia.no; s/d Nkr1020/1200) This is another good place with attractive rooms and it's just far enough removed from the centre to remind you that you're on the fringe of a wilderness area. You'll find it off the E136, about 2km northwest of the centre.

The main commercial complex in the centre includes the popular **Frich's Cafeteria** (☎ 61 24 10 23; Sentralplassen; 🕒 breakfast, lunch & dinner), which serves cheap if unimaginative meals. In the same complex is **Senter-Grillen** (☎ 61 24 18 33; Sentralplassen; 🕒 breakfast, lunch & dinner), which serves pizza.

Getting There & Away

Dombås lies on the railway line between Oslo (Nkr565, 3¾ hours) and Trondheim (Nkr352, 2½ hours). It is also the cut-off point for the spectacular Raumabanen line down Romsdalen to Åndalsnes (Nkr198, 1¼ hours, two or three daily). Nor-Way Bussekspress buses between Bergen (Nkr631, 11¼ hours) and Trondheim (Nkr315, 3¼ hours) call in twice daily in either direction. Cheaper Lavprisekspressen buses (from Nkr149) also pass through en route between Oslo and Trondheim.

The drive from Dombås to Åndalsnes, which also goes down the Romsdalen (107km), is spectacular.

DOVREFJELL-SUNNDALSFJELLA NATIONAL PARK

This 4367-sq-km national park, Norway's largest continuous protected area, protects the dramatic highlands around the 2286m-high Snøhetta and provides a suitably bleak habitat for Arctic foxes, reindeer, wolverines and musk oxen. Snøhetta can be ascended by hikers from Snøheim (allow six hours). The Knutshøene massif (1690m) section of the park, east of the E6, protects Europe's most diverse intact alpine ecosystem.

The **Fokstumyra marshes** are home to an astonishing array of bird life. Approximately 75 species nest in the area and up to 40 others are occasionally observed. Among the more unusual species breeding near the water are the ruff, great snipe, Temminck's stint, whimbrel, great northern diver (loon), lapwing, lesser white-fronted goose and hen harrier. Species that breed in the surrounding hills and forests include the snow bunting, ring ouzel, fieldfare, purple sandpiper, great grey shrike, dipper, brambling, peregrine falcon, dotterel, short-eared owl, raven and shore lark.

Many of these species can be viewed from the 7km-long marked trail near the Dombås end of the reserve; note that from May to July visitors are restricted to this trail to prevent disturbance of nesting birds.

For more information, visit the Dovrefjell National Park Centre (p177), while a variety of tours into the park are covered on p177.

To get there, you could also rent a bike from the Dombås tourist office (per hour/day Nkr35/100) or otherwise take a taxi (around Nkr170 one way).

Hikers will fare best with the Statens Kartverk map *Dovrefjell* (1:100,000). However it doesn't include the Knutshø section; for that you need Statens Kartverk's *Einunna 1519-I* and *Folldal 1519-II* topographic sheets.

Sleeping & Eating

The original DNT **Snøheim** hut was, thankfully judged to be too near the army's Hjerkinn firing range and was replaced by the new self-service **Reinheim** hut, 5km north and at 1341m, in Stroplsjødalen. DNT also maintains several other self-service huts in the adjacent Skrymtheimen region; keys are available from Dombås tourist office.

Kongsvold Fjeldstue (☎ 72 40 43 40; www.kongsvold.no; Kongsvold; d from Nkr650) Park information maps, meals and accommodation are available at this charming and historic place, 13km north of Hjerkinn on the E6. The intriguing early-18th-century timber buildings huddle deep in Drivdalen, 500m from tiny Kongsvold station (trains stop only on request). Every room is different.

Hjerkinn Fjellstue (☎ 61 24 29 27; www.hjerkinn.no in Norwegian; Hjerkinn; s/d from Nkr625/950) This cosy inn is about 1.5km east of Hjerkinn on Rv29. The rooms in the annexe are simple but fine and a lot cheaper than the main hotel building. There's also a restaurant and camping is available.

Getting There & Away

There's no public transport into the park, although tours from Dombås offer musk ox safaris (see p177). The only public transport between Dombås and Hjerkinn is by train (Nkr77, 25 minutes).

MUSK OX

Although a member of the family Bovidae, the musk ox *(Ovibos moschatus)* bears little resemblance to its nearest relations (sheep, goats and cattle) or indeed to any other animal. During the last ice age, it was distributed throughout the northern hemisphere's glaciated areas. Wild herds can now be found in parts of Greenland, Canada, Alaska and the Dovrefjell-Sunndalsfjella and Femundsmarka National Parks in Norway.

The musk ox, weighing between 225kg and 445kg, has incredibly high shoulders and an enormous low-slung head with two broad, flat horns that cross the forehead, curving outwards and downwards before twisting upwards and forwards. Its incredibly thick and shaggy coat, with a matted fleece of soft hair underneath, covers the whole body and hangs down like a skirt to almost reach the ground. Below this hair only the bottom part of the legs protrudes, giving the animal a solid, stocky appearance reminiscent of a medieval horse dressed for a joust. During the rutting season, when the males gather their harems, they repeatedly charge each other, butting their heads together with a crash that's often heard for miles around. This heated battle continues until one animal admits defeat and lumbers off.

Traditionally, the musk ox's main predator has been the wolf; its primary defence is to form a circle with the males on the outside and females and calves inside, trusting in the force of its collective horns to rip open attackers. This defence has proven useless against human hunters, especially the Greenlandic Inuit, and numbers have been seriously depleted. Only with restocking have they been able to thrive again.

In 1931 10 animals were reintroduced to Dovrefjell from Greenland. Musk oxen all but vanished during WWII, but 23 were transplanted from Greenland between 1947 and 1953. The herd has now grown to around 80 animals and some have shifted eastwards into Femundsmarka National Park to form a new herd.

Your best chance of seeing the musk ox is to take a musk ox safari, either from Oppdal (see the boxed text, p176) or Dombås (p177). You may also see them while hiking through the Røa and Mugga Rivers section of Femundsmarka National Park (p175) in summer.

Musk oxen aren't inherently aggressive toward humans, but an animal that feels threatened can charge at speeds of up to 60km/h and woe betide anything that gets in its way. Hikers should stay at least 200m away; if an animal seems agitated or paws at the ground don't run, but back off slowly until it relaxes.

OTTA

pop 3724

Set deep in Gudbrandsdalen, Otta occupies a strategic position at the confluence of the Otta and Lågen Rivers. Despite this promising location, it's not the region's prettiest town, although, to be fair, we were last there on a rainy Sunday and Monday when the town was not at its best. Otta's main attraction is as the gateway to Rondane National Park.

Rondane National Park Centre (☎ 61 08 08 70; otta@nasjonalparker.org; Johan Nygårdgata 17a; 10am-4pm Mon-Fri, 10am-2pm Sat)

Tourist office (☎ 61 23 66 50; www.visitrondane.com; Otta Skysstasjon; 8.30am-7pm Mon-Fri, 11am-6pm Sat & Sun mid-Jun–mid-Aug, shorter hrs rest-of-year)

Sights

The unusual 6m-high natural pillar formations of **Kvitskriuprestene** (White-scree Priests) resemble an assembly of priests and were formed by erosion of an Ice Age–moraine (deposit of material transported by a glacier). They're 4km east along the Nkr10 toll road from Sel towards Mysusæter, and a steep 20-minute hike uphill.

Sleeping

Otta Camping (☎ 61 23 03 09; www.ottacamping.no in Norwegian; Ottadalen; tent or caravan sites for 2 people Nkr130, 4-bed cabins Nkr350-550) The convenient and popular riverside Otta Camping is a 1.5km walk from the train and bus stations; cross the Otta bridge from the centre, turn right and continue about 1km upstream.

Killis Overnatting (☎ 61 23 04 92; Ola Dahlsgate 35; s/d/tr with shared bathroom Nkr250/280/325) The Killis Overnatting offers simple rooms (a shower cost Nkr5) and it is overseen by a delightful woman who will make you feel right at home.

GURI SAVES THE DAY

During the Kalmar War between Sweden and Denmark, when Norway was united with Denmark, 550 Scottish mercenaries arrived in Norway in August 1612 to aid the Swedes. Word spread through Gudbrandsdalen and local peasants armed themselves with axes, scythes and other farming implements. They stacked rocks and branches to block the track and, to set up a diversion, placed several older men across the river to fire their muskets at the column, using blanks.

As the Scots reached a narrow section of path between the river and a steep hillside at Høgkringom, 3km south of Otta, the heroic Pillarguri (Guri) dashed up the hill to announce their arrival by sounding her shepherd's birch-bark horn. The old farmers began to fire. The Scots fired back across the river, then responded to Guri's music by waving their hats and playing their bagpipes, unaware of the trap.

As Guri sounded her horn again, more rocks were tumbled across the trail behind the column, blocking any retreat. The farmers attacked with rocks and their crude weapons, savagely defeating the trapped contingent and making the river flow red with blood.

Only six farmers were killed in the battle. The victors intended to take the 134 surviving Scots as prisoners to Akershus Fortress in Oslo. However, during the victory celebrations at Kvam, the farmers, who had to get on with their harvest and couldn't be bothered with a tiresome march, executed the prisoners one by one.

The exploits of the peasant 'army' are still remembered in Otta, where the local *bunad* (national costume) is a distinctly un-Norwegian tartan and there's a statue of Pillarguri near the train station. There's also a war memorial at Kringom commemorating the victory, across the river from which rises the hill Pillarguri.

Grand Gjestegård (☎ 61 23 12 00; fax 61 23 04 62; Ola Dahlsgate; s/d Nkr610/840) Recently renovated and the busy hub of the little that happens in Otta, the Grand Gjestegård wins plaudits for its friendly welcome and pleasant rooms.

Norlandia Otta Hotell (☎ 61 21 08 00; www.norlandia.no/otta; Ola Dahlsgate 7; s/d Nkr820/1095) Don't be put off by the run-down 1980s exterior or that this place may be less personal than the other places; the rooms are large, comfortable and well-appointed.

Eating

In addition to the restaurants at the Grand Gjestegård and Norlandia Otta Hotell, there are two other decent options.

Milano Restaurant & Pizzeria (☎ 61 23 19 93; Storgata 17B; pasta Nkr90-109, small/large pizza Nkr90/180, other mains Nkr115-179; 🕑 1-11pm Sun-Thu, 1-11.30pm Sat) One of the most popular places in town, this Otta institution has more than 80 menu items to choose from and the outdoor balcony is the place to eat them in summer.

Pillarguri Kafé (☎ 61 23 01 04; Storgata 7; mains Nkr85-179) Another good choice of eatery, the Pillarguri promises a varied menu, with Norwegian fare (reindeer stew costs Nkr145) as well as sushi and a range of cheaper lunch specials.

Getting There & Away

Local buses to/from Lom (normal/express Nkr78/99, two/one hours) leave up to six times daily, less often on weekends. Nor-Way Bussekspress has buses to/from Lillehammer (Nkr180, two hours, up to five daily) and Oslo (Nkr410, five hours). Cheaper Lavprisekspressen buses (from Nkr149) also pass through once or twice daily. The town also lies on the Dovre rail line between Oslo (Nkr491, 3¼ hours) and Trondheim (Nkr426, three hours) and there are services to Bergen (Nkr964, 11 daily).

RONDANE NATIONAL PARK

Henrik Ibsen described the 963-sq-km **Rondane National Park** (www.visitrondane.com) as 'palace piled upon palace'. It was created in 1962 as Norway's first national park to protect the fabulous Rondane massif, regarded by many as the finest alpine hiking country in Norway. Ancient reindeer-trapping sites and burial mounds suggest that the area has been inhabited for thousands of years and the park is now one of the last refuges for the wild reindeer. Much of the park's glaciated and lichen-coated landscape lies above 1400m and 10 rough and stony peaks rise to over 2000m, including the highest, Rondslottet (2178m),

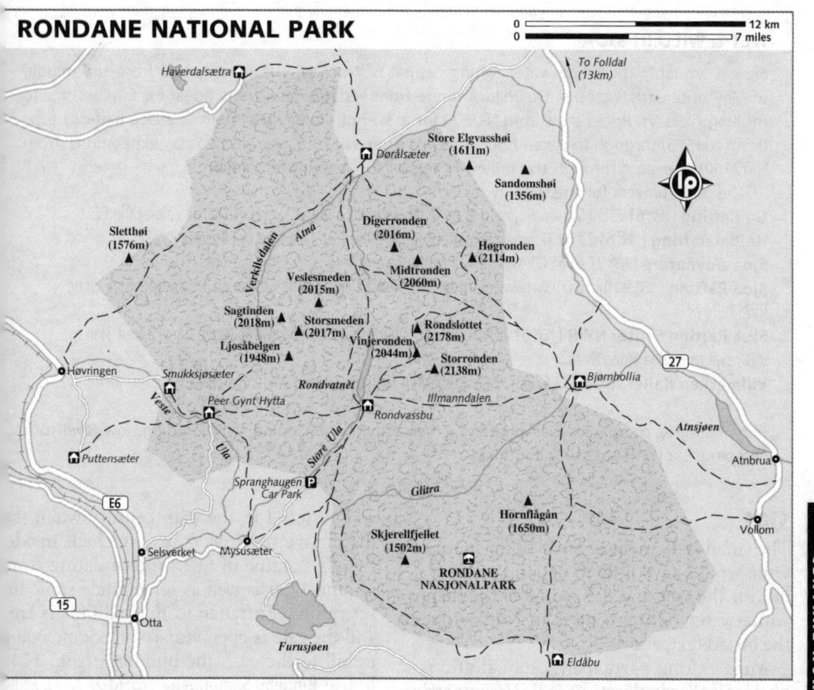

ınd Storronden (2138m). Rondane's range of wildlife includes 28 mammal species and 124 bird species.

If you're driving, the 87km-long Rv27 between Folldal and the E6 5km north of Ringebu is a stunningly beautiful route that runs along the Rondane range.

For hikers, Rondane provides ample opportunities for high-country exploration and the relatively dry climate is an added bonus, although the season only runs in July and August. The most accessible route into the park is from the Spranghaugen car park, about 13km uphill along a good road from Otta and via the toll road (Nkr10). From there, it's a straightforward 6km (1½ hour) hike to **Rondvassbu**, where there's a popular, staffed DNT hut; there are other DNT huts in the park.

From Rondvassbu, it's a five-hour return climb to the summit of Storronden. Alternatively, head for the spectacular view from the more difficult summit of **Vinjeronden** (2044m), then tackle the narrow ridge leading to the neighbouring peak, Rondslottet (about six hours return from Rondvassbu).

The best maps to use are Statens Kartverk's *Rondane* (1:100,000; Nkr99) and *Rondane Sør* (1:50,000).

Just down the hill from the 'Bom' (toll post) gate is a small shop selling staple provisions and supplies. Camping is permitted anywhere in the national park except at Rondvassbu, where you're restricted to the designated area.

Mysusæter Fjellstue (☎ 61 23 39 25; www.mysuseter rondane.no; Mysusæter; dm Nkr250, d with/without bathroom Nkr650/585) promises a basic roof over your head; while the **Rondane Spa Høyfjellshotell** (☎ 61 20 90 90; www.rondane.no; Mysusæter; per person with full board from Nkr850) is a comfortable upmarket option with good spa facilities, including pedicures for worn-out hikers' feet.

Getting There & Around

In summer, buses run twice daily between Otta and Mysusæter (Nkr29, 45 minutes), from where it's a further 4km to the car park.

From Rondvassbu, the ferry *Rondegubben* crosses the lake Rondvatnet to Nordvika (Nkr50, 30 minutes) three times daily from early July to late August.

WET & WILD IN SJOA

Sjoa is arguably the white-water rafting capital of Norway. The season runs from the middle of May until early October. Excursions range from sedate Class I runs (ideal for families) up to thrilling Class Vs. Prices start from Nkr500 for a 3½-hour family trip; there are also half-day trips (from Nkr565) through to seven-hour day trips (from Nkr790), or even two-day expeditions (from Nkr2150) that pass through the roiling waters of the Åsengjuvet canyon.

The main players for this activity include:

Go Rafting (☎ 61 23 50 00; www.gorafting.no in Norwegian) About 3.5km north of Sjoa along the E6.

Heidal Rafting (☎ 61 23 60 37; www.heidalrafting.no; Sjoa) Just 1km west of E6 along Rv257.

Sjoa Adventure (☎ 93 40 65 00; www.sjoaadventure.com; Sjoa)

Sjoa Rafting (☎ 90 07 10 00; www.sjoarafting.com; Nedre Heidal) Some 7.5km upstream from Sjoa along Rv257.

Sjoa Rafting Senter NWR (☎ 61 23 07 00; www.sjoaraftingsenter.no; Varphaugen Gård) About 3km upstream from Sjoa along Rv257.

Villmarken Kaller (☎ 90 52 57 03; www.villmarken-kaller.no) About 20km upstream from Sjoa along Rv257.

Most of these companies also organise other activities, including riverboarding, low-level rock climbing, canyoning, caving and hiking.

SJOA

The small settlement of Sjoa, 10km south of Otta, would have little to detain you were it not for the fact that this is one of the major white-water rafting centres in Norway (see the boxed text, above).

Most rafting participants stay at atmospheric **Sjoa Vandrerhjem** (☎ 61 23 62 00; www.heidalrafting.no; dm Nkr155-230, 2-bed r incl breakfast Nkr320-420; ⌚ mid-May–Sep), a hillside hostel. Dinner costs Nkr100 and is served in the wonderful 1747 log-farmhouse building.

The camp site at **Sæta Camping** (☎ 61 23 51 47; tent/caravan sites Nkr130/170, 1-5-bed hut per person from Nkr375) is down by the river bank. It's a pleasant grassy site with a front-row seat for some of the minor rapids.

Nor-Way Bussekspress bus routes between Oslo (Nkr400) and the western fjords pass through Sjoa three times daily.

RINGEBU

pop 4457

The southernmost small community of Gudbrandsdalen, the narrow river valley that stretches for 200km between lake Mjøsa and Dombås, Ringebu is worth a detour for its lovely **stave church** (☎ 61 28 43 50; adult/child Nkr40/20; ⌚ 8am-6pm Jul, 9am-5pm late May-Jun & Aug), 2km south of town and just off the E6. A church has existed on this site since the arrival of Christianity in the 11th century. The current version, which remains the local parish church, dates from around 1220, but was restored in the 17th century when the distinctive red tower was attached. Inside there's a statue of St Laurence dating from around 1250 as well as some crude runic inscriptions. Entrance to the grounds is free and the gate is open year-round. Some 300m uphill to the east, the buildings from 174[illegible] house **Ringebu Samlingene** (☎ 61 28 27 00; adult/child Nkr40/20; ⌚ 11am-5pm Tue-Sun mid-Jun–mid-Aug) which served as the vicarage until 1991.

For further information, contact the Ringebu **tourist office** (☎ 61 28 47 00; ⌚ 8am-6pm Mon-Thu, 8am-8pm Fri, 10am-1pm Sat, 5-8pm Sun mid-Jun–mid-Aug, shorter hrs rest-of-year).

Nor-Way Bussekspress bus routes between Oslo (Nkr355, five hours) and the western fjords stop in Ringebu three times daily. Cheaper Lavprisekspressen buses (from Nkr149) to Oslo or Trondheim also pass through one or two times a day. Trains to Oslo (Nkr403, 2¾ hours) or Trondheim (Nkr514, 3½ hours) stop in Ringebu four or five times daily.

WESTERN CENTRAL NORWAY

LOM

pop 2436

If you were to set up a town as a travellers gateway, you'd put it somewhere like Lom in the heart of some of Norway's most spectacular mountain scenery. Roads lead from

Lom to Geiranger (74km; p259) and the staggering Sognefjellet Road leads from here across the top of the Jotunheimen National Park (p184). Lom itself is picturesque with a lovely stave church.

Information

The helpful Lom **tourist office** (☎ 61 21 29 90; www.visitlom.com or www.visitjotunheimen.com; 9am-7pm Mon-Fri & 10am-7pm Sat & Sun mid-Jun–mid-Aug, shorter hrs rest-of-year), in the Norwegian Mountain Museum, dispenses advice and brochures. It also provides free internet access.

Sights

LOM STAVKYRKJE

This delightful 12th-century Norman-style **stave church** (☎ 97 07 53 97; adult/child Nkr45/free; 9am-8pm daily mid-Jun–mid-Aug, 10am-4pm mid-May–mid-Jun & mid-Aug–mid-Sep), in the centre of town on a rise by the water, is one of Norway's finest. Still the functioning local church, it was constructed in 1170, extended in 1634 and given its current cruciform shape with the addition of two naves in 1663. Guided tours explain the interior paintings and Jakop Sæterdalen's chancel arch and pulpit (from 1793). At night, the church is lit to fairy-tale effect. Entry to the grounds is free.

In the adjacent souvenir shop, there's a small **museum** (admission Nkr10; same hrs as church) about the stave church.

FOSSHEIM STEINSENTER

The **Fossheim Steinsenter** (☎ 61 21 14 60; www.fossheimsteinsenter.no; admission free; 9am-8pm Mon-Sat, 9am-7pm Sun mid-Jun–mid-Aug, shorter hrs rest-of-year) combines Europe's largest selection of rare and beautiful rocks, minerals, fossils, gems and jewellery for sale and it also includes a large museum of Norwegian and foreign geological specimens; we found stones from Gabon, Congo and Brazil.

The knowledgeable owners of the centre, both avid rock collectors, travel the world in search of specimens but they're especially proud of the Norwegian national stone, thulite. It was discovered in 1820 and is now quarried in Lom; the reddish colour is derived from traces of manganese.

NORWEGIAN MOUNTAIN MUSEUM

Acting as the visitors centre for Jotunheimen National Park, this worthwhile **mountain museum** (Norsk Fjellmuseum; ☎ 61 21 16 00; www.fjell.museum.no; adult/child Nkr50/free; 9am-7pm Mon-Fri, 10am-7pm Sat & Sun mid-Jun–mid-Aug, shorter hrs rest-of-year) contains mountaineering memorabilia, exhibits on natural history (the woolly mammoth is a highlight) and cultural and industrial activity in the Norwegian mountains. There's also an excellent 10-minute mountain slide show, a discussion of tourism and its impact on wilderness and, upstairs, a scale model of the park.

PRESTHAUGEN OPEN-AIR MUSEUM

Behind the mountain museum, this **museum** (Presthaugen Bygde-museum; ☎ 61 21 19 33; www.gbdmuseum.no; adult/child Nkr40/10; 11am-5pm late Jun–mid-Aug, guided tours 11.30am & 2.30pm Mon-Fri) is a collection of 19th-century farm buildings, several *stabbur* (elevated storehouses), an old hut (it's claimed that St Olav slept here) and a summer mountain dairy.

Activities

Although most of the serious trekking takes place in neighbouring Jotunheimen National Park, there are several **hiking trails** closer to town; ask the tourist office for maps, directions and its 'Footpaths in Lom' pamphlet. A popular route is the 3km return loop up Lomseggi (1289m) to the century-old stone cottage called Smithbue, with some excellent views of Ottadalen and Bøverdalen en route.

For something a touch more energetic, contact **Naturopplevingar** (☎ 61 21 11 55; www.naturopplevingar.no in Norwegian), which can organise ski tours and climbing. For an adrenaline rush contact **Skjåk Rafting** (☎ 99 77 50 88; www.skjak-rafting.no, in Norwegian; Skjåk); its base is in Skjåk, 18km upstream from Lom along Rv15.

For a full list (including prices) of hikes, glacier walks and ice-climbing in Jotunheimen National Park, pick up a copy of *Sognefjellet – Activities and Attractions* from the Lom tourist office.

Sleeping & Eating

Lom has three places to stay, all of which are recommended.

Nordal Turistsenter (☎ 61 21 93 00; www.nordalturistsenter.no; tent sites Nkr170-240, s/d/f Nkr660/950/1400, light meals from Nkr50) A busy, rambling place in the centre of town, the Nordal Turistsenter has something for everyone with comfy rooms, self-catering cabins and a camp site at the water's edge. It also has a casual cafeteria-style restaurant that serves simple meals, and a cosy pub.

our pick **Fossheim Turisthotell** (☎ 61 21 95 00; www.fossheimhotel.no; hotel s/d Nkr925/1250, hotel annexe s/d Nkr800/950, 4-bed apt Nkr1700) This historic family hotel at the eastern end of town is one of the best hotel-restaurant combinations in Norway. The all-wood rooms in the main hotel building are lovely (we especially like rooms 401 and 402 for the balconies and views), while there are also luxurious log cabins with modern interiors and simpler, cheaper rooms (some with good views) in the adjacent annexe. But this place is more famous for formerly being the home kitchen of the renowned Norwegian chef Arne Brimi (open 1pm to 3.30pm and 7pm to 10pm). Now under the care of Brimi's protégés, the traditional Norwegian food is exquisite. Specialities include wild trout, reindeer, elk and ptarmigan. The lunch buffets are highly recommended (from Nkr250), while the evening meals consist of three-/four-course set menus (Nkr250/495).

Fossberg Hotell (☎ 61 21 22 50; www.fossberg.no; s/d Nkr850/1150; 8am-10pm Mon-Sat, 10am-10pm Sun) Although not in the same league as the Fossheim Turisthotell, this is nonetheless an appealing place in the centre of town. The pine-clad rooms are tidy and pleasant and there's a gymnasium for guests. It also has a popular cafeteria (light meals from Nkr55, mains Nkr115 to Nkr215) where the food's nothing to write home about, but at least the outdoor tables are a pleasant place to do so.

Kafe Isbar (☎ 61 21 92 05; light meals Nkr79-125; 11am-9pm) Also in the centre of town, this informal café has an upstairs terrace with fine views.

Shopping

In addition to the shop at the Fossheim Steinsenter (p183), the small **Brimi Bue** (☎ 61 21 95 92; www.brimibue.no in Norwegian; 10am-8pm Jul, 10am-4pm Aug-Nov & Apr-Jun), next to the Fossheim Turisthotell, has cookbooks, organic foods and kitchenware inspired by Arne Brimi.

Getting There & Away

The thrice daily Nor-Way Bussekspress service between Oslo (Nkr470, 6½ hours) and Måløy (Nkr340, 4½ hours) passes through Lom. It's also on Ottadalen Billag's summer route between Otta (Nkr100, one hour) and Sogndal (Nkr230, 3½ hours, two daily), which serves Sognefjellet Rd from late June to early September. The *Sognefjellet – Activities and Attractions* brochure from the Lom tourist office has a timetable.

AROUND LOM

If eating at the Fossheim Turisthotell has you inspired by the food of Arne Brimi and you want to taste meals cooked by the man himself, **Vianvang** (☎ 90 50 24 69 or 41 93 11 11; www.brimiland.no in Norwegian; by appointment) is the master-chef's highland restaurant that he opens only by appointment. Here you can watch him work as he cooks up a gourmet meal. If you're coming from Lom along the Rv15, take the Rv51 towards Randsverk just before you reach Vågåmo (Vågå). Prices depend on the banquet and seasonal produce prices, but having arguably Norway's finest chef prepare a meal for you doesn't come cheap. It is, however, always worth it.

To stay nearby, **Brimisæter** (☎ 91 13 75 58; www.brimi-seter.no; per person around Nkr300) is a former summer mountain dairy with a simple but lovely rural family ambience and plenty of animals that kids will love. **Brimi-Fjellstugu** (☎ 61 23 98 12; www.brimi-fjellstugu.no; per person from Nkr475) offers higher levels of comfort in the same stirring mountain setting.

JOTUNHEIMEN NATIONAL PARK

The high peaks and glaciers of the Jotunheimen National Park (1151 sq km) make for Norway's best-loved and busiest wilderness destination. Hiking routes lead from ravine-like valleys and past deep lakes, plunging waterfalls and 60 glaciers to the tops of all the peaks in Norway over 2300m, including Galdhøpiggen (the highest peak in northern Europe at 2469m), Glittertind (2452m) and Store Skagastølstind (2403m). By one count, there are more than 275 summits above 2000m inside the park. DNT maintains staffed huts along most of the routes and there's also a choice of private lodges by the main roads.

For park information, contact Lom tourist office (p183).

Sights & Activities

SOGNEFJELLET ROAD

Snaking through the park (and providing access to many of the trailheads) is the stunningly scenic Sognefjellet Road (Rv55), billed as 'the road over the roof of Norway'

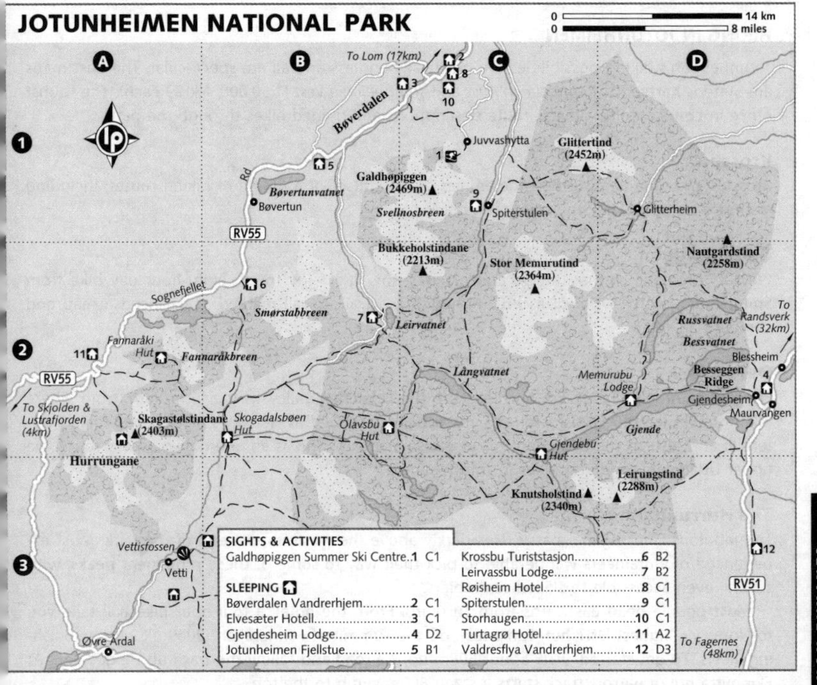

It connects Lustrafjorden with Lom and was constructed in 1939 by unemployed youths to a height of 1434m, making it the highest mountain road in northern Europe and providing those with a vehicle a taste of some of Norway's finest mountain panoramas. So fine is the road that it has been chosen as one of 18 'National Tourist Routes' (see the boxed text, p414); visit www.turistveg.no/index.asp?lang=eng for more information about the road.

Access from the southwest is via the multiple hairpin bends climbing up beyond the tree line to **Turtagrø**, with a wonderful vista of the **Skagastølstindane** mountains on your right. If you're coming from Lom, the ascent is more gradual, following beautiful **Bøverdalen**, the valley of the Bøvra River, with its lakes, glacial rivers, grass-roofed huts and patches of pine forest. The road summit on **Sognefjell** offers superb views.

The snow sometimes doesn't melt until at least early July, although the road is usually open from May to September. Even so, at higher elevations visitors should prepare for new snow at any time of year. The road can get very narrow and snow is often piled metres high on either side of the road. There are plenty of places to pull over and allow cars to pass (not to mention admire the spectacular view) and there are ample camping and other accommodation options lining the road (see p187).

Although this road is mainly traversed by motorised transport, the Sognefjellet Road also has legendary status among cyclists and frequently appears on lists of the world's most spectacular cycle routes. It's a serious undertaking that requires high levels of fitness and perfect brakes, but if you're a cyclist there are few finer roads in Norway.

From mid-June to late August, **Ottadalen Billag** (☎ 61 23 44 55; www.fjord1.no) has buses that run between Otta and Sogndal (Nkr230, 3½ hours, two daily) via Sognefjellet Road.

GALDHØPIGGEN SUMMER SKI CENTRE

Juvvashytta hut serves as the gateway to this **ski centre** (☎ 61 21 17 50; fax 61 21 21 72), at 1850m on the icy heights of Norway's highest mountain. From Galdesand on the Rv55, follow the Galdhøpiggen road (Nkr70 toll) to its end at

HIKING IN JOTUNHEIMEN

Jotunheimen's hiking possibilities are practically endless and all are spectacular. The best maps are Statens Kartverk's *Jotunheimen Aust* and *Jotunheimen Vest* (1:50,000; Nkr99 each). The tourist office in Lom can offer advice, route descriptions and guided hikes through the park.

Krossbu

Krossbu, near the head of Bøverdalen, lies at the outset of a tangle of hiking routes, including a short day trip to the Smørstabbreen glacier.

Galdhøpiggen

With its dramatic cirques, arêtes and glaciers, this is a fairly tough eight-hour day hike from Spiterstulen, with 1470m of ascent. Although the trail is well marked, you'll need a map and compass.

Øvre Årdal

From Øvre Årdal, head 12km northeast up the Utladalen valley to the farm Vetti, from where hiking tracks lead to Vettisfossen (275m), usually described as Norway's highest free-falling waterfall, and also to the unstaffed hut at Stølsmaradalen. This is an alternative access route, via upper Utladalen, to longer hikes in Jotunheimen.

The Hurrungane

The fabulous Hurrungane massif rises darkly above the westernmost end of the park. Most experienced mountaineers will be able to pick their way to some of these prominent peaks, with several even accessible to skilled scramblers.

Most people head eastwards from Turtagrø. From the hotel, a four-hour hike will take you to Norway's highest DNT hut, Fannaråki, on the summit of Fannaråken (2069m), with astonishing views. To get started, walk about 500m up the road and follow the track up Helgedalen. At Ekrehytta hut, a narrow track starts a steep 800m climb to the top.

1841m. The main season runs from June to mid-November. Apart from the skiing opportunities, this road takes you to the highest point reachable by road in Norway.

OTHER SCENIC DRIVES

Although most travellers will want to explore the following routes by car, serious cyclists will also enjoy the challenge.

Turtagrø to Øvre Årdal

The toll mountain road between Turtagrø and the industrial town of Øvre Årdal is one of Norway's most scenic short drives. Open from late May to October, it leads above the tree line through wild and lonely country. From late June to late August, the route is served by daily bus (Nkr100, one hour). The vehicle **toll** (Nkr50) is collected by an isolated gatekeeper at the pass (1315m).

Randsverk to Fagernes

Between Randsverk and Fagernes, the Rv51 climbs through the hilly and forested Sjodalen country onto a vast upland with far-ranging views of peaks and glaciers. It's one of Norway's most beautiful mountain routes and is used by lots of hikers heading for Jotunheimen's eastern reaches. En route it passes the DNT hut at **Gjendesheim**, the launching point for the popular day hike along the Besseggen ridge.

From mid-June to early September, two daily buses run between Otta and Gol, via Vågå, Randsverk, Gjendesheim, Valdresflya and Fagernes. You'll have to change at Gjendesheim. From Otta, the trip to Gjendesheim takes two hours and costs Nkr89. Valdresflya is just 15 minutes further.

Jotunheimvegen

Branching off the Rv51 at Bygdin, the 45km-long Jotunheimvegen (www.jotunheimvegen.no) to Skåbu is much quieter and every bit as picturesque. It's usually open from mid-June until October, depending on the weather, and you pay a Nkr100 toll, which seems expensive but it is the only way the authorities can make maintenance of the road viable. There's no

You can either return the way you came or descend the eastern slope along the well-marked track to Keisarpasset and thence back to Ekrehytta. To launch into a multiday trip, you can also descend Gjertvassdalen to Skogadalsbøen hut and then choose from one of many routes eastwards through Jotunheimen.

Besseggen

No discussion of hiking in Jotunheimen would be complete without mention of Besseggen ridge, the most popular hike in Norway. Indeed, some travellers find it *too* popular, with at least 30,000 hikers in the three months a year that it's passable. If you want to avoid the crowds, choose another route, but if you don't mind sacrificing solitude for one of Norway's most spectacular trips, you probably won't regret it. Henrik Ibsen wrote of Besseggen: 'It cuts along with an edge like a scythe for miles and miles…And scars and glaciers sheer down the precipice to the glassy lakes, 1600 feet below on either side.' So daunting did it appear to him, that one of Peer Gynt's mishaps was a plunge down to the lake on the back of a reindeer.

The day hike between Gjendesheim and Memurubu Lodge takes about six hours and climbs to a high point of 1743m. From Gjendesheim hut, follow the DNT-marked track towards Glitterheim for about 30 minutes, where a left fork strikes off up the Veltløyfti gorge, which leads upward onto the level Veslefjellet plateau.

After a short descent from the plateau the track leads you onto the Besseggen ridge, which slices between the deep-blue lake Bessvatnet and the 18km-long glacier-green lake Gjende, coloured by 20,000 tonnes of glacial silt that is dumped into it each year by the Memuru River.

Besseggen is never less than 10m wide and only from a distance does it look precarious. After passing the head of Bessvatnet, the route passes a small plateau lake, Bjørnbøltjørn, and shortly thereafter begins its descent to the modern Memurubu Lodge.

Once there, you can decide whether to take the boat M/S *Gjende* back to Gjendesheim (Nkr67, 30 minutes, five daily in summer), continue west to Gjendebu hut, either on foot or by boat (Nkr67, 30 minutes), or hike north to Glitterheim.

public transport along the route but there are camp sites at Beitostølen and Skåbu. The route also links up with Peer Gynt Vegen (see the boxed text, p168).

Sleeping & Eating

The following places all lie on, or are accessible from, the Sognefjellet Road, starting from those closest to Lom. Most open only from May to September, later if the weather permits.

Spiterstulen (☎ 61 21 14 80; www.spiterstulen.no; Spiterstulen; tent sites per person Nkr50, d with shared bathroom & without/with own bed linen Nkr410/305) The private Spiterstulen lodge, at an old *sæter* (summer dairy), is convenient for access to Galdhøpiggen. The toll road to Spiterstulen costs Nkr60 per vehicle. On foot, you can approach on the five-hour marked route from Leirvassbu hut, further west.

Bøverdalen Vandrerhjem (☎ /fax 61 21 20 64; boverdalen.hostel@vandrerhjem.no; Bøverdalen; dm Nkr160, s/d with shared bathroom Nkr250/380, breakfast Nkr65; ⏲ Jun-Sep) This fine riverside hostel has a small café, tidy rooms and delightful surrounds to enjoy once the day-trippers have returned home.

Røisheim Hotel (☎ 61 21 20 31; www.roisheim.no; Bøverdalen; s/d from Nkr1000/1200) This charming place combines rustic, historical buildings with modern comforts. Quite simply, it's a wonderful place to stay, although prices fluctuate and can soar once you include meals.

Storhaugen (☎ /fax 61 21 20 69; www.storhaugengard.no; Bøverdalen; cabin Nkr350-1500) A highly recommended upmarket alternative is this friendly farm run by Marit and Magner Slettede. It's a traditional-style timber farm with views of both the Jotunheimen heights and Bøverdalen. At Galdesand, turn south on the Galdhøpiggen road and continue 1.5km to the signposted turn-off for Storhaugen.

Elvesæter Hotell (☎ 61 21 20 00; www.elveseter.no; Bøverdalen; s/d Nkr750/975, 3-course dinner Nkr285) This comfortable hotel is high on novelty value, adjacent as it is to the Sagasøyla, a 32m-high carved wooden pillar tracing Norwegian history from unification in 872 to the 1814 constitution.

Leirvassbu Lodge (☎ 61 21 29 32; fax 61 21 29 21; dm DNT members/nonmembers Nkr150/160, s/d with bathroom Nkr650/990) Leirvassbu, a typical mountain lodge at 1400m and beside Leirvatnet lake, is a good hiking base; guided glacier walks on Smørstabbreen cost around Nkr600. Despite its large capacity, it can get crowded. The toll on the access road is Nkr50 per car.

Jotunheimen Fjellstue (☎ 61 21 29 18; www.jotunheimen-fjellstue.no; s/d Nkr845/1190, 3-course menu Nkr395) This modern mountain lodge has a lovely location, good rooms and decent food.

Krossbu Turiststasjon (☎ 61 21 29 22; www.krossbu.no in Norwegian; d with/without bathroom Nkr360/255) At this roadside lodge, the larger rooms have attached bath and dinner is available. Guided glacier hikes and courses cost Nkr300 (four to six hours) if there are enough people.

Turtagrø Hotel (☎ 57 68 08 00; www.turtagro.no; s/d Nkr1150/1670, tower r Nkr2050, full board from Nkr1340/2130; 💻) This historic hiking and mountaineering centre is a friendly and laid-back base for exploring Jotunheimen/Hurrungane. The main building was completely destroyed by fire in 2001, but a new building has arisen in its place, with wonderful views and supremely comfortable rooms. It also conducts week-long climbing courses and guided day trips (hiking, climbing and skiing). There's also a great bar full of historic Norwegian mountaineering photos. The dining room serves hearty meals (daily special Nkr89, available until late afternoon).

Across the mountains on the eastern side of the park, you'll find the popular **Gjendesheim Lodge** (☎ 61 23 89 10; www.gjendesheim.no; beds DNT members Nkr105-200, nonmembers Nkr170-265) and the quiet, well-run hostel **Valdresflya Vandrerhjem** (☎ 22 71 34 97; Valdresflya; dm/s/d Nkr150/250/310), about 15 minutes' drive south from Gjendesheim. The latter place prides itself on being the highest hostel in northern Europe (1389m). There's no guest kitchen but breakfast/dinner costs Nkr65/120 and there's a daytime café serving excellent waffles to passers-by.

HARDANGERVIDDA

The desolate and beautiful Hardangervidda plateau, part of the 3430-sq-km Hardangervidda National Park, ranges across an otherworldly tundra landscape that's the southernmost refuge of the Arctic fox and Norway's largest herd of wild reindeer (caribou). Long a trade and

HIKING THE HARDANGERVIDDA

Trekking through the Western Hardangervidda is possible only in July and August – for the rest of the time, snow and the possibility of sudden changes in weather conditions make setting out hazardous. Before exploring the park, visit the Hardangervidda Natursenter (p216), which is the best of its kind in Norway. It sells maps and the staff can offer advice on hiking routes, quite apart from have a wonderful exhibition on the park. Hikers and skiers will find the Turkart map *Hardangervidda* (Nkr125), at a scale of 1:100,000, to be the map of choice for locals. For an overview of trekking routes, get hold of its brochure *Eidfjord Tour Guide – Hardangervidda*. You should also pick up *Hytteringen Hardangervidda Nasjonalpark* (www.hardangerviddanett.no), which gives the run-down on mountain huts. The Bergen Turlag DNT office (p193) is another good source of information.

There are numerous trailheads, among them the waterfalls at Vøringfoss (p217) and Finse (opposite). Some of our favourites include:

- **Finse to Vøringfoss** (two days) The steepest hiking country of Hardangervidda, skirting the Hardangerjøkulen glacier and overnighting in Rembesdalsseter; you could also make the two-hour (one-way) detour to Kjeåsen Farm (p216).
- **Vøringfoss to Kinsarvik via Harteigen** (three to four days) To the picturesque mountain of Harteigen with it's panoramic views of Hardangervidda, then down the monk's stairway to Kinsarvik (p218).
- **Halne to Dyranut via Rauhelleren** (two days) Trails lead south off the Rv7 with strong chances of encountering reindeer herds.

There are also enticing options if you set out from Geilo (opposite) or Finse (opposite). For details of other adventure possibilities on the plateau, see the boxed text, p157.

RALLARVEGEN

The Rallarvegen, or Navvies' Road, was constructed as a supply route for Oslo–Bergen railway workers (the railway opened on 27 November 1909). Nowadays, this 80km route of asphalt and gravel extends from Haugastøl through Finse and all the way down to Flåm, and is only open to bicycle and foot traffic. To make the trip from Finse to Flåm means that you get the best of the stunning scenery of the emblematic Flåmsbana railway (p234) with the additional benefit of being able to stop whenever you like to enjoy the view. The popular stretch between Vatnahalsen and Flåm descends 865m in 29km, with an initial series of hairpin bends. Brakes on bikes usually have to be changed after just one descent!

Cyclists and hikers will find optimum conditions between mid-July and mid-September. Most people do the route from east to west due to the significant altitude loss.

To rent bikes (Nkr420 to Nkr820 depending on the date and type of bike) ready for the Rallarvegen challenge, contact **Finse 1222** (☎ 56 52 71 00; www.finse1222.no); bikes must be booked before arriving in Finse due to high demand in summer and prices include the return bike transportation fee on the train.

travel route connecting eastern and western Norway, it's now crossed by the main railway and road routes between Oslo and Bergen.

Reindeer numbers have dropped in recent years, from a high of around 19,000 in 1998 to around 7000. This fall in numbers is, however, part of a programme of resource management by the park's authorities as a ban on hunting until recently meant that herd numbers became too large and reindeer body weights began to fall dangerously due to a lack of sufficient fodder.

Old snow lingers here until early August and new snow is a possibility at any time of year. The perils of this wild country were brought home in March 2007 when two Scottish cross-country skiers died after being caught in snow and freezing fog.

GEILO

pop 3150

At Geilo (pronounced Yei-lo), midway between Oslo and Bergen, you can practically step off the train onto a ski lift. In summer, there's plenty of fine hiking in the area. A popular nearby destination is the expansive plateau-like mountain called Hallingskarvet, frosted with several small glaciers. For more information, contact the Geilo **tourist office** (☎ 32 09 59 00; www.geilo.no; 🕑 8.30am-9pm Mon-Fri, 9am-5pm Sat, 11am-5pm Sun Jul–mid-Aug, shorter hrs mid-Aug–Jun).

Geilo Aktiv (☎ 32 08 75 20; www.geiloaktiv.com in Norwegian) offers glacier trekking on Hardangerjøkulen (1862m) three times a week from July to mid-September. The standard 10-hour tour (including train to and from Finse) costs Nkr650 per person. The company also offers a variety of rafting tours, riverboarding and a two-hour moose safari that occurs once a week.

Sleeping & Eating

Geilo has dozens of accommodation choices, most of which are geared towards the adventure and outdoor-activity crowds. The tourist office has a full list.

Some of the more reasonable options include: **Øen Turistsenter & Geilo Vandrerhjem** (☎ 32 08 70 60; www.oenturist.no; Lienvegen 137; dm Nkr275, s/d Nkr470/650, breakfast Nkr60); **Haugen Hotell** (☎ 32 09 66 00; www.haugenhotell.no; Gamleveien 16; s/d from Nkr515/750); and **Ro Hotell & Kro** (☎ 32 09 08 99; www.rohotell.no; Geilovegen 55; s/d Nkr575/750, dinner mains from Nkr90).

Getting There & Away

Most visitors arrive on the train between Oslo (Nkr421, 3½ hours, five daily) and Bergen (Nkr378, three hours).

FINSE

Heading west from Geilo, the railway line climbs 600m through a tundra-like landscape of lakes and snowy peaks to Finse, lying at 1222m near the Hardangerjøkulen icecap. This region offers nordic skiing in winter and hiking in summer, not to mention what could be Norway's steepest mountain bike ride (see boxed text above).

East of Finse station, the **Finse Navvies Museum** (Rallarmuseet Finse; ☎ 56 52 69 66; adult/child Nkr50/20; 🕑 10am-8pm Jul-Sep) traces the history of the Oslo–Bergen railway and the 15,000 people who built this hard-won line in 2.5 million worker days.

Hiking

Finse is the starting point for some exceptional treks, including the popular four-hour trek to the Blåisen glacier tip of Hardangerjøkulen; some Norwegians-in-the-know claim this to be the most spectacular glacier walk in the country. Adding interest to your hike, remember that scenes of the planet Hof in the *Empire Strikes Back* were filmed around the glacier. It's also possible to walk around the glacier and down to Vøringfoss (see the boxed text, p188). The wonderful three- or four-day Finse–Aurland trek follows Aurlandsdalen down to Aurlandsfjorden and has a series of DNT and private mountain huts a day's walk apart. For more on this route, see p238.

Sleeping & Eating

Most budget travellers stay at the staffed DNT hut, **Finsehytta** (☎ 56 52 67 32; dm Nkr110-250), while the friendly **Finse 1222** (☎ 56 52 71 00; www.finse1222.no; full board Nkr900-1200) offers comfortable rooms in sight of the glacier, and a good three-course dinner; Finse 1222 is also the starting point and best source of information for many of the activities in the region.

Getting There & Away

Five daily trains run between Oslo (Nkr499, 4½ hours) and Bergen (Nkr299, 2¼ hours) via Finse.

Bergen & the Southwestern Fjords

Two beautiful, vibrant cities and some of Norway's most scenic fjord country make for a wonderful combination. If you're short on time (and even if you're not) and looking for the best that Norway has to offer, this could just be the region to visit.

Bergen is one of the world's most beautiful cities, laid out across harbours and hillsides. It's also rich in history and architecture, especially in the quayside Bryggen district. But this is a city that is anything but stuck in the past with a dynamic cultural life, great restaurants and nightlife. To the south, Stavanger may not match Bergen for architecture, but its old quarter, terrific museums and feel-good vibe make it a must-see.

Even better, both Bergen and Stavanger serve as gateways to the fjords you always dreamed of. Hardangerfjord and its tributaries are quite simply magnificent. Villages beneath precipitous cliffs find their most stunning manifestation in little Eidfjord where farms clinging to high ledges, dizzying waterfalls and Norway's best nature centre provide interest to add to the undeniable beauty. Ulvik, Utne and Kinsarvik also provide perfect vantage points onto this perfect world, while Stalheim allows you to look deep into the valley from its eyrie-like perch. If the plunging landscapes inspire you to do likewise, Voss should be high on your list, where a range of high-energy, high-altitude thrills await.

To the south, Lysefjord might just be Norway's most recognisable image, whether high on Pulpit Rock (Preikestolen) or balancing atop Kjeragbolten. These are places where a frisson of fear draws you to the edge, where you'll stand, amazed, at Norway's extraordinary beauty.

HIGHLIGHTS

- Stroll through the historic **Bryggen** (p195) in Bergen, a Unesco World Heritage site
- Climb to **Preikestolen** (p229) or **Kjeragbolten** (p231) overlooking Lysefjord
- Relax on a slow boat up **Hardangerfjord** (p215) from tranquil Ulvik
- Amble through cosmopolitan Stavanger, particularly the historic timber houses of **Old Stavanger** (p222)
- Wake up to the best hotel view in Norway at the **Stalheim Hotel** (p213)
- Climb up (or through) the mountain to **Kjeåsen Farm** (p216), high above Eidfjord

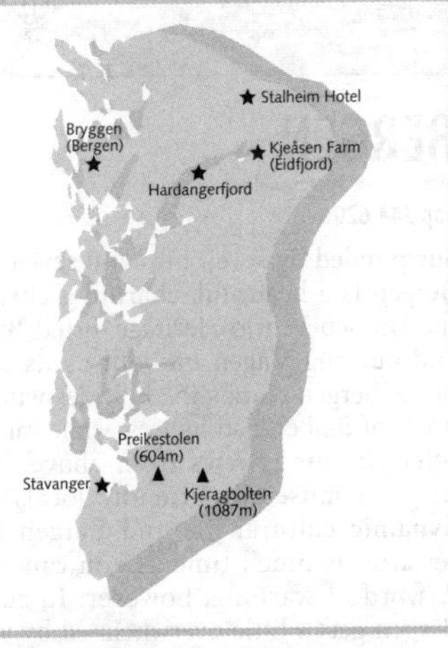

- POPULATION: 840,000
- HIGHEST ELEVATION: FOLGEFONN (1654M)

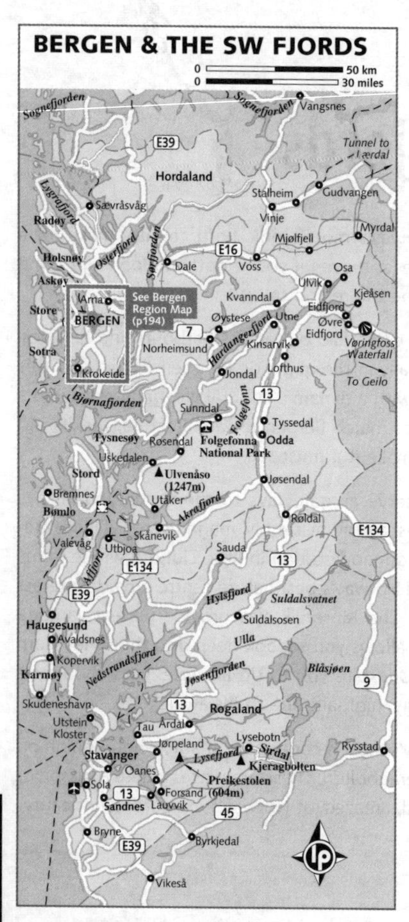

BERGEN

pop 244,620

Surrounded by seven hills and seven fjords, Bergen is a beautiful, charming city. With the Unesco World Heritage–listed Bryggen and buzzing Vågen harbour as its centrepiece, Bergen climbs the hillsides with hundreds of timber-clad houses, while cable cars offer stunning views from above. Throw in great museums, friendly locals and a dynamic cultural life and Bergen amply rewards as much time as you can give it. A word of warning, however: In summer Bergen gets a little overwhelmed by visitors (with a 25% increase in visitors in the last five years) and finding accommodation can be a problem so always book ahead.

HISTORY

During the 12th and 13th centuries, Bergen was Norway's capital and easily the country's most important city. By the 13th century, the city states of Germany allied themselves into trading leagues, most significantly the Hanseatic League with its centre in Lübeck. At its zenith, the league had over 150 member cities and was northern Europe's most powerful economic entity; the sheltered harbour of Bryggen drew the Hanseatic League's traders in droves. They established their first office here around 1360, transforming Bryggen into one of the league's four major headquarters abroad, with up to 2000 mostly German resident traders who imported grain and exported dried fish, among other products.

For over 400 years, Bryggen was dominated by a tight-knit community of German merchants who weren't permitted to mix with, marry or have families with local Norwegians. By the 15th century, competition from Dutch and English shipping companies, internal disputes and, especially, the Black Death (which wiped out 70% of Bergen's population) ensured the Hanseatic League's decline, (although Hamburg, Bremen and Lübeck are still called Hanseatic cities and Hamburg and Bremen retain city-state status).

By the early 17th century Bergen was nonetheless the trading hub of Scandinavia and Norway's most populous city with 15,000 people. During the 17th and 18th centuries, many Hanseatic traders opted to take Norwegian nationality and join the local community. Bryggen continued as an important maritime trading centre until 1899, when the Hanseatic League's Bergen offices finally closed.

ORIENTATION

Hilly greater Bergen has suburbs radiating out onto outlying peninsulas and islands, but the central area is compact and easily manageable on foot. Bergen's main attractions lie around the harbour at Vågen; Torgalmenningen, which runs southwest from the harbour to Øvre Ole Bulls plass, is a major commercial and shopping artery. The area south of Øvre Ole Bulls plass is a vibrant student quarter with great bars and restaurants. The bus and train stations lie a block apart on Strømgaten, a 10-minute walk southeast from the ferry terminals.

INFORMATION

Bookshops

Norli (Map p196; ☎ 55 21 42 91; www.norli.no; Torgalmenningen 8; ⏲ 9am-9pm Mon-Fri, 9am-6pm Sat May-Sep, shorter hrs rest-of-year) Great selection of travel and English-language books. There's another branch across the road at No 7.

Emergencies

Ambulance (☎ 113)
Police (☎ 112)

Internet Access

Bergen has plans to have universal wireless access throughout the city by the end of 2008 although most locals expect it to take longer. In the meantime, most hotels and some cafés have wireless access.

Accezzo (Map p196; Galleriet, Torgalmenningen 6; per hr Nkr70; ⏲ 9am-9pm Mon-Fri, 9am-6pm Sat Jun-Sep, shorter hrs rest-of-year)
Bergen Library (Map p196; ☎ 55 56 85 00; Strømgaten 6; ⏲ 10am-6pm Mon-Thu, 10am-4.30pm Fri, 10am-3pm Sat) Free, time-limited access.
Cyberhouse (Map p196; Hollendergaten 9; per hr Nkr60; ⏲ 9am-11pm)
Zoex (Map p196; Kong Oscars gate 13; per 15/30/60 mins Nkr20/40/70; ⏲ 10am-6pm Mon-Fri, 10am-2pm Sat)

Laundry

Jarlens Vaskoteque (Map p196; ☎ 55 32 55 04; Lille Øvregaten 17; wash/detergent/dry Nkr55/5/10; ⏲ 10am-6pm Mon, Tue & Fri, 10am-8pm Wed & Thu, 10am-3pm Sat) Full service (Nkr110) takes two hours.

Left Luggage

Lockers at the train and bus stations start at Nkr40.

Medical Services

Legevakten Medical Clinic (Map p196; ☎ 55 56 87 00; Vestre Strømkaien 19; ⏲ 24hr) Handles emergencies.
Pharmacy (Map p196; ☎ 55 21 83 84; bus station; ⏲ 8am-11pm Mon-Sat, 10am-11pm Sun)

Money

You can change money at the post office, tourist office (for much less than bank rates but no commission) or at any of the many banks (most have ATMs) dotted around the centre. One central bank that's good for changing money is **Sparebanken Vest** (Map p196; Nedre Korskirkeallmenning).

Post

Main post office (Map p196; Xhibition Shopping Centre, Småstrandgaten; ⏲ 8am-8pm Mon-Fri, 9am-6pm Sat mid-Jun–mid-Aug, shorter hrs rest-of-year)

Tourist Information

Bergen Turlag DNT office (Map p196; ☎ 55 32 22 30; www.bergen-turlag.no; Tverrgaten 4; ⏲ 10am-4pm Mon-Wed & Fri, 10am-6pm Thu, 10am-2pm Sat) Maps and information on hiking and hut accommodation throughout western Norway.
Tourist office (Map p196; ☎ 55 55 20 00; www.visitbergen.com; Vågsallmenningen 1; ⏲ 8.30am-10pm Jun-Aug, 9am-8pm May & Sep, 9am-4pm Mon-Sat Oct-Apr) One of the best and busiest in the country, Bergen's tourist office distributes the free and excellent *Bergen Guide* booklet.

Travel Agencies

Kilroy Travel (Map p196; ☎ 02633; www.kilroytravels.com; Vaskerelven 16; ⏲ 10am-5pm Mon-Fri, 11.30am-3pm Sat) Specialises in student tickets.

DANGERS & ANNOYANCES

Although Bergen is generally a safe city, pickpockets are known to operate around the fish market and Bryggen areas so, as in any tourist city, keep a close watch on your belongings.

Bergen's weather is something of a national joke (including for many people from Bergen) as it's one of the wettest cities in Norway – you can reliably expect rain on at least 275 days of the year. In 2006 the city almost broke the national record (held by the Oslo region) with 85 consecutive days of rain. A brolly is an essential accessory.

The sheer numbers of visitors in summer can be a little overwhelming. The sudden influx of cruise passengers (210,000 in 2006 alone) in particular can, without warning, change the atmosphere of this otherwise intimate city; as one local told us, 'cruise passengers from all over the world come to take pictures, buy a plastic troll and then leave on their massive cruise liners'. Many locals hope that a new local government tax on cruise ships will reduce the traffic a little.

SIGHTS & ACTIVITIES

Bergen has lots of quaint cobblestone streets lined with timber-clad houses; apart from Bryggen, some of the most picturesque are the quiet lanes climbing the hill behind

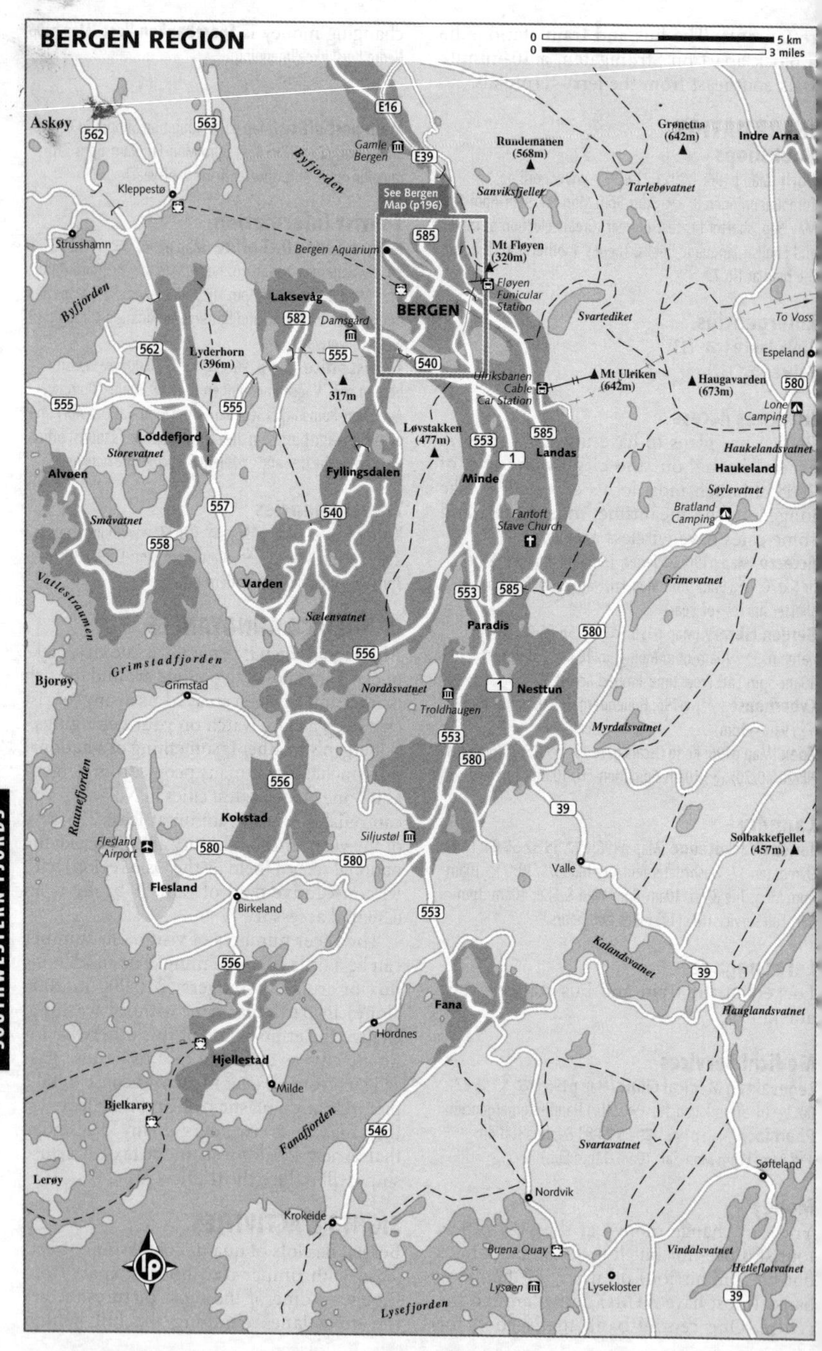

BERGEN REGION
0 5 km
0 3 miles
Askøy
Kleppestø
Strusshamn
Byfjorden
Gamle Bergen
See Bergen Map (p196)
Bergen Aquarium
Mt Fløyen (320m)
Fløyen Funicular Station
BERGEN
Laksevåg
Damsgård
Lyderhorn (396m)
317m
Rundemanen (568m)
Grønetua (642m)
Indre Arna
Sanviksfjellet
Tarlebøvatnet
Svartediket
To Voss
Espeland
Ulriksbanen Cable Car Station
Mt Ulriken (642m)
Haugavarden (673m)
Lone Camping
Løvstakken (477m)
Landas
Haukelandsvatnet
Haukeland
Søylevatnet
Bratland Camping
Loddefjord
Storevatnet
Alvøen
Småvatnet
Fyllingsdalen
Minde
Fantoft Stave Church
Vatlestraumen
Varden
Sælenvatnet
Paradis
Grimevatnet
Grimstadfjorden
Bjorøy
Grimstad
Nordåsvatnet
Troldhaugen
Nesttun
Myrdalsvatnet
Raunefjorden
Kokstad
Siljustøl
Flesland Airport
Flesland
Birkeland
Valle
Solbakkefjellet (457m)
Kalandsvatnet
Hauglandsvatnet
Fana
Hordnes
Hjellestad
Milde
Bjelkarøy
Fanafjorden
Svartavatnet
Søfteland
Lerøy
Nordvik
Krokeide
Buena Quay
Vindalsvatnet
Hetlefløtvatnet
Lysøen
Lysekloster
Lysefjorden

the Fløibanen funicular station, as well as in Nordnes (close to Kafe Kippers) and Sandviken (behind Bergenhus).

Bryggen

Bergen's oldest and most enchanting quarter runs along the eastern shore of Vågen Harbour. Once a major commercial centre for northern Europe (see p192), the long parallel rows of buildings with stacked-stone or wooden foundations and reconstructed rough-plank construction run back from gabled fronts facing the wharf.

Bryggen (see Map p196) has always been a work-in-progress and archaeological excavations suggest that the quay was once 140m further inland than where it now lies. The current 58 buildings (25% of the original, although some claim there are now 61) cover 13,000 sq metres and date from after the 1702 fire, although the building pattern dates back to the 12th century.

In the early 14th century, there were about 30 wooden buildings on Bryggen (whose name means 'The Wharf'), each of which was usually shared by several *stuer* (trading firms). They rose two or three storeys above the wharf and combined business premises with living quarters and warehouses. Each building had a crane for loading and unloading ships, as well as a large assembly room, or *schøtstue*, where employees met and ate. That atmosphere of an intimate waterfront community remains intact and losing yourself in Bryggen is one of Bergen's great pleasures.

For an excellent summary of Bryggen's history and threats to its existence, look out for the *Bryggen Guide*, available from the Bryggens Museum and elsewhere.

Hanseatic Museum

This terrific **museum** (Map p196; ☎ 55 54 46 90; www.museumvest.no; Finnegårdsgaten 1a; adult/child Nkr45/free mid-May–mid-Sep, Nkr25/free rest-of-year, also valid for Schøtstuene; 9am-5pm mid-May–mid-Sep, 11am-2pm Tue-Sat, 11am-4pm Sun rest-of-year) provides a window onto the world of Hanseatic traders. Housed in a rough-timber building from 1704, it starkly reveals the contrast between the austere living and working conditions of Hanseatic merchant sailors and apprentices, and the lifestyles of the management. Highlights include the manager's office, quarters, private liquor cabinet and summer bedroom; the apprentices' quarters where beds were shared by two men; the fish storage room, which pressed and processed over a million pounds (450,000kg) of fish a month; and the *fiskeskrue*, or fish press, which pressed the fish into barrels.

BERGEN CARD

The **Bergen Card** (www.visitbergen.com/bergencard; adult per 24/48 hrs Nkr170/250, child Nkr70/10) is worth considering given the rising admission fees, although it takes careful planning, an early start and a steady pace to make sure its economical. The card covers free travel on local buses and the Fløibanen funicular (Map p196); free entrance to some museums with discounted admission to the rest; free guided tours of Bergen; and discounts on city and boat sightseeing tours, concerts and cultural performances. The Bergen Card is available from the tourist office, some hotels, the bus terminal and online.

Schøtstuene

An essential complement to the Hanseatic Museum, **Schøtstuene** (Map p196; ☎ 55 31 60 20; Øvregaten 50; adult/child combined ticket with Hanseatic Museum Nkr45/free; 10am-5pm mid-May–mid-Sep, 11am-2pm Sun rest-of-year) is a reconstruction of one of the original assembly halls where the fraternity of Hanseatic merchants once met for their business meetings and beer guzzling.

Bryggens Museum

The archaeological **museum** (Map p196; ☎ 55 58 80 10; Dreggsallmenning 3; adult/child Nkr40/20, free with Bergen Card; 10am-5pm May-Aug, 11am-3pm Mon-Fri, noon-3pm Sat, noon-4pm Sun Sep-Apr) was built on the site of Bergen's first settlement, and the 800-year-old foundations unearthed during construction have been incorporated into the exhibits, which include medieval tools, pottery, skulls and runes. The permanent exhibition documenting Bergen in around 1300 is particularly interesting.

Theta Museum

This excellent one-room reconstruction of a clandestine Resistance headquarters, uncovered by the Nazis in 1942, is now Norway's tiniest **museum** (Map p196; Enhjørningsgården; adult/child Nkr20/5; 2-4pm Tue, Sat & Sun mid-May–mid-

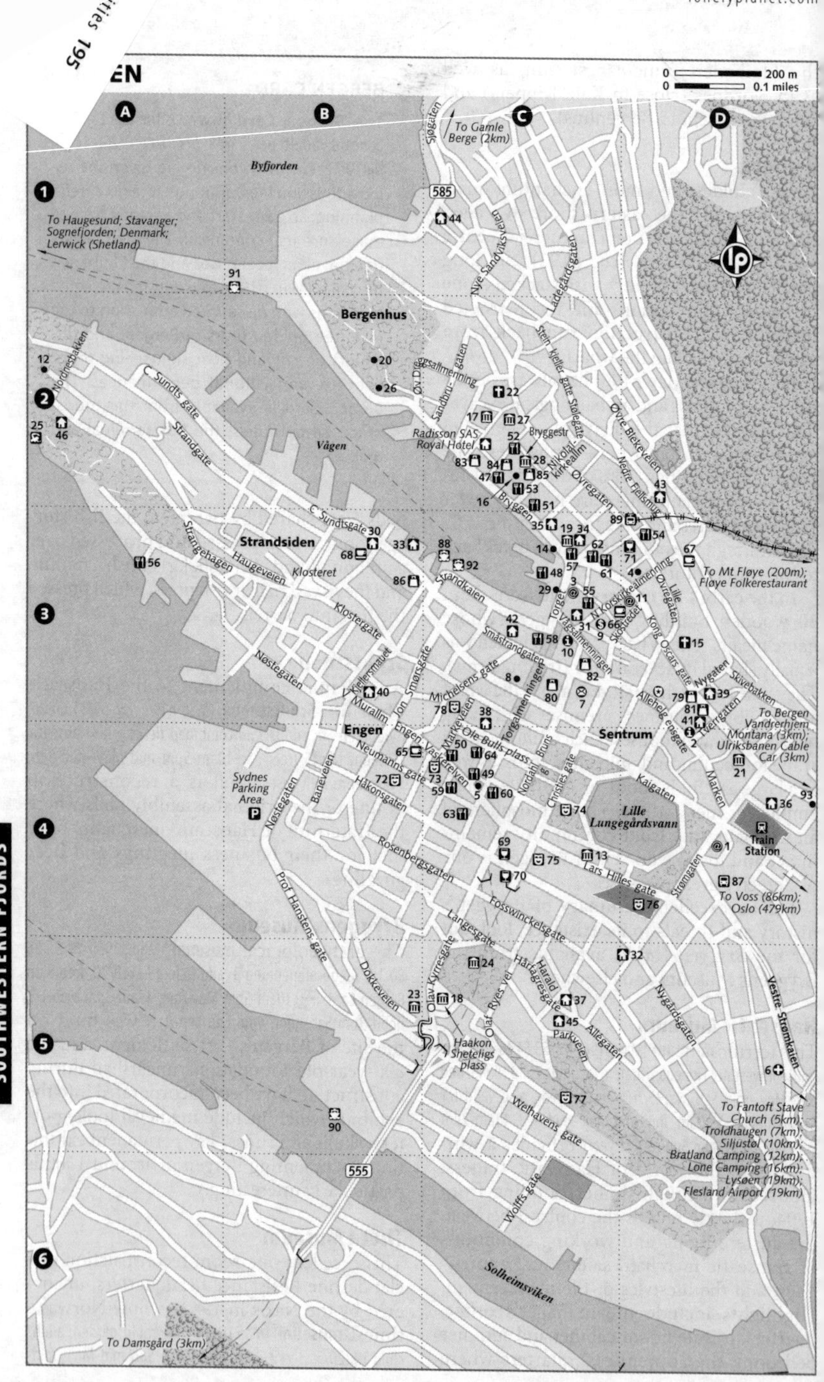
EN
0 200 m
0 0.1 miles
A
B
C
D
1
2
3
4
5
6
Byfjorden
To Haugesund; Stavanger; Sognefjorden; Denmark; Lerwick (Shetland)
To Gamle Berge (2km)
Sjøgaten
585
Nye Sandviksveien
Ladegårdsgaten
Bergenhus
Nordnesbakken
C Sundts gate
Strandgate
Vågen
Øv Dreggsallmenning
Sandbru- gaten
Radisson SAS Royal Hotel
Bryggestr
Stein Kjeller gate
Stølegate
Nikolaikirkeallm
Øvre Blekeveien
Nedre Fjellsmug
Øvregaten
Bryggen
C Sundtsgate
Strandsiden
Strangehagen
Haugeveien
Klosteret
Strandkaien
To Mt Fløye (200m); Fløye Folkerestaurant
Torget
N Korskirkealmenning
Skostredet
Lille Øvregaten
Vågsalmenningen
Klostergate
Småstrandgaten
Kong Oscars gate
Nøstegaten
Kjellersmauet
Jon Smørsgate
Michelsens gate
Torgalmenningen
Allehelgens gate
Nygaten
Skivebakken
Tverrgaten
To Bergen Vandrerhjem Montana (3km); Ulriksbanen Cable Car (3km)
Murallm
Engen
Marken
Vaskerelven
Ole Bulls plass
Sentrum
Neumanns gate
Håkonsgaten
Baneveien
Nordahl Bruns
Christies gate
Kaigaten
Lille Lungegårdsvann
Sydnes Parking Area
Nøstegaten
Train Station
Rosenbergsgaten
Lars Hilles gate
Strømgaten
To Voss (86km); Oslo (479km)
Fosswinckelsgate
Prof Hanstens gate
Langesgate
Olav Kyrresgate
Dokkeveien
Harald Hårfagresgate
Olaf Ryes vei
Haakon Sheteligs plass
Parkveien
Allégaten
Nygårdsgaten
Vestre Strømkaien
Welhavens gate
To Fantoft Stave Church (5km); Troldhaugen (7km); Siljustøl (10km); Bratland Camping (12km); Lone Camping (16km); Lysøen (19km); Flesland Airport (19km)
555
Wolffs gate
Solheimsviken
To Damsgård (3km)

INFORMATION
Accezzo (see 80)
Bergen Library 1 D4
Bergen Turlag DNT Office 2 D4
Cyberhouse 3 C3
Jarlens Vaskoteque 4 D3
Kilroy Travel 5 C4
Legevakten Medical Clinic 6 D5
Main Post Office 7 C3
Norli (see 80)
Norli 8 C3
Pharmacy (see 87)
Sparebanken Vest 9 C3
Tourist Office 10 C3
Zoex 11 D3

SIGHTS & ACTIVITIES
Bergen Aquarium 12 A2
Bergen Art Museum 13 C4
Bergens-Expressen Toy Train 14 C3
Bremen Cathedral (Domkirken) 15 D3
Bryggen Warehouses 16 C2
Bryggens Museum 17 C2
Cultural History Museum 18 C5
Hanseatic Museum 19 C3
Håkonshallen 20 B2
Leprosy Museum 21 D4
Mariakirken 22 C2
Maritime Museum 23 B5
Natural History Museum 24 C5
Nordnes Sjøbad 25 A2
Rosenkrantz Tower 26 B2
Schøtstuene 27 C2
Theta Museum 28 C2
Torget Fish Market 29 C3

SLEEPING
Augustin Hotel 30 B3
Bergen Vandrerhjem YMCA 31 C3
City Box 32 D5
Clarion Hotel Admiral 33 B3
Det Hanseatiske Hotel 34 C3
First Hotel Marin 35 C3
Grand Hotel Terminus 36 D4
Hotel Park Pension 37 C5
In City Hotel & Apartments 38 C4
Jacob's Apartments 39 D3
Kjellersmauet Gjestehus 40 B3
Marken Gjestehus 41 D3
Rica Strand Hotel 42 C3
Skansen Pensjonat 43 D2
Skuteviken Gjesthus 44 C1
Steens Hotell 45 C5
Villa Nordnes 46 A2

EATING
Baker Brun 47 C2
Baker Brun 48 C3
Bar Celona 49 C4
Bocca (see 38)
Boha 50 C4
Bryggeloftet & Stuene 51 C2
Bryggen Tracteursted 52 C2
Enhjørningen 53 C2
Escalon 54 D3
Finnegaards Stuene (see 34)
Godt Brød 55 C3
Kafe Kippers 56 A3
Kjøttbasarell 57 C3
Lido 58 C3
Naboen 59 C4
Pingvinen 60 C4
Pygmalion Økocafé (see 31)
Red Sun 61 C3
Sol Brød 62 C3
Stragiotti 63 C4
Sumo (see 63)
Torget Fish Market (see 29)
Wesselstuen 64 C4

DRINKING
Altona Vinbar (see 30)
Bocca (see 38)
Café Opera 65 B4
Capello 66 D3
Det Lille Kaffe Kompaniet 67 D3
Dromedar Kaffebar 68 B3
Fincken 69 C4
Jacob's Café (see 39)
Kafe Kippers (see 56)
Legal 70 C4
Naboen (see 59)
Onkel Lauritz (see 50)
Pingvinen (see 60)
To Glass Vinbar 71 D3
Vågen (see 61)

ENTERTAINMENT
Bergen Folklore (see 27)
Bergen Kino 72 B4
Calibar 73 C4
Fana Folklore Show Departure Point 74 C4
Garage 75 C4
Grieghallen 76 D4
Hulen 77 C5
Rick's 78 C3
USF Vertfet (see 56)

SHOPPING
Foto Video 79 D3
Galleriet Shopping Centre 80 C3
Gitarmaker 81 D3
Husfliden 82 C3
Juhls' Silver Gallery 83 C2
Kvams Flisespikkeri 84 C2
Læverkstedet 85 C2
Oleana 86 B3
Xhibition (see 7)

TRANSPORT
Bus Terminal 87 D4
Ferries to Rosendal 88 C3
Fløibanen Funicular Station 89 D3
Freileneskaien (Hurtigruten Terminal) 90 B5
Rødne Fjord Cruise (see 92)
Skoltegrunnskaien (International Ferry) 91 B1
Strandkaiterminal (Express Ferries) 92 C3
Sykkelbutikken 93 D4
Vågen Harbour Ferry (see 29)

Sep). Appropriately enough, finding it is still a challenge. It's behind the Enhjørningen restaurant; pass through the alley and up the stairs to the 3rd floor.

Torget

The waterfront fish market at Torget has a happy, bustling vibe that's hard to tear yourself away from. Here, fishy odours assault the olfactory senses, spilt effluent turns the quay into a slippery mess, and you'll find a range of tasty seafood snacks (see p204).

Mariakirken

This stone **church** (Map p196; ☎ 55 31 59 60; Dreggen; adult/child Nkr20/free mid-Jun–late-Aug, free rest-of-year & with Bergen Card; 9.30-11.30am & 1-4pm mid-Jun–late-Aug, 11am-12.30pm Tue-Fri rest-of-year), with its Romanesque entrance and twin towers, dates from the early 12th century and is Bergen's oldest building. The interior features 15th-century frescoes and a splendid baroque pulpit donated by Hanseatic merchants in 1676.

Rosenkrantz Tower

Built in the 1560s by Bergen governor Erik Rosenkrantz, this **tower** (Rosenkrantztårnet; Map p196; ☎ 55 31 43 80; Bergenhus; adult/child Nkr40/20, free with Bergen Card; 10am-4pm mid-May–Aug, noon-3pm Sun Sep–mid-May) was a residence and defence post. It also incorporates parts of the keep (1273) of King Magnus the Lawmender and the 1520s fortress of Jørgen Hansson. Spiral staircases lead past halls and sentry posts to a reasonable harbour view from the summit.

Håkonshallen

This large ceremonial **hall** (Map p196; ☎ 55 31 60 67; Bergenhus; adult/child Nkr40/20, free with Bergen Card; 10am-4pm daily mid-May–Aug, noon-3pm Fri-Wed, 3-6pm Thu Sep–mid-May), adjacent to the Rosenkrantz Tower, was constructed by King Håkon Håkonsson from 1247–61 and completed for his son's wedding and coronation. The roof was blown off in 1944 thanks to the explosion of a Dutch munitions boat, but extensive restoration has been carried out. There are hourly guided tours in summer.

SAVING BRYGGEN

So beautiful is Bryggen that it seems inconceivable that conservationists spent much of the 20th century fighting plans to tear it down.

Fire has destroyed Bryggen at least seven times (especially in 1702 and again in 1955 when one-third of Bryggen was destroyed). The notable tilt of the structures was caused in 1944, when a Dutch munitions ship exploded in the harbour, blowing off the roofs and shifting the pilings. The explosion and 1955 fire increased the already considerable clamour to tear down Bryggen once and for all; not only was it considered a dangerous fire hazard, but its run-down state was widely seen as an embarrassment. Plans for the redevelopment of the site included modern, eight-storey buildings, a bus station, shopping centre and car park.

What saved Bryggen were the archaeological excavations that took 13 years to complete after the 1955 fire and which unearthed over one million artefacts. In 1962 the **Bryggen Foundation** (www.stiftelsenbryggen.no) and Friends of Bryggen were formed. A lot of people and local politicians wanted to 'tear down the rat's nest after the fire in 1955', says Inger Marie Egenberg, manager of the Bryggen Project, which was founded in 2000 to oversee the restoration of Bryggen. After the Foundation of Bryggen was established, attitudes slowly changed. In 1979 Unesco inscribed Bryggen on its World Heritage list.

The buildings are privately owned. Ms Egenberg adds, 'The owners are permitted state funds for the safeguarding and preservation of the buildings, provided they follow the plans and the management guidelines'. Wherever possible, restorers use traditional craftsmanship and materials, although the restorations should also be 'readable', in that people should be able to distinguish between the original features and more recent works. Restorers have also learned that salt absorbed into the timbers in centuries past may have aided their preservation; restorers now soak timbers in sea water before using them in reconstruction.

Bergen Cathedral (DomkirkeN)

Bergen's **cathedral** (Map p196; ☎ 55 31 58 75; Domkirkeplass 1; admission free; 🕑 11am-4pm Mon-Fri mid-Jun–mid-Aug, 11am-12.30pm Tue-Fri rest-of-year), also known as St Olav's Church, is well worth a visit. The stonemasonry in the entrance hall is superb; it was carved by the same stonemasons as those who adorned Westminster Abbey's chapter house in London.

Bergen Art Museum

Beside the Lille Lungegårdsvann lake, this **art museum** (Bergen Kunstmuseum; Map p196; ☎ 55 56 80 00; www.bergenartmuseum.no; Rasmus Meyers Allé 3 & 7; adult/child/student Nkr50/free/35, free with Bergen Card; 🕑 11am-5pm mid-May–mid-Sep, 11am-5pm Tue-Sun rest-of-year) exhibits a superb collection of 18th- and 19th-century pieces by international and Norwegian artists, including Munch, Miró, Picasso, Kandinsky and Paul Klee.

University Museums

The two main university **museums** (www.museum.uib.no; adult/student or child combined ticket Nkr40/free, free with Bergen Card; 🕑 10am-4pm Tue-Fri, 11am-4pm Sat & Sun Jun-Aug, shorter hrs rest-of-year) include: the **Cultural History Collection** (Kultur-historik Samlinger; Map p196; ☎ 55 58 31 40; Haakon Sheteligs plass 10) with Viking weaponry, medieval altars, folk art, period furnishings, Inuit and Aleut cultures and displays covering everything from Henrik Ibsen to Egyptian mummies; and the **Natural History Collection** (Naturhistorisk Samlinger; Map p196; ☎ 55 58 29 20; Muséplass 3).

Maritime Museum

Bergen's **Maritime Museum** (Sjøfartsmuseet; Map p196; ☎ 55 54 96 00; Haakon Sheteligs plass 15; adult/student or child Nkr30/free; 🕑 11am-3pm Jun-Aug, 11am-2pm Sun-Fri Sep-May) is essential to understanding the history of this seafaring city. It features models of ships from Viking times to the present and exhibits tracing Norway's maritime history.

Bergen Aquarium

At the end of the Nordnes Peninsula, this **aquarium** (Bergen Akvariet; Map p196; ☎ 55 55 71 71; www.akvariet.com; Nordnesbakken 4; adult/child Nkr150/100, with Bergen Card Nkr115/75; 🕑 9am-7pm May-Aug, 10am-6pm Sep-Apr, feeding times noon, 3pm & 6pm May-Aug, noon & 3pm Sep-Apr) has a big outdoor tank with seals and penguins, as well as 70 indoor tanks. You'll never forget the loveable steinbit, the hideous anglerfish or the school of herring, which seems to function as a single entity.

Even with a greater awareness of conservation issues, mistakes have been made. As Ms Egenberg explains, when the Radisson SAS Royal Hotel and its underground car park were built at the northern end of Bryggen in 1982, 'it was necessary to drain out the groundwater under the building. Thus the cultural layers under the Bryggen site are supplied with too much oxygen, causing rot, compression and eventually damage to the foundation of the buildings and the buildings themselves. We just didn't know better, back then.' Talks between the Radisson hotel and the cultural-heritage authorities are ongoing in an effort to sort out what can be done to solve the problem.

There are numerous threats to the survival of Bryggen, says Ms Egenberg. 'Global warming, causing the ocean to reach higher levels, is a big threat, but I think if the resource plan (read money) fails, we will not be able to work according to the guidelines mentioned, and then the cultural significance of the site will eventually be lost.' Tourists, she says, do cause a 'certain wear and tear, but they also keep it alive'.

It is not only Bryggen that conservationists are seeking to preserve, but other old, timber-clad areas of Bergen. According to Sonja Krantz, who has been one of many locals lobbying the local government to protect such formerly working-class districts, 'the greatest threat comes from developers buying up houses and sometimes whole street quarters in order to deliberately run them down and destroy them'. In response, she says, 'people living in the old areas have organised in so-called *velforreninger,* informal, voluntary associations set up to protect their neighbourhoods'.

'Politicians are under great pressure to protect these fragile areas, both from the local associations and also the local newspaper,' says Ms Krantz. 'The attitude has changed.'

As told to Anthony Ham

On foot, you can get there from Torget in 20 minutes; alternatively, take the Vågen ferry (p209) or bus 11.

Gamle Bergen

The open-air **Old Bergen Museum** (Map p194; ☎ 55 39 43 00; www.bymuseet.no; Nyhavnsveien 4, Sandviken; adult/child Nkr50/25, free with Bergen Card; hourly tours 10am-5pm mid-May–early Sep), 4km north of the city centre, boasts a fine collection of 35 structures from the 18th and 19th centuries. A 30-minute walk from Torget will get you there or take a bus (No 20-23). Admission to the grounds is free and they are open all year.

Troldhaugen

This two-storey **home** (Map p194; ☎ 55 92 29 92; www.troldhaugen.com; Hop; adult/child Nkr60/free, Nkr20 with Bergen Card; 9am-6pm May-Sep, shorter hrs Oct-Apr) dates from 1885 and occupies an undeniably lovely setting on a lush and scenic peninsula by the coastal Nordåsvatnet lake, to the south of Bergen. Composer Edvard Grieg (see p50) and his wife Nina Hagerup spent every summer here from 1885 until Grieg's death in 1907. Today the house and grounds are open to the public, there's a multimedia Grieg exhibition and a 200-seat concert hall. Of particular interest are the Composer's Hut, where Edvard mustered his musical inspiration; the Steinway piano, which was a gift to celebrate Edvard and Nina's 50th wedding anniversary in 1892; and the couple's tombs, which are embedded in a rock face that overlooks Nordåsvatnet. It's an impressive place.

In summer, **concerts** (adult with/without Bergen Card Nkr160/220, children free) are held on Wednesday, Saturday and Sunday and during the Bergen International Festival; tickets and schedules are available at the tourist office.

Take any bus from platforms 19 to 21 to the Hopsbroen stop. From there, follow the signs to Troldhaugen; it's a 20-minute walk. There are free buses from outside the tourist office during the Bergen International Festival.

Siljustøl Museum

Another well-known Norwegian composer's home lies 3km south of Troldhaugen. Harald and Marie Sæverud lived in **Siljustøl** (Map p194; ☎ 55 92 29 92; www.siljustol.no; Siljustøl; adult/child/student Nkr60/free/20; noon-4pm Sun late-Jun–late-Sep), a simple timber home. It was constructed in the 1930s of natural stone and untreated wood in an attempt to create unity with the environment. Harald Sæverud's first symphony was completed in 1920 and he endeared himself to Norwegians everywhere when, during WWII, he wrote protest music against the Nazi occupation. In 1986 he was made official composer of the Bergen International Music Festival. When he died in March 1992, he was given a state funeral and buried at Siljustøl, as requested. To get there, take bus 30 from platform 20.

Damsgård

The 1770 **Damsgård manor** (Map p194; ☎ 55 58 80 10; www.vk.museum.no; Laksevåg; adult/child Nkr50/25, free with Bergen Card; ⏰ 11am-5pm late May-Aug, hourly tours 11am-4pm), 3km west of town, may well be Norway's (if not Europe's) finest example of 18th-century rococo timber architecture. The building's superb (even over-the-top) highlight is the baroque garden, which includes sculptures, ponds and plant specimens that were common 200 years ago. To get there, take bus 19 from the centre.

Lysøen

This beautiful **estate** (Map p194; ☎ 56 30 90 77; www.lysoen.no; Lysøen; adult/child incl guided tour Nkr30/10, free with Bergen Card; ⏰ noon-4pm Mon-Sat, 11am-5pm Sun mid-May–Aug, noon-4pm Sun Sep), on the island of the same name, was built in 1873 as the summer residence of renowned Norwegian violinist Ole Bull (see p49). After the death of Ole Bull's French-born wife, Felicité Villeminot, Bull purchased the 70-hectare Lysøen island, about 20km south of Bergen. Between 1872 and 1873, he and architect Conrad Fredrik von der Lippe constructed the fantasy villa 'Lysøen'. This 'Little Alhambra' took much of its extravagant inspiration from the architecture of Moorish Granada and integrated not only intricate frets and trellises, but also onion domes, romantic garden paths, Italian marble columns and a high-ceilinged music hall of Norwegian pine.

When Ole Bull died at the Lysøen property in August 1880, about 10,000 mourners accompanied the funeral procession to the Assistentkirkegården near Bergen's old city gate.

The grounds are crisscrossed with 13km of leisurely walks and there's a small café. From Bergen's bus station, take the Lysefjorden bus (566 and 567, return Nkr110) from platform 19 or 20 to Buena Quay, where there's a passenger ferry (adult/child Nkr50/20; hourly noon to 3pm, to 4pm Sun) to Lysøen.

Funiculars

FLØIBANEN

For an unbeatable view of the city, ride the 26-degree Fløibanen **funicular** (Map p196; ☎ 55 33 68 00; www.floibanen.no; Vetrlidsalmenning 21; adult/child return Nkr70/35, free with Bergen Card; ⏰ 8am-midnight May-Aug, 8am-11pm Mon-Sat & 9am-11pm Sun Sep-Apr) to the top of Mt Fløyen (320m), with departures every 15 minutes.

From the top, well-marked hiking tracks lead into the forest; the possibilities are mapped out on the free *Gledeskartet* or *Turløyper På Byfjellene Nord/Øst* (Nkr10) maps available from the Bergen tourist office. Track No 2 makes a 1.6km loop near Skomakerdiket Lake and track No 1 offers a 5km loop over hills, through forests and past several lakes. For a delightful 40-minute walk back to the city from Fløyen, follow track 4 clockwise and connect with track 6, which switchbacks down to the harbour.

ULRIKSBANEN

The Ulriksbanen **cable car** (Map p194; ☎ 55 20 20 20; www.ulriken.no; adult/child return Nkr80/40; ⏰ 9am-9pm Jun-Aug, shorter hrs rest-of-year) ascends to the radio tower and café atop Mt Ulriken (642m), offering a panoramic view of the city and surrounding fjords and mountains. The 'Bergen in a Nutshell' ticket (opposite) includes the cable car and a return bus from the tourist office. Otherwise, it's a 45-minute walk from the centre or a few minutes' ride on bus 2 or 31 from the post office or bus 50 from Bryggen.

A popular excursion is to ride up on the cable car and walk four to six hours north along a well-beaten track to the top of the Fløibanen funicular railway.

Fantoft Stavkirke

The Fantoft **stave church** (Map p194; ☎ 55 28 07 10; Paradis; adult/child/student Nkr30/12/20, free with Bergen Card; ⏰ 10.30am-2pm & 2.30-6pm mid-May–mid-Sep), in a lovely leafy setting (which goes by the name 'Paradise') south of Bergen, was built in Sognefjord around 1150 and moved to the southern outskirts of Bergen in 1883. It was burned down by a Satanist (and soon-to-be-released heavy metal musician) in 1992, but it has since been painstakingly reconstructed. The adjacent **cross**, originally from Sola in Rogaland, dates from 1050. From Bergen take any bus leaving from platform 20, get off at the Fantoft stop on Birkelundsbakken and walk uphill through the park for about five minutes.

Swimming Pools

If you fancy a swim but can't face wading into cold fjord waters, the outdoor heated pool (27°C) at the **Nordnes Sjøbad** (Nordnes Swimming Pool; Map p196; off Haugeveien; adult/child Nkr46/21; 7am-7pm Mon-Sat, 10am-7pm Sun mid-May–Aug) at the water's edge is good. For something a little cooler, there's a diving board to the open water.

TOURS

Bergen Fjord Sightseeing (☎ 55 25 90 00) operates a one-hour **harbour tour** (adult/child Nkr100/50, 3.30pm Jun–late-Aug), which offers good views of Bryggen and the surrounding hills. It also runs a four-hour **fjord tour** (adult/child Nkr400/200; 10am & 2.30pm Jul–late-Aug, 10am May & Jun, 10am Tue, Thu, Sat & Sun Sep). Boats depart from the waterfront next to the fish market.

A good way to reach the more outlying sights is to join one of the three-hour **Bergen Guided Tours** (☎ 05505; www.tide.no; adult/child Nkr280/180, discount with Bergen Card; 11am May-Sep), which take you to Fantoft Stave Church and Troldhaugen, among other sights.

Bergen wouldn't be a tourist town if it didn't have its **Bergens-Expressen toy train** (☎ 55 53 11 50; www.bergensexpressen.no; adult/child Nkr100/40; half-hourly 10am-5pm mid-Jun–mid-Aug & hourly 6pm & 7pm, shorter hrs May–mid-Jun & mid-Aug–Sep), which trundles along the Bryggen waterfront from opposite the Hanseatic Museum and up into some of the more interesting back streets. The trip takes one hour.

The **On&Off City Tour** (☎ 97 05 22 50; www.turistbuss.no; adult/child Nkr150/100, with Bergen Card Nkr100/70; hourly 9.30am-4.30pm Jun-Sep) does the usual hop-on, hop-off city circuit from Gamle Bergen to the aquarium.

The **'Bergen in a Nutshell' bus** (☎ 55 20 20 20; www.ulriken.no; adult/child Nkr150/75; hourly 9am-8pm Jun-Aug, 9am-5pm May & Sep) runs from next to the fish market, along the Bryggen waterfront, to the Ulriksbanen cable car and back again. Commentary is available in six languages.

Narrowing your focus a little, you could also take one of the excellent **Guided Tours of Bryggen** (☎ 55 58 80 10; adult/child Nkr80/free; 11am (German), 11am & 1pm (English), noon (Norwegian) Jun-Aug). They last 90 minutes, leave from Bryggens Museum and the commentary includes descriptions of life during Bergen's trading heyday. The ticket includes admission to Bryggens Museum, Schøtstuene and the Hanseatic Museum (you can revisit these museums later on the same day).

If you prefer to explore at your own pace, Bryggens Museum also has a (free) brochure entitled *Meeting Point Bryggen*, which allows **self-guided tours** covering 12 stops in the old town.

Bergen Guide Service (☎ 55 30 10 60; guide@visitbergen.com; adult/child/teenager Nkr95/free/45, with Bergen Card Nkr75/free/35; 3pm mid-Jun–mid-Aug) also does 90-minute walking tours of central Bergen.

From early June to early September, another popular excursion is the Sunday tour

FJORD TOURS FROM BERGEN

You can join any one of dozens of tours of Bergen and longer fjord tours; the tourist office has a full list and you can buy tickets there or purchase online in some cases. Most offer discounts if you have a Bergen Card.

Fjord Tours (☎ 81 56 82 22; www.fjordtours.com) has mastered the art of making the most of limited time with a series of tours into the fjords. Its popular and year-round **Norway in a Nutshell** tour is a great way to see far more than you thought possible in a single day. The day ticket (adult/child Nkr820/410) from Bergen combines a morning train to Voss, a bus to the Stalheim Hotel and then on to Gudvangen, from where a ferry takes you up the spectacular Nærøyfjord to Flåm, joining the stunning mountain railway to Myrdal, and a train back to Bergen in time for a late dinner (or you can continue on to Oslo to arrive around 10pm).

From May to September, it also runs train-bus-boat round-trips from Bergen such as the 10-hour **Explore Hardangerfjord** (Nkr645), which goes via Voss, Ulvik, Eidfjord and Norheimsund, as well as the nine-hour **World Heritage Tour** (Nkr830), which takes in Sognefjord, Nærøyfjord, Gudvangen and Voss.

Tide (☎ 55 23 87 00; www.tide.no) runs round trips by bus and boat to Eidfjord (p216; adult/child Nkr195/110).

by **veteran steam train** between Garnes and Midtun. It begins at 9am on the historic ferry M/S *Bruvik* from Bryggen to the **railway museum** (☎ 55 24 91 00) at Garnes and from there the teak-panelled train inches 18km to Midtun. The whole trip takes four hours (adult/child Nkr200/100). The train trip alone costs Nkr120/60 return.

FESTIVALS & EVENTS

The **Bergen International Festival** (☎ 55 36 55 66; www.fib.no), held for 14 days from late May until early June, is the big cultural festival of the year, with dance, music and folklore presentations throughout the city.

In late May, there's the **Seven Peaks Hike**, where all the local peaks must be visited on foot. It's an arduous 30km, with 2200m of ascent, but the record time is only 4½ hours!

Other highlights include:

Bergenfest (www.bergenfest.no) International music festival, late April to early May.

Bergen International Guitar Festival (www.bergenguitarfestival.com) Late June.

Bergen Food Festival (www.matfest.no) Early to mid-September. It showcases locally grown or caught food, which, sadly, includes whale meat.

Bergen International Film Festival (www.biff.no) Mid- to late October.

Night Jazz Festival (www.nattjazz.no) A happy festival as the city's large student population gets into the swing at the end of May.

For a full list of events, see the website www.visitbergen.com.

SLEEPING

Bergen has outstanding accommodation, but if we could leave you with only piece of advice, it would to book your accommodation before arriving in town, at least in the summer months. While we were there, the tourist office was sending tourists to Voss, one hour away, as Bergen was full.

The tourist office has an accommodation booking service (Nkr30 for walk-ins, Nkr50 for advance booking).

Budget

Lone Camping (Map p194; ☎ 55 39 29 60; www.lonecamping.no; Hardangerveien 697, Haukeland; tent sites Nkr130 plus per person Nkr20, cabins Nkr400-900) This lakeside camp site, 20km from town between Espeland and Haukeland, is a long way from Bergen's charms, although it's accessible by public transport; bus 900 runs to/from town (Nkr42, 30 minutes) every half-hour.

Bratland Camping (Map p194; ☎ 55 10 13 38; www.bratlandcamping.no; Bratlandsveien 6, Haukeland; tent sites Nkr110 plus per person Nkr15, cabins Nkr390-1200) Also accessible on bus 900, this well-equipped site is 4km south of Lone Camping.

Bergen Vandrerhjem YMCA (Map p196; ☎ 55 60 60 55; www.bergenhostel.no; Nedre Korskirkealmenning 4; dm Nkr155-230, bed linen Nkr50, breakfast Nkr55, d with bathroom, breakfast & bed linen Nkr750; 💻) Gone are the days when staying in a hostel meant a long hike into town; this friendly hostel could be Norway's most central. It has that unmistakeable hostel feel, same-sex or mixed dorms, kitchen facilities and a terrific rooftop terrace. Children under 14 pay half price and bookings are essential year-round.

Marken Gjestehus (Map p196; ☎ 55 31 44 04; www.marken-gjestehus.com; Kong Oscars gate 45; dm from Nkr160, s/d with shared bathroom Nkr395/500, with bathroom Nkr500/630) Midway between the harbour and the train station, this guesthouse has simple, but extremely well-kept rooms. The white walls and wooden floors give an attractive sense of light and space and the communal areas are clean and pleasant. It also has washing machine and bed linen/towels cost Nkr65/10 for those in dorms.

City Box (Map p196; ☎ 55 31 25 00; www.citybox.no; Nygårdsgaten 31; s/d with shared bathroom Nkr400/500, with bathroom Nkr500/600, breakfast Nkr59; 💻) The best hostel in Bergen, City Box is a place where the owners do simple things well, such as bright modern rooms with splashes of colour, free wireless access, a minimalist designer feel without the price tag and friendly young staff. For the rooms without a bathroom, there are two showers for every five rooms, most of the rooms have kitchen facilities and there's a laundry room. Let's hope the City Box idea catches on elsewhere in Norway.

Midrange

Villa Nordnes (Map p196; ☎ 92 44 03 80, 55 23 29 44; Haugeveien 34; s Nkr350-500, d Nkr650-750) This lovely rambling house out on the Nordnes Peninsula close to the aquarium is illuminated by a fine collection of antiques and by the friendly owner, Grethe Marthinussen. It's a good choice in a quiet location.

our pick Skansen Pensjonat (Map p196; ☎ 55 31 90 80; www.skansen-pensjonat.no; Vetrlidsalmenning 29; s Nkr375-500, d Nkr600-700, apt Nkr750) There are family-run guesthouses springing up all over Bergen, but this charming seven-room place is still our favourite. A wonderful location up behind the funicular station, a real attention to detail and many personal touches from the owners, Jannicke and Svein (who add much warmth to the place), make this a terrific choice. The rooms are light and airy, none more so than 'the balcony room', one of the nicest in Bergen. Prices for all but the largest apartments include breakfast.

Skuteviken Gjestehus (Map p196; ☎ 93 46 71 63; www.skutevikenguesthouse.com; Skutevikens Smalgang 11; s/d Nkr600/800, attic r Nkr900) This recently opened, authentic timber guesthouse, set on a small cobbled street, has traditional decoration (such as white wicker furniture and lace cushions) and a few modern touches. Painstakingly restored by two artists whose work adorns the rooms, the guesthouse is quite simply charming.

Kjellersmauet Gjestehus (Map p196; ☎ 55 96 26 08; www.gjestehuset.com; Kjellersmauet 22; 1-/2-/3-/4-bed apt from Nkr600/800/1350/1400) This oasis of hospitality and tradition in a delightful timber-clad street southwest of the centre is also outstanding. Run by the friendly Sonja, who goes the extra mile in taking care of her guests, the Kjellersmauet has a range of small, medium and large apartments in a building dating back to the 16th century. Wooden floors, traditional decoration and modern bathrooms make for a great stay.

Steens Hotell (Map p196; ☎ 55 30 88 88; www.steenshotel.no; Parkveien 22; s/tw/d with Fjord Pass Nkr700/850/970, otherwise s Nkr650-950, d Nkr880-1160; Ⓟ Nkr40 💻) This lovely 19th-century building oozes period charm, from the late-19th-century antiques to the gentle curve of the stairway; the bathroom facilities have recently been renovated. It's also a welcoming place. Most rooms are spacious and there's a wonderful dining room with stained-glass windows. It also boasts some of Bergen's cheapest parking.

Jacobs Apartments (Map p196; ☎ 98 23 86 00; www.apartments.no; Kong Oscars gate 44; dm Nkr165, s/d apt Nkr860/960, breakfast Nkr60; 💻) The owners are trying hard to present a designer apartment hotel and they almost succeed. The rooms have flat-screen TVs and some are spread over two levels, although these duplex rooms could do with a little more light.

Hotel Park Pension (Map p196; ☎ 55 54 44 00; www.parkhotel.no; Harald Hårfagresgate 35; s Nkr700-940, d Nkr970-1140; 💻) Filled with character and antiques, this family-run place spreads over two beautiful 19th-century buildings. Every room is different, although those in the building across the road from reception are more subtle; in the main building, expect antique writing desks and the corner rooms are gorgeous and filled with light. The location is quiet and just a 15-minute walk from the city centre.

First Hotel Marin (Map p196; ☎ 53 05 15 00; booking.marin@firsthotels.no; Rosenkrantz gate 8; s/d with Fjord Pass Nkr990/1150; 💻) A block back from the waterfront and with elegant hardwood floors, First Hotel Marin has a maritime theme and a great location. Some rooms have harbour views and there's a touch of class here that's sometimes lacking in chain hotels.

Clarion Hotel Admiral (Map p196; ☎ 55 23 64 00; www.admiral.no; C Sundtsgate 9; s Nkr990-1150, d Nkr1160-1555) With sweeping views across the water to Bryggen from the balconies of its harbour-facing rooms, this well-appointed hotel promises the best view to wake up to in Bergen if you can get a waterside room. The hotel also has a cigar and cognac salon and ice machines in the corridors.

In City Hotel & Apartments (Map p196; ☎ 53 23 16 13; www.incity.no; Øvre Ole Bulls plass 3; d/deluxe/penthouse/ste Nkr1190/1490/1690/1990; 💻) Modern, well-equipped apartments in the heart of town are the order of the day here. The rooms don't have a lot of personality but they're large and comfortable.

Top End

our pick **Det Hanseatiske Hotel** (Map p196; ☎ 55 30 48 00; www.dethanseatiskehotell.no; Finnegårdsgaten 2; s/d Nkr1195/1395, deluxe d Nkr1695-1895, ste up to Nkr4500; 💻) Now here's something special. The only hotel to be housed inside the old timber buildings of Bryggen itself, Det Hanseatiske Hotel is luxurious and like stepping back into a bygone Bergen age. Flat-screen TVs cohabit with antique bathtubs and some extraordinary architectural features from Bryggen's days as a Hanseatic port. Spread over two buildings and connected by a wonderful walkway, this is easily Bergen's most atmospheric hotel. If you're going to splash out, do it here.

Rica Strand Hotel (Map p196; ☎ 55 59 33 00; www.strandhotel.no; Strandkaien 2-4; s/d Nkr1200/1500; 💻) With rooms that range from a tight squeeze to those with views over Torget and towards Bryggen, the 1920s-era Rica Strand has an excellent central location.

Augustin Hotel (Map p196; ☎ 55 30 40 00; www.augustin.no; C Sundtsgate 22; s/d Nkr1450/1650; Ⓟ Nkr85 💻) Two things make this place stand out: first, as Bergen's oldest family-run hotel, it's renowned for the friendliness of its welcome. It's also one of very few hotels in Bergen that has met the exacting standards of environmental sustainability set by the Norwegian government (see p21). Modern artworks, blue-dominated, spacious rooms and Altona (opposite), a funky wine bar, round out a great package.

Grand Hotel Terminus (Map p196; ☎ 55 21 25 00; www.grand-hotel-terminus.no; Zander Kaaesgate 6; s/d from Nkr1450/1650, cheaper with Fjord Pass; P Nkr100) Opposite the train station, the Grand Hotel Terminus has historically been the hotel of choice for the city's well-heeled visitors. Some rooms are cramped and a little soulless, others are ornate and spacious, but the old-world charm (the building dates from 1928) and elaborate décor make this place stand out.

EATING

Bergen is the sort of place where international trends make their mark (sushi and tapas are all the rage) but you'll also find bastions of Norwegian tradition. There are plenty of restaurants in the Bryggen and Torget area, but many are targeted at a fairly undiscerning tourist market. There are exceptions as well as creative choices around and southwest of Øvre Ole Bulls plass.

Markets & Bakeries

our pick **Torget Fish Market** (Map p196; www.torgetibergen.no; Torget; 7am-7pm Jun-Aug, 7am-4pm Mon-Sat Sep-May) For price and atmosphere, it's hard to beat the fish market. Right alongside the harbour and a stone's throw from Bryggen, here you'll find everything from smoked whale meat (Nkr349 a kilo if you can live with your conscience) and salmon to calamari and chips (Nkr130), fish cakes (from Nkr89), prawn baguettes (Nkr45), local caviar and, sometimes, nonfishy reindeer and elk. Stallholders are usually happy to make up a take-away platter or prepare a sealed bag to take home.

Kjøttbasarell (Map p196; cnr Torget & Kong Oscars gate; 10am-5pm Mon-Wed & Fri, 10am-6pm Thu, 9am-4pm Sat) This lovely old food market is excellent if you're planning a picnic with cheeses, meats and all sorts of gourmet items.

Bakeries are in plentiful supply in Bergen. One delicacy to watch out for is Bergen's own *shillingsboller* (local pastry speciality shaped in a ball, which translates as shilling, ie the old currency unit) buns. Some of our favourite bakeries:

Baker Brun (Map p196; Zachariasbryggen Quay; 8am-8pm Mon-Sat, 11am-6pm Sun)

Godt Brød (Map p196; Nedre Korskirkealmenningen 12; 7am-6pm Mon-Fri, 7am-4.30pm Sat)

Sol Brød (Map p196; cnr Vetrlidsalmenning & Kong Oscars gate; 8am-5pm Mon-Fri, 8am-5.30pm Sat, 9am-4pm Sun)

Norwegian

Pygmalion Økocafé (Map p196; ☎ 55 32 33 60; Nedre Korskirkealmenning 4; ciabatta Nkr69-87, organic pancakes from Nkr86, salad from Nkr112; lunch & dinner; V) This very cool place has contemporary art adorning its walls, a downtempo vibe and tasty organic food. It's a great place at any time of the day and there are good choices for vegetarians.

our pick **Pingvinen** (Map p196; ☎ 55 60 46 46; Vaskerelven 14; mains Nkr63-135; 2pm-3.30am) Devoted to small-town Norwegian cooking and with a delightfully informal ambience, Pingvinen is terrific. Expect large servings of reindeer, elk, lamb and local fish but without the usual price tag and it's always obligatory to pay homage to Alma, the 'goddess chef'. As the night wears on and Alma heads home, the snacks menu comes out.

Lido (Map p196; ☎ 55 32 59 12; Torgalmenningen 1a; soup & mains Nkr69-169, children's menu Nkr35-89; lunch & dinner) Lido is an inexpensive cafeteria with good traditional grub. Its budget credentials get battered by the Nkr5 charge to go to the toilet, but it's nonetheless a good place for simple but hearty local food.

Bryggeloftet & Stuene (Map p196; ☎ 55 31 06 30; Bryggen 11; specials from Nkr89, mains Nkr89-275; lunch & dinner) Another Bryggen favourite for traditional Norwegian fare, this restaurant dates to the early 19th century, which is plenty of time to master the art of cooking reindeer, wolf-fish and lutefisk (dried whitefish).

Boha (Map p196; ☎ 55 31 31 60; Vaskerelven 6; starters Nkr95-135, mains Nkr210-255, 4-/6-course menu Nkr485/580; 4-10pm Mon-Thu, 4-11pm Fri, 5-11pm Sat) Famous for its seafood, this is the place to come for Kamchatka crab or monkfish. There's a thoughtfully chosen wine list and the retro décor works wonderfully well. The service is also attentive.

Wesselstuen (Map p196; ☎ 55 55 49 49; Øvre Ole Bulls plass 6; starters Nkr79-109, mains Nkr219-259; lunch & dinner) The richly decorated Wesselstuen evokes the wood-panelled dining halls of Bergen's past and is well known as the restaurant of choice for Bergen's intellectuals. The sirloin of reindeer (Nkr259) is excellent.

Bryggen Tracteursted (Map p196; ☎ 55 31 59 55; Bryggen; light meals Nkr95-145, starters Nkr82-145, mains

Nkr225-275; lunch & dinner May-Sep) This is one of the great Bryggen eating experiences. Housed in a 1708 building that ranges across the former stables, kitchen (note the stone floor, which meant that it was the only Bryggen building allowed to have a fire) and Bergen's only extant *schøtstuene* (dining hall), this fine restaurant does fish soup (Nkr98), steamed mussels (Nkr125) and a selection of Norwegian tapas. The food's good, but the atmosphere is the major drawcard.

ourpick **Enhjørningen** (Map p196; ☎ 55 32 79 19; Bryggen; starters Nkr95-135, mains Nkr275-310, 3-/4-course dinner Nkr490/550; noon-11pm Jun-Aug, 4-11pm Sep-May) The popular, upmarket Enhjørningen offers delicious fish and seafood in a rustic Bryggen setting. Known by locals for its unimpeachable excellence, this place is all about quality food and old-style elegance. We particularly like the scallops and scampi symphony (Nkr295) but everything's good.

Finnegaards Stuene (Map p196; ☎ 55 55 03 20; Finnegårdsgaten 2; 3-/5-/7-course dinner Nkr595/695/795; 6-11pm Mon-Sat) Part of the magnificent Det Hanseatiske Hotel, this high-class restaurant combines flavoursome traditional local dishes with the evocative architecture of 18th-century Bryggen.

Sushi & International

Red Sun (Map p196; ☎ 55 31 31 00; Kong Oscars gate 4; sashimi from Nkr47, makis from Nkr56, sushi combo Nkr270; lunch & dinner) The freshest seafood and stylish surrounds make for a great combination at Bergen's newest and most celebrated sushi bar. Upstairs is a more formal restaurant serving Vietnamese and Thai dishes.

ourpick **Kafe Kippers** (USF; Map p196; ☎ 55 31 00 60; Georgenes Verft 12; lunch mains Nkr58-81, dinner mains Nkr89-141; lunch & dinner) Away from the hubbub of downtown Bergen, this agreeable outdoor terrace is one of the best places for a meal or just a drink when the weather's warm. Attached to a cultural centre in an old sardine canning factory, it has an artsy vibe and serves plentiful lunch dishes such as linguini or sesame tuna salad.

Sumo (Map p196; ☎ 55 90 19 60; Neumanns gate 25; sushi from Nkr59, mains Nkr149-225; lunch & dinner) Sumo is another good sushi bar with a creative range of noodle dishes to complement all that sashimi and lovely outdoor tables.

Naboen (Map p196; ☎ 55 90 02 90; Neumanns gate 20; Swedish mains Nkr88-194; 4-11pm Mon-Sat, 4-10pm Sun) Although the cook does a range of Norwegian dishes here, Naboen is best known for its Swedish specialities, such as Swedish meatballs or the fillet of hare (Nkr194).

Bocca (Map p196; ☎ 55 32 64 50; Øvre Ole Bulls plass 3; 2-course lunch menu Nkr113-179, mains Nkr210-295; 7am-5pm Sun-Fri, 7am-4pm Sat Jun-Aug, 7am-4pm Mon-Sat Sep-May) Bocca has trendy décor and an upmarket brasserie feel and it's the sort of place where Bergen's young professionals come for Mediterranean food with a nod to Norwegian traditions.

Stragiotti (Map p196; ☎ 55 90 31 00; Vestre Torvgate 3; lunch specials Nkr59-139, mains Nkr129-279; lunch & dinner) This revamped Italian restaurant is stylish indoors, nice and breezy outside on the terrace and serves up authentic Italian food at very reasonable prices.

Tapas

ourpick **Escalon** (Map p196; ☎ 55 32 90 99; Vetrlidsalmenning 21; tapas Nkr56-98; 3pm-midnight Sun-Fri, 1pm-midnight Sat) Tapas has taken Bergen by storm and no-one does it better than Escalon. The friendly young waiters are happy to make suggestions on wine selection and the tapas are tasty and the closest you'll find in Bergen to what you'll get in Spain. Highly recommended.

Bar Celona (Map p196; ☎ 55 23 42 33; Vaskerelven 16-18; tapas Nkr39-79, mains Nkr174-228; 2pm-1am Mon-Thu, 2pm-2am Fri, noon-2am Sat) Another chic choice, this Spanish-inspired restaurant-bar has oodles of style with a friendly atmosphere. The outdoor tables are lovely on a fine afternoon and the food is excellent.

DRINKING

Bergen is a great place to go out. Although there's no hard-and-fast rule, the Bryggen area is where you'll find tourist-oriented bars (with tourist-oriented prices) while students and a discerning Bergen crowd hang out in places southwest of Øvre Ole Bulls plass; in the mainly student places, summer nights can be quieter than you might think as the main clientele is away on holiday. Bergen also has a thriving café culture.

Bars & Wine Bars

ourpick **Altona Vinbar** (Map p196; ☎ 55 30 40 30; C Sundtsgate 22; 6pm-12.30am Mon-Thu, 6pm-1.30am Fri & Sat) Possibly our favourite wine bar in town, Altona Vinbar is in an intimate warren of underground rooms that date from the 16th

LOCAL VOICE: ESPEN OLSEN

How long have you lived in Bergen? All my life, apart from one year overseas as an exchange student.

What's the best thing about living in Bergen? It feels like a small town but here you have everything you need. It's also a very cultural city and with the Bergen Wave a few years ago, many things that were new in Norwegian music and short or documentary film came from here; for a city of its size, Bergen has a variety of interesting cultural expressions.

What are people from Bergen like? We are a very proud people and we always say that we're not from Norway, we're from Bergen. We're also very talkative.

Does it annoy you that your city gets overrun with so many tourists? We like it, because we've always been a very international city. Tourism helped to save Bryggen and people now are very proud of it, but they almost tore it down in the 1970s...You should have seen Bergen back in the 1980s. It was quite ugly, but people have moved back into the city centre.

What makes you laugh about tourists in Bergen? In summer, when the weather is warm and everyone is outdoors, we get visitors who ask us what we're celebrating when we're just outdoors because it normally rains so much.

Best local tip? Take the Fløibanen up to the summit but walk back down.

Favourite places to go out at night? Altona (p205), Legal (below), Capello (opposite), Naboen (below), Pingvinen (below), Kafe Kippers (below) and Escalon (p205) where I work.

Best place for a coffee? Det Lille Kaffe Kompaniet (opposite) and Dromedar Kaffebar (opposite).

Favourite Bergen festivals Bergenfest, Night Jazz Festival and Bergen International Film Festival (see p202 for details on each).

Best things to do from Bergen? Hiking in the Stølsheimen mountains (p211), glacier walking from Finse (p190) and riding down to Flåm from Finse (see the boxed text p189).

As told to Anthony Ham

century. With a huge selection of international wines, soft lighting and music that ranges from jazz to rock but never drowns out conversation, it's hard to find fault with this place. If you've had a few glasses, take care with the impossibly low connecting doors!

Legal (Map p196; cnr Nygårdsgaten & Christies gate; 2pm-1.30am Sun-Thu, 2pm-2.30am Fri & Sat) One of the best student bars in Bergen, this laid-back place does retro décor and music that could be rock, but is more likely to be electronica or soft funk. Upstairs is a fine place to keep the night moving.

Fincken (Map p196; Nygårdsgaten 2A; 7pm-1.30am Wed & Thu, 7pm-2.30am Fri, 8pm-2.30am Sat) Just across the road from Legal, Fincken is one of few gay bars in Bergen.

To Glass Vinbar (Map p196; ☎ 55 32 90 99; Vetrlidsalmenning 19; 6pm-1am Mon-Thu, 6pm-2am Fri & Sat) If you're keen not to move too far from the centre, this trendy wine bar, next to the funicular station, gets a classier crowd than most bars on this street.

Bocca (Map p196; 1st fl, Øvre Ole Bulls plass 3; 11am-3.30am) Upstairs from the restaurant of the same name, Bocca draws a chic 30-something crowd who flock to the open balcony, or snuggle in the dimly lit retro salon. Music is usuall[y] lounge, with a DJ from Thursday to Saturday A San Miguel will set you back Nkr54 martinis cost Nkr59, while most cocktail[s] are Nkr93.

Other restaurants that double as cool bar[s] southwest of the centre:

Kafe Kippers (USF; Map p196; Georgenes Verft 12; 11am-12.30am Mon-Fri, noon-12.30am Sat & Sun) Great for an outdoor drink in summer.

Naboen (Map p196; Neumanns gate 20; 5pm-1.30am Sun-Thu, 5pm-2.30am Fri & Sat) Downstairs from the restaurant, this place is for those who love indie rock and jazz.

Onkel Lauritz (Map p196; Vaskerelven 6; 6pm-1am Sun-Thu, 6pm-2am Fri & Sat) Upstairs in Boha, this is good for a quiet conversation.

Pingvinen (Map p196; Vaskerelven 14; 2pm-3.30am) A funky, casual vibe and a friendly young crowd. Late-night snacks are good if you get the munchies.

Coffee Houses & Cafés

Café Opera (Map p196; ☎ 55 23 03 15; Engen 18 11am-12.30am Mon-Thu, 11am-3.30am Fri & Sat noon-12.30am Sun) By day, Café Opera has a literary- café feel with artworks and good coffee that attracts artists and students. O weekends, the crowd gets dancing until late with jazz seguing into electronica or classic club hits.

Det Lille Kaffe Kompaniet (Map p196; Nedre Fjellsmug 2; coffee or hot chocolate Nkr18-55; 10am-10pm Sun-Fri, noon-6pm Sat) In the past few years, this place has twice won a nationwide competition for the country's best coffee and two of its waiters are on Norway's national coffee team (kind of like a football team but with espresso machines). It's a lovely little place and it overflows onto the neighbouring stairs when the sun's out.

Dromedar Kaffebar (Map p196; ☎ 55 55 85 86; Strandgaten 79; 7.30am-6pm Mon-Fri, 10am-6pm Sat, 11am-6pm Sun) Bergen's coffee aficionados put this place not far behind Det Lille Kaffe Kompaniet for the city's best coffee.

Capello (Map p196; ☎ 55 96 12 11; Skostredet 14; noon-6pm Mon-Wed, noon-1am Thu-Sat, 1-6pm Sun) An engaging little café-bar that does smoothies, milkshakes, beer and pancakes, Capello is all about '50s and '60s décor and music downstairs (the juke box is filled with Elvis, the Monkeys, the Beatles and Bob Dylan). Upstairs the '70s take over.

Vågen (Map p196; Kong Oskars gate 10; 8.30am-9pm Mon-Fri, 8.30am-7pm Sat, 11am-9pm Sun) This quiet café is where old Norwegian meets Bob Marley, with traditional Norwegian decoration, rustic wooden tables and a chilled vibe helped by occasional Reggae tunes. It's a cool combination and provides a great backdrop to a lazy afternoon.

Jacobs Café (Map p196; Kong Oscars gate 44; 7.30am-1am Sun-Thu, 7.30am-2am Fri & Sat) Jacobs is a nice café with a beer garden and it draws a predominantly local crowd. There's occasionally live music in the evenings on weekends.

ENTERTAINMENT

Bergen has something for everyone, from high culture to late-night live-music venues. For some concerts and folklore performances, the Bergen Card (see p195) offers significant discounts.

Cinema

Bergen Kino (Map p196; ☎ 82 05 00 05; Neumanns gate 3; admission Nkr60-80) First-run movies are shown in their original languages at this multiscreen complex. It's also the base for the **Bergen International Film Festival** (www.biff.no) in October.

Concerts

Bergen has a busy programme of concerts throughout summer, many of them classical performances focusing on Bergen's favourite son, composer Edvard Grieg (see p50). Most of the concerts take place at evocative open-air venues such as **Troldhaugen** (Map p194; adult with/without Bergen Card Nkr160/220; Wed & Sat mid-Jun–Aug & Sun Sep & Oct) and **Siljustøl** (Map p194; Nkr200; 3pm Sun mid-April–mid-May), atop Mt Fløyen and in the park adjacent to Håkonshallen. For details and schedules, contact the tourist office. Tickets are sold by the tourist office or at the venue. There are free buses to the concerts from outside the tourist office, leaving one hour before starting time. From mid-June until late August, **Grieg concerts** (adult with/without Bergen Card Nkr140/180) also take place in the Grand Hotel Terminus (p204) at 9pm.

The renowned **Bergen Philharmonic Orchestra** (☎ 55 21 61 50; www.filharmonien.no) stages classical concerts at **Grieghallen** (Map p196; ☎ 55 21 61 00; www.grieghallen.no; Edvard Griegs plass) from September to May.

Grieghallen also hosts major rock and other modern music concerts. For upcoming concerts, check out www.bergenlive.no (in Norwegian).

Another place to watch out for concerts and exhibitions is **USF Vertfet** (☎ 55 31 55 70; www.usf.no; Georgenes Verft 12) on the Nordnes Peninsula.

Folklore

Fana Folklore (Map p194; ☎ 55 91 52 40; Fana church; tickets incl bus ride Nkr350; 7pm Fri Jun-Aug) If you're finding traditional Norwegian culture elusive, this folklore show in the Fana stave church may cut through the obscurity. Yes, it's tourist-oriented, but it's well done and a healthy proportion of the spectators is likely to be Norwegian. Fana Folklore buses pick up ticket holders at Festplassen at 7pm, returning at 10.30pm; tickets can be bought at the tourist office.

Bergen Folklore (Map p196; ☎ 55 55 20 06; adult/child Nkr100/free; 9pm Tue mid-Jun–mid-Aug) Another group performs traditional one-hour music and dance routines in the atmospheric Schøtstuene (see p195). Tickets are available from the tourist office or at the door.

Nightclubs & Live Music

Calibar (Map p196; www.calibar.no in Norwegian; Vaskerelven 1; 3pm-1am Mon-Thu, 3pm-3am Fri, noon-3am Sat) Funky! Calibar is hip in all the right places with stunning lighting and décor that fuses chic modern style with retro flair (it claims to have the oldest floor in Bergen). Upstairs is café and conversation, but downstairs is a sweaty nightclub for a 30-something crowd drawn by '80s music it can sing along to. You have to be 24 to get in and ready to pay Nkr96 for a cocktail.

Garage (Map p196; ☎ 55 32 19 80; Christies gate 14; 3pm-3.30am) Garage has taken on an almost mythical quality for music lovers across Europe. It does play live jazz and acoustic, but this is a rock venue at heart with well-known Norwegian and international acts drawn to the cavernous basement. If he's around, ask for Dennis, who's something of a local legend (he once played in the group Electric Rain) and he'll set you straight on the local music scene.

Hulen (Map p196; ☎ 55 55 31 31; www.hulen.no in Norwegian; Olaf Ryes vei 48; 9pm-3am Thu-Sat Sep–mid-Jun) Like Garage, Hulen enjoys a legendary status. Going strong since 1968, it's the oldest rock club in northern Europe and it's one of the classic stages for indie rock. Hulen means 'cave' and the venue is actually a converted bomb shelter. Sadly, it closes during summer when many of Bergen's students head off on holidays. It also hosts a heavy-metal festival in early November.

Rick's (Map p196; ☎ 55 55 31 31; Veiten 3; cover charge Nkr90; 1pm-3am Sun-Thu, 1pm-3.30am Fri & Sat) There's something for everyone at Rick's. At street level, 'Silver' is a superstylish wine bar and café with occasionally outrageous décor, while Rick's, downstairs and open from 10pm, is for live music, with an extra venue that serves as a popular disco. You have to be at least 24 to get in.

SHOPPING

Many of the shops along Bryggen are devoted to hideous fridge magnets, cheese slicers and trolls, but there's some higher quality stuff if you know where to look.

Juhls' Silver Gallery (Map p196; ☎ 55 32 47 40; juhls.bg@online.no; Bryggen 39; 9am-10pm mid-May–mid-Aug, 9am-6pm Mon-Fri & 1-7pm Sat & Sun rest-of-year) This wonderful jewellery shop sells exquisite silver jewellery crafted by Regine Juhls at her workshop high above the Arctic Circle (p365). Her 'Tundra' collection strongly evokes the icy wastes of the north.

Kvams Flisespikkeri (Map p196; ☎ 55 32 78 20; www.kvams-flisespikkeri.com; Bredsgården, Bryggen; 9am-6pm mid-May–mid-Sep, 11am-3pm Mon-Fri & noon-4pm Sat rest-of-year) Paintings, block prints and other artworks by Ketil Kvam adorn this lovely Bryggen gallery, with a range of cheaper prints available up to original artworks. Most have a Bergen theme.

Læverkstedet (Map p196; ☎ 55 31 45 73; Jacobsfjorden, Bryggen; 9am-7pm mid-May–mid-Aug, shorter hrs rest-of-year) One of the most popular shops in the lanes tucked away in Bryggen, this place sells the softest moose leather along with everything from jackets to bags and other knick-knacks.

Gitarmaker (Map p196; ☎ 55 31 07 01; www.hannokiehl.com in Norwegian; Kong Oscars gate 45; 11am-6pm Mon-Fri, 11am-2pm Sat) The engaging Hanno Kiehl hand-crafts top-notch acoustic guitars that seem very much at home in this most musical city. They don't come cheap (prices start at Nkr25,000) and they can take two months to make, but the quality is unquestionable.

Oleana (Map p196; ☎ 55 31 05 20; www.oleana.no; Strandkaien 2A; 9am-7pm Mon-Fri, 10am-4pm Sat, noon-6pm Sun) With textiles inspired by traditional folk costumes and a whole philosophy of storytelling through weaving, Oleana is all about vivid colours and beautiful clothes.

Husfliden (Map p196; ☎ 55 31 78 70; Vågsalmenningen 3; 9am-4.30pm Mon-Wed & Fri, 9am-7pm Thu, 9am-3pm Sat) If you're looking for the less creative but typically Norwegian souvenirs, Husfliden sells a broad selection of handicrafts, wooden toys and traditional clothing.

Foto Video (Map p196; ☎ 55 31 62 15; www.fotovideo.no in Norwegian; Nygaten 9; 9am-5pm Mon-Wed & Fri, 9am-7pm Thu, 9am-3pm Sat) This professional camera store is the place to come for all your photo and video needs.

Bergen has two stylish shopping centres in the centre of town. **Galleriet** (Torgalmenningen 8; 9am-8pm Mon-Fri, 9am-6pm Sat) spreads over five floors with everything from Benetton to the Body Shop, while **Xhibition** (Småstrandgaten 3; 9am-8pm Mon-Fri, 9am-6pm Sat) is home to an enormous H&M, as well as a supermarket and the post office.

GETTING THERE & AWAY

Air

Bergen airport (Map p194; ☎ 55 99 80 00) is at Flesland, about 19km southwest of the centre. **SAS Braathens** (☎ 81 52 00 00; www.sasbraathens.no) connects Oslo and Bergen (from Nkr265) six times daily. There are also direct flights to Trondheim (from Nkr560), Kristiansand (from Nkr560) as well as Stavanger (from Nkr520). **Coast Air** (☎ 81 54 44 42; www.coastair.no) also has a daily flight to Haugesund (from Nkr490).

For information on international flights to/from Bergen, see p403.

Boat

There are daily **Fylkesbåtane** (☎ 55 90 70 70; www fylkesbaatane.no) express boats to Balestrand (Nkr410, four hours), Flåm (Nkr552, 5½ hours), Måløy (Nkr595, 4½ hours), Selje (Nkr640, five hours) and Stavanger (one way/return Nkr620/710, four hours) from the Strandkaiterminal (Map p196).

The Hurtigruten coastal ferry leaves from the Frieleneskaien (Map p196), to the south of the university, at 8pm daily. See p412 for details.

International ferries to/from Bergen dock at Skoltegrunnskaien (Map p196), northwest of the Rosenkrantz tower. See p408 for details on international sailings.

Rødne Fjord Cruise (☎ 51 89 52 70; www.rodne no; Nkr285; May-Aug) has summer express boats from Bergen to Rosendal (p220) twice daily from Monday to Friday and once on Saturday and Sunday. It leaves just northwest of Strandkaiterminal.

Bus

The cheapest buses are with **Lavpriseksspressen** (www.lavprisekspressen.no in Norwegian), which runs services to Oslo (Nkr349, two on Saturday, Monday, Thursday and Friday). Otherwise, see below for details on Nor-Way Bussekspress destinations:

Destination	Departures	Cost	Duration
Ålesund	1 to 2 daily	Nkr610	10½hr
Kristiansand	1 daily	Nkr625	12hr
Oslo	3 daily	Nkr700	11½hr
Stavanger	8 daily	Nkr420	5¾hr
Stryn	3 daily	Nkr451	6½hr
Trondheim	2 daily	Nkr751	14¼hr

Train

The spectacular train journey between Bergen and Oslo (Nkr299 to Nkr728, 6½ to eight hours, five daily) runs through the heart of Norway. Local trains between Bergen and Voss (Nkr153, one hour) leave every hour or two; four of these run to/from Myrdal (Nkr232, 2¼ hours) for connections for the Flåmsbana railway.

GETTING AROUND

To/From The Airport

Flesland airport is serviced by **Flybussen** (www.fly bussen.no), which runs four times hourly between the airport, the Radisson SAS Royal Hotel, the main bus terminal and opposite the tourist office (adult/child Nkr75/free, 45 mins).

Bicycle

You can hire cycles from the downstairs workshop of **Sykkelbutikken** (Map p196; ☎ 55 36 18 80; Kong Oscars gate 81; per weekend from Nkr300, mountain bike per day/week Nkr200/700, bag/helmet Nkr40/50).

Bus

City buses (☎ 177) cost Nkr20, while fares beyond the centre are based on the distance travelled. Free bus 100 runs between Bryggen and the bus terminal.

Car & Motorcycle

In busy areas, metered parking is limited to 30 minutes or two hours; the parking areas at Sydnes allow up to nine hours (free at night). The largest and cheapest (Nkr75 per 24 hours) indoor car park is the 24-hour Bygarasjen at the bus terminal.

Boat

From late May to late August, the **Vågen Harbour Ferry** (Map p196; ☎ 55 56 04 00; one way/return adult Nkr40/50, child Nkr25/35; every 30 mins from 10am to 6pm) runs between the Torget fish market and Tollbodhopen at Nordnes (near the Bergen Aquarium).

VOSS

pop 13,786

Voss has built a world-renowned reputation as Norway's adventure capital and you'll be drawn here if you love the thrill of white-water rafting, bungee jumping and just about anything you can do from a parasail. For everyone else, Voss is little more than a staging post between Bergen and the fjords. It does have a pretty lakeside setting, but German bombing during WWII means that the architecture is largely modern and undistinguished.

INFORMATION

Bibliothek (☎ 56 51 94 70; 10am-4pm Mon-Wed & Fri, 10am-7pm Thu, 10am-2pm Sat) Free, time-limited internet access.

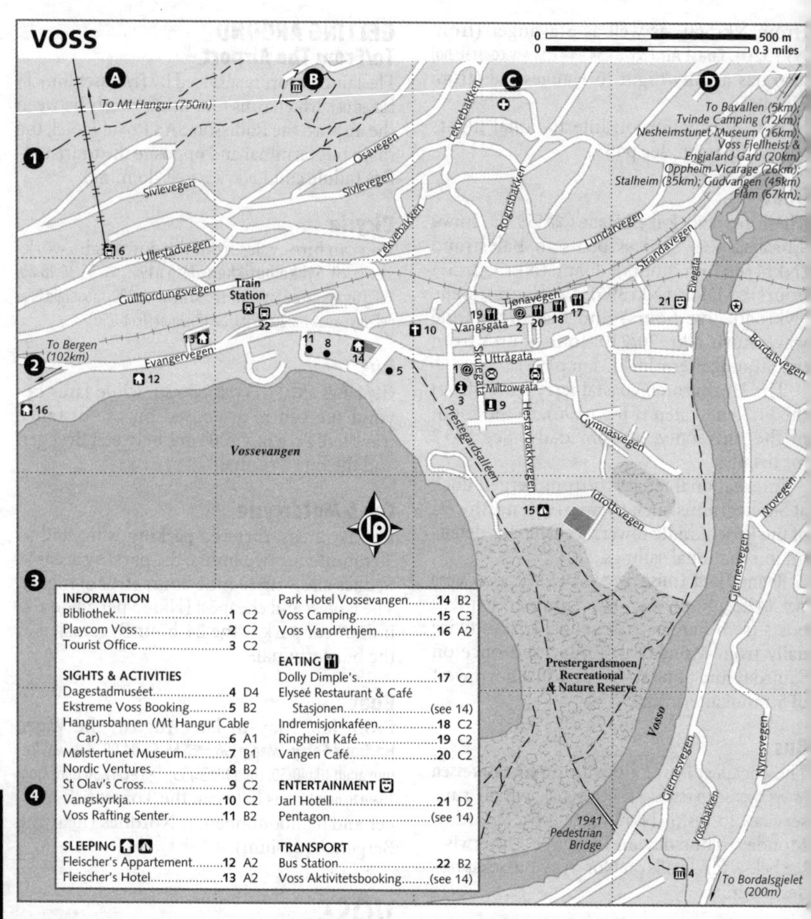

Playcom Voss (☎ 56 51 63 03; Vangsgata 36; per hr Nkr40; ⏲ 9am-10pm Mon-Fri, 10am-10pm Sat, 11am-10pm Sun) Internet access.

Tourist office (☎ 56 52 08 00; www.visitvoss.no; Uttrågata 9; ⏲ 8am-7pm Mon-Fri, 9am-7pm Sat & noon-7pm Sun Jun-Aug, 8.30am-3.30pm Sep-May)

SIGHTS

Vangskyrkja & St Olav's Cross

Voss' stone **church** (☎ 56 51 38 80; www.voss.kyrkjer.net; Uttrågata; adult/child Nkr15/free; ⏲ 10am-4pm Mon-Fri, 10am-2pm Sat, 2-4pm Sun Jun-Aug, shorter hrs rest-of-year) occupies the site of an ancient pagan temple. A Gothic-style stone church was built here in the mid-13th century. Although the original stone altar and unique wooden spire remain, the Lutheran Reformation of 1536 saw the removal of many original features. The 1923 stained-glass work commemorates the 900th anniversary of Christianity in Voss. Miraculously, the building escaped destruction during the intense German bombing of Voss in 1940.

In a field around 150m southeast of the tourist office stands a weathered **stone cross** erected by King Olav Haraldsson den Heilige (St Olav) in 1023 to commemorate the local conversion to Christianity. Just because it's close at hand, doesn't mean the tourist office knows where to find it.

Prestegardsmoen

The **Prestegardsmoen Recreational and Nature Reserve**, which extends south from Voss

Camping, is a series of hiking tracks through elm, birch and pine forests with 140 species of plants and 124 bird species.

Hangursbahnen

This **cable car** (☎ 56 53 02 20; adult/child Nkr90/55; 11am-5pm Jun-early Sep) whisks you to Mt Hangur, high above Voss, for stunning panoramic views over the town and the surrounding mountains.

Voss Folk Museum

The main portion of the Voss Folk Museum (Voss Folkemuseum) is the **Mølstertunet Museum** (☎ 56 51 15 11; Mølstervegen 143; adult/child Nkr45/free; 10am-5pm daily mid-May–mid-Sep, 10am-3pm Mon-Fri, noon-3pm Sun rest-of-year), on a hilltop at the farm Mølster high above Voss. The collection of 16 historic farm buildings once typical of the region dates from 1600 to 1870. There are guided tours on the hour, every hour.

The other two portions of the museum, the **Nesheimstunet Museum** (12 farm buildings, the oldest dating back to 1688) in Tvinne and the old wooden **Oppheim vicarage**, lie 16km and 26km from Voss respectively, along E16 to Gudvangen. Although the grounds are open, to see inside the buildings you'll need to ring ahead.

Dagestadmuséet

This **museum** (☎ 56 51 65 33; www.dagestadmuseet.no in Norwegian; Helgavangen 52; adult/child/student or senior Nkr40/free/30; 11am-2pm Tue-Sun Jun-Aug), 1.5km south of the town centre, was opened in 1950 by renowned local woodcarver Magnus Dagestad (1865–1957) and features his lifetime of carvings, drawings and traditional wooden furniture, as well as works by his wife, Helena. It's an unusual and worthwhile exhibit.

ACTIVITIES

From late June to mid-September, the tourist office arranges guided **half- or full-day hikes** (www.vossafjell.no) into the mountains surrounding Voss on Saturdays. It can also provide details of cycling routes and sells **fishing permits** (1-day/3-day/season Nkr50/75/250).

Voss Fjellhest & Engjaland Gard (☎ 56 51 91 66; www.vossfjellhest.no; Engjaland; 3hr/full day Nkr500/900) organises hiking and horse riding in the beautiful Stølsheimen mountains 20km north of Voss from July to late August. It also has full-board weekend accommodation for Nkr2500.

EXTREME SPORTS IN VOSS

If slow boats up the fjords seem like a pretty tame response to extraordinary Norwegian landscapes, Voss may be your antidote. This town lives and breathes extreme sports, never more so than in late June when adrenaline junkies converge on Voss for **Extremesport Week** (www.ekstremsportveko.com), a week-long festival that combines all manner of extreme sports (skydiving, paragliding and base jumping) with local and international music acts.

For bookings, contact **Ekstreme Voss Booking** (☎ 56 51 36 30; www.ekstremevoss.com; 10am-5pm Mon-Thu & Sun, 10am-8pm Fri & Sat May-Sep). You'll find it in the car park of the Park Hotel Vossevangen.

Paragliding, Parasailing & Bungee Jumping

Nordic Ventures (☎ 56 51 00 17; www.nordicventures.com; Apr–mid-Oct) is one of the best activity centres of its kind in Norway, offering tandem paragliding flights (Nkr1200), parasailing (Nkr450) and even 180m-high, 115km/h bungee jumps from a parasail (Nkr1600)! As its motto says: 'Be brave. Even if you're not, pretend to be. No-one can tell the difference.'

Watersports

If you're unable to take to the air, you don't need to be left behind. **Voss Rafting Senter** (☎ 56 51 05 25; www.vossrafting.no) has everything from white-water rafting (Nkr450 to Nkr750, or Nkr1600 per family), or canyoning (Nkr700) to waterfall abseiling (from Nkr800) and riverboarding (Nkr800). Rafters and riverboarders can choose between three very different rivers: the Stranda (Class III to IV), Raundalen (Class III to V) and Vosso (Class II). Not to be outdone in the motto stakes, its motto is: 'We guarantee to wet your pants'.

Nordic Ventures also runs sea-kayaking expeditions, ranging from lake tours (four to five hours, Nkr575) to one-/two-/three-day tours (Nkr895/1895/2595) on the stunning Nærøyfjord (p237).

The **ski season** in Voss usually lasts from early December until April. The winter action focuses on the cable-car route up Mt Hangur (p211) where there's a winter ski school. Those with vehicles can opt for Bavallen, 5km north of the centre, which is used for international downhill competitions. On the plateau and up the Raundalen Valley at Mjølfjell, you'll also find excellent cross-country skiing. For weather and snow conditions, call ☎ 56 51 94 88.

TOURS

The famous 'Norway in a Nutshell' tour (see boxed text p201), normally done from Oslo or Bergen, also works as a day tour from Voss. It involves rail trips from Voss to Myrdal and from there to Flåm, the boat to Gudvangen and the bus back to Voss (adult/child Nkr530/265, 6½ to 8½ hours). Book through the tourist office, any travel agency, or directly through **NSB** (☎ 56 52 80 07) at the train station.

The tourist office also organises 6½-hour day excursions to Ulvik (p215) and Eidfjord (p216) through a bus-ferry combination; tickets cost from Nkr300/250 per adult/child.

FESTIVALS

For Voss' **Extreme Sports Festival**, see the boxed text, p211.

On the last weekend of August, the **Voss Blues & Roots Festival** (☎ 56 51 63 03; www.vossblues.no in Norwegian; Fri/Sat day pass from Nkr400/500, festival pass Nkr850) is one of Norway's better music festivals. **Vossajazz** (www.vossajazz.no in Norwegian) is held in March.

The late-September **Sheep's Head Food Festival** (www.smalahovesleppet.no in Norwegian) involves exploring the culinary delights of sheep heads.

SLEEPING

Voss Camping (☎ 56 51 15 97; www.vosscamping.no; Prestegardsalléen 40; tent/caravan sites from Nkr140/190, cabins from Nkr500; Easter-Sep) The lakeside and centrally located Voss Camping has basic facilities. It can get a bit rowdy in summer but the location's a winner.

Tvinde Camping (☎ 56 51 69 19; www.tvinde.no; Tvinde; tent sites per person from Nkr110, cabins from Nkr375) If you don't mind being a bit out of town, this scenic alternative lies beside a waterfall about 12km north of town. Without a car, access is on the Voss–Gudvangen bus (Nkr35, 20 minutes).

Voss Vandrerhjem (☎ 56 51 20 17; www.vosshostel.com; Evangervegen 68; dm/s/d from Nkr150/455/590) The modern Voss hostel offers rooms with en suite and fine lake views; ask for a top-floor, lakeside room. Bicycles, canoes and kayaks can be hired here and there's a free sauna.

Fleischer's Appartement (☎ 56 52 05 00; www.fleischers.no; Evangervegen 13; 2-/4-bed apt Nkr990/1580; P) This lakeside annexe of Fleischer's Hotel offers small but adequate self-catering units.

Park Hotel Vossevangen (☎ 56 53 10 00; www.parkvoss.no; Uttrågata 1; s/d from Nkr825/1100; P) While this place lacks the elegance of Fleischer's Hotel, the modern rooms are nonetheless very comfortable and many overlook the lake Vossevangen.

our pick **Fleischer's Hotel** (☎ 56 52 05 00; www.fleischers.no; Evangervegen; s/d Nkr1195/1550, with Fjord Pass Nkr830/1230; P) For historic character, the beautiful Fleischer's Hotel, opened in 1888, oozes antique charm and is the best place in town. Some rooms have lake views. Edvard Grieg stayed here in 1901 if you're into celebrity hotel stays.

EATING

Café Stasjonen (☎ 56 53 10 17; Uttrågata 1; dishes Nkr35-175; 9.30am-midnight Sun-Thu, 9.30am-1am Fri & Sat) In the Park Hotel Vossevangen is this train-themed café, which offers snacks, light meals and a salad bar.

Fleischer's Hotel restaurant (Evangervegen; meals Nkr85-259; lunch & dinner) This restaurant is excellent with a salad buffet (Nkr110), light meals (from Nkr85) and main dishes (from Nkr179).

Dolly Dimple's (☎ 56 51 00 40; Vangsgata 52; pizzas from Nkr130; 2-10pm Mon-Thu, 2-11pm Fri, noon-11pm Sat, 1-10pm Sun) Dolly Dimple's serves more than 30 different pizzas.

our pick **Elysée** (☎ 56 53 10 09; Park Hotel Vossevangen, Uttrågata 1; mains Nkr130-275; lunch & dinner) The finest restaurant in Voss specialises in French and international cuisine and has a particularly extensive wine list. The Elysée also does set menus.

Traditional Norwegian food is served at **Indremisjonskaféen** (☎ 51 56 14 08; Vangsgata 46; snacks & light meals Nkr35-99; 9.30am-6pm Mon-Fri, 9.30am-3pm Sat, noon-6pm Sun). For cakes, snacks and reindeer roast, try **Vangen Café** (☎ 56 51 1[illegible] 05; Vangsgata 42; dishes Nkr49-115; 10am-6pm Mon-Fri, 10.30am-4pm Sat, 12.30-6pm Sun). You'll find a more varied menu at the **Ringheim Kafé** (☎ 56 51 13 65; Vangsgata 32; mains Nkr89-199; lunch & dinner), not to mention pleasant outdoor tables.

ENTERTAINMENT

Park Hotel Vossevangen (☎ 56 53 10 00; Uttrågata 1) has a piano bar, for those who like their music light, and the somewhat more energetic and popular Pentagon weekend disco. The pub in the **Jarl Hotell** (☎ 56 51 19 33; Elvegata 9) has a cellar disco that attracts the 18-to-25 crowd with house and techno.

GETTING THERE & AWAY

Buses stop at the train station, west of the centre. Frequent bus services connect Voss with Bergen (Nkr150, two hours) and Aurland (Nkr130, 1½ hours), via Gudvangen and Flåm.

The **NSB** (☎ 56 52 80 00) rail services on the renowned *Bergensbanen* to/from Bergen (Nkr153, one hour, hourly) and Oslo (Nkr199 to Nkr633, 5½ to six hours, five daily) connect at Myrdal (Nkr94, 50 minutes) with the scenic line down to Flåm (see p234).

GETTING AROUND

Bicycle hire is available for around Nkr250 per day from **Voss Aktivitetsbooking** (🕑 10am-5pm Mon-Thu & Sun, 10am-8pm Fri & Sat), beside the Park Hotel Vossevangen, or for Nkr150/250 per half/full day from the Voss Vandrerhjem (p212).

AROUND VOSS

Stalheim

This gorgeous little spot high above the valley is an extraordinary place.

Between 1647 and 1909, Stalheim was a stopping-off point for travellers on the Royal Mail route between Copenhagen, Christiania (Oslo) and Bergen. A road was built for horses and carriages in 1780. The mailmen and their weary steeds rested in Stalheim and changed to fresh horses after climbing up the valley and through the Stalheimskleiva gorge, flanked by the thundering Stalheim and Sivle waterfalls. Although a modern road winds up through two tunnels from the valley floor, the **old mail road** (marked as 'Stalheimskleiva' along the E16 from Gudvangen) climbs up at an astonishing 18% gradient.

At the top is the **Stalheim Hotel** (☎ 56 52 01 22; www.stalheim.com; s/d Nkr900/1380, half-board Nkr1195/1860, full-board Nkr1335/2140; 🕑 mid-May–early Oct), arguably Norway's most spectacularly sited hotel. Not surprisingly, the hotel (room 324 in particular) once featured in *Conde Nast's* 'best rooms-with-a-view'. The rooms are spacious and comfortable, but you'll scarcely be able to tear yourself away from the window to notice. Unfortunately, rooms without a view cost the same. Lunch/dinner buffets cost Nkr250/335, but lighter meals are available and meals work out cheaper if you pay half- and full-board rates.

If you're not staying at the hotel, the **terrace** (admission free; 🕑 9.30am-6pm mid-May–Sep) has breathtaking views down Nærøydalen.

The **Stalheim Folkemuseum** (☎ 56 52 01 22; Stalheim; adult/child Nkr50/free; 🕑 on request), near the hotel, includes folk exhibits and 30 log buildings laid out as a traditional farm. It only opens if there are 10 or more visitors; ask at the hotel for details.

There are two other options for sleeping in the Stalheim area. In summer, there are log cabins at **Stalheim Fjord og Fjellhytter** (☎ 56 51 28 47; www.stalheim.no; cabins from Nkr550) in the village just beyond the hotel, while **Stalheimsøy Gard** (☎ 56 52 00 22; www.stalheimsoy.no; d from Nkr700) is down in the valley far below.

To reach Stalheim from Voss (Nkr56, one hour, four to 11 daily), take any bus towards the towns of Gudvangen/Aurland, but you may have to hike 1.3km up from the main road unless you can persuade the bus driver to make the short detour.

Myrdal

Between towns of Voss and Finse, Myrdal is the junction of the Oslo–Bergen railway

A WALK ALONG THE PRECIPICE

Norwegians may seem to delight in building their homes in the most inaccessible places, but **Husmannsplassen Nåli** (the Cotter's Farm of Nåli), along the ledge from Stalheim high above Nærøydalen, may just win the prize. Built in 1870 when the first cotter moved there with two cows, four sheep and 11 goats, it was occupied until 1930. Now overgrown, it's an evocative spot, although the route there (two hours return) is not for the faint-hearted with the path beneath the cliff wall extremely narrow in parts and with nothing between you and the valley floor far below; don't even think of walking here after rain. As long as you don't suffer from vertigo, it's one of Norway's most beautiful walks. Ask directions from the reception of the Stalheim Hotel.

and the spectacularly steep Flåmsbana railway; it's also a famous stop on the 'Norway in a Nutshell' tour. From here, the dramatic Flåmsbana line twists 20km down to Flåm on Aurlandsfjorden, an arm of Sognefjorden. For more information, see p234.

HARDANGERFJORD

Running from the Atlantic to the steep wall of central Norway's Hardangervidda Plateau, Hardangerfjord is classic Norwegian fjord country. There are many beautiful corners, although our pick would probably be Eidfjord, Ulvik, Utne and Kinsarvik. Many people visit from Bergen, while the high-energy town of Voss makes a fine alternative and, if time permits, don't neglect to stay overnight in one of the small villages that cling to the water's edge. For details of exploring Hardangerfjord from Bergen, see the boxed text, p201, while www.hardangerfjord.com has plenty of useful information as well.

NORHEIMSUND

pop 3500

Quiet little Norheimsund serves as the gateway to Hardangerfjord. There are more beautiful places further into the fjord network, but it's a picturesque town nonetheless and makes for a pleasant introduction to what lies ahead.

Norheimsund tourist office (☎ 56 55 15 85; www.visitkvam.no; 🕑 10am-6pm Mon-Fri, 10am-4pm Sat, 3-8pm Sun mid-May–Aug) has information in summer. **Fjord Tours** (☎ 81 56 82 22; www.fjordtours.com) runs 'Explore Hardangerfjord' train-bus-and-boat tours from Bergen (p201) that you can just as easily catch in Norheimsund as Bergen.

Just 1km west of Norheimsund along Rv7 is the picturesque **Steinsdalsfossen waterfall**. It's a far cry from Norway's highest, but it does offer the chance to walk behind the water. Another attraction in Norheimsund is the unusual **Hardanger Boat-building Museum** (Hardanger Fartøyvernsenter; ☎ 56 55 33 50; www.fartoyvern.no; adult/child Nkr60/30; 🕑 10am-5pm daily end May-end Aug), where you'll find old wooden boats, restoration procedures, rope-making and exhibitions; children can also try their hand at building a boat. It sometimes also offers two-hour cruises on the fjord in a restored cutter.

Oddland Camping (☎ 56 55 16 86; oddland.camping@kvamnet.no; tent sites Nkr130, cabins from Nkr450) This well-equipped, family-run camp by the lake has good fjord views, simple cabins and the staff can rent out rowboats.

Sandven Hotel (☎ 56 55 20 88; www.sandvenhotel.no; s/d from Nkr790/1140; P 💻) Located right on the waterfront in the centre of Norheimsund, the atmospheric Sandven Hotel dates from 1857 and has loads of charm, expansive balconies and excellent views. You may also want to try the Crown Prince suite (Nkr2000) – this is where the future king of Norway once stayed.

Three to seven daily buses run between Voss and Norheimsund (Nkr138, two hours) via Øystese.

ØYSTESE

pop 2176

Øystese used to be little more than an adjunct to Norheimsund, but the **Kunsthuset Kabuso** (☎ 56 55 39 00; www.kabuso.no; adult/child Nkr50/free; 🕑 10am-5pm Tue-Sun Jun-Aug, 11am-3pm Tue-Sun Sep-May) has made it a destination in its own right. A showcase for contemporary and traditional art (it attracts artists of world renown, such as the UK's Damien Hirst in 2007), it's a terrific place that you just don't expect to find in a small village on the shore of a Norwegian fjord.

Also in town is the **Ingebrigt Vik Museum** (☎ 56 55 30 00; adult/child Nkr30/10; 🕑 10am-3pm Jun-Aug), an octagonal gallery dedicated to the renowned Norwegian sculptor of the same name (1867–1927).

Øystese tourist office (☎ 56 55 59 10; k-reise@online.no; 🕑 9am-8pm Mon-Fri, 9am-6pm Sat mid-May–Aug) has good information about the area if you're here in summer.

The best place to stay in town is the modern **Hardangerfjord Hotell** (☎ 56 55 63 00; www.hardangerfjord-hotell.no; s/d from Nkr700/1010; P 💻), which has pleasant rooms, a fjord-side location and a lovely heated swimming pool. It's opposite the Kunsthuset Kabuso.

Hardangerfjord is renowned as a fruit-growing region, especially its apples, and locals swear that the best apple pie (Nkr65) in all of Hardangerfjord is to be found at **Steinstø Fruit Farm** (Steinstø Fruktgard; ☎ 56 55 79 33; www.steinsto-fruktgard.no; Steinstø; 🕑 mid-Apr–mid-Oct), a short distance east of Øystese. It also runs guided farm visits (adult/child Nkr50/free) and serves lunch (by prior appointment; Nkr175) and great apple juice. Nearby, **Gamlastovo** (☎ 56 55 79 63; www.gamlastovo.no; Steinstø; set menu per person

EXPLORING HARDANGERFJORD FROM ULVIK

Little Ulvik is a terrific base from which to explore Hardangerfjord. The **Ulvik tourist office** (☎ 56 52 63 60; www.visitulvik.com) sells tickets to a range of self-guided day excursions that take in much of Hardangerfjord by boat, ferry and express boat from June to August. These include the following:

- Eidfjord (adult/child return Nkr219/110 Monday to Saturday) – via Bruravik and Brimnes; allows two hours each at Hardangervidda Nature Centre and Eidfjord; departs Ulvik 8.55am and arrives back at 3.10pm
- Eidfjord & Vøringfoss waterfall (adult/child boat only Nkr100/200, with tour of Hardangervidda Nature Centre and waterfall Nkr395/295 Monday to Saturday) – departs 11.10am and arrives back at 3.10pm
- Kinsarvik and Utne (adult/child Nkr217/110 Monday to Friday) – via Bruravik, Brimnes, Kvandal and Granvin with a visit to the Hardanger Folk museum in Utne. It departs Ulvik at 8.55am and arrives back 4.40pm
- Hardanger Grand Tour (adult/child Nkr320/160 Monday to Friday) – same as previous tour but also stops in Odda
- Norway in a Nutshell (adult/child Nkr668/335 Sunday to Friday) – Ulvik's own branch of the famous round trip leaves Ulvik at 8.55am and goes via Voss, Gudvangen, Flåm and Myrdal and returns to Ulvik at 6.40pm

kr80-250; by appointment) is similar, although it nly caters for groups; Arne Fykse sometimes lays the Hardanger fiddle for guests.

There are six to 12 buses that run each day rom Øystese to Bergen (Nkr145, 1¾ hours) ia Norheimsund.

LVIK

op 1137

here's something special about Ulvik, in the eart of Norway's apple-growing territory. ramed by hills and mountains and with wonlerful views up the fjord, Ulvik is bathed in ranquil silence once the tourist boats disapear. There's not a lot to see in Ulvik itself, but ou're in the heart of stunning fjord country vith plenty of cycling and hiking opportunities in the surrounding hills and farmstead isits possible. The wonderful Stream Nest omplex (right) is 10km away in Osa and he whole area in May is delightful when the lossoms are out.

The Ulvik **tourist office** (☎ 56 52 63 60; www isitulvik.com; 8.30am-5pm Mon-Sat, 1-5pm Sun midlay–mid-Sep, 8.30am-1.30pm Mon-Fri rest-of-year) has a ull list of local activities and hires **bicycles** (per /half-day/day Nkr40/90/160). It also organises **fruitarm visits** (Nkr150; Mon-Fri mid-Jun–mid-Aug).

leeping & Eating

lvik Fjordcamping (☎ 56 52 61 70; camping@ulvik rg; tent or caravan sites Nkr120, huts from s/d Nkr250/350) his convenient place, which lies 500m from the centre of town, is small and right by the water's edge.

Uppheim Gård (☎ 56 52 62 93; www.uppheim-farm .com; s/d Nkr650/800) This charming old timber farmhouse, 2km uphill and north of the village, has lovely accommodation and great views. Helen and Sjur will make you feel like one of the family.

Ulvik Fjord Hotel (☎ 56 52 61 70; www.ulvikfjord.no; s/d from Nkr650/860) Another excellent choice, this well-run guesthouse offers very comfortable rooms. It's across the road from the water, but some rooms have balconies terraces overlooking a bubbling stream.

Rica Brakanes Hotel (☎ 56 52 61 05; www.brakanes -hotel.no; s/d from Nkr990/1190; P) This huge modern hotel has a front-row seat to some of the best views in Hardangerfjord, although you pay an extra Nkr100 per person for a fjord view. The hotel serves meals (buffet dinner Nkr395, mains from Nkr135).

Getting There & Away

Buses run two to six times daily between Voss and Ulvik (Nkr85, 1¼ hours).

AROUND ULVIK

At the **Stream Nest complex** (☎ 56 52 69 90; Osa; adult/child Nkr40/free; 10.30am-4pm May-Aug), 10km east of Ulvik, highlights include the ecological herb garden, several artworks, including Allan Christensen's *Rambukk* (pile driver), and the odd eponymous log sculpture, *Stream*

Nest, originally conceived by Japanese artist Takamasa Kuniyasu for the 1994 Winter Olympics in Lillehammer. The sculpture, which consists of 3000 logs and 23,000 bricks, resounds with the tuba music of Geir Løvold, just as it did during the Games. It's a lovely spot.

EIDFJORD

pop 915

In the innermost reaches of Hardangerfjorden, Eidfjord wins our prize as the most beautiful town among many in this part of Norway. Dwarfed by sheer mountains and cascading waterfalls, accessible by spiral tunnels and close to charming farms perched on mountain ledges with great views, Eidfjord is simply magnificent. Eidfjord's beauty does, however, come at a price: in summer, cruise ships arrive on an almost daily basis and the town can get overwhelmed.

Over the next few years, Eidfjord will become even more accessible with a planned 1380m suspension bridge to replace the ferry between Bruravik and Brimnes along the Rv7/13. The project probably won't be finished during the life span of this book, but check out the website for **Vegdirektoratet** (www.vegvesen.no); follow the links to 'Roads' and then 'Road Projects'.

Information

Tourist office (☎ 53 67 34 00; www.visiteidfjord.no; 10am-8pm Mon-Fri, 10am-7pm Sat & Sun mid-Jun–mid-Aug, shorter hrs rest-of-year) In addition to dispensing tourist information, it also has internet (per 10 mins Nkr10)

Sights

Apart from the view from the water's edge, there are some wonderful sights in the Eidfjord vicinity. In addition to those listed below, the tourist office can point you in the direction of a number of nearby **Viking burial mounds**.

KJEÅSEN FARM

Above all other sights in the region, **Kjeåsen Farm**, 6km northeast of Eidfjord and close to the treeline 530m above the valley floor, should not be missed. According to some accounts, there has been a farm here for 400 years, although vehicle access was only possible with the construction of the road in 1975. Now one of Norway's top scenic locations, the wonderfully remote farm buildings are still inhabited by a woman who has lived alon there for 40 years – alone, that is, apart fron the busloads of tourists who visit the farn every day in summer. She sometimes show visitors around from 9am to 5pm. It's pos sible to climb up to the farm on foot (fou hours return), but it's steep and quite perilou involving at least one rope-bridge; ask th tourist office for directions. The vehicle roa goes through a one-way tunnel, driving up o the hour, down on the half-hour; ignore th signs that list the last time as 5.30pm as th road is open 24 hours. If Kjeåsen Farm ha piqued your curiosity, the booklet *Kjeåsen i Eidfjord*, by Per A Holst, tells the history o the farm and its inhabitants; it's available fo Nkr20 from the Eidfjord tourist office.

SIMA POWER PLANT

At the foot of the road leading up to the farm the **Sima Power Plant** (☎ 53 67 34 00; adult/chil Nkr55/45; guided tours at 10am, noon, 2pm daily mid Jun–mid-Aug, extra tour 3.30pm Jul), one of the larges hydroelectric power plants in Europe, run guided tours (one hour). The main hall run 700m inside the mountain.

HARDANGERVIDDA NATURSENTER

The exceptional **Hardangervidda Natursente** (☎ 53 66 59 00; www.hardangervidda.org; Øvre Eidfjor adult/child/family Nkr90/40/195; 9am-8pm Jun-Au 10am-6pm Apr, May, Sep & Oct) is a superlative in troduction to one of Norway's most beautifu national parks. The centre shows a must-se 19-minute movie with dramatic panorami footage of the park; if you can't visit the inne depths of the park on foot, this is the next bes thing. Otherwise, there are interactive dis plays, informative explanations of the region' natural history, fish tanks of mountain specie and interesting geology exhibits. The centr which is located 6.5km southeast of Eidfjor in Øvre Eidfjord, has detailed trekking map and staff can offer advice as to trekking an skiing in the park.

TROLL TRAIN

In summer, the cutesy **Troll Train** (☎ 53 67 34 0 adult one way/return Nkr55/70, child Nkr30/40; hour 10am-5.30pm Jun-Aug) runs from outside Eidfjord' tourist office to the waterfalls at Vøringsfosse 20km up through the steep Måbødalen, sto ping en route at Måbø Farm. Instead of takin Rv7 through the tunnels, it takes the olde more beautiful road up the valley. The jou ney takes about one hour and tickets must be purchased at the tourist office.

Activities

In addition to hiking up to Kjeåsen Farm (opposite) and trekking in the Hardangervidda National Park (see p188), climbing (half-day Nkr250), abseiling (per day Nkr1700), river- and sea-kayaking (half-day Nkr360 to Nkr400), power-kiting (half-day Nkr400) and guided, two-day glacier expeditions (Nkr1800) can be arranged through **Flat Earth** (☎ 47 60 68 47; www.flatearth.no; Øvre Eidfjord; 🕑 around May-Sep). You'll find it close to the Hardangervidda Natursenter in Øvre Eidfjord, 6.5km south-east of Eidfjord.

Sleeping & Eating

SæbøCamping (☎ 53 66 59 27; www.nafcamp.com/sabocamping; Øvre Eidfjord; tent sites Nkr120, cabins Nkr460-900; 🕑 mid-May–mid-Sep) This good camp site has a pretty lakeside location in Måbødalen just 500m from the Hardangervidda Natursenter. The owners promise freshly baked bread in the mornings.

Eidfjord Gjestegiveri (☎ 53 66 53 46; www.ovre-eidfjord.com; Øvre Eidfjord; hut Nkr325, s/d with shared bathroom & breakfast Nkr440/550; 💻) This delightful guest house run by Erik and Inge has a homely feel 6.5km from central Eidfjord; it's also close to the Hardangervidda Natursenter. Breakfasts are good and there's internet access. There are just four double rooms and one single; the six camping huts are only open from April to October.

our pick **Vik Pensjonat** (☎ 53 66 51 62; www.vikpensjonat.com; Eidfjord; d/f Nkr990/1340, cabins Nkr600-700) This appealing place in the centre of Eidfjord not far from the water's edge is set in a lovely, renovated old home. It offers a friendly welcome and an excellent range of cosy accommodation and there's a small café. The rooms with balconies (rooms 1 and 6) are our favourites.

Ingrid's Appartement (☎ 53 66 54 85; www.iapp.no; Eidfjord; d/f Nkr650/800, loft apt Nkr1050) This recommended, family-run place has well-kept apartments with bathroom and kitchen and some have good views.

Eidfjord Hotel (☎ 53 66 52 64; www.eidfjordhotel.no; Eidfjord; s/d with Fjord Pass from Nkr700/970) This modern hotel offers comfortable, if uninspiring rooms, some of which have partial views of the fjord. The garden terrace is a good place to chill and the restaurant (mains Nkr75 to Nkr179) is reasonable.

Quality Hotel Vøringfoss (☎ 53 67 41 00; www.choice.no; s/d May-Sep Nkr1290/1500, half-board Nkr1550/1900, s/d Oct-Apr from Nkr880/1000) This swish hotel opened in 2001 and offers extraordinary views from its fjord-facing rooms. This is a great place for a splurge and to wake up to an exceptional vista, unless, of course, a cruise ship has arrived blocking your view. Rooms are extremely comfortable. It also has a café that serves light meals and snacks; the wild boar burger with curry mayonnaise (Nkr139) makes a change from standard Norwegian kiosk food.

Getting There & Away

Buses run between Geilo and Odda via Vøringfoss, Øvre Eidfjord and Eidfjord once or twice daily, plus several extra runs daily except Sunday between Øvre Eidfjord, Eidfjord and Odda.

AROUND EIDFJORD

Eidfjord is a gateway to the **Hardangervidda Plateau** (p188), the largest mountain plateau in northern Europe and one of Norway's largest national parks. From Eidfjord, the Rv7 twists up through Måbødalen, including through a number of corkscrewing tunnels. At the summit after a steep 20km drive and where Hardangervidda begins, is the stunning, 182m-high **Vøringfoss waterfall**. There are actually numerous waterfalls here, which together are called Vøringsfossen, plunging over the plateau's rim and down into the canyon; the main section has a vertiginous drop of 145m. By some accounts, this is Norway's most-visited natural attraction, and it's hard to disagree given the endless stream of tour buses in summer (the record is 43 buses at any one time). The best views are from the lookout next to the Fossli Hotel (parking Nkr30) or from a number of lookouts (only one of which has a railing!) reached from the Vøringsfossen Cafeteria back down the valley on the Rv7. Buses between Geilo and Odda pass right by the falls.

If you'd like to fall asleep to the roar of cascading water, the **Fossli Hotel** (☎ 53 66 57 77; www.fossli-hotel.com; s/d Nkr690/1050, cheaper with Fjord Pass; 🕑 May-Sep) is set just back from the precipice. The views from the atmospheric and historic hotel are stunning and the rooms have character and modern parquet floors, but neither TV nor phones. Best of all, staying here allows you to enjoy the falls after the crowds disappear down the mountain. The hotel is run by Erik, whose great-grandfather built the hotel in the 1890s and who is a quiet but engaging host with a treasure-trove of stories from the Hardangervidda region; Erik cooks up delicious meals (Nkr180). Edvard Grieg composed his *Opus 66* in the hotel. The hotel is well signposted 1.3km off the Rv7.

KINSARVIK & LOFTHUS

pop 3416

The picturesque town of Kinsarvik and nearby Lofthus rest peacefully on the shore of Sørfjorden, an offshoot of Hardangerfjord in the heart of a region known as Ullensvang. Kinsarvik wasn't always so peaceful – it was the site of a settlement of up to 300 Vikings from the 8th to 11th centuries.

Kinsarvik tourist office (☎ 53 66 31 12; www.visitullensvang.no; per half-hr internet access Nkr25; 9am-7pm mid-Jun–mid-Aug, shorter hrs rest-of-year, closed December)

Lofthus tourist office (☎ 53 66 11 90; 11am-7pm mid-Jun–mid-Aug)

Sights & Activities

KINSARVIK

The small U-shaped patch of greenery opposite the Kinsarvik tourist office is all that remains of the former **Viking port.** Kinsarvik also boats one of Norway's oldest **stone churches** (admission free; 10am-7pm late-May–mid-Aug). First built in around 1180, it was restored in the 1960s and the walls still bear traces of lime-and-chalk paintings that depict the weighing of souls by Michael the Archangel with the devil trying to weigh down the scales. According to local legend, the church was built by Scottish invaders on the site of an earlier stave church.

Kinsarvik also offers an appealing access trail past the cooling **Husedalen waterfalls**, along what's known as the **Monk's Stairway,** and onto the network of tracks through the wild forest of **Hardangervidda National Park** (see the boxed text, p188).

For children, the **Familieparken Hardangertun** (☎ 53 67 13 13; www.hardangertun.no; day pass Nkr125; 10.30am-6.30pm daily late Jun–mid-Aug, 10.30am-6.30pm Sat & Sun mid-May–late Jun & mid-Aug-Sep) has water slides, minigolf and farm animals.

From May to September, the tourist office sells tickets for a **boat** (adult/child Nkr260/130) that leaves Kinsarvik at 10.25am and returns at 3.55pm, with three hours in Eidfjord. Given that you pay an extra Nkr195/110 if you want to take the sightseeing bus to the Hardangervidda Natursenter (p216) and Vøringsfossen (p217), it's only worth doing if you don't have your own wheels.

LOFTHUS

The main attraction in Lofthus is **Grieg's Hut** (24hr year-round), the one-time retreat of Norwegian composer Edvard Grieg. It's in the garden of Hotel Ullensvang. Lofthus also has a **stone church** (admission free; 10am-7pm late-May–mid Aug) dating back to 1250 (the tower was added in the 1880s) with fine stained-glass windows and it's surrounded by a cemetery with some graves from the Middle Ages.

Sleeping & Eating

KINSARVIK

Kinsarvik Camping (☎ 53 66 32 90; www.kinsarvikcamping.no; tent & caravan sites Nkr120 plus Nkr20 electricity, 4-bed cabins Nkr290-550) This simple, friendly place is right by the water's edge and has a waterslide for kids and the young at heart.

Kinsarvik Fjord Hotel (☎ 53 66 31 00; www.kinsarvikfjordhotel.no; s/d from Nkr890/1080;) This comfortable Best Western hotel just back from the shore in the centre of Kinsarvik is comfortable and it has a reasonable restaurant.

LOFTHUS

Lofthus Camping (☎ 53 66 13 64; www.lofthuscamping.com; tent & caravan sites Nkr130 plus Nkr35 electricity, 2-bed cabin Nkr360-480, 4-bed cabin Nkr450-590;) Another well-equipped fjord-side camp site with front-row views, Lofthus Camping has a heated indoor pool and can arrange boat rental.

Ullensvang Gjesteheim (☎ 53 66 12 36; www.ullensvang-gjesteheim.no; s/d/f from Nkr490/710/870) Kristin and Tor will make you feel right at home in this renovated 16th-century farmhouse. The rooms are simple but there's a warm feeling about this place.

Hotel Ullensvang (☎ 53 67 00 00; www.hotel-ullensvang.no; s/d from Nkr890/1350 with Fjord Pass, fjord view extra Nkr100; P) This enormous, luxurious place has exceptional views, supremely comfortable rooms and a good restaurant (buffet dinner Nkr375).

Getting There & Away

Buses run between Odda and Voss or Geilo on a semiregular basis and pass through Kinsarvik and Lofthus. A ferry connects Kinsarvik with Utne (per person/vehicle

BERGEN & THE SOUTHWESTERN FJORDS

Nkr28/77, 40 minutes) and on to Kvanndal (Nkr35/102, one hour) at least six times a day.

UTNE

One of the prettiest little villages you'll find Hardangerfjord, Utne is famous for its fruit-growing and for the excellent open-air **Hardanger Folk Museum** (☎ 53 67 00 40; www.hardanger.museum.no; adult/child Nkr50/free; ⏰ 10am-4pm May, 10am-5pm Jun-Aug, 10am-3pm Mon-Fri Sep-Apr), which acts as a repository for the cultural heritage of the Hardanger region. It comprises a collection of historic homes, boats, shops, outhouses and a school, plus exhibitions on Hardanger women, weddings, the famed Hardanger fiddle and fiddle-making, fishing, music, dance, orchard crops and the wood-carvings of local artist Lars Kinsarvik; it also bakes delicious local cakes on Tuesdays (noon to 3pm) in July.

There are also some good **walking trails** leading beyond the village; ask at the Utne Hotel for information.

Sleeping & Eating

Hardanger Gjestegård (☎ 53 66 67 10; www.hardangergjestegard.no; Alsåker; d from Nkr750) This atmospheric guesthouse, 10km west of Utne on Fv550, is in a pretty 1898 building with character-filled rooms brimming with cutesy folk touches. It offers good weekly rates.

Utne Hotel (☎ 53 66 64 00; www.utnehotel.no; Utne; s/d Nkr1135/1470; 💻) The historic wooden Utne Hotel was built in 1722 after the Great Nordic War, making it Norway's oldest hotel. Restored in 2003, it overflows with period touches from the 18th and 19th centuries. The hotel's fabulous décor makes it worth a look even if you're not staying and it also has the best restaurant (three-course evening buffet Nkr439) in town.

Getting There & Away

Ferries run between Utne, Kinsarvik (per person/vehicle Nkr28/77, 40 minutes) and Kvanndal (Nkr14/35, 20 minutes) at least six times a day.

ODDA

pop 7154

Frequently cited as Norway's ugliest town (it does battle with some pretty dire places in Finnmark), Odda is the Hardanger region's industrial, iron-smelting capital. What it does offer is a front-row view of one of Norway's finest landscapes: the innermost reaches of Hardangerfjord with a riotous waterfall and the icy heights of the fabulous Folgefonn glacier. Just try not to breathe in while you're admiring the view.

The Odda **tourist office** (☎ 53 65 40 05; www.visitodda.com; ⏰ 9am-8pm Mon-Fri, 10am-5pm Sat, 11am-6pm Sun mid-Jun–mid-Aug, 9.30am-4pm Mon-Fri rest-of-year; internet access per half-hr Nkr25) is near the Sørfjorden shore.

Sights

FOLGEFONN

Folgefonn is mainland Norway's third-largest icefield and offers summer skiing, snowboarding and sledding from mid-June to October. For more information, contact the **Folgefonn Sommar Skisenter** (☎ 53 66 80 28; www.folgefonn.no). Short tours to the ski centre leave from Jondal Quay at 10.30am from mid-June to mid-August and return at 3.30pm. From Odda, weekend glacier trips run to Odda Turlag's Holmaskjær mountain hut; contact the tourist office for details.

Anyone in good physical condition with warm clothing and sturdy footwear can take a guided hike up the lovely Buer valley followed by a glacier walk on the Buer arm of Folgefonn (minimum three persons, Nkr400 per person, including crampons and ice axes). For details contact **Hardanger Breføring** (☎ 90 64 49 75) or the tourist office. Transport to the starting point, at Buer, 8km west of Odda, isn't included in the price. For glacier hikes, you may also want to contact **Folgefonni Breførarlag** (☎ 95 11 77 92; www.folgefonni-breforarlag.no; Jondal).

TYSSESTRENGENE WATERFALL

About 5km east of town, in Skjeggedal, the 960m, 42-degree **Mågelibanen Funicular** (adult/child return Nkr120/60) runs on Wednesday and Friday; timings are variable so check with the Odda tourist office. Hikers can head for the top of the **Tyssestrengene waterfall** (646m) and the outrageous **Trolltunga rock feature** from either Skjeggedal (eight to 10 hours return) or the upper funicular station (six to eight hours return).

Sleeping & Eating

Odda Camping (☎ 41 32 16 10; www.oppleve.no/odda_camping; Odda; tent & caravan sites Nkr130; ⏰ mid-May–Aug) The most convenient camping is on the shores of the lake Sandvinvatnet, a 20-minute uphill walk south of the town centre.

Hardanger Hotel (☎ 53 64 64 64; www.hardangerhotel.no; Eitrheimsveien 17; s/d from Nkr790/950; P 💻) The upmarket Hardanger Hotel offers comfortable rooms with modern facilities and a reasonable restaurant-cafeteria.

Tyssedal Hotel (☎ 53 64 00 00; www.tyssedal-hotel.no; Tyssedal; s/d from Nkr950/1050) The highly recommended Tyssedal Hotel has great rooms with ensuite, parquet floors and a real sense of style, but this is above all a place for lovers of ghost stories – the hotel is reputedly haunted by the ghost of Eidfjord artist Nils Bergslien whose fantastic fairy-tale and Hardangerfjord landscape paintings adorn the hotel. The food is also terrific (mains around Nkr230) with fusion dishes based on local produce, such as reindeer in a blueberry sauce or mountain trout. The locally born owners are a mine of information on the area.

Getting There & Away

Between Odda and Jondal (Nkr149, 2½ hours), local buses operate one to three times daily. One to three daily Nor-Way Bussekspress buses run to/from Voss (Nkr215, 2½ hours) and Oslo (Nkr490, 7¼ hours).

ROSENDAL & AROUND

pop 1056

Just west of Folgefonn, scenic Rosendal can now be reached by an 11km-long road **tunnel** (car Nkr60; 🕓 6am-10pm) under the icefield from Odda. The **tourist office** (☎ 53 48 00 40; www.folgefonna.net; 🕓 9am-6pm Mon-Fri, 10am-5pm Sat, 11am-5pm Sun May-Sep) is by Rosendal Quay.

At Sunndal, 4km west of the tunnel, take the road up the Sunndal valley (drivable for 1km), then walk 2km on a good track to lake Bondhusvatnet, where there's a wonderful view of the glacier **Bondhusbreen**. In Uskedalen, 14km west of Rosendal, there's an extraordinary rock-slab mountain, Ulvenåso (1247m), offering some of the best **rock climbing** in Norway; contact the tourist office in Rosendal for details.

The 1665 **Baroniet Rosendal** (☎ 53 48 29 99; www.baroniet.no; Rosendal; adult/child Nkr75/10; 🕓 variable hrs May-Aug), Norway's only baronial mansion, features period interiors, a Renaissance rose garden, concerts and art exhibitions. You can even sleep here (single rooms Nkr350 to Nkr600, dorms Nkr600 to Nkr800) in one of the farm buildings, which makes for one of western Norway's most atmospheric stays.

In Sunndal, there's the reasonable **Sundal Camping** (☎ 53 48 41 86; www.sundalcamping.no; Sunndal; tent sites Nkr70, cabins Nkr400-600). It also rents canoes/bicycles for Nkr100/90 per day.

The ornate **Rosendal Gjestgiveri** (☎/fax 53 47 36 66; www.gjestgiveri.no in Norwegian; Skålagato 17; Rosendal; s/d with shared bathroom Nkr650/850) dates from 1887 and is an atmospheric B&B. The restaurant (mains Nkr89 to Nkr179) is probably the best in the area.

Buses run three to seven times daily between Rosendal and Odda via Sunndal. There are also two daily connections to Bergen via nearby Løfallstrand.

HAUGELANDET & RYFYLKE

North and east of Stavanger lies a region of low-lying hills and relatively flat coastal inlets and islands that are reminiscent of the northern Scottish Isles. Haugesund is the regional capital and its main calling cards are its festivals and waterfront café culture in summer.

HAUGESUND

pop 32,303

The North Sea port of Haugesund lies well off the beaten routes and is rarely visited by travellers. It's a base for the historically rich Haugelandet region with some interesting sights, while the Haugesund waterfront is lined with wooden buildings and has a real buzz about it in summer. The town also has a busy summer festival calendar.

The area around Haugesund carries huge historical significance for Norwegians. It was in the nearby Hafrsfjord that the decisive battle took place in 872 and Norway was first unified.

Information

Haugesund tourist office (☎ 52 01 08 30; www.visithaugelandet.no; Strandgata 171; 🕓 9am-5pm Mon-Fri, 10am-3pm Sat & Sun mid-Jun–end Aug, 10am-4.30pm Mon-Fri Sep–mid-Jun)

Quick Storkiosk (Haraldsgata 82; per hr Nkr40; 🕓 10am-11pm) Internet access.

Sights

Haugesund has retained many of its historical buildings, with the highlights including the **Rådhus** (town hall). About 75m south is the **Krosshaugen** mound and stone cross erected in celebration of Christian gatherings around 1000.

Haraldshaugen, the burial site of Viking King Harald Hårfagre, who died of plague at Avaldsnes on nearby Karmøy, is 1.5km north of Haugesund. The obelisk, erected in 1872, commemorates the decisive 872 battle.

Bizarrely, Haugesund claims to be the ancestral home of Marilyn Monroe, whose father, a local baker, emigrated to the USA. A **monument** on the quay, next to the Rica Maritim Hotel, commemorates the 30th anniversary of her death.

Festivals

Haugesund has two excellent festivals in August: **Silda Jazz** (Haugesund International Jazz Festival; early–mid-Aug) and the **Norwegian Film Festival** (mid-late Aug). For details, contact the tourist office.

Sleeping

Strandgaten Gjestgiveri (☎ 52 71 52 55; www.gjestgiveri.net; Strandgata 81; s/d Nkr545/750; 💻) On offer at Strandgaten Gjestgiveri are tidy rooms that are a cosy choice in the centre of Haugesund. There's also free wireless internet.

Comfort Hotel Amanda (☎ 52 80 82 00; www.choice.no; Smedasundet 93; s/d from Nkr945/1095; P Nkr90 💻) This hotel in the centre of town has the best waterfront location, an attractive early-20th-century building and large and luxurious rooms. Included in the price is a light evening buffet.

Rica Maritim Hotel (☎ 52 86 30 00; www.rica.no; Åsbygaten 3; s/d summer & weekend from Nkr860/1110, d summer & weekend with water view Nkr1250, s/d weekday mid-Sep–mid-Jun Nkr1200/1735; P Nkr100 💻) From its aquarium in the lobby to the luxuriously appointed rooms (one suite goes for Nkr10,000!), this recently renovated hotel is high class.

Eating

Haugesund's waterfront promenade, Smedasundet, is almost entirely given over to restaurants, giving the area an agreeable hum whenever the weather's warm. Any Haugesund restaurant worth its salt morphs into a bar as the night wears on.

NB Sørensen's Damskipsexpedisjon (☎ 52 70 00 50; Smedsundet 90; English breakfast Nkr99, lunch mains Nkr99-125, dinner mains Nkr229-295; ⏲ 11am-midnight Mon-Thu, 11am-2am Fri & Sat, 1-11pm Sun) One of the more architecturally distinguished buildings along Smedasundet, Sørensen's has Norwegian staples with creative twists such as fillet of monkfish with vegetarian lasagne or soy-and-honey-marinated pork neck.

Lothes Mat & Vinhus (☎ 52 71 22 01; Skippergata 4; mains Nkr145-279; ⏲ 11am-1.30am) With its lovely outdoor terrace overlooking the waterfront and period wood architecture, this long-standing Haugesund landmark is always full and deservedly so.

To Glass (☎ 52 70 74 00; Strandgata 169; light meals Nkr139-164, mains Nkr219-279; ⏲ 3-11pm Mon-Thu, 3pm-midnight Fri & Sat) There aren't many reasons to drag yourself away from the waterfront, but this achingly cool restaurant and wine bar is one of them. Try the entrecote sandwich (Nkr159) for a filling, but affordable meal.

Getting There & Away

SAS Braathens (☎ 81 52 00 00; www.sasbraathens.no) has up to five daily flights between **Haugesund airport** (☎ 52 85 79 00) and Oslo (from Nkr560). **Coast Air** (☎ 81 54 44 42; www.coastair.no) also has a daily flight to Haugesund (from Nkr490).

Nor-Way Bussekspress buses connect Haugesund with Stavanger (Nkr210, 2¼ hours) and Bergen (Nkr290, 3½ hours) almost hourly on weekdays and every second hour on weekends.

For details of international boat and air services to Haugesund, see p403.

AROUND HAUGESUND

Karmøy Island

Not content with playing a role in the family history of one American icon (Marilyn Monroe; see left), Haugesund was also essential to the founding of another. Copper from the mine at Visnes – now the **Visnes Mining Museum** (☎ 52 83 84 00; www.karmoy.kommune.no; Visnes; adult/child Nkr50/10; ⏲ 11am-5pm Mon-Fri, noon-5pm Sun mid-May–mid-Aug) – 4km west of Avaldsnes, was used to build the Statue of Liberty in New York.

About 5km south of central Haugesund, King Håkon Håkonsson's huge **stone church** (☎ 52 83 84 00; Avaldsnes; admission free; ⏲ 10am-5pm Mon-Sat, noon-5pm Sun Jun-Aug) was dedicated to St Olav in 1250. The adjacent 6.5m spire, known as the **Virgin Mary's Needle**, leans perilously towards the church wall and legend suggests that when it actually touches the wall, the Day of Judgment is at hand; it was close but still free-standing when we were there. Local legend has it that priests of little faith have, through the centuries, climbed the needle to chip bits away.

Down a short path from the church's car park is the new and outstanding **Nordvegen History Centre** (☎ 52 81 24 00; www.nordvegen.info; adult/child/student or senior Nkr80/40/60; ⏰ 10am-6pm Mon-Fri, 10am-5pm Sat, noon-6pm Sun Apr-Sep; 10am-4pm Mon-Fri, noon-5pm Sun Oct-Mar), which recreates the history of Harald Fair-Hair and other monarchs of the newly unified Nordvegen from the 10th century onwards.

The reconstructed **Viking farm** (☎ 52 83 84 00; www.nordvegen.info; Avaldsnes; adult/child Nkr30/10; ⏰ 10am-6pm Mon-Fri, noon-6pm Sun mid-Jun–mid-Aug) is beyond the church; you'll be guided by staff in period dress.

In early June, Karmøy Island hosts a **Viking Festival** (www.vikingfestivalen.no in Norwegian) with Viking feasts, processions and saga evenings.

In Vedavågen, on the island's west coast, the **Karmøy Fishery Museum** (☎ 52 81 74 55; www.museumsnett.no/karmoyfiskerimuseum in Norwegian; adult/child Nkr30/10; ⏰ 11am-5pm Mon-Fri, 2-6pm Sun mid-May–mid-Aug) will have fishing buffs enthralled with a state-of-the-art new building, fishing exhibits and a saltwater aquarium.

To reach Avaldnes from central Haugesund, catch bus 8, 9 or 10 (Nkr37) from next to the post office.

The wonderful settlement of **Skudeneshavn**, 37km south of Haugesund (on Karmøy), has many traditional wooden buildings and an extensive museum, **Mælandsgården** (☎ 52 84 54 60; adult/child Nkr50/10; ⏰ 11am-5pm Mon-Fri, 2-6pm Sun mid-May–mid-Aug), with excellent collections of household articles, rooms with period furnishings and agricultural and nautical exhibits.

Norneshuset (☎ 52 82 72 62; www.norneshuset.no in Norwegian; Nordnes 7, Skudeneshavn; s/d from Nkr550/750) is one of the most atmospheric and friendliest B&Bs in Norway; it's located in a former warehouse that was shipped from Riga, Latvia, in the 1830s.

STAVANGER & LYSEFJORD

Tucked away in Norway's southwest, the oil-rich city of Stavanger hums to an agreeable buzz. It also serves as the gateway to Lysefjord, the southernmost of Norway's signature fjords and home to one of its most recognisable vantage points – Pulpit Rock (Preikestolen).

STAVANGER

pop 117,315

Vibrant Stavanger ends up being many travellers' favourite city in Norway. With its centre arrayed around a pretty harbour with the quiet streets of the old town climbing up from the water's edge, it's a picturesque place. It's also home to almost two dozen museums. But Stavanger's appeal is as much about atmosphere as anything else. Most nights, especially in summer, the city's waterfront comes alive and can get quite rowdy in the best tradition of oil and port cities. By Sunday morning, it's quiet and charming, for this is a place that has never lost its small-town feel.

Orientation & Information

The bus and train stations are alongside each other on the southern shore of the lake Breiavann, about 10 minutes' walk from the harbour. Most sites of interest are within easy walking distance of the harbour.

Most major banks are represented along Olav V's gate and Håkon VII's gate. **Den Norske Bank** (Håkon VII's gate) and the adjacent **post office** (Håkon VII's gate) offer competitive exchange rates.

C@fe.com (☎ 51 55 41 20; Sølvberggata 15; ⏰ 11am-9pm Mon-Sat, noon-9pm Sun; per hr Nkr55) Well-run Skype-equipped internet café with good coffee.

Public library (Kulturhus; ⏰ 10am-4pm Mon-Wed & Fri, 10am-7pm Thu, 10am-2pm Sat) Free, time-limited internet access.

Stavanger Turistforening DNT (☎ 51 84 02 00; off Muségata; ⏰ 10am-5pm Mon-Wed & Fri, 10am-6pm Thu, 10am-2pm Sat) Information on hiking and mountain huts.

Tourist office (☎ 51 85 92 00; www.regionstavanger.com; Domkirkeplassen 3; ⏰ 9am-8pm Jun-Aug, 9am-4pm Mon-Fri, 9am-2pm Sat Sep-May) Local information and advice on Lysefjord and Preikestolen.

Sights

At last count, Stavanger had 23 museums; the tourist office has a full list.

OLD STAVANGER

Gamle (Old) Stavanger, above the western shore of the harbour, is a delight. The old town's cobblestone walkways pass between rows of 173 late-18th-century whitewashed wooden houses, all immaculately kept and adorned with cheerful, well-tended flowerboxes. It well rewards an hour or two's ambling.

NORWEGIAN EMIGRATION CENTRE

This **centre** (☎ 51 53 88 60; www.emigrationcenter.com; Strandkaien 31; 9am-3pm Mon-Fri) helps foreigners of Norwegian descent trace their roots. In mid-June it stages a popular Emigration Festival.

STAVANGER CATHEDRAL

This beautiful **cathedral** (Stavanger Domkirke; Håkon VII's gate; admission free; 11am-7pm Jun-Aug, 11am-4pm Tue-Thu & Sat Sep-May) is an impressive, but understated, medieval stone cathedral dating from approximately 1125; it was extensively renovated following a fire in 1272 and contains traces of Gothic, baroque, Romanesque and Anglo-Norman influences. Despite restoration in the 1860s and 1940, and the stripping of some features during the Reformation, the cathedral is, by some accounts, Norway's oldest medieval cathedral still in its original form. Its wonderful stone columns, tapestries, elaborate baroque pulpit and stained-glass window depicting the main events of the Christian calendar are a visual feast.

NORWEGIAN PETROLEUM MUSEUM

We could (and have) spend hours in this state-of-the-art **museum** (Norsk Oljemuseum; ☎ 51 93 93 00; www.norskolje.museum.no; Kjeringholmen; adult/child Nkr75/35; 10am-7pm daily Jun-Aug, 10am-4pm Mon-Sat, 10am-6pm Sun Sep-May), one of Norway's best. Filled with high-tech interactive displays, gigantic models and authentic reconstructions, its many highlights include a terrific 3-D film covering Norway's geological history, a documentary by former Lonely Planet TV presenter Ian Wright, simulators, a petrodome recreating millions of years of natural history and an amazing model of 'Ekofisk city'.

Tracing the history of oil formation and exploration in the North Sea from discovery in 1969 until the present, the museum nicely balances the technical side of oil exploration and extraction with archive footage and newspapers of significant moments in the history of Norwegian oil. Not least among these are: coverage of the *Alexander L Kielland* tragedy in 1980, when 123 oil workers were killed; the 1972 decision by Norway's parliament that Statoil should be based in Stavanger; and the 1950s declaration by a Norwegian government commission that 'the chances of finding oil on the continental shelf off the Norwegian coast can be discounted'. You'll spend longer here than you planned, especially if you have kids.

VALBERG TOWER & GUARD MUSEUM

The historic **tower** Valbergtårnet was constructed as a guards' lookout in 1850 and now contains this interesting **museum** (Vektermuseet; Valbergjet 2; adult/child Nkr20/free; 10am-4pm Mon-Sat). From behind the west side of the tower at ground level there are some reasonable views over the city towards the old town.

STAVANGER MUSEUM

The large **eight-part museum** (☎ 51 84 27 00; www.stavanger.museum.no), with its sites scattered around Stavanger, could easily fill a sightseeing day, but you'd have to keep up a brisk pace to fit them all in. The first museum you visit costs Nkr60/30 per adult/child, with each extra museum visited the same day costing Nkr20; student and senior prices are the same as for children. The children's museum has separate pricing. The other two museums we don't cover here are the **Norwegian Printing Museum** and the **Medical Museum**.

Stavanger Museum

The main **museum** (Muségata 16; 11am-4pm mid-Jun–mid-Aug, closed Mon rest-of-year) reveals nearly 900 years of Stavanger's history, 'From Ancient Landscape to Oil Town'. Features include evidence of Stone Age habitation, the medieval bishopric, the herring years and the development of the city into a modern oil capital. The Stavanger of the 1880s is described in a series of tableaux focusing on local author Alexander L Kielland.

Canning Museum

Don't miss this **museum** (Hermetikkmuseet; ☎ 51 52 65 91; Øvre Strandgate 88-90; 11am-4pm mid-Jun–mid-Aug, closed Mon rest-of-year); housed in an old cannery, it's one of Stavanger's most appealing museums. Before oil there were sardines and Stavanger was once home to more than half of Norway's canning factories; by 1922 the city's canneries provided 50% of the town's employment. Here you'll get the lowdown on canning brisling and fish balls and the exhibits take you through the whole 12-stage process from salting, through to threading, smoking, decapitating and packing. There are no labels but there's a handy brochure available at the entrance and guides are always on hand to answer your questions or crank up some of the old machines. Upstairs, there's a fascinating display of historical sardine-can labels (more than 40,000 designs were used and they became collectors' items). An

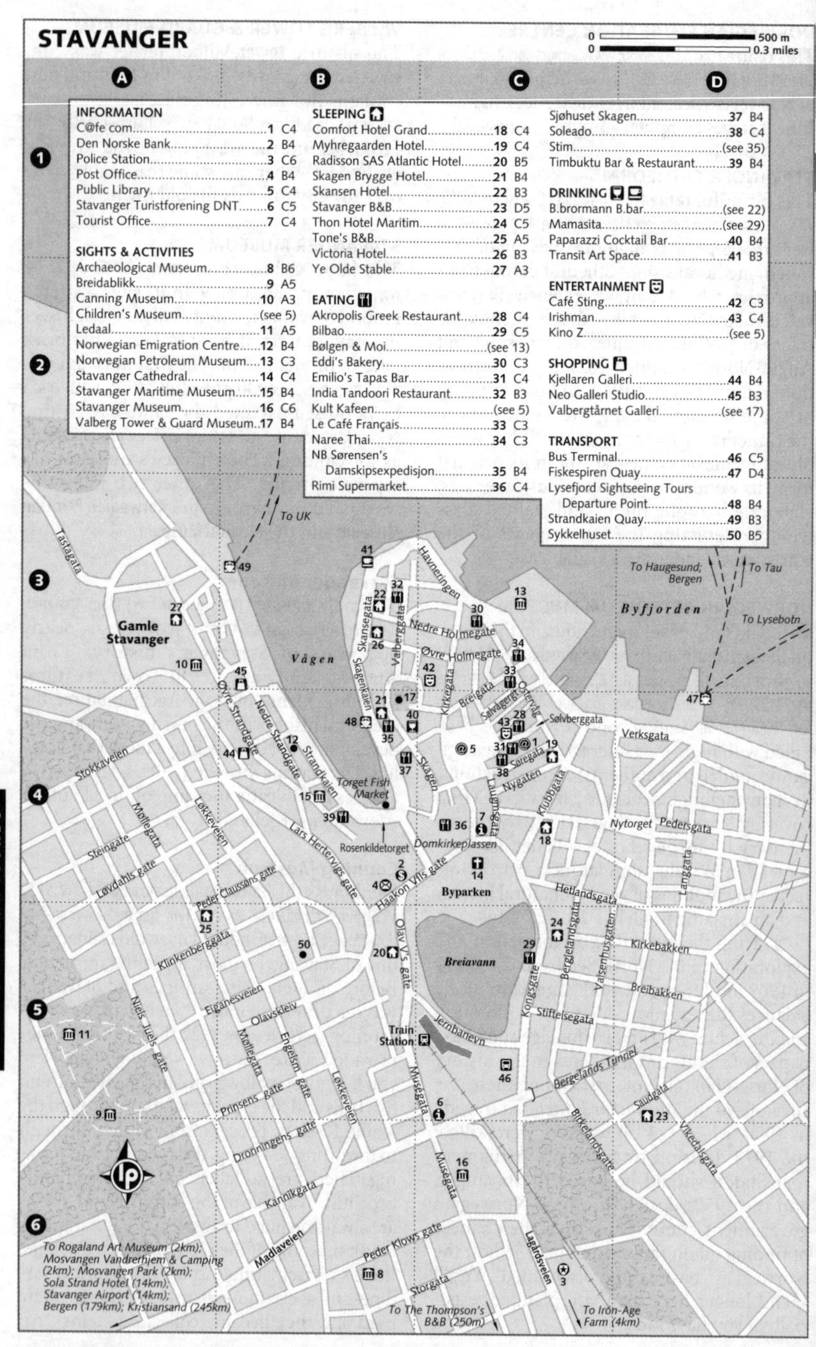
STAVANGER
0 500 m
0 0.3 miles
A
B
C
D
1
2
3
4
5
6
INFORMATION
C@fe com 1 C4
Den Norske Bank 2 B4
Police Station 3 C6
Post Office 4 B4
Public Library 5 C4
Stavanger Turistforening DNT 6 C5
Tourist Office 7 C4
SIGHTS & ACTIVITIES
Archaeological Museum 8 B6
Breidablikk 9 A5
Canning Museum 10 A3
Children's Museum (see 5)
Ledaal 11 A5
Norwegian Emigration Centre 12 B4
Norwegian Petroleum Museum 13 C3
Stavanger Cathedral 14 C4
Stavanger Maritime Museum 15 B4
Stavanger Museum 16 C6
Valberg Tower & Guard Museum 17 B4
SLEEPING
Comfort Hotel Grand 18 C4
Myhregaarden Hotel 19 C4
Radisson SAS Atlantic Hotel 20 B5
Skagen Brygge Hotel 21 B4
Skansen Hotel 22 B3
Stavanger B&B 23 D5
Thon Hotel Maritim 24 C5
Tone's B&B 25 A5
Victoria Hotel 26 B3
Ye Olde Stable 27 A3
EATING
Akropolis Greek Restaurant 28 C4
Bilbao 29 C5
Bølgen & Moi (see 13)
Eddi's Bakery 30 C3
Emilio's Tapas Bar 31 C4
India Tandoori Restaurant 32 B3
Kult Kafeen (see 5)
Le Café Français 33 C3
Naree Thai 34 C3
NB Sørensen's Damskipsexpedisjon 35 B4
Rimi Supermarket 36 C4
Sjøhuset Skagen 37 B4
Soleado 38 C4
Stim (see 35)
Timbuktu Bar & Restaurant 39 B4
DRINKING
B.brormann B.bar (see 22)
Mamasita (see 29)
Paparazzi Cocktail Bar 40 B4
Transit Art Space 41 B3
ENTERTAINMENT
Café Sting 42 C3
Irishman 43 C4
Kino Z (see 5)
SHOPPING
Kjellaren Galleri 44 B4
Neo Galleri Studio 45 B3
Valbergtårnet Galleri (see 17)
TRANSPORT
Bus Terminal 46 C5
Fiskespiren Quay 47 D4
Lysefjord Sightseeing Tours Departure Point 48 B4
Strandkaien Quay 49 B3
Sykkelhuset 50 B5
To UK
To Haugesund; Bergen
To Tau
Byfjorden
To Lysebotn
Tastagata
Gamle Stavanger
Vågen
Havneringen
Skansegata
Valberggata
Nedre Holmegate
Øvre Holmegate
Skagenkaien
Kirkegata
Breigata
Salvågeret
Østervåg
Sølvberggata
Verksgata
Øvre Strandgate
Nedre Strandgate
Strandkaien
Stokkaveien
Torget Fish Market
Skagen
Søregata
Nygaten
Klubbgata
Laugmsgata
Møllegata
Løkkeveien
Lars Hertervigs gate
Rosenkildetorget
Domkirkeplassen
Nytorget
Pedersgata
Steingate
Løvdahls gate
Haakon VIIs gate
Byparken
Langgata
Peder Claussøns gate
Hetlandsgata
Klinkenberggata
Olav V's gate
Breiavann
Bergjelandsgata
Vaisenhusgaten
Kirkebakken
Breibakken
Kongsgata
Stiftelsesgata
Niels Juels gate
Eiganesveien
Olavskleiv
Engelsm gate
Train Station
Jernbanevn
Bergelands Tunnel
Prinsens gate
Musegata
Saudgata
Birkelandsgata
Vikedalsgata
Dronningens gate
Kannikgata
Madlaveien
Peder Klows gate
Storgata
Lagårdsveien
To Rogaland Art Museum (2km); Mosvangen Vandrerhjem & Camping (2km); Mosvangen Park (2km); Sola Strand Hotel (14km); Stavanger Airport (14km); Bergen (179km); Kristiansand (245km)
To The Thompson's B&B (250m)
To Iron-Age Farm (4km)

adjoining building houses a café and restored workers' cottages furnished in 1920s and 1960s style. On the first Sunday of every month (and Tuesday and Thursday from mid-June to mid-August), the fires are lit and you can sample smoked sardines straight from the ovens.

Ledaal

The empire-style **Ledaal** (Eiganesveien 45; 11am-4pm mid-Jun–mid-Aug, 11am-4pm Sun rest-of-year) was constructed between 1799 and 1803 for wealthy merchant shipowner Gabriel Schanche Kielland. Now recently restored it serves as the local royal residence and summer home. You'll see the king's 250-year-old four-poster bed, unusual antique furniture and a pendulum clock from 1680.

Breidablikk

The excellent Breidablikk **manor** (Eiganesveien 40A; 11am-4pm mid-Jun–mid-Aug, 11am-4pm Sun rest-of-year) was constructed for another merchant shipowner, Lars Berentsen. These days, it allows you to see the opulent lifestyles of the rich and famous in late-19th-century Norway, displaying old farming implements, books and knick-knacks.

Stavanger Maritime Museum

This worthwhile **museum** (Sjøfartsmuseet; Nedre Strandgate 17-19; 11am-4pm mid-Jun–mid-Aug, closed Mon rest-of-year) covers 200 years of Stavanger's maritime history spread over two warehouses dating from around 1800. There's also a large collection of model boats, sailing vessels, a noisy wind-up foghorn, a reconstruction of a late-19th-century sailmaker's workshop, a shipowner's office and an excellent general store, as well as the merchant's living quarters. The museum also owns two historic sailing vessels, the 1848 *Anna of Sand* and the 1896 *Wyvern*, both on display.

Children's Museum

A great place to take the kids is this **museum** (Norsk Barnemuseum; ☎ 51 91 23 93; www.norskbarne.museum.no; Arneageren; adult/child Nkr80/40; 11am-3.30pm Tue-Sat, noon-4.30pm Sun), which has a range of activity-based exhibits (eg old toys, a labyrinth) centred around the themes of landscape, labyrinth, curiosity and theatre.

ARCHAEOLOGICAL MUSEUM

This well-presented **museum** (☎ 51 84 60 00; www.ark.museum.no; Peder Klows gate 30A; adult/child Nkr20/10; 11am-5pm Tue-Sun Jun-Aug, shorter hrs rest-of-year), traces 11,000 years of human history, including the Viking Age. Exhibits include skeletons, tools, a runestone and a description of the symbiosis between prehistoric humans and their environment. There's also a full programme of activities for kids (eg treasure hunts) in summer and it's making a welcome move to more interactive exhibits.

IRON-AGE FARM

The reconstruction of a 1500-year-old **Iron-Age Farm** (Jernaldergarden; ☎ 51 80 70 00; Ullandhaugvn 3, Ullandhaug; adult/child Nkr40/10; 11am-4pm daily Jun–mid-Aug, 11am-4pm Sun only May-Oct), 4km south of the centre, features various activities, staff in period dress and food preparation on Sunday. Take bus 25 or 26 towards Sandnes to Ullandhaug (Nkr27, 15 minutes).

ROGALAND ART MUSEUM

This **museum** (Rogaland Kunstmuseum; ☎ 51 53 09 00; Henrik Ibsensgate 55; adult/child Nkr50/30; 11am-4pm Tue-Sun), 2.5km south of the town centre, displays Norwegian art from the 18th century to the present, including the haunting *Gamle Furutrær* and other landscape paintings by Stavanger's own Lars Hertervig (1830–1902). A nine-sided annexe houses the largest assemblage of mid-20th-century Norwegian art, including work by Harald Dal, Kai Fjell, Arne Ekeland and others.

MOSVANGEN

The large forest **park** at Mosvangen is a popular place for locals to wander and picnic amid the greenery. The lake and its small attached lagoon, which are encircled by footpaths, attract large numbers of breeding ducks, geese, and sea birds, as well as songbirds. It's a pleasant 3km walk from the centre or 10 minutes on bus 130 (Nkr25).

Tours

From June to August, the tourist office runs **guided walking tours** (☎ 51 85 92 00; adult/senior, student or child Nkr200/125) of the city. They leave from the tourist office at 11am.

For details of tours to Lysefjord, see the boxed text, p231.

Festivals & Events

In early August, Stavanger plays host to its **International Chamber Music Festival** (www.icmf.no). Most concerts are held in the Stavanger

EUROPE'S CAPITAL OF CULTURE

Stavanger richly deserves its designation as Europe's Capital of Culture (an honour it shares in 2008 with Liverpool in the UK), so vibrant is its cultural life and so diverse are its cultural attractions. With a motto of 'Open Port', the year-long celebrations seem perfectly matched to this energetic port city, which is Norwegian to its core but open to cultural influences and visitors from all over the world. With more than 200 projects planned, chances are that there will be plenty of things happening to coincide with your visit if you're here during 2008. Themes around which the projects are based include cultural heritage, environment, architecture, youth and migration and 'Sounds from the Cathedral'. In practical terms, what that means is a continuous programme of concerts, exhibitions and street parties with Stavanger's signature landmarks as the backdrop. For more information on upcoming events, visit the website www.stavanger2008.com.

Cathedral and tickets range from Nkr100 to Nkr300. Other music festivals with Stavanger as their backdrop include the **May Jazz Festival** (www.maijazz.no in Norwegian; early to mid-May), the **Pulpit Rock Festival** (www.pulpit.no in Norwegian; mid-Aug) and **NuMusic** (www.numusic.no; early Sep).

In the middle of March, Stavanger shakes off the winter blues with the **Stavanger Vinfest** (www.stavangervinfest.no in Norwegian), a celebration of food and drink.

Sleeping

Accommodation in Stavanger is always snapped up well in advance during summer; book as far ahead as possible.

BUDGET

For the Mosvangen Vandrerhjem or Mossvangen Camping, take bus 78 or 79 (Nkr25) from opposite the cathedral to Ullandhaugveien, 3km to the south. Bus 4 also passes by.

Mosvangen Vandrerhjem (☎ 51 54 36 36; stavanger.hostel@vandrerhjem.no; Henrik Ibsensgate 19; dm/s/d with shared bathroom Nkr240/400/480, mid-May–mid-Sep) Stavanger's pleasant and simple lakeside hostel, 3km southwest of the city centre, charges Nkr60 for breakfast.

Mosvangen Camping (☎ 51 53 29 71; www.mosvangencamping.no/indexengelsk; Tjensvoll 1b; tent sites without/with car Nkr80/110, with caravan or camper Nkr120, 2-/4-person huts from Nkr350/500, mid-May–mid-Sep) During nesting season around Mosvangen lake, campers are treated to almost incessant birdsong amid the green and agreeable surroundings.

The tourist office distributes the *Bed & Breakfast Circle* leaflet and the seven places listed are all charming places to stay. Those in or close to the city centre:

Thompsons B&B (☎ 51 52 13 29; www.thompsonsbedandbreakfast.com; Muségata 79; s/d with shared bathroom Nkr250/450) Housed in a 19th-century home and with a warm family feel.

Tone's B&B (☎ 51 52 42 07; ton-bour@online.no; Peder Claussøns gate 22; s/d with shared bathroom Nkr280/450) An old Stavanger home close to Gamle Stavanger.

MIDRANGE & TOP END

Comfort Hotel Grand (☎ 51 20 14 00; www.choice.no; Klubbgata 3; d Fri-Sun & all week in summer Nkr590, s/d Mon-Thu rest-of-year Nkr1250/1450) Don't be put off by the grim exterior because this place promises modern, comfortable rooms in the heart of town.

our pick **Stavanger B&B** (☎ 51 56 25 00; www.stavangerbedandbreakfast.no; Vikedalsgata 1a; s/d with shared toilet Nkr625/740;) This quiet but popular place comes highly recommended by readers and it's not hard to see why. The simple rooms are tidy and come with satellite TV, shower and a smile from the friendly owners. Packed lunches are available for a bargain Nkr35, and at 9pm nightly, free coffee, tea and waffles are served.

our pick **Skansen Hotel** (☎ 51 93 85 00; www.skansenhotel.no; Skansegata 7; guesthouse s Nkr690-1030, d Nkr775-1190, hotel s Nkr790-1130, d Nkr875-1290;) This centrally located place, opposite the old customs house, has a more personal feel to it than Stavanger's larger hotels. The hotel is divided into an older guesthouse section with simple, comfortable rooms, and newer hotel rooms that are larger and more stylish. There's free wireless access throughout both sections.

Sola Strand Hotel (☎ 51 94 30 00; www.solastrandhotel.no; s/d from Nkr700/850) The recommended historic Sola Strand overlooks a quiet sandy beach 14km southwest of Stavanger. Many of the rooms are large and have sweeping coastal views. Breakfasts are also a highlight and the hotel contains an entire lounge from a former cruise ship.

Skagen Brygge Hotel (☎ 51 85 00 00; www.skagenbryggehotell.no; Skagenkaien 30; s/d Fri-Sun & all week in summer Nkr805/975, Mon-Thu rest-of-year Nkr1410/1520, ste Nkr1750-3100; 💻) This large and opulent hotel (part of the Fjord Pass network) offers good weekend and summer value from its superb location right by the water. There are a range of rooms to choose from, but your best bet is to ask for a room with a harbour view. Guests have access to a private gym, and bills from some restaurants around town can be added to your room bill to be paid at checkout. Internet rates (per 24 hours Nkr200) are extortionate.

Thon Hotel Maritim (☎ 51 85 05 00; www.thonhotels.no; Kongsgate 32; s/d Fri-Sun & all week in summer Nkr775/975, Mon-Thu rest-of-year Nkr1195/1395) Part of the consistently comfortable Thon chain of hotels, this modern hotel just back from the lakeshore keeps up the standard with spacious, well-appointed rooms.

Victoria Hotel (☎ 51 86 70 00; www.victoria-hotel.no; Skansegata 1; s/d Fri-Sun & all week in summer Nkr795/995, Mon-Thu rest-of-year Nkr1150/1350; 💻) Part of the Rica Hotels network, the Victoria has a somewhat baronial air with traditionally styled rooms.

Ye Olde Stable (☎ 51 52 53 46; www.gamlestallen.com; Øvre Strandgate 112; 4-/6-bed house Nkr1000/1400) Fifty sq metres all to yourself in one of Stavanger's oldest 18th-century homes.

Radisson SAS Atlantic Hotel (☎ 51 76 10 00; www.radissonsas.com; Olav V's gate 3; s/d from Nkr1295/1395; 💻) Arguably the most luxurious hotel in Stavanger, this outpost of the Radisson is supremely comfortable and staff are attentive to your every need. It's accredited as part of the system of Miljmerking good environmental practices.

Expected to open in 2008, the **Myhregaarden Hotel** (☎ 95 88 91 53; www.myhregaardenhotel.no; Nygaten 24) promises to be Stavanger's most stylish hotel.

Eating

Stavanger has an extensive choice of restaurants and, despite the hubbub around the harbour in the evening, many places lie in the streets beyond the waterfront. We're confident about our recommendations, but for a second opinion check out www.gardkarlsen.com, which gives a local view on many of Stavanger's eateries.

CAFÉS & BAKERIES

our pick **Le Café Français** (☎ 51 86 17 18; Østervåg 30-32; sandwiches from Nkr50; ⏰ 9am-5pm Mon-Wed & Fri, 9am-7pm Thu, 9am-4pm Sat, 11am-5pm Sun) With the widest range of pastries and other sweet goodies in town and outdoor tables on the pedestrian street outside, Le Café Français is a good place to wind down. It also serves sandwiches.

Eddi's Bakeri (☎ 51 53 90 00; Østervåg 39; ⏰ 9am-5pm Mon-Fri, 10am-3pm Sat) Some of Stavanger's freshest bread is found here; it also sells a small but delicious selection of pastries.

Kult Kafeen (☎ 51 89 16 00; Sølvberggata 14; pasta Nkr119-139, mains around Nkr135; ⏰ 10am-10pm Mon-Sat, noon-10pm Sun) Located in the Kulturhus in the centre of town, this cool place has won the affections of families and cool young professionals alike. It's relaxed with hints of minimalist style and serves a tasty fish burger (Nkr135) among the highlights.

NORWEGIAN

our pick **NB Sørensen's Damskipsexpedisjon** (☎ 51 84 38 20; Skagen 26; specials Nkr85-125, mains Nkr229-269; ⏰ lunch & dinner) One of the better places along the waterfront, this restaurant serves everything from red mullet to pork ribs, with a seasonal lunch menu that's excellent value. The atmospheric indoor dining area is ideal when the weather turns, and locals swear that the food and service is better upstairs.

Sjøhuset Skagen (☎ 51 89 51 80; Skagenkaien 16; lunch specials Nkr105-139, mains Nkr185-269; ⏰ lunch & dinner) Also along the waterfront, this 18th-century former warehouse is the venue for great seafood dishes, although the cooks also do meat dishes. The oven-baked salmon (Nkr245) would be our pick for mains. The outdoor tables are tempting, but inside has more character.

Bølgen & Moi (☎ 51 93 93 51; Norsk Oljemuseum, Kjerringholmen; lunch specials Nkr129-149, 3-/4-/5-course dinner menus Nkr465/525/595; ⏰ café 11am-6pm daily, bar & brasserie 5-11pm Tue-Sat) The imaginative menus in this stylish restaurant include monkfish, lamb and veal, while the lunch specials are huge – the shrimp sandwich in cilantro and lime marinade (Nkr139) can only be described as massive. Although there are set menus in the evenings, you can also choose à la carte.

INTERNATIONAL

Akropolis Greek Restaurant (☎ 51 89 14 54; Sølvberggata 14; specials Nkr59-129, mains from Nkr125, lunch buffet Nkr149; ⏰ lunch & dinner) This very popular place serves authentic Greek food at reasonable prices for those in search of great salads, tzatziki, grilled meats and moussaka. It also does a Sunday lunch buffet until 6pm.

Emilio's Tapas Bar (☎ 51 89 64 00; Sølvberggata 13; tapas Nkr55-125, mains from Nkr77; lunch & dinner Mon-Sat) Opposite the Akropolis and continuing on the Mediterranean theme, this pleasant Spanish tapas bar serves good Iberian food with friendly service at no extra cost.

Soleado (☎ 51 55 43 80; Sølvberggata 7; lunch specials Nkr59-162, dinner set menu from Nkr365; 11am-1am Mon-Sat) Better value for lunch than for dinner, Soleado does tasty dishes that include club sandwiches (Nkr92) and chicken curry (Nkr162).

Bilbao (☎ 51 53 33 00; Kongsgate 41; starters Nkr95-115, mains Nkr195-255, small/large tapas set menu Nkr195/345; dinner Tue-Sat) This elegant restaurant next to lake Breiavann serves high-quality Basque cuisine and other Spanish dishes such as paella (from Nkr195).

Timbuktu Bar & Restaurant (☎ 51 84 37 40; Nedre Strandgate 15; mains from Nkr235; 6pm-12.30am Mon & Tue, 6pm-1.30am Wed-Sat) This hip place attracts a young-and-trendy crowd for its excellent meat and well-chosen seafood as much as for the chic atmosphere.

Stim (☎ 51 85 00 16; Skagenkaien 28; starters Nkr89-129, mains Nkr169-265; 4pm-1am Mon-Fri, noon-1am Sat) The third place that's worth trying by the water, Stim is set in a refurbished 19th-century canning factory and has window tables on the 1st floor that we *really* like.

Also recommended:

India Tandoori Restaurant (☎ 51 89 39 35; Valberggata 14; mains Nkr115-225; 4pm-midnight Mon-Sat) Reasonably priced and extensive menu.

Naree Thai (☎ 51 89 05 10; Breigata 22; starters Nkr40-70, lunch mains from Nkr60, dinner mains around Nkr120; lunch & dinner) One of numerous Asian restaurants in town.

BERGEN & THE SOUTHWESTERN FJORDS

Drinking & Entertainment

Most of the livelier bars are right on the waterfront and cater to a younger crowd with a penchant for loud, energetic music. You'll hear them long before you see them and, as they're all similar, we think you're able to find them on your own.

Café Sting (☎ 51 89 32 84; Valbergjet 3; noon-midnight Mon-Thu, noon-3.30am Fri & Sat, 3-11pm Sun) Just up the hill but a world away, Café Sting is at once a mellow café and a funky cultural space with exhibitions, live jazz whenever the mood takes it and a weekend nightclub where the DJs keep you on your toes, spinning house, hip-hop and soul.

our pick **B.bromann B.bar** (☎ 51 93 85 00; Skansegata 7; 5pm-1am) One of Stavanger's coolest bars where you can actually hear the conversation and with contemporary artworks on the brick walls, this oddly named bar draws a discerning over-30s crowd and serves great-value half-litre beers (Nkr58) and spirits (Nkr76 to Nkr91). This is where we drink when we're in town.

Mamasita (☎ 51 53 33 00; Kongsgate 41; 10am-7pm Mon-Fri, 10am-3pm Sat) This appealing café-bar by the lake is wonderfully removed from the tourist scrum.

Transit Art Space (☎ 51 55 41 00; www.transitartspace.com; Skansekata; noon-4pm Tue-Sun) This sophisticated little café is an adjunct to a fine, small gallery of changing and often avant-garde exhibitions. It does good coffee and sells great art books. If you can't find it, look for the Mona Lisa baring her bottom on the wall outside.

Irishman (☎ 51 89 41 81; Hølebergsgata 9; 3pm-1am) Stavanger's friendly Irish pub has (free) live Irish folk music at least twice a week in summer.

Paparazzi Cocktail Bar (☎ 51 59 71 20; Skagen 27; 6pm-midnight Mon-Thu, 6pm-1.30am Fri & Sat) For more sophistication than most Stavanger bars can muster, this clean-lined place attracts a chic crowd most nights. It also has a restaurant.

For cinema features (some in English), try the eight-screen **Kino Z** (☎ 82 05 11 00; adult/child Nkr70/40) in the Kulturhus.

Shopping

Old Stavanger is home to dozens of artistic workshops, artists' studios and quiet little shops. If it's still around, get hold of the leaflet *The Old Town Stavanger – Art & Crafts*, which has advertisements and a map for some of these shops, although it's a little outdated. Of those that remain, **Kjellaren Galleri** (☎ 95 09 67 04; Øvre Strandgate 66; 10am-3pm) sells oils, watercolours and photos of old Stavanger, while **Neo Galleri Studio** (☎ 51 52 90 05; Nedre Strandgate 54; 10am-5pm Mon-Fri, 10am-2pm Sat) is a small studio that sells ceramics and glasswork.

In the Valberg Tower, you'll also find the excellent **Valbergtårnet Galleri** (☎ 93 65 30 41; www.valbergtaarnet.no; Valbergjet 4; 10am-4pm Tue, Wed & Fri, 10am-6pm Thu, 11am-3pm Sat & Sun), a gallery and showroom for high-quality artworks and handicrafts from across Norway.

Getting There & Away

AIR

Stavanger airport (☎ 51 65 80 00) is at Sola, 14km south of the city centre. **SAS Braathens** (☎ 81 52 00 00; www.sasbraathens.no) flies between Stavanger and Oslo (from Nkr560) and Bergen (from Nkr520) at least once daily. See p403 for international flights.

BOAT

From **Fiskepirterminalen** (☎ 51 86 87 80), **Flaggruten's** (☎ 51 86 87 80) boats leave for Bergen (Nkr620, 4½ hours, two daily Monday to Saturday, one on Sunday) and Haugesund (Nkr280, 80 minutes, four daily Monday to Friday, two daily Saturday and Sunday). For ferries to Lysefjord, see the boxed text, p230.

For ferries between Stavanger's Strandkaien Quay and England, see p409.

BUS

Buses run to the following places:

Destination	Departures	Cost	Duration
Bergen	every 2hr daily	Nkr420	5¾hr
Haugesund	every 2hr daily	Nkr210	2¼hr
Kristiansand	2-4 daily	Nkr355	4½hr
Oslo	up to 5 daily *	Nkr735	9½hr

* some services change at Kristiansand

CAR & MOTORCYCLE

Driving between Bergen and Stavanger along the direct E39 can be expensive, once you factor in two ferries, road tolls and city tolls. In all you'll end up paying around Nkr500. The toll to enter Stavanger for cars/motorcycles/campervans is Nkr13/free/26.

TRAIN

Trains run from Stavanger to Egersund (Nkr133, one hour, eight daily) and Oslo (Nkr846, eight hours, up to five daily) via Kristiansand (Nkr390, three hours), including an overnight service. For more information on cheaper *minipris* fares (from Nkr199), see p419.

Getting Around

TO/FROM THE AIRPORT

Between early morning and mid- to late evening, **Flybussen airport buses** (☎ 51 52 26 00) run every 20 minutes between the bus terminal and the airport at Sola (one way/return Nkr70/120). Alternatively, from Monday to Friday take city bus 9 (Nkr41), which runs hourly between early morning and midnight.

BICYCLE

You can hire mountain bikes at **Sykkelhuset** (☎ 51 53 99 10; Løkkeveien 33; per day/week Nkr75/280; 🕑 10am-5pm Mon-Wed & Fri, 10am-7pm Thu, 10am-2pm Sat).

LYSEFJORD

All along the 42km-long Lysefjord (Light Fjord), the granite rock glows with an ethereal, ambient light, even on dull days, all offset by almost-luminous mist. This is many visitors' favourite fjord, and there's no doubt that it has a captivating beauty. Whether you cruise from Stavanger, hike up to Preikestolen (604m), or drive the switchback road down to Lysebotn, it's one of Norway's must-sees. For visiting from Stavanger, see the boxed text, p230.

Information

Lysefjordsenteret (☎ 51 70 31 23; www.lysefjordsenteret.no; Oanes; adult/child Nkr50/25; 🕑 11am-8pm Jun-Aug, 11am-5pm Sep-May), in a fabulous setting north of the ferry terminal at Oanes, provides tourist information and presents Lysefjord in audio-visual displays. There are also geological and folk-history exhibits.

Also worth contacting is **Lysefjord Utvikling** (☎ 51 70 01 14; www.visitlysefjorden.no, in Norwegian) in Forsand.

Located at the trailhead for the hike up to Preikestolen, both the Preikestolhytta Vandrerhjem (p230) and the **kiosk** (☎ 97 16 55 51; 🕑 9.30am-8.45pm May–mid-Sep) at the entrance to the car park dispense information about Preikestolen and can sell walking guides of the region's various trails.

Preikestolen (Pulpit Rock)

The sight of people scrambling without fear to the edge of this extraordinary granite rock formation is one of Norway's emblematic images. Preikestolen, with astonishingly uniform cliffs on three sides plunging 604m to the fjord below, is a freak of nature which, despite the alarming crack where it joins the mountains, is likely to be around for a few more centuries. While looking down can be a bit daunting, you won't regret the magical view directly up Lysefjord. It's quite simply a remarkable place, a vantage point unrivalled anywhere in the world.

VISITING LYSEFJORD

The most spectacular aspect of visiting Lysefjord is the two-hour hike up to Preikestolen (Pulpit Rock; p229), although a ferry along Lysefjord is an alternative for those who can't make the hike. For general information on the region, check out www.lysefjordeninfo.no.

Preikestolen by Bus

Six ferries a day run from Stavanger's Fiskespiren Quay to Tau (adult/child foot passengers Nkr38/20) from late June to mid-August and just three daily the rest of summer; the first departure from Stavanger is at 8am (8.25am on Sunday). In summer, the ferries are met by a bus (Nkr55), which runs between the Tau pier and the Preikestolhytta Vandrerhjem. From there, the two-hour trail leads up to Preikestolen. The last bus from Preikestolhytta to Tau leaves at 8.10pm (7.50pm on Saturday).

Preikestolen by Car

If you've your own vehicle, you can take the car ferry from Stavanger's Fiskespiren Quay to Tau (car and driver Nkr125, 40 minutes, up to 24 departures daily). From the pier in Tau, a well-signed road (Rv13) leads 19km to Preikestolhytta Vandrerhjem (take the signed turn-off after 13km). It costs Nkr50/25 per car/motorcycle to park here.

An alternative route from Stavanger involves driving to Lauvik (via Sandnes along Rv13) from where a ferry crosses to Oanes (car and driver/adult foot passenger Nkr67/24, 10 minutes, departures almost every half-hour).

Either way, the trip between Stavanger and the trailhead takes around 1½ hours.

Lysebotn by Ferry

Ferry services from Stavanger to Lysebotn (opposite) were in a state of flux when we visited. The tourist office has plans to incorporate the Kjeragbolten (opposite) into the ferry service as visiting is difficult without a car. At the time of writing, the following companies were offering four-hour

There are no fences and those with vertigo will find themselves unable to go right to the edge (even watching the death-defying antics of people dangling limbs over the abyss can make the heart skip a beat). However, the local authorities assured us that there have been no reported cases of anyone accidentally falling off (even the French daredevil who balanced on the edge atop three chairs!). That said, please take all due care even if other people seemingly don't. Rocky trails also lead up the mountains behind, offering more wonderful views.

The two-hour, 3.8km trail up to Preikestolen leaves from Preikestolhytta Vandrerhjem. It begins along a steep but well-marked route, then climbs past a series of alternating steep and boggy sections to the final climb across granite slabs and along some windy and exposed cliffs to Preikestolen itself. The steepest sections are at the beginning and in the middle parts of the trail and can be challenging for those of low fitness.

The area also offers several other fabulous walks – the **Vatnerindane ridge circuit** (two hours), **Ulvaskog** (three hours), the **Refsvatnet circuit** (three hours) and summit of **Moslifjellet** (three hours) – all of which are accessible from the Preikestolhytta car park.

See above for detailed info on how to get to Preikestolen.

SLEEPING & EATING

Preikestolen Camping (☎ 51 74 97 25; www.preikestolencamping.no; Jørpeland; tent sites without/with car Nkr130/150 plus per person Nkr30; Apr-Oct) The closest camp site to Preikestolen (5km, or 1km off the Rv13) isn't anything to write home about but proximity is everything. Kitchen facilities are available, but you can also eat at the attached shop-restaurant.

Preikestolhytta Vandrerhjem (☎ 97 16 55 51; www.preikestolhytta.no; Jørpeland; dm incl breakfast Nkr250, d Nkr670-850) The fine turf-roofed hostel by a lake is adjacent to the start of the Preikestolen walking track. It's a well-run, fantastically situated place with a café (dishes Nkr35 to Nkr145), although it comes into its own when the crowds disappear for the night. It also rents out rowing boats.

car ferries (car/motorcycle & driver Nkr360/260, adult/child & senior foot passenger Nkr165/110) to Lysebotn. From Lysebotn, the road twists up the mountain from where you can continue on into the Setesdalen region (p159) and Oslo.

- **Veteran Fjord Cruise** (☎ 51 86 87 88; www.vfc.no or www.stavangerske.no; departures 10am daily Jun-Aug) Boat includes tourist commentary and stops for photos. Those travelling with a car should book *at least* two days in advance.
- **Kolumbus** (☎ 91 65 28 00; www.kolumbus.no) Normal car-and-passenger ferries that leave Stavanger at 1.30pm Monday, Wednesday and Friday and make eight stops en route to Lysebotn (arrival 3.25pm) but not at Preikestolen.

Lysebotn by Bus

Sirdalekspressen (☎ 51 59 90 60 or 51 86 87 88) buses from the Stavanger Fiskepirterminalen (departure 9.50am) or bus station (platform 6, departure 10am) to Lysebotn (arrival 2.20pm, one way/return Nkr250/490) depart daily from late June to mid-August.

Tours

At the time of writing, **Rødne Fjord Cruise** (☎ 51 89 52 70; www.rodne.no; adult/child/senior or student Nkr320/175/225; departures 10am & 2pm Sun-Wed, 10am, noon, 2pm & 6pm Thu-Sat Jul & Aug, noon daily May, Jun & Sep, noon Sat & Sun Oct-Apr) was offering 3½-hour cruises from Stavanger to the waters below Preikestolen and back.

Veteran Fjord Cruise (☎ 51 86 87 88; www.vfc.no; adult/senior or child Nkr300/200; departures 11.30am mid-Jun–late Aug) runs similar tours, sometimes under the banner of **Stavangerske** (www.stavangerske.no). It also runs eight-hour ferry-bus-hike tours from Stavanger to the top of Preikestolen that cost Nkr100/50 per adult/child. They depart at 8am daily from Stavanger Fiskepirterminalen from late May to early September.

Just down the road in Oanes (16km south of the Preikestolen turn-off along the Rv13) you'll find **Lysefjord Hyttegrend** (☎ 51 70 38 74; www.lysefjord-hyttegrend.no; 4-6-person cabins Nkr400-700, apt Nkr350-450), which has excellent chalets with en suite. Also in Oanes, **Lysefjordsenteret** (☎ 51 70 31 23; mains Nkr59-139, Sun buffet Nkr195) is a restaurant serving good, reasonably priced traditional meals.

Lysebotn

The ferry ride from Stavanger takes you to the fjord head at Lysebotn, where a narrow and much-photographed road corkscrews spectacularly 1000m up towards Sirdal in 27 hairpin bends. For more details on getting to Lysebotn, see opposite.

ACTIVITIES

After Preikestolen, the most popular Lysefjord walk leads to **Kjeragbolten**, an enormous oval-shaped boulder, or 'chockstone', lodged between two rock faces about 2m apart – you've surely seen it on postcards around Norway. The 10km return hike involves a strenuous 700m ascent from the Øygardsstølen Café car park (parking Nkr30), near the highest hairpin bend above Lysebotn.

The route trudges up and over three ridges and, in places, steep muddy slopes can make the going quite rough. Once you're at Kjeragbolten, actually reaching the boulder requires some tricky manoeuvring, including traversing an exposed ledge on a 1000m-high vertical cliff! From there, you can step (or crawl) directly onto the boulder for one of Norway's most astonishing views. The photo of you perched on the rock is sure to impress your friends.

If this doesn't provide sufficient thrills, then base jumping from Kjeragbolten could just be Norway's craziest sport; contact the **Stavanger Base Club** (☎ 51 88 12 10; www.basekjerag.com) for advice.

SLEEPING & EATING

Lysebotn Tourist Camp (☎ 90 83 20 35; www.lysebotn-touristcamp.com; tent/caravan sites Nkr130/150, dm Nkr250, 4-bed cabins Nkr650-950) If you can't face the daunting road up the mountain or, more likely, you can't bear to leave, Lysebotn Tourist Camp occupies an incredible setting at the head of the fjord. It's a lovely quiet spot to be after the ferry has left for the day.

Øygardsstølen Café (☎ 38 37 74 00; snacks & light meals Nkr45-129; 10am-6pm mid-Jun–mid-Sep) For views at this end of Lysefjord, you can't beat the 'eagle's nest', perched atop the cliff overlooking the hairpin twists down to Lysebotn. There's a viewing deck for those who don't wish to eat.

AROUND LYSEFJORD

The Rv13 road through the wild and lightly populated country north of Lysefjord is one of 18 roads designated as a 'National Tourist Route' (see the boxed text, p414). It's definitely the slow route between Stavanger and Bergen, but it's worth it if you have time. The finest scenery is around **Årdal**, **Jøsenfjorden**, **Suldalsosen** and **Suldalsvatnet**.

For considerable comfort and charm, the grand old **Sauda Fjord Hotel** (☎ 52 78 12 11; www.saudafjordhotel.no; Saudasjøen; s/d from Nkr690/990, half-board from Nkr850/1150), west off the Rv13, offers fine accommodation and good meals at reasonable prices. The hotel is part of the Fjord Pass network.

The best public transport is the ferry between Stavanger and Sauda (Nkr310, 2¼ hours, two or three daily), although Rv13 is best followed by private car.

The Western Fjords

The western fjords slit deeply into the two administrative regions of Sogn og Fjordane and, to its north, Møre og Romsdal. *National Geographic Traveler* magazine recently selected the Norwegian fjords as the world's best travel destination, ahead of other dream lands, such as the Alps, the Galapagos Islands, Australia's Great Barrier Reef and other comparable natural wonders, such as the fretted coastlines of Chile and New Zealand. It's easy to see why.

Scoured and gouged by ancient glaciers, of which a few vestigial traces still groan and creak, these formidable, deep, sea-drowned valleys are pincered by almost impossibly rugged terrain. Amazingly, this hasn't deterred Norwegians from settling and farming their slopes and heights for thousands of years. You'll find a confounding number of things to see and do, in the water, up the mountains or just on the level.

Ferries are fun. When planning your trip, bear in mind that these reliable work horses don't just lop off huge detours around a fjord; they're also an enjoyable part of the journey in their own right, offering great and otherwise inaccessible panoramas of the coastline around you.

Although you'll be hard pressed to find more than a few flat patches, the western fjords also make for great hiking country, whether in a guided group over one of the glaciers that are such a feature of the region or on one of the signed trails. And if, after so much fresh air and wide open space, you begin to crave a little small-town sophistication, drop into the charming coastal settlement of Ålesund.

HIGHLIGHTS

- Cruise between Geiranger and Hellesylt past the daunting cliffs of **Geirangerfjord** (p259)
- Ride the dramatic **Flåmsbana railway** (p234) between wild Hardangervidda and Flåm by gentle Aurlandsfjorden
- Buck over the spectacular **Trollstigen route** (p256) between Åndalsnes and Valldal
- Get your boots damp on but a tiny tongue of the vast **Jostedalsbreen icecap** (p244)
- Savour Art Nouveau architecture in the charming town of **Ålesund** (p262)
- Jazz it up at the **Molde Jazz Festival** (p268)

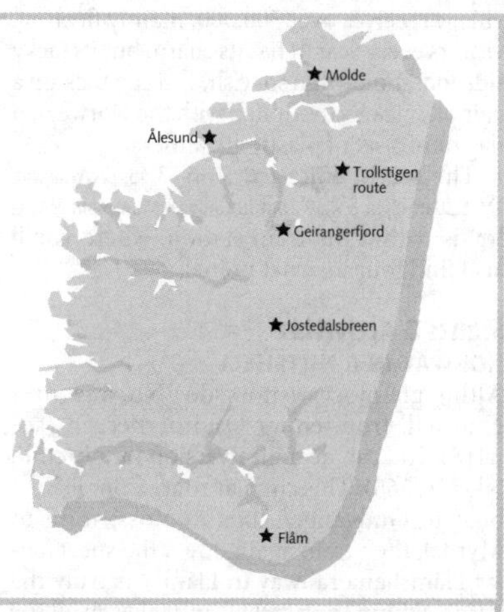

- POPULATION: 351,600
- HIGHEST ELEVATION: LODALSKÅPA (2083M)

SOGNEFJORDEN

Sognefjorden, the world's longest (203km) and Norway's deepest (1308m) fjord, cuts a deep slash across the map of western Norway. In places, sheer walls rise more than 1000m above the water while elsewhere a gentler shoreline supports farms, orchards and villages. The broad, main waterway is impressive but by cruising into its narrower arms, such as the deep and lovely Nærøyfjord to Gudvangen, you'll see idyllic views of abrupt cliff faces and cascading waterfalls.

For a good general website, consult www.sognefjord.no. For info on the towns of Flåm, Aurland and Lærdal, www.alr.no is a well-structured website.

Getting There & Away

Fjord1 (☎ 55 90 70 70; www.fjord1.no/fylkesbaatane) operates a daily express boat between Bergen and both Flåm (Nkr605, 5½ hours) and Sogndal (Nkr525, 4¾ hours), stopping along the way at 10 small towns including Vik (Nkr410, 3½ hours) and Balestrand (Nkr440, 3¾ hours). Several local ferries also link Sognefjord towns, and there's an extensive, if infrequent, bus network.

FLÅM

pop 550

Flåm, at the head of Aurlandsfjorden, sits in a truly spectacular setting. As a stop on the popular 'Norway in a Nutshell' tour, this tiny village receives over 500,000, mainly fleeting, visitors every year. It has its charm but its tacky side too; should you so wish, you can pick up a pair of knickers decorated with the Norwegian flag or of a set of plastic elk antlers.

The **tourist office** (☎ 57 63 33 13; www.alr.no; 🕑 8.30am-4pm & 4.30-8pm Jun-Aug, 8.30am-4pm May & Sep) is within the train station, where you'll also find four internet points.

Sights & Activities

NORWAY IN A NUTSHELL

Although most visitors do 'Norway in a Nutshell' from either Oslo or Bergen (see p418), you can do a miniversion (adult/child Nkr530/265). This circular route from Flåm – boat to Gudvangen, bus to Voss, train to Myrdal, then train again down the spectacular Flåmsbana railway to Flåm – is truly the kernel within the nutshell and takes in all the most dramatic elements.

FLÅMSBANA RAILWAY

The 20km **Flåmsbana railway** (☎ 57 63 21 00; www.flaamsbana.no; adult/child one way Nkr190/95, return Nkr290/190), an engineering wonder, hauls itself up 864m of altitude gain through 20 tunnels at a gradient of 1:18 up to Myrdal, on the bleak, treeless Hardangervidda plateau, past thundering waterfalls (there's a photo stop at awesome Kjosfossen). It runs year-round with up to 10 departures daily in summer.

Preface your trip with a brief visit to the **Flåmsbana museum** (☎ 57 63 23 10; admission free; 🕑 9am-5pm). It's not just about railways; it has fascinating photos of construction gangs and life in and around Flåm before the car era.

BOATING & CANOEING

To get out and about on the fjord, pass by Flåm Marina & Apartement, which hires out rowing boats and canoes (Nkr50 per hour) and motorboats (from Nkr150 per hour plus fuel).

Njord (☎ 91 32 66 28; www.fjordpaddlenorway.com) does a variety of sea-kayaking trips from Flåm, ranging from a two-hour induction (Nkr350) to a three-day hiking and kayaking sortie (Nkr2650).

HIKING & CYCLING

The tourist office produces an easy-to-interpret free sheet of local walks, varying from 45 minutes to five hours, with routes superimposed upon a couple of aerial photographs.

To meander along the shoreline or for something more strenuous, you can rent a bike from the tourist office (Nkr30/175 per hour/day) or Heimly Pensjonat (Nkr50/200 per hour/day).

For an exhilarating day ride, attack the **Rallarvegen**, the service road used by the navvies who constructed the railway that climbs to Myrdal and beyond. Nowadays a popular 80km cycle route, it begins on the main line at Haugastøl (988m), then heads northwest following the tracks via Finse (26km), at 1222m Norway's highest station, to Myrdal (62km), from where it drops to Flåm (80km) and fjord level in tandem with the Flåmsbana line. It's usually open from mid-July to September.

Sleeping

Flåm Camping & Youth Hostel (☎ 57 63 21 21; www.flaam-camping.no; camp sites Nkr85-150, dm Nkr145, s/d from Nkr300/450, cabins Nkr525-825; 🕑 May-Sep) This friendly camp site and hostel has good

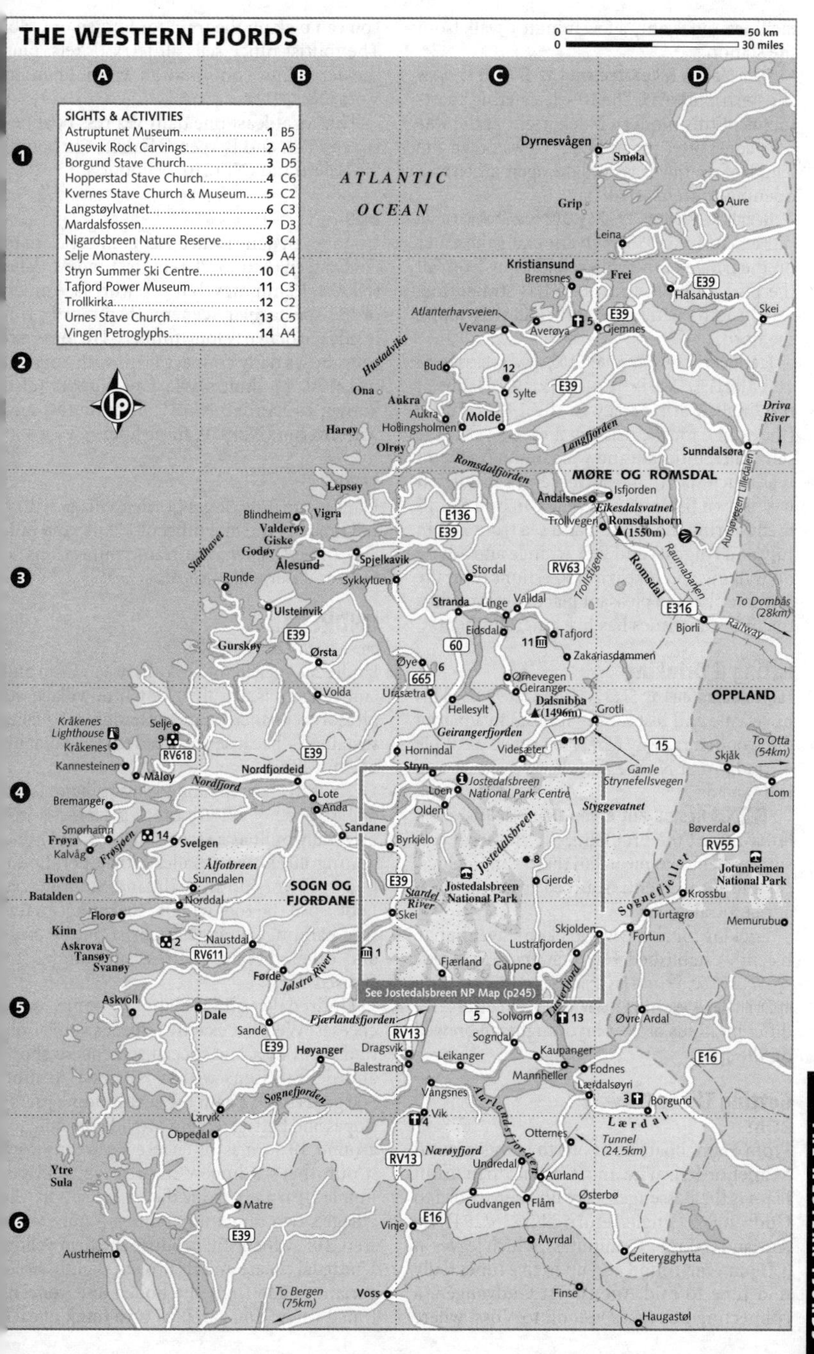
THE WESTERN FJORDS
0 50 km
0 30 miles
A
B
C
D
1
2
3
4
5
6
SIGHTS & ACTIVITIES
Astruptunet Museum....................1 B5
Ausevik Rock Carvings....................2 A5
Borgund Stave Church....................3 D5
Hopperstad Stave Church....................4 C6
Kvernes Stave Church & Museum....................5 C2
Langstøylvatnet....................6 C3
Mardalsfossen....................7 D3
Nigardsbreen Nature Reserve....................8 C4
Selje Monastery....................9 A4
Stryn Summer Ski Centre....................10 C4
Tafjord Power Museum....................11 C3
Trollkirka....................12 C2
Urnes Stave Church....................13 C5
Vingen Petroglyphs....................14 A4
ATLANTIC
OCEAN
Dyrnesvågen
Smøla
Grip
Aure
Leina
Kristiansund
Bremsnes
Frei
E39
Halsanaustan
Skei
Atlanterhavsveien
Vevang
Averøya
5
Gjemnes
Hustadvika
Bud
12
Sylte
Ona
Aukra
Molde
Harøy
Hollingsholmen
Olrøy
Langfjorden
Romsdalfjorden
Driva River
Sunndalsøra
MØRE OG ROMSDAL
Lepsøy
Åndalsnes
Isfjorden
Eikesdalsvatnet
Blindheim
Vigra
Valderøy
Giske
Godøy
E136
Trollvegen
Romsdalshorn
(1550m)
7
Aursjøvegen Lilledalen
Stadhavet
Ålesund
Spjelkavik
Stordal
RV63
Trollstigen
Romsdal
Raumabanen
Runde
Sykkyluen
Ulsteinvik
Stranda
Linge
Valldal
E316
Bjorli
To Dombås (28km)
Railway
Gurskøy
Eidsdal
11
Tafjord
Ørsta
60
Zakariasdammen
Øye
6
665
Ørnevegen
Geiranger
OPPLAND
Volda
Urasætra
Hellesylt
Dalsnibba
(1496m)
Grotli
Kråkenes Lighthouse
Selje
9
Kråkenes
RV618
Geirangerfjorden
10
Videsæter
15
To Otta (54km)
Skjåk
Kannesteinen
Måløy
Nordfjord
Nordfjordeid
Hornindal
Stryn
Gamle Strynefellsvegen
Lom
Jostedalsbreen National Park Centre
Loen
Bremanger
Lote
Anda
Olden
Styggevatnet
Smørhamn
Frøya
Kalvåg
Frøsjøen
14
Svelgen
Sandane
Byrkjelo
Jostedalsbreen
Bøverdal
RV55
Ålfotbreen
8
Jotunheimen National Park
Hovden
Sunndalen
SOGN OG FJORDANE
E39
Stardal River
Jostedalsbreen National Park
Gjerde
Sognefjellet
Krossbu
Batalden
Norddal
Florø
Skei
Turtagrø
Memurubu
Kinn
Naustdal
2
Skjolden
Fortun
Askrova
Tansøy
Svanøy
RV611
1
Lustrafjorden
Førde
Jølstra River
Fjærland
Gaupne
Lusterfjord
See Jostedalsbreen NP Map (p245)
Askvoll
Dale
Fjærlandsfjorden
5
Solvorn
13
Øvre Årdal
Sande
RV13
Sogndal
Dragsvik
Høyanger
Kaupanger
E16
Leikanger
Balestrand
Fodnes
Mannheller
Lærdalsøyri
Vangsnes
3
Borgund
Sognefjorden
Lærdal
Lavik
Vik
4
Aurlandsfjorden
Oppedal
Otternes
Tunnel (24.5km)
Nærøyfjord
Undredal
Ytre Sula
Aurland
Gudvangen
Flåm
Østerbø
Matre
Vinje
Myrdal
Austrheim
Geiterygghytta
To Bergen (75km)
Voss
Finse
Haugastøl

facilities and is only a few minutes' walk from the station.

Flåm Marina & Apartement (☎ 57 63 35 55, www.flammarina.no; d Nkr955) The 10 self-catering apartments of this modern block, right at the water's edge, offer magnificent views down the length of the fjord, as does the open-air terrace opening from its small bar.

Heimly Pensjonat (☎ 57 63 23 00; www.heimly.no; s/d incl breakfast from Nkr795/980) Overlooking the water on the fringe of the village and away from all the port hubbub, this place has straightforward rooms with a magnificent view along the fjord.

Fretheim Hotel (☎ 57 63 63 00; www.fretheim-hotel.no; s/d Nkr1195/1580; Feb–mid-Dec; P) Haunt of the English aristocracy in the 19th century (they came for the fishin'), the vast, yet at the same time intimate and welcoming Fretheim is as much sports and social centre as hotel. It has its own fishing reach (you can hire equipment during the salmon and sea trout run in July and August) and will arrange and advise on walking and bike trips. Exertions over, the 3rd-floor bar is a pleasant place to relax, while the pub sometimes has live entertainment.

Eating & Drinking

Togrestauranten (☎ 57 63 21 55; mains Nkr95-125) This novel café and restaurant, housed in a pair of old wooden railway carriages, offers a couple of traditional Norwegian dishes, snacks and leafy salads.

our pick **Restaurant Arven** (Fretheim Hotel; mains Nkr260-290) At the Fretheim, the chefs salt and smoke their own meat and there's an 'ecological and local' menu, sourced from the local agricultural college.

Looking for all the world like a stave church, recently established **Ægir Brewery** (Ægir Bryggeri; ☎ 57 63 20 60; core hrs noon-midnight Jun-Aug, 3pm-midnight May & Sep, Fri & Sat only rest-of-year) offers five different kinds of beer on draught, all brewed on the spot.

Getting There & Away

BOAT

From Flåm, boats head out to towns around Sognefjorden. The most scenic trip from Flåm is the passenger ferry up Nærøyfjord to Gudvangen (single/return Nkr215/294) via Aurland (Nkr68, 15 minutes), which leaves at 3.10pm year-round and up to five times daily mid-June to mid-August. At Gudvangen, a connecting bus takes you on to Voss, where you can pick up the train for Bergen or Oslo. The tourist office sells all ferry tickets, plus the ferry-bus combination from Flåm to Voss (Nkr291).

There's at least one daily express boat between Flåm and Bergen (Nkr605, 5½ hours) via Balestrand (Nkr210, 1¾ hours).

BUS

Up to seven daily local buses connect Flåm to Gudvangen (Nkr43, 20 minutes) and Aurland (Nkr29, 15 minutes) but you won't see much of the spectacular scenery; they mostly run inside particularly long tunnels. Up to six express buses daily connect Flåm with Sogndal (Nkr120, 1¾ hours) via Lærdalsøyri (also known as Lærdal; Nkr81, 45 minutes) and with Bergen (Nkr270, three hours).

TRAIN

Flåm is the only Sognefjorden village with a rail link, via the magnificent Flåmsbana railway (p234). There are train connections to Oslo and Bergen at Myrdal.

UNDREDAL

pop human 120, goats 500

Undredal, tucked mid-way between Flåm and Gudvangen, is a truly lovely little village, its pleasures enhanced – and its traditional quality sustained – because you need to make that bit of extra effort to get there.

The tiny, barrel-vaulted **village church** (adult/child Nkr30/free; core hrs noon-5pm mid-May–mid-Sep), originally built as a stave church in 1147 and seating 40, is the smallest still-operational house of worship in mainland Scandinavia. Look up at the roof with its charmingly naive roof paintings of angels, Christ on the cross and other biblical figures, surrounded by stylised stars.

Undredal's other claim to fame is its cheeses. Well not exactly fame, as you'll only find them in a few specialised cheese shops and delicatessens within Norway. Around 500 goats freely roam the surrounding grassy slopes and between them provide the milk for around 10 tonnes of cheese per year (work it out: that's a hugely impressive yield per nipple). Farmers from the valley supply the village's two remaining dairies – once there were 10 – which still produce the firm yellow Undredal cheese and its brown, slightly sweet variant, made from the boiled and concentrated whey. You can pick up a hunk of each at the village shop; it's the light blue building beside the shore.

Undredal is 6.5km north of the E16. The narrow road threads steeply downhill beside a hurtling torrent. If travelling by bus, get off at the eastern end of the 11km tunnel that leads to Gudvangen. By ferry, ask the captain to make the optional stop at Undredal's harbour. Best of all, take the bus out, walk down the spectacular valley along the lightly trafficked road and return by boat (press the switch beside the yellow blinking lamp on the café wall beside the jetty to alert the next passing ferry).

GUDVANGEN & NÆRØYFJORD

Nærøyfjord, its 17km length declared a Unesco world heritage site in 2006, lies west of Flåm. Beside the deep blue fjord (only 250m across at its narrowest point) are towering 1200m-high cliffs, isolated farms, and waterfalls plummeting from the heights. It can easily be visited as a day excursion from Flåm.

Kjelsfossen waterfall, one of the world's 10 longest, tumbles from the southern wall of Nærøydalen valley, above Gudvangen village. Notice too the **avalanche protection scheme** above Gudvangen. The powerful avalanches here typically provide a force of 12 tonnes per sq metre, move at 50m/second and, local legend reckons, can bowl a herd of goats right across the fjord!

A pair of camp sites flank the road, 1.3km from the ferry port: **Gudvangen Camping** (☎ 57 63 39 34; www.visitgudvangen.com; camp sites Nkr140, 2-/4-person cabins from Nkr350/400; ⏲ mid-Apr–Oct) and **Vang Camping** (☎ 57 63 39 26; promso@tele2.no; per person/site Nkr15/80, cabins Nkr300-950; ⏲ mid-May–mid-Sep). Each is beautifully situated at the base of sheer cliffs.

Gudvangen Fjordtell (☎ 57 63 39 29; www.gudvangen.com; s/d from Nkr780/1180; ⏲ May-Sep; P) has rooms in a cluster of buildings, both historical and sprucely contemporary, some of which have mini-kitchens. Most original are its 12 Viking rooms; with wooden swords and shields for wall decoration and pelts as bed covers – they teeter just the right side of naff. The restaurant is worth visiting for its gorgeous view down the fjord though the food (mains Nkr85 to Nkr120) is nothing to write postcards home about.

Scenic ferries between Gudvangen and Flåm (one way/return Nkr215/294) via Aurland run up to five times daily. A car ferry runs up to four times daily to/from Lærdal (car and driver/passenger Nkr210/500; three hours) via Kaupanger. Up to seven daily buses run to/from Flåm (Nkr43, 20 minutes), Aurland (Nkr58, 30 minutes) and Voss (Nkr81, one hour).

SNØVEGEN

The Snow Road climbs from sea level, twisting precipitously to the high plateau (1309m) that separates Aurland and Lærdalsøyri (Lærdal). This magnificent drive – strictly for summertime (snow banks line the road and tarns are still deep-frozen even in late June) – has been designated as a National Tourist Route so get there quickly before the coaches catch on. Even if you don't opt for the whole route, drive the first 8km from Aurland to the magnificent **observation point**. Projecting out over the fjord way below, pine-clad, simple and striking like the best of Norwegian design, it's almost as impressive as the magnificent panorama itself.

AURLAND

pop 600

Peaceful Aurland is so much less hectic and trodden than its neighbour, Flåm. It marks the end of the spectacular Aurlandsdalen hiking route. These days it's also renowned as one end of Lærdalstunnel, the world's longest road tunnel (24.5km long – 6km more than China's Zhongnanshan tunnel, its nearest rival). This essential link in the E16 highway that connects Oslo and Bergen (before its completion, traffic had to ferry-hop between Lærdal and Gudvangen) is a fast alternative to the beautiful but sinuous and seasonal 45km-long **Snøvegen** (⏲ Jun–mid-Oct). It's a choice between tunnel vision, speed and convenience set against a sometimes hair-raising ascent that offers inspirational views all the way up and down…

The Aurland **tourist office** (☎ 57 63 33 13; www.alr.no; ⏲ 9am-6pm Mon-Fri, 10am-5pm Sat & Sun Jun-Aug, 8am-3.30pm Mon-Fri rest-of-year) is beside the village church.

Between Flåm and Aurland, and high above the fjord perches the restored hamlet of **Otternes** (adult/child Nkr50/free; ⏲ 10am-6pm mid-May–Sep), a complex of 27 restored buildings, the earliest dating from the 17th century. To get full value from the visit, follow the one-hour guided tour (Nkr20 extra; available in English four times daily) and plan a rest break to lick a locally made organic ice cream or eat a bowl of *rømmegrøt,* a rich sour-cream porridge.

Activities

HIKING

The Aurland and Lærdal tourist offices have produced several walker-friendly sheets of local walks, where the route is superimposed upon an aerial photo.

The classic trek down Aurlandsdalen from Geiteryggen to Aurland follows a stream from source to sea as you tramp one of the oldest trading routes between eastern and western Norway. From mid-July, you can start this four-day walk in Finse, on the Oslo–Bergen rail line, with overnight stops at Geiterygghytta, Steinbergdalen and Østerbø. The final section from Østerbø (820m) to Vassbygdi (95m) is the most scenic and makes for a hugely enjoyable day hike (allow six to seven hours).

The lower sections of the walk are usually open between early June and late September. From Vassbygdi (15 minutes) and Østerbø (one hour), buses run to/from Aurland three times daily.

Sleeping & Eating

Lunde Gard & Camping (☎ 57 63 34 12; www.lunde-camping.no; per person/site Nkr30/110, cabins Nkr350-900; ⌚ May-Sep) This small camp site nestles agreeably beside a river, 1.2km up a side valley.

Vangsgaarden (☎ 57 63 35 80; www.vangsgaarden.no; d Nkr850, cabins Nkr750-1075; P) The complex embraces four 18th-century buildings, six cabins down at sea level and the Duehuset (Dovecot) Café & Pub. Most rooms are furnished in antique style; the dining room, for example, could be your grandmother's parlour.

Aurland Fjordhotell (☎ 57 63 35 05; www.aurland-fjordhotel.com; s/d/tr Nkr1145/1490/1785; P) At this friendly 30-room, family-owned hotel, most of the comfortable, well-furnished rooms have fjord views and there's a solarium, steam bath and sauna. To help you sleep, have a shot from the owner's huge collection of brandies and spirits in a couple of display cases beside reception.

Getting There & Away

Buses run up to seven times daily between Aurland and Flåm (Nkr29, 15 minutes) and one to three times daily between Aurland and Lærdal (Nkr62, 30 minutes). Express buses to/from Bergen (Nkr275, 3¼ hours) call in up to six times daily.

Watch out for the speed cameras in Lærdalstunnelen; they'll certainly have their eye on you…

LÆRDAL

Lærdalsøyri

pop 2150

The village of Lærdalsøyri, usually called simply Lærdal, is where the lovely green dale of the same name (whose fertile lower reaches produce the juiciest of cherries) meets the fjord.

Its **tourist office** (☎ 57 64 12 07; www.alr.no; Øyraplassen 7; ⌚ 9am-7pm mid-Jun–mid-Aug, 9am-4pm rest-of-year) occupies a lovely old clapboard house, once the town's bank, that's set back from the main street.

If you're planning to camp anywhere within the western fjords, this place, which locals claim is Norway's second-driest village, is your spot!

SIGHTS & ACTIVITIES

To learn all you'd ever want to know about Atlantic salmon and their unique migration and breeding habits, visit the **Wild Salmon Centre** (Norsk Villaks Senter; ☎ 57 66 67 71; www.norsk-villakssenter.no; adult/child Nkr75/40; ⌚ 10am-5pm, to 6pm or 7pm May-Sep). You can watch wild salmon and sea trout through viewing windows, see an excellent 20-minute film about the salmon's life cycle and learn to tie flies to increase the odds of you hooking one of your own.

The town makes for pleasant strolling beside well preserved 18th- and 19th-century timber homes, warehouses and fisherfolk's shacks. The tourist office has a free town map that describes the best of them and sets out a walking route. It will also lend you a free audioguide that takes you around the town's Top Eleven spots.

Lærdal Sport og Rekreasjon, which is based at the camp site (see opposite), rents row-

COMBINATION TICKET

To take in the valley's two principal sights, the Wild Salmon Centre and Borgund Stave Church, buy a combination ticket (adult/child/family Nkr115/70/250), which gives admission to both venues.

A FISHY COINCIDENCE

Helene Maristuen, managing director of the Wild Salmon Centre, tells of two bizarre coincidences that led her to mount the museum's most recent addition: an exhibition devoted to 'The English Era'. It commemorates the time when, in the early 20th century, members of the British aristocracy – including the then Prince of Wales – fished the creeks and rivers for giant salmon. Helene says 'I'd been planning to mount something on this theme for quite some time. Then, one day, quite by chance, a colleague put on my desk a copy of *A Valet's Diction*, the diary of an English valet who spent a season in Lærdal in the company of his master, edited with a commentary by his grandson, John Michael Wade. Then some months later, the author's brother, who was visiting our town, left three copies at reception. So I determined to track down the author, invited him over – and he inaugurated our latest permanent exhibition.'

As told to Miles Roddis

ing boats and canoes (Nkr45 per hour), motor boats (from Nkr100) and bikes (from Nkr40/150 per hour/day).

There's free **fishing** in the fjord and the upper reaches of the Lærdal river are good for trout (permits, available from the tourist office, cost Nkr50 per day).

For **hiking**, pick up the tourist office's free leaflet of walks in the area.

SLEEPING & EATING

Lærdal Ferie og Fritidspark (☎ 57 66 66 95; www.laerdalferiepark.com; camp site Nkr140, 2-/3-/4-bed cabins Nkr775/825/875) This camp site, almost at the water's edge, has sweeping views of the fjord. Its newest venture is the adjacent **motel** (s/d Nkr490/550), which has communal self-catering facilities and a common room with a broad picture window that gives a magnificent panorama of the fjord.

Lindstrøm Hotell (☎ 57 66 69 00; www.lindstroemhotel.no; s Nkr695-845, d Nkr950-1150, all incl breakfast; May-Sep; P) The most charming house of this five-unit complex, these days a protected building, is, alas, no longer used for accommodation. Ask for a room in the gabled building just behind it, constructed in 1899, renovated with all modern conveniences and a great second best. Cosy public areas in the main building (which houses reception) are attractively decorated and furnished in period style.

After the Lindstrøm Hotell, Lærdalsøyri's next best place for eating is the informal **Laksen Pub & Restaurant** (☎ 57 66 86 20; pizzas Nkr140-150, mains Nkr200-240) at the Wild Salmon Centre, which dispenses tempting snacks and sandwiches during the daytime, then morphs into a restaurant from 6pm to 9pm.

GETTING THERE & AWAY

If you're driving south, you have the choice between the world's longest road tunnel linking Aurland and Lærdal or, in summer, climbing up and over the mountain, following the Snøvegen. For details of both, see p237. Express buses run to/from Bergen (Nkr320, 3¾ hours) two to six times daily via the tunnel.

There are four daily car ferries that run to/from Gudvangen (passenger/car Nkr210/500, three hours).

Borgund Stave Church

Some 30km southeast of Lærdalsøyri along the E16, this 12th-century **stave church** (adult/child Nkr65/45; 8am-8pm mid-Jun–mid-Aug, 9.30am-5pm May–mid-Jun & mid-Aug–Sep) was raised beside one of the major trade routes between eastern and western Norway. Dedicated to St Andrew, it's one of the best-known, most-photographed – and certainly the best-preserved – of Norway's stave churches. Beside it is the only freestanding medieval wooden bell tower still standing in Norway. Buy your ticket at the visitors centre, which has a worthwhile exhibition (included in the price of your admission) on this peculiarly Norwegian phenomenon. If you enjoy walking, build in time to undertake the two-hour circular hike on ancient paths and tracks that starts and ends at the church.

VIK

pop 1600

On the southern outskirts of the village of Vik is the splendid **Hopperstad stave church** (adult/child Nkr50/free; 10am-5pm mid-May–mid-Jun & mid-Aug–mid-Sep, 9am-7pm mid-Jun–mid-Aug), about 1km from the centre. Built in 1130 and Norway's second oldest, it escaped demolition by a whisker in

STAVE CHURCHES

Stave churches, so typically Norwegian, are essentially wooden structures with roof-bearing posts (or staves) sunk deep into the earth. The majority of the 28 that survive from around a thousand originals date from the 12th and 13th centuries, although most have been much modified over the centuries.

First, horizontal sills, delineating the structure, were laid out above ground level on a raised stone foundation. On these, the upright, vertical plank walls rested. At each corner a vertical stave post – hence the name of the style – was pounded into the ground to hold together the sill below and a wall plate above.

Most stave church interiors are little more than a small nave and a narrow chancel. In some, nave and chancel combine into a single rectangular space, divided only by a chancel screen. The most elaborate stave church still standing, at **Borgund** (p239), also has a semicircular apse at its eastern end.

Typically, other freestanding posts, spaced about 2m apart and around 1m in from the walls, support the roof of the nave although smaller churches managed with just one central post. All today's stave churches are surrounded by outer walls, creating external galleries or protective passageways. It was these that, together with the use of tar on the roofs as a preservative, helped them to survive.

Interior walls are often painted in elaborate designs, including *rosemaling,* which are traditional rose paintings (for a 'modern' example of the genre, visit the flamboyantly decorated 18th-century church at **Stordal**, p259), and the complex roof lines are frequently embellished with scalloped wooden shingles and Viking-age dragon head finials, rather like those of Thai monasteries. Often, the most intricate decoration comes from the wooden carvings on the support posts, door frames and outer walls (especially at **Urnes**, p243), representing tendrils of stems, vines and leaves. They're frequently entwined with serpents, dragons and other fantasy creatures, thus meshing Norway's proud pagan past with newer Christian themes.

To learn more visit www.stavechurch.org, the website of architect and building historian, Dr Jurgen Jensenius.

the late 19th century. Inside, the original canopy paintings of the elaborately carved baldequin have preserved their freshness of colour. For an additional Nkr20 you can use the same ticket for the Hove stone church, 1km to the south, which dates from the same era.

BALESTRAND

pop 800

Balestrand sits comfortably beside the fjord, at its rear an impressive mountain backdrop. Genteel and low-key, it has been a tranquil, small-scale holiday resort ever since the 19th century. Its **tourist office** (☎ 57 69 12 55; www.midsogn.com; 7.30am-12.30pm & 1.30-6pm Mon-Sat, 10am-5pm Sun mid-Jun–mid-Aug; 8am-4pm Mon-Fri May-early Jun & mid-Aug–Sep) is opposite the ferry quay.

Sights & Activities

The road running south along the fjord, bordered by apple orchards and farmsteads, sees little motor traffic. Beside it, the **Church of St Olav** (1897) was constructed in the style of a traditional stave church at the instigation of English expat Margaret Green, who married a local hotel-owner. Should you find it closed, the owner of Midtnes Hotel (see opposite) has the key.

Less than 1km south along the fjord, excavation of two **Viking Age burial mounds** revealed remnants of a boat, two skeletons, jewellery and several weapons (no longer on site). One mound is topped by a statue of legendary **King Bele**, erected by Germany's Kaiser Wilhelm II, who was obsessed with Nordic mythology and regularly spent his holidays here prior to WWI (a similar monument, also funded by the Kaiser and honouring Fridtjof, the lover of King Bele's daughter, peers across the fjord from Vangsnes).

Near the ferry dock is the **Sognefjord Aquarium** (☎ 57 69 13 03; adult/child Nkr70/35 incl a free hr of canoe or rowing boat hire; 9am-11.30pm mid-Jun–mid-Aug, 9.30am-5pm May–mid-Jun & mid-Aug–Sep), which has an interesting audiovisual presentation and plenty of tanks in which saltwater creatures lurk.

HIKING

The 5km circular **Granlia forest nature trail** is a signed loop, beginning just above the Rv55 tunnel. For more suggestions about walks in the area, long and short, buy from the tourist office *Balestrand Turkart* (Nkr70), a good walking map at 1:50,000 with trails marked up.

Sleeping & Eating

Sjøtun Camping (☎ 57 69 12 23; www.sjotun.com; per person/site Nkr25/50, 4-/6-bed cabin Nkr250/320; ⏲ Jun–mid-Sep) At this place, a 15-minute walk south along the fjord, you can pitch a tent amid apple trees or rent a rustic cabin.

Vandrerhjem Kringsjå (☎ 57 69 13 03; www.kringsja.no; dm/d incl breakfast Nkr245/740; ⏲ mid-Jun–mid-Aug) Balestrand's HI-affiliated hostel, an outdoor activities centre during the school year, is a fine lodge-style place with a restaurant and self-catering facilities.

Midtnes Hotel (☎ 57 69 11 33; www.midtnes.no; s Nkr630-710, d Nkr690-960, all incl breakfast; ⏲ year-round; P 💻) Beside St Olav's church, this 32-room, family-run place has a breakfast room with great views of the water, an attractive terrace and a lawn that extends down to a jetty, where a rowing boat, free for guests, is moored.

Balestrand Hotell (☎ 57 69 11 38; www.balestrand.com; s Nkr590-665, d Nkr840-990, all incl breakfast; ⏲ Jun-Aug; P 💻) This summertime-only hotel, also family-run, is a friendly, jolly, intimate place that eschews the tour groups that fill so many beds elsewhere in town. As at the Midtnes, it's well worth paying that little extra for inspirational views over the fjord.

our pick Kvikne's Hotel (☎ 57 69 42 00; www.kviknes.no; s/d from Nkr1045/1590; ⏲ May-Sep; P 💻) The majestic pale-yellow, timber-built Kvikne's Hotel, on the point just south of the ferry landing, has lashings of mid-19th-century luxury, including exquisite antiques in its public areas. The newer building (whose rooms are comfortable to a fault) is a grotesque concrete pile by comparison. The hotel's Balholm Bar og Bistro is a reliable place for snacks and light meals. For a gastronomic delight, choose the main restaurant's set menu (Nkr530) or invest Nkr415 in their superb dinner buffet.

Café Galleri (salads Nkr50-70, snacks & sandwiches Nkr32-40) Next door but two to the tourist office, this quaint little place is integrated into a small art gallery. Outside, the tables of its small terrace are adorned with fresh cut flowers.

Getting There & Away

Express boats to/from Bergen (Nkr440, four hours) hurtle off twice daily, Monday to Saturday, and to/from Sogndal (Nkr140, one hour) once daily.

Between May and September, a car ferry departs at 8.05am and noon and follows the narrow Fjærlandsfjorden to Fjærland (one way/return Nkr175/263, 1¼ hours), gateway to the glacial wonderlands of Jostedalsbreen. For a great day tour, Nkr480/241 per adult/child will get you a return trip on the ferry, bus to the glacier museum, museum admission and a visit to the glacier itself. See p245 for more details.

Express buses link Balestrand and Sogndal (Nkr86, 1¼ hours, three daily).

The scenic Gaularfjellsvegen (Rv13) is an exciting drive to Førde, on Førdefjord, negotiating hairpin bends and skirting Norway's greatest concentration of roadside waterfalls.

Getting Around

The tourist office hires out bicycles for Nkr30/75/140 per hour/half-/full day.

SOGNDAL

pop 6050

Sogndal, though not the area's prettiest place, makes a good base for a trio of magnificent day drives: Jostedalen and Nigarsdsbreen (p246), Urnes and a circuit of Lustrafjord (p243) and the spectacular Sognefjellet circuit, p242.

Its **tourist office** (☎ 97 60 04 43; www.sognefjorden.no; Hovevegen 2; ⏲ 9am-6pm Mon-Fri, 10am-4pm Sat, 3-8pm Sun mid-Jun–mid-Aug, 10am-4pm Mon-Fri rest-of-year), a five-minute walk east of the bus station, can book accommodation for callers-in. To stretch your legs, ask for its booklet of hill walks (Nkr40). The town library, in the same building, has free internet access.

Sights & Activities

The extensive open-air **Sogn Folkmuseum** (☎ 57 67 82 06; Vestreim; adult/child Nkr60/30, audioguide Nkr20; ⏲ 10am-5pm Jun-Aug, 10am-3pm May & Sep) is in the hamlet of Vestreim between Sogndal and Kaupanger. Here, over 30 buildings have been brought from their original sites and embedded in the surrounding woods. In summer there are handicraft workshops, a traditional village shop, a section on children's lives and a typical farm, complete with its animals.

In **Kaupanger**, 2km southeast along the Rv5 and reachable by bus, the **Sogn Fjordmuseum**

THE SOGNEFJELLET CIRCUIT

A spectacular circular, day-long driving route runs beside one of Norway's loveliest fjords, climbs a sizable chunk of the magnificent Sognefjellet National Tourist Route, meanders along a lonely, lightly travelled single-lane road that threads across the heights, then plunges in a knuckle clenching descent, once more to fjord level. The trip can't be done by public transport and cyclists will need to be very fit to attempt it over a few days.

From Sogndal, head out on the Rv55 to the northeast as it hugs, for the most part, lovely Lustrafjord all the way to Skolden (opposite), at the head of the waters. About 5km beyond this tiny settlement, the road starts to seriously twist and climb. You're following an ancient highway where for centuries, when it was no more than a rough track, fish and salt would be hauled up from the coast, to be exchanged for iron, butter and hides from communities deep inland.

At Turtagrø, no more than a cluster of wind-battered shacks, you can continue along the Rv55, which runs alongside Jotunheimen National Park (p184) up and over northern Europe's highest road pass (1434m) and on to Lom (p182).

To return to Sogndal, turn right to leave the Rv55 and head for Årdal. The narrow road, known as Tindevegen, the Route of the Peaks, keeps climbing, just above the tree line, until the pass (1315m) and a toll booth (Nkr50 per vehicle).

Then, it's a plunge down through woods of spindly birch to the emerald green waters of Årdalsvatnet and the undistinguished village of Øvre Årdal. From here, the Rv53 takes you, via the ferry between Fodnes and Mannheller, back to Sogndal.

(admission free; 10am-5pm Jun-Aug) has a collection of 19th- and 20th-century fishing boats and equipment. From here, you can also rent a rowing boat (Nkr50 per hour) to explore the sound.

Kaupanger's main claim for your attention is its impressive **stave church** (adult/child Nkr30/20; 9.30am-5.30pm mid-Jun–mid-Aug). Constructed in 1184, its wonderfully ornate interior is shaped like an upturned Viking ship. The wall paintings feature musical annotation and the Celtic-style chancel arch is unique.

Sleeping & Eating

Kjørnes Camping (☎ 57 67 45 80; www.kjornes.no; per person/site Nkr30/90, cabin Nkr290-600, apt Nkr700; May-Sep) This camp site enjoys a pretty fjord-side setting, 3km from town off the Rv5.

Sogndal Vandrerhjem (☎ 57 62 75 75; sogndal.hostel@vandrerhjem.no; Helgheimsvegen 9-10; dm/s/d with shared bathroom Nkr200/280/550, d with bathroom Nkr650, all incl breakfast; mid-Jun–mid-Aug) This well-equipped, summertime-only HI-affiliated hostel, near the bridge that carries the Rv5, functions as a boarding school during the rest of the year.

Loftesnes Pensjonat (☎ 57 67 15 77; Fjøravegen; s/d/tr Nkr400/600/750) This small place, above the China House restaurant, is great value. Nine of its 12 rooms have complete bathrooms and there are self-catering facilities and a rooftop terrace. If no-one's around, take any room that has its key in the lock and sign the guest register. If no-one has turned up before you leave, pay the restaurant staff downstairs.

Hofslund Fjord Hotel (☎ 57 62 76 00; www.hofslund-hotel.no; s/d/tr Nkr890/1090/1330; P) This venerable 100-bed hotel, approaching its first century, has been run by the same family for four generations. Service is courteous and friendly and it enjoys a wonderful location. Most rooms have a balcony and view of the fjord, a neatly cropped lawn sweeps down to the water, the pool's heated and there are a couple of rowing boats and fishing gear, free on loan to guests.

Norlandia Park Hotel (☎ 57 62 84 00; www.norlandia.no/park; s Nkr915-1075, d Nkr1250-1550) They were still hammering and painting when we called by Sogndal's newest hotel. Its 28 rooms, with their parquet flooring and plasma TV, are particularly large (the smallest measures 31 sq metres) and each comes equipped with fridge, cooker and dishwasher.

In a town with limited gastronomic pleasures, your best bet is **Quality Hotel Sogndal** (☎ 57 62 77 00; Gravensteinsgata 5), which has three restaurants. Both its more intimate **Dr Hagen Café & Bar** (mains Nkr95-275) and main restaurant, Compagniet, have the same short à la carte list while the latter also does a copious dinner buffet (Nkr295) in summer. Its Dolly Dimple's does mainly pizzas, to eat in or take away.

Getting There & Away

Sogndal has Sognefjord's only **airport** (☎ 57 7 26 16) officially called Haukåsen, which has two daily flights to/from Bergen and five to/from Oslo.

Passenger boats connect Sogndal with Balestrand (Nkr140, 45 minutes, once or twice daily) and Bergen (Nkr525, four hours, once daily).

Daily buses run between Sogndal and Kaupanger (Nkr33, 20 minutes, up to eight), Fjærland (Nkr67, 30 minutes, three to six) and Balestrand (Nkr86, 1¼ hours, three). Twice daily buses (mid-June to late August) head northeast past Jotunheimen National Park to Lom (3¼ hours) and Otta (4¼ hours).

URNES & SOLVORN

The **stave church** (adult/child Nkr40/25; 10.30am-.30pm early Jun-Aug) at Urnes is famed for its unique and elaborate wooden carvings – animals locked in struggle, stylised intertwined bodies and abstract motifs.

This lovely structure, a Unesco's World Heritage Site, gazes out over Lustrafjord. Built in the 1130s, it has undergone several alterations through the ages; it's likely that much of the rich carving on its gables, pillars and door frames were transferred from an 11th-century building that previously stood here.

A car and passenger ferry (adult/child/car Nkr27/13/73, 20 minutes) shuttles roughly every hour between Solvorn and Urnes; many drivers prefer to leave their vehicles on the Solvorn bank. From the Urnes ferry landing, it's a 1km uphill walk to the stave church.

Solvorn has a splendid accommodation option.

our pick **Eplet** (☎ 41 64 94 69; www.eplet.net; camping per person Nkr80, dm Nkr120, d Nkr500; 💻) is run by Trond Erik Eplet, himself an environmental geologist, seasoned traveller, climber and seriously long-distance cyclist. It has magnificent views of Lustrafjord. Below are line upon line of raspberry bushes and apple trees (you won't get scurvy here), children can feed the lambs in season and there are self-catering facilities and a good library too. Not to speak of what must be the world's mini-est minigolf course on the handkerchief of a lawn. There are free bikes for guest use – ideal for slipping onto the ferry and exploring Urnes and Lustrafjord's east bank.

SKJOLDEN

pop 500

Skjolden, at the limit of Lustrafjord, is a charming little village. In Fjordstova, you'll find most that matters tucked under one roof: the **tourist office** (☎ 97 60 04 43; www.skjolden.com; 11am-7pm Jul–mid-Aug, 2-7pm Jun & late Aug), which has internet access (per 30 minutes Nkr25), a café, a swimming pool and even a climbing wall. The bit of industrial-looking junk on display outside is a turbine from the Norsk hydropower station.

For land- or water-based exercise, you can hire bicycles (Nkr75/100 per half/full day) and kayaks (Nkr75/150 per half/full day) at the tourist office, which can also supply you with a brochure (Nkr20) on signed walks in the area.

About 2km east of Skjolden, the Rv55 runs beside the lovely turquoise glacial lake **Eidsvatnet**. **Mørkridsdalen**, the valley that runs north of the village makes for some excellent hiking.

A little further along the Rv55, 3km from Skjolden, **Vassbakken Kro & Camping** (☎ 57 68 61 88; www.skjolden.com/vassbakken; per person/site Nkr20/100, 2-/4-bed cabins with outdoor bathroom Nkr380/480, 5-bed cabin Nkr770, May-Sep) is a smallish camp site, set beneath a surging waterfall.

Bus 153 connects Skjolden with Sogndal (Nkr100, 1¼ hours) and Fortun (Nkr27, 10 minutes) two to five times daily.

EXTREME SWIMMING

Most people think thrice before dipping even a toe into the cold waters of Sognefjord. Not so Lewis Pugh, an Anglo-South African lawyer, who, in 2004, plunged into the 6°C briney off Skjolden, then swam the entire length of Europe's longest fjord – all 204km of it. Gradually losing the extra 10kg that he'd gained as protection against the cold, he ploughed forward for five hours each and every day for three weeks. Three years later, he undertook what is, by comparison and strictly in terms of distance, a mere drop in the ocean – a 1km swim along a cleft in the ice at the geographic North Pole. Specialising in extreme swims, he uses the publicity his watery escapades generate to highlight the threat to the fragile ocean environment from global warming.

If you're heading north on Rv55, check your fuel gauge; Skjolden's petrol stations are the last for 77km.

JOSTEDALSBREEN

For years mighty Jostedalsbreen, many-tongued and mainland Europe's largest icecap, crept counter-current, still slowly advancing while most glaciers elsewhere in the world were retreating as a result, most scientists agree, of global warming. Now Jostedalsbreen herself has succumbed and, since 2006, has been withdrawing. Briksdalsbreen, which attracts day visitors by the coachload, is cracking and fissuring and, as always, you shouldn't venture onto the ice anywhere without a qualified guide.

With an area of 487 sq km and in places 600m thick, Jostedalsbreen rules over the highlands of Sogn og Fjordane county. The main icecap and several outliers are protected as the Jostedalsbreen National Park (for details of the park information centre, see p250).

The best hiking map for the region is Statens Kartverk's *Jostedalsbreen Turkart* at 1:100,000. The *Jostedalsbreen Glacier Walks* brochure, available at tourist offices and many other venues, gives a comprehensive list of glacier walks, their levels and guiding companies.

For more details on the gateway towns of Skei, Stryn, Olden and Loen, see p249.

FJÆRLAND

pop 300

The village of Fjærland (also called Mundal), at the head of scenic Fjærlandsfjorden, pulls in as many as 300,000 visitors each year. Most come to experience its pair of particularly accessible glacial tongues, Supphellebreen and Bøyabreen. Others come to bookworm. This tiny place, known as the 'Book Town' of Norway (www.bokbyen.no), is a bibliophile's nirvana, with a dozen shops selling a wide range of used books, mostly in Norwegian but with lots in English and other European languages. Its annual book fair, held on the Saturday nearest 21 June, attracts booksellers and antiquarians from around the country.

The village leaps to life in early May, when the ferry again runs and virtually hibernates from October onwards. Its **tourist office** (☎ 57 69 32 33; www.fjaerland.org; 10am-6pm May-Sep) is within the Bok & Bilde bookshop on the main street, 300m from the ferry point. It displays full list of accommodation options, togethe with prices, on the main door.

Sights & Activities

SUPPHELLEBREEN & BØYABREEN

You can drive to within 300m of th Supphellebreen glacier, then walk right u and touch the ice. Ice blocks from here wer used as podiums at the 1994 Winter Olympic in Lillehammer.

At blue, creaking Bøyabreen, more spectac ular than Supphellebreen, its brother over th hill, you might happen upon glacial calvin as a hunk tumbles into the meltwater lagoo beneath the glacier tongue.

NORWEGIAN GLACIER MUSEUM

For the story on flowing ice and how it ha sculpted the Norwegian landscape, visit thi superbly executed **museum** (Norsk Bremuseum ☎ 57 69 32 88; adult/child Nkr95/45; 9am-7pm Jun Aug, 10am-4pm Apr, May, Sep & Oct), 3km inland fron the ferry jetty.

The hands-on exhibits will delight children You can learn how fjords are formed, see a excellent 20-minute multiscreen audiovisua presentation on Jostedalsbreen (so impressiv that audiences often break into spontaneou applause at the end), wind your way through tunnel that penetrates the mock-ice and eve see the tusk of a Siberian woolly mammoth which met an icy demise 30,000 years ago There's also an exhibit on the 5000-year-ol 'Ice Man' corpse, which was found on th Austrian-Italian border in 1991.

The newest of the museum's themes is it multimedia (sounds, smoke, rumblings un derfoot and more) exhibition, *Our Fragil Planet*. It leads you from the earth's crea tion via a tertiary-era forest and the last ic age to the present – and on to the conse quences of our contemporary overuse of th world's resources. After a doomsday visua hypothesis, it ends on a note of qualifie optimism as the breathy voice of Sir Davi Attenborough urges responsible, personal ac tion to save our planet. In synopsis, it sound preachy. On the spot, it's stimulating an thought provoking.

BOOK BROWSING

As you saunter through this one-street vil lage, pause to browse a selection of its doze bookshops. Tusand og Ei Natt (Thousan

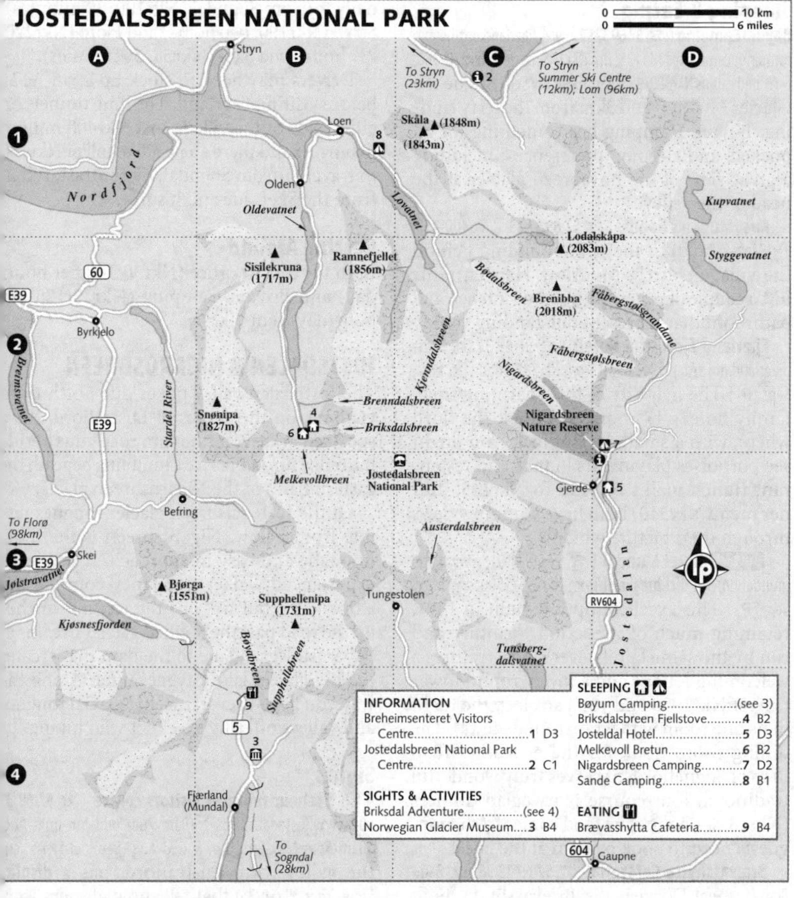

nd One Nights), the bookshop nearest to the erry jetty, has a 15m-long row, stacked seven helves high, of novels in English. If thrillers re your bedtime frisson, call by Onkel Mikkel Bokkafe, within Hotel Mundal.

HIKING

The tourist office's free leaflet, *Escape the Asphalt,* lists 13 walking routes, varying from 0 minutes to three hours. Supplement this with *Turkart Fjærland* (Nkr60) at 1:50,000, which comes complete with route descriptions and trails indicated, pull on your boots nd you're away. Most walks follow routes he local shepherds would have used until quite recently to lead their flocks to higher ummer pastures. After you complete four, the local sports association will register your achievement and issue a diploma, available through the tourist office!

Tours

A bus meets the twice-daily ferry from Balestrand, leaving the quayside at 9.35am (Nkr140) and 1.20pm (Nkr110). Both tours stop en route to allow visits to the interactive Glacier Museum (free with tour) and Bøyabreen glacier. The earlier tour also takes in the Supphellebreen glacier and leaves plenty of bookshop-browsing time before you catch the ferry back to Balestrand. Alternatively, a taxi from the Fjærland dock to Bøyabreen, with waiting time, costs about Nkr550 return.

Sleeping & Eating

Bøyum Camping (☎ 57 69 32 52; www.fjaerland.org/boyum camping; camp sites Nkr135, dm Nkr135, basic d Nkr270-340, 6-/8-bed cabins Nkr680/950; Jun-early Sep) Beside the Glacier Museum and 3km from the ferry landing, Bøyum Camping has something for all pockets and sleeping preferences, including a great view of the Bøyabreen glacier at the head of the valley.

Mrs Haugen's Rooms (☎ 57 69 32 43; d Nkr400-450; May–mid-Oct) In the white building behind the village church, Ms Alma Haugen rents just a couple of rooms with shared kitchen and bathroom that represent outstanding value.

Fjærland Fjordstue Hotell (☎ 57 69 32 00; www.fjaerland.no; s/d incl breakfast from Nkr785/1050; May-Sep; P) The majority of this charming small family hotel's 17 rooms overlook the fjord where, with a smattering of luck, you might see porpoises playing. Its lounge and restaurant (lunch mains Nkr130 to Nkr145, dinner menu Nkr340) both have stunning views through their picture windows.

our pick **Hotel Mundal** (☎ 57 69 31 01; www.hotelmundal.no; s/d incl breakfast from Nkr995/1500; May-Sep; P) This excellent option, built in 1891, retaining much of its period furniture and run by the same family ever since, features a welcoming lounge and a lovely round tower (invest Nkr1950 and you can sleep the night in its one room with wraparound views). The dining room (look for the evocative 1898 map of Sognefjorden) serves truly wonderful traditional four-course Norwegian dinners (Nkr485). Because the food comes fresh, non-guests need to book by 6pm at the latest.

Brævasshytta Cafeteria (☎ 57 69 32 96; 8am-8pm May-Sep) Do visit the Brævasshytta, built into the moraine of Bøyabreen's latest major advance, even if it's only for a cup of coffee. With the glacier right there and in your face, it's like eating in an IMAX cinema, but for real.

There's also a good cafeteria at the glacier museum.

Getting There & Away

Ferries run twice daily between Balestrand and Fjærland (Nkr175/263 one way/return, 1¼ hours) from May to September. The 9.40am departure connects in Balestrand with the boat to Flåm and the 3.25pm links with the Bergen-bound ferry.

Buses bypass the village and stop on the Rv5 near the glacier museum. Three to six run daily to/from Sogndal (Nkr100, 30 minutes), Stryn (Nkr190, two hours) and Florø (Nkr220, 2¾ hours) via Skei (Nkr58, 30 minutes).

Drivers may need to stock up at an ATM before visiting Fjærland. The long tunnels on either side of the village cost Nkr400 million to burrow and there's a punitive toll of Nkr160 to travel to/from Sogndal; by contrast, roll in from the Skei side and it's free.

Getting Around

Both the tourist office (Nkr30/140 per hour/day) and Bøyum Camping (Nkr25/125 per hour/day) rent bikes.

JOSTEDALEN & NIGARDSBREEN

The Jostedalen valley pokes due north from Gaupne, on the shores of Lustrafjord. It's a spectacular drive as the slim road runs beside the milky turquoise river, tumbling beneath the eastern flank of the Nigardsbreen glacier.

Of the Jostedalsbreen glacier tongues visible from below, Nigardsbreen is the most dramatic and easy to approach. If you're an experienced walker and fancy communing alone with (but not on) the ice, nip further up the road past the braided glacial streams at Fåbergstølsgrandane to the dam that creates the big glacial lake, Styggevatnet. Along the way you'll find several scenic glacial tongues and valleys offering excellent wild hiking.

Sights

The **Breheimsenteret visitors centre** (☎ 57 68 32 50; www.jostedal.com; 9am-7pm mid-Jun–mid-Aug, 10am-5pm May–mid-Jun & mid-Aug–Sep), 34km up the valley from Lustrafjord, has a **display** (adult/child Nkr50/35) that tells how glaciers were formed and how they sculpt the landscape. There's also a 20-minute film on the area and an exhibit on the girl Jostedalsrypa, the only villager to survive the Black Death. It also carries a worthwhile free pamphlet, *Walking in Jostedal,* that describes five short (one- to 2½-hour) walks.

Activities

You can book at the visitors centre for all these outfits.

Jostedalen Breførarlag (☎ 57 68 31 11; www.bfl.no) does several guided glacier walks. Easiest is the family walk to the glacier snout and briefly along its tongue (around one hour on the ice; adult/child Nkr170/80). Fees for the two-hour (Nkr370), three-hour (Nkr450) and five-hour

Nkr650) walks on the ice include the brief oat trip across Nigardsvatnet lake.

For a truly original glacial perspective, sign n for a guided kayak outing with **Ice Troll** (☎ 57 68 32 50; www.icetroll.com). Walking and kayaking tours of seven to eight hours (Nkr750), uitable for first-timers as well as the more xperienced, take you where those without addles never get. It also does overnight orties (Nkr1200).

Recently established **Leirdalen Bre og Juv** (Leirdal lacier & Canyon; ☎ 470 27 878; www.breogjuv.no) offers rout fishing (Nkr500), canyon clambering Nkr450) and day glacier hikes (Nkr550).

With **Moreld** (☎ 404 67 100; www.moreld.net) you an surge down the swift-flowing Jostedalen iver on one of their twice daily rafting rips (Nkr500).

Less strenuously, take a five-hour pony trip Nkr500) with **Raudskarvfjellet Turriding** (☎ 57 8 32 50; www.jostedal-horseguiding.no).

leeping & Eating

igardsbreen Camping (☎ 57 68 31 35; tent/caravan ites Nkr100/120, cabins Nkr350; late May-Sep) There's asic camping and cabins, near the entrance o the toll road leading to the glacier, 400m orth of the visitors centre.

Jostedal Hotel (☎ 57 68 31 19; www.jostedalhotel.no; /d incl breakfast Nkr700/950;) Just 2.5km south f the visitors centre, this friendly place has een run by the same family for three generations. Meat, milk and vegetables for the estaurant come, wherever possible, from he family farm. There are also family rooms Nkr1050) with self-catering facilities that can ccommodate up to five guests.

For a great view, enjoy a coffee or snack in he small café of the visitors centre.

ietting There & Around

eave the Rv55 Sognefjellet Road at Gaupne nd head north up Jostedal along the Rv604.

From late June to early September, ostedalsbrebussen (No 160) runs between ogndal (with connections from Flåm, alestrand and Lærdal) and the foot of the Nigardsbreen glacier, leaving at 8.45am and etting out on the return journey at 4.50pm.

From the visitors centre, a 3.5km-long toll oad (Nkr25 per vehicle) or a pleasant walk vith interpretive panels leads to the car park at Nigardsvatnet, the lagoon at the glacial snout. rom mid-June to August, a ferry shuttles over he lagoon to the glacier face (Nkr30 return).

BRIKSDALSBREEN

From the small town of Olden (p249) at the eastern end of Nordfjord, a scenic road leads 23km up Oldedalen past Brenndalsbreen, and from there on to the twin glacial tongues of Melkevollbreen and Briksdalsbreen. The more easily accessible, Briksdalsbreen, attracts hordes of tour buses. It's a temperamental glacier; in 1997 the tongue licked to its furthest point for around 70 years, then subsequently retreated by around 500m. Then, in 2005, the reaches where glacier walkers would clamber and stride cracked and splintered. For the moment, there are no guided hikes on Briksdalsbreen but she's a fickle creature and this may change.

Activities

Two companies offer a range of outdoor activities in Oldedalen and neighbouring valleys.

Briksdal Adventure (☎ 57 87 68 00; www.briksdal-adventure.com), also known as Briksdal Breføring, is based at Briksdalsbre Fjellstove, the end of the blacktop road. **Olden Activ** (☎ 57 87 38 88; www.oldenaktiv.no), which operates from the Melkevoll Bretun camp site, is a five-minute walk down the hill. Each organises a good range of treks, glacier hikes and climbs (that don't demand previous experience) in Oldendalen and adjacent valleys.

Both, for example, offer guided glacier walking on Brenndalsbreen (Nkr600), the next glacial tongue north of Briksdalsbreen. Treks last between six and seven hours, including around 2½ hours on the ice and depart daily between June and August.

It's about a 5km-return walk to the Briksdal glacier face, either up the steepish path or along the longer, gentler cart track. Alas, the traditional pony-carts that plied the route for over 100 years no longer transport visitors but **Oldedalen Skyss** (☎ 57 87 68 05) has 'troll cars', vehicles like giant golfing carts (Nkr170 per person). From their turnaround point, there's still a 15-minute hike on a rough path to see the ice. To breathe up close in the glacier's face, take a guided trip in an inflatable dinghy. Dinghies, operated by Briksdal Adventure, depart hourly in summer. We strongly recommend advance reservation for both troll cars and dinghies as places are often snapped up by tour groups.

The recently erected **activity tower** opposite Briksdalsbre Fjellstove offers a range of climbing activities for all ages.

Sleeping & Eating

our pick **Melkevoll Bretun** (☎ 57 87 38 64; www.melkevoll.no; per person/site Nkr40/90, dm Nkr90, basic cabins Nkr420, 6-bed fully equipped cabins Nkr750) You'll find accommodation for all pockets and gorgeous views whichever way you turn here. Look south and the Melkevollbreen glacier is sticking its tongue out towards you, spin west and the long, slim Volefossen waterfall cascades, turn north and the long reach of Oldevatnet lake shimmers, while eastwards, the Briksdalsbreen glacier blocks the horizon. There's a gorgeous green camp site with stacks of space between pitches. The larger cabins are particularly well furnished. For budget sleeping with attitude, spread your sleeping bag in the 'stone-age cave' (Nkr110).

Briksdalsbre Fjellstove (☎ 57 87 68 00; www.briksdalsbre.no; s/d Nkr650/900, 4-bed cabin Nkr800) This cosy mountain lodge run by Briksdal Adventure (see p247) has six comfortable rooms and a café-restaurant serving delicacies such as trout and reindeer.

Getting There & Away

Between June and August, a bus leaves Stryn for Briksdal (Nkr64, one hour) at 9.30am, calling by Loen and Olden. The return bus leaves Briksdal at 1.40pm. There's also a second departure at 3.45pm on weekdays from Stryn to Melkevoll Bretun.

If you park for the day at Melkevoll Bretun (Nkr40), there's a free sauna thrown in after your hike.

KJENNDALSBREEN & BØDALSBREEN

Lovely Kjenndalsbreen is 17km up Lodalen from the Nordfjord village of Loen (opposite). The least visited of the four best-known glacial tongues, it vies with Nigardsbreen for the most beautiful approach as you run parallel to the turquoise glacial lake of Lovatnet. Bødalsbreen, in a nearby side valley, provides good hiking possibilities.

Briksdal Adventure (☎ 57 87 68 00; www.briksdal-adventure.com; see p247) has on offer five- to six-hour guided glacier walks (your crampons crunch the ice for about half this time) on Bødalsbreen (Nkr600). It and **Olden Activ** (☎ 57 87 38 88; www.oldenaktiv.no; see p247) offer considerably more demanding 12-hour treks (Nkr750) to 2083m-high Lodalskåpa, the highest point on the Jostedal glacier. Tours set out from Sande camp site.

As you ascend the valley, notice the huge blocks of stone that dislodged from Ramnefjell and crashed down into the lake in 1905, 1936 and 1950 and prepare to duck; the first wave killed 63 people and deposited the lake steamer 400m inland, the second killed 72, while the third just left a bigger scar on the mountain. These are referred to as the Lovatnet disasters.

Sleeping

Sande Camping (☎ 57 87 45 90; www.sande-camping.no; Loen; camp sites Nkr110, 2-/4-bed cabin Nkr280/420, 4-/6-bed apt Nkr560/890) You could spend an active day or two in the lovely environs of Sande Camping near the northern end of Lovatnet, with its small restaurant, free sauna, rowing boats (Nkr85/270 per hour/day), canoes (Nkr30/100) and plenty of walking possibilities.

Getting There & Away

A wonderful way to approach Kjenndalsbreen is on the *Kjendal*, a boat that chugs up Lovatnet from Sande (adult/child under 10 years return Nkr180/free). The trip includes a return bus between Kjenndalstova Café, at the southern end of the lake, and the glacier car park. From here, it's a 2km walk to the glacier face. From June to August, the boat leaves Sande at 10.30am and Kjenndalstova at 1.30pm several days per week. For current sailings, ask at the Stryn tourist office or **Hotel Alexandra** (☎ 57 87 50 50) in Loen.

STRYN SUMMER SKI CENTRE

Nowhere near the town of Stryn, despite its name, this **ski centre** (Sommerskisenter; ☎ 9 25 83 33; www.strynefjellet.com; Videdalen; 10am-4pm Jun-Aug) is in fact on the Tystigen outlier of Jostedalsbreen, at its northernmost point. Here is Norway's most extensive and best known summer skiing, and most of those photos of bikini-clad skiers you see around were snapped here. There are six red runs, one blue and a black. The longest alpine run extends for 2100m with a drop of 530m and there are also 10km of cross-country ski tracks.

A ski bus runs from Stryn (Nkr150 return, one hour) at 9.15am and returns from the ski centre at 4.15pm, roughly between mid-June and mid-July, depending upon snow conditions. Drivers will enjoy the scenic Gamle Strynefjellsvegen, the old road that connects Grotli with Videsæter. Pick up a free leaflet at Stryn tourist office.

SOGNEFJORDEN TO NORDFJORD

For most travellers the 100km-long Nordfjord is but a stepping stone between Sognefjorden and Geirangerfjorden. These two popular fjords are linked by a road that winds around the head of Nordfjord past the villages of Byrkjelo, Olden and Loen to the larger town of Stryn. Both Olden and Loen make good bases for visiting the spectacular Briksdalsbreen and Kjenndalbreen glaciers (see p247).

SKEI

pop 400

The inland village of Skei lies near the head of lake Jølstravatnet at the junction of Rv5 and the E39. **Astruptunet museum** (☎ 57 72 67 82; adult/child Nkr40/free; 11am-4pm mid-May–mid-Jun & mid-Aug–late Sep, 10am-6pm mid-Jun–mid-Aug), 15km west of the village on the south side of the lake, is the former home of artist Nicolai Astrup (1880–1928) and includes a gallery plus open-air exhibits.

Jølster Rafting (☎ 90 06 70 70; www.jolster-rafting.no) does white-water rafting on the Stardal and Jølstra rivers. Shorter trips range from Nkr590 to Nkr750 while one- and two-day excursions are both Nkr1190.

Sporty **Skei Hotel** (☎ 57 72 78 00; www.skeihotel.no; s/d from Nkr1065/1510; P) has an indoor heated swimming pool, sauna, Jacuzzi, solarium, rowing boat (per hour Nkr25), cycles (per hour Nkr10) – and even a tennis court. Unappealing from the outside, it's much more attractive within and has a cosy bar and decent restaurant.

For good-value meals and snacks, drop into the cafeteria of **Audhild Vikens Vevstove** (☎ 57 72 81 25; pizza Nkr45, mains around Nkr100; 9am-5pm), Norway's largest store with tax-free facilities. Less than 100m from the road junction, it's a veritable emporium of souvenirs, clothing and Christmas products, sold year-round.

Many long-distance buses connect at Skei, including services to Fjærland (Nkr58, 30 minutes), Sogndal (Nkr115, 1¼ hours), Stryn (Nkr145, 1½ hours), Ålesund (Nkr340, six hours), Florø (Nkr180, two hours) and Bergen (Nkr335, 5¼ hours).

OLDEN

pop 550

Olden serves as a Jostedalsbreen gateway to Briksdalsbreen (p247) and has a seasonal **tourist office** (☎ 57 87 31 26; 11am-5pm mid-Jun–mid-Aug).

Galleri Cylindra (☎ 91 56 46 95; www.cylindra.net; May-Aug), opposite the cruise boat jetty, displays the works of Peter Opsvik, artist and industrial designer – photography, painting and sensuously rounded works in wood were executed by master craftsman Kjellbjørn Tusvik.

If you fancy a little fishing, the **Isabella** (☎ 91 35 10 42 or reserve via Olden or Stryn Tourist Office) does two- to three-hour trips (per person including gear Nkr200), leaving Olden marina at 4pm and 7.30pm, Monday to Friday.

For walks you can do in and around the valley, pick up the map *Olden og Oldendalen* (1:50,000), which indicates and describes 15 signed trails.

Sleeping & Eating

There are around 10 camp sites in the area, most of them along the route to Briksdalsbreen and several in stunningly pretty sites.

The automatic swing doors that purr open when you're still a couple of metres from the threshold of **Olden Fjordhotel** (☎ 57 87 34 00; www.olden-hotel.no; s Nkr970-1120, d Nkr1340-1640, all incl breakfast; May-Sep) are symptomatic of the warm welcome the Fjordhotel imparts. All of its comfortable rooms have views of the fjord, nearly all have balconies and the hotel does a fine Norwegian buffet dinner (Nkr385).

LOEN

pop 400

Loen, at the mouth of dramatic Lodalen, is, like Olden, a gateway to Jostedalsbreen, with a road service to the spectacular Bødalen and Kjenndalen glacial tongues (see opposite).

Like Olden too, it makes a good base for hikers. Arm yourself with *Walking in Loen & Lodalen* at 1:50,000, which describes 20 day walks. One great, though strenuous five- to six-hour hike leads to the Skålatårnet tower, near the 1843m-high summit of Skåla. The route begins near Tjugen farm, north of the river and immediately east of Loen.

Sleeping & Eating

Lo-Vik Camping (☎ 57 87 76 19; fax 57 87 78 11; per person/site Nkr25/110, 4-bed cabins with outdoors bathroom Nkr400, with bathroom Nkr600-950; ⏲ May-Sep) Install yourself at the furthest end, beside the fjord, where there's a peaceful green area, well away from the road and its traffic.

Hotel Loenfjord (☎ 57 87 50 00; www.loenfjord.no in Norwegian; s/d incl breakfast Nkr905/1370; P) The Loenfjord offers waterside accommodation that's a little less expensive than the Alexandra and altogether gentler on the eye. Less crowded, it offers a boat trip on Lovatnet and bicycle hire so you can really get away.

Hotel Alexandra (☎ 57 87 50 00; www.alexandra.no; s/d incl breakfast from Nkr1105/1710; P 💻) Loen's undisputed centre of action is as much a holiday centre as hotel and dominates tourism in the valley. It offers restaurants, bars, a nightclub, swimming pools (both indoors and open), a spa and fitness centre, a tennis court and marina. Although run as a family hotel since 1884, its current external architecture approaches the eyesore level. From the hotel you can book the Lovatnet boat, bicycles and other Jostedalsbreen excursions.

STRYN

pop 1700

The small town of Stryn, de facto capital of upper Nordfjord, is something of a sprawl. The helpful **tourist office** (☎ 57 87 40 40; www.nordfjord.no; ⏲ 8.30am-8pm Jul, 8.30am-6pm Jun & Aug, 8.30am-3.30pm Mon-Fri rest-of-year) is two blocks south of Tonningsgata, the main drag. It can arrange accommodation, charges Nkr1 per minute for internet access (wifi for Nkr40 per hour) and rents mountain bikes (Nkr50/190 per hour/day). Its booklet, *Guide for Stryn,* (Nkr10) includes local hikes. For more details, invest Nkr30 in *Kart over Fjallturar I Stryn*. This map of mountain walks in the Stryn region at a scale of 1:50,000 features a whole holiday's worth of hiking trails.

Sights & Activities

The **Jostedalsbreen National Park Centre** (Jostedalsbreen Nasjonalparksenter; ☎ 57 87 72 00; www.jostedalsbre.no; adult/child Nkr60/30; ⏲ 10am-4pm, to 6pm May-Aug) is at Oppstryn, 15km east of Stryn. It has glacier-oriented exhibits, a unique garden with 325 species of endemic vegetation and a lively audiovisual presentation. For good measure, it also covers avalanches, local minerals and meteorites and has a section on the Lovatnet disasters (see p248).

Sleeping

Stryn Camping (☎ 57 87 11 36; www.stryn-camping.no in Norwegian; Bøavegen 6; tent/caravan sites Nkr150/200, 4-bed cabin with outdoor bathroom Nkr350, 6-bed cabin Nkr890-1090; ⏲ year-round) The facilities are well maintained at trim Stryn Camping, at the eastern end of town and just two blocks uphill from the main street.

Stryn Vandrerhjem (☎ 57 87 11 06; Geilevegen 14; stryn.hostel@vandrerhjem.no; dm/s/d incl breakfast Nkr245/400/530; ⏲ late May–mid-Sep) This friendly HI-affiliated hostel, on the hillside and 2km by road from town, was once a Nazi military barracks.

our pick Visnes Hotel (☎ 57 87 10 87; www.visnes.no; Prestestegen 1; s Nkr650-925, d Nkr1150-1495 ⏲ mid-May–Sep) The Visnes, tautly run by the same family for six generations, occupies two magnificent listed properties, each with its own character. Most rooms are in the larger building, constructed in 1850. Higher room rates are for stunning fjord views and there are also a couple of large family rooms (Nkr1750). To feel like royalty, request a room in the smaller 1890 'dragon style' building that was occupied by King Rana V of Thailand during his 1908 tour, or the one where King Oscar of Sweden and Norway rested his head in 1913.

Stryn Hotel (☎ 57 87 07 00; www.strynhotel.no Visnesvegen 1; s/d Nkr995/1250; P 💻) Should the Visnes be full the Stryn, in the town itself and overlooking the fjord, is a decent alternative with a good restaurant.

Eating & Drinking

For wholesome, bog-standard eating, choose the cafeteria of the **Coop supermarket** (cnr Tonningsgata & Tinggata) or **Kafe Hjorten** (Tinggata), the café attached to the town cultural centre.

Stryn Vertshus (☎ 57 87 05 30; Tonningsgata 19 ⏲ 10am-4.30pm Mon-Sat; 💻) Both inside and on its flower-bedecked terrace, the Stryn Tavern serves tasty snacks and offers free wi-fi to customers.

Bryggja (☎ 90 16 81 34; Perhusvegen 11; mains Nkr165-235; ⏲ 2pm-midnight Jun-Sep) Dine on the outside terrace of this recently opened fish restaurant or simply pop in for a drink and savour its gorgeous riverside location. If it rains, the staff simply pull over the sail-shaped cover. Decorated in nautical style, it's an intimate place (there are only 30 seats) so you'll need to reserve.

Viknes Hotel restaurant (☎ 57 87 10 87; Prestestegen 1; menus Nkr350-450, mains Nkr195-235; 🕑 7-11pm) In the larger building of the hotel, it serves excellent gourmet food.

Base Camp (☎ 57 87 23 83; Tonningsgata 31) Also on the main street, Stryn's most popular bar sometimes operates as a disco too.

Getting There & Away

Stryn lies on the Nor-Way Bussekspress routes between Oslo (Nkr570, 8½ hours, three daily) and Måløy (Nkr180, two hours); Ålesund (Nkr235, 3¾ hours, two to three daily) and Bergen (Nkr425, six hours, four to six daily); and Bergen and Trondheim (Nkr530, 7½ hours, twice daily). Bergen-bound buses call in at Loen (Nkr29, 10 minutes) and Olden (Nkr38, 15 minutes). The Ålesund route passes Hellesylt (Nkr95, one hour), from where the ferry runs to Geiranger.

NORDFJORDEID

Above the village of Nordfjordeid, midway between Stryn and Måløy, are the stables of the **Norsk Fjordhestsenter** (☎ 57 86 48 00; www.norsk-fjordhestsenter.no), which specialises in rearing the stocky, handsome Norwegian fjord ponies with their bristle-stiff, Mohican manes and creamy-caramel hides. If you want a ride (Nkr250 for the first hour, Nkr100 for subsequent hours), do reserve since the ponies are often in demand for school groups and summer camps.

> **THE FLEETING HERRING**
>
> Florø, founded in 1860 as a herring port, prospered for a couple of decades from 'fishy silver'. But then the overfished shoals got wise, survivors simply swam away and Florø lost its prime industry. After a near moratorium on commercial fishing during WWII, the seas again glinted silver. But humankind is a slow learner, the seas were once again overexploited and a couple of decades later, the very last herring was hauled in, while the smarter survivors swam away to the relative sanctuary of the Barents Sea. Half a century later, after decades of strict control and limited fishing, herring stocks are almost back to the level of the 1950s.

FLORØ

pop 8300

Florø, Norway's westernmost town, is a pleasant if unexciting little place whose coat of arms features, appropriately, three herrings rampant.

Nowadays, wealth comes from the black gold of the oil industry. The large Fjord Base, just northeast of town, employs around 400 workers and serves the giant Snorreankeret offshore oil field. Florø is also enriched by fish farming, shipbuilding – and the return of the herring, the town's original raison d'être.

For a scenic overview, it's an easy 10-minute climb up the Storåsen hill from the Florø Ungdomsskule on Havrenesveien.

Information

Laundrette (Marina) Opposite Quality Hotel.
Library (Markegata 51; 🕑 core hrs 11am-3pm Mon-Fri) Has free internet access.
Tourist office (☎ 57 74 75 05; www.vestkysten.no; Strandgata 30; 🕑 8am-6pm Mon-Fri, 10am-4pm Sat, noon-4pm Sun mid-Jun–mid-Aug; 10am-2pm Mon-Fri rest-of-year)

Sights

SOGN OG FJORDANE COASTAL MUSEUM

The two main buildings of the **Kystmuseet** (☎ 57 74 22 33; Brendøyvegen; adult/child Nkr40/free; 🕑 11am-6pm Mon-Fri, noon-4pm Sat & Sun mid-Jun–Aug, 10am-3pm Mon-Fri, noon-3pm Sun Sep–mid-Jun) are chock-full of fishing exhibits and there's a model 1900 fishing family's home too. Also within the complex are several old warehouse buildings, moved from Florø and Måløy, and an old herring salt house. On a more contemporary theme, the Snorreankeret oil platform display illustrates the history, exploration and exploitation of the North Sea oil and gas fields.

THE OLD QUARTER

On and around Strandgata, the main street, the most significant 19th-century timbered houses are well signed and documented in both Norwegian and English.

OFFSHORE ISLANDS

Local ferries connect the mainland to the islands of Kinn, Svanøy, Batalden, Askrova and Tansøy from Fugleskjærskaia Quay. Schedules are intermittent and complicated; check for current information with the tourist office, which can reserve ferries and also advise on island accommodation.

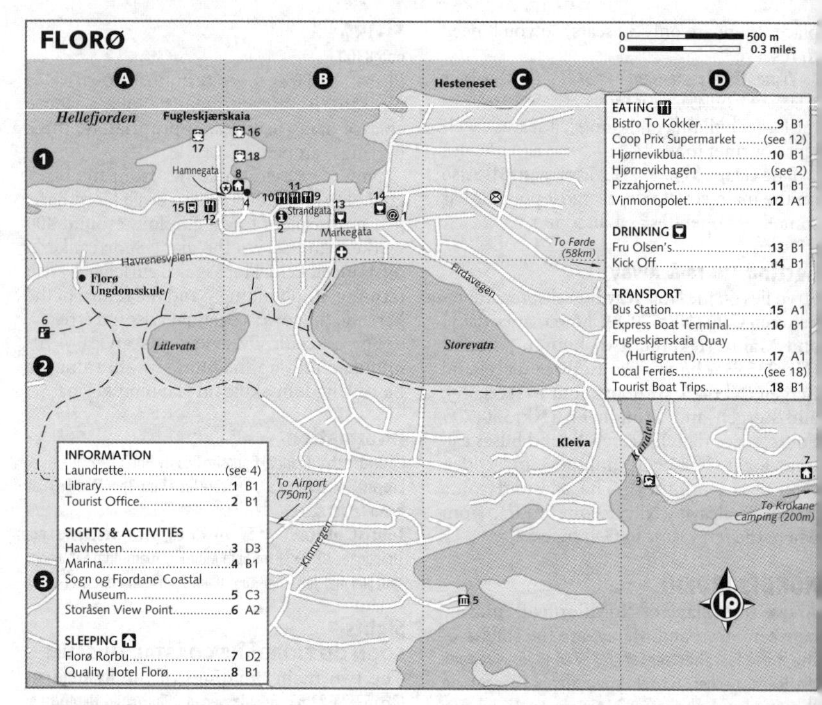

Kinn has a beautifully restored 12th-century **church**, believed to have been built by British Celts sheltering from religious persecution. On the second or third weekend in June, it's the site of the Kinnespelet pageant, which celebrates the history of the church on the island. Climbers and hikers will savour the dramatic landscapes, particularly the Kinnaklova cleft.

On **Svanøy**, you can hike and pass by the small **deer centre** (☎ 57 75 21 80), where the animals are fed at 11am and 8pm.

On **Batalden**, check out the gallery and small museum at **Batalden Havbu fishing cottages** (☎ 57 74 54 22), where you can overnight in their sensitively restored **cottages** (d Nkr880-940; ⏰ May-Sep).

Askrova has a prehistoric Troll Cave, whose deepest depths have never been explored. The highest point of adjoining **Tansøy**, connected to it by a bridge, at 233m offers great panoramic views over the surrounding archipelago.

Activities

BOATING

Florø Rorbu (opposite) hires motor boats (Nkr200 to Nkr400 per day) and sea kayaks (Nkr200 per day), while Krokane Camping (opposite) rents out rowing boats (Nkr50/100 per three hours/day) and motor boats (from Nkr200/300).

HIKING & CYCLING

The tourist office sells two useful booklets: *Cycling in Flora* (Nkr20) and *On Foot in Flora* (Nkr50).

SWIMMING

If the fjord's too chilly, visit **Havhesten** (☎ 57 75 67 20; adult/student/child Nkr80/65/50; ⏰ core hrs 11am-5pm late Jun–mid-Aug, 10am-8pm rest-of-year). Plunge into one of its three indoor heated pools and savour the fantastic view of the fjord as you bob up, work up a sweat in the gym, then get all aglow in the sauna. Everything, even the view, is included in your admission.

Tours

From late June to mid-August, the tourist office runs a number of tempting tours. On Friday, for example, its Lighthouse Safari (adult/child Nkr350/200 including snack lunch) takes you by boat to the offshore lighthouses at Stabben, Kvanhovden and the remote Ytterøyane (no landing at Ytterøyane, which is a bird sanctuary), passing by a seal colony. Another good option is its guided tour of Kinn (adult/child Nkr203/112), for which visits can be arranged daily.

Sleeping

Krokane Camping (☎ 57 75 22 50; www.krocamp.no; camp sites Nkr100, 2-/4-bed cabin Nkr450-500, 5-/6-bed cabin Nkr580-800; year-round) Krokane Camping occupies a wooded site on a peninsula 2.5km east of town. The shoreside meadow, though a trek to the toilets, is a tent camper's delight.

Florø Rorbu (☎ 57 74 81 00; www.florbu.com; Krokane Kai; 4-bed apt Nkr600-650, 6-bed apt Nkr750-800) These excellent, family-owned, fully furnished flats are right beside a tiny inlet and have their own moorings (you can hire a boat or kayak and putter around the fjord to celebrate sunset).

our pick **Quality Hotel Florø** (☎ 57 75 75 75; www.florahotel.no; Hamnegata 7; s/d Mon-Fri Nkr1390/1690, Sat & Sun Nkr995/1195; P) On the quayside, right beside the marina and constructed in the style of a dockside warehouse (the present banqueting area is a former fish store), this is Florø's best option. Rooms with sea views cost no extra and a couple have 'boat beds', made of recycled rowing boats.

Eating & Drinking

Bistro To Kokker (☎ 57 75 22 33; Strandgata 33; dishes Nkr65-145) This gloomy place where ageing bachelors stare into their cocoa does decent enough fare and portions are large. There's squid, salmon, monkfish and other seafood on the menu or, for more pedestrian palates, it has fish and chips (Nkr50 to Nkr60), burgers (Nkr45 to Nkr105), good salads (Nkr60 to Nkr84) and pizzas (Nkr115) too.

Hjørnevikbua (☎ 57 74 01 22; Strandgata 23; lunch Nkr65-125) The 2nd floor of the Hjørnevikbua pub and restaurant, with its ship-like interior, serves lunch that includes some mean fish soups (Nkr85). You can also eat outdoors on their barge that's moored to the quay, where smokers can puff at will.

Pizzahjornet (☎ 99 47 44 45; Strandgata 25; pizzas Nkr160-180) Pizzahjornet serves up decent pizzas, kebabs and shawarmas, to eat in or take away.

our pick **Hjørnevikhagen** (☎ 57 75 33 28; Strandgata 28; lunch mains Nkr75-100, dinner mains Nkr180-195; Mon-Sat) This recent addition to Florø's very limited dining options has style. Outside on the split-level terracing, furniture is smart, angular, of glass and metal, while the interior has good views of the marina. Dishes are well priced, tasty and attractively presented and it's also the most enticing spot in town for a quiet drink. It's just behind the tourist office.

Bryggekanten (Quality Hotel Florø, Hamnegata 7; mains Nkr195-25) The restaurant at Quality Hotel Florø sources most of its food locally and warrants a visit in its own right.

Vinmonopolet is in the same block as the Coop Prix supermarket, located next to the bus station.

THE WORLD'S LONGEST HERRING TABLE

OK, so the competition may not be all that extensive but a herring table 400m long is an impressive achievement in its own right. Each year, Florø and Haugesund, further down the coast, used to vie with each other for the year's largest and longest spread but, now that Haugesund has retired, there's no longer the same north–south rivalry and Florø has the field to itself.

Every second or third weekend in June, the table is erected in the heart of Florø. Just imagine a standard 400m running track, straightened out and laden with plates of herring, potatoes, bread and drinks, all free of charge, and you've got the scene.

Drinking & Entertainment

Kick Off (☎ 57 74 15 00; Strandgata 58; 3pm-midnight Mon-Thu, noon-midnight or 2.30am Fri-Sun) is, as you'd expect, a sports bar that shows all major football matches. It's also where the young folk of Florø head, drawn by its pool table, darts and massive music collection (make a request and test them out). It serves pizzas and snacks, there's free wi-fi and every Friday and Saturday are disco nights.

Fru Olsen's (☎ 57 74 10 00; Markegata 43), the pub at the Rica Victoria Hotell, is an altogether quieter drinking spot.

Getting There & Away

DAT (www.dat.dk) offers budget flights two to four times daily to/from both Oslo and Bergen from **Florø airport** (☎ 57 74 67 00).

Florø is the first stop on the Hurtigruten coastal ferry as it heads north from Bergen. Northbound, it calls by at about 2am (4.45am

KALVÅG

If you're travelling from Florø to Måløy via Bremanger island, do make the 5km detour from the ferry landing point at Smørhamn to the sensitively preserved fishing village of Kalvåg (population 370). Nowadays it's picture-postcard pretty and there's just one giant fish-processing factory on its outskirts. But at its peak Kalvåg had over 50 herring salt houses that employed a seasonal workforce of around 10,000. You can still visit one or two of them; ask at the friendly quayside **tourist office** (☎ 57 79 37 50; www.visitbremanger.no; ⏰ 10am-6pm Mon-Fri, 10am-4pm Sat, noon-4pm Sun Jul, 9am-3.30pm Mon-Fri rest-of-year), itself once a salt house.

mid-September to mid-April) and southbound, at 7.45am. Stops further north include Måløy, Ålesund and Trondheim.

Express boats call in twice daily on the run between Bergen (Nkr535, 3½ hours) and Måløy (Nkr190, one hour).

Florø is situated at the end of a Nor-Way Bussekspress route from Oslo (Nkr605, 12¼ hours, twice daily) via Stryn.

If you're driving, the most scenic way north to Måløy by road is via Bremanger island.

AROUND FLORØ

Ausevik Rock Carvings

These vivid rock carvings, featuring deer and other motifs from around 1000 BC, are a mere five-minute walk from the Fv611 (about 40 minutes' drive south of Florø). An upgrade, planned for 2008, will allow easier visitor access.

Vingen Petroglyphs

The 1500 early–Stone Age petroglyphs at Vingen, facing the sea from the slopes of Vingenfjellet south of Måløy, are northern Europe's largest concentration. They're thought to be the work of early Stone Age hunters, chipped into the rock between 6000 and 4000 BC. There's no road to the paintings, which are protected, but the Florø tourist office organises a weekly boat (adult/child Nkr270/140), departing from Florø and/or Bremanger between 1 July and mid-August.

MÅLØY

pop 3500

The little fishing town of Måløy, at the mouth of Nordfjord, lies on Vågsøy island. Nestling beneath a pair of rounded hills, for all the world like a pair of giant breasts, it's linked to the mainland by the graceful S-curve Måløybrua bridge.

Though there are no monuments or sights to make you gasp, it's a refreshingly real, alive place – when compared to the tourist toy-towns to its south – where commercial boats ply up and down. Also, Vågsøy island and neighbouring Selje are laced with sea-view hiking routes (pick up the 1:50,000 walking map *Outdoor Pursuits: Selje & Vågsøy Communes*). Three places are well worth a visit: the bizarre seaside rock, **Kannesteinen**, about 10km west of town, rising from the sea like a giant stone mushroom; **Refviksanden**, a 1.4km reach of pure white sand that ranks among Norway's top three finest beaches; and **Kråkenes Lighthouse** (see below), perched precariously on a rock shoulder. Sunny or stormy, it's a romantic spot with stunning views where you can have a meal, enjoy coffee and homemade cakes – and even spend the night.

Måløy's seasonal **tourist office** (☎ 57 84 50 77; Gate 1 No 53; ⏰ 9am-5pm Mon-Fri, 10am-4pm Sat & Sun Jul, 10am-4pm Mon-Sat mid–end Jun & early Aug) is on the main street. It has an internet point (Nkr1 per minute).

Sleeping & Eating

Steinvik Camping (☎ 57 85 10 70; oddbnyg@online.no; per person/site Nkr20/80, 2-bed cabin with toilet Nkr380, 4-bed cabin Nkr550, 4-bed self-catering apt Nkr480-650; ⏰ year-round) The nearest camp site to Måløy has spectacular views over the busy sea lane. To get there, cross the bridge to the east bank, turn right after 2km beside a school and follow the track downhill for 1.2km.

our pick **Kråkenes Lighthouse** (☎ 57 85 55 27; www.krakenesfyr.no; Kråkenes; d with shared bathroom Nkr600-800, with bathroom Nkr1200, 6-bed ste Nkr1900; ⏰ year-round) Take the Rv617 to the very tip of the promontory that runs northwards from Måløy to find this delightful, truly original overnighting option, run to a high standard by an enterprising German couple. You can either stay in the former lighthouse-keeper's house with self-catering facilities or enjoy the splendid top-floor suite, with bathroom, in the lighthouse itself. Meals are also available, if you order in advance. Even if you don't stay, drop by their café (open noon to 6pm mid-June to mid-August) to savour this isolated spot.

Norlandia Måløy Hotel (☎ 57 84 94 00; www norlandia.no; Gate 1 No 25; s/d Nkr825/1090) This large glass-fronted hotel is the centre of most tourist activity in town. Its Aquarius restaurant (open 7pm to 10pm) offers a three-course dinner (Nkr275) and a good à la carte selection.

Stormen Pub (☎ 57 85 11 25; Sjøgata) It's vast and a bit like eating in a station waiting room but this pub at the harbour opposite the Norlandia Måløy hotel lays on decent food and often has dancing on weekend evenings. Dine on its open-air terrace overlooking the sound.

Havfruen Fiskeutsalg (☎ 57 85 23 36; ⏲ 10am-4pm Mon-Fri, 10am-2pm Sat) The Mermaid, beside the express boat jetty, is both a wet fish shop ('Born to fish, forced to work' says the plaque on the wall) and small café, serving rich fish soups (Nkr50 to Nkr65), salmon sandwiches (Nkr25) and other fishy dishes.

Getting There & Away

The express boat from Bergen (Nkr645, 4½ hours) to Selje puts in at Måløy. The northbound Hurtigruten coastal ferry passes at 4.30am daily (7.30am mid-September to mid-April); the southbound one at 5.45am.

Nor-Way Bussekspress runs three times daily to/from Oslo (Nkr643, 11 hours), via Stryn (Nkr180, two hours, up to six buses daily).

SELJE & SELJA ISLAND

pop 700

Few visitors make it to Selje and therein lies the charm of this pleasant village on the western edge of Norway, with its strand of pristine, white beach. Vestkapp, 32km by road from Selje, isn't Norway's westernmost point despite the name but it still provides superb sea views.

Selje's **tourist office** (☎ 57 85 66 06; sunniva1@ start.no; ⏲ 9am-7pm Jul, core hrs 10am-4pm Jun & Aug, 8am-3.30pm Mon-Fri Apr, May & Sep, Mon-Tue Oct-Mar), at the harbour, keeps lists of cabins and apartments in the area and has internet access (Nkr1 per minute).

The haunting ruins of **Selja monastery** and the **church of St Sunniva** on Selja island date from the 11th and 12th centuries, respectively. You can climb the 40m-high tower for a splendid panorama. From mid-June to the end of August, there are one to three daily two-hour guided tours (adult/child Nkr150/75 including return boat trip). Reserve in advance through the tourist office and check the timetable, which may change when the current boatman retires.

The **Selje Hotel** (☎ 57 85 88 80; www.seljehotel.no; s Nkr925-1045, d Nkr1160-1550), a delightful wood and shaped-stone pile right beside the beach, is the village's only hotel. Within it is Spa Thalasso, a health centre with pool, Jacuzzi and a range of relaxing activities and treatments to tone you up – something you might welcome if you've stayed up late to enjoy the hotel's live-music duo.

From Måløy, you have two stunningly attractive ways of arriving – the splendid fjord-side drive along the Rv618 or aboard the twice-daily Nordfjord express boat route (Nkr67, 20 minutes). Local buses also run between Måløy and Selje (Nkr86, one hour) six times daily on weekdays and once at weekends.

THE NORTHERN FJORDS

It's yet more crinkly coastline and yet more deeply incised fjords as you push further northwards into the region of Møre og Romsdal. Geirangerfjord, recently declared a Unesco World Heritage site, a must on most tours and a favourite anchorage for cruise ships, staggers beneath its summer influx. Stray from this tour operators' mecca and you'll find the waterways and roads less crowded and the scenery almost as spectacular as further south. The coastal towns of Ålesund and Kristiansund each deserve an overnight stop – and the spectacular drive over the Trollstigen pass will have you checking your safety belt.

The region's official website, www.visitmr .com has a host of useful links.

ÅNDALSNES

pop 2500

There are two dramatic ways to approach Åndalsnes: by road through the Trollstigen pass or taking the spectacularly scenic Raumabanen, the rail route from Dombås, as it ploughs through a deeply cut glacial valley flanked by sheer walls and plummeting waterfalls. Badly bombed during WWII, the modern town, nestled beside Romsdalfjord, is nondescript, but the surrounding landscapes are magnificent.

The **tourist office** (☎ 71 22 16 22; www.visitandalsnes.com; 9am-6pm Mon-Sat, noon-6pm Sun mid-Jun–mid-Aug; 8am-3.30pm Mon-Fri rest-of-year) is at the train station. It has internet access (Nkr40 per 30 minutes) and rents bikes (Nkr50/170 per hour/day).

Sights

TROLLVEGGEN

Approaching from Dombås, the road and rail lines follow the dramatic 1800m-high Trollveggen (Troll Wall), first conquered in 1965 by a joint Norwegian and English team. The highest vertical mountain wall in Europe, its ragged and often cloud-shrouded summit, 1800m from the valley floor, is considered the ultimate challenge among mountaineers.

TROLLSTIGEN

The Trollstigen (Troll's Ladder), south of Åndalsnes, is a thriller of a road, completed in 1936 after eight years of labour, with 11 hairpin bends and a 1:12 gradient. To add an extra daredevil element, it's one lane practically all the way. On request, bus passengers get a photo stop at the thundering 180m-high Stigfossen waterfall, and a quick halt at the top for a dizzy view down the valley. If you have wheels and a camera, make sure you pause for photos of the dramatic peaks of Karitind, Dronningen, Kongen and Bispen – as well as Norway's only 'Troll Crossing' road sign.

More energetically, you can also take it at a slower pace and puff your way up and over the old horse trail, narrow and blazed with white spots, that was previously the only communication between the two valleys. Both routes are closed in winter.

At the pass, the small **Vegmuseum** (☎ 99 29 20 00; admission Nkr15; 9.30am-7pm late Jun–mid-Aug) tells the engineering history of this awesome road.

RAUMABANEN RAILWAY

Trains run daily year-round along this spectacular route, meeting the main line, after 114km, at Dombås. There's also a tourist train (adult/child/family return Nkr295/70/660) that runs intermittently in summer from the lakeside station up to Bjorli, at 600m. Book at the tourist office.

MARDALSFOSSEN

East of Åndalsnes, up Langfjorden and then past the dramatic lake, Eikesdalsvatnet, is Mardalsfossen – once the fifth-highest waterfall in the world. How did it lose this status? Well, in the 1970s, this two-level, 655m waterfall was sucked dry by a hydroelectricity project. Although environmentalists chained themselves together to prevent construction, it went ahead and Mardalsfossen now flows strictly for the tourists, from late June to mid-August.

For mountain thrills, take the bucking single-track mountain road **Aursjøvegen** (Nkr50 toll), open between late June and September and linking Mardalsfossen and Sunndalsøra.

Activities

HIKING

The pamphlet *Geiranger Trollstigen* (Nkr20) describes eight signed hiking trails in the Trollstigen area. You'll need to supplement this with the map *Romsdals-Fjella* at 1:80,000. The tourist office carries both.

An excellent day hike, signed by red markers, begins in town, 50m north of the roundabout before the Esso petrol station, and climbs to the summit of Nesaksla (715m), the prominent peak that rises above Åndalsnes. At the top, the payoff for a steep ascent is a magnificent panorama. In fine weather, the view extends up and down Romsdalen and into Isterdalen, rivalling any in Norway.

From the shelter at the top, you can retrace your steps or undertake the straightforward ascent to the summit of Høgnosa (991m) and trek on to Åkesfjellet (1215m). Alternatively, traverse along the marked route 5km eastward and descend to Isfjorden village, at the head of the Isfjord.

The tourist office can also arrange mountain walks of four to six hours with a qualified guide (Nkr250 to Nkr350).

CLIMBING

The best local climbs are the 1500m-high rock route on Trollveggen and the 1550m-high Romsdalshorn, but there are a wealth of others. Serious climbers should buy *Klatring i Romsdal* (Nkr280), which includes rock and ice-climbing infomation in both Norwegian and English; it's available from the tourist office.

FISHING

John Kofoed (☎ 71 22 63 54) runs three-hour fishing tours (Nkr300 per person, including rod hire) on Romsdalsfjorden three times daily in summer. Reserve directly or through the tourist office.

CANOEING

Trollstigen Hytteutleie (see below for detailed info) organises guided canoe trips, as well as mountain walks.

Festivals & Events

Norsk Fjellfestivalen (Norway Mountain Festival) in early July is a week-long jamboree for lovers of the great outdoors with plenty of folk events thrown in. The town's other big moot is **Rauma Rock** (www.raumarock.com), central Norway's largest pop gathering, held over two days in early August.

Sleeping

The tourist office keeps a list of a few private homes offering accommodation for around Nkr400.

Åndalsnes Camping (☎ 71 22 16 29; www.andalsnescamp.no; car/caravan sites Nkr125/140, 4-bed basic cabin with outdoor bathroom Nkr450, 6-7 bed cabins with bathroom Nkr880; May–mid-Sep;) Less than 2km from town, it enjoys a dramatic setting beside the River Rauma. There's internet access (Nkr60 per hour) and it hires canoes (Nkr50/200 per hour/day) and bikes (Nkr50/110 per hour/day).

Trollstigen Hytteutleie (☎ 71 22 68 99; www.trollstigen-hytteutleie.no; camp sites Nkr140, 4-/5-bed cabins from Nkr550/650) Recognisable by the strapping wooden troll at its entrance, this well-kept camp site is altogether quieter and has an equally scenic location, 2km along the Rv63 highway, direction Geiranger.

Åndalsnes Vandrerhjem Setnes (☎ 71 22 13 82; aandalsnes.hostel@vandrerhjem.no; dm/s/d incl breakfast Nkr245/450/650 mid-May–mid-Sep, dm only Nkr175 rest-of-year) This welcoming HI-affiliated and sod-roofed hostel is 1.5km from the train station on the E136, direction Ålesund. It's worth staying here for the pancakes-and-pickled-herring bumper breakfast alone. The Ålesund bus that meets the train passes right by.

Hotel Aak (☎ 71 22 71 71; www.hotelaak.no; s/d Nkr750/990; mid-Jun–mid-Aug; P) This charming place, the oldest tourist hotel in Norway, lies beside the E136, direction Dombås, 4km from town. Most of the 16 comfortable bedrooms are named after a mountain that you can see from the bedroom window (though in one or two you may have to poke your head out a little). Its restaurant (mains Nkr150 to Nkr190; open 4pm to 10pm) is equally impressive and offers excellent traditional cuisine. As it's so small, reserve in advance.

Grand Hotel Bellevue (☎ 71 22 75 00; www.grandhotel.no; Åndalgata 5; s/d Nkr850/1050 Jun-Aug, Nkr750/850 rest-of-year; P) This large whitewashed structure caps a hillock in the centre of town. Most of its 86 rooms have fine views, particularly those facing the rear. There's a public swimming pool only 100m away. Its restaurant (mains Nkr195 to Nkr285; open for dinner only) offers the town's most formal dining, but you can always nibble on a lighter dish for around Nkr100. Take a look at the vintage black-and- white photos in the corridor, including one of a very young and sprightly Cliff Richard. When we last visited, an annexe to contain the town library, cinema and auditorium was nearing completion.

Eating

For sandwiches, sweet treats and all things delicious, call by **Måndalen Bakeri** (Havnegate 5; 8.30am-5pm Mon-Fri, 8.30am-2pm Sat), on the waterfront near the train station.

Buona Sera (☎ 71 22 60 75; Romsdalsveien 6; dishes from Nkr80; core hrs 4-10.30pm) The Italian-oriented Buona Sera predictably specialises in pizzas and pasta, yet has much more character than most Norwegian pizza joints. All wood, with intimate crannies and friendly staff, it also does crispy salads (Nkr100) and juicy meat mains (around Nkr175).

Kaikanten (☎ 71 22 75 00; daily specials Nkr98, snacks Nkr35-78, mains Nkr120-155; 10am-11pm mid-May–Aug) Sit back and relax here at the jetty's edge and enjoy a drink, a snack and one of Norway's prettiest panoramas in this welcoming restaurant, run by the Grand Hotel.

Getting There & Away

BUS

Buses along the 'Golden Route' to Geiranger (Nkr197, three hours), via Trollstigen, the Linge-Eidsdal ferry and scenic Ørnevegen, run twice daily between mid-June and August. The Trollstigen pass is cleared and opens by at least 1 June; early in the season it's an impressive trip through a popular cross-country ski field, between high walls of snow. Buses leave Åndalsnes at 8.30am and 5.30pm daily, and from Geiranger at 1pm and 6.10pm. There are also services to Molde (Nkr120, 1½ hours, up to eight daily) and Ålesund (Nkr200, 2¼ hours, twice daily).

TRAIN

Trains to/from Dombås (Nkr198, 1½ hours) run up to six times daily, in synchronisation with Oslo–Trondheim trains. Trains connect in Åndalsnes twice daily with the express bus service to Ålesund via Molde.

VALLDAL & AROUND

Valldal

Valldal is a place that people tend to pass through, having driven over the famous Trollstigen pass from Åndalsnes or savoured the exquisitely beautiful ferry journey from Geiranger. Perched in a nick of Norddalsfjord, its agricultural surrounds lay claim to being Europe's northernmost orchards. Here apples, pears and even cherries thrive – and you'll also find strawberries in profusion, commemorated in an annual **Strawberry Festival**, usually on the last weekend in July.

To sample the goods, whatever the season, call by **Sylteøysbutikken** (☎ 70 25 75 11; Syltegata), on the road leading to the church. It has a healthy selection of jams and juices, pressed and simmered in the small factory behind the shop and sourced in the main from local farmers.

The **tourist office** (☎ 70 25 77 67; www.visitnorddal.com; 🕐 10am-7pm mid-Jun–mid-Aug, 10am-5pm Mon-Fri rest-of-year) rents bikes (Nkr25/100 per hour/day) and can also arrange motorboat hire (Nkr85/400 per hour/day). Invest Nkr20 in its useful booklet of signed walks, ranging from Geiranger to Trollstigen and lasting from 15 minutes to three hours. Each one sets out from a public car park.

From Valldal you can experience a four-hour white-water rush (Nkr590; 11am daily May to September) down the Valldøla River. Contact **Valldal Naturopplevingar** (☎ 90 01 40 35; www.valldal.no), whose headquarters is 200m from the tourist office. It also offers kayak hire and a variety of other outdoor activities such as wilderness camping and, in winter, moonlight ski trips.

SLEEPING & EATING

There's no shortage of camp sites, many overpopulated with caravans, parked semipermanently. For somewhere with more character, push on to **Gudbrandsjuvet Camping** (☎ 70 25 86 31; tent/caravan sites Nkr110/140, 4-bed cabins Nkr350; 🕐 late May–mid-Sep), 15km towards Åndalsnes up the Rv63, where the stream races through a tight gorge.

Fjellro Turisthotell (☎ 70 25 75 13; www.fjellro.no; s/d incl breakfast Nkr690/890; 🕐 May-Sep) At charming 'Mountain Peace', just behind (northeast of) Valldal's church, the welcome is warm and the rooms are well appointed. There's a café and restaurant (open 7pm to 11pm) that specialises in fish, and a pub on the ground floor that's open at weekends. At the rear is a tranquil garden with a small children's playground.

Lupinen Café (☎ 70 25 84 10; mains Nkr50-88) This café serves pizza, beef and fish dishes and puts on an inexpensive buffet (Nkr155).

Jordbærstova (☎ 70 25 76 58; 🕐 May-Sep) About 6km up the Åndalsnes road, Jordbærstova honours the valley's mighty strawberry. So stop in for a fat slice of their gooey, creamy *svele* (strawberry cake), the local pancake speciality that is served with strawberries and cream. It also offers light meals.

GETTING THERE & AWAY

Valldal lies on the 'Golden Route' bus service that runs from mid-June to August between Åndalsnes (Nkr88, 1¾ hours) and Geiranger (Nkr75, 1¼ hours), up and over the spectacular Trollstigen pass. If you're driving, pause too at Gudbrandsjuvet, 15km up the valley from Valldal, where the river slots through a 5m-wide, 20m-deep canyon.

Equally scenic is the spectacular ferry cruise (adult/child single Nkr160/80, return Nkr250/120, 2¼ hours) that runs twice daily between Valldal and Geiranger from late-June to mid-August.

Tafjord

In 1934 an enormous chunk of rock 400m high and 22m long – in all, a whopping eight million cu metres – broke loose from the hillside. It crashed into Korsnæsfjord and created a 64m-high tidal wave that washed up to 700m inland and claimed 40 lives in Fjørra and Tafjord.

The **Tafjord Power Museum** (Kraftverkmuseum; ☎ 70 17 56 00; www.tafjord.net/museum; admission free; 🕐 noon-5pm mid-Jun–mid-Aug), located within a now-defunct power station, shows how the advent of hydroelectric power changed the valley. The road that climbs from the village up to the Zakarias reservoir passes through a bizarre corkscrew tunnel and, a couple of kilometres higher up, a short walking route drops to the crumbling bridge at the dam's narrow base, where you feel at close range the stresses this 96m-high structure has to tolerate.

Stordal

If you're travelling between Valldal and Ålesund on the Rv650, do make a short stop at Stordal's **Rose Church** (Rosekyrkya; adult/child Nkr30/15; 11am-4pm mid-Jun–mid-Aug). Unassuming from the outside, it was constructed in 1789 on the site of an earlier stave church, elements of which were retained. Inside comes the surprise: the roof, walls and every last pillar are sumptuously painted with scenes from the Bible and portraits of saints in an engagingly naive interpretation of high baroque.

GEIRANGER

pop 250

Scattered cliffside farms, most long abandoned, still cling along the towering walls of twisting, 20km-long emerald-green Geirangerfjord, a Unesco World Heritage site. Down its near-sheer cliffs waterfalls – the Seven Sisters, the Suitor, the Bridal Veil and more – sluice and tumble. The one-hour scenic ferry trip along its length between Geiranger and Hellesylt is as much minicruise as means of transport – take it even if you've no particular reason to get to the other end.

If you arrive from Hellesylt, Geiranger village, at the head of the fjord, comes as a shock to the system, despite its fabulous site, as you mingle with the hordes of visitors, brought in by bus and ship. Every year Geiranger wilts under the presence of over 600,000 visitors and more than 150 cruise ships (three were moored offshore last time we visited, each polluting the pure air with dark fumes from its smokestack, while their bumboats belched diesel vapours at the jetty).

By contrast, if you drop from the north along the Rv63 from Åndalsnes and Valldal (called Ørnevegen, the Eagle's Way), you'll gasp as it twists down the almost sheer slope in 11 hairpin bends, each one giving a yet more impressive glimpse along the narrow fjord. And whichever way you're coming or going, in the evening, once the last cruise ship and tour bus has pulled out, serenity returns to this tiny port.

The **tourist office** (70 26 30 99; www.geiranger.no; 9am-7pm mid-Jun–mid-Aug, 9am-6pm mid-May–mid-Jun & mid-Aug–mid-Sep) is beside the pier.

Sights & Activities

GEIRANGER FJORD CENTRE

The **Geiranger Fjordsenter** (70 26 30 07; www.geirangerfjord.no; adult/child Nkr85/40; core hrs 9am-4pm May–mid-Sep, to 6pm Jul, to 10pm Aug) has tools, artefacts and even whole buildings that have been uprooted and brought here, illustrating the essential themes – the mail packet, avalanches, the building of early roads and the rise of tourism – that have shaped the land and its people.

FLYDALSJUVET

Somewhere you've seen that classic photo, beloved of brochures, of the overhanging rock Flydalsjuvet, usually with a figure gazing down at a cruise ship in Geirangerfjord. The car park, signposted to Flydalsjuvet, about 5km uphill from Geiranger on the Stryn road, offers a great view of the fjord and the green river valley, but doesn't exactly provide the postcard view. For that, you'll have to drop about 150m down the hill, then descend a slippery and rather indistinct track to the edge. Your intrepid photo subject will have to scramble down gingerly to the overhang about 50m further along…

CYCLING

Geiranger Downhill (47 37 97 71; www.geirangerdownhill.com) will drive you up to Djupvasshytta (1038m), from where you can coast for 17 gentle, scenically splendid kilometres by bike (Nkr195) down to the fjord; allow a couple of hours. Book at the sod-roofed cabin 50m above the harbour, which also rents bikes (Nkr50/200 per hour/day).

BOAT TOURS

Geiranger Fjordservice (70 26 57 86; www.geirangerfjord.no) does 1½-hour sightseeing **boat tours** (adult/child Nkr110/45, sailings 4 times daily Jun-Aug). Its kiosk is within the tourist office. From mid-June to August, it also operates a smaller, 15-seater boat (Nkr390/190) that scuds deeper and faster into the fjord.

SEA KAYAKING

Coastal Odyssey (91 11 80 62; www.coastalodyssey.com), based at Geiranger Camping, is run by Jonathan Bendiksen, a Canadian from the Northwest Territories who learnt to kayak almost before he could walk. He rents sea-kayaks (Nkr150/300/600 per hour/half-day/day) and does daily hiking and canoeing trips to four of the finest destinations around the fjord.

HIKING

Get away from the seething ferry terminal and life's altogether quieter. All around Geiranger there are great signed hiking routes to abandoned farmsteads, waterfalls and vista points. The stylised tourist office map features 13 such short walks leading from the village.

A popular longer trek begins with a ride on the Geiranger Fjordservice sightseeing boat. A steep 45-minute ascent from the landing at Skagehola brings you to Skageflå, a precariously perched hillside farm. You can retrace yours steps to the landing, where the boat stops (on request; tell the crew on the way out or just wave) or, to stretch your legs more, continue over the mountain and return to Geiranger via Preikestolen and Homlung.

Another recommended walk follows a sometimes muddy path to the Storseter waterfall, where the track actually passes behind the cascading water. Allow about 45 minutes each way from the starting point at the Vesterås farm.

Sleeping & Eating

Around the village, you'll find plenty of *rom* signs, indicating **private rooms and cabins** (s/d about Nkr300/500) for rent. Hotels are often booked out by package tours, but a dozen or so camping possibilities skirt the fjord and hillsides.

Below the Grande Ford Hotel are a couple of friendly, tranquil camp sites in unbeatable locations. Even if you're carrying a weighty pack, it's well worth the 2km walk northwestwards to get there. Both rent kayaks, rowing and motor boats and have internet access (Nkr60 per hour).

Grande Hytteutleige og Camping (☎ 70 26 30 68; www.grande-hytteutleige.no; per person/site Nkr20/90, 4-bed cabins with outdoors bathroom 350-450, with bathroom Nkr690-750, 5-/6-bed cabin Nkr720/920; Apr-Oct;) Take the smaller, northernmost of its two fields for the best views up the fjord. Has wi-fi.

Geirangerfjorden Feriesenter (☎ 95 10 75 27; www.geirangerfjorden.net; per person/site Nkr20/100, 4-bed cabins Nkr450-720, 5-bed cabins Nkr820-920; May–mid-Sep;) Right next door, this is another excellent camping option.

Geiranger Camping (☎ 70 26 31 20; www.geirangercamping.no; per person/site Nkr20/110; mid-May–mid-Sep;) A short walk from the ferry terminal, Geiranger Camping is sliced through by a fast-flowing torrent. Though short on shade it's pleasant and handy for an early morning ferry getaway. Has wi-fi.

Grande Fjord Hotel (☎ 70 26 94 90; www.grandefjordhotel.com; d Nkr980; P) This warmly recommended 48-room hotel does great buffet breakfasts and dinners. It's well worth paying an extra Nkr100 for a room with a balcony and magnificent view over the fjord. Take the shoreside Rv63, direction Åndalsnes, for 2km to find yourself half a world away from the ferry terminal bustle.

our pick **Villa Utsikten** (☎ 70 26 96 60; www.villautsikten.no; s Nkr890, d Nkr1290-1490; May-Oct; P) 'A temple to lift your spirits'. So observed the King of Siam when he stayed here in 1898 during his grand Norwegian tour. A century later, there's no reason to gainsay his judgement. High on the hill above Geiranger (take Rv63, direction Grotli) the venerable family-owned Utsiken, constructed in 1893, has stunning views over town and fjord. Aida, its recommended restaurant, offers splendid à la carte fare (mains around Nkr200) and is open to allcomers.

Union Hotel (☎ 70 26 83 00; www.union-hotel.no; s Nkr1150-1250, d Nkr1760-1960; Feb–mid-Dec; P) The large, spectacularly situated Union Hotel is high on the hill above town. It has a couple of pools (one indoor and heated). Even if you're not staying here, head up the hill, then roll back down after tucking into their gargantuan dinner buffet (Nkr415), which has a minimum of 65 dishes. The restaurant also offers à la carte (mains Nkr255 to Nkr375) and a four-course set menu (Nkr495).

Laizas (☎ 70 26 07 20; 10am-10pm mid-Apr–Sep) At the ferry terminal, just beside the tourist office, the young team at this airy, welcoming place put on a handful of tasty hot dishes, good salads and snackier items such as focaccia, wraps and sandwiches. There's also an internet terminal (Nkr1 per minute).

Getting There & Away

BOAT

The popular, hugely recommended run between Geiranger and Hellesylt (passenger/car with driver Nkr100/210, one hour) is quite the most spectacular scheduled ferry route in Norway. It has four to eight sailings daily between May and September (every 90 minutes, June to August). Almost as scenic is the ferry that runs twice daily between Geiranger and Valldal (adult/child single Nkr160/80, return

Nkr250/120, 2¼ hours) between late-June and mid-August.

From mid-April to mid-September, the Hurtigruten coastal ferry makes a detour from Ålesund to Geiranger (departs 1.30pm) on its northbound run only.

BUS

In summer, daily buses to Åndalsnes (Nkr197, three hours) via Valldal leave Geiranger at 1pm and 6.10pm. For Molde, change buses in Åndalsnes; for Ålesund, change at Linge.

HELLESYLT

pop 250

The old Viking port of Hellesylt, through which a roaring waterfall cascades, is altogether calmer, if less breathtaking, than Geiranger.

The **tourist office** (☎ 94 81 13 32; core hrs 10am-5pm mid-Jun–Aug) is in the Samfunnhuset (Community Centre) building. For hikers, it carries *Tafjardfjella,* a walking map at 1:50,000, and for cyclists, *Hellesylt Mountain Biking Map*. There's also an internet terminal (Nkr40 per hour).

The **Peer Gynt Galleriet** (adult/child Nkr50/free; 11am-7pm Jun-Aug) is a collection of fairly kitsch bas-relief wood carvings illustrating the Peer Gynt legend and fashioned by local chippy, Oddvin Parr. You may find the food at the complex's cafeteria more to your taste.

Sleeping & Eating

Hellesylt Camping (☎ 90 20 68 85; per person/site Nkr15/105) The absence of shade is more than compensated for by its fjord-side location and proximity to the ferry pier.

Hellesylt Vandrerhjem (☎ 70 26 51 28; hellesylt hostel@vandrerhjem.no; dm Nkr160, s/d with shared bathroom Nkr230/400, d with bathroom Nkr550, 4-bed cabin Nkr340; Jun–mid-Sep) This HI-affiliated hostel, perched on the hillside overlooking Hellesylt, is on the road towards Stranda, about 200m from the junction. Go for one of the cabins with stunning fjord views if you're in a group. If you're arriving by bus, ask the driver to drop you off to save a long slog back up the hill.

Getting There & Away

For details of the spectacular ferry ride to/from Geiranger see opposite.

Some ferries from Geiranger connect with buses to/from Stryn (Nkr95, one hour) and Ålesund (Nkr136, 2¾ hours).

NORANGSDALEN

Norangsdalen is one of the most inspiring yet little visited crannies of the Northern Fjords. This glorious hidden valley connects Hellesylt with the Leknes–Sæbø ferry, on the scenic Hjørundfjorden, via the village of Øye.

The boulder-strewn scenery unfolds among towering snowy peaks, ruined farmsteads and haunting mountain lakes. In the upper part of the valley at Urasætra, beside a dark mountain lake, are the ruins of several stone crofters' huts. Further on, you can still see the foundations of one-time farmhouses beneath the surface of the pea-green lake Langstøylvatnet, created in 1908 when a rock slide crashed down the slopes of Keipen.

Hikers and climbers will find plenty of scope in the dramatic peaks of the adjacent Sunnmørsalpane, including the lung-searingly steep scrambling ascent of Slogen (1564m) from Øye and the superb Råna (1586m), a long, tough haul from Urke.

Beside the road about 2km south of Øye, there's a monument to one CW Patchell, an English mountaineer who lost his heart to the valley.

The historic 1891 **Hotel Union** (☎ 70 06 21 00; www.unionoye.no; Øye; s/d Nkr865/1730; May-Sep) has attracted mountaineers, writers, artists and royalty for over a century. With period artwork and furnishings, panelled in wood and speaking old-world charm, it's a delight. Rooms are named after celebrities who have slept in them: Sir Arthur Conan Doyle, Karen Blixen, Kaiser Wilhelm, Edvard Grieg, Roald Amundsen, Henrik Ibsen, a host of kings and queens – even Coco Chanel. The restaurant serves one-/three-course lunches (Nkr195 to Nkr350) and a three-/five-course dinner costs Nkr475/595.

RUNDE

pop 150

The squat island of Runde, 67km southwest of Ålesund and connected to the mainland by a bridge, plays host to half a million sea birds of 230 to 240 species, including 100,000 pairs of migrating puffins that arrive in April, breed and stay around until late July. There are also colonies of kittiwakes, gannets, fulmars, storm petrels, razor-billed auks, shags and guillemots, plus about 70 other species that nest here.

ÅLESUND

pop 15,000

The coastal town of Ålesund is, for many, just as beautiful as Bergen, if on a much smaller scale, and it's certainly far less touristy.

After the sweeping fire of 23 January 1904, which left 10,000 residents homeless, the German emperor Kaiser Wilhelm II sent shiploads of provisions and building materials and Ålesund was rebuilt in record time. Teams of young, committed Norwegian architects, trained for the most part in Germany, designed the town in the characteristic Art Nouveau (Jugendstil) style of the time, while bringing to the movement traditional local motifs and ornamentation. Buildings graced with turrets, spires and gargoyles sprout throughout town. The best examples are along Apotekergata, Kirkegata, Øwregata, Løvenvoldgata and, especially, Kongensgata.

Ålesund is on a narrow, fishhook-shaped sea-bound peninsula. So tightly packed is the town centre that expansion would be impossible; today most of the townspeople live scattered across nearby islands and peninsulas.

Information

Internet access Available at the tourist Office (Nkr60 per hr). Log on for free at the library in the town hall or, for customers, at Lyspunket (p265; also has wi-fi) and Lille Løvenfold (p265; also has wi-fi).

Tourist office (☎ 70 15 76 00; www.visitalesund.com; Skaregata 1; 🕑 8.30am-7pm Mon-Fri, 9am-5pm Sat,

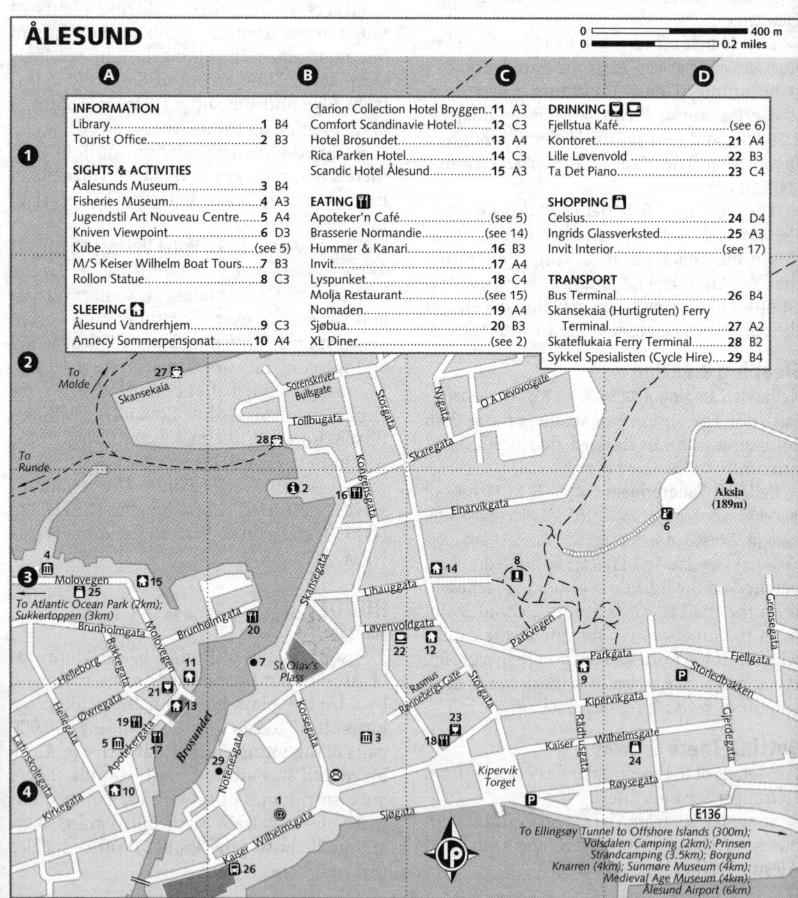

11am-5pm Sun Jun-Aug, 9am-4pm Mon-Fri Sep-May) Its free booklet *On Foot in Ålesund* details the town's architectural highlights in a walking tour.

Sights & Activities

SUNNMØRE MUSEUM

Ålesund's celebrated **Sunnmøre Museum** (☎ 70 17 40 00; www.sunnmoremuseum.no; Borgundgavlen; adult/child Nkr65/15; ⏰ 11am-5pm Mon-Sat, noon-5pm Sun late-Jun–Aug; 11am-3pm Mon, Tue & Fri, noon-4pm Sun rest-of-year) is 4km east of the centre. Here, at the site of the old Borgundkaupangen trading centre, active from the 11th to 16th centuries, over 50 traditional buildings have been relocated. Ship-lovers will savour the collection of around 40 historic boats, including replicas of Viking-era ships and a commercial trading vessel from around AD 1000. Take bus 618 or 624.

Should you coincide with its restricted opening hours, don't overlook – as many visitors often do – its **Medieval Age Museum** (Middelaldermuseet; ⏰ noon-3pm Tue-Thu & Sun mid-Jun–mid-Aug). Displayed around excavations of the old trading centre are well documented artefacts discovered onsite and reproductions of medieval illustrations depicting the way of life of the west Norwegian coastal folk who inhabited this thriving community. A pity that entry hours are so reduced…

ATLANTIC OCEAN PARK

At the peninsula's western extreme, sitting 3km from the centre, the **Atlantic Ocean Park** (Atlanterhavsparken; ☎ 70 10 70 60; Tueneset; adult/child Nkr90/55; ⏰ 10am-7pm Sun-Fri, 10am-4pm Sat Jun-Aug, 11am-4pm Tue-Sun rest-of-year) can merit a whole day of your life. It introduces visitors to the North Atlantic's undersea world with glimpses of the astonishing richness of coastal and fjord submarine life. Children will wow at the 'snails, seashells and weird marine animals' section, and can dangle a line for crabs or feed the fish in the touch pool while the whole family will gasp at the enormous four-million-litre aquarium. Be there at 1pm (also 3.30pm, June to August) when the largest ocean fish thrash and swirl as they're fed by human divers.

There's also a sanctuary for orphaned seals and the grounds offer superb coastal scenery, bathing beaches and walking trails. In summer, a special bus (adult/child Nkr27/14) leaves St Olav's Plass hourly from 9.55am to 3.55pm, Monday to Saturday.

JUGENDSTIL ART NOUVEAU CENTRE

Everyone from serious aesthetes to kids out for fun will get pleasure from this **art centre** (Jugendstil Senteret; ☎ 70 10 49 70; www.jugendstilsenteret.no; Apotekergata 16; adult/child Nkr50/25; ⏰ 10am-7pm Jun-Aug, 11am-5pm Tue-Fri, 11am-4pm Sat, noon-4pm Sun rest-of-year). The introductory Time Machine capsule presents 'From Ashes to Art Nouveau', a high-tech, very visual story of the rebuilding of Ålesund after the great fire, while the displays offer carefully selected textiles, ceramics and furniture of the genre. It's in and above a renovated chemist's shop that has retained its magnificent corkscrew staircase and 1st-floor dining room.

Drop into the one-time Bank of Norway building next door where **Kube**, Ålesund's most recent cultural asset, mounts quality temporary exhibitions of architecture, art and design.

AALESUNDS MUSEUM

The **town museum** (☎ 70 12 31 70; Rasmus Rønnebergs Gate 16; adult/child Nkr40/10; ⏰ 11am-4pm mid-Jun–mid-Aug; 11am-3pm rest-of-year, closed Sat & Sun Feb, Mar, Nov & Dec) illustrates the history of sealing, fishing, shipping and industry in the Sunnmøre region, the fire of 1904, the Nazi WWII occupation and the town's distinctive Art Nouveau architecture. There's also a collection of boats and ships, including the *Uræd* lifeboat (piloted across the Atlantic in 1904 by an intrepid Ole Brude), and an 1812 barn, converted into an old-time grocery.

The affiliated, much smaller **Fisheries Museum** (Ålesund Fiskerimuseet; ☎ 70 12 31 70; Molovegen 10; adult/child Nkr30/10; ⏰ 11am-4pm Mon-Sat, noon-4pm Sun & 6-8pm Wed-Fri mid-Jun–mid-Aug), in the 1861 Holmbua warehouse (one of the few to survive the 1904 fire), contains exhibits on fishing through the ages and a special section on drying stockfish and the processing of cod liver oil.

HARBOUR BOAT TOUR

If you're interested in a different perspective of the town, take the **M/S Keiser Wilhelm** (☎ 70 11 44 30; adult/child Nkr150/75), which does 1¼-hour tours of the harbour and nearby skerries four times daily.

For a more exotic sail, hop aboard the **Borgundknarren**, a replica Viking trading ship that leaves from Sunnmøre Museum for a one-hour cruise (adult/child Nkr50/20) at 1pm every Wednesday, from late June to early August.

AKSLA

The 418 steps up Aksla lead to the splendid **Kniven viewpoint** over Ålesund and the surrounding mountains and islands. Follow Lihauggata from the pedestrian shopping street Kongensgata to the start of the 20-minute puff to the top of the hill. There's also a road to the top; take Røysegata east from the centre, then follow the Fjellstua signposts up the hill.

Up top, the **Fjellstua Kafé** (☎ 70 10 74 00; mid-May–Aug) is a good place to recover your breath while enjoying a drink with a view.

SUKKERTOPPEN

A more challenging hike leading to an even wider-ranging view leads to the summit of Sukkertoppen (314m). It begins on the street Sukkertoppvegen, on the hook of Ålesund's peninsula. The track follows the easiest route, right up the east-pointing ridgeline. Take bus 618 from town and ask the driver to stop at Hessla school.

Tours

To really delve into Ålesund's Art Nouveau heritage, sign on for the tourist office's excellent 1½- to two-hour **guided town walk** (adult/child Nkr75/free; mid-Jun–mid-Aug), which leaves the office at noon.

Festivals & Events

Ålesund knows how to party. In late May or early June, there's the **Big Band Festival**. Yachties will be in seventh heaven at the **Ålesund Boat Festival** (www.batfestivalen.no), a week of watery pleasures in the first half of July, while the **Norwegian Food Festival** in the last week of August is a treat for all gourmets and gourmands.

Sleeping

The tourist office has a list of private rooms that start at about Nkr300 per person.

Volsdalen Camping (☎ 70 12 58 90; www.volsdalencamping.no; Volsdalsberga; car/caravan sites Nkr100/150, 2-/4-bed cabins with outdoor bathroom Nkr300/450, with bathroom Nkr800; year-round) Above the shore about 2km east of the centre, this particularly friendly camp site is the nearest to town. Mainly for caravans and motorhomers, it has a secluded grassy area for campers at its far end. Take bus 613, 614, 618 or 624.

Annecy Sommerpensjonat (☎ 70 12 96 30; Kirkegata 1b; basic s/d with shared bathroom Nkr360/390, d with bathroom Nkr490; mid-Jun–mid-Aug) This simple place is an excellent budget choice, letting out self-contained student rooms in summer.

Ålesund Vandrerhjem (☎ 70 11 58 30; aalesund.hostel@vandrerhjem.no; Parkgata 14; dm/s/d incl breakfast Nkr235/490/690; year-round;) This central, HI-affiliated hostel is in an attractive building (see the murals in the vast common room) that's just celebrated its first century. There are self-catering facilities and free internet, wi-fi and washing machine. Most doubles have en suite and, for those with a head for heights, bunk beds in the women's dorm are three tiers tall.

Scandic Hotel Ålesund (☎ 21 61 45 00; www.scandic-hotels.com; Molovegen 6; r Nkr890 mid-Jun–mid-Aug, s/d from Nkr1070/1270 Sun-Thu, Nkr870/1070 Fri & Sat rest-of-year, all incl breakfast; P) The Scandic has a lot going for it. Around 30% of its 150 rooms, all of which have parquet flooring, overlook the harbour, there's a free sauna and three rooms are equipped for the disabled. Guests – and those dropping in – also eat well; choices at the buffet breakfast are truly substantial and the dinner buffet (Nkr195) at its restaurant, the Molja, is a bargain. Families will welcome the children's play area and separate kids' buffet.

Hotel Brosundet (☎ 70 11 45 00; www.brosundet.no; Apotekergata 5; s/d from Nkr850/1070 mid-Jun–mid-Aug, Nkr990/1150 Sun-Thu, Nkr850/1070 Fri-Sun rest-of-year, all incl breakfast; P) Although no longer the splendid family concern that it recently superseded this revamped hotel, right on the waterfront retains its charm. An ex-warehouse and protected building, it was converted in the 1990s – just look at the wonderful old beams they've preserved, feel the way the floors list and slope and be careful not to crack your head on the huge pulleys, once used to haul up fish.

Rica Parken Hotel (☎ 70 12 50 50; www.rica.no; Storgata 16; s/d Nkr855/1070 Sun-Thu mid-Jun–mid-Aug & Fri & Sat year-round, Nkr1530/1745 Sun-Thu rest-of-year; P) Equipped to the usual high Rica chain standards, some of its attractive modern rooms have views of the town park. Its Brasserie Normandie (opposite) is a quality eating option.

Comfort Scandinavie Hotel (☎ 70 15 78 00; www.choice.no; Løvenvoldgata 8; s/d Nkr1255/1455 Sun-Thu, Nkr880/1030 Fri & Sat; P) This fine place, Ålesund's oldest hotel, was the first to be constructed after the fire of 1904. With touches and flourishes of Art Nouveau (the furniture is original and in keeping with this theme, and even the lobby flatscreen TV seems to blend in), it exudes style and confidence.

Clarion Collection Hotel Bryggen (☎ 70 12 64 00; www.choice.no; Apotekergata 1-3; s/d Nkr1475/1750 Mon-Thu, Nkr870/1150 Fri-Sun; 💻) This wonderful 130-room waterfront option occupies a converted fish warehouse, artfully decorated with former tools and equipment. Rates include a light evening meal and free waffles throughout the day. There's a sauna, free to guests, too.

Eating

A couple of attractive cafés gaze at each other from opposite sides of trendy Apotekergata.

Nomaden (☎ 97 15 89 85; 0 12; Apotekergata 10; 🕑 11am-5pm) Affiliated to the art gallery next door, this welcoming café, where cool jazz trills in the background, serves sandwiches, gooey cakes and fresh coffee and has its own changing art exhibition.

Invit (☎ 70 15 66 44; Apotekergata 9; 🕑 8.15am-4.30pm Mon-Fri, 10am-4.30pm Sat) Gosh, the style shows at this suave coffee bar, which also serves tasty snacks. Just what you'd expect from a place that runs the accompanying interior design boutique (see p266). You can also sip your espresso outside on their floating pontoon, where they considerately supply blankets if the wind whips up.

Apoteker'n Café (☎ 70 10 49 70; Apotekergata 16) Within the Jugendstil Art Nouveau Centre (p263) and completing a trio of tempting choices on the same street, this stylish, friendly little place rustles up good snacks, tempting cakes and great coffee.

our pick Hummer & Kanari (☎ 70 12 80 08; Kongensgata 19; mains Nkr100-275; 🕑 Mon-Sat) Behind the bar sit row upon row of liqueur and spirit bottles for mixers and shakers. Here at the downstairs bistro, you order at the counter. Upstairs, it's waiter service. But both call upon the same kitchen, which turns out ample portions of pasta (Nkr110 to Nkr130) and pizza (Nkr100). To save the decision-making, simply sit back, put yourself in the cook's capable hands and go for the best the sea can offer that day, 'Hummer & Kanari's selection of fish and shellfish.' (Nkr245).

Lyspunket (☎ 70 12 53 00; Kipervikgata 1; mains Nkr125-150; 🕑 Tue-Sun; 💻) There are a couple of internet points and free wi-fi for clients at this great-value, great-ambience, youthful place. Loll back in its deep sofas (though you might not want to sit directly beneath the magnificent swirls and pipes of the giant glass chandelier). There are free refills for coffee and soft drinks, and dishes, such as their turkey in a caramelised apple and curry sauce, are creative.

Brasserie Normandie (☎ 70 13 23 00; mains Nkr190-205) This brasserie, the main eating option at the Rica Parken Hotel, runs a short but impressive à la carte menu of local and international dishes.

XL Diner (☎ 70 12 42 53; Skaregata 1; mains around Nkr250; 🕑 dinner only) Nothing could be further from your traditional greasy diner than this 1st-floor fish restaurant overlooking the harbour. Bacalao is the house speciality. This quintessentially Norwegian dish is offered with a variety of sauces – Italian, Spanish, Portuguese, even Louisiana, and *Bacalao de Mirita Style* (sic), served in a zesty lime and mildly chilli sauce. Vegetables, still firm and crunchy, are cooked to perfection. Better not to request one of the tropical display fish that eye you apprehensively from their heated aquarium.

Sjøbua (☎ 70 12 71 00; www.sjoebua.no; Brunholmgata 1a; mains Nkr250-360; 🕑 4pm-1am Mon-Sat) In yet another converted wharfside building, stylish Sjøbua is one of northern Norway's finest fish restaurants, where you can choose your crustacean, wriggling and fresh, from the lobster tank.

For a simple snack from a bag, buy a scoop of fresh shrimps directly from the fishing boats that moor along the harbour front beside Skansegata.

Drinking

Ta Det Piano (☎ 70 10 06 99; Kipervikgata 1b; 🕑 from 11am) 'Take it Easy' is just that – a laid-back bar with a steep rear garden (live bands sometimes use its flat roof as a stage). Now in its second decade, it's the place to meet the town's younger movers and shakers.

Lille Løvenvold (☎ 70 12 54 00; Løvenvoldgata 2; 🕑 11am-midnight Mon-Thu, 11am-3am Fri & Sat) Here's a Jekyll and Hyde of a place. By day an intimate place for a coffee in relaxing surroundings, it morphs each evening into a bar where canned rock is the accompaniment to your beer. Also has free wi-fi.

Kontoret (☎ 70 10 05 80; Apotekergata 2; 🕑 6pm-late Mon-Sat) 'The Office', headquarters of the Ålesund chapter of Liverpool supporters club, packs 'em in with its hearty pub atmosphere.

Shopping

Ålesund has a couple of quality glass-blowing workshops.

Ingrids Glassverksted (☎ 70 12 53 77; www.ingridsglassverksted.no; Molovegen 15; 10am-5pm Mon-Fri, 10am-3pm Sat) You'll find everything from practical and stylish glasses, bowls and ornaments to quirky, multicoloured chickens with spiky coxcombs. Should you pass by out of hours, you can watch Ingrid at work on the DVD that plays in her window.

Celsius (☎ 70 10 01 16; Kaiser Wilhelmsgata 52; Tue-Sat) This small glass studio blows unconventional pieces in vivid colours. The kiln is at the front, the shop at the rear.

Invit Interior (☎ 70 15 66 44; Apotekergata 9) Appropriate for such a tasteful town, this shop-cum-gallery displays the very best of creative modern furniture and Scandinavian kitchenware and home appliances.

Getting There & Away

AIR

From Ålesund's **airport** (☎ 70 11 48 00), SAS has three daily flights serving Bergen, two to/from Trondheim and up to eight to/from Oslo. It also has two direct flights weekly between Ålesund and London (Gatwick).

BOAT

An express boat speeds down the coast daily to Bergen (8½ hours). Hurtigruten coastal ferries arrive/depart at 8.45am/6.45pm northbound and depart at 12.45am southbound. On its northbound run, there's a popular detour, mid-April to mid-September, via Geiranger – hence the large gap between arrival and departure times.

BUS

Nor-Way Bussekspress runs five times daily, Monday to Friday, to/from Hellesylt (Nkr149, 2½ hours) with three services continuing to Stryn (Nkr235, 3¾ hours). There's also one express bus daily to/from Bergen (Nkr580, 9¼ hours), three to/from Trondheim (Nkr500, 7½ hours) via Molde (Nkr131, 2¼ hours) and both a day and night run to/from Oslo (Nkr790, 10 hours). Local buses run to/from Åndalsnes (Nkr200, 2¼ hours, twice daily).

Getting Around

Ålesund's airport is located on Vigra island, connected to the town by an undersea tunnel. **Flybussen** (☎ 177) departs from Skateflukaia (Nkr70, 25 minutes) and the bus station one hour before the departure of domestic flights.

Town buses are run by **Nettbuss Møre** (☎ for timetables 177).

Drivers to the airport and offshore islands pay tunnel tolls totalling Nkr60 each way for a car and driver, plus Nkr19 per additional passenger.

Sykkel Spesialisten (☎ 70 12 28 20; Notenesgata 3) rents bicycles (Nkr140 per day).

For a taxi, call ☎ 70 10 30 00.

AROUND ÅLESUND

Offshore Islands

With wheels, you can take in the four offshore islands of Valderøy, Vigra, Giske and Godøy in a pleasant day trip from Ålesund. All offer excellent short hill or coastal walks.

At the furthest, northern extremity of the furthest island, **Godøy**, is the picturesque 1876 **lighthouse** (☎ 70 18 50 90; adult/child Nkr20/10; noon-6pm Jun-Aug) in the fishing station of **Alnes**. For that end-of-the-world feeling, climb to the circular balcony via the five floors of this all-wood structure, each displaying the canvases of renowned Norwegian artist and Godøy resident, Ørnulf Opdahl. Don't leave without sampling one of the delightful cakes, baked on the spot by Eva, the lighthouse custodian.

Giske was also the home of Gange-Rolv (known as Rollon in France; he's also claimed by Vigra), the Viking warrior who besieged Paris, subsequently founded the Duchy of Normandy in 911 and was an ancestor of England's William the Conqueror. Highlight of the island is its ornate 12th-century **church** (adult/child Nkr20/10 incl guided tour; 10am-5pm Mon-Sat, 1-7pm Sun mid-Jun–mid-Aug). Built largely of marble, its real jewels are the elaborately carved polychrome altarpiece and pulpit. The island's Makkevika marshes are a prime spot for bird-watching.

On **Valderøy**, the **Skjonghellaren caves** have revealed bones of Arctic fox, sea otter and ringed seal, plus evidence of human occupation at least 2000 years ago. In the northwest of the island, they're reached by a breezy 500m walk from the parking spot between cliff and shoreline, then a steep five-minute boulder scramble.

Vigra has Ålesund's airport and **Blindheimssanden** (also called Blimsand) a long white-sand beach.

MOLDE

pop 19,200

Molde, hugging the shoreline at the wide mouth of Romsdalsfjorden, is well known as the 'Town of Roses' for its fertile soil, rich vegetation and mild climate. But the town's chief claim to fame is its annual July jazz festival.

Modern Molde, though architecturally unexciting, is a pleasantly compact little place whose coastal landscapes recall New Zealand or Seattle's Puget Sound. To test the comparison, drive or trek up to the Varden overlook, 400m above the town.

Information

Dockside Pub (Torget) Internet access at a popular pub (see p268).
Laundrette (Guest Marina)
Library (Kirkebakken 1-3) Internet access.
Tourist office (☎ 70 20 10 00; www.visitmolde.com; Torget 4; ⏲ 9am-6pm Mon-Fri, 9am-3pm Sat, noon-5pm Sun mid-Jun–mid-Aug; 8.30am-3.30pm Mon-Fri rest-of-year) Sells *Molde Fraena* (1:50,000), the best hiking map of the area. Also offers free internet access.

Sights

ROMSDALEN FOLK MUSEUM

Sprawling across a large area within this open-air **museum** (Romsdalsmuseet; ☎ 71 20 24 60; Per Amdamsveg 4; admission free; ⏲ 8am-10pm) are nearly 50 old buildings, shifted here from around the Romsdal region. Highlights include Bygata (an early-20th-century town street) and a 'composite church', assembled from elements of now-demolished local stave churches. In summer, there are very worthwhile **guided tours** (adult/child Nkr60/free; ⏲ 11am-6pm Mon-Sat, noon-6pm Sun Jul, 11am-3pm Mon-Sat, noon-3pm Sun 15-30 Jun & 1-15 Aug), in English on request.

FISHERY MUSEUM

This **museum** (Fiskerimuseet; ☎ 93 42 54 06; adult/child Nkr60/free; ⏲ noon-5pm mid-Jun–mid-Aug), on Hertøya island, is a short ferry ride from the Torget terminal. Also open-air, its cod liver oil factory, cottages and fishermen's shacks, tiny schoolroom and collection of boats bring to life the coastal fishing cultures around the mouth of Romsdalsfjorden from the mid-19th century onwards. When it's open, **ferries** (☎ 99 54 98 94;

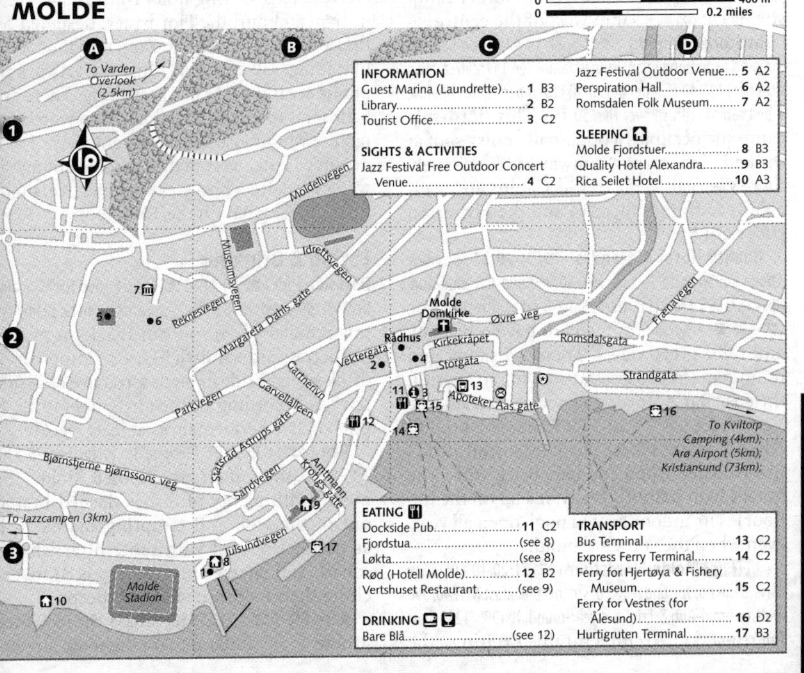

MOLDEJAZZ

Every year, Moldejazz pulls in up to 100,000 fans and a host of stars, mainly Scandinavian (in 2007 it included the intriguingly named Funky Butt) but with a sprinkling of the internationally famous (such as, in 2007, Steely Dan and Elvis Costello).

The town rocks all the way from Monday to Saturday in the middle of July. Of over 100 concerts, a good one-third are free, while big events are very reasonably priced at Nkr100 to Nkr280.

Trad jazz sweats it out in Perspiration Hall, while the big draws perform outdoors near the Romsdalsmuseet and there are plenty of free supporting events (including a daily street parade) from noon onwards in front of the Rådhus.

For the lowdown on this year's events, dial ☎ 71 20 31 50 or log onto www.moldejazz.no. You can book by credit card for a Nkr10 surcharge through **BillettService** (☎ 81 53 31 33).

adult/child Nkr50/25) run four times daily from Molde between 11am and 5.45pm.

Festivals & Events

Moldejazz, the Molde International Jazz Festival (see above) is a magnet for jazz fiends from all over Norway and further afield.

Sleeping

The tourist office has a number of private homes on its books, most with self-catering facilities and costing from Nkr150 to Nkr200 per person. During the Molde International Jazz Festival, there's a large temporary camp site, Jazzcampen, 3km west of the centre.

Kviltorp Camping (☎ 71 21 17 42; www.kviltorpcamping.no in Norwegian; Fannestrandveien 142; car/caravan sites Nkr120/140 plus per person Nkr10, 2-bed cabins Nkr400, 4-bed cabins with shower Nkr650-750) This fjord-side camp site occupies a potentially noisy spot at the end of the airport runway but fortunately there's very little air traffic. Cabins are available year-round. Bus 214 and the Flybussen pass right by.

Quality Hotel Alexandra (☎ 71 20 37 50; www.choice.no; Storgata 1-7; s/d Nkr750/960 mid-Jun–mid-Aug, Nk1475/1595 Mon-Thu, Nkr895/1050 Fri-Sun rest-of-year; P 🖳 🏊) Most rooms here have a balcony and offer great views. There's a sauna and mini-gym (free to guests) and, for an aperitif, the cosy Bar A. It runs a good restaurant, the Vertshuset (☎ 71 20 37 75; pizzas Nkr89 to Nkr205, mains Nkr185 to Nkr235), all attractive panelled wood and bare brickwork. The hotel's high point (literally: it's up on the top floor) is its indoor heated pool, open all year, even when the snow's around.

our pick **Molde Fjordstuer** (☎ 71 20 10 60; www.havstuene.no; Julsundvegen 6; s/d incl breakfast Nkr740/990 mid-Jun–mid-Aug & Fri & Sat year-round, Nkr990/1240 Sun-Thu rest-of-year) Architecturally exciting, the Fjordstuer replicates the squat, solid forms of typical fisherfolk cottages. Small and welcoming, half of its 18 rooms have fjord views. Enjoy the vista from its quality restaurant Fjordstua (open 4pm to 10.30pm, Monday to Saturday) with its picture windows, or snack on shrimps, fish soup and other delicacies from the sea at the equally stylish Løkta (open 11am to 7pm Monday to Saturday) on the quayside below.

Rica Seilet Hotel (☎ 71 11 40 00; www.rica.no; Gideonvegen 2; s/d Nkr1015/1115 mid-Jun–mid-Aug, Nk1500/1750 Mon-Fri, Nkr1015/1265 Sat & Sun rest-of-year; P 🖳). This soaring hotel contrasts with its near-neighbour, the Fjordstuer, designed by the same architect, as it juts out into the sound like a huge silver sail. Within, the artwork in public areas is particularly striking. There are bedrooms up to the 14th floor, each with large picture windows and magnificent views. For a dreamier vista, relax in the Glasgow Lounge at water level; for a bird's-eye perspective, shoot up to the Sky Bar on the 15th floor.

Eating & Drinking

Dockside Pub (☎ 71 21 93 90; Torget; soup Nkr45, mains Nkr150-190, salads Nkr82-99; 🕑 core hrs noon-12.30am) At this popular place you can snack on pizzas, baguettes and sandwiches, or simply sip a drink either inside or on its attractive quayside terrace, according to the air temperature. It puts on live performances at least weekly.

Rød (☎ 71 20 30 01; Storgata 19; mains Nkr175-230) At 'Red', the restaurant of Hotell Molde, the menu, with plenty of dishes flashed in and out of the wok and tempting mains such as its fillet of beef with sauté of artichoke, squash and cherry cream sauce, is more exciting than its run-of-the-mill décor.

Bare Blå (☎ 71 21 58 88; Storgata 19), in Hotel Molde, is a popular pub on the main street.

ietting There & Away

AIR

Molde's shoreside **Årø airport** (☎ 71 21 47 80) is ikm east of the city centre. Flybussen (Nkr35, l0 minutes) meets and greets all flights. There ire three to five services daily to/from Oslo ind two daily to/from both Trondheim ind Bergen.

BOAT

Northbound, the Hurtigruten coastal ferry eaves at 10pm (6.30pm mid-September to nid-April); southbound, at 9.30pm. Express 'erries also operate from Molde.

BUS

nland buses run to and from Kristiansund Nkr148, 1¾ hours, up to 12 daily). Also, nuch more attractive and scarcely longer s the coastal run that rolls along the Atlanterhavsveien (see right). Other regional services include Åndalsnes (Nkr120, 1½ ours, up to eight) and Ålesund (Nkr131, 2¼ hours, three daily).

CAR & MOTORCYCLE

Travelling northwards on the Rv64, the Tussentunnelen short cut (Nkr15) avoids a log's leg and lops off a good 15 minutes.

AROUND MOLDE

Ona

The beautiful, tiny outer island of Ona, with ts bare rocky landscapes and picturesque ighthouse, is home to an offshore fishing community. Its one major event was an enormous tidal wave that washed over it n 1670. It makes a popular day trip from Molde. En route, WWII buffs may want to stop off at **Gossen Krigsminnesamling** (☎ 71 17 15 0; Gossen; adult/child/family Nkr30/10/70; ⏰ noon-5pm ue-Sun late Jun-early Aug), a former Nazi wartime airstrip built by Russian POWs on the low sland of Gossen. The abandoned summer-house village of Bjørnsund, where a café and shop operate from June to August, also war-rants a brief stop.

Bud

The Rv63 coastal route between Molde and Kristiansund is a pleasant alternative to the 'aster, ferry-less E89. En route lies the lit-tle fishing village of Bud, huddled around ts compact harbour. In the 16th and 17th centuries it was the greatest trading centre between Bergen and Trondheim.

Serving as a WWII museum and memor-ial, **Ergan Coastal Fort** (Ergan Kystfort; ☎ 91 51 05 26; adult/child Nkr60/40; ⏰ 10am-6pm Jun-Aug) was hastily erected by Nazi forces in May 1940. Various armaments and a network of bunkers and soldiers' quarters are dispersed around the hill with the sick bay and store sunk deep inside the mountain.

PlusCamp Bud (☎ 71 26 10 23; www.budcamping.no in Norwegian; car/caravan sites Nkr150/175, 4-bed cabin with outdoor bathroom Nkr400, 8-bed cabin with bathroom Nkr950) lies beside a small marina, where you can hire canoes, rowing boats and motor boats.

Sjøbua Mat og Vinhus (☎ 71 26 14 00; Vikaveien; mains Nkr170-210; ⏰ daily mid-May–mid-Sep, Fri-Sun rest-of-year) is a fish restaurant that serves up the local catch in a harbourfront warehouse with wooden floorboards and a boat poised in the middle of the room.

Bus 352 travels regularly between Molde and Bud (one hour; four to seven times daily, except Sunday).

Trollkirka

If you're heading towards Bud and Atlanter-havsveien, it's worth making a short side trip to the Trollkirka (Trolls' Church) cave. Three white marble grottoes are connected by sub-terranean streams, and in one an impressive 14m waterfall tumbles. The entrance is a steep uphill walk (2.5km; allow two to three hours for the return trip) from the signed car park. You'll need a torch and good boots to explore the caves fully.

Atlanterhavsveien & Averøya

The eight storm-lashed bridges of the Atlantic Ocean Road, designated a National Tourist Route, buck and twist like so many sea ser-pents as it connects 17 islets between Vevang and the island of Averøya. In 2006, the UK's *Guardian* newspaper crowned it the 'world's best road trip'. That's going it a bit for a stretch of highway barely 8km long but it's certainly hugely scenic and in a storm you'll experience nature's wrath at its most dra-matic. Look out for whales and seals offshore along the route in season and perhaps make a short detour north of the main road to the isolated **Hestskjæret Fyr** lighthouse.

Well worth the detour too is **Kvernes stave church** (adult/child Nkr30/free; ⏰ 10am-5pm daily mid-Jun–mid-Aug, Sun only rest-of-year) on Averøya, dating from around the 14th century and rebuilt in the 17th. Inside are a large 300-year-old votive ship and a 15th-century Catholic-Lutheran hybrid altar screen. There's also a small open-air museum and a gallery/handicrafts outlet nearby.

Skjerneset Bryggecamping (☎ 71 51 18 94; www.skjerneset.com in Norwegian; per person/site Nkr25/90, cabins Nkr600-715, d with shared bathroom Nkr390, tr with bathroom Nkr530) is a hyperfriendly place, right beside the sea. At Sveggevika on Ekkilsøya, west of Bremsnes, it's at the end of a 1km dirt road. The owners, themselves former commercial fisherfolk, organise deep-sea trips in their own boat, or you can hire a motorboat and sling your own line. Rooms are in a former fish warehouse, which houses a fascinating family museum on the top floor.

Håholmen Havstuer (☎ 71 51 72 50; www.haholmen.no; s/d Nkr860/1270) is a former fishing station on an offshore islet north of the middle of the archipelago. The 49 rooms, scattered around the renovated complex, are simply and tastefully furnished in rustic style and Ytterbrugga, its restaurant, serves the freshest of fish. To transport you there, the *Kvitserk*, a replica of a Viking vessel, makes the 10-minute sea journey, leaving the roadside car park on the hour, between 11am and 9pm, late June to mid-August.

Year-round, buses of **Eide Auto** (90 77 30 63) link Molde and Kristiansund (Nkr123, 2¼ hours, two to four daily) via the coastal route and Atlanterhavsveien. For car drivers, there are frequent ferry connections between Bremsnes and Kristiansund.

KRISTIANSUND

pop 17,100

The historic cod-fishing and -drying town of Kristiansund ranges over three islands. Its best restaurants serve dishes from the deep, fishing boats – large and small – still moor alongside its quays while Mellemværftet, unkempt and chaotic, hangs on as a working boatyard.

Kristiansund looks both inland and to the sea for its wealth, even though the waters are no longer so bountiful – the huge hauls of yesteryear are now the source of tales as tall as any angler's. In addition to cod-processing (some 80% of the world's klippfisk is cured in and around the town), it remains an important port for the export of timber, hewn from the forests of the interior. And, as the most significant town between Trondheim and Stavanger for servicing Norway's North Sea oilfields, it takes its share of black gold.

Information

Ark bookshop (☎ 71 57 09 60; cnr Kaibakken & Nedre Enggate) Also good for maps.

Laundrette (Guest Marina)

Onkel og Vennene (Kaibakken 1) Free internet access at a popular place for a drink (see p272).

Tourist office (☎ 71 58 54 54; www.visitkristiansund.com; Kongens plass 1; ⏲ 9am-6pm Mon-Fri, 10am-3pm Sat, 11am-4pm Sun mid-Jun–mid-Aug, 9am-4pm Mon-Fri rest-of-year) Free internet access.

Sights

Kristiansund's **Gamle Byen** (Old Town) occupies part of Innlandet island, a few of whose clapboard buildings date back to the 17th century. The grandiose **Lossiusgården**, at the eastern end of the historic district, was the distinguished home of an 18th-century merchant. The venerable 300-year-old **Dødeladen Café** – where you can still get a decent meal and a drink – hosts cultural and musical events. The most convenient access from the centre is on the Sundbåt ferry (see p273) from Piren ferry port.

Kristiansund's monumental 1914 **Festiviteten** theatre, although plain enough from the outside, has an attractive Art Nouveau interior. Beside Piren, the **Klippfiskkjerringa statue**, by Tore Bjørn Skjøsvik, represents a fishwife carrying cod for drying.

MELLEMVÆRFTET

Something of a nautical junkyard, **Mellemværftet**, free and accessible any time, is best approached on foot along the quayside from the Smia Fiskerestaurant. It's difficult to make out what's what amid the agreeable clutter but it includes the remnants of Kristiansund's 19th-century shipyard, a forge and workshop, and workers quarters.

MUSEUMS

Kristiansund has several museums housed, for the most part, in historic buildings whose exteriors alone warrant a visit. Happily so since some have severely reduced opening hours – or none at all except by appointment. We detail here the situation as it was when we last visited and trust that things may have improved when you call by. The helpful tourist office will be au fait. Otherwise, try your luck on ☎ 71 58 70 00 the central phone number for all museums, or www.nordmore.museum.no.

Handelshuset (Freiveien; admission free; 11am-4pm daily mid-Jun–Aug, Sat & Sun only rest-of-year), formally a lively place serving traditional food, seems to have been overcome by the general cultural languor too. Its magnificent vintage jukebox, with old 45rpm hits by Presley, the Stones, the Beach Boys and other distant icons, may have played its last platter unless someone gets around to repairing it. But you can still browse among Handelshuset's old posters and signs, learn something of Kristiansund's commercial history and drink the freshest coffee, roasted on Norway's oldest operational coffee roaster.

The **Norwegian Klippfish museum** (Norsk Klippfiskmuseum; 71 58 30 14; adult/child incl Nkr50/free guided tour; noon-5pm late Jun–early Aug), in the 1749 **Milnbrygga warehouse** on Gomalandet peninsula, presents the 300-year history of the dried-cod export industry in Kristiansund and continues to produce modest quantities of *klippfisk* (salted cod) in the traditional way. From the town centre, take the Sundbåt ferry and ask to be dropped off.

Just north of this museum are **Hjelkrembrygga**, a former *klippfish* warehouse dating from 1835, and neighbouring **Woldbrygga**, a barrel factory constructed in 1875. Both are open only by appointment.

KIRKELANDET CHURCH

Architect Odd Østby's inspirational **church** (Langveien; 10am-6pm May-Aug, 10am-2pm rest-of-year) was built in 1964 to replace the one destroyed by Nazi bombs. The angular exterior, where copper and concrete alternate, is sober and measured. Inside, all lines direct the eye to the 320 panes of stained glass at the rear of the chancel. Moving upward from the earthy colours at the base, they become paler and, at the top, replicate the 'celestial light of heaven'.

Behind the church lies **Vanndammene Park,** with plenty of greenery, walking tracks and the eagle's eyrie Varden watchtower viewpoint.

Sleeping

Atlanten Camping & Kristiansund Vandrerhjem (71 67 11 04; www.atlanten.no; Dalaveien 22; car/caravan sites Nkr110/130 plus per person Nkr10, 4-bed cabin with outdoor bathroom Nkr380-485, with bathroom Nkr590, motel s/d Nkr530/630, hostel s/d with bathroom Nkr380/430) Occupying joint premises, this hostel, motel and camp site lie within 20-minutes walking distance of the centre. It's a friendly place and the well-equipped hostel kitchen boasts 17 fridges. Camping facilities could do with a revamp, however.

Utsyn Pensjonat (71 56 69 70; fax 71 56 69 90; Kongens Plass 4; s/d Nkr440/590) With only eight rooms, the Utsyn is a quiet, uncomplicated, bog-standard boarding house whose chief virtue is its price. Under new Asian ownership, its café offers both Norwegian and Chinese cooking.

Rica Hotel (71 57 12 00; www.rica.no; Storgata 41; s/d Nkr970/1160 mid-Jun–mid-Aug, Nkr1395/1645 Sun-Thu, Nkr910/1160 Fri & Sat rest-of-year; P) Fundamentally renovated in 2006, the fjord-side Rica has that almost-new feel to it. All rooms have a bathtub and most overlook the water. The view gets better – and best of all from its top-floor bar, open to all – the higher you rise. There's a free sauna and mini-gym for guest use.

Quality Hotel Grand (71 57 13 00; www.choice.no; Bernstorffstredet 1; s/d Nkr1310/1430 Sun-Thu, Nkr835/1050 Fri & Sat; P) With its 109 rooms, the Hotel Grand is Kristiansund's largest. Six rooms are equipped for the handicapped and 30 take into account guests with allergies. Rooms are comfortable and attractively furnished and the hotel's Edward Restaurant has an à la carte menu that's as good as anywhere in town.

Eating

For a café that's rich in atmosphere, go out of your way to visit Handelshuset (see left).

Bryggekanten (71 67 61 60; Storkaia 1; pizza Nkr115; Mon-Sat) This recently opened brasserie and bar sits right beside the harbour. It's a great choice, even if only for a drink. Even better, tuck into a pizza, bruschetta or creative sandwich (such as *bacalao* in tomato sauce, lightly spiced with chilli) on its broad terrace. Inside, where full dinners are served, is more intimate. Here, too, the menu is imaginative, taking traditional ingredients and giving them a new twist.

our pick **Smia Fiskerestaurant** (71 67 11 70; Fosnagata 30b; mains Nkr140-240; 1-11pm) The much garlanded Smia fish restaurant is in an old forge, adorned from wall to ceiling with bellows and blacksmith's tools – plus a couple of whale vertebrae and a hanging split cod. The fish soup (Nkr80) makes a great starter, or you can also have it as a main course (Nkr130).

Sjøstjerna (71 67 87 78; Skolegata 8; mains Nkr200-235; 5pm-midnight Mon-Fri, noon-midnight Sat) Here's

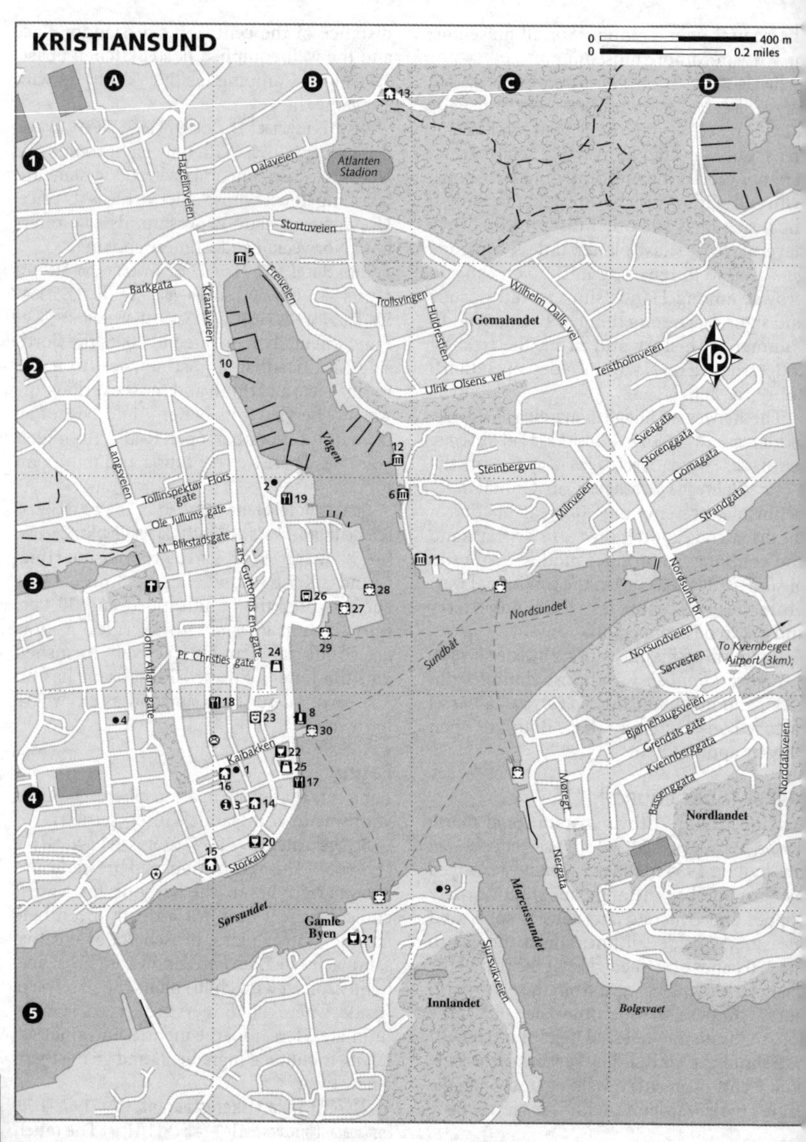

another recommended fish restaurant, which offers a similar menu and marine-themed interior. Eat inside or on its pleasant street-side terrace beside pedestrianised Skolegata.

Drinking & Entertainment

Onkel og Vennene (☎ 71 67 58 10; Kaibakken 1; 🖳) At 1st floor level it's a popular place for an evening beer or snack. It has great harbour views, whether inside or from the small veranda, where smokers can puff away. There's free internet for guests.

Christian's Bar (☎ 71 57 03 00; Storgata 17) On the 1st floor of Hotell Kristiansund, Christian's Bar is an attractive pub where the over-25s congregate.

Mucca (☎ 71 67 74 04; Hauggata 16; from 8pm Fri & Sat), located beside the Comfort Hotel Fosna, is where you'll find the town's younger crowd, while **J P Clausens** (☎ 71 57 12 00; Storgata 41-43), the piano and wine bar of the Rica Hotel, is more for slow waltzers.

Shopping

At **Klippfiskbutikken** (☎ 71 67 12 64, 95 20 26 30; Storkaia) genial Knut Garshol, a member of the international slow food ecogastronomy movement, will buttonhole you and enthusiastically proclaim the virtues of klippfish at this splendid temple to the mighty cod.

Kristiansund has a branch of **Vinmonopolet** (Storkaia), the state booze monopoly, which sits opposite Bryggekanten.

Getting There & Away

AIR

The town's Kvernberget **airport** (☎ 71 68 30 50) is on Nordlandet island. There are up to six flights daily to/from Oslo and two to three to/from Bergen.

Buses travel regularly to/from the airport (Nkr40, 15 minutes, up to eight daily) to meet incoming flights.

BOAT

For day trips to the eastern end of the Atlanterhavsveien and the Kvernes stave church, take the Bremsnes ferry (Nkr24, 20 minutes, every 20 to 30 minutes) from Holmakaia Quay.

Express boats connect Kristiansund with Trondheim (3½ hours, up to three daily from Nordmørskaia). The Hurtigruten coastal ferry also calls in daily at Holmakaia. The southbound ferry departs at 5pm, northbound at 1.45am (11pm mid-September to mid-April).

BUS

Inland buses run to/from Molde (Nkr148, 1¾ hours, up to 12 daily). The coastal run that rolls along the Atlanterhavsveien (see p269) is much more attractive and scarcely longer. Northwards, there are between one and three daily buses to Trondheim (Nkr375, 3¼ hours).

Getting Around

The **Sundbåt ferry** (adult/child Nkr20/10, day ticket Nkr50) is well worth the ride for its own sake and for the special perspective it gives of the harbour. It links the town centre and the islands of Innlandet, Nordlandet and Gomelandet, running every half hour, Monday to Saturday. The full circuit takes 20 minutes.

AROUND KRISTIANSUND

Grip

Crowded onto a tiny rocky island, the colourful village of Grip with its pastel painted houses sits amid an archipelago of 80 islets and skerries. In the early 19th century, after a drop in cod hauls and two powerful storms, the village was practically abandoned. It eventually bounced back and was for years Norway's smallest municipality before being appended to Kristiansund in 1964.

The island's **stave church**, much restored and open according to the ferry's arrival, was originally constructed in the late 15th century and has an interesting, manifestly Catholic altar cabinet. On an offshore skerry, the 47m-tall Bratthårskollen lighthouse, built in 1888, prods skywards.

From mid-May to late August, the **M/S Gripskyss** (☎ 71 58 26 16; www.gripskyss.no) plies the 14km between Kristiansund's Piren terminal and Grip (adult/child Nkr190/95 return, 30 minutes) once or twice daily.

Trøndelag

The Trøndelag is a region of rumpled hills, stippled with ox blood–coloured farmsteads and ruffled green with wheat and barley. Hay stands out to dry on distinctive long, low trellises like a line of shaggy yaks in procession, and always there's water near at hand, whether sea, a lake or an incised fjord.

Far and away the region's major draw is the attractive city of Trondheim, Norway's third-largest, and the most northerly place in Norway that merits the title 'city'. You can find fulfilment wandering the medieval streets and quays of this attractive town with its buzzing student life, pretty wharf-side restaurants and bars. Highlights include Nidaros Cathedral, Scandinavia's largest medieval structure, and the open-air Sverresborg Trøndelag Folk Museum.

The area also marks a couple of beginnings, one historical, the other contemporary. Stiklestad, site of the martyrdom of King Olav (St Olav) is at the heart of every Norwegian's sense of national identity. With its lovely little church, impressive visitors centre and open-air museum, it well deserves the minor detour from the Arctic Highway.

The town of Steinkjer marks the start of the ultrascenic Kystriksveien. Also called, more prosaically, the Rv17 (Steinkjer's tourist office, right beside the E6, is well endowed with information about this tempting alternative), this coastal route continues as far as Bodø Nordland, and offers a stimulating alternative to the Arctic Highway for those with spare time – and cash – for the extra ferry fares. Even if the chronometer or a krone shortfall precludes you from following the Kystriksveien, you can get the flavour of this alternative by diverting to the little coastal settlement of Namsos, then cutting back eastwards to rejoin the E6 at Grong.

HIGHLIGHTS

- Browse **Nidaros Cathedral** (p276), Trondheim, Norway's most sacred building
- Trundle a **trolley** (p288) along the no-longer-active Namsos–Skage railway line
- Explore the cultural centre at **Stiklestad** (p287), where St Olav was martyred
- Learn about coastal life at multimedia **Norveg** (p289) in Rørvik
- Tuck into Norwegian specialities in Trondheim's historical **Vertshuset Tavern** (p283)
- Hike in the wilderness of **Bymarka** (p281), right in Trondheim's backyard

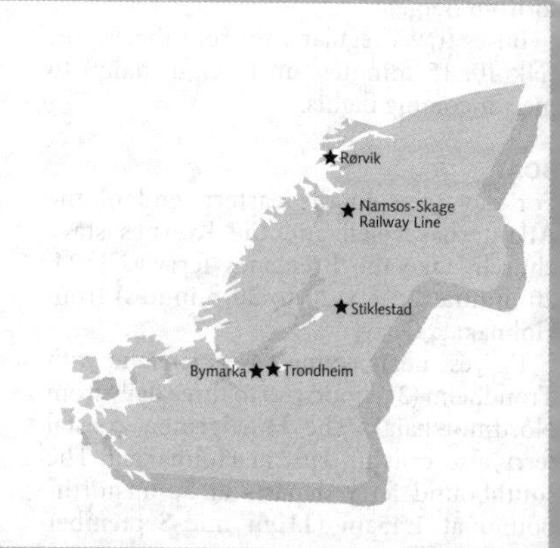

- POPULATION: 407,900
- HIGHEST ELEVATION: KRÅKVASSTIND (1699M)

TRONDHEIM

Pop 161,750

Trondheim, Norway's original capital, is nowadays the country's third-largest city after Oslo and Bergen. With its wide streets and partly pedestrianised heart, it's a simply lovely city with a long history. Fuelled by a large student population, it buzzes with life. Cycles zip everywhere, it has some good cafés and restaurants, and it's rich in museums. You *can* absorb it in one busy day, but it merits more if you're to slip into its lifestyle.

History

In 997, the Christian King Olav Tryggvason selected a broad sandbank at the River Nid estuary to moor his longboat. The natural harbour and strategic position made Nidaros (meaning 'mouth of the River Nid'), as the settlement was then called, especially useful for defence against the warlike pagan chiefs of Lade, who were a threat to Christianity and to the region's stability. One plausible theory has it that Leifur Eiríksson (or Leif Ericson as he's usually transcribed in English) visited the king's farm two years later and was converted to Christianity before setting sail for Iceland and Greenland and possibly becoming the first European to set foot in North America. (If you're from the USA, the Viking staring out to sea near the Hurtigruten quay may seem familiar. That's because he's an exact replica of the Ericson

TROND-*WHAT?*

Listen to Trondheimers talk about their city, and you may wonder whether they're all referring to the same place.

Since the late Middle Ages, the city has been called Trondhjem, pronounced 'Trond-yem' and meaning, roughly, 'home of the good life'. But in the early 20th century the fledgling national government was bent on making Norwegian city names more historically Norwegian; just as Christiania reverted to its ancient name of Oslo, on 1 January 1930 Trondhjem was changed back to Nidaros.

Some 20,000 locals took to the streets in protest and by 6 March the government relented – sort of. The compromise was 'Trondheim,' the etymologically Danish *'hj'* having been duly exorcised.

Nowadays the official pronunciation is 'Trond-haym', but many locals still say 'Trond-yem'. Thanks to the vagaries of the local dialect, still others call it 'Trond-yahm'. Typical of this tolerant city, any of these pronunciations is acceptable, as is the 'Trond-hime' that most English speakers hazard.

statue in Seattle that commemorates the tens of thousands of Norwegian emigrants to the New World.)

In 1030 another, now more famous, King Olav (Haraldsson) was martyred in battle at Stiklestad (p287), about 90km to the northeast, and canonised. Nidaros became a centre for pilgrims from all over Europe, its bishopric embracing Norway, Orkney, the Isle of Man, the Faroe Islands, Iceland and Greenland. It served as the capital of Norway until 1217, ruling an empire that extended from what is now western Russia to, possibly, the shores of Newfoundland. The cult of St Olav continued until the Reformation in 1537, when Norway was placed under the Lutheran bishopric of Denmark.

After a fire razed most of the city in 1681, Trondheim was redesigned with wide streets and Renaissance flair. The city's location became key once again in WWII, when German naval forces made it their base for northern Norway, although fortunately the city avoided major damage.

Orientation

Central Trondheim forms a triangular peninsula bordered by the river Nidelva to the southwest and east, and Trondheimsfjord to the north. The combined train station and bus terminal (Trondheim Sentralstasjon), and boat quays too are squeezed between the canal immediately north of the centre and Trondheimsfjord.

The epicentre of town is Torvet, the central square (also spelt 'Torget') with its statue of King Olav Tryggvason atop a column.

Just east of the centre, across the Gaml Bybro (Old Town Bridge), is the Bakklande neighbourhood, where, within old warehouse and renovated workers housing, are some c the city's most colourful places to eat an drink. Small Solsiden, even more recentl restored, is where you'll find Trondheim' trendiest cafés and wharf-side restaurants.

Information

Ark Bruns Bokhandel (☎ 73 51 00 22; Kongens gate 10) Carries a good selection of books in English.

Elefanten Vaskeri (🕑 10am-6pm Mon-Fri, 11am-4pm Sat) Wash your smalls and sip a coffee at this congenial café and laundrette, Norway's northernmost.

Library (Kongens gate; 🕑 9am-7pm Mon-Thu, 9am-4pm Fri, 10am-3pm Sat) Free internet access. Carries international press.

Main post office (Dronningens gate 10)

Spacebar (☎ 73 51 53 50; Kongens gate 19; per hr Nkr40; 🕑 10-midnight Sun-Thu, 24hr Fri & Sat) Internet café with entry on Prinsens gate.

Tourist office (☎ 73 80 76 60; www.trondheim.no; Torvet; 🕑 8.30am-8pm Mon-Fri, 10am-6pm Sat & Sun late Jun–mid-Aug; 8.30am-6pm Mon-Fri, 10am-4pm Sat & Sun late May-late Jun & mid–late Aug; 9am-4pm Mon-Fri, 10am-2pm Sat rest-of-year)

Trondheim is one of Europe's first wireless cit ies. If you're carrying your laptop, you can wi fi for free anywhere within the city centre.

Sights

NIDAROS CATHEDRAL & ARCHBISHOP'S PALACE

Nidaros Cathedral (Nidaros Domkirke; Kongsgårdsgata adult/child/family Nkr50/25/125, combined ticket to ca hedral, palace museum & crown jewels adult/child/family Nkr100/50/200; 9am-3pm Mon-Fri, 9am-2pm Sat, noon-4pm Sun May–mid-Jun & mid-Aug–mid-Sep, 9am-6pm Mon-Fri, 9am-2pm Sat, noon-4pm Sun mid-Jun–mid-Aug; noon-2.30pm Mon-Fri, 11.30am-2pm Sat, noon-4pm Sun rest-of-year), constructed in the late 11th century, s Scandinavia's largest medieval building. Outside, the ornately embellished west wall has top-to-bottom statues of biblical characters and Norwegian bishops and kings, sculpted in the early 20th century. Within, the cathedral is subtly lit (just see how the vibrantly coloured, modern stained-glass glows, especially in the rose window at the west end), so let your eyes attune to the gloom.

The altar sits over the original grave of St Olav, the Viking king who replaced the Nordic pagan religion with Christianity. The original cathedral was built in 1153, when Norway became a separate archbishopric. The current transept and chapter house were constructed between 1130 and 1180 and reveal Anglo-Norman influences (many of the craftsmen were brought in from England), while the Gothic choir and ambulatory were completed in the early 14th century. The nave, repeatedly ravaged by fire across the centuries, is mostly a faithful 19th-century reconstruction.

Down in the crypt is a display of medieval carved tombstones (the majority restored from fragments since many headstones were broken up and carted away to be recycled in domestic buildings). Look for one inscribed in English and dedicated to one William Miller, Shipmaster, of Dundee, Scotland, who met his end near Trondheim in the 18th century.

You can wander around freely but it's worthwhile joining a tour (a 15-minute canter or a more detailed 45-minute visit). Times vary but there are up to four daily in English (usually at 11am, noon, 1.30pm and 4pm). Music lovers may want to time their visit to take in a **recital** (admission free; 1pm Mon-Sat mid-Jun–mid-Aug) on the church's magnificent organ.

From mid-June to mid-August, you can climb the cathedral's **tower** for a great view over the city. There are ascents every half hour from its base in the south transept.

Admission to the cathedral also includes the complex of the adjacent 12th-century **Archbishop's Palace**, commissioned around 1160 and Scandinavia's oldest secular building. In the west wing, Norway's **crown jewels** (adult/child/family Nkr70/25/165) shimmer and flash. Its **museum** (adult/child/family Nkr50/25/125; 10am-3pm Mon-Sat, noon-4pm Sun May–mid-Jun & mid-Aug–mid-Sep; 10am-4pm Mon-Fri, 10am-3pm Sat, noon-4pm Sun Jun-Aug; core hrs 11am-2pm Wed-Sun rest-of-year) is in the same compound. After visiting the well-displayed statues, gargoyles and carvings from the cathedral, drop to the lower level, where only a selection of the myriad artefacts revealed during the museum's construction in the late 1990s are on show. Take in too its enjoyable 15-minute audiovisual programme.

The adjoining **National Military Museum** (admission free; 9am-3pm Mon-Fri, 11am-4pm Sat & Sun Jun-Aug), in the same courtyard, is full of antique swords, armour and cannons, and recounts the days from 1700 to 1900, when the Archbishop's Palace served as a Danish military installation. On the top floor is the **Hjemmesfront** (Home Front) museum, devoted to Trondheim's role in the WWII resistance.

SVERRESBORG TRØNDELAG FOLK MUSEUM

West of the centre, the **Folk Museum** (73 89 01 00; Sverresborg Allé 13; www.sverresborg.no; adult/concession/child/family Nkr80/55/30/195; 11am-6pm Jun-Aug, 11am-3pm Mon-Fri, noon-3pm Sat & Sun rest-of-year) is one of the best of its kind in Norway. The indoor exhibition, Livsbilder (Images of Life) in the main building, displays artefacts in use over the last 150 years – from clothing to school supplies to bicycles – and has a short multimedia presentation.

The rest of the museum, with over 60 period buildings, is open air, adjoining the ruins of King Sverre's castle and giving fine hilltop views of the city. Houses, the post office, the dentist's and other shops splay around the central market square in the urban section. There are farm buildings from rural Trøndelag, the tiny 12th-century Haltdalen stave church and a couple of small museums devoted to telecommunications (some great old phones) and skiing (with elaborately carved wooden skis). There are guided tours in Norwegian and English four times daily.

The museum's restaurant, **Vertshuset Tavern** (see p283), itself in a wonderfully preserved old building, is a great place to try Norwegian specialities. Take bus 8 (direction Stavset) from Dronningens gate.

OTHER MUSEUMS

The **Ringve Museum** (73 87 02 80; Lade Allé 60; adult/concession/child/family Nkr75/50/25/150; 11am-3pm May–mid-Jun, Aug & Sep, 11am-5pm mid-Jun–Jul, 11am-4pm Sun only rest-of-year) is Norway's national museum for

TRONDHEIM

A B C D

1 2 3 4 5 6

INFORMATION
Ark Bruns Bokhandel....1 F4
Library....2 F4
Main Post Office....3 F3
Spacebar....4 E4
Tourist Office....5 F4
Trondhjems Turistforening DNT Office....6 D3

SIGHTS & ACTIVITIES
Archbishop's Palace (Erkebispegården)....7 F5
Gregorius Kirke Ruins (Sparebanken)....8 F3
Hospitalkirken....9 D4
King Olav Tryggvason Statue....10 E4
Kristiansten Fort (Festning)....11 G4
Leif Erikson Statue....12 F1
Museum of Natural History & Archaeology (Vitenskapsmuseet NTNU)....13 D4
National Military Museum (Ruskammeret) & Home Front (Hjemmesfront) Museum....14 E5
National Museum of Decorative Arts (Nordenfjeldske Kunstindustrimuseum)....15 F4
Nidaros Cathedral (Domkirke)....16 F4
Olavskirken Ruins....(see 2)
Pirbadet Water Park & Pools....17 F1
Science Centre (Vitensenteret)....18 F4
Stiftsgården....19 E3
Sverresborg Trøndelag Folk Museum....20 A6
Synagogue & Jewish Museum....21 E5
Trondheim Art Museum (Trondheim Kunstmuseum)....22 E4
Trondheim Maritime Museum (Trondheims Sjøfartsmuseum)....23 G2

SLEEPING
Britannia Hotel....24 F3
Chesterfield Hotel....25 F3
Clarion Collection Hotel Grand Olav....26 F3
P-Hotel....27 F3
Pensjonat Jarlen....28 E4
Radisson SAS Royal Garden Hotel....29 G3
Singsaker Sommerhotel....30 H5
Thon Hotel Trondheim....31 E4
Trondheim InterRail Centre....(see 53)

EATING
Bakklandet Skydsstasjon....32 G4
Benitos....33 F4
Café ni Muser....(see 22)
Chablis....34 F4
Credo....35 F3
Dromedar....36 F3
Dromedar....37 F4
Edgar Café....(see 53)
Emilies....38 E4
Grønn Pepper....39 F2
Havfruen....40 F4
Persilleriet....41 E4
Ravnkloa Fish Market....42 E3
Sushi Bar....43 E3
To Rom og Kjøkken....44 F3
Vertshuset Tavern....45 A6
Zia Teresa....(see 33)
Ørens Kro....46 G3

DRINKING
Bare Blåbær....47 G3
Bruk Bar....48 E3
Den Gode Nabo....49 F4
Macbeth....50 F3
Metro....51 F4
Rick's Café....52 F3
Studentersamfundet....53 E6
Trondheim Microbryggeri....54 E3

ENTERTAINMENT
Dokkhuset....55 G3
Frakken....56 F3
Nova Kinosenter....57 F3
Olavshallen....(see 26)
Prinsen Kino....58 E5
Supa....(see 48)
Tiger Tiger....59 F2
Trøndelag Teater....60 E4

TRANSPORT
Bike Lift....61 G4
Express Boats to Kristiansund....(see 62)
Fast Ferry Quay....62 F1
Ferries to Munkholmen....63 E3
Intercity Bus Terminal (Rutebilstasjon)....64 F2
Local Bus Hub....65 E3
St Olavsgata Tram Station....66 E3
Tripps Estuary Cruises....(see 63)

Sandgate
Kongens gate
Nidelva
Gangbrua
Steinberget
To Bymarka (1km)
Fridtjof Nansens gate
Øya
Sverresborg Allé
To Gråkalbanen Tramway to Lian (15km); Trondheim Skisenter Granåsen (19km)

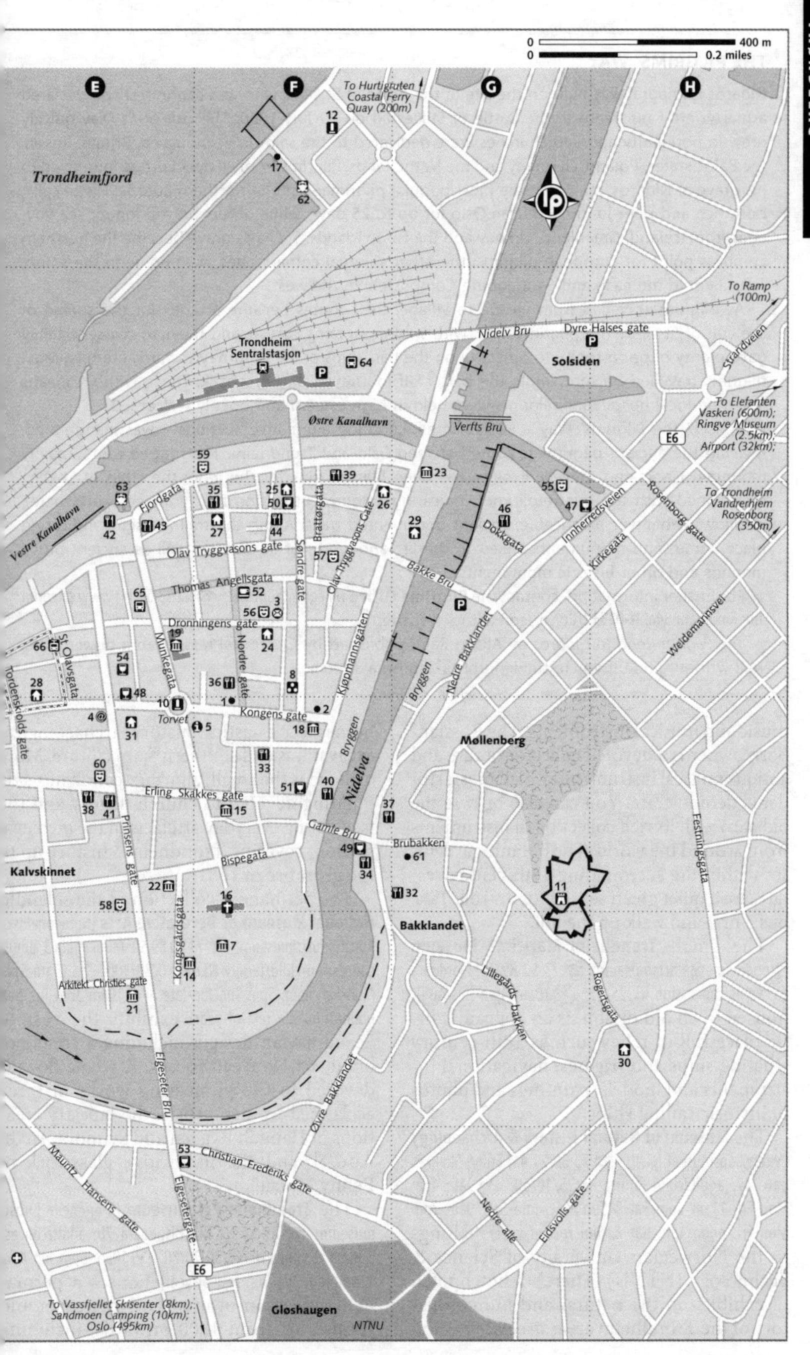
0 400 m
0 0.2 miles
E
F
G
H
Trondheimfjord
To Hurtigruten Coastal Ferry Quay (200m)
Trondheim Sentralstasjon
Østre Kanalhavn
Vestre Kanalhavn
Nidelv Bru
Dyre Halses gate
Solsiden
Strandveien
To Ramp (100m)
To Elefanten Vaskeri (600m); Ringve Museum (2.5km); Airport (32km)
To Trondheim Vandrerhjem Rosenborg (350m)
Verfts Bru
E6
Fjordgata
Olav Tryggvasons gate
Thomas Angellsgata
Dronningens gate
Søndre gate
Nordre gate
Brattørgata
Olav Tryggvasons Gate
Kjøpmannsgaten
Bakke Bru
Dokkgata
Innherredsveien
Rosenborg gate
Kirkegata
Weidemannsvei
Nedre Bakklandet
Bryggen
St Olavsgata
Tordenskiolds gate
Munkegata
Torvet
Kongens gate
Møllenberg
Nidelva
Erling Skakkes gate
Gamle Bru
Brubakken
Festningsgata
Bispegata
Kalvskinnet
Prinsens gate
Kongsgårdsgata
Bakklandet
Arkitekt Christies gate
Lillegårds bakken
Rogertsgata
Elgeseter Bru
Øvre Bakklandet
Christian Frederiks gate
Elgesetergate
Maurits Hansens gate
Nedre allé
Eidsvolls gate
To Vassfjellet Skisenter (8km); Sandmoen Camping (10km); Oslo (495km)
Gløshaugen
NTNU

THE PILGRIMS' WAY

Nidaros Cathedral was built on the site of the grave of St Olav, who was canonised and declared a martyr after his death at the Battle of Stiklestad on 29 July 1030. The cult of St Olav quickly grew in popularity and 340 churches were dedicated to the saint in Scandinavia, Britain, Russia, the Baltic states, Poland, Germany and the Netherlands. Pilgrims from all over Europe journeyed to his grave at Nidaros, making it the most popular pilgrimage site in northern Europe. Historically, both rich and poor journeyed from Oslo for up to 25 days, while others braved longer sea voyages from Iceland, Greenland, Orkney and the Faroe Islands. St Olav's grave became the northern compass point for European pilgrims; the other spiritual cornerstones were Rome in the south, Jerusalem in the east, and Santiago de Compostela in the west.

As pilgrims travelled from village to village, their routes became arteries for the spread of the cult of St Olav. The pilgrims' way, with wild mountains, forests and rivers to cross, certainly gave plenty of opportunity to reflect upon the hardships of life's journey towards eternity. Most pilgrims travelled on foot, while the better off journeyed on horseback. Those without means relied on local hospitality; pilgrims were held in high esteem and openly welcomed.

In 1997 the Pilgrims' Way – 926km in all, counting alternative sections – was inaugurated, reviving the ancient pilgrimage route between Oslo and Trondheim. The rugged route, mainly mountain tracks and gravelled roads, has been blazed (look for the logo: the cross of St Olav intertwined with the quatrefoil knot indicating a tourist attraction that you see everywhere). It follows, wherever practicable, ancient documented trails. Along the trail are signs indicating place names and monuments linked to the life and works of St Olav, as well as ancient burial mounds and other historic monuments.

For further information, contact the **Pilgrims Office** (Pilegrimskontoret; ☎ 22 33 03 11; www.pilegrim.no; Kirkegata 34a, N-0153 Oslo) or consult its website.

The Pilgrim Road to Nidaros by Alison Raju, published by Cicerone Press, is an indispensable, well-written guide if you're thinking of taking on a stretch.

music and musical instruments. The Russian-born owner is a devoted collector of rare and antique musical instruments, which music students demonstrate. You can also browse the old barn with its rich collection of instruments from around the world. The botanic gardens, set within the surrounding 18th-century estate, are a quiet green setting for a stroll. Take bus 3 or 4 and walk up the hill.

The small **Trondheim Maritime Museum** (Trondheims Sjøfartsmuseum; ☎ 73 52 89 75; Fjordgata 6a; adult/concession Nkr25/15; ⏲ 10am-4pm Jun-Aug), housed in an old prison, is an appealing little place full of relics such as 18th-century whaling ships and frigates, navigational instruments and models, paintings and photos of historic sailing ships.

The **Museum of Natural History & Archaeology** (Vitenskapsmuseet NTNU; ☎ 73 59 21 45; Erling Skakkes gate 47; adult/child/family Nkr25/10/50; ⏲ 9am-4pm Mon-Fri, 11am-4pm Sat & Sun May–mid-Sep, 9am-2pm Mon-Fri, noon-4pm Sat & Sun rest-of-year) belongs to the Norwegian University of Science & Technology (NTNU). There's a hotchpotch of exhibits on the natural and human history of the Trondheim area: streetscapes and homes, ecclesiastical history, archaeological excavations and southern Sami culture. More ordered is the small, alluring section in a side building devoted to church history and the fascinating everyday artefacts in the medieval section, covering Trondheim's history up to the great fire of 1681.

The permanent collection of the splendid **National Museum of Decorative Arts** (Nordenfjeldske Kunstindustrimuseum; ☎ 73 80 89 50; Munkegata 5; adult/concession/child/family Nkr60/40/30/100; ⏲ 10am-5pm Mon-Sat, noon-5pm Sun Jun-late Aug, 10am-3pm Tue-Sat, noon-4pm Sun rest-of-year) exhibits the best of Scandinavian design, including a couple of bijou Art Nouveau rooms. A whole floor is devoted to the pioneering works of three acclaimed women artists: the tapestry creations of Hannah Ryggen and Synnøve Anker Aurdal, and the innovative glasswork of Benny Motzfeldt.

The **Trondheim Art Museum** (Trondheim Kunstmuseum; ☎ 73 53 81 80; Bispegata 7b; adult/concession/child/family Nkr40/30/20/80; ⏲ 10am-5pm Jun-Aug, 11am-4pm Tue-Sun rest-of-year) houses a permanent collection of modern Norwegian and Danish art from 1800 onwards, including a hallway of Munch lithographs, and runs temporary exhibitions.

STIFTSGÅRDEN

Scandinavia's largest wooden palace, the late baroque **Stiftsgården** (☎ 73 84 28 80; Munkegata 23; adult/concession/child/family Nkr60/40/30/100; ⌚ 10am-4pm Mon-Sat, noon-4pm Sun Jun-late Aug) was constructed as a private residence in the late 18th century. It is now the official royal residence in Trondheim. Admission is by tour only, every hour on the hour.

HISTORIC NEIGHBOURHOODS

From **Gamle Bybro** (Old Town Bridge), there's a superb view of the **Bryggen**, colourful 18th- and 19th-century riverfront warehouses reminiscent of their better known counterparts in Bergen. To the east, the one-time working-class neighbourhoods of **Møllenberg** and **Bakklandet** are now gentrified latte-land, all cobbles, car-free alleys, trim houses in pastel shades and gardens scarcely bigger than a towel that burst with flowers.

The cobblestone streets immediately west of the centre are also lined with mid-19th-century wooden buildings, notably the octagonal 1705 timber church, **Hospitalskirken** (Hospitalsløkka 2-4), in the hospital grounds.

KRISTIANSTEN FESTNING

For a bird's-eye view of the city, climb 10 minutes from the Gamle Bybro to **Kristiansten Fort** (Festningsgata; admission free; ⌚ 10am-4pm daily Jun-Aug), built after Trondheim's great fire of 1681. During WWII the Nazis used it as a prison and execution ground for members of the Norwegian Resistance. The grounds are open year-round, whenever the flag is raised.

MUNKHOLMEN

During Trondheim's early years, the islet of Munkholmen (Monks' Island) 2km offshore was the town execution ground. Over the centuries it has been the site of a Benedictine monastery, a prison, a fort and finally a customs house. Today, it's a popular picnic venue. From mid-May to early September, ferries (Nkr50 trip) leave at least hourly between 10am and 4pm or 6pm from beside the Ravnkloa fish market.

MEDIEVAL CHURCH RUINS

During excavations for the library on Kongens gate, archaeologists found the ruins of a 12th-century church, thought to be **Olavskirken**, now visible beneath the courtyard, together with the skeletons of two adults and a child. In the basement of the nearby bank, **Sparebanken** (Søndre gate 4) are the ruins of the medieval **Gregorius Kirke**, also discovered during excavations. There's free access to both during regular business hours.

OTHER SIGHTS

Trondheim's **Synagogue** (☎ 73 52 94 34; Arkitekt Christies gate 1B; ⌚ 10am-4pm Mon-Thu, noon-3pm Sun) claims to be the world's northernmost. It has a small museum of the history of the local Jewish community (which was halved by the Holocaust).

Children will enjoy the hands-on experiments at the **Science Centre** (Vitensenteret; ☎ 73 59 61 23; Kongens gate 1; adult/concession/family Nkr65/45/140; ⌚ 10am-4pm Mon-Fri, 11am-5pm Sat & Sun mid-Jun–mid-Aug, to 5pm rest-of-year).

Activities

The free map, *Friluftsliv i Trondheimsregionen* (Outdoor Life in the Trondheim Region; text in Norwegian), available at the tourist office, shows all nearby outdoor recreation areas and walking trails.

HIKING

Two easy strolls within town are the steep but short ascent through the traffic-free lanes of Bakklandet to Kristiansten Fort (left) and the riverbank footpaths beside the Nidelva between Bakke Bru and Gangbrua bridges.

West of Trondheim spreads the Bymarka, a gorgeous green woodland area laced with wilderness footpaths and ski trails. Take the Gråkalbanen tram, in itself a lovely scenic ride through the leafy suburbs, from the St Olavsgata stop to **Lian**. There you can enjoy excellent views over the city and a good swimming lake, Kyvannet.

For more serious two-legged stuff, contact the local DNT office, **Trondhjems Turistforening** (☎ 73 92 42 00; Sandgate 30).

SKIING

The Vassfjellet mountains, south of town, offer both downhill and cross-country skiing. In season, a daily ski bus runs directly from Munkegata to the Vassfjellet Skisenter, only 8km beyond the city limits. The Bymarka also offers good cross-country skiing, as does the Trondheim Skisenter Granåsen, where the brave or foolhardy can launch themselves from the world's largest plastic-surfaced ski jump.

BOAT TRIPS

Tripps (☎ 73 52 87 15; adult/child Nkr140/55; ⌚ Tue-Sun late Jun–mid-Aug) runs a 1¼-hour cruise along the estuary of the River Nid and out into the fjord, sailing at noon and 2.30pm. Departures are from beside the Ravncloa fish market and you buy your ticket on the boat.

PIRBADET WATER PARK

On the Pirterminalen quay, **Pirbadet** (☎ 73 83 18 00; adult/child/concession Nkr125/85/105; ⌚ 11am-8pm Mon-Fri, 10am-6pm Sat & Sun Jun-Aug, core hrs 10am-10pm Sun-Fri, 10am-5pm Sat rest-of-year) is Norway's largest indoor water park with a wealth of liquid pleasures including a wave pool, sauna and 100m water slide.

Tours

Between late May and August, **Visit Trondheim** runs a two-hour guided city bus tour (adult/senior/child Nkr185/160/free), departing at 11am daily from opposite the tourist office, where you can make a reservation.

Festivals & Events

Olavsfestdagene, in honour of St Olav, is held during the week around his saint's day, 29 July. There's a medieval market and a rich programme of classical music, folk, pop and jazz (Sineád O'Connor topped the bill in 2007). The celebrations coincide with the annual **Trondelag Food Festival**, when stalls selling local fare pack Kongens gate, east of Torvet.

Kosmorama (www.kosmorama.no), Trondheim's international film festival, occupies an intensive week in late April, closely followed by the **Nidaros Blues Festival**, headed in 2007 by the late Ike Turner and Los Lobos.

Every other year in October and November, Trondheim's 25,000 university students stage the three-week **UKA** (www.uka.no, in Norwegian) celebration, Norway's largest cultural festival. It's a continuous party with concerts, plays, and other festivities based at the round, red Studentersamfundet (Student Centre; right and p284). It's next due to take the city by storm in 2009.

In February or March every second year, students put on **ISFiT** (www.isfit.org), an international student gathering with participants from over 100 countries. It's altogether more serious in tone and intent, but with plenty of concerts and events to occupy the leisure hours. The next moot is scheduled for 2009.

Sleeping

For a fee of Nkr30 the tourist office will book a room in a private house (singles Nkr250 to Nkr330, doubles Nkr400 to Nkr450).

Sandmoen Camping (☎ 72 88 61 35; www.sandmoen.no; camp sites Nkr150, 3-4-bed cabins Nkr400, with bathroom Nkr650-975; ⌚ mid-Jun–Aug; 💻) Offering shade (pitch your tent beneath mature pine trees) this place about 12km south of Trondheim is the nearest option for campers.

Trondheim InterRail Centre (☎ 73 89 95 38; www.tirc.no; Elgesetergate 1; dm incl breakfast Nkr150; ⌚ late Jun–mid-Aug; 💻) OK, so you're on a cot bed in a mixed dorm with between 15 and 35 sweating, snoring others but the advantages outweigh the downside at this convivial, excellent-value place, run by the Studentersamfundet. There's free internet access and luggage storage, frequent live music and curfew's an ugly word. Its Edgar Café serves inexpensive meals and beer (during backpacker evening, 8pm to 10pm every Tuesday and Friday, beers are only Nkr31). Should you hear strange shufflings, it's just the ghost of one S Møller, a student who mysteriously disappeared in the 1930s.

Pensjonat Jarlen (☎ 73 51 32 18; www.jarlen.no; Kongens gate 40; s/d Nkr450/560) There's nothing fancy about this central spot but it does have price, convenience and value for money on its side. All 25 rooms have full bathroom and all except the sole single have bunk beds, a fridge and self-catering facilities.

Singsaker Sommerhotel (☎ 73 89 31 00; Rogertsgata 1; dm/s/d with shared bathroom Nkr200/410/620, s/d with bathroom Nkr520/740, all incl breakfast; ⌚ mid-Jun–mid-Aug; 🅿) On a grassy knoll in a quiet residential neighbourhood, this imposing building, usually a student hostel, was originally built as a club for occupying German officers. It represents great value. Bus 63 from the train station passes by. If driving, take Klostergata eastwards from the Studentersamfundet and follow the signs.

Trondheim Vandrerhjem Rosenborg (☎ 73 87 44 50; www.trondheim-vandrerhjem.no; Weidemannsvei 41; dm Nkr230, s/d with shared bathroom Nkr490/620, with bathroom Nkr550/720, all incl breakfast; 🅿 💻) On a hillside 2km east of the train station, this hostel, no longer a member of HI, is overpriced. The few rooms in the newer part are pleasant enough; the majority, in the old wing, need some serious investment. Internet costs Nkr2 per minute.

Thon Hotel Trondheim (☎ 73 88 47 88; www.thonhotels.com; Kongens gate 15; s/d Nkr595/795; 💻) This central hotel offers pleasant, nothing-fancy accommodation at a reasonable price year round. Inside is more appealing than the plain, boxy exterior might suggest and rooms have a simple, trim design.

P-Hotel (☎ 73 80 23 50; www.p-hotels.no; Nordre gate 24; s/d incl breakfast Nkr695/795; 💻) This slick, modern hotel, part of an expanding Norwegian minichain, has 49 spruce rooms, each with beverage-making kit, that speak of good Scandinavian style. Someone pads by in the early morning and hangs your breakfast bag on the door.

Chesterfield Hotel (☎ 73 50 37 50; www.bestwestern.no; Søndre gate 26; s/d Nkr785/985 mid-Jun–mid-Aug, Nkr985/1095 Sun-Thu, Nkr775/1025 Fri & Sat rest-of-year; 💻) All 43 rooms at this venerable hotel are spacious. They were decorated and fundamentally renovated, with fresh beds and furniture, in 2006 following a major fire in the adjacent building. Those on the 7th (top) floor have huge skylights giving broad city views.

Britannia Hotel (☎ 73 80 08 00; www.britannia.no; Dronningens gate 5; s/d Nkr900/1100 mid-Jun–mid-Aug, Nkr1650/1850 Sun-Thu, Nkr995/1195 Fri & Sat rest-of-year; P 💻 ♿) This mastodon of a hotel with nearly 250 rooms is Trondheim's most venerable and was constructed in 1897. It exudes old-world grace from the mellow, wooden panelling from public areas to the magnificent oval Moorish-revival Palmehaven restaurant – but one of three places to eat – with its Corinthian pillars and central fountain. Relax or exert yourself in the brand new sauna or mini-gym.

Clarion Collection Hotel Grand Olav (☎ 73 80 80 80; www.choice.no; Kjøpmannsgaten 48; s/d from Nkr805/995 mid-Jun–mid-Aug & Fri & Sat year-round, from Nkr1045/1245 Sun-Thu rest-of-year) Two of Trondheim's finest hotels stare across the street at each other in perpetual competition. The Clarion offers sleek luxurious living above an airy shopping complex and the Olavshallen concert hall. It has 27 different styles among over a hundred rooms, so no guest can complain of lack of choice.

Radisson SAS Royal Garden Hotel (☎ 73 80 30 00; www.radissonsas.com; Kjøpmannsgaten 73; s/d Nkr1095/1195 Fri-Sun & mid-Jun–mid-Aug, Nkr1695/1945 Mon-Thu rest-of-year; P 💻 ♿) Opposite the Clarion, this first-class, contemporary river-side hotel (you can fish from your window in some rooms) is open, light and airy – and particularly family-friendly; children are accommodated for free when sharing a room with their parents and there's a summertime playroom.

Eating

RESTAURANTS

Persilleriet (☎ 73 60 60 14; Erling Skakkes gate 14; 🕑 noon-6pm Mon-Fri; V) This tiny lunchtime-only box of a place does tasty vegetarian fare, to eat in or take away.

Ramp (cnr Strandveien & Gregusgate; mains Nkr80-140; 🕑 noon-midnight) Well off the tourist route and patronised by in-the-know locals, friendly, alternative Ramp, both bar and restaurant, gets its raw materials, organic where possible, from local sources (its veg man, for example, calls by each morning). It's renowned for its juicy house burgers (Nkr100) filled with lamb, beef, fish or chickpeas.

Benitos/Zia Teresa (☎ 73 52 64 22; Vår Frue gate 4; mains from Nkr90) At these two related restaurants – fancy Italian trattoria and informal pizza and pasta joint – the gregarious, extrovert owner bears a striking resemblance to the late Luciano Pavarotti and may well burst into an aria.

our pick **Baklandet Skydsstasjon** (☎ 73 92 10 44; Øvre Bakklandet 33; mains Nkr115-200; 🕑 noon-1am) Within what began life as an 18th-century coaching inn are several cosy rooms with poky angles and listing floors. It's a hyper-friendly place where you can tuck into tasty mains, such as its renowned *bacalao* (cod stew or fish soup) for Nkr145, while always leaving a cranny for a gooey homemade cake (around Nkr50).

Grønn Pepper (☎ 73 53 26 30; Fjordgata 7; mains Nkr165-230) Bright Mexican blankets and – 'fraid so – sombreros add colour and life to the Pepper's architecturally staid interior. The food's Tex-Mex and you can slam down a tequila or two. Monday's special is four tacos with rice and salad (Nkr120).

our pick **Vertshuset Tavern** (☎ 73 87 80 70; Sverresborg Allé 11; mains Nkr110-270) Once in the heart of Trondheim, this historic (1739) tavern was lifted and transported, every last plank of it, to the Sverresborg Trøndelag Folk Museum (p277). Tuck into its rotating specials of traditional Norwegian fare or just peck at waffles with coffee in one of its 16 tiny rooms, each low-beamed, with sloping floors, candlesticks, cast iron stoves and lacy tablecloths.

Sushi Bar (☎ 73 52 10 20; Munkegata 39; mains Nkr175-240) The name says it all; the house speciality is sushi in multifarious forms. To savour the flavours, go for the 16-item *sushi moriawase* selection (Nkr198). It also does takeaway.

Chablis (☎ 73 87 42 50; Øvre Bakklandet 66; mains 180-220; 🕑 5-11pm) The Chablis is beside the river, indeed, part of it's on the water; reserve a table on its floating pontoon. Alternatively, the interior of this brasserie-style place is light and appealing and from the kitchen emerge the most delightful dishes, both Norwegian and international.

Ørens Kro (☎ 73 60 06 35; Dokkgata 8; mains around Nkr200) This characterful bar and restaurant was once a boat repair workshop. Tools of its former trade are arranged around the walls while part of the large external terrace straddles a former slipway, its rusting pulleys and hawsers still taut below. The menu's Norwegian and mainly fish, as befits its long waterside history.

To Rom og Kjøkken (☎ 73 56 89 00; Carl Johansgate 5; mains Nkr200-235; 🕑 Mon-Sat) At Two Rooms & a Kitchen, service is friendly, the ambience, with original, changing artwork on the walls, is bright and brisk, and prices are reasonable. Vegetables and meat are sourced locally, wherever feasible.

Emilies (☎ 73 92 96 41; Erling Skakkes gate 45; 2-6 courses Nkr350-595; 🕑 4pm-midnight Mon-Sat) The menu, carefully selected and constantly changing to reflect what's available locally, couldn't be shorter or sweeter at this sophisticated restaurant, its table linen and furniture an essay in contrasting blacks and whites.

Credo (☎ 73 53 03 88; Ørjaveita 4; 3-5-course menus Nkr465-580; 🕑 6-11pm) There's no need for a formal à la carte menu at this adventurous Spanish-influenced world-cuisine spot – the chef chooses the day's best items and serves them up in fine style. There's also a trendy bar upstairs.

Havfruen (☎ 73 87 40 70; Kjøpmannsgaten 7; meals Nkr455-785; 🕑 6pm-midnight Mon-Sat) This elegant riverside restaurant specialises in the freshest of fish. The quality, reflected in the prices, is excellent, as are the accompanying wines. The short menu, from which you select between three and eight courses, changes regularly according to what's hauled from the seas.

CAFÉS

Trondheim has plenty of lovely cafés for a light meal, coffee and cakes. Some stay open at night and turn into lively pubs.

Dromedar (☎ 73 50 25 02; Nedre Bakklandet 3) This longstanding local self-service favourite serves light dishes and very good coffee indeed, in all sizes, squeezes and strengths. Inside is cramped so, if the weather permits, relax on the exterior terrace bordering the cobbled street. There's a second **branch** (☎ 73 53 00 60; Nørdre gate 2), similar in style, also with a street-side terrace, that serves equally aromatic coffee.

Café ni Muser (☎ 73 53 25 50; Bispegata 9; light dishes Nkr60-85) For inexpensive light meals and an arty crowd, go to the café at the Trondheim Art Museum. On sunny afternoons, the outdoor terrace turns into a beer garden.

SELF-CATERING

For self-caterers, there's a grand little open-air fruit and veg market on Torvet each morning. You can munch on inexpensive fish cakes and other finny fare at the excellent **Ravnkloa fish market**.

Drinking

As a student town, Trondheim offers lots of through-the-night life. The free papers, *Natt & Dag* and *Plan B,* have listings, although mostly in Norwegian. Solsiden (Sunnyside) is Trondheim's trendiest leisure zone. A whole wharf-side of bars and restaurants nestle beneath smart new apartment blocks, converted warehouses and long-idle cranes.

Trondheim Microbryggeri (Prinsens gate 39) This splendid home-brew pub deserves a pilgrimage as reverential as anything accorded to St Olav from all committed *øl* (beer) quaffers. With up to eight of its own brews on tap and good light meals (around Nkr150) coming from the kitchen, it's a place to linger, nibble and tipple.

Macbeth (Søndre gate 22b) Homesick Scots will feel at home, Geordies with nostalgia can weep into their draught Newcastle Brown, and the rest of us can watch big-screen football or car racing (don't get yourself into the corner where the committed race-goers sit, though, or you'll be *persona*-really-*non-grata*). Absolutely everyone can enjoy a dram or two of its more than a dozen single malt whiskies…

Studentersamfundet (Student Centre; ☎ 73 89 95 38; Elgesetergate 1) During the academic year, it has 10 lively bars, a cinema and frequent live music, while in summer it's mostly a travellers' crash pad (p282).

Metro (☎ 73 52 05 52; Kjøpmannsgaten 12; ⏰ 10pm-2am Wed, Fri & Sat) Trondheim's only gay bar is also a pub, lounge, disco and friendly meeting place for both boys and girls.

Bare Blåbær (Innherredsveien 16; burgers & pizzas Nkr110-130, Tex-Mex around Nkr140) Join the throng that packs both the interior and dockside terrace of this popular place. It's renowned for preparing the finest pizzas in town, including the intriguing *chili bollocks* – presumably a wintertime special.

Den Gode Nabo (Øvre Bakklandet 66; mains Nkr174-194; ⏰ 1pm-1am) The Good Neighbour, dark and cavernous within and nominated more than once as Norway's best pub, enjoys a prime riverside location.

Bruk Bar (Kongens gate; ⏰ 11am-3am Mon-Sat, 1pm-3am Sun) Inside, candles flicker and designer lamps shed light onto the 30-or-so-year-olds who patronise this welcoming joint. The music is eclectic, varying at the whim of bar staff, but guaranteed loud. Outside, the street-side terrace, just off Torvet, is ideal for people-watching.

Rick's Café (Nordre gate 11; ⏰ from 11am) The original Rick's burnt down (at least one major conflagration over the years is almost a rite of passage in Norway) and this slick reconstruction opened in 2007. The ground floor is all edgy stainless steel while upstairs, more for quiet cocktails and lingering wines, has sink-down-deep leatherette sofas and armchairs. The weekend nightclub in the basement has two zones – one for rock, the other playing house.

Entertainment

Dokkhuset (⏰ 11am-1am Mon-Thu, 11am-3am Fri & Sat, 1pm-1am Sun) In an artistically converted former pumping station (look through the glass beneath your feet at the old engines), the Dock House is at once an auditorium (where if it's the right night you'll hear experimental jazz or chamber music), restaurant and café-bar. Sip a drink on the jetty or survey the Trondheim scene from its roof terrace.

Tiger Tiger (☎ 73 53 16 06; Fjordgata 56-58; ⏰ 11pm-3am Thu-Sat) The three storeys of this kitsch disco display a sub-Disney combination of artefacts, purportedly from South Africa, India and Polynesia. DJs cater to the masses, who flock in by the hundreds.

Supa (☎ 73 50 37 08; Kongens gate; ⏰ 10pm-3am Fri & Sat) The downstairs nightclub of Bruk Bar, once a wine cellar, continues the longstanding association with alcohol. DJs spin house, jungle, drum and bass with liberal lashings of R&B.

Frakken (☎ 73 52 24 42; Dronningens gate 12; ⏰ 6pm-3.30am) This multistorey nightclub and piano bar features both Norwegian and foreign musicians and has live music nightly.

Trondheim's main concert hall, **Olavshallen** (☎ 73 99 40 50; Kjøpmannsgaten 44), within the Olavskvartalet cultural centre, is the home base of the Trondheim Symphony Orchestra. However, it also features international rock and jazz concerts, mostly between September and May.

Trøndelag Teater (☎ 73 80 50 00; Prinsens gate 18-20), constructed in 1816 and handsomely refurbished, stages large-scale dance and musical performances.

The town's two main cinemas are **Nova Kinosenter** (☎ 82 05 43 33; Olav Tryggvasons gate 5) and **Prinsen Kino** (☎ 82 05 43 33; Prinsens gate 2b).

Getting There & Away

AIR

Værnes airport is located 32km east of Trondheim. SAS connects Trondheim to all major Norwegian cities, as well as Copenhagen. **Norwegian** (www.norwegian.no) flies to/from London (Stansted), Oslo and Bergen.

BOAT

The Hurtigruten coastal ferry stops in Trondheim leaving at noon (northbound) and 10am (southbound). Express passenger boats between Trondheim and Kristiansund (3½ hours) depart from the Pirterminalen quay up to three times daily.

BUS

The intercity bus terminal (Rutebilstasjon) adjoins Trondheim Sentralstasjon (train station, also known as Trondheim S).

As the main link between southern and northern Norway, Trondheim is a bus transport crossroads. Nor-Way Bussekspress services run up to three times daily to Ålesund (Nkr500, 7¾ hours), Namsos (Nkr320, 3¾ hours) and Oslo (Nkr575, 6½ hours). There's also an overnight bus to/from Bergen (Nkr751, 13¾ hours). If you're travelling by public transport to Narvik and points north, it's quicker – all is relative – to take the train

TRONDHEIM: CYCLE CITY

You have to admire the Kommune of Trondheim for its tenacity. A few years ago, it laid on around 200 green bicycles, available free of charge for use on the central peninsula. But they were soon stolen, wrecked or simply not returned. Undeterred, the municipality tightened up on security and tried again.

This time the distinctive bikes are red and widely used for short hops around town. You borrow one for a maximum of three hours before returning it to any of 10 racks around central Trondheim (including one at the train station). To join in, get a bike card (Nkr70 for up to four days plus a refundable deposit of Nkr200) from the tourist office, pick up a cycle from the nearest rack and jump into the saddle.

Other cycle-friendly measures include clear signing of cycle routes, often traffic-free and shared with pedestrians, a lane of smooth flagstones along cobbled streets that would otherwise uncomfortably judder your and the bike's moving parts – and Trampe, the world's only bike lift, a low-tech piece of engineering to which cyclists heading from the Gamle Bybro up the Brubakken hill to Kristiansten Fort can hitch themselves.

to Fauske or Bodø (the end of the line), then continue by bus.

CAR & MOTORCYCLE

There's an E6 bypass that avoids Trondheim – but why would you want to take it? The main route ploughs through the heart of the city. Drivers entering this central zone must pay a toll of Nkr25 (the motorway toll into town also covers the city toll, so keep your receipt). Use the 'Manuell' lane and pay up or you risk a steep fine.

Among car-hire options are **Avis** (Kjøpmannsgaten ☎ 73 84 17 90; Kjøpmannsgaten 34; airport ☎ 74 84 01 00), **Europcar** (Thonning Owesens ☎ 73 82 88 50; Thonning Owesens gate 36; airport ☎ 74 82 67 00) and **National** (Ladeveien ☎ 73 50 94 40; Ladeveien 24; airport ☎ 74 82 29 90).

TRAIN

For train information, phone ☎ 177. There are up to six daily trains to Oslo (Nkr810, 6¾ to 7¾ hours) and two head north to Bodø (Nkr937, 9¾ hours) via Mosjøen (Nkr648, 5½ hours), Mo i Rana (Nkr749, 6½ hours) and Fauske (Nkr905, nine hours). A *minipris* ticket (see p419) may considerably undercut these standard prices.

You can also train it to Steinkjer (Nkr217, two hours, hourly).

Getting Around

TO/FROM THE AIRPORT

Flybussen (☎ 73 82 25 00) runs every 15 to 20 minutes from 5am to 8pm (less frequently at weekends), stopping at major landmarks such as the train station, Studentersamfundet and Britannia Hotel (Nkr80; 40 minutes).

Trains run regularly (every two hours) between Trondheim Sentralstasjon and the Værnes airport station (Nkr68, 35 minutes).

CAR & MOTORCYCLE

Parking garages throughout town offer better rates and greater convenience than the krone-gobbling street-side meters.

PUBLIC TRANSPORT

The city bus service, **Team Trafikk** (☎ 73 50 28 70), has its central transit point, where all lines stop, on the corner of Munkegata and Dronningens gate. Bus and tram cost Nkr22 per ride (Nkr55 for a 24-hour ticket). You'll need the exact change.

Trondheim's tram line, the Gråkalbanen, runs west from St Olavsgata to Lian, in the heart of the Bymarka. Antique trolleys trundle along this route on Saturdays in summer. Transfers are available from city buses.

TAXI

To call a cab, ring **Trønder Taxi** (☎ 07373) or **Norgestaxi** (☎ 08000).

THE ROUTE NORTH

If you're heading north, from Steinkjer you have a choice of routes: the more frequented, inland Arctic Highway or the slower E17 Kystriksveien (Coastal Route). The railway line north to Bodø via Hell and Steinkjer more or less follows the Arctic Highway to Fauske.

HELL

Hell has little to offer but its name, meaning 'prosperity' in Norwegian. All the same, lots of travellers stop here for a cheap chuckle or at least to snap a photo of the sign at the train station. Forever after, whenever someone suggests you go here, you can honestly say you've already been and it wasn't all that bad.

STIKLESTAD

The site of Stiklestad commemorates what in terms of numbers was a small skirmish but which, in its impact, is at the heart of Norwegians' sense of national identity. They flock here by the thousands, some as pilgrims visiting the church associated with St Olav, but most come to picnic and enjoy the fresh air, open space and associated exhibitions.

On 29 July 1030 the larger and better-equipped forces of local feudal chieftains defeated a force of barely 100 men led by the Christian King Olav Haraldsson here in Stiklestad. Olav had been forced from the Norwegian throne by King Knut (Canute) of Denmark and England. He briefly escaped to Russia but on his return met resistance from local chiefs, who were disaffected by his destruction of pagan shrines and execution of anyone who persisted with heathen practices.

The Battle of Stiklestad marks Norway's passage between the Viking and medieval periods. Although Olav was killed, the battle is generally lauded as a victory for Christianity in Norway and the slain hero recalled as a martyr and saint.

St Olav developed a following all over northern Europe and his grave in Trondheim's Nidaros Cathedral became a destination of pilgrims from across the continent. The site, around most of which you can wander for free, is laid out rather like a sprawling theme park, with exhibits on the Battle of Stiklestad, an outdoor folk museum and, predating all, the 12th-century Stiklestad church.

Sights & Activities

The **Stiklestad National Cultural Centre** (Stiklestad Nasjonale Kultursenter; ☎ 74 04 42 00; www.stiklestad.no; ticket per adult/child Nkr95/40) is a grandiose wooden structure. Entry entitles you to visit **Stiklestad 1030**, an evocative exhibition about the battle with dioramas and plenty of shrieks and gurgles on the soundtrack; a 15-minute film on St Olav; a guided tour of the church; and a small WWII resistance museum. Within the complex too is a **restaurant** specialising in locally sourced food and a recently opened **hotel** (s/d incl breakfast Nkr690/790), its structure in the shape of St Olav's shield.

In the grounds there's a collection of over 30 historical buildings (admission free), ranging from humble crofts and artisans' workshops to the Molåna, a much grander farmhouse and, within it, a small, summertime café. In summer, actors in period costume bring several of the buildings to life.

Across the road is lovely Stiklestad **church** (⌚ core hrs 11am-6pm), built between 1150 and 1180 above the stone on which the dying St Olav reputedly leaned. The original stone was believed to have healing powers, but it was removed during the Reformation and hasn't been seen since.

The booklet *Stiklestad Yesterday & Today* (Nkr30), on sale at the centre, gives a succinct background to the site and its significance for Norwegians.

Festivals & Events

Every year during the week leading up to St Olav's Day (29 July) Stiklestad hosts the **St Olav Festival** with a medieval market, lots of wannabee Vikings in costume and a host of other folksy activities. The high point of the festival is an outdoor pageant (held over the last five days) dramatising the conflicts between the king and local farmers and chieftains. Some of Norway's top actors and actresses traditionally take the major roles while locals play minor parts and swell the crowd scenes.

STEINKJER & NORTH

pop 11,000

Medieval sagas speak of Steinkjer as a major trading centre and indeed it continues to be a crossroads, requiring a decision from northbound travellers: to opt for the more scenic Kystriksveien coastal route (Rv17) to Bodø or to continue northwards on the E6 (Arctic Highway).

The **tourist office** (☎ 74 16 36 17; www.visitinnherred.com; Namdalsvegen 11; ⌚ 9am-8pm Mon-Fri, 10am-7pm Sat, noon-8pm Sun mid-Jun–mid-Aug, 9am-4pm Mon-Fri rest-of-year) is beside the E6. From the train station take the foot tunnel. Doubling as the Kystriksveien Info-Center, it can book accommodation in town and along the coastal route. It also rents bikes (per hour/day Nkr30/150) and has free internet access.

Sights & Activities

Steinkjer's main attraction is its **Egge Museum** (☎ 74 16 31 10; Fylkesmannsgården; adult/child Nkr60/free; 🕑 11am-4pm mid-Jun–mid-Aug), an open-air farm complex 2.5km north of town. On the same hilltop site are several Viking burial mounds and stone circles.

To the north of Steinkjer, the E6 follows the north shore of the 45km-long, needle-thin lake **Snåsavatnet**, bordered by majestic evergreen forests. You may prefer to take the Rv763 along the quieter southern shore to see the **Bølarein**, a 5000- to 6000-year-old rock carving of a reindeer and several other incised carvings. Pass by the **Bølabua restaurant & gift shop** (☎ 45 42 65 88; 🕑 late Jun-early Aug), a short walk from the carving, for information.

Sleeping & Eating

Føllingstua (☎ 74 14 71 90; www.follingstua.com; E6, Følling; car/caravan sites Nkr100/160, cabins Nkr490-570, 3-4-bed r with shared bathroom Nkr450) Beside the E6 14km north of Steinkjer, near the lake's southwestern end, this lovely, welcoming camping ground may tempt you to linger for a day or two, fish in the lake or rent one of its boats and canoes.

Guldbergaunet Sommerhotel & Camping (☎ 74 16 20 45; g-book@online.no; Elvenget 34; camp sites Nkr160, d Nkr720, cabin Nkr375-480; 🕑 hotel mid-Jun–mid-Aug, cabins year-round) Normally student accommodation, this camp site and summer hotel is 2.3km from town amid a grassy area. A small river, ideal for paddling and bathing, flows right by.

Tingvold Park Hotel (☎ 74 14 11 00; www.tingvoldhotel.no; Gamle Kongeveien 47; s/d mid-Jun–mid-Aug & Fri & Sat year-round Nkr700/970, Sun-Thu rest-of-year Nkr1240/1530; P 💻) Beside an old Viking burial site, this secluded, good-value option overlooking Steinkjer has a pleasant lawn and garden.

Breidablikk (☎ 74 16 22 05; Kongens gate 22-24; mains around Nkr100; 🕑 9am-6pm Mon-Fri, noon-6pm Sun) Nothing fancy but friendly Breidablikk serves up honest, reliable Norwegian fare. Choose from its short à la carte selection or go for the dish of the day. Fish balls in white sauce, dessert and coffee for Nkr89? You won't find better value in all Norway.

Brod & Cirkus (☎ 74 16 21 00; Kongens gate 40; 🕑 Mon-Sat) On the main street 150m from the train station, it bakes its own bread daily and offers a range of tempting à la carte dishes. It'll even knock you up a six-tier wedding cake, if you've a happy event on the horizon…

NAMSOS

pop 9000

Namsos is considered the first port town of consequence on the northbound coastal route between Trondheim and Bodøl; it makes a pleasant overnight stop and has a couple of interesting diversions.

The **tourist office** (☎ 74 22 66 04; www.namsosinfo.no; Damskipskaia; 🕑 9am-6pm Mon-Fri, 10am-4pm Sat, noon-4pm Sun mid-Jun–mid-Aug; 9am-3.30pm rest-of-year) is at the quayside, co-located with the local bus and ferry company headquarters. It rents cycles (Nkr25/150 per hour/day) and also provides information about the Kystriksveien.

Cyberland Café (☎ 74 28 74 55; Kirkegata 11; 🕑 11am-10pm Mon-Sat, 1-10pm Sun) has several internet terminals (Nkr36 per hour).

Sights & Activities

An easy scenic 20-minute walk up Kirkegata from the centre will take you to the lookout atop the prominent loaf-shaped rock **Bjørumsklumpen** (114m) with good views over Namsfjorden, the town and its environs. About a third of the way up, a sign identifies a track leading to some impressive WWII Nazi bunkers hewn from solid rock.

For exercise both for the body and the sake of nostalgia, you can hire a **trolley** (single Nkr250, up to 4 riders Nkr350) from Namsos Camping (see opposite) and trundle it for 17km along the disused railway line between Namsos and Skage as it follows the gentle River Nansen.

If you're interested in wood chopping and chipping, check out the **Norsk Sagbruksmuseum** (☎ 74 27 13 00; Spillumsvika; admission free; 🕑 tours 10am, noon, 2pm & 4pm Tue-Sat Mid-Jun–mid-Aug, Mon-Fri rest-of-year), which is over the bridge 4km east of town and commemorates Norway's first steam-powered sawmill (1853).

The **Namdal Museum** (Namdalsmuseet; ☎ 74 27 40 72; Kjærlighetstien 1; adult/child Nkr30/free; 🕑 11am-3pm Tue-Sun mid-Jun–mid-Aug) has displays on local history, including the typical wooden sailing boats of the area, and is – hold on to your hat – 'Norway's only museum featuring exhibits of hospital equipment presented in chronological order'.

The **Oasen swimming hall** (☎ 74 21 90 40; Jarle Hildrums veg; adult/child/family Nkr80/35/190; 🕑 10am-8pm Mon-Fri, 10am-4pm Sat & Sun), about 1km east of town, has three heated pools and a 37m water slide built deep inside the mountain.

The **Namsos Candle Foundry** (Lysstøperiet; ☎ 74 21 29 00; Lokstallen; 🕑 10am-6pm Mon-Fri, 11am-4pm Sat) makes and sells lifelike sculpted candles (such as tropical flowers and – incongruously – ice), in a former train shed.

Sleeping & Eating

Namsos Camping (☎ 74 27 53 44; namsoscamp@online.no; tent/caravan Nkr150/185, 4-bed cabin with outdoor bathroom Nkr375-450, with bathroom Nkr800-850) This superior camp site has a large kitchen and dining room, playground and minigolf. Basic cabins are a bargain and the more expensive ones are well equipped. Alongside is a shallow lake that's ideal for children, who'll also enjoy communing with the romping squirrels and two tame goat kids. Take Rv17, direction Grong, then follow airport signs.

Borstad Hotel & Gjestgiveri (☎ 74 21 80 90; www.borstadhotel.no; Carl Gubransons gate 19; s/d Jul–mid-Aug & Fri & Sat year-round Nkr710/960, Sun-Thu rest-of-year from Nkr850/1090; P) Bright and friendly, this recently upgraded hotel has large sunny rooms and a pleasant outdoor garden. There's a cosy lounge and the huge oak dining table (over a century old and at which breakfast is served) was once used for company board meetings.

Tino's Hotell (☎ 74 21 80 00; www.tinoshotell.no in Norwegian; Verftsgata 5; s/d from Nkr950/1200 Sun-Thu, Nkr750/1000 Fri & Sat) Rooms are large and comfortable at this hotel, just a stone's throw from the waterside. Tino, the owner and Italian as they come despite many years in Norway, runs a great restaurant, La Sirenetta (mains around Nkr200; open 3pm to 11pm) that serves both international food and fine Italian cuisine (such as 25 varieties of pizza), a continent away from Norway's usual pizza and pasta joints.

Cyberland Café (☎ 74 28 74 55; Kirkegata 11; 🕒 11am-10pm Mon-Sat, 1-10pm Sun) It offers good burgers in three sizes, ciabattas and grills, all at very reasonable prices (Nkr45 to Nkr 106). While you're there you can check your email.

Aakervik (☎ 74 27 20 90; cnr Havnegata & Herlaugs gate 16; 🕒 core hr 9am-4.30pm Mon-Sat) A great shop for wild salmon and other fish, reindeer, roe deer and elk. The interior is a minimenagerie of stuffed animals and birds eyeing you glassily from all angles; pay your respects to the amiable brown bear.

Getting There & Away

Nor-Way Bussekspress runs twice daily between Namsos and Trondheim (Nkr320, 3¾ hours) and there are up to eight local buses to/from Steinkjer (Nkr120, 1½ hours).

RØRVIK

Tiny Rørvik buzzes when the northbound and southbound Hurtigruten coastal ferries meet each other here each day around 8.30pm. What gets passengers up early from the dinner table is the splendid multimedia **Norveg** (☎ 74 39 04 41; www.norveg.org; adult/child incl audioguide Nkr70/35; 🕒 10am-10pm mid-Jun–Jul, 10am-5pm rest-of-year & when the Hurtigruten's in port). Architecturally exciting and resembling a giant sailing ship, it recounts 10,000 years of coastal history through a variety of media, including an accompanying audioguide, available in English. It also runs a well-regarded gourmet restaurant.

A combined ticket (adult/child Nkr120/60), valid for two days, gives admission to Norveg, Berggården (an old trading house once typical of coastal communities) and several other historical buildings. Whether or not you go for the package, pick up from Norveg *Coastal Town Rørvik*, a useful free brochure that guides you around this small community's principal sites.

Buses run between Rørvik and Namsos (Nkr306, three hours) once or twice daily. If the day's right, it's swifter by express passenger boat (Nkr163, 1¼ hours, Monday, Friday and Sunday).

LEKA

pop 600

You won't regret taking a short side-trip to the wild and beautiful island of Leka; for hikers, the desert-like Wild West landscape is particularly enchanting. This prime habitat for the white-tailed sea eagle (hold on to your little ones; in 1932, a three-year-old girl was snatched away by a particularly cheeky specimen) also has several Viking Age burial mounds and Stone Age rock paintings.

Bed down at **Leka Motell og Camping** (☎ 74 39 98 23; www.leka-camp.no; tent/caravan sites Nkr80/120, cabin with outdoor bathroom Nkr250-700, d/q with bathroom & kitchen Nkr600/700). For comfort, reserve one of its well-equipped, reasonably priced motel rooms. For something different and more spartan, hire a sod-roofed stone hut (Nkr350), sleeping up to four in bunk beds.

Leka is accessed by hourly ferry from Gutvik (Nkr26/68 per person/car and driver, 20 minutes), which lies about 20 minutes off the Rv17 coastal road.

Nordland

There's a difficult choice to make as you head north. The spectacular Kystriksveien coastal route, ferry hopping and perhaps detouring to take in a glacier and offshore island or two? Or the almost-as-stunning inland Arctic Highway, more direct but still lightly trafficked?

Whichever you choose, try to build in time to take in Lofoten, a necklace of offshore islands with razor-sharp peaks and Caribbean-coloured bays. Here, cod is still king, as manifested in the small fishing museums, *rorbuer* (fishing cabins – literally 'rowers' dwellings') and rickety drying frames. Connected by bridges and with reasonable public transport, the islands are easy to hop around. Then again, you may want to linger and hire a bike or pull on your boots: the cycling can even be done by softies and the hiking is as gentle or as tough as you care to make it. Push further north to Andenes, at the northern tip of Andøya, a continuation of the Lofoten archipelago, and you'll enjoy the best whale watching in all Norway.

As you move northwards through the long, narrow Nordland region, the crossing of the Arctic Circle is almost palpable; fields give way to lakes and forests, vistas open up, summits sharpen and the tree line descends ever lower on the mountainsides. In summer, this is where northbound travellers get their first taste of the midnight sun; in winter, the northern lights slash the night sky.

In addition to Nordland, this chapter also includes the northeastern section of Vesterålen, a continuation of the Lofoten archipelago that belongs to the county of Troms.

HIGHLIGHTS

- Ferry hop and hug the splendid **Kystriksveien coastal route** (p303)
- Learn to respect eider ducks and feel their down float from your fingers at Vega's **E-Huset museum** (p304)
- Be a wide-eyed kid again at the **Norwegian Aviation Museum** (p307) in Bodø
- Linger in the tiny, preserved fishing village of **Å** (p320) in Lofoten
- Hike the coastal **Queen's Route** (p326) to Stø in Vesterålen
- Take time out to explore the historic **Sjøgata** (opposite) in Mosjøen, including its galleries, museum and cafés
- Get cold feet on one of the glaciers in **Saltfjellet-Svartisen National Park** (p296)

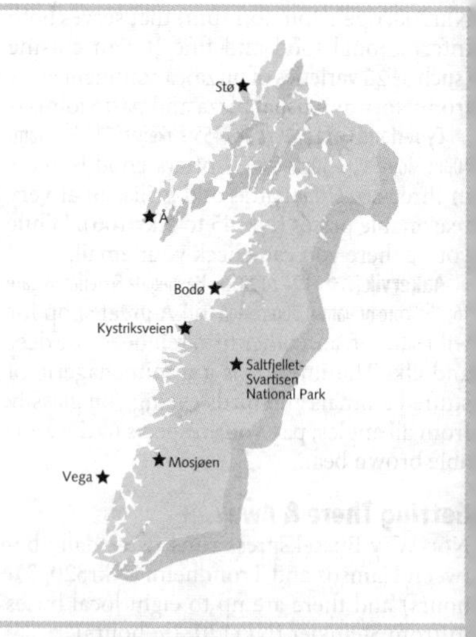

- POPULATION: 235,450
- HIGHEST ELEVATION: OKSSKOLTEN (1916M)

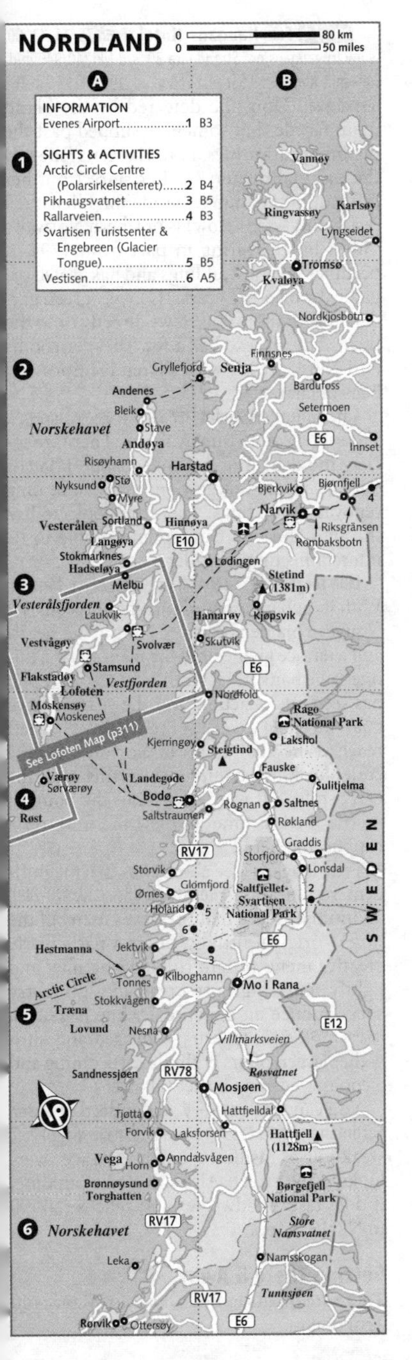

Getting There & Away

Although it's in Norwegian, you'll have no problem interpreting times and schedules on www.177nordland.com – a comprehensive listing, together with links, of all bus, boat, ferry, train and plane timetables throughout Nordland. Alternatively, phone ☎ 177 within Nordland or ☎ 75 77 24 10 beyond.

At Steinkjer, to the south in Trøndelag (p287), those with wheels have a binary choice: the swifter Arctic Highway to Narvik, or the slower, less-frequented, more expensive but much more beautiful E17, the 650km-long Kystriksveien (Coastal Route) with Bodø at its northern end. Go the latter if you can spare the time and cash. If you're without wheels, going along the Arctic Highway, by either bus or train, is the only practical choice.

ARCTIC HIGHWAY

MOSJØEN

pop 9900

When arriving in Mosjøen (pronounced moo-sher-en), along the E6, you may be put off by the industrial face of this aluminium-producing town. Don't be. About 1km south, along lake-like Vefsnfjorden, historic Sjøgata and a street or two nearby are among the most charming in northern Norway and well merit a browse.

The town has a strong historical connection with the UK; in the mid-19th century, five Englishmen imported technically advanced steam engines and sawmill machinery and established the North of Europe Land & Mining Company Ltd to provide timber for Britain's burgeoning industrial towns and cities. What was a tiny coastal settlement quickly became the region's first registered town.

Mosjøen's **tourist office** (☎ 75 11 12 40; www.visithelgeland.com; 🕑 9am-7pm Jul, 10am-5pm Mon-Fri Jun & Aug, 10am-3.30pm Mon-Fri rest-of-year) is at Sjøgata's southern end. It has internet access (per 15 minutes Nkr20).

Sights & Activities

SJØGATA

A stroll around the Sjøgata area, with over 100 listed buildings, takes you past galleries, coffee shops, restaurants and private homes in attractively renovated former warehouses, workshops and boat sheds. *The History of a*

Town (Nkr20), on sale at the museum and tourist office, is an excellent small booklet that brings Mosjøen's history to life.

VEFSN MUSEUM

A combined ticket (Nkr30) gives entry to both branches of Mosjøen's **museum** (☎ 75 11 01 10).

In Sjøgata, the **Jakobsensbrygga warehouse** (Sjøgata 31B; 10am-8pm Tue-Fri, 10am-3pm Sat Jul, 10am-3pm Tue-Fri rest-of-year) is an excellent small museum that portrays, via some particularly evocative photo blow-ups, the history of Mosjøen from the early 19th century onwards. There's an English guide-pamphlet for each section.

Northeast of the centre, the **rural building collection** (Bygdesamlinga; 10am-3pm Tue-Fri & Sun Jul only) features 12 farmhouses, shops and the like from the 18th and 19th centuries, which you can view from the exterior. It too has a pamphlet in English. Adjacent is the **Dolstad Kirke** (1735), built on the site of a medieval church dedicated to St Michael. If it's closed, ask for the key at the museum.

LAKSFORSEN

About 30km south of Mosjøen and a 600m detour from the E6, the roaring 17m-high Laksforsen **waterfall** has leaping salmon in season and makes a pleasant picnic spot, although it's a bit of a struggle to reach the shore below the torrent. The café here, a churlish place with its 'no photo' and 'guests only beyond this point' notices, is one place to avoid.

Sleeping & Eating

Mosjøen Camping (☎ 75 17 79 00; www.mosjoencamping.no; Mathias Bruuns gata 24; tent/caravan sites Nkr120/170, cabins Nkr390-1090) Beside the E6 about 500m southeast of the town centre, this camp site tends to be overcrowded with travellers doing the North Cape rush. In this land of superlatives, the sole urinal in the men's toilet must rank as Norway's, if not the world's, highest.

Mosjøen Hotell (☎ 75 17 11 55; www.mosjoencamping.no; Vollanveien 35; s/d with shared bathroom Nkr380/490, with bathroom s/d Nkr650/840 mid-Jun–mid-Aug, Nkr855/960 Sun-Thu, Nkr640/810 Fri & Sat rest-of-year; P) Under the same ownership as the camp site and about 100m north of the train station, this run-of-the-mill roadhouse offers cosy, good-value but unexceptional rooms.

our pick **Fru Haugans Hotel** (☎ 75 11 41 00; www.fruhaugans.no; Strandgata 39; s/d Nkr740/940 mid-Jun–mid-Aug & Fri & Sat year-round, Nkr1095/1295 Sun-Thu rest-of-year) Don't be deterred by the bland main façade that somehow slipped past the planning authorities. Frau Haugans (she was the original owner; see her stare from her portrait in the lounge beside the Ellenstuen restaurant – see below) is northern Norway's oldest hotel. Dating in part from 1794, it occupies several buildings and has grown organically over the years. Its lovely green garden gives panoramic views directly onto the fjord. The annexe has a few cheaper rooms (s/d Nkr450/650) with shared facilities and bags of character.

Café Kulturverkstedet (☎ 75 17 27 60; Sjøgata 22-24; 8am-4pm Mon-Sat) Run by the local heritage society, this delightful café enjoys, appropriately, one of Sjøgata's largest and most appealing renovated buildings. There are books to leaf through and you can sip and nibble in its interconnecting art gallery.

Lille Torget (☎ 75 17 04 14; Strandgate 24; Mon-Sat) With its pub interior (admire the gorgeous Art Nouveau maiden bearing a lamp at her heart) and a terrace giving onto the main square, this one-time bank, then clothing store, now pub has seen lots of action over the years. You're guaranteed an excellent brew; one of its staff reached the 2007 finals of Norway's annual coffee-making championship (this said, the early shift staff were languid to the point of inertia the last time we blew the froth off a cappuccino here).

Fru Haugans (see above) has two magnificent restaurants. **Ellenstuen** (mains Nkr220-240), an intimate place that preserves many of the hotel's original fittings, offers a particularly creative menu (might roasted stag fillet and lightly smoked grouse breast in a raspberry sauce induce an appetite?) while **Hagestuen** (mains Nkr165-245), tapestry-bedecked and altogether larger, offers both à la carte dining and a copious evening buffet (Nkr225).

You can also eat very well indeed at **Oksen Ferdinand** (☎ 75 11 99 91; Sjøgata 23; mains Nkr220-255) steakhouse, inside or on the terrace overlooking the street. Also a historic building, it does tasty sandwiches and snacks (Nkr90 to Nkr135), too.

Getting There & Away

There are flights to Bodø, via Mo i Rana, and Trondheim.

Buses run from Mosjøen to Brønnøysund (three hours, once or twice daily except Saturday) and Sandnessjøen (1¾ hours, three to five daily) and there's at least one service daily to/from Mo i Rana (1¾ hours).

Mosjøen lies on the rail line between Trondheim (Nkr648, 5½ hours) and Fauske (Nkr445, 3½ hours).

For drivers, a lovely detour follows the wild, scenic Villmarksveien route, which runs parallel to the E6 east of Mosjøen and approaches the bizarre 1128m peak Hatten (or Hattfjell). From the end of the nearest road, the hike to the top takes about two hours. However, taking this route cuts out Mosjøen itself.

MO I RANA

pop 5800

Mo i Rana (just plain Mo to those who know her) is the third-largest city in the north and gateway to the spruce forests, caves and glaciers of the Arctic Circle region. Its friendly reputation is often attributed to its rapid expansion due to the construction of the now-closed steel plant, which in its time employed over 1000 workers; nearly everyone here knows how it once felt to be a stranger in town.

Although Mo's predominant architectural style is boxy, the town is becoming lighter in tone now that heavy industry has given way to a tech-based economy.

The staff at the **tourist office** (☎ 75 13 92 00; www.arctic-circle.no; Ole Tobias Olsens gate 3; ⏰ 9am-8pm Mon-Fri, 9am-4pm Sat, 1-7pm Sun mid-Jun–mid-Aug; 9am-4pm Mon-Fri rest-of-year) are exceptionally helpful. There's free internet access and they can make reservations for activities around the region, such as visits to the Svartisen glacier and nearby caves.

Sights & Activities

A combined ticket (Nkr20) gives entry to Mo's two small **museums** (☎ 75 11 01 33; ⏰ 10am-4pm Mon-Fri, 10am-2pm Sat mid-Jun–mid-Aug), which merit a brief glance.

The **Rana Museum of Natural History** (Moholmen) illustrates the geology, ecology, flora and wildlife of the Arctic Circle region, and features several hands-on exhibits that will engage children. Highlight of its sister museum, the **Rana Museum of Cultural History** (☎ 75 14 61 70; Fridtjof Nansensgata 22), is a giant model of old Mo before the steelworks altered her complexion for ever.

At the **indoor water park** (Moheia Fritidspark; ☎ 75 14 60 60; Øvre Idrettsveien 1; adult/child Nkr75/50; ⏰ noon-8pm Mon-Fri, noon-6pm Sat & Sun), also called Badeland, you can dip into its four pools and three saunas – and zoom down its 42m-long water slide.

The oldest building in town, Mo's original **church** (Mo Kirke; ⏰ free guided tours 8-10pm Mon-Fri mid-Jun–mid-Aug) was constructed in 1724. With its steeply pitched roof and onion dome, it deserves to be open to visitors during more than the current brief hours. In the graveyard is a monument to Russian prisoners who died in captivity and the gravestones of eight British soldiers, killed in commando raids in May 1940.

Havmannen (Man of the Sea), a sculpture forever up to his knees in water, turns his back on the town and gazes resolutely out over the fjord. His clean lines and rounded profile are the work of iconic British sculptor Antony Gormley.

CAVES

The limestone and marble country northwest of Mo i Rana is riddled with caves and sinkholes, formed when river water dissolved

NORDLAND

ARCTIC MENU

To guarantee yourself a good meal in northern Norway, visit a restaurant affiliated to the Arctic Menu scheme. Members, who range from small, family-owned concerns to the restaurants of chain hotels, undertake to use the region's natural ingredients. It may be a sauce simmered with local berries; an Arctic char pulled from the icy waters; reindeer, seal, whale or, of course, cod – every last bit of it from the rich flesh to local delicacies such as the cheek, roe, liver, stomach or tongue.

You'll find such restaurants indicated within each town's Eating section. The scheme's **website** (www.arktiskmeny.no) has a full list of its 40 or so participants and most tourist offices carry its booklet. This comes complete with a few recipes so you can try a dish or two out back home – if, that is, you can get those fresh, northern Norway ingredients…

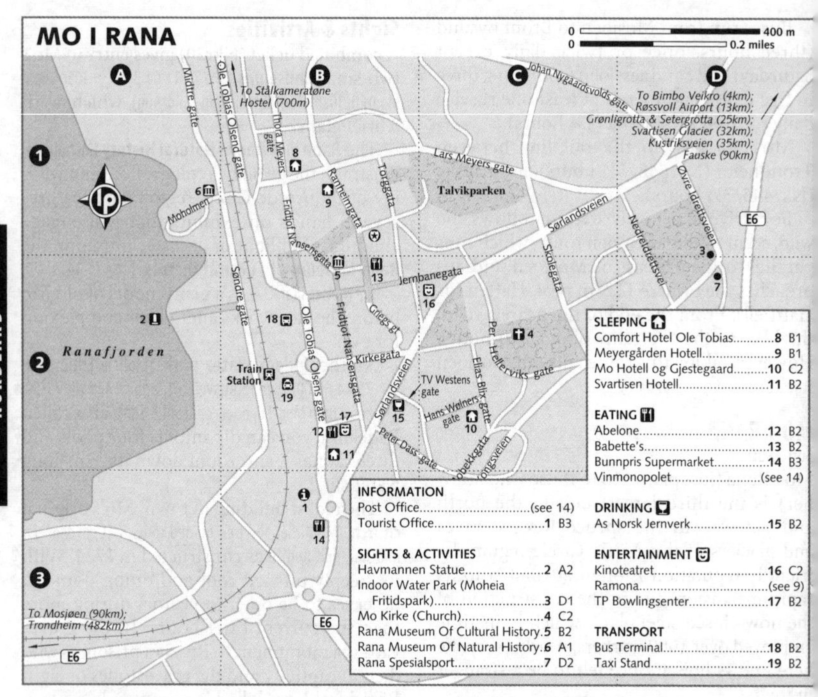

marble between layers of mica schist. Thanks to mineral deposits, the glacial water that runs into ponds and rivers as you approach the caves can change colour from green to grey to blue.

The most accessible and most visited cave is **Grønligrotta** (☎ 75 13 25 06; Grønli; adult/child Nkr100/50; ⌚ tours hourly 10am-7pm mid-Jun–Aug), 25km north of Mo. There's electric lighting (it's the only illuminated tourist cave in Scandinavia) and the 30-minute tour takes you along an underground river, through a rock maze and past a granite block torn off by a glacier and deposited in the cave by the brute force of moving water.

The two-hour trip through **Setergrotta** (☎ 75 16 23 50; Røvassdalen; adult/child Nkr265/235; ⌚ tours twice daily early Jun-late Aug) is altogether less dragooned and considerably more adventurous. Highlights include a couple of extremely tight squeezes and a thrilling shuffle between rock walls while straddling a 15m gorge. The operators provide headlamps, hard hats, gumboots and overalls.

The tourist office can make reservations for both.

OUTDOOR ACTIVITIES

Local operator **Rana Spesialsport** (☎ 75 12 70 88; Øvre Idrettsveien 35) puts on a range of sporty activities, including kayaking, guided hikes and glacier trekking.

Tours

Mo i Rana is the most convenient base for exploring the **fjords** to the west (although they are still some 110km away).

For tours to the **Svartisen glacier**, see p296. There's no public transport from Mo but you can hire a bike from the tourist office and pedal the 32km each way to the ferry point beside Svartisen lake to explore Østisen (see p296).

The tourist office does a pair of evening **guided walks** (Nkr80). Choose either the one-hour town walk or, for spectacular views, the 90-minute mountain walk (don't be put off by the term; it won't overtax you). Sign up by 4pm on the day.

Sleeping

Stålkameratøne (☎ 41 92 62 15; Stålbrakka, Søderlundmyra; per person Nkr200; ⌚ mid-Jun–mid-Aug; P 💻) Mo's biggest bargain is just off the

ARTSCAPE NORDLAND

You'll spot them on lonely promontories and windswept moorland, tucked beneath crags, in urban parks or lapped by the sea. As you travel through Nordland, follow the sign *Skulpturlandscap* to discover a work of creative modern sculpture, enhancing and in harmony with the landscape around it. In all, 33 works were commissioned from prominent sculptors in Norway, other Scandinavian countries and the wider international community. Representatives of 18 nations, including artists such as Antony Gormley, Anish Kapoor and Tony Cragg, have each left their very individual mark upon the Nordland countryside. For more on this ambitious project, see www.artscape.no.

first left bend of the E6, heading northwards. This hostel has four plainly furnished single rooms, occupied by students during the school year, and an eight-bed dorm. Facilities are in the corridor.

Mo Hotell og Gjestegaard (☎ 75 15 22 11; www.mo-gjestegaard.no in Norwegian; Elias Blix gate 5; s/d incl breakfast from Nkr550/700) Up the hill, this pleasant 15-room guesthouse is welcoming and impeccably kept. It's in a quiet location and has a small garden where you are welcome to sit and relax.

Svartisen Hotell (☎ 75 15 19 99; Ole Tobias Olsens gate 4; s/d from Nkr795/1095 mid-Jun–mid-Aug, Nkr940-1140 rest-of-year) The Comfort Hotel owners have recently taken over the Svartisen and renovated bathrooms and all public areas. Apartments are bright and have mini-kitchens. Those on the ground floor are particularly large and split-level, with the sleeping area upstairs. Choose a rear-facing room as the street can be noisy until the traffic dies down.

Meyergården Hotell (☎ 75 13 40 00; www.meyergarden.no in Norwegian; 28 Fridtjof Nansens gate; s/d Nkr835/1085 mid-Jun–mid-Aug, from Nkr1195/1445 Sun-Thu, Nkr730/980 Fri & Sat rest-of-year; P 💻) An affiliate of the Rica chain, Mo's longest-established hotel is full of character, with fine rooms, the Ramona nightclub and a highly regarded Arctic Menu restaurant. If price is a factor, go for one of the six economical rooms with shared facilities (s/d Nkr665/865) in the original – and much more atmospheric – late-19th-century wing.

Comfort Hotel Ole Tobias (☎ 75 12 05 00; www.ole-tobias.no; Thora Meyersgate 2; s/d from Nkr895/1195 mid-Jun–mid-Aug, from Nkr1305/1510 Sun-Thu, Nkr695/895 Fri & Sat rest-of-year) This railway-themed hotel – the corridor carpets simulate a railway track and each room has the name of a station – commemorates the local teacher and priest who convinced the government to build the Nordlandsbanen railway connecting Trondheim with Fauske and Bodø. As well as breakfast year-round, summer tariffs include a light evening meal.

Eating

Bimbo Veikro (☎ 75 15 10 01; Saltfjelletveien 34; mains Nkr75-200) Just 2km north of town, this roadhouse serves up the usual sandwiches, pizzas and grills and is also an Arctic Menu restaurant, offering more subtle fare. 'Bimbo' alludes to a nearby elephant-shaped rock formation, not the classy waitresses.

Babette's (☎ 75 15 44 33; Ranheimgata 2; mains Nkr174-194) Turkish-owned and set back in a pedestrianised square, Babette's has something for everyone. It's at once bar and café with a large, open terrace and a popular pizza, grills and kebab place.

Abelone (☎ 75 15 38 88; Ole Tobias Olsens gate 6; mains Nkr175-195) Abelone is your best dining option outside the hotels. It looks unprepossessing from the street but inside the cosy simulated log cabin makes for a congenial dining environment. Opt for one of its quality meat dishes.

For liquid picnics, both Bunnpris supermarket and Vinmonopolet are just south of the tourist office.

Drinking & Entertainment

As Norsk Jernverk (☎ 75 14 32 02; TV Westens gate 2; 🕑 6pm-2am daily) carries, not without irony, the name of Mo's long defunct steel-works. On the same premises as Big Horn Steakhouse, its narrow door is easy to miss. Not so for locals in the know, who congregate here to drink, chat and, if the mood takes them, dance.

Ramona (☎ 75 13 40 00; Fridtjof Nansensgata 28; 🕑 Thu-Sat) Within the Meyergården Hotell, this spot – and here comes another superlative – claims to be the largest nightclub in northern Norway.

Kinoteatret (☎ 75 14 60 50; Rådhusplass 1) The cinema at Mo i Rana's is located at the top of Jernbanegata.

TP Bowlingsenter (☎ 75 16 85 00; Fridtjof Nansensgata 1) You can go bowling here for Nkr50 per round at peak times.

Getting There & Away

Mo i Rana's Røssvoll airport, 14km northeast of town, has flights to/from Bodø and Trondheim, via Mosjøen. You'll enjoy an excellent panorama of the Svartisen icecaps unless it's misty down below.

By bus, options are fairly limited. There are three services daily except Saturday between Mo i Rana and Sandnessjøen (2¾ hours) and at least one daily run to/from Mosjøen (1¾ hours). For information about journeys to/from Umeå in Sweden, see p407.

Most visitors arrive at Mo i Rana's attractive octagonal **train station** (☎ 75 15 01 77) on the two to four daily trains from Trondheim (Nkr749, 6½ hours) or Fauske (Nkr298, 2¼ hours).

Getting Around

Flytaxi (☎ 90 16 21 57) does an airport run for all flights, calling by major hotels.

If you're driving, pick up a free visitors' parking permit from the tourist office, which also hires bicycles.

Call ☎ 7550 for a taxi.

SALTFJELLET-SVARTISEN NATIONAL PARK

The 2770-sq-km Saltfjellet-Svartisen National Park combines the Svartisen icecap, Norway's second-largest icefield, with its rugged peaks, a combined area of 369 sq km; and the high, rolling moorlands of the Saltfjellet massif near the Swedish border.

The best map for trekking is Staten's Kartverk's *Saltfjellet* at 1:100,000.

Northbound travellers on the Hurtigruten coastal ferry can visit the Svartisen glacier as an optional add-on to their journey (Nkr870).

Svartisen

The two Svartisen icecaps, separated by the valley Vesterdalen, straddle the Arctic Circle between Mo i Rana and the Meløy peninsula. At its thickest, the ice is around 600m deep. Its average height is about 1500m but some tongues lick down into the valleys and are the lowest-lying glaciers in mainland Europe. You can experience Svartisen from either its eastern or more spectacular western side. Most visitors to either just make a quick hop by boat, but hikers will find more joy approaching from the east.

Østisen, the eastern glacier, is more accessible from Mo. From the end of the Svartisdalen road, 20km up the valley from Mo i Rana's airport, **ferries** (☎ 75 16 23 79; adult/child return Nkr80/40; mid-Jun–Aug) cross Svartisen lake (Svartisvatnet) four times daily. From the ferry landing, it's a 3km hike to the beginning of the Austerdalsisen glacier tongue. There's a kiosk and camp site at the lake.

From the end of the road you can also trek up to the hut on the shore of the mountain lake Pikhaugsvatnet, which is surrounded by peaks and ice. This is an excellent base for day hikes up the Glomdal valley or to the Flatisen glacier.

For the western and more dramatic Svartisen icecap, see p305.

Saltfjellet

The broad upland plateaus of the Saltfjellet massif transcend the Arctic Circle, connecting the peaks surrounding the Svartisen icecap and the Swedish border. Within this relatively inhospitable wilderness are traces of several ancient Sami fences and sacrificial sites, some dating from as early as the 9th century.

A 15km walk to the east leads to Graddis, near the Swedish border, and the venerable **Graddis Fjellstue og Camping** (☎ 75 69 43 41; graddis@c2i.net; s Nkr450, d from 570-620; mid-Jun–mid-Aug). This cosy little guesthouse has been run by the same family since its establishment in 1867. It makes an excellent base to launch yourself into one of Norway's least tramped hiking areas. Camping is also available, and Methuselah, a 1000-year-old pine tree, is a nearby attraction.

By car, access to Saltfjellet is either along the E6 or the Rv77, which follows the southern slope of the Junkerdalen valley. Rail travellers can disembark at Lonsdal en route between Fauske and Trondheim, but you may have to request a stop.

ARCTIC CIRCLE CENTRE

Latitude 66°33' N marks the southernmost extent of the midnight sun on the summer solstice and the ragged edge of the polar night on the winter solstice. As the Arctic Highway between Mo i Rana and Fauske cuts across this imaginary line, it should be a magical moment.

But the **Polarsirkelsenteret** (☎ 75 12 96 96; E6, Rognan; optional exhibition adult/child/family Nkr50/20/100, ⌚ May–mid-Sep), beside the E6 and surrounded by the bleak moors that roll in from Saltfjellet-Svartisen National Park, is something of a tourist trap. There's an exhibition of stuffed wildlife and an audiovisual presentation on the Arctic regions, but the place exists mostly to stamp postcards with a special Arctic Circle postmark and sell certificates (Nkr50) for visitors to authenticate crossing the line. There's also boreal kitsch – miniature polar bears, trolls and other fluffy, furry things – by the basket load and, on the plus side, as its website chooses to highlight, 'very good lavatory facilities'. Altogether more sober and serious are the memorials to the Slav forced labourers who, during WWII, constructed the Arctic Highway for the occupying Nazi forces and died far from home.

Northbound travellers will feel spirits rising again as they leave these bleak uplands and descend into a relatively lush, green environment, which is much more typical of northern Norway.

FAUSKE

pop 7100

Fauske is known mainly for fine marble. Its 'Norwegian Rose' stone features in many a monumental building, including the Oslo Rådhus, the UN headquarters in New York and the Emperor's palace in Tokyo. The town is also the jumping-off point for Sulitjelma and the Rago National Park.

The seasonal **tourist office** (☎ 75 50 35 15; Sjøgata; ⌚ 9am-3pm mid-Jun–mid-Aug) shares its premises with the dominant building of Salten museum.

Sights include the marble-themed **town square**, and the park-like collection of historic buildings of the Fauske branch of **Salten museum** (Sjøgata; adult/child Nkr35/free; ⌚ 11am-5pm mid-Jun–mid-Aug), whose grounds are a lovely spot for a picnic.

Sleeping & Eating

Lundhøgda Camp & Café (☎ 75 64 39 66; lunghogda@c2i.net; Lundveien; camp site Nkr150, 4-bed cabin Nkr380-750; ⌚ May-Sep) This complex, 3km west of town, has superb views of the fjord and surrounding peaks.

Fauske Hotell (☎ 75 60 20 00; www.fauskehotell.no in Norwegian; Storgata 82; s/d Nkr700/950 mid-Jun–Aug, Nkr970/1220 Sun-Thu, Nkr825/1075 Fri & Sat rest-of-year) Fauske's only year-round upmarket choice has renovated, cheerful rooms although common areas feel decidedly dated. The restaurant does an Arctic Menu.

Brygga Hotell (☎ 75 60 20 00; s/d Nkr700/950; ⌚ mid-Jun–Jul) This less monolithic 30-room annexe of the Fauske Hotell, right beside the fjord, is an attractive alternative should you pass through town during the brief window when it's open.

Huset (☎ 75 64 41 01; Storgata 74; mains around Nkr200) This attractive eating choice on the main street does prime cuts of meat with garnishing, sold by weight, and other meaty mains. It also has an imaginative range of snacks and salads, plus the inevitable pizza.

Getting There & Away

BUS

There are four buses each day running to/from Bodø (Nkr106, 1¼ hours). The Nord-Norgeekspressen for Narvik (Nkr407, 4¾ hours) passes through Fauske twice daily and has fat discounts for holders of Inter-Rail and Eurail passes. You can also travel directly to Lofoten on the Fauske–Lofoten Ekspressen, which crosses to Sortland (Nkr370, five hours, twice daily). One of the two buses continues to Svolvær (Nkr507, nine hours). There's also a daily run to/from Harstad (Nkr343, 5½ hours).

TRAIN

Trains ply the Nordlandsbanen between Trondheim (Nkr905, nine hours) and Bodø (Nkr104, 45 minutes), via Fauske, twice daily and there are additional trains (up to five daily) between Fauske and Bodø. To continue further northwards, you've no option but to hop on a bus.

AROUND FAUSKE

Saltdal & Blood Road Museums

Saltdal Historical Village (☎ 75 68 22 90; adult/child Nkr30/free; ⌚ 9am-3pm Mon-Fri, 1-4pm Sat, 1-6pm Sun 20 Jun-20 Aug), just off the E6 near Saltnes, is a collection of rural and fishing-related buildings. Within the grounds is the **Blood Road Museum**. In an old German barracks, it reveals conditions for Allied prisoners of war who died building the highway between Saltnes and Saksenvik. The prisoners' cemetery, with the remains of some 7000 forced labourers, is about 3km north, in Botn.

Sulitjelma

As an interpretive panel just north of Fauske will confirm, you're exactly halfway along the E6 and it's an appropriate moment to break free from the Arctic Highway for a short while.

It's a gorgeous 40km run along the Rv830, up scenic Langvassdalen to the tiny community of Sulitjelma. It wasn't always such a backwater; in 1860 a Sami herder discovered copper ore in the forested country north of Langvatnet and suddenly the Sulitjelma region was attracting all sorts of opportunists from southern Norway. Large ore deposits were discovered and the Sulitjelma Gruber mining company was founded in 1891. By 1928 the wood-fuelled smelter had taken its toll on the surrounding birch forests, as did high concentrations of CO_2, a by-product of the smelting process. Nowadays, with the furnaces long since cold, the environment is well on its way to recovery.

SIGHTS & ACTIVITIES

A one-hour guided tour of the **Sulitjelma Show Mine** (Besøksgruve; adult/child Nkr125/50; 1pm mid-May–early Aug) includes a 1.5km rail ride deep into the mountain.

Alongside the fjord, the **Sulitjelma Mining Museum** (Gruvemuseum; 75 64 06 95; adult/child/family Nkr25/10/60; 10am-6pm Sun-Fri, noon-3pm Sat mid-Jun–early Aug) records the area's 100 years of mining history and displays some awesome rusting equipment.

The country east and south of Sulitjelma enjoys especially scenic glacial surroundings and there are ample hiking opportunities.

Rago National Park

The small (167 sq km), scarcely visited Rago National Park is a rugged chunk of forested granite mountain and moorland, riven with deep glacial cracks and capped by great icefields. Rago, together with the large adjoining Swedish parks, Pakjelanta, Sarek and Stora Sjöfjallet, belongs to a wider protected area of 5500 sq km. Wildlife includes not only beavers in the deep Laksåga (aka Nordfjord) river valley, but also wolverines in the higher areas. Along the relatively lush Storskogdalen valley, a series of foaming cascades and spectacular waterfalls tumble.

From the main trailhead at Lakshol, it's a three-hour, 7km walk up the valley to the free Storskogvasshytta and Ragohytta huts, then a stiff climb up and over the ridge into Sweden to connect with the well-established trail system over the border.

Maps to use are *Sisovatnet*, at 1:50,000, or *Sørfold*, at 1:75,000. To reach Lakshol, turn east off the E6 at the Trengsel bridge and continue about 6km to the end of the road.

NARVIK

pop 18,300

Narvik was established in 1902 as an ice-free port for the rich Kiruna iron mines in Swedish Lapland. Recently it's begun to capitalise on the unique sporting and sightseeing activities available in its majestic, wild and historic surroundings, including the spectacular Ofotbanen Railway to Sweden.

History

The Narvik region was inhabited as early as the Stone Age, as evidenced by the distinct rock carving of a moose found at Vassvik northwest of the centre.

During WWII control of this strategic port was essential to the Nazi war machine, intent upon halting iron supplies to the Allies and usurping the bounty. In April 1940, 10 German destroyers ploughed through a blizzard to enter the port and sink two Norwegian battleships. Next day five British destroyers arrived and a fierce naval battle resulted in the loss of two ships on each side. In May British, Norwegian, French and Polish troops disembarked and took back the town.

But the Nazis didn't retreat and the town was decimated, as evidenced by the remains of soldiers in the cemeteries and 34 ships of five nations (Norway, Britain, France, the Netherlands and Germany) in the harbour. On 8 June 1940 the Allies surrendered Narvik which remained under German control until 8 May 1945.

Although the town was admirably rebuilt downtown Narvik is less than prepossessing (some would say it's ugly). Still, the surrounding fjord, forest and mountain country borders on the spectacular in all directions and the trans-shipment facility bisecting the city still loads around 30 million tonnes of ore annually from train wagons onto ships.

Orientation & Information

Narvik is pincered by islands to the west and mountains in every other direction, while spectacular fjords stretch north and south

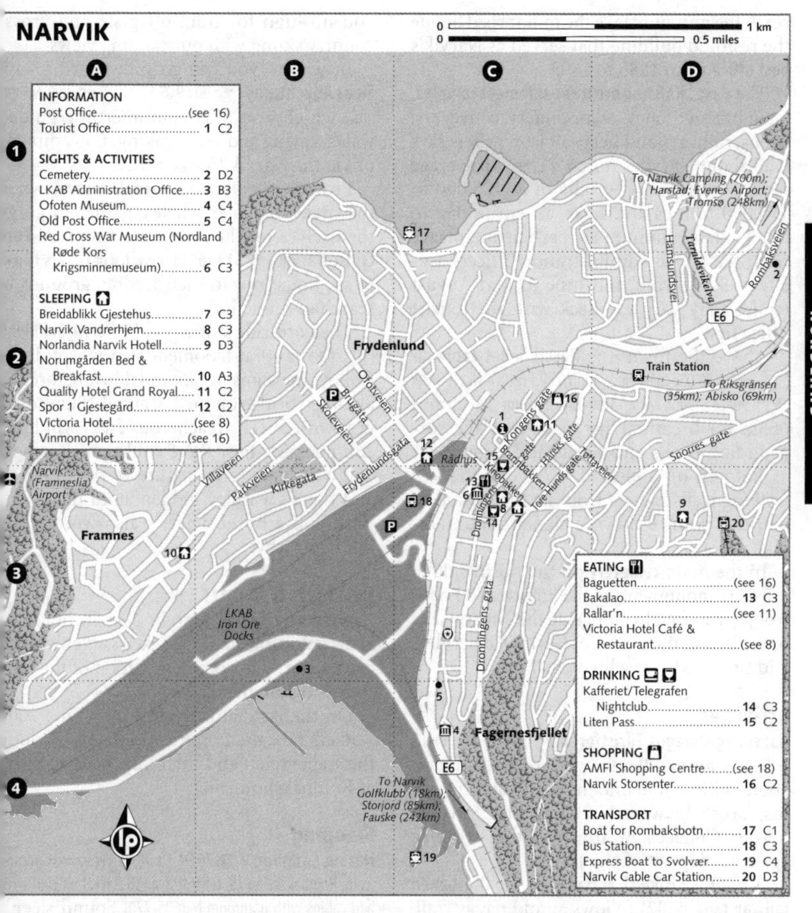

The E6 (Kongens gate) slices through the heart of town. The train station is at the north end of town and the bus station is just beside the AMFI shopping centre.

The **tourist office** (☎ 76 96 56 00; www.destinationnarvik.com; Kongens gate 57; 9am-7pm Mon-Fri, 10am-5pm Sat & Sun mid-Jun–mid-Aug; 9am-4pm May–mid-Jun, 9am-4pm Mon-Fri, 10am-2pm Sat mid-Aug–Sep, 9am-3.30pm Mon-Fri Oct-Apr) holds Narvik og Omegns Turistforening (NOT) cabin keys (Nkr100 deposit), has internet access (Nkr10 per 15 min) and rents bikes (Nkr200 per day).

Sights

Narvik's **Red Cross War Museum** (Nordland Røde Kors Krigsminnemuseum; ☎ 76 94 44 26; Kongens gate; adult/child Nkr50/25; 10am-9pm Mon-Sat, noon-6pm Sun early Jun–late Aug, 10am-4pm Mon-Sat, noon-4pm Sun May-early Jun & late Aug–mid-Sep, 11am-3pm Mon-Fri rest-of-year) illustrates the military campaigns fought hereabouts in the early years of WWII. The presentation may not be flash but it will still stun you.

The **Ofoten Museum** (☎ 76 96 00 50; Administrasjonsveien 3; adult/child/concession Nkr40/free/20; 10am-3pm Mon-Fri, noon-3pm Sat & Sun late Jun-early Aug, 10am-3pm Mon-Fri rest-of-year) tells of Narvik's farming, fishing, railway-building and ore trans-shipment heritage. There's a rolling film about the Ofotbanen Railway and children will enjoy pressing the button that activates the model train. Linger too over the display case of Sami costumes and artefacts and the collection of historic photos, contrasted with modern shots taken from the same angles. To reach the museum, take the minor road beside the restored building that served as Narvik's **post office** from 1888 to 1898.

The vast **LKAB iron ore trans-shipment complex**, an impressive tangle of machinery, conveyors, ovens, railways and heaps of iron pellets says it all about Narvik's *raison d'être*. An average tanker-load of ore weighs in at 125,000 to 175,000 tonnes and takes an entire day to fill. Tours (minimum six participants) leave from the LKAB administration offices, usually at 3pm, from mid-June to mid-August (times may vary so check with the tourist office first).

Above the town, the **Narvikfjellet cable car** (☎ 76 94 16 05; Mårveien; adult/child return Nkr100/80; 🕑 1-9pm early Jun & Aug, 1pm-1am mid-Jun–Jul) climbs 656m for breathtaking views over the surrounding peaks and fjords and even as far as Lofoten on a clear day. Several marked walking trails radiate from its top station or you can bounce down a signed mountain-bike route.

In the main **cemetery** on the north side of town are monuments to the French and Polish troops who fought alongside the Norwegians on land, and the graves of German defenders and British sailors who died at sea.

Activities

Narvik og Omegns Turistforening (NOT; www.narvikfjell.no) is an excellent source of information about hiking. It maintains more than 20 cabins, mostly between Narvik and the Swedish border. Collect keys from the tourist office against a deposit of Nkr100.

A popular hike that parallels the **Ofotbanen railway** (see p302) follows an old navvy trail, the **Rallarveien**. Few walkers attempt the entire way between Sweden's Abisko National Park and the sea, opting instead to begin at Riksgränsen, the small ski station just across the Swedish border, or Bjørnfell, the next station west. It's an undemanding descent as far as Katterat, from where you can take the evening train to Narvik. For more exertion, drop down to Rombaksbotn at the head of the fjord, the location of the main camp when the railway was being built (it's since returned to nature). From here, a **boat** (adult/child Nkr250/100) runs erratically to Narvik in summer. Check with the tourist office to avoid an unwelcome supplementary 10km at the end of the day.

From February to April, the Narvikfjellet cable car above town (see above) will whisk you up high for trail, off-piste and cross country skiing with outstanding views.

In winter, you can go snowshoeing witl **Sipas Adventures** (☎ 90 69 09 55; www.sipasadventure.no), which also offers summertime guide walks, caving and sea kayaking. Book directl or via the Narvik tourist office.

From November to mid-January, whe the orcas, or killer whales, gather to gorg themselves on the winter herring run, **For Cruise Narvik** (☎ 91 39 06 18; www.fcn.no) does four to six-hour trips to their feeding grounds i search of the action.

The fjord-side journey to the **Narvik Golfklub** (☎ 76 95 12 01) at Skjomendalen is wondrou (follow the signs to Skjomdal just before th Skjomen bridge on the E6, about 18km sout of town). Sheer, treacherous faces will leav you guessing how there could possibly be golf course here. Yet nature works wonders and there's a valley hidden amid the peaks Find golf a bore? There's also worthwhil hiking nearby.

Festivals & Events

Each year during March, Narvik holds it **Vinterfestuka**, an action-packed winter week o events, partly in commemoration of the nav vies who built the railway.

On the last Saturday in June, some 200 walkers take the train to various stops alon the Rallarveien and then hike back to part at Rombaksbotn.

Sleeping

Narvik Camping (☎ 76 94 58 10; www.narvikcampin.com; Rombaksveien 75; tent/caravan sites Nkr110/150; 4-/6 bed cabins with bathroom Nkr605/770) Sound sleep' not guaranteed at what's otherwise a perfectl adequate camp site, overlooking the fjord an E6, 2km northeast of the centre and Narvik' only choice. Trucks rumble along the highwa and long wagon trains clank by on the railway just above.

Spor 1 Gjestegård (☎ 76 94 60 20, 996 31 374; www.spor1.no; Brugata 2a; dm Nkr180-200, s/d 450/550) Th welcome at 'Trail 1' begins with the pots o fresh flowers flanking the entrance. In forme rail cabins by the tracks, it has a sauna, kitche and great pub with outdoor terrace, ope in the evenings from Tuesday to Saturday Hosts Brit and Bjørn Einar are themselve experienced backpackers.

Breidablikk Gjestehus (☎ 76 94 14 18; www.bre dablikk.no in Norwegian; Tore Hunds gate 41; dm/s/d fro

Nkr250/435/595; P 💻) It's a steep but worthwhile walk from the centre to this pleasant hillside guesthouse with its sweeping views over town and fjord. There's a cosy communal lounge and it serves a delicious buffet breakfast (Nkr50). Dorms have four beds. Some rooms (around Nkr200 extra) are freshly painted with sparkling new bathrooms.

our pick Norumgården Bed & Breakfast (☎ 76 4 48 57; http://norumgaarden.narviknett.no; Framnesveien 27; s/d Nkr350/500, d with kitchen Nkr600; 🕑 late Jan-Nov) This little treasure of a place (it has only four rooms so reservations are essential) is very special and offers excellent value. Used as a German officer's mess in WWII (the owner will proudly show you a 1940 bottle of Coca Cola, made under licence in Hamburg), it nowadays brims with antiques and character. Choose the Heidi room (it's the only one without a shower but the little balcony more than compensates) and you'll be sleeping in the bed once occupied by King Olav.

Narvik Vandrerhjem (☎ 76 96 22 00; narvik.hostel@vandrerhjem.no; Dronningens gata 58; dm Nkr270, s/d Nkr460/600, all incl breakfast; P 💻) Narvik's smart though by no means cheap HI hostel is a friendly place with a good café. Its 30 beds are quickly snapped up in summer so to reserve.

Victoria Hotel (☎ 76 96 28 00; www.victoria-hotel.net in Norwegian; s/d Nkr765/895 incl breakfast) This one shares premises with Narvik Vandrerhjem, and offers rooms with bathroom and more comfort.

Norlandia Narvik Hotell (☎ 76 96 48 00; www.norlandia.no; Skistuaveien 8; s/d Nkr725/970 mid-Jun–mid-Aug, Nkr850/1050 Sun-Thu, Nkr595/750 Fri & Sat rest-of-year; P 💻) This 90-room tour-group favourite, stretching long and low at the base of the cable car, offers great vistas. Accommodation is in comfortable chalet-type buildings.

Quality Hotel Grand Royal (☎ 76 97 70 00; www.choice.no; Kongens gate 64; s/d mid-Jun–mid-Aug Nkr700/1010, Nkr1250/1450 Sun-Thu, Nkr790/980 Fri & Sat rest-of-year; P 💻) Narvik's top-of-the-line hotel, although something of a monolith from the exterior, makes an attractive stopover. There's a beauty salon and a few disabled-equipped rooms.

Eating

Baguetten (☎ 76 95 25 00; Kongens gate 66; 🕑 Mon-Sat) Opposite Vinmonopolet on the top floor of the Narvik Storsenter, the Baguette will serve you rich cakes and Narvik's best coffee.

Bakalao (☎ 76 94 36 60; Kongens gate 42; mains Nkr174-194; 🕑 10am-4.15pm Mon-Fri) This tiny offshoot of Narvik's fish market offers tasty ready-to-eat dishes, such as fish cakes, *bacalao* and whale stew, to eat in or take away.

Rallar'n (☎ 76 97 70 77; Kongens gate 64) The pub/restaurant of Quality Hotel Grand Royal is all atmospheric low ceilings, bare brick and dark woodwork. Divided into intimate compartments, it offers pizza, pasta and creative mains (Nkr145 to Nkr245).

Victoria Hotel Café and Restaurant (☎ 76 96 28 00; Dronningens gata 58) Between 11am and 5pm, Monday to Friday, this light, pleasant, self-service café serves snacks. Then, from Tuesday to Saturday, it metamorphoses into Narvik's finest dining experience with a gourmet menu (Nkr425 for three courses, Nkr575 for five) that changes weekly.

The town's Vinmonopolet is on the 3rd floor of the Narvik Storsenter.

Drinking & Entertainment

Liten Plass (Dronningens gata; mains Nkr174-194) Prices are chalked in giant letters on the blackboard at the aptly named Little Place – a squeezebox of a bar, popular with a young crowd, where you're guaranteed human warmth on even the coldest night.

Kafferiet/Telegrafen Night Club (☎ 76 96 00 55; Dronningens gata 56) This popular hang-out, right beside the HI hostel, attracts the 20-to-35 crowd. It shows sport on wide-screen TV and has occasional live bands (with cover charge).

In winter you can tumble out of the cable car into the bar at the **Norlandia Narvik Hotell**, Narvik's leading après-ski venue.

Getting There & Away

AIR

Nearly all flights leave from Harstad/Narvik Evenes airport (p331), which is 1¼ hours away. Narvik's tiny Framneslia airport, about 3km west of the centre, serves only Bodø, Tromsø and Andenes.

BOAT

An express passenger boat runs to Svolvær on Lofoten (Nkr326, 3½ hours, daily except Saturday) from the Dampskipskaia dock on Havnegata, 1km south of the centre along Kongens gate.

SVARTABJØRN

No-one knows for sure whether there actually was a comely cook nicknamed Svartabjørn (Black Bear) who dished up meals for the navvies that built the railway of the Ofoten line. But her name certainly lives on in legend and in fiction. In his Malm trilogy, published in 1914, novelist Ernst Didring recounts some of the stories the navvies passed on to him.

It's said that this dark, beautiful girl, although still too young to be away from home, got on well with the rail workers and was a great little cook into the bargain. But she fell in love with the same man that another woman coveted and was beaten to death with a laundry paddle.

It's said that the navvies arranged for her burial at the Tornehamn cemetery. Today, the grave site bears the name of Anna Norge, but the date of death has been changed at least three times to fit different women who at different times have been assumed to be the genuine Svartabjørn.

BUS

Express buses run northwards to Tromsø (Nkr360, 4¼ hours, three daily) and also between Narvik and Bodø (Nkr497, 6½ hours, two daily) via Fauske (Nkr407, 4¾ hours). For Lofoten there are two buses daily between Narvik and Leknes (Nkr505, eight hours) via Sortland (Nkr294, four hours) and Svolvær (Nkr433, 6½ hours).

TRAIN

Heading for Sweden, there are at least two daily services between Narvik and Riksgränsen (one hour), on the border, and Kiruna (three hours). Trains continue to Lulea (7¼ hours) via Boden, from where you can pick up connections to Stockholm.

The route takes you up the spectacular Ofotbanen Railway and, in Sweden, past Abisko National Park, which offers excellent hiking and lovely Arctic scenery.

Getting Around

Narvik's Framneslia airport is 3km from the centre. Flybuss runs five to seven times daily between Narvik and Harstad/Narvik Evenes airport (Nkr180, 1¼ hours), 79km away. For a taxi, phone **Narvik Taxi** (☎ 07 550).

OFOTBANEN RAILWAY & RALLARVEIEN

The spectacular mountain-hugging **Ofotbanen railway** (☎ 76 92 31 21) trundles beside fjordside cliffs, birch forests and rocky plateaus as it climbs to the Swedish border. Constructed by migrant labourers (navvies) at the end of the 19th century to connect Narvik with the iron ore mines at Kiruna, in Sweden's far north, it was opened in 1903. Currently it transports around 15 million tonnes of iron ore annually and is also a major magnet for visitors.

The train route from Narvik to Riksgränsen, the ski resort just inside Sweden (one way/return Nkr80/160, including up to two children; one hour), features some 50 tunnels and snowsheds. Towards the Narvik end of the rail line, you'll be able to see the wreck of the German ship *Georg Thiele* at the edge of the fjord.

You can run the line as a day or half-day trip, leaving Narvik at 10.50am. The 12.33pm return train from Riksgränsen, just in Sweden, allows time for coffee and a quick browse or you can walk a trail in this stunning alpine country and catch the 6.05pm back to Narvik. For the best views, sit on the left side heading from Narvik.

Meteorologen Ski Lodge (☎ 46-7350 324 17 in Sweden; www.meteorologen.se; s/d Nkr900/1400; year round; P) Recently opened in what was originally a weather station, this is a very attractive option should you wish to overnight up high. Rooms all have large windows giving vistas of either lake or mountains and there's a pleasant dining room and restaurant, primarily for guests. It also manages self-catering apartments year-round (three/six-person Nkr695/965) in the vast adjacent winter hotel.

In Sweden, several long-distance trails radiate out from the railway, including the connecting route with Norway's Øvre Dividal National Park (see p343) and the world-renowned Kungsleden, which heads south from Abisko into the heart of Sweden.

Between late June and mid-August, bus 9 runs twice a day up the E10 to Riksgränsen (4 minutes) and on to Abisko and Kiruna.

‹YSTRIKSVEIEN – THE ⁏OASTAL ROUTE

,onger, yes, more expensive, yes (gosh, those erry tolls mount up). But if you've even a lay or two to spare, divert from the Arctic Iighway lemming run and enjoy the empty oads and solitary splendours of Kystriksveien, he coastal alternative. If the whole route seems launting, it's quite possible to cut in or out rom Steinkjer, Bodø or, midway, Mosjøen nd Mo i Rana. It's one to drive; don't even ttempt it by bus or you'll still be waiting when he first snows fall.

Off the coast are around 14,000 islands, ome little more than rocks with a few tufts of ,rass, others (such as Vega; see p304) supporting whole communities that for centuries have urvived on coastal fishing and subsistence griculture. The sea was the only highway and he living was harsh year-round – especially etween mid-January and Easter, when the nenfolk would be absent, working the fishing ,rounds off Lofoten for cod.

nformation

Ɩhe splendid free *Kystriksveien* (Coastal Ɍoute) booklet, distributed by tourist offices nd many lodgings along the way, is a mini-3ible. Its website, www.rv17.no, gives even nore detail. For greater depth, invest in *The ⁏oastal Road: A Travel Guide to Kystriksveien* Nkr298) by Olav Breen.

Click on www.rv17.no/sykkel for a recommended seven-day bike-and-ferry journey ,long the full length of the Kystriksveien. The ree brochure *Cycling from Steinkjer to Leka* ‹as detailed maps, and lists highlights and ›icycle-friendly accommodation.

For information on the southern part of ‹ystriksveien, see p287.

BRØNNØYSUND

›op 5000

Brønnøysund is flanked on one side by an archipelago of islets in a tropical-looking sea and ›n the other by rolling farm country. Its **tourist ›ffice** (☎ 75 01 80 00; www.visithelgeland.com; 9am-›pm Mon-Fri, 10am-6pm Sat, noon-6pm Sun mid-Jun–mid-›ug, 9am-4pm Mon-Fri rest-of-year), one block from the Iurtigruten quay, rents bicycles (per hour/day Nkr40/125). It also sells tickets for a spectacu-›ar daily minicruise (adult/child Nkr363/182) ›n the Hurtigruten. Leaving at 5pm, the coastal ferry passes Torghatten (see below) on its way south to Rørvik in Trøndelag – allowing an hour to explore the town and visit its splendid Norveg Centre for Coastal Culture and Industries before hopping aboard the northbound ferry and reaching Brønnøysund again at 1am.

Sights & Activities

Around 400 types of herb, 100 varieties of rose and 1000 species of cactus flourish at **Hildurs Urterarium** (☎ 75 02 52 12; adult/child Nkr40/free; 10am-5pm mid-Jun–mid-Aug). At Tilrem, about 6km north of Brønnøysund, it also produces its own wine. There are some rustic old farm buildings, a small art gallery and the shop carries locally grown products. The garden also makes a lovely spot for a lunch stop; dishes seasoned with locally grown herbs, of course.

Located some 15km south of Brønnøysund, **Torghatten** on Torget island is a significant local landmark. The peak, pierced by a hole 160m long, 35m high and 20m wide, is accessed from its base by a good 20-minute walking track. The best perspective of the hole is from the southbound Hurtigruten coastal ferry as it rounds the island. For the lowdown on the legend of Torghatten, see the boxed text, p49.

Sleeping & Eating

The Brønnøysund tourist office can book private farm cabins and *rorbuer* (Nkr600 to Nkr900) accommodating four to eight people.

Torghatten Camping (☎ 75 02 54 95; www.visittorghatten.no; tent/caravan sites Nkr90/130, 4-6-bed cabins with bathroom Nkr850, 6-bed apt Nkr950-1050) This lovely option with its small beach beside a man-made lake is great for children. Around 10km southwest of Brønnøysund, it's handy for an ascent of the Torghatten peak.

Galeasen Hotell (☎ 75 00 85 50; www.galeasen.com; Havnegata 32-36; s/d Nkr780/980 mid-Jun–mid-Aug & Fri & Sat year-round, Nkr1095/1295 Sun-Thu rest-of-year) The 22-room Galeasen sits right beside the quay and runs a small restaurant. It's an attractive spot even though reception is short on smiles. Ask for a room in the more recent main building, not the less attractive annexe, which occupies a converted fish processing plant.

Getting There & Away

There are at least two daily flights to/from both Trondheim and Bodø; the approach route passes right over Torghatten and the azure seas that lap around it.

Up to four buses run daily except Sunday between Brønnøysund and Sandnessjøen (Nkr180, three hours). Brønnøysund is also a port for the Hurtigruten coastal ferry.

VEGA

pop 1300

The island of Vega remains a very Norwegian destination (we were the only non-nationals on our ferry journeys to and from the island). It and the more than 6000 skerries, islets and simply large rocks that form the Vega archipelago are a Unesco World Heritage site. This distinction comes not for any grand building or monument, nor for their scenery (which is stunning, nevertheless) but for human endeavour. The evaluating committee stated that the archipelago reflects the way generations of fishermen/farmers have, over the past 1500 years, maintained a sustainable living in an inhospitable seascape. This lifestyle is based on the now unique practice of eider down harvesting, to which women make a major contribution. For more on these very special ducks and their down, visit the splendid little E-Huset (E-House) museum or click on www.verdensarvvega.no or www.lanan.no.

Vega's **tourist office** (☎ 75 03 53 88; www.visitvega.no in Norwegian; 🕑 10am-6pm Mon-Thu, 10am-8pm Fri, 10am-2pm Sat mid-Jun–mid-Aug, 9am-4pm rest-of-year) is in Gladstad, the island's largest hamlet.

E-Huset (☎ 95 04 44 59; admission Nkr30; 🕑 noon-4pm Tue-Sun mid-Jun–mid-Aug), in the tiny fishing hamlet of Nes, is a delightful, engagingly informative small museum that celebrates the eider duck and the way the birds were nurtured as domestic pets, when they returned – each one to its very same nesting box – after their winter migration. The E-House occupies a former trading post, which still retains its original counter and row upon row of goods that your great-grandparents used to buy.

Vega Camping (☎ 94 35 00 80; http://hjem.monet.no/camping in Norwegian; Floa; tent/caravan site Nkr100/120 plus per person Nkr15; d/q Nkr400/650; 🕑 mid-Jun–mid-Aug) The close-cropped green grass extending to the still water's edge make this simple camp site one of the prettiest in Norway. You can rent a boat or bike (Nkr250/100 per day) or go for a trot at the adjacent horse-riding school.

our pick **Vega Havhotell** (☎ 75 03 64 00; www.havhotellene.no in Norwegian; Viksås; s/d Nkr890/990 incl breakfast; 🕑 daily Apr-Sep, Tue-Sun Nov-Mar) This isolate getaway, down a dirt track at Vega's seclude northern limit, is tranquillity itself (you won' find a radio or TV in any of its 21 rooms). It' a place to unwind, go for breezy coastal stroll or simply watch the mother eider duck an her chicks pottering in the pool below.

Even if you don't stay overnight at Veg Havhotell, call by to enjoy the fine fare sourced locally for the most part, of its gour met **restaurant** (1/2/3 courses Nkr225/325/425), wher reservations are essential.

Express boats make the trip to/from bot Brønnøysund and Sandnessjøen, while ca ferries cross to Vega from the mainland a Horn and Tjøtta.

SANDNESSJØEN

pop 5750

Watching over Sandnessjøen, the main commercial centre of Nordland's southern coas is the imposing Syv Søstre (Seven Sisters range, just to its south. Hardy hikers can reac all seven summits (910m to 1072m) in a da and every several years there's a competitio taking in all the peaks. However, don't bust gut trying to crack the record of three hour 54 minutes.

Central Sandnessjøen's backbone is pedestrianised Torolv Kveldulvsons gate, one bloc from the harbour. The **tourist office** (☎ 75 04 4 00; www.helgelandskysten.com; 🕑 9am-7pm Mon-Fri, 10am 4pm Sat, noon-4pm Sun mid-Jun–mid-Aug, 9am-4pm Mon-F rest-of-year) is by the docks. It hires bicycles (pe hour/day Nkr40/125) and has internet acces (per minute Nkr1).

Hiking

The tourist office can suggest walks in th Syv Søstre range, reached most convenientl via the Rv17 at Breimo or Sørra, about 4kn south of town. From there it's a couple o kilometres' walk to its foot. Trails are blaze with red dots but pack *Alstahaug*, a reliabl map at 1:50,000. Sign your name in the boo at each summit, fill in a control card at th tourist office and be proud of the diploma i will award you.

Sleeping

Rica Hotel Sandnessjøen (☎ 75 06 50 00; www.rica.nc Torolv Kveldulvsons gate 16; s/d Nkr795/995 mid-Jun–mic Aug, Nk1290/1490 Sun-Thu, Nkr860/1060 Fri & Sat rest-of-yea Sandnessjøen's top-end choice, this large hote with its 69 recently renovated rooms offers a he comfort you'd expect from a member of he Rica chain.

Getting There & Away

Jp to four buses run daily except Sunday between Sandnessjøen and Brønnøysund Nkr180, three hours); and there are three o five services (Saturday excepted) to/from both Mosjøen (1¾ hours) and Mo i Rana (2¾ hours). Sandnessjøen is also a stop for the Hurtigruten coastal ferry.

TRÆNA & LOVUND

Træna is an archipelago of over 1000 small, flat skerries, five of which are inhabited.

Ferries from the mainland dock on the island of Husøy, which has most of Træna's population and lodgings, but the main sights are on the adjacent island of Sanna. Sanna is just over 1km long and a miniature mountain range runs along its spine, culminating at the northern end in the 318m spire, Trænstaven.

Near Sanna's southern end, archaeologists discovered a cemetery and artefacts (now at the Tromsø Museum) a good 9000 years old inside the cathedral-like **Kirkehelleren Cave**.

The steep-sided island of Lovund, where prolific bird colonies and 240 humans roost, rises 623m above the sea. Every 14 April the island celebrates Lundkommerdag, the day 200,000 puffins return to the island to nest until mid-August.

Express boats connecting Sandnessjøen and Træna and car ferries run three times per week.

STOKKVÅGEN TO STORVIK

If you do only one segment of the coastal highway, make it the part between Stokkvågen, west of Mo i Rana, and the broad sandy beach at Storvik, 100km south of Bodø. This stretch was recently declared a National Tourist Route, a designation awarded only to the most scenic of scenic roads.

From Mo i Rana to the coast, it's a dramatic run in its own right alongside pretty Ranafjord, where you can roam around the Nazi coastal fort of **Grønsvik** (admission free), one of more than 350 built along Norway's coastline.

The vistas will drain you of superlatives as you follow the coast northwards, cross the Arctic Circle and run within sight of islands, islets and skerries too numerous to count, as sea eagles wheel and peer for prey above you. Wildflowers show off their best in the relatively mild climate, warmed by the very last of the Gulf Stream's flow and for long stretches the highway rolls right beside the water. You catch enticing glimpses of the Svartisen glacier from the Kilboghamn–Jektvik and Ågskardet–Forøy ferries, supplemented by magnificent views from the road alongside Holandsfjorden.

From **Holand**, a **ferry** (☎ 47 99 40 30; adult/child return Nkr90/50) makes the 10-minute trip across Holandsfjorden roughly hourly. You can hire a bike (three/six hours Nkr40/60) to travel the 3km gravel track between the jetty and the tip of the Engebreen glacial tongue.

A 15-minute walk from the ferry landing takes you to the **Svartisen Turistsenter** (☎ 75 75 11 00; www.svartisen.no; ⏲ Jun–mid-Aug) with its café and shop. It does guided one- to two-hour glacier walks (Nkr400) and longer four- to five-hour treks (Nkr800) from the end of Engabrevatnet lake. Reserve in advance. You can also slog independently up the steep route along the glacier's edge to the Tåkeheimen hut (1171m), near the summit of Helgelandsbukken (1454m). Follow the 'T' markers and allow eight hours out and back.

Holand Hytter (☎ 75 75 00 16, 41 57 65 28; walterjoh@combitel.no; cabins Nkr500-800) has three attractive cabins, all with bathroom and kitchen. Two are within the woods and an easy walk from the Svartisen ferry jetty while the third, accommodating up to seven, is right beside it.

Furøy Camping (☎ 75 75 05 25; fax 75 75 03 36; Forøy; tent/caravan Nkr135/175, cabins Nkr490-900) Keep the children quiet as you work your way along the Kystriksveien with the promise of the five-star playground, complete with trampoline and minicabins, at this camp site, barely 1km from the Ågskardet–Føroy ferry terminal. Adults can soak in the hot tub (Nkr100 for up to six people) and everyone can savour the magnificent views of the Startisen glacier across the fjord. Do reserve your cabin in advance; a trail of vehicles heads from the ferry towards reception.

BODØ

pop 36,000

Bodø, Nordland's largest town, was founded in 1816 as a trade centre, then turned to fishing in 1860 during an especially lucrative herring boom. The town centre, rebuilt after being almost completely levelled by WWII

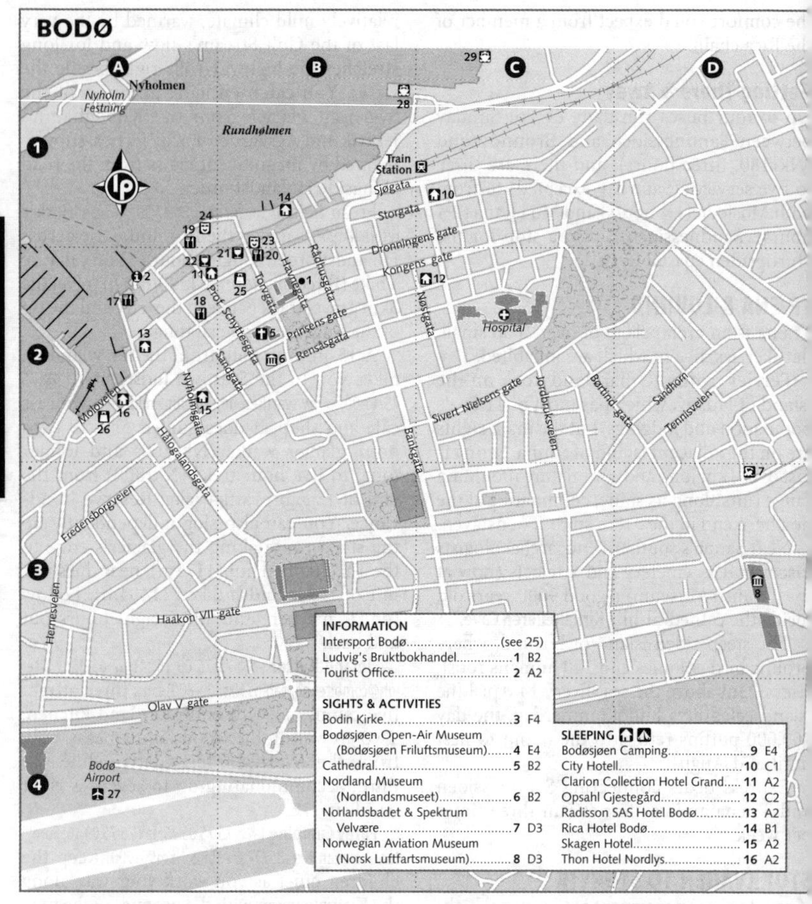

bombing, is unexciting architecturally – and in summer it can reek of the fish that sustain it – but it's open, tidy and has a pleasant marina. The city's main charm lies in its backdrop of distant rugged peaks and vast skies; while dramatic islands that support the world's densest concentration of white-tailed sea eagles – not for nothing is Bodø known as the Sea Eagle Capital – dot the seas to the north.

Many holidaymakers bypass Bodø in their rush to reach the far north or simply leap on a ferry to Lofoten. However, it's accessible and a great place to spend a day or two (it's only 63km west of Fauske on the Arctic Highway and is the northern terminus of the Nordlandsbanen railway).

Orientation & Information

Central Bodø slopes down a gradual hill towards the shoreline. The two main streets Sjøgata and largely pedestrianised Storgata run parallel, punctuated by the huge Glasshuset shopping mall. The tourist office, bus station and express boat terminal are all conveniently co-located a couple blocks west of the Glasshuset.

Intersport Bodø (☎ 75 54 98 50; 4th fl, Glasshuset) Sells walking maps and holds keys for Den Norske Turistforening (DNT) cabins.

Ludvig's Bruktbokhandel (Dronningens gate 42) Good selection of used books in English plus old LPs, comics and videos. A treasure trove for all addicted browsers.

Tourist office (☎ 75 54 80 00; www.visitbodo.com; Sjøgata 3; 9am-8pm Mon-Fri, 10am-6pm Sat, noon-8pm Sun mid-May–Aug, 9am-4pm Mon-Fri, 10am-3pm

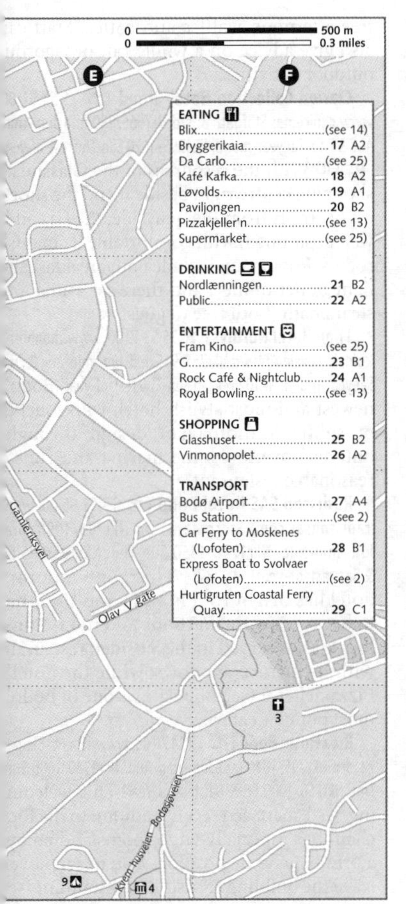

at rest-of-year) Publishes the excellent free *Bodø Guide* rochure, and has two internet terminals (per hr Nkr60). eside it are left-luggage lockers (Nkr20 to Nkr50).

ights

The **Norwegian Aviation Museum** (Norsk Luftfarts-nuseum; 75 50 78 50; Olav V gata; adult/concession/hild/family Nkr75/50/40/180; 10am-6pm mid-Jun–mid-ug, 10am-4pm Mon-Fri, 11am-5pm Sat & Sun rest-of-year) s huge fun to ramble around if you have even a passing interest in flight and aviation history. Allow at least half a day to roam ts 10,000 sq metres. If you're flying into Bodø for real, you'll see that, from above, he striking modern grey and smoked-glass nain museum building has the shape of an eroplane propeller.

Exhibits include a complete control tower and hands-on demonstrations. The affiliated Norwegian Air Force Museum has plenty of examples of historic military and civilian aircraft from the Tiger Moth to the U2 spy plane (the ill-fated US plane that was shot down over the Soviet Union in 1960, creating a major diplomatic incident, was en route from Peshawar in Pakistan to Bodø). Children and kids at heart will thrill and shudder at the small simulator, which, for an extra charge, takes you on some pretty harrowing virtual flights, including piloting a fighter jet.

The small **Nordland Museum** (Nordlandmuseet; 75 52 16 40; Prinsens gate 116; adult/child Nkr35/free; 9am-4pm Mon-Fri, 11am-4pm Sat & Sun May-Sep, 11am-4pm Mon-Fri rest-of-year) has a droll 20-minute film on the history of Bodø with English subtitles. Highlights of the collection are silver items from Viking times. Other exhibits cover Sami culture, the history of women in northern Norway, regional fishing culture and natural history.

The museum has an open-air component, the **Bodøsjøen Friluftsmuseum**, 3km from town near Bodøsjøen Camping. Here you'll find four hectares of historic homes, farm buildings, boat sheds, WWII German bunkers and the square-rigged sloop *Anna Karoline af Hopen*. You can wander the grounds for free but admission to the buildings is by appointment. Here too is the start of a **walking track** up the river Bodøgårdselva, which eventually leads to the wild, scenic Bodømarka woods.

Bodø's striking **cathedral** (Kongensgate; admission free; 9.30am-2.30pm mid-Jun–Aug), completed in 1956, has a soaring, freestanding tower and spire. Shaped like an inverted ship's hull, the walls of its nave are clad with tufty, multicoloured rugs and there's a fine stained-glass window.

The charming little onion-domed **Bodin Kirke** (Gamle Riksvei 68; 10am-3pm late-Jun–mid-Aug) stone church dates from around 1240. The Lutheran Reformation brought about substantial changes to the exterior, including the addition of a tower. A host of lively baroque elements – especially the elaborately carved altar – grace the interior.

Activities

Norlandsbadet & Spektrum Velvære (75 59 15 08; Plassmyrveien; adult/child/family Nkr130/90/390; core hrs 3-9pm Mon-Fri, 10am-6pm Sat & Sun) Here's a very superior place to relax, tone up and warm yourself if it's freezing outside. Exhaust yourself in its six swimming pools (you can zoom down an 85m water slide and splosh into one of them) then head upstairs to unwind in its six saunas (the one with therapy music and scents perhaps? Or does eucalyptus vapour tempt?). Soak yourself to the skin in the tropical rainforest shower or shiver in the ice grotto.

From Bodø you can visit the Svartisen glacier with a stop at the fishing village of Støtt on the return journey. A Hurtigruten express boat (Nkr645) with guide leaves at 6.45am, returning to Bodø at 2.30pm.

Festivals & Events

The **Nordlands Music Festival** in the first half of August is a full 10 days of music in its widest definition, with symphony orchestras, jazz, rock and folk.

Sleeping

Bodøsjøen Camping (☎ 75 56 36 80; bodocamp@yahoo.no; Kvernhusveien 1; tent/caravan sites Nkr100/200 plus per person Nkr30, cabins Nkr250-400, with bathroom Nkr630-840) At this waterside camp site, 3km from the centre, cabins are particularly well equipped. There's an attractive grassy area with picnic tables exclusively for tent campers. Buses 12 and 23 stop 250m away.

Opsahl Gjestegård (☎ 75 52 07 04; www.opsahlgjestegar.no in Norwegian; Prinsens gate 131; s/d Nkr430/600) On a quiet residential street, this guesthouse has 18 comfortable rooms whose décor ranges from flowery to less florid, and a small bar for guests.

City Hotell (☎ 75 52 04 02; johannsst@online.no; Storgata 39; s 590Nkr d Nkr690-890 plus Nkr150 per extra person; 💻) The paint was still fresh and the pipes of the fire-hazard sprinklers exposed when we visited this newly established hotel. Most of its 19 rooms are smallish but well priced. Beneath the eaves are a couple of very large family rooms and two rooms have a kitchenette. Reception is friendliness itself, management less so…

Skagen Hotel (☎ 75 51 91 00; www.skagen-hotel.no in Norwegian; Nyholmsgata 11; s/d Nkr650/800 mid-Jun–mid-Aug & Fri & Sat year-round, Nkr1290/1490 Sun-Thu rest-of-year, all incl breakfast; 💻) The Skagen occupies two buildings (one originally a butcher's though you'd never guess it). Facing each other, they're connected by a passage that burrows beneath the street. Rooms are attractively decorated and a continent away from chain-hotel clones. There's a bar and free afternoon waffles and coffee. Staff ca also give advice on a whole raft of vigorou outdoor activities.

Clarion Collection Hotel Grand (☎ 75 54 61 0 www.choice.no; Storgata 3; s/d Nkr665/880 mid-Jun–mi Aug & Fri & Sat year-round, Nk1395/1620 Sun-Thu rest-of-yea P 💻) With the resources of the Glasshuse shopping centre right beside it and the short est of strolls from the quayside, the Grand i well positioned, with comfortable if smallis rooms. Room rates include both breakfast an light buffet dinner, and there's a sauna an steam bath (both free to guests).

Thon Hotel Nordlys (☎ 75 53 19 00; www.thonhote .com; Moloveien 14; s/d Nkr755/955 mid-Jun–mid-Aug & Fri Sat year-round, Nk1025/1255 Sun-Thu rest-of-year) Bodø' newest and most stylish hotel, with touche of subtle Scandinavian design through out, also overlooks the marina and runs reasonable restaurant.

Radisson SAS Hotel Bodø (☎ 75 51 90 00; ww .radissonsas.com; Storgata 2; s/d Nkr795/1090 mid Jun–mid-Aug, Nkr1250-1450 Sun-Thu, Nkr795/995 F & Sat rest-of-year; P 💻) This contemporar hotel has bright rooms and a top-floor ba to better view the harbour and mountain Breakfast is served in the Sjøsiden restauran with its picture windows, while the hotel' Pizzakjeller'n (see opposite) is one of Bodø' most popular eateries.

Rica Hotel Bodø (☎ 75 54 70 00; www.rica.no; Sjøgat 23; s/d Nkr795/1046 mid-Jun–mid-Aug, Nkr1380/1680 Sun Thu, Nkr750/1000 Fri & Sat rest-of-year) This welcom ing, well-managed recent addition to the Ric chain has especially large rooms and enjoy a prime quayside position. You needn't eve leave the building to visit Blix restaurant (se opposite), Bodø's finest dining choice, wit which it interconnects.

Eating

Løvolds (☎ 75 52 02 61; Tollbugata 9; dishes Nkr35 105; 🕐 Mon-Sat) This popular historic quay side cafeteria, Bodø's oldest eating choice offers sandwiches, grills and hearty Nor wegian fare with quality quayside view thrown in to boot.

Kafé Kafka (☎ 75 52 35 50; Sandgata 5b; mains Nkr60 125, daily special Nkr78; 🕐 core hrs 11am-midnight Mon Sat, 3pm-midnight Sun) This stylish contemporar café does great coffee 11 different ways (you' smell the aroma before you even enter) an fresh juices. There's wi-fi and one interne terminal, free to clients. Some Saturdays i turns into a club with DJs.

Paviljongen (☎ 75 52 01 11; Torget; mains Nkr90-135) This great outdoor spot in the main square is the place to down a coffee or one of its three choices of draught beer; and perhaps nibble on an inexpensive lunch while watching the world pass (see how people adapt their pace to the rhythm of the buskers who strum and play nearby).

Pizzakjeller'n (☎ 75 51 90 00) The Radisson SAS Hotel's popular informal basement eatery is something of a misnomer. Yes, it serves up a long list of pizzas and other snacky and more substantial items, but for something more original, go for the daily special (Nkr110), which indeed changes daily, or its weekly equivalent (Nkr170).

Da Carlo (☎ 75 50 46 05; 2nd fl, Glasshuset) This pleasant, frondy place is popular with Bodø's younger movers and shakers, both as bar and restaurant, where you can down the usual snacks, pizza and burger fare. It partly occupies the sealed bridge above the shopping mall's main alley so you can snoop upon the shoppers below.

Bryggerikaia (☎ 75 52 58 08; Sjøgata 1; snacks around Nkr160, mains Nkr165-245) Not long on the Bodø drinking and dining scene, Bryggerikaia is already a firm favourite. You can dine well, snack, enjoy its lunch buffet (Nkr125) or quaff one of its beers, brewed on the premises. Enjoy your choice in its large pub-décor interior, on the street-side terrace or, best of all should you find a seat spare, on the veranda overlooking the harbour.

Blix (☎ 75 54 70 99; Sjøgata 25; mains around Nkr200) A favourite among Bodø's discerning diners, Blix has a justified reputation for fine cuisine and keeps a select wine list. Reserve a window table for great harbour views.

At the docks you can buy inexpensive fresh shrimp; the Vinmonopolet is just a couple of blocks further to the west. Inside the Glasshuset shopping centre you'll find a supermarket and several quick-service choices.

Drinking & Entertainment

Nordlænningen (Storgata 16; 🕒 noon-3.30am) This low-key basement pub beside the main square has occasional live music – see the signed posters of bands who've played here as you descend into the depths.

Public (Sjøgata 12; 🕒 core hrs 8pm-3.30am) Supersized stills from punk-rock shows line the walls of this minimalist bar with its black leather stools.

Rock Café & Nightclub (☎ 75 50 46 33; Tollbugata 13b; cover charge Nkr50; 🕒 9pm-3am Fri & Sat) This, the town's largest disco, can cram in over 500 punters. It puts on live bands about twice a month.

G (☎ 75 56 17 00; Sjøgata; 🕒 9pm-3am Fri & Sat) With its cave-like entrance on Sjøgata, below the main square, this *discoteka* packs in the over-25s.

Fram Kino (Storgata 8), near the entrance to the Glasshuset, is Bodø's cinema.

You can knock some pins down at **Royal Bowling** (☎ 75 52 28 80; Storgata 2), on the ground floor of the Radisson SAS Hotel.

Getting There & Away

AIR

From Bodø's airport, southwest of the city centre, there are up to eight daily flights to Oslo, 14 to Trondheim and 11 to Tromsø. Other destinations in northern Norway include Leknes (up to seven flights daily), Harstad (two) and Mo i Rana (four).

Norwegian has one daily flight to Oslo and two to Bergen.

BOAT

Bodø is a stop on the Hurtigruten coastal ferry. Car ferries sail five to six times daily in summer (less frequently during the rest of the year) between Bodø and Moskenes on Lofoten (adult/child/car Nkr149/74/538, 3½ hours). Most days at least one calls in at the southern Lofoten islands of Røst and Værøy. If you're taking a car in summer, it's wise to book in advance (an additional Nkr160) to avoid a long queue. There's also an express passenger ferry between Bodø and Svolvær (adult/child Nkr290/145, 3½ hours) once or twice daily.

BUS

The Nor-Way Bussekspress bus runs to/from Narvik (Nkr497, 6½ hours) via Fauske (Nkr106, 1¼ hours) twice daily.

TRAIN

From Bodø trains run to Fauske (Nkr104, 45 minutes, up to five daily), Mo I Rana (Nkr386, three hours, two to four daily) and Trondheim (Nkr937, 9¾ hours, two daily).

Getting Around

Local buses cost Nkr25 per ride. The tourist office rents bikes from Nkr100 per day.

NORDLAND BOATS

You're bound to come across the uniquely shaped, stubby Nordland boat, which has served local fishing communities from the earliest days of settlement. They're informal symbols of the tough, self-sufficient lifestyle of the hardy coastal folk here up north; and they're still in use from Namsos, in Trøndelag, right up to the Kola Peninsula in Arctic Russia, but the greatest concentrations are found in Lofoten.

The smallest versions are known as *færing*, measuring up to 5m, while larger ones are called *hundromsfæring* (6m), *seksring* (7m), *halvfjerderomning* (7.5m), *firroing* (8m), *halvfemterømming* (9m), *åttring* (10m to 11m) and *femboring* (11m to 13m).

Traditionally, the larger the boat, the greater was the status of its captain, or *høvedmann*. Whatever the size, Nordland boats are excellent for both rowing and sailing, even in rough northern seas. Until quite recently, sailing competitions, pitting fishing communities against each other, were one of the great social events of the year.

A good place to see museum-quality examples is in the harbour at Å in Lofoten.

AROUND BODØ

Kjerringøy

It's easy to see why this sleepy peninsula, washed by turquoise seas and with a backdrop of soaring granite peaks, is a regular location for Norwegian film makers. Some 40km north of Bodø, its principal man-made feature is the 19th-century trading station Kjerringøy. Here, the entrepreneurial – some would say exploitative – Erasmus Zahl family established an important trading post, providing local fishing families with supplies in exchange for their catches, and after making its fortune, expanded into mining, banking and steam-transport concerns.

Most of the timber-built historic district has been preserved as an **open-air museum** (☎ 75 50 35 00; adult/child Nkr45/free; 🕑 11am-5pm late May-Aug), where the spartan quarters and kitchens of the fishing families contrast with the sumptuous décor of the merchants' housing. There's also a 20-minute slide presentation, included in the museum price. Admission to the main building (adult/child Nkr35/20) is by guided tour.

Several buses connect Bodø and Kjerringøy daily (Nkr86, 1½ hours) and in summer it's possible to fit in a return trip on the same day. Check at Bodø's tourist office (p306) for the current timetable.

Whether by bus or car, the trip involves the ferry crossing between Festvåg and Misten. Along the way, you pass the distinctive profile of **Landegode island** (see the boxed text, p49), the white sandy beaches at **Mjelle** (whose car park is some 20 minutes' walk away) and the dramatic peak **Steigtind**, which rises a few kilometres south of Festvåg.

Saltstraumen Maelstrom

You need to plan your day to take in this natural phenomenon, guaranteed to occur four times every 24 hours. At the 3km-long, 150m-wide Saltstraumen Strait, the tides cause one fjord to drain into another, creating the equivalent of a waterfall at sea. The result is a churning, 20-knot watery chaos that shifts over 400 million cu metres of water one way, then the other, every six hours. It's an ideal environment for plankton, which in turn attracts an abundance of both fish and anglers. In spring, you can also see the squawking colonies of gulls that nest on the midstream island of Storholmen.

This maelstrom, claimed to be the world's largest, is actually a kinetic series of smaller whirlpools that form, surge, coalesce, then disperse. The experience is more immediate from the shoreline but for the best views, stand on the north side of the arching Saltstraumbrua bridge over the strait at its apex and watch as the waters swirl like emerald nebulae. At its best – which is most of the time – it's an exhilarating spectacle but if you're unlucky enough to hit an off day, it may recall little more than the water swirling around your bath plug.

Tide tables can be found in the tourist office in Bodø.

LOFOTEN

The pure air in your lungs (let's except the strong reek of fish in some of the small ports), daylight around the clock and summer's infinite shades of green and yellow: Lofoten

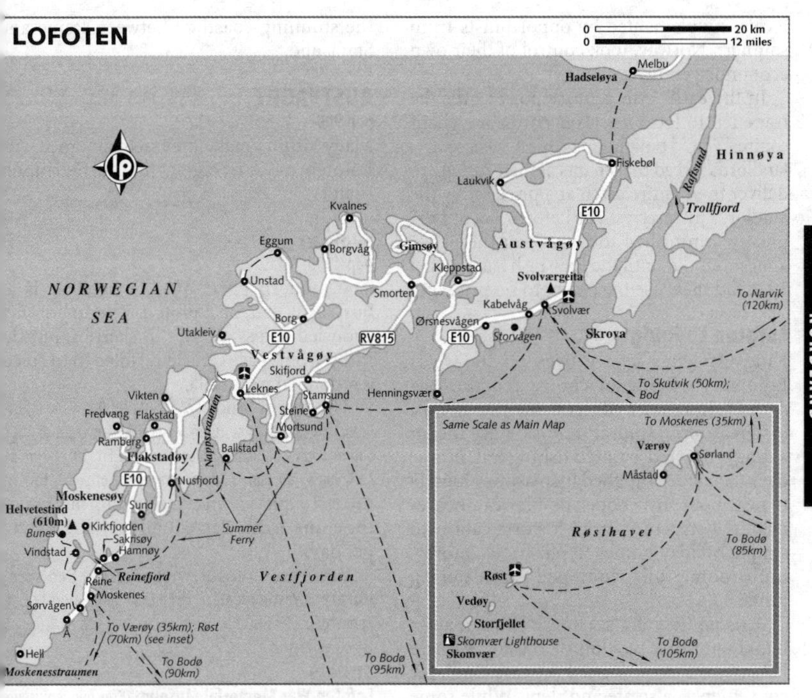

comes as a tonic. You'll never forget your first approach by ferry, especially if you've sailed from Bodø. The islands spread their tall, craggy physique against the sky like some spiky sea dragon and you wonder how humans eked a living in such inhospitable surroundings.

The main islands, Austvågøy, Vestvågøy, Flakstadøy and Moskenesøy, are separated from the mainland by Vestfjorden. On each are sheltered bays, sheep pastures and picturesque villages. The vistas (the whole of the E10 from tip to toe of Lofoten has recently been designated a National Tourist Route, a title bestowed only upon the most scenic roads) and the special quality of the Arctic light have long attracted artists, who are represented in galleries throughout the islands.

But Lofoten is still very much commercially alive. Each winter the meeting of the Gulf Stream and the icy Arctic Ocean draws spawning Arctic cod from the Barents Sea. For centuries, this in turn drew farmer-fishermen from the mainland's north coast. Although cod stocks have dwindled dramatically in recent years, fishing still vies with tourism as Lofoten's largest industry, as evidenced by the wooden drying racks that lattice nearly every village on the islands.

Both www.lofoten-tourist.no and www.lofoten.info take you to the same useful website, rich in information about the whole archipelago.

History

The history of Lofoten is essentially that of its fishing industry. Numerous battles have been fought over these seas, exceptionally rich in spawning cod ever since the glaciers retreated about 10,000 years ago. In 1120, King Øystein set up the first church and built a number of *rorbuer*, basic 4m by 4m wooden cabins for the fishermen with a fireplace, earthen floor and small porch area. It wasn't entirely philanthropy: in so doing, he took control of the local economy and ensured rich tax pickings for himself.

In the 13th century traders of the German Hanseatic League moved in and usurped power. Despite an increase in exports, the fisherfolk were left in poverty. By 1750, however, the trade monopoly lost its grip and locals, supplemented by opportunists from southern Norway, took control of their own economic ventures.

In the early 19th century power over the trade fell to local *nessekonger*, or 'merchant squires' who'd bought up property. These new landlords forced the tenants of their *rorbuer* to deliver their entire catch at a price set by the landlords themselves. The Lofoten Act of 1857 greatly diminished the power of the *nessekonger* but not until the Raw Fish Sales Act of 1936 did they lose the power to set prices.

Lofoten Lodging

King Øystein's legacy lives on today, as Lofoten's lodging of choice remains the *rorbu*, along with its cousin, the *sjøhus*. Whereas *rorbu* (plural *rorbuer*) once meant a dingy, tiny red-painted fishing hut, nowadays the name is applied increasingly loosely to just about any wooden ox-blood or ochre-coloured structure, from historic cabins to simple holiday homes to plush, two-storey, multiroom, fully equipped self-catering units.

A *sjøhus* (literally 'sea house') is normally a bunkhouse-style building on the docks where fishery workers processed the catch and, for convenience, also ate and slept. While some *sjøhus* retain this traditional feel, others have been converted into summer tourist lodges and apartments, usually of the simpler, less expensive kind.

Lofoten also has a few higher-end hotels and some wonderfully situated camp sites.

While summer prices tend to be lower in the rest of Norway, the opposite obtains in Lofoten; in hotels you can expect to pay Nkr250-plus per room above the rest-of-the-year prices, although the difference is less pronounced in *rorbuer* and *sjøhus*.

Getting Around

Getting around is easy. The four main islands are linked by bridge or tunnel, and buses run the entire E10 from the Fiskebøl–Melbu ferry in the north to Å at road's end in the southwest.

The *Sykkelguide* booklet (Nkr120), available from tourist offices, describes with full maps 10 delightful bicycle routes around Lofoten, each between 20km and 50km.

From June to August, the **Fosengutt** (☎ 93 49 74 45), with a capacity of only 12 passengers, runs a daily boat shuttle along the stunning coastline between Reine and Stamsund.

AUSTVÅGØY

pop 9000

Many visitors make their acquaintance with Lofoten on Austvågøy, the northernmost island.

Svolvær

pop 4300

The modern port town of Svolvær is as busy as it gets on Lofoten. The town once sprawled across a series of skerries, but the in-between spaces are being filled in to create a reclaimed peninsula.

The **tourist office** (☎ 76 06 98 00; www.lofoten.info; 9am-8pm or 10pm Mon-Sat, 10am-2pm or 10pm Sun mid-Jun–Jul, 9am-4pm or 8pm Mon-Fri, 10am-2pm Sat early Jun & Aug, 9am-3.30pm Mon-Fri rest-of-year), facing the ferry quays, can provide information on the entire archipelago. It hires bikes (Nkr200 per day).

You'll find free internet access at Svolvær's **library** (Vestfjordgata; 11am-3pm Mon-Fri, to 7pm Wed).

SIGHTS

Lofoten War Memorial Museum (Krigsminnemuseum; ☎ 91 73 03 28; Fiskergata 12; adult/child Nkr50/25; 10am-4pm & 6.15-10pm Jun-Sep, 6.15-10pm May & early Oct), privately and passionately run, is a fascinating place. Models in original military uniforms gaze down and there are plenty of artefacts and evocative, largely unpublished WWII-era photos.

Lofoten Nature (adult/child Nkr30/free; noon-10pm Tue-Sun mid-Jun–mid-Aug) displays, on two floors above the tourist office, the striking images of Lofoten wildlife photographer John Stenersen. The thoughtful, accessible text with its powerful ecological message is a stimulating condensed introduction to the ecosystems of the islands and their land-based and offshore wildlife. Warmly recommended.

Housed, appropriately, in what was once a fish-freezing plant, **Magic Ice** (☎ 76 07 40 11; Fiskergata 36; adult/child Nkr90/60; noon-10.30pm mid-Jun–mid-Aug, 6-10pm rest-of-year) is the ultimate place to chill out, perhaps with something to warm the spirit from the 7.5m-long bar. The 500 sq-metre space is filled with huge ice sculptures, illustrating Lofoten life. If you can't come back to northern Norway in winter here's a great, if brief, approximation.

The **North Norwegian Art Centre** (Nordnorsk Kunstnersenter; ☎ 76 06 67 70; Svinøya; adult/child Nkr60/free; 10am-6pm mid-Jun–mid-Aug, 10am-3pm rest-of-year) hosts changing exhibitions of paintings, sculpture, ceramics and more by artists from northern Norway. There's also a permanent exhibition of the works of the 19th-century Lofoten painter Gunnar Berg.

The **Lofoten Theme Gallery** (Lofoten Temagalleri; ☎ 76 07 03 36; Parkgata 12; adult/child Nkr50/free; 8am-10pm Jun-Aug) is very much the creation of one man, Geir Nøtnes, a keen photographer from a long fishing background. One room is devoted to cod fishing, another to whaling and there's a 20-minute DVD about Lofoten through the seasons.

ACTIVITIES

The island of **Skrova** is a fun day trip from Svolvær and offers a couple of short walks. The ferry between Svolvær and Skutvik, on the mainland, stops off twice daily in summer (Nkr31, 30 minutes from Svolvær).

XXLofoten (☎ 91 65 55 00; www.xxlofoten.no; Paulensgate 12) rents out sea kayaks (single up to three/eight hours Nkr400/500, double Nkr500/700) from late June and throughout July.

TOURS

There are several sailings daily in summer from Svolvær into the constricted confines of nearby Trollfjord, spectacularly steep and narrowing to only 100m. Take the three-hour cruise or sign on for a four-hour trip that includes the chance to dangle a line and bring home supper. Both tour options cost Nkr350/100 per adult/child and you can buy your ticket at the quayside.

Lofoten Seafari (☎ 47 90 29 40; per person Nkr350), based at the Rica Hotel, bounces over the waves in a Zodiac inflatable raft to Skrova and around the inlets in an exhilarating two-hour outing (Nkr400).

Among the summer activities of **Lofoten Activ** (☎ 76 07 89 10; www.lofoten-aktiv.no) are accompanied mountain walks (per person Nkr250 to Nkr700), a five-hour hike and bike trip (Nkr470 including cycle hire), and a four-hour guided sea-kayak safari (Nkr800). It also rents surf kayaks (Nkr700 per day) and runs a sea-kayak school, based at the Sandvika Fjord og Sjøhuscamp in Kabelvåg (see p316). In winter, it arranges snowshoe, cross-country and alpine ski outings.

FESTIVALS & EVENTS

The town's annual **Fish Festival**, a celebration of all things piscatorial, takes place in the last week in March. For three weeks in June, usually every other year (the next one will be in 2010), Svolvær hosts the **Lofoten Arts Festival**.

SLEEPING

Svolvær Sjøhuscamp (☎ 76 07 03 36; www.svolver-sjohuscamp.no; Parkgata 12; d/q Nkr440/720, d with kitchen Nkr490) This friendly sea house straddling the water is a convivial, excellent-value place to fetch up and meet fellow travellers. There's also a gem of an apartment with balcony and full facilities (Nkr1600) that sleeps up to six.

Svinøya Rorbuer (☎ 76 06 99 30; www.svinoya.no; Gunnar Bergs vei 2; 2-/4-/6-bed cabins from Nkr1000/1400/1700) Across a bridge on the islet of Svinøya, site of Svolvær's first settlement, are dozens of cabins, some historic, most contemporary, and all cosy and comfortable. Reception is a veritable museum, a restored and restocked *krambua* (general store), constructed in 1828, which was Svolvær's first shop.

Rica Hotel Svolvær (☎ 76 07 22 22; www.rica.no; Lamholmen; s/d Nkr950/1200 mid-Jun–mid-Aug, Nkr1004/1257

NORDLAND

ONE MAN'S OBSESSION

William Hakvaag, motive force behind Svolvær's war museum, is one of those passionate obsessives who enrich the world. 'I hear you have an original of Hitler's signature', I asked, following up a tip from a reader. 'Not only that,' he grinned, pulling out one of his desk drawers. '*This* was his magnifying glass. It arrived yesterday from a contact in Russia. I have influence in high places,' he says, eyes twinkling, 'things come my way.'

Things such as a stained, torn German sailor's shirt that had lain on the sea bed for almost 30 years. On it was a name, Hans O Shultz, and pinned to it was a letter of thanks from Herr Shultz, whom Hakvaag had tracked down. Injured when his destroyer was torpedoed, he was taken prisoner and sent to Britain, then Canada, where he finally settled and lived until his death a few years ago.

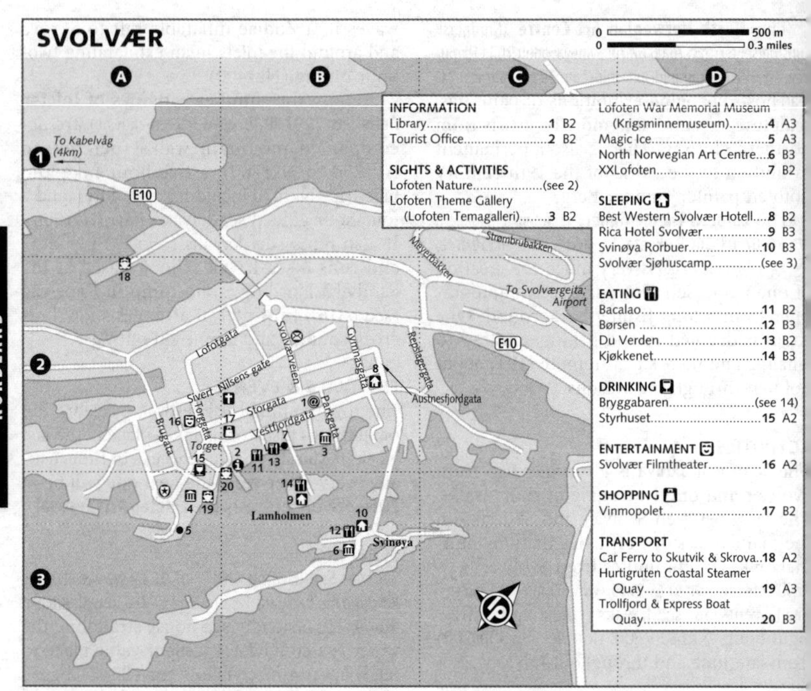

Sun-Thu, Nkr1100/1350 Fri & Sat rest-of-year) The Rica too is built on a tiny island, above the water and supported by piles. Some rooms have balconies, while room 121 has a hole in the floor so guests in the adjacent room can drop a fishing line directly into the briny. The restaurant (for great harbour views reserve a table in its bow window, shaped like a boat) has attractive lightweight wooden furnishings and does a gargantuan dinner buffet (Nkr295).

Best Western Svolvær Hotell (☎ 76 07 19 99; www.bestwestern.no; Austnesfjordgata 12; s/d Nkr1050/1250 Jun–mid-Aug, Nk970/1070 Sun-Thu, Nkr700/800 Fri & Sat rest-of-year; P 💻) Intimate (there are only 22 rooms) and in a residential neighbourhood away from the portside bustle, this is a comfortable, if unexceptional place. Some rooms have balconies, others come with kitchens. Public areas are decorated with prints of Edvard Munch – happily not at his most sombre – who was the owner's grand-uncle.

EATING

There's a pair of stylish places, near neighbours, on the quayside. Both have attractive, modern interiors and waterside terraces.

Bacalao (☎ 76 07 94 00) With its upbeat interior, Bacalao offers leafy, innovative salad (Nkr110 to Nkr130), sandwiches and som equally creative pasta dishes; the *hot rekepast* (hot shrimp pasta; Nkr150) will set your tast buds tingling. It also expresses what must b about the best coffee anywhere in Norway a country that so often settles for water black brews.

Du Verden (☎ 76 07 70 99; dinner mains aroun Nkr275) This smaller, hip restaurant with it clean, open lines and contemporary art work around the walls is a very congenia place for a relaxed dinner. The lunchtim dishes (Nkr45 to Nkr150) offer an excellen price-to-quality ratio.

Børsen (☎ 76 06 99 31; Svinøya; mains Nkr235 265) This Arctic Menu restaurant brim with character. A former fish house, it wa called the 'stock exchange' after the har bour-front bench outside, where the olde men of the town would ruminate endlessl over the state of the world. In its dinin room, with its cracked and bowed floor ing, you'll still catch the scent of tar an cod-liver oil.

Kjøkkenet (☎ 76 06 84 80; Lamholmen; mains around Nkr300) Kjøkennet, originally a shack for salting fish and nowadays furnished like an old-time kitchen, is a wonderfully cosy place to dine. The cuisine is just as traditional and the recommended menu choice is of course fish – try the kitchen's signature dish, *boknafisk* (Nkr270), cured cod with salted fat and vegetables.

DRINKING & ENTERTAINMENT

Styrhuset (OJ Kaarsbøs gate 5) Svolvær's oldest pub is all dark crannies that speak of sailors long gone.

Bryggabaren In the same complex as Kjøkennet, this low-beamed, cosy watering hole is bedecked with tools of all kinds. The bar is a lifeboat from a WWII Polish troop ship that washed up in Svolvær in 1946.

Svolvær Filmtheater (Storgata 28) Screens recent films and Hollywood blockbusters.

GETTING THERE & AROUND

From Svolvær's small airport there are four flights daily to Bodø.

Three sea routes connect Svolvær to the mainland. The shortest, most popular crossing is to/from Skutvik (adult/child Nkr73/36, car and driver Nkr251, two hours, eight to 11 daily). There's a daily express passenger boat to/from Bodø (Nkr290, 3½ hours) that calls by Skutvik (one hour), where you can connect by bus with Narvik. An express passenger boat also runs directly to Narvik (Nkr326, 3½ hours, Tueday to Friday and Sunday). Svolvær is also a stop on the Hurtigruten coastal ferry.

For Sortland on Vesterålen, bus 8 (2¼ hours) runs three to five times daily via Stokmarknes (1¾ hours). Bus 9 runs to Leknes (1½ hours), with connections to Å (3½ hours) four to six times daily.

For a taxi, call ☎ 76 07 06 00.

Kabelvåg

Kabelvåg, 5km southwest of Svolvær, is an altogether more intimate and cosy place. At its heart is a small square and tiny harbour while its Storvågen district, 2km off the E10 to the south, has an enticing trio of museums and galleries.

SIGHTS & ACTIVITIES

Behind the old prison in **Storvågen**, a trail climbs to the statue honouring King Øystein. In 1120 he ordered the first *rorbu* to be built to house fishermen, who previously had been sleeping beneath their overturned rowing boats. This wasn't just an act of kindness; His Majesty needed to keep his fisherfolk warm, dry and content since the tax on exported dried fish was the main source of his revenue.

A combination ticket (Nkr130) for three museums gives entry to Lofoten Museum, Lofoten Aquarium and Galleri Espolin, all in Storvågan. For children, it's more economical to pay at each museum.

Some of Kabelvåg's original *rorbuer* have been excavated as part of the **Lofoten Museum** (Lofotmuseet; ☎ 76 06 97 90; adult/child/concession Nkr50/15/40; 9am-6pm Jun-Aug; 9am-3pm Mon-Fri Sep-May plus 11am-3pm Sat & Sun May), on the site of what can be considered to be the first town in the polar region. The museum's main gallery was once the merchant's mansion where, typically, lived the man who hired out the *rorbuer* and sea houses to the fishermen and bought their catch. An easy, undulating and scenic 2km Heritage Path leads from the museum to the centre of Kabelvåg.

Nearby in the **Lofoten Aquarium** (Lofotakvariet; ☎ 76 07 86 65; adult/child/family Nkr80/40/220; 10am-7pm Jun-Aug, 11am-3pm Sun-Fri Feb-Apr & Sep-Nov, daily May), fish and sea animals of the cold Arctic waters swim and flap. Children will particularly enjoy the seal and sea otter feeding frenzies (noon, 3pm and 6pm) and there's a multimedia show five times daily on the hour.

Galleri Espolin (☎ 76 07 84 05; Storvågan; adult/child/concession Nkr60/25/45; 10am-6pm or 7pm Jun–mid-Aug, 11am-3pm rest-of-year) features the haunting etchings and lithographs of one of Norway's great artists, Kaare Espolin-Johnson (1907–94). Espolin – his work all the more astounding since he was nearly blind for much of his life – loved Lofoten and often featured its fisherfolk, together with other Arctic themes.

In Kabelvåg, **Vågan Church** (Vågan Kirke; admission Nkr20; 9.30am-6pm Mon-Sat, noon-6pm Sun late Jun–mid-Aug), constructed in 1898 and Norway's second-largest wooden church, rises above the E10 north of town. Built to minister to the influx of seasonal fisherfolk, its seating capacity of 1200 far surpasses Kabelvåg's current population.

Lofotdykk (☎ 99 63 91 66; www.lofotdykk.no; Kaiveien 15), based in a *rorbu* overlooking Kabelvåg's quayside, will take you diving between May and September and offers orca-watching safaris from October to December.

GLORY BE TO COD

For centuries, catching and drying cod has been a way of life in Lofoten and by far its biggest industry.

Although cod populations have been depleted by over-fishing, the overall catch is still substantial, 50,000 tonnes annually (30,000 tonnes without the heads). The fishing season peaks from January to April when the fish come from the Barents Sea to Vestfjorden to spawn. Around the end of March each year the unofficial World Cod Fishing Championship is held in Svolvær, attracting up to 300 entrants.

There are two ways to preserve cod. For saltfish, it's filleted, salted and dried for about three weeks. For *klipfish,* the saltfish is cleaned, resalted and dried, originally on cliffs (*klip* in Norwegian) and nowadays in large heated plants.

However, Lofoten is all about stockfish. In this ancient method, 15,000 tonnes of fish are decapitated each year, paired by size, then tied together and, dangling in pairs like sleeping bats, hung to dry over the huge wooden A-frames you see everywhere on the islands. The fish lose about 80% of their weight, and most are exported to Italy, with some to Spain and Portugal.

Stockfish stays edible for years, and it's often eaten raw (a trifle chewy but goes well with beer), salted or reconstituted with water. It's concentrated goodness; with a protein content of 80%, 1kg of stockfish has the same nutritional value as 5kg of fresh fish.

Even before drying, very little of a cod goes to waste: cod tongue is a local delicacy – children extract the tongues and are paid by the piece – and the roe is salted in enormous German wine vats. The heads are sent to Nigeria to form the basis of a popular spicy dish.

Then there is the liver, which produces the vitamin D-rich oil that has long been known to prevent rickets and assuage the depression brought on by the long, dark Arctic winters. In 1854

SLEEPING & EATING

A couple of inlets and 3km west of Kabelvåg, there are a couple of great camp sites, right beside each other.

Ørsvågvær Camping (☎ 76 07 81 80; www.orsvag.no in Norwegian; bike/car/caravan sites Nkr60/100/130, d Nkr550-650, 4-bed cabins Nkr650, 7-bed sea house apt Nkr950; ⏲ mid-May–mid-Aug) Most *rorbuer* and the sea house are right beside the fjord and offer splendid views. There's a sauna and you can rent a motorboat (per hour/day Nkr170/500).

Sandvika Fjord og Sjøhuscamp (☎ 76 07 81 45; www.lofotferie.no; camp sites Nkr145, cabin Nkr550, with bathroom from Nkr650, sea house apt Nkr650) This shoreside camp site has its own small beach. It rents motorboats (Nkr150 per hour) and is a base for sea-kayak trips. The camping area is significantly larger than its neighbour's.

Kabelvåg Vandrerhjem & Sommerhotell (☎ 76 06 98 80; kabelvag.hostel@vandrerhjem.no; Finnesveien 24; dm/s/d incl breakfast Nkr240/460/620; ⏲ Jun–mid-Aug; 💻) Less than 1km north of the centre, the Lofoten Folkehøgskole school becomes a hostel and hotel outside the teaching year. There's a kitchen for guest use. Hostel rooms have two, four and 10 beds.

One company owns Kabelvåg's two major hotels – and what a contrast they offer.

Kabelvåg Hotell (☎ 76 07 88 00; kabelvaag@dvg.no; Kong Øysteinsgate 4; s/d Nkr840/1240; ⏲ Jun-Jul) On a small rise close to the centre of Kabelvåg this imposing seasonal hotel was tastefully rebuilt in 1995 in its original Art Deco style. Rooms overlook either the port or mountains.

Nyvågar Rorbuhotell (☎ 76 06 97 00; www.nyvaagar.no; Storvåganveien 22; 4-bed rorbu incl breakfast from Nkr1770) At Storvågan, below the museum complex, this snazzy, modern seaside place owes nothing to history, but its strictly contemporary *rorbuer* are attractive and fully equipped. Guests can also rent bikes (Nkr50/190 per hour/day) and motorboats (Nkr190 per hour).

Præstenbrygga (☎ 76 07 80 60; Torget) In central Kabelvåg, this friendly pub with its all-wood interior and dockside terracing, front and rear, serves sandwiches, pizzas and tasty mains (around Nkr140), including a rich combination platter of marinated salmon, smoked whale, shrimps and salad. There's often live music and for Nkr20 you can drink coffee all day with free refills. Chase one down with a shot from its selection of nearly 100 whiskies and ryes.

Two hotels have good restaurants: at Kabelvåg Hotell there's the **Krambua restau**

Lofoten pharmacist Peter Møller decided to introduce this magic-in-a-bottle to the world and constructed a cauldron for steam-boiling the livers. The oil he skimmed received honours at trade fairs in Europe and abroad. Even after skimming, the livers were steamed in large oak barrels and then pressed to yield every last, profitable drop. Every summer, thousands of barrels of it were shipped to Europe, and the smell pervaded the village of Å, whose inhabitants liked to comment that it was the scent of money.

And what of cod-liver oil's notorious taste? Locals will tell you that it tastes bad only when it becomes rancid. Fresh cod-liver oil can be quite nice, like salad oil with a slightly fishy bouquet.

Modern Norwegian fishing folk are vociferously protective of this asset – in certain northern districts as many as 90% of votes were against EU membership. For if Norway joined the EU, the Spanish fishing fleet and others would have access to Norway's inshore waters – a potential modern-day Armada that Norway's fisherfolk are determined to repel. There have even been skirmishes with Icelandic trawlers over territorial fishing rights.

Fun cod fact: one in 20,000 cod is a king cod; the distinctive lump on its forehead is said to indicate intelligence and bring good luck to the fishing family that catches it. King cod are often dried and hung on a string from the ceiling; as the string expands and contracts with humidity, the fish rotates like a barometer, hence the nickname 'weather cod'.

The latest news from the world of cod involves the fishes' mating calls; it seems that the grunts they use to attract mates can be loud enough to block submarines' sonar devices, making underwater navigation almost impossible!

Mark Kurlansky's book *Cod* (1999) is an excellent, thoroughly entertaining study of this piscatorial powerhouse.

rant (mains around Nkr210), which specialises in fish; and the acclaimed **restaurant** (mains Nkr120) at Nyvågar Rorbuhotell serves primarily local specialities, including a lip-smacking reindeer stew.

Henningsvær

A delightful 8km shore-side drive southwards from the E10 brings you to the still-active fishing village of Henningsvær, perched at the end of a thin promontory. Its nickname, 'the Venice of Lofoten', may be a tad overblown but it's certainly the lightest, brightest and trendiest place in the archipelago. It's also the region's largest and most active fishing port.

SIGHTS & ACTIVITIES

Ocean Sounds (☎ 76 07 18 28; Hellandsgata 63; www.ocean-sounds.com; adult/child Nkr85/free; ⏰ 10am-8pm Jul & Aug, 10am-6pm Tue-Sun Jun, Sep & Oct), a not-for-profit centre, is the initiative of one hugely determined young biologist, Heike Vester. Enjoy a multimedia presentation about cod, whales and other Arctic marine mammals, supplemented by a 25-minute film about Lofoten. Or get out and about on a three- to four-hour marine safari in the Zodiac research boat (Nkr500, departures 10am and 5pm). From November to January, you can join a researcher on a whale-observing trip (Nkr1000).

Engelskmannsbrygga (☎ 76 07 52 85; Dreyersgate 1; admission free; ⏰ 10am-8pm mid-Jun–early Aug, noon-4pm Tue-Sun rest-of-year), or 'Englishman's Wharf', is the open studio and gallery of three talented local artists: potter Cecilie Haaland, photographer John Stenersen (see p312) and glassblower Kari Malmberg, with whom you can try a hand at blowing your own glass (Nkr150; 5pm to 7pm Monday to Thursday).

The **North Norwegian Climbing School** (Nord Norsk Klatreskole; ☎ 90 57 42 08; www.nordnorskklatreskole.no in Norwegian; Misværveien 10; ⏰ Mar-Oct) offers a wide range of technical climbing and skiing courses all around northern Norway. Climbing the peaks with an experienced guide costs Nkr2000, including equipment, for up to four people. For ideas, check out the 320-page *Climbing in the Magic Islands* by Ed Webster, the last word on climbing in Lofoten and sold at the attached mountaineering shop.

Lofoten Opplevelser (☎ 90 58 14 75; www.lofoten-opplevelser.no; ⏰ mid-Jun–mid-Aug), which is based in Henningsvær, offers a sea-eagle safari (Nkr350, 1½ hours) and two-hour snorkelling trips (Nkr600, equipment provided). From

November to mid-January, it organises three-hour whale safaris (Nkr850).

The **Lofoten Hus Gallery** (☎ 76 07 15 73; Hjellskjæret; adult/child/concession Nkr75/35/60; 9am-7pm Jun-Aug, 10am-6pm late May & early Sep), in a former fish-processing house, displays a fine collection of paintings from what is known as the Golden Age of Norwegian painting, between 1870 and 1930, plus canvases by contemporary Norwegian artist Karl Erik Harr. Admission includes an 18-minute slide show of photos by Frank Jenssen, shown on the hour. Revealing the people and landscapes of Lofoten throughout the seasons, it's marred only by the trite, syrupy background music.

SLEEPING & EATING

The **North Norwegian Climbing School** (see p317; dm/d Nkr175/500, 4-bed apt Nkr1200) The climbing school's café and hostel (reservation recommended) face each other down a side alley. Both friendly and informal, they cross a Lofoten *rorbu* with an English pub and a Himalayan trekkers' lodge. Some doubles have bathroom.

Johs H Giæver Sjøhus og Rorbuer (☎ 76 07 47 50; www.giaever-rorbuer.no; Hellandsgata 790; rorbu from Nkr650, sea house r Nkr450-700) In summer, workers' accommodation in a modern sea house belonging to the local fish plant is hired out to visitors. Spruce rooms have shared facilities, including a large kitchen and dining area, and are good value. The company also has three *rorbuer* with bathroom and balcony in the heart of town.

Henningsvær Bryggehotel (☎ 76 07 47 50; www.henningsvaer.no; Hjellskjæret; s/d from Nkr1070/1400) Overlooking the harbour, this attractive hotel is Henningsvær's finest choice. It's modern, with comfortable rooms furnished in contemporary design, yet constructed in a traditional style that blends harmoniously with its neighbours.

Klatrekafeen café (dishes Nkr75-130) At the North Norwegian Climbing School, it serves up snacks and a small selection of good-value homemade dishes.

Bluefish restaurant (mains Nkr195-285) The award-winning restaurant at Henningsvær Bryggehotel is equally stylish; it serves Arctic Menu dishes and does succulent sorbets, using fresh berries in season.

Fiskekrogen (☎ 76 07 46 52; Dreyersgate 29; mains Nkr235-265) At the end of a slipway overlooking the harbour, this dockside restaurant, a favourite of the Norwegian royal family, is Henningsvær's other culinary claim to fame. Try, in particular, the outstanding fish soup (Nkr145).

GETTING THERE & AWAY

Bus 510 shuttles between Svolvær (40 minutes), Kabelvåg (35 minutes) and Henningsvær three to five times daily.

VESTVÅGØY

pop 10,750

The E10 snakes its way through the heart of Vestvågøy island. A more attractive route follows the alternative, less travelled and only slightly longer Rv815, which runs northeastwards for 28km from Leknes amid stunning coastal and mountain scenery.

The island's **tourist office** (☎ 76 08 75 53; Storgata 31; 9am-7pm Mon-Fri, 10am-2pm Sat & Sun mid-Jun–early Aug, 9am-3.30pm Mon-Fri rest-of-year) is in the lacklustre town of Leknes.

Sights & Activities

LOFOTR VIKING MUSEUM

In 1981 at Borg, near the centre of Vestvågøy a farmer's plough hit the ruins of the 83m-long dwelling of a powerful Viking chieftain the largest building of its era ever discovered in Scandinavia.

The **Lofotr Viking Museum** (☎ 76 08 49 00; www.lofotr.no; adult/child incl guided tour Nkr100/50; 10am-7pm Jun-Aug, 11am-5pm May & Sep), 14km north of Leknes, offers a glimpse of life in Viking times You can walk 1.5km of trails over open hilltops from the replica of the chieftain's longhouse (the main building, shaped like an upside-down boat) to the Viking-ship replica on the water. Costumed guides conduct multilingual tours and, inside the chieftain's hall, artisans explain their trades.

The Svolvær–Leknes bus passes the museum's entrance.

UNSTAD TO EGGUM HIKE

A popular hike connects these two tiny villages on the island's west coast. A 9km coastal track winds past several headlands, a solitary lighthouse, superb seascapes and the ruins of a fortress by the ocean.

Take care after rain as the trail, particularly around Unstad, can be slick with mud plus, if you're very unlucky and as one reader attests, sheep dip. Eggum and Unstad are both about 9km from the main road and are served infrequently by buses.

STAMSUND

Galleri 2 (☎ 90 95 65 46; www.galleri2.no; admission free; 12.30-4pm & 6.30-8.30pm), 175m from the Hurtigruten quay, is the gallery of Lofoten painter Scott Thoe displaying the works of a number of contemporary Norwegian artists, including his own grand-scale projects.

Located 14km northeast of Stamsund along the Rv815, **Brustranda Sjøcamping** (☎ 76 08 71 00; www.brustranda.no; Rolvsfjord; car/caravan sites Nkr120/145, 2-/4-bed cabin Nkr220/385, with bathroom Nkr660-1100) is a well-tended, beautifully situated seaside camp site, which stretches around a tiny harbour.

The island's HI-affiliated youth hostel **Justad Rorbuer og Vandrerhjem** (☎ 76 08 93 34; fax 76 08 97 39; dm/s/d Nkr120/300/400, 4-bed cabins Nkr500-800; Mar–mid-Oct) is a 1.2km walk from the Hurtigruten quay and has its regular clientele who come back year after year – one particularly loyal guest has stayed here over 50 times – so be sure to reserve. It's right beside the water in an old fishing complex. Roar Justad, the friendly owner, dispenses information about local hiking routes, rents bicycles (Nkr80 to Nkr100 per day) and lends rowing boats and fishing lines for free.

Skjaerbrygga Sjøhus (☎ 76 05 46 00; pub food from noon, dinner 5-10pm), low-beamed, large yet cosy, is right at the water's edge. Both café and restaurant, it has a limited dinner menu (three starters, three fish dishes and two meat mains) that includes all the local favourites such as roast king crab, smoked whale (both Nkr135) and tender Lofoten lamb (Nkr235).

Getting There & Away

Up to seven flights daily connect Leknes airport with Bodø. Leknes has bus connections to Å (1½ hours, four to five daily), Stamsund (25 minutes, three to seven daily) and Svolvær (1½ hours, four to six daily). Stamsund is the island's port for the Hurtigruten coastal ferry.

FLAKSTADØY

pop 1450

Most of Flakstadøy's residents live along its flat north shore, around the town of Ramberg, but the craggy south side provides the most dramatic scenery. Many visitors just zip through but it's worth stopping to sun yourself (sandy beaches are the exception in Lofoten) and perhaps to build in a detour to the arty village of Nusfjord.

The island's seasonal **tourist office** (☎ 76 09 31 10; henkirk@online.no; 9am-7pm mid-Jun–late Aug) is in Ramberg's Galleri Steinbiten.

Sights

NUSFJORD

A spectacular 6km diversion southwards from the E10 and beneath towering bare crags brings you to Nusfjord (www.nusfjord.no), sprawled around its tiny, tucked-away harbour. Many artists consider it to be the essence of Lofoten but be warned: so do tour operators. And the locals are smart: it costs Nkr30 just to walk around plus a further Nkr30 to see *The People & The Fish*, a 12-minute video about Nusfjord, past and present. In the country store that has just celebrated its centenary, upper shelves are crammed with vintage cans, bottles and boxes while the lower ones are stocked with contemporary fare. There's the old cod-liver oil factory, boat house, sawmill and a cluster of *rorbuer*, most of them modern. The most original feature is **Krismar** (☎ 76 09 33 99), the workshop of Italian Michele Sarno and his intricate creations in silver.

RAMBERG & FLAKSTAD

Imagine an arch of surfable tropical white sand fronting a sparkling blue-green bay with a backdrop of snowcapped Arctic peaks. That's pretty much **Ramberg** and **Flakstad** beaches, on the north coast, when the sun shines kindly on them. Should you hit such a day, no-one back home will believe that your holiday snaps of this place were taken north of the Arctic Circle, but you'll know it if you stick a toe in the water.

Set back from Flakstad beach and bypassed these days by the E10, the red onion-domed **Flakstad Kirke** (admission Nkr20; 11am-3pm late Jun-early Aug) was built in 1780 but has been extensively restored over the years. Most of the original wood was ripped out of the ground by the Arctic-bound rivers of Siberia and washed up here as driftwood.

GLASSHYTTA

You can make a 4km side trip to Vikten to visit the **gallery** (☎ 76 09 44 42; 10am-7pm mid-Jun–mid-Aug) of glassblower Åsvar Tangrand, designer of the Lofoten Rune, the region's seven-pronged logo, which evokes a longboat.

SUND FISKERIMUSEUM

This **fishery museum** (☎ 76 09 36 29; adult/child Nkr45/10; ⌚ 10am-4pm or 6pm mid-May–Aug) lies 3km south of the bridge linking Flakstadøy and Moskenesøy. In one dim shack, there's an astounding clutter of boats, ropes and floats while within another is an unlabelled yet fascinating jumble of pots, pans, skis, old valve radios and the like. All this to the throb and fumes curling from the collection of permanently beached ships' diesel engines. Tor-Vegard Mørkved, the young resident blacksmith, bashes out cormorants in iron (the cheapest, around Nkr300 but Nkr1700 for something you'd be proud to have on your mantelpiece).

Sleeping & Eating

Ramberg Gjestegård (☎ 76 09 35 00; www.ramberg-gjestegard.no; E10; car/caravan site Nkr120/135, 2-/4-bed cabins Nkr800/1000) At this welcoming camp site, right on the beach, you can rent a kayak or rowing boat (per hour/day Nkr25/100), upgrade to a motorboat (Nkr100/350) or explore the island by bike (Nkr25/100). There's a justifiably popular Arctic Menu restaurant (mains Nkr180 to Nkr220) that does mainly fish dishes and its own splendid Flakstad Menu (cod, cured roast lamb and rhubarb compote for dessert). It also offers cheaper but still very tasty lunch specials (Nkr80 to Nkr170).

MOSKENESØY

pop 1150

The 34km-long island of Moskenesøy, a spiky, pinnacled igneous ridge rising directly from the sea and split by deep lakes and fjords, could almost have been conceived by Tolkien. A paradise for mountaineers, some of the tight gullies and fretted peaks of this tortured island – including its highest point, Hermannsdalstind (1029m) – are accessible to ordinary mortals as well.

ORIENTATION & INFORMATION

The E10 runs along the island's south coast, past the communities of Hamnøy, Sakrisøy and Reine, before reaching the functional village of Moskenes and its ferry terminal. The route ends at the museum-like village of Å. But for a few short coastal skirts, mountains occupy the rest of the island.

The island's **tourist office** (☎ 76 09 15 99; www.lofoten-info.no; ⌚ 10am-7pm mid-Jun–mid-Aug, 10am-5pm Mon-Fri May–mid-Jun & late Aug, 10am-2pm Mon-Fri rest-of-year) is at Moskenes harbour. It publishes the free, informative *Moskenes Guide*, has an internet point (per hour Nkr60) and makes reservations for a variety of tours and activities.

ACTIVITIES

The *Moskenes Guide* has 14 suggestions for **hikes** of between one and 10 hours and the youth hostel in Å carries a free information sheet describing six walks of between two and seven hours. You'll need to supplement these with Staten Kartverk's *Lofoten* at 1:100,000.

You can **deep-sea fish** (Nkr400-500) for three to four hours using traditional long lines and hand lines. From the *Hellvåg* in Å and the *Carina* in Reine, both working cod-fishing vessels in winter, you're all but guaranteed a fat catch. Other options include fishing the Reinefjord, off Nusfjord, or near the maelstrom off Å.

At sea, there's excellent **bird-watching** and the possibility of **whale sightings** in season.

GETTING THERE & AWAY

Car ferries sail five to six times daily in summer (less frequently during the rest of the year) between Moskenes and Bodø (adult/child/car Nkr149/74/538, 3½ hours). At least one calls in daily at the tiny southern Lofoten islands of Røst and Værøy.

Four to five buses connect Leknes and Å (1½ hours) daily in summer, stopping in all major villages along the E10.

Å

At the tail end of Moskenesøy, the bijou village of Å (appropriately, the last letter of the Norwegian alphabet), sometimes referred to as Å i Lofoten, is truly a living museum – a preserved fishing village with a shoreline of red *rorbuer*, cod drying racks and picture-postcard scenes at almost every turn. It's an almost feudal place, carved up between two families, now living very much from tourism but in its time a significant fishing port (upwards of 700,000 cod would be hung out to dry right up to WWII).

Do the village a favour and leave your vehicle at the car park beyond a short tunnel and walk in.

SIGHTS

Fourteen of Å's 19th-century boathouses, storehouses, fishing cottages, farmhouses and commercial buildings constitute the **Norwegian**

FISHY MEDICINE

Remember the breakfast tantrums, the spoon being forced into your mouth and that strong fishy flavour, overcoming the nutty taste of cornflakes, as your parents forced the fluid down your throat to stave off winter colds?

It wasn't always so. *Tran,* cod-liver oil, was originally used as fuel for lamps or in the tanning process for skins and nobody would have dreamed of imbibing it. But gradually its medicinal properties were understood and, in an early example of deliberate – and highly successful – marketing, cod-liver oil became the preventative of choice throughout Europe. It's a bit like olive oil; the first pressing, the virgin oil, is considered the purest while steam cooking – a technological advance that reduced production costs and enhanced yield – enables much more of the oil to be used.

Early hunch is nowadays backed up by objective medical evidence. Cod-liver oil, rich in vitamins A and D, plus omega-3 fatty acids, is good for your heart and blood circulation, eyesight, skin, bone development and brain.

So take a breath, pinch your nostrils, join one in three of all Norwegians and take your medicine like a man/woman…

Fishing Village Museum (Norsk Fiskeværs Museum; ☎ 76 09 14 88; adult/child Nkr50/25; ⌚ 10am-5.30pm mid-Jun–mid-Aug, 11am-3.30pm Mon-Fri rest-of-year). Highlights (pick up a pamphlet in English at reception) are Europe's oldest cod-liver oil factory, where you'll be treated to a taste of the wares and can pick up a bottle (Nkr40) to stave off those winter sniffles; the smithy, who still makes cod-liver oil lamps; the still-functioning bakery, established in 1844; the old *rorbuer* with period furnishings; and a couple of traditional Lofoten fishing boats.

At the nearby **Lofoten Stockfish Museum** (Lofoten Tørrfiskmuseum; ☎ 91 15 05 60; adult/child/concession Nkr40/free/25; ⌚ 10am-5pm mid-Jun–mid-Aug, 11am-4pm early Jun & late Aug), in a former fish warehouse, you'll be bowled over by Steinar Larsen, its enthusiastic, polyglot owner, who meets and greets every visitor. This personal collection, a passionate hobby of his, illustrates well Lofoten's traditional mainstay: the catching and drying of cod for export, particularly to Italy. Displays, artefacts and a DVD programme take you through the process, from hauling the fish out of the sea through drying, grading and sorting to despatch.

Beyond the camp site just south of Å, there's an excellent hillside view of Værøy island, across the Moskenesstraumen strait. The mighty **maelstroms** created by tidal flows between the two islands were first described 2000 years ago by Pytheas and later appeared as fearsome adversaries on fanciful early sea charts. They also inspired tales of maritime peril by Jules Verne and Edgar Allan Poe, and are still said to be among the world's most dangerous waters. This formidable expanse is exceptionally rich in fish and attracts large numbers of sea birds and marine mammals.

SLEEPING & EATING

Moskenesstraumen Camping (☎ 76 09 11 48; camping for 1/2/3 persons Nkr90/110/120, caravans Nkr140, 2-/4-bed cabins Nkr380/500, with bathroom Nkr500/700; ⌚ Jun-Aug) This wonderful cliff-top camp site, just south of the village, has flat, grassy pitches between the rocks, just big enough for your bivouac. Cabins too have great views, as far as the mainland on clear days.

Å Vandrerhjem og Rorbuer (☎ 76 09 11 21; www.lofoten-rorbu.com; hostel dm Nkr180, d/tr in sea house per person Nkr250, rorbuer Nkr850-1550) There's accommodation for all budgets, dispersed throughout Å's historic buildings, the more expensive ones fully equipped and furnished with antiques. Very much the hub of the village, the office provides general tourist information and also hires out bikes (per day Nkr200), rowing boats (Nkr150) on Lade Åvannet, a short walk away, and motorboats (Nkr1000 plus petrol). It also rents *rorbuer* in the nearby and more tranquil hamlet of Tind, 1km to the north.

Å-Hamna Rorbuer & Hennumgården (☎ 76 09 12 11; www.lofotenferie.com; 2-4-bed r per person Nkr100, 4-8-bed rorbuer Nkr450-1000) You can stay here in restored fishing huts or the hostel-style Hennumgårdensjøhus. Prices drop significantly outside high summer.

Brygga restaurant (☎ 76 09 15 72; mains Nkr95-170; ⌚ Jun-Sep) Hovering above the water, this is Å's one decent dining choice. The menu, as is right and proper in a village with such a strong fishing tradition, is mainly of things with fins. It's also a great little spot simply for a drink as the water sloshes below your feet.

Sørvågen

Alongside the E10 in Sørvågen and south of Moskenes, the **Norwegian Telecommunications Museum** (☎ 76 09 14 88; adult/child Nkr40/20; core hrs noon-4pm Jun–mid-Aug) presents itself as a study in 'cod and communications'. Granted, it's not an immediately winning combination but in fact this small museum commemorates a huge advance in fishing techniques. In 1906, what was Norway's second wireless telephone station was established in this tiny hamlet. From that day on, weather warnings could be speedily passed on and fishing vessels could communicate with each other, pass on news about where the shoals were moving and call up the bait boats.

our pick **Maren Anna** (☎ 76 09 20 50; mains around Nkr200) is at once a pub, restaurant and café. Serving its mainstay of fish, portions are generous and hyperfresh (our coley had been hauled out of the sea by the chef herself barely two hours earlier). For a table with views over the fishing boats below and what's claimed, tongue in cheek, to be Norway's smallest beach, reserve ahead. The menu's only in Norwegian but the staff readily translate.

Moskenes

In a bleak location yet with great waterside views, **Moskenes Camping** (☎ 99 48 94 05; kra-ri@online.no; tent/caravan sites Nkr100/140; May-Sep) is gravel surfaced yet also has a sheltered grassy area for tent campers. Facilities have been recently upgraded and it's convenient for an early getaway from the ferry terminal, only 400m away.

Reine

Reine is a characterless place but gosh, it looks great from above, beside its placid lagoon and backed by the sheer rock face of Reinebringen. You get a great view from the road that drops to the village from the E10 but for a truly exceptional panorama, hike up the precipitous track to Reinebringen's summit (670m). It starts at the tunnel entrance about 1.2km south of the Reine turnoff from the E10, and climbs very steeply to the ridge (448m).

From Reine, you can choose among several worthwhile boat tours between June and August. The most popular is a six-hour excursion (adult/child Nkr800/400). It takes you via the maelstrom to the cave **Refsvikhula**, a 115m-long, 50m-high natural rock cathedral. Around midsummer, the midnight sun shines directly into the mouth of the cave and illuminates a panel of Stone Age stick figures marching across the walls, thought to have been painted at least 3000 years ago.

Alternatively, you can take a three-hour bird- and marine mammal-watching **safari** (adult/child Nkr600/350) into the fish-rich Moskstraumen maelstrom.

Both tours are run by run by **Moskstraumen Adventure** (☎ 90 77 07 41).

Around Reine

In summer ferries run between Reine and Vindstad (adult/child return Nkr100/50, 15 minutes, three daily) through scenic Reinefjord. From Vindstad, it's a one-hour hike across the ridge to the abandoned beachside settlement of **Bunes**, in the shadow of the brooding 610m Helvetestind rock slab.

Sakrisøy

In Sakrisøy, Dagmar Gylseth has collected more than 2500 dolls, antique teddy bears and historic toys over 20 years for her **Museum of Dolls & Toys** (Dagmars Dukke og Leketøy Museum; ☎ 76 09 21 43; adult/child/concession Nkr50/25/40; 10am-6pm or 8pm late May-Aug). There's also an affiliated antique shop upstairs.

Reserve at the Doll Museum for **Sakrisøy Rorbuer** (☎ 76 09 21 43; www.lofoten.ws; Nkr675-1250), a relatively authentic complex of ochre-coloured cottages hovering above the water. You can also hire motorboats (Nkr400 to Nkr550 per day).

For self-catering, the fish stall **Sjømat** (Sakrisøy), across the street from the Doll Museum, is famous for its fish cakes, smoked salmon, prawns, whale steaks and – go on, be adventurous – seagulls' eggs.

Hamnøy

our pick **Hamnøy Mat og Vinbu** (☎ 76 09 21 45; Hamnøy; mains Nkr155-205; Jun-early Sep) is a welcoming restaurant run by three generations of the same family (the teenage boys are coopted for washing-up duties). It's well regarded for local specialities, including whale, *bacalao* and cod tongues. Grandmother takes care of the traditional dishes – just try her fish cakes – while her son is the main chef. Its fish is of the freshest catch, bought daily from the harbour barely 100m away.

SOUTHERN ISLANDS

This remote pair of islands is superb for bird-watching. Værøy, mainly high and rugged, and Røst, flat as a pancake, both offer good walking and relative solitude in well-touristed Lofoten.

Værøy

pop 500

Craggy Værøy, its handful of residents hugely outnumbered by over 100,000 nesting sea birds – fulmars, gannets, Arctic terns, guillemots, gulls, sea eagles, puffins, kittiwakes, cormorants, eiders, petrels and a host of others – is a mere 8km long with white-sand beaches, soaring ridges, tiny, isolated villages, granite-gneiss bird cliffs and sparkling seas.

The **tourist office** (☎ 76 05 15 00; ⏰ 10am-3pm Mon-Sat mid-Jun–mid-Aug) is near the ferry landing at Sørland, the main village. It's open additional hours whenever the car ferry is in port.

SIGHTS & ACTIVITIES

Walking routes approach some of the major sea-bird rookeries. The most scenic and popular trail begins at the end of the road around the north of the island, about 6km from Sørland and 300m beyond the former airstrip. It heads southward along the west coast, over the Eidet isthmus to the mostly abandoned fishing village of Måstad, on the east coast, where meat and eggs from the puffin colonies once supported 150 people.

Fit hikers who relish a challenge may also want to attempt the steep climb from Måstad to the peak of Måhornet (431m), which takes about an hour each way. Alternatively, from the quay at Sørland you can follow the road (or perhaps the more interesting ridge scramble) up to the NATO installation at Håen (438m).

SLEEPING & EATING

Gamle Prestegård (Old Vicarage; ☎ 76 09 54 11; www.prestegaarden.no in Norwegian; s/d Nkr400/600, with bathroom Nkr475/690, all incl breakfast) Værøy's smartest lodging and dining is on the island's north side. It's the large house with a flagpole in the garden beside the church, just where you'd expect the vicar to have lived.

Kornelius Kro (☎ 76 09 52 99; korn-kro@online.no; Sørland; 1-/2-/4-bed cabins Nkr550/820/1500) The island's only nightlife option (there's live music most Saturdays) has a pub, restaurant (mains Nkr75 to Nkr170) and five cabins at the rear.

GETTING THERE & AWAY

There's a **helicopter flight** (☎ 77 60 83 00) between Bodø and Værøy once or twice daily, February to October. The rest of us take the car ferry that runs daily except Saturday from Bodø (passenger/car Nkr139/493), directly or via Moskenes. The ferry also links Værøy with Røst (passenger/car Nkr73/251).

Røst

pop 600

The 356 islands and skerries of Røst form Lofoten's ragged southern edge. Røst stands in sharp contrast to its rugged neighbours to the north, and were it not for a small pimple in the middle, the main pond-studded island of Røstlandet would be dead flat. Thanks to its location in the heart of the Gulf Stream, this cluster of islets basks in one of the mildest climates in Norway and attracts 2.5 million nesting sea birds to some serious rookeries on the cliffs of the outer islands.

An unusual view of medieval life on the island is provided in the accounts of a shipwrecked merchant of Venice, one Pietro Querini, who washed up on Sandøy in 1432 and reputedly introduced stockfish to Italy. The **tourist office** (☎ 76 05 05 00; ⏰ mid-Jun–mid-Aug), a short walk from the ferry dock, has a sheet outlining the tale.

TOURS

From June to mid-August the MS *Inger Helen*, belonging to Kårøy Rorbucamping (see left), does five-hour boat tours (adult/child Nkr300/125) that cruise past several bird cliffs, including the Vedøy kittiwake colony. Weather permitting, the boat makes a stop for a short walk to the 1887 Skomvær lighthouse or, if you prefer, you can try a little fishing (lines provided).

SLEEPING & EATING

Kårøy Rorbucamping (☎ 76 09 62 38; www.karoy.no; per person Nkr150; ⏰ May-Aug) Rooms sleep two, four or six at this authentic *rorbu*. Bathrooms are communal and there are self-catering facilities. This great budget choice is on the minuscule island of Kårøy; phone from the ferry and a boat will be sent to collect you.

Røst Bryggehotel (☎ 76 05 08 00; www.rostbryggehotell.no; d Nkr750 Jul–mid-Aug, Nkr900 rest-of-year) This modern development in traditional style is right on the quayside. It has 16 comfortable doubles, and hires out both bikes and fishing tackle.

Querini Pub og Restaurant (☎ 76 09 64 80) Named after the shipwrecked merchant from Venice, this is a reliable choice among Røst's few eating options.

GETTING THERE & AWAY

Røst, like Værøy, is served by the car ferry (daily except Saturday) that runs between Bodø and Moskenes.

VESTERÅLEN

pop 28,300

Administratively, the islands of Vesterålen, the northern continuation of the archipelago that includes Lofoten, are divided between the counties of Nordland and Troms but, for convenience, we cover the entire area in this chapter. Although the landscapes here aren't as dramatic as those in Lofoten, they tend to be much wilder and the forested mountainous regions of the island of Hinnøya are a unique corner of Norway's largely treeless northern coast.

An Encounter with Vesterålen – Culture, Nature & History (Nkr170), sold at tourist offices, gives a good introduction to the region, its sights and walking routes.

HADSELØYA

pop 8050

Vesterålen's link to Lofoten is the southernmost island of Hadseløya, connected by ferry from the port of Melbu to Fiskebøl on Austvågøy. The other main town, Stokmarknes, is best known as the birthplace of the Hurtigruten coastal ferry.

The island's **tourist office** (☎ 76 16 46 60; 🕑 10am-5pm Mon-Sat, 11am-4pm Sat & Sun mid-Jun–mid-Aug only) is on the waterfront in Stokmarknes.

Stokmarknes

The Hurtigruten coastal ferry was founded in Stokmarknes in 1893 by Richard With. Originally a single ship, the S/S *Vesterålen*, it called on nine ports between Trondheim and Hammerfest, carrying post, passengers and vital supplies. Now the line boasts 11 ships, carries half a million passengers annually, serves 35 towns and villages and is a vital link for Norway, providing transport for locals and a scenic cruise experience for tourists.

The **Hurtigruten Museum** (Hurtigrutemuseet; ☎ 76 11 81 90; Markedsgata 1; museum admission adult/child Nkr80/30, M/S Finnmarken Nkr40/20, combined admission Nkr80/30; 🕑 noon-4pm mid-May–mid-Jun & mid-Aug–mid-Sep, 10am-6pm mid-Jun–mid-Aug, 2-4pm Mon-Fri, noon-4pm Sat rest-of-year) portrays the history of the line in text and image. Hitched to the quayside is the retired ship M/S *Finnmarken*, claimed to be the world's largest museum piece, which plied the coastal route between 1956 and 1993.

Hurtigrutenshus (☎ 76 15 06 00; www.hurtigrutenshus.com; Markedsgata 1; s/d Nkr840/1280; 🕑 Jun–mid-Aug) is a luxurious hotel, conference and arts complex, where rooms represent good value for your krone. In the same complex as the museum, it's one of the few places where it's more fun to be alone than accompanied; single rooms are furnished to resemble ships' cabins.

Hurtigrutenshus Turistsenter (☎ 76 15 29 99; s/d Nkr670/840 mid-Jun–mid-Aug, Nkr995/1280 rest-of-year) is found over the bridge and has more conventional cabins and rooms. It's a friendly extension to the Hurtigruten complex.

Just across from the Hurtigruten Museum, **Rødbrygge Pub** (☎ 76 15 26 66; Markedgata 6a; mains Nkr60-190; 🕑 11am-3am) is an all-wood place that does good grills, seafood and pizzas at more modest prices (including a mean fish soup for Nkr75).

our pick **Isqueen** (☎ 76 15 29 99; mains Nkr235-290; 🕑 6-11pm) sits within the Turistcenter grounds. This one-time whaler, forever beached, is now an excellent Arctic Menu restaurant. You can dine within its hull, in the grafted-on restaurant with its wraparound windows or up top on the outdoor terrace with fine views over the sound.

Melbu

In an abandoned herring oil factory (romantically named Neptune despite its stark functionality), the **National Fishing Industry Museum** (Norsk Fiskerindustrimuseum; ☎ 76 15 98 25; Neptunveien; adult/child Nkr50/20; 🕑 9am-3pm Mon-Fri) traces the life of a fish from the deep sea to the kitchen table. There's also a children's exhibition about the goings-on on the sea floor. Across the harbour from the ferry pier, it's 750m from the E10 along a pocked causeway. In summer there are guided visits, included with the admission fee.

The **Sommer-Melbu festival**, held each July, is one of northern Norway's liveliest cultural festivals with seminars, lectures, music of all genres, theatre and art exhibitions.

Getting There & Around

Of course, the Hurtigruten coastal ferry still makes a detour stop in its home port of Stokmarknes...

Buses between Melbu and Stokmarknes run several times daily on weekdays and twice daily at weekends.

LANGØYA

pop 14,700

The high points, both literally and figuratively, of Langøya, Vesterålen's central island, are the historic, little-visited fishing villages at its northern tip. Should you be passing through Sortland around bedtime, you'll find some decent lodging options that also offer good dining.

The annual 170km **Arctic Sea Kayak Race** (www.askr.no), held over five days in July, is one of the ultimate challenges in competitive sea-kayaking. Lesser beings can opt for a shorter option or an introductory course in sea-kayaking. You can register online.

Sortland

pop 5000

Sortland, Vesterålen's commercial centre and transit hub, occupies a nick in the island's east coast. Its mostly chunky, rectangular buildings are painted a soothing sea-blue. The helpful **tourist office** (☎ 76 11 14 80; www.visitvesteralen.com; Kjøpmannsgata 2; 🕑 9am-6pm Mon-Fri, 10am-4pm Sat, noon-4pm Sun mid-Jun–mid-Aug, 8am-4pm Mon-Fri rest-of-year) covers the whole of the Vesterålen region.

Sortland Jazz is a couple of weeks of jazz that the town hosts in September.

A family-run camp site, **Sortland Camping og Motell** (☎ 76 11 03 00; www.sortland-camping.no; Vestervegen 51; car/caravan sites Nkr200/225, cabins Nkr350-450, for 5-7 persons with bathroom Nkr1200) is the only option in town. It's 1.3km from the centre and offers home cooking, strong on northern-Norway cuisine. Occupying an extensive, semiwooded area, it produces a useful information sheet about the area.

Located precisely 1.4km north of the bridge, **SjøhusSenteret** (☎ 76 12 37 40; sjoehus@online.no; Ånstadsjøen; d/tr Nkr630/785, 3-/5-bed cabin Nkr1330/1630) has both comfortable rooms and waterside cabins with views. You can fish from the end of the private jetty (you can borrow a rod) and rent a bike (Nkr30/160 per hour/day), rowing boat (Nkr75/140) or motorboat (Nkr390/1200). Its Sjøstua restaurant, where the chef produces a delightful range of à la carte dishes, is worth a visit in its own right.

Strand Hotell (☎ 76 11 00 80; www.strandhotell.no; Strandgata 34; s/d 750/900 mid-Jun–mid-Aug, Nk970/1150 Mon-Thu, Nkr700/910 Fri &Sat rest-of-year; Ⓟ 💻) is a waterside, family-run hotel. It has 37 cheery, upscale rooms, each decorated with prints by local artist Tove Hov Jacobsen.

Spisestua (☎ 76 12 28 78; mains Nkr240-285) is the top-floor Arctic Menu restaurant of Strand Hotell, and equally impressive. There's freshly baked homemade bread for breakfast, and free coffee and waffles all day long.

GETTING THERE & AWAY

Two to four daily buses run north from Sortland to Risøyhamn (one hour) and Andenes (two hours). Buses to/from Harstad (2¼ hours) run one to four times daily. You can also take the twice-daily express bus to Narvik (Nkr294, four hours) on the mainland or Svolvær (Nkr248, 2¼ hours), to which three to five local buses also run daily. The express bus between Fauske (Nkr370, 5¼ hours) and Svolvær stops in daily too.

Sortland is also a stop on the Hurtigruten coastal ferry.

Myre

Myre, where the roads for Nyksund and Stø split, has a seasonal **tourist office** (☎ 76 18 50 50; 🕑 core hrs 10am-4pm Mon-Sat mid-Jun–mid-Aug).

Nyksund

A dramatic drive along a narrow ribbon of road that hugs the shoreline brings you to this long-abandoned fishing village that's been reborn as an artists' colony. From the crumbling old structures to the faithfully renovated commercial buildings, it's picture-perfect. It's hard to imagine that, until recently, Nyksund was a ghost town.

The bakery and post office, heart of any community, shut up shop in the 1960s and nearly everyone else left in 1975 after a storm

NORDLAND

RECLAIMED & RECYCLED

Ssemjon Gerlitz, the sparky German owner of Holmvik Brygge, has lived year-round in Nyksund for a decade and more. Over the years, he and his team of helpers have gleaned, picked and scavenged what could be salvaged from Nyksund's crumbling buildings and incorporated them into higgledy-piggledy Holmvik Brygge, where every room's different, each with its own personality.

Two things in particular keep him here, at the road's end. Modulating his rat-a-tat delivery for just a millisecond, he slows to speak of the lure of silence, nothing but the rhythm of wind and waves for most of the year. Then, changing a gear, of his sense of communion with long-gone fisherfolk ('Every rusty nail I pull out was hammered in by someone who lived and worked here') and, once again in overdrive, of the sheer energy of this splendid place where mountains tumble to the sea.

destroyed the mole. The last inhabitant, blacksmith Olav Larsen, packed his bags in 1977.

Sheep and vandals took over but slowly, over the decades, life has been breathed back into this charming, remote settlement. Nowadays, modern Nyksund boasts a summer population of around 60 and some half-dozen hardy souls hack it throughout the harsh winters.

our pick **Holmvik Brygge** (☎ 76 13 47 96; www.nyksund.com; r per person Nkr225; ⌚ year-round) is a cosy, hugely welcoming guesthouse and café, and in itself justifies the detour. You can either cater for yourself or enjoy a snack (from Nkr55), a drink or a filling dinner (Nkr85 to Nkr150) at its Kai Café.

Stø

The small, distinctive fishing village of Stø clings to Langøya's northernmost tip. From July to September, **Arctic Whale Tours** (☎ 76 13 43 00; www.arcticwhaletours.com) mount daily seven-hour whale-watching cruises (adult/child Nkr780/500), leaving at noon. On the way to the sperm whales' feeding grounds, it pauses to view sea bird and seal colonies.

Departing from both Stø and Nyksund, **Island Adventure** (☎ 48 17 31 64; www.islandadventure.no) organises both seal- and bird-watching trips and fishing outings. You can reserve at Stø Bobilcamp.

The walk over the headland between Nyksund and Stø, waymarked with red letter T's, merits a short day of your life. Most hikers sweat a little on the outward leg of this five-hour circular trek via the 517m Sørkulen, then breathe easy, returning via the simpler sea-level route. Called the **Queen's Route**, its name derives from a hike taken by Norway's Queen Sonja in 1994. The Myre and Sortland tourist offices carry a free guide leaflet.

Small, waterside **Stø Bobilcamp** (☎ 76 13 25 30; www.stobobilcamp.com; camp site Nkr140, cabins Nkr700-850; ⌚ mid-May–mid-Aug) is stark indeed and a windy spot to pitch your tent but it does run an unpretentious little restaurant, serving primarily fish.

Of the one to four daily buses between Sortland and Myre (one hour), two continue to Stø (1¼ hours) on weekdays.

ANDØYA

pop 6000

Andøya, long, narrow and flat except for the mountains on its western flank, is atypical of Vesterålen. The 1000m-deep, dark, cold waters of its northwestern shore attract abundant stocks of squid, including some very large specimens indeed, and these in turn attract the squid-loving sperm whales. The result is fairly reliable whale-watching, centred on the town of Andenes at the island's northern end. Andenes is the only place of any size but other nature safaris depart from the tiny ports of Bleik and Stave, about 10km and 25km southwest of the town.

Andenes

pop 2700

This straggling village has a rich fishing history and is northern Norway's main base for whale-watching. The harbour front is a charming jumble of wooden boat sheds and general nautical detritus.

Its **tourist office** (☎ 76 14 12 03; www.andoyturist.no; Hamnegata 1; ⌚ 10am-6pm mid-Jun–Aug, 9am-4pm Mon-Fri rest-of-year) covers the whole island and shares premises with the Hisnakul Natural History Centre. It produces a leaflet in English, *Andanes Vær* (Nkr35), which outlines a walking tour of the old quarter. There's internet access (Nkr60 per hour) and it rents bikes (Nkr100/175 per three-hours/day).

Yanthi (☎ 75 91 75 75; Storgata 2) has three internet terminals (Nkr25 per 30 minutes) and brews good coffee.

SIGHTS & ACTIVITIES

The tourist office sells a combined ticket (adult/child Nkr100/50) that gives access to all sights below except the Whale Centre.

The **Hisnakul Natural History Centre** (☎ 76 14 12 03; Hamnegata 1; adult/concession Nkr50/25; 10am-6pm mid-Jun–Aug, 9am-4pm rest-of-year) shares a restored wooden warehouse with the tourist office. It showcases the natural history of northern Norway, including sea birds, marine mammals, topography, farming, fisheries and local cultures.

Next door, the **Northern Lights Centre** (adult/child Nkr40/20; 10am-6pm late Jun-late Aug) is an impressive high-tech aurora borealis exhibition that first featured at the 1994 Winter Olympics in Lillehammer.

The **Whale Centre** (Hvalsenter; ☎ 76 11 56 00; Havnegate 1; adult/child Nkr60/30; 8.30am-4pm or 7pm late May–mid-Sep) provides a perspective for whale-watchers, with displays on whale research, whaling and whale life cycles. Most people visit here in conjunction with a whale-watching tour (see below).

The quaint, Arctic-themed **Polar Museum** (☎ 76 11 54 32; Havnegate; adult/child Nkr30/free; 10am-6pm mid-Jun–mid-Aug) has displays on local hunting and fishing traditions. There's extensive coverage of the 38 winter hunting expeditions in Svalbard undertaken by local explorer Hilmar Nøis, who also collected most of the exhibits.

The town's landmark red **Andenes Fyr** (lighthouse), automated for many years, opened in 1859 and still shines on. **Guided visits** (adult/child Nkr35/10; late Jun–Aug), which require a climb up 40m and 148 steps, take place hourly, on the hour between noon and 4pm.

TOURS

The island's biggest outfit, **Whale Safari** (☎ 76 11 56 00; www.whalesafari.no), which operates the Whale Centre, runs popular cruises (adult/child/concession Nkr795/ 500/700) between late May and mid-September. The tour begins with a guided visit to the Centre and slide show, followed by a three- to six-hour boat trip. If you fail to sight at least one sperm whale, your next trip is free. There's also a chance of spotting minke, pilot and humpback whales and, towards the end of the season, killer whales (orcas). Trips depart at least once daily (at 11am) with up to six sailings in high summer. Your fee includes a light lunch, if you can face it – staff pass around the seasickness pills, just like airline boiled sweets before takeoff. A tip: weather and high seas only rarely prevent a sailing but try to build in an extra day on the island, just in case you're unlucky.

THE ROAD LESS TRAVELLED

Unless you leave Andøya by the seasonal ferry from Andenes to Gryllefjord, there's no way of avoiding the 100km drive the length of the island's slim northern finger, poking up from Sortland. To avoid repetition, but all the more so because it's a spectacular drive in its own right, take the minor, lightly trafficked west coast road from Risøyhamn as you head northwards. Designated a National Tourist Route, it offers magnificent coastal panoramas as it threads along the shoreline. Returning by the Rv83, notice the giant hillocks of peat, extracted, dried and ready to be transported to garden centres around the world.

SLEEPING & EATING

Andenes Camping (☎ 76 11 56 00; car/caravan sites Nkr130/190; late May–mid-Sep) This basic camp site, 3.5km from town, is on a gorgeous seaside meadow, green and smooth as a golf course.

Andenes Vandrerhjem (☎ 76 14 28 50; fax 76 14 28 55; Havnegata 31; per person Nkr150; Jun-Aug) This last-resort seasonal hostel, no longer an HI-affiliate, is severely run-down. Near the harbour, it's also part of the Norlandia empire, to which it does no credit.

Hisnakul Natural History Centre (see left; dm/s/d Nkr100/225/325) has well-priced budget rooms above its gallery. The bathroom is in the corridor and there are self-catering facilities. There are only 14 beds so phone to reserve.

Den Gamle Fyrmesterbolig (☎ 76 14 10 27; Richard Withs gate 11; r Nkr400) In the shadow of Andenes' resplendent lighthouse, this charming option occupies what was once the lighthouse keepers' cottage. There are only two rooms and it doesn't take advance reservations, but if you ring up on the day it'll hold one for you.

Norlandia Andrikken Hotell (☎ 76 14 12 22; www.norlandia.no/andrikken; Storgata 53; s/dNkr790/1070

FARGEKLATTEN

Fargeklatten, meaning splashes of colour, is a very special place, the creation of Grethe Kvalvik. For years, Grethe was the receptionist at Andrikken Hotell until she lost her sight. After two long years of blindness, partial vision returned and she could again perceive shapes and, above all, colours.

Determined to live a full life anew, she rescued Fargeklatten, at the time earmarked for demolition to make way for a car park. This complex of historical buildings now houses a couple of small galleries displaying the art and crafts of northern Norway, a simple café and also a **boarding house** (r Nkr600-700), furnished in antique style. Next step, she enthused as we met, is to restore a 17th-century fisherfolk's cottage.

mid-Jun–mid-Aug, Nkr1180/1390 Sun-Thu, Nkr850/1145 Fri & Sat rest-of-year; P) Norlandia's house-brand lodging – dull stuff and boxy from the outside – has rooms that, once you penetrate, are comfortable and well equipped. It also runs a decent restaurant (mains Nkr170 to Nkr240).

Fargeklatten (☎ 97 76 00 20; Sjøgata 38A; 11am-2pm & 6-8pm May-Sep, 11am-2pm Mon-Fri rest-of-year) Enjoy coffee and cakes within this small, recently established art gallery (see above).

Lysthuset (☎ 76 14 14 99; Storgata 51; pizzas Nkr125-190, mains Nkr145-250) The Lysthuset is the best of Andenes' limited dining options. In front, it's your typical takeaway burgers, pizzas and other speedy stuff. Behind, the restaurant proper offers altogether more subtle fare. For dessert, indulge in a little 'Sex on the Mountain' – an orgasmic confection of ice cream, cream, blackberries and cloudberries, all doused in eggnog.

GETTING THERE & AROUND

The flight between Andenes and Tromsø, via Narvik or Bodø, is a contender for the world's most scenic flight with spectacular aerial views of the landscapes, seas and agricultural patterns.

Two to four daily buses run south to Sortland (two hours) via Risøyhamn, where a bus to/from Andenes meets and greets the Hurtigruten. From late May to mid-August, a car ferry connects Andenes with the port of Gryllefjord (two hours, two to five daily) on the island of Senja (see p342), passing magnificent coastal scenery.

Around Andenes

From **Stave**, 18km southwest of Andenes, **Seal Safari** (☎ 97 68 00 18; www.sealsafari.no) leads two- to three-hour boat tours between late May and mid-August. These sail close to Norway's largest common seal colony before chugging on to the bird sanctuary on Bleiksøya, where auks, puffins, kittiwakes and other gulls teem.

Puffin Safari (☎ 76 14 57 75; www.puffinsafari.no), based in Bleik, also does daily 1½-hour birdwatching **boat trips** (adult/child Nkr300/150; 1pm & 3pm May–mid-August) off Bleiksøya and four-hour **deep-sea fishing trips** (adult/child Nkr400/200; 5pm Jun–mid-Aug).

SLEEPING

Stave Camping (☎ 76 14 65 62; stavecamping@c2i.net; car/caravan site Nkr130/140, 2-/4-bed cabins Nkr340/500, with bathroom Nkr550-660; mid-May–mid-August) Camp at the water's edge overlooking the fjord or set back and more sheltered at this friendly option with its cosy café.

Havhusene Bleik (☎ 76 14 57 40; www.norlandia.no; Fiskeværsveien, Bleik; 2-/4-/6-bed cabins Nkr1075/1270/1500) These well-equipped modern sea houses within the quiet harbour of Bleik are a very comfortable way to rough it.

HINNØYA

Administratively, Hinnøya, the largest island off mainland Norway, splits between the two counties of Troms and Nordland. Contrasting with the islands to the south, it's mostly forested green upland punctuated by snowcaps and deeply indented by stunning fjords. Off Hinnøya's west coast, Vesterålen is divided from Lofoten by the narrow Raftsund strait and even narrower, hugely scenic Trollfjorden, whose sheer walls plunge to the water, dwarfing all below.

Harstad

pop 19,400

On a hillside close to the northern end of Hinnøya, Harstad is the Vesterålen region's largest town, even though technically it tumbles within Troms county. It's a small industrial and defence-oriented place, full of docks, tanks and warehouses. Contrasting with so many tourism-'n'-fishing towns to the south, it pulsates with a certain purposeful bustle.

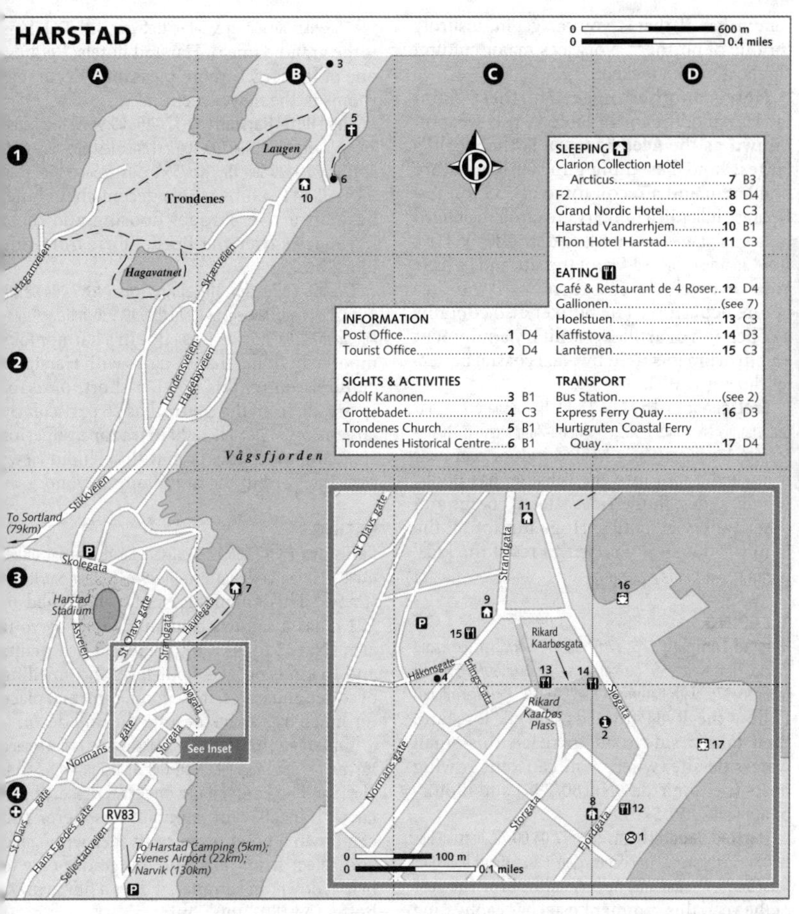

The **tourist office** (☎ 77 01 89 89; www.visitharstad com; 8am-6pm Jun–mid-Aug, 8am-3pm rest-of-year) shares premises with the bus station.

SIGHTS & ACTIVITIES

Most sights are on the **Trondenes Peninsula**, north of town.

The **Trondenes Historical Centre** (Trondenes Historiske Senter; ☎ 77 01 83 80; Trondenesveien 122; adult/child/concession Nkr70/50/25; 11am-5pm mid-Jun–mid-Aug, Sun only rest-of-year) has well-mounted and equally well-documented displays and artefacts illustrating the social history of the area from Viking days to the present.

Trondenes Church (Trondenes Kirke; guided tours in English adult/child Nkr40/20; tours 5pm Jun-early Aug), just north of the historical centre, was built by King Øystein around 1150, after Viking chieftains lost the battle against the unification of Norway under a Christian regime. For ages it was the northernmost church in Christendom – and still lays claim to being Norway's northernmost *stone* church. Originally of wood, the current stone structure replaced it around 1250 and quickly came to double as a fortification against Russian aggression. Its jewels are the three finely wrought altars at the east end, all venerating Mary. Most interesting is the central one of the Virgin surrounded by her extended family with infants in arms and children tugging at skirts on all sides. Glance up too at the pair of trumpet-wielding cherubs, precariously perched atop the main pillars of the rood screen. Entry is free between tour visits – if, that is, you can get in; absurdly for one of northern Norway's major cultural sights, it's often locked.

Here's another biggest/furthest claim for Harstad: the formidable WWII weapon known as the **Adolf Kanonen** is the world's largest land-based big gun, with a calibre of 40.6cm and a recoil force of 635 tonnes. Because it lies in a military area, you're obliged to take a **guided tour** (adult/child Nkr60/30; 11am, 1pm & 3pm mid-Jun–mid-Aug) of the site and to have your own vehicle. Just turn up 10 minutes before departure. The bunker also contains a collection of artillery, military equipment and instruments used by Nazi coastal batteries during WWII.

Grottebadet (77 04 17 70; Håkonsgate 7; adult/child/family Nkr130/95/300; noon-8pm Mon-Fri, 10am-6pm Sat, 11am-6pm Sun), a heated indoor complex tunnelled 150m into the hillside, has pools, rapids, slides, flume rides, steam rooms and other watery activities. Huge fun for all the family – but steel yourself to resist the kids' pleas for a *grottyburger*.

SLEEPING

Harstad Camping (77 07 36 62; www.harstad-camping.no; Nesseveien 55; car/caravan sites Nkr150/175 4-bed cabin Nkr375, with bathroom Nkr700-950; year-round) Follow the Rv83 towards Narvik for 4km, then take a side road to reach this small waterside site, where you can rent rowing boats (per hour/day Nkr80/290) and motorboats (Nkr150/570).

Harstad Vandrerhjem (77 04 00 78; harstad.hostel@vandrerhjem.no; Trondenesveien 110; s/d incl breakfast Nkr365/590; Jun–mid-Aug) A school for the rest of the year, this summer hostel has captivating harbour views from most rooms. Take bus 12 from the bus station.

F2 (77 00 32 00; www.f2hotel.no in Norwegian; Fjordgata 2; s/d Nkr545/690 mid-Jun–mid-Aug, from Nkr850/1000 Sun-Thu, Nkr595/960 Fri & Sat rest-of-year, all incl breakfast) Freshly renovated, F2's smart 88 rooms all have flat-screen TV, microwave, kettle and large windows that let in plenty of light. Bathrooms, however, are a little cramped. For guests, it rents cycles (per day Nkr100) and quads too. Faces in the photos that decorate rooms and public areas may seem familiar; they feature staff in a variety of poses, from mountain summit on the top floor to feet-in-the-sea at reception.

Grand Nordic Hotel (77 00 30 00; www.nordic.no; Strandgata 9; s/d Nkr590/790 mid-Jun–mid-Aug, Nk1345/1555 Sun-Thu, Nkr590/960 Fri & Sat rest-of-year; P) This is the grand dame of Harstad hotels. Request one of the larger, more pleasantly decorated rooms in the newer section.

Thon Hotel Harstad (77 00 08 00; www.thonhotels.com; Sjøgata 11; s/d Nkr700/900 incl breakfast mid-Jun–mid-Aug, Nk920/1120 Sun-Thu, Nkr755/955 Fri & Sat rest-of-year;) All 141 rooms at this decent chain hotel have attractive parquet flooring and most have views over the fjord, albeit from one block back.

Clarion Collection Hotel Arcticus (77 04 08 00; www.choice.no; Havnegata 3; s/d Nkr710/930 mid-Jun–mid-Aug, from Nk795/995 rest-of-year; P) In a harmonious modern building that it shares with Harstad's cultural centre, this hotel, a short, pleasant jetty walk from the centre, has 75 particularly large rooms. It's Nkr200 extra for a superior standard, waterside room with splendid views over the fjord to the mountains beyond.

EATING

Kaffistova (77 06 12 57; Rikard Kaarbøsgata 6; dishes Nkr40-135; 8am-6pm Mon-Thu, 9am-3.30pm Sat, noon-5pm Sun) This amenable spot, established in 1913, has a sandwich menu as long as your arm (Nkr62 to Nkr78), meat and fish mains and 16 kinds of cake. Split-level and smelling of coffee and cakes, it's a good, informal place for lunch or a snack despite the dull décor.

Lanternen (77 00 30 30; Hakons gate; mains around Nkr120; 2pm-midnight Mon-Thu, 1pm-2am Fri & Sat, 4-11pm Sun) The Lantern is a cheerful place, popular with locals, with a pub atmosphere. You can down a good pizza or burger with salad and select from its ample range of beers to help it down. In summer, it does a filling pizza buffet (Nkr80) until 7pm.

Café & Restaurant de 4 Roser (77 01 27 50; Torvet 7; mains Nkr160-320; café 10am-midnight, restaurant 6-11pm Mon-Sat) The Four Roses offers a great gourmet experience, whether you drop into the café for something simple or linger over a tempting item from the restaurant's creative à la carte selection.

Hoelstuen (77 06 55 00; Rikard Kaarbøs Plass 4; mains Nkr250-285; 5-11pm Mon-Sat) This trim place rivals the 4 Roser for the title of best restaurant in a town of limited eating opportunities. Its cuisine has flair. Dig your fork, for example, into the fillet of stag with chestnuts and thyme-flavoured glaze. It also does a particularly rich and creamy fish soup (Nkr100).

Gallionen (77 04 08 00; mains Nkr245-265) The restaurant of Clarion Collection Hotel Arcticus is an Arctic Menu establishment that also does a tempting daily special (around Nkr150). Fish dishes are its forte, particularly the grilled fillet of wolf-fish (Nkr260). Views, whether through the dining room's picture windows or from the quayside deck, will have you gasping.

GETTING THERE & AWAY

The Harstad-Narvik airport at Evenes has direct SAS flights to Oslo, Bodø, Tromsø and Trondheim. **Norwegian** (www.norwegian.no) also flies directly to/from Oslo, Bergen and Stavanger.

If you're heading for Tromsø, the easiest and most scenic option is by boat. There are two to four express passenger ferries daily between Harstad and Tromsø (2¾ hours), via Finnsnes (1½ hours).

There's also a year-round express passenger ferry (daily except Monday and Wednesday) between Harstad and Skrolsvik (1¼ hours), at the southern end of Senja island, where you'll find bus connections to Finnsnes and then on to Tromsø. Harstad is also a stop on the Hurtigruten coastal ferry.

Buses to/from Sortland (2¼ hours) run one to four times daily. There's one weekday bus to/from Narvik (three hours) and a daily service between Harstad and Fauske (Nkr343, 5½ hours).

GETTING AROUND

Flybussen (Nkr130, 50 minutes) shuttles between the town centre and Evenes airport several times daily.

Buses (Nkr25, 10 minutes, hourly, Monday to Friday only) connect Trondenes with the central bus station.

Parking may not be easy to find but – God bless the good burghers of Harstad – it's free in public car parks for vehicles with non-Norwegian licence plates.

For a taxi, call ☎ 77 04 10 00.

Møysalen National Park

Møysalen, scarcely 50 sq km in area, was set up to preserve a stretch of pristine alpine coastal scenery. The third-smallest of Norway's national parks, it's also one of the least visited.

The Far North

Norway's northernmost counties of Troms and Finnmark arc across the very top of Europe
Here in this undervisited terrain, broad horizons share the land with dense forest. Part o
the thrill is simply the sheer effort of getting where few others go.

Tromsø, the area's only town of any size, well merits a couple of days to catch your breatl
before pushing deeper into the sparsely inhabited lands to the north and east. It's a sparky
animated, self-confident place whose museums will orient you for the Arctic lands beyond
It makes a great base for winter sports and summer hiking – or a diversion to the lovely
unspoilt island of Senja, every bit as dramatic as Lofoten and 10 times less crowded.

The goal of so many travellers is Nordkapp, North Cape, nearer to the North Pole than to
Oslo and the European mainland's most northerly point. Or very nearly so; to reach the *rea*
point of no return, pack your boots and enjoy an 18km round trek across the tundra. The
plateaus of Inner Finnmark and the wild northeastern coast are the Norwegian heartlanc
of the Sami people, whose territory, traditionally known as Lapland, straddles the frontier
with Sweden, Finland and Russia. Build in a stop at Karasjok, the Sami 'capital', to visit its
Sápmi Park, the more academic Sami National Museum and the architecturally stunning
all-wood Sami Parliament.

Tiny Kirkenes is the last port of call of the Hurtigruten coastal ferry. With all the feel of a
frontier town, its signs are in both Norwegian and Cyrillic script and you'll hear almost as
much Russian as Norwegian on the streets. Within Norway, you can go no further…

HIGHLIGHTS

- Reaching dramatic **Nordkapp** (p350) after the long haul northwards, then leaving the crowds behind to hike to **Knivskjelodden** (p352), continental Europe's northernmost point
- Learning about the unique Sami culture in **Karasjok** (p367) and **Kautokeino** (p365)
- Exploring **Alta's Stone-Age rock carvings** (p344), a Unesco World Heritage site, and learning more at its award-winning museum
- Dog-mushing through the snow and bruise-blue winter light near **Karasjok** (p369)
- Cycling the spectacular, lightly trafficked northern coast of the island of **Senja** (p342)
- Listening to an organ recital as the midnight sun peeks through the windows of Tromsø's **Arctic Cathedral** (p335)

- POPULATION: 226,800
- HIGHEST ELEVATION: NJUNES (1713M)

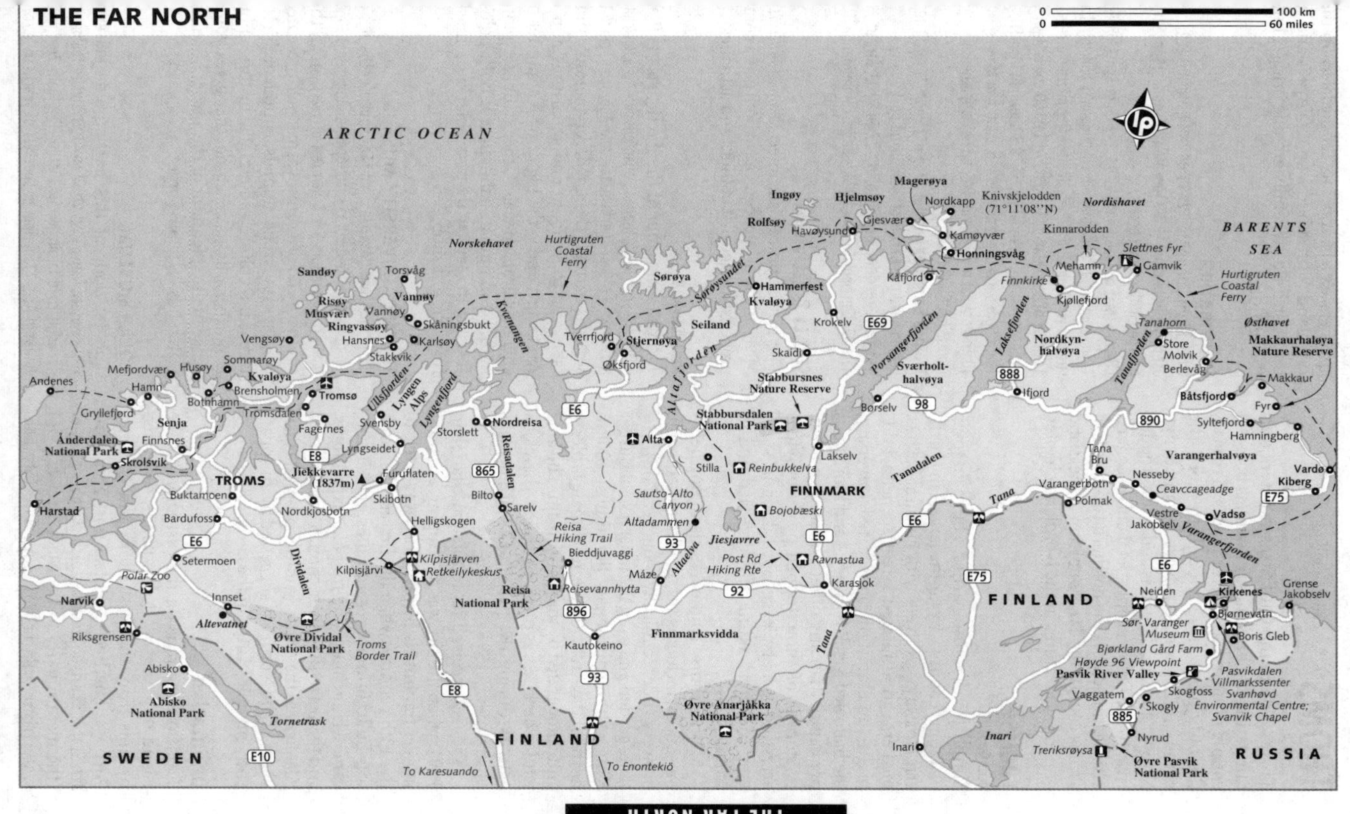
THE FAR NORTH
0 100 km
0 60 miles
ARCTIC OCEAN
BARENTS SEA
Nordishavet
Norskehavet
Østhavet
Hurtigruten Coastal Ferry
Hurtigruten Coastal Ferry
Magerøya
Nordkapp
Knivskjelodden (71°11'08''N)
Ingøy
Hjelmsøy
Rolfsøy
Gjesvær
Havøysund
Kamøyvær
Honningsvåg
Kinnarodden
Slettnes Fyr
Gamvik
Mehamn
Finnkirke
Kjøllefjord
Kåfjord
Sørøya
Sørøysundet
Hammerfest
Kvaløya
Krokelv
Seiland
Sandøy
Torsvåg
Vannøy
Risøy
Musvær
Vannøy
Skåningsbukt
Ringvassøy
Hansnes
Karlsøy
Stakkvik
Vengsøy
Sommarøy
Mefjordvær
Husøy
Kvaløya
Brensholmen
Andenes
Hamn
Botnhamn
Tromsø
Gryllefjord
Senja
Tromsdalen
Fagernes
Ullsfjorden
Lyngen Alps
Lyngenfjord
Svensby
Kvænangen
Tverrfjord
Stjernøya
Øksfjord
Altafjorden
Skaidi
Stabbursnes Nature Reserve
Stabbursdalen National Park
Porsangerfjorden
Sværholthalvøya
Børselv
Laksefjorden
Nordkynhalvøya
Ifjord
Tanahorn
Tanafjorden
Store Molvik
Berlevåg
Makkaurhaløya Nature Reserve
Makkaur
Båtsfjord
Fyr
Syltefjord
Hamningberg
Varangerhalvøya
Vardø
Kiberg
Ånderdalen National Park
Finnsnes
Skrolsvik
Harstad
TROMS
Buktamoen
Bardufoss
Lyngseidet
Jiekkevarre (1837m)
Furuflaten
Skibotn
Nordkjosbotn
Storslett
Nordreisa
Reisadalen
Alta
Stilla
Reinbukkelva
Lakselv
Tanadalen
Tana Bru
Nesseby
Ceavccageadge
Varangerbotn
Polmak
Vestre Jakobselv
Vadsø
Varangerfjorden
FINNMARK
Tana
Bilto
Sarelv
Sautso-Alto Canyon
Altadammen
Bojobæski
Helligskogen
Reisa Hiking Trail
Bieddjuvaggi
Jiesjavrre
Post Rd Hiking Rte
Ravnastua
Karasjok
Setermoen
Dividalen
Kilpisjärven Retkeilykeskus
Kilpisjärvi
Máze
Altaelva
Reisa National Park
Reisevannhytta
Polar Zoo
Narvik
Innset
Altevatnet
Øvre Dividal National Park
Troms Border Trail
Riksgrensen
Abisko
Abisko National Park
Tornetrask
Kautokeino
Finnmarksvidda
Tana
FINLAND
Neiden
Kirkenes
Grense Jakobselv
Bjørnevatn
Sør-Varanger Museum
Boris Gleb
Bjørkland Gård Farm
Høyde 96 Viewpoint
Pasvik River Valley
Pasvikdalen Villmarkssenter
Svanhøvd Environmental Centre; Svanvik Chapel
Skogfoss
Vaggatem
Skogly
Nyrud
Inari
Inari
Treriksrøysa
Øvre Pasvik National Park
Øvre Anarjåkka National Park
FINLAND
SWEDEN
RUSSIA
To Karesuando
To Enontekiö
E6
E8
E10
E69
E75
E75
92
93
93
98
865
885
888
890
896
THE FAR NORTH

TROMS

Troms, where the Gulf Stream peters out, mitigating the harshness of winter, boasts a couple of near-superlative places: Tromsø, the only place large enough to merit the name 'city' in northern Norway, and Senja, Norway's second-largest island, a less trodden rival to the Lofotens for spectacular scenery. This section covers the northern two-thirds of Troms county; the Troms portion of the island of Hinnøya features in the Nordland chapter.

TROMSØ

pop 65,000

Simply put, Tromsø parties. The main town of Troms county – by far the largest in northern Norway – is lively with cultural bashes, buskers, an animated street scene, a midnight-sun marathon, a respected university, the hallowed Mack Brewery – and more pubs per capita than any other Norwegian town. Its corona of snow-topped peaks provides arresting scenery, excellent hiking in summer and great skiing and dog-sledding in winter.

Many Tromsø landmarks claim northernmost titles, including the university, cathedral, brewery (not technically – but read on), botanic garden and even the most boreal Burger King. Although the city lies almost 400km north of the Arctic Circle, its climate is pleasantly moderated by the Gulf Stream. The long winter darkness is offset by round-the-clock activity during the perpetually bright days of summer.

Tromsø received its municipal charter in 1794, when the city was developing as a trading centre, but its history goes way back to the 13th century, when the first local church was built. In more recent times, the city became a launching point for polar expeditions, and thanks to that distinction, it's nicknamed 'Gateway to the Arctic' (more appropriate than 'Paris of the North', as suggested by an apparently myopic visitor in the early 1900s).

Orientation

Tromsø's centre is on the east shore of the island of Tromsøya (Map p335), separated by hills from the west shore and Langnes Airport. The lively, central port area runs from the Skansen docks, south past Stortorget (the main square) to the Mack Brewery and waterfront Polaria museum. The city also spills across a channel to Tromsdalen on the mainland, with suburbs on Kvaløya island to the west. Two gracefully arching bridges link the sections.

Information

Dark Light (Map p336; ☎ 77 68 74 44; Stortorget 1, 1st fl; per hr Nkr60; ⏰ 3-11pm Mon-Fri, noon-11pm Sat, 6-11pm Sun) Internet access.

Library (Map p336; Grønnegata 94; ⏰ 11am-5pm Mon-Fri, 11am-3pm Sat) In a magnificent contemporary building that streams with light and airiness, it offers free internet access.

Tourist office (Map p336; ☎ 77 61 00 00; www.destinasjontromso.no; Kirkegata 2; ⏰ 8.30am-6pm Mon-Fri, 10am-5pm Sat & Sun late May-Aug; 9am-4pm Mon-Fri, 10am-2pm Sat rest-of-year) Pick up its comprehensive *Tromsø InfoGuide* booklet.

Tromsø Bruktbokhandel (Map p336; ☎ 77 68 39 40; behind Kirkegata 6) Lots of secondhand books.

Via Ferieverden (Map p336; ☎ 77 64 80 02; Strandgata 32) Can book Svalbard flights and accommodation.

Sights & Activities

The tourist office's summer *Tromsø Activity Menu* and its winter equivalent both give a comprehensive checklist of tours and activities.

POLARIA

Tromsø's museum of the Arctic, **Polaria** (Map p336; ☎ 77 75 01 00; Hjalmar Johansens gate 12; adult/child Nkr90/45; ⏰ 10am-7pm mid-May–mid-Aug, noon-5pm rest-of-year) is daringly designed. A panoramic film takes you to Svalbard and aquariums house Arctic fish and – the big draw – a quintet of energetic bearded seals. Other exhibits explore nature and human habitation at both poles. Just try to leave without a polar-bear mask from the gift shop.

TROMSØ UNIVERSITY MUSEUM

This **museum** (Map p335; ☎ 77 64 50 00; Lars Thøringsvei 10; adult/child Nkr40/20; ⏰ 9am-6pm Jun-Aug; 9am-3.30pm Mon-Fri, 11am-5pm Sat & Sun rest-of-year), near the southern end of Tromsøya, has well-presented displays on Arctic animals, church architecture, Sami culture and regional history – plus a 'northern lights machine' that gives you a sense of the splendour of the aurora borealis. Catch bus 28 from Torget.

POLAR MUSEUM

The 1st floor of this harbourside **museum** (Polarmuseet; Map p336; ☎ 77 68 43 73; Søndre Tollbugata 11; adult/child/family Nkr50/10/100; ⏰ 10am-7pm mid-Jun–mid-Aug, 11am-3pm or 5pm rest-of-year), in a restored early 19th-century customs house near the colourful Skansen docks, illustrates early polar research, especially the ventures of Nansen and Amundsen. Downstairs there's a well-mounted exhibition about the hunting and trapping of fuzzy Arctic creatures on Svalbard before coal became king there. Note the nasty exploding harpoons outside; the whale didn't stand much of a chance.

CABLE CAR

You get a fine view of the city and midnight sun by taking the **Storsteinen Fjellheis** (Map p335; ☎ 77 63 87 37; adult/child/family return Nkr85/40/200; 🕑 10am-1am late May–mid-Aug, 10am-5pm Apr-late May & mid-Aug–Sep), 420m up Mt Storsteinen (421m). There's a restaurant at the top, from where a network of hiking routes radiates. Take bus 26. A combination bus/cable car ticket costs Nkr90/45 per adult/child.

MACK BREWERY

OK, this **brewery** (Mack Ølbryggeri; Map p336; ☎ 77 62 45 80; Storgata 5) isn't really the world's northernmost – a microbrewery in Honningsvåg (p353) takes that title – but it's still a venerable institution that merits a pilgrimage. Established in 1877, it nowadays produces 18 kinds of beer, including the very quaffable Macks Pilsner, Isbjørn, Haakon and several dark beers. At 1pm year-round – plus 3pm, June to August – tours (Nkr130, including a beer mug, pin and pint) leave from the brewery's own Ølhallen Pub (p339), Monday to Thursday.

GLASS-BLOWING

Blåst (Map p336; ☎ 77 68 34 60; Peder Hansens Gate 4; admission free). Pass by the world's most northerly glass-blowing workshop to see the young team puffing their cheeks and perhaps to pick up an item or two.

CHURCHES

The 11 arching triangles of the **Arctic Cathedral** (Ishavskatedralen; Map p335; ☎ 77 64 76 11; Hans Nilsensvei 41; adult/child Nkr25/free; 🕑 9am-7pm Mon-Sat, 1-7pm Sun Jun–mid-Aug), as the Tromsdalen Church is styled, suggest glacial crevasses and auroral curtains. The magnificent glowing stained-glass window that occupies almost the whole of the east end depicts Christ redescending to earth. Look back toward the west end and the contemporary organ, a work of steely art

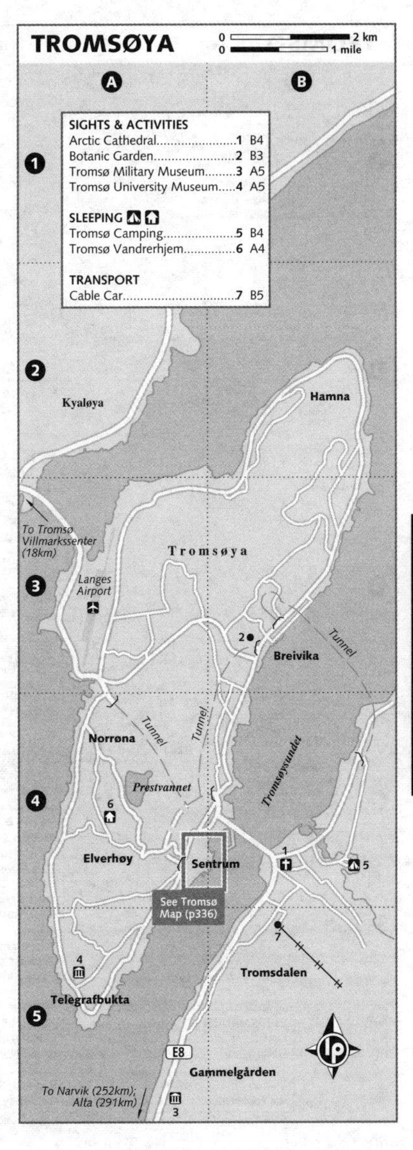

in itself, then up high to take in the lamps of Czech crystal, hanging in space like icicles.

The Church of Norway's **Tromsø Cathedral** (Domkirke; Map p336; Storgata 25; 🕑 noon-4pm Tue-Sat) is one of Norway's largest wooden churches. Its opening hours are erratic. Up the hill is the town's **Catholic Church** (Map p336; Storgata 94;

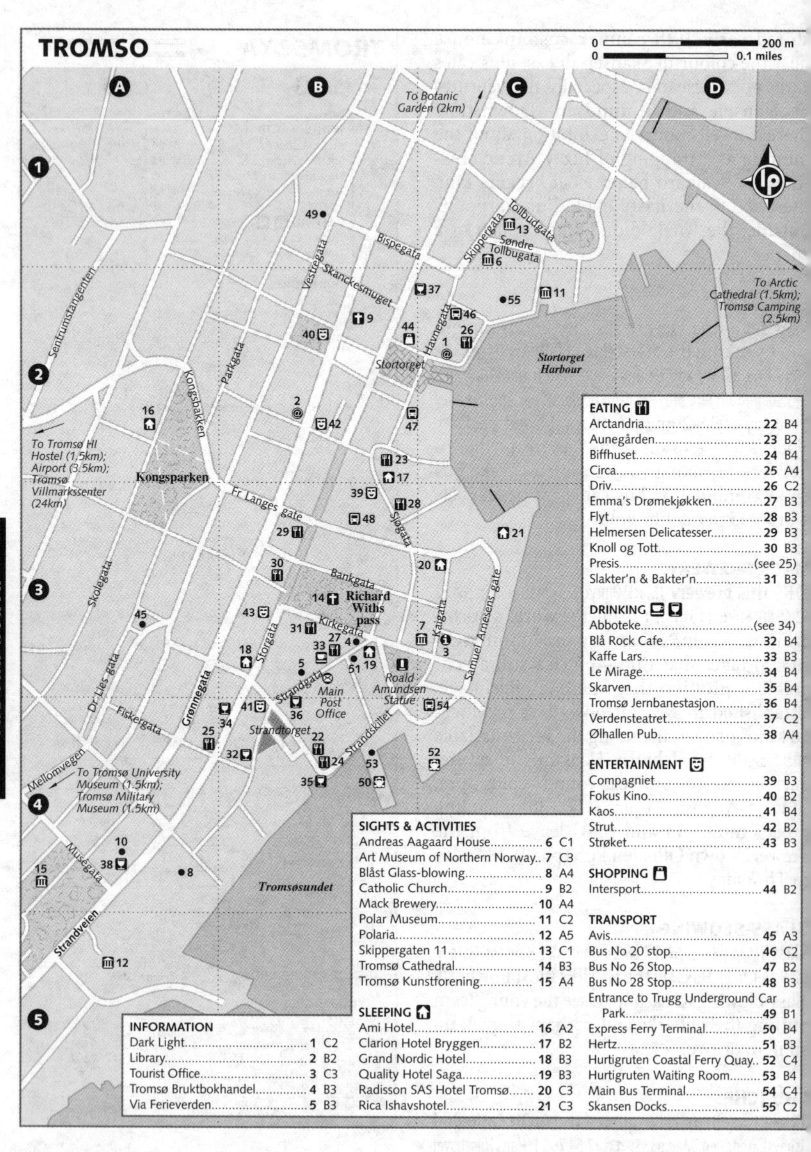

9am-7.30pm). Both were built in 1861 and each lays claim to be – here comes yet another superlative – 'the world's northernmost bishopric' of its sect.

HISTORIC BUILDINGS

The booklet *Town Walks*, on sale at the tourist office (Nkr50), is a well-illustrated, exhaustive run-down of Tromsø's historic buildings.

You'll find lots of early-19th-century timber buildings around the centre. **Andreas Aagaard House** (Map p336; Søndre Tollbugate 1), constructed in 1838, was the first building in town to be electrically lit. Explore too the stretch of 1830s shops and merchants' homes along Sjøgata.

ART MUSEUM OF NORTHERN NORWAY

The **Nordnorsk Kunstmuseum** (Map p336; ☎ 77 64 0 20; Sjøgata 1; adult/child/family Nkr30/20/70; ⏰ core rs noon-5pm Tue-Sun) exhibits mainly 19th- to 21st-century sculpture, photography, painting and handicrafts by artists from northern Norway, and runs an active programme of emporary exhibitions.

TROMSØ KUNSTFORENING

The Tromsø branch of this national conemporary **art foundation** (Map p336; ☎ 77 65 58 7; Muségata 2; adult/child Nkr30/free; ⏰ noon-5pm Tue-un) makes the most of its late-19th-century premises and promotes rotating exhibitions of contemporary art.

TROMSØ MILITARY MUSEUM

The southern end of Tromsø's mainland was irst developed by the Nazis in 1940 as a coastal artillery battery, complete with six big guns. The cannons have been restored as the basis of he **Tromsø Forsvarsmuseum** (Map p335; ☎ 77 62 88 36; olstrandveien; adult/child Nkr40/20; ⏰ noon-5pm Wed-Sun un-Aug, Sun only May & Sep), which also includes a estored commando bunker and an exhibiion on the giant German battleship *Tirpitz,* unk at Tromsø on 12 November 1944. Take bus 12 or 28.

BOTANIC GARDENS

Within the Arctic and alpine landscapes of Tromsø's **Botanisk Hage** (Map p335; ☎ 77 64 50 00; reivika; admission free; ⏰ 24hr) grows flora from all over the world's colder regions. And yes, t's the world's northernmost…Take bus 20.

WINTER ACTIVITIES

Several companies offer trips out of town to prime northern lights observing sites. You can book lessons in both cross-country (around own are some 70km of groomed trails) and downhill skiing (including that very Norwegian variant, Telemark) at the tourst office. **Intersport** (Map p336; Storgata 87) rents ski equipment.

Tromso Villmarkssenter (☎ 77 69 60 02; www villmarkssenter.no) offers dog-sled excursions, ranging from a one-day spin (Nkr1220) o a four-day trek with overnight camping Nkr8000). The centre, 24km south of town on Kvaløya island, also offers a range of summer activities such as trekking and sea-kayaking.

Natur i Nord (☎ 77 66 73 66; Nansenveien 34) puts on snowmobile trips (five hours, Nkr1400), ice fishing (four hours, Nkr1200), cross-country ski tours (four to eight hours, from Nkr750) and snowshoe treks (three hours, Nkr750).

Tours

The *Cetacea* does a two-hour scenic **cruise** (adult/child Nkr450/200; ⏰ noon Mon-Thu mid-Jun–mid-Aug) around Tromsø island, sailing at noon.

You can fish from the *Signe I,* then have your catch sizzled on board. Built in 1908, she sails on three-hour evening **fishing trips** (adult/child Nkr350/200; ⏰ 6pm Mon-Sat late Jun–mid-Aug).

For both outings, reserve at the tourist office.

Festivals & Events

The classic **Midnight Sun Marathon** (☎ 77 67 33 63; www.msm.no), held on a Saturday in June, has something for all levels of fitness. In addition to the full-monty 42km marathon, there's also a half-marathon and a children's race.

However, Tromsø's two big annual bashes both take place in deepest winter. The **Northern Lights Festival** (www.nordlysfestivalen.no) is six days of music of all genres, held in late January. It's followed closely in early February by **Sami Week**, which includes the national reindeer sledge championship, where Sami teams whoop and crack the whip along the main street.

MUSICAL RECITALS

In July and August the Arctic Cathedral has nightly organ recitals (Nkr50) at 7.30pm and musical concerts (Nkr80) at 11.30pm. The swelling organ and the light of the midnight sun streaming through the huge west window can be one of the great sensory moments of your trip.

At 5.30pm in July, the Church of Norway cathedral has daily concerts (Nkr80) of classical music and both Norwegian and Sami folk tunes.

Sleeping

Atypically, Tromsø's peak tourist time is June, when the university's still in full throe and when reservations are essential. For a fee of Nkr30, the tourist office can book accommodation (including rooms in private homes, where singles/doubles average around Nkr350/500) for callers-in.

Tromsø Camping (Map p335; ☎ 77 63 80 37; www.tromsocamping.no; Tromsdalen; car/caravan sites Nkr175/220,

2-bed cabin with outside bathroom Nkr450, 4-bed Nkr550-650, 4-/6-bed with bathroom Nkr950;) Tent campers enjoy leafy green camp sites beside a slow-moving stream. However, bathroom and cooking facilities at this veritable village of cabins are stretched to the limit. There's internet access (per 30 minutes Nkr20) and bike rental (a bargain Nkr50 per day). Take bus 20 or 24.

Tromsø Vandrerhjem (Map p335; 77 65 76 28; tromso.hostel@vandrerhjem.no; Åsgårdveien 9; dm/s/d Nkr150/290/380; mid-Jun–mid-Aug) This summertime HI-affiliated hostel occupies university-student residences 1.5km west of the town centre. It accepts only Norwegian credit cards and signing from town is inadequate. To get there, go west along Fredrik Langes gate and up Kirkegårdsveien, turning into Holtveien where Kirkegårdsveien turns abruptly right, then turn right down Asgårdveien. There are lovely views from most bedrooms, though, and good self-catering kitchens. Bus 26 runs within 100m.

Ami Hotel (Map p336; 77 62 10 00; www.amihotel.no; Skolegata 24; s/d without bathroom Nkr495/595, with bathroom Nkr595/695, all incl breakfast; P) Beside a traffic-free road and park, this is a quiet, friendly, family-owned choice. There's a well-equipped kitchen for self-caterers and a couple of communal lounges, each with TV, internet access and free tea and coffee (nibble on something more substantial and simply pop Nkr20 in the honesty box).

Clarion Hotel Bryggen (Map p336; 77 78 11 00; www.choice.no; Sjøgata 19/21; s/d Nkr795/995 mid-Jun–mid-Aug, Nkr1400/1500 Sun-Thu, Nkr1200/1300 Fri & Sat rest-of-year, all incl breakfast; P) This stylish 121-room waterside hotel, poking towards the sea like the prow of a ship, is architecturally stunning with its odd angles, aluminium trim, images on bedroom ceilings, sauna – and a top-floor Jacuzzi where you can savour the picturesque harbour and mountain views as you bubble and boil in the hot tub.

Grand Nordic Hotel (Map p336; 77 75 37 77; www.nordic.no in Norwegian; Storgata 44; s/d Nkr845/995 mid-Jun–mid-Aug, Nkr1400/1500 rest-of-year; P) The Grand Nordic is Tromsø's oldest hotel. There's little that's antique inside, however, since the place has twice burnt to the ground. Both bedrooms and public areas have been recently renovated. Rates include a particularly ample breakfast with fresh fruit and hot dishes.

Quality Hotel Saga (Map p336; 77 60 70 00; www.sagahotel.no/international; Richard Withs plass 2; s/d Nkr885/1095 mid-Jun–mid-Aug; Nkr1475/1675 Sun-Thu Nkr885/1095 Fri & Sat rest-of-year; P) This comfortable option offers free afternoon waffle and 67 modern rooms, each with tea- and coffee-making facilities plus – when did you last come across this particular feature? – a trouser press.

Radisson SAS Hotel Tromsø (Map p336; 77 6 00 00; www.radissonsas.com; Sjøgata 7; s/d Nkr806/103 mid-Jun–mid-Aug, Nkr1200/1650 Sun-Thu, Nkr1000/1200 Fr & Sat rest-of-year; P) What a change since our last visit! Bedrooms have been comprehensively renovated and onto the solid, dul rectangular block of the original building ha been grafted an attractive new wing. Of its 26 rooms (it's worth the Nkr100 extra for one in the new wing), around half have harbou views and eight are handicapped-equipped Reception, with two staff and two desks to receive arrivals, is swift, smart and friendly It runs a decent pub, the Rorbua, and a fine Arctic Menu restaurant, the Aurora (open 3pm to 10pm).

our pick **Rica Ishavshotel** (Map p336; 77 66 6 00; www.rica.no; Fredrik Langes gate 2; s/d Nkr900/1150 mid Jun–mid-Aug, Nkr1740/2015 Sun-Thu, Nkr1030/1230 Fri & Sa rest-of-year;) Occupying a prime quayside position with fishing boats and freighters almos at arm's length, this hotel is immediately recognisable by its tall spire resembling a ship's mast. It sometimes swallows as many as seven tour groups per day so summer reservation are essential. Of its 180 attractive rooms, 74 including many singles, have superb view of the sound.

Eating

In Tromsø, the line is blurry between restaurants, cafés and pubs and many places function in all three modes, simultaneously or a different times of the day.

Helmersen Delikatesser (Map p336; 77 65 40 50 Storgata 66) This great little delicatessen carries a good range of cheeses, cold meats and salady items to fill your sandwich.

Slakter'n & Baker'n (Map p336; 77 61 06 65 Kirkegata 12) Long established 'Butcher & Baker is the place to stock up on your picnic fare To the left, meat balls, cold cuts, hanks o sausages, salads and dips. To the right, richly scented breads and tempting pastries.

Knoll og Tott (Map p336; 77 66 68 80; Storgata 62; 10am-6pm Mon-Fri, 10am-4pm Sat) Run by a cheerful young team, this popular upstairs downstairs place with its fresh salads, crisp aguettes and house pies is ideal for a filling nidday snack.

Driv (Map p336; ☎ 77 60 07 76; Tollbugata 3; mains kr85-120; 11am-7pm mid-Jun–mid-Sep, 2pm-2am rest f year) This student-run converted warehouse erves meaty burgers, great salads (Nkr95), ocaccias with a variety of fillings (Nkr85) nd a vegetarian pasta (Nkr95). It organ-ses musical and cultural events (notably the elf-styled Fucking North Pole Festival) and ometimes has a disco. In winter you can teep yourself in good company within its pen-air hot tub.

Flyt (Map p336; ☎ 77 69 68 00; Sjøgata 25; mains Nkr120-65) Build your own burger at this friendly estaurant and bar, picking the size of your neat, fish or veggie filling and selecting its xtras and trimmings. With an outdoor activi-ies theme, its beer's ice-cold and the music's eavy metal and rock. The intimate upstairs ocktail bar fills to capacity after midnight on ridays and Saturdays.

Brasseriet (Map p336; ☎ 77 66 64 00; mains Nkr190-280) lica Ishavshotel's excellent restaurant serves reative dishes, such as reindeer with puréed arrot and blueberry sauce (Nkr280).

our pick **Aunegården** (Map p336; ☎ 77 65 12 34; øgata 29; mains Nkr120-150, cakes around Nkr65; Mon-at) You can almost lose yourself in this won-erful café-cum-restaurant that's all intimate rannies and cubby holes. In a 19th-century uilding that functioned as a butcher's shop ntil 1996, it's rich in character and serves xcellent salads (from Nkr117), sandwiches from Nkr75) and mains. If you don't fancy full meal, drop by just to enjoy a coffee nd one of its melt-in-the-mouth cakes.

Circa (Map p336; ☎ 77 68 10 20; Storgata 36; mains kr174-194) Circa (Approximately) and its up-tairs neighbour Presis (Precisely), under the ame ownership, complement each other. Circa, downstairs, cavernous, both bar and ight-meal venue, has free wi-fi. It serves asty pastas, salads and sandwiches (Nkr90 to Nkr100) until 4pm. Thereafter, its cool jazz nd electronic music attracts a 25- to 35-ear-old crowd. There's occasional live music lus, at weekends, a live DJ. Wednesday, vine night, is normally packed.

Presis (Map p336; ☎ 77 68 10 20; Storgata 36; tapas kr70-90; kitchen core hrs 6-11pm Tue-Sat, bar until very te Tue-Sat) Step upstairs, above Circa, to snack n Presis' great range of Nordic-style tapas. The air's calmer here, in a more rarefied at-nosphere, furnishings are hip and original, and frequently changing artwork decorates the walls.

Kaffe Lars (Map p336; ☎ 77 63 77 30; Kirkegata 8; Mon-Sat) This cosy café is another example of Tromsø flexibility: it serves great coffee and mouthwatering pastries by day, then metamorphoses into an intimate pub on the dot of 6pm.

Emma's Drømekjøkken (Map p336; ☎ 77 63 77 30; Kirkegata 8; mains Nkr270-325; 6-10pm Mon-Sat) Upstairs from Kaffe Lars, this stylish and highly regarded place pulls in discriminating diners with its imaginative cuisine. Advance booking is essential.

There's one common entrance to Arctandria, Biffhuset and the much more pubby-style Skarven (p340).

Arctandria (Map p336; ☎ 77 60 07 25; Strandtorget 1; mains Nkr205-260, menus Nkr395-460; from 4pm Mon-Sat) Upstairs and upscale, Arctandria serves filling and supremely fresh ocean catches, includ-ing a sample starter of whale steak and seal (Nkr85). Save a cranny for its crême brulée with cloudberries dessert.

Biffhuset (Map p336; ☎ 77 60 07 28; Strandtorget 1; mains Nkr175-330; from 3.30pm) On two floors, wood-panelled and low-beamed, the Beef House is a seriously meaty place, strictly for ardent carnivores. Just tick/check your menu card, indicating size, cut and accom-panying sauce, hand it to the server and sit back.

You can buy fresh boiled shrimp from fish-ing boats at the Stortorget waterfront.

Drinking

At Mack Brewery's **Ølhallen Pub** (Map p336; 9am-5pm Mon-Thu, 9am-6pm Fri, 9am-3pm Sat) you can sample its fine ales right where they're brewed. Perhaps the world's only, never mind most northerly, watering hole to be closed in the evening, it carries eight varieties on draught.

Blå Rock Café (Map p336; ☎ 77 61 00 20; Strandgata 14/16; core hrs 11.30am-2am) The loudest, most raving place in town has theme evenings, over 50 brands of beer, occasional live bands and weekend DJs. The music's rock, naturally.

Le Mirage (Map p336; ☎ 77 68 52 34; Storgata 42; core hrs noon-1.30am) A less rowdy crowd, many of them seasoned regulars, gather at Le Mirage, with its deep leather armchairs and a gilded cherub gazing benignly down. It also serves reasonably priced sandwiches, salads, pastas and casseroles.

HARD DRINKING, TROMSØ STYLE

It takes stamina to stay the course. With work over, friends will meet for *Fredagpils;* Friday drinks to plan the campaign ahead. Then it's time for *Vorspiel,* or foreplay, a preliminary oiling at a friend's house before setting off around midnight for a club or bar. At the statutory throwing-out time of 3.30am, it's *Fyllemat,* fill-up time, when you pick up a burger, kebab or hot dog from one of the street stalls that lurk outside major venues before heading once more to a friend's pad for a few hours' *Nachspiel,* or afterplay.

By now it's bed for middle-distance runners while the marathon crowd stamp its feet outside Ølhallen's, waiting for the sliding of bolts that marks its 9am opening. 'If you can stand, we'll serve you', is the bar staff's rule of thumb.

Abboteke (Map p336; ☎ 77 68 21 50; Storgata 42; 8pm-3am Wed & Thu, 6pm-3am Fri & Sat) At this retro cocktail bar (the music's bebop, big band or bland Ray Connif), upstairs from Le Mirage, the barman shakes a selection of award-winning cocktails. Behind him shimmer over 40 brands of single malt whisky and an equally impressive range of rums and brandies. There's also a reputable restaurant open for dinner Monday to Saturday.

Skarven (Map p336; ☎ 77 60 07 43; Strandtorget 1; from 6pm Tue-Sat) Companion to Arctandria and Biffhuset, Skarven has an extensive waterfront terrace and offers fine bar meals and well-priced fish dishes – unsurprisingly since it includes selections from these two choice restaurants.

Tromsø Jernbanestasjon (Map p336; ☎ 77 61 23 48; Strandgata 33; core hrs 3pm-2am) This engaging railway-themed pub is typical local humour – Tromsø has never, ever had a railway station.

Verdensteatret (Map p336; ☎ 77 75 30 90; Storgata 93b) Norway's oldest film house will satisfy both cinephiles and thirsters after great cafés. The bar is a hip place with free wi-fi, occasional live music and weekend DJs. At other times, the barperson spins from its huge collection of vinyl records, so expect anything from classical to deepest underground. Peek into the magnificent cinema, its walls painted roof to ceiling with early 20th-century murals. It shows art house and independent films on an ad hoc basis.

Entertainment

Tromsø has plenty of thriving nightspots. On Friday and Saturday, most stay open until 3.30am and many also serve light meals.

Strut (Map p336; ☎ 77 68 46 00; Grønnegata 81; 10pm-3am Fri & Sat) This is a place of contrasts. Downstairs, with beers on draught and pool tables, is pubby while upstairs where 1970s and '80s disco music pounds, i decidedly retro.

Kaos (Map p336; ☎ 77 63 59 99; Strandgata 22; co hrs 8pm-2am Mon-Sat, 3-11pm Sun) A cool basemen hangout with low beams and bare brick walls Kaos engages arthouse and underground DJ (Friday and Saturday) and bands (up to thre times weekly). Carrying UK and Norwegia football, it also has a faithful following c armchair sporting regulars. Capacity is 9(squeezed close, so show up early for big game and band nights.

Compagniet (Map p336; ☎ 77 66 42 22; Sjøgata 1. 9pm-3.30am Fri & Sat) Both a bar and nightclub this is another lively weekend venue.

Strøket (Map p336; ☎ 77 68 44 00; Storgata 5. 9pm-2am Wed, 9pm-3.30am Fri & Sat) This plac attracts a young, post-acne crowd and get down and dirty on weekend nights. Climb t the top of its three levels to watch the masse writhing below.

Fokus Kino (Map p336; ☎ 77 75 63 00; Grønnega 94) Tromsø's new six-screen cinema share premises with the town hall.

Getting There & Away

AIR

Destinations with direct SAS flights to/fror Tromsø's **Langnes Airport** (Map p335; ☎ 77 64 8 00), the main airport for the far north, in clude Oslo, Bergen, Narvik/Harstad, Bodø Trondheim, Alta, Hammerfest, Kirkene and Longyearbyen.

Norwegian (www.norwegian.no) flies to and fror London (Stansted) and Oslo.

BOAT

Express boats connect Tromsø and Harsta (2¾ hours), via Finnsnes (1¼ hours), two t four times daily. Tromsø is also a major sto on the Hurtigruten coastal ferry route.

BUS
The main bus terminal (sometimes called Prostneset) is located on Kaigata. Nor-Way Bussekspress has at least two daily express buses to/from Narvik (Nkr360, 4¼ hours) and at least one to/from Alta (Nkr469, 6¼ hours), where you can pick up a bus for Honningsvåg, and from there, on to the Nordkapp.

CAR & MOTORCYCLE
A two- or four-wheeled vehicle is the best way to negotiate Norway's far-northern reaches. Among car-hire companies are **Avis** (Map p336; ☎ 90 74 90 00; Strandskillet 5), **Europcar** (☎ 77 67 56 ·0; Alkeveien 5), **Hertz** (Map p336; ☎ 77 62 44 00; Richard Withs plass 4) and **Budget** (☎ 77 65 19 00). All have desks at the airport. Contrasting with steep rates in summer (when it's essential to reserve in advance), car rental can be very reasonable in winter.

Getting Around
TO/FROM THE AIRPORT
Tromsø's airport is about 5km from the centre, on the western side of Tromsøya island. The **Flybuss** (☎ 77 67 75 00; Nkr45) service runs between the airport and Radisson SAS Hotel, connecting with arriving and departing flights and stopping by other major hotels along the way. Alternatively, take city bus 40 or 42 (Nkr23); when you arrive, wait for it on the road opposite the airport entrance.

Metered taxis between the airport and centre cost around Nkr125.

BICYCLE
You can hire town bikes from **Intersport** (Map p336; ☎ 77 66 11 00; Storgata 87; per day/weekend/week Nkr175/400/1000).

CAR & MOTORCYCLE
Tromsø has ample paying parking in the centre. There's also the huge Trygg underground car park tunnelled into the hill, its entrance on Vestregata (closed to trailers and caravans).

PUBLIC TRANSPORT
Local buses cost Nkr23 per ride – purchase your ticket on board. For a **taxi**, call ☎ 77 ·0 30 00.

AROUND TROMSØ
Sommarøy & Kvaløya
From Tromsø, this half-day trip is more for the drive than the destination. It's an extraordinarily pretty, lightly trafficked run across Kvaløya, much of it down at wet-your-feet shore level as far as the small island of Sommarøy. Here you can grab a drink or a snack and even overnight at **Sommarøy Kurs & Feriesenter** (☎ 77 66 40 00; www.sommaroy.no; s/d Nkr875/1095 mid-Jun–mid-Aug, Nkr1215/1465 Sun-Thu, Nkr1090/1340 Fri & Sat rest-of-year, 6-8-person cabins Nkr1490-1800; P 🖳) with its restaurant, bar, small children's playground, hot tub and sauna.

If you're arriving from Senja (p342) by the **Botnhamn–Brensholmen ferry** (www.senjafergene.no), the vistas as you cross Kvaløya island, heading westwards for Tromsø, are equally stunning.

Karlsøy
pop 2350

After WWII, the population of this historic fishing community declined drastically until by 1970 there remained only 45 mostly elderly people. Then an emergent counterculture recognised the appeal of this remote island. Over the next decade, young people from elsewhere in Norway and abroad moved to the island to create a sort of Arctic utopia, complete with communes, 'flower power' and an artists' colony. New farmland was cultivated and a fresh economy emerged, based on the arts, tourism and the production of goats' milk. For the full story on Karlsøy, see the booklet *Among Church Cottages & Goats in Alfred Eriksen's Kingdom* (Nkr60), available at the tourist office in Tromsø.

While you're in the area, you may also want to visit nearby Vannøy island, with its sandy beaches, classic lighthouse and wild coastline. You can reach the port of Skåningsbukt by car ferry daily from Hansnes and several times weekly from Karlsøy.

Lyngen Alps
Some of the most rugged alpine peaks in all Norway ruck up to form the spine of the heavily glaciated Lyngen Peninsula, east of Tromsø; you get the best views of them from the eastern shore of 150km-long Lyngenfjord. The peaks, the highest of which is Jiekkevarre (1833m), offer plenty of opportunities for climbers but this challenging glacial terrain is strictly for the experienced.

The Lyngsdalen Valley, above the industrial village of Furuflaten, is an altogether more accessible and popular hiking area. The usual route begins at the football pitch south of the bridge over the Lyngdalselva and climbs up the valley to the tip of the glacier Sydbreen, 500m above sea level.

The best map for hiking is Statens Kartverk's *Lyngenhalvøya* at 1:50,000.

SENJA

pop 16,500

Senja, Norway's second-largest island, rivals Lofoten for natural beauty yet attracts a fraction of its visitors (we meandered the length of its northern coastline and saw only one non-Norwegian vehicle).

A broad agricultural plain laps at Innersida, the island's eastern coast facing the mainland. By contrast, birchwoods, moorland and sweetwater lakes extend beneath the bare craggy uplands of the interior. Along the northwestern coast, Yttersida, knife-ridged peaks rise directly from the Arctic Ocean. Here, the Rv86 and Rv862, declared a National Tourist Route, link isolated, still-active fishing villages such as Hamn and Mefjordvær and traffic is minimal. The now flat, now mildly bucking road, almost always within sight of the shore, is a cyclist's dream. On the way, pause at the Tunganeset viewing point and scramble over the broad slabs of weathered rock to savour the spiky peaks to the west and, eastwards, more gently sculpted summits.

The helpful **tourist office** (☎ 77 85 07 30; www.visittroms.no; Storgata 17; 9am-5pm Mon-Fri, 10am-3pm Sat Jun-Aug, 9am-4pm Mon-Fri rest-of-year) in Finnsnes, on the mainland just across the bridge for Senja, has plenty of information and sells *Opplev Midt Troms* (Nkr20), an invaluable map of the island and its environs.

Sleeping

Hamn i Senja (☎ 77 85 98 80) A restored fishing hamlet, Hamn i Senja was until recently a delightful get-away-from-it-all place. Following an extensive and disastrous fire it promises to be so again, once it's up and running in late 2008. Nearby is the small dam that held back the waters for what is claimed to be the world's first hydroelectric plant, established in 1882.

Getting There & Away

Two to three daily buses run from Finnsnes to Tromsø (2¾ hours) and Narvik (three hours) with a connection in Buktamoen.

Express ferries connect Finnsnes with Tromsø (1¼ hours) and Harstad (1½ hours) two to three times a day. A summertime ca ferry connects Skrolsvik, on Senja's south coast to Harstad (1½ hours, two to four daily).

With the completion of a final tunnel ir 2006, it's now possible to drive the whole o the northwest coast from Grylleford (linkec by car ferry with Andenes) to Botnhamn with its car ferry link to Brensholmen, wes of Tromsø.

Finnsnes is also a stop for the Hurtigruter coastal ferry.

BARDU

pop 3850

The rural district of Bardu is located soutl of Tromsø.

Setermoen

The wooded town of Setermoen is the com mercial centre for the Bardu district anc a staging point for visits to Øvre Divida National Park (opposite). Visitors to its **tour ist information point** (☎ 77 18 53 00; 8am-3pn Mon-Fri) in the town hall are greeted by a stuffec wolf with a dejected-looking lamb in its jaws The village is best known to Norwegians a a military training centre and venue fo NATO exercises.

In the porch of Setermoen's early-19th century **church** (10am-5pm Mon-Sat late Jun-earl Aug) is a bell dating from 1698. The ingen ious heating system, with wood stoves anc hot-water pipes beneath the pews, mus encourage attendance during even the longest sermons.

Those who are aroused by war game will have fun at the **Troms Defence Museun** (Forsvarsmuseum; ☎ 77 18 56 50; adult/child Nkr40/free 10am-6pm Tue-Fri, noon-4pm Sat & Sun mid-Jun–mid Aug, 10am-3pm Mon-Fri rest-of-year) with its evoca tive interior dioramas and over 20 militar vehicles to explore outside.

SLEEPING

Bardu Camping & Turistsenter (☎ 77 18 15 58, 91 3 60 90; tent/caravan sites Nkr100/175 plus per person Nkr1C 2-/3-/4-bed cabin with outdoor bathrooms Nkr300/450/55C with bathroom Nkr800-1000; Jun-Aug;) At the northern limit of Setermoen, dad can slope of for a little river fishing while the kids splasl in the pool and zoom down the waterslide o this well-tended camp site.

Bardu Hotell (☎ 77 18 59 40; barduhotell@bard.online.no; Toftakerlia 1; s/d Nkr800/950 mid-Jun–mid-Auç Nkr1050/1200 rest-of-year; P) The lobby vith pelts splayed across its walls, has a hunt-ng-lodge feel while rooms are decorated in variety of twee themes such as spring and ummer, Adam and Eve. With plenty of char-cter, it's popular with adventure tour groups nd visiting military, not least for the comfort-ble bar and its restaurant Trollstua. There's sauna, Jacuzzi and year-round heated pool, ll free to guests.

olar Zoo

The **Polar Zoo** (☎ 77 18 66 30; adult/child/family kr135/70/340; ⏲ 9am-6pm Jun-Aug, 9am-4pm May & Sep) eatures wildlife of the boreal taiga in spacious nclosures that, but for the metal fencing, re virtually indistinguishable from the sur-ounding birch forests. Here you can watch nd photograph those elusive faces that peer ut from postcards all over Norway: brown ears, deer, musk oxen, reindeer, wolves, ynx, wolverines, badgers and both red and olar fox. Follow the keeper around at feed-ng time (noon or 2pm; check at reception). The zoo is 23km south of Setermoen and .3km east of the E6, where the express bus etween Narvik and Tromsø passes three to our times daily.

VRE DIVIDAL NATIONAL PARK

Between Setermoen and the Swedish and Finnish borders lies the wild, roadless, lake-tudded Øvre Dividal National Park. While he park lacks the spectacular steep-walled cenery of coastal Norway, this remote, semi-orested, 750-sq-km upland wilderness still oasts plenty of challenging peaks and fine iews.

ctivities

The most popular hike is the eight-day **Troms order Trail**, linking seven unstaffed DNT huts. The route begins along the northern shore of he artificial lake, Altevatnet, about 3km east of the settlement of Innset, and twists north-astward, curling in and out of Sweden before winding up near the point where Sweden, Finland and Norway meet. At the easternmost ut, Galdahytta, the track splits. Here, you can ead for either Helligskogen in Norway or etter-equipped Kilpisjärvi in Finland. Many ikers also use the trail between the western nd of Altevatn, in Øvre Dividal, and Abisko National Park, in northern Sweden, where ou'll find the start of Sweden's renowned Kungsleden hiking route.

The map to use for the Troms Border Trail and the Abisko Link is Statens Kartverk's *Turkart Indre Troms*, at a scale of 1:100,000. In summer, the mosquitoes will drive you to distraction; use a head net, smear yourself liberally with repellent and swat every single last buzzing bastard you can, in the interests of those who follow your footsteps.

Tours

Winter visitors can join a dog-sled trip through Arctic Norway led by renowned musher **Bjørn Klauer** (☎ 77 18 45 03; www.husky adventure.com) and colleagues. In addition to tours through the national park he runs expe-ditions into Sweden; typical all-inclusive costs are Nkr15,000 for eight days and Nkr21,000 for 11 days.

In summer he and his team organise cycle and canoe tours, or you can do your own thing and hike any of several signed trails that pass nearby. His farm (below) is also a delightful place to stay.

Sleeping

Seven unstaffed DNT huts run the length of the main hiking route through Øvre Dividal: Gaskashytta, Vuomahytta, Dividalshytta, Dærtahytta, Rostahytta, Gappohytta and Galdahytta.

Klauerhytta (☎ 77 18 45 03; www.huskyadventure.com; adult/child Nkr200/80) At the village of Innset, 35km southeast of Setermoen, dog-musher Bjørn Klauer runs a lovely, rustic hut plus a cabin for hikers and other travellers. There's a sauna, a well-equipped kitchen for guest use and you can hire bikes and canoes.

Helligskogen Fjellstua (☎ 77 71 54 60; helligskogen.hostel@vandrerhjem.no; dm/d Nkr175/345; ⏲ mid-Jun–mid-Aug) Near the eastern end of the park on the E8, 30km east of Skibotn, this hos-tel is surrounded by wild open highlands. It's handy for travel between Norway and Finland, and serves hikers finishing the Troms Border Trail.

Kilpisjärven Retkeilykeskus (☎ 358-16 537 771; Kilpisjärvi, Finland; d Nkr510, 4-bed cabins Nkr590; ⏲ Mar-Sep) Just over the Finnish border, this friendly, inexpensive place anchors the eastern end of the Troms Border Trail. It has simple rooms, a good-value café and cooking fa-cilities for guest use. You can arrange boat trips across Lake Kilpisjärvi and take a choice of scenic hikes through Finland's highest mountains.

WESTERN FINNMARK

Norway's northernmost mainland county, Finnmark has been inhabited for up to 12,000 years, first by the Komsa hunters of the coastal region and later by Sami fishing cultures and reindeer pastoralists, who settled on the coast and in the vast interior, respectively.

Finnmark's wild northern coast, dotted with fishing villages, is deeply indented by grand fjords, while the vast interior is dominated by the broad Finnmarksvidda plateau, a stark wilderness with only two major settlements, Karasjok and Kautokeino.

Virtually every Finnmark town was decimated at the end of WWII by retreating Nazi troops, whose scorched-earth policy aimed to delay the advancing Soviets. Towns were soon reconstructed in the most efficient, yet boxy, building style. So, in contrast to the spectacular natural surroundings, present-day Finnmark towns are architecturally uninspiring.

Dangers & Annoyances

Do keep an eye out for reindeer on the road. They're not dangerous and they're more charming than annoying but they might slow your progress and bring you to a very abrupt halt if you hit one at speed. Sometimes wandering alone, now and again in herds, they might not be fazed by your inanimate car. If they refuse to budge, just get out, walk towards them and they'll amble away.

ALTA

pop 14,000

Although the fishing and slate-quarrying town of Alta lies at latitude 70°N, it enjoys a relatively mild climate. The Alta Museum, with its ancient petroglyphs, is a must-see and the lush green Sautso-Alta Canyon (see p346), a quick hop away, is simply breathtaking.

The river Altaelva, which runs east of town, was once a Sami fishery and a popular haunt of sporting 19th-century English aristocrats. In the late 1970s, it became an environmental cause célèbre when, despite fierce local and national opposition, a 100m-high dam, the Altadammen, was built to exploit this rich salmon-spawning stream for hydroelectric power.

Orientation & Information

Alta, stretching along some 15km of coastline has a large footprint. Its two main centres are about 2km apart: hilly Bossekop to the west, and Sentrum in – well, just that – with its uninspiring blocks and parking lots and a pleasant enough traffic-free central square.

Studentbokhandelen (Sentrumsparken 2) Maps and a selection of books in English.

Tourist office (☎ 78 44 95 54; www.altatours.no; Parksentret Bldg, Sentrum; 8.30am-4pm Mon-Fri, 10am-2pm Sat)

Tourist office (☎ 78 44 50 50; Sorekskriverveien, Bossekop; 10am-6pm Mon-Fri Jun & Aug, 10am-8pm daily Jul) Has internet access (per min Nkr1).

Sights

Alta Museum (☎ 78 45 63 30; Altaveien 19; adult/child Nkr75/free; 8am-9pm Jun-Aug, 9am-6pm May & Sep, 9am-3pm Mon-Fri, 11am-4pm Sat & Sun rest-of-year) is in Hjemmeluft, at the western end of town. The cliffs around it, a Unesco World Heritage site, are incised with around 5000 late-Stone Age carvings, dating from 6000 to 2000 years ago. As the sea level decreased after the last ice age, carvings were made at progressively lower heights. Themes include hunting scenes, fertility symbols, bears, moose, reindeer and crowded boats. The works have been highlighted with red-ochre paint (thought to have been the original colour) and are connected by 3km of boardwalks that start at the main building. The short loop (1.2km; allow around 45 minutes, including viewing time) is the most visited. You can also graft on a second loop (total distance 2.1km), a pleasant seaside walk that takes in more sites.

Inside, the superb award-winning museum features exhibits and displays on Sami culture, Finnmark military history, the Alta hydroelectric project and the aurora borealis (northern lights).

Festivals & Events

The **Borealis Alta** winter festival in March is five days of concerts and culture, designed to dispel winter's gloom. It also marks the start of the **Finnmarksløpet 1000km dog-sled endurance race** (www.finnmarkslopet.no), Europe's longest. In late May the **Alta blues and soul festival** (www.altasoulogblues.no) brings in top Norwegian bands and stars from afar (Nazareth topped the bill in 2006).

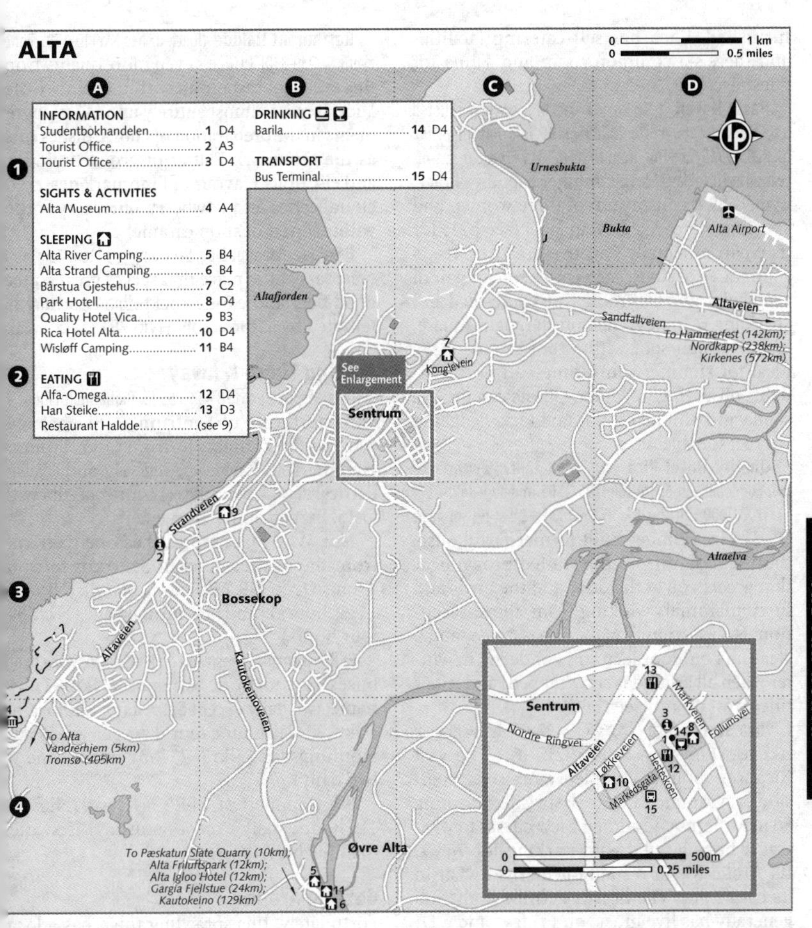

Sleeping

You'll find three excellent riverside camp sites, open year-round, in Øvre Alta, 3.5km south of the E6 along the Rv93 to Kautokeino.

Alta River Camping (☎ 78 43 43 53; www.alta-river camping.no; car/caravan site Nkr120/150, cabin with outside bathroom Nkr500-700, 6-bed with bathroom Nkr1200) Special features are its sauna, from which you can plunge straight into the river, and a couple of cute little barbecue huts, furnished with skins.

Wisløff Camping (☎ 78 43 43 03; www.wisloeff.no in Norwegian; per person/site Nkr20/150, 2-bed cabin with outside bathroom Nkr400, 4-bed with bathroom Nkr750) Declared Norwegian Camping Club 'campground of the year' in 2000, it still well deserves the accolade.

Alta Strand Camping (☎ 78 43 40 22; www.alta camping.no; site for 2/4 persons Nkr160/190, 2-/4-bed cabin with outdoor bathroom Nkr360/440, with bathroom Nkr650-750; self-catering apt s/d Nkr600/750) This spacious camp site has mountain views, table football (a cultural rarity east of Tromsø) and a small children's playground.

Alta Vandrerhjem (☎ 48 24 11 69; alta.hostel@van drerhjem.no; dm/s/d Nkr250/350/600; ⌚ Jun-Aug) Alta's youth hostel has recently changed premises and is now at Kvenvik, off the E6 and around 5km west of town.

Bårstua Gjestehus (☎ 78 43 33 33; www.baarstua .no; Kongleveien 2a; s/d incl breakfast Nkr760/900) This friendly, recently opened B&B lies right beside the E6. Its eight rooms, decorated with striking photographs, are spruce and well furnished. Each has self-catering facilities and there's a common room and sauna for guest use.

Park Hotell (☎ 78 45 74 00; www.parkhotell.no; Markedsgata 6; s/d Nkr895/1195 mid-Jun–mid-Aug; Nkr1235/1345 Sun-Thu, from Nkr860/1075 Fri & Sat rest-of-year, all incl breakfast) Here's another friendly choice, owned by a consortium of three women and sporting the coveted Swan label (see p21) for its environmentally sensitive practices. Its 34 rooms are spacious, each with a sofa or pair of armchairs, and bathrooms are white-tiled and sparkling. Although just off the main square, it's a tranquil spot with a roof terrace that's ideal for summer sunbathing and northern-lights observing in winter. Guests can use the sauna and rent bikes, skis and kick-sledges at very reasonable rates.

Quality Hotel Vica (☎ 78 48 22 22; www.choice.no; Fogdebakken 6; s/d Nkr1295/1505 mid-Jun–mid-Aug, Nkr1200/1400 Sun-Thu, Nkr1070/1180 Fri & Sat rest-of-year; P 💻) In a timber-built former farmhouse, the Vica, right from the stuffed brown bear that greets you at the door and the birds and furry mammals winking from above reception, is a welcoming place. It has a free sauna, steaming outdoor Jacuzzi (wonderful in winter when all around is snowcapped) and Alta's finest restaurant (see right).

Rica Hotel Alta (☎ 78 48 27 00; www.rica.no; Løkkeveien 61; s/d from Nkr1035/1235; P) The vast Rica was about to complete a massive extension programme when we last visited, creating 86 new rooms and adding a few curves to what was a boring cube with parking-lot views. Its Arctic Menu restaurant merits a visit in its own right. The hotel's Pernille nightclub generally has live music on Fridays and a DJ every Saturday.

Eating & Drinking

Apart from the Vica and Rica hotel restaurants, pickings are slim indeed.

Alfa-Omega (☎ 78 44 54 00; Markedsgata 14-16; mains Nkr85-120; 🕑 Mon-Sat) As its name suggests, this place has two parts: Omega, its contemporary café, open 11am to midnight, serves salads, sandwiches, pastas and cakes. Alfa, a pleasant, casual bar, comes into its own from 8pm. There's also a terrace, ideal for taking a little summer sunshine, overlooking Alta's bleak central square.

Han Steike (☎ 78 44 08 88; Løkkeveien 2) This steakhouse, all dark wood and grey flagstones, is the place if you're after something red and raw.

Restaurant Haldde (lunch dishes Nkr110-170, dinner mains Nkr230-330) There's even more quality from this excellent restaurant within Quality Hotel Vica. It relies almost entirely upon local ingredients in the preparation of choice dishes such as the Finnmark Platter of grouse, reindeer and elk, or its Flavour of Finnmark dessert of cloudberries and cowberry-blueberry sorbet within a nest of spun caramel.

Barila (Parksentret Bldg, Sentrum; 🕑 11am-1am) is a chic, sassy little place that serves great coffee, good beer and exotic cocktails. You may be tempted by a 'Blow Job' (Nkr78).

Getting There & Away

Alta's **airport** (☎ 78 44 95 55 for flight information) is 4km northeast of Sentrum at Elvebakken. SAS has direct flights to/from Oslo, Tromsø, Hammerfest, Kirkenes, Lakselv and Vadsø. **Norwegian** (www.norwegian.no) connects Alta with Oslo, Bergen and Stavanger.

Nor-Way Bussekspress has one daily run from the bus terminal in Sentrum to/from Tromsø (Nkr449, 6¼ hours), Narvik (Nkr656, 11½ hours) and Honningsvåg (Nkr367, four hours).

FFR (Finnmark Fylkesrederi og Ruteselkap; www.ffr.no) buses run to/from Karasjok (Nkr391, 4¾ hours, two daily except Saturday), Kautokeino (Nkr220, 2¼ hours, four days per week) and Honningsvåg (Nkr367, four hours, one to two daily).

For Hammerfest, FFR's fast ferry (Nkr230, 1½ hours, daily except Saturday) is swifter than the bus.

Getting Around

Fortunately, this sprawling town has a local bus to connect its dispersed ends. On weekdays, buses run more or less hourly between the major districts and to the airport. Services are less frequent on Saturday and don't run at all on Sunday.

Taxis (☎ 78 43 53 53) cost about Nkr100 from airport to town.

AROUND ALTA

Sights

SAUTSO-ALTA CANYON

The Altaelva hydroelectric project has had very little effect on the most scenic stretch of river, which slides through 400m-deep Sautso, northern Europe's grandest canyon. The easiest way to see this impressive forested gorge is to take the four-hour tour (Nkr500)

THE FAR NORTH

hat the tourist office organises each Monday, Wednesday and Friday in July, leaving at 4pm, numbers permitting (minimum five people). In addition to spectacular views of the Sauto-Alta Canyon, the tour also includes a pass through the Alta Power Station dam and a snack.

KÅFJORD

Kåfjord's **Tirpitz Museum** (☎ 92 09 23 70; www.tirpitz museum.no; adult/child/concession Nkr60/30/50; 🕑 10am-6pm Jun-Aug) is the achievement of local resident Even Blomkvist, who has single-handedly collected, bought, begged and borrowed the artefacts, uniforms, memorabilia and nearly 1000 evocative photographs relating to what was the world's largest battleship, its time in Kåfjord, where it hid from March 1943 to October 1944, and its eventual sinking near Tromsø.

At its peak in the 1840s, this tiny settlement 18km west of Alta was a prosperous town of over 1000 inhabitants thanks to the copper works (Kåfjord Kobberverk), which were then Norway's largest. You can follow an easy 1.3km signed trail around the little that remains (you'll find plenty more information in Alta Museum). Half hidden in the grass opposite the explanatory panel is a plaque in memory of three British midget submarines that entered the fjord and severely damaged the *Tirpitz* in 1943.

To the right of the E6, a 9km cart track begins 250m north of the parish church and leads past copper-mine tailings up to the observatory at the summit of Mt Haldde (904m), a mountain venerated by the Sami.

PÆSKATUN SLATE QUARRY

Some 13km south of town in Pæskatun, the **Alta Skiferprodukter** is one of Alta's economic mainstays. In summer, you can visit the quarry and historical exhibits, enjoy a fine view over the canyon – and have a little hands-on experience with the slate cutting tools. It also sells a range of Finnmark minerals and souvenirs made of slate. Contact the tourist office for current times and tariffs.

Activities

HIKING

For experienced hikers, Alta makes a good launching pad for long-distance hiking trails that follow historic routes across the Finnmarksvidda plateau to the south. Alta's tourist office can advise and you can pick up hiking maps at Studentbokhandelen (p344).

BOAT TRIPS

From **Alta Friluftspark** (☎ 78 43 33 78; www.ice-alta .no), beside the Altaelva river, 16km south of town then a further 6.5km off the Rv93, you can choose from several riverboat rides, lasting from 20 minutes to three hours and costing between Nkr195 and Nkr495 per person. They leave at 1pm and 3pm daily from June to August.

WINTER ACTIVITIES

Alta Friluftspark has 80 snowmobiles, the largest such herd in northern Norway. It offers guided outings, and, your exertions over, you can relax in its steaming hot tub. You can also scud over the snow with **Gargia Fjellstue** (see below), then replenish your energy with a hot Sami meal. **Holmen Hundesenter** (www.hol menhundesenter.no) specialises in dog-sledding with outings ranging from three hours to five days. For all, reserve directly or through the tourist office.

Sleeping

Alta Igloo Hotel (☎ 78 43 33 78; www.ice-alta.no; per person incl breakfast Nkr2195; 🕑 mid-Jan–mid-Apr) This seasonal hotel with a capacity for 80 guests is constructed block by block each winter within Alta Friluftspark. It's Norway's first lodging made entirely of snow and ice, right down to the drinking glasses.

Gargia Fjellstue (☎ 78 43 33 51; www.gargia-fjellstue.no in Norwegian; s/d Nkr775/990, cabin Nkr600 with outdoor bathroom, with bathroom Nkr875) Around 25km south of Alta, direction Kautokeino, this mountain lodge offers a forest getaway and a range of summer and winter outdoor activities, including the best foot access to the Sautso-Alta Canyon.

HAMMERFEST

pop 6800

Because of its strategic location and excellent harbour, Hammerfest has long been an important way station for shipping, fishing and Arctic hunting. In its heyday, ladies wore the finest Paris fashions and in 1890 Europe's first electric street lighting was installed. Nowadays it proudly claims to be the world's northernmost town (other Norwegian communities, while further north, are, Hammerfest vigorously argues, too small to qualify as towns!).

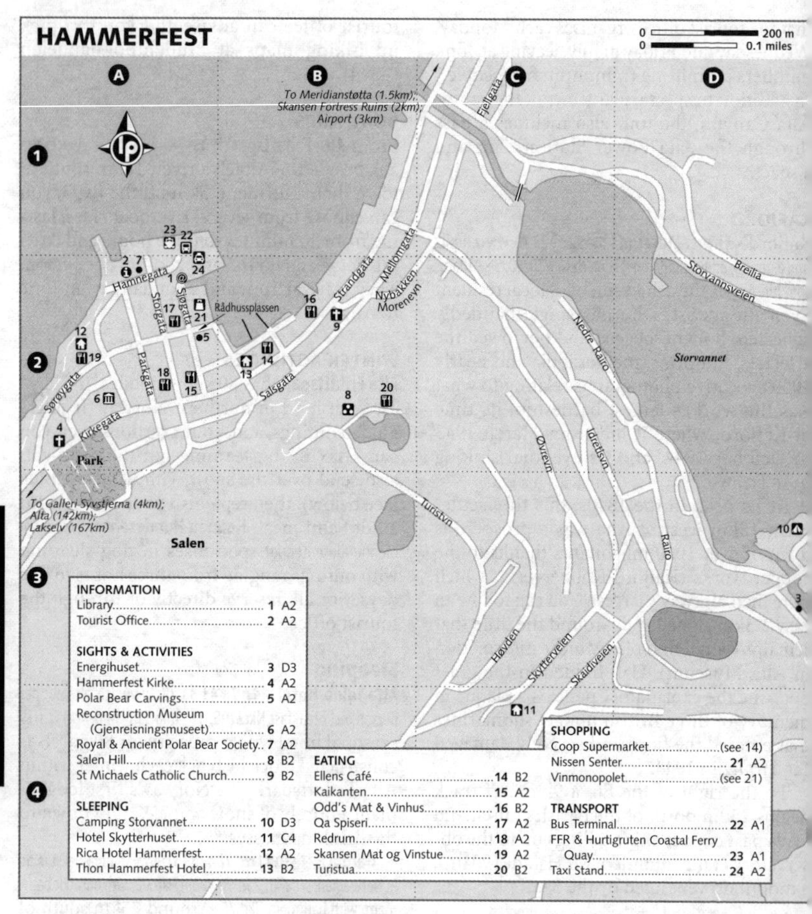

Neither man nor nature have been kind to the town: it was decimated in a gale in 1856, burned severely in 1890, then burned again by the Nazis in 1944. Its parish church has gone up in flames five times over the centuries. All the same God may at last be smiling on the town in a way that is having a huge impact. The world's longest undersea pipeline runs for 143km from the huge Snøhvit natural gas fields in the Barents Sea to the small island of Melkøya out in the bay. With estimated reserves of 193 billion (yes, *billion*) cu metres, the pumps, which came on tap in 2007, are expected to pound for at least 25 years.

If you're arriving on the Hurtigruten coastal ferry, you'll have only a couple of hours to pace around, pick up an Arctic souvenir and scoff some fresh shrimp at the harbour. For most visitors that will suffice.

Information

Library (Bibliotek; Sjøgata; 10am-3.30pm Mon-Fri) Has free internet access.

Tourist office (☎ 78 41 31 00; www.hammerfest-turist.no; Hamnegata 3; 9am-5pm daily mid-Jun–mid-Aug, 9am-3pm Mon-Fri, 10.30am-1.30pm Sat & Sun rest-of-year)

Sights

GJENREISNINGSMUSEET

Hammerfest's **Reconstruction Museum** (☎ 78 40 29 30; Kirkegata 21; adult/child/concession Nkr40/15/30; 9am-4pm Mon-Fri, 11am-2pm Sat & Sun mid-Jun–mid-Aug, 11am-2pm rest-of-year) recounts the forced evacuation and decimation of the town during the Nazi retreat in 1944; the hardships that its citizens endured through the following winter; and Hammerfest's post-war reconstruction and regeneration.

ENERGIHUSET

The **Energy House** (☎ 78 42 82 00; adult/child Nkr45/20; 10am-2pm Mon-Fri mid-Jun–mid-Aug), a new interactive centre, explains natural gas extraction, which is bringing increasing wealth to Hammerfest, and also alternative energy sources such as wind and tidal power. Coincidentally, it's on the site of northern Europe's first hydropower station.

ROYAL & ANCIENT POLAR BEAR SOCIETY

Dedicated to preserving Hammerfest culture, the **Royal & Ancient Polar Bear Society** (adult/child Nkr40/free) features exhibits on Arctic hunting and local history and shares premises with the tourist office. The place is, it must be said, a bit of a come-on (the Norwegian name, Isbjørklubben, simply Polar Bear Club, lacks the portentousness of the English but is nearer the mark). For Nkr160, you can become a life member and get a certificate, ID card, sticker and pin. For Nkr195, you also receive a schnapps glass and, as the demure young receptionist will explain without blanching, get dubbed with the bone from a walrus's penis. It's well worth that extra Nkr35 for the conversation this unique honour will generate down the pub, once you're home.

FUGLENES

On this peninsula, just across the harbour, are the foundations of the **Skansen Fortress**, which dates from the Napoleonic Wars, when the British briefly held and plundered the town; and the **Meridianstøtta**, a marble column commemorating the first survey (1816–52) to determine the arc of the global meridian and thereby calculate the size and shape of the earth.

HAMMERFEST KIRKE

Behind the altar of Hammerfest's contemporary **church** (Kirkegata 33; 7.15am-3pm Mon-Fri, 11am-3pm Sat, noon-1pm Sun mid-Jun–mid-Aug), consecrated in 1961, the glorious stained-glass window positively glows in the summer sun. The wooden frieze along the organ gallery depicts highlights of the town's history. The chapel in the cemetery across the street is the only building in town to have survived WWII.

SALEN HILL

For panoramic views over the town, coast and mountains (there's a free pair of binoculars for you to sweep the bay), climb **Salen Hill** (86m), topped by the Turistua restaurant (see p350), a couple of Sami turf huts and a lookout point. The 15-minute uphill trail begins at the small park behind the Rådhus.

GALLERI SYVSTJERNA

Local artist Eva Arnesen designed the Nobel Peace Prize diploma that was awarded to Jody Williams and the campaign to ban land mines. Her **gallery** (☎ 78 41 01 60; Fjordaveien 27; 10am-5pm Mon-Fri, 10am-3pm Sat) is about 4km south of town, opposite the Statoil petrol station. Arnesen's paintings evoke the colours of the region from the northern lights to the bright palette of summer. The handsome pair of carved and silvered polar bears on Rådhus Plass was fashioned by her husband, woodcarver Knut Arnesen.

ST MICHAELS CATHOLIC CHURCH

With a strong claim to be the world's most northerly catholic church, **St Michaels** (cnr Strandgata & Mellomgata), serving a congregation of barely 90 souls, is immediately recognisable by the striking mosaic of the eponymous saint that extends the length of its facade.

Sleeping

Camping Storvannet (☎ 78 41 10 10; storvannet@yahoo.no; Storvannsveien; car/caravan sites Nkr140/185, 2-/3-bed cabin Nkr360/410; late May-late Sep) Beside a lake and overlooked by a giant apartment complex, this pleasant site, Hammerfest's only decent camping option, is small so do book your cabin in advance.

Hotel Skytterhuset (☎ 78 41 15 11; www.skytterhuset.no; Skytterveien 24; s/d Nkr795/995 Sun-Thu, Nkr595/795 Fri & Sat; P) The three spurs of this secluded hotel, overlooking the town, look decidedly barrackslike from the outside and with good reason; it was originally built as living quarters for summertime fishwives from Finland who worked in the large Findus processing factory. Long ago converted to a friendly, cosy hotel (reindeer frequently hop over the fence to browse the garden and seek a stretch of shade), it's a good option with free sauna and solarium.

Rica Hotel Hammerfest (☎ 78 41 13 33; www.rica.no; Sørøygata 15; s/d Nkr852/1102 mid-Jun–mid-Aug; Nkr1320/1525 Sun-Thu, Nkr835/1085 Fri & Sat rest-of-year; P) Constructed in agreeable mellow brick, this hotel has an attractive bar and lounge and well-furnished rooms, most with harbour views. Its Arctic Menu restaurant, Skansen Mat og Vinstue, serves excellent local fare.

Thon Hotel Hammerfest (☎ 78 42 96 00; www.thonhotels.com; Strandgata 2-4; s/d Nkr1190/1390 mid-Jun–mid-Aug, Nkr1400/1600 Sun-Thu, Nkr850/1050 Fri & Sat rest-of-year; P) Overlooking the fjord and only a stone's throw from the cruise-ship jetty, this hotel has bags of character, three bars, free sauna and solarium and Bernoni, its tempting restaurant. Rooms overlooking the fjord come at no extra cost. Those in the newer wing replicate a ship's cabins, complete with bunk beds, dark woodwork and nautical décor.

Eating & Drinking

Ellens Café (Strandgata 14-18; mains Nkr65-75; 9am-5pm Mon-Sat) Upstairs from the Coop Supermarket, this is an unpretentious, inexpensive cafeteria.

Kaikanten (☎ 78 41 49 00; Sjøgata 19) An appealing café that serves light meals by day, the Quayside becomes a popular evening pub serving pizzas. Nautically themed (the backdrop to the bar represents old Hammerfest's dockside, and sail canvases billow beneath the ceiling), it has a pool table and comfy sofas into which you sink deep.

Redrum (☎ 78 41 00 49; Storgata 23; 11am-5pm Mon-Thu, 11am-3am Fri & Sat) Just around the corner and similarly split in character, Redrum, with its attractive contemporary décor, saves its energy for weekend wildness, when there's regularly live music.

Turistua (☎ 78 42 96 00; Salen; mains Nkr145-190) From atop Salen Hill, Turistua offers great views over the town and sound. The off-putting name is for a lady named Turi, though 'turist' buses often stop here too.

Qa Spiseri (☎ 78 41 26 12; Sjøgata 8; mains Nkr150-265; Mon-Sat) Run by a young team, this welcome recent addition to Hammerfest's limited dining options offers reliable cuisine with a great price-to-quality ratio, whether you opt for a main course or one of its lunchtime snacks (Nkr90 to Nkr110). Whichever, save a cranny for a hunk of one of its mouthwatering homemade cakes.

our pick **Odd's Mat & Vinhus** (☎ 78 41 37 66; Strandgata 24; mains Nkr245-355; Mon-Sat) Drop downstairs to one of the finest restaurants in all Norway, offering dishes such as grouse steak, fillet of hare and salmon marinated in gin. Hanks of plaited rope are festooned from ceiling and windows, and there's plenty of attractive dark woodwork. Reservations are all but essential.

Vinmonopolet, for wine and hooch, is within the Nissen Senter shopping complex.

Getting There & Around

Buses run to/from Alta (Nkr229, 2½ hours, two daily), Honningsvåg (Nkr321, 3¼ hours, one to two daily) and Karasjok (Nkr344, 4¼ hours, twice daily except Saturday), with one service extending to Kirkenes (Nkr831, 10 to 12 hours) via Tana Bru (Nkr616, 7½ to 10 hours) four times weekly.

For Alta, FFR's fast ferry (Nkr230, 1½ hours, daily except Saturday) is faster than the bus alternative. The Hurtigruten coastal ferry also stops in Hammerfest for 1½ hours in each direction.

To call a taxi, ring ☎ 78 41 12 34.

NORDKAPP & MAGERØYA

pop 3300

Nordkapp is the one attraction in northern Norway that everyone seems to visit even if it is a tourist trap. Billing itself as the northernmost point in continental Europe, it sucks in visitors by the busload, some 200,000 each summer.

Nearer to the North Pole than to Oslo, Nordkapp sits at latitude 71° 10' 21"N, where the sun never drops below the horizon from mid-May to the end of July. Long before other Europeans took an interest, it was a sacrificial site for the Sami, who believed it had special powers.

Richard Chancellor, the English explorer who drifted here in 1553 in search of the Northeast Passage, first gave it the name North Cape. Much later, after a highly publicised visit by King Oscar II in 1873, Nordkapp became a pilgrimage spot for Norwegians. It's also, bizarrely, one for Thais, of all people, thanks to a visit by King Chulalongkorn in 1907.

Now here's a secret: Nordkapp isn't continental Europe's northernmost point. That award belongs to Knivskjelodden, an 18km round-trip hike away, less dramatic, inacces-

FRIDTJOF NANSEN

Fridtjof Nansen (1861–1930), the Norwegian all-rounder, explorer and diplomat, pushed the frontiers of human endurance and human compassion.

Growing up in rural Store Frøen outside Oslo, he enjoyed a privileged childhood. An excellent athlete, he won a dozen or so national nordic skiing championships and broke the world one-mile skating record. Studies in zoology at the University of Christiania led to a voyage aboard the sealing ship *Viking* to study ocean currents, ice movements and wildlife. His first tantalising glimpses of Greenland planted the dream of travelling across its central icecap.

He didn't hang around; in 1888 Nansen, still only 27, headed a six-man expedition. He over-wintered in Greenland and his detailed observations of the Inuit (Eskimo) people formed the backbone of his 1891 book, *Eskimo Life*.

In June 1893, aboard the 400-tonne, oak-hulled, steel-reinforced ship *Fram*, Nansen's next expedition left Christiania (current-day Oslo) for the Arctic with provisions for six whole years. Nansen left behind his wife Eva and six-month-old daughter Liv, not knowing when, if ever, he'd return.

On 14 March 1895, he and Hjalmar Johansen set out in the *Fram* (see p102) for the North Pole and journeyed for five months, including 550km on foot over the ice, before holing up for nine winter months in a tiny stone hut they'd built on an island. On heading south, they encountered lone British explorer Frederick Jackson (for whom Nansen later, magnanimously, named the island where they'd spent the winter). Having given up on reaching the Pole, all three headed back to Vardø.

In 1905 a political crisis arose as Norway sought independence from Sweden. Nansen, by then a national hero, was dispatched to Copenhagen and Britain to represent the Norwegian cause.

Upon independence, Nansen was offered the job of prime minister but declined in order to keep exploring (he's also rumoured to have turned down offers to be king or president). He did, however, accept King Håkon's offer to serve as ambassador to Britain. In 1907, after the sudden death of his wife, he abandoned his dreams of conquering the South Pole and – again with a generosity untypical of the competitive world of polar exploration at the time – allowed fellow Norwegian explorer Roald Amundsen to take over the *Fram* for an expedition north of Siberia.

After WWI Nansen threw himself into large-scale humanitarian efforts: the new League of Nations, repatriating half a million German soldiers imprisoned in the Soviet Union and an International Red Cross programme against famine and pestilence in Russia. When some two million Russians and Ukrainians became stateless after fleeing the 1917 Bolshevik revolution, 'Nansen Passports' enabled thousands of them to settle elsewhere. Perhaps Nansen's greatest diplomatic achievement was the resettlement of several hundred thousand Greeks and Turks after the massive population shifts in the eastern Mediterranean following WWI.

In 1922 Nansen received the Nobel Peace Prize – then gave it all away to international relief efforts. After 1925 he concentrated on disarmament and lobbying for a non-Soviet homeland for Armenian refugees. Although this never happened, he is still revered among Armenians worldwide.

On 13 May 1930, Nansen died quietly at his home in Polhøgda, near Oslo, and was buried in a garden nearby.

The standard biography of this extraordinary man is *Nansen* by Roland Huntford.

sible by vehicle – and to be treasured all the more for that.

Nordkapp & Around

NORDKAPPHALLEN

So you've finally made it to Europe's northernmost rip-off – an opinion shared by the regular letters we receive from readers who've felt exploited. To reach the tip of the continent, by car, by bike, on a bus or walking in, you have to pay a **toll** (adult/child/student/family Nkr195/60/110/390). This allows unlimited entry over two days but it's small compensation for the vast majority who simply roll in, look quickly around, take a snap or two and roll out.

This vast bunker of a place, topped by a giant, intrusive golf ball, is a love/hate kind of place. Within are a tediously detailed account of WWII naval actions off the cape, a cafeteria and restaurant, the striking Grottan bar with views of Europe's end through its vast glass wall, a one-room Thai museum, the St Johannes chapel ('the world's northernmost ecumenical chapel'), a post office (for that all-important Nordkapp postmark) and an appropriately vast souvenir shop. A five-screen, 120-degree theatre runs an enjoyable 17-minute panoramic film.

But it's the view that thrills the most. In fair weather – which is a lot of the time – you can gaze down at the wild surf 307m below, watch the mists roll in and simply enjoy the moment.

KNIVSKJELODDEN

The continent's real northernmost point, Knivskjelodden, is mercifully inaccessible to vehicles and devoid of tat. You can hike to the tip of this promontory from a marked car park 6km south of the Nordkapp toll booth. The 9km track isn't difficult despite some ups and downs, but it's best to wear hiking boots since it can be mucky after precipitation. When you get to latitude 71° 11' 08"N, at sea level, sign the guest book. Should you wish, note down your reference number from the book and you can buy – nothing but the hike comes free on this island – a certificate (Nkr50) authenticating your achievement from Nordkapp Camping or the tourist office. Allow about five hours return.

SLEEPING

Astoundingly, you can spend the night in your motor home or caravan at Nordkapp itself (fill up on water and electricity though, because you won't find any there for the taking).

Nordkapp Camping (☎ 78 47 33 77; www.nordkappcamping.no; E69, Skipsfjorden; person/site Nkr30/100, d Nkr550, 2-/4-bed cabin with outdoor bathroom Nkr500/550, with bathroom Nkr950-1150; ⏲ May–mid-Sep) The well-equipped communal kitchen, friendly service and variety of lodging options more than compensate for the stark location of this place, north of Skipsfjord.

Kirkeporten Camping (☎ 78 47 52 33; www.kirkeporten.no; Storvannsveien 2, Skarsvåg; person/site Nkr25/150, cabin with outdoor bathroom Nkr475-550, 5-/6-bed with bathroom from Nkr775/850; ⏲ mid-May–Aug) Just outside the hamlet of Skarsvåg, this is another welcoming camp site, a favourite of British adventure tour groups. Its claim to be the 'world's northernmost camping' stands up; there's a rival on Svalbard but it's without cabins. The cosy café does reindeer (Nkr115) and a fresh-fish dish daily special (Nkr130 to Nkr145).

Honningsvåg

pop 2500

Honningsvåg is by far the island's largest settlement. Magerøya's **tourist office** (☎ 78 47 70 30; www.visitnorthcape.com; Fiskeriveien 4B; ⏲ 8.30am-8pm Mon-Fri, noon-8pm Sat & Sun mid-Jun–mid-Aug, 8.30am-4pm Mon-Fri rest-of-year), beside the harbour, has one internet point (per 15 minutes Nkr23).

SIGHTS & ACTIVITIES

Honningsvåg's small **Nordkapp Museum** (☎ 78 47 72 00; www.nordkappmuseet.no; Fiskeriveien 4; adult/child Nkr30/5 incl guided tour in English; ⏲ 10am-7pm Jun–mid-Aug, noon-4pm rest-of-year), co-located with the tourist office, illustrates the impact of early visitors to the cape, Sami culture, the hard days in the immediate aftermath of WWII and the daily life of a town that, until the advent of tourism, lived from the sea.

The 19th-century **church** (Kirkegata; ⏲ 8am-10pm Jun–mid-Sep) was the only building in town to survive the Nazis' scorched-earth retreat in 1944. For a time it was a communal dwelling until the first new houses were hastily erected.

SLEEPING

Northcape Guesthouse (☎ 47 25 50 63; www.northcapeguesthouse.com; Elvebakken 5a; dm Nkr200, d/q Nkr520/880; ⏲ May-Sep) A 15- to 20-minute walk from the Hurtigruten quay, this bright, modern hostel is an excellent budget choice. There's a cosy lounge, washing machine, well-equipped kitchen for self-caterers – and great views over the town below. Relatively new but already with a reputation, it's often full so do reserve well in advance.

Honningsvåg Brygge (☎ 78 47 64 64; Vågen 1a; s/d Nkr1150/1300; ⏲ year-round) This family-owned renovated former fishing warehouse has unbeatable views from its pier location. Rooms with harbour views come at no extra cost but you'll need to book ahead to reserve one. Its excellent restaurant is for hotel guests only.

EATING & DRINKING

Corner (☎ 78 47 63 40; Fiskerveien 1; mains Nkr145-175) This café serves seafood and pizza and also has a bar with an inviting outdoor terrace overlooking the water. Enjoy crispy cod tongues (Nkr145), whale (Nkr145) or, more conventionally, fried halibut (Nkr160).

Arctico (☎ 78 47 15 00; Sjøgata 1a; adult/child Nkr120/free; ⏲ 10am-9pm Apr-Sep) For a shiver in summer and sense of how Nordkapp must hit the senses in winter, visit this ice bar. Owner José Milares, himself a polar adventurer, talks with passion of the shapes, bubbles and inadvertent abstract art in the pure ice that he garners freshly each season and there's an igloo for the kids to crawl in.

Bryggerie (☎ 78 47 26 00; Nordkappgate 1) The splendid Mack Brewery in Tromsø has been supplanted as the world's northernmost by Honningsvåg's microbrewery. Among beers brewed on the spot is Ole Anton (Uncle Anton), named after the uncle of one of the owners.

Nøden Pub (☎ 78 47 27 11; Larsjorda 1; ⏲ 8pm-2am Tue-Sun) This local favourite near the Rica Hotel often has live music.

Gjesvær

pop 130

It's a stunning drive to the remote fishing village of **Gjesvær**, 34km northwest of Honningsvåg. Rolling taiga, punctuated by dark pools and cropped by reindeer, gives way to a stark, rocky landscape, and then a sudden view of low skerries and the Gjesværstappan islands.

Bird Safari (☎ 41 61 39 83; www.birdsafari.com; adult/child/youth under 12 Nkr450/free/225) sails two to three times daily between June and late August to the offshore bird colony on the Gjesværstappan islands. There are an estimated three *million* nesting birds, including colonies of puffins, skuas, razorbills, kittiwakes, gannets and white-tailed eagles. Reserve this 1½-hour tour directly or at the Honningsvåg tourist office. Bird Safari can also arrange **accommodation** (s/d with shared bathroom & kitchen Nkr350/40, cabins Nkr750; ⏲ Jun-Aug).

Stappan Sjøprodukter (☎ 95 03 77 22; www.stappan.no) is an altogether smaller concern. Fisherman Roald Berg will take you bird-watching (Nkr1000 for up to two passengers, Nkr450 each for three to six) in his small boat. Or join him for a fishing expedition (Nkr2000 per hour, maximum four passengers). He also runs a splendid waterside summer **café** (⏲ core hrs 11am-5pm) offering delights such as smoked wild salmon sandwiches (Nkr75), cloudberries and cream (Nkr75) and waffles with home-made blueberry jam (Nkr40); he runs a well-furnished **apartment** (d/tr/q Nkr850/1000/1250).

Kamøyvær

A short detour from the E69 brings you to this tiny, sheltered fishing hamlet, its pastel-shaded cottages and cabins encircling the small harbour.

our pick **Arran** (☎ 78 47 51 29; www.arran.as; s/d from Nkr700/1050; ⏲ mid-May–Aug; P) has 44 rooms spread over three quayside buildings. The Sami family who run it bake their own bread and the menu is always the freshest of fish, hauled from the sea, often by its own boat. To vary the cuisine it also offers a reindeer special (Nkr140).

If you find it full, several other houses in the village advertise rooms. And should you fancy a cultural diet, call by **The Gallery East of the Sun** (⏲ noon-10pm mid-May–mid-Aug), featuring the sinuous shapes and bright canvases of artist Eva Schmutterer.

Getting There & Away

The Hurtigruten coastal ferry makes calls at Honningsvåg. Its 3½-hour northbound stop allows passengers a quick buzz up to Nordkapp (Nkr645).

An express bus connects Honningsvåg with Alta (Nkr367, four hours, one or two daily) and there's also a run to/from Hammerfest (Nkr321, 3¼ hours, one to two daily).

The road approach from the E6 is via Olderfjord, where the E69 branches northwards. The one-way toll for the 6.8km-long Nordkapptunnelen is a swingeing Nkr145 for a saloon car and driver plus Nkr47/24 per adult/child passenger.

Getting Around

CAR & MOTORCYCLE

Until the blacktop road to Nordkapp was constructed in the mid-1950s, all access was by boat. Nowadays, the route winds across a rocky plateau past herds of grazing reindeer. Depending upon snow conditions, it's open to private traffic from April to mid-October. In fringe months, ring the tourist office if the weather looks dicey.

A taxi to/from Nordkapp from Honningsvåg costs around Nkr1050, including an hour of waiting at the cape – plus that Nkr195 admission charge per passenger.

In Honningsvåg, **Avis** (☎ 78 47 62 22) has a special five-hour deal on car hire for Nkr850, including petrol and insurance. The **Shell petrol station** (☎ 78 47 60 60) offers a similar four-hour deal for Nkr600.

PUBLIC TRANSPORT

Between June and late August, a local bus (adult/child Nkr90/45, 45 minutes) runs daily at 10.45am and 9.30pm between Honningsvåg and Nordkapp, setting off back from the cape at 1.15pm and 12.15am (so that you can take in the midnight sun at midnight). If you're on a budget, scan carefully the terms of any inclusive tours, which probably charge considerably more for similar services. And bear in mind that even if you arrive by bus, you still get dunned for that Nkr195 entry fee.

LAKSELV & AROUND

pop 3000

The plain fishing village of Lakselv, at the head of long, slim Porsangerfjord, has little to detain you. The name means 'salmon stream', which reflects its main appeal for Norwegian holidaymakers.

The **tourist office** (☎ 78 46 07 00; www.arctic-active.no; 9am-5pm Mon-Fri, 10am-5pm Sat & Sun early Jun–mid-Aug, 8.30am-4pm Mon-Fri rest-of-year) is in the lugubrious Porsanger Vesthus hotel.

Its products may not be from the juice of the grape but **North Cape Wine** (☎ 78 46 23 73; Meieriveien 11) is the world's northernmost winery, making its own special vintages from Arctic berries. Ring the winery or tourist office for a tour and tasting, or pick up a bottle at the Vinmonopolet in the Torgsenteret shopping centre.

Sleeping & Eating

Lakselv Vandrerhjem (☎ 78 46 14 76; lakselv.hostel@vandrerhjem.no; dm Nkr200, d Nkr450, cabins with bathroom & kitchen Nkr500-600; Jun-Aug) This HI-affiliated hostel is in a secluded site amid the trees and surrounded by small lakes. It makes a great base for gentle strolls and has self-catering facilities. Follow the E6 southwards from Lakselv for 6km, then take a dirt road to the left for 2km.

Lakselv Hotell (☎ 78 46 54 00; www.lakselvhotell.no; Karasjokveien; s/d Nkr910/1175 mid-Jun–mid-Aug; from Nkr940/1290 Sun-Thu, Nkr795/50 Fri & Sat rest-of-year; P) Just 2km south of town beside the E6, it has cosy rooms, hilltop fjord views, a sauna that's free for guests and a restaurant that does a good summertime dinner buffet (Nkr280). Guests can rent bikes (per day Nkr80).

our pick **Bungalåven Vertshus** (☎ 95 77 82 11; www.bungalaaven.com; Børselv; basic d Nkr350-450) Some 40km up the Rv98 northeast of Lakselv, take a signed turning to reach this convivial converted farmhouse after 2km. It serves dinner in summer with traditional food for a bargain Nkr150. The lounge is a cosy haven and the owner plays a mean squeezebox so you may find yourself up and dancing. There are also a couple of simple cabins (Nkr350), a big one with bathroom (Nkr900) and a small camping space too (car/caravan site Nkr75/100).

Don't expect anything fancy to eat in Lakselv itself. Your best of few options is **Åstedet Café & Bistro** (☎ 78 46 13 77), beside Porsanger Versthus and the tourist office. Both pub and café-restaurant, it serves a range of decent meaty mains (around Nkr150) plus the usual burgers, pizzas and salads.

Getting There & Away

Lakselv's North Cape Airport, an important link for central Finnmark, has up to three daily flights to/from Tromsø.

Buses run to/from Alta (Nkr275, 3½ hours), Karasjok (Nkr123, 1¼ hours) and Honningsvåg (Nkr266, 3¼ hours) once or twice daily except Saturday. In summer, a daily bus running between Nordkapp and Rovaniemi via Ivalo (both in Finland) calls by.

STABBURSNES

At Stabbursnes, 16km north of Lakselv and beside one of the most attractive sectors of Porsangerfjord, there are a couple of important protected areas.

Stabbursnes Nature Reserve

The Stabbursnes Nature Reserve extends over the wetlands and mudflats at the estuary of the River Stabburselva. Bird-watchers come to observe the many species of duck, plus geese, divers and sandpipers that rest in the area while migrating between the Arctic and more temperate zones. Among the more exotic species are the bar-tailed godwit, dunlin, knot and the increasingly rare lesser white-fronted goose. Coastal marshes are closed to visitors during the nesting season (May and June) and also from mid-August to mid-September.

A signed nature trail (2.8km one way) leads along the estuary and beside the shore of Porsangerfjord. Ask at the visitors centre for its useful trail description in English.

The **Stabbursnes Naturhus og Museum** (☎ 78 46 47 65; ⏰ 9am-8pm mid-Jun–mid-Aug, 11am-6pm early Jun & late Aug, noon-3pm Tue-Thu rest-of-year) serves both the nature reserve and national park. It sells field guides, maps and fishing permits and has a well-mounted **exhibition** (adult/child/concession Nkr50/10/40 incl a 20min DVD) about the birds, animals and geology of the interior high plateau, river valleys and coast.

Stabbursdalen National Park

No roads cross through the 747 sq km of Stabbursdalen National Park, which offers a spectacular glacial canyon and excellent hiking in the world's most northerly pine forest. For hikers, there are two mountain huts, Rørkulphytta and Ivarstua, as well as a turf hut. For longer treks, consult the Stabbursnes visitors centre, which carries the relevant walking maps: Statens Kartverk's *Stabbursdalen* and *Laksdal*, both at 1:50,000. Less arduously, there are three signed trails, the longest requiring around four hours.

Sleeping

Stabbursdalen Feriesenter (☎ 78 46 47 60; www.stabbursdalen.no; car/caravan site Nkr120/160 plus per person Nkr20, 2-bed cabin with outdoor bathroom Nkr450, 2-6 bed with bathroom Nkr650-850; ⏰ mid-May–mid-Sep) Beside the salmon-rich River Stabburselva and packed with gumbooted fisherfolk in quest of The Big One (the café's TV relays live, real-time images from the riverbed), this extensive camp site enjoys a beautiful position. Facilities, however, are stretched in high season.

EASTERN FINNMARK

Relatively little visited, Eastern Finnmark, heartland of the Eastern Sami culture, has some charming coastal villages and a unique frontier history that embraces Finns, explorers and wartime destruction.

NORDKYN PENINSULA

The church-shaped rock formation known as the **Finnkirke** marks the entrance to the village of Kjøllefjord and provides a majestic introduction to this remote corner of Finnmark, a treasure trove for collectors of 'northernmosts'.

Across the peninsula, the tiny coastal village of Gamvik claims the world's northernmost museum. The **Latitude 71 Museum** (☎ 78 49 79 49; Strandveien 94; adult/child/concession Nkr50/10/25; ⏰ 9am-4.30pm mid-Jun–mid-Aug, 9am-4pm Mon-Fri rest-of-year), in a former fish-drying shed, reveals the fishing cultures of these far-flung environs. Nearby, a bird-watchers' trail runs through the **Slettnes Nature Reserve**, frequented by nesting and migrating ducks and wading birds (accessible only on foot or by private vehicle), and **Slettnes Fyr** is the world's northernmost mainland lighthouse.

In the centre are **Kinnarodden**, the northernmost point of mainland Europe (Nordkapp is, technically, on an island) and the town of **Mehamn**, unremarkable except as the site of one of Norway's earliest environmental movements. In 1903 troops were brought in to subdue local fishermen, who protested that whaling was exterminating the whales that had historically made fishing easy by driving cod towards the shore.

Alone beside the seashore, **Gamvik Gjestehus** (☎ 78 49 62 12; Strandveien 78, Gamvik), a renovated fishermen's cabin, has a good restaurant serving king crab and fresh fish.

Kjøllefjord and Mehamn are both brief stops on the Hurtigruten coastal ferry.

BERLEVÅG

pop 1100

This pint-sized fishing village has produced one big thing, the **Berlevåg Mannsangforening**, a male voice choir that was the subject of Knut Erik Jensen's 2001 documentary *Heftig og Begeistret* (Cool and Crazy). Something of a Nordic *Buena Vista Social Club*, the film caused a national sensation when it was released and earned international respect.

Sights & Activities

The **Harbour Museum** (Havnemuseum; ☎ 78 78 20 55; Havnegate; adult/child Nkr40/10; ⏰ 10am-6pm Mon-Fri, 1-6pm Sat & Sun mid-Jun–mid-Aug, noon-3pm Mon-Fri rest-of-year) has the usual maritime displays as well as an unusual old expedition dory, the *Berlevåg II*.

About 12km away is a **Sami sacrificial site** atop the 269m Tanahorn, with a wonderful view over the Arctic Ocean. The 8km return walk begins 9km west of town, along the gravel road towards the evocative abandoned fishing village of Store Malvik (20km west of Berlevåg).

Berlevåg Trolling & Deep Sea Fishing (☎ 78 98 18 80; www.trollingnorway.com; Storgata 13) runs four-hour fishing trips (Nkr1180) and two-hour king crab safaris (Nkr980) aboard a genuine deep-sea fishing boat.

Sleeping

Berlevåg Pensjonat og Camping (☎ 78 98 16 10; www.berlevag-pensjonat.no; Havnegate 8b; person/site Nkr15/130, s/d Nkr500/600) This friendly, well-kept complex also houses the tourist office. Between them, they can arrange a visit to a fish farm, scuba diving and fishing excursions; and you can rent a bike here.

Getting There & Away

Buses run from Tana Bru (Nkr215, 2½ hours) and Båtsfjord (Nkr151, 1¾ hours) at least once a day except Saturday. The run takes you by the spectacular, polychrome folded sedimentary layers in the Gamasfjellet cliffs, along the eastern shore of Tanafjord. Berlevåg is also a stop on the Hurtigruten coastal ferry route.

BÅTSFJORD

pop 2100

If Berlevåg is rustic, its neighbour, the small port of Båtsfjord, has a much more bustling, industrial feel to it.

The main site in town is the **Båtsfjord church** (🕑 mid-Jun–mid-Aug). Constructed in 1971, its mundane exterior contrasts sharply with the view from within of its glowing 85 sq metres of stained glass.

A 25km hike eastward along the fjord's southern shore leads to Makkaur, an **abandoned fishing village** that dates from medieval times and escaped bombing during WWII. There are all sorts of interesting junk to poke around, including the remains of a German POW camp.

Båtsfjord's best accommodation choice is **Polar Hotell** (☎ 78 98 31 00; www.polarhotel.no; s/d Nkr1050/1350; 🕑 Apr-Oct). It's trim and tidy with a bar and restaurant. Beside it there's limited **camping** (site Nkr150) with access to the hotel's facilities.

Getting There & Away

Flights run from the airport, 5km from town, to Tromsø and Kirkenes, offering excellent views of the Arctic landscape, complete with grazing reindeer.

Buses connect Båtsfjord with Tana Bru (Nkr174, two hours) once or twice daily except Saturday. Båtsfjord is also a stop on the Hurtigruten coastal ferry.

TANA BRU

pop 600

Tiny Tana Bru takes its name from the picturesque bridge over the great Tana River. Here, on one of Europe's best salmon reaches, locals use the technique of constructing barrages to obstruct the upstream progress of the fish; the natural barrage at Storfossen falls, about 30km upstream, is one of the finest fishing spots in all Norway. Test its waters, though you'll need singular good luck to pull out anything to compare with the record 36kg specimen that was once played ashore.

Tana Gull og Sølvsmie (☎ 78 92 80 06; www.tanagullogsolv.com) was established over 30 years ago as eastern Finnmark's first gold- and silversmith. Andreas Lautz creates some very fine gold, silver and bronze jewellery, inspired by traditional Sami designs. The shop also displays quality textiles, ceramics and glassware.

You'll find camping, comfortable rooms, a restaurant, bar and the summertime tourist office at **Hotel Tana** (☎ 78 92 81 98; camp sites Nkr150; s/d Nkr695/795 mid-Jun–mid-Aug, Nkr1095/1345 rest-of-year; Ⓟ), a convenient staging post where the Rv98 meets the E6/E75. Hotel prices include breakfast and a light evening meal, and the new owners have grand plans for development and expansion.

There are daily services to/from Kirkenes (Nkr229, 2¼ hours) and Vadsø (Nkr114, 1¼ hours). Local buses run to/from Berlevåg (Nkr215, 2½ hours) and Båtsfjord (Nkr174, two hours) daily except Saturday. Westbound, the Kirkenes to Alta bus passes through four times weekly.

SAMI MUSEUMS

Between Tana Bru and Vadsø are two Sami treasures, each worth a brief visit.

At **Varangerbotn**, the **Varanger Sami Museum** (Várjjat Sámi Musea; ☎ 78 95 99 20; adult/child Nkr40/20; 🕑 10am-6pm mid-Jun–mid-Aug, 10am-3pm Mon-Fri rest-of-year) mounts temporary exhibitions on Sami culture and history, and displays art by contemporary Sami artists. There's also a small permanent open-air display of Sami turf huts, fishing equipment and domestic life.

SAMI CULTURE & TRADITIONS

Sami life was for centuries based on hunting and fishing, then sometime during the 16th century reindeer were domesticated and the hunting economy transformed into a nomadic herding economy. While reindeer still figure prominently in Sami life, only about 15% of Sami people are still directly involved in reindeer herding and transport by reindeer sledge. These days, a mere handful of traditionalists continue to lead a truly nomadic lifestyle. The majority these days fish or are engaged in tourist-related activities.

A major identifying element of Sami culture is the *joik* (or *yoik*), a rhythmic poem composed for a specific person to describe their innate nature and considered to be owned by the person it describes (p43). Other traditional elements include the use of folk medicine, Shamanism, artistic pursuits (especially woodcarving and silversmithing) and striving for ecological harmony.

The Sami national dress is the only genuine folk dress that's still in casual use in Norway, and you might see it on the streets of Kautokeino and Karasjok. Each district has its own distinct features, but all include a highly decorated and embroidered combination of red-and-blue felt shirts or frocks, trousers or skirts, and boots and hats. On special occasions, the women's dress is topped off with a crown of pearls and a garland of silk hair ribbons.

To learn more, look out for *The Sami People* published by Davvi Girji (1990) or *The Sami: Indigenous People of the Arctic* by Odd Mathis Hælta, both available in English translation. *The Magic of Sami Yoik* by Dejoda is one of several CDs devoted to this special genre, while the tracks on *Eight Seasons* by Mari Boine, a Karasjok singer, offer a greater variety of Sami music.

On the E75, about 15km east of Verangerbotn is an affiliated site: the **Ceavccageadge** (Fish Oil Stone; Mortensnes; admission free; noon-6pm mid-Jun–late Aug), where you can stroll towards the shore amid traces of 10,000 years of Sami culture. At the western end, past burial sites, the remains of homesteads and a reconstructed turf hut, is the namesake *ceavccageadge*, a pillar standing near the water, which was smeared with cod-liver oil to ensure luck while fishing. On a hill to the east the Bjørnstein, a rock resembling a bear, was revered by early Sami inhabitants.

VADSØ

pop 5500

The administrative centre of Finnmark, Vadsø was the site of large-scale immigration from Finland; in the mid-19th century the town's population was 50% Kven, as the Fins were known. A monument at the north end of Tollbugata commemorates this cultural heritage. Vadsø is also renowned as a site for polar exploration, with several expeditions having started or ended here. Like other Finnmark towns, it was badly mauled, by both Russian bombers and retreating Nazi troops, in WWII.

In the cemetery on Vadsø island, across a short bridge from the mainland, rest the remains of several Pomors, Russian traders and fisherfolk from the White Sea area, who prospered here in the 17th century. There are also traces of several protected prehistoric turf huts. If visiting in early summer, watch for the rare Steller's eider, a duck that nests here.

The **tourist office** (☎ 78 94 04 44; www.varanger.com; 10am-6pm Mon-Fri, 10am-4pm Sat & Sun mid-Jun–mid-Aug, 9am-3pm Mon-Fri rest-of-year) is at Kierkegate 15.

Sights

The **Vadsø Museum** (☎ 78 94 28 90; 9am-7pm Mon-Fri, 9am-4pm Sat & Sun mid-Jun–mid-Aug, 10am-3pm Mon-Fri rest-of-year) has three elements. The **Tuomainengården** (Tuomainen estate, Slettengate 21) is a mid-19th-century Finnish farmhouse, with its own bakery, sauna and blacksmith. From the same era, **Esbensengården** (Esbensen estate, Hvistendalsgata), just around the corner, is an altogether more opulent merchant's dwelling, complete with stable and servants' quarters. Admission to each costs Nkr30 (Nkr40 for both sites) and children are free.

The third site, the **Kjeldsen Fish Plant** (adult/child Nkr30/free; noon-6pm mid-Jun–mid-Aug) is at Ekkerøy, 15km east of town. It retains its old stores and lodgings, a mass of arcane fishing equipment, the old shrimp processing and bottling room and – to make you wince at childhood memories – a vast black vat and boiler for extracting cod-liver oil. Plan to arrive when hunger is beginning to bite and you can enjoy an excellent fish meal in the **Havhesten Restaurant** (☎ 90 50 60 80; mains

Nkr120-180; core hrs 2-10pm Tue-Sun), housed in one of the outbuildings. Its maritime artefacts could be an extension of the museum and, if the wind isn't whipping, you can dine on the jetty with the sea sloshing beneath you.

The oil-rig-shaped **Luftskipsmasta** (airship mast) on Vadsø island was built in the mid-1920s as an anchor and launch site for airborne expeditions to the polar regions. The expedition of Roald Amundsen, Umberto Nobile and Lincoln Ellsworth, which flew via the North Pole to Alaska in the airship *Norge N-1,* first used it in April 1926. Two years later it was the launch site for Nobile's airship, *Italia,* which attempted to repeat the journey but crashed on Svalbard. Amundsen – together with 12 steamships, 13 planes and 1500 men – joined the rescue expedition and disappeared in the attempt, becoming a national martyr as well as a hero. It's well worth the breezy 600m stroll across the grass flats with a rich variety of aquatic birds that quack and croak in the small lake just beyond.

As so often in these small Finnmark communities, the **church** (Amtmannsgate 1b; 8.30am-3pm Mon-Fri mid-Jun–mid-Aug) is the most interesting structure architecturally – and all too often the only building to have survived the devastation wreaked by retreating Nazi forces. Vadsø's didn't. Built anew in 1958, it's simple enough yet rich in symbolism. The twin peaks are intended to recall an iceberg, the Orthodox-inspired altarpiece looks metaphorically over the frontier and the rich stained glass depicts the seasons.

Sleeping & Eating

Vestre Jakobselv Camping (78 95 60 64; Lilledalsveien; person/site Nkr10/115, 4-/5-bed cabins Nkr350/420, 4-/6-bed r Nkr350/500, 3-bed r with bathroom & kitchen Nkr700; May-Sep) Rooms and cabins are very reasonably priced at Vadsø's nearest camp site, 17km west of town. Only 200m from a fast-flowing salmon river, it's a popular venue for fisherfolk.

Vadsø Apartments (78 95 44 00, 92 06 86 03; Tibergveien 3; s/d Nkr400/600) The town's only mid-range choice is three blocks from the harbour. It's an excellent deal. The five singles and three doubles are furnished in homely style and have both bathroom and mini-kitchen. Capacity is limited, so book in advance.

Nobile Hotell (78 95 33 35; www.nobilehotell.no; Brugata 2, Vadsøya island; s/d Nkr700/1000 Jun-Jul Nkr850/1250 Sun-Thu, Nkr800/1000 Fri & Sat rest-of-year all incl breakfast; P) Named after the Arctic explorer – blown-up photos of him and his contemporaries gaze down at you from the walls – the Nobile is a short stroll from the Hurtigruten quay. Ask for room 217, slightly larger than the rest and with good views over town and sound.

Rica Hotel Vadsø (78 95 25 50; www.rica.no; Oscarsgate 4; s/d Nkr650/900 mid-Jun–mid-Aug, Nk1395/1645 Mon-Thu, Nkr1125/1395 Fri & Sat rest-of-year, all incl breakfast; P) Plumb in the centre, the friendly Rica has recently renovated rooms with parquet flooring. Complete with free sauna and mini-gym, it represents Vadsø's best choice.

Oscar Mat og Vinhus restaurant (mains Nkr188-317; 4-10pm) at the Rica Hotel Vadsø is the town's finest, offering a great buffet breakfast and a daily fish or meat special (Nkr145).

Hildonen Café (78 95 15 06; Kirkegata 20) The aroma of warm bread and sweet cakes draws you into this bakery and café, hugely popular with locals and bang opposite the tourist office.

Påls Matopplevelser (78 95 33 84; Hvistendalsgata 6b; 9am-5pm Mon-Fri, 10am-3pm Sat) Pål dishes up tasty baguettes (Nkr33 to Nkr50) and salads (Nkr50 to Nkr90) and does a fresh-fish daily special (Nkr100 to Nkr140), all to eat in or take away.

Indigo (78 95 16 81; Tollbugata 12; mains Nkr150-255; Tue-Sat) It makes no such claim but surely the long-established Indigo must rank as Europe's, if not the world's, northernmost Indian restaurant. Its related takeaway adjunct is something of a culinary UN, dishing up kebabs, burgers, pizzas and Tex-Mex as well as curries.

Getting There & Away

Vadsø is a stop only on the northbound Hurtigruten coastal ferry, which heads for Kirkenes at 8.15am. There are at least two buses daily to/from Tana Bru (Nkr114, 1¼ hours) and Vardø (Nkr128, 1½ hours).

VARDØ

pop 2100

It's a pancake-flat 75km drive between Vadsø and Vardø, well off the beaten track for all but the most die-hard travellers. But the ribbon of road has a lonely charm as it threads its way between the shoreline, hardy grasses and tough, low shrubs.

Vardø qualifies as Norway's easternmost town. Although this butterfly-shaped island

HAMNINGBERG

A warmly recommended 88km round trip northwards from Vardø along the coast brings you to the tiny, semi-abandoned, timber-built settlement of Hamningberg.

The wisp of a single-lane road runs through some of northern Norway's most fascinating geology: inky tarns, copses of scrubby bushes clinging to the meagre topsoil for dear life, flecks of snow even in late July and looming, lichen-covered eroded stone pillars, the remnants of sedimentary layers turned on end. En route, you'll pass reindeer herds and several sandy beaches. Save the bucket-and-spading, though, until the return journey when, 7.3km south of Hamningberg, you can walk to the broadest beach through the small nature reserve of **Sandfjordneset**, with its protected sand dunes set back from the shoreline.

What makes the village special is that, being so remote, it was saved from the general destruction of the Nazi retreat in WWII. Only one house was destroyed – and that by a Russian bomber. The rest, abandoned in the 1960s except for summer visitors, still stand as living reminders of what was once one of eastern Finnmark's largest fishing villages. Here where the road ends, there's a small **café** (10am-6pm Jun-Aug).

is connected to the mainland by the 2.9km-long Ishavstunnelen (Arctic Ocean tunnel), locals maintain that theirs is the only 'mainland' Norwegian town lying within the Arctic climatic zone (its average temperature is below 10°C). Once a stronghold of trade with the Russian Pomors, it's now a major fishing port and home to many Russian and Sri Lankan immigrants.

The **tourist office** (78 98 69 07; www.varanger.com; 10am-7pm Mon-Fri, noon-7pm Sat & Sun Jun–mid-Aug) is in a smart wooden building beside the Hurtigruten quay.

Sights & Activities

In summer the tourist office runs **boat trips** (Nkr200 return; hourly 9am-3.30pm) to the island of **Hornøya** with its picturesque lighthouse and teeming bird cliffs. To be all alone after the last shuttle pulls out, reserve one of the only three beds at the lighthouse (Nkr250).

The star-shaped **Vardøhus Festning** (Vardøhus Fortress; 78 98 85 02; Festningsgate 20; admission Nkr30; 8am-9pm mid-Apr–mid-Sep, 10am-6pm rest-of-year) – yes, of course it's the world's most northerly – was constructed in 1737 by King Christian VI. For a fortress, it's painted in gentle fairy-tale colours. On a nice, sunny day it's pleasant to stroll around the flower-festooned bastions, past turf-roofed buildings and Russian cannons. You pay the admission fee either at the guard office or by dropping it into the WWII sea mine that guards the entrance.

Vardø's recently established **Pomor Museum** (78 98 80 75; Kaigata; adult/child Nkr40/20; 11am-5pm mid-Jun–mid-Aug, 4-5pm Mon-Fri rest-of-year) recalls the historic trade between Russia and Norway, which involved bartering fish against corn. This lasted until the Bolshevik Revolution in 1917.

Between 1621 and 1692, around 90 Vardø women were accused of witchcraft and burned; a sign and flag at Kristian IV gate 24 commemorate the site. On **Domen**, a hill about 2km south of town on the mainland, is the cave where they were supposed to have held their satanic rites and secret rendezvous with the devil.

And those huge spheres on Vardø's hilltops? The official version is that they're space-tracking equipment.

Tours

Hexeria (78 98 84 04; www.hexeria.no; Kaigata 12) organises bird-watching and fishing trips and also rents boats and bikes.

Sleeping

Hexeria (see above; s/d from Nkr300/450; Jun-Aug) Rents student hostel rooms during the summer vacation, and also has apartments (from Nkr650) on its books. Hostel rooms have corridor bathrooms and self-catering facilities,

Kiberg Bed & Boat (41 32 86 79; www.kibergbedandboat.com; Ordfører Halvaris Gate 11, Kiberg; s/d Nkr350/490) We recommend this quirky place in Kiberg, 13km south of Vardø, with a degree of diffidence. Genial owner Ronny Larsen and most of his guests were happily out of their skulls on wine when we overnighted as it was the night in the year when the community celebrates the return of the salmon from the deep ocean. So we'd welcome your feedback about this renovated fisherfolk's sleeping quarters with its lounge and well-equipped guest kitchen. Rooms are trim and tidy with corridor facilities and there's no better place in all Norway to suck on the limbs of a giant king crab (Nkr350). Ronny can organise four-hour fishing trips (Nkr1500 per boat) and bird-watching walks (Nkr150). Reception is open between the hours of 6pm and midnight.

Vardø Hotell (☎ 78 98 77 61; www.vardohotel.no; Kaigata 8; s/d Nkr490/590 mid-Jun–mid-Aug, Nk1070/1170 Mon-Thu, Nkr860/960 Fri & Sat rest-of-year) The staff are willing and cheerful at Vardø's only hotel. However, rooms and corridors are decidedly threadbare and passé. On the plus side, summer prices are very reasonable, many rooms overlook the harbour and a couple are handicapped-equipped.

Eating & Drinking

Asia Burger Café (☎ 78 94 46 00; Kristian IV gate 4; mains Nkr130; ⌚ Tue-Sun Feb-Nov) Disregard the off-putting name, shun the burgers and order a dish of tasty, authentic Thai cooking in – you've guessed it – mainland Europe's most northerly Thai restaurant. Accompany this with one of the 36 kinds of bottled beer on offer, including equally authentic Thai Singha beer.

Nordpol Kro (☎ 78 98 75 01; Kaigata 21; ⌚ 10am-midnight) No, despite the name, the Northpole Pub isn't another 'northernmost'. But, dating from 1858 with wooden boards and antique bric-a-brac, each telling a story about the island, it does lay good claim to be northern Norway's oldest. Your friendly landlord, Bjørn Bredesen, has what must be just about anywhere's most comprehensive collection of beer mats. Pick the right night and you can enjoy live music too.

Getting There & Away

Vardø is a stop on the Hurtigruten coastal ferry route. Buses do the scenic seaside run between Vadsø and Vardø (Nkr128, 1½ hours) at least twice daily.

KIRKENES

pop 4600

This is it: you're as far east as Cairo, further east than most of Finland, a mere 15km from the border with Russia – and at the end of the line for the Hurtigruten coastal ferry. This tiny, nondescript place, anticlimactic for many, has a distinct frontier feel. You'll see street signs in Norwegian and Cyrillic script and hear Russian spoken by trans-border visitors and fishermen, who enjoy better prices for their catch here than in their home ports further to the east.

The town reels with over 100,000 visitors per annum, most stepping off the Hurtigruten to spend a couple of hours in the town before travelling onward. But you should linger a while here, not primarily for the town's sake but to take one of the many excursions and activities offered by the useful one-stop tourist office.

History

The district of Sør-Varanger, with Kirkenes as its main town, was jointly occupied by Norway and Russia until 1926, when the Russian, Finnish and Norwegian borders were set.

In 1906 iron ore was discovered nearby and Kirkenes became a major supplier of raw materials for artillery during WWI. Early in WWII the Nazis coveted its resources and strategic position near the Russian port of Murmansk, occupied the town and posted 100,000 troops there. As a result, tiny Kirkenes was, after Malta, the most bombed place during WWII, with at least 320 devastating Soviet raids. The town was also an internment site for Norwegians from all over the country who did not cooperate with the Nazi occupiers.

The retreating Nazis burned to the ground the little left of Kirkenes before advancing Soviet troops liberated its ruins in October 1944. Subsequently rebuilt, it continued to supply iron ore to much of Europe but costs were too high to sustain the industry and in 1996 the mines closed down.

Information

Library (Bibliotek; ☎ 78 99 32 51; Town Sq; ⌚ core hrs 9.30am-3pm Mon-Fri) Has internet access.

Tourist office (☎ 78 99 25 44; www.kirkenesinfo.no; Presteveien 1; ⌚ 8.30am-6pm Mon-Fri, 10am-5pm Sat & Sun Jun-Aug, 8.30am-4pm Mon-Fri rest-of-year)

Dangers & Annoyances

Don't even think about stepping across the Russian border for a photo. Nowadays, in addition to vestiges of old Cold War neuroses on both sides, Norway, as a Schengen Agreement country, is vigilant in keeping illegal immi-

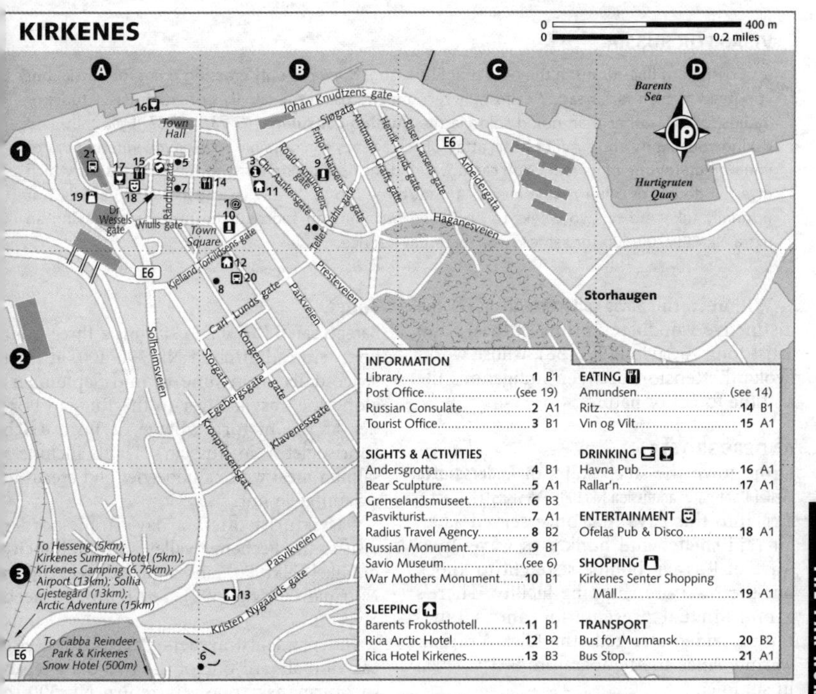

grants from entering. Both Norwegian and Russian sentries are equipped with surveillance equipment and the fine for any illegal crossings, even momentary ones, starts at a whopping Nkr5000. Greeting people on the other side, tossing anything across, using telephoto or zoom lenses or even a tripod all qualify as violations. As the guidance document sternly warns: 'any attempts at violations will be punished as if they had been carried out'.

Sights & Activities

For such a tiny place, Kirkenes offers a wealth of tours and activities in and around town. For an overview according to season, pick up one of the tourist office's comprehensive brochures, *Summer Activities* and *Winter Activities*.

Principal tour agencies are:

Arctic Adventure (☎ 95 15 07 55; www.arctic-adventure.no; Jarfjordbotn)

Pasvikturist (☎ 78 99 50 80; www.pasvikturist.no; Dr Wessels gate 9)

Radius (☎ 78 97 05 40; www.radius-kirkenes.com; Kongensgate 1-2)

Summer activities, in addition to the ones we describe following, include:

- Visiting a Russian trawler (Nkr275)
- Helicopter flights to the Russian border (Nkr895)
- King crab safaris (Nkr990)
- Visiting the old iron-ore mine (adult/child Nkr400/200)
- Half-day tours of the Pasvik Valley (adult/child Nkr650/350)

Winter fun includes:

- snowmobile safaris (from Nkr1150)
- ice fishing (Nkr790)
- dog-sledding (from Nkr1250)

You can book all through the tourist office or directly with the operators.

GRENSELANDSMUSEET

This well-presented **frontier museum** (☎ 78 99 48 80; Førstevannslia; adult/child/concession Nkr40/free/30; 🕑 10am-6pm early Jun–mid-Aug, 10am-3.30pm rest-of-year), 1km from the centre, presents the geography and culture of the border region with special displays on WWII and mining.

THE FAR NORTH

VISAS FOR RUSSIA

It's possible to pass through the border at Storkskog, Norway's only crossing point for Russia, but you need to plan far ahead. We strongly recommend using the services of either Pasvikturist or Radius (p361), rather than going solo via the **Russian consulate** (☎ 78 99 37 37, if you insist) and risking your sanity and a minor heart attack. Each agency can obtain a visa for you whether or not you sign on for one of its tours. You can download the application form from their websites, which give full details of other requirements. A one-/three-/up-to-29-day visa costs Nkr500/675/825. It normally takes up to two weeks to be issued but you can shortcut the process by paying an extra Nkr800/700/600 for same-/two-/three-day service.

Within it, the **Savio collection** displays the distinctive woodblock prints of local Sami artist John A Savio (1902–38), whose works evoke the tension between indigenous life and the forces of nature.

ANDERSGROTTA

Drop down the steep stairs of **Andersgrotta** (Tellef Dahlsgate; admission Nkr100; visits 11.30am & noon) into this cave that once served as an air-raid shelter and bunker as wave upon wave of Russian bombers sought to knock out the Nazi ore shipping facility. There's a multilingual presentation and a nine-minute video also tells the tale. Wrap up warmly since the temperature is 3°C, even in summer.

MONUMENTS & SCULPTURES

Up a short hill, the **Russian Monument** is dedicated to the Red Army troops who liberated the town in 1944. The **War Mothers Monument** in the town square commemorates women's efforts during the war and there's an engaging little **sculpture** of a bear mounting – in every sense of the word, it would appear – a lamppost outside the Russian consulate.

GABBA REINDEER PARK

This **reindeer safari park** (admission Nkr275; tours 2pm daily) may not be so much of a treat for the children if you've been driving in Eastern Finnmark and stopped to relate to browsing roadside reindeer but it's worth the visit if you've rolled in on the Hurtigruten.

RUSSIAN MARKET

On the last Thursday of most months, Russian merchants set up shop around the town centre, selling everything from crafts and knitted tablecloths to binoculars. Prices aren't as cheap as in Russia, but they're still a bargain for Norway.

Tours

Barents Safari (☎ 90 19 05 94) runs a three-hour boat trip (adult/child Nkr790/400, at least twice daily from June to mid-September) along the Pasvik River to the Russian border at the historic village of Boris Gleb (Borisoglebsk in Russian). Tariffs include a salmon meal with cloudberries and cream in a Sami-style hut.

Pasvikturist offers a day's trans-border visit to the Pechenga valley and mining city of Nikel (Nkr990), and a guided weekend in Murmansk (Nkr1690). For both you need a visa.

Independent travellers armed with a visa can hop aboard one of the two daily buses to Murmansk (one way/return Nkr300 to to Nkr800, five hours). See Lonely Planet's *Russia & Belarus* for more information.

Sleeping

Kirkenes Camping (☎ 78 99 80 28; Maggadalen, Hesseng tent/caravan sites Nkr90/140 plus per person Nkr25, 4-bed cabins Nkr370-770; Jun-Aug) Beside the E6 and 8km west of Kirkenes, this friendly spot is the sole option for campers. Reception opens only between 9am and 8pm (no way to run a campsite in high season) so reserve in advance if you're after a cabin.

Kirkenes Summer Hotel (☎ 78 97 05 40; www.radius-kirkenes.com; Hesseng; s/d Nkr440/890; late Jun–mid-Aug; P) In the village of Hesseng, 4km southwest of Kirkenes along the E6, this option serves as student accommodation during the academic year. Singles have corridor bathrooms while all doubles are en suite.

Barents Frokosthotell (☎ 78 99 32 99; gcelius@frsurf.no; Presteveien 3; basic s/d Nkr500/700, with bathroom Nkr650/800) Reception and most of your fellow guests will probably be Russian at this unpretentious place. Right beside the tourist office, its 14 bog-standard rooms are fresh and comfortable.

our pick **Sollia Gjestegård** (☎ 78 99 08 20; www.storskog.no; 2-6-bed cabins Nkr500-950, d Nkr750) The Sollia, 13km southeast of Kirkenes, is a wonderful getaway haven, offering both cabins and apartments. The whole family can sweat it out in the sauna while the children will enjoy communing with the resident huskies.

Rica Arctic Hotel (☎ 78 99 29 29; www.rica.no; Kongensgate 1-3; s/d Nkr895/1145 mid-Jun–mid-Aug; Nkr1415/1665 Sun-Thu, Nkr880/1130 Fri & Sat rest-of-year; P) The Rica Arctic, a pleasing modern block, boasts Norway's most easterly swimming pool, heated and open year-round. The other special attribute, its Arctic menu restaurant (summer buffet Nkr295), is one of the best of Kirkenes's hotel dining options.

Rica Hotel Kirkenes (☎ 78 99 14 91; www.rica.no; Pasvikveien 63; s/d Nkr895/1145 mid-Jun–mid-Aug, Nkr1355/1605 Sun-Thu, Nkr825/1075 Fri & Sat rest-of-year, all incl breakfast) This Rica really does feel like an overspill hotel, similarly priced to the Rica Arctic yet with none of the latter's charm. All the same it's comfortable enough, and being above town, has panoramic views from the restaurant and many bedrooms.

Eating

Ritz (☎ 78 99 34 81; Dr Wessels gate 17; pizzas Nkr160-186; core hrs 3-11.30pm) Kirkenes' pizza place has an all-you-can-eat dinnertime taco buffet (Nkr110) on Wednesday and pizza buffet (Nkr105) each Friday.

Amundsen (☎ 78 99 34 80; core hrs 8.30am-4pm) A neat little café attached to Ritz with a good selection of sandwiches, salads and cakes. It's equally pleasant inside or, the wind willing, outdoors on the terrace flanking pedestrianised Dr Wessels gate.

Sollia Gjestegård (mains Nkr220-340; Tue-Sun) This hotel also runs a 1st-class restaurant, offering a grand panorama of the Russian frontier from its broad picture windows.

Vin og Vilt (☎ 78 99 38 11; Kierkegata 5; mains Nkr270-475; 6-11pm) This gourmet choice, its décor simulating an elegant hunting lodge, has an enticing à la carte menu, where reindeer, hare and grouse (in season) plus Arctic char all feature.

Drinking & Entertainment

Havna Pub (Johan Knudtzens gate 1; 3pm-1am Wed-Sun), an earthy sailors' hang-out overlooking the harbour and a rusting Russian hulk, is a great place to play pool or darts. **Rallar'n** (☎ 78 99 18 73; Storgata 1), while by no means snooty, is less rough-and-ready.

Ritz (☎ 78 99 34 81; Dr Wessels gate 17) is a disco and pub attracting a mainly younger crowd. **Ofelas Pub & Disco** (Dr Wessels gate 3) pulls in a slightly older clientele. Both open on Friday and Saturday nights.

Getting There & Away

From **Kirkenes airport** (☎ 78 97 35 20), there are direct flights to Oslo and Tromsø. Savvy locals save money by flying in/out of Ivalo, Finland, in summer, when a daily bus (see below) runs the 250km between Kirkenes and Ivalo's airport.

Buses run to Karasjok (Nkr504, 5¼ hours), Hammerfest (Nkr831, 10 to 12 hours), Alta (Nkr876, 15 hours) and many points in between three or four times weekly. From late June to mid-August, **Lapin Linjat** (www.eskelisen-lapinlinjat.com) runs once daily to Ivalo town and airport (Nkr320, 4½ hours).

Kirkenes is the terminus of the Hurtigruten coastal ferry, which heads southwards again at 12.45pm daily. A bus meets the boat and runs into town (Nkr25) and on to the airport (Nkr70).

Getting Around

The airport, 13km southwest of town, is served by the Flybuss (Nkr70, 20 minutes), which connects the bus terminal and Rica Arctic Hotel with all arriving and departing flights. **Kirkenes Taxi** (☎ 78 99 13 97) charges Nkr225/305 for a day/evening run between town and airport.

Hourly buses (less frequent at weekends) run between the centre and Hesseng (Nkr20, 15 minutes).

Car rental agencies include **Hertz** (☎ 78 99 39 73) and **Avis** (☎ 78 97 37 05), both in Hesseng and both prepared to deliver a car to your hotel.

PASVIK RIVER VALLEY

Even when diabolical mosquito swarms make life hell for warm-blooded creatures, the remote lakes, wet tundra bogs and Norway's largest stand of virgin taiga forest lend appeal to little Øvre Pasvik National Park, in the far reaches of the Pasvik River valley.

Some 100km south of Kirkenes and 200 sq km in area, this last corner of Norway seems more like Finland, Siberia or even Alaska. Here, wolves, wolverines and brown bears still roam freely. The park is also home to elk and a host of relatively rare birds that

OPORINIA AUTUMNATA

Throughout Finnmark and over the border in Finland too, you'll come across desolate forests of birch, leafless, their trunks blackened as though fire had swept through. But the culprit is something smaller, slower, more insidious and just as destructive.

The *Oporinia autumnata* moth is dowdy and looks harmless; the caterpillars come bright green, up to 2cm long and hungry as hell, devouring the leaves and swinging on gossamer threads to their next chlorophyll meal.

Eventually, they'll eat themselves out of house and home and numbers will drop but until that time, their impact can be devastating for fragile taiga forest. What's needed for them to be eradicated is at least two consecutive days of temperatures below –35°C. But, while winters are harsh up here, years can go by before it gets *that* bitter.

includes the Siberian jay, pine grosbeak, redpoll and smew.

The Stone-Age Komsa hunting culture left its mark here in the form of hunters' pitfall traps around lake Ødevann and elsewhere in the region; some date from as early as 4000 BC.

Information

The **Øvre Pasvik National Park Centre** (☎ 46 41 36 00; 🕒 8am-8pm Mon-Fri, 10am-8pm Fri & Sat mid-Jun–mid-Sep, 8am-3.30pm Mon-Fri rest-of-year) is set in lovely gardens about 40km south of Kirkenes.

Sights & Activities

It's worth a stop at the Strand branch of the **Sør-Varanger Museum** (☎ 78 99 48 80; 🕒 Jul–mid-Aug), which preserves Norway's oldest public boarding school and illustrates the region's ethnic mix. Visit, too, the timber-built **Svanvik chapel** dating from 1934, and a couple of 19th-century farms, **Bjørklund** and **Nordre Namdalen**.

The Cold War lookout tower **Høyden 96** offers a view eastward to the Russian mining town of Nikel.

HIKING

Douse yourself liberally in mosquito repellent before heading off into the wilds. The most accessible route is the poor road that turns southwest 1.5km south of Vaggatem and ends 9km later at a car park near the northeastern end of Lake Sortbrysttjørna. There, a marked track leads southwestward for 5km, passing several scenic lakes, marshes and bogs to end at the Ellenvannskoia hikers' hut, beside the large lake, Ellenvatn.

Also from the Ødevasskoia car park, it's about an 8km walk due south to Krokfjell (145m) and the **Treriksrøysa**, the monument marking the spot where Norway, Finland and Russia meet. Although you can approach it and take photos, you may not walk around the monument, which would amount to an illicit border crossing!

The topographic sheet to use is Statens Kartverk's *Krokfjellet,* which conveniently covers the entire park at 1:25,000.

Sleeping & Eating

There are several hunting and fishing huts scattered around the park but the only one that's practical for casual hikers is Ellenvannskoia, which is free.

Øvre Pasvik Café & Camping (☎ 78 99 55 30; www.pasvik-café.no in Norwegian; Vaggetem; cabin Nkr300-570 This place rents canoes and bicycles, and provides information on local wilderness and attractions.

Pasvik Taiga Restaurant (☎ 78 99 54 44; www.pasvik-taiga.no in Norwegian; Skogfoss; 3-4 course dinner Nkr500 This highly acclaimed place presents a range of gourmet fish and game dishes prepared using local herbs and berries. There are only seven rooms (per person including breakfast Nkr800), so it's essential to book ahead – for the restaurant, too, since all food is freshly prepared on the day.

Getting There & Away

A weekday bus leaves Kirkenes for Skogfoss (Nkr100, 1½ hours) and continues to Vaggetem (Nkr156, 2½ hours) on Monday, Wednesday and Friday.

GRENSE JAKOBSELV

The first settlement at Grense Jakobselv probably appeared around 8000 years ago, when the sea level was 60m lower than it is today Only a small stream separates Norway and Russia here, and along the road you can see the border obelisks on both sides. The only real attraction – apart from the chance to

;aze over the magic line – is the 1869 stone :hurch. It was constructed within sight of the ;ea to cement Norway's territorial claims after ocal people complained to the authorities that Russian fishing boats were illegally trespassing nto Norwegian waters; it was thought that the ntruders would respect a church and change :heir ways.

During school holidays, you can make a day :rip between Kirkenes and Grense Jakobselv (Nkr105, 1½ hours) on Monday, Wednesday ınd Friday. The bus leaves at 9am and returns ıt 11.30am, allowing an hour to explore.

INNER FINNMARK

Nestled against the Finnish border, Norway's big sky country' is a place of lush greenery and epicentre of the semi-political entity known ıs Sápmi, the 'land of the Sami'. Kautokeino, ı one-street town if ever there was one, is :he traditional heart of the region, although Karasjok is altogether livelier and has more Sami institutions.

KAUTOKEINO

pop 2000

While Karasjok has made concessions to Norwegian culture, Kautokeino, the traditional winter base of the reindeer Sami (as opposed to their coastal kin), remains more emphatically Sami; some 85% of the townspeople have Sami as their first language and t's not uncommon to see a few nontourist-industry locals in traditional costume. The *kommune,* or municipality, is Norway's argest, covering nearly 10,000 sq km. That's ın awful lot of forest and lake. The town is, frankly, dull in summer since so many of its people are up and away with the reindeer n their warm-weather pastures (in winter, by contrast, around 100,000 reindeer live hereabouts). What makes a visit well worthwhile is Juhls' Silver Gallery, just out of town ınd a magnificent repository of the best of Scandinavian jewellery design.

From as early as 1553, during the gradual transition between nomadic and sedentary ifestyles, records reveal evidence of permanent settlement. Christianity took hold early ınd the first church was built in 1641.

The **tourist office** (☎ 78 48 65 00; www.kautokeino nu; 🕑 10am-5pm Mon-Sat, noon-4pm Sun mid-Jun–mid-Aug) is on the ground floor of the all-purpose complex beside the main road that also houses a bank, the town post office and the Coop supermarket.

Sights & Activities

JUHLS' SILVER GALLERY

Juhls' Sølvsmie (Silver Gallery) is a wonderful building, all slopes and soft angles, designed and built by owners Regine and Frank Juhls,

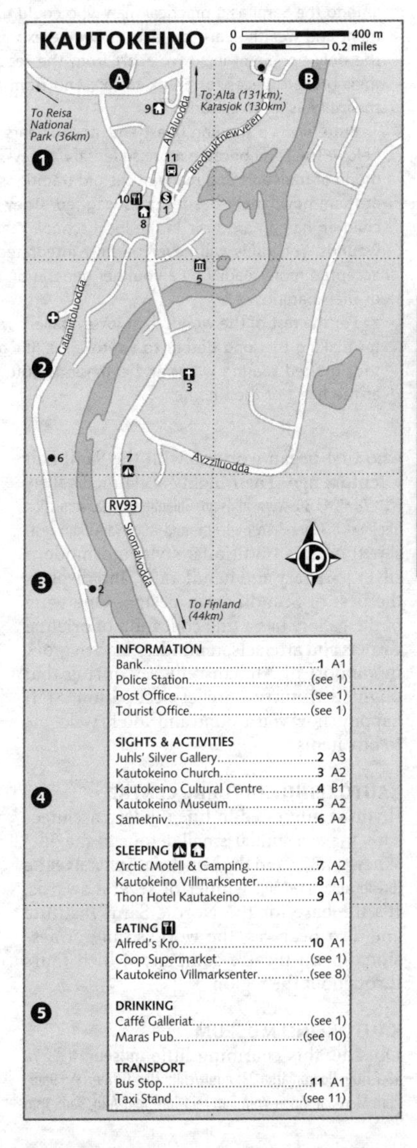

REGINE & FRANK JUHLS

It's over half a century since Frank Juhls, despairing of the incestuous art scene in his native Copenhagen, travelled alone to Sami country. 'I've always looked eastwards, never to the west', he says, sipping a coffee as the light of summer streams through the windows of his gallery. And it's nearly as long since his wife, Regine, fetched up here. A slip of a girl aged only 18, she too came alone, leaving her native Germany to spend her early months as maidservant to an itinerant Sami family. Frank hunted, painted and built himself a log cabin – and a reputation among the Sami as a practical man who could fix anything. Silver for the Sami was both adornment and wealth – 'art to wear', as Regine expresses it, recalling the early days when they were the only non-Sami in town, apart from the teachers at the local school, 'so they would bring their broken pieces for Frank to fix'. And from the Sami the Juhls first derived inspiration for their exquisite silverwork.

But envy is a snarling beast and, as the years passed, jealous eyes looked up from the valley below. The Sami became more sedentary. Snow-scooters replaced reindeer sleds as the preferred mode of transport and many of the old traditions faded away. 'They came with nothing and look at them now,' malicious tongues wagged. 'They patronise us', spat Sami radicals and the Juhls' children had a hard time in the local school. Years have gone by since then and time heals raw wounds. The Juhls will never be fully integrated but the couple who live on the hill are now accepted more readily by a younger generation who have sloughed off some of the complexes of their parents.

For the rest of the world, their lovely gallery with its soft, sweeping angles is the prime reason for making the long detour to Kautokeino. 'It's grown organically', says Regine, explaining how they grafted soaring wings and extensions onto the original simple wooden cabin that remains at the heart of their home.

who first began working with the Sami half a century ago. Their highly acclaimed **gallery** (☎ 78 48 43 30; www.juhls.no; Galaniitoluodda; admission free; 🕑 8.30am-8pm mid-Jun–mid-Aug, 9am-6pm rest-of-year) creates traditional-style and modern silver jewellery and handicrafts, and displays the best of Scandinavian design. One wing of the gallery has a fine collection of oriental carpets and artefacts, reminders of their work in support of Afghan refugees during that blighted country's Soviet occupation. Staff happily show you around and you're welcome to buy items.

KAUTOKEINO CULTURAL CENTRE

If you're interested in fine modern architecture, make a similar small detour to the outskirts of town and the **Kautokeino Cultural Centre** (Bredbuktnesveien 50), winner of several awards. It's the base for the Nordic Sami Institute and also Beaivváš, the world's only professional Sami theatre company, which tours throughout the region.

KAUTOKEINO MUSEUM

Outside, this charming little **museum** (☎ 78 48 71 00; Boaronjárga 23; adult/child Nkr30/free; 🕑 9am-7pm Mon-Sat, noon-7pm Sun mid-Jun–mid-Aug, 9am-3pm Mon-Fri rest-of-year) presents a traditional Sam settlement, complete with an early home temporary dwellings and outbuildings such as the kitchen, sauna, and huts for storing fish potatoes and lichen (also called 'reindeer moss and prime reindeer fodder). Inside are Sam handicrafts, farming and reindeer-herding implements, religious icons and artefacts, and winter transport gear.

KAUTOKEINO KIRKE

The timbered Kautokeino **church** (Suomalvodda 🕑 9am-9pm Jun–mid-Aug), which dates from 1958 is one of Norway's most used, particularly at Easter. Its cheery interior, alive with bright Sam colours, has some fixtures salvaged from the earlier 1701 church that was torched in WWII.

SAMEKNIV

Samekniv (☎ 78 48 62 84; Galaniitoluodda; admission free; 🕑 9am-8pm Jun-Aug, 9am-4pm rest-of-year) is the gallery of local Sami knifesmith Josef Per Buljo.

CANOEING

Between June and August you can hire canoes (per day Nkr300) to potter around on the river. Ask at Alfred's Kro (see opposite).

Festivals & Events

Easter week is a time for weddings and an excuse for a big gathering to mark the end of the dark season, before folk and flocks disperse to the summer grazing. It's celebrated with panache: the reindeer racing world championships, the Sami Grand Prix – no, not a souped-up snowmobile race but the premier *yoik* (rhythmic poem) contest – and other traditional Sami and religious events. Check out www.saami-easterfestival.org for more details and programme information.

Sleeping & Eating

When we last passed by, pile-drivers were pounding, laying the foundations of a new hotel belonging to the Thon chain that's projected to open in late summer, 2008.

Arctic Motell & Camping (☎ 78 48 54 00; www.kauto.no; Suomaluodda 16; car/caravan sites Nkr130/150, cabin with outdoor bathroom Nkr400, with bathroom Nkr750-1400, motel r Nkr600) Campers and cabin dwellers have access to a communal kitchen at this friendly place. Its Sami *lavvo* (tepee) is a warm and cosy spot to relax by a wood fire and sip the steaming coffee, laid on nightly at 8pm. If you ask, the small café will also rustle up *bidos*, the traditional reindeer meat stew served at Sami weddings and other rites of passage.

Kautokeino Villmarksenter (☎ 78 48 76 02; isakmathis@hotmail.com; Hannoluohkka 2; s/d Nkr610/810, 4-bed cabins Nkr500) Set above the main road, this is a functional, cheerless sort of place whose main asset is its café-restaurant (mains Nkr90 to Nkr160) with an attractive open-air deck.

Alfred's Kro (☎ 78 48 61 18; Hannoluohkka 4) With Mack beer on draught, this amiable self-service café does a whole range of traditional Finnmark dishes such as pike fishcakes and – its speciality – juicy reindeer steak. A buffet plus main dish and coffee cost around Nkr150, representing outstanding value.

Drinking

Caffé Galleriat, above the tourist office and with its principal entrance on the main drag, is a convivial little place for a relaxing coffee.

Tucked away below Alfred's Kro, **Maras Pub** (🕑 8pm-midnight or 2am Thu-Sun) is an animated dive that sometimes has live music, both pop and traditional. Once the ale starts flowing, patrons are quite likely to spontaneously break into a *yoik* or two.

Getting There & Away

Public transport is slim. FFR buses run between Kautokeino and Alta (Nkr220, 2¼ hours) four times weekly. From June to mid-August, the Finnish Lapin Linjat bus connects Kautokeino with Alta (1¾ hours) and Rovaniemi (eight hours), in Finland once daily.

REISA NATIONAL PARK

Although technically in Troms county, Reisa National Park is most readily accessible by road from Kautokeino. For hikers, the 50km route through this remote Finnmarksvidda country is one of Norway's wildest and most physically demanding challenges. The northern trailhead at Sarelv is accessible on the Rv865, 47km south of Storslett, and the southern end is reached on the gravel route to Reisevannhytta, 4km west of Bieddjuvaggi on the Rv896, heading northwest from Kautokeino.

Most people walk from north to south. From Bilto or Sarelv, you can either walk the track up the western side of the cleft that channels the Reisaelva river or hire a riverboat for the three-hour 27km trip upstream to Nedrefoss, where there's a DNT hut. En route, notice the 269m Mollesfossen waterfall, east of the track on the tributary stream Molleselva. From Nedrefoss, the walking route continues for 35km south to the Reisavannhytta hut on lake Reisajävri, near the southern trailhead.

KARASJOK

pop 1500

It's a lovely drive between Kautokeino and Karasjok, following, for the most spectacular stretch, the River Ješjokka.

Kautokeino may have more Sami residents, but Karasjok (Kárásjohka in Sami) is Sami Norway's indisputable capital. It's home to the Sami Parliament and library, NRK Sami Radio, a wonderful Sami museum and an impressive Sami theme park. Karasjok is also the site of Finnmark's oldest timber church, **Gamlekirke**, constructed in 1807 and the only Karasjok building to survive WWII destruction. Only 18km from the border with Finland, the town pulls in coaches, caravans and cars by the hundred, all heading for Nordkapp.

The **tourist office** (☎ 78 46 88 10; www.koas.no; 🕑 9am-7pm Jun–mid-Aug, 9am-4pm Mon-Fri rest-of-year) is in Sápmi Park, near the junction of the E6 and the Rv92. It will change money if you're

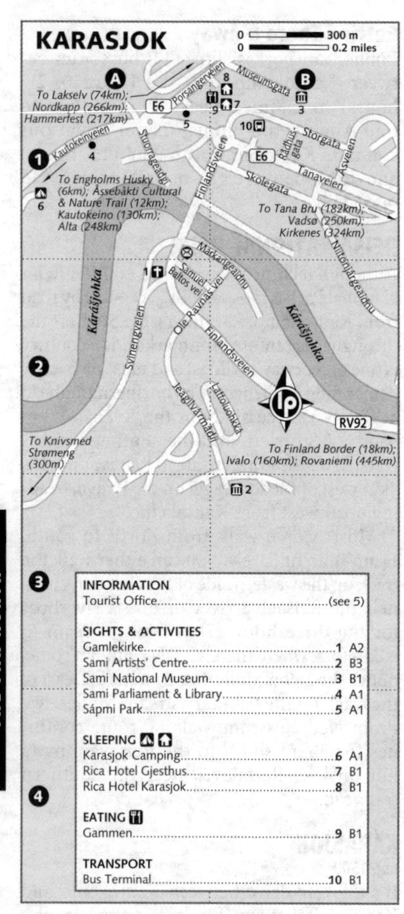

stuck with euros after crossing the border from Finland.

Sights & Activities

SÁPMI PARK

Sami culture is big business here, and it was only a matter of time before it was consolidated into a **theme park** (☎ 78 46 88 00; Porsangerveien; adult/child/family Nkr100/60/270; 🕑 9am-7pm Jun–mid-Aug, 9am-4pm Mon-Fri rest-of-year). There's a wistful, high-tech multimedia introduction to the Sami in the 'Magic Theatre', plus Sami winter and summer camps and other dwellings in the grounds, and of course, a gift shop and café. It's actually very good and presents the Sami as the normal fellow human beings they are rather than as exotic anachronisms.

If you want more substance, the smaller Sami museums in Karasjok and Kautokeino are less flash and more academic.

SAMI PARLIAMENT

The **Sami Parliament** (Sámediggi; ☎ 78 47 40 00; Kautokeinoveien 50; admission free) was established in 1989. In 2000 it moved into a glorious new building, encased in mellow Siberian wood, with a birch, pine and oak interior. The main assembly hall is shaped like a Sami tent, and the **Sami library**, lit with tiny lights like stars, houses over 35,000 volumes plus other media. From late June to mid-August, there are 30-minute tours leaving hourly between 8.30am and 2.30pm (except 11.30am), Monday to Friday. The rest of the year, tours are at 1.30pm on weekdays. There are similar Sami parliaments in Finland and Sweden.

SAMI NATIONAL MUSEUM

The **Sami National Museum** (Sámiid Vuorká Dávvirat; ☎ 78 46 99 50; Museumsgata 17; admission Nkr70; 🕑 9am-6pm Mar-Oct, 9am-3pm Mon-Fri rest-of-year) is also called the Sami Collection. Smaller and more serious, it's been rather upstaged by the genial razzmatazz down the road. Devoted to Sami history and culture, it has displays of colourful, traditional Sami clothing, a bewildering array of tools and artefacts and works by contemporary Sami artists. Outdoors, a homestead reveals the simplicity of traditional Sami life. Signing is only in Norwegian and Sami and the English guide sheet is difficult to follow.

SAMI ARTISTS' CENTRE

This dynamic **gallery** (☎ 78 46 90 02; Jeagilvármádi 54; 🕑 10am-3pm Mon-Fri, noon-5pm Sun) mounts temporary exhibitions by contemporary Sami artists and is well worth the short journey to the limits of town.

ÁSSEBÁKTI CULTURAL & NATURE TRAIL

On the Rv92, 12km south of Karasjok heading for Kautokeino, this 3.5km trail (signed 'Kulturminner' on the highway) is well worth undertaking for a taste of the forest even though, despite its name, it doesn't actually have much that's cultural. This said, around 25 minutes out (allow two hours for the full out-and-back route), there are traces of trappers' pits, store mounds and, across the river, turf huts.

ours

ngholm's Husky, in the lodge bearing the ame name (below), offers winter dog-sled nd cross-country skiing tours, as well as ummer walking tours with a dog to carry our pack – or at least some of it. All-inclu-ive expeditions range from one-day dog-sled ours (per person Nkr1100) to eight-day, off-iste Arctic safaris (Nkr11,500). Consult the vebsite, www.engholm.no, for the full range f activities.

leeping & Eating

arasjok Camping (☎ 78 46 61 35; halonen@online no; Kautokeinoveien; person/site Nkr10/110, dm Nkr150, abin with outdoor bathrooms Nkr275-450, with bathroom kr650-990) Friendly Karasjok Camping oc-upies a hillside site with river views and a ange of cabins. Lay back on reindeer skins o the crackle of the nightly birch-wood fire n the cosy *lavvo* or cook your own thing in he equally relaxing barbecue hut.

our pick **Engholm's Design Lodge** (☎ 91 58 66 5; www.engholm.no; cabins Nkr300-400 plus per person kr200) About 6km from Karasjok along the v92, Sven Engholm, the owner of Engholm's Iusky, has built from nothing this wonder-ul haven in the forest. Each rustic cabin is ndividually furnished with great flair, all ave kitchen facilities and two have bath-ooms. You sink into sleep to the odd bark nd yelp from the sled dogs. A plentiful din-er costs Nkr250. Signed trails lead through he forest and barely a five-minute stroll way there's a salmon stream with a fine each, where you can rent a double canoe Nkr350 per day). Sven's place also serves s Karasjok's HI-affiliated youth hostel dorms/singles/doubles Nkr175/355/500).

Rica Hotel Karasjok (☎ 78 46 88 60; www.rica no; Porsangerveien; s/d Nkr950/1165 mid-Jun–mid-Aug, k1375/1625 Sun-Thu, Nkr830/1080 Fri & Sat rest-of-year; P) Adjacent to Sápmi Park, this is Karasjok's premier lodging, with handsome rooms and Sami motifs throughout, plus an impressive Arctic Menu restaurant. In addition to wi-fi, there's an internet point for guests which, at Nkr3 per minute, may rank as the world's most expensive. The hotel's **Gjestehus** (s/d Nkr590/700 mid-Jun–mid-Aug, Fri & Sat year-round Nkr645/860 Sun-Thu rest-of-year) is substantially cheaper and also in the park grounds, and has corridor bathrooms.

Gammen (☎ 78 46 88 60; mains Nkr215-310; 10am-11pm mid-Jun–mid-Aug) It's very much reindeer or reindeer, with a token trout dish, at this rustic complex of four large interconnected Sami huts run by the Rica Hotel. Although it may be busy with bus tour groups, it's an atmospheric place to sample traditional Sami dishes from reindeer stew to fillet of reindeer or simply to drop in for a coffee or beer. And hey, although cigarettes are banned from all Norwegian eateries, tenacious puffers may derive more than cold comfort from this dark, smoky environment.

Shopping

Knivsmed Strømeng (☎ 78 46 71 05; Badjenjárga; Mon-Fri) This craft shop calls on five generations of local experience to create unique and original handmade Sami knives for everything from outdoor to kitchen use.

Getting There & Away

Twice-daily buses (except Saturday) connect Karasjok with both Alta (Nkr391, 4¾ hours) and Hammerfest (Nkr344, 4¼ hours). There's a service to Kirkenes (Nkr504, 5¼ hours) three times weekly.

A daily Finnish Lapin Linjat bus runs to Rovaniemi (Nkr500, eight hours) via Ivalo (Nkr200, 3½ hours), in Finland; it also runs from Karasjok, year-round.

Svalbard

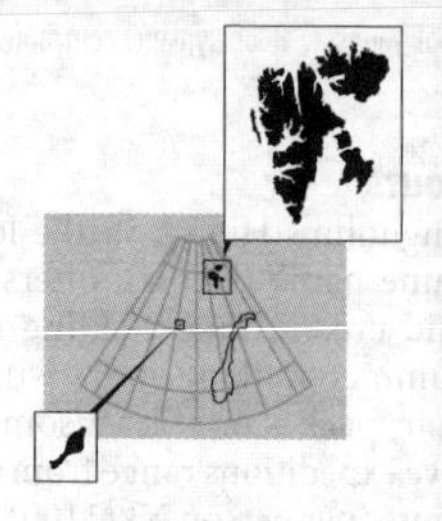

Svalbard is an assault on the senses. This wondrous archipelago is the world's most readil accessible bit of the polar north and one of the most spectacular places imaginable. Vas icebergs and floes choke the seas, and icefields and glaciers frost the lonely heights. Bu under close scrutiny, the harsh conditions reveal tiny gems as the Arctic desert soil, howeve barren-looking, manages to sustain lichens, miniature grasses and delicate little flowers The environment supports larger creatures too: whales, seals, walruses, Arctic foxes, squa Svalbard reindeer – and polar bears aplenty, outnumbering us humans for the moment.

Svalbard doesn't come easy – especially on the pocket. It's nearly a 1000km flight fron the nearest major airport on the mainland and budget accommodation is very much at a premium. The independent traveller is a rare sight on islands; the vast majority of visitors arrive on an organised tour. We recommend signing up for group visits once arriving ir Longyearbyen, the usual point of independent entry.

Don't discount a winter visit. There are plenty of outdoor activities to keep you rosy cheeked and you'll get more of a feel for Longyearbyen as a living community with a *raisor d'être* of its own.

What really bumps the cost up is the price of organised tours and activities. Since trave outside Longyearbyen is difficult at best and can be downright dangerous, you miss out on a lot if you don't sign up for one or two. So, when you're doing your pre-holiday sums, budge for a glacier walk, a boat trip or a mine visit and see if you can still make ends meet.

HIGHLIGHTS

- Crunch your crampons on accessible **Longyearbreen glacier** (p379), then fossick for fossils
- Experience pristine Arctic nature on an **organised hiking expedition** (p373)
- Penetrate deep into disused **Mine No 3** (p376) outside Longyearbyen and be glad you're not a collier
- Visit the former Russian mining village of **Barentsburg** (p380)
- Spend a sunny morning surrounded by the brilliant glaciers and turquoise waters of **Magdalenefjord** (p384)

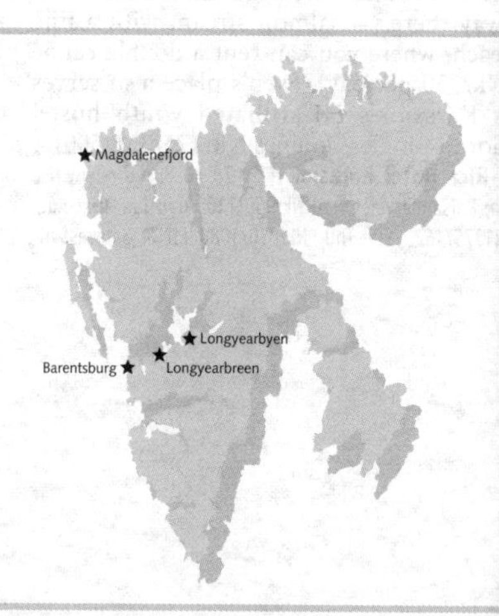

- POPULATION: 2800
- HIGHEST ELEVATION: NEWTONTOPPEN (1713M)

istory

'he first mention of Svalbard occurs in an celandic saga from 1194. Officially, however, he Dutch voyager Willem Barents, in search f a northeast passage to China, is regarded as he first visitor from the European mainland 1596). He named the islands Spitsbergen, r 'sharp mountains'. The Norwegian name, valbard, comes from the Old Norse for cold coast'; ancient Norse sagas referred o 'a land in the far north at the end of the cean'. Today, Spitsbergen is the name of valbard's largest island. In 1920 the Svalbard 'reaty granted Norway sovereignty over the slands and restricted military activities. nitially signed by nine nations, it now has ver 40 adherents, whose citizens enjoy the ame rights and obligations on the islands as Norwegians themselves.

OLAR EXPLORATION

ongyearbyen is precisely 1338km from the North Pole (or not quite precisely; by the time ou read this, it will be fractionally nearer s Svalbard inches northwards by 2mm per ear). In the late 19th and early 20th centuries, series of explorers attempted to reach the North Pole using airships and balloons, and nost met with failure. Roald Amundsen and Jmberto Nobile were successful in 1926, but wo years later Amundsen and his crew died while on a rescue mission to find Nobile, who ad disappeared on a similar expedition and was later rescued.

VHALING & HUNTING

At the time of Barents' discovery, the archipelago was uninhabited, as the early Inuit nigrations eastward from Siberia and Alaska alted in Greenland. There's archaeological vidence of Russian overwintering around he beginning of the 17th century but the irst confirmed western European activities n Svalbard didn't begin until a decade later. From 1612 to 1720 English, Dutch, French, Norwegian and Danish ships engaged in whaling off the western coast of Spitsbergen island; t's estimated that the Dutch alone slaughtered 0,000 whales.

An English group undertook the first nown overwintering at Bellsund in 1630, ollowed by a Dutch group at Smeerenburg hree years later; the following winter, however, scurvy took its toll and the settlement was abandoned for winter, leaving behind a small caretaker team, who all perished. From the early 18th century, Russian Pomor (coast-dwelling) hunters and traders focused their attentions on Svalbard, hunting walruses, moose, seals and belugas. From around 1795 Norwegians exploited the islands' wildlife resources and began hunting both polar bears and Arctic foxes.

COAL MINING

Perhaps as early as 1612 whalers had discovered coal at Ny Ålesund (p382), but the first modern mine wasn't opened until 1906, when the Arctic Coal Company (ACC) began extracting coal from a rich seam. The settlement that grew up around this mine was named for the ACC's US owner, John Munroe Longyear. In 1916 ACC sold out to the Store Norske Spitsbergen Kull Compani (SNSK). Over the next few years, two other Norwegian companies set up operations on the archipelago's southernmost island, Bjørnøya, and the Kings Bay Kull Compani opened a mine at Ny Ålesund.

Mining was halted during WWII and on 3 September 1941 the islands were evacuated. Even so, the Nazis bombed Longyearbyen and the settlements of Barentsburg and Sveagruva (Mine No 2, on the hillside just east of Longyearbyen, was shelled and set alight and continued to burn for 14 years). When the Nazis surrendered in 1945, Norwegian civilians returned, Longyearbyen was rebuilt and the Russians resettled and again mined in Pyramiden and Barentsburg.

Ny Ålesund also re-opened, but was closed down after a mine explosion in 1962 and converted into a scientific post.

Mine No 7 has been in operation for nearly 40 years and nowadays is the only one around Longyearbyen still producing; it yields around 70,000 tonnes per year for firing the town's power station or for export to Germany.

The big one these days is the Svea Nord coalfield, 44km southeast of Longyearbyen. The scale of operation boggles the mind. It produces around three million tonnes annually – extracting more in two days than Mine No 7 does in a year. There are estimated reserves of over 30 million tonnes and the project will extend until at least 2013. At the other end of the scale, the workforce, based in Longyearbyen and flown into Sveagruva for three-week shifts, is small, operating colossal,

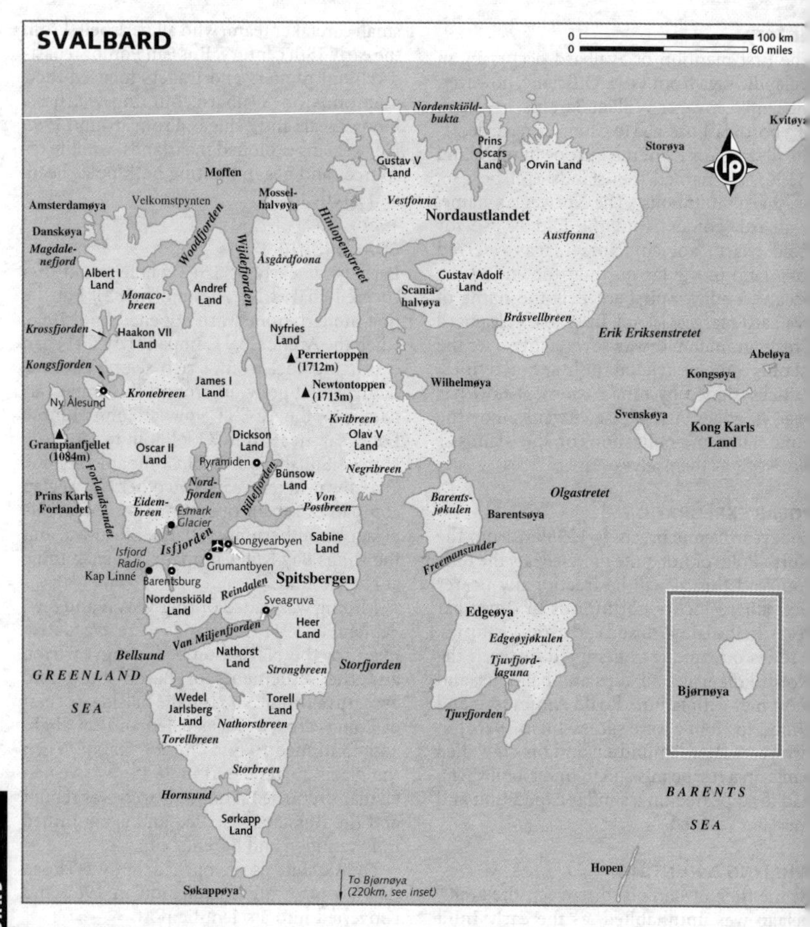

state-of-the-art machinery that chews its way through the mountain.

OTHER NATURAL RESOURCES

The most sanguine predictions of Svalbard's gold reserves beneath the Arctic soil put them on a level with South Africa's. There are also indications of rich oil and gas deposits, which will become more easily and economically accessible if global warming continues.

Geography & Climate

Svalbard is 13% vegetation, 27% barren stone and a massive 60% glacier. Summer, the brief season when you're most likely to visit, is a period of hectic growth for plants, mammals and birds alike. The land's sparse, stunted, ground-hugging vegetation contrasts with the bounty of the surrounding seas, where everything from microscopic plankton to beluga whales flourish.

The archipelago is about the size of Ireland and consists mainly of glaciated and eroded sedimentary layers that were deposited beneath the sea up to 1.2 billion years ago. It's difficult to imagine but between 300 million and 60 million years ago, Svalbard was lush and tropical. Rich layers of organic matter built up on the surface, then metamorphosed under great heat and pressure into coal. Continental drift shifted it to its present polar location, and most present-day landforms were created during the ice ages of the past two million years. Its high

DON'T DISTURB SVALBARD!

'We realise it's not possible to be an invisible tourist, but we appreciate your trying', says the tourist literature. In addition to treading lightly, you will also be making your modest contribution to the preservation of Svalbard in another way. A levy of Nkr150 per visitor is added to the price of your plane or cruise-ship ticket. The income this raises is ring-fenced to support environmental measures across the archipelago.

Any pre-1946 remains of human activity are classified as 'cultural monuments' and aren't to be touched. This is understandable, particularly where it relates to evidence of distant whalers and hunters or old graves. But it's a very grandiose term when applied to the rusting machinery, scruffy pylons and tumbling wooden piles and gantries around Longyearbyen – industrial detritus that authorities elsewhere would be compelling companies to have removed.

st points are Newtontoppen (1713m) and Perriertoppen (1712m).

Svalbard's latitude ranges from 74°N at Bjørnøya in the south to over 80°N on northern Spitsbergen and Nordaustlandet. In Longyearbyen the midnight sun lasts from 19 April to 23 August, while it never even peeks above the horizon between 28 October and 14 February.

The archipelago enjoys a brisk polar-desert climate, with only 200mm to 300mm of precipitation annually. Although the west coast remains ice-free for most of the summer, pack ice hovers just north of the main island year-round, and sheets and rivers of ice cover approximately 60% of the land area. Snow and frost are possible at any time of year; the mean annual temperature is -4°C, and in July, it's only 6°C. On occasion, however, you may experience temperatures of up to 20°C. In January the mean temperature is -16°C, but temperatures of -30°C aren't uncommon.

Given current global concern about the fate of polar bears as the Arctic icecap melts, it's an encouraging thought, especially for bears, that, at least for the moment, the current human population of Svalbard of around 2800 is still exceeded by the number of bears, estimated between 3000 and 3500.

Dangers & Annoyances

In real life Svalbard's symbol, the polar bear, is not the cute fuzzy thing you see in the zoo. Even one bear at close quarters is one too many. While it's most unlikely that you'll have a Close Encounter of the Furred Kind in the environs of Longyearbyen, the best advice is, if you're trekking, go with an organised tour. Walk leaders carry a gun and know how to use it. Standard equipment too, especially if you're camping, are trip wires with flares and distress flares too – to fire at the ground in front of the bear, not to summon help, which could be hours away.

If, despite this, you're determined to set out without a guide, carry the same equipment; several places in town rent out kits – and make sure you get in some practice shooting before you travel if one end of a gun is much the same as another to you.

Don't get alarmed; the last bear fatality was in 1995 – but it happened only 2km from Longyearbyen…

Tours

For reasons of security and sheer logistics, it's almost impossible to arrange independent trips on Svalbard and we endorse the governor's advice that you should book organised tours through recognised operators. Fortunately, there's a huge range of options from winter dog-sledding or snowmobiling day trips to two-week excursions to the North Pole. The official **tourist information website** (www.svalbard.net) lists dozens of tours and we detail but a sample of the most popular ones below. For more day-trip ideas, see p377.

SPITSBERGEN TRAVEL

One of the giants of the Svalbard travel scene, **Spitsbergen Travel** (☎ 79 02 61 00; www.spitsbergentravel.no) runs three-day guided cruises between mid-June and mid-September aboard the former Hurtigruten coastal steamer *Nordstjernena,* putting ashore at both Barentsburg and Ny Ålesund. Prices, not including airfare, start at Nkr7930/12,875 per person without/with private shower. It also offers seven-day cruises with the smaller *Polar Star,* which penetrates more deeply into Svalbard's so lightly travelled areas. Prices begin at Nkr32,600 per double cabin.

POLAR BEARS UNDER THREAT

Polar bear numbers had been in decline since the late 19th century, when intensive hunting began. But ever since the 1973 treaty for the Conservation of Polar Bears and their Habitat, signed by all the countries whose lands impinge upon the Arctic, polar bear numbers have been gradually increasing again. But nowadays there's a new, less direct and more pervasive threat that can't be controlled by legislation.

Polar bears, for town- and temperate-climate dwellers, are almost a symbol of the Arctic wilderness – loners, immensely strong and survivors in one of the world's most extreme environments. But for all the bears' raw power, some scientists predict that they could be extinct by the end of this century if the world continues to heat up. As in so much of the globe's cold parts, Svalbard's glaciers are retreating. The ice sheet, their natural habitat and prime hunting ground for seals, mainstay of their diet (an adult bear needs to eat between 50 and 75 seals every year), is shrinking. Some computer models suggest that it might even disappear entirely from the North Pole in summertime. Although polar bears are powerful swimmers (in fact, they're classified as marine mammals), many risk drowning as they attempt to reach fresh ice floes. Less sea ice also means that some populations will become isolated and inbred, their genetic stock weakened. The birth rate may fall since females need plenty of deep snow to dig the dens in which they will whelp. And hungry bears, on the prowl and desperate for food, could lead to increasing confrontations with humans, where the bear stands little chance of coming off best.

Your chances of seeing one, unless you're on a cruise and observing from the safety of a ship, are minimal. Otherwise, contact is actively discouraged, both for your and the bear's sake (if a snowmobiler irresponsibly gives chase, for example, he or she will be in for a stiff fine). Bears under pressure, apart from being stressed out, quickly overheat under their shaggy coats and may even die of heat exhaustion if pursued.

Should you be unlucky enough to come within sight of one on land, don't even think of approaching it. An altogether safer way to track polar bears is to log onto www.panda.org/polar bears, managed by the World Wildlife Fund. Here, you can track the movements of four bears that scientists have equipped with a collar and satellite transmitter. You'll also learn a whole lot more about how these magnificent, resilient creatures survive in such tough conditions.

SVALBARD WILDLIFE SERVICE

Offering many of the usual and several unusual trips, **Svalbard Wildlife Service** (☎ 79 02 56 60; www.wildlife.no; 9am-4pm Mon-Fri) can take you on three days of camping, hiking and kayaking around the Esmark glacier (Nkr6400), or seven days among the glaciers, seals and walruses of Prins Karls Forlandet island (Nkr13,500).

SPITSBERGEN TOURS

The owner of **Spitsbergen Tours** (☎ 79 02 10 68; www.terrapolaris.com), Andreas Umbreit, with 20 years experience on the archipelago, has written the standard guide in English about Svalbard (see the boxed text, p378).

The range of adventurous options includes an Arctic week in three versions, based in Longyearbyen: during the long, dark polar night (Nkr10,200), in April's wintry springtime (Nkr13,800), or during the summer high season, when prices range from Nkr7650 if you camp to Nkr19,000 in single room accommodation. The price includes day excursions from the settlements (for exampl two days of dog-sledding, a snow-machin tour, boat cruises and walks, according t season). Winter dog-sledding tours cos around Nkr2000 per day and it's advisabl to book well in advance. For the hardy, ther are also winter snowshoe and hiking week (Nkr12,800) with accommodation in tent (make sure you bring a four-season sleepin bag) and the opportunity to build – and slee in, if you choose – an igloo.

Spitsbergen Tours also organises modula hiking tours, within the capacity of anyon who's reasonably fit, that mix day walks wit linear treks. All-in prices for one/two/thre weeks are Nkr7900/13,200/22,000.

GUIDED CRUISES

Among travel operators who can arrang guided cruises around the archipelago are, i the UK, **Discover the World** (☎ 01737-218 800; ww.discovertheworld.co.uk; Arctic House, 8 Bolters Lane, Banstea Surrey SM7 2AR) and the Canadian-based compan

GAP Adventures (www.gapadventures.com; Canada 19 Charlotte St, Toronto, Ontario M5V 2H5; North America ☎ 1-800-708-7761; UK ☎ 0870 999 0144; Australia ☎ 1300 796 618).

POLI ARCTICI

Poli Arctici (☎ 79 02 17 05; www.poliartici.com) is the rading name of Stefano Poli, originally from Milan and with 13 years as a Svalbard wilderness guide under his belt. Specialising in nultiday treks, he also offers guided day hikes ınd, in winter, snowmobile sorties.

BASECAMP SPITSBERGEN

Basecamp Spitsbergen (☎ 79 02 46 00; www.baseampexplorer.com) mainly offers winter activities, ncluding a stay aboard the *Noorderlicht,* a Dutch sailing vessel that's set into the fjord ce as the long freeze begins each autumn. It ılso offers winter and summer stays at Isfjord Radio, the ultimate remote getaway on an ıpgraded, one-time radio station at the northwestern tip of Spitsbergen island.

SVALBARD VILLMARKSSENTER

The experts in dog mushing are **Svalbard Villmarkssenter** (☎ 79 02 17 00; www.svalbardvillmarksenter.no), whether by sledge over the snow or – OK, it's not the same thing but it gives you a eel of what a wintertime dog-sled experience nust be like – on wheels during summer.

LONGYEARBYEN

pop 1500

Svalbard's only town – indeed, only centre vith more than a handful of inhabitants – Longyearbyen (literally the 'LongYear Town') s these days a base for tourism. But its gritty coal-mining roots still show through, commemorated in the statue of a grizzled miner ınd his pick near the Lompensenteret. For lecades, Store Norsk, owner of the pits, possessed the communal mess, company shop, ransport in and out, and almost the miners' souls. Then in 1976 the Norwegian state stepped in to bale the company out from bankruptcy. Today, most of the few people hat live here year-round enjoy one-year taxree contracts.

The modern town, fringed by abandoned nining detritus, enjoys a superb backdrop ncluding two glacier tongues, Longyearbreen ınd Lars Hjertabreen. Construction here akes into account the harsh Arctic climate; nost structures are built on pilings to prevent ıeated buildings from melting the permafrost that's never more than a metre deep, then simply sinking into it. The heavily insulated plumbing pipes also run above ground.

Reflecting the days when miners would remove their coal-dust-encrusted boots at the threshold, local decorum still dictates that people take off their shoes upon entering most buildings in town. Exceptions include the majority of shops and places to eat.

Information

Basecamp Spitsbergen (per 10min Nkr20) One internet terminal.

Library (Lompensenteret; 🕐 11am-6pm Mon-Thu) Free internet.

Longyearbyen Hospital casualty clinic (☎ 79 02 42 00)

Sparebanke 1 Norge Bank & ATM in the post office building.

Tourist office (☎ 79 02 55 50; www.svalbard.net; 🕐 10am-5pm May-Sep, noon-5pm rest-of-year) Within the Gateway to Svalbard complex. Produces the comprehensive *Guide Longyearbyen* and a weekly activities list of the infinite range of outdoor pursuits.

Sights & Activities

SVALBARD MUSEUM

Museum is the wrong word for this impressive, recently inaugurated exhibition space. Themes include the life on the edge formerly led by whalers, trappers, seal and walrus hunters and, more recently, miners. It's an attractive mix of text, artefacts and birds and mammals, stuffed and staring. There's a cosy book-browsing area too where you can lounge on sealskin cushions and rugs.

HELLO SUNSHINE

Some 50m south of Svalbard's church stand five weathered wooden steps, all alone, and a barely legible sign, 'Sykhustrappa' (Hospital Stairs). They're all that remain of Longyearbyen's first hospital and they have a special significance for the town's residents.

Traditionally, a week of celebrations to dispel the weeks of winter darkness would begin once the first of the spring sun's rays touched the top step. The hospital is long demolished but this little piece of solar timekeeping has been preserved and the tradition continues.

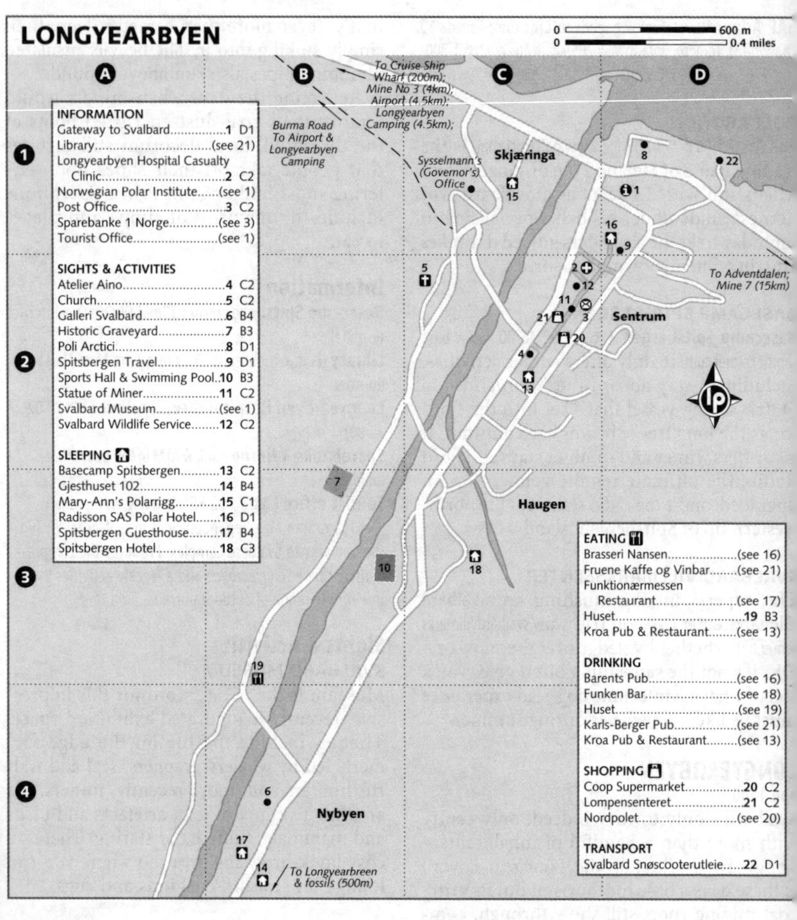

MINE NO 3

Sign on for a three-hour journey deep into **Mine No 3** (admission incl transport from your lodging Nkr590, minimum age 14). Productive from 1971 to 1996, this was the last shaft to be worked manually, thrusting itself 5.5km deep into the heart of the mountain. The side spurs, from whose veins the coal was hacked, were only 80cm high. You can crawl into one to sense what life at the coal face was really like.

MINE NO 7

In summer **Svalbard Explorer** (☎ 90 76 29 33; www.svalbardexplorer.no in Norwegian) runs trips (Nkr590) once or twice daily to Longyearbyen's last producing coal mine, 15km east of the town.

HISTORIC GRAVEYARD

This haunting little graveyard with its simple white, wooden crosses dates from the early 20th century. In a few days in October 1918 seven young men in Longyearbyen were struck down by the Spanish flu, a virus that killed 40 million people in Europe, Asia and North America.

GALLERI SVALBARD

Galleri Svalbard (☎ 79 02 23 40; adult/child/concession Nkr50/20/40; 11am-5pm) features the Svalbard-themed works of Norwegian artist Kåre Tveter, so pure and cold they make you shiver; reproductions of early maps of Svalbard; and a 10-minute film, *The Arcti*

Vature of Svalbard, which gives a glimpse of ›valbard's other, winter persona.

ATELIER AINO

Atelier Aino (admission free; 11am-5pm Mon-Fri, 1am-3pm Sat) Follow the sign directing you off the main pedestrian street to the gallery and workshop of Danish artist Aino Grib. A resident of Svalbard, she captures in her canvases the hues and tones of the Arctic easons.

BIRD-WATCHING

Flocks of birds nest on Svalbard each summer and large numbers call by during their annual migration as well. Among the many species on show are puffins, little auks, purple sandpipers, Brünnich's guillemots, red-throated divers, various gulls and skuas, and many geese species, including barnacle, pink-footed and Brent.

SWIMMING

f you've energy left at the end of the day, plunge into Longyearbyen's heated pool at he Sports Hall.

Tours

You'll be disappointed if you restrict yourself o scruffy Longyearbyen and you'll leave with ittle sense of the sheer majesty of Svalbard's wilderness. Fortunately, there's a dizzying array of short trips and day tours that vary with the season, including fossil hunting (Nkr300), mine tours (Nkr590), boat trips o Barentsburg (Nkr990), dog-sledding (Nkr800), glacier walking (from Nkr490), ce-caving (from Nkr520), kayaking (from Nkr550), horse riding (Nkr550) and snowmobiling (Nkr1000 to Nkr1400). The tourist office's weekly activities list details many more. All outings can be booked through individual operators (directly or via their websites) or online at the tourist office.

For further information on longer tours, see p373.

Sleeping

Longyearbyen Camping (☎ 79 02 10 68; www.longyearbyen-camping.com; per person Nkr90; mid-Jun–mid-Sep) Near the airport on a flat stretch of turf, this particularly friendly camp site overlooks Isfjorden and the glaciers beyond and has a kitchen and showers. It's about an hour's walk from town or you can rent a bicycle (per day for campers Nkr100). You can also hire a tent (per night Nkr100), mattress (Nkr20) and sleeping bag (first/subsequent nights Nkr50/30). There are no cabins.

Poli Arctici (☎ 79 02 17 05, 91 38 34 67; www.poliarctici.com; s/d Nkr700/800) Seasoned Arctic guide Stefano Poli has four good-value apartments, each with bathroom and self-catering facilities, in the centre of Longyearbyen.

Longyearbyen has a couple of reasonably priced – for the island – options in Nybyen, at the southern extremity of town, about a 20-minute walk from the centre. Formerly miners' accommodation, they have corridor bathrooms, a kitchen for self-caterers and small lounge. Prices include breakfast.

Gjesthuset 102 (☎ 79 02 57 16; 102@wildlife.no; dm/s/d Nkr300/495/850; Mar-Nov) Guesthouse 102 (which, to confuse things, occupies building 7) belongs to Svalbard Wildlife Service and was once sardonically nicknamed 'Millionaire's Residence'.

Spitsbergen Guesthouse (☎ 79 02 63 00; www.spitsbergentravel.no; dm/s/d Nkr295/500/850; mid-Mar–Sep) This guesthouse is a subsidiary of Spitsbergen Travel spread over four buildings, one of which houses the large breakfast room (once the miners' mess hall), and can accommodate up to 136.

our pick **Mary-Ann's Polarrigg** (☎ 79 02 37 02; www.polarriggen.com; Skjæringa; s/d with shared bathroom Nkr595/875, d Nkr2000) Run by the ebullient Mary-Ann and adorned with mining and hunting memorabilia, the Polarrigg brims with character. Betraying its origins as a workers' billet from without, it's cosiness itself within. In the main wing, rooms have corridor bathrooms

BRINGING THE ARK TO THE ARCTIC: SVALBARD GLOBAL SEED VAULT

Deep inside the mountain, down beneath the permafrost, a vast man-made cavern, already dubbed the Doomsday Vault or a vegetarian Noah's Ark, was completed in early 2008. It's a repository with a capacity for up to four million different seeds, representing the botanical diversity of the planet. Samples from seed banks and collections all over the world are to be kept here at a constant temperature of –18°C so that, should a species become extinct in its native habitat, it can be revived and won't be lost for eternity.

SVALBARD BOOKS

Spitsbergen: Svalbard, Franz Josef Land, Jan Mayen by long-time Svalbard resident Andreas Umbreit is a splendid guide to the whole archipelago.

The Norwegian Polar Institute's *Birds and Mammals of Svalbard* and its *Marine Mammals of Svalbard,* both fully illustrated with photos, are sound and very readable. *Flowers of Svalbard* by Olav Gjœrevoll and Olaf Rønning is also well illustrated with colour photos. *The Flora of Svalbard* by Olaf Rønning, alone is more complete but less comprehensively illustrated.

Svalbard & the Life in Polar Oceans by Bjorn Gulliksen and Erling Svensen deals specifically with the marine life and ecology of the region, but it's also of interest to the more general reader and has stacks of stunning photos.

The Governor of Svalbard's office publishes some excellent booklets in English, both for guiding and for background reading. *Isfjorden* by Kristin Prestvold is an impressive guide to the fjord that runs between Longyearbyen, Barentsburg and west to the headland of Kap Linné. More general titles include *Smeerenburg & Gravneset,* the fascinating history of a whaling community; and *Virgohamna,* an equally compelling description of this one-time base for North Pole expeditions.

and doubles come with bunk beds. There's a large, comfortably furnished lounge with sink-into armchairs and another with billiards, darts and a guitar to strum on. In the smart annexe, rooms have every comfort.

Spitsbergen Hotel (☎ 79 02 62 00; www.spitsbergentravel.no; s/d Nkr1200/1390; mid-Feb–mid-Oct;) This comfortable place (sink yourself low into the leather armchairs of its salon), where the mine bosses once lived, contrasts to this day with the two Nybyen guesthouses, previously the miners' more spartan quarters.

Radisson SAS Polar Hotel (☎ 79 02 34 50; www.radissonsas.com; s/d Nkr1290/1510;) This 95-room chain hotel ('the world's northernmost full-service hotel') is the town's most luxurious. Rooms are stylishly furnished and it's well worth paying Nkr200 extra for one with views of the fjord and Hiorthfjellet mountain beyond. Its annexe was originally accommodation for the Lillehammer Winter Olympic Games, then transported here.

our pick **Basecamp Spitsbergen** (☎ 79 02 46 00; www.basecampexplorer.com; s/d Nkr1750/1960;) Imagine a re-created sealing hut, built in part from recycled beams, planks and flotsam. Add artefacts and decorations, culled from the local refuse dump and mining castoffs. Graft on 21st-century plumbing and design flair and you've got this place, also known as Trapper's Lodge. Its 16 cabin-like rooms are cosiness and comfort defined and the breakfasts are splendid.

Eating

Fruene Kaffe og Vinbar (☎ 79 02 76 40; Lompensenteret; core hrs 10am-5pm) 'The Missus', run by three sprightly young women, is a welcomin café, serving decent coffee, baguettes, pizz and snacks.

Mary-Ann's Polarrigg (☎ 79 02 37 02) The world' most northerly Thai restaurant dishes up spic rice dishes in a wonderful glasshouse setting festooned with living plants that, unlike thei native Svalbard counterparts, entwine an climb much more than 2cm high.

Longyearbyen has two excellent hotel restaurants: **Brasseri Nansen** (3-/4-course dinner Nkr350/42 summer buffet Nkr295) at the Radisson SAS Pola and Funktionærmessen Restaurant in th Spitsbergen Hotel. These apart, locals will te you that the two best places to eat and drin are the pub and the house. But not just any ol pub or house…

our pick **Kroa** (The Pub; ☎ 79 02 13 00; mains aroun Nkr200) This pub and restaurant was reconstructed from the elements of a buildin brought in from Russian Barentsburg (th giant white bust of Lenin peeking from behind the bar – and sporting a Liverpool F scarf when we were last here – gives a clue Service is cheerful and mains verge on th gargantuan. Starters are more modest in size Try, for example, the cured seal (Nkr78) o Arctic char (Nkr92).

Huset (The House; ☎ 79 02 25 00) It's something o a walk to work up an appetite for the Huset' highly regarded restaurant, on whose menu (Nkr495) reindeer and grouse feature regularly. The bar serves up pizzas (Nkr85 t Nkr100), whale in pepper sauce (Nkr165 and seal stew (Nkr155) and its signatur *hamburger med alt* (Nkr96) – a meaty burge vith all the trimmings, so juicy, a researcher old us, that lonely scientists in their tents lream of it. A curiosity for a place so far from he nearest vineyard: its wine cellar has over 0,000 bottles.

The Coop Supermarket in Svalbardbutikken carries a good selection of groceries.

Drinking & Entertainment

Bustling Kroa, its metal bar stools fashioned from old mine stanchions, is normally the choice of younger locals. More formal are the Radisson's Barents Pub and Funken Bar at the Spitsbergen Hotel.

Huset is your all-purpose night spot, with a bar and weekend nightclub (cover charge Nkr50). It also houses the town cinema, which screens feature films a couple of nights a week.

Enter **Karls-Berger Pub Café** (☎ 79 02 25 11; Kompensenteret; 🕑 5pm-2am), put on your shades and prepare to be dazzled at the sight of over 1000 bottles of whiskies, brandies and sundry spirits shimmering behind the bar of this snug pub.

Although alcohol is duty-free in Svalbard, it's rationed for locals and visitors must present a valid onward airline ticket in order to buy it. The Nordpolet booze outlet is at the back of the Coop Supermarket.

Getting There & Away

In clear weather, the descent to Longyearbyen gives otherworldly views of glaciers and ice floes. SAS flies to/from Oslo directly in summer (three flights weekly) or via Tromsø year-round, making the 957km flight once or twice daily. There are as many as 11 different tariffs; book early to avoid paying the 11th least expensive.

Getting Around

Svalbard Maxi Taxi (☎ 79 02 13 05) and **Longyearbyen Taxi** (☎ 79 02 13 75) charge Nkr80 to Nkr120 for the journey between town and airport. The airport bus (Nkr40) connects with flights and runs up to the two guesthouses at the southern extremity of town, calling by hotels.

Possibilities for car hire include **Longyearbyen Bilutleie** (☎ 78 02 11 88) and **Svalbard Auto** (☎ 79 02 49 30). You'll tank up on the cheapest petrol in Norway but there is only 45km of road and not much to see from a vehicle.

Bicycles would be a better bet, and you can rent them from **Poli Arctici** (☎ 79 02 17 05; Nkr150 per day) or **Basecamp** (☎ 79 02 46 00; Nkr280 per day).

To scoot around Svalbard on a snowmobile in winter, you'll need to flash your home driving licence. Check with the tourist office; many areas are off limits for snowmobiles to allow wildlife a little peace and quiet. Rental agencies include **Svalbard Snøscooterutleie** (☎ 79 02 16 66; www.scooterutleie.svalbard.no) and **Svalbard Reiser Kroa** (☎ 79 02 56 50). Daily rates are from Nkr1000 to Nkr1400.

AROUND LONGYEARBYEN

Platåberget & Bjørndalen

The extensive upland region that overlooks Longyearbyen to the west is known as Platåberget (commonly called The Plateau) and makes for a popular day hike. Either ascend a steep, scree-covered route from near the governor's office or, preferably, sneak up Blomsterdalen, not far from Mine No 3. You can also get onto Platåberget via Bjørndalen (yes, it means 'bear valley'), south of the airport. Once on the plateau it's possible to continue to the summit of Nordenskiöldsfjellet (1050m), where a Swedish observatory is said to have once operated.

Longyearbreen

The prominent glacier tongues licking at the upper, southwestern outskirts of Longyearbyen have scoured and gouged through many layers of sedimentary material, including fossil layers, created when Svalbard enjoyed a more tropical climate. The terminal moraine churns up plant fossils – leaves and twigs that left their marks 40 to 60 million years ago. Several guided walks build in time for a little foraging.

To get there under your own steam, pass the Huset and head up the river's true left bank, past the abandoned mine buildings, and onto a rough track. After the remains of a bridge (on your left), you'll approach the terminal moraine and cross a stream that flows down from your left. The track then traverses some steep slopes, crosses the river (sometimes there's a bridge) and continues upstream to its end at the fossil fields. The 5km return hike from Huset takes about 1½ hours, not counting fossicking time.

Burma Road

The Burma Rd, which is now a walking track, follows the old coal-mine Taubanen cableway

SVALBARD'S REINDEER

Svalbard's reindeer are genetically akin to their distant Canadian cousins and some have been found bearing Russian tags, proving that they walked in over the ice. Unlike their cousins on the mainland, they don't live in herds but in family groups of two to six animals. Since they have no predators – they're too fleet over other than short distances for polar bears, which are quick out of the traps but incapable of sustaining speed – they thrive and the estimated population of around 8000 is kept constant by an annual cull of 250. Most Svalbard reindeer starve slowly to death when they're about eight years old, their teeth having been ground to stumps by the stones and pebbles they mouth along with sprigs of edible matter.

to the processing plant and Mine No 3, near the airport. It makes an easy half-day hike.

Adventdalen

Stark, wide-open Adventdalen beckons visitors with wild Arctic landscapes. There's pleasant hiking, but as you'll sense from the polar bear crossing sign at the town end of the valley, you should carry a firearm.

After leaving town, you'll pass the pungent husky kennels; Isdammen, a freshwater lake that provides drinking water for Longyearbyen, then a northern lights station. With a car or bike, you can also cruise out to the defunct **coal mine Nos 5 and 6** and pass **No 7** (the only one that still functions).

BARENTSBURG

pop 600

The first thing you see of Barentsburg, Svalbard's only remaining Russian settlement, is its power-station chimney, belching dark black smoke into the blue sky. This isolated village continues to mine coal against all odds and still produces up to 350,000 tonnes per year, though selling it on the open market is a constant problem and stockpiles are huge. Everything's a bit run-down, dishevelled and sooty. With its signing in Cyrillic script, a still-standing bust of Lenin and murals of muscly workers in heroic pose, it feels further east and of the last century.

History

Barentsburg, on Grønfjorden, was first identified as a coal producing area around 1900 when the Kullkompaniet Isefjord Spitsbergen started operations. Several other companies also sank shafts and in 1920 the town was founded by the Dutch company Nespico. Twelve years later it passed to the Soviet Trust Arktikugol.

Like Longyearbyen, Barentsburg was partially destroyed by the British Royal Navy in 1941 to prevent it falling into Nazi hands (ironically, the German navy itself finished the job later). In 1948 it was rebuilt by Trust Arktikugol and embarked on a period of growth, development and scientific research that lasted until the fall of the Soviet Union.

Barentsburg, like every other pit on Svalbard, has known tragedy. In 1996 many of those who perished in a plane crash during a blizzard near Adventdalen (left) were miners' families from the Ukraine. Then in 1997, only a year later, 23 miners died in a devastating mine explosion and fire.

These days, most of Trust Arktikugol's coal shipments go directly to the west, notably to power stations in the Netherlands. Pay cheques are now being eaten up by Russian inflation and obsolete mining equipment is breaking down. The scientific community is reduced though a small team of geophysicists, meteorologists and glaciologists still researches and the town's population has dwindled to around 600.

Supplies are sparse and Barentsburg continues to grow some of its own produce, including tomatoes, onions and peppers. However, most of the former pig farm has ended up in the cooking pot – though you may see a few of the community's very last cows clomping around. For most people, conditions here are preferable to those at home in Russia (or the Ukraine, home to around half of Barentsburg's people) and quite a lot choose to remain in Barentsburg beyond their standard initial two-year contracts.

Sights & Activities

You'll almost certainly be visiting Barentsburg as part of an organised tour. Once the guiding is over, do rush around in the short time left before the boat weighs anchor and fit in a visit to the following.

The simple, appealing little **Pomor museum** (☎ 79 02 18 14; admission Nkr40; ⏰ when tour boats are

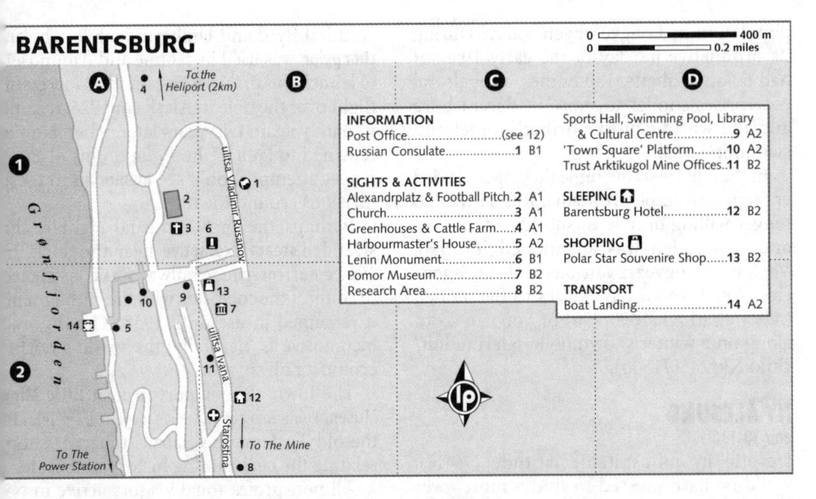

n port) outlines (in Russian only) the historic Pomor trade with mainland Russia, plus Russian mining and history on Svalbard. Especially worthwhile are the excellent geological exhibits and the collection of artefacts suggesting Russian activity in Svalbard prior to the archipelago's accepted European 'discovery' by Willem Barents.

The small wooden Orthodox **chapel** commemorates the twin disasters of 1996 and 1997 (see opposite). Above the football pitch and set aside from the community's other buildings, it merits poking your nose inside.

Sleeping & Eating

Barentsburg Hotel (☎ 79 02 10 80, 79 02 18 14; d Nkr550) The Barentsburg Hotel (the settlement's only accommodation for visitors) serves traditional Russian meals, featuring such specialities as boiled pork with potatoes and Arctic sorrel, parsley and sour cream. If you're overnighting, sign on for the gourmet dinner, offering both Russian and Ukrainian cuisine, lubricated with Russian champagne and vodka.

In the bar, you can enjoy a deliciously affordable and generous slug of vodka or a Russian beer. It also sells large tins of the Real McCoy caviar at prices you'll never find elsewhere in the West, let alone Norway.

Shopping

Polar Star Souvenire Shop is conveniently positioned as you begin to descend the 238 steps to the quayside. It's worth dropping into if you should be after a babushka doll, Lenin lapel badge or some Soviet army surplus.

Getting There & Away

Several tour operators (p373) do summertime nine- to 10-hour **boat trips** (adult/child Nkr1190/890) to Barentsburg from Longyearbyen. The cruise, which is half the fun, sails past the one-time Russian colliery of Grumantbyen, abandoned in the 1960s, and also heads across the fjord to the vast Esmark glacier on the homeward journey. The price includes a light lunch and around 1½ hours in Barentsburg, mostly occupied by a guided tour. Most longer cruises also call in at Barentsburg.

In winter, you can belt across the snow and ice on a **snowmobile guided tour** (adult/child Nkr2150/1200). The record for the trip between Longyearbyen and Barentsburg is precisely 22 minutes but tours stretch the journey to a more leisurely, much more enjoyable three hours each way.

PYRAMIDEN

Formerly Russia's second settlement in Svalbard, Pyramiden was named for the looming pyramid-shaped mountain that rises nearby. In the mid-1910s coal was discovered here and operations were set up by the same Swedish concern that exploited Sveagruva. In 1926 it was taken over by a Soviet firm, Russkiy Grumant, which sold out to the Soviet Trust Arktikugol, exploiters of Barentsburg, in 1931. In the 1950s there were as many as 2500 Russian residents, well exceeding the population of Longyearbyen today. During its productive heyday in the early 1990s it had 60km of shafts, 130 homes, agricultural enterprises similar to those in Barentsburg and the world's most northerly hotel and swimming pool.

In the late 1990s the mine no longer yielded enough coal to be profitable, Russia was no longer willing or able to subsidise the mine and Pyramiden was abandoned in 1998. Various Longyearbyen-based tour agencies offer 10-hour day cruises to Pyramiden (adult/child Nkr1090/790) or you can scoot along on a winter snowmobile safari (adult/child Nkr2450/1500).

NY ÅLESUND

pop 30-130

Despite its inhospitable latitude (79°N), you'd be hard pressed to find a more awesome backdrop anywhere on earth than the scientific post of Ny Ålesund, 107km northwest of Longyearbyen. Founded in 1916 by the Kings Bay Kull Compani, Ny Ålesund likes to claim that it's the world's northernmost permanently inhabited civilian community (although you could make a case for three other equally minuscule spots in Russia and Canada).

Throughout much of the 20th century Kings Bay mined for coal. As many as 300 people once lived and worked here but, after the last of several lethal explosions resulted in 21 deaths, mining stopped in 1963. Ny Ålesund has since recycled itself as a prominent scientific post with research stations of several nations, including Japan, France, the British Antarctic Survey and, since July 2004, China (bizarrely in this land of polar bears and Arctic foxes, two marble lions stand watch over the Chinese quarters). India's first team was about to arrive when we were last on Svalbard. There's a hardy year-round population of around 30 scientists, rising to 130 in summer (never more since that's the number of beds available) as researchers from about 15 countries fly in.

Sights

There's a 1.5km trail with multilingual interpretive panels that takes you around the main sites of this tiny settlement.

In the early 20th century several polar explorers set off from Ny Ålesund, including the likes of Roald Amundsen, Lincoln Ellsworth, Admiral Byrd and Umberto Nobile. The **anchor pylon** was used by Nobile and Amundsen to launch the airship *Norge* on their successful flight over the pole to Alaska in 1926; it came in handy again two years later, when Nobile returned to launch the *Italia* on his ill-fated repeat attempt. You'll see **memorials** to these missions around town.

Perhaps the most unusual sight is the stranded **steam locomotive** near the dock. In 1917 a narrow-gauge railway was constructed to connect the coalfields with the harbour and it remained in use until 1958. The restored locomotive is, naturally, the world's northernmost railway relic.

The town also supports a neat little **Mine Museum** (Gruvemuseum; donation suggested; 24hr) in the old Tiedemann's Tabak (tobacco) shop relating the coal-mining history of this area.

All non-professional visitors arrive in Ny Ålesund on tourist cruises and linger for an hour or two.

AROUND NY ÅLESUND

Kongsfjorden

Ny Ålesund's backdrop, Kongsfjorden (the namesake for the Kings Bay Kull Compani) spectacularly contrasts bleak grey-brown shores with expansive white icefields. The distinctive Tre Kroner peaks, Dana (1175m), Svea (1226m) and Nora (1226m) – named in honour of Denmark, Sweden and Norway, respectively – jut from the ice and are among Svalbard's most recognisable landmarks.

Blomstrandhalvøya

Gravelly Blomstrandhalvøya was once a peninsula but, in the early 1990s, it was released from the icy grip on its northern end and it's now an island. In summer the name Blomstrand, or 'flower beach', would be appropriate, but it was in fact named for a Norwegian geologist. Ny London, at the southern end of the island, recalls one Ernest Mansfield of the Northern Exploration Company who attempted to quarry marble in 1911 only to discover that the stone had been rendered worthless by aeons of freezing and thawing. A couple of buildings and some forlorn machinery remain.

AROUND SPITSBERGEN

Sveagruva

Coal was first discovered at Sveagruva in the early 1910s and exploited by a Swedish

ROALD AMUNDSEN

If Fridtjof Nansen (see the boxed text, p351) had the biggest heart of any polar explorer, fellow Norwegian Roald Amundsen had the most determination and grit. Born into a family of shipowners and captains in 1872 at Borge, near Sarpsborg, he dreamed of becoming a polar explorer and devoured every bit of literature he could find on the subject. Following his mother's wishes, he dutifully studied medicine, but when she died in 1893 he returned to his polar dreams and never looked back.

By 1897 he was sailing to the Antarctic as first mate on the Belgian *Belgica* expedition. Their ship froze fast in the ice near Peter I Island and became – unintentionally – the first expedition to overwinter in the Antarctic. When the captain fell ill with scurvy, Amundsen took command, displaying his ability in a crisis.

Having gained a reputation as a captain, Amundsen set his sights on the Northwest Passage and study of the Magnetic North Pole. The expedition set out from Oslo in June 1903 aboard the 47-tonne sloop *Gjøa* and overwintered in a natural harbour on King William Island, which they named Gjøahavn. For two years they built observatories, took magnetic readings establishing the position of the Magnetic North Pole, studied the lives of the Inuit and learned how to drive dog teams. By August 1905 they emerged into waters that had been charted from the west, becoming the first vessel to navigate the Northwest Passage. When the *Gjøa* again froze fast in the ice, Amundsen and an American companion set off by dog-sled to the telegraph station at Eagle, Alaska, over 900km away, to announce their success.

Amundsen had wanted to be the first man to reach the North Pole, but in April 1909 Robert Peary took that honour. So in 1910 Amundsen headed instead for the South Pole, only to learn that Britain's Robert Falcon Scott's *Terra Nova* expedition was setting out from New Zealand with the same goal.

Amundsen's ship dropped anchor in January 1911 at Roosevelt Island, 60km closer to the South Pole than Scott's base. With four companions and four 13-dog sleds, Amundsen reached the South Pole on 14 December 1911. Scott – who, together with four members of his expedition, died of cold and starvation on the return journey – arrived on 17 January 1912 to discover the Norwegian flag already flying.

In 1925 Amundsen attempted to become the first to fly over the North Pole. The American Lincoln Ellsworth sponsored the expedition and two planes took off from Svalbard bound for Alaska, but faulty equipment forced them to land on sea ice about 150km from the pole. The pilot, Hjalmar Riiser-Larsen, hewed a runway with hand tools, managed to take off with all six crew members and returned one plane to Nordaustlandet, in Svalbard, where they ditched at sea but were rescued.

Never one to give up, Amundsen tried again the following year aboard the airship *Norge*, this time with Ellsworth, Riiser-Larsen and the Italian explorer Umberto Nobile. They left Spitsbergen on 11 May 1926 and, 16 hours later, dropped the Norwegian, American and Italian flags on the North Pole. On 14 May they landed triumphantly at Teller, Alaska, having flown 5456km in 72 hours – the first ever flight between Europe and North America.

In May 1928 Nobile attempted another expedition in the airship *Italia* and, when it crashed in the Arctic, Amundsen joined the rescue. Although Nobile and his crew were subsequently rescued, Amundsen's last signals were received just three hours after takeoff. His body has never been found.

company. The colliery changed hands several times, survived a fire and was yielding 400,000 tonnes of coal annually by the time SNSK took it over in 1934. The operations were levelled by a submarine attack in 1944 but activity snapped back after the war and by the late 1970s Sveagruva had grown into a settlement of 300 workers.

Over the following years increased production around more-accessible Longyearbyen led to a decline at the original Sveagruva pit; and by the mid-1990s it had dwindled to just a handful of miners and administrators. Nowadays, the nearby Svea Nord (see p371) has taken over its mantle and is one of Europe's biggest producing mines.

Magdalenefjord

The lovely blue-green bay of Magdalenefjord in Nordvest Spitsbergen, flanked by towering peaks and intimidating tidewater glaciers, is the most popular anchorage along Spitsbergen's western coast. In the 17th century, this area saw heavy Dutch whaling; at Graveneset, near the mouth of the fjord, you can still see the remains of two stoves used to boil the blubber. There are numerous protected graves of 17th- and mid-18th-century whalers.

Prins Karls Forlandet

On the west coast of Spitsbergen, the oddly shaped 86km-long island of Prins Karls Forlandet is a national park set aside to protect breeding walruses, seals and sea lions.

Krossfjorden

Thanks to Lillehöökbreen (its grand tidewater glacier) and several cultural relics, Krossfjorden also attracts quite a few cruise ships. At Ebeltoftbukta, near the mouth of the fjord, you can see several whalers' graves as well as a heap of leftover junk from a 1912 German telegraph office that was shifted wholesale to Ny Ålesund after only two years of operation. Opposite the entrance rise some crowded bird cliffs overlooking one of Svalbard's most verdant spots, with flowers, moss and even grasses.

Danskøya

One of the most intriguing sites in northwest Spitsbergen is Virgohamna, on the bleak, gravely island of Danskøya, where the remains of several broken dreams now lie scattered across the lonely beach. Among them are the ruins of three blubber stoves from a 17th-century whaling station, as well as eight stone-covered graves from the same era. You'll also find the remains of a cottage built by English adventurer Arnold Pike, who sailed north in his yacht *Siggen* and spent a winter subsisting on polar bears and reindeer.

The next adventurer at Virgohamna was Swedish engineer Salomon August Andrée who in the summer of 1897 set off from Virgohamna in an airship, hoping to reach the North Pole. The fate of his expedition wasn't known until 1930, when sailors from a seal-hunting ship put ashore and stumbled across their last site on Kvitøya.

Then, in 1906, journalist Walter Wellman, who was sponsored by a US newspaper, attempted to reach the North Pole in an airship but failed. Next year, when he returned to try again, his ship was badly damaged in a storm. On his third attempt, in 1909, he floated to within 60km of the pole, met with technical problems and gave up for good; mainly because he'd heard that Robert Peary had already reached the pole anyway. All of the remaining junk (including dozens of rusted 44-gallon fuel drums) is protected. Erosion damage, caused by the few visitors who manage to get here, has been considerable so do the right thing and stick strictly to the marked paths.

Amsterdamøya & Fairhaven

The island of Amsterdamøya was the site of the large Smeerenburg (meaning 'blubber town' in Dutch) whaling station. Co-founded in 1617 by Dutch and Danish concerns, all that remains of it today are seven ovens and some graves. There are more whalers' graves, scattered around the nearby sound, Fairhaven.

Moffen Island

Most tourist cruises attempt to approach flat, gravelly Moffen Island, known for its walrus population, but are often turned back by pack or drift ice. In any case, between mid-May and mid-September, boats are not allowed to approach within 300m of the island, lest they disturb the walruses' breeding activities.

Directory

CONTENTS

ACCOMMODATION

Norway offers a wide range of accommodation, from camping, hostels and pensions to international-standard hotels. You'll pay a lot more for what you get compared with other countries, but standards are high. Remember that if you're making enquiries in advance about prices, they're often quoted *per person*, so always check. Most hotels have wi-fi access for those lugging computers; see p398 for more details.

Throughout this book, quoted prices are for a room with private bathroom unless stated otherwise, except for hostels and camping where you can expect most rooms to come with a shared bathroom. Budget accommodation ranges from Nkr80 to Nkr150 (camping per site) and up to Nkr350/550 for singles/doubles in other types of accommodation. Midrange accommodation, usually in hotels, costs up to Nkr990/1200, while for top-end accommodation the sky's the limit.

BOOK YOUR STAY ONLINE

For more accommodation reviews and recommendations by Lonely Planet authors, check out the online booking service at www.lonelyplanet.com/hotels. You'll find the true, insider lowdown on the best places to stay. Reviews are thorough and independent. Best of all, you can book online.

A handy source of information (and discounts) for budget travellers is **VIP Backpackers** (☎ 90 62 16 44; www.vipbackpackers.no).

By law, all bars and restaurants and 50% of hotel bedrooms must be nonsmoking but in reality it's rare to find hotels that still offer smoking rooms.

Many tourist offices can help you find accommodation, usually for a fee of around Nkr30 to Nkr50; apart from in some larger tourist offices, this service usually operates only if you're physically present in the tourist office and not for advance bookings.

B&Bs, Pensions & Private Homes

Tourist offices in many towns have lists of private rooms, which are among the cheapest places to stay. In some cases, they allow you to stay with a Norwegian family, a far more intimate option than the hostel or hotel experience. Prices vary, but you'll rarely have to pay more than Nkr300/400 for a single/double; breakfast isn't normally included. Showers sometimes cost Nkr10 extra.

Some places operate as B&Bs, where prices start from single/double Nkr250/450 and can go up to Nkr500/800. These options can be tracked down through **Bed & Breakfast Norway** (www.bbnorway.com), which has extensive online listings for B&Bs throughout Norway; it also sells *The Norway Bed & Breakfast Book*, with listings throughout the country.

Many towns also have *pensjonat* (pensions) and *gjestehus* (guesthouses). Prices usually start at Nkr350/550, but linen and/or breakfast will only be included at the higher-priced places. Some of these are excellent.

Along highways, you'll also see a few *rom* signs, indicating informal accommodation typically costing from Nkr150 to Nkr275 per room (without breakfast); those who bring their own sheets or sleeping bags may get a discount.

Camping

Norway has more than 1000 camp sites. Tent space ordinarily costs from Nkr80 at basic camp sites up to Nkr150 for those with better facilities or in popular or expensive areas, such as Oslo and Bergen. Quoted prices usually include your car, motorcycle or caravan. A per-person charge is also added in some places, electricity often costs a few kroner extra and almost all places charge Nkr10 for showers.

Most camp sites can also rent simple cabins with cooking facilities starting at around Nkr250 for a very basic two- or four-bed bunkhouse. Bring a sleeping bag, as linen and blankets are provided only at an extra charge (anywhere from Nkr50 to Nkr100).

Unless you opt for a more expensive deluxe cabin with shower and toilet facilities (Nkr500 to Nkr1100), you'll also have to pay for showers and washing water (there are a few enlightened exceptions). Normally, cabin occupants must clean their cabin before leaving or pay an additional cleaning charge (around Nkr120).

Note that although a few complexes remain open year-round, tent and caravan sites are closed in the off season (normally early September to mid-May).

PRACTICALITIES

- Like most of Western Europe (but not the USA), Norway uses the PAL (Region 2) DVD system.
- Electricity sockets use 220V AC and 50Hz (train sleeping cars 110V or 220V AC) with round, continental-style, two-pin plugs.
- Major international newspapers and magazines are available a day after publication in cities.
- Government-run NRK (one TV and four radio channels) competes with TV2 and TV Norge networks and satellite broadcasts of TV3. Foreign-language programmes are subtitled. Hotels often have cable TV.
- Norway uses the metric system. Watch out for the use of *mil* (mile), which is a Norwegian mile (10km).

For a comprehensive list of Norwegian camp sites, pick up a copy of the free *Camping* (available at most tourist offices) or visit www.camping.no.

DNT & Other Mountain Huts

Den Norske Turistforening (DNT; Norwegian Mountain Touring Club; Map pp96-7; ☎ 22 82 28 22; www.turistforeningen.no; Storgata 7, Oslo) maintains a network of over 440 mountain huts or cabins located a day's hike apart along the country's 20,000km of well-marked and maintained wilderness hiking routes. These range from unstaffed huts (over 400 around the country) with two beds, to 42 large staffed lodges with more than 100

ALLEMANNSRETTEN

Anyone considering camping or hiking in Norway should be aware of *allemansretten* (every man's right, often referred to as 'right of access'). This 1000-year-old law, in conjunction with the modern Friluftsleven (Outdoor Recreation Act), entitles anyone to: camp anywhere for up to two days, as long as it's more than 150m from a dwelling (preferably further and out of sight); hike or ski across uncultivated wilderness areas, including outlying fields and pastures (except in fields with standing crops and close to people's houses); cycle or ride on horseback on all paths and roads; and canoe, kayak, row and sail on all rivers and lakes. However, these freedoms come with responsibilities, among the most important of which are the prohibition against fires between 15 April and 15 September and the requirement that you leave the countryside, any wildlife and cultural sights as pristine as you found them. For more on what these responsibilities mean in practice, see the boxed text, p390.

beds and renowned standards of service. All unstaffed huts offer cooking facilities, but in most places you must have your own sleeping bag or hostel-style sleeping sheet; sleeping sheets are often sold or included in the price at staffed huts. Staffed lodges don't normally have cooking facilities for guests, but a self-service section with cooking facilities is available at some lodges when unstaffed.

At staffed huts, which are concentrated in the south, you can simply turn up and pay your fees. In compliance with international mountain hospitality, no-one is turned away, even if there's only floor space left; DNT members over 50 years of age are guaranteed a bed, even if it means displacing a younger hiker! Huts tend to be packed at Easter and consistently busy throughout summer.

For details of becoming a DNT member, see p392.

In the staffed huts, nightly fees for DNT members/nonmembers in a room with one to three beds are Nkr205/270; rooms with four to six beds Nkr165/235; dorms Nkr105/170; and overflow on the floor Nkr75/140. Lodging and full board (for DNT members only) in one- to three-bed rooms/dorms costs Nkr535/495 in low season, Nkr555/515 in summer and Nkr605/565 during Easter; these prices apply to people staying three nights or more. Otherwise, a full breakfast (members/nonmembers Nkr85/110) or dinner (Nkr200/250) is available, as are sandwiches (Nkr10/15), a thermos of tea or coffee (Nkr25/40) and lighter dinners (Nkr125/145). Dinners, often including local specialities, can be excellent. A sleeping sheet costs Nkr55/70.

Members/nonmembers who prefer to camp outside the huts and use the facilities will pay Nkr50/60.

For unstaffed huts, you must pick up keys (Nkr100 to Nkr150 deposit) in advance from a DNT office or a staffed hut. To pay, fill out a Once-Only Authorisation slip and leave either cash or a valid credit-card number in the box provided. There are two classes of unstaffed huts. Self-service chalets are stocked with blankets and pillows and have wood stoves, firewood, gas cookers and a wide range of tinned or freeze-dried food supplies for sale (on the honour system). In these, DNT members/nonmembers pay Nkr165/265 for a bed. At other unstaffed huts, users must carry in their own food. Visit the DNT website for a full list of prices.

Most DNT huts are open from 16 February to 14 October. Staffed DNT lodges also open from the Saturday before Palm Sunday until Easter Monday, but staffed huts along the Oslo-Bergen railway and a few others open for the cross-country ski season as early as late February. DNT can provide lists of opening dates for each hut.

There are also numerous private hikers' huts and lodges peppered around most mountain areas, but not all are open to the public. Some offer DNT members a discount.

Hostels

In Norway, reasonably priced hostels *(vandrerhjem)* offer a dorm bed for the night, plus use of communal facilities that usually include a self-catering kitchen (you're advised to take your own cooking and eating utensils), internet access and bathrooms. Hostels vary widely in character, but increasingly, they're open longer hours and family-run places have largely replaced those presided over by 'wardens' with a sergeant-major mentality; consumption of alcohol on most hostel premises is prohibited. That said, the designation 'hostel', even when HI-affiliated, can be a loosely interpreted term. While some hostels have quite comfortable lodge-style facilities and are open year-round, some are used for school accommodation except during summer months and others are the cheaper wing of a hotel; occasionally prices work out more expensive than a cabin or budget hotel. In most hostels, guests must still bring their own sleeping sheet and pillowcase, although most hire sleeping sheets for a one-off Nkr50 fee regardless of the number of nights.

Several hostel guides are available, including HI's annually updated Europe guide. The Norwegian hostelling association, **Norske Vandrerhjem** (☎ 23 12 45 10; www.vandrerhjem.no), also publishes the free *Hostels in Norway*, which contains a full listing of hostels and updated prices.

Most hostels have two- to six-bed rooms and beds cost from Nkr140 to Nkr240. The higher-priced hostels usually include a buffet breakfast, while other places may charge from Nkr50 to Nkr70 for breakfast. Some also provide a good-value evening meal for around Nkr110.

In summer, reservations are recommended, particularly for popular destinations. Most places in Norway accept phone reservations and are normally happy to book beds at your next destination for a small fee (around Nkr20). Note, however, that popular hostels in Oslo and Bergen are often heavily booked in summer.

Prices listed in this book are those for non-HI members; members pay 15% less. Contact **Hostelling International** (www.hihostels.com) to find its office in your home country so that you can join and qualify for members' prices in Norway.

There are very few private hostels in Norway.

Hotels

Although hotel prices are high, most hotels offer substantially discounted rates on weekends and in summer (usually mid-June to mid-August, but sometimes July only), which are slow periods for business travel.

Although a few Norwegian hotels have consistent year-round prices, most charge exorbitant rates (singles/doubles from around Nkr1200/1500) from Monday to Thursday outside the summer months. This is largely because the only people travelling are businesspeople on expense accounts. If you're travelling at this time, ask the hotel about special offers to see if discounts are available. In summer and on weekends, prices can drop by around 40%. The some-time exception to this rule is the southern Norwegian coast where beach resorts raise their prices to cash in on the school-holiday influx. Be aware also that listed prices for hotels in particular are representative only as many establishments have almost as many different prices as there are days in the year.

Nationwide chains or hotel networks sometimes offer chain-hotel passes, which can entitle you to a free night if you use the chain enough times; some passes only operate in summer. The main nationwide chains (whose discounts sometimes also apply in other Scandinavian countries) include:

Best Western (www.bestwestern.no) Free pass at Best Western's 15 Norwegian hotels from June to August; entitles you to third consecutive night at same hotel free.

Choice Hotels (www.choice.no) Covering Choice, Clarion Collection and Comfort Hotels, the Choice Club can add up to free nights. There's also the Choice Hotel Cheque (12 nights for Nkr11,940). In some Comfort Hotels, you get a light evening buffet included in the price.

Fjord Pass (www.fjordpass.no) Probably the pick (and certainly the largest) of the hotel passes, the Fjord Pass costs Nkr120 (valid for two adults and any children under 15) and is available at 150 hotels year-round; no free nights, but the discounts on nightly rates are considerable.

Rica Feriepass (www.rica.no) Offers a free pass at 90 Rica hotels in Norway and Sweden; earns bonus points that can add up to the 10th night free at any Rica hotel.

Thon Hotels (www.thonhotels.com) Free membership that qualifies you for discounts or free nights.

One other worthwhile network (although it offers no discounts) is **De Historiske Historic Hotels and Restaurants** (☎ 55 31 67 60; www.dehistoriske.no), which links Norway's most character-filled old hotels. The quality on offer is consistently high, every hotel is architecturally distinguished and many are family-run. Admittedly, they can be expensive, but are almost always worth it.

Summer Homes & Cabins

Most tourist offices in popular holiday areas keep lists of private huts, cabins and summer homes that are rented out to holidaymakers when the owners aren't using them; these arrangements sometimes also apply in the ski season. The price for a week's rental starts from around Nkr1200 for a simple place in the off season to about Nkr14,000 for the most elaborate chalet in midsummer. Most cabins sleep at least four people, and some accommodate as many as 12; if you have a group, it can be an economical option. Advance booking is normally required, and you'll probably have to pay a deposit of around Nkr500 or 20% of the total fee, whichever is less.

For further information, contact **Novasol** (☎ 23 35 62 70; www.novasol.com), which publishes an English-language photo catalogue describing nearly 2000 self-catering cabins and chalets in Norway. A similar scheme is offered by the Danish company **Dansommer** (in Denmark ☎ 86 17 61 22; www.dansommer.com).

ACTIVITIES

Norway is one of the world's premier wilderness destinations and it has a world-class adventure industry to match. Just about anything's possible and each of these activities is covered in the relevant regional chapters, but what follows here is an overview to whet your appetite.

Cycling

Whether you're keen for a two-wheeled amble around the flat shoreline of your favourite

TOP FIVE CYCLING EXPERIENCES

- Sognefjellet Road, through the Jotunheimen National Park (p184)
- The exhilarating descent from Finse down to Flåm along the Rallarvegen (see the boxed text, p189)
- Lofoten (p312) offesr leisurely cycling through some wonderful, rugged scenery
- Across the Hardangervidda Plateau near Rjukan (see the boxed text, p157)
- The high country around Trysil (p171)

fjord or a serious cyclist with your sights set on the ultimate Norwegian challenge, Norway won't disappoint. For the ambler, many tourist offices and some bicycle shops rent out bicycles for casual cyclists, while Trondheim has taken this to a whole new level with free bicycles; for details see the boxed text, p286. For the serious cyclist, there are some extraordinary routes that the world cycling community raves about; some of our favourites are covered in the boxed text, above, while the National Tourist Routes (p414) are another possibility.

An excellent website with route descriptions of some of the better long-distance cycling routes in Norway is www.bike-norway.com. It also sells online nine different cycling maps, some with route descriptions, for Nkr120 to Nkr298; click on 'Brochure' on its home page. For further information on long-distance cycling routes and tunnels, contact **Syklistenes Landsforening** (Map pp96-7; ☎ 22 47 30 30; www.slf.no; Storgata 23d, Oslo), the main contact point for Norway's cycling clubs. The map *Sykkelruter i Norge* (Nkr120) is sold by Syklistenes Landsforening; it's only available in Norwegian, but the English-text *Sykkelguide* series of booklets with maps are available for Nkr125 each and include Lofoten, Rallarvegen, the North Sea Cycleway from the Swedish border at Svinesund to Bergen, and other routes.

Most tourist offices can offer advice on cycling trails (and sometimes maps) in their local area, while Syklistenes Landsforening is good for maps and advice for longer expeditions.

For the practicalities of cycling and bicycle hire in Norway, turn to p411.

Dog-sledding

This Inuit means of transport readily transfers to the Norwegian wilds, and several operators can take you on a range of winter adventures. While some people are content with just a half-day taster – Alaska Husky Expeditions in Røros organises short expeditions (p173) – keen prospective 'mushers' can jump in the deep end and opt for a two-week dog-sled safari through Øvre Dividal National Park (p343), Tromsø (p337), Karasjok (p369),

11 COMMANDMENTS FOR ANGLERS

1. Foreigners may fish for free on the Norwegian coast but can't sell their catch.
2. Fishing is prohibited within 100m of fish farms, or cables and nets that are anchored or fastened to the shore.
3. Anyone who damages fishing equipment must pay compensation.
4. Anchoring is prohibited close to drift nets or line-fishing sites.
5. It's forbidden to shoot off firearms or make noises that can disturb the fish.
6. Fishing with live bait is prohibited.
7. It's forbidden to abandon fishing tackle or other rubbish that can disturb, delay or damage fish catches or fishing boats.
8. Only Norwegian citizens or permanent residents may catch lobsters.
9. Salmon, trout and char fishing with a rod is permitted year-round. For rivers with fishing bans, you may still fish within 100m of the river mouth. From 1 June to 4 August, between 6pm on Friday and 6pm on Monday, you can fish for salmon, trout and char with a hook and troll. All anglers for these fish must have a national fishing permit, and must also follow other local fishing regulations (which may include compulsory disinfection of fishing equipment).
10. All anglers from boats must wear life jackets.
11. Don't throw rubbish or pollute the waters in any way.

around Alta (p347), Kirkenes (p361) and Svalbard (p374). Tour operators, some of which offer dog-sledding, are covered on p409, while dog-sled endurance races take place in January from Røros (p173) and in March from Alta (p344).

Fishing

Norway's rivers and lakes have drawn avid anglers since the 19th century. Norway's salmon runs are still legendary and, in June and July, you can't beat the rivers of Finnmark; try Tana Bru (p356) for starters. In addition to salmon, 41 other fish species inhabit the country's 200,000 rivers and lakes. In the south, you'll find the best fishing from June to September, and in the north, in July and August. In Svalbard, the best fishing holes are well-kept secrets, but Arctic char inhabit some rivers and lakes. The 175-page book *Angling in Norway*, available from tourist offices for Nkr185, details the best salmon- and trout-fishing areas, fees and regulations.

Regulations vary between rivers but, generally, from mid-September to November fish under 20cm must be thrown back. At other times between August and May, the limit is 30cm.

All river and lake fishing in Norway requires an annual licence (Nkr225 for salmon, trout and char and Nkr110 for other fish), which is sold at post offices. A weekly licence is also available for Nkr55. To fish on private land, you must also purchase a local licence (Nkr55 to Nkr375 per day), which is available from sports shops, hotels, camp sites and tourist offices. Some areas require a compulsory equipment disinfection certificate (Nkr110).

RESPONSIBLE HIKING

To help preserve the ecology and beauty of Norway, consider the following tips when hiking:

Rubbish

- If you've carried it in, you can carry it back out – *everything,* including empty packaging, citrus peel and cigarette butts, can be stowed in a dedicated rubbish bag, as can rubbish left by others.
- Never bury your rubbish: Digging disturbs fragile soil and ground cover and encourages erosion. Buried rubbish may take years to decompose and will likely be dug up by animals, who may be injured or poisoned by it.
- Minimise waste by taking minimal packaging and no more food than you'll need. Take reusable containers or stuff sacks.
- Sanitary napkins, tampons, condoms and toilet paper should be carried out despite the inconvenience. They burn and decompose poorly.

Fires & Low-Impact Cooking

- Don't depend on open fires for cooking. The cutting of wood for fires in popular trekking areas causes rapid deforestation; use only dead, fallen wood. Cook on a light weight kerosene, alcohol or Shellite (white gas) stove and avoid those powered by disposable butane gas canisters.
- If trekking with a guide and porters, supply stoves for the whole team. In alpine areas, ensure all members are outfitted with enough clothing so that fires aren't a necessity for warmth.
- If you patronise local accommodation, select places that don't use wood fires to heat water or cook food.
- Fires may be acceptable below the tree line in areas that get very few visitors. If you light a fire, use an existing fireplace. Don't surround fires with rocks. Remember the adage 'the bigger the fool, the bigger the fire'. Use minimal wood, just what you need for cooking. In huts, leave wood for the next person.
- Ensure that you fully extinguish a fire after use. Spread the embers and flood them with water.

Flying & Helicopter Trips

If the sight of a helicopter or light plane circling over the fjords makes you wonder just how this extraordinary landscape looks from above, ask at your nearest tourist office to see if it's possible to board a short, often 45-minute flight. Prices start from around Nkr700 per person. Some of the more spectacular places where this is possible include Bergen and Ulvik, but options abound throughout Norway's fjord country.

Glacier Hiking

One of Norway's most rewarding outdoor activities is glacier hiking. As it's a potentially perilous undertaking, you should only set out on such a venture with an experienced local guide. The best places include: Jotunheimen National Park (see the boxed text, p186), which has more than 60 glaciers; the otherworldly Hardangerjøkulen glacier on Hardangervidda (p189 or p190); Folgefonn (p219); Nigardsbreen (p246); Briksdalsbreen (p247); Bødalsbreen (p248); Saltfjellet-Svartisen National Park (p296); Lyngen Alps (p341); and Svalbard (p374).

If you find yourself captivated by glaciers, the Norwegian Glacier Museum (Norsk Bremuseum; p244) or the Breheimsenteret (p246), which serves as the visitors centre for Nigardsbreen, should both be on your itinerary.

Hiking

Norway has some of Europe's best hiking, including a network of around 20,000km of marked trails that range from easy strolls through the green zones around cities, to long treks through national parks and wilderness areas. Many of these trails are maintained by

Water Pollution

- Don't use detergents or toothpaste in or near streams or lakes; even it they are biodegradable they can harm fish and wildlife.
- For personal washing, use biodegradable soap and a water container (or even a lightweight, portable basin) at least 50m away from the watercourse. Disperse the waste water widely to allow the soil to filter it fully.
- Wash cooking utensils 50m from watercourses using a scourer, sand or snow instead of detergent.
- Contamination of water sources by human faeces can lead to the transmission of all sorts of nasties. Where there is a toilet, please use it. Where there is none, bury your waste. Dig a small hole 15cm deep and at least 100m from any watercourse. Cover the waste with soil and a rock. In snow, dig down to the soil.

Erosion

- Always stick to existing trails and avoid short cuts to minimise erosion.
- If a well-used trail passes through a mud patch, walk through the mud so as not to increase the size of the patch.
- Avoid removing the plant life that keeps topsoils in place.

Wildlife Conservation

- Don't engage in or encourage hunting.
- Don't attempt to exterminate animals in huts. In wild places, they are likely to be protected native animals.
- Discourage the presence of wildlife by not leaving food scraps behind you. Place gear out of reach and tie packs to rafters or trees.
- Don't feed the wildlife as this can lead to animals becoming dependent on hand-outs, to unbalanced populations and to diseases.

WEATHER WARNING

Always check weather and other local conditions before setting out cross-country. This applies whenever traversing any exposed area, but is particularly an issue for cross-country skiers (two Scottish cross-country skiers died after being caught in snow and freezing fog in March 2007 on the Hardangervidda Plateau despite, according to some reports, being warned by local experts not to set out). The only months that favourable conditions can be almost guaranteed for hiking are July and August. You should always be prepared for sudden inclement weather and stay aware of potential avalanche dangers, which are particularly rife in Jotunheimen but are a possibility anywhere in Norway's high country. Also, never venture onto glacial ice without the proper equipment and experience. And trust the advice of locals who understand the conditions better than even the most experienced out-of-town hikers – if they say not to go, don't go.

DNT and are marked either with cairns or red Ts at 100m or 200m intervals.

The hiking season runs roughly from late May to early October, with a much shorter season in the higher mountain areas and the far north. In the highlands, the snow often remains until June and returns in September, meaning that many routes are only possible in July and August. The most popular wilderness hiking areas are the Jotunheimen (see the boxed text, p186) and Rondane (p180) National Parks and the Hardangervidda Plateau (see the boxed text, p188). If you're after a wilder experience, try such national parks as Dovrefjell-Sunndalsfjella (p178), Øvre Dividal (p343), Stabbursdalen (p355), Rago (p298), Reisa (p367), Saltfjellet-Svartisen (p296) and/or any of the vast number of unprotected areas throughout the country, such as Trollheimen (p177). Avid hikers will never run out of options!

There are many excellent books for hikers in Norway. Erling Welle-Strand's 1993 *Mountain Hiking in Norway* includes hiking itineraries, sketch maps and details on trail huts. More recent is Constance Roos' *Walking in Norway* (2003) and *Walks and Scrambles in Norway* by Anthony Dyer et al (2006). A good choice for avid hikers is probably *Norwegian Mountains on Foot* by DNT, which is the English edition of the Norwegian classic, *Til Fots i Fjellet*.

For a full list and description of Norway's major national parks, see p70.

DEN NORSKE TURISTFORENING

Den Norske Turistforening (DNT) and its various chapters maintain a network of over 440 mountain huts and lodges throughout the country. For details and prices for the use of these huts, see p386.

If you're going to do lots of hiking, it's certainly worth joining DNT. The standard annual membership starts at Nkr465, including seven *Fjell og Vidde* magazines; the *DNT Yearbook* costs an extra Nkr50. Memberships for 13 to 18-year-old/student/senior cost Nkr150/265/355; members' families pay Nkr210 per person. For further information, contact **DNT** (☎ 22 82 28 22; www.turistforeningen.no). DNT also sells hiking maps and topographic sheets (see p399).

Paragliding, Parasailing, Bungee & Base Jumping

Those who either have no fear or would simply love a bird's-eye view of some of Europe's most spectacular country have three main options. The first is to head to Voss, which has the widest range of possibilities such as paragliding, parasailing and bungee jumping from a parasail, most of which are organised by **Nordic Ventures** (☎ 56 51 00 17; www.nordicventures.com). True adrenaline junkies will want to be in Voss in late June for Extremesport Week when skydiving and base jumping are added to the rush; see the boxed text, p211, for more information.

The second option, although for bungee jumping only, is in Rjukan (see the boxed text, p156), home to the highest land-based bungee jump in Norway.

Finally, if plummeting towards the earth at breakneck speed is your thing, base jumping is possible from the precipitous cliffs of Lysefjord at Kjeragbolten (p231). Remember, however, that base jumping is fraught with risk – three people have died while base jumping in Norway since 2005.

Rock Climbing & Mountaineering

Norway's astounding vertical topography is a paradise for climbers interested in rock, ice and alpine pursuits. In fact, outside the Alps, Norway is probably Europe's finest climbing venue, although Norway's climatic extremes mean that technical climbers face harsh conditions, short seasons and strict restrictions. The most popular alpine venues in Norway include the area around Åndalsnes (p256), the Lyngen Alps (p341), Bondhusbreen (p220) and Lofoten (p317); the latter has a good climbing school that organises expeditions. In addition to having wonderful surrounding peaks, Åndalsnes has a very popular mountaineering festival, Norsk Fjellfestivalen (p257). Lom also has the Norwegian Mountain Museum (p183) that's worth checking out.

For general information on climbing in Norway, contact **Norsk Tindeklub** (☎ 22 50 54 56; www.ntk.no; c/o Egil Fredriksen, Sorkedalsveien 202b, N0754, Oslo).

In addition to the rock climbers' classic *Climbing in the Magic Islands* by Ed Webster, which describes most of the feasible routes in Lofoten look for *Ice Fall in Norway* by Sir Ranulph Fiennes, which describes a 1970 sojourn around Jostedalsbreen. The more practical *Scandinavian Mountains* by Peter Lennon introduces the country's finest climbing venues.

Skiing

'Ski' is a Norwegian word and thanks to aeons-old rock carvings depicting hunters travelling on skis, Norwegians make a credible claim to having invented the sport. Interest hasn't waned over the years and these days, it's the national pastime. Most skiing is of the cross-country (nordic) variety, and Norway has thousands of kilometres of maintained cross-country ski trails. However, visitors should only set off after closely studying the trails/routes (wilderness trails are identified by colour codes on maps and signposts) and ensuring that they have appropriate clothing, sufficient food and water, and emergency supplies, such as matches and a source of warmth. You can either bring your own equipment or rent on site.

Most towns and villages provide some illuminated ski trails, but elsewhere it's still worth carrying a good torch, as winter days are very short and in the north there's no daylight at all in December and January. The ski season generally lasts from early December to April. Snow conditions vary greatly from year to year and region to region, but February and March, as well as the Easter holiday period, tend to be the best (and busiest) times.

There are also scores of resorts with downhill runs, but these are quite expensive due to the costs of ski lifts, accommodation and the après-ski drinking sessions. The spring season lasts longer than in the Alps and the snow is better quality too.

Popular skiing spots include the Holmenkollen area (p106) near Oslo, Geilo (p189) on the Oslo–Bergen railway line, Voss (p211), Lillehammer (p168), Trysil (p171) and Hovden (p161). Summer skiers can head for Stryn (p248), Folgefonn (p219), or Jotunheimen National Park (p185).

For general information on skiing in Norway, contact DNT (p386), or visit the website www.skiingnorway.com.

THE TELEMARK MANOEUVRE

The Telemark region of Norway has lent its name to the graceful turn that has made nordic (cross-country) skiing popular around the world. nordic ski bindings attach the boot at the toes, allowing free movement of the heel; to turn, one knee is dropped to the surface of the ski while the other leg is kept straight. The skis are positioned one behind the other, allowing the skier to smoothly glide around the turn in the direction of the dropped knee.

Whale-Watching

One of the best places for watching whales is from Stø (p326) on Vesterålen, while the waters off nearby Andenes (p327) are equally good and there's also a whale centre (p327) to add context to your trip. Trips are also possible from Narvik (p300), Henningsvær (p317) and Kabelvåg (p315).

White-Water Rafting & Sea-Kayaking

Norway's steep slopes and icy, scenic rivers create an ideal environment for avid rafters, and a number of reputable operators offer trips, primarily in central Norway. These range from short, Class II doddles to Class III and IV adventures and rollicking Class V punishment. Most are guaranteed to provide a thrill, and the rates include all requisite equipment and waterproofing. Among the finest venues are Evje (Setesdalen; see the boxed text, p159), Sjoa (Heidalen; see the boxed text, p182), Oppdal (Drivadalen; see the boxed text, p176) and Voss (see the boxed text, p211).

Norges Padleforbund (☎ 21 02 98 35; www.padling.no; Service boks 1, Ullevål stadion, 0840 Oslo) provides a comprehensive list of rafting operators in Norway, many of which can also organise sea-kayaking and river-boarding.

If you're into sea-kayaking, you may want to be in Langøya for the 170km Arctic Sea Kayak Race in July (see p325); the event sponsors introductory and more advanced courses.

BUSINESS HOURS

Offices, including most post offices, are open from 9am to 5pm Monday to Friday and 10am to 2pm Saturday. Post offices in larger cities open from 8am to 8pm Monday to Friday and 9am to 6pm Saturday and shorter hours in other places. For opening hours for shops, supermarkets, banks and restaurants, see the Quick Reference inside the front cover of this book. The opening hours for tourist offices are listed under each city throughout the book.

CHILDREN

Travelling through Norway with children couldn't be easier, although successful travel with young children requires planning and effort. Don't try to overdo things; packing too much into the time available causes problems, even for adults. Make sure the planning includes kids as well; if they've helped to work out where you're going, chances are they'll still be interested when you arrive. Lonely Planet's *Travel with Children* by Cathy Lanigan is a useful source of information.

Practicalities

Car-rental firms hire out children's safety seats at a nominal cost, but it's essential that you book them in advance. The same goes for highchairs and cots (cribs); they're standard in many restaurants and hotels, but numbers may be limited. Norway offers a relatively wide choice of baby food, infant formulas, soy and cow's milk, disposable nappies (diapers) etc; after the supermarkets close, you'll have to resort to more expensive convenience stores.

Children aged under two travel for 10% of the full fare (or free on some airlines), as long as they don't occupy a seat. They don't get a baggage allowance. 'Skycots', baby food and nappies should be provided by the airline if requested in advance. Children aged between two and 12 can usually occupy a seat for half to two-thirds of the full fare and get a standard baggage allowance.

Hotels, HI hostels, camp sites and other accommodation options often have 'family rooms' or cabins that accommodate up to two adults and two children. In hotels, this may cost little more than the price of a regular double.

Many restaurants have children's menus with servings designed to satisfy a child's appetite and prices to avoid sending the parents bankrupt. For more information, see p60.

Sights & Activities

In many ways, Norway is a children's country and most towns have attractions and museums specifically targeted for the younger crowd. Domestic tourism is often organised around children's interests: regional museums invariably have a children's section with toys and activities, and there are also numerous public parks for kids to play at. Most attractions are generous and allow free admission for young children up to six years of age and half-price (or substantially discounted) admission for those aged up to 16. Family tickets are available at Norway's sights.

For a list of the some of the best places in Norway for kids, see p20.

CLIMATE CHARTS

Although Norway covers the same latitude range as Alaska (and much further north when you include Svalbard), most of the country enjoys a surprisingly temperate climate. For this you can thank the Gulf Stream, which flows north along the coast. Average maximum temperatures for July hover around 16°C in the south (although they can be double that) and around 13°C in the north. In January, the average maximum temperature is 1°C and -3°C respectively. Bergen, on the southwest coast, is the wettest city, with 2250mm of annual precipitation, while Rondane and Gudbrandsdal, protected by coastal mountain ranges from the moisture-laden prevailing southwesterly winds, are among the driest districts of Norway, with less than 500mm of precipitation annually. Alta in the country's far north receives less rain than the Sahara!

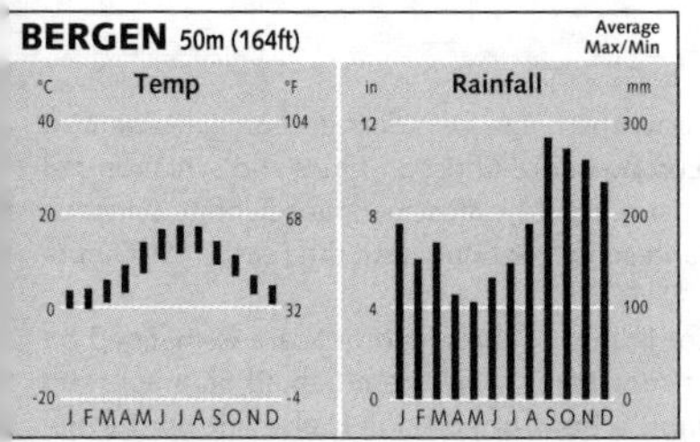

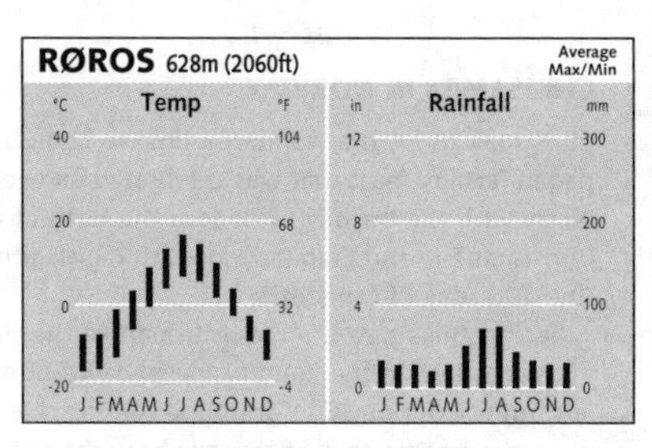

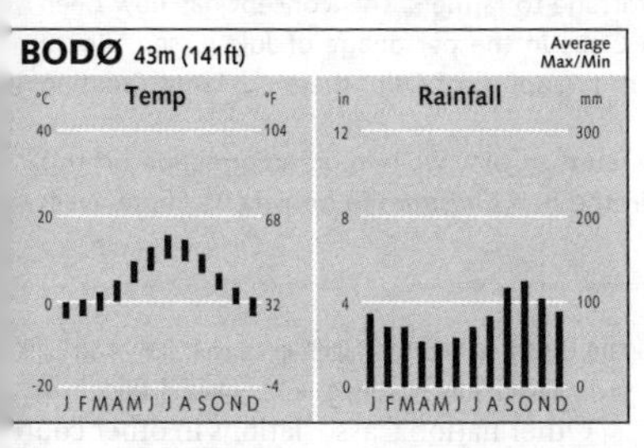

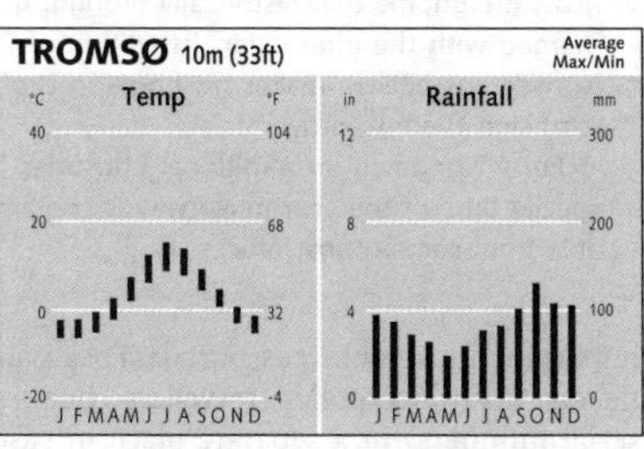

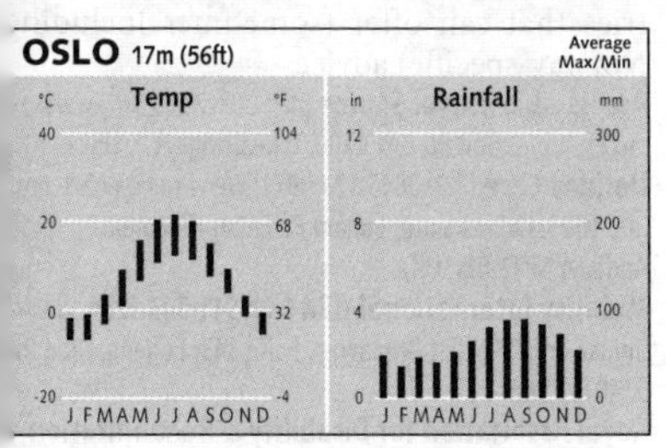

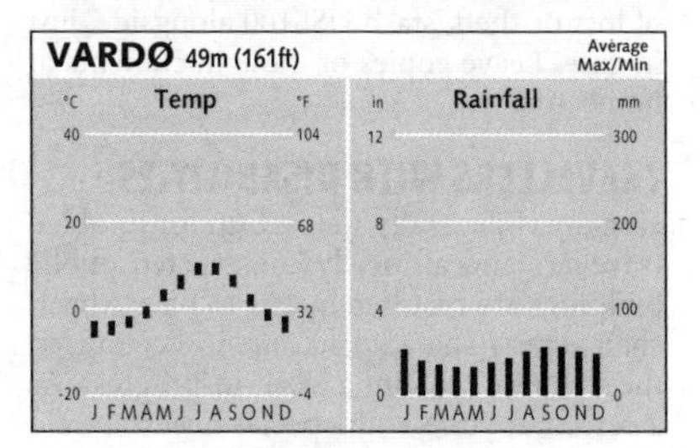

Extreme temperatures are possible even in the Arctic region. In July 1998, even Narvik rose above 30°C and Svalbard positively soared to over 20°C a month later. At the other end of the scale, winter temperatures can plummet (in January 1999, the temperature in Kirkenes dropped to a chilly -56°C) and snow up to 10m deep can accumulate in the mountains; a mere 2m to 3m is more usual in the lower areas.

The **Norwegian Meteorological Institute** (www.dnmi.no) has the latest weather information.

CUSTOMS

Alcohol and tobacco are extremely expensive in Norway. To at least get you started, it's worth importing your duty-free allotment: 1L of spirits and 1L of wine (or 2L of wine), plus 2L of beer per person. Note that drinks with an alcohol content of over 60% may be treated as narcotics! You're also allowed to import 200 cigarettes duty-free. Importation of fresh food and controlled drugs is prohibited.

DANGERS & ANNOYANCES

Your personal belongings are safer in Norway than in most people's home countries, and the cities – even east Oslo, which has a relatively poor reputation – are reasonably safe at all hours of the night. However, don't become blasé about security: be careful near the nightclubs in the Rosenkrantz gate area of Oslo and beware of pickpockets around the Torget area of Bergen. Normally, the greatest nuisance value will come from drug addicts, drunks and/or beggars (mainly in Oslo) who can spot a naive tourist a block away. Oslo and other larger cities suffer from a growing drug problem. Although dope may be readily available in places, it isn't legal.

While the risk of theft in Norway is minimal, it's wise to keep photocopies of all your

CHRISTMAS IN NORWAY

Christmas, or *jul*, is a wonderful time to be in Norway. The name *jul* is derived from *joulu* or *lol*, a pagan fertility feast that was celebrated all over Europe in pre-Christian times and synchronised nicely with the holiday to honour the birth of Christ. Currently, most people celebrate between Christmas Eve and Epiphany, or 12th night, although some continue until the Feast of St Canute (the 20th day of Christmas).

A Christmas tree is a requisite part of the décor in most homes, and gifts are exchanged on Christmas Eve. In the countryside, sheaves of oats known as *julenek* are mounted on a pole and left out for the birds. In gratitude for past blessings, a bowl of porridge is also left out for the *nisse*, the gnome that historically brought good fortune to farmers. This concept has now been merged with the international tradition of Santa Claus in the personage of Jule-nissen, whom Norwegians believe makes his home in Drøbak (p117), south of Oslo; there's a Santa Crossing road sign there to prove it!

For a run-down on traditional Christmas foods, turn to p59, while more information on this special time of the year in Norway is contained in the free *Christmas in Norway* brochure available from some tourist offices.

important documents (passport data page, air tickets, insurance policy, travellers cheques serial numbers) in a separate place in case of loss or theft; stash US$100 alongside, just in case. Leave copies of these documents at home, too.

TRAVELLERS WITH DISABILITIES

Norway is generally well set up for disabled travellers and all newly constructed public buildings are required by law to have wheelchair access. That said, like in most countries, the situation remains a work-in-progress. As a result, anyone with special needs should plan ahead.

Most Norwegian tourist offices carry lists of wheelchair-accessible hotels and hostels – for an excellent example, go to the English-language section of the website of **Bergen tourist office** (www.visitbergen.com) and click on 'For the physically disabled' – but your best bet is to contact the Norwegian Association for the Disabled (see below). Nearly all street crossings are equipped with either a ramp or a very low kerb (curb), and crossing signals produce an audible signal – longer beeps when it's safe to cross and shorter beeps when the signal is about to change. Most (but not all) trains have carriages with space for wheelchair users and many public buildings have wheelchair-accessible toilets.

Organisations

For information on disabled travel and sites of special interest to disabled travellers in Norway, contact the **Norwegian Association for the Disabled** (Norges Handikapforbund; ☎ 24 10 24 00; www.nhf.no; Schweigaards gate 12, Grønland, Oslo).

Other national associations in other countries that can offer (sometimes including Norway-specific) advice:

Access-able Travel Source (☎ 303-232 2979; www.access-able.com; PO Box 1796, Wheatridge, CO, USA)

Holiday Care (☎ 0845 124 9971; www.holidaycare.org.uk; The Hawkins Suite, Enham Pl, Enham Alamein, Andover SP11 6JS, UK)

Mobility International USA (☎ 541-343 1284; www.miusa.org; 132 East Broadway, Suite 343, Eugene, Oregon 97401, USA)

Royal Association for Disability & Rehabilitation (Radar; ☎ 020-7250 3222; www.radar.org.uk; 12 City Forum, 250 City Rd, London, EC1V 8AF, UK) Publishes a useful guide called *Holidays & Travel Abroad: A Guide for Disabled People.*

Society for Accessible Travel and Hospitality (☎ 212-447 7284; www.sath.org; 347 5th Ave, Ste 610, New York, NY 10016, USA)

Tours

A number of tour companies offer tailored trips to Norway for travellers with a disability, with a special focus on wheelchair travellers.

Accessible Journeys (☎ 800 846-4537; www.disabilitytravel.com; 35 West Sellers Ave, Ridley Park, PA 19078, USA)

Accessible Travel & Leisure (☎ 01452-729739; www.accessibletravel.co.uk; Avionics House, Naas Lane, Quedgeley, Gloucester GL2 2SN, UK) Claims to be the biggest UK travel agent dealing with travel for the disabled and encourages people with a disability to travel independently.

Easy Access Adventures (www.easyaccessadventures.com)

Flying Wheels Travel (☎ 507-451 5005; www.flyingwheelstravel.com; 143 W Bridge St, Owatonna, MN 55060, USA)

DISCOUNT CARDS

For details on benefits of purchasing a HI card before you leave home, see p387.

Senior Cards

Honnør (senior) discounts are the same as those for students and are normally available to those aged 67 years or over for admission to museums, public pools, transport etc. The discounts are usually less than for children (entry usually amounts to 75% of the full price). You don't require a special card, but those who look particularly youthful may, apart from enjoying the compliment, need proof of their age to qualify, as the ever-friendly Norwegian ticket sellers won't believe you're a day over 50.

Student Cards

The most useful student card is the International Student Identity Card (ISIC), a plastic ID-style card with your photograph. Some travellers have reported being refused access with their normal university cards (unless it's from a Norwegian university) so the ISIC card is a good investment. It can provide discounts on many forms of transport (including airlines, international ferries and local public transport) and in some internet cafés, reduced or free admission to museums and sights, and cheap meals in some student restaurants.

EMBASSIES & CONSULATES

Embassies & Consulates in Norway

Australia The nearest Australian embassy is in Copenhagen; contact the British embassy in an emergency.

Canada (Map pp96-7; ☎ 22 99 53 00; www.canada.no; Wergelandsveien 7, N-0244 Oslo)

Denmark (Map p91; ☎ 22 54 08 00; www.ambosloum.dk; Olav Kyrres gate 7, N-0244 Oslo)

Finland (Map p93; ☎ 22 12 49 00; www.finland.no; Thomas Heftyes gate 1, N-0244 Oslo)

France (Map p93; ☎ 22 28 46 00; www.ambafrance-no.org; Drammensveien 69, N-0244 Oslo)

Germany (Map pp96-7; ☎ 22 27 54 00; www.oslo.diplo.de; Oscars gate 45, N-0244 Oslo)

Ireland (Map pp96-7; ☎ 22 01 72 00; osloembassy@dfa.ie; 4th fl, Håkon VII's gate 1, N-0212 Oslo)

Japan (Map pp96-7; ☎ 22 99 16 00; www.no.emb-japan.go.jp; Wergelandsveien 15, N-0244 Oslo)

Netherlands (Map p93; ☎ 23 33 36 00; www.netherlands-embassy.no; Oscars gate 29, N-0244 Oslo)

New Zealand The British embassy handles consular affairs; the nearest New Zealand embassy is in The Hague.

Russia (Map p93; ☎ 22 55 32 78; www.norway.mid.ru; Drammensveien 74, N-0271 Oslo)

Sweden (Map p91; ☎ 24 11 42 00; www.sverigesambassad.no; Nobelsgata 16, N-0244 Oslo)

UK (Map p93; ☎ 23 13 27 00; www.britain.no; Thomas Heftyes gate 8, N-0244 Oslo)

USA (Map pp96-7; ☎ 22 44 85 50; www.usa.no; Henrik Ibsens gate 48, N-0244 Oslo)

FESTIVALS & EVENTS

Norway is chock-a-block with special festivals, which take place at all times of year in every city, town and village. Large and popular ones are covered on p22 and in the regional chapters of this book.

FOOD

For a comprehensive insight into eating in Norway for both carnivores and vegetarians, see p56. Throughout this book, restaurants are open for lunch and dinner unless otherwise stated, the timings of which are given in the Quick Reference inside the front cover of this book. Only significant deviations from these general times are listed in full.

GAY & LESBIAN TRAVELLERS

Norwegians are generally tolerant of alternative lifestyles, and Norway, along with several neighbouring countries, allows gay and lesbian couples to form 'registered partnerships' that grant every right of matrimony, except access to church weddings, adoption and artificial insemination. There's an ongoing debate at a public and political level as to whether adoption rights should be extended to gay couples and whether the Church should continue to be exempt from Norway's strong anti-discrimination laws. There have been numerous gay or lesbian members of parliament and Oslo's mayor at the time of writing is openly gay.

That said, public displays of affection are not common practice, except perhaps in some areas of Oslo. Oslo is generally the easiest place to be gay in Norway, although even here there have been occasional recent attacks on gay couples holding hands, especially in the central-eastern areas of the capital. You're most likely to encounter difficulties wherever conservative religious

MAY I SEE YOUR ID, PLEASE?

For the record:

- The legal age for drinking beer is 18, but for spirits and wine it's 20; some bars won't let you in unless you're 24 or over.
- The legal age for voting is 18.
- You can drive when you are 18, but not necessarily rent a vehicle.
- The legal age of sexual consent is 16 (heterosexual or homosexual).

views predominate, whether among newly arrived Muslim immigrant communities or among devoutly Lutheran communities in rural areas.

For information on gay issues, contact **Landsforeningen for Lesbisk og Homofil frigjøring** (LLH; Map pp96-7; ☎ 22 36 19 48; www.llh.no in Norwegian; Kongensgate 12, Oslo), the Norwegian National Association of Lesbian and Gay Liberation. Other good sources of information (if you speak Norwegian) include the website for the gay-and-lesbian magazine **Blikk** (www.blikk.no in Norwegian) or the website for the **Oslo Pride Festival** (www.skeivedager.no), which runs in late June or early July.

Gay and lesbian travellers can find gay entertainment spots in larger cities and towns. The *Spartacus International Gay Guide*, published by Bruno Gmünder Verlag (Berlin), is an excellent international directory of gay entertainment venues, but it's now well out of date and best used in conjunction with up-to-date listings in local papers. More accessible for English speakers is the Oslo-specific 'Gay Guide' section of the excellent *Streetwise* booklet published annually by Use-It (p92).

Oslo has the liveliest gay scene (see the boxed text, p114).

INSURANCE

You should seriously consider taking out travel insurance that covers not only medical expenses and luggage theft or loss, but also cancellation or delays in your travel arrangements (due to illness, ticket loss, industrial action etc). It's a good idea to buy insurance as early as possible, as late purchase may preclude coverage of industrial action in force before you bought the policy. Note that some policies specifically exclude 'dangerous activities' such as motorcycling, skiing mountaineering, scuba diving or even hiking. Make sure the policy covers ambulances and an emergency flight home. A policy that pays doctors or hospitals directly may be preferable to one where you pay on the spot and claim later. If you have to claim later, make sure you keep all documentation.

In Norway, EU citizens may be required to pay a service fee for emergency medical treatment, but presentation of an E111 form will certainly expedite matters and minimise the amount of paperwork involved. Inquire about these at your national health service or travel agent well in advance.

For health insurance see p420, and for car insurance see p415.

INTERNET ACCESS

Apart from in larger towns, there are fewer internet cafés around Norway than you might expect; young waiters, waitresses and students are good people to ask if you need to find one. However, the scarcity of internet cafés is compensated for by having free internet access available in most municipal libraries. As it's a popular service, you may have to reserve a time slot earlier in the day; in busier places, you may be restricted to a half-hour slot. At private internet cafés, expect to pay around Nkr55 to Nkr70 per hour; students sometimes receive a discount. Internet access is also available at some tourist offices around the country for a fee.

If your laptop has a wireless internet facility, connecting couldn't be easier as most hotels, and even some hostels and guesthouses offer wireless access; most often this is free for guests, although some hotels charge around Nkr120 per 12 hours. Unless you're using a web-based email service such as **Yahoo** (www.yahoo.com), **Hotmail** (www.hotmail.com) or **Gmail** (www.gmail.com), ask your internet service provider (ISP) if they have local Norwegian access numbers.

For useful Norwegian, travel-related websites see p19.

LAUNDRY

Myntvaskeri (coin laundries) can be expensive and hard to find, with two exceptions. The guest-harbour facilities in most towns along Norway's coast (particularly in the south) have coin-operated machines (Nkr45 to Nkr60 per wash-and-dry). In addition, hostels and camp sites often have coin-operated washers and dryers available to guests.

In both Oslo (p90) and Bergen (p193), laundries provide detergent, and will wash, dry and even fold your clothes nicely; expect to pay anywhere between Nkr75 and Nkr110 for the full service. Some places also let you do it yourself, which works out cheaper. Unless you're on an expense account, avoid hotel laundry and dry-cleaning services.

MAPS

One of the best maps of Norway for general travellers is the colourful and popular *Bilkart over Norge*, published by Nortrabooks. This detailed map includes useful topographic shading and depicts the entire country on one sheet at a scale of 1:1,000,000.

Statens Kartverk covers the country in 21 sheets at a scale of 1:250,000, and also produces 1:50,000 hiking maps. You'll find details at http://showcase.netins.net/web/travelgenie/norway.htm.

Most local tourist offices distribute user-friendly and free town plans.

Hiking Maps

The best source of hiking maps is **Den Norske Turistforening** (DNT; Norwegian Mountain Touring Club; Map pp96-7; ☎ 22 82 28 22; www.turistforeningen.no; Storgata 7, Oslo) and hikers can pick up topographic sheets at any DNT office, although the offices in larger cities have a wider selection beyond the local area. National-park centres and nearby tourist offices are also good sources for the excellent Turkart or Statens Kartverk hiking maps.

Map Shops

General road maps are available in Norway in bookshops, Narvesen kiosks, rural general stores, DNT offices, larger petrol stations and from most large tourist offices. If you want to pick up maps before leaving home, the following have comprehensive catalogues and some allow you to order online:

Map Land (☎ 03-9670 4383; www.mapland.com.au; 372 Little Bourke St, Melbourne, Vic 3000, Australia)

Map Shop (☎ 01684-593146; www.themapshop.co.uk; 15 High St, Upton-upon-Severn, Worcester, WR8 0HJ, UK)

Omni Resources (☎ 336-227 8300; www.omnimap.com; 1004 S Mebane St, Burlington, NC 27216-2096, USA)

Stanfords (☎ 020-7836 1321; www.stanfords.co.uk; 12-14 Long Acre, London, WC2E 9LH, UK)

Travel Bookshop (☎ 02-9261 8200; www.travelbooks.com.au; shop 3, 175 Liverpool St, Sydney, NSW 2000, Australia)

Road Maps

The best road maps are the Cappelens series, which are sold in Norwegian bookshops for Nkr95. There are three maps at 1:335,000 scale: *No1 Sør-Norge Sør, No2 Sør-Norge Nord* and *No3 Møre og Trøndelag*. Northern Norway is covered in two sheets at 1:400,000 scale: *No4 Nordland og Sør-Troms* and *No5 Troms og Finnmark*. The *Veiatlas Norge* (Norwegian Road Atlas; Nkr235), published by Statens Kartverk (the national mapping agency), is revised every two years. Another reasonable map is Michelin's *711-Scandinavia & Finland* (1:500,000).

MONEY

The Norwegian krone is most often represented either as Nkr (preceding the number, as in this book), NOK (preceding the number) or simply kr (following the amount). One Norwegian krone (Nkr1) equals 100 øre. Coins come in 50 øre and Nkr1, Nkr5, Nkr10 and Nkr20 denominations, and notes are worth Nkr50, Nkr100, Nkr200, Nkr500 and Nkr1000.

For exchange rates at the time of publication, see the Quick Reference inside the front cover of this book.

ATMs

Norwegian ATMs allow you to access cash in your home account with an ATM card from your home bank. 'Mini-Banks' (the Norwegian name for ATMs) are found adjacent to many banks and around busy public places, such as shopping centres. They accept major credit cards as well as Cirrus, Visa Electron and/or Plus bank cards, although check with your bank before leaving about which banks charge the lowest withdrawal fees.

Cash & Travellers Cheques

Don't assume that all banks will change money and in some places you may need to shop around to find one that does. Post offices, some tourist offices and banks exchange major foreign currencies and accept all brands of travellers cheques, which command a better exchange rate than cash by about 2%. Rates at post offices and tourist offices are generally poorer than at banks, but can be convenient for small amounts outside banking hours. Post offices charge a service fee of Nkr15 per travellers cheque or Nkr30 per cash transaction. Some banks, including Kreditkassen and Den Norske Bank, have slightly higher fees but similar exchange rates. Other banks tend to charge steeper travellers cheque commissions (1% to 5%).

Credit Cards

Visa, Eurocard, MasterCard, Diners Club and American Express cards are widely accepted throughout Norway. Although credit or debit cards allow you to avoid the fees charged for changing cash or travellers cheques, such gains can be cancelled out by bank fees and not all places accept debit cards. Credit cards can be used to buy train tickets and are accepted on some (eg Hurtigruten), but not all, domestic ferries.

If your card is lost or stolen in Norway, report it immediately:

American Express (☎ 22 96 08 00)
Diners Club (☎ 21 01 50 00)
Eurocard/MasterCard (☎ 21 01 52 22)
Visa (☎ 08989)

Tipping

Service charges and tips are included in restaurant bills and taxi fares and tipping on an American scale is not expected. It is, however, customary (and always greatly appreciated by often poorly paid service staff) to round up the bill. If the service has been particularly helpful, feel free to leave more.

PHOTOGRAPHY

For digital and other photographic supplies, Japan Photo is a good nationwide chain, while you'll find other well-stocked shops around the country, particularly in larger towns.

Although few Norwegians are camera-shy, it's still a courtesy to first ask permission. This is especially important in Sami areas, where you may encounter some camera sensitivity, as well as in villages where whaling is a mainstay (people may be concerned that the photos will be used against them in environmental pieces).

Due to the clear northern light and glare from water, ice and snow, photographers may want to use a UV or skylight filter and a lens shade. In winter, you may want to polar oil your camera so that the mechanism doesn't freeze up. In temperatures below around -20°C, digital cameras may fail altogether.

For comprehensive advice on taking terrific photos, Lonely Planet's *Travel Photography*, *Landscape Photography*, *Urban Photography* and *People Photography* are designed to take on the road.

POST

Norway has an efficient postal service, but postal rates have soared in recent years. Postcards and letters weighing up to 20g cost Nkr7 within Norway, Nkr9 to elsewhere in Europe and Nkr11 to the rest of the world. For larger parcels, the good-value Verdenspakke rate (up to 20kg) will provide delivery anywhere in the world within 15 working days. Poste restante services are available at all but a handful of Norwegian post offices.

For post office opening hours, see p394.

SHOPPING

Given the prices, few people would consider a shopping holiday in Norway, although there are some specialty items, including some that you won't find anywhere else in the world. Look for items such as wool sweaters and other hand-knitted clothing, pewter ware, intricate silver jewellery, Sami sheath knives, reindeer-leather products, troll figurines, wooden toys and woodwork adorned with *rosemaling* (painted or carved floral motifs). Some of the best shopping (especially in larger cities) is covered in the relevant regional chapters, while the online **Shopping Guide** (www.guide4you.no) lists a range of shops in Oslo, Bergen, Stavanger, Trondheim and Tromsø. Items in shops are mostly high quality, but beware of cheaper kitsch in tourist areas.

Taxes & Refunds

The 25% MVA (the equivalent of value-added or sales tax), locally known as MOMS, is normally included in the marked prices for goods and services, including meals and accommodation. One exception is car hire, where quoted rates may not include MVA.

At shops marked 'Tax Free for Tourists', goods exceeding Nkr315 (Nkr285 for foodstuffs) are eligible for an MVA refund, less a service charge (11% to 19% of the purchase price). At the point of sale, ask the shop for a 'Tax-Free Shopping Cheque', which should be presented along with your purchases at your departure point from the country (ferry passengers normally collect their refund from the purser during limited hours once the boat has sailed).

Most tourist offices and some tourist shops have the brochure *How to Shop Tax Free in Norway,* which explains the procedure and lists border crossings at which refunds can be collected. Alternatively, visit www.globalrefund.no.

TELEPHONE & FAX

All Norwegian phone numbers have eight digits. Most pay phones accept Nkr1, Nkr5, Nkr10 and Nkr20 coins and will return unused coins but won't give change. To call anywhere in the country costs a fixed national rate (Nkr8 plus Nkr0.65 during peak times). National calls get a 33% discount on standard phone rates between 5pm and 8am on weekdays, and any time on weekends. Directory assistance (☎ 180) is available throughout the country and costs Nkr9 per minute. Numbers starting with '800' usually indicate a toll-free number, while those beginning with '9' are mobile or cell-phone numbers.

International calls can be prohibitively expensive. Card phones accept Telenor phonecards and most also accept credit cards. Card and coin phones are found at post offices, transport terminals, kiosks and other public places, but they're not as ubiquitous elsewhere as you might expect. Telekort (Telenor phonecards) are sold in Nkr40, Nkr90 and Nkr140 denominations and work out slightly cheaper than using coins, but they're still expensive. Cards can be purchased at post offices and Narvesen kiosks.

For making international calls, you're best bet is to forsake Telenor altogether and go for one of the phonecards issued by private companies. Usually costing Nkr100, they allow you to make over six hours of calls using a scratch PIN number on the back and a local access number. The only drawback is that they can be difficult to find – some kiosks sell them, but the easiest place to look is an 'ethnic' grocery store.

Otherwise, internet-connected calls (eg www.skype.com) are the way to go, although unfortunately if you're not travelling with a laptop, not many internet cafes are Skype-enabled; you cannot make phone calls from municipal library computers.

To make international calls from Norway call ☎ 00. If you're calling from outside Norway, the country code is ☎ 47.

Fax

Faxes can be received and sent from most hotels, but it's considerably cheaper to send one from any post office.

Mobile Phones

There aren't too many places where you can't get GSM mobile access with coverage for close to 90% of the country. This doesn't, of course, apply to wilderness areas and the hiking trails of most national parks. There are two main service providers: **Telenor Mobil** (☎ 81 07 70 00; www.telenor.com) and **NetCom** (☎ 23 88 80 00; www.netcom.no in Norwegian).

If you want to use your home-country mobile in Norway, always check with your carrier about the cost of roaming charges to avoid a nasty surprise when your next bill arrives; although agreements between European countries have substantially reduced calling costs in recent years, prices remain high.

If you wish to use your mobile, but with a Norwegian SIM card, check with your network before leaving home as some phones sold by some networks (eg Vodafone) are blocked from using other carriers. If your phone will accept a foreign SIM card, these can be purchased from any 7-Eleven store and some Narvesen kiosks. However, as the connection instructions are entirely in Norwegian, you're better off purchasing the card from any Telehuset outlet, where they'll help you connect on the spot. SIM cards start from Nkr200, which includes Nkr100 worth of calls.

Mobile-phone rental isn't currently possible in Norway.

TIME

Time in Norway is one hour ahead of GMT/UTC, the same as Sweden, Denmark and most of Western Europe. Clocks go forward one hour on the last Sunday in March and back an hour on the last Sunday in October.

When telling the time, Norwegians use 'half' as signifying *half before* rather than half past. Always double-check unless you want to be an hour late!

TOILETS

Most towns (and many roadside stops) have public facilities. However, at many shopping malls, train stations, bus terminals and even some (but not many) restaurants you may have to pay up to Nkr10. If you resent paying for an entirely necessary and natural bodily function, hang on until lunchtime or until you reach your hotel.

TOURIST INFORMATION

It's impossible to speak highly enough of tourist offices in Norway. Most serve as one-stop clearing houses for general information and bookings for accommodation and activities. Nearly every city and town – even the tiniest place – has its own tourist office. Most tourist offices publish comprehensive annual booklets giving the complete, up-to-date lowdown on their town.

Offices in smaller towns may be open only during peak summer months, while in cities they're open year-round but with shorter hours in the off season. Opening hours and contact details are listed under each city throughout the book.

Tourist offices operate under a variety of names – *turistkontor* and *reiseliv* are among the most common – but all have the information symbol (i) prominently displayed outside and are easy to identify and find.

For general information on travelling in Norway, contact the **Norwegian Tourist Board** (Norges Turistråd; ☎ 24 14 46 00; www.visitnorway.com; PO Box 722, Sentrum, N-0105 Oslo).

Outside Norway, tourist offices are usually attached to Norwegian embassies, but there's so much information available on the internet that you're unlikely to need to visit one.

VISAS

Citizens of Denmark, Finland, Iceland and Sweden may enter Norway freely without a passport. Citizens of EU and other European Economic Area (EEA; essentially EU countries, plus Switzerland, Liechtenstein, Greenland and the Faroe Islands) countries, the USA, Canada, the UK, Ireland, Australia, New Zealand most Latin American and Commonwealth countries need a valid passport to visit Norway, but do not need a visa for stays of less than three months. Norway belongs to the Schengen group of countries (named after the treaty that allows free movement within EU countries), so there are only limited border controls at Norwegian frontiers. For more information on entering Norway, see opposite.

WOMEN TRAVELLERS

Women travellers will have few worries in Norway, and sober Norwegian men are normally the very picture of decorum. While alcohol-impaired men may become tiresome or obnoxious, they're probably no different from the same breed you'll encounter in your home country.

Norway's main feminist organisation is **Kvinnefronten** (Women's Front; Map pp96-7; ☎ 22 20 6[illegible] 00; www.kvinnefronten.no; Osterhaugsgt 27, Oslo). Women who have been attacked or abused can contact the **Krisesenter** (☎ 23 01 03 41; www.krisesenter.com) in Oslo or dial ☎ 112 nationwide.

First-time women travellers should track down the eminently practical *Handbook for Women Travellers* by Maggie and Gemma Moss, although remember that most of the situations described are no more likely to confront you in Norway than they are in your home country.

Of the general websites dedicated to women travellers, **Journeywoman** (www.journeywoman.com) is outstanding. There's also a women's page on Lonely Planet's **Thorn Tree** (www.lonelyplanet.com).

WORK

In order to work in Norway, knowledge of basic Norwegian is required at the very least. As a member of the EEA, Norway grants citizens of other EEA countries the right to look for work for a three-month period without obtaining a permit; those who find work have the right to remain in Norway for the duration of their employment. For other foreigners, it's very difficult and an application for a work permit must be made through the Norwegian embassy or consulate in your home country before entering Norway.

For help with looking for work, the best places to start are the **Norwegian Labour & Welfare Organisation** (www.nav.no), which distributes two free booklets, *Looking for Work in Norway* and *Norway – Access to Job Vacancies*, or Use-It (p92).

Transport

CONTENTS

GETTING THERE & AWAY

ENTERING THE COUNTRY

Crossing most borders into Norway is usually hassle-free, particularly if you're arriving by road, although if you're from a non-Western country you may find yourself and your baggage under greater scrutiny than other travellers. If arriving in Norway from a non-EU country, expect your papers to be checked carefully.

For visa requirements info, see opposite.

AIR

Airports

For a full list of Norwegian airports, visit www.avinor.no. The main international Norwegian airports:

Ålesund, Vigra Airport (airport code AES; ☎ 70 11 48 00; fax: 70 18 37 38)
Bergen, Flesland Airport (airport code BGO; ☎ 55 99 80 00; infosenteret.bergen@avinor.no)
Haugesund, Karmøy Airport (airport code HAU; ☎ 52 85 79 00; haugesund.lufthavn@avinor.no)
Kristiansand, Kjevik Airport (airport code KRS; ☎ 38 06 56 00; fax 38 06 31 22)
Oslo, Gardermoen Airport (airport code OSL; ☎ 81 55 02 50; www.osl.no)

THINGS CHANGE....

The information in this chapter is particularly vulnerable to change. Check directly with the airline or a travel agent to make sure you understand how a fare (and ticket you may buy) works and be aware of the security requirements for international travel. Shop carefully. The details given in this chapter should be regarded as pointers and are not a substitute for your own careful, up-to-date research.

Sandefjord, Torp Airport (airport code TRF; ☎ 33 42 70 00; www.torp.no)
Stavanger, Sola Airport (airport code SVG; ☎ 51 65 80 00; stavanger.lufthavn@avinor.no)
Tromsø Airport (airport code TOS; ☎ 77 64 84 00; fax 77 64 84 93)
Trondheim, Værnes Airport (airport code TRD; ☎ 74 84 30 00; info.vaernes@avinor.no)

Airlines

Airlines that use Norway as their primary base:

Coast Air (☎ 52 84 85 00; www.coastair.no) Flies to Copenhagen from Haugesund.
Norwegian (☎ 81 52 18 15; www.norwegian.no) Low-cost airline flying from 28 European cities to Oslo, Bergen, Stavanger, Trondheim and Tromsø.
SAS Braathens (☎ 91 50 54 00; www.sasbraathens.no) Flies from many Norwegian airports to 30 destinations around Europe, and with hundreds more cities around the world.
Widerøe (☎ 81 00 12 00; www.wideroe.no) Flies to Aberdeen, Edinburgh, Newcastle and Copenhagen, mostly from Bergen and Stavanger.

Other international airlines that fly to/from Norway:

Aeroflot (☎ 22 35 62 00; www.aeroflot.aero)
Air France (☎ 23 50 20 01; www.airfrance.com)
Austrian Airlines (☎ 81 52 10 52; www.aua.com)
British Airways (☎ 81 53 31 42; www.british-airways.com)
British Midland Airways (www.flybmi.com)
Brussels Airlines (☎ 23 16 25 68; www.brusselsairlines.com)
City Star Airlines (☎ 51 65 81 65; www.citystarairlines.com) Flies to Oslo, Stavanger and Kristiansund from Aberdeen.

CLIMATE CHANGE & TRAVEL

Climate change is a serious threat to the ecosystems that humans rely upon, and air travel is the fastest-growing contributor to the problem. Lonely Planet regards travel, overall, as a global benefit, but believes we all have a responsibility to limit our personal impact on global warming.

Flying & Climate Change

Pretty much every form of motorised travel generates CO_2 (the main cause of human-induced climate change) but planes are far and away the worst offenders, not just because of the sheer distances they allow us to travel, but because they release greenhouse gases high into the atmosphere. The statistics are frightening: two people taking a return flight between Europe and the USA will contribute as much to climate change as an average household's gas and electricity consumption over a whole year.

Carbon Offset Schemes

Climatecare.org and other websites use 'carbon calculators' that allow travellers to offset the level of greenhouse gases they are responsible for with financial contributions to sustainable travel schemes that reduce global warming – including projects in India, Honduras, Kazakhstan and Uganda.

Lonely Planet, together with Rough Guides and other concerned partners in the travel industry, support the carbon offset scheme run by climatecare.org. Lonely Planet offsets all of its staff and author travel.

For more information check out our website: www.lonelyplanet.com.

TRANSPORT

Danish Air Transport (☎ 57 74 67 00; www.dat.dk) Flies to Stavanger from Esjberg and Billund.
Finnair (☎ 81 00 11 00; www.finnair.fi)
Fly Nordic (☎ 24 14 87 58; www.flynordic.com)
Iberia (www.iberia.com)
Icelandair (☎ 22 03 40 50; www.icelandair.com)
Jet 2 (www.jet2.com) Flights between Bergen and Newcastle.
KLM-Royal Dutch Airlines (☎ 22 64 37 52; www.klm.com)
Lufthansa (☎ 22 33 09 00; www.lufthansa.com)
Ryanair (☎ 82 00 07 20; www.ryanair.com) Flies to Sandefjord.
Spanair (☎ 91 50 54 00; www.spanair.com)
Sterling (☎ 81 55 88 10; www.sterling.dk) Budget airline with dozens of destinations from Oslo.
TAP Portugal (☎ 81 00 00 15; www.flytap.com)
Welcome Air (www.welcomeair.com)
Wizz Air (www.wizzair.com) Flights between Polish cities and Sandefjord.

For details of these and other airline safety records, visit www.airsafe.com or www.waasinfo.net.

Tickets

For bargain air fares, your first option should be shopping around on the internet. If you plan on flying with a national airline (as opposed to a budget or no-frills carrier), you should also check for cheaper fares with a travel agent who knows about special deals and can offer advice on other aspects of your trip. Reliable online flight-booking sites:
Cheap tickets (www.cheaptickets.com)
eBookers (www.ebookers.com)
Expedia (www.expedia.com)
Lowest Fare (www.lowestfare.com)
Opodo (www.opodo.com)
Orbitz (www.orbitz.com)
Plane Simple (www.planesimple.co.uk)
STA (www.sta.com)
Travel.com (www.travel.com.au)
Travelocity (www.travelocity.com)

The only intercontinental flights to Norway are from the USA, so the first step for everyone else is to get to Europe where you'll find plenty of deals to Norway from European 'gateway' cities, particularly London, Paris, Frankfurt, Berlin or Copenhagen.

Another possibility to consider is an open jaw ticket, which allows you to fly into one city and leave from another at no extra cost. SAS Braathens, with its extensive network of Norwegian routes, is particularly useful in this regard. You could for example fly into Ålesund and fly out from Bergen, Oslo or a number of other cities in Norway or elsewhere in Scandinavia.

frica

Nairobi and Johannesburg are the best places n Africa to buy tickets to Europe. Several Vest African countries offer cheap charer flights to France, and charter fares from Morocco can be incredibly cheap if you're ucky enough to find a seat.

Rennies Travel (www.renniestravel.com) and **STA ravel** (www.statravel.co.za) have offices throughout outhern Africa.

sia

TA Travel (www.statravel.com; Bangkok ☎ 02-236 262; www.statravel.co.th; Singapore ☎ 6737 7188; www statravel.com.sg; Japan ☎ 03-5391 2922; www.statravel o.jp) proliferates in Asia, with branches just bout everywhere. Another resource in Japan s **No 1 Travel** (☎ 03-3205 6073; www.no1-travel.com); n Hong Kong try **Four Seas Tours** (☎ 2200 777; www.fourseastravel.com).

In India, **STIC Travels** (www.stictravel.com; Delhi ☎ 11-233 57 468; Mumbai ☎ 22-221 81 431;) has ofices in dozens of cities.

ustralia & New Zealand

f you're coming from Australasia, there's a large difference between low- and higheason fares. From Australia, flights to Oslo usually require a couple of stopovers on the way, usually Singapore or Bangkok and another European city. Good deals are often to be found with Air France, Qantas, KLM or Cathay Pacific. From New Zealand, Lufthansa offers some of the best deals for ravel to Oslo.

Both **STA Travel** (☎ 134 782; www.statravel.com au) and **Flight Centre** (☎ 133 133; www.flightcentre com.au) have offices throughout Australia. For online bookings, try www.travel.com.au.

In New Zealand, both **Flight Centre** (☎ 0800 243 544; www.flightcentre.co.nz) and **STA Travel** (☎ 0800 474 400; www.statravel.co.nz) have branches hroughout the country. The site www.travel co.nz is recommended for online bookings.

ontinental Europe

There's not much variation in air fare prices or departures from the main European ities.

In France there is a student travel agency, **Voyages Wasteels** (☎ 01 55 82 32 33; www.wasteels.fr n French), which has offices around the country and specialises in student and youth travelers. **Voyageurs du Monde** (☎ 08 92 23 56 56; www.vdm com in French) and **Nouvelles Frontières** (☎ 08 25 00 07 47; www.nouvelles-frontieres.fr in French) are also recommended. Online agencies include **Lastminute** (www.fr.lastminute.com in French).

In Germany **STA Travel** (☎ 069-743 032 92; www .statravel.de in German) is an ever-reliable agency, with offices across Germany. Online agencies are **Lastminute** (☎ 01805 284 366; www.lastminute.de in German) and **Expedia** (www.expedia.de in German).

Dutch travellers will find **Airfair** (☎ 0900 771 7717; www.airfair.nl) to be a reliable source of discounted tickets.

Travellers from Italy should check out **CTS Viaggi** (www.cts.it), while Spaniards could consider **Barcelo Viajes** (☎ 902 116 226; www.barcelo viajes.com); good online Spanish booking agencies include **Atrapalo** (www.atrapalo.com) and **Despegar** (www.despegar.es).

UK

Travellers from the UK have the widest range of options for flying to/from Norway with services from London and many other cities in England and Scotland. In addition to internet fares (see opposite), recommended travel agencies include **Flight Centre** (☎ 0870 499 0040; flightcentre.co.uk) and **STA Travel** (☎ 0871 230 0040; www.statravel.co.uk).

USA & Canada

The North Atlantic is the world's busiest long-haul air corridor and the flight options are bewildering. Thanks to the large ethnic Norwegian population in Minnesota, Wisconsin and North Dakota, you may find small local agencies specialising in travel to Norway and offering good-value charter flights.

Some of the best deals are offered by Icelandair, which flies to Bergen and Oslo via Reykjavík, from a number of US cities; on some of its transatlantic flights it allows a three-day stopover in Reykjavík. If you're planning on flying within Norway (or around Scandinavia), SAS Braathens has some interesting regional discounts available to passengers who fly on its transatlantic flights.

Airhitch (www.airhitch.org) specialises in cheap stand-by tickets to Europe, but you'll need a flexible schedule.

Recommended agencies include **Air-Tech** (www.airtech.com) and **Educational Travel Centre** (☎ 800 747-5551; www.edtrav.com). In Canada, try **Travel Cuts** (☎ 1866-246-9762; www.travelcuts.com), Canada's national student travel agency.

LAND

Border Crossings

Border crossings between Norway and Sweden or Finland are straightforward; half the time you aren't even aware that you've crossed a border. If you're travelling by bus, some bags may be checked by customs, but you'll rarely stop for more than a few minutes. For Russia, however, everyone needs a visa and travellers face greater scrutiny.

Bus

For almost all international bus services to/from Norway, the best website is www.eurolines.nu, which acts as a feeder for national companies. For some country-specific information, see opposite.

Train

Train travel is possible between Oslo and Stockholm, Gothenburg, Malmö and Hamburg, with less frequent services to northern and central Swedish cities from Narvik and Trondheim. For more details, see opposite.

TRAIN PASSES

The ScanRail pass is no more. Instead, Eurail has expanded its coverage to include a pass that covers Norway only, as well as a pass that covers either three, four or five countries covered by Eurail that share a common border. Inter-Rail passes are also an option. In addition to the websites listed in the following sections, details about rail passes can also be found at www.railpass.com.

Eurail passes (www.eurailpass.com) can only be bought by residents of non-European countries (residents of Turkey and Russia are also excluded), and are supposed to be purchased before arriving in Europe, although passes can be purchased within Europe if your passport proves you've been there for less than six months; the passes are, however, more expensive than getting them outside Europe. Try the **Oslo S train station** (Map pp96-7; ☎ 23 15 24 48) if you've arrived in Europe without one.

Eurail Global Passes

Eurail Global Passes (often referred to as the Eurailpass) are valid for unlimited travel on national railways and some private lines in 20 European and Scandinavian countries. The passes do not cover the UK or the Baltic countries. Eurail is also valid for som international ferries.

The Global Passes offer reasonable valu to people aged under 26. A Youthpass i valid for unlimited 2nd-class travel for 1 days (US$485), 21 days (US$639), one mont (US$779), two months (US$1099) or thre months (US$1359).

For those aged over 26, a standard 1st class Eurailpass is valid for 15 days (US$745) 21 days (US$965), one month (US$1199) two months (US$1695) or three month (US$2089). Two to five people travelling together can get good discounts on a Saverpass which works like the standard Eurailpass. A 15-day Saverpass costs US$629 per person fo 15 days of continual travel and up to US$178 for three months. Children under four year travel free, and those between four and 1 pay half price.

There is also a Global Flexi option that al lows 10/15 days travel within a two-mont period for US$879/1155 for people aged 2 or over.

Eurail Select Passes

Eurail Select Passes allow travel within thre to five bordering countries by rail or sea Select Passes now includes all Scandinavia countries. They cover between five and 1 days travel (15 days for the five-country op tion) over two months and the pass must b used within six months of purchase. The cos is US$459/505/599/695 for five/six/eight/1 days of travel in three countries for a perso aged 26 and over in 1st class. There are greate discounts for people under 26 years of ag (US$335/365/425/485 in 2nd class) and peo ple in groups of two to five people can use th Eurail Select Saverpass (US$435/479/555/63 in 1st class). Reservations are required. Th pass also offers some free ferry crossing within the selected region and also variou discounts on other ferry crossings, selecte bus services and car rental.

Note that Norway and Finland are not con sidered to be bordering countries as they ar not adjoined by rail or ship.

Eurail Norway Passes

The Norway passes cover from three to eigh days of 2nd-class travel within one month Sample costs for a person aged 26 year or over are US$279/299/379/425 for three four/six/eight days. For those aged unde

26 years the costs are US$209/229/289/319. There is also a Saverpass for groups of two or more. These passes offer discounts on selected bus services as well as international ferry services.

Inter-Rail

Inter-Rail passes (www.inter-rail.com) are available to European residents of six-months standing (passport identification and evidence is required). Terms and conditions vary, but in the country of origin there's a discount of around 50% on normal fares.

Travellers over 26 can get the Inter-Rail 26+, valid for unlimited rail travel in many European and Scandinavian countries. The pass also gives 30% to 50% discounts on various other ferry routes (more than covered by Eurail) and certain river and lake services. A one-country pass for Norway costs UK£291/216 in 1st/2nd class for eight days of travel during a one-month period. An all-zone, one-month pass costs UK£583/431/288 for 1st/2nd/youth class, while all-zone Flexi Passes are also available.

Denmark

Nor-Way Bussekspress (www.nor-way.no) buses travel between Copenhagen and Oslo (Dkr340, eight hours, at least twice daily) via Göteborg, Malmö and the Øresund bridge. Three **Swebus Express** (☎ 8070 3300; www.swebusexpress.se) buses also run to/from Copenhagen each day (from Skr323).

A cheaper alternative is **Lavprisekspressen** (www.lavprisekspressen.no in Norwegian), which sells tickets over the internet for as little as Nkr49 for Oslo to Copenhagen, although Nkr149 or Nkr199 is more common; it all depends on how early you book.

Finland

BUS

The E8 highway extends from Tornio, in Finland, to Tromsø, and secondary highways connect Finland with the northern Sami towns of Karasjok and Kautokeino. Regular buses serve all three routes.

The Finnish company **Eskelisen Lapin Linjat** (☎ 016-342 2160; www.eskelisen-lapinlinjat.com) has cross-border services (one daily service only), some of which are covered in the table, right; some services run only in summer.

BUS TRAVEL FROM FINLAND

From	To	Price	Duration
Rovaniemi	Tana Bru	€74.40	7hr
Rovaniemi	Alta	€80.70	8hr
Rovaniemi	Karasjok	€61.80	7hr
Rovaniemi	Lakselv	€73.80	12½hr
Rovaniemi	Nordkapp	€113.70	12hr
Ivalo	Kirkenes	€39.50	3¼hr
Helsinki	Tromsø	€126.30	21½hr

Germany

BUS

Nor-Way Bussekspress (www.nor-way.no) buses connect Berlin with Oslo (€97, 15¼ hours) each day, via Rostock, Germany and Gothenburg (Göteborg), Sweden.

TRAIN

Hamburg is the central European gateway for Scandinavia; with up to three daily trains to Oslo, you may need to change in Malmö. For these services and online booking, contact **Deutsche Bahn** (www.bahn.de).

Berlin Night Express (www.berlin-night-express.com) has a daily overnight train from Berlin to Malmö in Sweden (bed in single/double compartments €250/125, 17¾ hours). Travelling to/from Oslo requires changing trains in Malmö, and in Gothenburg from late August until mid-June.

Russia & Asia

BUS & TRAIN

Russia has a short border with Norway and buses run daily between Kirkenes and Murmansk. The rail link to/from eastern Asia via Russia can work out at about the same price as flying, depending on how much time and money you spend along the way, and it can be a lot more fun. Russian trains run as far as Murmansk (from St Petersburg).

For more details on overland travel to Russia, see p362. Check out Lonely Planet's *Trans-Siberian Railway* for detailed information on trans-Siberian travel.

Sweden

BUS

Lavprisekspressen (www.lavprisekspressen.no, in Norwegian), which sells cheap tickets over the internet, operates a service that runs from Oslo to Copenhagen making stops in Gothenburg (Göteborg) and Malmö. Fares can be as low as Nkr49 or Nkr199, depending on how early you book.

Otherwise, the cheapest fares are with **Swebus Express** (☎ 0200 218 218; www.swebusexpress.se). Up to five daily buses run between Stockholm and Oslo (from Skr348, eight hours), with four each to Gothenburg (Göteborg; from Skr128, 4½ hours, four daily) and Malmö (from Skr210, eight hours, four daily).

There are also buses between Bodø and Skellefteå (Skr565, 8¾ hours, once daily except Saturday) and along the Blå Vägen, or 'Blue Highway', between Mo i Rana and Umeå (Skr282, eight hours, once daily).

TRAIN

After three years of uncertainty, regular rail services have finally resumed between Oslo and Stockholm (Nkr454, six hours). Two trains run in each direction daily (one requiring a change in the Swedish city of Karlstad) from Monday to Friday and once daily on weekends. For more information, visit either **Norwegian Railways** (NSB; ☎ 81 50 08 88; www.nsb.no) or **Swedish Railways** (SJ; ☎ in Sweden 0771-75 75 99; www.sj.se).

There are also daily trains from Stockholm to Narvik (Skr1650, 18¾ hours). Journeys from Trondheim to Sweden via Storlien and Östersund require changing trains at the border. Trains also run between Oslo and Malmö (Skr733, 8¼ hours, twice daily), via Gothenburg (Skr573, four hours, four daily).

UK

BUS

Given that slow travel doesn't necessarily equate to environmentally sound travel, and given that it's cheaper to fly, it's difficult to see why you'd take the bus journey from London to Oslo (from UK£120, 36 hours, five weekly) via Brussels, Copenhagen and Gothenburg. Should you discover a good reason, contact **National Express** (☎ 0870 580 8080; www.nationalexpress.com) or **Nor-Way Bussekspress** (☎ 81 54 44 44; www.nor-way.no).

TRAIN

Travelling by train from the UK to Oslo (29 hours) can also be more expensive than flying, although it is much better for the environment. For tickets, contact **Euro Railways** (☎ 1-866-768 8927; www.eurorailways.com).

SEA

Transatlantic Passenger Ships

Regular, long-distance passenger ships disappeared with the advent of cheap air travel and were replaced by a small number of luxury cruise ships. **Cunard Line** (www.cunardline.com; USA ☎ 800 728-6273; UK ☎ 0845 071-0300;) has sailings between New York and Southampton; summer cruises (late April to mid-August) operate from Southampton to the Norwegian coast (even into the fjords at Flåm) and back again. Basic prices for seven-day cruises start at UK£937 from Southampton.

Ferry

Ferry connections between Norway and Denmark, Germany, Iceland, the Faroe Islands, Sweden and also the UK provide straightforward links. Most ferry operators offer package deals that include taking a car and passengers, and most lines offer substantial discounts for seniors, students and children. Taking a bicycle incurs a small extra fee.

If you're travelling by international ferry, consider picking up your maximum duty-free alcohol allowance on the boat.

DENMARK

The following companies operate ferries between Norway and Denmark.

Color Line (www.colorline.com; Denmark ☎ 99 56 19 77; Norway ☎ 81 00 08 11)

DFDS Seaways (www.dfdsseaways.com; Denmark ☎ 33 42 30 82; Norway ☎ 21 62 13 00)

Fjord Line (www.fjordline.com; Norway ☎ 81 53 35 00; Denmark ☎ 97 96 14 01)

Stena Line (☎ in Norway 02010; www.stenaline.no)

The table opposite lists the possible routes. Listed fares are for high season (mid-June to mid-August); at other times, fares can be half the high-season price but departures are much less frequent.

On all of the Color Line routes in the table (p409) except Bergen–Hirtshals, a car with up to five people costs €198/231 on weekdays/weekends, while DFDS Seaways charges €195, including two passengers. On Stena Line, a car with driver includes costs from €122, while to Bergen with Fjord Line costs around €120, including driver and one passenger.

GERMANY

Color Line (www.colorline.com; Germany ☎ 0431-7300 300; Norway ☎ 81 00 08 11;) has a daily ferry link between Kiel and Oslo (20 hours). From mid-June to mid-August, reclining chairs start at

FERRY ROUTES BETWEEN DENMARK & NORWAY

To	From	Fare per person	Duration	Times per week	Ferry operator
Bergen	Hanstholm	€20-160	18hr	3	Fjord Line
Bergen	Hirtshals	€74-80	22½hr	3	Color Line
Egersund	Hanstholm	€10-160	6¾hr	7	Fjord Line
Haugesund	Hanstholm	€20-160	13¼hr	3	Fjord Line
Kristiansand	Hirtshals	€54-60	4½hr	6	Color Line
Larvik	Fredrikshavn	€54-60	6¼hr	11	Color Line
Larvik	Hirtshals	€54-60	5¾hr	7	Color Line
Oslo	Copenhagen	€184	16hr	7	DFDS Seaways
Oslo	Fredrikshavn	from €24	12hr	7	Stena Line & Color Line
Oslo	Hirtshals	€54-60	8½hr	4	Color Line
Stavanger	Hirtshals	€54-60	11hr	3	Color Line

€98 (Sunday to Thursday) or €108 (Friday and Saturday). Cars cost €80. Outside high season, one-way/return packages are available for a car and basic cabin for two people for €328/350.

ICELAND & THE FAROE ISLANDS

Smyril Line (www.smyril-line.fo; in the Faroes ☎ 345900; Norway ☎ 55 59 65 20;) runs once weekly from May to mid-September between Bergen and Seyðisfjörður (Iceland), via Lerwick (Shetland, Scotland) and the Faroe Islands. One-way fares from Bergen begin at €195 to Tórshavn (25 hours) in the Faroes, and €295 to Seyðisfjörður (46 hours).

SWEDEN

Color Line (www.colorline.com; Sweden ☎ 0526-62000, Norway ☎ 81 00 08 11) operates ferry services between Sandefjord and Strömstad (€22, 2½hr, twice daily).

UK

Smyril Line (www.smyril-line.fo; UK ☎ 01595-690845; Norway ☎ 55 59 65 20;) sails between Lerwick (Shetland) and Bergen, from May to mid-September, and takes at least 10½ hours. Couchette fares in low/high-season are UK£53/73 and cars up to 5m long are priced at UK£42/61.

The popular **DFDS Seaways** (www.dfdsseaways.com; UK ☎ 01255-240240; Norway ☎ 22 41 90 90) operates services from Newcastle to Bergen (with/without car from UK£149/80, 27 hours, twice weekly), Stavanger (with/without car from UK£225/167, 19½ hours, three weekly) and Haugesund (with/without car from UK£297/167, 22½ hours, twice weekly).

TOURS

Given the expenses involved in Norwegian travel, it may be worth looking into an organised tour. Several reputable operators offer affordable itineraries. For details of some Norwegian operators, see p418.

Australia

Bentours International (☎ 02-9251 1574; www.bentours.com.au; Level 7, 189 Kent St, Sydney) is one of the few Australian travel agencies specialising in Scandinavia.

France

Grand Nord Grand Large (☎ 01 40 46 05 14; www.gngl.com in French; 15 rue du Cardinal Lemoine, F-75005 Paris) seeks out the locations and activities that are noticed by only a handful of other companies. In Norway, it offers cruises and hiking in Svalbard and Lofoten, among other destinations.

North America

Backroads (☎ 800 462-2848; www.backroads.com; 801 Cedar St, Berkeley, CA 94710-1800) offers upmarket cycling tours of Lofoten and the Vesterålen archipelago as well as a six-day hiking, rail and ferry tour between Geilo and Sognefjorden.

Borton Overseas (☎ 800 843-0602; www.bortonoverseas.com; 5412 Lyndale Ave S, Minneapolis, MN 55419) specialises in adventure travel with dozens of Norwegian tours including hiking, cycling and cross-country skiing.

Brekke Tours (☎ 800 437-5302; www.brekketours.com; 802 N 43rd St, Grand Forks, ND 58203) caters mainly for North Americans of Norwegian descent, and has both excellent escorted and independent tours.

Destination Wilderness (☎ 1800 423-8868; www.wildernesstrips.com; PO Box 1965 Sisters, OR 97759) promises medium-level hiking in the Jotunheimen and Rondane national parks among others.

Scanam World Tours & Cruises (☎ 800 545-2204; www.scanamtours.com; 108 N Main St, Cranbury, NJ 08512) organises cruises and shorter upmarket tours, including an eight-day fjord tour.

Scantours (☎ 800 223-7226; www.scantours.com) has an extensive range of short tours in Norway, from one day around Sognefjord ('Norway in a Nutshell') to 12 days aboard the Hurtigruten coastal ferry.

UK

Arctic Experience (☎ 01737-218800, www.arctic-experience.co.uk; 8 Bolters Lane, Banstead, Surrey SM7 2AR) is one of the most popular tour operators for Scandinavia and offers a range of hiking tours, skiing expeditions, snowmobile safaris and short breaks, mostly in Svalbard.

Arcturus Expeditions (☎ 1432-850 886; www.arcturusexpeditions.co.uk; PO Box 41, Hereford, HR1 9DP) is one of Britain's most inventive operators and organises tours through the furthest reaches of the polar regions. In Norway, it offers hiking and dog-sledding in Finnmark and Dividalen, and icebreaker cruises and trekking in and around Svalbard.

Go Fishing Worldwide (☎ 0208-742 1552; www.gofishingworldwide.co.uk; 2 Oxford House, 24 Oxford Rd N, London, W4 4DH) organises tailor-made fishing trips to Norway.

Scantours (☎ 020-7554 3530; www.scantoursuk.com; 73 Mornington St., London NW1 7QE) offers a wide range of options throughout Norway and Svalbard, lasting from five to 13 days.

Taber Holidays (☎ 01274-594 642; www.taberhols.co.uk; Tofts House, Tofts Rd, Cleckheaton, West Yorkshire BD19 3WX) offers highlight-oriented, and all-inclusive tours around Norway, including cruises, coach and self-drive tours.

Tangent Expeditions International (☎ 01539-822363; www.tangent-expeditions.co.uk; Glebe House, Crook, Kendal, Cumbria LA8 8LG) runs well-organised ski and mountaineering trips to Svalbard.

Waymark Holidays (☎ 0870-9509800; www.waymarkholidays.com; First Choice House, London Rd, Crawley, West Sussex, RH10 9GX) specialises particularly in Nordic skiing and hiking holidays in the Gol and Oslo areas.

For more information on tours at Svalbard, see p373.

GETTING AROUND

Norway's has an extremely efficient public transport system and its trains, buses and ferries are often timed to link with each other. The handy *NSB Togruter*, available free at most train stations, details rail timetables and includes information on connecting buses. Boat and bus departures vary with the season and the day (services on Saturday are particularly sparse, although less so in the summer high season), so pick up the latest *ruteplan* (timetables) from regional tourist offices.

Rail lines reach as far north as Bodø (you can also reach Narvik by rail from Sweden); further north you're limited to buses and ferries. Inter-Rail and Eurail pass holders are entitled to discounts on some northern routes. Some express boats and buses offer a 50% discount for the second person when two people travel together. A fine alternative to land travel is the Hurtigruten coastal ferry, which calls in at every sizable port between Bergen and Kirkenes.

One thing that you should always watch out for, whether you're travelling by bus, train or air, are cheaper *minipris* tickets; they're usually available only if you book early and/or over the internet.

AIR

Airlines in Norway

Norway has nearly 50 airports with scheduled commercial flights, from Kristiansand in the south to Longyearbyen and Ny Ålesund (Svalbard) in the north. For a full list visit www.avinor.no. Due to the time and distances involved in overland travel, even budget travellers may want to consider a segment or two by air.

The five airlines operating on domestic routes:

Coast Air (☎ 52 84 85 00; www.coastair.no)
Danish Air Transport (☎ 57 74 67 00; www.dat.dk)
Norwegian (☎ 81 52 18 15; www.norwegian.no)
SAS Braathens (☎ 91 50 54 00; www.sasbraathens.no)
Widerøe (☎ 81 00 12 00; www.wideroe.no)

The major Norwegian domestic routes are quite competitive, meaning that it is possible (if you're flexible about departure dates and book early) to travel with SAS Braathens from Oslo to Bergen (from Nkr461), Ålesund (from Nkr380), Stavanger (from Nkr380), Tromsø (from Nkr547) and Trondheim (from Nkr461) for little more than the equivalent train fare. That said, fares vary widely – for example, on the Bergen–Oslo route, you could pay anywhere from Nkr461 to Nkr1724.

Although their coverage is not quite as extensive, both Widerøe (a subsidiary of SAS) and Norwegian usually offer cheaper fares (eg Oslo–Bergen with Norwegian starts at Nkr320, while the cheapest fare we found with Widerøe was Nkr361). Coast Air, based in Haugesund, flies small planes and has a much smaller network, which includes Haugesund–Bergen (from Nkr399), Haugesund–Sandefjord (from Nkr490) and Oslo–Røros (Nkr499).

Danish Air Transport has flights to Florø from Bergen and Oslo; one-way fares start at Nkr353.

Air Passes

Air passes have become less important in recent years as most airline companies have slashed the prices of their regular one-way or return tickets. As always, keep an eye out for *minipris* return tickets, which can cost just 10% more than full-fare one-way tickets. There are also sometimes promotional fares that make return tickets even cheaper than one-way tickets. In addition, spouses (including gay partners), children aged two to 15 and senior citizens over 67 years of age are eligible for 50% discounts. Both SAS Braathens and Widerøe offer significant discount deals for travellers aged under 26 (and students aged under 32).

BICYCLE

Given Norway's great distances, hilly terrain and narrow roads, only serious cyclists engage in extensive cycle touring, but those who do rave about the experience. Assuming you've steeled yourself for the challenge of ascending mountain after mountain, the long-distance cyclist's biggest headache will be tunnels (see the boxed text, p416), and there are thousands of them. Most of these, especially in the Western Fjords, are closed to nonmotorised traffic; in many (although not all) cases there are outdoor bike paths running parallel to the tunnels. If no such path exists, alternative routes may involve a few days' pedalling around a long fjord or over a high mountain pass.

Rural buses, express ferries and nonexpress trains carry bikes for various additional fees (around Nkr100), but express trains don't allow them at all and international trains treat them as excess baggage (Nkr250). Nor-Way Bussekspress charges half the adult fare to transport a bicycle!

There are also opportunities for those who see cycling as more a hobby than a mode of transport. For details of possible cycling routes in Norway, turn to p388; our favourite cycling routes are covered in the boxed text, p389.

The Norwegian government takes cycling seriously enough to have developed an official **Cycling Strategy** (www.sykkelby.no), among the primary goals of which are to increase cycling in larger Norwegian cities.

Hire

Although there are few dedicated bicycle hire places outside larger towns, most tourist offices and many hostels and camping grounds rent out bicycles. Bicycle shops are another good place to ask. Rental usually starts at around Nkr50 for an hour and is rarely more than Nkr250 per day, although prices drop if you rent for a few days.

BOAT

Norway's excellent system of ferries connects otherwise inaccessible, isolated communities with an extensive network of car ferries crisscrossing the fjords; express boats link the country's offshore islands to the mainland. Most ferries accommodate motor vehicles, but express coastal services normally take only foot passengers and cyclists, as do the lake steamers.

Highway ferries are subsidised and therefore aren't overly expensive (at least in a Norwegian context), but long queues and delays are possible at popular crossings in summer. They do, however, run deep into the night, especially in summer, and some run around the clock, although departures in the middle of the night are less frequent. Details on schedules and prices for vehicle ferries and lake steamers are provided in the timetables published by the Norwegian Tourist Board, or *Rutebok for Norge*. Tourist offices can also provide timetables for local ferries.

Canal Trips

Southern Norway's Telemark region has an extensive network of canals, rivers and lakes. There are regular ferry services or you can travel using your own boat. See the boxed text, p152 for details.

Hurtigruten Coastal Ferry

For more than a century, Norway's legendary **Hurtigruten coastal ferry** (☎ 810 30 000; www.hurtigruten.com) has served as a lifeline linking coastal towns and villages and it's now one of the most popular ways to explore Norway. Year in, year out, one of 11 Hurtigruten ferries heads north from Bergen almost every night of the year, pulling into 35 ports on its six-day journey to Kirkenes, where it then turns around and heads back south. The return journey takes 11 days and covers a distance of 2500 nautical miles. In agreeable weather (which is by no means guaranteed) the fjord and mountain scenery along the way is nothing short of spectacular. Most of the ships are modern, others are showing their age; the oldest ship dates from 1982, but all were substantially remodelled in the 1990s.

If you're travelling as a deck-class passenger, there are baggage rooms, a shower room, a 24-hour cafeteria and a coin laundry. Meals are served in the dining room and you can buy snacks and light meals in the cafeteria. At night, some people roll out a sleeping bag on the floor in one of the lounges, but all-night activity will mean short nights of little sleep, especially in the 24-hour summer daylight; at least one Lonely Planet author enjoyed a blissful sleep curled up in a cupboard.

Summer fares, which run from mid-April to mid-September, are considerably more expensive than winter prices. Sample summer/winter deck-class fares from Bergen are Nkr1705/1194 to Trondheim, Nkr2708/1895 to Bodø, Nkr3499/2449 to Tromsø and Nkr5426/3798 to Kirkenes. Cars can also be carried for an extra fee. Children aged four to 16, students, and seniors over the age of 67, all receive a 50% discount, as do accompanying spouses and children aged 16 to 25. Ask also about cheaper, 21-day coastal passes if you're aged between 16 and 26 years.

If you prefer an en suite cabin you'll pay an additional Nkr210 to Nkr3380. Cabins are extremely popular; book well in advance.

You may want to break up the trip with shore excursions, especially if you're travelling the entire route. The possibilities, which are organised by the shipping company, include the following (northbound/southbound excursions are denoted by N/S): an overland tour between Geiranger and Ålesund or Molde (N; three or seven hours); a short tour of Trondheim (S; two hours); a day trip to Svartisen (N; six hours); spins around

HURTIGRUTEN – READER'S TIP

Australian travellers Bruce and Jo praise the Hurtigruten coastal steamer service as being very pleasant and well organised, but provide the advice that 'pressure is exerted to sign up for a 'water plan' that provides still/sparkling water in bottles in the dining room that you can take to your cabins.' Be aware that this option is expensive and the quality of water from taps is fine. They note that tap water is served in the dining room if the staff are pushed. They also note that, on their trip at least, the pay phones on board did not return your money if you failed to get a connection.

THE HURTIGRUTEN – SLOW TRAVEL?

Although the Hurtigruten route is a marvellous journey, some travellers are keen to emphasise that it's more useful as a means of getting from one town to the next than it is for sightseeing at towns along the route as the ferry usually only stops in ports for 15 to 60 minutes and these times can be cut shorter if the ferry is behind schedule. As David, a traveller from Australia noted: 'There was only one stop which gave any opportunity to visit a town, Trondheim, but that was at 6am till 9.30am... The attitude of the ship was geared to meeting the route times.'

It is important to keep in mind that even though the majority of passengers are tourists, the Hurtigruten is a regular ferry service not a tour. David also notes 'There are few activities on the boat – passengers need to take plenty of books to read.'

Lofoten (S; three hours) and Vesterålen (S; four hours); a haul from Honningsvåg up to Nordkapp (N; four hours); an overland tour between Honningsvåg and Hammerfest, via Nordkapp (S; seven hours); and a tour from Kirkenes, at the end of the route, to the Russian border (two hours). These offer fairly good value (contact the operators for prices) but, in some cases, you'll miss segments of the coastal scenery.

The Hurtigruten website carries a full list of international sales agents. You can also purchase tickets through **Fjord Tours** (☎ 81 56 82 22; www.fjordtours.no).

Yacht

Exploring the Norwegian coastline aboard your own yacht is one of life's more pleasurable experiences, although harsh weather conditions may restrict how far north you go. Almost every town along Norway's southern coast has an excellent *gjestehavn* (guest harbour) where the facilities include showers, toilets, electricity and laundries as a bare minimum, while some offer bicycle hire and wireless internet. Standard mooring fees generally range from Nkr100 to Nkr150 per 24 hours.

BUS

Buses on Norway's extensive long-distance bus network are comfortable and make a habit of running on time.

Nor-Way Bussekspress (☎ 82 02 13 00; www.nor-way.no) operates the largest network of express buses in Norway, with routes connecting most towns and cities, from Mandal in the far south to Alta in the far north. There are also a number of independent long-distance companies that provide similar prices and levels of service.

Considerably cheaper are buses operated by **Lavprisekspressen** (☎ 67 98 04 80; www.lavprisekspressen.no in Norwegian), which sells tickets over the internet. At the time of writing, it only operates along routes from Oslo to Bergen, Trondheim and Kristiansand, but let's hope that the number of routes expands and that the competition drives down the prices of other companies. In the meantime, Oslo to Bergen costs as little as Nkr149 with Lavprisekspressen; the cheapest fare with Nor-Way Bussekspress is Nkr700.

In northern Norway, there are several Togbuss (train-bus) routes, while elsewhere there's also a host of local buses, most of which are confined to a single *fylke* (county). Most local and even some long-distance bus schedules are drastically reduced everywhere in Norway on Saturday, Sunday and in the low (usually mid-August to mid-June).

To get a complete listing of bus timetables (and some prices) throughout the country, pick up a copy of the free *Rutehefte* from any reasonably sized bus station and some tourist offices. All bus stations and tourist offices have smaller timetables for the relevant routes passing through town.

Costs & Reservations

Advance reservations are almost never required in Norway and Nor-Way Bussekspress even has a 'Seat Guarantee – No Reservation' belief in its ability to get you where you want to go at the time of your choosing. That said, you're more likely to find cheaper fares the further in advance you book.

Buying tickets over the internet is usually the best way to get the cheapest fare. Tickets are also sold on most buses or in advance at the bus station, and fares are based on the distance travelled, averaging around Nkr165 for the first 100km. Some bus companies quote bus fares excluding any ferry costs so always check.

Many bus companies offer student, child, senior and family discounts of 25% to 50%, so it pays to inquire when purchasing. Groups (including two people travelling together) may also be eligible for discounts. In northern Norway, holders of Inter-Rail and Eurail passes (see p406) are also often eligible for discounts on some routes.

In summer, special *minipris* tickets are frequently offered for some of the more popular long-distance services if you book early.

CAR & MOTORCYCLE

There are no special requirements for bringing your car to Norway. For details on ferry services to Norway from other European countries, see p408.

Automobile Associations

By reciprocal agreement, members affiliated with AIT (Alliance Internationale de Tourisme) national automobile associations are eligible for 24-hour breakdown recovery assistance from the **Norges Automobil-Forbund** (NAF; ☎ 08505, 22 34 14 00; www.naf.no). NAF patrols

NATIONAL TOURIST ROUTES

By 2015, the Norwegian Public Roads administration plans to have 18 specially designated roads (covering 1850km) known as 'National Tourist Routes' (www.turistveg.no/index.asp?lang=eng), each one passing through signature Norwegian landscapes. The plan is to set up regular lookouts and information points along these pre-existing routes. Of most interest to visitors of this scheme is the easy identification of some of Norway's most scenic routes, and help in planning and making the most of your trip along Norway's most picturesque drives.

Of the 18 roads, a handful are already up-and-running:

- Sognefjellet Road (Rv55; p184)
- Rv86 and Rv862 on the island of Senja (p342)
- Kystriksveien Coastal Route between Stokkvågen, west of Mo i Rana, and Storvik, south of Bodø (p305)
- E10 through Lofoten (p310)
- west coast road through Vesterålen from Risøyhamn to Andenes (see the boxed text, p327)
- Gamle Strynefjellsvegen between Grotli in Oppland and Videseter in Sogn og Fjordane (Rv258)
- two routes through Hardanger from Halne in the east to Steinsdalsfossen (Rv7) and Jondal (Rv550) in the west.

ply the main roads from mid-June to mid-August. Emergency phones can be found along motorways, in tunnels and at certain mountain passes.

If you break down call **Falken Redningskorps** (☎ 80 03 38 80, 22 95 00 00) or **Viking Redningstjeneste** (☎ 80 03 29 00, 22 08 60 00).

Driving Licence

Short-term visitors may hire a car with only their home country's driving licence. Also ask your automobile association for a *lettre de recommendation* (letter of introduction), which entitles you to services offered by affiliated organisations in Norway, usually free of charge. These services may include touring maps and information, help with breakdowns, technical and legal advice etc.

Fuel

Leaded and unleaded petrol and diesel are available at most petrol stations. Although prices fluctuate in keeping with international oil prices, prevailing prices at the time of research ranged from Nkr10.90 per litre up to Nkr11.90. Diesel usually costs around Nkr1 per litre less. Credit cards are accepted at most places. In towns, petrol stations may be open until 10pm or midnight, but there are some 24-hour services. In rural areas, many stations close in the early evening and don't open at all on weekends. Some have 24-hour automatic pumps operated with credit cards.

Hire

Norwegian car hire is costly and geared mainly to the business traveller. Walk-in rates for a compact car with 200km free start are typically over Nkr1000 per day (including VAT, but insurance starts at Nkr60 per day extra).

You'll get a better daily rate the longer you rent. In summer, always ask about special offers, as you may be able to get the smallest car (eg VW Polo) for a three- to five-day period for Nkr500 per day with 50km free, or Nkr600 per day with 200km free; each extra kilometre costs Nkr2.50, which quickly adds up.

Some major rental agencies also offer weekend rates, which allow you to pick up a car after noon on Friday and keep it until 10am on Monday for around Nkr1200 – be sure it includes unlimited kilometres.

All major firms, such as Hertz, Avis, Budget and Europcar, have desks at many airports around the country and some city centres. Any speed-camera tickets are automatically paid through your credit card; always scrutinise your credit-card statements for months afterwards.

In general, local companies will offer better deals than larger international firms, although their offers aren't always as good.

ROAD DISTANCES (KM)

	Ålesund	Alta	Bergen	Bodø	Florø	Hammerfest	Harstad	Kautokeino	Kirkenes	Kristiansand	Kristiansund	Lillehammer	Narvik	Odda	Oslo	Røros	Stavanger	Tromsø	Trondheim
Ålesund	---																		
Alta	1701	---																	
Bergen	384	2071	---																
Bodø	1008	814	1378	---															
Florø	201	1970	248	1277	---														
Hammerfest	1845	144	2215	959	2114	---													
Harstad	1186	557	1556	300	1455	701	---												
Kautokeino	1827	131	2197	941	2096	276	684	---											
Kirkenes	2215	519	2585	1329	2484	498	1072	451	---										
Kristiansand	811	2226	492	1533	652	2370	1711	2352	2740	---									
Kristiansund	142	1609	517	916	329	1753	1094	1735	2123	867	---								
Lillehammer	382	1756	439	1063	466	1900	1241	1882	2270	473	396	---							
Narvik	1190	511	1560	304	1459	655	119	637	1025	1715	1098	1245	---						
Odda	416	2064	159	1371	320	2208	1549	2190	2578	333	549	362	1553	---					
Oslo	533	1909	478	1216	512	2053	1394	2035	2423	322	562	168	1398	357	---				
Røros	401	1569	635	876	535	1713	1054	1695	2083	704	327	263	1058	624	382	---			
Stavanger	603	2251	179	1558	426	2395	1736	2377	2765	245	736	587	1740	187	453	836	---		
Tromsø	1440	290	1810	554	1709	435	296	417	805	1965	1348	1495	250	1803	1648	1308	1990	---	
Trondheim	287	1414	657	721	556	1558	899	1540	1928	812	195	342	903	650	495	155	837	1153	---

The following is a partial list:

Avis (☎ 81 56 30 44; www.avis.no in Norwegian)
Bislet Bilutleie (☎ 22 60 00 00; www.bislet.no)
Budget (☎ 81 56 06 00; www.budget.no in Norwegian)
Europcar (☎ 22 83 12 42; www.europcar.no in Norwegian)
Hertz (☎ 67 16 80 00; www.hertz.no)
Rent-a-Wreck (☎ 81 52 20 50; www.rent-a-wreck.no)

If you'll be using the car for a while, you should seriously consider hiring your car in Sweden and either return it there afterwards, or negotiate a slightly more expensive one-way deal. One of the best online rental agencies is **Auto Europe** (www.autoeurope.com), which acts as a clearing house for cheap rates from major companies and offers a host of pick-up and drop-off options in Norway and across Europe.

Insurance

Third-party car insurance (unlimited cover for personal injury and Nkr1,000,000 for property damage) is compulsory and, if you're bringing a vehicle from abroad, you'll have fewer headaches with an insurance company Green Card. Ensure that your vehicle is insured for ferry crossings.

Road Conditions

If Norway was Nepal they'd have built a road to the top of (or underneath) Mt Everest. There are roads that can inspire nothing but profound admiration for the engineering expertise involved. The longest tunnels link adjacent valleys, while shorter tunnels drill

IS THE ROAD OPEN?

Main highways, such as the E16 from Oslo to Bergen and the entire E6 from Oslo to Kirkenes, are open year-round; the same cannot be said for smaller, often more scenic mountain roads that generally only open from June to September, snow conditions permitting. **Vegmeldingssentralen** (☎ 175), Statens Vegvesen's 24-hour Road User Information Centre, provides up-to-date advice on road closures and conditions throughout the country.

through rocky impediments to straighten routes. To get an idea of just how hard-won were Norway's roads and tunnels through the mountains, visit the Norwegian Museum of Road History (p168) outside Lillehammer.

Most tunnels are lit and many longer ones have exhaust fans to remove fumes, while others are lined with padded insulation to absorb both fumes and sound. Motorcyclists must be wary of fumes in longer tunnels and may want to avoid them.

We do, however, have two complaints. For all their considerable expertise in road-building, Norway's transport authorities seem incapable of understanding the frustration of sitting behind a slow vehicle for an hour or more. More overtaking lanes please!

Which brings us to our other complaint. When you've spent four hours going just 200km along a major, though single-lane, highway, it's galling to say the least to have to pay a toll (up to Nkr150) for the privilege. Road tolls are particularly common in the south, where you should always keep a stack of coins handy. New segments of highway and recently built tunnels and bridges must be paid off in user tolls. In theory, the tolls are dropped when the construction project is paid off, although some privately funded facilities become quite lucrative so this doesn't always happen. Then again, by one estimate, one-quarter of the road construction budget comes from tolls. Oslo, Bergen, Tønsberg Trondheim, Stavanger, Kristiansand and little Evje also impose tolls on drivers every time they cross the city limits. Note that there's a Nkr350 fine if you use a lane reserved for vehicles with *abonnement* (subscription) passes. Motorcycles aren't subject to the tolls.

A good guide for those wanting to know more is Erling Welle-Strand's concise *Motoring in Norway*.

Road Hazards

Older roads and mountain routes are likely to be narrow, with multiple hairpin bends and very steep gradients. Although most areas are accessible by car (and very often tour bus) some of the less-used routes have poor or untarred surfaces only suitable for 4WD vehicles and some seemingly normal roads can narrow sharply with very little warning. On some mountain roads, caravans and campervans are forbidden or advisable only for experienced drivers, as it may be necessary to reverse in order to allow approaching traffic to pass. Restricted roads for caravans are outlined on a map published by **Vegdirektoratet** (☎ 02030; www.vegvesen.no; Brynsengfaret 6A, 0667 Oslo); it also has a handy route planner at www.visveg.no/norguide/.

TUNNELS IN NORWAY

In November 2000, after nearly six years of construction, the world's longest road tunnel, from Lærdal to Aurland (24.51km long, 7.59km longer than the St Gotthard tunnel in Switzerland), was completed at a total cost of Nkr1082 million. There are no tolls to use the tunnel as it was paid for entirely by the national government. The two-lane tunnel, part of the vital E16 road connecting Oslo and Bergen, reduces the difficulties of winter driving and replaces the lengthy Gudvangen–Lærdal ferry route. It was drilled through very hard pre-Cambrian gneiss, with over 1400m of overhead rock at one point. There's a treatment plant for dust and nitrogen dioxide in the tunnel, 34 gigantic ventilation fans, emergency phones every 500m and three bizarre 'galleries' with blue lighting to 'liven up' the 20-minute trip.

Motorists should tune into NRK radio (p386) when driving through the tunnel (yes, there are transmitters inside!) in case of emergency.

Norway has three out of the 10 longest road tunnels in the world, and other long road tunnels in Norway include: Gudvangentunnelen in Sogn og Fjordane (11.43km, also on the E16); Folgefonntunnelen in Hardanger (11.15km, on Rv551 and passing beneath the Folgefonn icecap); Steigentunnelen in Nordland (8.06km, on Rv835); and Svartisentunnelen in Nordland (7.61km, on Rv17 and passing beneath the Svartisen icecap).

Norway also has a number of undersea tunnels, which typically bore around 40m below the sea bed. The longest ones include Oslofjordtunnelen (7.2km, on Rv23, south of Oslo), Nordkapptunnelen (6.87km, on the E69 and connecting Magerøya Island to the mainland) and Byfjordtunnelen (5.86km, on the E39 just north of Stavanger).

HASTE MAKES WASTE

The national speed limit is 80km/h on the open road, but pass a house or place of business and the limit drops to 70km/h or even 60km/h. Through villages limits range from 50km/h to 60km/h and, in residential areas, they're 30km/h. A few roads have segments allowing 90km/h, and you can drive at 100km/h on a small part of the E6 – bliss! The speed limit for caravans (and cars pulling trailers) is usually 10km/h less than for cars.

The lethargy-inspiring national speed limits may seem laborious by your home standards, but avoid the temptation to drive faster as they're taken very seriously. Mobile police units lurk at the side of the roads. Watch for signs designating *Automatisk Trafikkontrol,* which means that there's a speed camera ahead; these big and ugly grey boxes have no mercy at all.

You'll be nabbed for even 5km/h over the limit – there's no leniency, no compromises, and fines range from Nkr1000 to well over Nkr10,000. Norwegian nationals risk losing their driving licences and could even land in jail.

If you're expecting snowy or icy conditions, ıse studded tyres or carry snow chains. In)slo, snow chains can be hired from **Hakres** (☎ 35 51 48 57; fax 35 51 52 50) for Nkr1000/1500 'or one/two weeks, including changing of yres. Your ordinary tyres are kept as a de-)osit. Snow chains can also be obtained in the JK from **Snowchains Europroducts** (☎ 01732-884 408; www.snowchains.co.uk).

One reader wrote to us that 'Norwegian drivers treat speed limits with utter contempt', that 'all Norwegian drivers are wannabe rally drivers' and told of being tailgated, overtaken on blind turns, experiencing general lack of courtesy and leaving Norway 'a nervous wreck'. Our only explanation for such an experience is that he must have encountered a Lonely Planet author succumbing to a sudden rush of blood in frustration at the sedate pace of Norwegian driving. In all our years of driving on Norwegian roads, we have far more often encountered politeness and a general adherence to speed limits.

Road Rules

In Norway, traffic keeps to the right. At road junctions, you must give way to cars coming from the right, which are liable to shoot across your bows 'like a troll from a box', as one Norwegian told us. The use of seat belts is obligatory at all times and children under the age of four must have their own seat or safety restraint. The use of dipped headlights (including on motorcycles) is required at all times and right-hand–drive vehicles must (in theory) have beam deflectors affixed to their headlight in order to avoid blinding oncoming traffic. Drivers must carry a red warning triangle to use in the event of a breakdown; motorists must always give way to pedestrians at zebra crossings; and vehicles from other countries should bear an oval-shaped nationality sticker on the back. Motorcycles may not be parked on the pavement (sidewalk) and are subject to the same parking regulations as cars.

Drink-driving laws are strict in Norway: the maximum permissible blood alcohol content is 0.02% and violators are subject to severe fines and/or imprisonment. Because establishments serving alcohol may legally share liability in the case of an accident, you may not be served even a small glass of beer if the server or bartender knows you're driving.

UK-registered vehicles must carry a vehicle registration document (Form V5), or a Certificate of Registration (Form V379, available from the DVLA in the UK). For vehicles not registered in the driver's name, you'll require written permission from the registered owner.

Most road signs are international, but a white M on a blue background indicates a passing place on a single-track road (the 'm' stands for *møteplass*). *All Stans Forbudt* means 'No Stopping', *Enveiskjøring* is 'One Way'; *Kjøring Forbudt* is 'Driving Prohibited' or 'Do Not Enter'; *Parkering Forbudt* is 'No Parking'; and *Rekverk Mangler* is 'Guardrail Missing'.

For more detail than you probably need, there's a downloadable PDF of Norway's road rules on the website for **Vegdirektoratet** (www.vegvesen.no); follow the links to 'Road Users', then 'Traffic Rules'.

Vehicle Ferries

While travelling along the scenic but mountainous and fjord-studded west coast may be spectacular, it also requires numerous ferry crossings that can prove time-consuming and costly. For a complete list of ferry schedules and fares, get hold of the Nkr225 *Rutebok for Norge,* a phone book–sized transport guide sold in bookshops and larger Narvesen kiosks. Otherwise, order directly from **Norsk Reiseinformasjon** (☎ 22 47 73 40; www.reiseinfo.no; Karl Johans gate 12A, 0154 Oslo), or download it at www.rutebok.no.

HITCHING

Hitching isn't entirely safe and we don't recommend it. Travellers who decide to hitch should understand they're taking a potentially serious risk. People who choose to hitch will be safer if they travel in pairs and let someone know where they're planning to go.

If you're determined to hitch, you'll find Norwegians generally friendly, and they understand that not all foreigners enjoy an expense-account budget or earn Norwegian salaries. Your chances of success are better on main highways, but you still may wait for hours in bad weather. One good approach is to ask for rides from truck drivers at ferry terminals and petrol stations; that way, you'll normally have a place to keep warm and dry while you wait.

LOCAL TRANSPORT

Bus

Nearly every town in Norway supports a network of local buses, which circulate around the town centre and also connect it with outlying areas. In many smaller towns, the local bus terminal is adjacent to the train station, ferry quay and/or long-distance bus terminal. Fares range from Nkr16 to Nkr25 per ride. Day- or multitrip tickets are also available.

Taxi

Taxis are best hailed around taxi ranks, but you can also reserve one by phone. If you're phoning for a taxi immediately, remember that charges begin at the moment the call is taken. Daytime fares, which apply from 6am to 7pm on weekdays and from 6am to 3pm on Saturday, cost from Nkr31.20 at flagfall (more in larger cities), plus Nkr12 to Nkr19 per kilometre. Weekday evening fares are 22% higher, and in the early morning, on Saturday afternoon and evening, and on Sunday, they're 30% higher. On holidays, you'll pay 45% more. In some places, you may find 'maxi-taxis', which can carry up to eight passengers for about the same price.

TOURS

Norway has some outstanding local tours that enable you to make the most of limited time and which save the hassle of having to arrange your own transport. In every tourist office you'll find an exhaustive collection of leaflets, folders and brochures outlining their offerings in the immediate area.

Fjord Tours

NORWAY IN A NUTSHELL

An extremely popular option is the almost legendary, year-round 'Norway in a Nutshell' tour, organised through travel agencies, NSB rail services and tourist offices around southern and western Norway. To find out more, contact **Fjord Tours** (☎ 81 56 82 22; www.fjordtours.no). Itineraries vary, but most involve a one- or two-day excursion taking in the rail line between Bergen or Oslo and Myrdal, the Flåmsbana line to Flåm, a cruise along Nærøyfjord to Gudvangen, a bus to Voss and then rail trips to Bergen or to Oslo on the overnight train. The full tour from Oslo to Bergen costs Nkr1165/1896 one-way/return. The cheaper (and shorter) options from Bergen/Voss cost Nkr820/530.

OTHER TOURS

Fjord Tours also organises a number of other, similar self-guided tours around southern and western Norway. These include: the Triangle Tour (from Oslo to Stavanger with a 'Norway in a Nutshell' itinerary en route; Nkr1770); the Golden Route (round trip to/from Oslo via Otta, Geiranger, Åndalsnes, Trondheim and Dombås; from Trondheim/Oslo Nkr1530/1760); Explore Hardangerfjord (round trip to/from Bergen via Voss, Ulvik, Eidfjord and Norheimsund; Nkr645); and a host of other one- to five-day tours, some of which include the Hurtigruten Coastal Ferry. Each of these tours can, like 'Norway in a Nutshell', be taken in whole or in part. Full details are available on the Fjord Tours website or from most larger tourist offices.

Other companies that offer fjord tours include **Norway Fjord Cruise** (☎ 57 65 69 99; www.fjordcruise.no) whose offerings include Lofoten and Sognefjord, and **Fjord1** (☎ 55 90 70 70; www.fjord1.no/fylkesbaatane), which runs a range of tours and ferries.

MINIPRIS – A TRAVELLER'S BEST FRIEND

If you plan to travel on longer routes by train through Norway and know your itinerary in advance, the following information will save you hundreds of kroner. On every route, for every departure, Norwegian State Railways sets aside a limited number of tickets known as *minipris*. Those who book the earliest can get just about any route for just Nkr199. Once those are exhausted, the next batch of *minipris* tickets goes for Nkr299 and so on. These tickets cannot be purchased at ticket counters and must instead be bought over the internet (www.nsb.no) or in ticket-vending machines at train stations. The other catch is that *minipris* tickets may only be purchased in advance (minimum one day). One NSB official told us that in peak seasons (especially from mid-June to mid-August) on popular routes, you may need to book up to three weeks in advance to get the cheapest fares, which may reduce the appeal of the *minipris* system. That said, the savings are considerable.

For more information on touring the Western Fjords, see the boxed texts, p201 and p215.

Den Norske Turistforening

Den Norske Turistforening (DNT; Norwegian Mountain Touring Club; ☎ 22 82 28 22; www.turistforeningen.no; Storgata 3) organises hundreds of year-round adventure trips in the Norwegian mountains, including cycling, fishing, hiking, skiing, glacier hiking, rock and ice-climbing, family activities, hut-to-hut trekking, Svalbard tours, and so on. Information on the tours is available on the DNT website, or you can pick up the brochure *Norwegian Summer* from any DNT office.

TRAIN

Norwegian State Railways (Norges Statsbaner; NSB; ☎ 81 50 08 88; www.nsb.no) operates an excellent, though limited, system of lines connecting Oslo with Stavanger, Bergen, Åndalsnes, Trondheim, Fauske and Bodø; lines also connect Sweden with Oslo, Trondheim and Narvik. Most train stations offer luggage lockers for Nkr20 to Nkr50 and many also have baggage storage rooms.

Most long-distance day trains have 1st- and 2nd-class seats and a buffet car or refreshment trolley service. Public phones can be found in all express trains and most Inter-City trains. Doors are wide and there's space for bulky luggage, such as backpacks or skis.

Reservations cost an additional Nkr35 and are mandatory on a number of long-distance routes, including between Oslo and Bergen.

Classes & Costs

On long-distance trains, 2nd-class carriages provide comfortable reclining seats with footrests. First-class carriages, which cost 50% more, offer marginally more space and often a food trolley, but they're generally not worth the extra expense.

Travelling by train in Norway is (like everything else) expensive. Indeed, the fact that it often costs less to fly than it does to catch a train puts a serious dint in Norway's otherwise impressive environmental credentials. However, if you learn how to work the *minipris* system (see the boxed text, above), or the train passes (see p406), train travel suddenly becomes affordable. And think of the scenery...

There's a 50% discount on rail travel for people aged 67 and older and for children under 16. Children under four travel free. Students get a 60/40% discount on departures marked green/white in timetables.

Second-class sleepers offer a good, cheap sleep: a bed in a three-berth cabin costs Nkr135; two-berth cabins cost Nkr240/295 per person in old/new carriages.

Train Passes

For details of rail passes that can be used in Norway (but which should be bought before you arrive in the country), see p406. Eurail now has a pass that includes only Norway.

Health

CONTENTS

Travel health depends on your predeparture preparations, your daily health care while travelling and how you handle any medical problem that does develop. If you do fall ill while in Norway you will be very well looked after as health care is excellent.

Norway is, in general, a very healthy place and no special precautions are necessary when visiting. The biggest risks are likely to be viral infections in winter, sunburn and insect bites in summer, and foot blisters from hiking.

For a medical emergency dial ☎ 113; visit a local pharmacy or medical centre if you have a minor medical problem and can explain what it is. Hospital casualty wards will help if the problem is more serious. Nearly all health professionals in Norway speak English; tourist offices and hotels can make recommendations.

BEFORE YOU GO

Prevention is the key to staying healthy while abroad. A little planning before departure, particularly for pre-existing illnesses, will save trouble later – see your dentist before a long trip, carry a spare pair of contact lenses and glasses, and take your optical prescription with you. You will have no problem getting new glasses or contact lenses made up quickly and competently in Norway, but you will pay for the privilege. Bring medications in their original, clearly labelled containers. A signed, dated letter from your physician describing your medical conditions and medications is also a good idea. Most medications are available in Norway, but may go by a different name than at home, so be sure to have the generic name as well as the brand name. If carrying syringes or needles, be sure to have a physician's letter documenting their medical necessity.

TRAVEL HEALTH WEBSITES

It's usually a good idea to consult your government's travel-health website (if available) before departure:

Australia www.dfat.gov.au/travel
Canada www.travelhealth.gc.ca
UK www.doh.gov.uk/traveladvice
USA www.cdc.gov/travel

INSURANCE

If you're an EU citizen, an E111 form (available from health centres, or post offices in the UK) covers you for most medical care, except nonemergencies or emergency repatriation home. Citizens from other countries should find out if there is a reciprocal arrangement for free medical care between their country and Norway. If you do need health insurance, strongly consider a policy that covers you for the worst possible scenario, such as an accident requiring an emergency flight home. If you're planning on engaging in activities such as hiking, dog-sledding, skiing, rock climbing or more high-speed pursuits such as bungee jumping, make sure that your insurance policy doesn't exclude such 'dangerous' activities. Find out in advance if your insurance plan will make payments directly to providers or reimburse you later for overseas health expenditures. The former option is generally preferable, as it doesn't require you to pay out of pocket in a foreign country.

RECOMMENDED VACCINATIONS

The World Health Organization (WHO) recommends that all travellers should be covered

MEDICAL KIT CHECK LIST

Following is a list of items you should consider including in your medical kit – consult your pharmacist for brands available in your country.

- antibiotics – consider including these if you're travelling well off the beaten track; see your doctor, as they must be prescribed, and carry the prescription with you
- antifungal cream or powder – for fungal skin infections and thrush
- antihistamine – for allergies, eg hay fever; to ease the itch from insect bites or stings; and to prevent motion sickness
- antiseptic (such as povidone-iodine) – for cuts and grazes
- aspirin or paracetamol (acetaminophen in the USA) – for pain or fever
- bandages, Band-aids (plasters) and other wound dressings
- calamine lotion, sting-relief spray or aloe vera – to ease irritation from sunburn and insect bites or stings
- cold and flu tablets, throat lozenges and nasal decongestant
- eye drops
- insect repellent
- loperamide or diphenoxylate – 'blockers' for diarrhoea
- multivitamins – consider for long trips, when dietary vitamin intake may be inadequate
- prochlorperazine or metaclopramide – for nausea and vomiting
- rehydration mixture – to prevent dehydration, which may occur, for example, during bouts of diarrhoea; particularly important when travelling with children
- scissors and tweezers
- sunscreen and lip balm
- thermometer – note that mercury thermometers are prohibited by airlines
- water purification tablets or iodine

for diphtheria, tetanus, measles, mumps, rubella and polio, regardless of their destination. Since most vaccines don't produce immunity until at least two weeks after they're given, visit a physician at least six weeks before departure.

ONLINE RESOURCES

The WHO's publication *International Travel and Health* is revised annually and is available online at www.who.int/ith. Other useful websites include www.mdtravelhealth.com (travel-health recommendations for every country, updated daily), www.fitfortravel.scot.nhs.uk (general travel advice), www.ageconcern.org.uk (advice on travel for the elderly) and www.mariestopes.org.uk (information on women's health and contraception).

FURTHER READING

Health Advice for Travellers (currently called the 'T6' leaflet) is an annually updated leaflet by the Department of Health in the UK available free in post offices. It contains some general information, legally required and recommended vaccines for different countries, reciprocal health agreements and an E111 application form. Lonely Planet's *Travel with Children* includes advice on travel health for younger children. Other recommended references include *Traveller's Health* by Dr Richard Dawood (Oxford University Press), and *The Traveller's Good Health Guide* by Ted Lankester (Sheldon Press).

IN TRANSIT

DEEP VEIN THROMBOSIS (DVT)

Blood clots may form in the legs during plane flights, chiefly because of prolonged immobility – the longer the flight, the greater the risk. The chief symptom of DVT is swelling or pain of the foot, ankle or calf, usually but not always on just one side.

When a blood clot travels to the lungs, it may cause chest pain and breathing difficulties. Travellers with any of these symptoms should immediately seek medical attention.

To prevent the development of DVT on long flights you should walk about the cabin, contract and move leg muscles by completing exercises while sitting, drink plenty of fluids and avoid alcohol and tobacco.

JET LAG & MOTION SICKNESS

To avoid jet lag (common when crossing more than five time zones) try drinking plenty of nonalcoholic fluids and eating light meals. Upon arrival, get exposure to natural sunlight and readjust your schedule (for meals, sleep and so on) as soon as possible.

Antihistamines such as dimenhydrinate (Dramamine) and meclizine (Antivert, Bonine) are usually the first choice for treating motion sickness. A herbal alternative is ginger.

IN NORWAY

AVAILABILITY & COST OF HEALTH CARE

Good health care is readily available in Norway, and for minor, self-limiting illnesses, pharmacists can dispense valuable advice and over-the-counter medication. They can also advise when more specialised help is required. The standard of dental care is usually good; however, it is sensible to have a dental checkup before a long trip. Remember that, like almost everything else, medical care can be prohibitively expensive in Norway.

INFECTIOUS DISEASES

Tick-borne encephalitis is spread by tick bites. It is a serious infection of the brain and vaccination is advised for those in risk areas who are unable to avoid tick bites (such as campers, forestry workers and hikers). Two doses of vaccine will give a year's protection; three doses up to three years.

TRAVELLER'S DIARRHOEA

Stomach upsets are as possible in Norway as they are at home and the same rules apply. Take great care when eating fish or shellfish (for instance, cooked mussels that haven't opened properly can be dangerous). As autumn approaches, collecting mushrooms is a favourite pastime in this part of the world, but don't eat any mushrooms unless they have been positively identified as safe by someone qualified to know.

If you develop diarrhoea, be sure to drink plenty of fluids, preferably an oral rehydration solution (eg dioralyte). A few loose stools don't require treatment, but if you start having more than four or five stools a day, you should start taking an antibiotic (usually a quinoline drug) and an antidiarrhoeal agent (such as loperamide). If diarrhoea is bloody, persists for more than 72 hours or is accompanied by fever, shaking, chills or severe abdominal pain, you should seek medical attention.

ENVIRONMENTAL HAZARDS

Giardia

Giardia is an intestinal parasite that lives in the faeces of humans and animals, and is normally contracted through drinking water. Problems can start several weeks after you've been exposed to the parasite and symptoms may sometimes remit for a few days and then return; this can go on for several weeks or even longer.

The first signs are a swelling of the stomach, followed by pale faeces, diarrhoea, frequent gas and possibly headache, nausea and depression. If you exhibit these symptoms you should visit a doctor for treatment.

Tap water is always safe to drink in Norway, but it's wise to beware of drinking from streams, as even the clearest and most inviting water may harbour giardia and other parasites. For extended hikes where you must rely on natural water, the simplest way of purifying water is to boil it thoroughly. Vigorous boiling should be satisfactory; however, at high altitude water boils at a lower temperature, so germs are less likely to be killed. Boil it for longer in these environments (up to 10 minutes).

If you cannot boil water it should be treated chemically. Chlorine tablets (Puritabs, Steritabs or other brands) will kill many pathogens, but not giardia and amoebic cysts. Iodine is more effective in purifying water and is available in tablet form (such as Potable Aqua). Follow the directions carefully and remember that too much iodine can be harmful.

Although some unpopulated lands in Norway serve as sheep pastures, there seems to be little giardia. However, while most people have no problems drinking untreated surface water, there's still a possibility of contracting it.

Hypothermia & Frostbite

Proper preparation will reduce the risks of getting hypothermia. Even on a hot day in the mountains, the weather can change rapidly – carry waterproof garments and warm layers, and inform others of your route.

Acute hypothermia follows a sudden drop of temperature over a short time. Chronic hypothermia is caused by a gradual loss of temperature over hours.

Hypothermia starts with shivering, loss of judgment and clumsiness. Unless rewarming occurs, the sufferer deteriorates into apathy, confusion and coma. Prevent further heat loss by seeking shelter; wearing warm, dry clothing; drinking hot, sweet drinks; and by sharing body warmth.

Frostbite is caused by freezing and subsequent damage to bodily extremities. It is dependent on wind-chill, temperature and length of exposure. Frostbite starts as frostnip (white, numb areas of skin) from which complete recovery is expected with rewarming. As frostbite develops, the skin blisters and becomes black. Loss of damaged tissue eventually occurs. Wear adequate clothing, stay dry, keep well hydrated and ensure you have adequate calorie intake to prevent frostbite. Treatment involves rapid rewarming. Avoid refreezing and rubbing the affected areas.

Insect Bites & Stings

In northern Norway, the greatest nuisances are the plagues of blackflies and mosquitoes that swarm out of tundra bogs and lakes in summer. Fortunately, malaria is unknown, but the mental risks can't be underestimated, as people have literally been driven insane by the ravenous hordes. Midsummer is the worst, and regular mosquito coils and repellents are scarcely effective; hikers must cover exposed skin and may even need head nets to keep the little buggers from making kamikaze attacks on eyes, nose, ears and throat. If you're camping, a tent with mosquito netting is essential. Most people get used to the mosquito bites after a few days as their bodies adjust and the itching and swelling become less severe. An antihistamine cream should help alleviate the symptoms. Use a DEET-based insect repellent.

Bees and wasps cause real problems only to those with a severe allergy (anaphylaxis.) If you have such an allergy, make sure you carry EpiPen or similar adrenaline injections at all times.

Rabies

Rabies, caused by a bite or scratch by an infected mammal, is found in Svalbard and (occasionally) in eastern Finnmark. Dogs are a noted carrier, but cats, foxes and bats can also be infected. Any bite, scratch or even lick from a warm-blooded, furry animal should be cleaned immediately and thoroughly. Scrub with soap and running water, and then apply alcohol or iodine solution. If you've been infected by a rabid animal, medical help should be sought immediately.

Snakes

Snakes are rarely seen in Norway and adders (the only poisonous variety) don't exist north of Tysfjorden in Nordland. To minimise your chances of being bitten always wear boots, socks and long trousers when walking through undergrowth where snakes may be present. Don't put your hands into holes and crevices, and be careful when collecting firewood.

Adder bites aren't normally fatal and antivenins are available. Immediately wrap the bitten limb tightly, as you would for a sprained ankle, and then attach a splint to immobilise it. Keep the victim still and seek medical help, if possible with the dead snake for identification; don't attempt to catch the snake if there is a possibility of being bitten again. Tourniquets and sucking out the poison are now comprehensively discredited.

Sunburn

You can get sunburnt surprisingly quickly, even through cloud. Use a sunscreen, a hat, and a barrier cream for your nose and lips. Calamine lotion or Stingose are good for mild sunburn. Protect your eyes with good-quality sunglasses, particularly if you will be near water, sand or snow.

Ticks

Check your body after walking through tick-infested areas, as ticks can cause skin infections and other more serious diseases.

If a tick is found, press down around its head with tweezers, grab the head and gently pull upwards. Avoid pulling the rear of the body as this may squeeze the tick's gut contents through the attached mouth parts into the skin, increasing the risk of infection and disease.

TRAVELLING WITH CHILDREN

All travellers with children should know how to treat minor ailments and when to seek medical treatment. Make sure the children are up-to-date with routine vaccinations and discuss possible travel vaccines well before departure, as some vaccines are not suitable for children under the age of one.

Remember to avoid contaminated food and water. If your child has vomiting or diarrhoea, lost fluid and salts must be replaced. It may be helpful to take rehydration powders for reconstituting with boiled water.

Children should be encouraged to avoid and mistrust any dogs or other mammals because of the risk of rabies and other diseases; see p423 for further advice.

SEXUAL HEALTH

Condoms are widely available at *apótek* (pharmacies). When buying condoms, look for a European CE mark, which means they have been rigorously tested, and then keep them in a cool, dry place or they may crack and perish.

Emergency contraception is most effective if taken within 24 hours after unprotected sex. The **International Planned Parent Federation** (www.ippf.org) can advise about the availability of contraception in different countries.

Language

CONTENTS

LANGUAGES OF NORWAY

Bokmål & Nynorsk

Norway's two official languages, Bokmål (BM) and Nynorsk (NN), are quite similar and spoken or understood by all Norwegians. However, rural regional dialects vary tremendously and people from one side of the country may have difficulty understanding people from the other side.

Bokmål, literally 'book-language' (also known as Riksmål, the 'national language') is the modern urbanites' version of the language of the former Danish rulers. As the predominant language in Norwegian cities, it's used by over 80% of the population. It's also the language of instruction for most school children and the predominant language of the media.

Nynorsk or 'New Norwegian' (as opposed to Old Norwegian, the language used prior to Danish rule) predominates in the Western Fjords and parts of central Norway; it also serves as a lingua franca (common language) in those regions that may have one or more dialects. Prior to WWII, Nynorsk was the first language of nearly one-third of all Norwegian school children; growing urbanisation has seen this figure reduced to about 15% today.

Perhaps the most striking oddity of Norway's linguistic dichotomy is that many words and place names have two or more authorised spellings. Today, Nynorsk is the official administrative language in the counties of Møre og Romsdal and Sogn og Fjordane. Interestingly, the national government has decreed that a certain percentage of television subtitles be translated into Nynorsk.

Fortunately for most visitors, English is also widely spoken in Norway, even in rural areas. Nevertheless, it's still a good idea to learn a few Norwegian phrases to help you establish contact with people – and if you're having obvious trouble with your Norwegian, most people will be happy to switch to English.

Sami

In northern Norway, quite a few people speak Sami, a language of the Finno-Ugric group. It's related to Samoyed (among other northern Russian ethnic dialects), Finnish, Estonian and Hungarian.

Sami is spoken by around 20,000 people in Norway (there are also Sami speakers in Finland, Sweden and Russia). Although most of them can also communicate in Norwegian (and some even speak English), visitors who know even a few words of the local language will be able to access this unique culture more readily (see p431 for some basic Sami words and phrases).

There are three distinct Sami dialects in Norway – the Fell (also called Eastern or Northern) Sami, Central Sami and South Sami – but a total of 10 different dialects are used within the Sápmi region: Ume, Pite, Lule, Inari, Skolt, Kildin and Ter (see the map on p431). Fell Sami is considered the standard Sami language.

NORWEGIAN

While Norway has two official languages, in this guide we've used Bokmål only – it's by far the most common language that travellers to Norway will encounter.

Lonely Planet's *Scandinavian Phrasebook* offers a more comprehensive guide to Norwegian. A number of Norwegian language course books are available internationally – most also come with audio cassettes. If you're interested in learning Bokmål, the two best Norwegian books are *Ny i Norge* and *Bo i Norge*; both are available locally.

The Norwegian alphabet has 29 letters: those used in English, plus the vowels **æ**, **ø** and **å** (which are listed at the end of the alphabet). While the consonants **c**, **q**, **w**, **x**, and **z** are included, they are used mainly in foreign words. In many Norwegian place names, the definite article 'the' – which may be masculine *(-en)*, feminine *(-en/-a)* or neuter *(-et)* – is appended to the end, eg Jotunheim becomes Jotunheimen, and Horningdalsvatn becomes Horningdalsvatnet. Plurals of nouns are usually formed by adding the suffix *-e* or *-er*.

PRONUNCIATION

Norwegian pronunciation is a complex affair for native English speakers. We've included pronunciation guides in this chapter to simplify things, but the best way to improve your pronunciation is to employ the 'listen and learn' method.

Vowels

As in English, Norwegian vowels can have many permutations. The length of vowels is a very important feature in the pronunciation of Norwegian. When occurring in a stressed syllable every vowel has both a (very) long and a (very) short counterpart. Generally, a vowel is short when followed by one consonant, and when followed by two or more consonants, it's long.

LANGUAGE

	Pronunciation Guide
a	**a/aa** – short, as the 'u' in 'cut'; long, as in 'father'
å	**o/aw** – short, as the 'o' in 'pot'; long, as in 'law'
e/æ	**e/ay/ə** – short, as in 'bet'; long, as in 'whey'; with unstressed syllables, as the 'a' in 'ago'
i	**i/ee** – very short, as in 'police'; long, as in 'seethe'
o	**o/oo/u/or** – short, as in British 'pot'; long, as in 'zoo'; short, as the 'u' in put; long, as in 'or'
ø	**er** – as the 'e' in 'her'
u	**u/oo** – short, as in 'put'; long, as in 'soon'
y	**ew/y** – produced as if pursing your lips and saying 'ee'

Consonants & Semivowels

	Pronunciation Guide
d	**d** – often silent at the end of a word or when between two vowels
g	**g/y** – as in 'go' except before **ei**, **i**, **j**, **øy** and **y** when it's pronounced as the 'y' in 'yard'
h	**h** – as in 'her'; silent before **v** and **j**
j	**y** – always as the 'y' in 'yard'
k	**k/ch** – a hard sound, as in 'kin'; before the letters or combinations **ei**, **i**, **j**, **øy** and **y** it's mostly pronounced as the 'ch' in 'chin'. (In many areas, these combinations are pronounced as the 'h' in 'huge', or as 'ch' in Scottish *loch*.)
l	**l/ll** – pronounced thinly, as in 'list' except after 'ah', 'aa', 'o' and 'or' sounds, when it's like the 'll' in 'all'
ng	**ng** – in most areas, as the 'ng' in 'sing'
r	**r** – trilled, like Spanish 'r'; in southwest Norway the **r** has a guttural pronunciation, as in French *rien*. The combinations **rd**, **rl**, **rn**, **rt** sound a little as they do in American 'weird', 'earl', 'earn' and 'start', but with a much weaker 'r'. The combination **rs** is pronounced 'sh' as in 'fish'.
s	**s/sh** – as in 'so'; when **sk** is followed by **ei**, **i**, **j**, **øy** and **y**, it's pronounced as 'sh', eg the Norwegian word *ski* sounds like English 'she'
t	**t** – as in 'top', except in two cases where it's silent: in the Norwegian word *det* (it, that) – roughly pronounced like British English 'dare' – and in the definite singular ending *-et* of Norwegian neutral nouns
v	**v** – a cross between English 'v' and 'w' but without rounding the lips

ACCOMMODATION

I'm looking for a ...
Jeg leter etter ...
yay le·tər et·tər ...

campground	
camping-plass	kam·ping plaas

guesthouse
gjestehus yes·tə·hoos
hotel
hotell hu·tel
youth hostel
vandrehjem vun·dra·hyem

Where is a cheap hotel?
Hvor er et billig hotell? voor ar et bil·li hu·tel?
What is the address?
Hva er adressen? vaa ar a·dres·en?
Could you write it down, please?
Kan du skrive det ned? kan do skree·va də ned?
Do you have any rooms available?
Har du ledige rom? har du lay·di·ə rum?

I'd like a ...
Jeg vil gjerne ha ...
yay vil yar·nə haa ...
bed
en seng en seng
single room
et enkeltrom et eng·kəlt·rum
double-bed
en dobbeltseng en dob·elt·seng
room
et rom et rom
double room
et dobbeltrom et dob·əlt·rum
room with a bathroom
et rom med bad et rom med baad

I'd like to share a dorm.
Jeg vil gjerne ligge på sovesalen.
yay vil yar·nə lig·gə paw sor·və·saa·lən

How much is it ...?
Hvor mye er det ...?
voor mew·yə kos·tər de ...
per night
pr dag par daag
per person
pr person par pa·shoon

May I see it?
Kan jeg få se det? kan yay for se de?
Where is the toilet?
Hvor er toalettene/wc? voor ar too·a·let·tə·nə/ve·se?
I'm leaving now/tomorrow.
Jeg reiser nå/i morgen. yay ray·sər nor/i·mo·rn

CONVERSATION & ESSENTIALS

Hello.
Goddag. gud·daag
Goodbye.
Ha det. ha·de
Yes.
Ja. yaa
No.
Nei. nay
Thank you.
Takk. taak
You're welcome.
Ingen årsak. ing·ən aw·shaak
Excuse me.
Unnskyld. un·shewl
Sorry.
Beklager. bek·laga
What's your name?
Hva heter du? vaa hay·tə du?
My name is ...
Jeg heter ... yay hay·tər ...
Where are you from?
Hvor er du fra? voor ar du fraa?
I'm from ...
Jeg er fra ... yay ar fraa ...
I like ...
yay lee·kər ... *Jeg liker ...*
I don't like ...
yay lee·kər ik·kə ... *Jeg liker ikke ...*
Just a minute.
Vent litt; vent lit;
Et øyeblikk. et ə·yew·blik

DIRECTIONS

Where is ...?
Hvor er ...? voor ar ...?
Go straight ahead.
Det er rett fram. de ar ret fraam
Turn left.
Ta til venstre. taa til vens·trə
Turn right.
Ta til høyre. taa til hə·yew·rə
at the next corner
ved neste hjørne ve nes·tə yayr·nə
at the traffic lights
ved lyskrysset ve lews·krew·sə

SIGNS

Inngang	Entrance
Utgang	Exit
Opplysninger	Information
Åpen	Open
Stengt	Closed
Forbudt	Prohibited
Politistasjon	Police Station
Toaletter	Toilets
Herrer	Men
Damer	Women

behind	*bak*	bak
in front of	*foran*	fo·raan
far	*langt*	laangt
near (to)	*nær*	nar
opposite	*overfor*	or·vər·for

beach	*strand*	straan
bridge	*bru*	broo
castle	*slott*	slot
cathedral	*katedral*	ka·te·draal
church	*kirke*	chir·kə
island	*øy*	əy
lake	*vann/vatn*	vunn/vutt·en
main square	*(stor)torget*	(stoo·r)·to·rgə
market	*torget*	to·rgə
old city (town)	*gammel by*	gam·məl bew
palace	*slott*	slot
quay	*brygge*	brew·gə
riverbank	*elvebredd*	el·və bred
ruins	*ruiner*	roo·ee·nər
sea	*sjø*	shə
square	*torget*	tor·gə
tower	*tårn*	torn

EMERGENCIES

Help!
Hjelp! yelp!

It's an emergency!
Det er en nødsituasjon! de aa en nərd·see·tyoo·ay·shon!

There's been an accident!
Det har skjedd en ulykke! de haar shed en oo·lew·kə!

I'm lost.
Jeg har gått meg vill. yay haar gawt me vil

Go away!
Forsvinn! fo·shvin!

Call ...!	*Ring ...!*	ring ...!
a doctor	*ein lege*	ayn lay·gə
the police	*politiet*	pu·li·tee·ə

HEALTH

I'm ill.
Jeg er syk. yay ar sewk

It hurts here.
Dette gjør vondt. de yer·r vunt har

I'm ...
Jeg har ...
yay haar ...

asthmatic	*astma*	aast·ma
diabetic	*sukkersyke*	suk·kər·sew·kə
epileptic	*fallesyke*	faal·lə·sew·kə

I'm allergic to ...
Jeg er allergisk mot ...
yay ar a·ler·gisk moot ...

antibiotics	*antibiotika*	aan·ti·byoo·ti·ka
penicillin	*penicillin*	pen·ni·si·leen
bees	*bier*	bee yər
nuts	*nøtter*	nə tər
peanuts	*peanøtter*	pee·ya·nə tər

antiseptic
sårsalve so·ar sal·va

aspirin
aspirin/parasett/dispril a·spe·reen/pa·ra·set/dis·preel

condoms
kondomer kon·dom·ma

contraceptive
prevensjons middel pre ven·syons mi·del

contraceptive pill
P-Pille peh pil·lə

diarrhoea
diare dee·ya·ray

medicine
medisin me·dee·sin

nausea
kvalm kvarm

sunblock cream
solfaktor sool fak·tor

tampons/pads
tamponger/bind tam·pon·gər/bind

LANGUAGE DIFFICULTIES

Do you speak English?
Snakker du engelsk?
sna·kə du eng·əlsk?

Does anyone here speak English?
Er det noen som snakker engelsk?
ar de noon som sna·kər eng·əlsk?

How do you say ... in Norwegian?
Hva heter ... på norsk?
vaa hay·tər ... por noshk?

What does ... mean?
Hva betyr ...?
vaa bə·tewr ...?

I understand.
Jeg forstår.
yay for·shtawr

I don't understand.
Jeg forstår ikke.
yay for·shtawr ee·kə

Could you speak more slowly, please?
Kan du snakke sakte?
kan du sna·kər sak·tə?

Can you show me (on the map)?
Kan du vise meg (på kartet)?
kan du vee·sə ma (po kaar·tə)?

NUMBERS

0	*null*	nul
1	*en*	en
2	*to*	too
3	*tre*	tre
4	*fire*	fee·rə
5	*fem*	fem
6	*seks*	seks
7	*sju/syv*	shu/sewv
8	*åtte*	ot·tə
9	*ni*	nee
10	*ti*	tee
11	*elleve*	el·və
12	*tolv*	tol
13	*tretten*	tre·ten
14	*fjorten*	fyor·ten
15	*femten*	fem·ten
16	*seksten*	seks·ten
17	*sytten*	sew·ten
18	*atten*	at·ten
19	*nitten*	ni·ten
20	*tjue*	chu·ə
21	*tjueen*	chu·en
30	*tretti/tredve*	tret·te/tred·və
40	*førti*	fer·rti
50	*femti*	fem·ti
60	*seksti*	seks·ti
70	*sytti*	sew·ti
80	*åtti*	ot·ti
90	*nitti*	nit·ti
100	*hundre*	hun·drə
1000	*tusen*	tus·ən

PAPERWORK

name
navn naavn
nationality
nasjonalitet naa·shu·naa·li·tayt
date of birth
fødselsdato fert·səls·daa·tu
place of birth
fødested fayr·də·stay
sex/gender
kjønn chern
passport
pass paas
visa
visum vee·sum

QUESTION WORDS

Who?	*Hvem?*	vem?
What?	*Hva*	vaa?
What is it?	*Hva er det?*	vaa ar de?
When?	*Når?*	nor?
Where?	*Hvor?*	vor?
Which?	*Hvilken?*	vil·ken?
Why?	*Hvorfor?*	vor·for?
How?	*Hvordan?*	vor·dan?

SHOPPING & SERVICES

I'd like to buy ...
Jeg kan få ... yay kan faw ...
How much is it?
Hvor mye koster det? vor mew·yə kos·tər de?
I don't like it.
Det liker jeg ikke. de lee·kər yay ik·kə
May I look at it?
Kan jeg få se på det? kan yay for say po de?
I'm just looking.
Jeg bare ser meg rundt. yay ba·rə sayr ma roont
I'll take it.
Jeg tar det. yay taar de

Do you accept ...?
Tar du imot ...?
taar du i·moot ...?
credit cards
kredittkort kray·dit·kort
travellers cheques
reise-sjekk ray·se shek

more	*mer*	mer
less	*mindre*	min·drə
small	*liten*	lee·tən
big	*stor*	stoor

I'm looking for ...
Jeg leter etter ...
yay le·tər et·tər ...
a bank
banken baang·kən
the church
kirken chir·kən
the city centre
sentrum sen·trum
the ...embassy
den ... ambassade den ... am·ba·saa·də
the hospital
sykehus sew·kə·hoos
the market
torget tor·gə
the museum
museet mu·say·ə
the police
politiet pu·lee·tee·ə
the post office
postkontoret post·kun·too·rə
a public toilet
et offentlig toalett et of·fənt·lee too·a·let

the tourist office
turistinformasjon tu·rist·in·for·ma·shoon

TIME & DATES

What time is it?
Hva er klokka? vaa ar klok·ka?
It's ... o'clock.
Klokka er ... klok·ka ar ...
in the morning
om formiddagen um for·mid·daa·gən
in the afternoon
om ettermiddagen um et·tər·mid·daa·gən
in the evening
om kvelden um kve·lən

When?	*Når?*	nawr?
today	*i dag*	i·daag
tomorrow	*i morgen*	i·mor·ən
yesterday	*i går*	i·gawr

Monday	*mandag*	man·daa(g)
Tuesday	*tirsdag*	teesh·daa(g)
Wednesday	*onsdag*	uns·daa(g)
Thursday	*torsdag*	toosh·daa(g)
Friday	*fredag*	fre·daa(g)
Saturday	*lørdag*	lər·daa(g)
Sunday	*søndag*	sərn·daa(g)

January	*januar*	ya·noo·waar
February	*februar*	feb·roo·waar
March	*mars*	maash
April	*april*	a·pril
May	*mai*	maa·i
June	*juni*	yoo·ni
July	*juli*	yoo·li
August	*august*	ow·gust
September	*september*	sep·tem·bər
October	*oktober*	uk·too·bər
November	*november*	no·vem·bər
December	*desember*	de·sem·bər

TRANSPORT

Public Transport

What time does the ... leave/arrive?
Når går/kommer ...?
naw gaw/kom·mər ...?

boat	*båten*	baw·tən
(city) bus	*(by)bussen*	(bew)bu·sən
plane	*flyet*	flew·yə
train	*toget*	tor·gə
tram	*trikken*	trik·kən

I'd like a ... ticket.
Jeg vil gjerne ha ... billett.
yay vil ya·rnə haa ... bil·let

one·way	*enkelt*	en·kelt
return	*tur-retur*	too·rə·toor
1st class	*første klasse*	fərsh·tə klaa·sə
2nd class	*annen klasse*	aan·ən klaa·sə

I want to go to ...
Jeg skal til ...
yay skaal til ...
The train has been delayed/cancelled.
Toget er forsinket/innstilt.
tor·gə ar fo·shing·ket/in·stilt

the first	*første*	fersh·tə
the last	*siste*	sis·tə
next	*neste*	nes·tə
platform	*perrong*	pə·rong
ticket office	*billettluka*	bi·let·lu·ka
timetable	*tidtabell*	teed·taa·bel
train station	*stasjon*	sta·shoon

Private Transport

Where can I rent ...?
Hvor kan jeg leie ...?
voor kan yay lay·ə ...?

a car	*en bil*	en beel
a 4WD	*firehjulstrekk*	fee·rə·hyools·trek
a motorbike	*(motor)sykkel*	(maw·tor·)sew·kel
a bicycle	*tråsykkel*	traw·sew·kel

ROAD SIGNS

Vikeplikt	Give Way
Parkering Forbudt	No Parking
Omkjøring	Detour
Inngang	Entry
Utgang	Exit
Selvbetjent	Self Service
Veiarbeid	Roadworks

Is this the road to ...?
Er dette veien til ...?
ar de·tə vay·yən til ...?
Where's the next service station?
Hvor er nærmeste bensinstasjon?
voor ar nar·məs·tə ben·seen·sta·shoon?

diesel
diesel dee·sel
(unleaded) petrol
blyfri blew·free

(How long) Can I park here?
(Hvor lenge) Kan bilen min stå her?
(voor leng·ə) kan bee·lən min staw har?

Where do I pay?
Hvor betaler jeg?
voor be·ta·lər yay?

I need a mechanic.
Jeg trenger en bilmekaniker.
yay treng·ər en bil·me·kaa·ni·kər

The car/motorbike has broken down at ...
Bilen/Sykkelen har fått motorstopp ...
bee·lən/sew·ke·lən har fawt mo·tor·stop ...

The car/motorbike won't start.
Bilen/Sykkelen starter ikke.
bee·lən/sew·ke·lən star·tər ik·kə

I have a flat tyre.
Hjulet er punktert.
yoo·lə aar pung·tayrt

I've run out of petrol.
Jeg er tom for bensin.
yay ər tom for ben·seen

I've had an accident.
Jeg har vært i en ulykke.
yay haar vart ee en u·lew·kə

TRAVEL WITH CHILDREN

Is there (a/an) ...?
Finnes det ...?
fin·nes de ...?

I need (a/an) ...
Jeg trenger ...
yay tren·ga ...

baby change room	
et stellerom	et stel·la·room
car baby seat	
et barnesete	et bar·na·say·tə
child-minding service	
en barnevakt	en bar·nə·vaakt
children's menu	
en barnemeny	en baar·nə·me·new
disposable nappies/diapers	
bleier	blay·yər
formula	
morsmelktillegg	mors·melk·til·eg
(English-speaking) babysitter	
en engelsktalende barnevakt	en en·gelsk·ta·len·də bar·na·vaakt
highchair	
en høy barnestol	en həy bar·na·stool
potty	
en potte	en po·tə
stroller	
en sportsvogn	en spawts·von

Do you mind if I breastfeed here?
Kan jeg amme her? kan yay am·mə haar?

Are children allowed?
Er det tillat for barn? aar de til·lat faw baarn?

Also available from Lonely Planet: *Scandinavian Phrasebook*

SAMI

Although written Fell Sami includes several accented letters, it still doesn't accurately represent the spoken language – even some Sami people find the written language difficult to learn. For example, *giitu* (thanks) is pronounced '*gheech*-too', but the strongly aspirated 'h' is not written.

Here are a few Sami phrases. To learn the correct pronunciation, it's probably best to ask a local to read the words aloud.

Hello.	*Buorre beaivi.*
Hello. (reply)	*Ipmel atti.*
Goodbye. (to person leaving)	*Mana dearvan.*
Goodbye. (to person staying)	*Báze dearvan.*
Thank you.	*Giitu.*
You're welcome.	*Leage buorre.*
Yes.	*De lea.*
No.	*Li.*
How are you?	*Mot manna?*
I'm fine.	*Buorre dat manna.*

1	*okta*
2	*guokte*
3	*golbma*
4	*njeallje*
5	*vihta*
6	*guhta*
7	*cieza*
8	*gávcci*
9	*ovcci*
10	*logi*

Glossary

You may encounter some of the following terms and abbreviations during your travels in Norway. See also p61 for some food-related Norwegian words and the Language chapter (p425) for other useful words and phrases. Note that although the letters ø and å fall at the end of the Norwegian alphabet, we have included them under 'o' and 'a' respectively to make things easier for non-Norwegian-speaking readers.

abonnement – subscription
allemannsretten – 'every man's right'; a tradition/law allowing universal access to private property (with some restrictions), public lands and wilderness areas
apótek – pharmacy
Arctic Menu – scheme to encourage the use of the region's natural ingredients in food served by restaurants
arête – a sharp ridge between two valley glaciers
arsamerit – name given by Inuit (Eskimos) to aurora borealis
aurora borealis – northern lights
automatisk trafikkontrol – speed camera

bakke – hill
berg – mountain
bibliotek – library
billett – ticket
bilutleie – car-hire company
blodveien – literally 'blood road'; nickname given to Arctic Highway during construction due to high number of worker fatalities
bokhandel – bookshop
bru, bro – bridge
brygge – quay, wharf
bryggeri – brewery
bukt, bukta – bay
bunad – the Norwegian national costume; each region has its own version
by – town

calving – breaking off of icebergs from tidewater glaciers
cirque – an amphitheatre scoured out by a glacier
crevasse – a fissure in moving ice, which may be hidden under snow

dal – valley
DNT – Den Norske Turistforening (Norwegian Mountain Touring Club)
domkirke – cathedral
dressin – rail bikes or bicycles on bogies

elg – elk, moose
elv, elva – river

Fata Morgana – Arctic phenomenon whereby distant features do not appear out of focus
ferje – ferry
festning – fort, fortress
fiskeskrue – fish press
fjell, fell, fjall – mountain
fjord – drowned glacial valley
fonn – glacial icefield
forening – club, association
foss – waterfall
friluft – outdoor, open-air
Fv – Fylkesvei; county road
fylke – county
fyr, fyrtårn – lighthouse

galleriet – gallery, shopping arcade
gamle, gamla, gammel – old
gamlebyen – the 'old town'
gamma, gammen – Sami tent or turf hut, sometimes partially underground
gård, gard – farm, courtyard
gate, gata – street (often abbreviated to g or gt)
gatekjøkken – literally 'street kitchen'; street kiosk/stall/grill
gjestehavn – 'guest harbour'; the area of a port town where visiting boats and yachts moor
gjestehus – guesthouse
gravlund, gravplass – cemetery
grønlandssel – harp seal
gruve, gruva – mine

hage – garden
halvøya – peninsula
Hanseatic League – association of German traders that dominated trade in Bergen from the 12th to 16th centuries
hav – ocean
havn – harbour
honnør – senior citizen
hulder – elusive mythical Norwegian creature who steals milk from summer pastures
Hurtigruten – literally 'the Express Route'; system of coastal steamers plying the route between Bergen and Kirkenes
hus – house
husmannskost – traditional Norwegian food; home-cooking
hval – whale
hvalross – walrus

hytte – cabin, hut or chalet
hytteutleie – hut-hire company

ice floe – a flat chunk of floating sea ice or small iceberg
icecap, icefield – a stable zone of accumulated and compressed snow and ice, and a source of valley glaciers. An icecap generally covers a larger area than an icefield.
iddis – colourful sardine tin label; Stavanger dialect for 'etikett' or label
isbjørn – polar bear

jarls – earls
jernbanestasjon – train station
jerv – wolverine
joik – 'song of the plains'; religious Sami tradition
jul – Christmas

kai, kaia – quay
kanoutleie – canoe-hire company
kappleiker – dance competitions
kart – map
kirke, kirkja, kirkje, kerk – church
knörr – small cargo boats (plural *knerrir*)
kort – card
krambua – general store
krone – Norwegian currency unit
Kulturhus – a large complex containing cinemas, public library, museums etc
kvadraturen – the square grid pattern of streets measuring six long blocks by nine shorter blocks
kyst – coast

landsmål – Norwegian dialect
lavvo, lavvu – tepee; Sami tent dwelling
legevakten – clinic
leikarringer – folk dancers
lemen – lemmings
libris – books; indicates a bookshop
lufthavn – airport
lundefugl – puffins

magasin – department store
marka – the forested hills around Oslo
mil – Norwegian mile measuring 10km
minipris – cheaper fares, usually for transport
MOMS – Value Added Tax/sales tax
moskus-okse – musk oxen
M/S – motorskip or motor ship; designates ship names
museum, museet – museum
MVA – see *MOMS*
myntvaskeri – coin laundry

nasjonalpark – national park
naturreservat – nature reserve
navvy – railway worker
nord – north
nordlys – northern lights, aurora borealis
Norge – Norway
Norges Turistråd – Norwegian Tourist Board, formerly NORTRA
Norsk – Norwegian
Norway in a Nutshell – a range of tours that give high-speed travellers a glimpse of the best of Norway in one or two days
NSB – Norges Statsbaner (Norwegian State Railways)
ny – new
Nynorsk – see *landsmål*

og – and
ølutsalg – beer sales outlet
øst – east
oter – otter
øvre – upper
øy – island

pack ice – floating ice formed by frozen seawater, often creating an impenetrable barrier to navigation
pensjonat – pension, guesthouse
plass – plaza, square
polarsirkelen – Arctic Circle; latitude 66°33'N
Polynya – Russian word referring to an area of open water surrounded by pack ice
Pomor – Russian trading and fishing community from White Sea, which prospered in northern Norway in the 17th century
postkontor – post office

rådhus – town hall
reinsdyr – reindeer
reiseliv – local tourist office
riksdaler – old Norwegian currency
rødruss – see *russ*
rom – signs on roads indicating private rooms/cabins for rent
rorbu – cabin/fishing hut
rosemaling – painted floral motifs
russ – to run amuck; students graduating from high-school dress in a red beret and overalls and have permission to get into mischief
rutebilstasjon – bus terminal
ruteplan – transport timetable
Rv – Riksvei; national highway

sæter – summer dairy
schøtstue – large assembly room where employees of the Hanseatic League met and ate
selskap – company
sentrum – town centre
siida – small Sami communities or bands that hunted and trapped together

sild – herring
sjø – sea
sjøhus – fishing bunkhouse on the docks; many are now available for tourist accommodation
skalds – metaphoric and alliterative works of Norwegian court poets in the 9th and 10th centuries
skerries – offshore archipelago of small rocky islets
skog – forest
sla låm – slope track
slott – castle, palace
snø – snow
solarsteim – Viking navigational tool used when the sky was overcast or the sun below the horizon
sør – south
søyle – column, pillar
spekkhogger – killer whales or orcas
stabbur – raised storehouse
stasjon – station
Statens Kartverk – State Mapping Agency
stavkirke – stave church
steinkobbe – harbour seal
stige – ladder
storting – parliament
strand – beach
stuer – trading firm
sund – sound, strait
Svalbard rein – Svalbard caribou
Sverige – Sweden
svømmehall, svømmebad – swimming pool
sykehus – hospital
sykkel – bicycle
sykkelutleie – bicycle-hire company

taiga – marshy forest
tårn – tower
teater – theatre
telekort – Telenor phone cards
tog – train
togbuss – bus services in Romsdalen and Nordland run by NSB to connect railheads with other popular destinations
torget, torvet – town square
turistkontor – tourist office

ulv – wolves
utleie – hire company

vandrerhjem – youth hostel
vann, vatn, vannet, vatnet – lake
vaskeri – laundry
vei, veg – road (often abbreviated to v or vn)
vest – west
vetter – mythical Norwegian guardian spirits of the wildest coastline
vidde, vidda – plateau
vinmonopolet – government-run shop selling wine and liquor

yoik – see *joik*

The Authors

ANTHONY HAM

Coordinating Author, Southern & Central Norway, Bergen, Southwestern Fjords

More often found exploring Africa, the Middle East or his adopted home in Spain, Anthony nonetheless fell in love with Norway the first time he laid eyes on her. Like the altogether more clamorous destinations that he usually frequents, Norway's hospitable people and the drama of its landscapes call him back to Norway time and again. In addition to more than 30 guidebooks for Lonely Planet, including the previous edition of this book, Anthony works as a photojournalist for newspapers and magazines around the world with a particular focus on travel and the environment.

KARI LUNDGREN

Oslo

With a stewardess mother, pilot father and Viking roots, Kari began exploring at an early age, sailing up the coast of Norway to 80 degrees north when she was aged 12 and across the Atlantic at 15. Now based in London, she returns home whenever she can to ski, bask in the midnight summer sun and drink the occasional glass of aquavit. She is the author of the Norway chapter in Lonely Planet's *The Europe Book*.

MILES RODDIS

Western Fjords, Trøndelag, Nordland, Far North, Svalbard

A distant camping holiday deep in the forests of Finland, an even more distant Swedish girlfriend and two stimulating months in the vast lands north of the Arctic Circle, researching the previous edition of this guide: such were the irresistible pulls that drew Miles back once more to this land of dramatic cliffs, fretted fjords and lush, green grass. Miles, who has written or contributed to 40 Lonely Planet guidebooks and walking guides, usually writes about Mediterranean lands these days. So these chill breaths of Scandinavian air came as a tonic and reminder of his northern European roots.

LONELY PLANET AUTHORS

Why is our travel information the best in the world? It's simple: our authors are independent, dedicated travellers. They don't research using just the internet or phone, and they don't take freebies in exchange for positive coverage. They travel widely, to all the popular spots and off the beaten track. They personally visit thousands of hotels, restaurants, cafés, bars, galleries, palaces, museums and more – and they take pride in getting all the details right, and telling it how it is. Think you can do it? Find out how at lonelyplanet.com.

Behind the Scenes

THIS BOOK

This 4th edition of *Norway* was coordinated by Anthony Ham, who also wrote the introductory chapters and colour chapters, as well as the Directory, Transport, Health, Southern Norway, Central Norway and Bergen & The Southwestern Fjords chapters. He was assisted by co-authors Kari Lundgren, who wrote the Oslo chapter for this edition, and Miles Roddis, who wrote the Western Fjords, Trøndelag, Nordland, The Far North and Svalbard chapters of this book. The Health chapter was adapted from material originally written by Dr Caroline Evans. Anthony and Miles compiled the 3rd edition of the book. This guidebook was commissioned in Lonely Planet's London office, and produced by the following:

Commissioning Editor Ella O'Donnell
Coordinating Editor Evan Jones
Coordinating Cartographer Jolyon Philcox
Coordinating Layout Designer Yvonne Bischofberger
Colour Layout Designer Jacqui Saunders
Managing Editors Geoff Howard, Brigitte Ellemor
Managing Cartographer Mark Griffiths
Managing Layout Designer Celia Wood
Assisting Editors David Andrew, Victoria Harrison, Andrew Bain, Stephanie Ong
Assisting Cartographers Tony Fankhauser, Ross Butler, Julie Sheridan
Assisting Layout Designers Indra Kilfoyle, Cara Smith
Cover Designer Marika Mercer
Project Manager Eoin Dunlevy
Language Content Coordinator Quentin Frayne

Thanks to Lisa Knights, Wayne Murphy, Mark Germanchis, John Mazzocchi, Adam McCrow, Valentina Kremenchutskaya, James Hardy, Adrian Persoglia, Csanad Csutoros, Trent Paton

THANKS

ANTHONY HAM

Special thanks to Henriette Westhrins and Paul Hofseth (Ministry of the Environment), Espen Larsen, Bjørn Krag Ingul (Innovation Norway), Bernt Erik Pedersen (Dagsavisen), Sonja Krantz, Inger Marie Egenberg (Bryggen Project) and Espen Olsen who all gave generously of time and insight for the interviews in this book. Thanks also to: Kjetil Svorkmo Bergmann, Jon Berg and Terje Devold. Others who were extremely helpful include: Erik Garen, Frode Bjelland, Fredrik Sevheim, Inger-Sigrun Slagstad Vik, Karina Dahlum, Odd Løver, Hege Næss, Anita Tapio, Øistein Saugerud Chit, Johannes Aicher, Kristin G Løcken, Trine Nordkvelle, Jannicke Alvær, Svein Skjøtskift and Helen Siverstøl. At Lonely Planet, Ella O'Donnell was a fount of common sense and wisdom, not to mention

THE LONELY PLANET STORY

Fresh from an epic journey across Europe, Asia and Australia in 1972, Tony and Maureen Wheeler sat at their kitchen table stapling together notes. The first Lonely Planet guidebook, *Across Asia on the Cheap,* was born.

Travellers snapped up the guides. Inspired by their success, the Wheelers began publishing books to Southeast Asia, India and beyond. Demand was prodigious, and the Wheelers expanded the business rapidly to keep up. Over the years, Lonely Planet extended its coverage to every country and into the virtual world via lonelyplanet.com and the Thorn Tree message board.

As Lonely Planet became a globally loved brand, Tony and Maureen received several offers for the company. But it wasn't until 2007 that they found a partner whom they trusted to remain true to the company's principles of travelling widely, treading lightly and giving sustainably. In October of that year, BBC Worldwide acquired a 75% share in the company, pledging to uphold Lonely Planet's commitment to independent travel, trustworthy advice and editorial independence.

Today, Lonely Planet has offices in Melbourne, London and Oakland, with over 500 staff members and 300 authors. Tony and Maureen are still actively involved with Lonely Planet. They're travelling more often than ever, and they're devoting their spare time to charitable projects. And the company is still driven by the philosophy of *Across Asia on the Cheap*: 'All you've got to do is decide to go and the hardest part is over. So go!'

great company in Bergen. My co-authors, Miles, a long-standing companion of the road, and Kari were a privilege to work with. Thanks also to Ron, Jan, Lisa, Greg, Alex, Greta, Damien, Marina and Alberto. To Marina: *te quiero, te quiero, te quiero*. And to my special Carlota who was born during the writing of this book: may your life always carry you towards the horizon and may your world be a wonderful, wonderful place.

KARI LUNDGREN

Tusen takk to Eyvind Hellstrøm, Geir Lundestad and Ivar Kraglund for their insight on Norwegian food, the Nobel Peace Prize and WWII history; to cousins Morten and Trine for numerous warm welcomes and Sidsel and Torbjørn for walking me through Oslo's medieval history. Thanks to aunts Kate, Kajo, Nusse, uncle Finn and my mum; my trusted guides on all things Norwegian. Not to mention Oslo locals Eivind Vad Petersson, Espen Sommerfelt, Julie Lodrup, Magnus Nome, Marte Christensen, Øyvind Gjengaar and Per-Ivar Nikolaisen. And to Ella, Anthony, Mark and Miles for your guidance throughout. Finally, my brother Tor for keeping me company during my research and for simply being the best brother a little sister could ever hope for.

MILES RODDIS

Miles' chapters are all for Caleb in the hope that he'll come to love mountains, wild lands and greenness as much as his Ya Yo does. Huge thanks, as always, to Ingrid for driving me the length and most of the breadth of this long, slim land, cooking nightly and cajoling and inspiring me constantly.

My friend Anthony Ham was a genial, wise and tolerant colleague, while Ella O'Donnell remains my favourite commissioning editor for her cheerful enthusiasm and readiness to bend the rules where common sense dictates.

Thanks too to readers Peter & Thérèse O'Neill for their particularly thoughtful email comments. Also to Anne-Katrin Grube for some much-appreciated tips about Norway's furthest northern reaches.

Unfailingly, hyper-efficient tourist office staff pitched in enthusiastically with information. Many were themselves avid, seasoned Lonely Planet travellers in their vacation time, so we would immediately find ourselves on the same wavelength. Some were outstandingly helpful. Especial thanks to ebullient Knut Hansvold (Tromsø), Nicola Mulryan (Narvik), Elise Hannaas (Longyearbyen), Ann-Helen Blakset & Andreas Bergset (Stryn), Bente Saxon & Britt Giske Andersen (Ålesund), Frode Lindberg (Steinkjer), Sigrid Haarberg (Sandnessjøen), Birgitte Bjørkmo (Mo i Rana), Agata Gasior (Moskenes), Elisabeth Müller (Finnsnes), Anders Lauridsen (Vardø) and Lisbeth Fallan with Monica Selnes (Trondheim).

Warmest appreciation too to Tanna Gjeraker and Mari Skjerdal Lysne (Lærdal), Anja-Therese Fardal (Sogndal), Laura (Fjærland), all the team in Florø, Inger-Marie Aarsheim (Selje), Tom Christian Nekstad (Åndalsnes), Helene Ottestad (Molde), Cathrine Husby (Kristiansund), Anne Berit Flo (Namsos), Thomas Gregersen (Bodø), Tonje Ulriksen (Svolvær), Gro Dagsvold (Harstad), Lásse Juhán Helander (Kautakeino), Olga Polezhaeva (Alta), Piera Kirstte Jovsset (Karasjok), Sarah Marie Aronsen (Vadsø), Ina Heline Olsen (Honningsvåg), Jill Tingvold & Ida Ekerhovd (Hammerfest) – and to Tim Dassler at Mack Brewery, Tromsø, for a sprightly run through of Norwegian drinking habits.

OUR READERS

Many thanks to the travellers who used the last edition and wrote to us with helpful hints, useful advice and interesting anecdotes:

Hans Petter Aalmo, Maddy Aldis-Evans, Rachel Allen, Denys Alves, Ben Andrew, Bolaji Balslev, Robert Blackwood, Arris Blom, Line T Boerve, Christopher Bourne, Ross Brown,

SEND US YOUR FEEDBACK

We love to hear from travellers – your comments keep us on our toes and help make our books better. Our well-travelled team reads every word on what you loved or loathed about this book. Although we cannot reply individually to postal submissions, we always guarantee that your feedback goes straight to the appropriate authors, in time for the next edition. Each person who sends us information is thanked in the next edition – and the most useful submissions are rewarded with a free book.

To send us your updates – and find out about Lonely Planet events, newsletters and travel news – visit our award-winning website: **www.lonelyplanet.com/contact**.

Note: we may edit, reproduce and incorporate your comments in Lonely Planet products such as guidebooks, websites and digital products, so let us know if you don't want your comments reproduced or your name acknowledged. For a copy of our privacy policy visit www.lonelyplanet.com/privacy.

Simone Busetti, Celine Campana, Claudia De Carvalho, Nicole Coulom, Peter Courtney, Lindis Davidsen, Edwin Deventer, Cam Donaldson, Hans Eggink, Cindy Ensink, Catherine Fleming, James Foster, Stefanie Franz, Aslaug Moi Frøysnes, Leon Furness, Jane Galea-Singer, Anne-Katrin Grube, Alv Haagaard Gustavsen, Søren Vestergaard Hansen, Paul Harlow, Ira Hartmann, Jackie Hartnell, Michelle Hogan, Anne Hughes, Kevin Hughes, Timothy Johnson, Christine Kaaløy, Frida Kalbakk, Julie Knutson, Hilde Leversund, Ruth Mair, Lizette De Man, Patrick McGowan, Petter Muri, Tracy Newton, Tracy Flox Nieva, Svein Roar Nilsen, Marek Nohejl, Peter & Thérèse O'Neill, Bernd Oswald, Morten Øvestad, Gloria Pamplona, Daniel Peña, Spencer Plaitin, Steve Pottinger, Steven Price, Isabelle Pronovost, Neil Purcell, Michael Raffaele, Jan Rondeel, Jackie Ross, Laura Marie Levorson Rueslåtten, Carrie Ryder, Nick Sanders, Iliyan Savov, Bastian Schnabel, Wencke Shishido, Sietse Snel, And & Odd Sorensen, Emile Spanjer, Suzanne Stuijfzand, Ueli Stähli, Helen Travis, Jamie Umaña, Maartje van Kregten, Mieke Der van Wenden, Margo Dedert, Arjan van den Hul Ronald van den Tol, Valerie Vella, Tor Wathne, Redma Woudstra

ACKNOWLEDGMENTS

Many thanks to the following for the use of thei content:

Globe on title page ©Mountain High Maps 1993 Digital Wisdom, Inc.

Internal photographs by ©Arco Images/Alamy p7 (#7); All other photographs by Lonely Planet Images and by Adina Tovy Amsel p9 (#2); Anders Blomqvist p5, p6 (#2), p7 (#4), p9 (#4); Christian Aslund p6 (#6), p10 (#4), p11 (#3), p12; Craig Pershouse p11 (#1); Jan Stromme p8

Index

000 Map pages
000 Photograph pages

INDEX

000 Map pages
000 Photograph pages

000 Map pages
000 Photograph pages

GreenDex

GOING GREEN

With some of Europe's most dramatic landscape on the doorstep, including its largest icecap, Norway is well aware of its responsibility as an environmental citizen. Consequently, recycling is almost universal and most places go about their business with a high regard for the environment. The following listings have been selected by our authors because they demonstrate a strong commitment to sustainability. We've selected some places for their support of local producers and use of seasonal and organic food. We've also chosen independently owned accommodation options deemed to be especially environmentally friendly, for example those showing real commitment to energy conservation. Attractions are listed because they're involved in environmental education or have won ecological awards.

For information on 'green' activities and locations such as hiking, cycling and national parks, see the general index. For more tips on travelling responsibly in Norway, turn to the Getting Started chapter (see p19).

We want to develop our sustainable-travel content further so if you think we've omitted someone who should be listed, or if you disagree with our choices, email us at talk2us@lonelyplanet.com.au. For more information about sustainable tourism and Lonely Planet, see www.lonelyplanet.com/responsibletravel. For further details on Norway's environmental policies see p74.

Stavangar

- Mountain Preikestolen (Pulpit Rock)
- Lyser fjorden (cruises 3h)
- Boatrip to Bergen
- Sights of old Stavanger
- Cathedral (Domkirken)

ferry to Tau &
bus to Preikestolenpal
4km each way
300m climb

- old wooden house area near dom
- Ulstein Kloster

Fjords:
- Naeroyfjord → easier by public transport
- Geiranger → need car

Romsdal Valley drive (E136 from Dombas)
→ stop in
- Verma
- Monge
- Trollveggen
- bridge where head to Trollstigen (63)

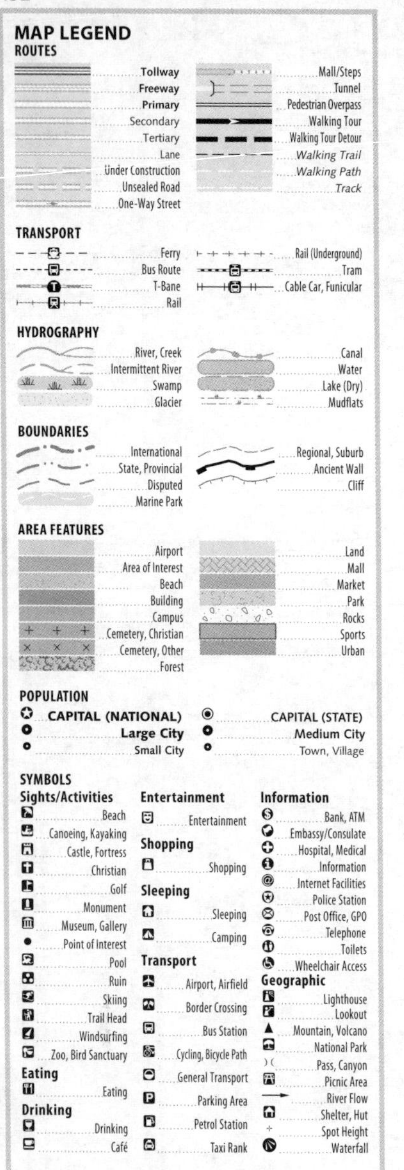

LONELY PLANET OFFICES

Australia

Head Office
Locked Bag 1, Footscray, Victoria 3011
☎ 03 8379 8000, fax 03 8379 8111
talk2us@lonelyplanet.com.au

USA

150 Linden St, Oakland, CA 94607
☎ 510 893 8555, toll free 800 275 8555
fax 510 893 8572
info@lonelyplanet.com

UK

2nd Floor, 186 City Road,
London ECV1 2NT
☎ 020 7106 2100, fax 020 7106 2101
go@lonelyplanet.co.uk

Published by Lonely Planet Publications Pty Ltd
ABN 36 005 607 983

Cover photograph: The icecaps of Jostedalsbreen from acro Oldevatnet lake, Briksdalsbreen, Sogn og Fjordane, Norway, Lesl Garland/LGPL/Photolibrary. Many of the images in this guide ar available for licensing from Lonely Planet Images: www.lonelyplan images.com.

Printed by Hang Tai Printing Company.
Printed in China.